DIGITAL SIGNAL PROCESSING

AF653786

B KUMAR
MTech., PhD
Formerly Director
Netaji Subhas Institute of Technology, Delhi (1996-97)
GPM College of Engineering, Delhi (2000-02)
HMR Institute of Technology and Management, Delhi (2005-06)

Publishing Globally

NEW AGE INTERNATIONAL (P) LIMITED, PUBLISHERS
LONDON • NEW DELHI • NAIROBI
Bangalore • Chennai • Cochin • Guwahati • Hyderabad • Kolkata • Lucknow • Mumbai
Visit us at **www.newagepublishers.com**

Copyright © 2015, New Age International (P) Ltd., Publishers
Published by New Age International (P) Ltd., Publishers
First Edition: 2015
Reprint: 2020

All rights reserved.
No part of this book may be reproduced in any form, by photostat, microfilm, xerography, or any other means, or incorporated into any information retrieval system, electronic or mechanical, without the written permission of the publisher.

GLOBAL OFFICES

- **New Delhi** **NEW AGE INTERNATIONAL (P) LIMITED, PUBLISHERS**
7/30 A, Daryaganj, New Delhi-110002, (INDIA)
Tel.: (011) 23253771, 23253472, **Telefax:** 23267437, 43551305
E-mail: contactus@newagepublishers.com • Visit us at www.newagepublishers.com
- **London** **NEW AGE INTERNATIONAL (UK) LTD.**
27 Old Gloucester Street, London, WC1N 3AX, UK
E-mail: info@newacademicscience.co.uk • Visit us at www.newacademicscience.co.uk
- **Nairobi** **NEW AGE GOLDEN (EAST AFRICA) LTD.**
Ground Floor, Westlands Arcade, Chiromo Road (Next to Naivas Supermarket)
Westlands, Nairobi, KENYA, **Tel.:** 00-254-713848772, 00-254-725700286
E-mail: kenya@newagepublishers.com

BRANCHES

- **Bangalore** 37/10, 8th Cross (Near Hanuman Temple), Azad Nagar, Chamarajpet, Bangalore- 560 018
Tel.: (080) 26756823, **Telefax:** 26756820, **E-mail: bangalore@newagepublishers.com**
- **Chennai** 26, Damodaran Street, T. Nagar, Chennai-600 017, **Tel.:** (044) 24353401, **Telefax:** 24351463
E-mail: chennai@newagepublishers.com
- **Cochin** CC-39/1016, Carrier Station Road, Ernakulam South, Cochin-682 016, **Tel.:** (0484) 2377303, **Telefax:** 4051304
E-mail: cochin@newagepublishers.com
- **Guwahati** Hemsen Complex, Mohd. Shah Road, Paltan Bazar, Near Starline Hotel, Guwahati-781 008,
Tel.: (0361) 2513881, **Telefax:** 2543669, **E-mail: guwahati@newagepublishers.com**
- **Hyderabad** 105, 1st Floor, Madhiray Kaveri Tower, 3-2-19, Azam Jahi Road, Near Kumar Theater, Nimboliadda Kachiguda, Hyderabad-500 027, **Tel.:** (040) 24652456, **Telefax:** 24652457
E-mail: hyderabad@newagepublishers.com
- **Kolkata** RDB Chambers (Formerly Lotus Cinema) 106A, 1st Floor, S N Banerjee Road, Kolkata-700 014
Tel.: (033) 22273773, **Telefax:** 22275247, **E-mail: kolkata@newagepublishers.com**
- **Lucknow** 16-A, Jopling Road, Lucknow-226 001, **Tel.:** (0522) 2209578, 4045297, **Telefax:** 2204098
E-mail: lucknow@newagepublishers.com
- **Mumbai** 142C, Victor House, Ground Floor, N.M. Joshi Marg, Lower Parel, Mumbai-400 013
Tel.: (022) 24927869, **Telefax:** 24915415, **E-mail: mumbai@newagepublishers.com**
- **New Delhi** 22, Golden House, Daryaganj, New Delhi-110 002, **Tel.:** (011) 23262368, 23262370, **Telefax:** 43551305
E-mail: sales@newagepublishers.com

ISBN: 978-81-224-3609-9
C-19-05-12107

Printed in India at Ajit Printing Press, Delhi.
Typeset at Goswami Associates, Delhi.

NEW AGE INTERNATIONAL (P) LIMITED, PUBLISHERS
7/30 A, Daryaganj, New Delhi-110002
Visit us at **www.newagepublishers.com**
(CIN: U74899DL1966PTC004618)

Dedicated to

My Sweetest Grand-daughter

AMAYA

Preface

Due to its wide applications and efficacy, the subject of Digital Signal Processing (DSP) is included in the curricula of many engineering and science courses, such as Electronics & Communication Engg., Electrical Engg., Control & Instrumentation Engg., Computer and Information Technology, Mechanical Engg., Civil Engg., and even Chemical Engg. (to mention a few). This book aims at imparting sound knowledge of DSP. The student is assumed to have good mathematical background covering Integration/Differentiation and Laplace Transform. The other essential mathematical topics, needed to understand the subject, have been appropriately covered in the book to enable the student grasp the subject clearly.

Chapter 1 covers the basics of Signals and Systems, both for continuous-time as well as for discrete-time systems. Chapters 2 and 3 cover Discrete-time Fourier Series and Discrete-time Fourier Transform (DTFS and DTFT); Z-Transform (ZT) and Discrete-time LTI Systems. Realization of digital systems, in various forms of structures, has been covered in Chapter 4. Chapter 5 introduces the response of Pole-zero systems, along with a brief on solution of Difference Equations. Chapter 6 explains the important topics of DFT, FFT and other related algorithms. Sampling Theorem and Signal Reconstruction have been covered in Chapter 7. Various design approaches for FIR and IIR filters are covered in Chapters 8 and 9. Chapter 10 explains, in detail, the Quantization Effects. Chapter 11 highlights the basics of Random Variables and Signals, which are necessary in Digital Communication and Digital Control Systems, in particular. Chapter 12 has been devoted to cover the theory and application of Multirate Digital Signal Processing (MDSP). Chapter 13 explains the Signal Flow Graphs and Tellegen's Theorem. Finally, Chapter 14 gives important applications of DSP.

The concept of DSP has been elucidated, backed by essential mathematical proofs for better apprehension of the subject. A large number of solved examples and problems (with answers), totalling over 500, and a list of Reference Books would be very useful for the reader.

I hope the book in its present form will meet my expectations. The author will be too glad to receive any suggestions and feedback for further improvement of this book at my e-mail: bkumar 35@yahoo.com

BALBIR KUMAR

Acknowledgements

The completion of this book is due to the blessings and encouragement of several individuals. I wish to extend my sincere gratitude to them.

My wife, Mrs. Shashi Kala, retired Principal, has been the prime inspiration for writing this book. No words can match her devotion and contribution. She deserves my foremost salutation. During my stay in Canada (Dec. 2011 to Nov. 2012), where the major part of this book was written, I had developed serious health problems. It was my fifteen-month-old grand-daughter (AMAYA) who would support my stick while I relearnt walking and balancing. My heart-felt prayers and kind blessings are for tender AMAYA whose contribution is unique.

I am also grateful to my sons Pankaj and Niraj as well as my daughters-in-law: Rachna and Archana for extending tremendous support in completing this book.

I am thankful to all members of New Age International Publishers for bringing out this book.

Contents

CHAPTER 1

Signals and Systems

(A) SIGNALS

In this chapter, we have focussed on signals, classification and transformation of independent variables. Systems, their properties, analysis and identification/deconvolution is covered. Mention of continuous-time signals and systems has also been made to appreciate the connection to the discrete-time signals and systems.

1.1 INTRODUCTION—A SIGNAL

A signal is a piece of information. In olden times, the signals were conveyed by burning fire (fire flame attached to a pole is seen from a long distance) or by drum beats (sound of drum can also be heard at a large distance) or by somaphore (signal sent by different coloured flags), and by various other means. As the technology developed, we needed long or complex variety of various signals and those which can be easily sent to long distances. The ideal choice is the electrical signals. Once the signal is complicated and intricate we require a suitable system to process such signals to extract the information contained in the signal. The development of different systems to cater to the processing needs of different signals is obvious. In this chapter, we shall introduce the mathematical representation of various signals and systems, together with their classifications. Basic signals have also been defined, which are needed to formulate complex signals.

1.2 CLASSIFICATION OF SIGNALS

A signal represents some physical quantity or a parameter. In general, a signal gives the behaviour of a phenomenon which in turn depends on time. Mathematically, signals are denoted by symbols such as: $x, y, z, f, g, h, \ldots$, etc. and are functions of time t or may be constant.

A signal $x(t)$ is a *continuous-time signal* if the independent variable t (t is usually time) is continuous. If the time is not continuous, but has discrete values: $0, T, 2T, \ldots, nT$ etc., we write the signal as $x(nT)$, $n = 0, 1, 2, \ldots$. It is customary to write $x\,(nT)$, which we call *discrete-time signal*, by the symbol, $x[n]$, which implies $x[0], x[1], \ldots, x[n]$. Also, the other symbols used for discrete signals $x[n]$ are:

$$x_n = x\,[n] = x\,[nT] \qquad \ldots(1.1)$$

or $\quad x_0, x_1, x_2, \ldots, x_n$

At times, we ignore T (*i.e.*, assume T as unity) and $x[n]$ would automatically mean $x[nT]$; given $x[5]$, for example, we know it means $x\,[5T]$. We shall see that assuming $T = 1$ will simplify most of the calculations. We call $x[n]$ as samples, since, it is the value of parameter x at discrete times nT and nT are the sampling instants. In this book, we shall, at times, also use $x(n)$ to indicate a discrete signal, as it is still very popularly used by some authors.

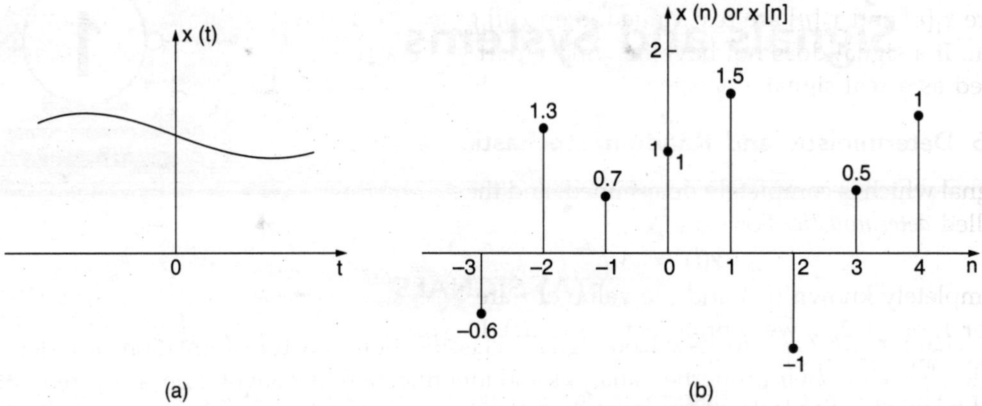

Fig. 1.1. The signals (*a*) a continuous-time signal $x(t)$ (*b*) a discrete-time signals $x[n]$ or $x(n)$

Figure 1.1 shows typically a continuous-time signal $x(t)$, and a discrete-time signal $x[n]$. Note that $x(t)$ is a continuous curve. If there are finite number of breaks in the curve $x(t)$, we still call it continuous signal with zero values at the breaks. Time t can take any value from $-\infty$ to $+\infty$. The discrete signal $x[n]$ may be written as:

$$x[n] = \{\ldots, -0.6, 1.3, 0.7, \underset{\uparrow}{1}, 1.5, -1, 0.5, 1, \ldots\}$$

The arrow below the value 1 in above sequence shows that $n = 0$ here. Note that $x[n]$ can be easily defined though by a lengthy sequence. But $x(t)$ *cannot* be written in this fashion, except when $x(t)$ has a curve which can be expressed in a mathematical expression, such as $x(t) = \sin 2t$ or $x(t) = 1 - t^2$ ..., etc. It is this property of $x[n]$ which makes it computer friendly, since, we can readily store all the samples $x[n]$ in the computer memory. A continuous signal $x(t)$ cannot be exactly stored in a computer hard disc except by taking infinitely many values of x at close points t.

Now we classify the signals in a broad sense.

1.2.1 Analog and Digital Signals (Continuous-time and Discrete-time Signals)

A typical signal $x(t)$, where the argument t is continuous time and t can assume values in the range $-\infty \le t \le \infty$, is an analog signal. $x(t)$ shown in Fig. 1.1(*a*) is an analog signal.

The signal $x[n]$, where the argument n assumes discrete values, is an example of a discrete-time signal. If we quantize the signal values $x[n]$, it is called a digital signal. Such digital signals can be easily stored in a computer. In general, n can take only finite discrete value. $x[n]$ shown in Fig. 1.1 (*b*) is a digital (or discrete-time) signal.

1.2.2 Real and Complex Signals

Let $$x(t) = x_1(t) + j\,x_2(t) \qquad ...(1.2)$$

where $j = \sqrt{-1}$ and $x_1(t)$ and $x_2(t)$ are real valued, then $x(t)$ is a complex analog signal. Similarly, if

$$x[n] = x_1[n] + j\,x_2[n] \qquad ...(1.3)$$

where $x_1[n]$ and $x_2[n]$ are real valued, then $x[n]$ given by (1.3) is an example of a complex digital signal. If a signal does not have imaginary part *i.e.*, if $x_2(t)$ and $x_2[n]$ are zero, then the signal is termed as a real signal.

1.2.3 Deterministic and Random/Stochastic Signals

A signal which is completely determined, and there is no uncertainty about its value or behaviour is called *deterministic.* For example,

$$x(t) = A\,e^{-5t} \qquad ...(1.4)$$

is completely known if A and the value of t are known. If we are not sure what A is, may be it is 0 or 1, or – 0.2,..., we cannot determine $x(t)$. In general, deterministic signals are used in most of the computer applications.

If a signal is not fully determined at any instant of time t or n, the signal is called *random or stochastic.* For example, in a digital signal

$$x(n) = n^2 + 5n \qquad ...(1.5)$$

if n = number of heads, when a coin is tossed, say, 100 times, then the value of n is not exactly known. It could be 30, 41, 71, or any value. In such a case, the value of $x(n)$ in Eqn. (1.5), is not exactly calculable. This is the case of a random signal. Such signals play important role in communication and control. We shall also deal with random signals in this book. Note that the random signals are usually defined by a few important properties such as mean, variance, auto and cross correlations etc.

1.2.4 Periodic and Aperiodic Signals

If $x(t) = x(t + kT)$, $k = 0, \pm 1, \pm 2, \pm 3, ...$ ...(1.6)

then $x(t)$ is a *periodic signal with period T.* It implies that if in the argument t of $x(t)$ we add or subtract integral multiples of T, the signal value remains the same. $x(t)$ shown in Fig. 1.2 is periodic with period T. After and before time T the signal repeats. As we cannot draw infinite segments of basic $x(t)$, we show three dots (...) on both sides of one or two segments of $x(t)$, as shown in Fig. 1.2.

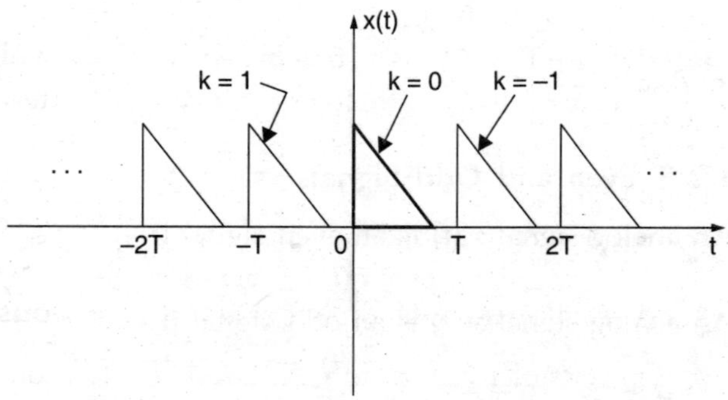

Fig. 1.2. A periodic analog signal $x(t)$ with period T

Similarly, we can also have periodic digital signals.

Here, $$x[n] = x[n + kN],\ k = 0, \pm 1, \pm 2, ..., \qquad ...(1.7)$$

$x[n]$ is periodic with period N samples. A periodic digital signal is shown in Fig. 1.3 with period $N = 3$. Note that $x[0] = x[-3] = x[3] = 3.5$. Similarly, $x[-2] = x[1] = x[4] = 2$. We also add three dots (...) to avoid drawing a long periodic sequence $x[n]$.

We can generate a periodic signal, given one "lobe" (or one basic expression) of the signal as follows :

Continuous-time periodic signal $x_p(t) = \sum_{i=-\infty}^{\infty} x(t - iT_0)$ ...(1.8)

where $x(t)$ is one lobe of the complete periodic signal $x_p\,(t)$ and T_0 is it's period.

Similarly, discrete-time periodic signal $x_p[n]$ is given by

$$x_p[n] = \sum_{i=-\infty}^{\infty} x\,[n - iN] \quad ...(1.9)$$

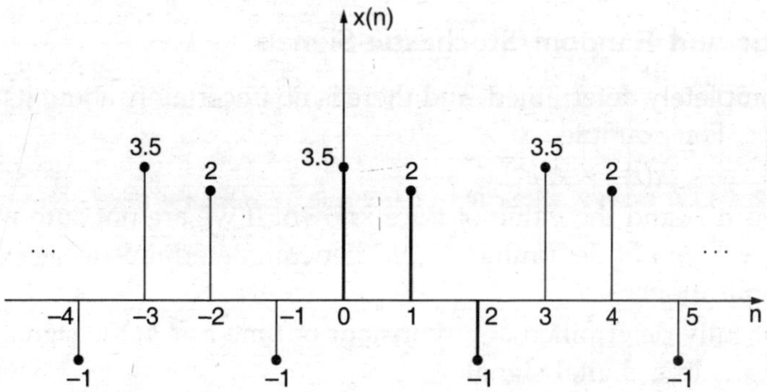

Fig. 1.3. A digital periodic signal $x[n]$ with period $N = 3$

where $x[n]$ is the signal for one period (N samples) and $x_p[n]$ is the periodic version of $x[n]$ with period N.

For example

$x(t) = A \sin\,(2\pi\omega_0 t)$ is periodic in t with period $1/\omega_0$ sec, since $A \sin\left(2\pi\left(t + \frac{1}{\omega_0}\right)\right) = A \sin\,(2\pi\omega_0 t + 2\pi) = A \sin\,(2\pi\omega_0 t)$.

Similarly,

$x[n] = B \sin\left[\frac{2\pi n}{N}\right]$ is periodic in n with period N samples, since, $B \sin\left[\frac{2\pi\,(n+N)}{N}\right]$ reduces to $B \sin\left[\frac{2\pi\, n}{N}\right]$

1.2.5 Even and Odd Signals

An analog signal $x_e(t)$ is an even signal if

$$x_e(t) = x_e\,(-\,t) \quad ...(1.10a)$$

An analog signal $x_o(t)$ is an odd signal if

$$x_o(t) = -\,x_o(-\,t) \quad ...(1.10b)$$

Thus, for even signals making the argument t negative does not affect the signal whereas in odd signal, the signal value $x_o(t)$ becomes $-\,x_o(t)$ when t is changed to $(-\,t)$.

Similar definitions can be extended to digital sequence *i.e.*,

$$x_e[n] = x_e[-\,n] \quad \text{for even signal } x_e[n] \quad ...(1.10c)$$

$$x_o[n] = -\,x_o[-\,n] \quad \text{for odd signal } x_o[n] \quad ...(1.10d)$$

Note that we have used subscript e or o to $x(t)$ and $x[n]$ to indicate that $x_e(t)$ and $x_o(t)$ are even and odd signals, respectively.

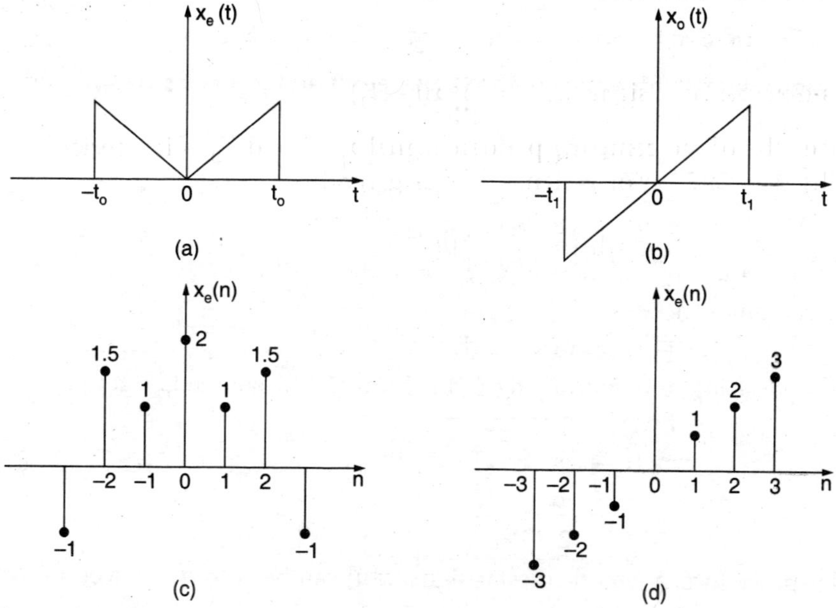

Fig. 1.4. Examples of even [$x_e(t)$, $x_e[n]$] and odd [$x_0(t)$, $x_0[n]$] signals

Note Important

We may also note some additional properties of even and odd signals, as follows:

1. (odd function) + (odd function) = odd function
2. (even function) + (even function) = even function
3. (odd function) × (odd function) = even function
4. (even function) × (even function) = even function
5. (even function) × (odd function) = odd function
6. For an even function $x_e(t)$

$$\int_{-t_0}^{t_0} x_e(t)\,dt = 2\int_0^{t_0} x_e(t)\,dt \qquad \text{...(1.11}a\text{)}$$

7. For an odd function $x_o(t)$

$$\int_{-t_0}^{t_0} x_o(t)\,dt = 0 \qquad \text{...(1.11}b\text{)}$$

8. For discrete even signal $x_e[n]$

$$\sum_{n=-n_0}^{n_0} x_e[n] = 2\sum_{n=0}^{n_0} x_e[n] - x_e[0] \quad \text{(Note the relation)} \qquad \text{...(1.11}c\text{)}$$

9. For discrete odd signal $x_o[n]$

$$\sum_{n=-n_0}^{n_0} x_o[n] = 0 \qquad \text{...(1.11}d\text{)}$$

1.2.6 Derivation of Even and Odd Parts of a Generic Signal

Let a generic signal be $x(t)$, for which we are required to find its even part $x_e(t)$ and odd part $x_o(t)$.

We can write

$$x(t) = x_e(t) + x_o(t) \quad ...(1.12)$$

change t to $-t$ or both sides of Eq. (1.12). Therefore,

$$x(-t) = x_e(-t) + x_o(-t) \quad ...(1.13)$$

But $x_e(-t) = +x_e(t)$ and $x_0(-t) = -x_o(t)$ due to Eq. (1.10), (*i.e.* by definition).

Using these values in Eq. (1.13), we get

$$x(-t) = x_e(t) - x_o(t) \quad ...(1.14)$$

adding (1.12) and (1.14), and subtracting (1.14) from (1.12), we readily get

$$x_e(t) = \frac{1}{2}[x(t) + x(-t)] \quad ...(1.14a)$$

$$x_o(t) = \frac{1}{2}[x(t) - x(-t)] \quad ...(1.14b)$$

By similar procedure, a generic digital signal $x[n]$ can be split in its even part $x_e[n]$ and odd part $x_o[n]$ by

$$x_e[n] = \frac{1}{2}(x[n] + x[-n]) \quad ...(1.15a)$$

$$x_o[n] = \frac{1}{2}(x[n] - x[-n]) \quad ...(1.15b)$$

Note that the odd functions $x_o(t)$ and $x_o[n]$ must have zero value at argument $t = 0$ or $n = 0$ *i.e.*,

$$x_o(t)|_{t=0} = x_o(0) = 0 \quad ...(1.16a)$$

$$x_o(n)|_{n=0} = x_o(0) = 0 \quad ...(1.16b)$$

$\text{sinc}(x) = \frac{\sin x}{x}$ is an even function, since, $\frac{\sin(-x)}{-x} = \frac{\sin x}{x}$ we shall see in later chapters that calculations of various transforms becomes easy if a signal is purely even or odd.

1.2.7 Energy Signals and Power Signals

Let $v(t)$ and $i(t)$ be the voltage and current, respectively, across a resistance, then the power $p(t)$ per ohm is defined as

$$p(t) = \frac{v(t)\cdot i(t)}{R} = i^2(t) = v^2(t) \quad ...(1.17)$$

Total energy, E, and average power P on a per-ohm is

$$\text{Energy } E = \int_{-\infty}^{\infty} i^2(t)\,dt \text{ joule} \quad ...(1.18)$$

$$\text{Power } P = \lim_{T\to\infty}\frac{1}{T}\int_{-T/2}^{T/2} i^2(t)\,dt \text{ watt} \quad ...(1.19)$$

For an arbitrary continuous $x(t)$, we extend this concept and define

$$\text{Normalised energy content of } x(t) = E \,\Delta \int_{-\infty}^{\infty} |x(t)|^2\,dt \quad ...(1.20)$$

and

Normalised average power P of $x(t)$ is defined as

$$P \triangleq \lim_{T \to \infty} \frac{1}{T} \int_{-T/2}^{T/2} |x(t)|^2 \, dt \qquad ...(1.21)$$

Extending similar concept for digital signal $x[n]$, we have

Normalised energy content E of $x[n]$ defined as

$$E \triangleq \sum_{n=-\infty}^{\infty} |x[n]|^2 \qquad ...(1.22)$$

and normalised power P of $x[n]$ is defined as

$$P \triangleq \lim_{N \to \infty} \frac{1}{2N+1} \sum_{n=-N}^{N} |x[n]|^2 \qquad ...(1.23)$$

1.2.8 Tests for Energy Signals and Power Signals

We categorise the signals as energy/power signal by using the following tests:

1. If $x(t)$ or $x[n]$ have $0 < E < \infty$ and $P = 0$, then $x(t)$ or $x[n]$ are the **Energy signals.**
2. If $x(t)$ or $x[n]$ have $0 < P < \infty$, and therefore $E = \infty$, then $x(t)$ or $x[n]$ are the **Power signals.**
3. If the signals $x(t)$ or $x[n]$ do not satisfy above properties then these signals are neither energy nor power signals.
4. If a signal is periodic with finite energy content per period, then it is a power signal. Its average power P is the average power of one period only.

EXAMPLE 1.1: *Which of the following signals are periodic, and if one is, what is its fundamental period.*

SOLUTION: (*a*) $g(t) = 7 \sin(400\pi t)$ (given signal)

If the argument of sine function is increased/decreased by 2π, or their integral multiples, the value remains the same.

Here, if t is increased by $\frac{1}{200}$, then argument becomes

$$400\pi\left(t + \frac{1}{200}\right) = 400\,t + 2\pi$$

$\therefore$ $g(t)$ is periodic with $T_0 = \frac{1}{200}$ **Ans.**

(*b*) $g(t) = 3 + t^2$ (given signal)

As $g(t)$ increases monotonically, $g(t)$ is not periodic. **Ans.**

(*c*) $g(t) = \cos 60\pi t - j \sin 60\pi t$ (given signal)

$= e^{-j\,60\pi t}$ (by Euler's theorem)

$$T_0 = \frac{1}{30} \quad \because \quad 60\pi\left(t + \frac{1}{30}\right) = 60\pi t + 2\pi \quad \text{and} \quad e^{\pm j2\pi} = 1$$

$\therefore$ $g(t)$ is periodic with period $T_0 = \frac{1}{30}$ **Ans.**

(*d*) $g(t) = 10 \sin(12\pi t) + 4 \cos(18\pi t)$ (given signal)

$$T_{01} = \frac{1}{6}, \quad T_{02} = \frac{1}{9}$$ (T_{01} and T_{02} are determined as in part (*a*))

LCM of $\frac{1}{6}, \frac{1}{9}$ *i.e.*, of $\frac{3}{18}$ and $\frac{2}{18}$ which is $\frac{6}{18} = \frac{1}{3}$

$g(t)$ is periodic with period $T_0 = \frac{1}{3}$ **Ans.**

(Check by changing t to $\left(t + \frac{1}{3}\right)$ in the given signal, we get back $g(t)$)

(*e*) $g(t) = 10 \sin(12\pi t) + 4 \cos(8t)$ (given signal)

$$T_{01} = \frac{1}{6}, \quad T_{02} = \frac{\pi}{4}$$

$\therefore$ $T_{01}/T_{02} = \frac{1}{6} \Big/ \frac{\pi}{4} = \frac{2}{3\pi}$, an irrational value $\therefore$ $g(t)$ is not periodic.

EXAMPLE 1.2: *Let $x(t) = e^{j\omega_0 t}$ and $x[n] = x(nT_S) = e^{j\omega_0 nT_s}$. Find the condition on value of T_S, so that $x[n]$ is periodic.*

SOLUTION: Let $x[n]$ be periodic with fundamental period N_0

i.e., $x[n + N_0] = x[n]$

i.e., $e^{j\omega_0 (n+N_0)T_S} = e^{j\omega_0 nT_S}$

$$e^{j\omega_0 nT_S} \cdot e^{j\omega_0 N_0 T_S} = e^{j\omega_0 nT_S}$$

$\therefore$ $e^{j\omega_0 N_0 T_S} = 1$

or $\omega_0 N_0 T_S = m \cdot 2\pi$ (a multiple of 2π)

$\therefore$ $(2\pi f_0) N_0 T_S = m \cdot 2\pi$ (cancel 2π both sides)

$\therefore$ $\frac{1}{T_0} N_0 T_S = m$ $\left(\because f_0 = \frac{1}{T_0}\right)$

$\therefore$ $\boxed{\frac{T_S}{T_0} = \frac{m}{N_0} = \text{rational number}}$ (because, m and N_0 are both integers)

Thus, $x[n]$ is periodic with period N_0, if $\frac{T_s}{T_0}$ or $\frac{\text{Sampling interval}}{\text{Fundamental period}}$ is a rational number. Note that the above condition is also true for sinusoidal signal $x(t) = \cos(\omega_0 t + \theta)$.

EXAMPLE 1.3: *If $x_1(t)$ and $x_2(t)$ are periodic signals with fundamental periods T_1 and T_2, respectively, under what conditions $x(t) = x_1(t) + x_2(t)$ is periodic. What is the fundamental period of $x(t)$?*

SOLUTION: Given $x_1(t + T_1) = x_1(t)$, periodic with fundamental period T_1

and $x_2(t + T_2) = x_2(t)$, periodic with fundamental period T_2

Also, $x_1(t) = x_1(t + mT_1)$, m an integer

and $x_2(t) = x_2(t + kT_2)$, k an integer

$\therefore$ $x(t) = x_1(t) + x_2(t)$

i.e., $x(t) = x_1(t + mT_1) + x_2(t + kT_2)$ ...(*A*)

Let $x(t)$ has a fundamental period of T

Then $\quad x(t+T) = x_1(t+T) + x_2(t+T) \quad \text{...(B)}$

Comparing (*A*) and (*B*), we must have

$$T = mT_1 = kT_2$$

$$\boxed{\frac{T_1}{T_2} = \frac{k}{m} = \text{rational number}} \qquad \therefore \; k \text{ and } m \text{ are integers.}$$

The fundamental period T of sum of two periodic signals $x_1(t)$ and $x_2(t)$ is LCM of T_1 and T_2, if T_1/T_2 is rational. If $\frac{T_1}{T_2}$ is an irrational number then $x(t) = x_1(t) + x_2(t)$ cannot be periodic. This is so, because, we cannot find the LCM of T_1 and T_2 if T_1/T_2 is an irrational number.

EXAMPLE 1.4: *Consider the sinusoidal signal $x(t) = \cos 15t$*

(a) Find the value of sampling interval T_S such that $x[n] = x(nT_S)$ is periodic sequence.

(b) Find the fundamental period of $x[n] = x(nT_S)$ if $T_s = 0.1\,\pi$ second.

SOLUTION: Since, $x(t) = \cos 15t$, replace t by nT_S, and get $x[n]$

(*a*) As $\quad x[n] = x(nT_S)$

$$\therefore \quad x[n] = \cos(15\,nT_S)$$

Let N_0 be the period of $x[n]$. Then we have

$$x[n+N_0] = x[n]$$

$$\therefore \quad \cos(15(n+N_0)T_S) = \cos(15nT_S)$$

or $\quad \cos[15nT_S + 15N_0T_S] = \cos(15nT_S)$

$$\therefore \quad 15\,N_0\,T_S = 2\pi\,m, \quad m \text{ an integer}$$

or $\quad T_S = \dfrac{n}{N_0}\dfrac{2\pi}{15}$ **Ans.** $\qquad$ *i.e.*, $N_0 = \left(\dfrac{2\pi}{15\,T_S}\right)$ multiple

(*b*) If $\;T_0 = 0.1\pi$, then from above result

$$0.1\pi = \frac{m}{N_0}\frac{2\pi}{15}, \quad m \text{ and } N_0 \text{ integers}$$

$$\therefore \quad \frac{N_0}{m} = \frac{2}{15}\times\frac{1}{0.1} = \frac{4}{3}$$

$$N_0 = \frac{4}{3}\,m, \quad m \text{ an integer}$$

as N_0 must be an integer, hence, the smallest value of $m = 3$.

Then $N_0 = 4$ **Ans.** $\qquad$ *i.e.*, fundamental period of $\cos(1.5\pi\,n)$ is $N_0 = 4$

EXAMPLE 1.5: *Test whether discrete signals given in (a), (b), (c) and (d) are periodic or not. If periodic, find their periods.* *(IP Univ. 2007, 2008)*

SOLUTION:

(*a*) $\quad x[n] = e^{j(\pi/4)n}$ (given signal)

$$x[n] = e^{j\omega_0 n} \quad \text{where } \omega_0 = \frac{\pi}{4}$$

$$N_0 = \frac{2\pi}{\omega_0} = \frac{2\pi}{\pi/4} = 8 \quad \therefore \; x[n] \text{ is periodic with } N_0 = 8 \quad \textbf{Ans.}$$

(*b*) $x_1[n] = \cos\left(\frac{1}{4}n\right);\ x_2(n) = \sin\left(\frac{1}{4}n\right)$ (given signals)

As $x_1[n] = \cos\omega_0 n$ where $\omega_0 = \frac{1}{4}$

$$\text{"}N_0\text{"} = \frac{2\pi}{\omega_0} = \frac{2\pi}{1/4} = 8\pi \text{ an irrational number}$$

$\therefore$ $x_1[n]$ is non-periodic. Similarly, $x_2(n) = \sin\left(\frac{n}{4}\right)$ is not periodic. **Ans.**

(*c*) $x[n] = \cos\frac{\pi}{3}n + \sin\frac{\pi}{4}n$ (given signal)

Let $x[n] = \cos\omega_{01}n + \sin\omega_{02}n$

where $\omega_{01} = \frac{\pi}{3}$ and $\omega_{02} = \frac{\pi}{4}$

$$N_{01} = \frac{2\pi}{\omega_{01}} = \frac{2\pi}{\pi/3} = 6 \text{ and } N_{02} = \frac{2\pi}{\omega_{02}} = \frac{2\pi}{\pi/4} = 8;\ \frac{N_{01}}{N_{02}} = \frac{6}{8} \text{ (rational)}$$

LCM of N_{01} and N_{02} *i.e.*, of 6 and 8 is 24.

$\therefore$ $x[n]$ is periodic with $N_0 = 24$. **Ans.**

(*d*) $x[n] = \cos^2\frac{\pi}{8}n$ (given signal)

As
$$x[n] = \frac{1}{2}\left(1 + \cos\frac{\pi}{4}n\right)$$
$$= \frac{1}{2}\left((1)^n + \cos\frac{\pi}{4}n\right)$$

Period $N_{01} = 1$ period $N_{02} = \frac{2\pi}{\pi/4} = 8$

LCM of 1 and 8 is 8

$x[n]$ is periodic with period $N_0 = 8$ **Ans.**

EXAMPLE 1.6: *Let x[n] be a discrete-time sequence and let*

$$y_1[n] = x[2n];\quad \text{and } y_2[n] = \begin{cases} x[n/2], & n \text{ even} \\ 0, & n \text{ odd} \end{cases}$$

Determine whether the following statements are true or false. Give reasons

(*i*) *If $x[n]$ is periodic, then $y_1[n]$ is also periodic*

(*ii*) *If $y_1[n]$ is periodic, then $x[n]$ is periodic*

(*iii*) *If $y_2[n]$ is periodic, then $x[n]$ is also periodic*

(*iv*) *If $x[n]$ is periodic, then $y_2[n]$ is also periodic.*

SOLUTION:

(*i*) Given $y_1[n] = x[2n]$

Let $x[n] = x[n + N_x]$ (*i.e.* $x[n]$ is periodic with period N_x) (given) ...(*A*)

$\therefore$ $x[2n] = x[2n + N_x]$ replacing n by $2n$ in (*A*)

or
$$y_1[n] = x\left[2\left(n + \frac{N_x}{2}\right)\right] = y_1\left[n + \frac{N_x}{2}\right] \quad ...(B)$$

Also $\quad x(n) = x(n + 2N_x)$, we can add or subtract multiple of period, here, N_x in the argument n

$\therefore \quad x(2n) = x(2n + 2N_x)$

$\therefore \quad y_1(n) = x[2(n + N_x)] = y_1(n + N_x) \quad ...(C)$

Period of $y_1[n]$ is $\frac{N_x}{2}$ if N_x is even (as $N_x/2$ is an integer only if N_x is even), due to (B) and period of $y_1(n)$ is N_x if N_x is odd, due to (C). So, the statement (i) is true.

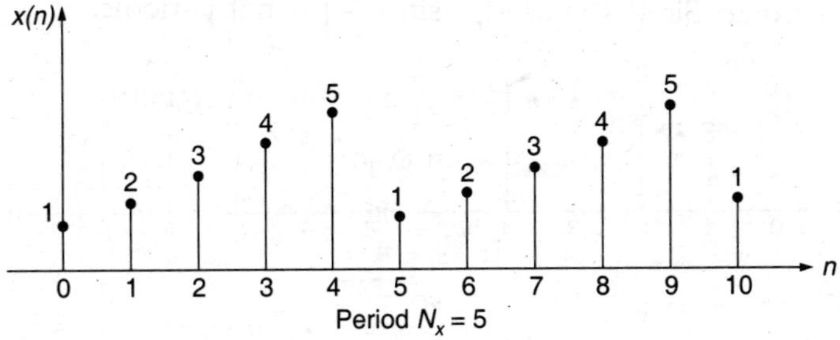

Fig. (a) $x(n)$ periodic with period N_x, N_x odd

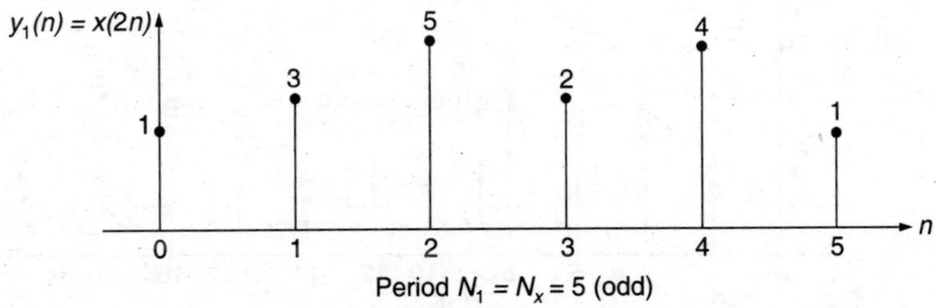

Fig. (b) $y_1(n) = x(2n)$ is periodic in n with period N_x if N_x is odd

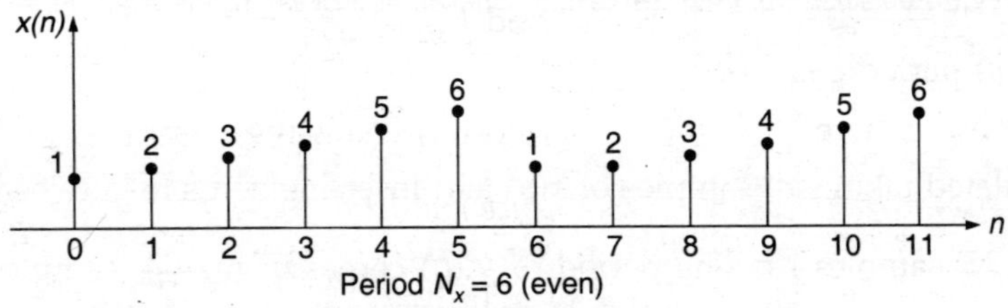

Fig. (c) $x(n)$ periodic with period N_x, N_x even

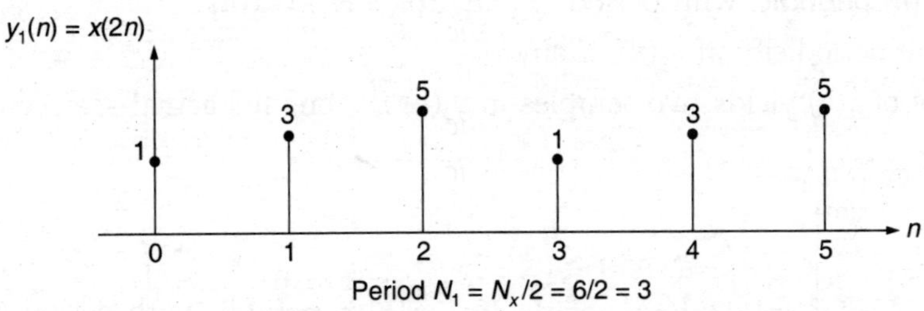

Fig. (d) $y_1(n) = x(2n)$ is periodic in n with period $N_x/2$ if N_x is even

(*ii*) Given $y_1(n) = y_1(n + N_1)$ *i.e.*, $y_1(n)$ is periodic with period N_1 (given).

Then, $x(n)$ is NOT necessarily periodic. When we derive $y_1(n)$, we ignore samples of $x(n)$ when n is odd. $x(n)\mid_{n \text{ odd}}$ may take any arbitrary value. (see samples of $x(n)$ at $n = 1, 3, 5, 7$, in *Fig. (a) and (c)...*). Only $x(n)\mid_{n \text{ even}}$ (which contribute to $y_1(n)$) can be a periodic sequence as shown in $y_1(n)$ here (see Fig. (*f*)). Thus, $y_1(n)$ may be periodic, but $x(n)$ may not be periodic. **Ans.**

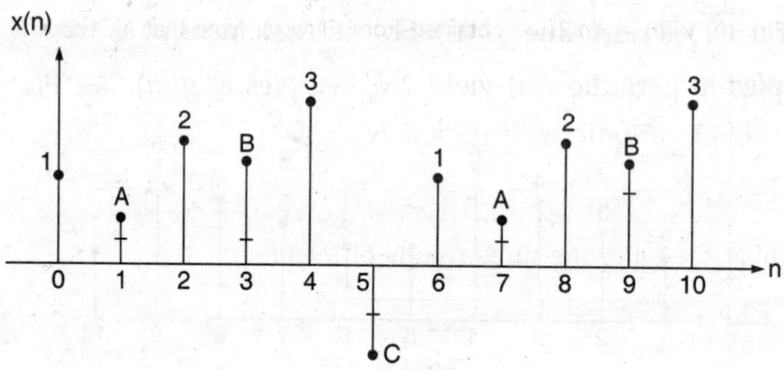

Fig. (*e*) $x(n)$ from where we obtain $x(n/2)$ *i.e.* $y_1(n) = x(n/2)$ and samples at $n = 1, 3, 5, ...,$ are ignored to obtain $y_1(n)$

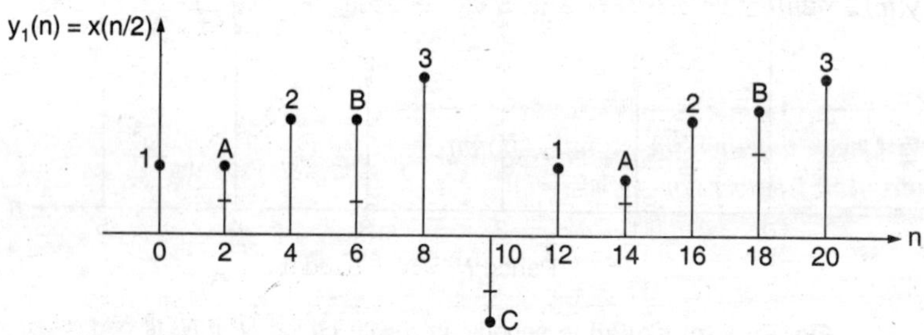

Fig. (*f*) $y_1(n)$ obtained from Fig. (*e*) taking samples of $x(n)$ when n is even. $N_1 = 2$ here

(*iii*) Given $y_2(n)$ periodic *i.e.*

$y_2(n) = y_2(n + N_2)$, where N_2 is $y_2(n)$'s period (N_2 is always even)

$y_2(n)$ is formulated taking all samples of $x(n)$ and inserting zeros in between samples for odd n for $y_2(n)$. Thus, N_2 samples *i.e.*, one period of $y_2(n)$ comes from $\frac{N_2}{2}$ samples of $x(n)$.

Thus, if $y(n)$ is periodic with period N_2, then $x(n)$ is ALSO periodic with period $N_2/2$. **Ans.**

(*iv*) Given $x(n)$ periodic, with period N_x. *i.e.*, $x(n + N_x) = x(n)$

To determine periodicity of $y_2(n)$, if any

Each sample of $x(n)$ yields two samples in $y_2(n)$ *i.e.*, one the actual sample of $x(n)$ followed by a zero.

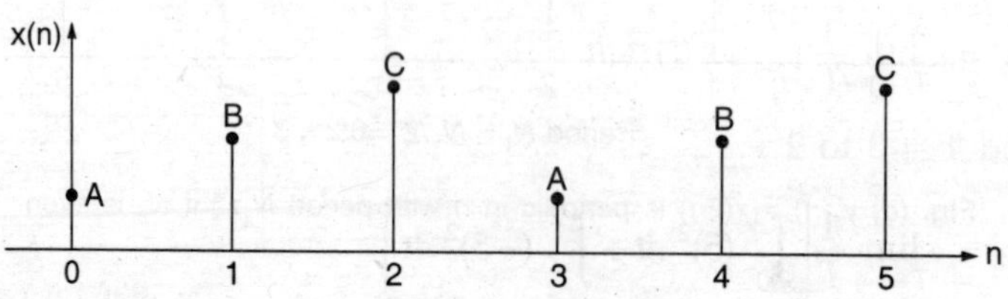

Fig. (*g*) The sequence $x(n)$, from where we obtained $y_2(n) = x(n/2)$, $N_x = 3$ here

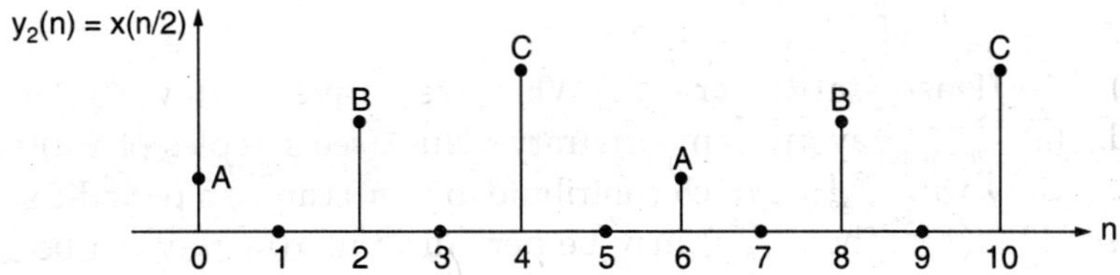

Fig. (*h*) $y_2(n) = x(n/2)$ as obtained from Fig. (*g*). Note that $N_2 = 2 \times N_x = 6$

Thus, N_x samples in periodic $x(n)$ yield $2N_x$ samples in $y_2(n)$. See Fig. (*h*)

Thus, $y_2(n)$ is ALSO periodic with period $N_2 = 2N_x$ **Ans.**

Note Important

It is useful to remember the following three results of integration

$$\int_0^{2\pi} \sin m\theta \cdot \cos n\theta \, d\theta = 0$$

$$\left.\begin{matrix} \dfrac{1}{2\pi}\displaystyle\int_0^{2\pi} \sin m\theta \cdot \sin n\theta \, d\theta \\ \dfrac{1}{2\pi}\displaystyle\int_0^{2\pi} \cos m\theta \cdot \cos n\theta \, d\theta \end{matrix}\right] = \left\{\frac{1}{2}\delta(m-n)\right. \quad \text{...(1.24)}$$

EXAMPLE 1.7: *Check whether the signals shown in Fig. (a), (b) are energy signals or power signals. Calculate the energy and power for each signal.*

SOLUTION: (*a*)

$$E_\infty = \lim_{T\to\infty} \int_{-T}^{T} |x(t)|^2 \, dt$$

$$= \lim_{T\to\infty} \int_{-1}^{1} (5)^2 \, dt = 25\Big[t\Big]_{-1}^{1} = 50$$

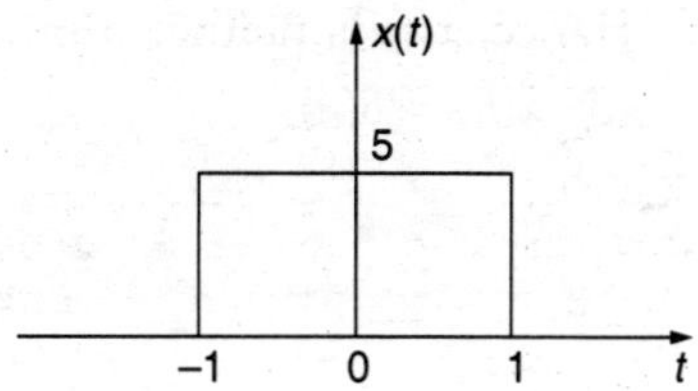

Fig. (*a*) The given signal

$x(t)$ given in Fig. (*a*) is an **energy signal**

Here $P_\infty = 0$ **Ans.** $\left(\because\ P_\infty = \lim_{T\to\infty} \dfrac{E_\infty}{T} = \lim_{T\to\infty} \dfrac{50}{T} = 0\right)$

(*b*) Since, the signal $x(t)$ exists for infinite time, its energy $E_\infty = \infty$

$$P_\infty = \lim_{T\to\infty} \frac{1}{2T} \int_{-T}^{T} |x(t)|^2 \, dt$$

We have $x(t) = \begin{cases} +5, 0 < t < 1 \\ -5, 1 < t < 2 \end{cases}$ for one period

$$\therefore \quad P_\infty = \lim_{T\to\infty} \frac{1}{T} \int_0^T |x(t)|^2 \, dt$$

we take one period $T = 0$ to 2

$$= \lim_{T\to\infty} \frac{1}{T}\left[\int_0^1 (5)^2 \, dt + \int_1^2 (-5)^2 \, dt\right]$$

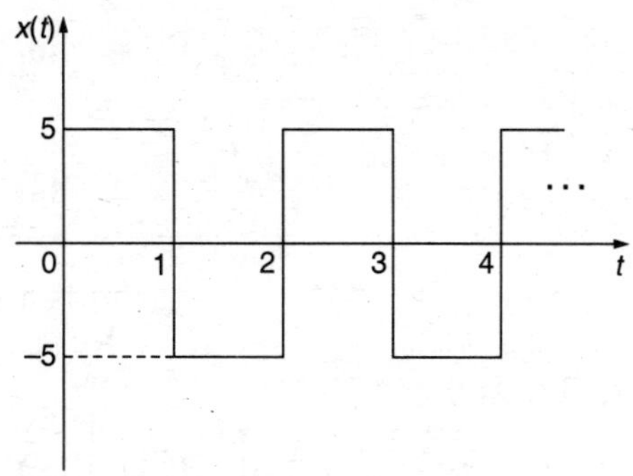

Fig. (*b*) The given signal

$$= \lim_{T\to\infty} \frac{1}{T}\left[25\left(t\right)_0^1 + 25\left(t\right)_1^2\right]$$

$$= \lim_{T\to\infty} \frac{1}{T}[50] \qquad T = 2 \text{ here for one period}$$

$$= \lim_{T\to\infty} \frac{1}{2}(50) = 25 < \infty \text{ (finite)}$$

$\therefore$ $x(t)$ is a **power signal.** **Ans.**

EXAMPLE 1.8: *Check if the following signals are energy signals or power signals.*

(IP Univ. 2007)

(*a*) $x(t) = t^2\, u(t)$, (*b*) $x(n) = \delta(n)$, (*c*) $x(n) = \frac{1}{2} u(n)$, (*d*) $x(n) = e^{\frac{j\pi}{6}n}$

SOLUTION: (*a*) $P_\infty = \lim_{T\to\infty} \frac{1}{T}\int_{-T/2}^{T/2} |x(t)|^2\, dt = \lim_{T\to\infty} \frac{1}{T}\int_0^{T/2} t^4\, dt \qquad (\because\ t^2u(t) = 0 \text{ for } t < 0)$

$$= \lim_{T\to\infty} \frac{1}{T}\left(\left(\frac{T}{2}\right)^5 \Big/ 5\right) = \lim_{T\to\infty} \frac{1}{160}\left(\frac{T^5}{T}\right) = \infty$$

$\therefore$ $P_\infty = \infty$ $\therefore$ not a power signal

As, $E_\infty = \lim_{T\to\infty} \int_{-T/2}^{T/2} |x(t)|^2\, dt = \lim_{T\to\infty} \frac{1}{160}(T^5) = \infty$, $\therefore$ not an energy signal

Hence, $x(t)$ is neither a power signal nor an energy signal. **Ans.**

(*b*) $x(n) = \delta(n)$

$$P_\infty = \lim_{N\to\infty} \frac{1}{2N+1}\sum_{n=-N}^{N} |x(n)|^2 = \lim_{N\to 0} \frac{1}{2N+1}\sum_{n=0}^{N} |\delta(n)|^2 = 0 < \infty$$

$$E_\infty = \lim_{N\to\infty} \sum_{n=-N}^{N} |x(n)|^2 = \lim_{n=0} \sum_{n=0}^{N} |\delta(n)|^2 = 1$$

$\therefore$ $x(n)$ is an energy signal. **Ans.**

(*c*) $x(n) = \left(\frac{1}{2}\right) u(n)$

$$P_\infty = \lim_{N\to\infty} \frac{1}{2N+1}\sum_{n=-N}^{N} |x(n)|^2 = \lim_{N\to\infty} \frac{1}{2N+1}\sum_{n=0}^{N} \frac{1}{4}$$

$$= \lim_{N\to\infty} \frac{1}{4(2N+1)}\sum_{n=0}^{N} 1 = \lim_{N\to\infty} \frac{N+1}{4(2N+1)} = \frac{1}{8} < \infty$$

$\therefore$ $x(n)$ is a power signal (Clearly, E_∞ will be ∞) **Ans.**

(*d*) $x(n) = e^{j\frac{\pi}{6}n}$

$$P_\infty = \lim_{N\to\infty} \frac{1}{2N+1}\sum_{n=-N}^{N} |x(n)|^2 = \lim_{N\to\infty} \frac{1}{2N+1}\sum_{n=-N}^{N} \left|\left[e^{j(\pi/6)n}\right]^2\right|$$

$$= \lim_{N\to\infty} \frac{1}{2N+1} \sum_{n=-N}^{N} 1 = \lim_{N\to\infty} \frac{1}{2N+1}(2N+1) = 1 < \infty$$

$\therefore$ $x(n)$ is a power signal. **Ans.**

EXAMPLE 1.9: *Determine the values of P_∞ and E_∞ for each of the following signals given in (a) to (f).* *(IP Univ. 2006)*

SOLUTION: (*a*) $x_1(t) = e^{-2t}\, u(t)$: $\quad E_\infty = \int_{-\infty}^{\infty} |x_1(t)|^2\, dt = \int_0^{\infty} e^{-4t} dt = \left[\frac{1}{-4} e^{-4t}\right]_0^{\infty} = \frac{1}{4}$

As $E_\infty < \infty$ $\therefore$ $P_\infty = 0$. This is an **energy signal.** **Ans.**

(*b*) $x_2(t) = e^{-j\,(2t + \pi/4)}$: $E_\infty = \int_{-\infty}^{\infty} |(e^{-j(2t+\pi/4)})^2|\, dt = \int_0^{\infty} 1 dt = \infty$

$$P_\infty = \lim_{T\to\infty} \frac{1}{2T} \int_{-T}^{T} |x_2(t)|^2\, dt = \lim_{T\to\infty} \frac{1}{2T} \int_{-T}^{T} 1\cdot dt = 1 \text{ (finite)}$$

$\therefore$ $x_2(t)$ is a **power signal.** **Ans.**

(*c*) $x_3(t) = \cos t$: $E_\infty = \int_{-\infty}^{\infty} (\cos^2 t)\, dt = \int_{-\infty}^{\infty} \frac{1}{2}(1 + \underbrace{\cos 2t}_{\text{gives zero finite value}})\, dt = \infty$ (N.T.S.)

$$E_\infty = \lim_{T\to\infty} \int_0^T \cos^2 t\, dt = \lim_{T\to\infty} \frac{1}{2} \int_0^T (1 + \cos 2t)\, dt = \lim_{T\to\infty} \frac{1}{2}\ [T + \text{finite value}] = \infty$$

$$P_\infty = \lim_{T\to\infty} \frac{1}{2T} \int_{-T}^{T} (\cos^2 t)\, dt = \lim_{T\to\infty} \frac{1}{2T} \int_{-T}^{T} \frac{1}{2}(1 + \cos 2t)\, dt = \frac{1}{2} < \infty$$

$\therefore$ $x_3(t)$ is a **power signal** **Ans.**

(*d*) $x_4(n) = \left(\frac{1}{2}\right)^n u(n)$ $\therefore$ $E_\infty = \sum_{n=0}^{\infty} \left(\frac{1}{2}\right)^{2n} = \sum_{n=0}^{\infty} \left(\frac{1}{4}\right)^{n} = \frac{1}{1-\frac{1}{4}} = \frac{4}{3} < \infty$

$P_\infty = 0$, because, $E_\infty < \infty$. Therefore, $x_4\,(n)$ is an **energy signal. Ans.**

(*e*) $x_5(n) = e^{j(\pi/2n\, +\, \pi/8)}$ $\therefore$ $E_\infty = \sum_{n=-\infty}^{\infty} |x_5(n)|^2 = \sum_{n=\infty}^{\infty} 1 = \infty$

$$P_\infty = \lim_{N\to\infty} \frac{1}{2N+1} \sum_{n=-N}^{N} |x_5(n)|^2 = \lim_{N\to\infty} \frac{1}{2N+1} \sum_{n=-N}^{N} 1 = 1 \text{ (finite)}$$

$\therefore$ $x_5\,(n)$ is a **power signal.** **Ans.**

(*f*) $x_6(n) = \cos\left(\frac{\pi}{4} n\right)$: $E_\infty = \sum_{n=-\infty}^{\infty} |x_6(n)|^2 = \sum_{n=-\infty}^{\infty} \cos^2 \frac{\pi}{4} n = \sum_{n=-\infty}^{\infty} \frac{1}{2}\left(1 + \underbrace{\cos\frac{\pi n}{2}}_{\text{gives finite sum}}\right) = \infty$

$$P_\infty = \lim_{N\to\infty} \frac{1}{2N+1} \sum_{n=-N}^{N} \frac{1}{2}\left(1 + \cos\frac{\pi n}{2}\right) = \frac{1}{2} + \underbrace{\lim_{N\to\infty} \frac{1}{2N+1} \underbrace{\sum_{n=-N}^{N} \frac{1}{2} \cos\frac{\pi n}{2}}_{\text{finite}}}_{=0}$$

$\therefore$ $P_\infty = \frac{1}{2}$, hence $x_6(t)$ is a **power signal. Ans.**

EXAMPLE 1.10: *Determine whether the following signals are energy signals, power signals or neither.*

(*IP Univ. 2006, 2007, 2008*)

(*a*) $x(n) = (-0.5)^n\, u(n)$ (*b*) $x(n) = u(n)$ (*c*) $x(n) = 2e^{j3n}$

(*d*) $x(t) = \sin 2t$ (*e*) $x(t) = \sin(5/2\, t)$ (*f*) $x(t) = e^{-at}u(t)$

SOLUTION: (*a*) $E_\infty = \sum_{n=-\infty}^{\infty} |x(n)|^2 = \sum_{n=0}^{\infty}(-0.5)^{2n} = \sum_{n=0}^{\infty}(0.25)^n = \frac{1}{1-0.25} = \frac{4}{3} < \infty$

$\therefore$ P_∞ would be $< \infty$ $(\because E_\infty < \infty)$

Hence $x(n)$ is an **energy signal.** **Ans.**

(*b*) $x(n) = u(n)$

$$P_\infty = \lim_{N\to\infty} \frac{1}{2N+1} \sum_{n=-N}^{N} |x(n)|^2 = \lim_{N\to\infty} \frac{1}{2N+1} \sum_{n=-N}^{N} |u(n)|^2$$

$$= \lim_{N\to\infty} \frac{1}{2N+1} \sum_{n=0}^{N} 1 = \lim_{N\to\infty} \frac{N+1}{2N+1} = \frac{1}{2} < \infty$$

$\therefore$ $x(n) = u(n)$ is a **power signal.** **Ans.**

(*c*) $x(n) = 2e^{j3n}$

$$P_\infty = \lim_{N\to\infty} \frac{1}{2N+1} \sum_{n=-N}^{N} |x(n)|^2$$

$$= \lim_{N\to\infty} \frac{1}{2N+1} \sum_{n=-N}^{N} 4 = \lim_{N\to\infty} \frac{4(2N+1)}{2N+1} = 4 < \infty$$

$\therefore$ $x(n) = 2e^{j3n}$ is a **power signal.** **Ans.**

(*d*) $x(t) = \sin 2t$

It is periodic in t with period π. Power over one period is

$$P = \frac{1}{4\pi}\int_0^{\pi} (\sin^2 2t)\, dt = \frac{1}{2\pi}\int_0^{\pi} (1 - \cos 4t)\, dt = \frac{1}{2\pi}[t]_0^{\pi} = \frac{1}{2} < \infty$$

$\therefore$ It is a **power signal.** **Ans.**

(*e*) $x(t) = \sin((5/2)t)$

It is a periodic signal with period $T_0 = 4\pi$. Power over one period is

$$P = \frac{1}{4\pi}\int_0^{4\pi} \sin^2(5/2t)\, dt = \frac{1}{8\pi}\int_0^{4\pi} (1 - \cos 5t)\, dt = \frac{1}{8\pi}[t]_0^{4\pi} = \frac{1}{2} < \infty$$

$\therefore$ It is a **power signal.** **Ans.**

(*f*) $x(t) = e^{-at}\, u(t)$

If a is +ve, $E_\infty = \int_0^{\infty} e^{-2at}\, dt = \left[\frac{e^{-2at}}{-2a}\right]_0^{\infty} = \frac{1}{2a} < \infty$ $\therefore$ It is an energy signal as in part (*a*) **Ans.**

If a is –ve, let $a = -b$, with b +ve

$$E_\infty = \int_0^\infty e^{2bt}\,dt = \left[\frac{e^{2bt}}{2b}\right]_0^\infty = \infty \quad \therefore \text{ not an energy signal}$$

$$P_\infty = \lim_{T\to\infty}\frac{1}{2T}\int_0^\infty e^{2bt}\,dt = \frac{1}{4b}\lim_{T\to\infty}(e^{2bT}-1) = \infty \quad \therefore \text{ not a power signal.} \quad \textbf{Ans.}$$

Hence, if a is –ve then $x(t)$ is neither an energy signal nor a power signal.

1.3 BUILDING BLOCKS FOR CONTINUOUS–TIME SIGNALS (BASIC CONTINUOUS—TIME FUNCTIONS)

We shall now define some basic continuous time signals, which play a vital role in formulating and analysing the continuous time signals. Amongst these $\delta(t)$ is the most useful one.

1.3.1 Unit Impulse Function [$\delta(t)$]: Dirac Delta Function

Consider a rectangle with x-axis width $2T$ and y-axis height $1/2T$. Therefore, area of this rectangle is $2T \times \frac{1}{2T} = 1$. Now make the width from $-\frac{T}{2}$ to $\frac{T}{2}$ *i.e.*, T and the height $\frac{1}{T}$. The area is again unity $\left(\text{because } T\times\frac{1}{T}=1\right)$. If we go on narrowing the width and appropriately increasing the height such that the area under the "rectangle" is always unity, a stage comes that the width is, say, $-\varepsilon$ to $+\varepsilon$ where ε tends to zero. This would result a narrowest sharp pulse, called impulse (immediate pulse *i.e.*, time–wise almost zero width, but height tends to infinity). Note that when we integrate such an impulse from $-\varepsilon$ to ε, we must get an area of unity. Note that an impulse can also be derived by taking a triangle (instead of a rectangle) and narrowing the triangle.

Aforementioned curve (width zero seconds and height almost infinite is called unit *impulse function, denoted by* $\delta(t)$. Then we have

$$\int_{-\varepsilon}^{\varepsilon} \delta(t)\,dt = 1 \qquad ...(1.25a)$$

or

$$\int_{-0}^{+0} \delta(t)\,dt = 1 \qquad ...(1.25b)$$

We can also write

$$\delta(t) = \begin{cases} 0, & t \neq 0 \\ \infty, & t = 0 \end{cases} \qquad ...(1.26)$$

The definition (1.25) is more useful, since, area of $\delta(t)$ is an unity and $\delta(t)$ spreads from -0 to $+0$, we can assume that (see Fig. 1.6)

$$\int_a^b \phi(t)\cdot\delta(t)\,dt = \phi(0) \qquad ...(1.27)$$

Equation (1.27) is obviously true, if zero lies in between the range $[a, b]$. More rigorously:

$$\int_a^b \phi(t)\cdot\delta(t)\,dt = \begin{cases} \phi(0), & a<0<b \\ 0, & a,b<0 \text{ or } a,b>0 \end{cases} \qquad ...(1.28)$$

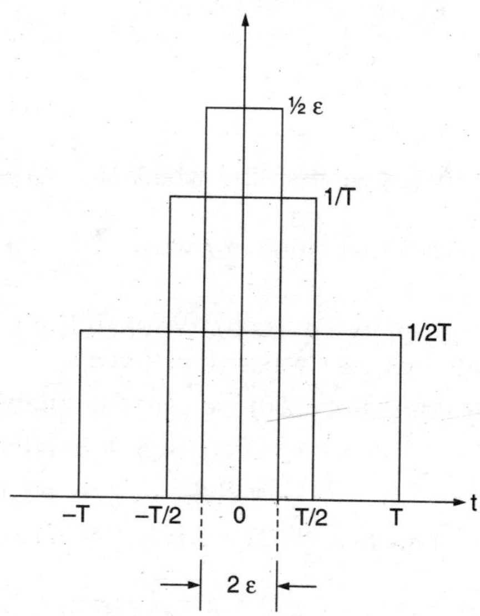

Fig. 1.5 Concept of unit impulse function $\delta(t)$

For $a = b = 0$, above integral cannot be defined.

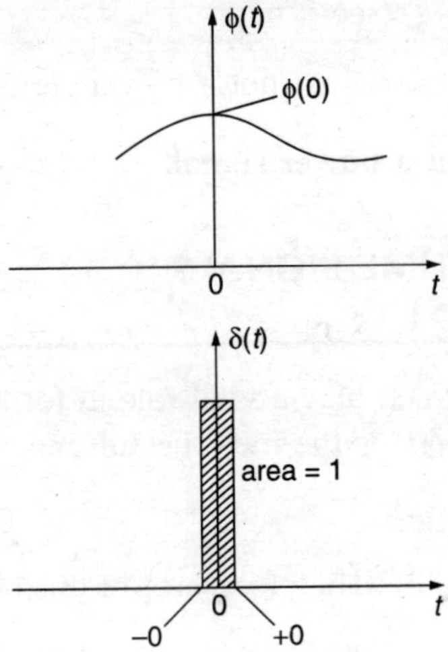

Fig. 1.6. Showing $\int_{-0}^{+0} \phi(t)\,\delta(t) = \phi(0)$

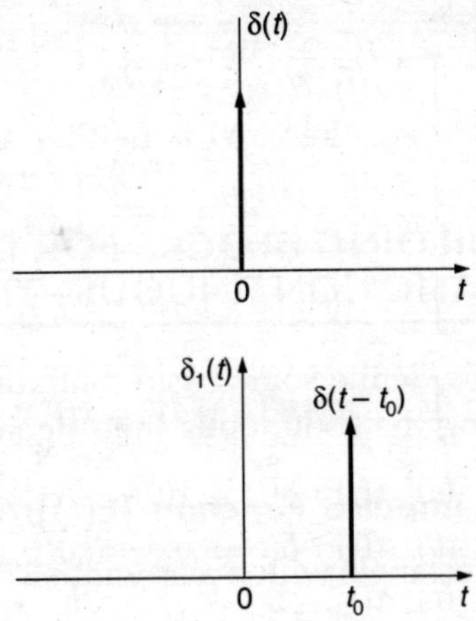

Fig. 1.7. Showing that $\delta(t - t_0)$ is shifted to right side, by t_0, $\delta_1(t) = \delta(t - t_0)$

It may be inferred that $\delta(t)$ has unit area around $t = 0$ (rigorously from $t = -0$ to $t = +0$). Similarly, the function

$$\delta(t - t_0) = \begin{cases} 1, & t = t_0 \\ 0, & \text{otherwise} \end{cases} \qquad ...(1.29)$$

Hence, we can write

$$\boxed{\int_{-\infty}^{\infty} \phi(t) \cdot \delta(t - t_0)\, dt = \phi(t_0)} \qquad ...(1.30)$$

Thus, in short, the value of $\int_{-\infty}^{\infty} \phi(t) \cdot \delta(t - t_0)\, dt$ assumes that value of $\phi(t)$, where $\delta(t - t_0)$ is unity *i.e.*, we first find where $\delta(t - t_0)$ is unity (which is at $t = t_0$ here), and then replace argument t in $\phi(t)$ that value of t where $\delta(t - t_0)$ is unity. It is at $t = t_0$ in this case, hence $\phi(t)\Big|_{t = t_0}$ is $\phi(t_0)$, as given by Eq. (1.30). We shall learn, as we progress, that $\delta(t - t_0)$ implies shifting $\delta(t)$ to right side by t_0, on x-axis (time axis).

By using Eq. (1.30) we can also infer that

$$\phi(t) \times \delta(t) = \phi(0) \qquad (\because \delta(t) = 1 \text{ at } t = 0) \qquad ...(1.31)$$

$$\phi(t)\,\delta(t - t_0) = \phi(t_0) = \phi(t_0)\,\delta(t - t_0) \qquad ...(1.32)$$

Equation (1.32) holds if $\phi(t)$ is continuous at $t = t_0$, otherwise $\phi(t_0)$ is meaningless.

Table 1.1 Summary of Some Important Properties of $\delta(t)$

1.	$\int_{-\infty}^{\infty} \delta(t)\, dt = 1$ (By definition of $d(t)$,	(see 1.25)
2.	$\int_{-\infty}^{\infty} x(t) \cdot \delta(t)\, dt = x(0)$	(see 1.27)
3.	$\int_{a}^{b} x(t) \cdot \delta(t)\, dt = \begin{cases} x(0), & a < 0 < b \\ 0, & a, b < 0 \text{ or } a, b > 0 \end{cases}$	(see 1.28)
4.	$\int_{-\infty}^{\infty} x(t) \cdot \delta(t - t_0)\, dt = x(t_0)$	(see 1.30)
5.	$\int_{-\infty}^{\infty} x(\tau)\, \delta(t - \tau)\, d\tau = x(t) * \delta(t) = x(t)$	(Convolution Property)
6.	(*a*) $x(t) \cdot \delta(t) = x(0)$ (*b*) $x(t) \cdot \delta(t - t_0) = x(t_0)$ (*c*) $x(t_0) \cdot \delta(t - t_0) = x(t_0)$	(see 1.31) (see 1.32) (see 1.32)
7.	$\delta(at) = \frac{1}{\lvert a \rvert} \delta(t)$, a is a constant, +ve or – ve	(see 1.37)
8.	$\int_{t_1}^{t_2} x(t)\, \delta^{(n)}(t - t_0)\, dt = (-1)^n x^{(n)}(t_0)$, for $t_1 < t_0 < t_2$, where suffix (n) means n^{th} derivative.	(see 1.40)

We shall prove the property 7 after defining the Equivalence Property as follows.

1.3.2 Equivalence Property

Two functions $f_1(t)$ and $f_2(t)$ are equal *i.e.*, $f_1(t) = f_2(t)$ if and only if

$$\int_{-\infty}^{\infty} \phi(t)\, f_1(t)\, dt = \int_{-\infty}^{\infty} \phi(t)\, f_2(t)\, dt \qquad ...(1.33)$$

for suitably defined function $\phi(t)$ and $\tau(t)$ not being zero.

1.3.3 To show that $\delta(at) = \frac{1}{|a|} \delta(t)$ (Property 7 of Table 1.1)

Case 1. Let a be positive

$$\text{Let} \quad \int_{-\infty}^{\infty} \phi(t) \cdot \delta(at)\, dt = F(t) \qquad ...(1.34)$$

Putting $at = \tau$ and, therefore, $dt = \frac{1}{a}\, d\tau$ in (1.34), we get

$$F(t) = \int_{-\infty}^{\infty} \phi\left(\frac{\tau}{a}\right) \cdot \delta(\tau) \cdot \frac{1}{a}\, d\tau$$

$$= \frac{1}{a} \int_{-\infty}^{\infty} \phi\left(\frac{\tau}{a}\right) \delta(\tau)\, d\tau$$

$$= \frac{1}{a}\, \phi(0) \qquad \text{(due to property 2 of Table 1.1)}$$

$$= \frac{1}{|a|}\, \phi(0) \qquad ...(1.35)$$

Case 2. Now let a be negative

Let $a = -b$ where b is +ve

$$\therefore \quad F(t) = \int_{-\infty}^{\infty} \phi(t) \cdot \delta(at)\, dt$$

$$= \int_{-\infty}^{\infty} \phi(t)\, \delta(-bt)\, dt \qquad (\because \; a = -b, \text{ assumed above})$$

Put $-bt = \tau \quad \therefore \quad dt = -\dfrac{1}{b}\, d\tau$ and limits of integration gets reversed.

$$\therefore \quad F(t) = \int_{+\infty}^{-\infty} \phi\left(-\frac{\tau}{b}\right) \delta(\tau) \left(\frac{-1}{b}\, d\tau\right)$$

$$= \frac{1}{b} \int_{-\infty}^{\infty} \phi\left(-\frac{\tau}{b}\right) \delta(\tau)\, d\tau$$

$$= \frac{1}{b} \cdot \phi(0) \qquad \text{(due to property 2 of Table 1.1)}$$

$$= \frac{1}{|a|}\, \phi(0) \qquad \left|\; \begin{array}{l} \because \; a = -b, \; (b \text{ –ve}) \\ \therefore \; |a| = b \end{array}\right. \qquad ...(1.36)$$

From (1.35) and (1.36), we infer that

$$\int_{-\infty}^{\infty} \phi(t)\, (\delta(at))\, dt = \frac{1}{|a|}\, \phi(0)$$

$$= \int_{-\infty}^{\infty} \phi(t) \left(\frac{1}{|a|}\, \delta(t)\right) dt \qquad ...(1.37)$$

Using Equivalence Property in Eq. (1.37), we get

$$\boxed{\delta(at) = \frac{1}{|a|}\, \delta(t)} \qquad \text{(Q.E.D.)}$$

(**Note:** Q.E.D. is an abbreviation for Quod Erat Demonstrandum meaning "which was to be proved". This a Latin wording).

1.3.4 To show that $\int_{t_1}^{t_2} x(t)\, \delta^{(n)}(t - t_0)\, dt = (-1)^n\, x^{(n)}(t_0),\; t_1 < t_0 < t_2$

(Property 8 of Table 1.1)

We know that

$$\frac{d}{dt}\left[x(t) \cdot \delta(t - t_0)\right] = x(t) \times \delta^{(1)}(t - t_0) + x^{(1)}(t) \times \delta(t - t_0), \qquad t_1 < t_0 < t_2 \qquad ...(1.38)$$

where suffix implies degree of derivative $\left(\text{i.e., } f^{(n)}(t) = \dfrac{d^n f(t)}{dt^n}\right)$.

Integrate (1.38) on both sides between the time limits $t_1 < t_0 < t_2$. We, therefore, obtain

$$\int_{t_1}^{t_2} \frac{d}{dt}\left[x(t) \cdot \delta(t - t_0)\right] dt = \int_{t_1}^{t_2} x(t)\, \delta^{(1)}(t - t_0)\, dt + \int_{t_1}^{t_2} x^{(1)}(t)\, \delta(t - t_0)\, dt$$

i.e.,

$$\left[x(t) \cdot \delta(t - t_0)\right]_{t_1}^{t_2} = \int_{t_1}^{t_2} x(t) \cdot \delta^{(1)}(t - t_0)\, dt + \int_{t_1}^{t_2} x^{(1)}(t)\, \delta(t - t_0)\, dt \qquad ...(1.39)$$

The L.H.S. term $= x(t_2)\, \delta(t_2 - t_0) - x(t_1)\, \delta(t_1 - t_0)$

As $\delta(t_2 - t_0) = 0$ and $\delta(t_1 - t_0)$ also zero, since, the function $\delta(t)$ is non-zero only when its argument $t = 0$, and here $t_0 \neq t_1$ or $t_0 \neq t_2$, since, $t_1 < t_0 < t_2$ (given condition).

But $(t_2 - t_0)$ and $(t_1 - t_0)$ are not zero arguments, since, $t_1 < t_0 < t_2$, hence $\delta(t_2 - t_0) = \delta(t_1 - t_0) = 0$ makes L.H.S. of (1.39) equal to zero. Hence (1.39) reduces to

$$0 = \int_{t_1}^{t_2} x(t)\,\delta^{(1)}(t - t_0)\,dt + \int_{t_1}^{t_2} x^{(1)}(t)\,\delta(t - t_0)\,dt$$

$$\therefore \quad \int_{t_1}^{t_2} x(t)\,\delta^{(1)}(t - t_0)\,dt = (-1)\int_{t_1}^{t_2} x^{(1)}(t)\cdot\delta(t - t_0)\,dt = (-1)\,x^{(1)}(t_0)$$

(due to property 4 in Table 1.1)

If we repeat *i.e.*, take second derivative of $\delta(t - t_0)$ *i.e.*, use $\delta^{(2)}(t - t_0)$ and try to calculate $\int_{t_1}^{t_2} x(t)\cdot\delta^{(2)}(t - t_0)\,dt$ starting from $\frac{d}{dt}\left[x(t)\,\delta^{(1)}(t - t_0)\right]$, we would obtain

$$\int_{t_1}^{t_2} x(t)\cdot\delta^{(2)}(t - t_0)\,dt = (-1)^2\,x^{(2)}(t_0)$$

and so on. Generalising the aforementioned results, we would get

$$\boxed{\int_{t_1}^{t_2} x(t)\,\delta^{(n)}(t - t_0)\,dt = (-1)^n\,x^{(n)}(t_0),\; t_1 < t_0 < t_2} \quad ...(1.40)$$

which is the property 8 listed in Table 1.1.

1.3.5 Signum Function [sgn(*t*) ; sgn(*n*)]

$$\text{sgn } t \triangleq \begin{cases} 1, & t > 0 \\ -1 & t < 0 \end{cases} \quad \text{(see Fig. } (a))$$

$$\text{sgn } [n] \triangleq \begin{cases} 1, & n > 0 \\ -1 & n < 0 \end{cases} \quad \text{(see Fig. } (b))$$

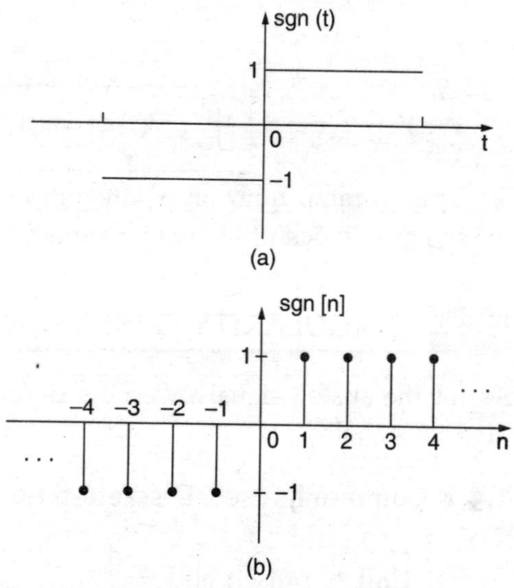

Fig. (*a*) sgn (*t*), (*b*) sgn [*n*].

1.3.6 Unit Step Function (Heaviside Function)

We define unit step function (for analog signals) by

$$u(t) \triangleq \begin{cases} 0, & t < 0 \\ 1, & t \geq 0 \end{cases} \quad ...(1.41)$$

$u(t)$ is also called Heaviside function. $u(t)$ is shown in Fig. (1.8).

Some books define $u(t)$ by

$$u(t) = \begin{cases} 0, & t < 0^- \\ 1/2, & t = 0 \\ 1, & t > 0^+ \end{cases} \quad ...(1.42)$$

The definition (1.42) is not very popular. We shall assume $u(t) = 1$ for $t = 0$ and for $t > 0^+$, as in (1.41).

It is easy to visualise that

$$u(t) = \int_{-\infty}^{t} \delta(t)\,dt \quad ...(1.43)$$

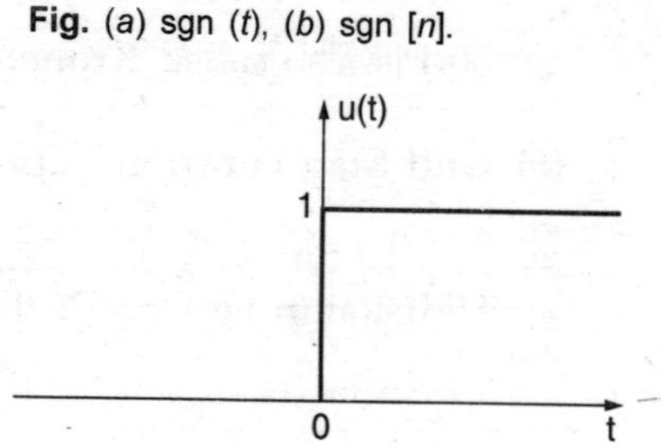

Fig. 1.8. Graph of unit step function *u(t)*.

1.3.7 Unit-Ramp Function : $r(t)$

Unit ramp fanction $r(t)$ is defined by

$$r(t) \triangleq \begin{cases} t, & t \geq 0 \\ 0, & t < 0 \end{cases} \quad \text{...(1.44)}$$

and is shown in Fig. 1.9.

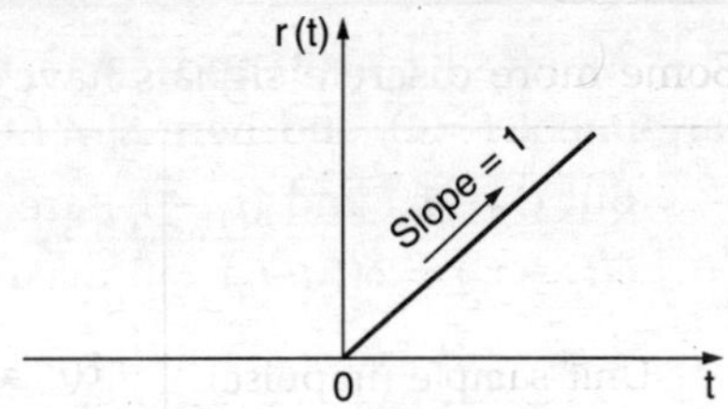

Fig. 1.9. Graph of unit ramp functions $r(t)$.

Note that

$$\int_{0^-}^{0^+} \delta(t)\,dt = 1$$

$$\int_{-\infty}^{0^+} \delta(t)\,dt = 1 \quad \text{...(1.45)}$$

$$\int_{-\infty}^{\alpha} \delta(t)\,dt = 1 \quad \text{from } t = 0 \text{ to } t = \alpha, (\alpha \text{ +ve})$$

$$\int_{-\infty}^{\alpha} \delta(t)\,dt = u(\alpha) \text{ i.e., a unit step function for } 0 \leq t \leq \alpha \quad \text{...(1.46)}$$

$$\therefore \int_{\alpha=-\infty}^{t} \left(\int_{\tau=-\infty}^{\alpha} \delta(\tau)\,d\tau \right) d\alpha = \int_{\alpha=-\infty}^{t} u(\alpha)\,d\alpha = \int_0^t 1 \cdot d\alpha$$

$$= t \text{ for } 0 < t \leq \infty \quad = r(t), t \geq 0 \quad \text{...(1.47)}$$

We may write : $\int_{-\infty}^{t} \delta(\tau)\,d\tau = u(t)$, and $\int_{-\infty}^{t} u(\tau)\,d\tau = r(t), t \geq 0$ {(1.45), (1.46)}

Thus, a ramp function is integration of $u(t)$ and $u(t)$ is the integration of $\delta(t)$. Hence, $\delta(t)$ is the building block of all analog signals.

1.4 SINGULARITY/BASIC FUNCTIONS FOR DISCRETE-TIME SIGNALS

As for the analog signals, we now define some basic sequences which are used in analysis of discrete signals.

1.4.1 Commonly used Discrete-time Basic Signals

(*a*) **Unit Impulse :** $\delta[n] = \begin{cases} 1, & n = 0 \\ 0, & \text{otherwise} \end{cases}$ ...(1.48)

$\delta(n)$ is also called **Kronecker delta**

(*b*) **Unit Step Function :** $u[n] = \begin{cases} 1, & n \geq 0 \\ 0, & n < 0 \end{cases}$ ...(1.49)

(*c*) **Unit Ramp Function :** $r[n] = \begin{cases} n, & n \geq 0 \\ 0, & n < 0 \end{cases}$ ...(1.50)

Some more discrete signals have been shown in Fig. 1.10.

Unit sample (impulse)	$\delta(n) = \begin{cases} 1, & n = 0 \\ 0, & n \neq 0 \end{cases}$	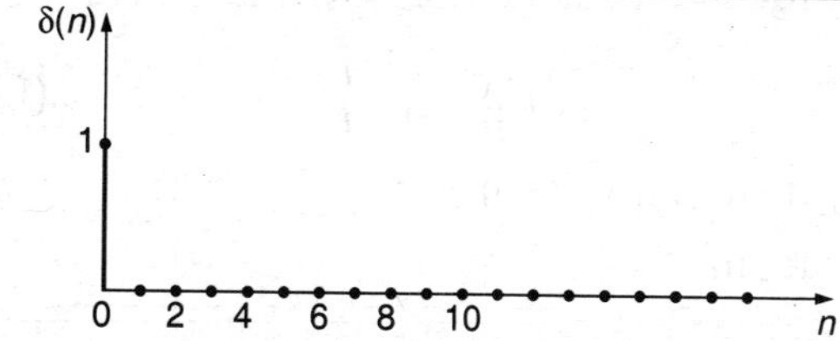
Unit step	$u(n) = \begin{cases} 1, & n \geq 0 \\ 0, & n < 0 \end{cases}$	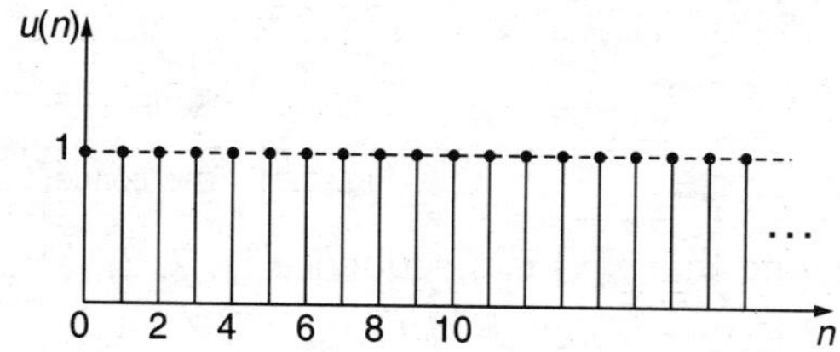
Unit ramp	$r(n) = \begin{cases} n, & n \geq 0 \\ 0, & n < 0 \end{cases}$	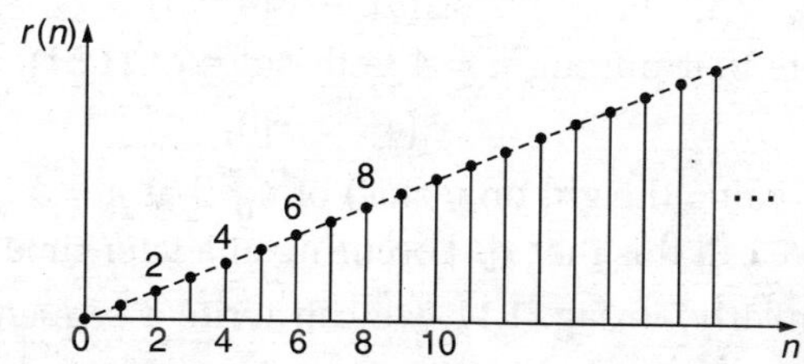
Exponential	$e^{\alpha n}\, u(n)$	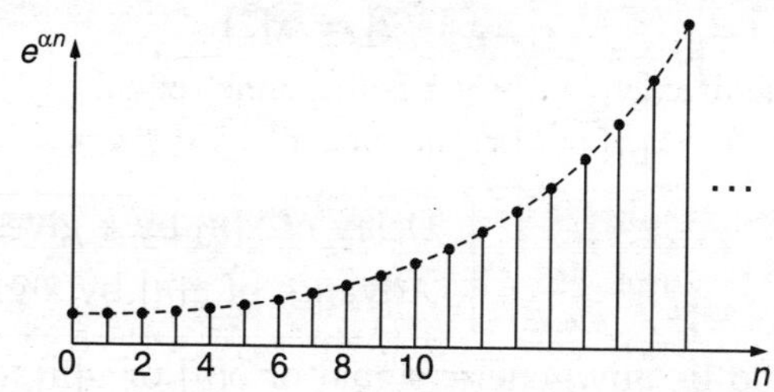
Sinusoid	$\sin n\omega$	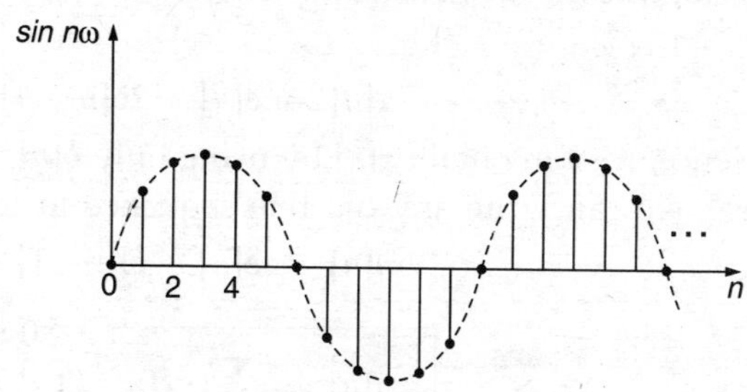

Fig. 1.10. Showing some basic discrete signals with definitions and graphs.

1.4.2 δ(*n*): The Building Block of All Sequences

We first define sequence $x(n-k)$, and derive it from $x(n)$

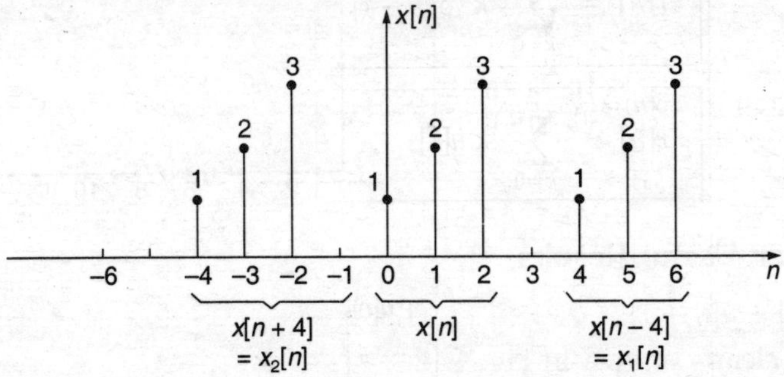

Fig. 1.11. The concept of delay and advance.

Assume that $x[n]$ is a sequence $\{\underset{\uparrow}{1}, 2, 3\}$, as shown in Fig. 1.11 for $n = 0, 1, 2$. If we shift $x[n]$ to right side, say, by 4 on n-axis, then the shifted sequence, denoted by $x_1[n]$ is written as

$$x_1[n] = x[n-4] \qquad \text{...(1.51)}$$

Note that putting $n = 4$ both sides of (1.51), we get

$$x_1[4] = x[0] \qquad \text{...(1.52)}$$

i.e., the value (height on y-axis) of $x_1[n]$ at $n = 4$ is the same as value of $x[n]$ at $n = 0$, which is 1 here. We call this that $x[n]$ occuring at a later time (n-axis) *i.e.*, $x[n]$, has been "delayed" by 4 here.

Similarly, in Fig. 1.11, we can write a sequence $x_2[n]$ by

$$x_2[n] = x[n+4] \qquad \text{...(1.53)}$$

Note that putting $n = -2$ both sides of (1.53), we get

$$x_2[-2] = x[2]$$

i.e., value of $x_2[n]$ at $n = -2$ is the same (equal to 3) as that of $x[n]$ at $n = +2$. This implies that $x_2[n]$ occurs before $x[n]$ or $x[n]$ "advanced" by 4 gives as $x_2[n]$. In general,

Delay of $x[n]$ by k gives a signal $x[n-k]$ Advance of $x[n]$ by k gives a signal $x[n+k]$	...(1.54)

$x[n]$ could be any generic signal or $\delta[n]$ or $u[n]$, or any other sequence.

It may be noted that $x[n]$ as shown in Fig. 1.11 has 3 samples, occuring at $n = 0, 1, 2$. These samples form the sequence $x[n] = \{\underset{\uparrow}{1}, 2, 3\}$ or by the argument of delay given above, it implies that

$$x[n] = \delta[n] + 2\delta[n-1] + 3\delta[n-2] \qquad \text{...(1.55)}$$

Hence, we can obtain $x[n]$ by using only $\delta[n]$, after appropriate delays and scaling factors. In general, we can write any discrete sequence in terms of $\delta[n]$. For example,

$$u[n] = \delta[n] + \delta[n-1] + \delta[n-2] + \ldots$$

$$\therefore \qquad \boxed{u[n] = \sum_{k=0}^{\infty} \delta[n-k]} \qquad \text{...(1.56)}$$

Similarly,

$$\boxed{r[n] = \sum_{k=0}^{\infty} k \cdot \delta[n-k]} \qquad ...(1.57a)$$

or

$$\boxed{r[n] = \sum_{k=0}^{n} k\, u[k]} \qquad ...(1.57b)$$

1.4.3 Some Other Useful Results

(a) $\delta[n] = u[n] - u[n-1]$ ...(1.58)

This has been clearly shown in Fig. 1.12.

(b) $u[n] - u[n-k]$ = a sequence of values 1 from $n = 0$ to $n = k - 1$ ...(1.59)

From example,

$$x[n] = \{1, 1, 1, 1, 1\}$$
$$\uparrow$$
$$= u[n] - u[n-5]$$

(c) Since, $u(t) = \int_{-\infty}^{t} \delta(t)\, dt$

$$\therefore \quad \frac{d}{dt} u(t) = \delta(t) \qquad ...(1.60)$$

(d) Since, $r(t) = \int_{-\infty}^{t} u(t)\, dt$

$$\therefore \quad \frac{d}{dt} r(t) = u(t) \qquad ...(1.61)$$

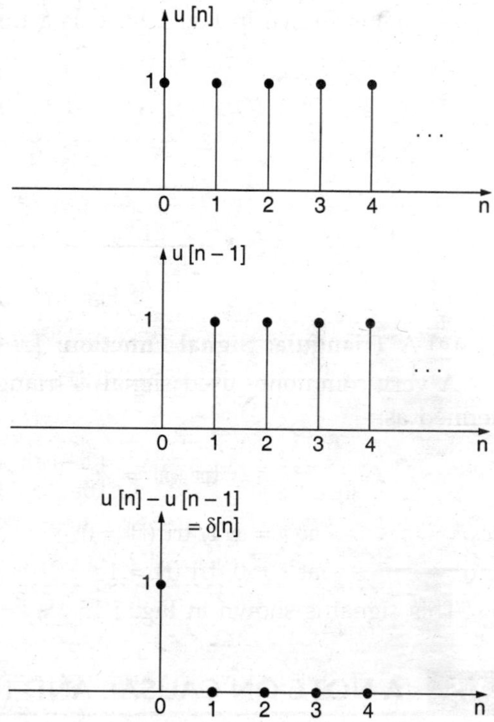

Fig. 1.12. Derivation of $\delta[n]$ from $u[n]$ and $u[n-1]$.

(e) **Unit Doublet :** Think of $\delta(t)$ as shown in Fig. 1.13(a). We have drawn $\delta(t)$ spanning from $-\varepsilon$ to $+\varepsilon$ intentionally to make clear the differentiation of $\delta(t)$. Differentiation of curve *AB* is $+\infty$, and that of curve *CD* is $-\infty$. When $\varepsilon \to 0$, the two derivatives at *AB* and *CD* look like $\delta'(t)$ shown in Fig. 1.13(b). Such a function is called a Doublet.

i.e.,

$$\boxed{\frac{d}{dt}\delta(t) = \delta'(t) \; : \; a \text{ doublet}} \qquad ...(1.62a)$$

$$\int \delta'(t)\, dt = \delta(t) \; : \; a \text{ delta function} \qquad ...(1.62b)$$

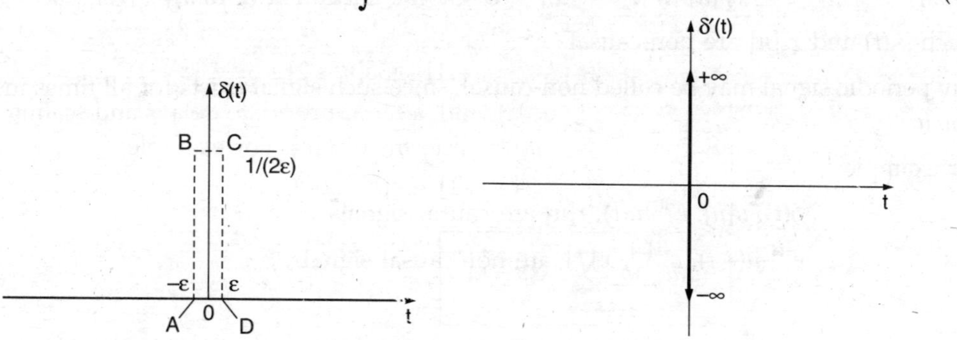

Fig. 1.13. Derivation of a Doublet $\delta'(t)$ from $\delta(t)$. In Fig. (a) when $\varepsilon \to 0$, rectangle becomes $\delta(t)$.

(*f*) **A Gate Function:** $G_{a,b}(t)$

Just as we obtained a sequence, say, from $n = 0$ to $n = k - 1$ by using $u[n] - u[n-k]$ on (1.59), similarly we define a

Gate function $$G_{a,b}(t) = \begin{cases} 1, & a \le t \le b \\ 0, & \text{otherwise} \end{cases} \quad ...(1.63)$$

Clearly, $$\boxed{G_{a,b}(t) = u(t-a) - u(t-b)} \quad ...(1.64)$$

$G_{a,b}(t)$ is shown in Fig. 1.14. It is a time window of width $(b - a)$ in time

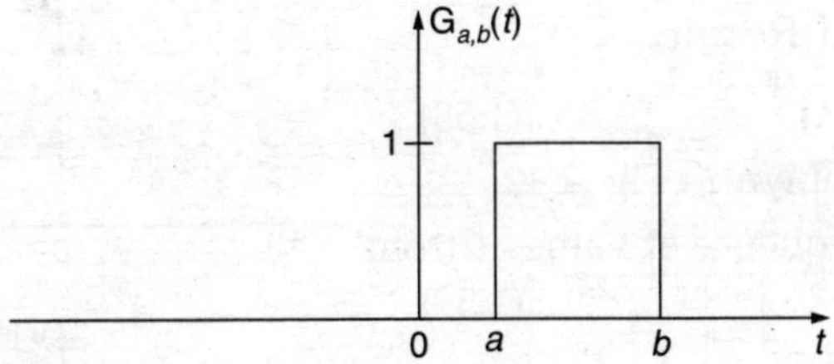

Fig. 1.14. A Gate function $G_{a,b}(t)$.

(*g*) **A Triangular Signal Function:** *Tri* (t)

A very commonly used signal is triangular : tri (t) and defined as:

$$\text{tri}(t) = \begin{cases} 1 - |t| & |t| \le 1 \\ 0, & |t| \ge 1 \end{cases} \quad ...(1.65)$$

i.e., at $t = \pm 1$, tri $(t) = 0$

and at $t = 0$, tri $(t) = 1$

This signal is shown in Fig. 1.15.

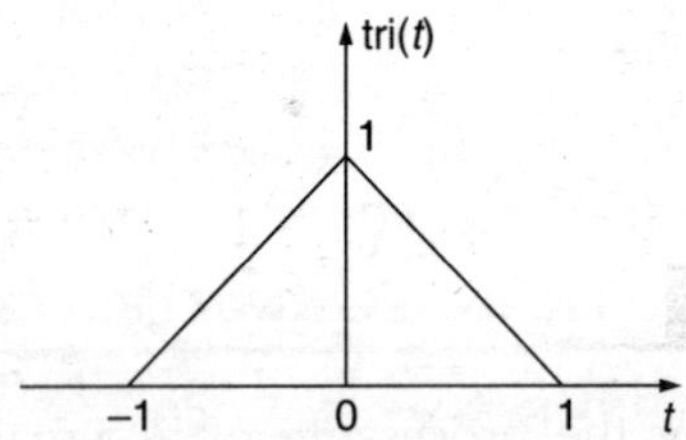

Fig. 1.15. Graph of a triangular signal tri (t).

1.5 A NOTE ON CAUSAL AND NON-CAUSAL SIGNAL

If a signal does not exist for $t < 0$, or for $n < 0$ it is called causal *i.e.*, if

$$x_1(t) = 0 \quad \text{for} \quad t < 0 \quad \text{[See Fig. 1.16(a)]}$$

or $$x_1[n] = 0, \quad \text{for} \quad n < 0 \quad \text{[See Fig. 1.16(c)]} \quad ...(1.66)$$

then such $x_1(t)$ and $x_1[n]$ are causal. If

$$x_2(t) \ne 0 \quad \text{for} \quad t < 0 \quad \text{[See Fig. 1.16(b)]}$$

or $$x_2[n] \ne 0 \quad \text{for} \quad n < 0 \quad \text{[See Fig. 1.16(d)]} \quad ...(1.67)$$

then such $x_2(t)$ and $x_2[n]$ are non-causal.

Any periodic signal may be called non-causal, since such signal exists for all times including –ve t or n.

For example:

$\delta(t)$, $u[n]$, $e^{-at}\,u(t)$, $r[n]$ are causal signals

$e^{-bt}\,u(-t)$, $a^{-a[n]}$, $x\,|t|$ are non-causal signals.

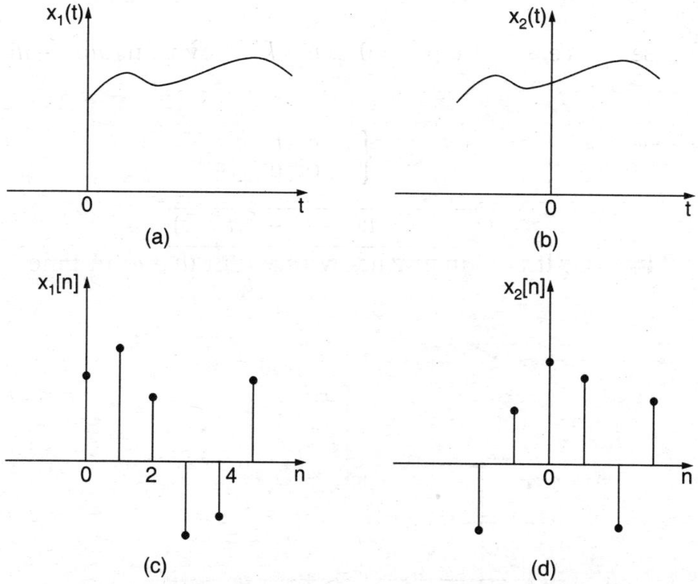

Fig. 1.16. Examples of causal and non-causal signals.
Signals (*a*) and (*c*) are causal. Signals (*b*) and (*d*) are non-causal.

1.6 TRANSFORMATION OF INDEPENDENT VARIABLE

During the processing of a signal $x(t)$ or $x[n]$. We do various manipulations involving the independent variable t or n. The signal's appearance looks changed, although the information which the 'changed' signal gives is the same as given by the original signal. Various manipulations help us for simplifying the signal processing. These, so called manipulations, can be also reversed when so needed. It is easy to study the various transformations of the independent variable t of the analog signals. The same concept will be easily extended for the discrete signals $x[n]$. The most commonly used transformations are:

(*i*) Time-shifting (*ii*) Amplitude scaling
(*iii*) Time-scaling (*iv*) Time-inversion or Time-folding.

1.6.1 Time-Shifting

Consider a signal $x(t)$ as shown in Fig. 1.17(*a*)

Then $x(t)\,|_{t=0} = 1$, *i.e.*, $x(0) = 1$ and

$$x(1) = 1,\ x(2) = 1,\ x(3) = 1/2,\ x(4) = 0.$$

In Fig. 1.17(*b*)

$$x_1(t) = x(t-1) \text{ (i.e., delaying } x(t) \text{ by 1)}$$

Check, putting $t = 0, 1, 2, 3, 4, 5$ in $x_1(t)$

$\therefore$
$$x_1(0) = x(-1) = 0$$
$$x_1(1) = x(0) = 1$$
$$x_1(2) = x(1) = 1$$
$$x_1(3) = x(2) = 1$$
$$x_1(4) = x(3) = 1/2$$
$$x_1(5) = x(4) = 0$$

All the values of $x_1(t)$ match with $x(t-1)$ when argument of $x_1(t)$ is 1 more than the argument of $x(t)$. So, $x_1(t)$ is delayed by 1.

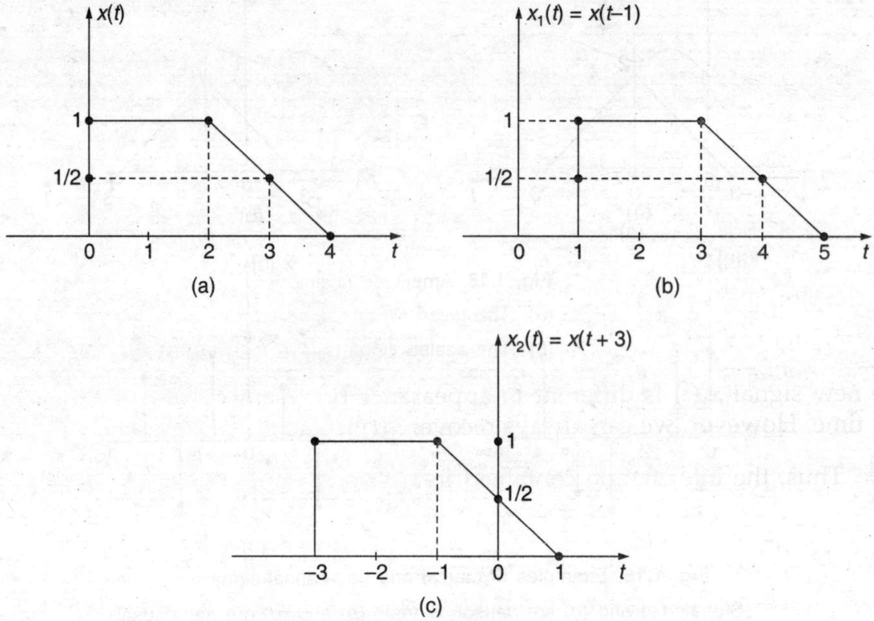

Fig. 1.17. Time shifting of a signal $x(t)$

(*a*) The given signal $x(t)$

(*b*) $x_1(t) = x(t-1)$ *i.e.*, $x(t)$ delayed by 1. We shift $x(t)$ to right on time axis by 1.

(*c*) $x_2(t) = x(t+3)$ *i.e.*, $x(t)$ advanced by 3. We shift $x(t)$ to left on time axis by 3.

In Fig. 1.17 (*c*),

$$x_2(t) = x(t+3) \quad (\text{i.e., advancing } x(t) \text{ by } 3)$$

We call $x(t)$ advanced by 3. Advancement means shifting the given signal $x(t)$ by the advancement needed (it is 3 here) to left on time axis. Check that

$$\begin{aligned} x_2(-3) &= x(-3+3) = x(0) = 1 \\ x_2(-2) &= x(-2+3) = x(1) = 1 \\ x_2(-1) &= x(-1+3) = x(2) = 1 \\ x_2(0) &= x(0+3) = x(3) = 1/2 \\ x_2(1) &= x(1+3) = x(4) = 0 \end{aligned}$$

The values of $x_2(t)$ are the same as those of $x(t)$, when we use the argument t in $x_2(t)$ less than 3 to the corresponding argument of $x(t)$. This is called advancing the signal $x(t)$ by 3. In general, we can write, for t_0 positive:

$$\text{Delay } x(t) \text{ by } t_0 \text{ gives } x(t-t_0) \qquad ...(1.68a)$$
$$\text{Advance } x(t) \text{ by } t_0 \text{ gives } x(t+t_0) \qquad ...(1.68b)$$

Note that the shape of $x(t)$ *does not change* when we delay $x(t)$ or advance $x(t)$. To delay $x(t)$, it is shifted to rightside and to advance $x(t)$ it is shifted to left side.

1.6.2 Amplitude-Scaling

Here, the signal's amplitude gets affected. Scaling $x(t)$ to, say, $kx(t)$ will amplify $x(t)$ to $k \times x(t)$. If $k = -1$ then the signal $kx(t) = -x(t)$ is reversed (negated) along the y-axis.

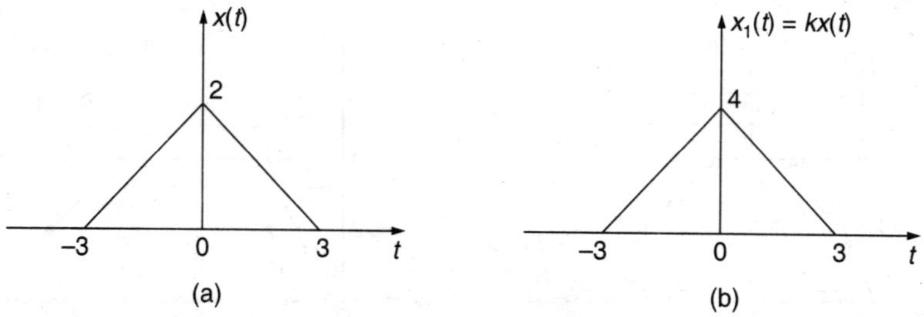

Fig. 1.18. Amplitude scaling.

(*a*) The given signal *x*(*t*).

(*b*) The scaled signal $x_1(t) = kx(t)$ with $k = 2$ here.

Here, the new signal $x_1(t)$ is different in appearance being amplified to k times values at each instant of time. However, we can always recover $x(t)$ from $kx(t)$ *i.e.*, from $x_1(t)$ by inverse scaling $x_1(t)$ by $\frac{1}{k}$. Thus, the information contained in $x(t)$ and $kx(t)$ is the same.

1.6.3 Time Scaling

Figure 1.19 (*a*) shows the given signal $x(t)$, which we wish to time-scale. In Fig. 1.19(*b*), $x_1(t) = x(2t)$ check, putting $t = T_1/2$ on both sides of $x_1(t) = x(2t)$ we get

$$x_1(T_1/2) = x(2 \times T_1/2)$$
$$= x(T_1)$$

Values of $x_1(T_1/2)$ on Fig. 1.19(*b*) (which is zero here) is the same as $x(T_1)$ in Fig. 1.19(*a*) (again equal to zero)

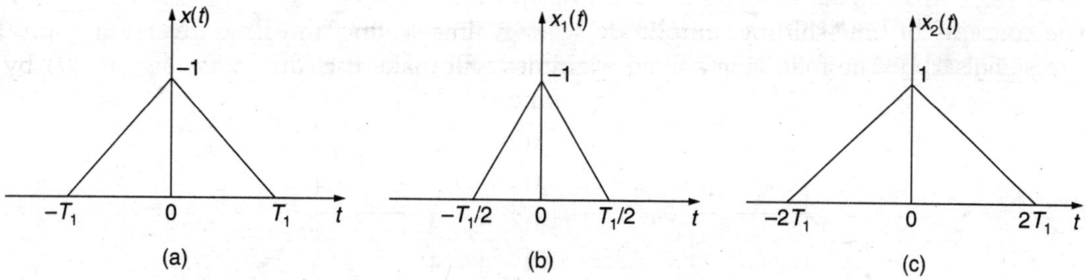

Fig. 1.19. The concept of time scaling:

(*a*) The given signal *x*(*t*)

(*b*) $x_1(t) = x(2t)$ (time scale contracted)

(*c*) $x_2(t) = x(t/2)$ (time scale expanded).

Similarly, Fig. 1.19(*c*) shows

$$x_2(t) = x(t/2)$$

Here time scale of Fig. 1.19(*a*) gets expanded (elongated or dilated) as shown in Fig. 1.19(*c*).

To draw new signal $x(kt)$, given a signal $x(t)$, we divide each point of t-axis for $x(t)$ by k *i.e.*, replace each t in $x(t)$ by t/k. Call the y-axis as $x(kt)$ in lieu of $x(t)$. Thus, we have obtained $x(kt)$ from $x(t)$.

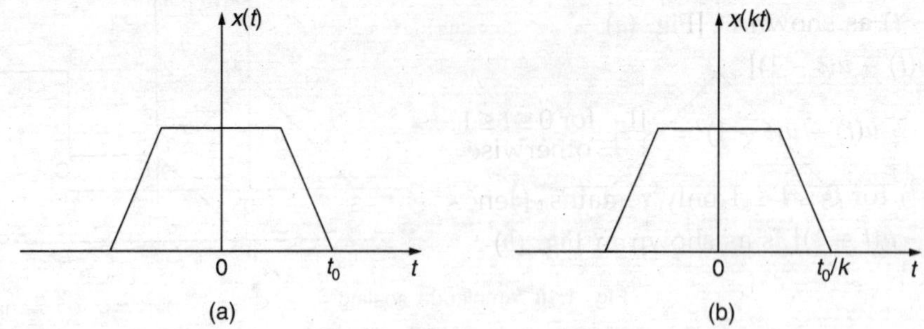

Fig. 1.20. To obtain $x(kt)$ from $x(t)$.

(*a*) Given $x(t)$. (*b*) Call each point of (*a*) as t/k *i.e.*, t_0 is called t_0/k. Write $x(kt)$ on the vertical axis. We have obtained $x(kt)$.

Note that if $k = 3$, say *i.e.*, $k \geq 1$, t_0 on Fig. 1.20(*a*) gets replaced by $t_0/k = t_0/3$. If, say, $k_1 = 1/3$, *i.e.*, $k_1 \leq 1$, then following the same rule, t_0 gets replaced by $t_0/k_1 = 3t_0$.

Also, note that k has been assumed positive. We shall in the next section, see what transformation is needed when k is negative.

1.6.4 Time Inversion/Time Folding

In this case, we derive signal

$$x_1(t) = x(-t).$$

To do so, the signal $x(t)$ is flipped around vertical axis $t = 0$.

In this case, to obtain $x(-t)$, we flip the signal $x(t)$ around y-axis (which is $t = 0$ axis).

Note that $x(-t)$ is a special case of time-scaling $x(kt)$, where $k = -1$ here.

The concepts of time-shifting, amplitude scaling, time-scaling and time inversion apply to discrete signals $x[n]$. The following solved examples will make it clear.

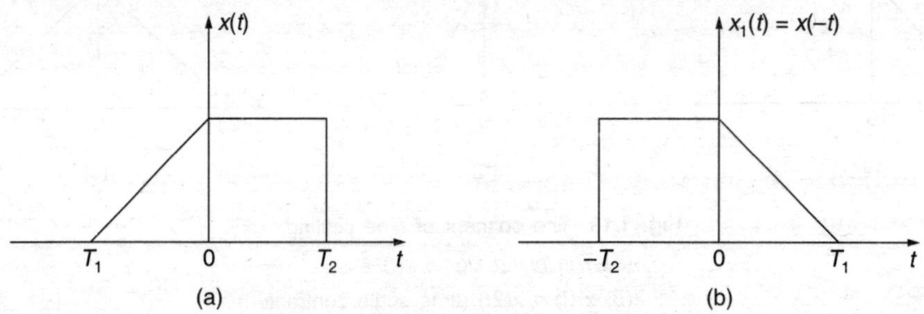

Fig. 1.21. Time Inversion of a signal:
(*a*) The given signal $x(t)$
(*b*) The signal $x_1(t)$ equalling $x(-t)$.

EXAMPLE 1.11: *A continuous time signal $x(t)$ is shown below. Sketch and label (a) $x(t) \cdot u(1-t)$ (b) $x(t)\,[u(t) - u(t-1)]$ (c) $x(t) \cdot \delta\left(t - \frac{3}{2}\right)$.*

SOLUTION: (*a*) $x(t) \,.\, u(1-t)$

Since, $\quad u(1-t) = 1$ for $t < 1$

$\therefore$ Part of $x(t)$ which is for $t < 1$ is $x(t) \times u(1-t)$ as shown in [Fig. (*a*)

(*b*) $x(t)\ [u(t) - u(t-1)]$

As, $$u(t) - u(t-1) = \begin{cases} 1, & \text{for } 0 \le t \le 1 \\ 0, & \text{otherwise} \end{cases}$$

Part of $x(t)$ for $0 \le t \le 1$ only remains. Hence, $x(t)\ [u(t) - u(t-1)]$ is as shown in Fig. (*b*)

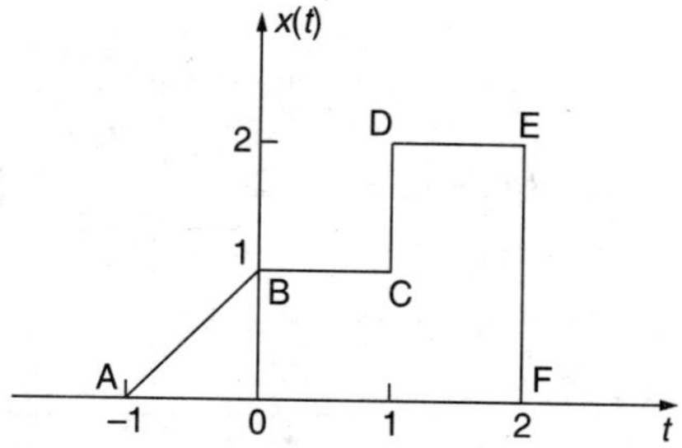

Fig. (*a*) The given signal $x(t)$.

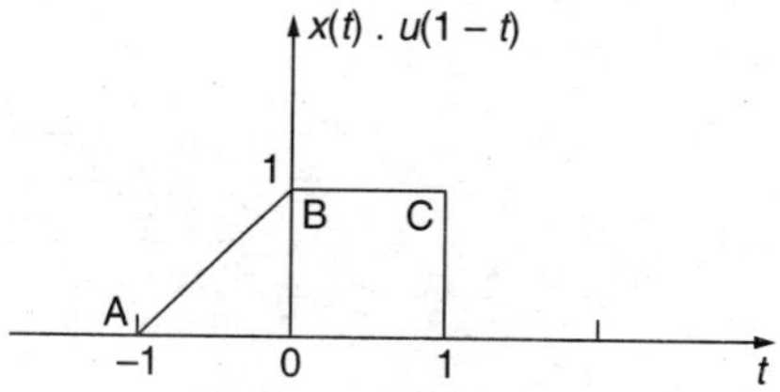

Fig. (*a*) $x(t)\ u(1-t)$

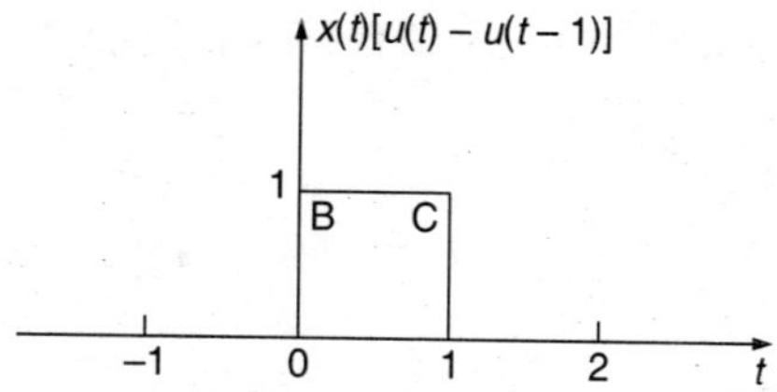

Fig. (*b*) $x(t)\ [u(t) - u(t-1)]$

(*c*) $x(t) \times \delta\left(t - \frac{3}{2}\right)$

As $\delta\left(t - \frac{3}{2}\right) = 1$ around $t = \frac{3^-}{2}$ to $\frac{3^+}{2}$

$\therefore$ Part or sample of $x(t)$ at $\frac{-3}{2}$ to $\frac{3^+}{2}$

i.e., at $t = \frac{3}{2}$ is the signal $x(t) \times \delta\left(t - \frac{3}{2}\right)$ see Fig. (*c*).

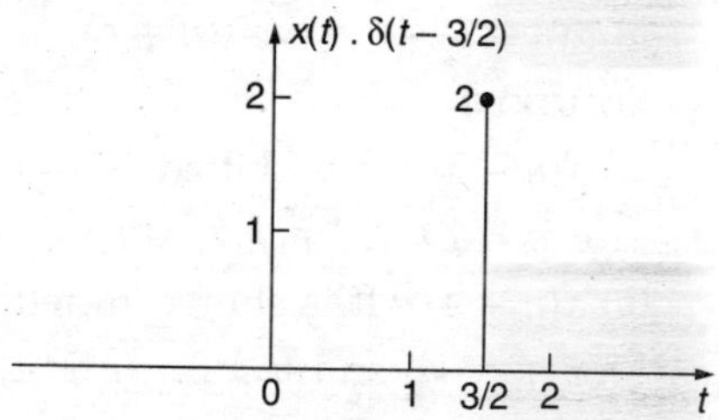

Fig. (*c*) $x(t)\ \delta(t - 3/2)$

EXAMPLE 1.12: *A discrete-time signal x[n] is shown. Sketch and table the signals*

(*a*) $x[n]\ u[1-n]$ (*b*) $x[n]\ \{u[n+2] - u[n]\}$, (*c*) $x(n)\ \delta(n-1)$.

SOLUTION:

(*a*) As $u[1-n] = 1$ for $n = 1, 0, -1, -2, \ldots,$

$\therefore$ $x(n)\ u[1-n]$ has $x(n)$'s samples for $n = 1, 0, -1, -2, \ldots,$

See Fig. (*a*) for $x[n]\ u(1-n)$ sequence.

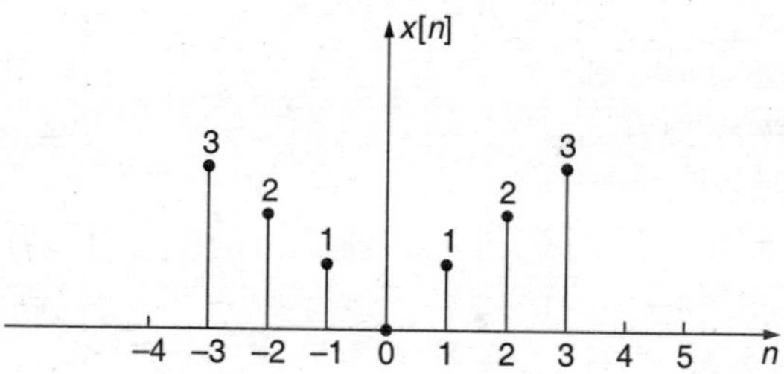

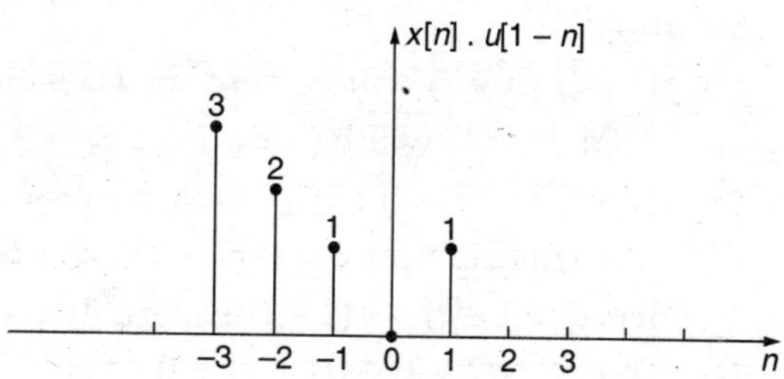

Fig. (a) $x[n] \cdot u[1-n]$

(*b*) $u[n+2]-u[n] = \begin{cases}1, & \text{for } n=-2,-1\\0, & \text{otherwise}\end{cases}$

$\therefore$ Only samples at $n = -1, -2$ appear

or $x[n]\,\{u[n+2]-u[n]\}$ as shown in Fig. (*b*)

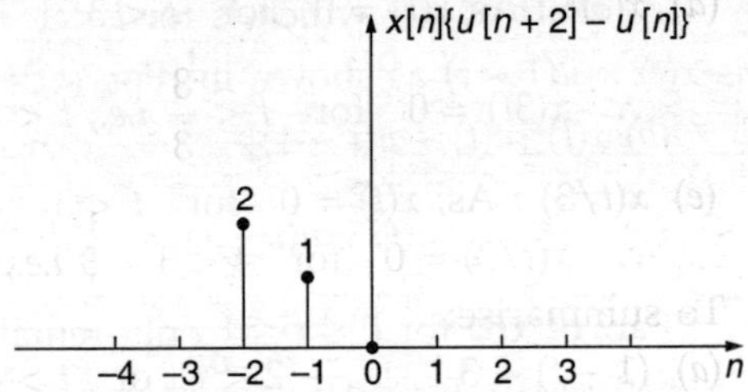

Fig. (*b*) $x(n)\,[u(n+2)-u(n)]$

(*c*) $x(n)\,.\,\delta(n-1)$

As $\delta(n-1) = \begin{cases}1, & n=1\\0, & \text{otherwise}\end{cases}$

So only one sample of $x(n)$ at $n = 1$ appears in $x(n) \times \delta(n-1)$. See Fig. (*c*)

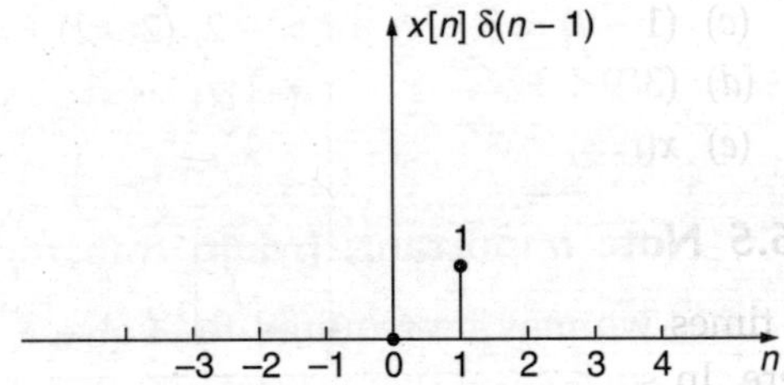

Fig. (*c*) $x(n) \times \delta(n-1)$

EXAMPLE 1.13: *Let $x(n)$ be a signal with $x(n) = 0$ for $n < -2$, and $n > 4$. For each signal given below, (a) to (e), determine the values of n for which it is guaranteed to be zero.*

(*a*) $x(n-3)$, (*b*) $x(n+4)$, (*c*) $x(-n)$, (*d*) $x(-n+2)$, (*e*) $x(-n-2)$

SOLUTION:

(*a*) $x(n-3)$: It is shifted to right by 3, $\therefore$ $n < (-2+3)$ and $n > (4+3)$

i.e., for $n < 1$ or $n > 7$, $x(n-3)$ is guaranteed zero. **Ans.**

(*b*) $x(n+4)$: It is shifted to left by 4 $\therefore$ $n < (-2-4)$ and $n > (4-4)$

i.e., for $n < -6$ and $n > 0$, $x(n+4)$ is guaranteed zero. **Ans.**

(*c*) $x(-n)$: It is $x(n)$ flipped $\therefore$ $n < -2$ yields $-n < -2$ *i.e.*, $n > 2$ and $n > 4$ yields $(-n) > 4$ *i.e.*, $n < -4$.

Hence, for $n > 2$ and $n < -4$, the signal $x(-n)$ is guaranteed zero. **Ans.**

(*d*) $x(-n+2)$: It is $x(-n)$ shifted right by 2 (delayed by 2)

$\therefore$ $n > (2+2)$ and $n < (-4+2)$ *i.e.*, $n > 4$ or $n < -2$ guarantees $x(-n+2)$ to be zero. **Ans.**

(*e*) $x(-n-2)$: It is $x(-n)$ shifted left 2 *i.e.*, advanced.

$\therefore$ $n > (2-2)$ and $n < (-4-2)$ *i.e.* $n > 0$, $n < -6$, guarantees $x(-n-2)$ to be zero. **Ans.**

EXAMPLE 1.14: *Let $x(t)$ be a signal with $x(t) = 0$ for $t < 3$. For each signal given below determine the values of t for which it is guaranteed to be zero.*

SOLUTION:

(*a*) $x(1-t)$: $x(-t)$ will be zero for $t > -3$

$\therefore$ $x(-t+1)$ will be zero for $t > (-3+1)$ *i.e.*, $t > -2$. **Ans.**

(*b*) $x(1-t) + x(2-t)$: $x(1-t)$ is zero for $t > -2$

$x(2-t)$ is zero for $t > (-2+1)$ *i.e.*, $t > -1$

Hence, $x(1-t) + x(2-t)$ is zero guaranteed for $t > -1$. **Ans.**

(*c*) $x(1-t)\,.\,x(2-t)$: $x(1-t) = 0$ for $t > -2$

$x(2-t) = 0$ for $t > -1$

$\therefore$ $x(1-t)\,.\,x(2-t) = 0$ for $t > -2$ **Ans.**

(*d*) $x(3t)$: As $x(t) = 0$ for $t < 3$

$\therefore \quad x(3t) = 0 \quad$ for $\quad t < \frac{3}{3}$ *i.e.*, $t < 1$. **Ans.**

(*e*) $x(t/3)$: As, $x(t) = 0$ for $t < 3$

$\therefore \quad x(t/3) = 0 \quad$ for $\quad t < 3 \times 3$ *i.e.*, $t < 9$. **Ans.**

To summarise:

(*a*) $(1 - t) < 3 \quad \therefore \quad -2 < t$ or $t > -2$ **Ans.**

(*b*) $(1 - t) < 3 \quad \therefore \quad t > -2$; $(2 - t) < 3 \quad \therefore \quad -1 < t$ or $t > -1 \quad \therefore \quad t > -1$ **Ans.**

(*c*) $(1 - t) < 3 \quad \therefore \quad t > -2$, $(2 - t) < 3 \quad \therefore \quad t > -1 \quad \therefore \quad t > -2$ **Ans.**

(*d*) $(3t) < 3 \quad \therefore \quad t < 1$ **Ans.**

(*e*) $x(t/3) < 3 \quad \therefore \quad t < 9$. **Ans.**

1.6.5 Note Important: (Multi transformations)

At times we may be required to evolve a new signal where more than one transformation are there. In such cases, we proceed as explained below.

To find $3x\left(-\frac{1}{2}t+1\right)$ from $x(t)$, for example, we must proceed in a certain sequence. The derivation of $3x\left(-\frac{1}{2}t+1\right)$ requires amplitude scaling (by 3), time scaling $\left(\text{by } \frac{1}{2}\right)$, time-shifting (by + 1) and time inversion (because of –ve sign with t). We proceed in the following sequence:

1. Draw $x(t)$ the given function. (Fig. 1.22*a*)
2. Advance $x(t)$ by 1 to get $x_1(t) = x(t + 1)$. (Fig. 1.22*b*)
3. Scale $x_1(t)$ to get $x_2(t) = x_1(t/2)$. Renumber each t of $x_1(t)$ by doubling each t. (Fig. 1.22*c*)
4. Flip $x_2(t)$ to get $x_3(t) = x_2(-t)$

Also scale appropriately to get $x_3(t) = 3x_2(-t)$. (Fig. 1.22*d*)

Then $x_3(t) = 3x\left(-\frac{1}{2}t+1\right)$

This may be readily checked by calculating values of $x_3(t)$ at various values of t.

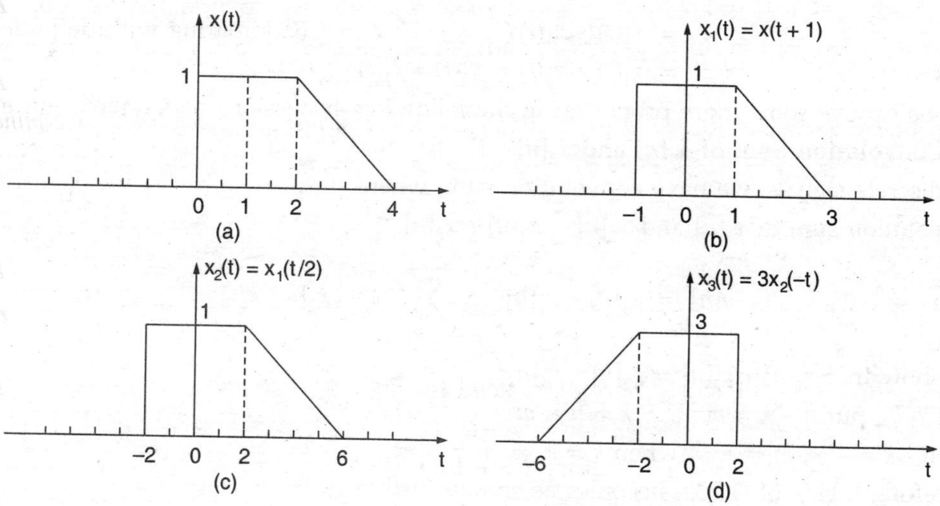

Fig. 1.22. Obtaining $3x\left(-\frac{1}{2}t+1\right)$ at given $x(t)$.

In short, to get $Ax(Bt + C)$ from $x(t)$, we perform the required transformation as necessary due to C, B and A, *in that order*. C requires time-shifting; B requires time-scaling, if B is –ve, first scale by $|B|$ and then do time-inversion; and A requires magnitude scaling. We follow similar procedure to get $Ax[Bn + C]$ from $x[n]$.

1.7 CONVOLUTION INTEGRAL AND CONVOLUTION SUM

As we progress to study the behaviour of a system (Part B of the chapter), we shall, in general, deal with more than two signals say $x_1(t)$, $x_2(t)$ or $x_1[n]$ and $x_2[n]$.

A few operations performed on them are as follows:

(*a*) **Convolution Integral of $x_1(t)$ and $x_2(t)$ is defined**

as
$$y(t) = x_1(t) * x_2(t)$$

$$y(t) = x_1(t) * x_2(t) \triangleq \int_{-\infty}^{\infty} x_1(\tau)\, x_2(t-\tau)\, d\tau \qquad ...(1.69)$$

The sign * used in (1.69) is meant to show that $x_1(t)$ convolved with $x_2(t)$. It can be shown from (1.69) that

$$x_1(t) * x_2(t) = x_2(t) * x_1(t) \qquad ...(1.70)$$

Proof : In (1.69), put $t - \tau = t'$, $\therefore$ $\tau = t - t'$

$\therefore$ $d\tau = -dt'$

when $\tau = +\infty,\ t' = -\infty$

when $\tau = -\infty,\ t' = +\infty$

$\therefore$ (1.69) reduces to

$$y(t) = \int_{t'=+\infty}^{t'=-\infty} x_1(t-t') \cdot x_2(t') \cdot (-dt')$$

$$= \int_{t'=-\infty}^{\infty} x_1(t-t') \cdot x_2(t')\, dt' \qquad \text{(inversion of time limits)}$$

$$= \int_{\tau=-\infty}^{\infty} x_2(\tau) \cdot x_1(t-\tau)\ dt \qquad \text{(Replacing } t' \text{ by } \tau \text{ in above equation)}$$

$$= x_2(t) * x_1(t) \qquad \text{(Comparing with definition 1.69)}$$

Thus, $y(t) = x_1(t) * x_2(t) = x_2(t) * x_1(t)$ Q.E.D.

We shall prove some more properties in the following discussions on Convolution Integral.

(*b*) **Convolution Sum of $x_1[n]$ and $x_2[n]$**

For discrete signals, we have convolution sum, where:

Convolution sum of $x_1[n]$ and $x_2[n] = x_1[n] * x_2[n]$ ...(1.70*a*)

Then
$$y[n] = x_1[n] * x_2[n] \triangleq \sum_{k=-\infty}^{\infty} x_1[k]\, x_2[n-k] \qquad ...(1.70b)$$

[To show that $x_1[n] * x_2[n] = x_2[n] * x_1[n]$

In (1.70*b*), put $n - k = m$ $\therefore$ $k = n - m$

When $k = -\infty$, $m = +\infty$, when $k = +\infty$, $m = -\infty$.

Therefore, R.H.S. of (1.70*b*) becomes as shown further

$$y[n] = \sum_{m=+\infty}^{m=-\infty} x_1[n-m]\,x_2\,[m]$$

$$= \sum_{m=-\infty}^{\infty} x_2[m]\cdot x_1[n-m] \qquad \text{(Summation is commutative}$$

$\therefore$ summation order can be changed)

i.e., $y[n] = x_2[n] * x_1[n]$ (Comparing with definition (1.70*b*))

Hence, $$y[n] = x_1[n] * x_2[n] = x_2[n] * x_1[n] \qquad ...(1.71)$$

As we discuss the properties of a Linear System, in part B of this Chapter, we shall extensively use the concept of Convolution Integral and Convolution Sum for various results.

(*c*) **Differentiation/Difference**

For analog signal $x(t)$, we shall often require its differentiation (also called derivative) given by

$$y(t) = \frac{dx(t)}{dt} \triangleq x^{(1)}(t) \equiv \dot{x}(t) \qquad ...(1.72a)$$

$$\frac{dy(t)}{dt} = \frac{d^2x(t)}{dt^2} \triangleq x^{(2)}(t) \equiv \ddot{x}(t) \qquad ...(1.72b)$$

Continuing we can write

$$\frac{d^n x(t)}{dt^n} \triangleq x^{(n)}(t) \qquad ...(1.72c)$$

Similarly, for discrete signals, we have first difference (instead of first derivative for analog signal $x(t)$).

First difference of signal $x[n]$ is written as

$$y[n] = x[n] - x[n-1] \qquad ...(1.73)$$

Note that $$y[n-1] = x[n-1] - x[n-2] \qquad ...(1.74)$$

is equivalent to (1.73). If we put $n - 1 = m$ in (1.74) we can write

$$y[m] = x[m] - x[m-1] \qquad ...(1.75a)$$

Or renaming m as n. (1.75*a*) gives us

$$y[n] = x[n] - x[n-1] \qquad ...(1.75b)$$

Clearly, equations (1.74), (1.75*a*) and (1.75*b*) are equivalent.

In this part, we have defined the types of various signals, their specific properties like even/odd, periodic/aperiodic, causal/non-causal both for analog as well as for digital (*i.e.*, discrete) signals. The basic building blocks $\delta(t)$ and $\delta[n]$ have been defined. Other useful signals such as $u(t)/u[n]$, $r(t)/r[n]$ have been derived from $\delta(t)/\delta[n]$. Various useful transformations such as amplitude scaling, time scaling, time reversal, dealy and advance and most important operation *viz.* convolution has been studied.

The next part deals with the systems, wherein the signals will be processed for various requirements.

(A) UNSOLVED PROBLEMS WITH ANSWERS

A-1.1. Determine the even and odd components of the signals

(a) $x(t) = u(t)$ $\left[\textbf{Ans. } x_e(t) = \frac{1}{2}, x_o(t) = \frac{1}{2}\,\text{sgn}\,t\right]$

(b) $x(t) = \sin\left(\omega_0 t + \frac{\pi}{4}\right)$ $\left[\textbf{Ans. } x_e(t) = \frac{1}{\sqrt{2}}\cos\omega_0 t, x_o(t) = \frac{1}{\sqrt{2}}\sin\omega_0 t\right]$

(c) $x[n] = e^{j(\omega_0 n + \pi/2)}$ [**Ans.** $x_e[n] = j\cos\omega_0 n$, $x_o[n] = -\sin\omega_0 n$]

(d) $x[n] = \delta[n]$ [**Ans.** $x_e[n] = \delta[n]$, $x_o[n] = 0$]

A-1.2. If $x(t) = x_e(t) + x_o(t)$, where $x_e(t)$ and $x_o(t)$ are its even part and odd part of $x(t)$, respectively, show that

$$\int_{-\infty}^{\infty} x^2(t)\,dt = \int_{-\infty}^{\infty} x_e^2(t)\,dt + \int_{-\infty}^{\infty} x_o^2(t)\,dt.$$

A-1.3. If $x[n]$ is periodic with period N then show that

(a) $\sum_{k=n_0}^{n} x[k] = \sum_{k=n_0+N}^{n+N} x[k]$ (b) $\sum_{k=0}^{n} x[k] = \sum_{k=n_0}^{n_0+N} x[k]$.

A-1.4. Show that

(a) $\delta(2t) = \frac{1}{2}\delta(t)$ (b) $\delta[2n] = \delta[n]$.

A-1.5. Determine the values of

(a) $\int_{-\infty}^{t} (\cos\tau)\cdot u(\tau)\,d\tau$ [**Ans.** $\sin t$]

(b) $\int_{-\infty}^{t} (\cos\tau)\cdot\delta(\tau)\,d\tau$ $\left[\textbf{Ans. } \begin{cases}1, & t>0\\ 0, & t<0\end{cases} \text{at } t = 0\text{, function is not defined}\right]$

(c) $\int_{-\infty}^{\infty} (\cos t)\cdot u(t-1)\cdot\delta(t)\,dt$ [**Ans.** 0]

(d) $\int_{0}^{2\pi} t\sin\frac{t}{2}\,\delta(\pi - t)\,dt$. [**Ans.** π]

A-1.6. Determine the values of P_∞ and E_∞ for the signals

(a) $x(t) = e^{-2t}\,u(t)$

(b) $x(t) = A\sin(\omega_0 t + \theta_0)$

(c) $x[n] = \left(\frac{1}{2}\right)^n u[n]$

(d) $x[n] = 2e^{j3n}$ $\left[\textbf{Ans. } (a)\ P_\infty = 0, E_\infty = \frac{1}{4}; (b)\ P_\infty = 1, E_\infty = \infty; (c)\ P_\infty = 0, E_\infty = 4/3; (d)\ P_\infty = 4, E_\infty = \infty\right]$

A-1.7. Show that $x_1(t) = e^{j\omega_0 t}$ and $x_2(t) = \cos(\omega_0 t + \theta)$ are periodic with fundamental periods $2\pi/\omega_0$.

A-1.8. Show that $\lim_{a\to 0}\int_{-\infty}^{\infty} x(t)\,dt$ for the signal $x(t)$ as shown is equivalent to $\delta(t)$.

$\left[\textbf{Hint: } \int_{-\infty}^{\infty} x(t)\,dt = \int_{0}^{\infty} \frac{1}{a}e^{-t/a}\,dt = 1.\right]$

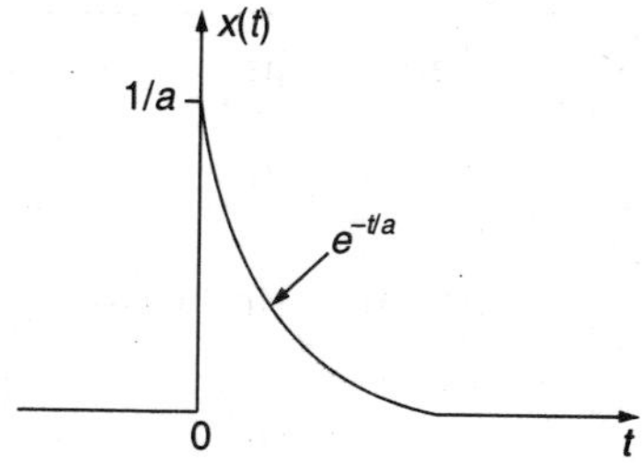

Fig. Prob. 1.8.

A-1.9. Find the period of

(a) $x_1(t) = \cos\left(\frac{\pi}{3}t\right).\sin\left(\frac{\pi}{4}t\right)$

(b) $x_2(n) = e^{j(\pi+2)n}$

[**Hint:** (a) $x_1(t) = \cos\left(\frac{\pi}{3}t\right)\cdot\sin\left(\frac{\pi}{4}t\right)$

$\uparrow$ $T_{01} = 6$ $\quad$ $\uparrow$ $T_{02} = 8$

LCM of 6, 8 = 24

$\therefore$ Period of $x_1(t) = 24$

Otherwise $x_1(t) = \frac{1}{2}\left[\sin\frac{7\pi t}{12} - \sin\frac{\pi t}{12}\right]$

Clearly, period = $T_0 = 24$ **Ans.**

(b) $x_2(n) = e^{j(\pi+2)n}$

$= e^{j\pi n} \cdot e^{j2n}$

$e^{j\pi n}$: periodic; e^{j2n}: non-periodic as n is an integer

Hence, $x_2(n) = e^{j(\pi+2)n}$ is not periodic. **Ans.**]

A-1.10. Show that $x(t) = \cos(\omega_0 t + \theta)$ is periodic with period T if $\frac{T}{T_0}$ is a rational number, where $T_0 = 1/f_0$ and $\omega_0 = 2\pi f$.

(B) SYSTEMS

In this part of the chapter, we cover the properties of a discrete-time system. In some cases, important similarity with continuous-time systems is also given for better comprehension of the subject.

1.8 A SYSTEM

We are concerned mainly with signal processing systems. A system is an entity or processing device which acts on one or more inputs or excitations and produces one or more responses or outputs. A typical block diagram for a system is shown in Fig. 1.23.

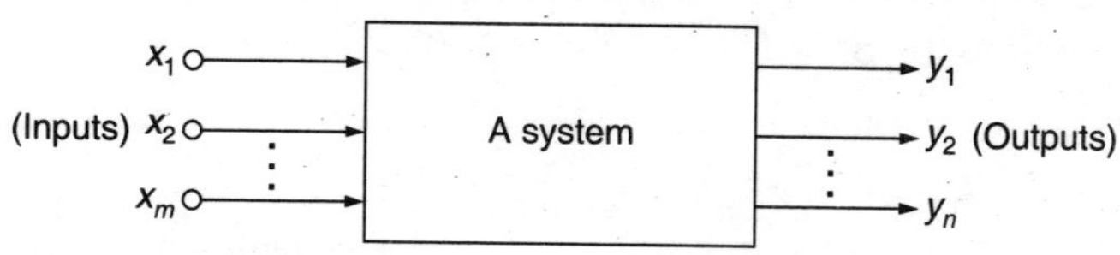

Fig. 1.23. Block diagram for a typical system:
$x_1, x_2, ..., x_m$ are inputs/excitation/perturbation
$y_1, y_2, ..., y_n$ are outputs/response/reaction.

It has some inputs, say, $x_1, x_2, ..., x_m$ which have many other names (such as excitation, perturbation or action signals) and the system produces outputs $y_1, y_2, ..., y_n$ (also called reaction, response). We shall assume $x_1, ...$ and $y_1, ...$ as electric signals. The inside design of the system will determine what type of output is possible. The system design is a fairly involved technique and it requires a good knowledge of various aspects which we shall learn during the course of this book.

Linear-time invariant (LTI) systems are most useful, which will be covered, in detail, in this chapter. A typical system could be analog or discrete, meant for processing an analog or a discrete/digital signal.

1.8.1 A Discrete-time System: $h[n]$ or $H(z)$

For a discrete-time system, various parameters are as shown in Fig. 1.24.

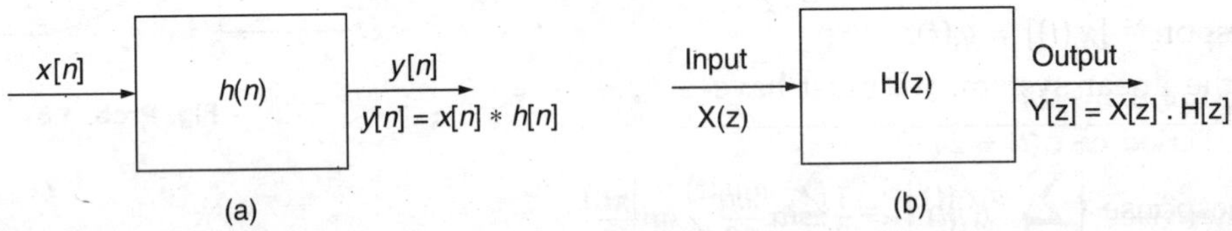

Fig. 1.24. Representation of a discrete-time system: (*a*) in time-domain mol (*b*) in *z*-transform domain.

Here $h[n]$: is called impulse response or unit sample response of the system

i.e., when $x[n] = \delta[n]$, then $y[n] = h[n]$.

$H(z)$ = *z*-transform of $h[n]$, and is called the system function of the discrete time system.

We shall learn *z*-transform in Chapter 3, and show that

$$\left.\begin{aligned} Y(z) &= X(z) \,.\, H(z) \\ y[n] &= x[n] * h[n] \end{aligned}\right\} \qquad \text{...(1.76)}$$

The symbol $*$ between $x[n]$ and $h[n]$ indicates the convolution of $x[n]$ and $h[n]$.

1.9 PROPERTIES OF SYSTEMS

Practical systems to be useful must have some desirable properties. We shall study the properties of systems in general and then determine which of these properties are necessary to make the system useful.

1.9.1 Linear and Non-linear Systems

For a system, shown by $h(t)$ in Fig. 1.25, for input $x_1(t)$ to it, the output is $y_1(t)$ in Fig. 1.25(*a*). In Fig. 1.25(*b*), the system output is $y_2(t)$ for input $x_2(t)$. Then the system is linear if an input $ax_1(t) + bx_2(t)$ to it gives output $ay_1(t) + by_2(t)$, as shown in Fig. 1.25(*c*). Here a and b are some constants (*i.e.*, a and b are not functions of time t).

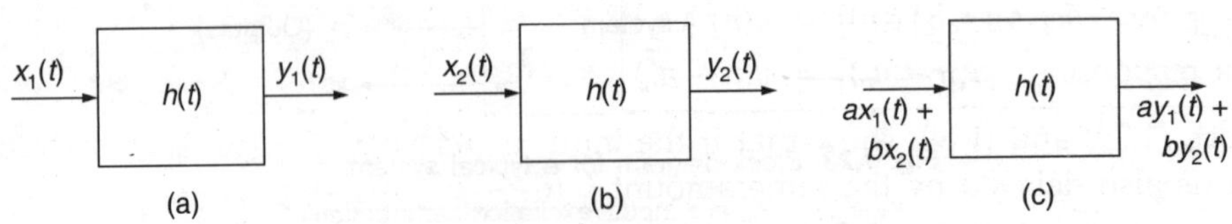

Fig. 1.25. A linear system: (*a*) input is $x_1(t)$ and output is $y_1(t)$, (*b*) input is $x_2(t)$ and output is $y_2(t)$ and (*c*) input is $ax_1(t) + bx_2(t)$ then output is $ay_1(t) + by_2(t)$ if the system is linear.

The linearity property is very useful. Suppose a system cannot handle a "large signal", say, $(ax_1(t) + bx_2(t))$. We input $x_1(t)$ to the system and find its output $y_1(t)$. Then we input $x_2(t)$ to the system and find the output $y_2(t)$. It has been assumed that the system can handle small signals *i.e.*, $x_1(t)$ or $x_2(t)$. If the system is linear, then a composite input signal $(ax_1(t) + bx_2(t))$ should give $(ay_1(t) + by_2(t))$ from the system as its output. The linearity concepts help us to realize an equivalent "bigger system's" operation whereas we are using only a "smaller system". Here, we take outputs from the smaller system by inputting parts of the given "large signal", and then addition of all the individual outputs will be the desired overall output for the composite input signal.

Putting mathematically the concept of linearity, we can write

For the continuous time/analog system

If response $[x_i(t)] = y_i(t)$, ...(1.77*a*)

then for the linear system, we must have

$$\text{Response}\left[\sum_i a_i x_i(t)\right] = \sum_i a_i y_i(t) \quad \text{...(1.77}b\text{)}$$

Similarly, a discrete system will be a linear discrete system if the following conditions hold.

If response for $[x_i(n)] = y_i(n)$, ...(1.78*a*)

then

$$\text{Response}\left[\sum_i a_i x_i(n)\right] = \sum_i a_i y_i(n) \quad \text{...(1.78}b\text{)}$$

In short, **the superposition property holds good when a system is linear.** Equations (1.77*b*) and (1.78*b*) indicate the validity of superposition property.

1.9.2 Time-invariant/Time-variant Systems

Time-invariance (TI) means that system which does not vary (does not change or does not alter) in performance as time passes. Suppose you have a TV system. If its performance does not degrade as time passes, then your TV is time-invariant system *i.e.*, passage of time has no effect on its performance. More rigorously, we should have the following properties for the system to be time-invariant *i.e.*,

$$\begin{array}{ll} \text{If response} & [x(t)] = y(t) \\ \text{then response} & [x(t - t_0)] = y(t - t_0) \end{array} \quad \text{...(1.79)}$$

Similarly, for discrete/digital system, the system is time invariant if it satisfies the conditions:

$$\begin{array}{ll} \text{If response} & [x(n)] = y(n) \\ \text{then response} & [x(n - n_0)] = y(n - n_0) \end{array} \quad \text{...(1.80)}$$

In short, (1.79) and (1.80) show that if the input is delayed by t_0 (or n_0 in discrete signals), the output is also delayed by the same amount t_0 (or n_0).

On the other hand, if the equations (1.79) or (1.80) are not satisfied the system is not time-invariant, *i.e.*, then the system is *time-variant*. In discrete systems, the time-invariant or time-variant is also termed as *shift-invariant* or *shift-variant*, respectively, since, variance of n is "shift" in n.

A system which is both the linear as well as time-invariant is termed as the *linear-time invariant system* (LTI). Most of the practical systems are LTI systems. A few examples which follow will make the concept of LTI systems clear. We need some tips for quick recognition, as follows:

Important Hints. (Aid to recognize an LTI system)

1. Let input be $x(t)$ (or $x[n]$). If the system equation specifying $y(t)$ and $x(t)$ (or $y[n]$ and $x[n]$) is of the form:
   (*i*) $y(t) = a\ |x\ (t - t_0)|$ *i.e.*, mod operation, the system in non-linear
   (*ii*) $y(t) = x^p\ (t - t_0)$, $p \neq 0$ or 1, then the analog system is non-linear. For example, the systems characterized by:
   $$(i)\ y(t) = 7|x(t)|\ ; \quad (ii)\ y(t) = 3\ \frac{1}{[x(t)]} = 3\ [x(t)]^{-1}, \text{ are non-linear systems}$$
   (*iii*) $y(t) = 5\ x^2(t)$ is a non-linear system.
2. If $y(t) = t^p\ x(t - t_0), p \neq 0$ or $y(t) = x(kt), k \neq 1$
   the specified system is time variant. It implies that if the signal $x(t)$ or $x(t - t_0)$ is multiplied by a function of t, (it was t^p here), or if the argament t is multiplied by any constant k, $k \neq 1$, then the system would be time variant. For example, the systems characterized by: (*i*) $y(t) = a(t)\ .\ x(t - t_0)$; or (*ii*) $y(t) = t^2\ x(t - 3)$, (*iii*) $y(t) = x(2t)$, or (*iv*) $y(t) = x(-t)$ are time-variant.
3. Logic as given in serials 1 and 2 also holds for discrete systems. For example,
   (*i*) $y[n] = b\ |x[n - n_0]|$ (mod operation)
   (*ii*) $y[n] = x^3[n - n_1]$
   (*iii*) $y[n] = x^{1/2}\ [n - n_2]$
   are non-linear systems. Again, the systems characterized by equations
   (*i*) $y[n] = n^2\ x[n - n_0]$
   (*ii*) $y[n] = a[n]\ .\ x[n - n_1]$
   (*iii*) $y[n] = x[kn]$, $k \neq 1$
   (*iv*) $y[n] = x[-2n]$
   are time-variant as the multiplying factors n^2 or $a[n]$ are functions of time n, which are time dependent, or the argument n of $x[n]$ is by multiplied by $k(\neq 1)$

EXAMPLE 1.15: *Check if the analog systems characterized by the equations given below, are for linear or non-linear systems*

(*a*) $y(t) = x(t - 3)$ (*b*) $y(t) = x^2(t - 2)$

(*c*) $y(t) = 3\ |x(t)|$.

SOLUTION: (*a*) As $y(t) = x(t - 3)$

Let inputs be $x_1(t)$, $x_2(t)$ and $x_3(t) = ax_1(t) + bx_2(t)$

$\therefore$ for input $x_1(t)$, output $y_1(t) = x_1(t - 3)$

for input $x_2(t)$, output $y_2(t) = x_2(t - 3)$

for input $x_3(t)$, output $y_3(t) = x_3(t - 3)$

$= ax_1(t - 3) + bx_2(t - 3)$

$= ay_1(t) + by_2(t)$

It is seen that the superposition property holds here,

i.e., response to $ax_1(t) + bx_2(t) = a$ [response to $x_1(t)$] $+ b$ [response to $x_2(t)$]

$\therefore$ The system is a linear system. **Ans.**

(*b*) As $y(t) = x^2(t - 2)$

Let the inputs be $x_1(t)$, $x_2(t)$ and $x_3(t) = ax_1(t) + bx_2(t)$

$\therefore$ For input $x_1(t)$, output $y_1(t) = x_1^2(t-2)$

for input $x_2(t)$, output $y_2(t) = x_2^2(t-2)$

for input $x_3(t)$, output

$$y_3(t) = x_3^2(t+2) = (ax_1(t) + bx_2(t))^2 = a^2x_1^2(t) + 2abx_1(t).x_2(t) + b^2x_2^2(t)$$

Clearly, $y_3(t) \neq ay_1(t) + by_2(t)$

$\therefore$ The system is non-linear. **Ans.**

(c) As $y(t) = 3\,|x(t)|$ (*i.e.*, it is mod operation)

Let input be $x_1(t)$, output $y_1(t) = 3\,|x_1(t)|$

Assuming $x(t)$ is + ve for all values of t, then

$$y_1(t) = 3\,|x_1(t)| = 3x_1(t)$$

Let input be $x_2(t) = -x_1(t)$, $\therefore$ $x_1(t)$ is – ve for all t.

$\therefore$

$$y_2(t) = 3\,|x_2(t)| = 3\,|-x_1(t)| = 3x_1(t)$$

Now assume a, b be two + ve constants and $x_1(t)$ and $x_2(t)$, also + ve for all t.

Let input $x_3(t) = ax_1(t) - bx_2(t)$

then

$$y_3(t) = 3\,|x_3(t)| = 3\,|ax_1(t) - bx_2(t)| = 3ax_1(t) + 3bx_2(t) \neq ay_1(t) - by_2(t)$$

$\therefore$ The system is non-linear. **Ans.**

1.9.3 Static and Dynamic Systems

A system, where the output $y(t)$ or $y[n]$ does not depend on past or future values of the input signal is called static or *Instantaneous system*. If the output $y(t)$ or $y[n]$ depends on past or future value of the signal $x(t)$ or $x[n]$, then such a system is called *Dynamic system*. Hence, a time equation of a static system cannot have delays or advances. For example,

(*i*) $y(t) = ax(t) + bx(t-1)$ is a dynamic system

↗ delay of 1

(*ii*) $y(t) = cx(t)$ is a static system (no delay or advance)

(*iii*) $y[n] = ax[n] + bx[n+2]$ is a dynamic system

↗ this is an advance of 2

(*iv*) $y[n+2] = 5x[n+2]$ is equivalent to

$y[n] = 5x[n]$, hence a static system.

Note that we want to determine an advance or a delay in the system equation, we must refer it w.r.t. $y(t)$ or $y[n]$. Hence in part (*iv*) of example we first transform $y[n+2]$ to $y[n]$ (by replacing $n + 2$ to n' on both sides and then dropping dashes (′)). Then we see R.H.S. to detect delay or advance.

1.9.4 Causal and Non-causal Systems

A system is causal if its output $y(t)$ or $y[n]$ at any time depends on only the present value of the input $x(t)$ or $x[n]$ or the past values of the input *i.e.*, $x(t - t_0)$, $x[n - n_0]$, where t_0 and n_0 are + ve values. **A causal system is non-anticipative** *i.e.*, it does not depend on the future values of the signal.

A system is non-causal, if its output $y(t)$ or $y[n]$ depends on the future values of the signal $x(t)$ or $x[n]$. Thus, such a system is rightly called an **anticipative system.**

Note that the spelling is causal (from cause). Many students misspell it as casual (as a casuality ward in a hospital). The system is not hospitalised, we are of course dealing with healthy systems ! A memory less system has no delays or advances and is, therefore, always a causal system. But a causal system is not always memoryless, since, it can contain delays.

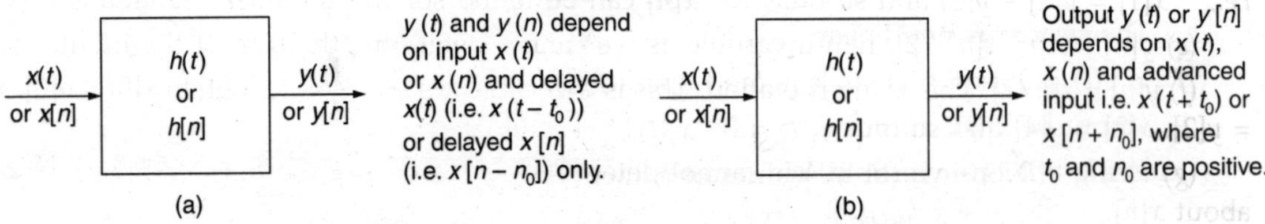

Fig. 1.26. Explaining input /output signals for: (*a*) causal, and (*b*) non-causal systems.

To be more specific, for a causal system its impulse response $h(t)$ or $h[n]$, which is the output when the signal input is $\delta(t)$ or $\delta[n]$, has zero value when $t < 0$ or $n < 0$, since, the signal is applied only at $t = 0$ (or $n = 0$) onward. The system cannot yield output before the signal is inputted. In other words, a causal system cannot give output in anticipation of application of the input signal. This is exactly the reason that we call the causal systems as non-anticipatory. In practice, only the causal systems are most useful, since, they "obey the order" of input signal and perform as per their assigned design.

1.9.5 Invertible and Non-invertible Systems

Suppose that input $x(t)$ to system-1, shown in Fig. 1.27, results in output $y(t)$. Now we let $y(t)$ be input of system-2 and let output of system-2 be $w(t)$. If $w(t)$ is a constant times $x(t)$, *i.e.*, we have obtained $k\ x(t)$, where k is a constant ($k \neq 0$), then the system-1 is *Invertible*. It implies that it is possible to undo (by using a system-2) what system-1 did. Such systems find extensive use in Communication, Control and Automation. For example, in communication, a message is coded (using system-1, say), then at the receiving end the message is decoded/recovered (by using system-2, say). We say that a coder is an invertible system, because, we can always decode (*i.e.*, undo the coding). CODEC is a practical example of an invertible system.

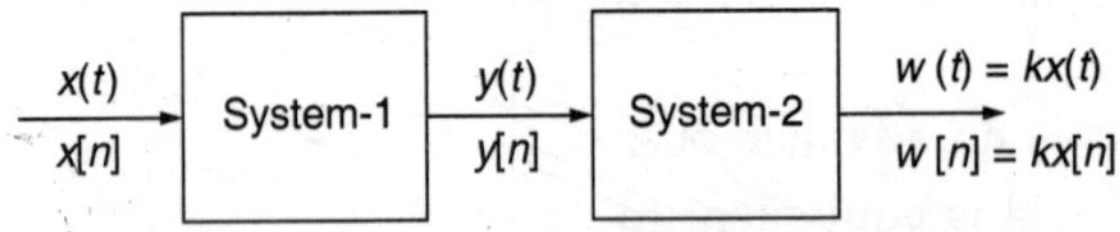

Fig. 1.27. Concept of Invertible system. System-2 does the reverse function that of System-1.

EXAMPLE 1.16: *For each of the following input-output relationships, check whether the corresponding system is invertible or not.*

SOLUTION: (*a*) $y(t) = 2\ x(t)$, is invertible, as $x(t) = \frac{1}{2}\ y(t)$

(*b*) $y(t) = x^2(t)$, non-invertible, as we cannot determine the sign of input $\because\ x(t) = \pm\ y(t)$

(*c*) $y(t) = \dfrac{dx(t)}{dt}$, non-invertible

$\because \quad x(t) = \int y(t)\, dt + a$ constant. Knowledge of constant with $x(t)$ is lost when we take its differentiation.

(*d*) $y[n] = \sum_{k=-\infty}^{n} x[k]$, invertible. As $y[0] = \sum_{k=-\infty}^{0} x[k]$, $y[1] = \sum_{k=-\infty}^{1} x[k] = y[0] + x[1]$

i.e., $x[1] = y[1] - y[0]$ and so on. $\therefore$ $x[n]$ can be found solving the linear equations.

(*e*) $y[n] = x[n]\, x[n-2]$, non-invertible as we cannot determine the sign of the input.

(*f*) $y[n] = x[n/2]$, This is interpolation. This is invertible system. We can obtain $x[0] = y[0]$, $x[1] = y[2]$, $x[2] = y[4]$ and so on.

(*g*) $y[n] = 0$, Non-invertible. We cannot determine $x[n]$ from zero output. Nothing is known about $x[n]$.

(*h*) $y[n] = \cos x[n]$, Non-invertible, since, output $y[n]$ is periodic. We cannot find $x[n]$ uniquely.

(*i*) $y[n] = x[2n]$. This is decimation. In this decimation, the alternate sample values of $x[n]$ *i.e.,* of $x[1]$, $x[3]$, $x[5]$ ..... are lost. We cannot recover full $x[n]$. Hence, it is non-invertible system.

1.9.6 Stable and Unstable Systems

A system is called BIBO (bounded input bounded output) if the output $y(t)$ or $y[n]$ is bounded for bounded input $x(t)$ or $x[n]$, respectively. We shall learn in this chapter that the following conditions emerge for a system to be BIBO stable.

(*a*) **For analog system:** $h(t)$ or $H(s)$, to be BIBO stable we must have

$$\int_{-\infty}^{\infty} |\, h(t)\, |\, dt < \infty \qquad \text{...(1.81)}$$

or $H(s)$ has its poles with their real parts to be negative. In other words, if $H(s) = \frac{N(s)}{D(s)}$ the roots of $D(s) = 0$ all lie strictly on left hand side of *s*-plane, as shown in Fig. 1.28.

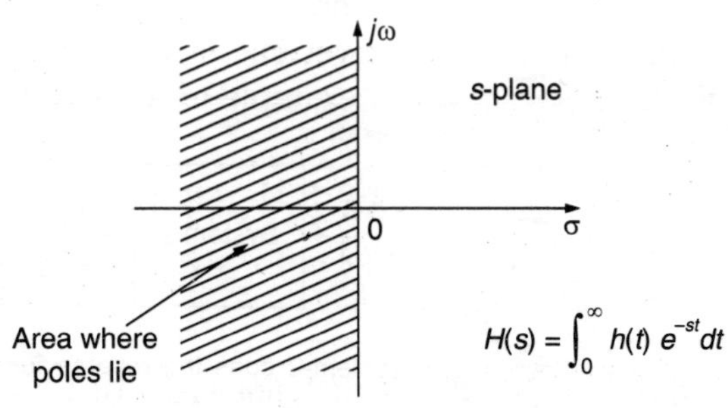

Fig. 1.28. Roots of $D(s) = 0$ lie strictly in shaded region *i.e.,* on L.H.S. of *s*-plane if $H(s) = \frac{N(s)}{D(s)}$ represents a stable system. Roots cannot lie on $j\omega$ axis.

(*b*) **For discrete system:** $h[n]$ or $H(z)$ will be BIBO stable if and only if

$$\sum_{n=-\infty}^{\infty} |h[n]| < \infty \qquad \text{...(1.82)}$$

We shall prove (1.82), when we learn about convolution operation [see Eq. (1.109)].

Equation (1.82) is equivalent to that for a causal system represented by $H(z)$, $H(z)$ must have its poles strictly inside the unit circle $|z| = 1$ in z-plane. This is as shown in Fig. 1.29.

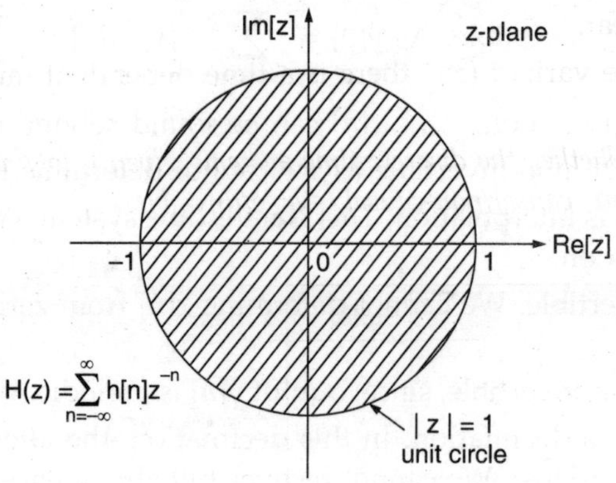

Fig. 1.29. If $H(z)$ is system function of a causal, BIBO stable system, then poles of $H(z)$ must strictly lie inside the unit circle $|z| = |e^{j\omega}| = 1$.

The poles cannot lie on the circumference of the unit circle $|z| = 1$. Note the region where the poles of $H(z)$ can lie is the shaded area and it does not include the circumference of $|z| = 1$ circle. We shall prove this in Chapter 3 (z-transform).

EXAMPLE 1.17: *Consider a discrete-time LTI system whose input x[n] and the output y[n] are related by*

$$y[n] = \sum_{k=-\infty}^{n} 2^{k-n}\, x[k+1]$$

Is the system causal? Also, check if the system is stable, linear and time-invariant or not (see also Example 1.33).

SOLUTION: As

$$y[n] = \sum_{k=-\infty}^{n} 2^{k-n}\, x(k+1)$$

$$= \sum_{k=-\infty}^{\infty} 2^{k-n}\, x(k+1)\,.\,u(n-k)$$

Put $k + 1 = k'$

$$\therefore \quad y[n] = \sum_{k'=-\infty}^{\infty} 2^{k'-1-n}\, x(k')\,.\,u(n-(k'-1))$$

i.e.,

$$y[n] = \sum_{k'} \underbrace{2^{-(n+1-k')}\, u(n+1-k')}\,.\,x(k'), \quad \left(\text{Form } ``\sum_{k} h(n-k)\,.\,x(k)"\right)$$

By inspection

$$h(n) = 2^{-(n+1)}\,.\,u(n+1) \quad \therefore \quad y[n] = h[n] * x[n] \text{ (Note this step)}$$

(*a*) The system is NOT causal as $h(n) \neq 0$ for $n = -1$

(*b*) As $\sum_{n} |h(n)| = \sum_{n=-\infty}^{\infty} 2^{-(n+1)} u(n+1) = \sum_{n=-1}^{\infty} 2^{-(n+1)} = \frac{1}{1-2^{-1}} = 2 < \infty$

$\therefore$ The system is stable.

(*c*) The system is linear.

(*d*) The system is time variant ($\because$ there is a time dependent multiplier $2^{-(n+1)}$ in the input-output equation).

EXAMPLE 1.18: *Check whether the discrete-time systems given below are static/dynamic, linear/non-linear, shift variant/invariant, causal/non-causal, stable/unstable.* (*IP Univ. 2006, 2008*)

SOLUTION:

	Static	**Linear**	**Shift invariant**	**Causal**	**Stable**
(*a*) $y(n) = \cos[x(n)]$	√	×	√	√	√
(*b*) $y(n) = (\cos \omega n)\, x(n)$	√	√	×	√	√
(*c*) $y(n) = x(-n)$	×	√	×	×	√
(*d*) $y(n) = x(n) + nx(n+1)$ *(bounded I.P. $x(n) = u(n)$ produces unbounded O/P)	×	√	×	×	× (see *)
(*e*) $y(n) = x(-n+3)$	×	√	×	×	√
(*f*) $y(n) = e^{x(n)}$	√	×	√	√	√
(*g*) $y(n) = 2x(n) + 6$	√	×	√	√	√
(*h*) $y(n) = x^2(-n)$	×	×	×	×	√
(*i*) $y(n+1) = 3x(n+1) + 2$ ($\therefore$ $y(n) = 3x(n) + 2$)	√	×	√	√	√
(*j*) $y(n) = x(n) \cdot x(n-1)$	×	×	√	√	√
(*k*) $y(n) = x^2(n+1) + x(n-1)$	×	×	√	×	√

The symbols √ means yes and × means no. For part (g), also see Example 1.30(*f*)

EXAMPLE 1.19: *For each of the following systems, determine whether or not the system is (i) stable, (ii) causal, (iii) linear, (iv) shift invariant.*

(*a*) $y(n) = g(n) \cdot x(n)$, (*b*) $y(n) = \sum_{k=n_0}^{n} x(k)$

(*c*) $y(n) = \sum_{k=n-n_0}^{n+n_0} x(k)$, (*d*) $y(n) = x(n - n_0)$

(*e*) $y(n) = e^{x(n)}$, (*f*) $y(n) = ax(n) + b$.

SOLUTION: (*a*) Let $|x(n)| \le M$ then $|y(n)| = g(n) \cdot M$ $\therefore$ it is stable if $|g(n)|$ is bounded. $y(n) = g(n) \cdot x(n)$, R.H.S. contains no advances $\therefore$ causal if $x(n)$ causal, also R.H.S is product of $x(n)$ $\therefore$ $y(n)$ is linearly connected with $x(n)$. Also, $y(n)$ is shift variant as $g(n)$, the scaling factor is n dependent.

Hence, the system is BIBO stable, causal, linear and shift variant. **Ans.**

(*b*) Let $|x(n)| \le M$ then $y(n) = \sum_{k=n_0}^{n} x(k) \le (n - n_0 + 1) M \rightarrow \infty$ if $n \rightarrow \infty$

$\therefore$ system not BIBO stable

As $\quad y(n) = x(n_0) + x\,(n_0 + 1) + ...\, x(0) + x(1) + ... + x(n).$

If $n < n_0$, then system is not causal, as $y(n)$ depends on future value of $x(n)$.

If $n \geq n_0$, then system is causal.

The system is linear and shift invariant. **Ans.**

(c) $y(n) = \sum_{k=n-n_0}^{n+n_0} x(k) \leq M\,(2n_0 + 1)$ for $|x(n)| \leq M$ $\therefore$ system is stable as n_0 is finite. $y(n)$ is non-causal as it depends on future value $x\,(n+n_0)\big|_{n_0+ve}$ or $x\,(n-n_0)\big|_{n_0-ve}$. Clearly, the system is linear and shift invariant as $y(n)$ depends on linear additions of $x(n)$ or its delayed/advanced versions. **Ans.**

(d) $\quad y(n) = x(n - n_0)$

If $|x(n)| \leq M$ then $|y(n)| \leq M$ $\therefore$ system is stable.

It is clearly linear.

If n_0 is +ve, it is causal, otherwise non-causal, if $n_0 < 0$

It is also shift invariant as no multiplier which is time dependent. **Ans.**

(e) $\quad y(n) = e^{x(n)}$

If $|x(n)| \leq M$ then $|y(n)| < \infty$ $\therefore$ It is a stable system.

As $y(n)$ does not depend on future values of $x(n)$ $\therefore$ it is causal.

Clearly, it is a non-linear system since:

$$y_1(n) + y_2(n) = e^{x_1(n)} + e^{x_2(n)} \neq e^{x_1(n) + x_2(n)}.$$

Hence, the system is stable, causal and non-linear. **Ans.**

(f) $\quad y(n) = ax(n) + b$

If $|x(n)| \leq M$, then $|y(n)| < \infty$ $\therefore$ the system is stable if a, b are finite.

$$y_1(n) = ax_1(n) + b$$
$$y_2(n) = ax_2(n) + b$$
$$y_1(n) + y_2(n) = 2b + a[x_1(n) + x_2(n)] \quad \therefore \text{ the system is non-linear.}$$

The system is causal and shift invariant by inspection. **Ans.**

Putting the answers in compact form, we write

System Equation	Stable	Causal	Linear	Shift invariant
$y(n) = g(n) \,.\, x(n)$	√	√	√	×
$y(n) = \sum_{k=n_0}^{n} x(k)$	×	$n > n_0$ √ $n < n_0$ ×	√	√
$y(n) = \sum_{k=n-n_0}^{n+n_0} x(k)$	√	×	√	√
$y(n) = x(n - n_0)$	√	n_0 + ve, √ n − ve ×	√	√
$y(n) = e^{x(n)}$	√	√	×	√
$y(n) = ax(n) + b$	√	√	×	√

EXAMPLE 1.20: *Examine whether the following systems are (i) static or dynamic, (ii) linear or non-linear, (iii) time invariant or time variant, (iv) causal or non-causal, (v) stable or unstable.* (IP 2004)

SOLUTION:

(*a*) $y(n) = \cos[x(n)]$

(*b*) $y(n) = \sum_{k=-\infty}^{n+1} x(k)$

If $x(k) = u(k)$ a bounded input, output

$$\sum_{k=-\infty}^{n+1} u(k) = \begin{cases} 0, & n < -1 \\ n+2, & n \geq -1 \end{cases}$$

As $n \to \infty$, $y(n) \to \infty$

∴ the system is BIBO unstable

(*c*) $y(n) = x(n) \cos(w_0 n)$

(*d*) $y(n) = x(-n+2)$

∴ ($y(-1) = x(3)$ ∴ non-causal)

(*e*) $y(n)$ = Truncation of $x(n)$

(*f*) $y(n)$ = Rounded $[x(n)]$

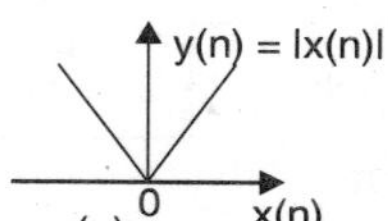

(g)

(*g*) $y(n) = |x(n)|$

(*h*) $y(n) = x(n) \cdot u(n)$ [$u(n) = 0$ or 1 *i.e.*, constant]
similar to (*k*)

(*i*) $y(n) = x(n) + nx(n+1)$
[**Note.** bounded I/P $x(n) = u(n)$
produces unbounded O/P]

(*j*) $y(n) = x(2n)$ (see Proof below*)

(*k*) $y(n) = \begin{cases} x(n), & x(n) \geq 0 \\ 0, & x(0) < 0 \end{cases}$

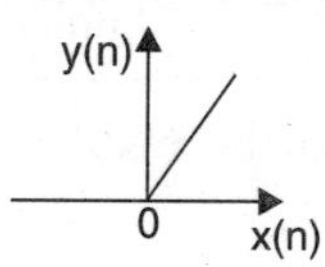

(*l*) $y(n) = x(-n)$
∴ $y(-1) = x(1)$ (dynamic, non-causal)

(*m*) $y(n) = \text{sign}[x(n)]$

(*n*) $x(n) = x_a(t)|_{t=nT}$, $-\infty < n < \infty$

	Static	Linear	Time invariant	Causal	Stable
(*a*)	√	×	√	√	√
(*b*)	×	√	√	×	×
(*c*)	√	√	×	√	√
(*d*)	×	√	×	×	√
(*e*)	√	×	√	√	√
(*f*)	√	×	√	√	√
(*g*)	√	×	√	√	√
(*h*)	√	×	√	√	√
(*i*)	×	√	×	×	×
(*j*)	×	√	×	×	√
(*k*)	√	×	√	√	√
(*l*)	×	√	×	×	√
(*m*)	√	×	√	√	√
(*n*)	√	√	√	√	√

*** To show that y(n) = x(2n) is time variant.**

The given system is such that $x(n)$ gets transformed to what we call as $y(n)$

i.e., $x(n)$ → System T → $x(2n)$ called $y(n)$

We write $x(n) \xrightarrow{T} = x(2n) = y(n)$

$$\therefore \quad \underset{\text{delay by } n_0}{x(n-n_0)} \xrightarrow{T} = x(2n-n_0) = x\left(2\left(n-\frac{n_0}{2}\right)\right)$$

$$= y\left(n-\frac{n_0}{2}\right), \quad \because \text{argument of } y \text{ is half the argument of } x.$$

$\therefore$ Delaying $x(n)$ by n_0 does not cause delaying $y(n)$ by n_0. Here delaying $x(n)$ by n_0 has produced $y(n)$ delayed by $\frac{n_0}{2}$.

$\therefore$ $y(n) = x(2n)$ is not time-invariant.

By similar argument, $y(n) = x(n/2)$ or $y(n) = x(-n)$ are time-variant systems.

1.9.7 Recursive or Feedback Systems

In most of the applications feedback principle is used to obtain efficient system. Here, there is a signal flow from output ($y(t)$ or $y[n]$) which is added (or subtracted) to $x(t)$ or $x[n]$, such a system is called recursive or feedback system. A typical recursive system in digital domain may be expressed as a difference equation as follows:

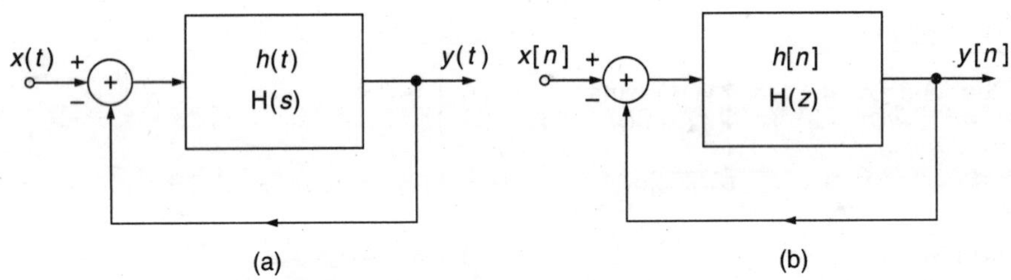

Fig. 1.30. Feedback systems: (*a*) analog system and (*b*) discrete system.

$$y[n] = 1 + a_0\, x[n] + a_1\, x[n-1] + \ldots\ldots + b_1\, y[n-1] + b_2\, y[n-2]\ldots.$$

$$= 1 + \sum_{i=0}^{N} a_i\, x[n-i] + \sum_{i=1}^{N} b_i\, y[n-i] \qquad \ldots(1.83)$$

We shall deal with similar difference equations when we deal system function $H(z)$ in z-domain.

If $b_i = 0$ for all i in (1.83) the feedback vanishes, and the resulting equation of the type

$$y[n] = 1 + \sum_{i=0}^{N} a_i\, x[n-i] \qquad \ldots(1.84)$$

is called *a non-recursive system's* difference equation.

In the analog systems also feedback methodology is applied. An LTI analog system is often described by a differential equation such as the following:

$$\sum_{k=0}^{n} a_k \frac{d^k y(t)}{dt^k} = \sum_{k=0}^{m} b_k \frac{d^k x(t)}{dt^k} \qquad \ldots(1.85)$$

The differential equation of the type (1.85) can be easily solved by transforming it to Laplace transform domain.

EXAMPLE 1.21: *Find the impulse response h(n) for each of the LTI discrete-time systems given by the difference equations as given. Indicate whether each system is an FIR or an IIR system. Assume the systems causal.*

SOLUTION: (a) $y(n) = x(n) - 2x(n-2) + x(n-3)$ (given difference equation)

$\therefore\ h(n) = \delta(n) - 2\,\delta(n-2) + \delta(n-3)$ [changing $x(n)$ to $\delta(n)$ and $y(n)$ to $h(n)$]

$\therefore\ h(n) = \{\underset{\uparrow}{1}, 0, -2, 1\}$ The system is FIR **Ans.**

(b) $y(n) + 2y(n-1) = x(n) + x(n-1)$ (given difference equation)

$\therefore\ h(n) = -2h(n-1) + \delta(n) + \delta(n-1)$ (changing $x(n)$ to $\delta(n)$ and $y(n)$ to $h(n)$)

Since, the system is causal, h(– 1) = 0 (this assumption is given)

$$\begin{aligned}
\therefore\quad h(0) &= -2h(-1) + \delta(0) + \delta(-1) = -0 + 1 + 0 = 1\\
h(1) &= -2\,h(0) + \delta(1) + \delta(0) = -2 + 0 + 1 = -1 \;= (-1)^1\, 2^{1-1}\\
h(2) &= -2h(1) + \delta(2) + \delta(1) = -2h(1) = -2(-1) = 2 = (-1)^2\, 2^{2-1}\\
h(3) &= -2h(2) = -2(2) = -2^2 = (-1)^3\, 2^{3-1}\\
&\vdots
\end{aligned}$$

$$h(n) = \underbrace{(-1)^n \cdot 2^{n-1}}_{\text{for } n\ge 1} + \underbrace{\delta(n)}_{\text{for } n=0} = \delta(n) + ((-1)^n\, 2^{n-1})\, u(n-1) \text{ system is IIR.}$$ **Ans.**

(c) $y(n) = \frac{1}{2}\, y(n-2) + 2x(n) - x(n-2)$ (given difference equation)

$\therefore\ h(n) = \frac{1}{2}\, h(n-2) + 2\delta(n) - \delta(n+2)$ (changing $x(n)$ to $\delta(n)$ and $y(n)$ to $h(n)$)

System is causal, therefore, assume $h(-1) = 0$ (this assumption is given)

$$\begin{aligned}
h(0) &= \frac{1}{2}\, h(-2) + 2\delta(0) - \delta(-2) = 0 + 2 - 0 = 2\\
h(1) &= \frac{1}{2}\, h(-1) + 2\delta(1) - \delta(-1) = 0 + 0 - 0 = 0\\
h(2) &= \frac{1}{2}\, h(0) + 2\delta(2) - \delta(0) = \frac{1}{2}(2) - 1 = 0\\
h(3) &= \frac{1}{2}\,(0) + 0 - 0 = 0,
\end{aligned}$$

$\therefore\ h(n) = \{\underset{\uparrow}{2}, 0, 0, \ldots\}$ *i.e.*, $h(n) = 2\delta(n)$ $\quad\therefore$ the system is FIR. **Ans.**

EXAMPLE 1.22: *The input x[n] and output y[n] are related by* *(IP Univ. 2007)*

$$y[n] = \sum_{k=-\infty}^{\infty} 2^{k-n}\, x[k+1]$$

(i) Find out whether the system is linear, time invariant, stable and causal.

(ii) Find the impulse response of the system.

(iii) Is the system stable ?

SOLUTION: As $\quad y[n] = \sum_{k=-\infty}^{\infty} 2^{k-n}\, x[k+1]$

$$= \sum_{k'=-\infty}^{\infty} 2^{k'-1-n} x[k'] \qquad \text{Putting } k+1 = k' \quad \therefore \quad k = k'-1$$

$$= \sum_{k=-\infty}^{\infty} 2^{-(n+1-k)} . x[k] \qquad \left(\text{Form } \text{“}\sum_{k} h(n-k) . x(x)\text{”}\right) \quad \text{(Note this step)}$$

By inspection, we have

(*i*) $h(n) = 2^{-(n+1)}$. **Ans.**

(*ii*) $h(n) \neq 0$ for $n < 0$, $\therefore$ the system is not causal

The system is linear. **Ans.**

The system is time-variant ($\because$ $h(n)$ contains a multiplier depending on n)

(*iii*) As $\sum_{n=-\infty}^{\infty} |h(n)| = \frac{1}{2} \sum_{n=-\infty}^{\infty} 2^{-n} \to \infty$

$\therefore$ The system is unstable. **Ans.**

(B) UNSOLVED PROBLEMS WITH ANSWERS

B-1.11. Consider a continuous-time system with input-output relation

$$y(t) = \frac{1}{T} \int_{t-T/2}^{t+T/2} x(\tau)\, d\tau$$

(*a*) Is the system linear ? (*b*) Is the system time-invariant ?

(*c*) Is it causal? [**Ans.** (*a*) linear, (*b*) time-invariant, (*c*) non-causal]

B-1.12. Given a discrete-time systems with input-output relation

(*a*) $y[n] = x^2[n]$ (*b*) $y[n] = nx[n + 2]$

(*c*) $y(n) = 5x(-n - 1)$

Check if these systems are linear, time-invariant and causal.

[**Ans.** (*a*) non-linear, time-invariant, causal
(*b*) linear, time-variant, non-causal
(*c*) linear, time-variant, non-causal]

B-1.13. Determine if each of the following systems is invertible or not. Also give the inverse system:

(*a*) $y(t) = 6x(t)$ (*b*) $y(t) = x^3(t)$

(*c*) $y(t) = \int_{-\infty}^{t} x(p)\, dp$ (*d*) $y[n] = \sum_{k=-\infty}^{n} x[k]$

(*e*) $y[n] = n\, x[n]$ (*f*) $y[n] = \cos [n]$

[**Ans.** (*a*) invertible, $x(t) = \frac{1}{6} y(t)$, (*b*) not-invertible, (*c*) invertible, $x(t) = \frac{dy(t)}{dt}$,
(*d*) invertible, $x[n] = y[n] - y[n - 1]$, (*e*) not-invertible, (*f*) non-invertible]

B-1.14. Check whether the following systems are stable or not:

(*a*) $y[n] = x^2[n]$ (*b*) $y[n] = x[n] \cos w_0 n$

(*c*) $y[n] = x[2n]$ (*d*) $y(t) = \frac{dx(t)}{dt}$

(e) $y(t) = Ax(t/2)$ (f) $y(t) = \int_{-\infty}^{t} u(p)\, dp$

[**Ans.** (a) stable, (b) stable, (c) stable, (d) stable, (e) stable, (f) unstable]

B 1.15. Find the inverse systems for the given systems:

(a) $y_1(t) = 3\, x(t)$ (b) $y_1[n] = \sum_{k=-\infty}^{n} x[k]$

$\left[\right.$**Ans.** (a) $y_2(t) = \frac{1}{3} y_1(t)$, Note that $y_2(t) = x(t)$ (b) $y_2[n] = y_1[n] - y_1[n-1]$

Note that $y_1[n] - y_1[n-1] = x[n]$. $\left.\right]$

(C) LINEAR TIME-INVARIANT (LTI) SYSTEMS

In this part of the chapter, we cover important properties of an LTI system, including response, convolution and deconvolution. These will form the bases for topics covered in all the subsequent chapters.

1.10 INTRODUCTION

In the last chapter, we have studied about the properties of various systems. It was mentioned there that linear time-invariant (LTI) systems form the most useful class of practical systems. They obey the superposition property (*i.e.*, these are linear systems) and they act only when the signal is available (*i.e.*, their output is caused by the available signal data, hence called CAUSAL). We shall, in this chapter, learn more about the operation and properties of LTI systems. We shall learn in what way and how the input signal $x(t)$ or $x[n]$ gets converted to the output signal $y(t)$ or $y[n]$.

1.11 ANALYSIS OF CONTINUOUS-TIME LTI SYSTEMS

We first learn about the convolution operation between two signals which an LTI system performs. It will be easier to understand the convolution principle in discrete domain using two discrete signals, say $x[n]$ and $h[n]$.

1.11.1 The Convolution of $x[n]$ and $h[n]$ (Understanding the Operation of Discrete-time Convolution Sum)

Consider a system $h[n]$ with internal detail shown in Fig. 1.31 (b). The delay time T means an input signal $x[n]$ becomes $x[n-1]$ after a delay of T. Similarly, an input $x[n-1]$ becomes $x[n-2]$ after a delay of T again. With this understanding, an input $\delta[n]$ becomes $\delta[n-1]$ after delay by time T, it becomes $\delta[n-2]$ after another delay of time T, and so on. In the system Fig. 1.31 (b), the various sequences available are summed up at the block shown by summer Σ after getting multiplied en-route. $\delta[n]$ becomes $2\delta[n]$ after getting multiplied by 2, $\delta[n-2]$ becomes $-3\delta[n-2]$ after getting multiplied by (–3) and so on. Since, the various inputs *i.e.*, $2\delta[n]$, $\delta[n-1]$, $-3\delta[n-2]$ and $4\delta[n-3]$ being fed to the summer Σ are at different instants of time (respectively, at $n = 0$, $n = 1$, $n = 2$ and $n = 3$) they will appear as shown in Fig. 1.31 (*c*). Thus, we have obtained a response for input $\delta[n]$. This is, therefore, called impulse response, because, input is an impulse $\delta[n]$, and is denoted by $h[n]$. $h[n]$ is also called the Unit Sample Response.

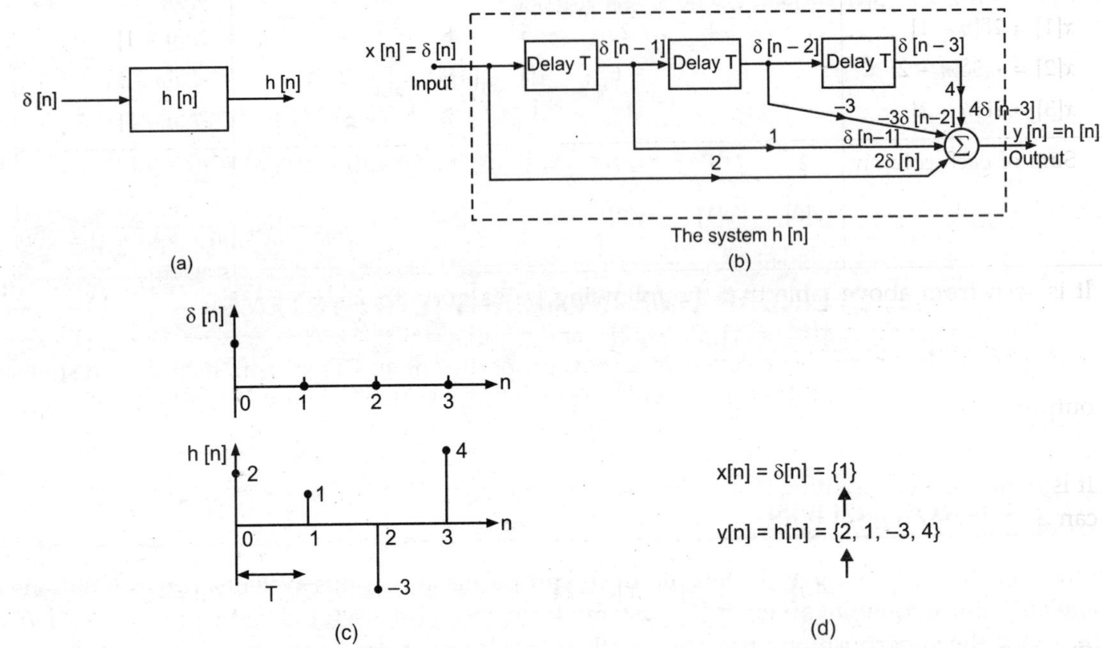

Fig. 1.31. (*a*) Block diagram of a system, (*b*) Internal details of the system (*a*), (*c*) Input $\delta[n]$ and output $h[n]$ shown on time axis, (*d*) $x[n] = \delta[n]$ and $y[n] = h[n]$ shown as the sequences.

Had we inputted $a\delta[n]$ (and not $\delta[n]$), the output would be a times the values of each sample of $h[n]$. *i.e.*, for input $5\delta[n]$, output will be $5h[n] = [\underset{\uparrow}{10}, 5, -15, 20]$.

Let us assume that the input to the system shown in Fig. 1.31 (*b*) is a generic signal $x[n]$ and not necessarily $\delta[n]$. The output will then be named as $y[n]$. Let, for example,

$$x[n] = \{1, 2, -3, 2\} \qquad \text{...(1.86)}$$

We wish to determine the sequence $y[n]$. Clearly the input is

$$x[n] = \delta[n] + 2\delta[n-1] - 3\delta[n-2] + 2\delta[n-3] \qquad \text{...(1.87)}$$

hence the output $\quad y[n] = h[n] + 2h[n-1] - 3h[n-2] + 2h[n-3] \qquad$ ...(1.88)

Note that the system has been assumed linear, hence the output $y[n]$ is the addition of outputs due to various segments ($\delta[n]$, $2\delta[n-1]$, $-3\delta[n-2]$ and $2\delta[n-3]$) of the input. The time invariance implies that delay in input causes the same delay in output (Remember if $x[n] \xrightarrow{gives} y[n]$), then in time invariant system $x[n-n_0] \xrightarrow{gives} y[n-n_0]$. Putting all these facts mathematically we get the following table:

Inputs ↓	Outputs at various times							Output is equal to
	$n = 0$	$n = 1$	$n = 2$	$n = 3$	$n = 4$	$n = 5$	$n = 6$	
$x[0] = \delta[n]$	2	1	– 3	4				$h[n]$
$x[1] = 2\delta[n-1]$		4	2	– 6	8			$2h[n-1]$
$x[2] = -3\delta[n-2]$			– 6	– 3	9	– 12		$-3h[n-2]$
$x[3] = 2\delta[n-3]$				4	2	– 6	8	$2h[n-3]$
Sum of each column	2	5	– 7	– 1	19	– 18	8	
	$y[0]$	$y[1]$	$y[2]$	$y[3]$	$y[4]$	$y[5]$	$y[6]$	$= \sum_{k=0}^{3} x(k)\, h(n-k)$

It is seen from above table that the following holds good for

$$x[n] = \{\underset{\uparrow}{1}, 2, -3, 2\} \quad \text{and} \quad h[n] = \{\underset{\uparrow}{2}, 1, -3, 4\} \qquad \text{...(1.89}a\text{)}$$

output

$$y[n] = \{\underset{\uparrow}{2}, 5, -7, -1, 19, -18, 8\} \qquad \text{...(1.89}b\text{)}$$

It is quite time-consuming, if we draw table to compute the output $y[n]$ each time. Note that we can also obtain output $y[n]$ in this example by the series

$$y[n] = \sum_{k=0}^{3} x[k] \cdot h[n-k], \quad n = 0, 1, ..., 6 \qquad \text{...(1.90)}$$

Check, by expanding the series given in (1.90). Putting $n = 0$ on both sides of (1.90), we get

$$y[0] = \sum_{k=0}^{3} x[k]\, h[0-k]$$

$$= x[0] \cdot h[0] = 1 \times 2 = 2$$

Putting $n = 1$ on both sides of (1.90), we get

$$y[1] = \sum_{k=0}^{3} x[k] \cdot h[1-k]$$

$$= x[0] \cdot h[1] + x[1] \cdot h[0]$$

$$= 1 \times 1 + 2 \times 2 = 1 + 4 = 5$$

Similarly,

$$y[2] = \sum_{k=0}^{3} x[k] \cdot h[2-k]$$

$$= x[0]\, h[2] + x[1]\, h[1] + x[2]\, h[0]$$

$$= 1 \times (-3) + 2 \times 1 + (-3) \times 2 = -3 + 2 - 6 = -7$$

Putting $n = 3$ both sides of (1.90), we have

$$y[3] = \sum_{k=0}^{3} x[k] \cdot h[3-k]$$

$$= x[0] \cdot h[3] + x[1] \cdot h[2] + x[2] \cdot h[1] + x[3] \cdot h[0]$$

$$= 1 \times 4 + 2 \times (-3) + (-3) \times 1 + 2 \times 2$$
$$= 4 - 6 - 3 + 4 = -1$$

and so on. It can be readily verified that all the values of the sequence $y[n]$ obtained at the output of the system shown in Fig. 1.31 (*b*) and calculated in the table can be computed by a generic convolution sum:

$$\boxed{y[n] = \sum_{k=-\infty}^{\infty} x[k] \cdot h[n-k]} \quad ...(1.91)$$

If we put $n - k = m$ in (1.91), then we obtain

$$\boxed{y[n] = \sum_{m=-\infty}^{\infty} x[m-k] \cdot h[m]} \quad ...(1.92)$$

We express convolution of two sequences $x_1[n]$ and $x_2[n]$ by the symbol $*$ between them and define it by

$$x_1[n] * x_2[n] \triangleq \sum_k x_1[k] \cdot x_2[n-k] \quad ...(1.92a)$$

$$= \sum_k x_1[n-k] \cdot x_2[k] \quad ...(1.92b)$$

Thus, in the above example $x_1[n]$ was $x[n]$ and $x_2[n]$ was $h[n]$. We can now express for the discrete-time system $h[n]$, input $x[n]$ and output $y[n]$ as in Fig. 1.32

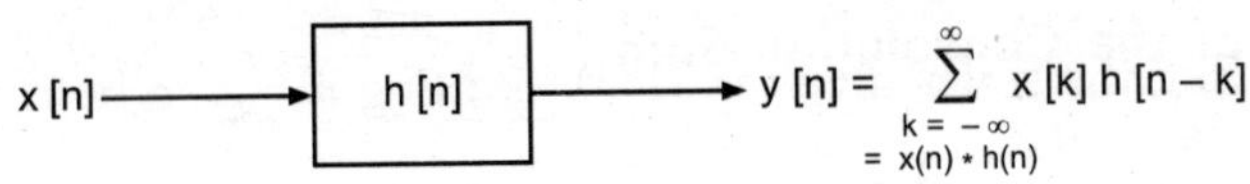

Fig. 1.32. Input-Output for a discrete-time system

Extending this concept on analog system, the summation series becomes integral, n becomes t, k becomes τ, and we get the *Convolution Integral:*

$$x_1(t) * x_2(t) \triangleq \int_{-\infty}^{\infty} x_1(\tau) \cdot x_2(t-\tau)\, d\tau \quad ...(1.93a)$$

$$= \int_{-\infty}^{\infty} x_1(t-\tau) \cdot x_2(\tau)\, d\tau \quad ...(1.93b)$$

We can show for an analog system, Fig. 1.33, the input $x(t)$ and $y(t)$ as indicated

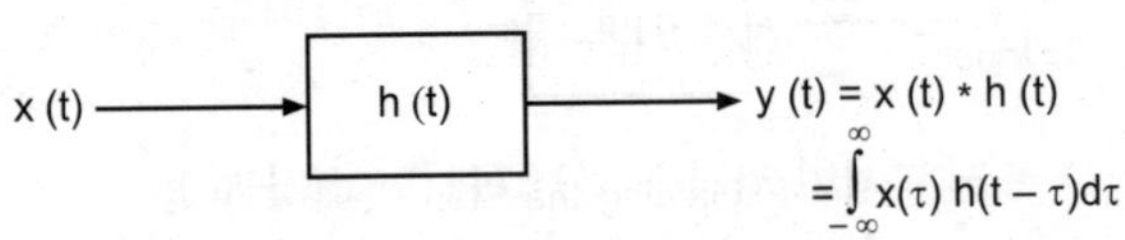

Fig. 1.33. Input-Output for an analog system

Replacing $x(t)$ as the input continuous-time signal, then the system with impulse response $h(t)$ will result output $y(t)$, as follows:

$$\boxed{y(t) = x(t) * h(t) = \int_{-\infty}^{\infty} x(\tau)\, h(t-\tau)\, d\tau} \quad ...(1.94)$$

1.11.2 Graphical Computation of Convolution Integral

The convolution integral (1.94) involves the following operations:

1. The impulse response $h(\tau)$ is time reversed, by reflecting about the origin , $\tau = 0$ axis, to obtain $h(-\tau)$. If we shift $h(-\tau)$ right by t we get $h[-(\tau - t)]$ *i.e.,* $h(t - \tau)$. This is a function of τ with parameter t as the shift.
2. The signal $x(\tau)$ and $h(t - \tau)$ is multiplied together for all values of τ with t fixed.
3. The product $x(\tau) \cdot h(t - \tau)$ is integrated from $\tau = -\infty$ to $\tau = t$. This integration yields $y(t)$.
4. Steps 1 to 3 are repeated as t varies from $-\infty$ to $+\infty$.

1.11.3 The Convolution Sum by Graphical Method

The Convolution sum determined in (1.91) *i.e.,*

$$y[n] = \sum_{k=-\infty}^{\infty} x[k] \cdot h(n-k)$$

can be found by graphical method as (as for analog case)

1. Time reverse $h[k]$ to get $h[-k]$ by reflecting about the origin. Shift $h[-k]$ by n to form $h[-(k - n)] = h[n - k]$ which is a function of k with parameter n as the shift.
2. Multiply sequences $x[k]$ and $h[n - k]$ for all values of k with n fixed at some value.
3. Product $x[k] \cdot h[n - k]$ is summed up for all k to produce a single output $y[n]$.
4. Steps 1 to 3 are repeated as n varies over $-\infty$ to $+\infty$ to produce the entire output $y[n]$.

1.11.4 Properties of the Convolution Sum (for proof see solved Example 1.35)

1. **Commutative Property:**

$$x_1[n] * x_2[n] = x_2[n] * x_1[n] \quad ...(1.95)$$

2. **Associative Property:**

$$\{x_1[n] * x_2[n]\} * x_3[n] = x_1[n] * \{x_2[n] * x_3[n]\} \quad ...(1.96)$$

3. **Distributive Property:**

$$x_1[n] * \{x_2[n] + x_3[n]\} = x_1[n] * x_2[n] + x_1[n] * x_3[n] \quad ...(1.97)$$

1.11.5 Definition of Step Response

When the input is $u[n]$ *i.e.,* a unit step, then the system output is called unit step response, as shown in Fig. 1.34. Hence,

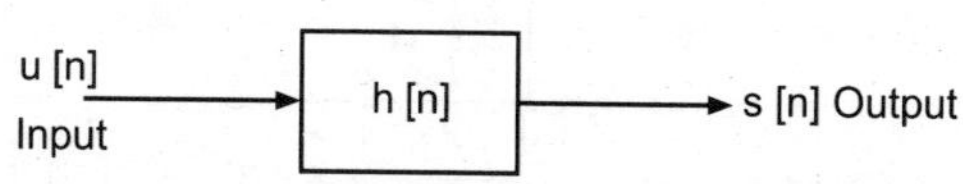

Fig. 1.34. Explaining the Step Response $s[n]$

$$s[n] = u[n] * h[n] \quad ...(1.98)$$

$$= \sum_{k=-\infty}^{\infty} h[k]\, u[n-k]$$

$$= \sum_{k=-\infty}^{n} h[k] \quad (\because u[n-k] = 0 \text{ for } k > n)$$

$$\therefore \qquad s[n-1] = \sum_{k=-\infty}^{n-1} h[k] = \sum_{k=-\infty}^{n} h[k] - h[n]$$

or
$$s[n] - s[n-1] = h[n] \qquad \text{...(1.99)}$$

EXAMPLE 1.23: *$x(n)$ and $h(n)$ are shown in Fig. Evaluate $y(n) = x(n) * h(n)$ by (a) analytical method, and (b) by graphical method.*

SOLUTION:

By Graphical Method

(*a*) Given $h(n)$ and $x(n)$, also drawn as $h(k)$ and $x(k)$

(*b*) $h[-k]$ advanced by 2 *i.e.*, $n = -2$ *i.e.*, $h[-(k+2)]$

(*c*) $h[-(k+1)]$ *i.e.*, $h(-k)$ advanced by 1

(*d*) $h[-k]$ *i.e.*, $n = 0$

(*e*) $h[-(k-1)]$ *i.e.*, $h(-k)$ delayed by 1

(*f*) $h[-(k-2)]$ *i.e.*, $h(-k)$ delayed by 2

(*g*) $h[-(k-3)]$ *i.e.*, $h(-k)$ delayed by 3

(*h*) $h[-(k-4)]$ *i.e.*, $h(-k)$ delayed by 4

(*i*) $h[-(k-5)]$ *i.e.*, $h(-k)$ delayed by 5

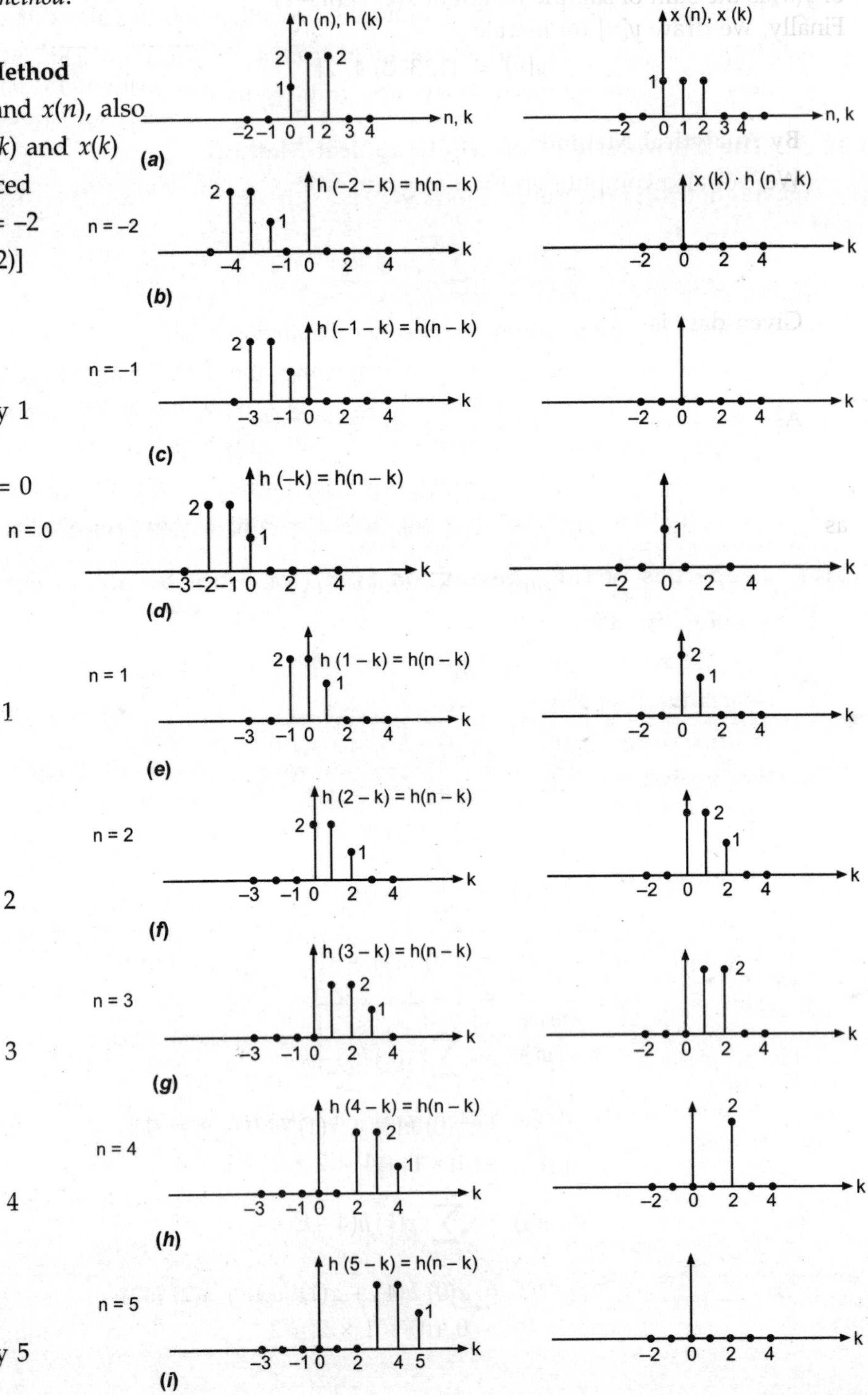

RHS sequences for (*b*) to (*i*) are $x(k) \cdot h(n-k)$ for $n = -2, -1, ..., 5$.

We first draw $h(-k)$ see Fig. (*d*). Then advance or delay $h(-k)$ by shifting this sequence to left or to right, as shown or LHS figures (*b*) to (*i*). The value of $y(n)$ is the sum of sample height of $x(k) \cdot h(n-k)$. Finally, we draw $y[n]$ on n-scale.

$$y[n] = \{\underset{\uparrow}{1}, 3, 5, 4, 2\}$$

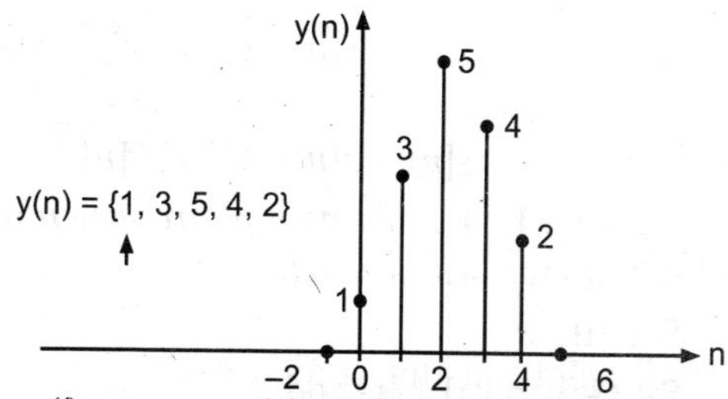

(*j*) sequence $x(n) * h(n)$ drawn on n as x-axis

Fig. Ex. 1.34. Explaining $x(n) * h(n)$

By Analytical Method

We can also compute $y(n) = x(n) * h(n)$ from the convolution sum given by Eq. (1.91)

$$y(n) = \sum_{k=-\infty}^{\infty} x(k) \cdot h(n-k), \quad n = -2, -1, ..., 5$$

Given data is $x(n) = \{\underset{\uparrow}{1}, 1, 1\}, \quad h(n) = \{\underset{\uparrow}{1}, 2, 2\}$

As $y(n) = \sum_{k=0}^{2} x(k)\, h(n-k)$ (since, $x(k)$ is non-zero only for $k = 0, 1$ and 2)

$\therefore$ $y(-1) = y(-2) = ... = 0$

as $h(n-k) = 0$ for $n = -1, -2, ...,$ and $k = 0, 1, 2,...$

$$y(0) = \sum_{k=0}^{2} x(k)\, h(-k)$$

$$= x(0) \cdot h(0) = 1 \times 1 = 1$$

$$y(1) = \sum_{k=0}^{2} x(k)\, h(1-k)$$

$$= x(0)\, h(1) + x(1)\, h(0)$$

$$= 1 \times 2 + 1 \times 1 = 3$$

$$y(2) = \sum_{k=0}^{2} x(k)\, h(2-k)$$

$$= x(0)\, h(2) + x(1)\, h(1) + x(2)\, h(0)$$

$$= 1 \times 2 + 1 \times 2 + 1 \times 1 = 5$$

$$y(3) = \sum_{k=0}^{2} x(k)\, h(3-k)$$

$$= x(0)\, h(3) + x(1)\, h(2) + x(2)\, h(1)$$

$$= 1 \times 0 + 1 \times 2 + 1 \times 2 = 4$$

$$y(4) = \sum_{k=0}^{2} x(k)\, h(4-k)$$

$$= x(0)\, h(4) + x(1)\, h(3) + x(2)\, h(2)$$

$$= 0 + 0 + 1 \times 2 = 2$$

$$y(5) = \sum_{k=0}^{2} x(k)\, h(5-k)$$
$$= x(0)\, h(5) + x(1)\, h(4) + x(2)\, h(3)$$
$$= 0 + 0 + 0 = 0$$

and so on $\quad y(n) = 0$ for $n = 5, 6, \ldots$

Also $\quad y(n) = 0$ for $n = -1, -2, \ldots$

Total length of the sequence = 5, $y(n) = \{1, 3, 5, 4, 2\}$ as expected.
$\uparrow$

> **Important Note:**
>
> ***(i)* If $x_1(n)$ and $x_2(n)$ are both causal then $x_1(n) * x_2(n)$ is also causal.** ...(1.100)
>
> ***(ii)* If $x_1(n)$ is of length N_1 and $x_2(n)$ is of length N_2, then their convolution $y(n) = x_1(n) * x_2(n)$ has length $N_1 + N_2 - 1$**

EXAMPLE 1.24: *Verify that:*

(*a*) $x(n) * h(n) = h(n) * x(n)$ (*b*) $\{x(n) * h_1(n)\} * h_2(n) = x(n) * \{h_1(n) * h_2(n)\}$

SOLUTION: (*a*) As by definition

$$x(n) * h(n) = \sum_{k=-\infty}^{\infty} x(k) \cdot h(n-k)$$

Put $\quad n - k = m$

$\therefore$ when $\quad k = -\infty, \quad m = +\infty$

$\quad k = +\infty, \quad m = -\infty$

$$\therefore \quad x(n) * h(n) = \sum_{m=-\infty}^{\infty} x(n-m) \cdot h(m)$$

$$= \sum_{m=-\infty}^{\infty} h(m) \cdot x(n-m) = h(n) * x(n)$$

Hence, $\quad \boxed{x(n) * h(n) = h(n) * x(n)}$ **Q.E.D.**

(*b*) Let $\quad x(n) * h_1(n) = f_1(n)$

and $\quad h_1(n) * h_2(n) = f_2(n)$ **N.T.S.****

$$\therefore \quad f_1(n) = \sum_{k=-\infty}^{\infty} x(k) \cdot h_1(n-k) \qquad \text{...(A)}$$

$$\text{and} \quad f_2(n) = \sum_{k=-\infty}^{\infty} h_1(k) \cdot h_2(n-k) \qquad \text{...(B)}$$

** N.T.S. ≡ Note this step. We have written N.T.S. at various places where we think that the student should note the mathematical manipulation with care.

and $\{x(n) * h_1(n)\} * h_2(n) = f_1(n) * h_2(n)$

$$= \sum_{m=-\infty}^{\infty} f_1(m) \cdot h_2(n-m)$$

$$= \sum_{m=-\infty}^{\infty} \left[\sum_{k=-\infty}^{\infty} x(k)\, h_1(m-k) \right] \cdot h_2(n-m)$$

[(*A*) replace n by m to get $f_1(m)$]

$$= \sum_{k=-\infty}^{\infty} x(k) \sum_{m=-\infty}^{\infty} h_1(m-k) \cdot h_2(n-m) \qquad \textbf{N.T.S.}$$

(interchanging the order of summation)

Put $m - k = r$, interchanging order of summation

$$\text{RHS} = \sum_{k=-\infty}^{\infty} x(k) \cdot \underbrace{\sum_{r=-\infty}^{\infty} h_1(r) \cdot h_2(n-k-r)}_{= f_2(n-k) \text{ due to } (B)}$$

$$= \sum_{k=-\infty}^{\infty} x(k) \cdot f_2(n-k) = x(n) * f_2(n) = x(n) * \{h_1(n) * h_2(n)\}$$

Hence,

$$\{x(n) * h_1(n)\} * h_2(n) = x(n) * \{h_1(n) * h_2(n)\} \qquad \textbf{Q.E.D.}$$

EXAMPLE 1.25: *Show that*

(*a*) $x(n) * \delta(n) = x(n)$

(*b*) $x(n) * \delta(n - n_0) = x(n - n_0)$

(*c*) $x(n) * u(n) = \sum_{k=-\infty}^{n} x(k)$

(*d*) $x(n) * u(n - n_0) = \sum_{k=-\infty}^{n-n_0} x(k)$ (*IP Univ. 2009*)

SOLUTION:

(*a*)
$$x(n) * \delta(n) = \sum_{k=-\infty}^{\infty} x(k) \cdot \delta(n-k)$$

$$= x(n) \qquad \because \delta(n-k) = 1 \text{ for } k = n, \text{ otherwise zero}$$

(*b*)
$$x(n) * \delta(n - n_0) = \sum_{k=-\infty}^{\infty} x(k)\, \delta(n - n_0 - k)$$

$$= x(n - n_0) \qquad \because \delta(n - n_0 - k) = 1 \text{ for } k = n - n_0, \text{ otherwise zero}$$

(*c*)
$$x(n) * u(n) = \sum_{k=-\infty}^{\infty} x(k) \cdot u(n-k)$$

But $u(n - k) = 0$ for $k > n$ $\quad \therefore$ take limits of $k \le n$

$$\therefore \quad x(n) * u(n) = \sum_{k=-\infty}^{n} x(k)$$

(d) $$x(n) * u(n-n_0) = \sum_{k=-\infty}^{\infty} x(k)\cdot u(n-n_0-k)$$

But $u(n-n_0-k) = 0$ for $k > n - n_0$ $\therefore$ take limits of $k \le n - n_0$

$$\therefore \quad x(n) * u(n-n_0) = \sum_{k=-\infty}^{n-n_0} x(k)$$

EXAMPLE 1.26: *Given step response s(n) of a discrete-time system, with impulse response h(n), find h(n) in terms of s(n).*

SOLUTION:

As $$s(n) = h(n) * u(n)$$

$$= \sum_{k=-\infty}^{\infty} h(k)\, u(n-k)$$

$$\therefore \quad s(n) = \sum_{k=-\infty}^{n} h(k) \qquad ...(A) \qquad \because u(n-k) = 0 \text{ for } k > n$$

Hence, $$s(n-1) = \sum_{k=-\infty}^{n-1} h(k) \qquad ...(B) \qquad (\text{Changing } n \text{ to } n-1 \text{ in (A)})$$

Subtracting (B) from (A), we have

$$s(n) - s(n-1) = \sum_{k=-\infty}^{n} h(k) - \sum_{k=-\infty}^{n-1} h(k)$$

$$= \left(h(n) + \sum_{k=-\infty}^{n-1}\right) - \sum_{k=-\infty}^{n-1} h(k) = h(n)$$

$$\therefore \quad \boxed{h(n) = s(n) - s(n-1)} \qquad ...(1.101)$$

Also directly:

As $$\delta(n) = u(n) - u(n-1)$$

$$\therefore \quad \delta(n) * h(n) = u(n) * h(n) - u(n-1) * h(n) \qquad ...(A)$$

$$\therefore \quad h(n) = s(n) - s(n-1), \text{ as expected}$$

The second term on RHS of (A) is due to the following steps

$$\because \quad s(n) = \sum_{k=-\infty}^{\infty} h(k)\, u(n-k)$$

$$\therefore \quad s(n-1) = \sum_{k=-\infty}^{\infty} h(k)\, u\big((n-1)-k\big) = u(n-1) * h(n)$$

$$= u(n-1) * h(n)$$

EXAMPLE 1.27: *The step response s[n] of a discrete-time LTI system is given by*

$$s[n] = \alpha^n u[n], 0 < \alpha < 1$$

Find the impulse response h[n] of the system.

SOLUTION: Given $s[n] = \alpha^n u[n]$, $0 < \alpha < 1$

We know that

$$h[n] = s[n] - s[n-1]$$

$$= \alpha^n u[n] - \alpha^{n-1} u[n-1]$$

$$= \alpha^n \cdot [\delta[n] + \underbrace{\delta[n-1] + \delta[n-2] + \ldots}_{u[n-1]}] - \alpha^{n-1} u[n-1] \quad \text{(N.T.S.)}$$

$$= \underbrace{\alpha^n \delta[n]}_{=\delta[n]} + \alpha^n u[n-1] - \alpha^{n-1} u[n-1]$$

$$= \delta[n] + \alpha^{n-1} (\alpha - 1) u[n-1]$$

$$\therefore \quad h[n] = \delta[n] - (1 - \alpha) \alpha^{n-1} . u[n-1]$$ **Ans.**

1.12 IMPORTANT PROPERTIES OF A DISCRETE-TIME LTI SYSTEM

(*a*) **System with or without memory:** If the system time equation is of the form

$$y[n] = kx[n] \quad \text{...(1.102a)}$$

i.e.,

$$h[n] = k\delta[n] \quad \text{...(1.102b)}$$

then the discrete-time LTI system is memoryless. Here, $y[n]$ depends only on the present values $x[n]$ of the input signal.

If the system equation is of the form

$$y[n] = k_1 x[n] + k_2 x[n - n_0] \quad \text{...(1.103a)}$$

i.e.,

$$h[n] = k_1 \delta[n] + k_2 \delta[n - n_0] \quad \text{...(1.103b)}$$

then the discrete-time LTI system is with memory if $n_0 \neq 0$. If n_0 is +ve, then $x[n - n_0]$ is the past or delayed value of the signal $x[n]$. If n_0 is –ve, then $x[n - n_0]$ is the future value of $x[n]$.

(*b*) **Causality of discrete-time LTI systems:** If $h[n] = 0$, for $n < 0$, ...(1.104)

then the system is causal

In such systems (*i.e.*, causal systems)

$$y[n] = x[n] * h[n]$$

$$= \sum_{k=0}^{\infty} h[k] \cdot x[n-k] \quad \text{...(1.105a)}$$

because $h[k] = 0$, for $k < 0$

Alternatively, for causal systems (1.105*a*) reduces to

$$y[n] = \sum_{k=-\infty}^{n} x[k] \cdot h[n-k] \quad \text{...(1.105b)}$$

(*c*) **Anticausal discrete systems:**

If $h[n] = 0$, for $n > 0$ ...(1.106)

the discrete system is anticausal

Also, if $\qquad x[n] = 0, \text{ for } n > 0$ ...(1.107)

the sequence $x[n]$ is anticausal.

Note that anticausal systems may have causal or anticausal output sequence $y[n]$. For example, when $x[n]$ is causal and $h[n]$ anticausal, then $y[n]$ can have values on both sides of $n = 0$. Other combinations are as given below.

$x[n]$	$h[n]$	$y[n] = x[n] * h[n]$
causal	causal	causal
causal	anticausal	$y[n]$ may extend on both sides of $n = 0$
anticausal	anticausal	anticausal
anticausal	causal	$y[n]$ may extend on both sides of $n = 0$

In fact, it is only when $x[n]$ and $y[n]$ are both causal, only then the output $y[n]$ is causal. As the causal systems are practically more useful, (due to their realizability), we always prefer a causal signal $x[n]$ and a causal system $h[n]$, to obtain a causal output $y[n]$.

(*d*) **Stability of a discrete-time system:** We have defined *BIBO* (bounded input bounded output) stability in Section 1.9.6. Let the system be characterized by $h[n]$ (may be causal or anticausal), and $x[n]$ be the bounded input, then we have

$$y[n] = x[n] * h[n] \qquad \text{...(1.108}a\text{)}$$

i.e.,

$$y[n] = \sum_{k=-\infty}^{\infty} h[k]\cdot x[n-k] \qquad \text{...(1.108}b\text{)}$$

For $x[n]$ to be bounded, we can always assume that $|x[n]| \le k_1$ *i.e.,* no sample of $x[n]$ has the magnitude exceeding k_1 ($k_1 < \infty$). If the output $y[n]$ is bounded then we must have $|y[n]| < \infty$. Applying these conditions on (1.108*b*), we have

$$|y[n]| = \left|\sum_{k=-\infty}^{\infty} h[k]\cdot x[n-k]\right| < \infty$$

As

$$\left|\sum_{k=-\infty}^{\infty} h[k]\cdot k_1\right| < \infty$$

$\therefore$

$$\left|\sum_{k=-\infty}^{\infty} h[k]\right| < \infty$$

$\therefore$

$$\boxed{\sum_{k=-\infty}^{\infty} |h[k]| < \infty} \qquad \text{...(1.109)}$$

which is the condition of the system $h[n]$ to be *BIBO* stable.

(*e*) **Eigen functions of discrete-time LTI systems:** Before we define the eigen function of a discrete-time system, it is necessary to understand the significance of eigen value and eigen function.

1.12.1 A Short Note on Eigen Function and Eigen Value

Consider an $N \times N$ matrix **A**.

If $$\boxed{\mathbf{A}\,\mathbf{X} = \lambda\,\mathbf{X}} \quad ...(1.110)$$

where λ is scalar constant and **X** is a non-zero column matrix, then

X is called eigen function or eigen vector of **A** associated with λ. ...(1.111*a*)

λ is called eigen value of **A** ...(1.111*b*)

Some books refer λ as *the characteristic value of* **A**. Note that there can be N different or multi eigen values λ. To determine the values of λ, we solve the characteristic equation

$$\boxed{|\lambda\,\mathbf{I} - \mathbf{A}| = 0} \quad ...(1.112)$$

where **I** is a unit matrix of degree N (*i.e.*, degree of the matrix **A**). For example, let the matrix **A** be

$$\mathbf{A} = \begin{bmatrix} 2 & 5 \\ 1 & 6 \end{bmatrix}$$

To find its eigen values, we solve the determinant equation

$$\begin{vmatrix} 2-\lambda & 5 \\ 1 & 6-\lambda \end{vmatrix} = 0$$

i.e., $$(2-\lambda)(6-\lambda) - 5 = 0$$

i.e., $$\lambda^2 - 8\lambda + 7 = 0 \quad \therefore \quad \lambda = 1, 7$$

Then the eigen values are $\lambda_1 = 1$, $\lambda_2 = 7$ for the given matrix **A**. It can be readily confirmed that

$$[A]\begin{bmatrix} x_1 \\ x_2 \end{bmatrix} = 1 \cdot \begin{bmatrix} x_1 \\ x_2 \end{bmatrix} \quad \text{for all values of } x_1 \text{ and } x_2.$$

and also,

$$[A]\begin{bmatrix} x_1 \\ x_2 \end{bmatrix} = 7 \cdot \begin{bmatrix} x_1 \\ x_2 \end{bmatrix} \quad \text{for all values of } x_1 \text{ and } x_2.$$

We, in our discrete-time system $h[n]$, also have some input signals $x[n]$ which result output of the form $\lambda x[n]$, λ and $x[n]$ could be both complex valued. In our case, the system function $h[n]$ will be equivalent to **A**. Consider the Z-transform $H(z)$ of $h[n]$ given by

$$H(z) = \sum_{k=-\infty}^{\infty} h[k]\, z^{-k} \quad ...(1.113)$$

(We shall learn, in detail, about the Z-transform in Chapter-3, $h[n]$ is called the system's impulse response and $H(z)$ is called the system function)

Let input $x(n) = z^n$ and output $y(n)$ for an LTI system

Then

$$\begin{aligned} y(n) &= x(n) * h(n) \\ &= \sum_{k=-\infty}^{\infty} h(k) \cdot x(n-k) \\ &= \sum_{k=-\infty}^{\infty} h(k) \cdot z^{n-k} \qquad \because x(n-k) = z^{(n-k)} \end{aligned}$$

$$= z^n \sum_{k=-\infty}^{\infty} h(k)\, z^{-k}$$

$$= z^n \cdot H(z), \text{ using relation (1.113)}$$

Hence, $\boxed{y(n) = H(z) \cdot z^n \text{ for input } x(n) = z^n}$ ...(1.114)

Thus, z^n is the eigen function of an LTI system because

Response $\{z^n\} = H(z) \cdot z^n$ have form

$$\mathbf{A\,X} = \lambda\,\mathbf{X}$$

Here $\mathbf{X} = z^n$, $\lambda = H(z)$ and (**note that** $y(0) = H(z)$ from Eq. (1.114))

$$\mathbf{A} = \text{Response}$$

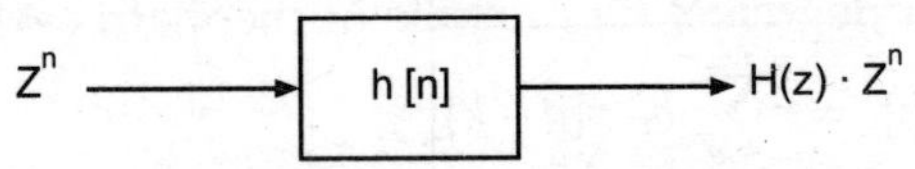

Fig. 1.35. Concept of eigen function of the system $h[n]$. Here z^n, is the eigen function and $H(z)$ is the eigen value

EXAMPLE 1.28: *Let T represents a discrete-time LTI system. Then show that*

$$T\{z^n\} = \lambda\, z^n$$

where z is a complex variable and λ is a complex constant.

SOLUTION: Given: $T\{x(n)\} = y(n)$ ...(A)

For $x(n) = z^n$

$$T\{z^n\} = y(n) \quad \text{...(B)}$$

Since, the system is time-invariant, we have, for an arbitrary n_0

$$T\left\{z^{n+n_0}\right\} = y(n+n_0)$$

i.e., $T\left\{z^{n_0} \cdot z^n\right\} = y(n+n_0)$ ...(C)

i.e., $z^{n_0}\, T\left\{z^n\right\} = y(n+n_0)$ ∵ the system is linear time invariant

Hence, $z^{n_0} \cdot y(n) = y(n+n_0)$

or $y(n+n_0) = z^{n_0} \cdot y(n)$ ...(D)

Setting $n = 0$, we have $y(n_0) = y(0) \cdot z^{n_0}$ from (D). Since n_0 is arbitrary, change n_0 to n in (D), we get

$$y(n) = \lambda\, z^n \quad \text{where } \lambda = y(0) = H(z)$$

Thus $T\{z^n\} = \lambda\, z^n$ **Q.E.D.**

Mathematically:

If $T\{x(\cdot)\} = \lambda\, x(\cdot)$

(LTI system) (Eigen value) (Eigen function)

then $x(\cdot)$ is called an eigen function (or characteristic function) of operator T.

1.13 DESCRIPTION OF DISCRETE-TIME LTI SYSTEMS BY DIFFERENCE EQUATIONS

In continuous-time systems, we use *differential equations* to describe an LTI system. Similarly, we use *difference equations* to describe an LTI discrete-time system. We briefly explain a discrete-time LTI in terms of difference equations.

1.13.1 Linear, Constant-Coefficient Difference Equation

An *N*-th order linear, constant-coefficient difference equation is of the form

$$a_0\, y[n] + a_1\, y[n-1] + a_2\, y[n-2] + \ldots + a_N\, y[n-N]$$
$$= b_0\, x[n] + b_1\, x[n-1] + b_2\, x[n-2] + \ldots + a_M\, x[n-M] \quad \ldots(1.115a)$$

i.e.,

$$\boxed{\sum_{k=0}^{N} a_k\, y[n-k] = \sum_{k=0}^{M} b_k\, x[n-k]} \quad \ldots(1.115b)$$

For a causal system, we must have $M \geq N$. Also, the coefficients a_i and b_i are all constant in the above difference equations. Moreover, $y[n] = 0$ at $n < 0$ or the system is initially at rest.

1.13.2 Recursive and Non-recursive System

In equation (1.115*a*) taking all terms $y[n-1]$, $y[n-2]$... onwards to RHS, we obtain

$$a_0\, y[n] = b_0\, x[n] + b_1\, x[n-1] + \ldots + b_M\, x[n-M]$$
$$- \{a_1\, y[n-1] + a_2\, y[n-2] + \ldots. + a_N\, y[n-N]\} \quad \ldots(1.116a)$$

we get,

$$y[n] = \frac{1}{a_0}\left\{\sum_{k=0}^{M} b_k\, x[n-k] - \sum_{k=1}^{N} a_k\, y[n-k]\right\} \quad \ldots(1.116b)$$

(*a*) In equation (1.116 *b*), if any a_k is non-zero, the equation (1.116*b*) is for a *recursive* discrete-time system.

(*b*) If all $a_1, a_2, \ldots, a_N$ are zero, then (1.116*b*) reduces to

$$\boxed{y[n] = \frac{1}{a_0}\sum_{k=0}^{M} b_k\, x[n-k]} \quad \ldots(1.117)$$

Equation (1.117) represents a *non-recursive* discrete-time system because, $y[n]$ is explicitly expressed in terms of scaled $x[n]$ with delays. To compute $y[n]$ we do not require the previous values $y[n-1]$, $y[n-2]$... etc. Hence, in this case, the auxiliary (additional) conditions are not needed to compute $y[n]$.

1.13.3 Impulse Response *h*[*n*], from Difference Equation

We know that output $y[n] = h[n]$ when input $x[n] = \delta[n]$. Hence

(*a*) **For Recursive system:** In equation (1.116*b*), replacing $y[n]$ by $h[n]$ and $y[n-1]$ by $h[n-1]$ and so on, and replacing $x[n]$ by $\delta[n]$ and $x[n-1]$ by $\delta[n-1]$ and so on, we get

$$h[n] = \frac{1}{a_0}\left\{\sum_{k=0}^{M} b_k\, \delta[n-k] - \sum_{k=1}^{N} a_k\, h[n-k]\right\} \quad \ldots(1.118)$$

It appears that calculation of $h[n]$ from equation (1.118) is quite involved. Yes, it is really so. We shall learn, after learning Z-transform, that this equation will get reduced to

$$H(z) = \frac{1}{a_0}\left\{\sum_{k=0}^{M} b_k Z^{-k} - \sum_{k=1}^{N} a_k \cdot Z^{-k} H(z)\right\}$$

Putting $a_0 H(z) = (a_0 Z^0) H(z)$ and shifting $H(z)$ terms on LHS, we get

$$H(z)\left\{\sum_{k=0}^{N} a_k Z^{-k}\right\} = \sum_{k=0}^{M} b_k Z^{-k}$$

Hence,

$$\boxed{H(z) = \frac{\sum_{k=0}^{M} b_k Z^{-k}}{\sum_{k=0}^{N} a_k Z^{-k}} = \frac{\sum_{k=0}^{M} b_k Z^{-k}}{a_0 + \sum_{k=1}^{N} a_k Z^{-k}}} \quad ...(1.119)$$

(*b*) **For Non-recursive system:** In equation (1.117), we replace $x[n]$ by $\delta[n]$ *i.e.*, $x[n-k]$ by $\delta[n-k]$ and $y[n]$ by $h[n]$. This readily gives us the equation.

$$h[n] = \frac{1}{a_0}\sum_{k=0}^{M} b_k\, \delta[n-k] \quad ...(1.120a)$$

Or

In the Z-transform domain, equation (1.120*a*) becomes

$$\boxed{H(z) = \frac{1}{a_0}\sum_{k=0}^{M} b_k Z^{-k}} \quad ...(1.120b)$$

From equation (1.120*a*), it is clear that

$$\boxed{h[n] = \begin{cases} b_n/a_0, 0 \le n \le M \\ 0, \text{otherwise} \end{cases}} \quad ...(1.121)$$

As the terms in $h[n]$ (see equation 1.120*a*) are finite, (which are $M + 1$ here), such an impulse response is also called *finite impulse response* (*FIR*).

Having developed various operations and properties of discrete-time systems, it will now be easy to extend these operations to continuous-time systems. The summation in discrete-time systems becomes integration in time domain for continuous-time systems.

EXAMPLE 1.29: *Find the impulse response h(n) for each of the LTI discrete-time systems given by the difference equations as given. Indicate whether each system is an FIR or an IIR system. Assume the systems causal.*

(*a*) $y(n) = x(n) - 2x(n-2) + x(n-3)$

(*b*) $y(n) + 2y(n-1) = x(n) + x(n-1)$

(*c*) $y(n) = \frac{1}{2}\, y(n-2) + 2x(n) - x(n-2)$

SOLUTION:

(*a*)
$$y(n) = x(n) - 2x(n-2) + x(n-3) \text{ (given)}$$
$$\therefore \quad h(n) = \delta(n) - 2\delta(n-2) + \delta(n-3) \text{ (replacing } x(n) \text{ by } \delta(n) \text{ and } y(n) \text{ by } h(n))$$
$$\therefore \quad h(n) = \{\underset{\uparrow}{1}, 0, -2, 1\}. \text{ The system is } FIR$$
Ans.

(*b*)
$$y(n) + 2y(n-1) = x(n) + x(n-1) \text{ (given)}$$
$$\therefore \quad h(n) = -2h(n-1) + \delta(n) + \delta(n-1) \text{ (replacing } x(n) \text{ by } \delta(n) \text{ and } y(n) \text{ by } h(n))$$

Since the system is causal, $h(-1) = 0$ (This assumption is given)

$$\therefore \quad h(0) = -2h(-1) + \delta(0) + \delta(-1) = -0 + 1 + 0 = 1$$
$$h(1) = -2h(0) + \delta(1) + \delta(0) = -2 + 0 + 1 = -1 = (-1)^1\, 2^{1-1}$$
$$h(2) = -2h(1) + \delta(2) + \delta(1) = -2h(1) = -2(-1) = 2 = (-1)^2\, 2^{2-1}$$
$$h(3) = -2h(2) = -2(2) = -2^2 = (-1)^3\, 2^{3-1}$$
$$\vdots$$
$$h(n) = \underbrace{(-1)^n \cdot 2^{n-1}}_{\text{for } n \geq 1} + \underbrace{\delta(n)}_{\text{for } n=0} = \delta(n) + [(-1)^n\, 2^{n-1}]\, u(n-1)$$

Hence, the system is *IIR*. **Ans.**

(*c*)
$$y(n) = \frac{1}{2} y(n-2) + 2x(n) - x(n-2) \text{ (given)}$$
$$\therefore \quad h(n) = \frac{1}{2} h(n-2) + 2\delta(n) - \delta(n-2) \text{ (replacing } x(n) \text{ by } \delta(n) \text{ and } y(n) \text{ by } h(n))$$

System is causal, therefore, assume $h(-1) = 0$ (this assumption is given)

$$h(0) = \frac{1}{2} h(-2) + 2\delta(0) - \delta(-2) = 0 + 2 - 0 = 2$$
$$h(1) = \frac{1}{2} h(-1) + 2\delta(1) - \delta(-1) = 0 + 0 - 0 = 0$$
$$h(2) = \frac{1}{2} h(0) + 2\delta(2) - \delta(0) = \frac{1}{2}(2) - 1 = 0$$
$$h(3) = \frac{1}{2}(0) + 0 - 0 = 0, \text{ and so on}$$

Finally, we get $x(n) = 2\delta(n)$. Hence, the system is *FIR*. **Ans.**

EXAMPLE 1.30: *Show that if the input $x(n)$ to a discrete-time LTI system is periodic then the output $y(n)$ is also periodic.* (*GGS IP Univ. 2007*)

SOLUTION: Let $x(n)$ be periodic with period N $\quad \therefore x(n) = x(n + N)$

$$y(n) = x(n) * h(n)$$
$$= \sum_{k=-\infty}^{\infty} h(k)\, x(n-k) \qquad \text{...}(A)$$

Put $n = m + N$ on both sides of (A)

$$\therefore \quad y(m + N) = \sum_{k=-\infty}^{\infty} h(k) \cdot x(m + N - k)$$

But $x(m-k+N) = x(m-k)$ $\quad$ $x(n)$ being periodic with period N

$$\therefore \quad y(m+N) = \sum_{k=-\infty}^{\infty} h(k)\cdot x(m-k)$$

$$= y(m)$$

As $y(m+N) = y(m)$

i.e. $y(n+N) = y(n)$ $\quad$ $\therefore$ the output $y(n)$ is periodic with period N

Q.E.D.

EXAMPLE 1.31: *(a) Define periodic convolution of two sequences $x_1[n]$ and $x_2[n]$ each being periodic with period N. (b) Show that $y[n] = x_1[n] * x_2[n]$ is also periodic with period N.*

SOLUTION: If $x_1[n]$ is periodic then $x_1[n] = x_1[n+kN]$, $k = 0, \pm1, \pm2, \ldots$. Similarly, if $x_2[n]$ is periodic then $x_2[n] = x_2[n+kN]$, $k = 0, \pm 1, \pm 2, \ldots$

As,

$$\text{“}y[n] = x_1[n] * x_2[n]\text{”}$$

A convolution between two periodic sequences $x_1(n)$ and $x_2(n)$ is defined by $x_1(n) \otimes x_2(n)$.

Hence, $y[n] = x_1[n] \otimes x_2[n]$

$$= \sum_{k=0}^{N-1} x_1[k]\cdot x_2[(n-k)_N] \quad \ldots(A)$$

where, $x\left[((\cdot))_N\right]$ is mod operation which means we can add or subtract which multiples of N from the argument of x

$$y(n) = \sum_{k=0}^{N-1} x_1[k]\cdot x_2[n+N-k] \quad \ldots(B) \because \; x_2[(n-k)_N] = x_2[n-k+N]$$

But *RHS* of (B) $= y\,(n+N)$ $\quad$ convolution for one period N

$$\therefore \quad y[n] = y[n+N]$$

Thus, $y[n]$ is periodic with period N.

> **Important Note:**
>
> When the sequences are periodic, it makes no sense to take limits of summation for k varying from $-\infty$ to $+\infty$. We take only one period samples, preferably k varying from 0 to $N-1$ (*i.e.*, N samples). ...(1.122)

1.14 SYSTEM IDENTIFICATION AND DECONVOLUTION

1.14.1 System Identification [to find $h(n)$, given $x(n)$ and $y(n)$]

The computation of unit sample response $h(n)$ of an unknown system by suitable measurement made at input ($x(n)$) and output ($y(n)$) is known as *system identification*. As for LTI system with finite length of its $h(n)$ and assuming $h(n)$ causal, we have

$$y(n) = \sum_{k=0}^{n} h(k)\, x\,(n-k) \quad \ldots(A)$$

$$\therefore \quad y(n) = h(0)\; x(n) + h(1)\; x\;(n-1) + \ldots + h(n)\; x(0) \quad \ldots(B)$$

Putting $n = 0$, both sides of (A), we get

$$y(0) = \sum_{k=0}^{0} h(k)\, x(0-k)$$

$$= h(0) \cdot x(0)$$

$$\therefore \quad \boxed{h(0) = \frac{y(0)}{x(0)},\ x(0) \neq 0} \qquad \text{...(1.123)}$$

We can write (*B*) as

$$y(n) = \sum_{k=0}^{n-1} h(k)\, x(n-k) + h(n)\, x(0) \quad \text{for } n \geq 1$$

$$\therefore \quad \boxed{h(n) = \frac{1}{x(0)}\left[y(n) - \sum_{k=0}^{n-1} h(k)\, x(n-k)\right];\ \begin{matrix} n \geq 1, x(0) \neq 0 \\ n = 1, 2, ..., n \end{matrix}} \qquad \text{...(1.124)}$$

We can compute $h(n)$ iteratively by using equations (1.123) and (1.124).

1.14.2 Deconvolution [to find $x(n)$, given $h(n)$ and $y(n)$]

The procedure for computing the input signal $x(n)$, given the unit-sample response, $h(n)$, and the output signal $y(n)$, is called the *Deconvolution*. The procedure is almost similar to the one for system identification (where we compute $h(n)$, given $x(n)$ and $y(n)$). We know that

$$y(n) = \sum_{k=0}^{n} h(k)\, x(n-k) \qquad \text{...(A)}$$

We have assumed an LTI causal system with FIR impulse response $h(n)$

From (*A*), separating the first term, we can write

$$y(n) = h(0)\, x(n) + \sum_{k=1}^{n} h(k)\, x(n-k) \qquad \text{...(B)}$$

We know that

$$y(0) = x(0) \cdot h(0) \qquad \text{(Note this step)}$$

i.e.

$$\boxed{x(0) = \frac{y(0)}{h(0)}, \qquad h(0) \neq 0} \qquad \text{...(1.125)}$$

From (B), we can write

$$\boxed{x(n) = \frac{1}{h(0)}\left[y(n) - \sum_{k=1}^{n} h(k) \cdot x(n-k)\right];\ \begin{matrix} n = 1, 2, ..., n \\ h(0) \neq 0 \end{matrix}} \qquad \text{...(1.126)}$$

Hence, $x(n)$ can be determined iteratively, for $n = 1, 2, ..., n$ by using Eqs. (1.125) and (1.126). This procedure is called Deconvolution.

EXAMPLE 1.32: *An unknown discrete-time causal LSI system yields $y(n) = \{1, 3, 6, 10, 12, 12, 10, 6, 3, 1\}$ for input $x(n) = \{1, 1, 1, 1\}$. Identify the system i.e. find $h(n)$ for this system.*

SOLUTION:

Given $\qquad x(n) = \{\underset{\uparrow}{1}, 1, 1, 1\}$ and $y(n) = \{\underset{\uparrow}{1}, 3, 6, 10, 12, 12, 10, 6, 3, 1\}$

From Eq. (1.123), we have

$$h(0) = \frac{y(0)}{x(0)} = \frac{1}{1} = 1 \neq 0 \qquad h(0) = 1$$

Again from Eq. (1.124), we have

as $$h(n) = \frac{1}{x(0)}\left[y(n) - \sum_{k=0}^{n-1} h(k)\cdot x(n-k)\right], \quad n = 1, 2, \ldots,$$

We expect $h(n)$ of length = length of $y(n)$ – length of $x(n)$ + 1 = 7 (Note this step)

∴ We find $h(n)$ for $n = 0, 1, 2, \ldots, 6$

$$h(1) = \frac{1}{1}\left[y(1) - \sum_{k=0}^{0} h(k)\, x(1-k)\right] = 3 - (1\times 1) = 2 \qquad \therefore h(1) = 2$$

$$h(2) = \frac{1}{1}\left[y(2) - \sum_{k=0}^{1} h(k)\, x(2-k)\right] = [6 - (1\times 1 + 2\times 1)] = 3 \qquad \therefore h(2) = 3$$

$$h(3) = \frac{1}{1}\left[y(3) - \sum_{k=0}^{2} h(k)\, x(3-k)\right] = [10 - (1\times 1 + 2\times 1 + 3\times 1)] = 4 \qquad \therefore h(3) = 4$$

$$h(4) = \frac{1}{1}\left[y(4) - \sum_{k=0}^{3} h(k)\cdot x(4-k)\right] = [12 - (1\times 0 + 2\times 1 + 3\times 1 + 4\times 1)] = 3$$

$$\therefore h(4) = 3$$

$$h(5) = \frac{1}{1}\left[y(5) - \sum_{k=0}^{4} h(k)\, x(5-k)\right] = [12 - (1\times 0 + 2\times 0 + 3\times 1 + 4\times 1 + 3\times 1)] = 2$$

$$\therefore h(5) = 2$$

$$h(6) = \frac{1}{1}\left[y(6) - \sum_{k=0}^{5} h(k)\, x(6-k)\right] = [10 - (1\times 0 + 2\times 0 + 3\times 0 + 4\times 1$$

$$+ 3\times 1 + 2\times 1)] = 10 - 9 = 1$$

$$\therefore h(6) = 1$$

Hence, $h(n) = \{\underset{\uparrow}{1}, 2, 3, 4, 3, 2, 1\}$ **Ans.**

Note that we do not use $y(n)$ values beyond $y(6)$, as $h(n)$ has been computed for seven length sequence.

(C) UNSOLVED PROBLEMS WITH ANSWERS

C-1.16. Show that if $y(t) = x(t) * h(t)$, then

$$\left[\frac{dy(t)}{dt}\right] = \left[\frac{dx(t)}{dt}\right] * h(t) = x(t) * \left[\frac{dh(t)}{dt}\right]$$

C-1.17. Show that

$$x_1[n] \otimes x_2[n] = \sum_{k=n_0}^{n_0+N-1} x_1[k]\cdot x_2[n-k]$$

where ⊗ shows circular convolutions and $x_1(n)$ and $x_2(n)$ are periodic with period N.

C-1.18. A discrete-time LTI-system has impulse response

$$h[n] = \left(\frac{1}{2}\right)^n u[n-1]$$

(*a*) Is the system causal?

(*b*) Is the system stable?

[**Ans:** (*a*) Yes, causal, (*b*) Yes, stable]

C-1.19. Consider a discrete-time LTI-system with impulse response

$$h[n] = \begin{cases} 1, & n = 0, 1 \\ 0, & \text{otherwise} \end{cases}$$

Find the input-output relationship of the system.

[**Ans:** $y[n] = x[n] + x[n-1]$]

C-1.20. Compute the convolution sum $y(n) = x(n) * h(n)$

(*a*) $x(n) = u(n)$, $h(n) = 2^n\, u(-n)$

(*b*) $x(n) = \left(\frac{1}{2}\right)^n u(n),\ h(n) = \delta(n) - \frac{1}{2}\delta(n-1)$

[**Ans:** (*a*) $y(n) = 2^{1-n}\, u(-n)$, (*b*) $y(n) = \delta(n)$]

C-1.21. Given $x(t) = 5 \cos t$ and $y(t) = 2e^{-|t|}$, find $x(t) * y(t)$

[**Ans:** $10 \cos t,\ -\infty < t < \infty$]

C-1.22. Identify the system $h(n)$ if the input $x(n) = \left\{\underset{\uparrow}{1}, 2, -1\right\}$ and output $y(n) = \left\{2, \underset{\uparrow}{4}, 0, 4, -2\right\}$

(Identification problem) [**Ans:** $h(n) = \left\{2, \underset{\uparrow}{0}, -2\right\}$].

C-1.23. Given $y(n) = \left\{2, \underset{\uparrow}{4}, 0, 4, -2\right\}$ and $h(n) = \left\{2, \underset{\uparrow}{0}, -2\right\}$.

(Deconvolution problem) [**Ans:** $x(n) = \left\{\underset{\uparrow}{1}, 2, -1\right\}$]

CHAPTER 2

Discrete-Time Fourier Series and the Discrete-Time Fourier Transform (DTFS and DTFT)

2.1 INTRODUCTION

We know the representation of continuous-time periodic and aperiodic signals in terms of continuous-time Fourier series (CTFS) and continuous-time Fourier transform (CTFT), respectively. In this chapter, we extend the Fourier analysis for periodic and aperiodic discrete-time signals. For computer-oriented applications, discrete signals form the basis of any system. Even an analog signal $x(t)$ is first converted into an appropriate discrete signal $x(nT)$ so as to adopt it to computer processing.

2.1.1 An Important Result

We first give an important result which will be used in many mathematical calculations, when we deal with the discrete-time signals. We will show that

$$\sum_{k=0}^{N-1} e^{jkm(2\pi/N)} = N\,\delta(m) \qquad \text{...(2.1)}$$

Proof.

$\sum_{k=0}^{N-1} e^{jkm(2\pi/N)}$ is a geometric progression (GP) with 'r' = $e^{jm(2\pi/N)}$, the first term being 1 and the last term being $e^{j(N-1)\,m(2\pi/N)} = r^{N-1}$

The summation

$$\sum_{k=0}^{N-1} r^k = \frac{1-r^N}{1-r} \qquad \text{...(2.2)}$$

i.e.,

$$\sum_{k=0}^{N-1} e^{jkm(2\pi/N)} = \frac{1-e^{jNm\,2\pi/N}}{1-e^{jm2\pi/N}} \qquad \text{...(2.3}a\text{)}$$

$$= \frac{1 - e^{j2\pi m}}{1 - e^{j2\pi m/N}} \quad ...(2.3b)$$

$$= 0, \quad m \neq 0 \quad ...(2.3c)$$

For $m = 0$, (2.3b) assumes the form $\frac{0}{0}$. So, we apply l' Hospital Rule to evaluate RHS of (2.3b). We differentiate the numerator and the denominator w.r.t. m, and then put $m = 0$. Doing so we obtain

$$\lim_{m \to 0} \frac{1 - e^{j2\pi m}}{1 - e^{j2\pi m/N}} = \lim_{m \to 0} \frac{(-j2\pi)e^{j2\pi m}}{\left(-j\frac{2\pi}{N}\right)e^{j2\pi m/N}}$$

$$= N \quad \text{for } m = 0 \quad ...(2.3d)$$

Hence, we can write

$$\sum_{k=0}^{N-1} e^{jkm(2\pi/N)} = \begin{cases} 0 \text{ for } m \neq 0 & \text{(due to 2.3}c\text{)} \\ N \text{ for } m = 0 & \text{(due to 2.3}d\text{)} \end{cases}$$

i.e.,

$$\boxed{\sum_{k=0}^{N-1} e^{jkm(2\pi / N)} = N\delta(m)} \quad ...(2.4)$$

Note that m and k are integers. For example,

$$\sum_{k=0}^{N-1} e^{jk(l - m)(2\pi/N)} = N\delta(l - m) \quad ...(2.5)$$

Here "m" $= l - m$, an integer if l and m are both integers. We can also prove that

$$\sum_{k=0}^{N-1} e^{-jkm(2\pi / N)} = N\delta(m) \quad ...(2.6)$$

2.1.2 Fundamental Period (N) and Fundamental Frequency (ω_0) of a Periodic Signal $x(n)$

A discrete-time signal/sequence $x(n)$ is periodic if

$$x(n) = x(n + kN) \quad \text{for all } k = 0, \pm 1, \pm 2, ..., \quad ...(2.7)$$

We define the fundamental frequency by

$$\omega_0 = \frac{2\pi}{N} \quad ...(2.8)$$

Note that in the case of periodic analog signal $x(t)$ with period T, we had the following definitions

$$x(t) = x(t + kT), \quad k = 0, \pm 1, \pm 2, ..., \quad ...(2.9a)$$

$$\omega_0 = \frac{2\pi}{T} \quad \text{(fundamental frequency)} \quad ...(2.9b)$$

Also, we note that a signal $x(n)$ given by

$$x(n) = e^{j\omega n} = e^{j(\omega + 2\pi k)\, n} \quad ...(2.10)$$

Hence, $e^{j\omega n}$ is a periodic sequence, periodic in ω with period 2π. Also, if

$$x(n) = e^{jn\frac{2\pi}{N}} = e^{j(n+kN)\frac{2\pi}{N}} \quad ...(2.11a)$$

then $\qquad x(n + kN) = x(n), \quad k = 0, \pm 1, \pm 2...,$ ...(2.11b)

Here $x(n)$ is periodic in n with period N.

2.2 REPRESENTATION OF A PERIODIC SEQUENCE $x(n)$ AS A FOURIER SERIES (DTFS)

If $x(n)$ is periodic with period N,

then $$x(n) = \sum_{k=\langle N\rangle} a_k\, e^{jk\omega_0 n}, \; \omega_0 = \frac{2\pi}{N} \quad ...(2.12a)$$

(*synthesis equation*)

and $$a_k = \frac{1}{N}\sum_{n=\langle N\rangle} x(n)\, e^{-jk\omega_0 n}, \; \omega_0 = \frac{2\pi}{N} \quad ...(2.12b)$$

(*analysis equation*)

Equation (2.12*a*) is called the *synthesis equation*. It builds up (synthesizes) the signal $x(n)$ from the coefficients a_k, $k = 0, 1, 2, ... , N - 1$ *i.e.*, totalling N coefficients. Equation (2.12*b*) is called the *analysis equation*. The coefficients a_k, also called the Fourier coefficients, form the N bases to construct $x(n)$. a_k are also called the spectral coefficients of $x(n)$. These coefficients form the decomposed version of $x(n)$ into N harmonically related orthogonal exponentials. The meaning of $x = \langle N\rangle$ is that n varies over one period of n. (May be $n = 0, 1, ..., N - 1$; or $n = n_0, n_0 + 1, n_0 + 2, ..., N + n_0 - 1$, and so on). We shall use this notation in the various derivations.

Proof. (Derivation of a_k)

Assume that equation (2.12*a*) is true *i.e.*,

$$x(n) = \sum_{k=\langle N\rangle} a_k\, e^{jk\omega_0 n}, \quad \omega_0 = \frac{2\pi}{N} \quad ...(2.13)$$

Consider the series

$$\frac{1}{N}\sum_{n=\langle N\rangle} x(n)\, e^{-jk\omega_0 n} = \frac{1}{N}\sum_{n=\langle N\rangle}\left(\sum_{l=\langle N\rangle} a_l\, e^{jl\omega_0 n}\right) e^{-jk\omega_0 n} \quad ...(2.14)$$

We have replaced the expression for $x(n)$ from (2.13) on LHS of (2.14). As k is a dummy variable in (2.13), we have renamed it as l. This has been done, since, k already appears in the term $e^{-jk\omega_0 n}$ of LHS of (2.14). Had we used $a_k\, e^{jk\omega_0 n}$ (and not $a_l\, e^{jl\omega_0 n}$) in L.H.S. of (2.14), then $e^{-jk\omega_0 n}$ and $e^{jk\omega_0 n}$ would cancel each other giving $\left(e^{-jk\omega_0 n}\right)\left(e^{jk\omega_0 n}\right) = 1$. RHS of (2.14) can be manipulated by interchanging the order of summation. Doing so (2.14) gives us:

$$\frac{1}{N}\sum_{n=\langle N\rangle} x(n)\, e^{-jk\omega_0 n} = \frac{1}{N}\sum_{l=\langle N\rangle} a_l \sum_{n=\langle N\rangle} e^{j(l-k)\,\omega_0 n}$$

$$= \frac{1}{N}\sum_{l=\langle N\rangle} a_l \sum_{n=\langle N\rangle} e^{j(l-k)\left(\frac{2\pi}{N}\right)n} \qquad \left(\because \omega_0 = \frac{2\pi}{N}\right)$$

$$= \frac{1}{N} \sum_{l=\langle N \rangle} a_l \, N\delta(l-k) \quad \text{(using (2.4))}$$

$$= \sum_{l=\langle N \rangle} a_l \, \delta(l-k)$$

$$= a_k \qquad (\because \delta(l-k) = 1 \text{ only when } l = k)$$

Then $$a_k = \frac{1}{N} \sum_{n=\langle N \rangle} x(n) \, e^{-jk\omega_0 n}, \quad \omega_0 = \frac{2\pi}{N}$$

which is same as (2.12*b*). **Q.E.D.**

2.2.1 Periodicity of a_k

We show that a_k is periodic with period N, *i.e.*,

$$\boxed{a_k = a_{k+lN}, \quad l = 0, \pm 1, \pm 2, \ldots} \qquad \text{...(2.15)}$$

Proof.

From (2.12b), we have

$$a_k = \frac{1}{N} \sum_{n=\langle N \rangle} x(n) \, e^{-jk\left(\frac{2\pi}{N}\right)n}$$

$$\therefore \quad a_{k+lN} = \frac{1}{N} \sum_{n=\langle N \rangle} x(n) \, e^{-j(k+lN)\frac{2\pi}{N}n} \quad \text{(replacing } k \text{ by } k + ln)$$

$$= \frac{1}{N} \sum_{n=\langle N \rangle} x(n) \, e^{-jk\left(\frac{2\pi}{N}\right)n} \times e^{-j2\pi ln} = a_k \quad (\because e^{-j2\pi ln} = 1 \text{ for all } n) \quad \text{Q.E.D.}$$

2.3 PROPERTIES OF DTFS

We shall now prove some important properties of discrete-time Fourier series. These will enable us to tackle practical problems. Thereafter, we shall evolve discrete-time Fourier transform (DTFT) for the aperiodic discrete-time sequence $x(n)$ with $N \to \infty$.

2.3.1 Linearity

$$\boxed{\begin{array}{c} \text{If } x(n) \xleftrightarrow{DTFS} a_k \text{ and } y(n) \xleftrightarrow{DTFS} b_k \\ \text{then } Ax(n) + By(n) \xleftrightarrow{DTFS} Aa_k + Bb_k \end{array}} \qquad \text{...(2.16)}$$

Proof.

Given $$a_k = \frac{1}{N} \sum_{n=\langle N \rangle} x(n) \, e^{-jk\omega_0 n} \text{ and } b_k = \frac{1}{N} \sum_{n=\langle N \rangle} y(n) \, e^{-jk\omega_0 n} \qquad \text{...(2.17)}$$

Let $$A\,x(n) + B\,y(n) \xleftrightarrow{DTFS} d_k \qquad \text{...(2.18)}$$

then $$d_k = \frac{1}{N} \sum_{n=\langle N \rangle} [A\,x(n) + B\,y(n)] \, e^{-jk\omega_0 n}$$

$$= \frac{A}{N} \sum_{n=\langle N \rangle} x(n) \, e^{-jk\omega_0 n} + \frac{B}{N} \sum_{n=\langle N \rangle} y(n) \, e^{-jk\omega_0 n}$$

$$= A\,a_k + B\,b_k \quad \text{using (2.17)}$$

i.e., $$A\,x(n) + B\,y(n) \xleftrightarrow{DTFS} A\,a_k + B\,b_k$$ **Q.E.D.**

2.3.2 Time-Reversal

$$\boxed{\text{If } x(n) \xleftrightarrow{DTFS} a_k, \text{ then } x(-n) \xleftrightarrow{DTFS} a_{-k}} \quad ...(2.19)$$

Proof.

Let $$x(-n) \xleftrightarrow{DTFS} b_k$$

Then $$b_k = \frac{1}{N}\sum_{n=\langle N\rangle} x(-n)\,e^{-jk(2\pi/N)\,n} \quad \text{(by definition)} \quad ...(2.20)$$

Put $$n = -n'$$

If n varies from n_1 to $n_1 + N$ then $-n$ varies from $-n_1$ to $-(n_1 + N)$. Addition being commutative, n' will vary for one time period N. Hence,

$$b_k = \frac{1}{N}\sum_{n'=\langle N\rangle} x(n')\,e^{jk(2\pi/N)\,n'}$$

$$= \frac{1}{N}\sum_{n'=\langle N\rangle} x(n')\,e^{-j(-k)(2\pi/N)\,n'} = a_{-k}$$

$\therefore$ $$b_k = a_{-k}$$

i.e., $$x(-n) \xleftrightarrow{DTFS} a_{-k}$$ **Q.E.D.**

2.3.3 Conjugation

$$\boxed{\text{If } x(n) \xleftrightarrow{DTFS} a_k, \text{ then } x^*(n) \xleftrightarrow{DTFS} a^*_{-k}} \quad ...(2.21)$$

Proof.

Let $$x^*(n) \xleftrightarrow{DTFS} b_k$$

then $$b_k = \frac{1}{N}\sum_{n=\langle N\rangle} x^*(n)\,e^{-jk(2\pi/N)\,n} \quad ...(2.22)$$

$$= \left[\frac{1}{N}\sum_{n=\langle N\rangle} x(n)\,e^{-j(-k)(2\pi/N)\,n}\right]^* = [a_{-k}]^*$$

$\therefore$ $$b_k = a^*_{-k}, \text{ which implies that } x^*(n) \xleftrightarrow{DTFS} a^*_{-k}$$ **Q.E.D.**

2.3.4 Time-Shifting

$$\boxed{\text{If } x(n) \xleftrightarrow{DTFS} a_k, \text{ then } x(n - n_0) \xleftrightarrow{DTFS} a_k \cdot e^{-jk(2\pi/N).\,n_0}} \quad ...(2.23)$$

Proof.

Let $$x(n - n_0) \xleftrightarrow{DTFS} b_k$$

then $$b_k = \frac{1}{N}\sum_{n=\langle N\rangle} x(n - n_0)\,e^{-jk\frac{2\pi}{N}n} \quad ....(2.24)$$

↗ Put $n - n_0 = n'$

$\therefore$ when $n = \langle N\rangle$, n' also $= \langle N\rangle$ (Note this step)

$$= \frac{1}{N} \sum_{n'=\langle N \rangle} x(n')\, e^{-jk\frac{2\pi}{N}(n'+n_0)}$$

$$\therefore \quad b_k = e^{-jk\left(\frac{2\pi}{N}\right)n_0} \cdot \frac{1}{N} \sum_{n'=\langle N \rangle} x(n')\, e^{-jk\frac{2\pi}{N}\cdot n'} = a_k \cdot e^{-jk\frac{2\pi}{N}n_0}$$ Q.E.D.

2.3.5 Frequency-Shifting

$$\boxed{\text{If } x(n) \xleftrightarrow{DTFS} a_k, \text{ then } e^{jm\left(\frac{2\pi}{N}\right)n} x(n) \xleftrightarrow{DTFS} a_{k-m}} \quad ...(2.25)$$

Proof.

Let $e^{jm(2\pi/N)n}\, x(n) \xleftrightarrow{DTFS} b_k$

then
$$b_k = \frac{1}{N} \sum_{n=\langle N \rangle} x(n).\, e^{jm(2\pi/N)n} .\, e^{-jk(2\pi/N)n} \quad ...(2.26)$$

$$= \frac{1}{N} \sum_{n=\langle N \rangle} x(n).\, e^{-j(k-m)(2\pi/N)n}$$

$$= a_{k-m} \,(\equiv a_{k'}) \quad \because a_k = \frac{1}{N} \sum_{n=\langle N \rangle} x(n)\, e^{-jk(2\pi/N)n}$$

$\therefore$ $b_k = a_{k-m}$. Hence, $e^{jm(2\pi/N)n}\, x(n) \xrightarrow{DTFT} a_{k-m}$ **Q.E.D.**

2.3.6 Time-Scaling

If $x(n) \xleftrightarrow{DTFS} a_k$ then $x\left(\frac{n}{M}\right) \xleftrightarrow{DTFS} \frac{1}{M} a_k$
Period of $x\left(\frac{n}{M}\right)$ is NM, ω_0' for $x\left(\frac{n}{M}\right)$ is $\omega_0' = \frac{2\pi}{MN}$

...(2.27)

Proof.

Let $x\left(\frac{n}{M}\right) \xleftrightarrow{DTFS} b_k$

then
$$b_k = \frac{1}{N'} \sum_{n=\langle N' \rangle} x\left(\frac{n}{M}\right) e^{-jk\left(\frac{2\pi}{N'}\right)n} \quad ...(2.28)$$

where $N' = MN$, the period of time scaled signal $x\left(\frac{n}{M}\right)$. Note that sequence length N of $x(n)$ elongates to NM for the signal $x\left(\frac{n}{M}\right)$. Putting $N' = MN$ is (2.28) we get

$$b_k = \frac{1}{MN} \sum_{n=\langle MN \rangle} x(n/M)\, e^{-jk\left(\frac{2\pi}{MN}\right)n} \quad ...(2.29)$$

Put $\frac{n}{M} = n'$ $\therefore$ when $n = MN$, then $n' = N$

Hence, (2.29) gives us

$$b_k = \frac{1}{M} \cdot \frac{1}{N} \sum_{n'=\langle N \rangle} x(n').\, e^{-jk\left(\frac{2\pi}{N}\right)n'}$$

$$\therefore \qquad b_k = \frac{1}{M} a_k, \quad \omega_0' = \frac{2\pi}{NM}$$

with ω_0' for $x(n/M)$ is ω_0/M *i.e.*, $2\pi/NM$. Hence, the result as given in (2.27).

2.3.7 Multiplication

$$\text{If } x(n) \xleftrightarrow{DTFS} a_k \text{ and } y(n) \xleftrightarrow{DTFS} b_k$$

$$\text{then } x(n) \cdot y(n) \xleftrightarrow{DTFS} \sum_{l=\langle N \rangle} a_l\, b_{k-l} \triangleq d_k \qquad \text{...(2.30)}$$

Proof.

Given
$$x(n) = \sum_{k=\langle N \rangle} a_k\, e^{jk\left(\frac{2\pi}{N}\right)n} \qquad \text{...(2.31)}$$

and
$$y(n) = \sum_{k=\langle N \rangle} b_k\, e^{jk\left(\frac{2\pi}{N}\right)n} \qquad \text{...(2.32)}$$

Let
$$x(n) \cdot y(n) \xleftrightarrow{DTFS} d_k$$

$$\therefore \qquad d_k = \frac{1}{N} \sum_{n=\langle N \rangle} [x(n) \cdot y(n)]\, e^{-jk\left(\frac{2\pi}{N}\right)n}$$

$$= \frac{1}{N} \sum_{n=\langle N \rangle} \left[\sum_{l=\langle N \rangle} a_l\, e^{jl\left(\frac{2\pi}{N}\right)n} \right] y(n)\, e^{-jk\left(\frac{2\pi}{N}\right)n}$$

[Putting value of $x(n)$ from (2.31) after changing dummy variable k *to* l]

$$= \sum_{l=\langle N \rangle} a_l \cdot \frac{1}{N} \sum_{n=\langle N \rangle} y(n)\, e^{-j(k-l)\left(\frac{2\pi}{N}\right)n}$$

(interchanging summation order)

$$= \sum_{l=\langle N \rangle} a_l \cdot b_{k-l} \qquad \left(\because\ b_k = \frac{1}{N} \sum_{n=\langle N \rangle} e^{jk\left(\frac{2\pi}{N}\right)n} \right)$$

i.e.,
$$x(n) \cdot y(n) \xleftrightarrow{DTFS} \sum_{l=\langle N \rangle} a_l\, b_{k-l} \triangleq d_k \qquad \textbf{Q.E.D.}$$

2.3.8 A Note on Periodic Convolution

We have earlier defined the convolution operation of two aperiodic sequences $x(n)$ and $h(n)$ as

$$x(n) * h(n) = \sum_{m=-\infty}^{\infty} x(m)\, h(n-m)$$

Similarly, when two analog signals $x(t)$ and $h(t)$ are aperiodic, their convolution has been defined as

$$x(t) * h(t) = \int_{\tau=-\infty}^{\infty} x(\tau)\, h(t-\tau)\, d\tau$$

When the signals are periodic then their summation or integration will result in ∞ or $-\infty$, in general. We, in such cases, use periodic convolutions, for the periodic signals for one period N.

Let $x_1(n)$ and $x_2(n)$ be both periodic with period N.

The periodic convolution of periodic signals $x_1(n)$ and $x_2(n)$ is defined as

$$\boxed{\text{Periodic convolution: } x_1(n) \otimes x_2(n) \triangleq \sum_{m=\langle N\rangle} x_1(m)\, x_2(n-m)} \quad \text{...(2.33)}$$

If $x_1(n) \otimes x_2(n) = x_3(n)$, then $x_3(n)$ is also periodic with period N.

Similarly, for periodic signals $x_1(t)$ and $x_2(t)$ with period T, we define periodic convolution of $x_1(t)$ and $x_2(t)$ by

$$\boxed{\text{Periodic convolution: } x_1(t) \otimes x_2(t) \triangleq \int_T x_1(\tau)\, x_2(t-\tau)\, d\tau} \quad \text{...(2.34)}$$

2.3.9 Periodic Convolution

$$\boxed{\text{If } x(n) \xleftrightarrow{DTFS} a_k, \text{ and } y(n) \xleftrightarrow{DTFS} b_k \text{ then } \sum_{r=\langle N\rangle} x(r)\, y(n-r) \xleftrightarrow{DTFS} Na_k b_k} \quad \text{...(2.35)}$$

Proof.

Let
$$\sum_{r=\langle N\rangle} x(r)\cdot y(n-r) \xleftrightarrow{DTFS} d_k$$

then
$$d_k = \frac{1}{N}\sum_{n=\langle N\rangle}\left[\sum_{r=\langle N\rangle} x(r)\cdot y(n-r)\right].\, e^{-jk(2\pi/N)n} \quad \text{...(2.36)}$$

$$= \frac{1}{N}\sum_{r=\langle N\rangle} x(r).\, \underbrace{\sum_{n=\langle N\rangle} y(n-r).\, e^{-jk(2\pi/N)(n-r)}}_{=N\, b_k} .\, e^{-jk(2\pi/N)\,r}$$

$$= b_k \sum_{r=\langle N\rangle} x(r)\, e^{-jk(2\pi/N)\,r} = b_k \cdot Na_k$$

$$\therefore \quad d_k = Na_k b_k$$

Q.E.D.

2.3.10 First Difference

$$\boxed{\text{If } x(n) \xleftrightarrow{DTFS} a_k, \text{ then } [x(n) - x(n-1)] \xleftrightarrow{DTFS} (1 - e^{-jk(2\pi/N)})\, a_k} \quad \text{...(2.37)}$$

Proof.

Let
$$x(n) - x(n-1) \xleftrightarrow{FS} d_k$$

then $$x(n) - x(n-1) = \sum_{k=\langle N\rangle} a_k\, e^{jk(2\pi/N)n} - \sum_{k=\langle N\rangle} a_k . e^{-jk(2\pi/N).1} . e^{jk(2\pi/N)n} \qquad \text{...(2.38)}$$

$$\left(\because\ x(n-n_0) \overset{FS}{\longleftrightarrow} a_k .\, e^{-jk(2\pi/N)n_0} \text{ here } n_0 = 1\right)$$

$$= \sum_{k=\langle N\rangle} a_k\,(1 - e^{-jk(2\pi/N)})\, e^{+jk(2\pi/N)n}$$

$$\triangleq \sum_{k=\langle N\rangle} d_k \cdot e^{jk(2\pi/N)n}$$

where $$d_k = (1 - e^{-jk(2\pi/N)})\, a_k$$

Q.E.D.

2.3.11 Parseval's Relation

If $x(n) \overset{DTFS}{\longleftrightarrow} a_k$, where $x(n)$ is periodic with period N

then $$\frac{1}{N}\sum_{n=\langle N\rangle} |x(n)|^2 = \sum_{k=\langle N\rangle} |a_k|^2 \qquad \text{...(2.39)}$$

Proof.

If $x(n)$ is periodic with period N, then we have

$$x(n) = \sum_{k=\langle N\rangle} a_k .\, e^{jk(2\pi/N)n}$$

and $$a_k = \frac{1}{N}\sum_{n=\langle N\rangle} x(n)\, e^{-jk(2\pi/N)n}$$

Now $$\frac{1}{N}\sum_{n=\langle N\rangle} |x(n)|^2 = \frac{1}{N}\sum_{n=\langle N\rangle} x^*(n)\, x(n) \qquad \text{...(2.40)}$$

$$= \frac{1}{N}\sum_{n=\langle N\rangle} x^*(n).\left(\sum_{k=\langle N\rangle} a_k\, e^{jk(2\pi/N)n}\right), \text{ [series in bracket is } x(n)]$$

$$= \sum_{k=\langle N\rangle} a_k \frac{1}{N}\sum_{n=\langle N\rangle} x^*(n)\cdot e^{jk(2\pi/N)n}$$

(interchanging summation order)

$$= \sum_{k=\langle N\rangle} a_k .\left[\frac{1}{N}\sum_{n=\langle N\rangle} x(n)\cdot e^{-jk(2\pi/N)n}\right]^*$$

$$= \sum_{k=\langle N\rangle} a_k .\, a_k^*$$

$$\boxed{\frac{1}{N}\sum_{n=\langle N\rangle} |x(n)|^2 = \sum_{n=\langle N\rangle} |a_k|^2}$$ Parseval's Relation for discrete periodic series $x(n)$, period N.

This relation shows that average power of a periodic signal $x(n)$ is equal to the sum of power of its N Fourier series coefficients a_k.

2.3.12 Properties of a_k for $x(n)$ Real

If $x(n)$ is real, (*i.e.*, $x(n) = x^*(n)$), and $x(n) \longleftrightarrow a_k$
then
$$a_k = a^*_{-k} \quad \text{due to (2.21)}$$
$$|a_k| = |a_{-k}|$$
$$\text{Re}\,[a_k] = \text{Re}\,[a_{-k}]$$
$$I_m\,[a_k] = -I_m\,[a_{-k}] \quad ...(2.41)$$

Proof.

Given
$$x(n) = \sum_{k=\langle N\rangle} a_k\, e^{jk\left(\frac{2\pi}{N}\right)n} \quad ...(2.42a)$$

and
$$a_k = \frac{1}{N}\sum_{k=\langle N\rangle} x(n)\, e^{-jk\left(\frac{2\pi}{N}\right)n} \quad ...(2.42b)$$

Let
$$x^*(n) \xleftrightarrow{DTFS} d_k$$

then
$$d_k = \frac{1}{N}\sum_{n=\langle N\rangle} x^*(n)\, e^{-jk\left(\frac{2\pi}{N}\right)n}$$
$$= \left[\frac{1}{N}\sum_{n=\langle N\rangle} x(n)\, e^{-j(-k)\left(\frac{2\pi}{N}\right)n}\right]^*$$

$\therefore$
$$d_k = [a_{-k}]^* \quad ...(2.43)$$

Hence,
$$x^*(n) \xleftrightarrow{FS} a^*_{-k} \quad \text{(we also proved this in (2.21))}$$

But
$$x(n) = x^*(n) \quad [x(n) \text{ is real, given}]$$

$\therefore$
$$a_k = a^*_{-k} \quad ...(2.44a)$$

i.e.,
$$|a_k| = |a_{-k}| \quad \text{(Mod values are same for the conjugates)} \quad ...(2.44b)$$

As
$$a_k = a^*_{-k}$$

$\therefore$
$$\text{Real part of } a_k = \text{Real part of } a_{-k}$$

i.e.,
$$\text{Re}\,[a_k] = \text{Re}\,[a_{-k}] \quad ...(2.44c)$$

i.e., the real part of a_k is an **even function** of k.

Also, (2.44*a*) implies that imaginary part of a_k and imaginary part of a_{-k} must be equal and opposite. Hence,
$$I_m\,[a_k] = -I_m\,[a_{-k}] \quad ...(2.44d)$$

i.e., the imaginary part of a_k is an **odd function** of k.

We have proved all the four results of (2.41) and these are given in (2.44*a*) to (2.44*d*).

2.3.13 $x(n)$ Real and Even

If $x(n)$ is real and even function, then
If $x(n) \xleftrightarrow{FS} a_k$, then a_k is real and even ...(2.45)

Proof.

$$\left.\begin{array}{llr} \text{If} & x(n) \xleftrightarrow{FS} a_k & ...(A) \\ \text{then} & x(-n) \xleftrightarrow{FS} a_{-k} & ...(B) \end{array}\right\} \text{(due to (2.19))}$$

If $x(n)$ is real, then

$$a_k = a^*_{-k} \quad ...(C) \quad \text{(due to (2.44a))} \qquad ...(2.46)$$

As $x(n) = x(-n)$ and $x(n)$ is real, therefore,

$$a_k = a_{-k} = a^*_{-k}$$

The first two conditions give that a_k is even ($a_k = a_{-k}$) and the last two conditions give that a_{-k} is purely real. But $a_{-k} = a_k$, hence a_k is purely real. As such a_k is real and even function when $x(n)$ is real and even function.

2.3.14 *x*(*n*) Real and Odd

If $x(n)$ is real and an odd function, then If $x(n) \longleftrightarrow a_k$, then a_k is purely imaginary and odd

...(2.47)

Proof.

If $\quad x(n) \longleftrightarrow a_k \quad ...(A)$ (by definition)

$\quad x(-n) \longleftrightarrow a_{-k} \quad ...(B)$ (time reversal)

As $x(n)$ is real, therefore,

$$a_k = a^*_{-k} \quad ...(C) \quad \text{[proved in (2.41)]}$$

Here, $x(n) = -x(-n)$ and $x(n)$ is real, therefore, using (A) and (B), we get

$$a_k = -a_{-k} \quad \text{Hence, } a_k \text{ is an odd function of } k$$

As $\quad -a_{-k} = a^*_{-k}$ due to (C) and using $[-x(-n)] \longleftrightarrow -a_{-k}$

$\therefore$ a_{-k} is purely imaginary *i.e.*, a_k is purely imaginary. Hence,

a_k is purely imaginary and an odd function when $x(n)$ is real and odd function.

2.3.15 Even-odd Decomposition of a Real Signal

If $x(n)$ is real its decomposition $x_e(n) = \text{Even}\,[x(n)] \xleftrightarrow{FS} \text{Re}\,[a_k]$ $x_o(n) = \text{Odd}\,[x(n)] \xleftrightarrow{FS} j\,I_m\,[a_k]$

...(2.48)

Proof.

As $x(n)$ is real, therefore, $a_k = a^*_{-k}$ $\qquad (\because x^*(n) \xleftrightarrow{FS} a^*_{-k}$ (2.21))

Let $\quad x(n) = x_e(n) + x_o(n)$

Then $\quad x_e(n) = \frac{1}{2}[x(n) + x(-n)]$ [due to (1.15*a*)]

and $\quad x_o(n) = \frac{1}{2}[x(n) - x(-n)]$ [due to (1.15*b*)]

We know that

$$x(n) \xleftrightarrow{FS} a_k$$

$$x(-n) \xleftrightarrow{FS} a_{-k} \quad \text{[due to (2.19)]}$$

$$\therefore \qquad x_e(n) \xleftrightarrow{FS} \frac{1}{2}[a_k + a_{-k}]$$

$$= \frac{1}{2}[a_k + a_k^*] \quad [a_k = a_{-k}^* \ \therefore\ a_{-k} = a_k^* \text{ for } x(n) \text{ real, using (2.44a)}]$$

$$= \text{Re}\,[a_k]$$

$$x_o(n) \xleftrightarrow{FS} \frac{1}{2}[a_k - a_{-k}]$$

$$= \frac{1}{2}[a_k - a_k^*] \qquad (\because a_{-k} = a_k^*)$$

$$= j\,I_m\,[a_k]$$

2.3.16 Running Sum

> If $x(n) \xleftrightarrow{FS} a_k$, then $\sum_{r=-\infty}^{n} x(r) \xleftrightarrow{FS} \dfrac{a_k}{1 - e^{-jk(2\pi/N)}}$
>
> If $x(r)$ is finite valued and periodic and $a_0 = 0$ ...(2.49)

Proof.

We know that a finite valued periodic series, $x(n)$ with period N has Fourier series coefficient *i.e.,*

$$x(n) \xleftrightarrow{FS} a_k$$

Let
$$y(n) = \sum_{r=-\infty}^{n} x(r) \qquad ...(A)$$

Put $r = n' + n$ $\quad \therefore$ when $r = -\infty$, $n' = -\infty$

when $r = n$, $n' = 0$

Hence, (A) gives us

$$y(n) = \sum_{n'=-\infty}^{0} x(n' + n)$$

Put
$$n' = -n''$$

$$\therefore \qquad y(n) = \sum_{n''=0}^{\infty} x(n - n'')$$

But
$$x(n - n'') \xleftrightarrow{FS} e^{-jn''\left(\frac{2\pi}{N}\right)k} a_k$$

$$\therefore \qquad y(n) \xleftrightarrow{FS} \sum_{n''=0}^{\infty} a_k \cdot e^{-jn''\left(\frac{2\pi}{N}\right)k} \qquad ...(B)$$

We have used the linearity condition in (B)

But
$$\sum_{n''=0}^{\infty} a_k \cdot e^{-jn''\left(\frac{2\pi}{N}\right)k} = a_k \sum_{n''=0}^{\infty} e^{-jn''\left(\frac{2\pi}{N}\right)k} \qquad ...(C)$$

RHS of (C) is a GP and is summable provided $|r| < 1$.

If $k \neq 0$, then "r" $= e^{-j(2\pi/N)\,k}$ has mod value less than 1, and the series would be summable. For $k = 0$, it has been given that $a_0 = 0$. Therefore, the case when "r" = 1 is excluded. Hence, (C) gives us

$$a_k \sum_{n''=0}^{\infty} e^{-jn''\left(\frac{2\pi}{N}\right)k} = a_k \frac{1}{1 - e^{-j(2\pi/N)\,k}}$$

Hence, $$\sum_{r=-\infty}^{n} x(r) \xleftrightarrow{FS} \frac{a_k}{1 - e^{-j(2\pi/N)\,k}}$$ Q.E.D.

We have proved all the properties of discrete-time Fourier series (DTFS) as given in Table 2.1.

Table 2.1 Properties of Discrete-time Fourier Series (DTFS)

S.N.	Sequence "$x(n)$"		"a_k"	
1	$x(n)$, $x(n)$ periodic in n period $= N$, $\omega_0 = 2\pi/N$		$a_k = \frac{1}{N} \sum_{n=\langle N \rangle} x(n)\, e^{-jk(2\pi/N)\,n}$	(2.12)
2	$A\, x(n) + B\, y(n)$	(Linearity)	$A\, a_k + B\, b_k$	(2.16)
3	$x(-n)$	(Time reversal)	a_{-k}	(2.19)
4	$x^*(n)$	(Conjugation)	a^*_{-k}	(2.21)
5	$x(n - n_0)$	(Time shifting)	$e^{-jk(2\pi/N)\,n_0}\, a_k$	(2.23)
6	$e^{jM(2\pi/N)\,n} \cdot x(n)$	(Frequency shifting)	a_{k-M}	(2.25)
7	$x\left(\frac{n}{M}\right)$	(Time-scaling)	$\frac{1}{M} a_k$ and $\omega'_0 = \frac{1}{M} \omega_0$	(2.27)
8	$x(n) \cdot y(n)$	(Multiplication)	$\sum_{l=\langle N \rangle} a_l\, b_{k-l} = d_k$	(2.30)
9	$x(n) * y(n)$	(Periodic-convolution)	$N\, a_k \cdot b_k$	(2.35)
10	$\frac{1}{N} \sum_{n=\langle N \rangle} \lvert x(n) \rvert^2$	(Parseval's relation)	$\sum_{k=\langle N \rangle} \lvert a_k \rvert^2$	(2.39)
11	$x(n) - x(n-1)$	(First difference)	$[1 - e^{-jk(2\pi/N)}]\, a_k$	(2.37)
12	If $x(n)$ is real *i.e.*, $x(n) = x^*(n)$		(*i*) $a_k = a^*_{-k}$ (*ii*) Re $[a_k]$ = Re $[a_{-k}]$ (*iii*) $I_m\,[a_k] = -I_m\,[a_{-k}]$ (*iv*) $\lvert a_k \rvert = \lvert a_{-k} \rvert$	(2.44*a*) (2.44*c*) (2.44*d*) (2.44*b*)
13	$x(n)$ real and even		a_k real and even	(2.45)
14	$x(n)$ real and odd		a_k purely imaginary and odd	(2.47)
15	Generic $x(n)$ and real (*a*) $x_e(n)$ = Even $[x(n)]$ (*b*) $x_o(n)$ = Odd $[x(n)]$		a_k = Re $[a_k] + j\, I_m\,[a_k]$ Re $[a_k]$ $j\, I_m\,[a_k]$	 (2.48)

16	$\sum_{r=-\infty}^{n} x(r)$ (Running sum if $a_0 = 0$) $x(n)$ periodic	$\dfrac{a_k}{1 - e^{-jk(2\pi/N)}}$	(2.49)

2.3.17 Examples on Discrete-time Fourier Series (DTFS)

EXAMPLE 2.1: *Determine the Fourier coefficients for the periodic sequence $x(n) = \{0, 1, 2, 3\}$, with period $N = 4$.*

SOLUTION: Given $N = 4 \therefore \omega_0 = \dfrac{2\pi}{4},\ e^{-j\omega_0} = e^{-j\pi/2} = -j$

We know that

$$C_k = \frac{1}{N}\sum_{n=0}^{N-1} x(n)\, e^{-jk\omega_0 n}$$

$$= \frac{1}{4}\sum_{n=0}^{3} x(n)(-j)^{kn} \quad (\because\ e^{-j\omega_0} = -j \text{ found above})$$

$\therefore$

$$C_0 = \frac{1}{4}\sum_{n=0}^{3} x(n) = \frac{1}{4}(0+1+2+3) = \frac{3}{2}$$

$$C_1 = \frac{1}{4}\sum_{n=0}^{3} x(n)(-j)^n = \frac{1}{4}[(0)(1) + (1)(-j) + (2)(-1) + (3)(j)]$$

$$= -\frac{1}{2} + j\frac{1}{2}$$

$$C_2 = \frac{1}{4}\sum_{n=0}^{3} x(n)(-j)^{2n} = \frac{1}{4}\sum_{n=0}^{3} x(n)(-1)^n$$

$$= \frac{1}{4}[(0)(1) + (1)(-1) + (2)(1) + (3)(-1)] = -\frac{1}{2}$$

$$C_3 = \frac{1}{4}\sum_{n=0}^{3} x(n)(-j)^{3n} = \frac{1}{4}\sum_{n=0}^{3} x(n)(j)^n$$

$$= \frac{1}{4}[(0)(1) + (1)(j) + (2)(-1) + (3)(-j)]$$

$$= -\frac{1}{2} - j\frac{1}{2}$$

Hence,

$$\left.\begin{array}{l} C_0 = \dfrac{3}{2},\ C_1 = \dfrac{1}{2}(-1+j) \\ C_2 = -\dfrac{1}{2},\ C_3 = \dfrac{1}{2}(-1-j) \end{array}\right\}$$

Ans.

EXAMPLE 2.2: *Find the discrete-time Fourier series for*

$$x(n) = \cos\left(\frac{\pi}{4}n + \phi\right), \text{ and plot } a_k$$

SOLUTION:

$$x(n) = \cos\left(\frac{\pi}{4}n + \phi\right) \quad \text{form } \cos(\omega_0 n + \phi)$$

$$\therefore \qquad \omega_0 = \frac{\pi}{4} \quad \therefore N = \frac{2\pi}{\omega_0} = \frac{2\pi}{(\pi/4)} = 8$$

We can write

$$x(n) = \frac{1}{2}\left[e^{j\left(\frac{\pi}{4}n + \phi\right)} + e^{-j\left(\frac{\pi}{4}n + \phi\right)}\right]$$

$$= \underbrace{\frac{1}{2}e^{-j\phi}}_{a_{-1}} . e^{j(-1)\underbrace{\frac{\pi}{4}n}_{\omega_0 n}} + \underbrace{\frac{1}{2}e^{j\phi}}_{a_{-1}} . e^{j(+1)\underbrace{\frac{\pi}{4}n}_{\omega_0 n}} \qquad ...(A)$$

$$= \sum_{k=\langle N \rangle} a_k \, e^{jk\omega_0 n} \qquad ...(B)$$

Clearly, $a_{-1} = \frac{1}{2}e^{-j\phi}, \; a_1 = \frac{1}{2}e^{j\phi}$ [by inspection from (*A*) and (*B*)]

i.e., $$x(n) \xleftrightarrow{FS} a_k = \begin{cases} \frac{1}{2}e^{-j\phi}, & k = -1 \\ \frac{1}{2}e^{j\phi}, & k = 1 \\ 0, & -3 \le k \le 4, \; k \ne \pm 1 \end{cases}$$ **Ans.**

We need to find only N a_k's as a_k is periodic in k with period N.

As a_k has a period of $N = 8$

$$\therefore \qquad a_{-1} = a_7 = a_{15} = ... = \frac{1}{2}e^{-j\phi}$$

$$a_1 = a_9 = a_{17} = ... = \frac{1}{2}e^{-j\phi}$$

The amplitude $|a_k|$ and the phase Arg (a_k) is shown in Fig. Ex. 2.2.

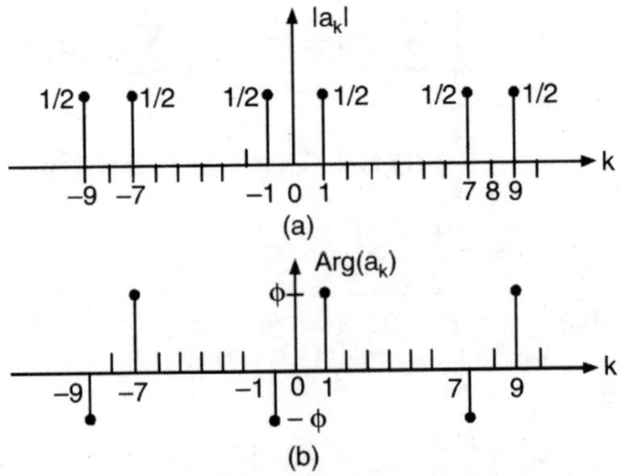

Fig. Ex. 2.2. (*a*) Amplitude spectrum
(*b*) Phase spectrum

EXAMPLE 2.3: *Calculate the Fourier-series coefficients a_k for the signal*

$$x(n) = \sin \omega_0 n, \text{ and plot } a_k.$$

SOLUTION: $x(n) = \sin \omega_0 n$ is periodic with period N if $N = \dfrac{2\pi}{\omega_0}$ is an integer

As
$$\sin \omega_0 n = \frac{1}{2j}\left[e^{j\omega_0 n} - e^{-j\omega_0 n}\right]$$
$$= \sum_{k=\langle N\rangle} a_k\, e^{jk\omega_0 n} = \sum_{k=\langle N\rangle} a_k\, e^{jk\left(\frac{2\pi}{N}\right)n}$$
$$= -\frac{1}{2j}\, \underset{\uparrow_{k=-1}}{e^{j(-1)\,\omega_0 n}} + \frac{1}{2j}\, \underset{\uparrow_{k=1}}{e^{j(1)\omega_0 n}}$$

$\therefore$
$$a_{-1} = \frac{-1}{2j} = j\frac{1}{2} \quad \text{and} \quad a_1 = \frac{1}{2j} = -j\frac{1}{2}$$

(*i*) **Suppose $N = 5$** *i.e.,* $\omega_0 = \dfrac{2\pi}{5}$ and $x(n) = \sin\left(\dfrac{2\pi}{5}\right)n$

The Fourier series coefficients a_k are periodic with period $N = 5$ and are as shown *i.e.,*
$$a_1 = a_6 = a_{11} = \ldots, \quad \text{and} \quad a_{-1} = a_{-6} = a_{-11} = \ldots,$$

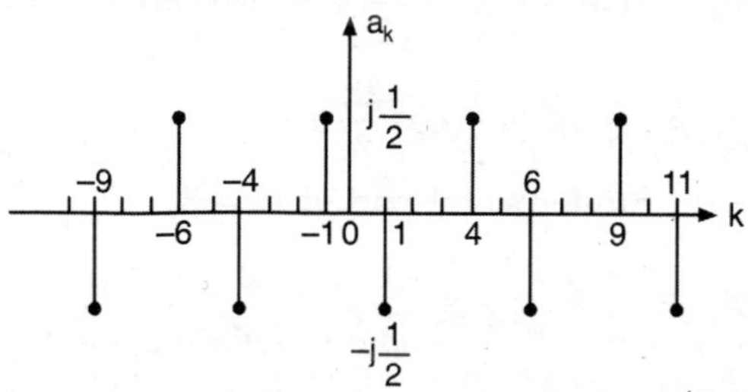

Fig. Ex. 2.3 (*a*) Fourier series coeffs. a_k for $\sin\left(\dfrac{2\pi}{5}n\right)$

(*ii*) **Suppose** $\dfrac{2\pi}{\omega_0} = \dfrac{N}{M}$ (N, M relative prime) $\because \sin \dfrac{2\pi M}{N} n$ has period N

Then
$$\omega_0 = \frac{2\pi}{N/M} = M\left(\frac{2\pi}{N}\right).$$
$$x(n) = -\frac{1}{2j}\, \underset{\substack{\uparrow \\ k=-M}}{e^{+j(-M)\left(\frac{2\pi}{N}\right)}} + \frac{1}{2j}\, \underset{\substack{\uparrow \\ k=M}}{e^{j(M)\left(\frac{2\pi}{N}\right)n}}$$

$\therefore$
$$a_{-M} = -\frac{1}{2j} = j\frac{1}{2}$$
$$a_M = \frac{1}{2j} = -j\frac{1}{2}$$

Suppose $M = 3$, $N = 5$

$\therefore$
$$a_{-3} = j\frac{1}{2}$$
$$a_3 = -j\frac{1}{2}$$

i.e., $a_3 = a_8 = a_{13} \ldots,$
and $a_2 = a_7 = a_{12} \ldots,$

as $a_k = a_{k+N}$ and $N = 5$

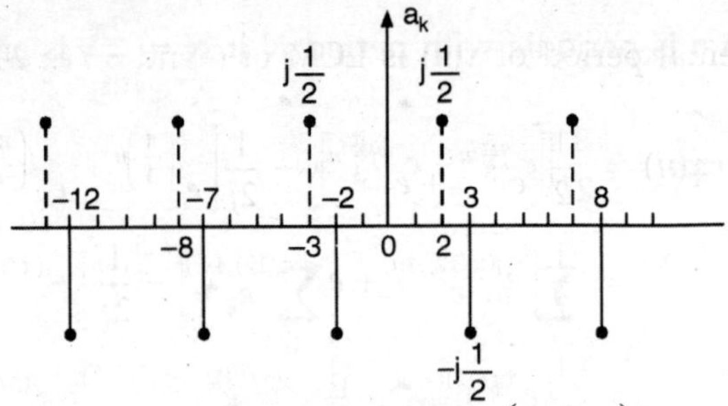

Fig. Ex. 2.3. (*b*) Fourier series coeffs a_k for sin $\left(3 \cdot \frac{2\pi}{5} n\right)$ for $M = 3$, $N = 5$

EXAMPLE 2.4: *Determine the discrete Fourier series representation of the following signals*

(*a*) $x(n) = \cos^2\left(\frac{\pi}{8} n\right)$

(*b*) $x(n) = \cos\left(\frac{\pi}{3} n\right) + \sin\left(\frac{\pi}{4} n\right)$

SOLUTION: (*a*) $$x(n) = \cos^2\left(\frac{\pi}{8} n\right) = \frac{1}{2}\left[1 + \cos\frac{\pi}{4} n\right]$$

$$= \frac{1}{2}(1)^n + \frac{1}{2}\cos\frac{2\pi}{8} n \qquad \text{(Note this step)}$$

$\therefore$ $x(n)$ is periodic in n with fundamental period $N = 8$.

As $$x(n) = \frac{1}{2} + \frac{1}{4}\left[e^{j\frac{2\pi}{8}n} + e^{-j\frac{2\pi}{8}n}\right]$$

$$= \frac{1}{2} e^{j\frac{2\pi}{8} \times 0 \times n} + \frac{1}{4}\left[e^{j\frac{2\pi}{8} \times n \times 1} + e^{j\frac{2\pi}{8} \times n \times (-1)}\right]$$

$\therefore$ By inspection

$$C_0 = \frac{1}{2}, C_1 = \frac{1}{4}, C_{-1} = \frac{1}{4}$$

$$C_7 = C_{8-1} = C_{-1} = \frac{1}{4}$$

Other $$C_k = 0 \quad \text{for} \quad k = 2, 3, 4, 5, 6$$

$$x(n) = \sum_{k=0}^{7} C_k \, e^{j\left(\frac{2\pi}{8}\right)nk}$$

i.e, $$x(n) = C_0 + C_1 e^{j\frac{2\pi}{8} n} + C_7 e^{j\left(\frac{2\pi}{8}\right)7\pi}, \quad \omega_0 = \frac{2\pi}{8} \text{ here}$$

$\therefore$ $$x(n) = \frac{1}{2} + \frac{1}{4} e^{j\omega_0 n} + \frac{1}{4} e^{j\omega_0 7n}$$ **Ans.**

(*b*) $$x(n) = \cos\left(\frac{\pi}{3} n\right) + \sin\left(\frac{\pi}{4} n\right)$$

$$= \cos\left(\frac{2\pi}{6} n\right) + \sin\left(\frac{2\pi}{8} n\right)$$

Clearly, the fundamental period of $x(n)$ is LCM of 6 and 8 *i.e.*, 24 *i.e.*, $\omega_0 = \frac{2\pi}{N} = \frac{2\pi}{24} = \frac{\pi}{12}$.

As
$$x(n) = \frac{1}{2}\left[e^{j\frac{\pi}{3}n} + e^{-j\frac{\pi}{3}n}\right] + \frac{1}{2j}\left[e^{j\left(\frac{\pi}{4}\right)n} - e^{-j\left(\frac{\pi}{4}\right)n}\right]$$
$$= \frac{1}{2}\left[e^{j(\pi/12)\,4n} + e^{-j(\pi/12)\,4n}\right] + \frac{1}{2j}\left[e^{j(\pi/12)\,3n} - e^{-j(\pi/12)\,3n}\right]$$
$$= \frac{1}{2}\,e^{j(\pi/12)(4)\,n} + \frac{1}{2}\,e^{j(\pi/12)(-4)\,n} + \frac{1}{2j}\,e^{j(\pi/12)(3)\,n} - \frac{1}{2j}\,e^{j(\pi/12)(-3)\,n}$$

$\therefore$ By inspection
$$C_4 = \frac{1}{2},\ C_{-4} = \frac{1}{2},\ C_3 = \frac{1}{2j},\ C_{-3} = -\frac{1}{2j}$$

We now cover all C_k for $k = 0$ to $k = 24$

i.e.,
$$C_0 = C_1 = C_2 = 0,\ C_3 = \frac{-j}{2},\ C_4 = \frac{1}{2},\ C_5 = C_6 = \ldots C_{19} = 0,$$
$$C_{20} = C_{24-4} = C_{-4} = \frac{1}{2}$$
$$C_{21} = C_{24-3} = C_{-3} = j\left(\frac{1}{2}\right)$$
$$C_{22} = C_{23} = 0$$

Hence,
$$x(n) = -\frac{j}{2}\,e^{j3\omega_0 n} + \frac{1}{2}\,e^{j4\omega_0 n} + \frac{1}{2}\,e^{j20\omega_0 n} + \frac{j}{2}\,e^{j21\omega_0 n}$$ **Ans.**

EXAMPLE 2.5: *The following information about a sequence $x(n)$ is given*

1. *$x(n)$ is periodic with period $N = 6$*
2. $\sum_{n=0}^{5} x(n) = 2$
3. $\sum_{n=2}^{7} (-1)^n\, x(n) = 1$
4. *$x(n)$ has the minimum power per period among the set of signals satisfying the preceding conditions. Determine the sequence $x(n)$.*

SOLUTION:

As
$$a_k = \frac{1}{N}\sum_{n=0}^{N-1} x(n)\, e^{-jk\left(\frac{2\pi}{N}\right)n}$$ $\boxed{N = 6 \text{ (given)}}$

$\therefore$
$$a_0 = \frac{1}{N}\sum_{n=0}^{N-1} x(n)$$

Due to condition 2, we obtain
$$a_0 = \frac{1}{6}(2) \quad \therefore a_0 = \frac{1}{3}$$ $\boxed{a_0 = \frac{1}{3}}$

As
$$(-1)^n = e^{-j\pi n} = e^{-j(2\pi/6).\,3n}$$ (Note this step)

∴ The condition 3 gives us

$$a_3 = \frac{1}{N}\sum_{n=\langle N\rangle} x(n)\cdot e^{-j(2\pi/6)n\times 3}$$

$$= \frac{1}{6}\sum_{n=\langle N\rangle} x(n)(-1)^n$$

$$= \frac{1}{6}\times 1 = 1/6 \qquad \boxed{a_3 = \frac{1}{6}}$$

From Parseval's relation, we know that the average power of the signal $x(n)$ is given by

$$P = \frac{1}{N}\sum_{n=\langle N\rangle} |x(n)|^2 = \sum_{n=\langle N\rangle} |a_k|^2 \quad \text{[see (2.39)]}$$

Each non-zero coefficient a_k contributes to positive amount of power. We have found non-zero a_k as

$$a_0 = \frac{1}{3}, \text{ and } a_3 = \frac{1}{6}$$

The power P will be minimum if we choose $a_1 = a_2 = a_4 = a_5 = 0$. With this choice

$$x(n) = \sum_{n=\langle N\rangle} a_k\, e^{jk(2\pi/N)\,n}$$

$$= \sum_{n=0}^{5} a_k\, e^{jk\left(\frac{2\pi}{6}\right)n} = a_0 + a_3\, e^{j3\left(\frac{\pi}{3}\right)n} \quad (\because a_1 = a_2 = a_4 = a_5 = 0)$$

$$= \frac{1}{3} + \frac{1}{6}(-1)^n \quad (\because e^{j\pi} = -1)$$

Hence,

$$x(0) = \frac{1}{2},\; x(1) = \frac{1}{3} - \frac{1}{6} = \frac{1}{6},\; x(2) = \frac{1}{3} + \frac{1}{6} = \frac{1}{2}$$

$$x(3) = \frac{1}{3} - \frac{1}{6} = \frac{1}{6},\; x(4) = \frac{1}{3} + \frac{1}{6} = \frac{1}{2},\; x(5) = \frac{1}{3} - \frac{1}{6} = \frac{1}{6}$$

$x(n)$ is as shown for one period

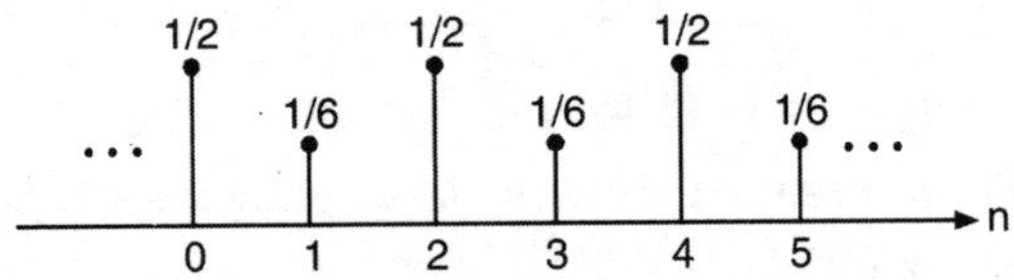

Ans.

Fig. Ex. 2.5: Sequence $x(n)$ period $N = 6$

EXAMPLE 2.6: *A signal x(n) is periodic with period N and its discrete-time Fourier coefficients* a_k *satisfy the following*

1. $x(n)$ *is real,*
2. $a_l = 1$
3. $\sum_{n=0}^{N-1} |x(n)|^2 = 3N$, *and*
4. $\sum_{n=0}^{N-1} x(n) = N.$

Find x(n). *(GGS IP Univ. 2007)*

SOLUTION: As $x(n)$ is periodic and real, therefore

$$a_k = a_{-k}^* \quad \text{(property (2.4a))}$$

and a_k is periodic *i.e.*, $a_k = a_{N+K} = a_{k-N}$

As $a_1 = 1 \quad \therefore \quad a_{-1} = (1)^* = 1$ $\boxed{a_1 = a_{-1} = 1}$

$$a_k = \frac{1}{N}\sum_{n=0}^{N-1} x(n)\, e^{-jk\left(\frac{2\pi}{N}\right)n}$$

$$\therefore \quad a_0 = \frac{1}{N}\sum_{n=0}^{N-1} x(n) = \frac{1}{N} \times N = 1 \qquad \boxed{a_0 = 1}$$

Now by Parseval's relation

$$\frac{1}{N}\sum_{n=\langle N\rangle} |x(n)|^2 = \sum_{k=\langle N\rangle} |a_k|^2$$

$$\therefore \quad \frac{1}{N}(3N) = \sum_{k=\langle N\rangle} |a_k|^2 = \sum_{k=-1}^{N-2} |a_k|^2 \quad \text{(Note this step)}$$

i.e., $|a_{-1}|^2 + |a_0|^2 + |a_1|^2 + \sum_{k=2}^{N-2} |a_k|^2 = 3$

As $a_{-1} = a_0 = a_1 = 1$, therefore, $a_2 = a_3 = \ldots\, a_{N-2} = 0$

$$\therefore \quad x(n) = \sum_{k=-1}^{N-2} a_k\, e^{jk\left(\frac{2\pi}{N}\right)n}$$

$$= a_{-1}\, e^{-j\left(\frac{2\pi}{N}\right)n} + a_0 + a_1\, e^{j\left(\frac{2\pi}{N}\right)n} + 0 + 0$$

$$= e^{-j\left(\frac{2\pi}{N}\right)n} + 1 + e^{j\left(\frac{2\pi}{N}\right)n}$$

$$x(n) = 1 + 2\cos\left(\frac{2\pi}{N}\, n\right) \qquad \textbf{Ans.}$$

Note that if $N = 3$, then $x(n) = \{3, 0, 0\}$ for one period $\left(\because\ 2\cos\frac{2n\pi}{3} = -1 \text{ for } n = 1, 2\right)$.

i.e., $x(n) = \{\ldots, 3, 0, 0, 3, 0, 0\}$

EXAMPLE 2.7: *For sequence* $x(n) \xleftrightarrow{FS} a_k$ *and* $y(n) \xleftrightarrow{FS} b_k$ *and each periodic with* $N = 4$*, find the Fourier series coefficients of the signal* $x(n)\cdot y(n)$*. Given* $a_0 = a_3 = \frac{1}{2}a_1 = \frac{1}{2}a_2 = 1$ *and* $b_0 = b_1 = b_2 = b_3 = 1$.

SOLUTION: By multiplication property

$$x(n)\cdot y(n) \xleftrightarrow{FS} \sum_{l=\langle N\rangle} a_l\, b_{k-l}, \text{ say, } C_k$$

$$C_k = \sum_{l=0}^{3} a_l\, b_{k-l}$$

$$= a_0\, b_k + a_1\, b_{k-1} + a_2\, b_{k-2} + a_3\, b_{k-3}$$

As $a_0 = 1,\ a_1 = 2,\ a_2 = 2,\ a_3 = 1$

$$\therefore \qquad C_k = (1)\, b_k + (2)\, b_{k-1} + (2)\, b_{k-2} + (1)\, b_{k-3}$$
$$= b_k + 2\,(b_{k-1} + b_{k-2}) + b_{k-3}$$

Since, $b_k = 1$ for all k, $\therefore \quad C_k = 1 + 2\,(1 + 1) + 1 = 6$ for all k

$\therefore \qquad C_k = 6,\ k = 1, 2, 3, 4$ **Ans.**

EXAMPLE 2.8: *Find the Fourier coefficients a_k of the discrete-time periodic square waveform shown:*

$$x(n) = \begin{cases} 1, & |n| \le N_1 \\ 0, & N_1 < |n| \le N/2 \end{cases}$$

SOLUTION:

$$a_k = \frac{1}{N} \sum_{n=\langle N \rangle} x(n)\, e^{-jk\left(\frac{2\pi}{N}\right)n}$$

$$= \frac{1}{N} \sum_{n=-N_1}^{N_1} 1\, e^{-jk\left(\frac{2\pi}{N}\right)n}$$

Put $\qquad m = n + N_1$

$$\therefore \qquad a_k = \frac{1}{N} \sum_{m=0}^{2N_1} e^{-jk\left(\frac{2\pi}{N}\right)(m - N_1)}$$

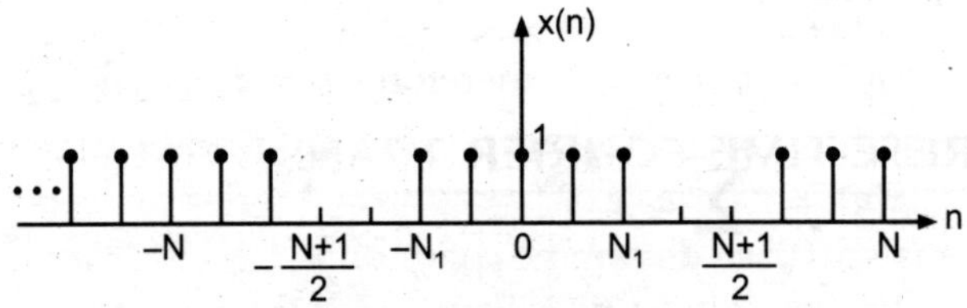

Fig. Ex. 2.8 (*a*) Periodic series $x(n)$ period N, N odd (in one period N, 1's are odd and zeros are even, in number)

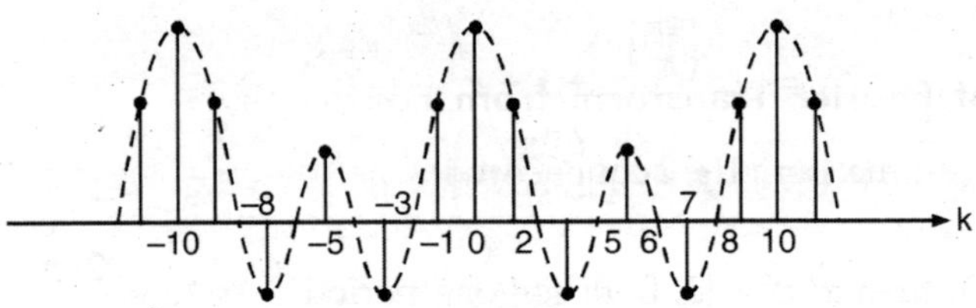

Fig. Ex. 2.8 (*b*) Coeffs. a_k for $N_1 = 2$, $N = 5$

$$= \frac{1}{N}\, e^{jk\left(\frac{2\pi}{N}\right)N_1} \cdot \sum_{m=0}^{2N_1} e^{-jk\left(\frac{2\pi}{N}\right)m}$$

$$= \frac{1}{N}\, e^{jk\left(\frac{2\pi}{N}\right)N_1}\, \frac{1 - e^{-jk\left(\frac{2\pi}{N}\right)(2N_1+1)}}{1 - e^{-jk\left(\frac{2\pi}{N}\right)}}$$

$$= \frac{1}{N}\, e^{jk\left(\frac{2\pi}{N}\right)N_1} \cdot \frac{\left[e^{-jk\left(\frac{2\pi}{N}\right)\left(\frac{2N_1+1}{2}\right)}\right]}{e^{-jk\left(\frac{2\pi}{N}\right)\cdot\frac{1}{2}}} \frac{\left(e^{jk\left(\frac{2\pi}{N}\right)\left(\frac{2N_1+1}{2}\right)} - e^{-jk\left(\frac{2\pi}{N}\right)\left(\frac{2N_1+1}{2}\right)}\right)}{\left(e^{jk\left(\frac{2\pi}{N}\right)\cdot\frac{1}{2}} - e^{-jk\left(\frac{2\pi}{N}\right)\cdot\frac{1}{2}}\right)}$$

$$= \left(\frac{1}{N}\right) \cdot \frac{\sin\left(k\left(\frac{2\pi}{N}\right)\left(\frac{2N_1+1}{2}\right)\right)}{\sin\left(k\left(\frac{2\pi}{N}\right)\frac{1}{2}\right)}$$

$$= \frac{1}{N} \cdot \frac{\sin\left(2\pi k\left(N_1 + \frac{1}{2}\right)/N\right)}{\sin\frac{\pi k}{N}}. \; k \neq 0, \pm N, \pm 2N$$

For $k = 0, \pm N, \pm 2N, \ldots$ we get **(by L' Hospital Rule)**

$$a_k = \frac{1}{N} \frac{2\pi\left(N_1 + \frac{1}{2}\right)/N}{\frac{\pi}{N}} = \frac{2N_1 + 1}{N} \text{ for } k = 0, \pm N, \pm 2N, \ldots,$$

$$\text{Generic } a_k = \frac{2N_1 + 1}{N} \frac{sinc\left(\frac{2\pi k}{N}\left(N_1 + \frac{1}{2}\right)\right)}{sinc\left(\frac{\pi k}{N}\right)}, \; k = 1, 2, \ldots, N - 1$$

Note that when N is even, then in one period (N) the number of 1's and zeros are both even or odd.

2.4 THE DISCRETE-TIME FOURIER TRANSFORM (DTFT)

For continuous-time signals $x(t)$, we determine continuous-time Fourier transforms (CTFT). CTFT theory was evolved from the continuous-time Fourier series expressing a periodic signal $x(t)$ with time periodic T, and letting the time period T tend to infinity. We shall proceed similarly here, to obtain a result for DTFT.

2.4.1 Derivation of Fourier Transform from Fourier Series

Let $x_p(n)$ be a discrete-time periodic sequence with period N. Then the Fourier-series relations derived by us are

$$x_p(n) = \sum_{k=<N>} a_k e^{jk\left(\frac{2\pi}{N}\right)n} \quad \ldots(2.50a)$$

$$a_k = \frac{1}{N} \sum_{k=<N>} x_p(n)\, e^{-jk\left(\frac{2\pi}{N}\right)n} \quad \ldots(2.50b)$$

Define $$\omega_0 = \frac{2\pi}{N} \quad \ldots(2.50c)$$

Let $x(n)$ be the sequence for one period of $x_p(n)$, and let

$$x(n) = \begin{cases} x_p(n), n = 0, 1, \ldots, N-1 \\ 0, \text{ otherwise} \end{cases} \quad \ldots(2.51a)$$

i.e. $x(n)_p$, $n = 0, 1, \ldots, N - 1 \equiv x(n)$ for all n from $-\infty$ to ∞ ...(2.51b)

Thus, the Fourier series coefficients a_k given by

$$a_k = \frac{1}{N}\sum_{k=<N>} x_p(n)\, e^{-jk\omega_0 n}$$

are equivalent to
$$a_k = \frac{1}{N}\sum_{n=-\infty}^{\infty} x(n)\, e^{-jk\omega_0 n} \quad \text{[due to (2.51}a\text{)]} \qquad ...(2.52)$$

Define
$$X(e^{j\omega}) = \sum_{n=-\infty}^{\infty} x(n)\, e^{-j\omega n} \qquad ...(2.53)$$

$$\therefore \quad \frac{1}{N} X(e^{jk\omega_0}) = \frac{1}{N}\sum_{n=-\infty}^{\infty} x(n)\, e^{-j(k\omega_0)n} \quad \text{(replace } \omega \text{ by } k\omega_0\text{, on both sides of (2.53))}$$

$$= a_k \quad \text{(due to 2.52)}$$

Putting
$$a_k = \frac{1}{N} X(e^{jk\omega_0}) \text{ in (2.50}a\text{), we get} \qquad ....(2.54)$$

$$x_p(n) = \sum_{k=<N>}\left[\frac{1}{N} X(e^{jk\omega_0})\right] . \, e^{jk\omega_0 n} \qquad ...(2.55)$$

Put
$$N = \frac{2\pi}{\omega_0} \text{ in (2.55), and we obtain}$$

$$x_p(n) = \frac{1}{2\pi}\sum_{k=<N>} X(e^{jk\omega_0}) . \, e^{jk\omega_0 n} . \, \omega_0 \qquad ...(2.56)$$

Take limit on both sides of (2.56) as $N \to \infty$, therefore,

$$\left.\begin{aligned} \lim_{N\to\infty} x_p(n) &= x(n) \\ \lim_{N\to\infty} \omega_0 &= \lim_{N\to\infty} \frac{2\pi}{N} \to d\omega \text{ (infinitesimal small)} \\ \lim_{N\to\infty} k\omega_0 &= \omega \quad \text{(as } k \text{ is an integer and takes any value, and so is } \omega\text{)} \end{aligned}\right\} \qquad ...(2.57)$$

$$\therefore \quad \lim_{N\to\infty} x_p(n) = \lim_{N\to\infty} \frac{1}{2\pi}\sum_{k=<N>} X(e^{jk\omega_0})\, e^{jk\omega_0 n}\omega_0 \qquad ...(2.58)$$

becomes
$$x(n) = \frac{1}{2\pi}\int_{-\pi}^{\pi} X(e^{j\omega})\, e^{j\omega n}\, d\omega \qquad ...(2.59)$$

because summation becomes integration, as $N \longrightarrow \infty$.

Then $\omega_0 = 2\pi/N$ added N time gives total interval $\omega = 2\pi$, since, k takes only N values in (2.58).

Finally, writing (2.53) and (2.59) as a pair of equations, we have

$$X(e^{j\omega}) = \sum_{n=-\infty}^{\infty} x(n)\, e^{-j\omega n} \quad ...(2.60a)$$

$$x(n) = \frac{1}{2\pi}\int_{-\pi}^{\pi} X(e^{j\omega})\, e^{j\omega n}\, d\omega \quad ...(2.60b)$$

This is Fourier-transform pair of an aperiodic sequence $x(n)$.

2.4.2 Why the Notation $X(e^{j\omega})$ for Fourier-transform of $x(n)$

As $$X(e^{j\omega}) = \sum_{n=-\infty}^{\infty} x(n)\, e^{-j\omega n} \quad \text{[by definition see (2.53)]}$$

The argument $e^{j\omega}$ of $X(e^{j\omega})$ is periodic in ω with period 2π, since,

$$e^{j\omega} = e^{j(\omega + 2\pi k)},\ k = 0, \pm 1, \pm 2, ...,$$

and so is the function $X(e^{j\omega})$. Note that

$$X(e^{j(\omega + 2\pi k)}) = \sum_{n=-\infty}^{\infty} x(n)\, e^{-j(\omega + 2\pi k)n}$$

gives us, replacing $e^{j(\omega + 2\pi k)}$ by $e^{j\omega}$ on RHS, we obtain

$$X(e^{j(\omega + 2\pi k)}) = \sum_{n=-\infty}^{\infty} x(n)\, e^{-j\omega n} \quad \text{(as desired for a periodic function)}$$

Hence, the notation $X(e^{j\omega})$ is generally used as it gives us the information at a glance that $X(e^{j\omega})$ is a periodic function, periodic in ω, with period 2π. Some authors prefer $X(e^{i\Omega})$ or $X(\Omega)$ or $X(\omega)$ as the notation.

The use of Ω is generally preferred for analog signals by many authors. However, we shall, in this book, use the notation: $FT[x(n)] = X(e^{j\omega})$, or $X(\omega)$.

2.4.3 Conjugate Symmetric and Antisymmetric Signals

A conjugate symmetric sequence, $x_e(n)$, is defined as a sequence such that

$$x_e(n) = x_e^*(-n) \text{ Conjugate symmetry} \quad ...(2.61)$$

A conjugate antisymmetric sequence, $x_0(n)$, is defined as a sequence such that:

$$x_o(n) = -x_o^*(-n) \text{ Conjugate antisymmetry} \quad ...(2.62)$$

If $x(n)$ is a real sequence then $x^*(n) = x(n)$. Hence we have:

$$\begin{aligned} x_e(n) &= x_e(-n) \text{ Symmetric for } x_e(n) \text{ real} \\ x_o(n) &= -\,x_o(-n)\text{: Antisymmetric for } x_o(n) \text{ real} \end{aligned} \quad ...(2.63)$$

Computation of $x_e(n)$ and $x_o(n)$ given $x(n)$

Let $$x(n) = x_e(n) + x_o(n) \quad ...(2.64a)$$

$\therefore$ $$x^*(-n) = x_e^*(-n) + x_o^*(-n)$$

i.e. $$x^*(-n) = x_e(n) - x_o(n) \qquad \because x_e^*(-n) = x_e(n),\ x_o^*(-n) = -\,x_o(n) \quad ...(2.64b)$$

Adding and subtracting (2.64*a*) and (2.64*b*) gives us

$$x_e(n) = \frac{1}{2}\left[x(n) + x^*(-n)\right]$$
$$x_o(n) = \frac{1}{2}\left[x(n) - x^*(-n)\right] \quad ...(2.65)$$

2.5 PROPERTIES OF DISCRETE-TIME FOURIER TRANSFORM (DTFT)

We now prove some important properties of DTFT of sequences.

2.5.1 Periodicity

As $$X(e^{j\omega}) = \sum_{n=\infty}^{\infty} x(n)\, e^{-jn\omega}$$

$\therefore$ $$X(e^{j(\omega+2\pi l)}) = \sum_{n=-\infty}^{\infty} x(n\, e^{-jn(\omega+2\pi l)})$$
$$= \sum_{n=-\infty}^{\infty} x(n)\cdot e^{-jn\omega} = X(e^{j\omega})$$

$\therefore$ $X(e^{j\omega})$ is periodic in ω with period 2π ...(2.66)

2.5.2 Linearity

If $x(n) \xleftrightarrow{FT} X(e^{j\omega})$ and $y(n) \xleftrightarrow{FT} Y(e^{j\omega})$

then $ax(n) + by(n) \xleftrightarrow{FT} aX(e^{j\omega}) + bY(e^{j\omega})$ ...(2.67)

Proof.

$$FT[ax(n) + by(n)] = \sum_n [ax(n) + by(n)]\, e^{-j\omega n} \quad \text{(by definition of } FT\text{)}$$
$$= a\sum_n x(n)\, e^{-j\omega n} + b\sum_n y(n)\, e^{-j\omega n}$$
$$= aX(e^{j\omega}) + bY(e^{j\omega})$$

Q.E.D.

2.5.3 Time-Shifting

If $x(n) \xleftrightarrow{FT} X(e^{j\omega})$, then $x(n-n_0) \xleftrightarrow{FT} e^{-j\omega n_0}\, X(e^{j\omega})$ ...(2.68)

Proof.

$$FT[x(n-n_0)] = \sum_{n=-\infty}^{\infty} x(n-n_0)\, e^{-j\omega n} \quad \text{(by definition of FT)}$$

Put $n - n_0 = n'$

$\therefore$ $n = n' + n_0$. Limits of summation are $n' = -\infty$ to ∞

$$\therefore \quad FT[x(n-n_0)] = \sum_{n'=-\infty}^{\infty} x(n')\, e^{-j\omega(n'+n_0)}$$

$$= e^{-j\omega n_0} \sum_{n=-\infty}^{\infty} x(n')\, e^{-j\omega n'}$$

$$= e^{j\omega n_0} \cdot X(e^{j\omega})$$

Q.E.D.

2.5.4 Frequency Shifting

$$\boxed{\text{If } x(n) \xleftrightarrow{FT} X(e^{j\omega}), \text{ then } e^{j\omega_0 n} x(n) \xleftrightarrow{FT} X(e^{j(\omega-\omega_0)})} \qquad ...(2.69)$$

Proof.

$$FT[e^{j\omega_0 n}\, x(n)] = \sum_{n=-\infty}^{\infty} [e^{j\omega_0 n} x(n)]\, e^{-j\omega n} \quad \text{(by definition of FT)}$$

$$= \sum_{n=-\infty}^{\infty} x(n)\, e^{-j(\omega-\omega_0)n}$$

$$= X\left(e^{j(\omega-\omega_0)}\right)$$

Q.E.D.

2.5.5 Conjugation

$$\boxed{\text{If } x(n) \xleftrightarrow{FT} X(e^{j\omega}), \text{ then } x^*(n) \xleftrightarrow{FT} X^*(e^{-j\omega})} \qquad ...(2.70)$$

Proof.

$$FT[x^*(n)] = \sum_{n} x^*(n)\, e^{-j\omega n} \quad \text{(by definition of } FT\text{)}$$

$$= \left(\sum_{n} x(n)\, e^{-j(-\omega)n}\right)^* \quad \text{(taking conjugation outside the series)}$$

$$= X^*(e^{-j\omega})$$

Q.E.D.

2.5.6 Time-Reversal

$$\boxed{\text{If } x(n) \xleftrightarrow{FT} X(e^{j\omega}), \text{ then } x(-n) \xleftrightarrow{FT} X(e^{-j\omega})} \qquad ...(2.71)$$

Proof.

$$FT[x(-n)] = \sum_{n=-\infty}^{\infty} x(-n)\, e^{-j\omega n} \quad \text{(by definition of } FT\text{)}$$

Put $-n = n'$

$\therefore$ limits of n' in summation are $n' = -\infty$ to ∞

$$\therefore \quad FT[x(-n)] = \sum_{n'=-\infty}^{\infty} x(n')\, e^{-j(-\omega)n'}$$

$$= X(e^{-j\omega})$$

Q.E.D.

2.5.7 Time Expansion (Interpolation)

$$\text{If } x(n) \xleftrightarrow{FT} X(e^{j\omega}), \text{ then } x\left(\frac{n}{M}\right) \xleftrightarrow{FT} X(e^{jM\omega}) \qquad ...(2.72)$$

Proof.

Note that: Interpolated signal

$$x\left(\frac{n}{M}\right) \triangleq \begin{cases} x(n/M), \text{if } n \text{ is multiple of } M \\ 0, \text{if } n \text{ is not multiple of } M \end{cases}$$

$$FT\left[x\left(\frac{n}{M}\right)\right] = \sum_{\substack{n=-\infty \\ n=kM}}^{\infty} x\left(\frac{n}{M}\right) e^{-j\omega n}$$

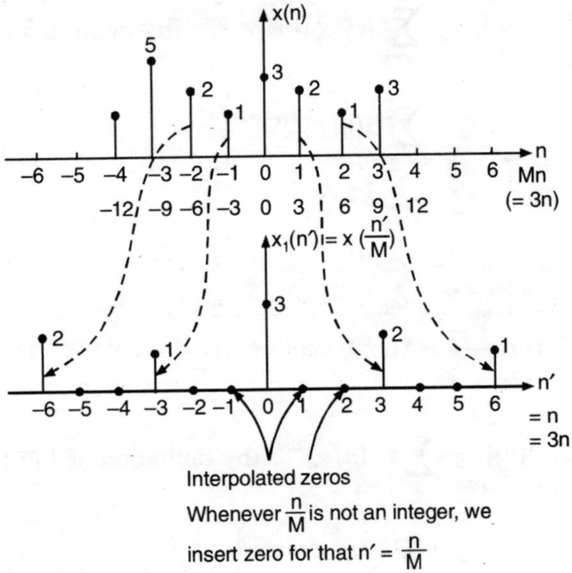

Fig. 2.1. Showing $x(n)$ and $x\left(\frac{n}{M}\right)$ for M = 3

Put $\quad \frac{n}{M} = n'$

$\therefore \quad n' = -\infty$ to ∞

$$\therefore \quad FT\left[x\left(\frac{n}{M}\right)\right] = \sum_{n'=-\infty}^{\infty} x(n')\, e^{-j\omega n' M}$$

$$= \sum_{n'=-\infty}^{\infty} x(n')\, e^{-j(M\omega)n'} = X(e^{jM\omega}) \qquad \text{Q.E.D.}$$

2.5.8 Differentiation-in-Time (Cf. Differentiation in CTFT)

$$\text{If } x(n) \xleftrightarrow{FT} X(e^{j\omega}), \text{ then } x(n) - x(n-1) \xleftrightarrow{FT} (1 - e^{-j\omega})\, X(e^{j\omega}) \qquad ...(2.73)$$

Proof.

$$FT[x(n) - x(n-1)] = FT[x(n)] - FT[x(n-1)]$$

$$= X(e^{j\omega}) - e^{-j\omega 1} X(e^{j\omega}) \qquad \because FT[x(n-n_0)] = e^{-j\omega n_0} X(e^{j\omega})$$

here $n_0 = 1$

$$= (1 - e^{-j\omega}) X(e^{j\omega})$$

Q.E.D.

2.5.9 Differentiation in Frequency

$$\text{If } x(n) \xleftrightarrow{FT} X(e^{j\omega}), \text{ then } n\,x(n) \xleftrightarrow{FT} j\frac{dX(e^{j\omega})}{d\omega} \qquad \text{...(2.74)}$$

Proof.

We know that $$X(e^{j\omega}) = \sum_{n=-\infty}^{\infty} x(n)\,e^{-j\omega n} \qquad \text{...(A)}$$

Differentiating both sides of (A) w.r.t. ω, we shall get

$$\frac{dX(e^{j\omega})}{d\omega} = \sum_{n=-\infty}^{\infty} (-jn)\,x(n)e^{-j\omega n}$$

or $$j\frac{dX(e^{j\omega})}{d\omega} = \sum_{n=-\infty}^{\infty} [nx(n)]\,e^{-j\omega n}$$

which implies that $nx(n) \xleftrightarrow{FT} j\dfrac{dX(e^{j\omega})}{d\omega}$

Q.E.D.

2.5.10 Accumulation

$$\text{If } x(n) \xleftrightarrow{FT} X(e^{j\omega}), \text{ then } \sum_{k=-\infty}^{n} x(k) \xleftrightarrow{FT}, \frac{X(e^{j\omega})}{1-e^{-j\omega}} + \pi X(e^{jo}) \sum_{k=-\infty}^{\infty} \delta(\omega - 2\pi k) \qquad \text{...(2.75)}$$

Proof.

Let $$y(n) = \sum_{k=-\infty}^{n} x(k)$$

$$= \sum_{k=-\infty}^{n} x(k)\cdot u(n-k) = x(n) * u(n) \qquad \text{(Note this step)}$$

$\therefore$ $$Y(e^{j\omega}) = X(e^{j\omega}) \cdot U(e^{j\omega}) \qquad \text{(Convolution property)}$$

$$= X(e^{j\omega})\left[\frac{1}{1-e^{-j\omega}} + \sum_{k=-\infty}^{\infty} \pi\delta(\omega - 2\pi k)\right] \qquad \text{(due to 2.94)}$$

$$= \frac{X(e^{j\omega})}{1-e^{-j\omega}} + \pi X(e^{j2\pi k}) \sum_{k=-\infty}^{\infty} \delta(\omega - 2\pi k)$$

$$= \frac{X(e^{j\omega})}{1-e^{-j\omega}} + \pi X(e^{j0}) \sum_{k=-\infty}^{\infty} \delta(\omega - 2\pi k)$$ **Q.E.D.**

2.5.11 Convolution

$$\text{If } x(n) \xleftrightarrow{FT} X(e^{j\omega}), \text{ and } y(n) \xleftrightarrow{FT} Y(e^{j\omega}), \text{ then } x(n) * y(n) \xleftrightarrow{FT} X(e^{j\omega}) \cdot Y(e^{j\omega}) \quad ...(2.76)$$

Proof.

$$FT[x(n) * y(n)] = \sum_{n=-\infty}^{\infty} [x(n) * y(n)]\, e^{-j\omega n}$$

$$= \sum_{n=-\infty}^{\infty} \left[\sum_{k=-\infty}^{\infty} x(k)\, y(n-k) \right] \cdot e^{-j\omega n}$$

$$= \sum_{k=-\infty}^{\infty} x(k) \sum_{n=-\infty}^{\infty} y(n-k) \cdot e^{-j\omega n}$$ (Interchanging the order of summation)

$\uparrow$ Put $n - k = m$

$$= \sum_{k=-\infty}^{\infty} x(k) \sum_{m=-\infty}^{\infty} y(m)\, e^{-j\omega(m+k)}$$

$$= \sum_{k=-\infty}^{\infty} x(k)\, e^{-j\omega k} \underbrace{\sum_{m=-\infty}^{\infty} y(m) \cdot e^{-j\omega m}}_{=Y(e^{j\omega})}$$

$$= \sum_{k=-\infty}^{\infty} x(k)\, e^{-j\omega k} \cdot Y(e^{j\omega})$$

$$= X(e^{j\omega}) \cdot Y(e^{j\omega})$$ **Q.E.D.**

2.5.12 Multiplication

$$\text{If } x(n) \xleftrightarrow{FT} X(e^{j\omega}), \text{ and } y(n) \xleftrightarrow{FT} Y(e^{j\omega}), \text{ then } x(n) \cdot y(n) \xleftrightarrow{FT} \frac{1}{2\pi} \int_{2\pi} X(e^{j\theta})\, Y\left(e^{j(\omega-\theta)}\right) d\theta$$

$$= \frac{1}{2\pi} X(e^{j\omega}) * Y(e^{j\omega}) \quad ...(2.77)$$

Proof.

$$FT\,[x(n) \cdot y(n)] = \sum_{n=-\infty}^{\infty} [y(n) \cdot x(n)] e^{-j\omega n}$$

$$= \sum_{n=-\infty}^{\infty} [y(n) \cdot e^{-j\omega n}] \cdot \left(\frac{1}{2\pi} \int_{2\pi} X(e^{j\theta})\, e^{j\theta n}\, d\theta \right)$$ $\leftarrow$ This is IFT of $X(e^{j\omega})$ equalling $x(n)$

$$= \frac{1}{2\pi} \int_{2\pi} X(e^{j\theta}) \left(\sum_{n=-\infty}^{\infty} [y(n) \cdot e^{-j(\omega-\theta)n}] \right) d\theta$$

$$= \frac{1}{2\pi} \int_{2\pi} X(e^{j\theta}) \cdot Y(e^{j(\omega-\theta)})\, d\theta$$

$$= \frac{1}{2\pi} X(e^{j\omega}) * Y(e^{j\omega}) \qquad \text{Q.E.D.}$$

2.5.13 Parseval's Relation

$$\text{If } x(n) \xleftrightarrow{FT} X(e^{j\omega}), \text{ then } \sum_{n=-\infty}^{\infty} |x(n)|^2 = \frac{1}{2\pi} \int_{2\pi} |X(e^{j\omega})|^2 d\omega \qquad ...(2.78)$$

Proof.

$$\sum_{n=-\infty}^{\infty} |x(n)|^2 = \sum_{n=-\infty}^{\infty} x^*(n) \cdot x(n)$$

$$= \sum_{n=-\infty}^{\infty} x^*(n) \cdot \left(\frac{1}{2\pi} \int_{2\pi} X(e^{j\omega})\, e^{j\omega n} d\omega \right) \leftarrow \text{This is } x(n) \text{ due to IFT of } X(e^{j\omega})$$

$$= \frac{1}{2\pi} \int_{2\pi} X(e^{j\omega}) \cdot \left(\sum_{n=-\infty}^{\infty} x^*(n) \cdot e^{j\omega n} \right) d\omega$$

$$= \frac{1}{2\pi} \int_{2\pi} X(e^{j\omega}) \cdot \left(\sum_{n=-\infty}^{\infty} x(n) \cdot e^{-j\omega n} \right)^* d\omega$$

$$= \frac{1}{2\pi} \int_{2\pi} X(e^{j\omega}) \cdot X^*(e^{j\omega})\, d\omega = \frac{1}{2\pi} \int_{2\pi} |X(e^{j\omega})|^2\, d\omega \qquad \text{Q.E.D.}$$

This relation shows that the total energy in the signal $x(n)$ can be determined by integrating the energy per unit frequency $|X(e^{j\omega})|^2/2\pi$, over a full 2π interval of distinct discrete-time frequencies.

2.5.14 Conjugate Symmetry for Real Signals

If $x(n)$ is real signal and $x(n) \xleftrightarrow{FT} X(e^{j\omega})$, then

(*a*) $\text{Re}\,[X(e^{j\omega})] = \text{Re}[X(e^{-j\omega})]$;

(*b*) $I_m[X(e^{j\omega})] = -I_m[X(e^{-j\omega})]$

(*c*) $X(e^{j\omega}) = X^*(e^{-j\omega})$;

(*d*) $|X(e^{j\omega})| = |X(e^{-j\omega})|$

(*e*) $\text{Arg } X(e^{j\omega}) = -\text{Arg } X(e^{-j\omega})$ ...(2.79)

Proof.

If $x(n)$ is real then $x(n) = x^*(n)$

$$X(e^{j\omega}) = X^*(e^{-j\omega}) \quad ...(A) \qquad \left(\because x^*(n) \xleftrightarrow{FT} X^*(e^{-j\omega}) \text{ see } (2.70)\right)$$

It readily follows that

$$\mathrm{Re}[X(e^{j\omega})] = \mathrm{Re}[X(e^{-j\omega})] \quad ...(B)$$

$$I_m[X(e^{j\omega})] = -I_m[X(e^{-j\omega})] \quad ...(C)$$

$$|X(e^{j\omega})| = |X(e^{-j\omega})| \quad ...(D)$$

Q.E.D.

As Real parts of $X(e^{j\omega})$ and $X(e^{-j\omega})$ are equal but imaginary parts have opposite sign, therefore, $\mathrm{Arg}\ X(e^{j\omega}) = -\mathrm{Arg}\ X(e^{-j\omega})$. ...(E)

2.5.15 Symmetry for Real Signals

(*a*) If $x(n)$ is real and even, then $X(e^{j\omega})$ is real and even
(*b*) If $x(n)$ is real and odd, then $X(e^{j\omega})$ is purely imaginary and odd ...(2.80)

Proof.

We know that, for all types of sequences $x(n)$, the following holds.

$$x(n) \xleftrightarrow{FT} X(e^{j\omega}) \quad \text{(by definition)} \quad ...(a)$$

$$x^*(n) \xleftrightarrow{FT} X^*(e^{-j\omega}) \quad \text{(conjugation property)} \quad ...(b)$$

$$x(-n) \xleftrightarrow{FT} X(e^{-j\omega}) \quad \text{(time reversal property)} \quad ...(c)$$

If $x(n)$ is real *i.e.* $x(n) = x^*(n)$, then due to (*a*) and (*b*) above

$$X(e^{j\omega}) = X^*(e^{-j\omega}) \quad ...(d)$$

(*a*) If $x(n)$ is even then $x(n) = x(-n)$, then combining (*c*) and (*d*)

$$X(e^{-j\omega}) = X^*(e^{-j\omega})$$

or $$X(e^{j\omega}) = X^*(e^{j\omega}) \quad \text{(changing } -\omega \text{ to } \omega \text{ on both sides)} ...(e)$$

$\therefore X(e^{j\omega})$ is purely real

From (*d*),

$$\mathrm{Re}\,[X(e^{j\omega})] = \mathrm{Re}\,[X(e^{-j\omega})] \text{ i.e.}$$

i.e. $X(e^{j\omega})$ is an even function of ω ...(*f*)

Combining (*e*) and (*f*), we can say that

if $x(n)$ is real and even, then $X(e^{j\omega})$ is also real and even.

(*b*) If $x(n)$ is real and odd *i.e.*, $x(n) = -x(-n)$ then from (*d*) and (*c*), we get

$$X(e^{j\omega}) = X^*(e^{-j\omega}) = -X(e^{-j\omega}) \quad ...(g)$$

The first two terms of (*g*) give us

$$X(e^{j\omega}) = X^*(e^{-j\omega})$$

i.e. $$I_m[X(e^{j\omega})] = -I_m[X(e^{-j\omega})] \quad ...(h)$$

The last two terms of (*g*) give us

$$X(e^{-j\omega}) = -X^*(e^{-j\omega})$$

or $$X(e^{j\omega}) = -X^*(e^{j\omega}) \quad \text{(changing } -\omega \text{ to } \omega \text{ both sides)}$$

i.e. $X(e^{j\omega})$ is purely imaginary ...(*i*)

Combining (*g*) and (*i*), we can say that if $x(n)$ is real and odd then $X(e^{j\omega})$ is purely imaginary and odd. Q.E.D.

2.5.16 Symmetric and Antisymmetric Conjugate Parts of $x(n)$

$$\text{If } x(n) \overset{F}{\longleftrightarrow} X(e^{j\omega}), \text{ then } x_e(n) \overset{F}{\longleftrightarrow} \text{Re}[X(e^{j\omega})], \text{ and } x_o(n) \overset{F}{\longleftrightarrow} j\,I_m[X(e^{j\omega})] \quad ...(2.81)$$

Proof.

As $$FT[x^*(-n)] = \sum_{n=-\infty}^{\infty} x^*(-n)\,e^{-j\omega n} = \left(\sum_{n=-\infty}^{\infty} x(-n)\,e^{j\omega n}\right)^* \quad \text{Put } n=-m$$

$$= \left(\sum_{m=-\infty}^{\infty} x(m)\,e^{-j\omega m}\right)^* = X^*(e^{j\omega})$$

Thus, $$x_e(n) = \frac{1}{2}[x(n)+x^*(-n)]$$

$\therefore$ $$x_e(n) \overset{F}{\longleftrightarrow} \frac{1}{2}[X(e^{j\omega})+X^*(e^{j\omega})] = \text{Re}[X(e^{j\omega})] \quad \text{Q.E.D.}$$

and $$x_o(n) = \frac{1}{2}[x(n)-x^*(-n)]$$

$\therefore$ $$x_o(n) \overset{F}{\longleftrightarrow} \frac{1}{2}[X(e^{j\omega})-X^*(e^{j\omega})] = jI_m[X(e^{j\omega})] \quad \text{Q.E.D.}$$

2.5.17 Conjugate Symmetric and Conjugate Antisymmetric Parts of $X(e^{j\omega})$

$X(e^{j\omega})$ in terms of $X_e(e^{j\omega})$ and $X_o(e^{j\omega})$ can be derived as follows

Let

$$X(e^{j\omega}) = X_e(e^{j\omega}) + X_o(e^{j\omega}) \quad ...(2.82)$$

$X_e(e^{j\omega})$ ↗ called conjugate symmetric part; $X_o(e^{j\omega})$ ↖ conjugate antisymmetric part

then $$\left.\begin{aligned} X_e(e^{j\omega}) &= X_e^*(e^{-j\omega}) \\ X_o(e^{j\omega}) &= -X_o^*(e^{-j\omega}) \end{aligned}\right\} \text{ by definition of conjugate symmetric and conjugate antisymmetric functions} \quad ...(2.83)$$

Changing ω to $-\omega$ and taking conjugate on both sides of (2.82), we get

$$X^*(e^{-j\omega}) = X_e^*(e^{-j\omega}) + X_o^*(e^{-j\omega})$$

i.e. $$X^*(e^{-j\omega}) = X_e(e^{j\omega}) - X_o^*(e^{j\omega})$$ [due to properties of X_e and X_o] ...(2.84) see (2.83)

Adding/subtracting (2.82) and (2.84), we get

$$X_e(e^{j\omega}) = \frac{1}{2}\left[X(e^{j\omega})+X^*(e^{-j\omega})\right]$$

$$X_o(e^{j\omega}) = \frac{1}{2}\left[X(e^{j\omega})-X^*(e^{-j\omega})\right] \quad ...(2.85)$$

where $X(e^{j\omega}) = X_e(e^{j\omega}) + X_o(e^{j\omega})$, with $X_e(e^{j\omega})$ the 'even' part and $X_o(e^{j\omega})$ the 'odd' part which gives the decomposition of $X(e^{j\omega})$ into its conjugate symmetric part $X_e(e^{j\omega})$ and conjugate antisymmetric part $X_o(e^{j\omega})$.

> **Important Note:**
> $$FT \text{ of } x_e(n) \neq X_e(e^{j\omega})$$
> Similarly, $$FT \text{ of } x_o(n) \neq X_o(e^{j\omega})$$

Relation between $x_e(n)$, $x_o(n)$, $X_e(e^{j\omega})$, $X_o(e^{j\omega})$

(*a*) As $$x_e(n) = \frac{1}{2}[x(n) + x^*(-n)]$$

Taking *FT* both sides, we have

$$FT[x_e(n)] = \frac{1}{2}\left[X(e^{j\omega}) + X^*(e^{j\omega})\right] \quad \because x^*(-n) \xrightarrow{FT} X^*(e^{j\omega})$$

or $$\boxed{FT[x_e(n)] = \text{Re}[X(e^{j\omega})]} \quad \text{...(2.86)}$$

(*b*) Again $$x_o(n) = \frac{1}{2}[x(n) - x^*(-n)]$$

$\therefore$ $$FT[x_o(n)] = \frac{1}{2}\left[X(e^{j\omega}) - X^*(e^{j\omega})\right]$$

or $$\boxed{FT\ [x_o(n)] = j\ I_m[X(e^{j\omega})]} \quad \text{...(2.87)}$$

(*c*) $$\text{Re}[x(n)] = \frac{1}{2}[x(n) + x^*(n)]$$

$$FT[\text{Re}\ x(n)] = \frac{1}{2}\left[X(e^{j\omega}) + X^*(e^{-j\omega})\right] \quad \because x^*(n) \xrightarrow{FT} X^*(e^{-j\omega})$$

$$= \frac{1}{2}\left(X_e(e^{j\omega}) + X_o(e^{j\omega})\right) + \left(X_e^*(e^{-j\omega}) + X_o^*(e^{-j\omega})\right)$$

$$= X_e(e^{j\omega}) \qquad = -X_o(e^{j\omega}) \qquad \textbf{(N.T.S.)}$$

$$= \frac{1}{2}[2\,X_e(e^{j\omega})] = X_e(e^{j\omega})$$

$\therefore$ $$\boxed{FT\ \{\text{Re}[x(n)]\} = X_e(e^{j\omega})} \quad \text{...(2.88)}$$

(*d*) $$jI_m\ [x(n)] = \frac{1}{2}(x(n) - x^*(n))$$

$$FT\ [jI_m\ x(n)] = \frac{1}{2}\left(X(e^{j\omega}) - X^*(e^{-j\omega})\right)$$

$$= \frac{1}{2}\left[(X_e(e^{j\omega}) + X_o(e^{j\omega})) - (X_e^*(e^{-j\omega}) + X_o^*(e^{-j\omega}))\right]$$

$$= X_e(e^{j\omega}) \qquad -X_o(e^{j\omega})$$

$\therefore$ $$\boxed{FT\ \{jI_m\ [x(n)]\} = X_o(e^{j\omega})} \quad \text{...(2.89a)}$$

We have listed all the properties in a tabular form in Table 2.2 for ready reference.

Table 2.2 Properties of Discrete-time Fourier Transform (DTFT)

S.N.	Property	Signal	$X(e^{j\omega}) = \sum_{n=-\infty}^{\infty} x(n)\, e^{-j\omega n}$	
1.	Periodicity	: $x(n), y(n)$	$X(e^{j\omega}) = X(e^{(j\omega + 2\pi)}), Y(e^{j\omega}) = Y(e^{j(\omega + 2\pi)})$	(2.66)
2.	Linearity	: $ax(n) + by(n)$	$aX(e^{j\omega}) + bY(e^{j\omega})$	(2.67)
3.	Time-shifting	: $x(n - n_0)$	$e^{-j\omega n_0}X(e^{j\omega})$	(2.68)
4.	Frequency-shifting	: $e^{j\omega_0 n}\, x(n)$	$X(e^{j(\omega - \omega_0)})$	(2.69)
5.	Conjugation	: $x^*(n)$	$X^*(e^{-j\omega})$	(2.70)
6.	Time-reversal	: $x(-n)$	$X(e^{-j\omega})$	(2.71)
7.	Time-expansion	: $x\left(\frac{n}{M}\right)$(interpolation)	$X(e^{jM\omega})$	(2.72)
8.	Differentiation in time	: $x(n) - x(n-1)$	$(1 - e^{-j\omega})\, X(e^{j\omega})$	(2.73)
9.	Differentiation in frequency	: $n\, x(n)$	$j\frac{d}{d\omega}X(e^{j\omega})$	(2.74)
10.	Accumulation	: $\sum_{k=-\infty}^{n} x(k)$	$\frac{1}{1-e^{-j\omega}} X(e^{j\omega}) + \pi X(e^{j0}) \sum_{k=-\infty}^{\infty} \delta(\omega - 2\pi k)$	(2.75)
11.	Convolution	: $x(n) * y(n)$	$X(e^{j\omega}) \cdot Y(e^{j\omega})$	(2.76)
12.	Multiplication	: $x(n) \cdot y(n)$	$\frac{1}{2\pi}\int_{2\pi} X(e^{j\theta})\cdot Y(e^{j(\omega-\theta)})d\theta \equiv \frac{1}{2\pi}X(e^{j\omega}) * Y(e^{j\omega})$	(2.77)
13.	Parseval's relation	: $\sum_{n=-\infty}^{\infty} \lvert x(n)\rvert^2$	$\frac{1}{2\pi}\int_{2\pi} \lvert X(e^{j\omega})\rvert^2\, d\omega$	(2.78)
14.	Conjugate symmetry for real signals	: $x(n)$ real	$X(e^{j\omega}) = X^*(e^{-j\omega})$ $\text{Re}[X(e^{j\omega})] = \text{Re}[X(e^{-j\omega})]$; $\lvert X(e^{j\omega})\rvert = \lvert X(e^{-j\omega})\rvert$; $I_m[X(e^{j\omega})] = -I_m[X(e^{-j\omega})]$	(2.79)
15.	Symmetry for real signals	: $x(n)$ real, even	$X(e^{j\omega})$ real and even	(2.80)
16.	Symmetry for real signals	: $x(n)$ real, odd	$X(e^{j\omega})$ purely imaginary and odd	(2.80)
17.	Symmetric conjugate part	: $x_e(n) = \frac{1}{2}[x(n) + x^*(-n)]$	$\text{Re}[X(e^{j\omega})]$	(2.81)
18.	Antisymmetric conjugate part	: $x_o(n) = \frac{1}{2}[x(n) - x^*(-n)]$	$jI_m[X(e^{j\omega})]$	(2.81)

In most of the practical applications, $x(n)$ is a real sequence. It may be even function of n or an odd function of n. In case $x(n)$ is not real or odd but a generic real sequence, we can decompose $x(n)$ in its odd part $x_e(n)$ and its even part $x_o(n)$ by using the formulas given below, for $x(n)$ real

$$x(n) = x_e(n) + x_o(n) \quad ...(2.89b)$$

$$x_e(n) = \frac{1}{2}[x(n) + x(-n)] \quad ...(2.90)$$

$$x_o(n) = \frac{1}{2}[x(n) - x(-n)] \quad ...(2.91)$$

Then apply the results of Fourier-transform to $x_e(n)$ or $x_o(n)$. Table 2.3 gives various useful relations when $x(n)$ is a real sequence.

Also, the duality between $x(n)$ and Fourier transform as given by Eqns. (2.86–2.89) is worth noting, when $x(n)$

$$x_e(n) \xrightarrow{FT} \text{Re}[X(e^{j\omega})], \qquad X_e(e^{j\omega}) \xrightarrow{FT} \text{Re}[x(n)]$$

$$x_o(n) \xrightarrow{FT} jI_m[X(e^{j\omega})], \qquad X_o(e^{j\omega}) \xrightarrow{FT} jI_m[x(n)]$$

Table 2.3 Summary of Results When x(n) is a Real Sequence

If $x(n)$ is a real sequence, then				
1.	$x^*(n)$	=	$x(n)$ (given condition)	
2.	$x(n)$	≜	$x_e(n) + x_o(n)$	...(2.89)
where	$x_e(n)$	=	$\frac{1}{2}[x(n)+x(-n)]$; $x_o(n)=\frac{1}{2}[x(n)-x(-n)]$	...(2.90), (2.91)
3.	$X(e^{j\omega})$	=	$X^*(e^{-j\omega})$ *i.e.* FT is conjugate symmetric	...(2.79)
4.	$\text{Re}[X(e^{j\omega})]$	=	$\text{Re}[X(e^{-j\omega})]$ *i.e.* Real part of FT is an even function of ω	...(2.79)
5.	$I_m[X(e^{j\omega})]$	=	$-I_m[X(e^{-j\omega})]$ *i.e.* imaginary part of FT is an odd function of ω	...(2.79)
6.	$\lvert X(e^{j\omega})\rvert$	=	$\lvert X(e^{-j\omega})\rvert$: Magnitude is even function of ω	...(2.79)
7.	$\text{Arg}\, X(e^{j\omega})$	=	$-\text{Arg}\, X(e^{-j\omega})$: Phase is odd function of ω	...(2.79)
8.	$x_e(n)$	⟷	$\text{Re}[X(e^{j\omega})]$ *i.e.* even part of $x(n)$ transforms to real part of $X(e^{j\omega})$	...(2.79)
9.	$x_o(n)$	⟷	$jI_m[X(e^{j\omega})]$ *i.e.* odd part of $x(n)$ transforms to $j\times$ imaginary part of $X(e^{j\omega})$	...(2.86)
10.	In general, for any real function of time, such as $x(n)$ here, the spectral function $F(\omega)$ satisfies the relation			
	$F^*(\omega)$	=	$F(-\omega)$, $\lvert F(\omega)\rvert = \lvert F(-\omega)\rvert$	...(2.87)

Note: **Result at serial 6 above implies that the magnitude function of *FT* of a real sequence *x(n)* is an even function of ω *i.e.* if there is an impulse at $\omega = \omega_0$, then there must be an impulse at $\omega = -\omega_0$ too. This is the case for signals like sin $\omega_0 n$ and cos $\omega_0 n$.**

2.6 DERIVATIONS OF DISCRETE-TIME FOURIER TRANSFORMS OF STANDARD SIGNALS

In order to tackle various problems, using DTFT, it is useful to derive and memorise the Fourier transforms of standard sequences $x(n)$. In derivation of DTFTs of various sequences in this section, we shall use the properties of DTFT's given in Table 2.2 which must also be mastered to understand various algebraic manipulations during the derivations.

2.6.1 Fourier Transform of $\delta(n)$

$$FT[\delta(n)] = \sum_{n=-\infty}^{\infty} \delta(n).e^{-j\omega n}$$

$$= 1 \quad \text{as } \delta(n) = \begin{cases} 1, n=0 \\ 0, \text{otherwise} \end{cases}$$

$$\therefore \quad \boxed{\delta(n) \xrightarrow{FT} 1} \qquad ...(2.92)$$

2.6.2 Fourier Transform of $a^n u(n)$, $|a| < 1$

$$FT[a^n u(n)] = \sum_{n=0}^{\infty} a^n e^{-j\omega n} \qquad (\because u(n) = 0 \text{ for } n \text{ negative})$$

$$= \sum_{n=0}^{\infty} \left(a e^{-j\omega}\right)^n \qquad (\text{a } GP \text{ with 'r'} = ae^{-j\omega} \text{ and } |r| < 1)$$

$$= \frac{1}{1 - ae^{-j\omega}}$$

$$\therefore \quad \boxed{a^n u(n) \xrightarrow{FT} \frac{1}{1 - ae^{-j\omega}}, \ |a| < 1} \qquad ...(2.93)$$

2.6.3 Fourier Transform of $u(n)$

Let $\qquad u(n) \longleftrightarrow U(e^{j\omega}) \qquad ...(A)$

But $\qquad u(n) - u(n-1) = \delta(n) \qquad ...(B)$

Taking FT on both sides of (B), we have

$$1 = (1 - e^{-j\omega})\, U(e^{j\omega}) \quad (\because \delta(n) \xleftrightarrow{FT} 1,\ u(n-1) \xleftrightarrow{FT} e^{-j\omega}U(e^{j\omega}) \ ...(C)$$

The equation (C) fails for $\omega = 0$, since, $(1 - e^{-j\omega})$ factor gives 0 at $\omega = 0$. To remove this disparity, $U(e^{j\omega})$ must be of form (note this step) as given below.

$$U(e^{j\omega}) = A\delta(\omega) + \frac{1}{1 - e^{-j\omega}} \qquad ...(D)$$

By using $U(e^{j\omega})$ as given in (D), equation (C) gets modified to:

$$1 = (1 - e^{-j\omega})\left(A\delta(\omega) + \frac{1}{1 - e^{-j\omega}}\right) \qquad ...(E)$$

Note that for $\omega = 0$, (E) is now satisfied. To determine the constant A, we proceed as follows.

Even part of $\qquad u(n) = u_e(n) = \frac{1}{2}[u(n) + u(-n)] = \frac{1}{2}[1 + \delta(n)] \qquad ...(F)$

Odd part of $\qquad u(n) = u_o(n) = \frac{1}{2}[u(n) - u(-n)]$

Also,
$$u_o(n) = u(n) - u_e(n)$$
$$= u(n) - \frac{1}{2}[1 + \delta(n)] \quad \text{due to } (F)$$
$$\therefore \quad u_o(n) = u(n) - \frac{1}{2}\delta(n) - \frac{1}{2} \qquad \ldots(G)$$

Take FT on both sides of (G). Therefore,

$$U_o(e^{j\omega}) = \left(A\delta(\omega) + \frac{1}{1-e^{-j\omega}}\right) - \frac{1}{2}(1) - \frac{1}{2}(2\pi\delta\omega) \quad (\because \text{FT }[1] = 2\pi\delta(\omega) \text{ see 2.6.7})$$
$$= A\delta(\omega) - \pi\delta(\omega) + \left(\frac{1}{1-e^{-j\omega}} - \frac{1}{2}\right)$$
$$= (A-\pi)\,\delta(\omega) + \frac{1+e^{-j\omega}}{2(1-e^{-j\omega})}$$
$$= (A-\pi)\delta(\omega) + \frac{1}{2}\frac{e^{-j\omega/2}\,(e^{j\omega/2} + e^{-j\omega/2})}{e^{-j\omega/2}(e^{j\omega/2} - e^{-j\omega/2})}$$
$$= (A-\pi)\delta(\omega) + \frac{1}{2}\frac{1}{j\tan\omega/2}$$
$$= (A-\pi)\delta(\omega) - \frac{j}{2}\cot\omega/2 \qquad \ldots(H)$$

But $u_o(n)$ is an odd part of a real sequence $u(n)$.

$\therefore$ $U_o(e^{j\omega})$ must be purely imaginary. This is only possible if the real part on RHS of (H) is zero. Hence, $A = \pi$. Putting $A = \pi$ in (D), we finally get

$$\boxed{u(n) \xleftrightarrow{FT} \frac{1}{1-e^{-j\omega}} + \pi\sum_{k=-\infty}^{\infty}\delta(\omega - 2\pi k)} \qquad \ldots(2.94)$$

We have made necessary amendment to (D) so that $U(e^{j\omega})$ is periodic in ω with period 2π.

2.6.4 Fourier Transform of $\delta(n - n_0)$

We know that

$$\delta(n) \xleftrightarrow{FT} 1$$

and using the property

$$x(n - n_o) \xleftrightarrow{FT} e^{-j\omega n_o} X(e^{j\omega})$$

we readily get

$$\boxed{FT[\delta(n - n_o)] = e^{-j\omega n_0}} \qquad \ldots(2.95)$$

2.6.5 Fourier Transform of $(n + 1)\, a^n\, u(n)$, $|a| < 1$

We know that

$$FT[a^n u(n)] = \frac{1}{1 - ae^{-j\omega}} \quad \text{for } |a| < 1 \qquad \ldots(A)$$

$$\therefore \quad FT[na^n u(n)] = j\frac{d}{d\omega}\left[\frac{1}{1-ae^{-j\omega}}\right] \quad \text{(differentiation in frequency property)}$$

$$= j\frac{-1}{(1-ae^{-j\omega})^2}(0+aje^{-j\omega})$$

$$= \frac{ae^{-j\omega}}{(1-ae^{-j\omega})^2} \qquad ...(B)$$

Adding (A) and (B), we get

$$FT[a^n u(n) + na^n u(n)] = \frac{1}{1-ae^{-k_0}} + \frac{ae^{-j\omega}}{(1-ae^{-j\omega})^2}$$

$$\therefore \quad \boxed{(n+1)\,a^n u(n) \xleftrightarrow{FT} \frac{1}{(1-ae^{-j\omega})^2}, |a|<1} \qquad ...(2.96)$$

2.6.6 To Show that ${}^{n+r-1}C_n\, a^n u(n) \xleftrightarrow{FT} \frac{1}{(1-ae^{-j\omega})^r}$, $|a| < 1$ ...(2.97)

(Proof by induction)

Define a function $x_r(n)$ by

$$x_r(n) = {}^{n+r-1}C_n\, a^n u(n) = \frac{(n+r-1)!}{n!(r-1)!}a^n u(n), |a|<1 \qquad ...(A)$$

Suppose

$$x_r(n) \xleftrightarrow{FT} \frac{1}{(1-ae^{-j\omega})^r}, \quad |a|<1 \qquad ...(B)$$

is true. Then we first show that (B) is true for $r = 1$.

For $r = 1$, from (A), we get

$$x_1(n) = a^n u(n)$$

Putting $r = 1$, in (B)

$$x_1(n) = a^n u(n) \xleftrightarrow{FT} \frac{1}{(1-ae^{-j\omega})}, \quad |a|<1 \qquad ...(C)$$

which is true, see (2.93). Hence, (B) holds (is true) for $r = 1$. Let us find whether (B) is true for $x_{r+1}(n)$ also if it is true for $x_r(n)$.

From equation (A), changing r into $r + 1$ both sides, we have

$$x_{r+1}(n) = \frac{(n+r)!}{n!r!}a^n u(n), \quad |a|<1$$

$$= \frac{(n+r)(n+r-1)!}{n!\,r.(r-1)!}a^n u(n)$$

$$= \frac{n}{r}\left[\frac{(n+r-1)!}{n!(r-1)!}a^n u(n)\right] + \frac{(n+r-1)!}{n!(r-1)!}a^n u(n) \qquad ...(D)$$

Then taking FT on both sides of (D), we get

$$x_{r+1}(n) \xleftrightarrow{FT} FT\left[\frac{n}{r}x_r(n)\right] + FT[x_r(n)]$$

$$= \frac{1}{r}\left[j\frac{d}{d\omega}(FT\, x_r(n))\right] + FT[x_r(n)]$$

$$= \frac{1}{r}\, j\frac{d}{d\omega}\left[\frac{1}{(1-a\,e^{-j\omega})^r}\right] + \frac{1}{(1-a\,e^{-j\omega})^r} \quad \text{[due to (B) assumed true]}$$

$$= \frac{j}{r}\frac{(-r)(a\,j\,e^{-j\omega})}{(1-a\,e^{-j\omega})^{r+1}} + \frac{1}{(1-a\,e^{-j\omega})^r}$$

$$= \frac{1}{(1-a\,e^{-j\omega})^{r+1}}\left[a\,e^{-j\omega} + (1-a\,e^{-j\omega})\right]$$

i.e.,

$$x_{r+1}(n) \xleftrightarrow{FT} \frac{1}{(1-a\,e^{-j\omega})^{r+1}},\quad |a| < 1 \qquad \text{...}(E)$$

It is seen from (*B*) and (*E*) that if the Fourier transform of $x_r(n)$ is true as given in (*B*), for some arbitrary integer r, then it is also true for higher integer $r + 1$. But (*B*) is true for $r = 1$, as shown by (*C*). Therefore, (*B*) is true for $r = 2, 3, \ldots$, and so on. Hence, relation (*B*) is true for all values of integer $r > 0$, and $|a| < 1$. Q.E.D.

2.6.7 Fourier Transform of $x(n) = 1$

Consider the inverse Fourier transform of

$$X(e^{j\omega}) = 2\pi\delta(\omega)$$

$$\therefore \quad x(n) = \frac{1}{2\pi}\int_{-\pi}^{\pi} X(e^{j\omega})\, e^{j\omega n}\, d\omega \quad \text{(definition of FT)}$$

$$= \frac{1}{2\pi}\int_{-\pi}^{\pi} 2\pi\delta(\omega)\, e^{j\omega n}\, d\omega$$

$$= \frac{1}{2\pi}(2\pi\times 1) \qquad (\because \delta(\omega) = 1 \text{ only for } \omega = 0 \text{ and } e^{j0n} = 1)$$

i.e.,

$$x(n) = 1 \text{ transforms to } 2\pi\delta(\omega) \qquad \text{...}(A)$$

But Fourier transform $X(e^{j\omega})$ must be periodic in ω with period 2π. With this condition inserted in (*A*), we get

$$\boxed{x(n) = 1 \xleftrightarrow{FT} 2\pi\sum_{k=-\infty}^{\infty}\delta(\omega - 2\pi k)} \qquad \text{...}(2.98)$$

Note the method of proof by *indirect approach.* A direct approach would be quite involved.

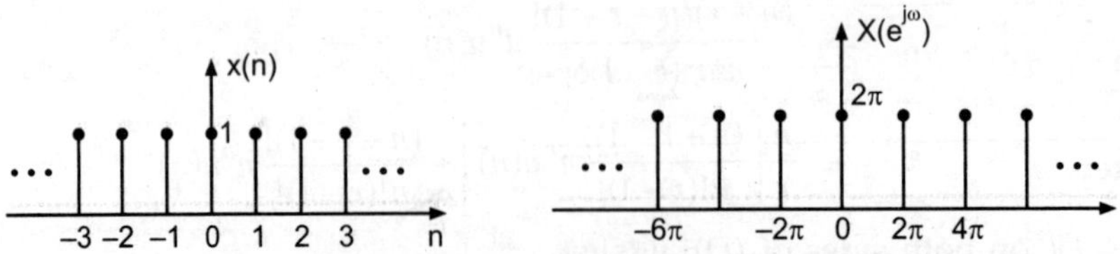

Fig. 2.2. Showing $x(n) = 1$ and its Fourier transform

2.6.8 Fourier Transform of $x(n) = e^{j\omega_0 n}$

We know that $$1 \xleftrightarrow{FT} 2\pi \sum_{l=-\infty}^{\infty} \delta(\omega - 2\pi l) \text{ see (2.98)}$$

$$x(n) = e^{j\omega_0 n} = (e^{j\omega_0 n}) \times 1$$

$\therefore$ $X(e^{j\omega})$ = FT of 1 with ω changed into $\omega - \omega_0$ (Frequency shifting property)

Hence, $$\boxed{e^{j\omega_0 n} \xleftrightarrow{FT} 2\pi \sum_{l=-\infty}^{\infty} \delta(\omega - \omega_0 - 2\pi l)} \qquad ...(2.99)$$

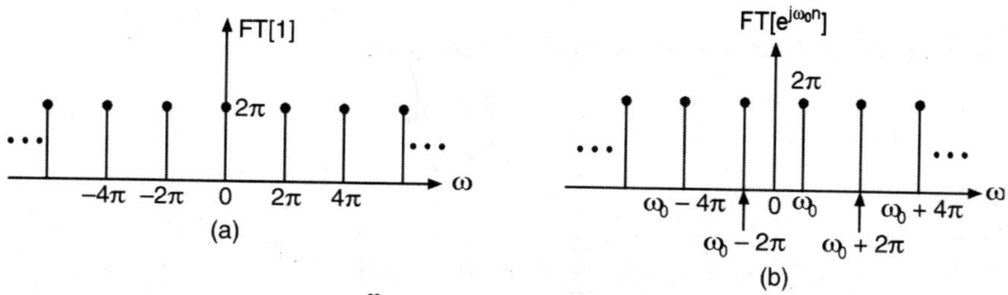

Fig. 2.3. Showing $FT\,[1] = 2\pi \sum_{l=-\infty}^{\infty} \delta(\omega - 2\pi l)$ shown in (a) gets shifted to RHS by ω_0 for $FT[e^{j\omega_0 n}] = 2\pi \sum_{l=-\infty}^{\infty} \delta(\omega - \omega_0 - 2\pi l)$ shown in (b)

2.6.9 Fourier Transform of $x(n) = \sum_{k=\langle N\rangle} a_k e^{jk(2\pi/N)n}$

Given $$x(n) = \sum_{k=\langle N\rangle} a_k\, e^{jk(2\pi/N)\,n} \qquad ...(A)$$

Hence, $x(n)$ is a periodic sequence with period N and a_k is also periodic with period N ($\because a_k = a_{k+lN}$)

As $$e^{j\omega_0 n} \xleftrightarrow{FT} 2\pi \sum_{k=-\infty}^{\infty} \delta(\omega - \omega_0 - 2\pi k)$$

$$= 2\pi\delta(\omega - \omega_0) \text{ and periodic with period } 2\pi$$

$\therefore$ $$\sum_{k=\langle N\rangle} a_k\, e^{j\left(k\frac{2\pi}{N}\right)n} \xleftrightarrow{FT} \left.\begin{array}{c} 2\pi \displaystyle\sum_{k=\langle N\rangle} a_k \delta\left(\omega - \frac{2\pi k}{N}\right) \\ \text{periodic with period } 2\pi \end{array}\right\} \qquad ...(B)$$

Hence, $$\boxed{\sum_{k=\langle N\rangle} a_k\, e^{jk(2\pi/N)\,n} \xleftrightarrow{FT} 2\pi \sum_{k=-\infty}^{\infty} a_k \delta\left(\omega - \frac{2\pi k}{N}\right)} \qquad ...(2.100)$$

How this step

In (B), for $k = 1$, say, we get a term $2\pi a_1 \delta\left(\omega - \frac{2\pi}{N}\right)$

In (2.100) also for $k = 1$, we get a term $2\pi a_1 \delta\left(\omega - \frac{2\pi}{N}\right)$

In (2.100) for $k = N + 1$, we get a term $2\pi a_{N+1}\delta\left(\omega - \frac{2\pi(N+1)}{N}\right)$

which equals $2\pi a_1 \delta\left(\omega - \frac{2\pi}{N} - 2\pi\right)$, as $a_{N+1} = a_1$,

which is term $2\pi a_1 \delta\left(\omega - \frac{2\pi}{N}\right)$ delayed by 2π.

Thus, in the series given by both sides of (2.100) periodicity is there. After every N terms in RHS of (2.100), the same term appears with delay or advance of 2π *i.e.*, it is periodic in ω with period 2π. Hence, the *FT* of $x(n)$ is indeed periodic as derived.

2.6.10 To Find Fourier Transform of $x(n) = \cos \omega_0 n$

As $$\cos \omega_0 n = \frac{1}{2}\left[e^{j\omega_0 n} + e^{-j\omega_0 n}\right]$$

We know that

$$e^{j\omega_0 n} \xleftrightarrow{FT} 2\pi \sum_{l=-\infty}^{\infty} \delta(\omega - \omega_0 - 2\pi l) \quad ...(A)$$

and

$$e^{-j\omega_0 n} \xleftrightarrow{FT} 2\pi \sum_{l=-\infty}^{\infty} \delta(\omega + \omega_0 - 2\pi l) \quad ...(B)$$

Adding (*A*) and (*B*) and divide by 2, we obtain

$$\cos \omega_0 n \xleftrightarrow{FT} \pi \sum_{l=-\infty}^{\infty} \{\delta(\omega - \omega_0 - 2\pi l) + \delta(\omega + \omega_0 - 2\pi l)\} \quad ...(2.101)$$

2.6.11 To Find Fourier Transform of $x(n) = \sin \omega_0 n$

As $$\sin \omega_0 n = \frac{1}{2j}[e^{j\omega_0 n} - e^{-j\omega_0 n}]$$

Subtract (*B*) from (*A*) and divide by $2j$, we get

$$\sin \omega_0 n \xleftrightarrow{FT} \frac{\pi}{j} \sum_{l=-\infty}^{\infty} \{\delta(\omega - \omega_0 - 2\pi l) - \delta(\omega + \omega_0 - 2\pi l)\} \quad ...(2.102)$$

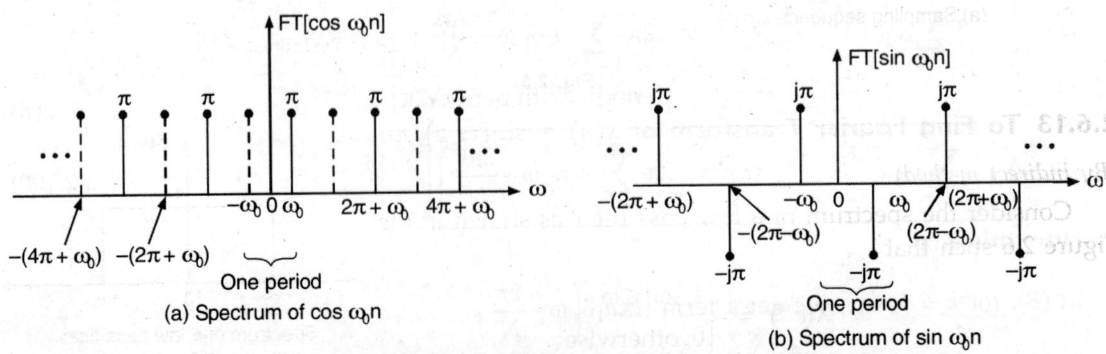

Fig. 2.4. Showing spectra of cos $\omega_0 n$ and sin $\omega_0 n$

2.6.12 Fourier Transform of $x(n) = \sum_{k=-\infty}^{\infty} \delta(n-kN)$

$$x(n) = \sum_{k=-\infty}^{\infty} \delta(n-kN)$$

is a periodic sequence with period N. Let

$$x(n) = \sum_{k=\langle N\rangle} a_k\, e^{jk(2\pi/N)n} \qquad \text{[DTFS of } x(n)]$$

then

$$a_k = \frac{1}{N}\sum_{n=\langle N\rangle} x(n)\, e^{-jk(2\pi/N)n}$$

$$= \frac{1}{N}\sum_{n=\langle N\rangle} \delta(n)\, e^{-jk(2\pi/N)n} \qquad (\text{as } \delta(n) \text{ appears for } -N/2 < n \le N/2)$$

$$= \frac{1}{N}$$

Hence

$$x(n) = \frac{1}{N}\sum_{n=\langle N\rangle} e^{jk(2\pi/N)n}$$

Putting $a_k = \frac{1}{N}$, we readily get

$$FT\left[\frac{1}{N}\sum_{k=\langle N\rangle} e^{jk(2\pi/N)m}\right] = \frac{2\pi}{N}\sum_{k=-\infty}^{\infty} \delta(\omega - k\omega_0),\ \omega_0 = \frac{2\pi}{N}$$

Hence,

$$\boxed{\sum_{k=-\infty}^{\infty} \delta(n-kN) \xleftrightarrow{FT} \omega_0 \sum_{k=-\infty}^{\infty} \delta(\omega - k\omega_0),\ \omega_0 = \frac{2\pi}{N}} \qquad \text{...(2.103)}$$

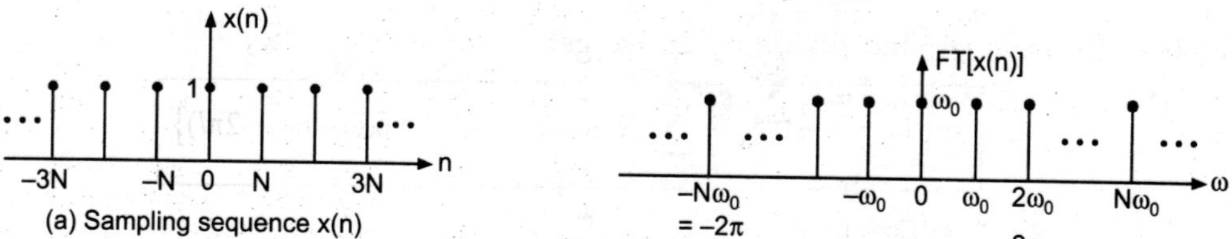

(a) Sampling sequence x(n)

(b) FT [x(n)]; $\omega_0 = \frac{2\pi}{N}$

Fig. 2.5.

2.6.13 To Find Fourier Transform of $x(n) = \sin(\omega_c n)/\pi n$

(By indirect method)

Consider the spectrum of a low pass filter as shown in the Figure 2.6 such that

$$X(e^{j\omega}) = \begin{cases} 1, |\omega| \le \omega_c \\ 0, \text{otherwise} \end{cases}$$

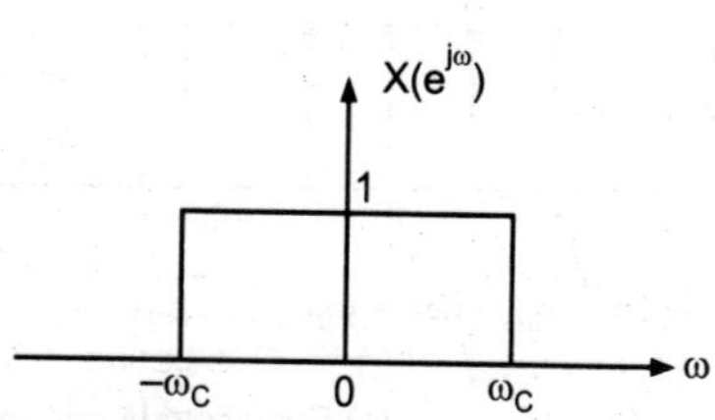

Spectrum of a low pass filter with cut off frequency ω_c

Fig. 2.6. Showing ideal LPF spectrum

The sequence $x(n)$ which Fourier transforms to above spectrum is given by taking Inverse Fourier transform of $X(e^{j\omega})$ *i.e.,*

$$x(n) = \frac{1}{2\pi}\int_{-\pi}^{\pi} X(e^{j\omega})\, e^{j\omega n}\, d\omega \quad \text{[due to (2.60)]}$$

$$= \frac{1}{2\pi}\int_{-\omega_c}^{\omega_c} 1.e^{j\omega n}\, d\omega$$

$$= \frac{j}{2\pi}\left[\frac{e^{j\omega n}}{jn}\right]_{-\omega_c}^{\omega_c} = \frac{1}{j2\pi n}(e^{j\omega_c n} - e^{-j\omega_c n}) = \frac{\omega_c}{\pi}\frac{\sin\omega_c n}{\omega_c n}$$

Hence,

$$\boxed{\frac{\omega_c}{\pi}\text{sinc}\,\omega_c n = \frac{\sin\omega_c n}{\pi n} \xleftrightarrow{FT} \begin{cases} 1, & |\omega| < \omega_c \\ 0, & \text{otherwise}\end{cases}} \qquad \text{...(2.104)}$$

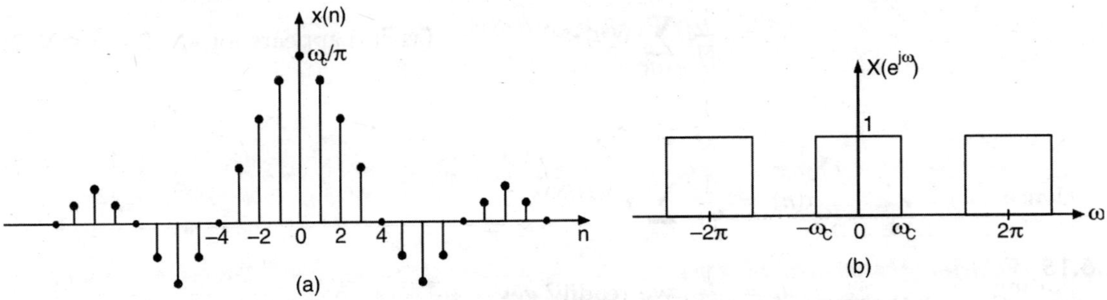

Fig. 2.7. (*a*) a sinc function and (*b*) $X(e^{j\omega})$, a rectangular pulse spectrum

2.6.14 Fourier Transform of $x(n) = \begin{cases} 1, & |n| \le N_1 \\ 0, & \text{otherwise}\end{cases}$, $N = 2N_1 + 1$ = length

Given an aperiodic sequence with length $N = 2N_1 + 1$

$$X(e^{j\omega}) = \sum_{n=-\infty}^{\infty} x(n)\, e^{-j\omega n}$$

$$= \sum_{n=-N_1}^{N_1} e^{-j\omega n} \qquad \text{...}(A)$$

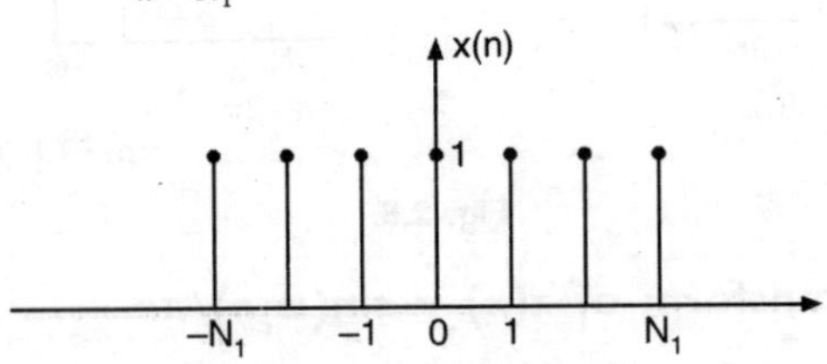

Fig. 2.8. A square pulse $x(n)$ sequence of unit height

Put $n' = n + N_1$ on RHS of (*A*)

$$\therefore \quad X(e^{j\omega}) = \sum_{n'=0}^{2N_1} e^{-j\omega(n' - N_1)}$$

$$= e^{j\omega N_1}\sum_{n=0}^{2N_1} e^{-j\omega n} \quad \text{(drop dashes)}$$

$$= e^{j\omega N_1}\frac{1-e^{-j\omega(2N_1+1)}}{1-e^{-j\omega}}$$

$$= e^{j\omega(N-1)/2}\frac{[1-e^{-j\omega N}]}{e^{-j\omega/2}(e^{j\omega/2}-e^{-j\omega/2})} \qquad \because 2N_1 + 1 = N \text{ and } N_1 = (N-1)/2$$

$$= \frac{e^{j\omega N/2}(1-e^{-j\omega N})}{e^{j\omega/2}-e^{-j\omega/2}} = \frac{e^{j\omega N/2}-e^{-j\omega N/2}}{e^{j\omega/2}-e^{-j\omega/2}}$$

$$= \frac{(2j)\sin N\omega/2}{(2j)\sin \omega/2}$$

$$\therefore \quad x(n) = \begin{cases}1, & |n|\le N_1\\ 0, & \text{otherwise}\end{cases}, N = 2N_1+1 \xleftrightarrow{FT} \frac{\sin(N\omega/2)}{\sin(\omega/2)} \qquad ...(2.105)$$

2.6.15 Fourier Transform of $x(n) = \begin{cases}1, & |n|\le N_1\\ 0, & N_1<|n|\le N/2\end{cases}$, $x(n) = x(x + N)$ i.e., $x(n)$ Periodic with period $N > N_1$

Note that $x(n)$ is periodic here with period N and $x(n) = 1$ for $-N_1 \le n \le N_1$

$$a_k = \frac{1}{N}\sum_{n=-N_1}^{N_1} 1.\, e^{-jk(2\pi/N)n}$$

Putting $m = n + N_1$, we obtain

$$a_k = \frac{1}{N}\sum_{m=0}^{2N_1} e^{-jk(2\pi/N)(m-N_1)} = \frac{1}{N}e^{jk(2\pi/N)N_1}\sum_{m=0}^{2N_1} e^{-jk\frac{2\pi}{N}.m}$$

$$= \frac{1}{N}e^{jk(2\pi/N)N_1}.\frac{1-e^{-jk(2\pi/N)(2N_1+1)}}{1-e^{-jk\,2\pi/N}}$$

$$= \frac{1}{N}e^{jk(2\pi/N)N_1}\frac{e^{-jk(\pi/N)(2N_1+1)}\left[e^{jk\frac{2\pi}{N}\left(N_1+\frac{1}{2}\right)}-e^{-jk\frac{2\pi}{N}\left(N_1+\frac{1}{2}\right)}\right]}{e^{-jk\pi/N}[e^{jk\pi/N}-e^{-jk\pi/N}]}$$

$$a_k = \frac{1}{N}\frac{\sin\left[2\pi k\left(N_1+\frac{1}{2}\right)/N\right]}{\sin[k\pi/N]}, \; k \ne 0, \pm N, \pm 2N, ...$$

for $k = 0, \pm N, \pm 2N, ...$

$$a_o = \frac{1}{N}\times\frac{2\pi k\left(N_1+\frac{1}{2}\right)/N}{k\pi/N} = \frac{1}{N}(2N_1+1), \; k = 0, \pm N, \pm 2N, ...$$

(using L' Hospital's Rule)

As $$x(n) = \sum_{k=\langle N\rangle} a_k e^{jk\left(\frac{2\pi}{N}\right)n}$$

$$\therefore \quad X(e^{j\omega}) = \sum_{k=-\infty}^{\infty} a_k \delta\left(\omega - \frac{2\pi k}{N}\right)$$

where $$a_k = \left(\frac{1}{N}\right)\frac{\sin\left(2\pi k\left(N_1 + \frac{1}{2}\right)/N\right)}{\sin(k\pi/N)}, k \neq 0, \pm N, \pm 2N\ldots, \qquad \ldots(2.106)$$

$$a_k = (2N_1 + 1)/N, \quad k = 0, \pm N, \pm 2N, \ldots,$$

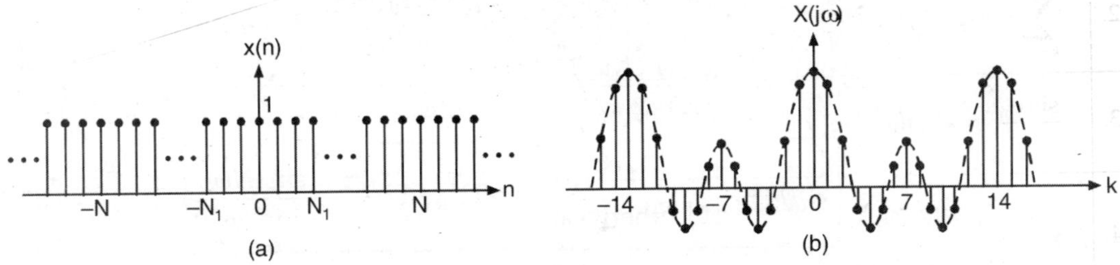

Fig. 2.9. (*a*) The periodic signal $x(n)$, non-zero from $n = -N_1$ to N_1 period N (*b*) Its Fourier transform

The signal $x(n)$, a periodic sequence, given here, is shown in Fig. 2.9(*a*) and its Fourier transform is shown in Fig. 2.9(*b*) for $N_1 = 3$ and $N = 14$.

The various derivations of DTFT have given us useful results which the student is advised to memorise. Therefore, all these results have been given in Table 2.4 for ease of reference by the students.

Table 2.4 Basic Discrete-time Fourier Transform (DTFT) Pairs

S.N.	$x(n)$	$X(e^{j\omega}) = \sum_{n=-\infty}^{\infty} x(n)\, e^{-j\omega n}$	
1.	$\delta(n)$	1	(2.92)
2.	$u(n)$	$\frac{1}{1-e^{-j\omega}} + \sum_{k=-\infty}^{\infty} \pi\delta(\omega - 2\pi k)$	(2.94)
3.	$a^n u(n), \lvert a \rvert < 1$	$\frac{1}{1-ae^{-j\omega}}$	(2.93)
4.	$\delta(n - n_0)$	$e^{-j\omega n_0}$	(2.95)
5.	$(n + 1)\, a^n u(n), \lvert a \rvert < 1$	$\frac{1}{(1-ae^{-j\omega})^2}$	(2.96)
6.	$\frac{(n+r-1)!}{n!(r-1)!} a^n u(n), \lvert a \rvert < 1$	$\frac{1}{(1-a e^{-j\omega})^r}$	(2.97)
7.	$x(n) = 1$	$2\pi \sum_{k=-\infty}^{\infty} \delta(\omega - 2\pi k)$	(2.98)

8.	$e^{j\omega_0 n}$	$2\pi \sum_{l=-\infty}^{\infty} \delta(\omega - \omega_0 - 2\pi l)$ (2.99)
9.	$\sum_{k=\langle N\rangle} a_k e^{jk(2\pi/N)n}$ $x(n)$ periodic with period N	$2\pi \sum_{k=-\infty}^{\infty} a_k \delta\left(\omega - \frac{2\pi k}{N}\right)$, periodic with period 2π (2.100)
10.	$\cos \omega_0 n$	$\pi \sum_{l=-\infty}^{\infty} \{\delta(\omega - \omega_0 - 2\pi l) + \delta(\omega + \omega_0 - 2\pi l)\}$ (2.101)
11.	$\sin \omega_0 n$	$\frac{\pi}{j} \sum_{l=-\infty}^{\infty} \{\delta(\omega - \omega_0 - 2\pi l) - \delta(\omega + \omega_0 - 2\pi l)\}$ (2.102)
12.	$\sum_{k=-\infty}^{\infty} \delta(n - kN),\ \omega_0 = \frac{2\pi}{N}$	$\frac{2\pi}{N} \sum_{k=-\infty}^{\infty} \delta\left(\omega - \frac{2\pi k}{N}\right) \equiv \omega_0 \sum_{k=-\infty}^{\infty} \delta(\omega - k\omega_0)$ (2.103)
13.	$\frac{\sin \omega_0 n}{\pi n} = \frac{\omega_c}{\pi} \text{sinc}\ \omega_c n$	$X(e^{j\omega}) = \begin{cases} 1, & 0 \le \lvert\omega\rvert \le \omega_c \\ 0, & \omega_c \le \lvert\omega\rvert \le \pi \end{cases}$ (a *LPF*) (2.104)
14.	$x(n) = \begin{cases} 1, & \lvert n\rvert \le N_1 \\ 0, & \text{otherwise} \end{cases}$ Aperiodic square pulse, length $N = 2N_1 + 1$	$\frac{\sin(2N_1+1)\,\omega/2}{\sin(\omega/2)} = \frac{\sin\frac{N\omega}{2}}{\sin\frac{\omega}{2}},\ N = 2N_1 + 1$ (2.105)
15.	$\left[\begin{array}{l} x(n) = \begin{cases} 1, & \lvert n\rvert \le N_1 \\ 0, & N_1 < \lvert n\rvert \le N/2 \end{cases} \\ x(n) = x(n+N): \text{Periodic} \\ \qquad\qquad \text{square wave} \end{array}\right.$	$2\pi \sum_{k=-\infty}^{\infty} a_k \delta\left(\omega - \frac{2\pi k}{N}\right)$ $a_k = \frac{1}{N} \sum_{n=-N_1}^{N_1} 1.e^{-jk\left(\frac{2\pi}{N}\right)n}$ $= \frac{2N_1+1}{N} \cdot \frac{\text{sinc}\left(\frac{2\pi k}{N}\left(N_1 + \frac{1}{2}\right)\right)}{\text{sinc}\left(\frac{\pi k}{N}\right)},\ k = 1, 2, ..., N-1, k \ne 0, + N.$ $a_k = \frac{2N_1+1}{N}, k = 0, \pm N, \pm 2N$ (2.106)

2.7 THE FREQUENCY RESPONSE OF DISCRETE-TIME SYSTEMS

We can usefully exploit the Fourier-transform (DTFT) for analysing the discrete-time systems

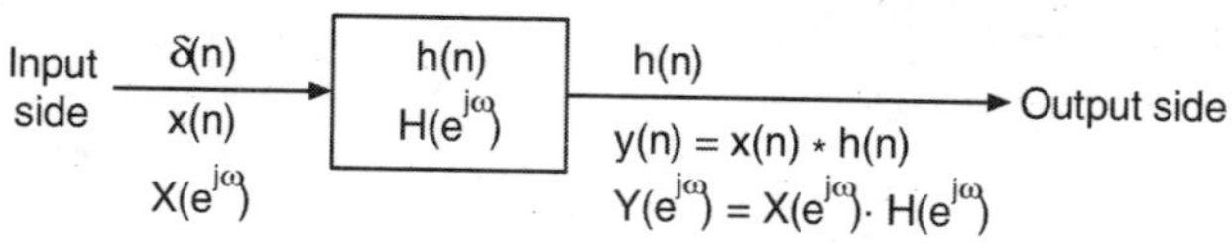

Fig. 2.10. Shows the relationships between inputs and outputs for an LTI discrete-time system

If input $x(n)$ is applied to a discrete-time system $h(n)$, we get output $y(n)$. By applying convolution property, we have

$$y(n) = x(n) * h(n) \qquad ...(2.107a)$$

Hence,

$$Y(e^{j\omega}) = X(e^{j\omega}) \cdot H(e^{j\omega}) \qquad ...(2.107b)$$

$$\therefore \quad \boxed{H(e^{j\omega}) = \frac{Y(e^{j\omega})}{X(e^{j\omega})}} \qquad ...(2.108)$$

$H(e^{j\omega})$ is called the discrete-time system's Frequency Response. $H(e^{j\omega})$ is, in general, a complex function. Hence, we can write

$$H(e^{j\omega}) = |H(e^{j\omega})|\, e^{j\theta(\omega)} \qquad ...(2.109)$$

Then

$|H(e^{j\omega})|$ is called magnitude response of the system
$\theta(\omega)$ is called phase response of the system ...(2.110)

For example, a system characterized by the difference equation.

$$\sum_{k=0}^{N} a_k\, y(n-k) = \sum_{k=0}^{M} b_k\, x(n-k) \qquad ...(2.111)$$

can be easily solved by taking Fourier-time on both sides of (2.111) which gives us

$$\sum_{k=0}^{N} a_k\, Y(e^{j\omega})\cdot e^{-jk\omega} = \sum_{k=0}^{M} b_k\, X(e^{j\omega})\cdot e^{-jk\omega}$$

$$H(e^{j\omega}) = \frac{Y(e^{j\omega})}{X(e^{j\omega})} = \frac{\sum_{k=0}^{M} b_k\, e^{-jk\omega}}{\sum_{k=0}^{N} a_k\, e^{-jk\omega}} \qquad ...(2.112)$$

Thus, we have found for the given system (characterized by difference equation (2.111)), the systems Frequency Response $H(e^{j\omega})$. We shall use the analysis technique, using DTFT, in Chapters 8 and 9.

2.8 EXAMPLES ON DISCRETE-TIME FOURIER TRANSFORMS

EXAMPLE 2.9: *Find the Fourier transforms of the sequences as given*

(a) $x_1(n) = \left(\frac{1}{2}\right)^{n-1} u(n-1);$

(b) $x_2(n) = \left(\frac{1}{2}\right)^{|n-1|},$

(c) $x_3(n) = \delta(n-1) + \delta(n) + \delta(n+2);$

(d) $x_4(n) = u(n-2) - u(n-6)$

SOLUTION:

(a)
$$x_1(n) = \left(\frac{1}{2}\right)^{n-1} u(n-1)$$

$$X_1(e^{j\omega}) = \frac{e^{-j\omega}}{1-\left(\frac{1}{2}\right)e^{-j\omega}} \text{ by inspection } \left(\because u(n) \xleftrightarrow{FT} \frac{1}{1-e^{-j\omega}}\right) \qquad \textbf{Ans.}$$

(b)
$$x_2(n) = \left(\frac{1}{2}\right)^{|n-1|}$$

$$\therefore \quad X_2(e^{j\omega}) = \sum_{n=-\infty}^{\infty} \left(\frac{1}{2}\right)^{|n-1|} e^{-j\omega n} = \sum_{n=1}^{\infty} \left(\frac{1}{2}\right)^{n-1} e^{-j\omega n} + \sum_{n=-\infty}^{0} \left(\frac{1}{2}\right)^{-(n-1)} e^{-j\omega n}$$

Put $n = -m$ (N.T.S)

$$= \sum_{n=1}^{\infty} \left(\frac{1}{2}\right)^{n-1} e^{-j\omega n} + \sum_{m=0}^{\infty} \left(\frac{1}{2}\right)^{m+1} e^{j\omega m}$$

$$= \frac{e^{-j\omega}}{1-\left(\frac{1}{2}\right)e^{-j\omega}} + \frac{\frac{1}{2}}{1-\frac{1}{2}e^{j\omega}} = \frac{e^{-j\omega}\left(1-\frac{1}{2}e^{j\omega}\right)+\frac{1}{2}\left(1-\frac{1}{2}e^{-j\omega}\right)}{1-\frac{1}{2}(e^{j\omega}+e^{-j\omega})+\frac{1}{4}}$$

$$= \frac{0+e^{-j\omega}-\frac{1}{4}e^{-j\omega}}{\frac{5}{4}-\cos\omega} = \frac{3\,e^{-j\omega}}{5-4\cos\omega}$$ **Ans.**

(c) $$x_3(n) = \delta(n-1) + \delta(n) + \delta(n+2)$$

$$X_3(e^{j\omega}) = \sum_{n=-\infty}^{\infty} [\delta(n-1)+\delta(n)+\delta(n+2)]\, e^{-j\omega n}$$

$$= e^{-j\omega(1)} + e^{-j\omega(0)} + e^{-j\omega(-2)} = e^{-j\omega} + 1 + e^{j2\omega}$$ **Ans.**

(d) $$x_4(n) = u(n-2) - u(n-6)$$

$$\therefore \quad X_4(e^{j\omega}) = \sum_{n=-\infty}^{\infty} [u(n-2)-u(n-6)]\, e^{-j\omega n}$$

$$= \frac{e^{-j2\omega}-e^{-j6\omega}}{1-e^{-j\omega}} = \frac{e^{-j4\omega}(e^{j2\omega}-e^{-j2\omega})}{e^{-j\omega/2}(e^{j\omega/2}-e^{-j\omega/2})} = e^{-j\frac{7}{2}\omega}\,\frac{\sin 2\omega}{\sin(\omega/2)}$$ **Ans.**

EXAMPLE 2.10: *Determine the Fourier transform of each of the following sequences*

(a) $x_1(n) = k\,x(n)$, *k constant,*

(b) $x_2(n) = x(n - n_0)$, n_0 *a real integer*

(c) $x_3(n) = x(2n)$,

(d) $x_4(n) = \begin{cases} x(n/2), & n \text{ even} \\ 0, & n \text{ odd} \end{cases}$

(e) $x_5(x) = x^2(n)$ *(I.P. Univ. 2004)*

SOLUTION:

(a) $$X_1(e^{j\omega}) = FT\,[kx(n)] = k\sum_{n=-\infty}^{\infty} x(n)\, e^{-j\omega n} = kX(e^{j\omega})$$ **Ans.**

(b) $$X_2(e^{j\omega}) = FT\,[x(n-n_0)] = \sum_{n=-\infty}^{\infty} x(n-n_0)\, e^{-j\omega n}$$

Put $$n' = n - n_0 \;\therefore\; n = n' + n_0$$

$$= \sum_{n'=-\infty}^{\infty} x(n')\cdot e^{-j\omega(n'+n_0)} = e^{-j\omega n_0}\, X(e^{j\omega})$$ **Ans.**

(c) $$X_3(e^{j\omega}) = FT\,[x(2n)] = \sum_{n=-\infty}^{\infty} x(2n)\cdot e^{-j\omega n}$$

Put $$2n = n' \Rightarrow \sum_{n'\,\text{even}} x(n')\,e^{-j\omega\left(\frac{n'}{2}\right)}$$ or dropping dashes.

$$X_3(e^{j\omega}) = \sum_{n\,\text{even}} x(n)\cdot e^{-j\omega\left(\frac{n}{2}\right)}$$

$$= \sum_{n=-\infty}^{\infty} \frac{1}{2}[x(n)+(-1)^n\, x(n)]\,e^{-j\omega\frac{n}{2}}$$ (Note this step)

$$= \frac{1}{2}\left[\sum_{n=-\infty}^{\infty} x(n)\cdot e^{-j\frac{\omega}{2}n} + \sum_{n=-\infty}^{\infty} x(n)\,e^{j\frac{\omega}{2}n}\right]$$

$$= \frac{1}{2}\left[X\left(e^{j\frac{\omega}{2}}\right) + X\left(e^{-j\frac{\omega}{2}}\right)\right]$$ **Ans.**

(d) $$X_4(e^{j\omega}) = FT\,[x(n/2)]\Big|_{n\,\text{even}} = \sum_{n=-\infty}^{\infty} x(n/2)\Big|_{n\,\text{even}} e^{-j\omega n} = \sum_{\substack{n=-\infty\\ \ldots,-2,0}}^{2,4,\ldots,-\infty} x(n/2)^{e^{-j\omega n}}$$

Put $$\frac{n}{2} = n' \quad \therefore\ n = 2n'$$

$$= \sum_{n'=-\infty,\ldots,-2,-1,0}^{1,2,3,\ldots,\infty} x(n')\,e^{-j\omega(2n')} = \sum_{n=-\infty}^{\infty} x(n)\,e^{-j2\omega n} = X(e^{j2\omega})$$ **Ans.**

(e) $$FT\,[x^2(n)] = FT\,[x(n)\cdot x(n)] = X(e^{j\omega}) * X(e^{j\omega})$$

$$= \frac{1}{2\pi}\int_{-\pi}^{\pi} X(e^{j\theta})\,X(e^{j(\omega-\theta)})\,d\theta$$ **Ans.**

EXAMPLE 2.11: *Find the Fourier transforms for the sequences*

(a) $x_1(n) = 2^n \sin\left(\frac{\pi}{4}\right)n\cdot u(-n)$,

(b) $x_2(n) = \begin{cases} n, & -3\le n\le 3,\\ 0, & \text{otherwise}\end{cases}$

(c) $x_3(n) = (-1)^n\, u(-n)$

SOLUTION: (a) $$x_1(n) = 2^n \sin\left(\frac{\pi}{4}n\right) u(-n)$$

$$X(e^{j\omega}) = \sum_{n=-\infty}^{\infty}\left[2^n \sin\left(\frac{\pi}{4}n\right)\cdot u(-n)\right] e^{-j\omega n}$$

$$= \sum_{n=-\infty}^{0} 2^n \left(\frac{e^{j\frac{\pi}{4}n} - e^{-j\frac{\pi}{4}n}}{2j}\right) e^{-j\omega n}$$

$$= \sum_{m=0}^{\infty}\left(\frac{1}{2j}\right)\left(\frac{1}{2}\right)^m e^{-j\frac{\pi}{4}m} e^{j\omega m} - \sum_{m=0}^{\infty}\left(\frac{1}{2j}\right)\left(\frac{1}{2}\right)^m e^{j\frac{\pi}{4}m} \cdot e^{j\omega m}$$

$$= \frac{1}{2j}\left[\sum_{m=0}^{\infty}\left(\frac{1}{2}\cdot e^{-j\frac{\pi}{4}}\cdot e^{j\omega}\right)^m - \sum_{m=0}^{\infty}\left(\frac{1}{2}e^{j\frac{\pi}{4}} e^{j\omega}\right)^m\right]$$

$$= \frac{1}{2j}\left[\frac{1}{1-\frac{1}{2}e^{-j\frac{\pi}{4}}e^{j\omega}} - \frac{1}{1-\frac{1}{2}e^{j\frac{\pi}{4}}e^{j\omega}}\right]$$

$$= \frac{1}{j2}\left[\frac{\left(1-\frac{1}{2}e^{j\frac{\pi}{4}}e^{j\omega}\right)-\left(1-\frac{1}{2}e^{-j\frac{\pi}{4}}e^{j\omega}\right)}{1-\frac{1}{2}(e^{-j\pi/4}e^{j\omega}+e^{j\pi/4}e^{j\omega})+\frac{1}{4}e^{j2\omega}}\right]$$

$$= \frac{1}{j2}\left[\frac{-\frac{1}{2}e^{j\omega}\left(e^{j\frac{\pi}{4}}-e^{-j\frac{\pi}{4}}\right)}{\left(1-\cos\frac{\pi}{4}\cdot e^{j\omega}+\frac{1}{4}e^{j2\omega}\right)}\right] = \frac{-\frac{1}{2}\cdot\left(\sin\frac{\pi}{4}\right)e^{j\omega}}{1-\frac{1}{\sqrt{2}}e^{j\omega}+\frac{1}{4}e^{j2\omega}}$$

$$= -\frac{1}{2\sqrt{2}}\left(\frac{e^{j\omega}}{\left(1-\frac{1}{\sqrt{2}}e^{j\omega}+\frac{1}{4}e^{j2\omega}\right)}\right)$$ **Ans.**

(b)
$$x_2(n) = \begin{cases} n, & -3 \le n \le 3 \\ 0, & \text{otherwise}\end{cases}$$

$$X_2(e^{j\omega}) = \sum_{n=-3}^{3} n e^{-j\omega n}$$

$$= -3e^{j3\omega} - 2e^{j2\omega} - e^{j\omega} + 1 + e^{-j\omega} + 2e^{-j2\omega} + 3e^{-j3\omega}$$

$$= 1 - j2(\sin\omega + 2\sin 2\omega + 3\sin 3\omega)$$ **Ans.**

(c)
$$x_3(n) = (-1)^n u(-n)$$

$$X_3(e^{j\omega}) = \sum_{n=-\infty}^{\infty}(-1)^n u(-n)\cdot e^{-j\omega n}$$

$$= \sum_{n=-\infty}^{0}(-1)^n e^{-j\omega n} = \sum_{m=0}^{\infty}(-1)^{-m} e^{j\omega m}$$ (Putting $n = -m$)

$$= \sum_{m=0}^{\infty}(-e^{j\omega})^m = \frac{1}{1+e^{j\omega}}$$ **Ans.**

EXAMPLE 2.12: *Calculate Fourier transform of the discrete signal*

$$x(n) = a^{|n|}, 0 < a < 1$$ (*IP Univ. 2004, Delhi Univ. 1997*)

SOLUTION:

$$X(e^{j\omega}) = \sum_{n=-\infty}^{\infty} x(n)\, e^{-j\omega n} = \sum_{n=-\infty}^{\infty} a^{|n|}\, e^{-j\omega n}$$

$$= \sum_{n=0}^{\infty} a^{n}\, e^{-j\omega n} + \sum_{n=-\infty}^{-1} a^{-n}\, e^{-j\omega n}$$

$$= \sum_{n=0}^{\infty} a^{n}\, e^{-j\omega n} + \sum_{m=1}^{\infty} a^{m}\, e^{j\omega m}$$

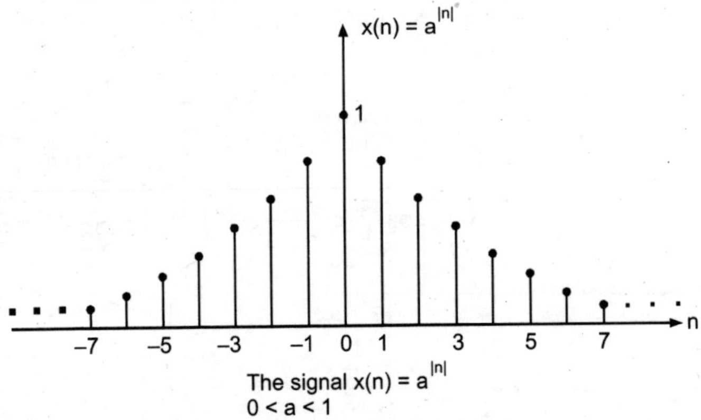

Fig. Ex. 2.12. (*a*) Showing the signal *x*(*n*)

$$= \frac{1}{1-ae^{-j\omega}} + \frac{ae^{j\omega}}{1-ae^{j\omega}}$$

$$= \frac{1-ae^{j\omega} + ae^{+j\omega}(1-ae^{-j\omega})}{1-a(e^{j\omega}+e^{-j\omega})+a^2}$$

$$\therefore \quad X(e^{j\omega}) = \frac{1-a^2}{1-2a\cos\omega + a^2}$$ **Ans.**

$$X(e^{j0}) = \frac{1-a^2}{1-2a+a^2} = \frac{1+a}{1-a}$$

$$X(e^{j\pi}) = \frac{1-a^2}{1+2a+a^2} = \frac{1-a}{1+a}$$

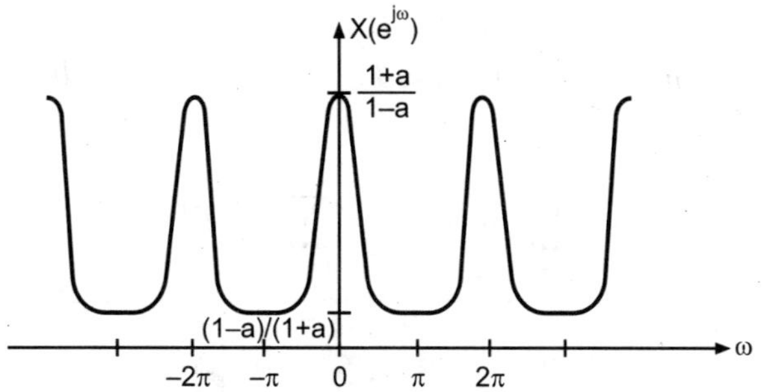

Fourier transform of $x(n) = a^{|n|}$, $0 < a < 1$

Fig. Ex. 2.12. (*b*) Showing the spectrum $X(e^{j\omega})$

The spectrum $X(e^{j\omega})$ is as shown. Note that $x(n)$ is real and even and hence $X(e^{j\omega})$ is also real and even, see property (2.80).

EXAMPLE 2.13: *Find and plot the DTFT of periodic signals*

(*a*) $x_1(n) = \frac{1}{2\pi} \sin \omega_0 n,$ (*b*) $x_2(n) = \cos\left(\frac{\pi}{2} n\right)$

SOLUTION:

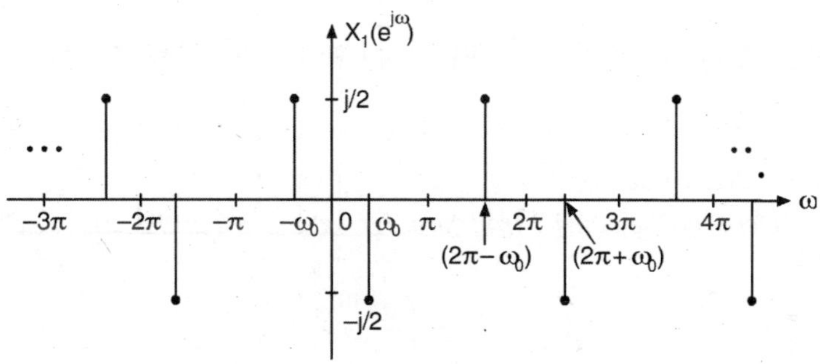

Fig. Ex. 2.13. (*a*) Showing the spectrum of $FT\left[\frac{1}{2\pi}\sin \omega_0 n\right]$

(*a*)

$$x_1(n) = \frac{1}{2\pi} \sin \omega_0 n$$

$$= \frac{1}{2\pi}\frac{1}{2j}\left[e^{j\omega_0 n} - e^{-j\omega_0 n}\right]$$

$\therefore$

$$X_1(e^{j\omega}) = \frac{1}{2j}\left[\delta(\omega-\omega_0) - \delta(\omega+\omega_0)\right]$$

$$= -\frac{j}{2}\delta(\omega-\omega_0) + \frac{j}{2}\delta(\omega+\omega_0)$$

Draw $X_1(e^{j\omega})$ and repeat at a period of 2π as shown in Fig. Ex. 2.13(*a*) above

(*b*)

$$x_2(n) = \cos\frac{\pi}{2} n$$

$$= \frac{1}{2}[e^{j(\pi/2)n} + e^{-j(\pi/2)n}]$$

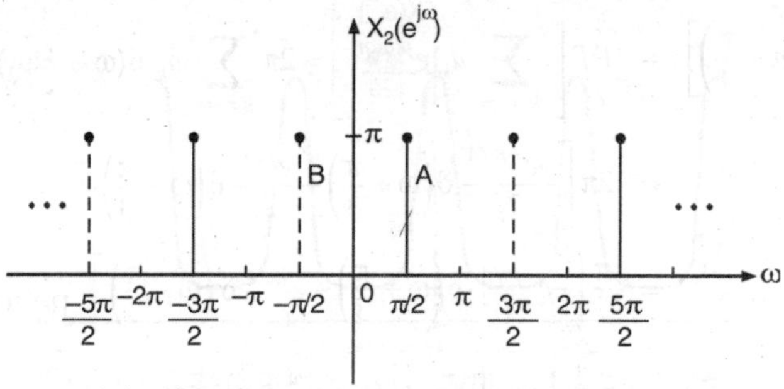

Fig. Ex. 2.13. (*b*) Showing the spectrum of $FT\left[\cos\frac{\pi}{2}n\right]$

$$X_1(e^{j\omega}) = 2\pi\left[\frac{1}{2}\sum_k \delta\left(\omega-\frac{\pi}{2}-2\pi k\right)+\frac{1}{2}\sum_k \delta\left(\omega+\frac{\pi}{2}-2\pi k\right)\right]$$

$$= \pi\sum_{k=-\infty}^{\infty} \delta\left(\omega-\frac{\pi}{2}-2\pi k\right)+\pi\sum_{k=-\infty}^{\infty} \delta\left(\omega+\frac{\pi}{2}-2\pi k\right)$$

First draw $\pi\delta\left(\omega-\frac{\pi}{2}\right)$ as plot *A* and $\pi\delta\left(\omega+\frac{\pi}{2}\right)$ as plot *B*. Then repeat plots *A* and *B* with a period of 2π *i.e.* on both sides of *y*-axis $\omega = 0$. The plot showing the Fourier transform of $\cos\left(\frac{\pi}{2}n\right)$ as shown in Fig. Ex. 2.13(*b*) above.

EXAMPLE 2.14: *Determine the Fourier transform for* $-\pi < \omega < \pi$ *in the case of each of the given periodic signals*

(*a*) $\sin\left(\frac{\pi n}{3}+\frac{\pi}{4}\right)$; (*b*) $2+\cos\left(\frac{\pi n}{6}+\frac{\pi}{8}\right)$

SOLUTION: We know that if $x(n)$ is a periodic signal with period *N* *i.e.* $\omega_0 = \frac{2\pi}{N}$, then

> *FT* of a periodic signal
>
> $$X(e^{j\omega}) = \sum_{l=-\infty}^{\infty} 2\pi\, a_k\, \delta(\omega-2\pi l-k\omega_0)$$
>
> $$= 2\pi\, a_k\, \delta(\omega-k\omega_0) \text{ periodic with period } 2\pi$$

(*a*)

$$\sin\left(\frac{\pi n}{3}+\frac{\pi}{4}\right) = \frac{1}{2j}\left[e^{j\left(\frac{\pi}{4}+\frac{\pi}{3}n\right)}-e^{-j\left(\frac{\pi}{4}+\frac{\pi}{3}n\right)}\right]=\frac{1}{2j}\left[e^{j\frac{\pi}{4}}\cdot e^{j\omega_0 n}-e^{-j\frac{\pi}{4}}e^{-j\omega_0 n}\right],\ \omega_0=\pi/3$$

($\frac{\pi n}{3}$ = $\omega_0 n$)

$$= a_{-1}\, e^{+j(-1)\omega_0 n}+a_1\, e^{+j(1)\omega_0 n},\ \omega_0=\pi/3$$

with $$a_{-1} = \frac{-e^{-j\pi/4}}{2j},\quad a_1=\frac{e^{j\pi/4}}{2j},\quad \text{and}\quad \omega_0=\pi/3$$

i.e. $$\sin\left(\frac{\pi}{3}n+\frac{\pi}{4}\right) = \sum_{k=-\infty}^{\infty} a_k\, e^{jk\omega_0 n}$$

$$\therefore \quad FT\left[\sin\left(\frac{\pi}{3}n+\frac{\pi}{4}\right)\right] = FT\left[\sum_{k=-\infty}^{\infty} a_k\, e^{jk\omega_0 n}\right] = 2\pi \sum_{k=-\infty}^{\infty} a_k\, \delta(\omega - k\omega_0)$$

$$= 2\pi\left[\frac{-e^{-j\pi/4}}{2j}\,\delta\left(\omega+\frac{\pi}{3}\right) + \frac{e^{j\pi/4}}{2j}\,\delta\left(\omega-\frac{\pi}{3}\right)\right]$$

$$= \frac{\pi}{j}\left[-e^{-j\pi/4}.\delta\left(\omega+\frac{\pi}{3}\right) + e^{j\pi/4}\,\delta\left(\omega-\frac{\pi}{3}\right)\right], \text{ periodic with period } 2\pi$$

Ans.

(b) $$2 + \cos\left(\frac{\pi}{6}n+\frac{\pi}{8}\right) = 2 + \frac{1}{2}\left[e^{j\left(\omega_0 n+\frac{\pi}{8}\right)} + e^{-j\left(\omega_0 n+\frac{\pi}{8}\right)}\right] \text{ with } \omega_0 = \pi/6$$

$$\therefore \quad a_0 = 2,\ a_{-1} = \frac{1}{2}e^{-j\frac{\pi}{8}},\ a_1 = \frac{1}{2}e^{j\frac{\pi}{8}}$$

$$\therefore \quad FT\left[2+\cos\left(\frac{\pi}{6}n+\frac{\pi}{8}\right)\right] = 2\pi\left[2.\delta(\omega) + \frac{1}{2}e^{-j\frac{\pi}{8}}\,\delta(\omega+\omega_0) + \frac{1}{2}e^{j\frac{\pi}{8}}\,\delta(\omega-\omega_0)\right],\ \omega_0 = \frac{\pi}{8}$$

$$= 4\pi\,\delta(\omega) + \pi\left[e^{-j\pi/8}\,\delta\left(\omega+\frac{\pi}{6}\right) + e^{j\pi/8}\,\delta\left(\omega-\frac{\pi}{6}\right)\right].$$

Ans.

periodic with period 2π

EXAMPLE 2.15: *By using Fourier transform and its properties, calculate the numerical value of*

$$A = \sum_{n=0}^{\infty} n\cdot\left(\frac{1}{2}\right)^n$$

SOLUTION: Let $x(n) = \left(\frac{1}{2}\right)^n u(n)$

$$\therefore \quad X(e^{j\omega}) = FT\,[x(n)] = \frac{1}{1-\frac{1}{2}e^{-j\omega}} \quad \text{...(A)}$$

We know that $nx(n) \xrightarrow{FT} j\frac{d}{d\omega}X(j\omega)$

$$\therefore \quad \sum_{n=\infty}^{\infty}\left[n\cdot\left(\frac{1}{2}\right)^n u(n)\right]e^{-j\omega n} = j\frac{d}{d\omega}\left[\frac{1}{1-\frac{1}{2}e^{-j\omega}}\right]$$

$$= j\frac{-\frac{1}{2}j\,e^{-j\omega}}{\left(1-\frac{1}{2}e^{-j\omega}\right)^2} = \frac{\frac{1}{2}e^{-j\omega}}{\left(1-\frac{1}{2}e^{-j\omega}\right)^2}$$

$$\text{i.e.} \quad \sum_{n=-\infty}^{\infty} n\left(\frac{1}{2}\right)^n u(n)\,e^{-j\omega n} = \frac{\frac{1}{2}e^{-j\omega}}{\left(1-\frac{1}{2}e^{-j\omega}\right)^2} \quad \text{...(B)}$$

Put $\omega = 0$ in (*B*), we get

$$\sum_{n=0}^{\infty} n\left(\frac{1}{2}\right)^n = \frac{\frac{1}{2}}{\left(1-\frac{1}{2}\right)^2} = 2$$

Ans.

EXAMPLE 2.16: *For the resulting system shown in the Figure,* $H(e^{j\omega}) = \dfrac{-12+5\,e^{-j\omega}}{12-7e^{-j\omega}+e^{-j2\omega}}$, *and given* $h_1(n) = \left(\dfrac{1}{3}\right)^n u(n)$, *calculate* $h_2(n)$.

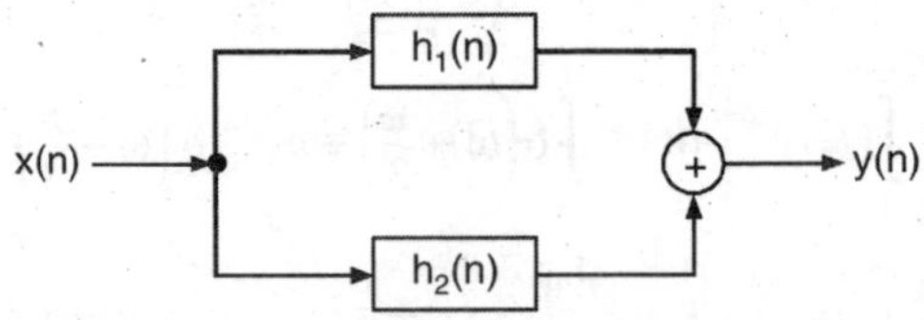

Fig. Ex. 2.16.

SOLUTION:

$$H(e^{j\omega}) = H_1(e^{j\omega}) + H_2(e^{j\omega}) \quad \text{and } H_1(e^{j\omega}) = FT\left[\left(\frac{1}{3}\right)^n u(n)\right] = \frac{1}{1-\left(\frac{1}{3}\right)e^{-j\omega}}$$

$$\therefore \quad H_2(e^{j\omega}) = \frac{-12+5e^{-j\omega}}{12-7e^{-j\omega}-e^{-j2\omega}} - \frac{1}{1-\left(\frac{1}{3}\right)e^{-j\omega}}$$

$$= \frac{-12+5e^{-j\omega}}{12\left(1-\frac{1}{3}e^{-j\omega}\right)\left(1-\frac{1}{4}e^{-j\omega}\right)} - \frac{1}{1-\frac{1}{3}e^{-j\omega}} = \frac{-12+5e^{-j\omega}-(12-3e^{-j\omega})}{12\left(1-\frac{1}{3}e^{-j\omega}\right)\left(1-\frac{1}{4}e^{-j\omega}\right)}$$

$$= \frac{-24\left(1-\frac{1}{3}e^{-j\omega}\right)}{12\left(1-\frac{1}{3}e^{-j\omega}\right)\left(1-\frac{1}{4}e^{-j\omega}\right)} = -2\frac{1}{1-\frac{1}{4}e^{-j\omega}}$$

Taking inverse Fourier transform, we get

$$h_2(n) = -2\left(\frac{1}{4}\right)^n u(n)$$

Ans.

2.9 EXAMPLES ON INVERSE DTFT AND APPLICATIONS OF DTFT

EXAMPLE 2.17: *Determine the Inverse Fourier transform of:*

(*a*) $X_1(e^{j\omega}) = \sum_{l=-\infty}^{\infty}\left\{2\pi\,\delta(\omega-2\pi l)+\pi\,\delta(\omega-\frac{\pi}{2}-2\pi l)+\pi\,\delta\left(\omega+\frac{\pi}{2}-2\pi l\right)\right\}$

(*b*) $X_2(e^{j\omega}) = \begin{cases} j2, & 0<\omega\le\pi \\ -j2, & -\pi<\omega\le 0 \end{cases}$ –(*Hilbert transformer with scaling factor-2*)

(*c*) $X_3(e^{j\omega}) = \cos^2\omega + \sin^2 3\omega$

SOLUTION:

(*a*)
$$x_1(n) = \frac{1}{2\pi}\int_{2\pi} X_1(e^{j\omega})\,e^{j\omega n}\,d\omega$$

$$= \frac{1}{2\pi}\int_{2\pi}\sum_{l=-\infty}^{\infty}\left\{2\pi\,\delta(\omega-2\pi l)+\pi\delta\left(\omega-\frac{\pi}{2}-2\pi l\right)+\pi\delta\left(\omega+\frac{\pi}{2}-2\pi l\right)\right\}e^{j\omega n}\,d\omega$$

$$= e^{j(2\pi l)n} + \frac{1}{2} e^{j\left(\frac{\pi}{2} + 2\pi l\right)n} + \frac{1}{2} e^{j\left(\frac{-\pi}{2} + 2\pi l\right)n}$$

$$\therefore \quad x_1(n) = 1 + \frac{1}{2}\left[e^{j\frac{\pi}{2}n} + e^{-j\frac{\pi}{2}n}\right] = 1 + \cos\frac{\pi}{2}n \qquad \textbf{Ans.}$$

(b)
$$x_2(n) = \frac{1}{2\pi}\left[\int_0^{\pi} (j2)\, e^{j\omega n}\, d\omega + \int_{-\pi}^{0} (-j2)\, e^{j\omega n}\, d\omega\right]$$

$$= \frac{1}{2\pi}\left[(j2)\frac{e^{j\omega n}}{jn}\right]_0^{\pi} + \frac{1}{2\pi}\left[(-j2)\frac{e^{j\omega n}}{jn}\right]_{-\pi}^{0}$$

$$= \frac{1}{2\pi}\left[\frac{2}{n}(e^{j\pi n} - 1) - \frac{2}{n}(1 - e^{-j\pi n})\right] = \frac{2}{\pi n}[\cos \pi n - 1]$$

$$\therefore \quad x_2(n) = -\frac{4}{\pi n}\sin^2\frac{\pi n}{2} \qquad \textbf{Ans.}$$

(c)
$$X_3(e^{j\omega}) = \left[\frac{1}{2}(e^{j\omega} + e^{-j\omega})\right]^2 + \left[\frac{1}{j2}(e^{j3\omega} - e^{-j3\omega})\right]^2$$

$$= \frac{1}{4}\left[(e^{j2\omega} + e^{-j2\omega} + 2) - (e^{j6\omega} + e^{-j6\omega} - 2)\right]$$

$$= -\frac{1}{4}\left[e^{j6\omega} - e^{j2\omega} - e^{-j2\omega} + e^{-j6\omega} - 4\right]$$

Taking Inverse Fourier transform, we get

$$x_3(n) = -\frac{1}{4}[\delta(n+6) - \delta(n+2) - \delta(n-2) + \delta(n-6) - 4\,\delta(n)] \qquad \textbf{Ans.}$$

EXAMPLE 2.18: *Find the Inverse Fourier transform for the Frequency response*

(a) $X(e^{j\omega}) = \begin{cases} 0, & 0 \le |\omega| \le \omega_0 \\ 1, & \omega_0 \le |\omega| \le \pi \end{cases}$ *(a high pass filter)*

(b) $X(e^{j\omega}) = \cos^2\omega.$ *(Delhi Univ. 1999)*

SOLUTION: (a)
$$x(n) = \frac{1}{2\pi}\int_{-\pi}^{\pi} X(e^{j\omega})\, e^{+j\omega n}\, d\omega$$

$$= \frac{1}{2\pi}\left[\int_{-\pi}^{-\omega_0} 1\cdot e^{j\omega n}\, d\omega + \int_{\omega_0}^{\pi} 1\cdot e^{j\omega n}\, d\omega\right]$$

$$= \frac{1}{2\pi}\left[\int_{\omega_0}^{\pi}\left(e^{j\omega n} + e^{-j\omega n}\right) d\omega\right] \qquad ...(A)$$

(change ω into $-\omega'$ in the first term and simplify)

$$= \frac{1}{\pi}\int_{\omega_0}^{\pi} \cos \omega n\, d\omega = \frac{1}{\pi}\left[\frac{\sin n\omega}{n}\right]_{\omega_0}^{\pi}$$

$$x(0) = \frac{1}{\pi}[\omega]_{\omega_0}^{\pi} = \frac{\pi - \omega_0}{\pi}$$ [putting $n = 0$ on both the sides of (A),

we get $x(0) = \frac{1}{\pi}\int_{\omega_0}^{\pi} d\omega$]

$$x(n)\big|_{n\neq 0} = \frac{1}{\pi . n}[\sin n\pi - \sin n\omega_0] = -\frac{\sin n\omega_0}{n\pi}, \; n > 0$$

$\therefore$
$$x(n) = \delta(n)\left[\frac{\pi-\omega_0}{\pi}\right] - \frac{\sin n\omega_0}{n\pi}u(n-1)$$ **Ans.**

(b) As
$$X(e^{j\omega}) = \cos^2\omega = \left(\frac{e^{j\omega}+e^{-j\omega}}{2}\right)^2$$
$$= \frac{1}{4}(e^{2j\omega}+2+e^{-2j\omega})$$

$\therefore$
$$x(n) = \frac{1}{2\pi}\cdot\frac{1}{4}\int_{-\pi}^{\pi}(e^{j2\omega}+e^{-j2\omega}+2)\,e^{jn\omega}\,d\omega$$
$$= \frac{1}{8\pi}\int_{-\pi}^{\pi}(e^{j(n+2)\omega}+e^{+j(n-2)\omega}+2)\,d\omega$$

**Proof

$$\int_{-\pi}^{\pi} e^{j(n+k)\omega}\,d\omega = \frac{1}{j(n+k)}\left[e^{j(n+k)\omega}\right]_{-\pi}^{\pi}$$
$$= \frac{e^{j(n+k)\pi}-e^{-j(n+k)\pi}}{j(n+k)}$$
$$= \frac{2\sin((n+k)\pi)}{(n+k)}$$
$$= 0, \quad (n+k)\neq 0$$
$$= 2\pi\delta(n+k) \quad \text{if } n+k=0$$

$$= \frac{1}{8\pi}[2\pi\,\delta(n+2)+2\pi\,\delta(n-2)+4\pi\,\delta(n)] \quad \text{(See **)}$$
$$= \frac{1}{4}[\delta(n+2)+\delta(n-2)+2\delta(n)]$$ **Ans.**

EXAMPLE 2.19: *Determine the Inverse DTFT of the frequency domain representation shown in the Figure.*

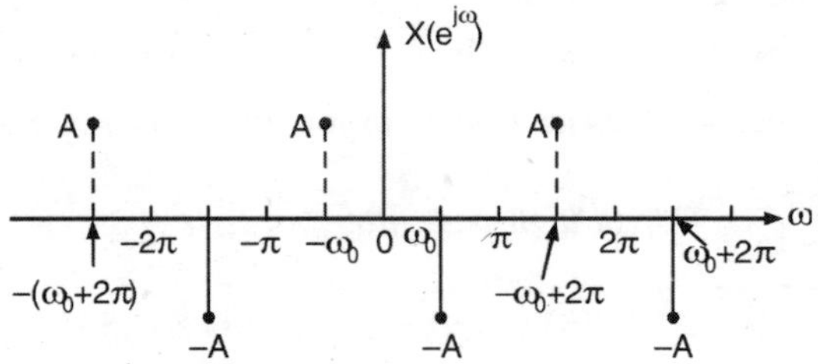

Fig. Ex. 2.19. The given spectrum

SOLUTION: In the frequency period $-\pi \le \omega \le \pi$, we have

$$X(e^{j\omega}) = A\delta(\omega+\omega_0) - A\delta(\omega-\omega_0)$$

$\therefore$
$$x(n) = \frac{1}{2\pi}\int_{-\pi}^{\pi}\cdot X(e^{j\omega})\,e^{j\omega n}\,d\omega$$
$$= \frac{1}{2\pi}\int_{-\pi}^{\pi}[A\,\delta(\omega+\omega_0) - A\,\delta(\omega-\omega_0)]\,e^{j\omega n}\,d\omega$$
$$= \frac{A}{2\pi}\left[e^{-j\omega_0 n} - e^{j\omega_0 n}\right]$$
$$= \frac{A}{2\pi}(-2j\sin\omega_0 n) = \frac{-jA}{\pi}\sin\omega_0 n$$ **Ans.**

EXAMPLE 2.20: *By using the convolution theorem, find the Inverse Fourier transform of* $X(e^{j\omega}) = \dfrac{1}{(1-ae^{-j\omega})^2}$, $|a| < 1$.

SOLUTION: We know that $a^n u(n) \xleftrightarrow{FT} \dfrac{1}{1-ae^{-j\omega}}$

As
$$X(e^{j\omega}) = \frac{1}{1-ae^{-j\omega}} \times \frac{1}{1-ae^{-j\omega}}$$

$\therefore$
$$x(n) = a^n\, u(n) * a^n\, u(n)$$
$$= \sum_{k=-\infty}^{\infty} a^k\, u(k).\, a^{n-k}\, u(n-k)$$
$$= a^n \sum_{k=0}^{n} \cdot 1, \quad n + ve$$
$$= a^n.\,(n+1)\cdot u(n)$$

Hence,
$$\frac{1}{(1-ae^{-j\omega})^2} \xleftrightarrow{IFT} (n+1)\, a^n u(n), \text{ as expected. See (2.96)}$$
Ans.

EXAMPLE 2.21: *Determine the inverse transforms for*

(i) $H_1(e^{j\omega}) = \dfrac{2-e^{-j\omega}}{\left(1+\frac{1}{2}e^{-j\omega}\right)}$; (ii) $H_2(e^{j\omega}) = \dfrac{1}{1-\frac{1}{2}e^{-j\omega}+\frac{1}{4}e^{-j2\omega}}$

If $H_1(e^{j\omega})$ and $H_2(e^{j\omega})$ are cascaded, what would be the overall system's transfer function $H(e^{j\omega})$?

(IP Univ. 2008)

SOLUTION: (*i*) As
$$H_1(e^{j\omega}) = \frac{2-e^{-j\omega}}{1+\frac{1}{2}e^{-j\omega}} = \frac{2}{1+\frac{1}{2}e^{-j\omega}} - \frac{e^{-j\omega}}{1+\frac{1}{2}e^{-j\omega}}$$

$\therefore$
$$h_1(n) = 2\cdot\left(\frac{-1}{2}\right)^n u(n) - \left(\frac{-1}{2}\right)^n u(n) \Big| \text{ change } n \text{ to } n-1$$
$$= 2\left(-\frac{1}{2}\right)^n u(n) - \left(\frac{-1}{2}\right)^{n-1} u(n-1)$$
Ans.

(*ii*) Now
$$H_2(e^{j\omega}) = \frac{1}{1-\frac{1}{2}e^{-j\omega}+\frac{1}{4}e^{-j2\omega}} = \frac{4}{e^{-j2\omega}-2e^{-j\omega}+4}$$
$$= \frac{4}{(e^{-j\omega}-a)\,(e^{-j\omega}-b)} \text{ (say)}$$
$$= \frac{4}{a-b}\left[\frac{1}{(e^{-j\omega}-a)} + \frac{-1}{(e^{-j\omega}-b)}\right]$$
$$= \frac{4}{a-b}\left[\frac{-1}{a}\frac{1}{1-\frac{1}{a}e^{-j\omega}} + \frac{1}{b}\frac{1}{1-\frac{1}{b}e^{-j\omega}}\right]$$

roots of $e^{-j2\omega} - 2e^{-j\omega} + 4 = 0$

are $a, b = \dfrac{2 \pm \sqrt{4-16}}{2}$
$= 1 \pm j\sqrt{3}$

$\therefore\ a = 1+j\sqrt{3},\ \ b = 1-j\sqrt{3}$

$\therefore$
$$h_2(n) = \frac{4}{a-b}\left[\left(\frac{-1}{a}\right)\left(\frac{1}{a}\right)^n u(n) + \left(\frac{1}{b}\right)\left(\frac{1}{b}\right)^n u(n)\right]$$

$$= \frac{4}{(a-b)}\left[\left(\frac{1}{b}\right)^{n+1} - \left(\frac{1}{a}\right)^{n+1}\right] u(n), \quad (a-b) = j\,2\sqrt{3}$$ **Ans.**

If $H_1(e^{j\omega})$ and $H_2(e^{j\omega})$ are cascaded then

$$H(e^{j\omega}) = H_1(e^{j\omega}).\, H_2(e^{j\omega}) = \frac{2 - e^{-j\omega}}{\left(1 + \frac{1}{2}e^{-j\omega}\right)\left(1 - \frac{1}{2}e^{-j\omega} + \frac{1}{4}e^{-j2\omega}\right)}$$ **Ans.**

EXAMPLE 2.22: *The input $x(n)$ and the output $y(n)$ of a causal stable LTI system are related as $y(n) - \frac{1}{6}\, y(n-1) - \frac{1}{6}\, y(n-2) = x(n)$.*

(i) Calculate the frequency response $H(e^{j\omega})$, and (ii) the impulse response $h(n)$ of the system.

(IP Univ. 2007, 2009)

SOLUTION: Taking FT, we get $Y(e^{j\omega})\left[1 - \frac{1}{6}e^{-j\omega} - \frac{1}{6}e^{-j2\omega}\right] = X(e^{j\omega})$

or $$H(e^{j\omega}) = \frac{1}{1 - \frac{1}{6}e^{-j\omega} - \frac{1}{6}e^{-j2\omega}}$$ **Ans.**

$$= \left[\frac{6}{6 - e^{-j\omega} - e^{-j2\omega}} = \frac{6}{(2 - e^{-j\omega})(3 + e^{-j\omega})}\right.$$

$$= \frac{6/5}{(2 - e^{-j\omega})} + \frac{6/5}{(3 + e^{-j\omega})} = \frac{3/5}{\left(1 - \frac{1}{2}e^{-j\omega}\right)} + \frac{2/5}{1 + \frac{1}{3}e^{-j\omega}}$$

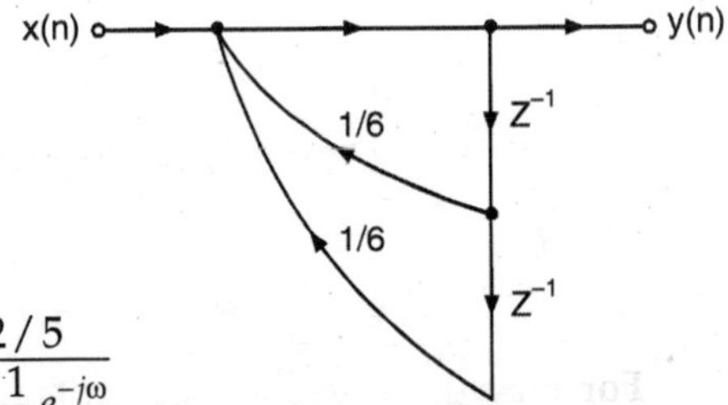

Fig. Ex. 2.22. The system realization

$$\therefore \quad h(n) = \left[\frac{3}{5}\left(\frac{1}{2}\right)^n + \frac{2}{5}\left(-\frac{1}{3}\right)^n\right] u(n)$$ **Ans.**

EXAMPLE 2.23: *The system function $H(z)$ of a causal discrete-time LTI system is given by*

$$H(z) = \frac{b + z^{-1}}{1 - az^{-1}}, \quad a \text{ is real and } |a| < 1$$

Find the value of b so that $|H(e^{j\omega})| = 1$ for all ω i.e. $H(z)$ is an all pass filter.

SOLUTION: $H(e^{j\omega}) = H(z)\big|_{Z = e^{j\omega}} = \dfrac{b + e^{-j\omega}}{1 - ae^{-j\omega}}$

$$|H(e^{j\omega})| = \left|\frac{b + e^{-j\omega}}{1 - ae^{-j\omega}}\right| = 1$$

$$\therefore \quad (b + \cos\omega)^2 + \sin^2\omega = (1 - a\cos\omega)^2 + (a\sin\omega)^2$$

or $$1 + 2b\cos\omega + b^2 = 1 + a^2 - 2a\cos\omega \qquad \text{...(A)}$$

$$\therefore \quad b = -a \quad \text{(by inspection of (A))}$$

Hence, for $b = -a$, $H(z) = \dfrac{-a + z^{-1}}{1 - az^{-1}}$ is an all pass filter **Ans.**

EXAMPLE 2.24: *An FIR filter is described by the difference equation*

$$y(n) = x(n) + x(n - 10)$$

(a) Compute and sketch its magnitude and phase response

(*b*) Determine its response to the inputs

(*i*) $x(n) = \cos\frac{\pi}{10}n + 3\sin\left(\frac{\pi}{3}n + \frac{\pi}{10}\right), -\infty < n < \infty$

(*ii*) $x(n) = 10 + 5\cos\left(\frac{2\pi}{5}n + \frac{\pi}{2}\right), -\infty < n < \infty$ (*IP Univ. 2002, Delhi Univ. 1999*)

SOLUTION: (*a*) As $y(n) = x(n) + x(n - 10)$

$$\therefore \quad Y(z) = X(z)\,[1 + z^{-10}]$$

$$Y(e^{j\omega}) = X(e^{j\omega})\,(1 + e^{-j\omega 10})$$

$$\therefore \quad H(e^{j\omega}) = \frac{Y(e^{j\omega})}{X(e^{j\omega})} = 1 + e^{-j\omega/10}$$

$$= e^{-j\omega 5}\,(e^{+j5\omega} + e^{-j5\omega})$$

$$= (2\cos 5\omega)\,e^{-j5\omega}$$

$$|H(e^{j\omega})| = 2\cos 5\omega$$

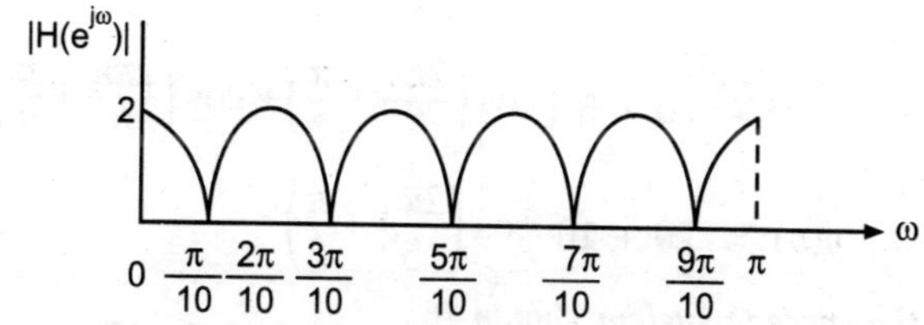

Fig. Ex. 2.24. (*a*) Magnitude response

For magnitude response: see Fig. Ex. 2.24(*a*)

For phase response: $\omega = 0$ to $\pi/10$, $\cos 5\omega$ is +ve

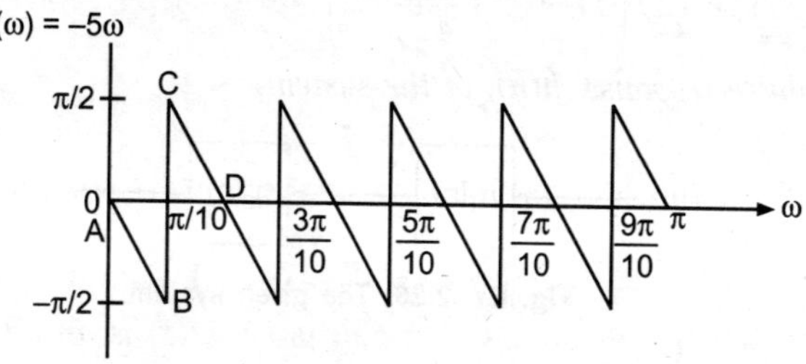

Fig. Ex. 2.24. (*b*) Phase response

$\therefore \quad \phi(\omega) = +(-5\omega)$, a straight line

at $\quad \omega = 0, \ \phi(\omega) = 0,$

at $\quad \omega = \pi/10, \ \phi(\omega) = -\pi/2$ (*AB*)

as $\quad \frac{\pi}{10} < \omega < \frac{2\pi}{10}$, $\cos 5(\omega)$ is –ve

$\therefore$ $\phi(\omega)$ is +ve and is a straight line (*CD*).

Then again $\phi(\omega)$ is –ve. The overall curve of phase response as shown in Fig. Ex. 2.24(*b*).

(*b*) (*i*) As $y(n) = x(n) + x(n - 10)$ is the given system equation,

put $\quad x(n) = \cos\frac{\pi}{10}n + 3\sin\left(\frac{\pi}{3}n + \frac{\pi}{10}\right)$

$$\therefore \quad y(n) = \cos\left(\frac{\pi}{10}n\right) + \cos\left(\frac{\pi}{10}(n-10)\right) + 3\left[\sin\left(\frac{\pi}{3}n + \frac{\pi}{10}\right) + \sin\left(\frac{\pi}{3}(n-10) + \frac{\pi}{10}\right)\right]$$

$$= 2\cos\left(\frac{\pi}{10}n - \frac{\pi}{2}\right)\cdot\cos\frac{\pi}{2} + 6\left[\sin\left(\frac{\pi}{3}n + \frac{\pi}{10} - \frac{5\pi}{3}\right)\cos\frac{5\pi}{3}\right]$$

$\cos\frac{\pi}{2} = 0$ (Use $\cos A + \cos B = 2\cos\frac{A+B}{2}\cos\frac{A-B}{2}$)

$$\therefore \quad y(n) = 6\cos\frac{5\pi}{3}\sin\left(\frac{\pi n}{3} + \frac{\pi}{10} - \frac{5\pi}{3}\right) \quad (\sin A + \sin B = 2\sin\frac{A+B}{2}\cos\frac{A-B}{2})$$ **Ans.**

(*ii*) Here $x(n) = 10 + 5\cos\left(\frac{2\pi n}{5} + \frac{\pi}{2}\right)$

$$\therefore \quad y(n) = 10 + 5\cos\left(\frac{2\pi n}{5} + \frac{\pi}{2}\right) + 10 + 5\cos\left(\frac{2\pi(n-10)}{5} + \frac{\pi}{2}\right)$$

$$= 20 + 5\left[\cos\left(\frac{2\pi n}{5} + \frac{\pi}{2}\right) + \cos\left(\frac{2\pi n}{5} + \frac{\pi}{2} - 4\pi\right)\right]$$

$$= 20 + 5\left[\cos\left(\frac{2\pi n}{5} + \frac{\pi}{2}\right) + \cos\left(\frac{2\pi n}{5} + \frac{\pi}{2}\right)\right]$$

i.e.
$$y(n) = 20 + 10\cos\left(\frac{2\pi n}{5} + \frac{\pi}{2}\right)$$ **Ans.**

EXAMPLE 2.25: *For the cascade system shown if*

$$h_1(n) = 2\left(-\frac{1}{2}\right)^n u(n) - \left(-\frac{1}{2}\right)^{n-1} u(n-1), \text{ and}$$

$$H_2(e^{j\omega}) = 2\Big/\left(1 - e^{-j\omega} + \frac{1}{4}e^{-j2\omega}\right)$$

find the overall impulse response, h(n), of the system. (*I.P. Univ. 2007*)

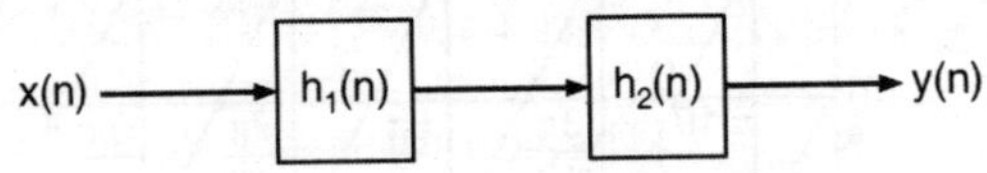

Fig. Ex. 2.25. The given system

SOLUTION: $h_1(n) = 2\left(-\frac{1}{2}\right)^n u(n) - \left(\frac{-1}{2}\right)^{n-1} u(n-1)$

$$\therefore \quad H_1(e^{j\omega}) = \left.\frac{2 - z^{-1}}{1 + \frac{1}{2}z^{-1}}\right|_{z=e^{j\omega}}$$

$\left(\because a^n u(n) \xleftrightarrow{ZT} \frac{1}{1 - az^{-1}}, \text{ here } a = -\frac{1}{2}\right.$ and $\left. a^{n-1}u(n-1) \xleftrightarrow{ZT} \frac{z^{-1}}{1 - az^{-1}}\right)$

$$= \frac{2 - e^{-j\omega}}{1 + \frac{1}{2}e^{-j\omega}}$$

$$H(e^{j\omega}) = H_1(e^{j\omega}) \cdot H_2(e^{j\omega})$$

$$= \left(\frac{2 - e^{-j\omega}}{1 + \frac{1}{2}e^{-j\omega}}\right)\left(\frac{2}{1 - e^{-j\omega} + \frac{1}{4}e^{-j2\omega}}\right)$$

$$= 2 \times 2 \frac{1-\frac{1}{2}e^{-j\omega}}{1+\frac{1}{2}e^{-j\omega}} \times \left(\frac{1}{\left(1-\frac{1}{2}e^{-j\omega}\right)^2}\right)$$

$$= 4. \frac{1}{\left(1+\frac{1}{2}e^{-j\omega}\right)\left(1-\frac{1}{2}e^{-j\omega}\right)}$$

$$= 4\left[\frac{1/2}{1+\frac{1}{2}e^{-j\omega}} + \frac{1/2}{1-\frac{1}{2}e^{-j\omega}}\right] \quad \text{(by partial fractions)}$$

$$\therefore \quad h(n) = 2\left[\left(-\frac{1}{2}\right)^n + \left(\frac{1}{2}\right)^n\right]u(n) \qquad \textbf{Ans.}$$

EXAMPLE 2.26: *An LTI, causal, second order discrete-time system is described by the difference equation*

$$y(n) - 6y(n-1) + 8y(n-2) = 16x(n).$$

Calculate its step response s(n) *(IP Univ. 2008)*

SOLUTION: Taking *FT* on both sides, we get

$$Y(e^{j\omega})\,[1 - 6e^{-j\omega} + 8e^{-j2\omega}] = 16\,X(e^{j\omega})$$

$$\therefore \quad H(e^{j\omega}) = \frac{Y(e^{j\omega})}{X(e^{j\omega})} = \frac{16}{(1-6e^{-j\omega}+8e^{-j2\omega})}$$

$$\therefore \quad H(e^{j\omega}) = \frac{16}{(1-2e^{-j\omega})(1-4e^{-j\omega})} = 16\left[\frac{-1}{1-2e^{-j\omega}} + \frac{2}{1-4e^{-j\omega}}\right]$$

$$\therefore \quad h(n) = 16\,[-(2)^n + 2.\,(4)^n]\,u(n)$$

$$S(e^{j\omega}) \cdot H(e^{j\omega}) = \left[\frac{16}{(1-2e^{-j\omega})(1-4e^{-j\omega})}\right]\left(\frac{1}{1-e^{-j\omega}} + \pi\delta(\omega)\right)$$

[The second factor is the *FT* of unit step function $u(n)$]

$$= \frac{16}{(1-2e^{-j\omega})(1-4e^{-j\omega})(1-e^{-j\omega})} + \frac{16}{3}\pi\,\delta(\omega)$$

$$= \frac{-32}{(1-2e^{-j\omega})} + \frac{128/3}{(1-4e^{-j\omega})} + \frac{16/3}{(1-e^{-j\omega})} + (16/3)\,\pi\,\delta(\omega)$$

$$\therefore \quad s(n) = IFT\,[S(e^{j\omega}) \cdot H(e^{j\omega})]$$

$$= -32\,(2)^n\,u(n) + \frac{128}{3}(4)^n\,u(n) + \frac{16}{3}u(n)$$

$$= 16\left[-2^{n+1}u(n) + \frac{8}{3}4^n\,u(n) + \frac{1}{3}u(n)\right]$$

$$\therefore \quad s(n) = 16\left[-2\cdot(2)^n + \frac{8}{3}(4)^n + \frac{1}{3}\right]u(n) \qquad \textbf{Ans.}$$

EXAMPLE 2.27: *Consider a system described by*

$$H(e^{j\omega}) = \frac{1}{1-\frac{5}{6}e^{-j\omega}+\frac{1}{6}e^{-j2\omega}}$$

Determine the response of the system to the input $x(n) = \delta(n) - \frac{1}{2}\delta(n-1)$. *(IP Univ. 2005)*

SOLUTION:

$$H(e^{j\omega}) = \frac{1}{\left(1-\frac{1}{2}e^{-j\omega}\right)\left(1-\frac{1}{3}e^{-j\omega}\right)} = \frac{-2}{1-\frac{1}{3}e^{-j\omega}} + \frac{3}{\left(1-\frac{1}{2}e^{-j\omega}\right)}$$

$$\therefore \quad h(n) = \left(-2\left(\frac{1}{3}\right)^n + 3\left(\frac{1}{2}\right)^n\right)u(n)$$ **Ans.**

$$X(e^{j\omega}) = FT\left[\delta(n) - \frac{1}{2}\delta(n-1)\right] = 1-\frac{1}{2}e^{-j\omega}$$

$$\therefore \quad Y(e^{j\omega}) = X(e^{j\omega})\cdot H(e^{j\omega}) = \frac{1}{\left(1-\frac{1}{3}e^{-j\omega}\right)\left(1-\frac{1}{2}e^{-j\omega}\right)} \times \frac{\left(1-\frac{1}{2}e^{-j\omega}\right)}{1} = \frac{1}{1-\frac{1}{3}e^{-j\omega}}$$

$$\therefore \quad y(n) = \left(\frac{1}{3}\right)^n u(n)$$ **Ans.**

EXAMPLE 2.28: *An LTI discrete-time system is described by the difference equation*

$$y(n) - \frac{1}{4}y(n-1) = x(n).$$

Calculate (a) unit sample response h(n). (b) step response of the system s(n). (c) response y(n) to input $x(n) = \left(\frac{1}{2}\right)^n u(n)$.

SOLUTION: (*a*) Clearly $H(e^{j\omega}) = \frac{1}{1-\frac{1}{4}e^{-j\omega}}$ $\quad \therefore h(n) = \left(\frac{1}{4}\right)^n u(n)$ **Ans.**

(*b*)

$$S(e^{j\omega}) = H(e^{j\omega}).\,[U(e^{j\omega})] = \frac{1}{1-\frac{1}{4}e^{-j\omega}}\cdot\left(\frac{1}{1-e^{-j\omega}} + \pi\,\delta(\omega)\right)$$

$$= \frac{1}{\left(1-\frac{1}{4}e^{-j\omega}\right)\left(1-e^{-j\omega}\right)} + \frac{\pi\cdot\delta(\omega)}{1-\frac{1}{4}\times 1} = \frac{1}{\left(1-\frac{1}{4}e^{-j\omega}\right)\left(1-e^{-j\omega}\right)} + \frac{4}{3}\pi\,\delta(\omega)$$

$$= \frac{-(1/3)}{\left(1-\frac{1}{4}e^{-j\omega}\right)} + \underbrace{\frac{(4/3)}{(1-e^{-j\omega})} + \frac{4}{3}\pi\,\delta(\omega)}_{\equiv 4/3\,u(n)}$$

$$\therefore \quad s(n) = \frac{4}{3}\left(1-\left(\frac{1}{4}\right)^{n+1}\right)u(n)$$ **Ans.**

(*c*) $Y(e^{j\omega}) = H(e^{j\omega})\cdot X(e^{j\omega}) = \frac{1}{1-\frac{1}{4}e^{-j\omega}}\cdot\frac{1}{1-\frac{1}{2}e^{-j\omega}}$

$$= \frac{-1}{1-\frac{1}{4}e^{-j\omega}} + \frac{2}{1-\frac{1}{2}e^{-j\omega}} \quad \text{(by partial fractions)}$$

Taking *IFT*, we get

$$y(n) = \left[-\left(\frac{1}{4}\right)^n + 2\left(\frac{1}{2}\right)^n\right]u(n) = \left[2\left(\frac{1}{2}\right)^n - \left(\frac{1}{4}\right)^n\right]u(n) \qquad \textbf{Ans.}$$

EXAMPLE 2.29: *The frequency response of a causal LTI discrete-time system is given by*

$$H(e^{j\omega}) = e^{-j\omega}\left(1-\frac{1}{2}e^{j\omega}\right)\Big/\left(1-\frac{1}{2}e^{-j\omega}\right).$$

Show that (a) $|H(e^{j\omega})|$ *is unity at all frequencies i.e. the system is an all pass system.*

(b) $\measuredangle H(e^{j\omega}) = -\omega - 2\tan^{-1}\dfrac{\frac{1}{2}\sin\omega}{1-\frac{1}{2}\cos\omega}$

(c) The group delay is given by $\tau_g(\omega) = \dfrac{3/4}{\frac{5}{4}-\cos\omega}$ *(IP Univ. 2008)*

SOLUTION: It is easy to show that the given system is described by

$$y(n) - \frac{1}{2}y(n-1) = -\frac{1}{2}x(n) + x(n-1)$$

(a)
$$|H(e^{j\omega})| = |e^{-j\omega}|\left|\frac{1-\frac{1}{2}(\cos\omega + j\sin\omega)}{1-\frac{1}{2}(\cos\omega - j\sin\omega)}\right| = \left|\frac{\left(1-\frac{1}{2}\cos\omega\right)-j\frac{1}{2}\sin\omega}{\left(1-\frac{1}{2}\cos\omega\right)+j\frac{1}{2}\sin\omega}\right| = 1 \quad \text{QED}$$

(b)
$$\measuredangle H(e^{j\omega}) = \measuredangle e^{-j\omega} + \measuredangle\left(1-\frac{1}{2}e^{j\omega}\right) - \measuredangle\left(1+\frac{1}{2}\cos\omega\right)$$

$$= -\omega + \measuredangle\left[\left(1-\frac{1}{2}\cos\omega\right) - j\frac{1}{2}\sin\omega\right] - \measuredangle\left[\left(1-\frac{1}{2}\cos\omega\right) + j\frac{1}{2}\sin\omega\right]$$

$$= -\omega - \tan^{-1}\frac{\frac{1}{2}\sin\omega}{\left(1-\frac{1}{2}\cos\omega\right)} - \tan^{-1}\frac{\frac{1}{2}\sin\omega}{\left(1-\frac{1}{2}\cos\omega\right)}$$

or
$$\theta(\omega) = -\omega - 2\tan^{-1}\left[\left(\frac{1}{2}\sin\omega\right)\Big/\left(1-\frac{1}{2}\cos\omega\right)\right] \qquad \textbf{Ans.}$$

(c)
$$\tau_g(\omega) = -\frac{d\theta(\omega)}{d\omega}$$

$$= -\frac{d}{d\omega}\left[-\omega - 2\tan^{-1}\frac{\frac{1}{2}\sin\omega}{1-\frac{1}{2}\cos\omega}\right]$$

$$= 1 + 2\cdot\frac{1}{1+\left(\dfrac{\frac{1}{2}\sin\omega}{1-\frac{1}{2}\cos\omega}\right)^2}\cdot\frac{d}{d\omega}\frac{\frac{1}{2}\sin\omega}{1-\frac{1}{2}\cos\omega}$$

$$= 1 + \frac{2\left(1-\frac{1}{2}\cos\omega\right)^2}{\left(1-\frac{1}{2}\cos\omega\right)^2+\left(\frac{1}{2}\sin\omega\right)^2} \cdot \frac{\left(1-\frac{1}{2}\cos\omega\right)\frac{1}{2}\cos\omega-\frac{1}{2}\sin\omega\left(\frac{1}{2}\sin\omega\right)}{\left(1-\frac{1}{2}\cos\omega\right)^2}$$

$$= 1 + 2\frac{-\frac{1}{4}+\frac{1}{2}\cos\omega}{1+\frac{1}{4}-\cos\omega} = 1 + \frac{2\left(\frac{-1}{4}+\frac{1}{2}\cos\omega\right)}{\frac{5}{4}-\cos\omega}$$

$$= \frac{\frac{5}{4}-\cos\omega-\frac{2}{4}+\cos\omega}{\frac{5}{4}-\cos\omega} = \frac{3/4}{\frac{5}{4}-\cos\omega}$$ **Ans.**

EXAMPLE 2.30: *A causal, stable LTI system produces output*

$y(n) = n\left(\frac{4}{5}\right)^n u(n)$ to the input $x(n) = \left(\frac{4}{5}\right)^n u(n)$.

Calculate : (a) the frequency response $H(e^{j\omega})$ of the system

(b) the impulse response $h(n)$ of the system

(c) a difference equation relating any input $x(n)$ and the output $y(n)$.

SOLUTION: As $X(e^{j\omega}) = FT\,[x(n)] = FT\left[\left(\frac{4}{5}\right)^n u(n)\right] = \dfrac{1}{1-\left(\frac{4}{5}\right)e^{-j\omega}}$

and $$Y(e^{j\omega}) = FT\,[y(n)] = FT\left[n\left(\frac{4}{5}\right)^n u(n)\right] = j\frac{d}{d\omega}\left[\frac{1}{1-\left(\frac{4}{5}\right)e^{-j\omega}}\right]$$

$$= j\left[-\frac{\frac{-4}{5}(-j)e^{-j\omega}}{\left(1-\frac{4}{5}e^{-j\omega}\right)^2}\right] \qquad \left[\because \text{if } x(n) \xrightarrow{F} x(e^{j\omega}) \text{ then } nx(n) \xrightarrow{F} j\frac{d}{d\omega}X(e^{j\omega})\right]$$

$$= \frac{(4/5)e^{-j\omega}}{\left(1-\frac{4}{5}e^{-j\omega}\right)^2}$$

(a) $$H(e^{j\omega}) = \frac{Y(e^{j\omega})}{X(e^{j\omega})} = \frac{(4/5)\,e^{-j\omega}}{\left(1-\frac{4}{5}e^{-j\omega}\right)^2} \times \frac{\left(1-\frac{4}{5}e^{-j\omega}\right)}{1} = \frac{(4/5)\,e^{-j\omega}}{\left(1-\frac{4}{5}e^{-j\omega}\right)}$$ **Ans.**

(b) $$h(n) = IFT\,[H(e^{j\omega})] = IFT\left[\frac{(4/5)\,e^{-j\omega}}{\left(1-\frac{4}{5}e^{-j\omega}\right)}\right] = \frac{4}{5}\left(\frac{4}{5}\right)^n u(n)\Big|_{\text{change } n \text{ to } n-1}$$

$\therefore$ $$h(n) = \left(\frac{4}{5}\right)^n u(n-1)$$ **Ans.**

(c) From part (a), $\dfrac{Y(e^{j\omega})}{X(e^{j\omega})} = \dfrac{(4/5)\,e^{-j\omega}}{1-\frac{4}{5}e^{-j\omega}}$

$$\therefore \quad Y(e^{j\omega})\left[1-\frac{4}{5}e^{-j\omega}\right] = X(e^{j\omega})\left[\frac{4}{5}e^{-j\omega}\right]$$

Taking *IFT* on both sides, we get

$$y(n)-\frac{4}{5}y(n-1) = \frac{4}{5}x(n-1)$$

Ans.

EXAMPLE 2.31: *An LTI, causal, second-order discrete-time system described by the difference equation*

$$y(n) - \frac{3}{4}y(n-1) + \frac{1}{8}y(n-2) = 2x(n)$$

Calculate (a) its impulse response h(n); (b) its step response s(n); (c) if $x(n) = \left(\frac{1}{4}\right)^n u(n)$*, find the output y(n).* *(IP Univ. 2000, 2006, 2008)*

SOLUTION:

(a) Clearly,
$$H(e^{j\omega}) = \frac{2}{1-\frac{3}{4}e^{-j\omega}+\frac{1}{8}e^{-j2\omega}} = \frac{2}{\left(1-\frac{1}{2}e^{-j\omega}\right)\left(1-\frac{1}{4}e^{-j\omega}\right)}$$

$$= 2\left[\frac{2}{\left(1-\frac{1}{2}e^{-j\omega}\right)}+\frac{-1}{\left(1-\frac{1}{4}e^{-j\omega}\right)}\right]$$

$$\therefore \quad h(n) = \left[4\left(\frac{1}{2}\right)^n - 2\left(\frac{1}{4}\right)^n\right]u(n)$$

Ans.

(b) As $u(n) \xleftrightarrow{FT} \dfrac{1}{1-e^{-j\omega}} + \pi\,\delta(\omega)$ (Note this step)

$$\therefore \quad S(e^{j\omega}) = \frac{2}{\left(1-\frac{1}{2}e^{-j\omega}\right)\left(1-\frac{1}{4}e^{-j\omega}\right)}\left[\frac{1}{1-e^{-j\omega}}+\pi\delta(\omega)\right]$$

$$= \frac{2}{\left(1-\frac{1}{2}e^{-j\omega}\right)\left(1-\frac{1}{4}e^{-j\omega}\right)\left(1-e^{-j\omega}\right)} + \frac{2\pi\,\delta(\omega)}{\left(1-\frac{1}{2}\right)\left(1-\frac{1}{4}\right)}$$

$$= 2\left[\frac{-2}{1-\frac{1}{2}e^{-j\omega}}+\frac{1/3}{1-\frac{1}{4}e^{-j\omega}}+\frac{8/3}{1-e^{-j\omega}}\right]+\frac{16}{3}\pi\;\delta(\omega) \xrightarrow{IFT} \frac{16}{3}u(n)$$

$$\therefore \quad s(n) = -4\left(\frac{1}{2}\right)^n u(n)+\frac{2}{3}\left(\frac{1}{4}\right)^n u(n)+\frac{16}{3}u(n)$$

Ans.

due to $\left(\frac{1}{4}\right)^n u(n)$

(c)
$$Y(e^{j\omega}) = X(e^{j\omega})\cdot H(e^{j\omega}) = \frac{2}{\left(1-\frac{1}{2}e^{-j\omega}\right)\left(1-\frac{1}{4}e^{-j\omega}\right)}\times\frac{1}{\left(1-\frac{1}{4}e^{-j\omega}\right)}$$

$$= \frac{2}{\left(1-\frac{1}{2}e^{-j\omega}\right)\left(1-\frac{1}{4}e^{-j\omega}\right)^2} \equiv \frac{A}{\left(1-\frac{1}{2}e^{-j\omega}\right)} + \frac{Be^{-j\omega}+C}{\left(1-\frac{1}{4}e^{-j\omega}\right)^2}$$

[To find A, B, C]

$$2 = A\left(1-\frac{1}{4}e^{-j\omega}\right)^2 + \left(Be^{-j\omega}+C\right)\left(1-\frac{1}{2}e^{-j\omega}\right)$$

$$\begin{cases} 2 = A + C & \text{(comparing constants on both sides)} \\ 0 = -\frac{1}{2}A + B - \frac{1}{2}C & \text{(comparing } e^{-j\omega} \text{ on both sides)} \\ 0 = \frac{1}{16}A - \frac{1}{2}B & \text{(comparing } e^{-j2\omega} \text{ on both sides)} \end{cases}$$

Solve for A, B, C $\therefore A = 8, B = 1, C = -6$

$$\therefore \quad Y(e^{j\omega}) = \frac{8}{\left(1-\frac{1}{2}e^{-j\omega}\right)} + \frac{e^{-j\omega}-6}{\left(1-\frac{1}{4}e^{-j\omega}\right)^2} = \frac{8}{\left(1-\frac{1}{2}e^{-j\omega}\right)} + \frac{-4\left(1-\frac{1}{4}e^{-j\omega}\right)-2}{\left(1-\frac{1}{4}e^{-j\omega}\right)^2}$$

$$= \frac{8}{\left(1-\frac{1}{2}e^{-j\omega}\right)} - \frac{4}{\left(1-\frac{1}{4}e^{-j\omega}\right)} - \frac{2}{\left(1-\frac{1}{4}e^{-j\omega}\right)^2}$$

$$\therefore \quad y(n) = \left[8\left(\frac{1}{2}\right)^n - 4\left(\frac{1}{4}\right)^n - 2(n+1)\left(\frac{1}{4}\right)^n\right]u(n)$$ **Ans.**

$$\because (n+1)\,a^n\,u(n) \xrightarrow{FT} \frac{1}{(1-ae^{-j\omega})^2}$$

EXAMPLE 2.32: *(a) Determine the Inverse Fourier transforms*

$$h_1(n) = IFT\left[(2-e^{-j\omega})\Big/\left(1+\frac{1}{2}e^{-j\omega}\right)\right]$$

$$h_2(n) = IFT\left[1\Big/(1-e^{-j\omega}+\frac{1}{4}e^{-j2\omega})\right]$$

(b) If the systems $h_1(n)$ and $h_2(n)$ are cascaded, what would be the overall system's Transfer function $H(e^{j\omega})$? *(IP Univ. 2008)*

SOLUTION: (a) $H_1(e^{j\omega}) = \dfrac{2-e^{-j\omega}}{1+\frac{1}{2}e^{-j\omega}} = \dfrac{2}{1+\frac{1}{2}e^{-j\omega}} - \dfrac{e^{-j\omega}}{1+\frac{1}{2}e^{-j\omega}}$

$$\therefore \quad h_1(n) = 2\left(-\frac{1}{2}\right)^n u(n) - \left(\frac{-1}{2}\right)^{n-1} u(n-1)$$ **Ans.**

$$H_2(e^{j\omega}) = \frac{1}{1-\frac{1}{2}e^{-j\omega}+\frac{1}{4}e^{-j2\omega}} = \frac{1}{\left(1-\frac{1}{2}e^{-j\omega}\right)^2}$$

$$\therefore \quad h_2(n) = (n+1)\left(\frac{1}{2}\right)^n u(n) \quad \therefore (n+1)\,a^n\,u(n) \xrightarrow{FT} \frac{1}{(1-ae^{-j\omega})^2}$$ **Ans.**

(b) $H(e^{j\omega}) = H_1(e^{j\omega}) \cdot H_2(e^{j\omega})$

$$= \frac{2 - e^{-j\omega}}{1 + \frac{1}{2}e^{-j\omega}} \cdot \frac{1}{\left(1 - \frac{1}{2}e^{-j\omega}\right)^2}$$

$$= \frac{2}{\left(1 + \frac{1}{2}e^{-j\omega}\right)\left(1 - \frac{1}{2}e^{-j\omega}\right)}$$

$$= \frac{1}{1 + \frac{1}{2}e^{-j\omega}} + \frac{1}{1 - \frac{1}{2}e^{-j\omega}}$$

$\therefore$ $$h(n) = \left[\left(-\frac{1}{2}\right)^n + \left(\frac{1}{2}\right)^n\right] u(n)$$ **Ans.**

EXAMPLE 2.33: *For the discrete-time system described by*

$y(n) - \frac{1}{2}\, y(n-1) = x(n) + \frac{1}{2}\, x(n-1)$

(a) determine the system function $H(e^{j\omega})$

(b) find the impulse response h(n) of the system

(c) determine the output y(n) for input $x(n) = \cos \frac{\pi}{2} n$

SOLUTION: (a) Taking FT on both sides of the given difference equation, we get

$$Y(e^{j\omega})\left[1 - \frac{1}{2}e^{-j\omega}\right] = X(e^{j\omega})\left[1 + \frac{1}{2}e^{-j\omega}\right]$$

$\therefore$ $$H(e^{j\omega}) = \frac{Y(e^{j\omega})}{X(e^{j\omega})} = \frac{1 + \frac{1}{2}e^{-j\omega}}{1 - \frac{1}{2}e^{-j\omega}}$$ **Ans.**

(b) As $$H(e^{j\omega}) = \frac{1}{1 - \frac{1}{2}e^{-j\omega}} + \frac{1}{2}\frac{e^{-j\omega}}{1 - \frac{1}{2}e^{-j\omega}}$$

(partial fractions of RHS of above equation)

$\therefore$ $$h(n) = \left(\frac{1}{2}\right)^n u(n) + \frac{1}{2} \cdot \left(\frac{1}{2}\right)^n u(n)\Big|_{n \text{ to } n-1}$$

$$= \left(\frac{1}{2}\right)^n u(n) + \frac{1}{2}\left(\frac{1}{2}\right)^{n-1} \cdot u(n-1)$$

$$= \left(\frac{1}{2}\right)^n [u(n) + u(n-1)]$$

$$h(0) = \left(\frac{1}{2}\right)^0 [1 - 0] = 1$$

For $n \geq 1$, $$h(n) = \left(\frac{1}{2}\right)^n [1 + 1] = \left(\frac{1}{2}\right)^{n-1}$$

Hence, $$h(n) = \begin{cases} 1, & n=0 \\ \left(\frac{1}{2}\right)^{n-1}, & n \geq 1 \end{cases}$$ **Ans.**

(c) As $$x(n) = \cos\frac{\pi}{2}n \quad \text{(form } \cos\omega_0 n)$$

$\therefore$ $$X(e^{j\omega}) = \pi\left[\delta\left(\omega-\frac{\pi}{2}\right)+\delta\left(\omega+\frac{\pi}{2}\right)\right] . |\omega| \leq \pi$$

$$Y(e^{j\omega}) = X(e^{j\omega}) \cdot H(e^{j\omega})$$

$$= \pi\left[\delta\left(\omega-\frac{\pi}{2}\right)+\delta\left(\omega+\frac{\pi}{2}\right)\right] \cdot \frac{1+\frac{1}{2}e^{-j\omega}}{1-\frac{1}{2}e^{-j\omega}}$$

$$= \pi\left[\frac{1+\frac{1}{2}e^{-j\pi/2}}{1-\frac{1}{2}e^{-j\pi/2}}\right]\delta\left(\omega-\frac{\pi}{2}\right)+\pi\left[\frac{1+\frac{1}{2}e^{j\pi/2}}{1-\frac{1}{2}e^{j\pi/2}}\right]\delta\left(\omega+\frac{\pi}{2}\right)$$

$$= \pi\left[\frac{1-\frac{1}{2}j}{1+\frac{1}{2}j}\right]\delta\left(\omega-\frac{\pi}{2}\right)+\pi\left[\frac{1+\frac{1}{2}j}{1-\frac{1}{2}j}\right]\delta\left(\omega+\frac{\pi}{2}\right)$$

$$Y(e^{j\omega}) = \pi\,\delta\left(\omega-\frac{\pi}{2}\right)e^{-j2\tan^{-1}\left(\frac{1}{2}\right)}+\pi\,\delta\left(\omega+\frac{\pi}{2}\right)e^{j2\tan^{-1}\left(\frac{1}{2}\right)} \quad \text{....}(A)$$

Taking inverse FT on both the sides of (A) and using the result $e^{j\omega_0 n} \xleftrightarrow{FT} 2\pi\delta(\omega-\omega_0)$ (see (2.99)), we get

$$y(n) = \frac{1}{2}e^{j(\pi/2)n} \cdot e^{-j2\tan^{-1}\left(\frac{1}{2}\right)}+\frac{1}{2}e^{-j(\pi/2)n}\,e^{j2\tan^{-1}\left(\frac{1}{2}\right)}$$

$$= \frac{1}{2}\left[e^{j(\pi/2)n-\theta}+e^{-j(\pi/2)n+\theta}\right], \text{ where } \theta = 2\tan^{-1}\frac{1}{2}$$

$\therefore$ $$y(n) = \cos\left(\frac{\pi}{2}n - 2\tan^{-1}\frac{1}{2}\right)$$ **Ans.**

UNSOLVED PROBLEMS WITH ANSWERS

2.1. Show that $\sum_{k=-\infty}^{n} x(k) \xleftrightarrow{FT} \pi X(e^{j0})\,\delta(\omega)+\frac{1}{1-e^{-j\omega}}X(e^{j\omega})$

2.2. If $x(n)$ is a real periodic sequence with fundamental period N and Fourier coefficients $C_k = a_k + jb_k$ with a_k and b_k both real.

(a) show that $a_{-k} = a_k$ and $b_k = -b_{-k}$

(b) If N is even then $C_{N/2}$ is real

2.3. Calculate Fourier transforms of

(a) $x_1(n) = \left(\frac{1}{2}\right)^{-n} u(-n-1)$ (b) $x_2(n) = \left(\frac{1}{2}\right)^{n} u(n-1)$

(c) $x_3(n) = u(n) - u(n-2)$ (d) $\left(\frac{1}{2}\right)^{|n|} u(-n-2)$

[Ans. (a) $\left(\frac{1}{2}\right)e^{j\omega}\Big/\left(1-\frac{1}{2}e^{j\omega}\right)$ (b) $\frac{1}{2}e^{-j\omega}\Big/\left(1-\frac{1}{2}e^{-j\omega}\right)$

(c) $\left(1-e^{-j2\omega}\right)\Big/\left(1-e^{-j\omega}\right)$ (d) $\frac{1}{4}e^{j2\omega}\Big/\left(1-\frac{1}{2}e^{j\omega}\right)$

2.4. Let $x(n) \xleftrightarrow{FT} X(e^{j\omega})$, then determine the DTFT for the signals given below in terms of $X(e^{j\omega})$

(a) $x_1(n) = x(n+1) + x(n-1)$

(b) $x_2(n) = (n-1)^2\, x(n)$

(c) $x_3(n) = \frac{1}{2}\left[x(n) + x^*(-n)\right]$

(d) $x_4(n) = \left(\frac{1}{3}\right)^{|n|} u(-n-2)$

[Ans. (a) $X_1(e^{j\omega}) = 2\cos\omega \cdot X(e^{j\omega})$

(b) $X_2(e^{j\omega}) = -\dfrac{d^2X(e^{j\omega})}{d\omega^2} - j2\dfrac{dX(e^{j\omega})}{d\omega} + X(e^{j\omega})$

(c) $X_3(e^{j\omega}) = \text{Re}\,[X(e^{j\omega})]$

(d) $X_4(e^{j\omega}) = \left(\frac{1}{3}\right)^2 e^{j2\omega}\Big/\left(1-\frac{1}{3}e^{j\omega}\right)]$

2.5. $f(n)$ and $g(n)$ are real, causal and stable sequences with $f(n) \xleftrightarrow{FT} F(e^{j\omega})$ and $g(n) \longleftrightarrow G(e^{j\omega})$.

Show that $\dfrac{1}{2\pi}\displaystyle\int_{-\pi}^{\pi} F(e^{j\omega})\cdot G(e^{j\omega})\,d\omega = \left\{\frac{1}{2\pi}\int_{-\pi}^{\pi} F(e^{j\omega})\,d\omega\right\}\left\{\frac{1}{2\pi}\int_{-\pi}^{\pi} G(e^{j\omega})\,d\omega\right\}$ *(IP Univ. 2004, DU 1997, 1999)*

2.6. The cascade system shown with two LTI systems $h_1(n)$ are $h_2(n)$ such that

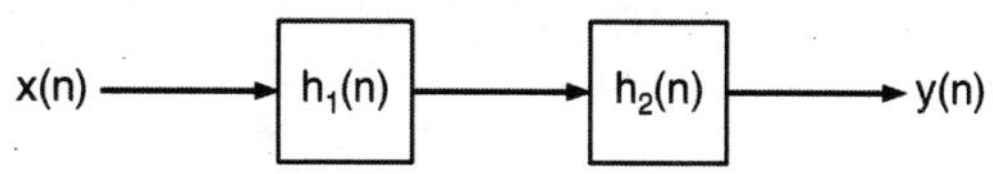

Fig. Prob. 2.6.

$$H_1(e^{j\omega}) = (2-e^{-j\omega})\Big/\left(1+\frac{1}{2}e^{-j\omega}\right)$$

$$H_2(e^{j\omega}) = 1\Big/\left(1-\frac{1}{2}e^{-j\omega}+\frac{1}{4}e^{-j2\omega}\right)$$

(a) Find the overall impulse response of the cascaded system

(b) Give the difference equation characterizing the cascade system

[Ans. (a) $h(n) = 2\,(1/8)^{n/3}\, u\left(\frac{n}{3}\right) - \left(\frac{1}{8}\right)^{(n/3-1)} \cdot u\left(\frac{n}{3}-1\right)$

(b) $y(n) + \frac{1}{8}y(n-3) = 2x(n) - x(n-1)$ **]**

2.7. A causal LTI system is described by the difference equation

$$y(n) - ay(n-1) = x(n) - bx(n-1)$$

Determine the value of b ($b \neq a$), such that this system is an all pass system *i.e.* the magnitude of its frequency response $H(e^{j\omega})$ is constant for all frequencies. *(DU 1988, 1997)*

[Ans. $b = \dfrac{1}{a^*}$ **]**

2.8. For the system input-output relation given by $y(n) = \frac{1}{L+1}\sum_{k=0}^{L} x(n-k)$, show that the system frequency response is given by $H(e^{j\omega}) = \frac{1}{L+1}e^{-jL\omega/2}$ [sin (L+1) ω/2/sin(ω/2)]

2.9. An LTI system described by its frequency response

$$H(e^{j\omega}) = \left(1+\frac{1}{2}e^{-j\omega}\right)\Big/\left(1-\frac{1}{2}e^{-j\omega}\right)$$

(*a*) Determine the system difference equation

(*b*) Find the impulse response $h(n)$ of the system

(*c*) Determine the output $y(n)$ for input $x(n) = \cos\frac{\pi}{2}n$

[Ans. (*a*)$y(n) = \frac{1}{2}y(n-1) + x(n) + \frac{1}{2}x(n-1)$

(*b*) $h(n) = \begin{cases} 1, & n=0 \\ \left(\frac{1}{2}\right)^{n-1}, & n\geq 1 \end{cases}$

(*c*) $y(n) = \cos\left(\frac{\pi}{2}n - 2\tan^{-1}\frac{1}{2}\right)$]

2.10. Given a periodic signal $x(n)$ with the following information

1. $x(n)$ is a real and even signal
2. $x(n)$ has period $N = 10$ and Fourier coefficients a_k
3. $a_{11} = 5$
4. $\frac{1}{10}\sum_{n=0}^{9}|x(n)|^2 = 50$

Find $x(n)$.

[Hint: Since, $x(n)$ is real and even, hence, a_k is also real and even (see (2.45)). ∴ $a_1 = a_{-1} = a_{11}$ (a_k being periodic)]

∴ $$a_1 = a_{-1} = a_{11} = 5.$$

Also $$\frac{1}{10}\sum_{n=0}^{9}|x(n)|^2 = 50$$

i.e., $$\sum_{k=0}^{9}|a_k|^2 = 50 \quad \text{(due to Parseval's relation)}$$

∴ $$\sum_{k=-1}^{8}|a_k|^2 = 50$$

or $$|a_{-1}|^2 + |a_0|^2 + |a_1|^2 + \sum_{k=2}^{8}|a_k|^2 = 50$$

or $$5^2 + |a_0|^2 + 5^2 + \sum_{k=2}^{8}|a_k|^2 = 50$$

Hence, $$a_0 = a_2 = a_3 = \dots = a_8 = 0$$

$$\therefore \quad x(n) = \sum_{k=-1}^{8} a_k\, e^{jk(2\pi/10)n} = 5e^{j(-1)\frac{\pi}{5}n} + 5e^{j(1)\frac{\pi}{5}n}$$

$$= 10\cos\left(\frac{\pi}{5}n\right)]$$ **Ans.**

2.11. For the two discrete-time periodic signals $x(n)$ and $y(n)$, given by

$$x(n) = 1+\cos\left(\frac{\pi}{3}n\right), \quad y(n) = \sin\left(\frac{\pi}{3}n+\frac{\pi}{4}\right)$$

(*a*) Determine the Fourier series coefficients a_k for $x(n)$ and b_k for $y(n)$

(*b*) Determine the Fourier series coefficients c_k for $z(n) = x(n)\cdot y(n)$

(*c*) Find $z(n)$.

Hint:

(*a*) $a_0 = 1,\ a_1 = a_{-1} = \frac{1}{2},\ b_1 = b_{-1}^* = (e^{-j\pi/4})/2$

(*b*) $C_0 = \frac{1}{2}\cos(\pi/4), C_1 = C_{-1}^* = \frac{1}{2}(e^{-j\pi/4})$

$C_2 = C_{-2}^* = \frac{1}{4}e^{-j\pi/4}$

(*c*) $z(n) = \sin\left(\frac{\pi}{3}n+\frac{\pi}{4}\right)+\frac{1}{2}\left[\sin\left(\frac{2\pi}{3}n+\frac{\pi}{4}\right)+\sin\frac{\pi}{4}\right]$

2.12. If $x_1(n)$ and $x_2(n)$ are two periodic signals, each of period N, show that

$$\frac{1}{N}\sum_{n=0}^{N-1} x_1(n)\cdot x_2(n) = \sum_{k=0}^{N-1} a_k\, b_{-k}$$

where a_k and b_k are the Fourier series coefficients of the signals $x_1(n)$ and $x_2(n)$, respectively.

[Hint: Let $x_1(n)\cdot x_2(n) \xleftrightarrow{FS} c_k$

Then $$c_k = \frac{1}{N}\sum_{n=0}^{N-1} x_1(n)\cdot x_2(n)\, e^{-jk(2\pi/N)} = \sum_{l=0}^{N-1} a_l\, b_{k-l}$$

Put $k = 0$ in the last two expressions to obtain

$$\frac{1}{N}\sum_{n=0}^{N-1} x_1(n)\, x_2(n) = \sum_{l=0}^{N-1} a_l\, b_{-l}\text{, hence, the result.]}$$

2.13. A discrete-time signal is given as $x(n) = a^n\, u(n)$, $|a| < 1$, determine the energy density spectrum (EDS), $\psi(e^{j\omega})$ for this signal.

[Hint: $$X(e^{j\omega}) = \frac{1}{1-ae^{-j\omega}}$$

$$\psi(e^{j\omega}) = \left|X(e^{j\omega})\right|^2 = X(e^{j\omega}).X^*(e^{j\omega})$$

$$= \frac{1}{(1-ae^{-j\omega})(1-ae^{j\omega})} = \frac{1}{1-2a\cos\omega + a^2}\ ]$$ **Ans.**

2.14. The DTFT of a sequence $x(n)$ is $X(e^{j\omega}) = \cos^3(3\omega)$. Find the value of $\sum_{n=-8}^{\infty} (-1)^n\, x(n)$ **[Ans: –1]**

CHAPTER 3

The z-Transform and Discrete-Time LTI Systems

3.1 INTRODUCTION

We know that the Laplace transform is a useful tool for analysing analog continuous-time systems. For the discrete-time systems, the corresponding tool is the z-transform. The discrete-time signals $x(n)$ are transformed to z-domain. The LTI discrete-time systems can be easily analysed, designed and realized by using z-transforms. (z is a complex variable like s is in Laplace domain.) Many properties of Laplace transform hold good for z-transform. Whereas the Laplace transform converts integral/differential equations into linear algebraic, the z-transform converts difference equations (involving delays and advances) into algebraic equations, which are easy to manipulate and solve.

3.2 THE z-TRANSFORM (ZT)

There are two versions of z-transforms, and are defined as follows:

(*a*) **Bilateral z-transform [$X(z)$]**

For a discrete-time signal $x(n)$, its bilateral z-transform is defined as

$$ZT[x(n)] = X(z) \triangleq \sum_{n=-\infty}^{\infty} x(n)\, z^{-n} \qquad ...(3.1)$$

Bilateral z-transform

(*b*) **Unilateral z-transform [$\widetilde{X}(z)$]**

For a discrete-time signal $x(n)$, its unilateral z-transform is defined as

$$ZT_1[x(n)] = [\widetilde{X}(z)] \triangleq \sum_{n=0}^{\infty} x(n)\, z^{-n} \qquad ...(3.2)$$

Unilateral z-transform

Thus, for a causal signal $x(n)$, $X(z) = \widetilde{X}(z)$, *i.e.*, the bilateral z-transform and the unilateral z-transform are equal.

Note that z is a complex variable. It can be expressed in polar form as

$$\boxed{z = re^{j\omega}} \qquad ...(3.3)$$

In (3.3), r is the magnitude of z and ω its phase angle in radians. We shall, as we progress, call ω as the angular frequency. Note that the discrete time Fourier transforms are periodic in ω with period 2π. This was explained in Chapter 8. As the phase angle in (3.3) is ω which is also periodic (as $e^{j\omega} = e^{j(\omega + 2\pi)}$) with period 2π, this similarity will help us to associate ω in (3.3), when $r = 1$ as the angular frequency in discrete-time signals and systems. Also, we shall write the expression

$$x(n) \xleftrightarrow{ZT} X(z) \qquad ...(3.4)$$

to signify that $x(n)$ z-transforms to $X(z)$, and $X(z)$ has inverse z-transform $x(n)$.

3.2.1 Relationship between z-Transform and Fourier Transform

We define z-transform as

$$X(z) = \sum_{n=-\infty}^{\infty} x(n)\, z^{-n} \qquad ...(3.5)$$

Put $z = re^{j\omega}$, (due to (3.3)) in (3.5) and we get

$$X(z)\big|_{z = re^{j\omega}} = \sum_{n=-\infty}^{\infty} x(n)\, r^{-n}\, e^{-j\omega n} \qquad ...(3.6)$$

$$\therefore \quad X(re^{j\omega}) = \sum_{n=-\infty}^{\infty} x(n)\, r^{-n}\, e^{-j\omega n} \qquad ...(3.7)$$

Put $r = 1$ on both the sides of (3.7). This gives us

$$X(z)\big|_{z = e^{j\omega}} = \sum_{n=-\infty}^{\infty} x(n)\, e^{-j\omega n} \qquad ...(3.8)$$

But R.H.S. of (3.8) is the definition of Fourier transform of a discrete-time signal. Hence, we can say that $X(z)$ with $z = e^{j\omega}$ converts $X(z)$ into Fourier transform for discrete-time signal $x(n)$. As

$$z = e^{j\omega} \text{ implies } |z| = 1 \qquad ...(3.9a)$$

Hence,

$$\boxed{X(z)\big|_{|z|=1} \longrightarrow X(e^{j\omega})} \qquad ...(3.9b)$$

Or evaluation of *ZT* on the unit circle $|z| = 1$, *i.e.*, for $z = e^{j\omega}$, gives the *DTFT* of that sequence $x(n)$. In other words, *ZT* is more generic function and *FT* is its special case when $|z| = 1$ everywhere.

3.2.2 The Region of Convergence (ROC)

We have learnt in Laplace transform where a Laplace parameter was used (to form an expression $\int x(t) \cdot e^{-st} dt$, while defining the Laplace transform) that the transform function has some region of conversion. In this region, the transform is finite *i.e.*, it converges. Similarly, for z-transform, the z-region when $X(z)$ will result a finite/converging value (*i.e.*, non-infinite value) is called the region of convergence (ROC) of the $X(z)$. This concept will be clear by the following example.

Note also that the ROC cannot have a pole within it. The very meaning of ROC is that the function has finite value at every point in the ROC. At a pole point a function has infinite value. Thus, $X(z)$ cannot have its poles in its ROC.

EXAMPLE 3.1: *Find the z-transform of*

$$x(n) = a^n\, u(n),\ a,\ \text{real}.$$

SOLUTION:

$$X(z) = \sum_{n=-\infty}^{\infty} x(n)\, z^{-n} = \sum_{n=-\infty}^{\infty} a^n\, u(n)\, z^{-n}$$

$$= \sum_{n=-\infty}^{\infty} (a^n z^{-n})\, u(n)$$

$$= \sum_{n=0}^{\infty} a^n\, z^{-n}$$

$$= \sum_{n=0}^{\infty} (az^{-1})^n \qquad \text{(a G.P. with 'r' = } az^{-1})$$

$$= 1 + (az^{-1}) + (az^{-1})^2 + \ldots + (az^{-1})^k + \ldots \infty \qquad \ldots(3.10)$$

If $|az^{-1}| < 1$, *i.e.*, if $\left|\frac{a}{z}\right| < 1$, *i.e.*, if $|z| > |a|$

then the series in (3.10) converges and

$$X(z) = \frac{1}{1-(az^{-1})} = \frac{z}{z-a} \qquad \textbf{Ans.}$$

$X(z)$ has a zero at $z = 0$

a pole at $z = a$

Thus, *ZT* for $x(n) = a^n\, u(n)$ to converge, the parameter z can be anywhere, in the ROC shown by shaded area in Fig. 3.1. The ROC's will take different profiles depending upon the sequence $x(n)$.

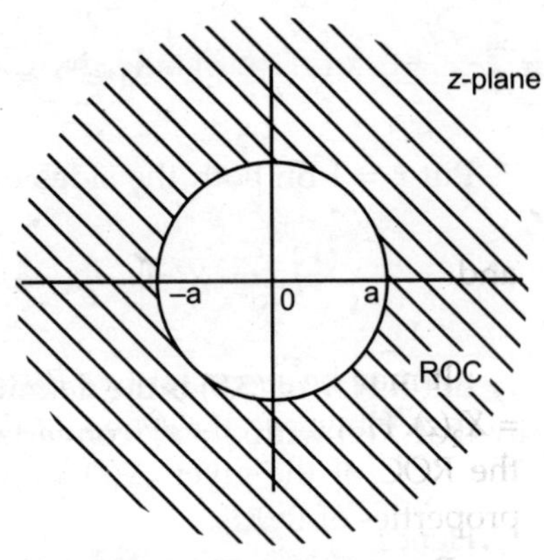

Fig. 3.1. Region of Convergence (ROC) for ZT X(z) of x(n) = a^n u(n)

To emphasise the significance of region of convergence (ROC) one more example is necessary, as follows:

EXAMPLE 3.2: *Find the z-transform of*

$$x(n) = -\,a^n\, u(-n-1),\ \text{for } |a| < 1, \text{ and } |a| > 1.$$

SOLUTION:

$$X(z) = \sum_{n=-\infty}^{\infty} x(n)\, z^{-n}$$

$$= \sum_{n=-\infty}^{\infty} [-\,a^n\, u(-n-1)]\, z^{-n}$$

$$= -\sum_{n=-\infty}^{-1} (a^{-1}z)^{-n} \qquad \text{(N.T.S.)}$$

Put $\quad n' = -n - 1$

$\therefore$ limits of n' become $n' = 0$ to ∞

$$\therefore \quad X(z) = -\sum_{n'=0}^{\infty} (a^{-1}z)^{n'+1}$$

$$= -(a^{-1}z)\sum_{n=0}^{\infty} (a^{-1}z)^{n}$$

If $|a^{-1}z| < 1$, *i.e.*, $|z| < |a|$, then the above series converges and we get

$$X(z) = \frac{-(a^{-1}z)}{1-a^{-1}z} = \frac{1}{1-az^{-1}}, \quad \text{ROC: } |z| < |a|$$

$\therefore$ ROC can take the shapes as shown in Fig. 3.2. For $|a| < 1$, ROC is a circle of radius $|a|$, *i.e.*, inside the unit circle $|z| = 1$, as shown in Fig. 3.2(*a*). For $|a| > 1$, the ROC crosses the unit circle $|z| = 1$, as shown in Fig. 3.2(*b*).

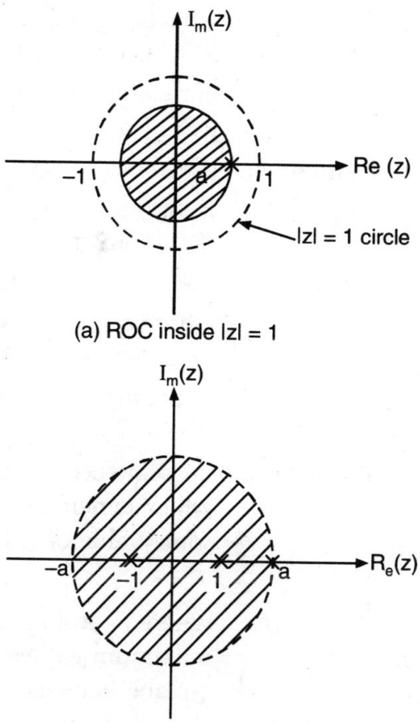

(a) ROC inside |z| = 1

(b) ROC extends upto |a| i.e. crosses |z| =1

Fig. 3.2. ROC for cases: (*a*) $|a| < 1$, (*b*) $|a| > 1$.

3.2.3 Properties of Region of Convergence (ROC)

The previous two examples show that

$$x_1(n) = a^n\, u(n) \text{ gives } X_1(z) = \frac{1}{1-az^{-1}},$$

$$\text{ROC: } |z| > |a|$$

and $\quad x_2(n) = -a^n\, u(-n-1)$ gives $X_2(z) = \dfrac{1}{1-az^{-1}}$, ROC: $|z| < |a|$.

It may be seen that two different signals $x_1(n)$ and $x_2(n)$ give the same *z*-transforms *i.e.*, $X_1(z) = X_2(z)$. However, these two *ZTs* have different ROCs. Thus, to find the inverse *ZT*, we must specify the ROC of the given $X(z)$ so as to determine a unique $x(n)$. Now, we study some important properties of ROCs:

Property 1: The region of convergence (ROC) does not contain any pole of $X(z)$.

Property 2: If $x(n)$ is a finite length sequence, *i.e.*, $x(n) = 0$ beyond some interval $N_1 \le n \le N_2$ (N_1, N_2 being finite), then $X(z)$ converges for all values of z, and ROC is the entire z-plane, *i.e.*, z can lie anywhere except, in some cases, $z = 0$ and $z = \infty$ does not form the ROC region.

[For example : a sequence $x_1(n) = \{\underset{\uparrow}{1}, 2, 3\}$ has $X_1(z) = 1 + 2z^{-1} + 3z^{-2}$ has a pole at $z = 0$. Or another sequence $x_2(n) = \{2, \underset{\uparrow}{1}, 3, 5\}$ has $X_2(z) = 2z + 1 + 3z^{-1} + 5z^{-2}$ has poles at $z = 0$ and $z = \infty$]

Property 3: If $x_1(n)$ is a right-sided sequence, *viz.*, $x_1(n) = 0$ for some $n < N_1 < \infty$, and if $X_1(z)$ converges for some value of z, then the ROC is of the form

$$|z| > r_{max} \quad \text{or} \quad \infty > |z| > r_{max}$$

where r_{max} is the largest magnitude out of all the poles of $X(z)$. Hence, in this case ROC is exterior to the circle $|z| = r_{max}$ in the z-plane.

For example, in Example 3.1, the sequence $x_1(n) = a^n\, u(n)$ was right-sided, and ROC was $|z| > |a|$ *i.e.*, the ROC was exterior to the circle $|z| = |a|$.

Property 4: (Dual of Property 3)

If $x_2(n)$ is a left-sided sequence, *viz.*, $x_2(n) = 0$ for some $n > N_2 > -\infty$, and its ZT $X_2(z)$ converges for some value of z, then the ROC is of the form

$$|z| < r_{min} \quad \text{or} \quad 0 < |z| < r_{min}$$

where r_{min} is the smallest magnitude out of all the poles of $X_2(z)$. Hence, in this case, the ROC is the interior of the circle $|z| = r_{min}$ in the z-plane.

In Example 3.2, the sequence $x_2(n) = -a^n\, u(-n-1)$ was a left-sided and the ROC was $|z| < |a|$.

Property 5: If a sequence $x(n)$ is a two-sided sequence *viz.*, $x(n)$ is an infinite-duration sequence which is neither right-sided nor left-side and its z-transform $X(z)$ converges for some value of z, then the ROC is of the form

$$r_1 < |z| < r_2$$

where r_1 and r_2 are the magnitudes of two poles of $X(z)$ giving minimum and maximum values of magnitudes. The ROC in this case is an annular ring in the z-plane between the circles $|z| = r_1$ and $|z| = r_2$ not containing any pole.

In Example 3.3(b) where $x(n) = \left(\frac{1}{3}\right)^n u(n) + \left(\frac{1}{2}\right)^n u(-n-1)$ is a two-sided sequence of infinite length. Here, ROC is an annular ring $\frac{1}{3} < |z| < \frac{1}{2}$.

Note Important. It is not necessary that the z-transform of all sequences must have finite ROC. In some sequences the series giving ZT of $x(n)$ never converges, hence, here $X(z)$ will have no ROC. See Example 3.3(c) to understand this statement.

EXAMPLE 3.3: *Find the z-transform X(z) and sketch the pole-zero plot with the ROC for the sequences*

(a) $x(n) = \left(\frac{1}{2}\right)^n u(n) + \left(\frac{1}{3}\right)^n u(n)$

(b) $x(n) = \left(\frac{1}{3}\right)^n u(n) + \left(\frac{1}{2}\right)^n u(-n-1)$

(c) $x(n) = \left(\frac{1}{2}\right)^n u(n) + \left(\frac{1}{3}\right)^n u(-n-1)$. *(GGSIP Univ. 2009)*

SOLUTION: We know that

$$\left(\frac{1}{2}\right)^n u(n) \xleftrightarrow{ZT} \frac{1}{1-\frac{1}{2}z^{-1}} = \frac{z}{z-\frac{1}{2}}, \qquad |z| > \frac{1}{2}$$

$$\left(\frac{1}{3}\right)^n u(n) \xleftrightarrow{ZT} \frac{1}{1-\frac{1}{3}z^{-1}} = \frac{z}{z-\frac{1}{3}}, \qquad |z| > \frac{1}{3}$$

and

$$\left(\frac{1}{3}\right)^n u(-n-1) \xleftrightarrow{ZT} -\frac{1}{1-\frac{1}{3}z^{-1}} = \frac{-z}{z-\frac{1}{3}}, \qquad |z| < \frac{1}{3}$$

(a) $ZT[x(n)] = \frac{z}{z-\frac{1}{2}} + \frac{z}{z-\frac{1}{3}}$,

ROC: $|z| > \frac{1}{2}$ and $|z| > \frac{1}{3}$, *i.e.*, $|z| > \frac{1}{2}$.

It exists as shown in (*a*).

(b) $ZT[x(n)] = \frac{z}{z-\frac{1}{3}}, \; |z| > \frac{1}{3}$

$-\frac{z}{z-\frac{1}{2}}, \; |z| < \frac{1}{2}$

$\therefore \quad \frac{1}{3} < |z| < \frac{1}{2}$ exists as shown in (*b*).

(c) $ZT[x(n)] = \frac{z}{z-\frac{1}{2}}, \; |z| > \frac{1}{2}$

$+\frac{-z}{z-\frac{1}{3}}, \; |z| < \frac{1}{3}$

As ROC: $|z| < \frac{1}{3}$ and $|z| > \frac{1}{2}$, these two conditions cannot be fulfilled together. Hence, no ROC exists in this case *i.e.*, we will have no *ZT* of $x(n)$.

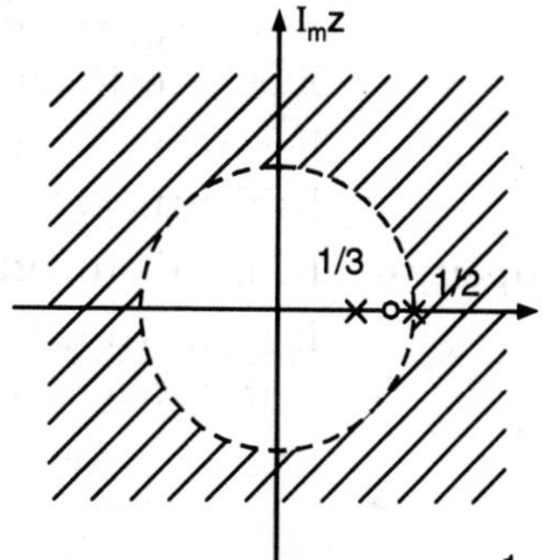

(a) ROC – Shaded area $|z| > \frac{1}{2}$

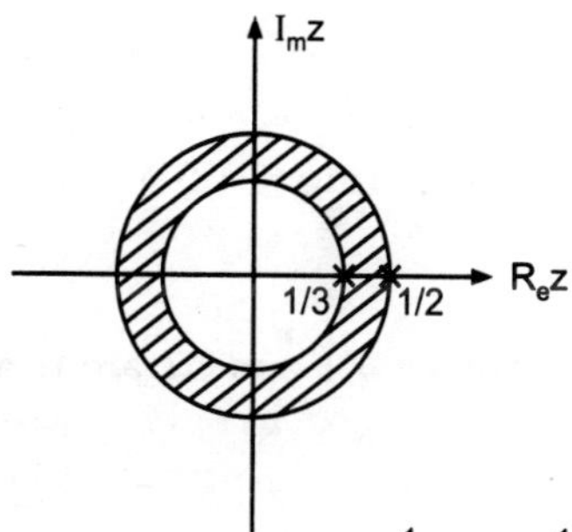

(b) ROC : Shaded area $\frac{1}{3} < |z| < \frac{1}{2}$

Fig. Ex. 3.3.

3.2.4 Relationship between the z-Transform and the Laplace Transform

A continuous signal $x_a(t)$ has its sampled version $x_a(nT)$, $n = 0, \pm 1, \pm 2, \ldots$,

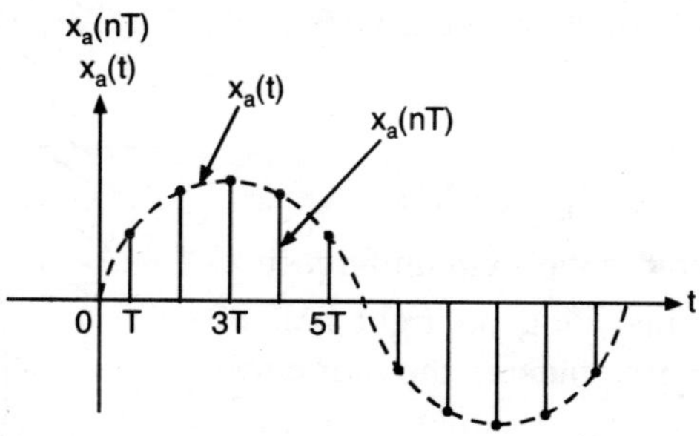

Fig. 3.3. (a) Showing $x_a(t)$ and its discrete samples $x_a(nT)$.

At any instant, say, $t = nT$, we can say that $x_a(nT)\,\delta(t - nT)$ is value of $x_a(t)$. Fully, sampled sequence is given by

$$x_a(t)\Big|_{sampled} = \sum_{n=-\infty}^{\infty} x_a(nT)\,\delta(t-nT) \qquad \ldots(3.11)$$

Laplace transform

$$\alpha\left[x_a(t)\Big|_{sampled}\right] = \alpha\left[\sum_{n=-\infty}^{\infty} x_a(nT)\,\delta(t-nT)\right]$$

$$= \sum_{n=-\infty}^{\infty} (x_a nT)\, L[\delta(t-nT)]$$

$$\therefore \quad L\left[x_a(t)\big|_{sampled} \right] \triangleq \bar{X}(s) = \sum_{n=-\infty}^{\infty} x_a(nT) e^{-snT} \qquad (\because \; LT \text{ of } \delta(t-nT) = e^{-nTs}) \qquad ...(3.12)$$

But ZT of $x(n)$ is given by

$$X(z) = \sum_{n=-\infty}^{\infty} x(n)\, .\, z^{-n} \qquad \text{(by definition of } ZT) \qquad ...(3.13)$$

Replacing $x(n)$ by $x_a(nT)$ in (3.13), we get

$$X(z) = \sum_{n=-\infty}^{\infty} x_a(nT)\, z^{-n} \qquad ...(3.14)$$

Comparing (3.12) and (3.14), we have

$$X(z) = ZT\,[x_a(nT)] \xrightarrow{z = e^{sT}} LT\left[x_a(t)\big|_{sampled} \right] \qquad ...(3.15)$$

Hence, ZT and LT are related by the relation given below

$$\boxed{z = e^{sT}} \qquad ...(3.16)$$

As
$$z = e^{sT}$$
$$= e^{(\sigma + j\omega)T} \qquad (\because \; s = \sigma + j\omega)$$
$$|z| = |e^{\sigma T}|\, .\, |e^{j\omega T}|$$
$$|z| = |e^{\sigma T}| \quad \because \; |e^{j\omega T}| = 1$$

When σ is –ve *i.e.*, point in left half of *s*-plane maps inside the unit circle $|z| = 1$, since, σ –ve gives $|e^{\sigma T}| < 1$.

When $s = j\omega$, $\sigma = 0$

then $|z| = |e^{(0 + j\omega)T}| = 1$

Thus, $j\omega$ axis maps on unit circle's circumference.

When σ is +ve, *i.e.*, points lying on right half of *s*-plane. These points map to area outside the unit circle $|z| = 1$.

Figure 3.3 (*b*) shows how LHS of *s*-plane (shaded area) maps inside the unit circle $|z| = 1$ in *z*-plane. The $j\omega$ axis in *s*-plane maps to the circumference of the unit circle. The RHS of *s*-plane (unshaded) maps outside the unit circle $|z| = 1$ of *z*-plane. Note that we have considered the *LT* of an analog signal $x(t)$ and the *ZT* of sampled version of the same signal. We shall consider in Chapter 7 the method of obtaining $x(nT)$ from $x(t)$ and the constraints on the choice of sampling period T such that $x(nT)$ and $x(t)$ contain the same information.

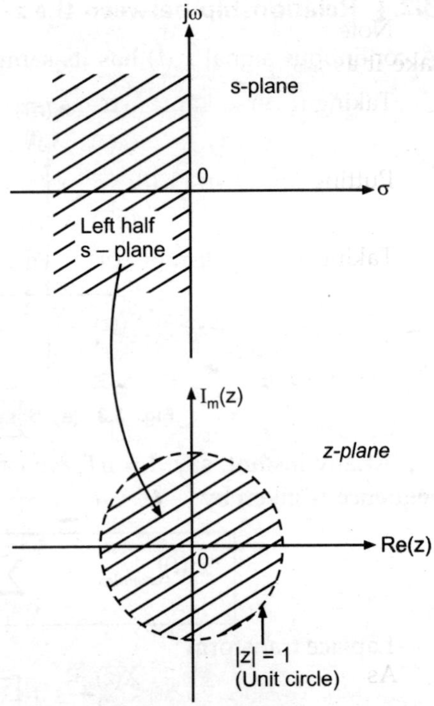

Fig. 3.3. (b) Mapping $Z = e^{sT}$.

3.2.5 Mapping of Samples of $x(t)$ *i.e.* of $x(nT)$

We are interested in knowing in what way the Laplace transform, $X(s)$, of an analog signal $x(t)$ maps its important points from s-plane when we take z-transform, $X(z)$, of sampled version $x(nT)$ of $x(t)$.

For simplicity, take an analog signal $x(t)$ such that its Laplace transform is

$$X(s) = \frac{A}{s+\alpha}, \quad A, \text{ constant} \qquad ...(3.17)$$

Then $X(s)$ has a pole at $s = -\alpha$.

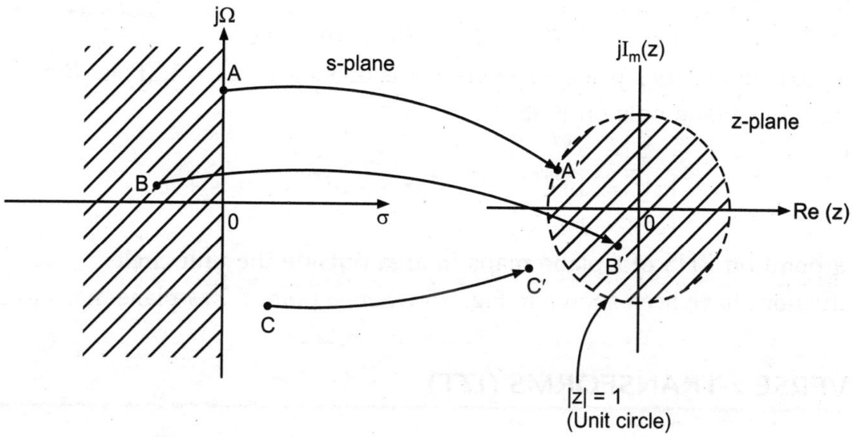

Fig. 3.4. (*i*) Points on LHP of s-plane map inside the unit circle (B maps to B').
(*ii*) Points on $j\Omega$ axis of s-plane map on the unit circle (A maps to A').
(*iii*) Points on RHS of $j\Omega$ axis of s-plane map outside the unit circle (C maps to C')

Note that it is customary to show the vertical axis of s-plane by $j\Omega$, though some authors also take it as $j\omega$.

Taking inverse Laplace transform of $X(s)$, (3.17) yields

$$x(t) = Ae^{-\alpha t}\, u(t) \qquad ...(3.18)$$

Putting $t = nT$ in (3.18) we obtain sampled version of $x(t)$ *i.e.*, $x(nT)$, given by

$$x(nT) = Ae^{-\alpha(nT)}\, u(nT) \qquad ...(3.19)$$

Taking z-transform of $x(nT)$, we get

$$X(z) = zT[x(nT)] = \sum_{n=-\infty}^{\infty} x(nT)\, z^{-n}$$

$$= \sum_{n=-\infty}^{\infty} [Ae^{-\alpha nT}\, u(nT)]\, z^{-n} \qquad \text{[Due to (3.19)]}$$

$$= \sum_{n=0}^{\infty} A\, [e^{(-\alpha T)}\, z^{-1}]^{n} \qquad (\because\ u(nT) = 0 \text{ for } n \text{ -ve})$$

$$= A\, \frac{1}{1 - e^{-\alpha T}\, z^{-1}}$$

As

$$X(z) = \frac{A}{1 - e^{-\alpha T}\, z^{-1}} \qquad ...(3.20)$$

$X(z)$ has a pole at $z = e^{-\alpha T}$

Hence, **A pole of $H(s)$ at $s = -\alpha$ maps to a pole of $H(z)$ at $z = e^{-\alpha T}$** ...(3.21)

To analyse, how a pole $s = -\alpha$ of $H(s)$ transforms in z-domain we consider the three possible situations.

(a) If $\alpha = 0$, then $z = e^{-(0)T} = 1$ or $|z| = 1$

i.e. a point on $j\Omega$ axis in s-plane maps to unit circle $|z| = 1$ in the z-plane. (Point A maps to point A')

(b) If α is +ve (s-plane pole on LHS)

Then
$$z = e^{-\alpha T}$$
$$|z| = |e^{-\alpha T}| < 1 \qquad \text{Since, } \alpha \text{ is +ve}$$

i.e., a point on LHS of s-plane maps inside the unit circle $|z| = 1$. (Point B maps to point B')

(c) If α is –ve (s-plane pole on RHS)

Then
$$z = e^{-\alpha T}$$
$$|z| = |e^{-\alpha T}| \qquad \because \alpha \text{ is –ve } \therefore -\alpha \text{ is +ve}$$

or
$$|z| > 1$$

i.e., a point on RHS of s-plane maps in area outside the unit circle.

Above situations have been shown in Fig. 3.5 where a point C in s-plane maps to C' in z-plane.

3.3 INVERSE z-TRANSFORMS (IZT)

In order to find inverse z-transform, we need a result from Cauchy's Theorem.

3.3.1 Cauchy's Theorem

It states that

$$\frac{1}{2\pi j}\oint_C z^{k-1}\,dz = \begin{cases} 1, & k = 0 \\ 0, & k \neq 0 \end{cases} = \delta(k) \qquad ...(3.22)$$

where C is counter-clockwise contour that encircles the origin.

As by definition,

$$X(z) = \sum_{n=-\infty}^{\infty} x(n)\, z^{-n} \qquad ...(3.23)$$

Multiply both sides of (3.22) by z^{k-1} and take integral with a counter-clockwise contour around the origin, such that the contour encloses the origin, and lies in the ROC of $X(z)$, we get

$$\frac{1}{2\pi j}\oint_C X(z)\, z^{k-1}\,dz = \frac{1}{2\pi j}\oint_C \sum_{n=-\infty}^{\infty} x(n)\, z^{-n} \,.\, z^{k-1}\,dz$$

$$= \sum_{n=-\infty}^{\infty} x(n) \,.\, \underbrace{\frac{1}{2\pi j}\oint_C z^{-n+k-1}\,dz}_{\substack{= 1 \text{ only when } -n+k=0 \\ i.e., \text{ for } n=k \text{ (Cauchy's theorem)} \\ i.e. = \delta(k-n)}}$$

$$= \sum_{n=-\infty}^{\infty} x(n) \,.\, \delta(k-n)$$

$$= x(k) \qquad ...(3.24)$$

Hence,

$$x(n) = \frac{1}{2\pi j} \oint_C X(z)\, z^{n-1}\, dz \quad \text{(Inverse ZT relation)}$$

where C is counterclockwise closed contour in the ROC of $X(z)$ encircling the origin of z-plane. ...(3.25a)

3.3.2 The Residue Theorem

If $f(z)$ is a single-valued function which is analytic inside a simply closed path C and on C, except for finitely many singular points $a_1, a_2, ..., a_m$ inside C then

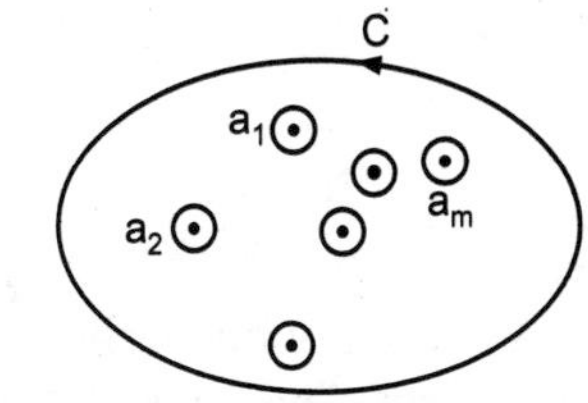

$$\frac{1}{2\pi j} \oint_C f(z)\, dz = \sum_{\substack{i=1 \\ Z = a_i}}^{m} \text{Residue } f(z) \qquad ...(3.25b)$$

i.e. the sum of residues of poles enclosed by the contour C.

We, in general, evaluate the integral on RHS of (3.25*a*) by using the Residue Theorem, as suggested in what follows:

By Residue theorem in complex variable, it can be shown that:

(*i*) If $f(z)$ has a pole at $z = a$ *i.e.* $f(z) \triangleq \Psi(z)/(z - a)$

then $$\operatorname*{Res}_{z=a} f(z) \triangleq \frac{1}{2\pi j} \oint_C f(z)\, dz = \Psi(a) \qquad ...(3.26a)$$

(*ii*) If $$f(z) = \frac{p(z)}{q(z)}, \quad \operatorname*{Res}_{z=a} f(z) = \frac{p(a)}{q'(a)}, \text{ where } q'(z) = \frac{d}{dz} q(z) \qquad ...(3.26b)$$

(*iii*) If $$f(z) = \frac{S(z)}{(z-a)T(z)}, \quad \operatorname*{Res}_{z=a} f(z) = \frac{S(a)}{T(a)} \qquad ...(3.26c)$$

(*iv*) If $$f(z) = \frac{\Psi(z)}{(z-a)^m}, \quad \operatorname*{Res}_{z=a} f(z) = \frac{1}{(m-1)!} \lim_{z \to a} \frac{d^{m-1}\, \Psi(z)}{dz^{m-1}} \qquad ...(3.26d)$$

(*v*) If $f(z)$ has no poles, then the residues of $f(z)$ are zero. ...(3.26*e*)

We find residues at each pole of $f(z)$ and then add them to obtain $\sum_{i=1}^{m}$ (Residue at $z = a_i$). This will give us LHS of (3.25*a*). For finding inverse ZT of $X(z)$ our function $f(z) = X(z)\,.\, z^{n-1}$.

3.4 PROPERTIES OF z-TRANSFORMS

We now give some properties of z-transforms, which will prove useful in solving various problems.

3.4.1 Linearity

If a and b are arbitrary constants and

if $$ZT[x_1(n)] = X_1(z), \quad \text{ROC: } R_1$$

$$ZT[x_2(n)] = X_2(z), \qquad \text{ROC: } R_2$$

then

$$ZT\,[ax_1(n) + bx_2(n)] = aX_1(z) + bX_2(z) \qquad ...(3.27)$$
$$R' = R_1 \cap R_2$$

Proof:

$$ZT[ax_1(n) + bx_2(n)] = \sum_{n=-\infty}^{\infty} [ax_1(n) + bx_2(n)]\, z^{-n} \quad \text{(by definition of } ZT\text{)}$$

$$= a \sum_{n=-\infty}^{\infty} x_1(n)\, z^{-n} + b \sum_{n=-\infty}^{\infty} x_2(n)\, z^{-n}$$

$$= aX_1(z) + bX_2(z) \qquad \text{Q.E.D.}$$

As mentioned earlier, ROC is an important parameter which we must specify with the z-transform. The revised ROC R' for the z-transform $[aX_1(z) + bX_2(z)]$ is the common ROC between $X_1(z)$'s ROC and $X_2(z)$'s ROC. We write this by

$$R' = R_1 \cap R_2 \qquad \text{(i.e., intersection of } R_1 \text{ and } R_2\text{)}$$

Various results of the properties are shown in Table 3.1 for ready reference.

3.4.2 Time Shifting

If $\quad x(n) \xleftrightarrow{ZT} X(z), \quad$ ROC: R

then $\quad x(n - n_0) \xleftrightarrow{ZT} z^{-n_0}X(z), \quad$ ROC: $R' = R \qquad ...(3.28)$

Proof: $\quad ZT[x(n - n_0)] = \sum_{n=-\infty}^{\infty} x(n - n_0)\, z^{-n} \qquad$ (by definition) $\quad ...(3.29)$

Put $n - n_0 = n'$ and $\therefore$ $n = n' + n_0$ on RHS of (3.29).

The limits of summation will be for $n' = -\infty$ to ∞

$$ZT\,[x(n - n_0)] = \sum_{n'=-\infty}^{\infty} x(n') \cdot z^{-(n' + n_0)}$$

$$= z^{-n_0} \sum_{n'=-\infty}^{\infty} x(n')\, z^{-n'}$$

$$\therefore \qquad x(n - n_0) \xleftrightarrow{ZT} z^{-n_0}\, X(z)$$

ROC R' for ZT of $x(n - n_0)$ will be the same as that of $X(z)$. However, in the new ROC R', origin may be added or deleted. For example, if $X(z) = b_2z^2 + b_1z + 1$.

Its ROC, R is the entire z-plane except $z = \infty$.

If $n_0 = 1$, say, then $ZT[x(n - 1)] = b_1z^1 + b_1z^0 + z^{-1}$.

This ZT has its value ∞ at $z = 0$. Hence, ROC R' for this ZT does not contain origin, as well as $z = \infty$. So, here origin has been deleted in the new ROC R'.

3.4.3 Scaling in z-Domain

If	$x(n)$	$\xleftrightarrow{ZT}$	$X(z)$, ROC: R
then	$z_0^n x(n)$	$\xleftrightarrow{ZT}$	$X(z/z_0)$, ROC: $R' = \lvert z_0 \rvert \cdot R$

...(3.30)

Proof:

$$ZT[z_0^n x(n)] = \sum_{n=-\infty}^{\infty} [z_0^n\, x(n)]\, z^{-n} = \sum_{n=-\infty}^{\infty} x(n)(z/z_0)^{-n}$$

$$\therefore \quad X_1(z) = ZT\left[z_0^n\, x(n)\right] = X(z/z_0) \qquad ...(3.31)$$

ROC of $X_1(z)$ is $R' = \lvert z_0 \rvert R$

Explanation. From (3.31), it is clear that any value of z of $X_1(z)$ is equivalent to z/z_0 of $X(z)$. It means that z_0 in $X_1(z)$ is equivalent to 1 of $X(z)$ or $\lvert z_0 \rvert R$ in $X_1(z)$ is equivalent to R of $X(z)$.

Hence, ROC: R of $X(z)$ is mapped to ROC: R' equalling $\lvert z_0 \rvert R$.

Versions of Scaling Factor z_0^n

z_0 can be purely phase function $e^{j\omega}$ or can be purely real equal to 'a' (+ve or –ve). In such cases, the scaling in z-domain yields, putting $z_0^n = e^{j\omega_0 n}$ or $z_0^n = a^n$, the following are the two more versions:

$e^{j\omega n}x(n)$	$\xleftrightarrow{ZT}$	$X(e^{-j\omega_0}z)$, ROC: $R' = R$
$a^n x(n)$	$\xleftrightarrow{ZT}$	$X(a^{-1}z)$, ROC: $R' = \lvert a \rvert R$

...(3.32)

3.4.4 Time Reversal

If	$x(n)$	$\xleftrightarrow{ZT}$	$X(z)$, ROC: R
then	$x(-n)$	$\xleftrightarrow{ZT}$	$X\left(\frac{1}{z}\right)$, ROC: $R' = \frac{1}{R}$

...(3.33)

Proof: $$ZT[x(-n)] = \sum_{n=-\infty}^{\infty} x(-n) \cdot z^{-n} \quad \text{(by definition)} \qquad ...(3.34)$$

Put $n = -n'$ in (3.34), the limits of n' will be $n' = +\infty$ to $n' = -\infty$. Summation being commutative, we get

$$ZT[x(-n)] = \sum_{n'=-\infty}^{\infty} x(n')\, z^{n'} = \sum_{n'=-\infty}^{\infty} x(n')\, (z^{-1})^{-n'}$$

$$\therefore \quad X_1(z) = X(z^{-1}) = X\left(\frac{1}{z}\right)$$

Clearly, ROC of $X_1(z)$ is R' such that $R' = \dfrac{1}{R}$

3.4.5(*a*) A Note on Interpolation and Decimation

(A) Interpolation $\left[x\left(\frac{n}{k}\right)\right]$

The concept of continuous-time scaling cannot be directly extended in discrete time, as in discrete-time the sequence is defined only at integer values of n. When there is no signal available we insert a zero. In Fig. 3.5, we assume $k = 3$ for explanation. To draw $x\left(\frac{n}{3}\right)$ in Fig. 3.5(*b*) whenever $\frac{n}{3}$ is an integer, such as for $n = 3$, $n/3 = 1$, we use sample $x(1)$ and draw at $n = 3$ for $x\left(\frac{n}{3}\right)$ signal [Fig. 3.5(*b*)]. At $n = 1, 2, 4, 5, ...$ of $x\left(\frac{n}{3}\right)$, we do not get an integer, so, we insert zero at $n = 1, 2, 4, 5, ...$ in Fig. (*b*). In general, we insert $(k - 1)$ zeroes in between samples in drawing sequence $x\left(\frac{n}{k}\right)$.

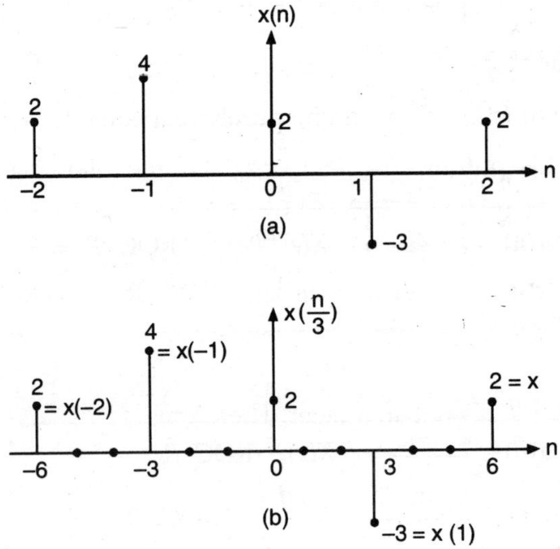

Fig. 3.5. (*a*) a sequence $x(n)$, (*b*) sequence $x\left(\frac{n}{k}\right)$ for $k = 3$ when $n/3$ is not an integer, insert zero.

This process is also called Interpolation and is the time expansion version in discrete-time domain. This type of signal transformation is often used in multirate digital signal processing.

(B) Decimation [$x(kn)$]

Here, we contract the time scale of $x(n)$ to obtain $x(kn)$.

If $k = 2$, say, then we can only choose sequence values $x(0)$, $x(2)$, $x(4)$, ..., $x(-2)$ etc. of $x(n)$ to be drawn as $x(2n)$ in Fig. 3.6(*b*). Here, half the samples of $x(n)$ are lost, when we choose $x(2n)$.

Decimation means to weaken. In general, $(k - 1)$ samples are lost when we obtain $x(kn)$ from $x(n)$. Fig. 3.6 shows $x(n)$ and $x(2n)$, *i.e.*, decimation for $k = 2$. We shall learn more on Interpolation and Decimation in Chapter 12.

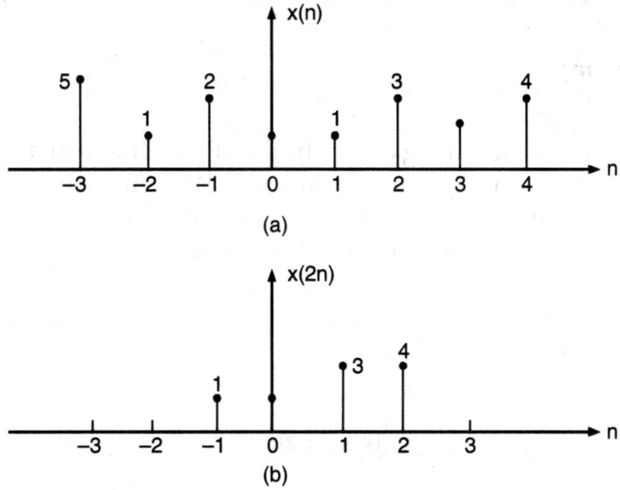

Fig. 3.6. Showing decimation, for $k = 2$.

3.4.5(*b*) Time Expansion

If	$x(n) \xleftrightarrow{ZT} X(z)$,	ROC: R
then	$x\left(\frac{n}{k}\right) \xleftrightarrow{ZT} X(z^k)$,	ROC: $R' = R^{1/k}$

...(3.35)

Proof:
$$ZT\left[x\left(\frac{n}{k}\right)\right] = \sum_{n=-\infty}^{\infty} x\left(\frac{n}{k}\right) z^{-n} \quad \text{(by definition)} \quad ...(3.36a)$$

But $x\left(\frac{n}{k}\right) = 0$ when $\left(\frac{n}{k}\right)$ is not an integer. Therefore, in RHS of (3.36*a*), $x\left(\frac{n}{k}\right)z^{-n}$ terms, when $\frac{n}{k}$ is not an integer, are zero. Hence are need n to vary only as a multiple of k *i.e.*,

$$ZT\left[x\left(\frac{n}{k}\right)\right] = \sum_{\substack{n=-\infty \\ n \text{ multiple of } k}}^{\infty} x\left(\frac{n}{k}\right) z^{-n} \quad \text{(Note this step)} \quad ...(3.36b)$$

Put $\frac{n}{k} = m$ in (3.36*b*), it gives m varying continuously from $-\infty$ to ∞ and we get

$$ZT\left[x\left(\frac{n}{k}\right)\right] = \sum_{\substack{m=-\infty \\ m \text{ integer}}}^{\infty} x(m)\, z^{-km} = \sum_{m=-\infty}^{\infty} x(m)(z^k)^{-m}$$

Hence, $\quad x_1(n) \xleftrightarrow{ZT} X_1(z) = X(z^k), \quad$ where $x_1(n) = x\left(\frac{n}{k}\right)$

If ROC of $X(z)$ is R, the ROC of $X(z^k)$ is $R' = R^{1/k}$

(Note that $X_1(z^{1/k}) = X(z)$, *i.e.*, a pole of $X(z)$ at $z = a$, gives a pole of X_1 at $a^{1/k}$. Hence, all points lying in R for $X(z)$ map to points in $R^{1/k}$)

3.4.6 Conjugation

If	$x(n) \xleftrightarrow{ZT} X(z)$, ROC: R	...(3.37)
then	$x^*(n) \xleftrightarrow{ZT} X^*(z^*)$, ROC: $R' = R$	

Proof:

$$ZT[x^*(n)] = \sum_{n=-\infty}^{\infty} x^*(n)z^{-n} \quad \text{(by definition)}$$

$$= \left[\sum_{n=-\infty}^{\infty} x(n)\,(z^*)^{-n}\right]^* \quad \text{(Note this step)}$$

$$= [X(z^*)]^*$$

$$\therefore \quad x^*(n) \xleftrightarrow{ZT} X^*(z^*)$$

ROC of $X(z)$ is R (given)

$\therefore$ ROC of $X(z^*)$ is also R (a pole at $z = a$ also means a pole at z^*)

Hence, ROC of $X^*(z^*)$ is also R

Note that at a pole point, the magnitude of that function is infinite. Conjugation has no effect on the magnitude. So, if $z = a$ is a pole point, then $z = a^*$, is also a pole for that function. When we talk of a region R then region R^* is the same as the region R.

3.4.7 Convolution (Real Convolution)

If	$x_1(n) \xleftrightarrow{ZT} X_1(z)$, ROC: R_1	
	$x_2(n) \xleftrightarrow{ZT} X_2(z)$, ROC: R_2	...(3.38)
then	$x_1(n) * x_2(n) \xleftrightarrow{ZT} X_1(z) \cdot X_2(z)$, ROC: $R' = R_1 \cap R_2$	

Proof:

$$ZT[x_1(n) * x_2(n)] = \sum_{n=-\infty}^{\infty} [x_1(n) * x_2(n)] \cdot z^{-n} \quad \text{(by definition)}$$

$$= \sum_{n=-\infty}^{\infty} \left[\sum_{k=-\infty}^{\infty} x_1(k) \cdot x_2(n-k)\right] \cdot z^{-n} \quad \text{(using definition of convolution)}$$

$$= \sum_{k=-\infty}^{\infty} x_1(k) \sum_{n=-\infty}^{\infty} x_2(n-k)\, z^{-n} \quad \text{(by change of summation order)}$$

$$= \sum_{k=-\infty}^{\infty} x_1(k) \cdot z^{-k} \underbrace{\sum_{n=-\infty}^{\infty} x_2(n-k)\, z^{-(n-k)}}_{=X_2(z)} \quad \text{(Note this step)}$$

$$= X_2(z) \underbrace{\sum_{k=-\infty}^{\infty} x_1(k) \cdot z^{-k}}_{=X_1(z)}$$

$$\therefore \quad ZT[x_1(n) * x_2(n)] = X_1(z) \cdot X_2(z)$$

ROC of $X_1(z) \cdot X_2(z)$ must be common to both ROC's R_1 and R_2.

$\therefore$ ROC of $X_1(z) \cdot X_2(z) = R_1 \cap R_2$ (intersection of R_1 and R_2)

Note: This is the case of real convolution. We shall also explain complex convolution, in the next section.

3.4.8 First Difference

$$\text{If} \quad x(n) \xleftrightarrow{ZT} X(z), \quad \text{ROC: } R$$
$$\text{then} \quad x(n) - x(n-1) \xleftrightarrow{ZT} (1 - z^{-1})\, X(z), \quad \text{ROC: } R' = R \cap \{|z| > 0\} \qquad ...(3.39)$$

Proof: We know that

$$x(n) \xleftrightarrow{ZT} X(z), \quad \text{ROC: } R$$
$$x(n-1) \xleftrightarrow{ZT} z^{-1}X(z) \qquad \text{(using time shifting here, } n_0 = 1)$$

The function $z^{-1}X(z)$ has one additional pole at $|z| = 0$, besides all the poles of $X(z)$. Therefore, ROC of $z^{-1}X(z)$ must exclude $|z| = 0$ from R. As z^{-1} converges for $|z| > 0$. Hence,

$$\text{ROC of } z^{-1}X(z) = R \cap \{|z| > 0\}$$
$$ZT\,[x(n) - x(n-1)] = X(z) - z^{-1}X(z)$$
$$\therefore \quad x(n) - x(n-1) \xleftrightarrow{ZT} (1 - z^{-1})\, X(z)$$

and its ROC $= R' = R \cap \{|z| > 0\}$

3.4.9 Accumulation

$$\text{If} \quad x(n) \xleftrightarrow{ZT} X(z), \quad \text{ROC: } R$$
$$\text{then} \quad \sum_{k=-\infty}^{n} x(k) \xleftrightarrow{ZT} \frac{1}{1 - z^{-1}}\, X(z), \quad \text{ROC: } R' = R \cap \{|z| > 1\} \qquad ...(3.40)$$

Proof:

$$\sum_{k=-\infty}^{n} x(k) = \sum_{k=-\infty}^{\infty} x(k) \cdot u(n-k)$$

$\because$ $u(n-k) = 0$ for $k > n$ (Note this step)

$$= x(n) * u(n) \qquad \text{(definition of convolution)}$$

$$\therefore \quad ZT\left[\sum_{k=-\infty}^{n} x(k)\right] = ZT[x(n) * u(n)]$$
$$= X(z) \cdot U(z)$$

(where $U(z) = ZT$ of $u(n)$ and we use convolution theorem)

$$= X(z) \cdot \frac{1}{1 - z^{-1}}$$

$$\text{ROC of } X(z) = R$$
$$\text{ROC of } \frac{1}{1 - z^{-1}} = |z| > 1$$

Hence, intersection of above two ROCs gives overall ROC

$$R' = R \cap \{|z| > 1\}$$

3.4.10 Differentiation in z-Domain

If	$x(n)$	$\xleftrightarrow{ZT}$	$X(z)$,	ROC: R
then	$nx(n)$	$\xleftrightarrow{ZT}$	$-z\dfrac{dX(z)}{dz}$,	ROC: $R' = R$ ...(3.41)

Proof: As
$$X(z) = \sum_{n=-\infty}^{\infty} x(n)\, z^{-n} \quad \text{(by definition)} \quad ...(A)$$

Differentiate both the sides of (A) w.r.t. z

$$\therefore \quad \frac{dX(z)}{dz} = \frac{d}{dz}\left[\sum_{n=-\infty}^{\infty} x(n)\, z^{-n}\right]$$

$$= \sum_{n=-\infty}^{\infty} x(n)\, \frac{d}{dz}(z^{-n})$$

(Take differentiation inside the summation sign)

$$= \sum_{n=-\infty}^{\infty} x(n)(-n)\, z^{-n-1}$$

$$= -z^{-1} \sum_{n=-\infty}^{\infty} [nx(n)]\, z^{-n}$$

$$\therefore \quad -z\frac{dX(z)}{dz} = \sum_{n=-\infty}^{\infty} [nx(n)]\, z^{-n} \quad \text{[Standard form of } ZT \text{ function } nx(n)]$$

i.e.,
$$nx(n) \xleftrightarrow{ZT} -z\frac{dX(z)}{dz}$$

If ROC of $X(z)$ is R

then ROC of $\left(-z\dfrac{dX(z)}{dz}\right)$ will also be R.

3.4.11 Initial Value Theorem

For a causal sequence $x(n)$, $\quad x(0) = \lim_{z\to\infty} X(z)$ ...(3.42)

This helps us to find initial value $x(0)$ directly from ZT of $x(n)$

Proof:
$$X(z) = \sum_{n=-\infty}^{\infty} x(n)\, z^{-n} \quad \text{(by definition)}$$

$$= \sum_{n=0}^{\infty} x(n)\, z^{-n} \quad [x(n) \text{ being causal}]$$

$$X(z) = x(0) + x(1)\, z^{-1} + x(2)\, z^{-2} + ... \quad ...(3.43)$$

Take limits on both the sides of (3.43) for $z \to \infty$

$$\therefore \quad \lim_{z\to\infty} X(z) = x(0) \quad \text{(as other terms canceled)}$$

3.4.12 Final Value Theorem

For a causal $x(n)$, $x(\infty) = \lim_{n \to \infty} x(n) = \lim_{z \to 1} (1 - z^{-1}) X(z)$ ...(3.44)

Proof: $x(n) - x(n-1) \xleftrightarrow{ZT} (1 - z^{-1})X(z)$ (the first differences property)

$$\therefore \quad \sum_{n=0}^{\infty} [x(n) - x(n-1)] z^{-n} = (1 - z^{-1}) X(z) \qquad ...(3.45)$$

Let $z \to 1$, then LHS of (3.45) can be written as

$$\lim_{z \to 1} \sum_{n=0}^{\infty} [x(n) - x(n-1)]z^{-n} = \lim_{m \to \infty} \sum_{n=0}^{m} [x(n) - x(n-1)]$$

$$= \lim_{m \to \infty} \big[(x(m) - x(m-1)) + (x(m-1) - x(m-2)) + ...$$

$$+ (x(1) - x(0)) + (x(0) - x(-1))\big]$$

$$= x(\infty) \qquad \because \; x(-1) = 0, \text{ as } x(n) \text{ is causal}$$

Hence, $x(\infty) = \lim_{n \to \infty} x(n) = \lim_{z \to 1} (1 - z^{-1}) X(z)$

EXAMPLE 3.4: *If $X(z) = 1 + 2z^{-1} + z^{-2}$, determine the initial and final values of the corresponding sequence, $x(n)$.*

SOLUTION: By Initial Value Theorem:

$$x(0) = \lim_{z \to \infty} [X(z)]$$

$$= \lim_{z \to \infty} [1 + 2z^{-1} + z^{-2}] = 1 \qquad \textbf{Ans.}$$

By Final Value Theorem:

$$x(\infty) = \lim_{z \to 1} [(1 - z^{-1}) X(z)]$$

$$\therefore \quad x(\infty) = \lim_{z \to 1} [(1 - z^{-1})(1 + 2z^{-1} + z^{-2})]$$

$$= \lim_{z \to 1} [1 + z^{-1} - z^{-2} - z^{-3}]$$

$$= 1 + 1 - 1 - 1 = 0 \quad \therefore \quad x(\infty) = 0 \qquad \textbf{Ans.}$$

Note. The above results can be confirmed by inspection.

The initial value is the coefficient of z^0, which is 1. The final value is the coefficient of z^{∞}, which is obviously 0 in the given $X(z)$.

EXAMPLE 3.5: *Determine the initial and final values of the discrete-time signal $x(n)$ having its z-transform $X(z) = 3 + 5z^{-1} + 7z^{-2}$.*

SOLUTION:

We know that $x(0) = \lim_{z \to \infty} X(z)$

$$= \lim_{z \to \infty} \left[3 + 5z^{-1} + 7z^{-2}\right] = 3 \qquad \textbf{Ans.}$$

Final value is $x(\infty) = \lim_{z \to 1} (1 - z^{-1}) X(z) = \lim_{z \to 1} (1 - z^{-1})(3 + 5z^{-1} + 7z^{-2}) \quad \because \; z^{-1}\big|_{z=1} = 1$

$$= \lim_{z \to 1} \left[3 + 2z^{-1} + 2z^{-2} - 7z^{-3}\right] = 0 \qquad \textbf{Ans.}$$

3.5 COMPLEX CONVOLUTION

The inverse z-transform of a product of z-transforms can be formed by using the real convolution in time domain. By the same analogy, the z-transform of a product of two time-domain functions can be formed by using the complex convolution.

Theorem : Complex Convolution Theorem

If
$$ZT[f(n)] \triangleq F(z) = \sum_{n=-\infty}^{\infty} f(n)\, z^{-n}$$

$$ZT[g(n)] \triangleq G(z) = \sum_{n=-\infty}^{\infty} g(n)\, z^{-n}$$

If
$$y(n) = f(n) \cdot g(n)$$

then
$$Y(z) = ZT[y(n)] = \frac{1}{2\pi j} \oint_{C_1} F(v)\, G\left(\frac{z}{v}\right) v^{-1} dv$$

$$= \frac{1}{2\pi j} \oint_{C_2} F\left(\frac{z}{v}\right) G(v)\, v^{-1} dv \qquad ...(3.46)$$

where C_1 and C_2 are the contours in common convergence regions of $F(v)$ and $G(z/v)$ $\left(\text{or } F\left(\frac{z}{v}\right) \text{ and } G(v)\right)$, respectively.

Proof:

$$Y(z) = ZT[y(n)] = ZT[f(n) \cdot g(n)]$$

$$= \sum_{n=-\infty}^{\infty} \left(f(n) \cdot g(n)\right) z^{-n}$$

$$= \sum_{n=-\infty}^{\infty} f(n) \left[\frac{1}{2\pi j} \oint_{C_2} G(v)\, v^{n-1}\, dv\right] \cdot z^{-n}$$

$$= \frac{1}{2\pi j} \oint_{C_2} \left[\sum_{n=-\infty}^{\infty} f(n) \left(\frac{z}{v}\right)^{-n}\right] G(v)\, v^{-1}\, dv$$

$$\therefore \quad ZT[f(n) \cdot g(n)] = \frac{1}{2\pi j} \oint_{C_2} F\left(\frac{z}{v}\right) G(v) \cdot v^{-1}\, dv \qquad ...(3.47a)$$

Similarly, we can show that

$$ZT[f(n) \cdot g(n)] = Y(z) = \frac{1}{2\pi j} \oint_{C_1} F(v)\; G\left(\frac{z}{v}\right) v^{-1}\, dv \qquad ...(3.47b)$$

Parseval's Relation

where C_1 is in the ROC of common ROC's between $F(z)$ and $G\left(\frac{z}{v}\right)$.

Note that if C_1 is a circle in the ROC and if

$$v = \rho e^{j\theta},\ z = re^{j\omega} \quad \therefore \quad dv = \rho je^{j\theta}d\theta = jvd\theta$$

Putting these values in (3.47*b*), we get

$$Y(re^{j\omega}) = \frac{1}{2\pi j}\int_0^{2\pi} F(\rho e^{j\theta})\cdot G\left(\frac{r}{\rho}e^{j(\omega-\theta)}\right)v^{-1}(jvd\theta)$$

$$= \frac{1}{2\pi}\int_0^{2\pi} F(\rho e^{j\theta})\cdot G\left(\frac{r}{\rho}e^{j(\omega-\theta)}\right)d\theta \qquad ...(3.48)$$

which is recognized as a convolution integral. Note that if $\rho = r = 1$, then (3.48) reduces to (2.77).

3.6 ONE-SIDED z-TRANSFORM (UNILATERAL z-TRANSFORM)

As explained in Section 3.2, we have two versions of z-transforms. Two-sided z-transform which is more popular and useful has been dealt with so far. We have explained its properties. We shall see that some properties of unilateral z-transform will be different from those of the bilateral z-transform. We define unilateral *i.e.*, one sided z-transform by

$$\text{Unilateral } ZT[x(n)] \text{ or } Z_1[x(n)] \triangleq \sum_{n=0}^{\infty} x(n)\,z^{-n} \equiv \tilde{X}(z) \qquad ...(3.49)$$

Note that when $x(n) = 0$, $n < 0$, *i.e.*, $x(n)$ is a causal sequence

then $$X(z) = \tilde{X}(z),\ x(n) \text{ causal} \qquad ...(3.50)$$

We now develop the properties of unilateral z-transform.

3.6.1 Linearity

$$Z_1[ax_1(n) + bx_2(n)] = az_1[x_1(n)] + bz_1[x_2(n)]$$

$$= a\tilde{X}_1(z) + b\tilde{X}_2(z)$$

The proof is trivial.

3.6.2 Translation

If $$x(n) \overset{Z_1}{\longleftrightarrow} \tilde{X}(z)$$

then $$x(n+m) \overset{Z_1}{\longleftrightarrow} z^m\left[\tilde{X}(z) - \sum_{k=0}^{m-1} x(k)z^{-k}\right],\ m \geq 0 \qquad ...(3.51)$$

$$x(n-m) \overset{Z_1}{\longleftrightarrow} z^{-m}\left[\tilde{X}(z) + \sum_{k=1}^{m} x(-k)z^{k}\right],\ m \geq 0$$

Proof:

(*i*) **Signal $x(n + m)$, $m \geq 0$**

$$Z_1[x(n+m)] = \sum_{n=0}^{\infty} x(n+m)\,z^{-n} \qquad \text{(by definition of one sided } ZT)$$

Put $n + m = n'$, limits of summation will be $n' = m$ to ∞

$$\therefore \quad Z_1[x(n+m)] = \sum_{n'=m}^{\infty} x(n')\, z^{-(n'-m)}$$

$$= z^m \left[\sum_{n'=m}^{\infty} x(n')\, z^{-n'} \right]$$

$$= z^m \left[\sum_{n'=0}^{\infty} x(n')\, z^{-n'} - \sum_{n'=0}^{m-1} x(n')\, z^{-n'} \right]$$

$$= z^m \left[\tilde{X}(z) - \sum_{k=0}^{m-1} x(k)\, z^{-k} \right] \qquad \text{...(A)}$$

(*ii*) **Signal $x(n - m)$, $m \geq 0$**

$$Z_1[x(n-m)] = \sum_{n=0}^{\infty} x(n-m)\, z^{-n} \qquad \text{(by definition of one sided } ZT\text{)}$$

Putting $n - m = n'$, the limits of summation will be

$$n' = -m \text{ to } \infty$$

$$\therefore \quad Z_1[x(n-m)] = \sum_{n'=-m}^{\infty} x(n')\, z^{-(n'+m)}$$

i.e.

$$Z_1[x(n-m)] = z^{-m} \left[\sum_{n'=-m}^{\infty} x(n')\, z^{-n'} \right]$$

$$= z^{-m} \left[\sum_{n'=0}^{\infty} x(n')\, z^{-n} + \sum_{n'=-m}^{-1} x(n')\, z^{-n'} \right]$$

Putting $n' = -k$ in the second term in the bracket on RHS, we get

$$Z_1[x(n-m)] = z^{-m} \left[\tilde{X}(z) + \sum_{k=1}^{m} x(-k)\, z^{k} \right] \qquad \text{(as expected)} \qquad \text{...(B)}$$

Note that if $x(n)$ is a causal sequence then second term on RHS of above expression is zero, and (*B*) reduces to

$$Z_1[x(n-m)] = z^{-m}\, \tilde{X}(z), \; x(n) \text{ causal} \qquad \text{...(C)}$$

For example:

$$ZT \text{ of } x(n-1) = z^{-1}\, \tilde{X}(z) + z^0 x(-1)$$

$$ZT \text{ of } x(n-2) = z^{-2}\, \tilde{X}(z) + z^{-1}\, x(-1) + z^0 x(-2)$$

$$ZT \text{ of } x(n-3) = z^{-3}\, \tilde{X}(z) + z^{-2}\, x(-1) + z^{-1}\, x(-2) + z^0 x(-3)$$

i.e.,

$$ZT[x(n-m)] = z^{-m}\, \tilde{X}(z) + \sum_{k=1}^{m} x(-k) z^{-m+k}$$

For $m = 3$, we get

$$Z_1[x(n-3)] = z^{-3}\,\tilde{X}(z) + \sum_{k=1}^{3} x(-k)z^{-3+k}$$

$$= z^{-3}\,\tilde{X}(z) + x(-2)\,z^{-1} + x(-2)\,z^{-1} + x(-3)z^{0}$$

3.6.3 Complex Scale Change (Same Result as in General ZT Case)

$$\boxed{Z_1[\omega^{-n}\,x(n)] = \tilde{X}(\omega z)} \qquad \text{...(3.52)}$$

Proof:

$$Z_1[\omega^{-n}\,x(n)] = \sum_{n=0}^{\infty} \omega^{-n}\,x(n)\,(\omega z)^{-n} \qquad \text{(by definition)}$$

$$= \sum_{n=0}^{\infty} x(n)\,(\omega z)^{-n}$$

$$= \tilde{X}(\omega z)$$

3.6.4 Complex Differentiation (Same Result as in General ZT Case)

$$\boxed{Z_1[n\,x(n)] = -z\frac{d\tilde{X}(z)}{dz}} \qquad \text{...(3.53)}$$

Proof:

$$Z_1[n\,x(n)] = \sum_{n=0}^{\infty} n\,x(n)\,z^{-n} \qquad \text{(by definition)}$$

$$= -z\sum_{n=0}^{\infty} x(n)\cdot(-n)\,z^{-n-1}$$

$$= -z\sum_{n=0}^{\infty} x(n)\frac{dz^{-n}}{dz} \qquad \text{(Note this step)}$$

$$= -z\frac{d}{dz}\sum_{n=0}^{\infty} x(n)\,z^{-n} \qquad \text{(interchanging summation and differentiation order)}$$

$$= -z\frac{d}{dz}\tilde{X}(z)$$

3.6.5 Real Convolution [Same Result as in General (Bidirectional) z-Transform]

$$\boxed{Z_1\left[\sum_{k=0}^{\infty} x(k)\,y(n-k)\right] = Z_1\left[\sum_{k=0}^{\infty} x(n-k)\,y(k)\right] = \tilde{X}(z)\,\tilde{Y}(z) \quad \text{if } x(n) \text{ and } y(n) \text{ are causal sequences}} \qquad \text{...(3.54)}$$

Proof:

$$Z_1\left[\sum_{k=0}^{\infty} x(k)\,y(n-k)\right] = \sum_{n=0}^{\infty}\left[\sum_{k=0}^{\infty} x(k)\,y(n-k)\right]z^{-n} \qquad \text{[for } x(n) \text{ and } y(n) \text{ causal]}$$

$$= \sum_{k=0}^{\infty} x(k) \cdot z^{-k} \sum_{n=0}^{\infty} y(n-k)\, z^{-(n-k)}$$

Put $n - k = n'$
$$= \sum_{k=0}^{\infty} x(k)\, z^{-k} \sum_{n'=-k}^{\infty} y(n')\, z^{-n'}$$

$$= \sum_{k=0}^{\infty} x(k) \cdot z^{-k} \sum_{n'=0}^{\infty} y(n')\, z^{-n}$$

[$\because$ $y(n) = 0$ for $n < 0$, since, $y(n)$ is causal]

$$= \sum_{k=0}^{\infty} x(k)\, z^{-k}\, \tilde{Y}(z) = \tilde{Y}(z) \sum_{k=0}^{\infty} x(k)\, z^{-k}$$

$$= \tilde{Y}(z) \cdot \tilde{X}(z) = \tilde{X}(z) \cdot \tilde{Y}(z)$$

So, it may be seen that the property of Time-shifting (also called Translation) is slightly different from that in two-sided ZT. However, when the signals are causal (as is usually true in most of the practical situations), the properties given in Table 3.1 for two-sided ZT can be used without any error.

3.7 PERIODIC SEQUENCE AND z-TRANSFORM

If $x_p(n)$ is a periodic sequence and repeats every N samples and if $ZT[x(n)] = X(z)$, where $x(n) = x_p(n)$ over the one period and ROC of $X(z)$ is R, then $x_p(n)$ z-transforms to

$$X_p(z) = X(z)\left[\frac{z^N}{z^N - 1}\right], \text{ROC; } R' = R \qquad \text{...(3.55)}$$

Proof.

Let $x_p(n)$ be a given periodic sequence with one period $x(n)$

Then
$$X(z) = \sum_{n=0}^{N-1} x(n)\, z^{-n}$$
{assuming $x_p(n)$ and $x(n)$ causal sequences]

Clearly, $x(n) = x_p(n)\,[u(n) - u(n-N)]$ (Note this step)

Take ZT on both the sides in the above equation

$$X(z) = ZT[u(n) \cdot x_p(n)] - ZT\,[\underbrace{x_p(n) \cdot u(n-N)}_{=x_p(n-N) \text{ being periodic}}]$$

$$= X_p(z) - z^{-N} X_p(z) = X_p(z)\left[1 - z^{-N}\right]$$

$$\therefore \quad X_p(z) = X(z)\frac{1}{1 - z^{-N}}$$

i.e., $X_p(z)$
$$= X(z)\left[\frac{z^N}{z^N - 1}\right] = X(z)\frac{1}{1 - z^{-N}} \qquad \text{...(3.55a)}$$

We shall use these results to retrieve the signal $x_p(n)$ when we do Discrete Fourier Transform (DFT). Some additional results concerning z-transform are given in Table 3.2.

Table 3.1 Properties of z-Transforms

S.No.	Property	Signal	z-Transform	ROC
		$x(n)$	$X(z)$	R
		$x_1(n)$	$X_1(z)$	R_1
		$x_2(n)$	$X_2(z)$	R_2
1.	Linearity (3.27)	$ax_1(n) + bx_2(n)$	$aX_1(z) + bX_2(z)$	$R' = R_1 \cap R_2$ (intersection of R_1 and R_2)
2.	Time shifting (3.28)	$x(n - n_0)$	$z^{-n_0}X(z)$	$R' = R$ (origin may be added or deleted)
3.	Scaling in z-domain	$e^{j\omega_0 n}\, x(n)$	$X(e^{-j\omega_0} z)$	$R' = R$
	(3.30) to (3.32)	$z_0^n\, x(n)$	$X(z/z_0)$	$R' = \|z_0\| R$
		$a^n\, x(n)$, a real	$X(a^{-1} z)$	$R' = \|a\| R$
4.	Time reversal (3.33)	$x(-n)$	$X\left(\frac{1}{z}\right)$	$R' = \frac{1}{R}$
5.	Time expansion (3.35)	$X\left(\frac{n}{k}\right) = \begin{cases} x(r), & n = rk \\ 0, & \frac{n}{k} \text{ not integer} \end{cases}$	$X(z^k)$	$R' = R^{1/k}$
6.	Conjugation (3.37)	$x^*(n)$	$X^*(z^*)$	$R' = R$
7.	Convolution (3.38)	$x_1(n) * x_2(n)$	$X_1(z) \cdot X_2(z)$	$R' = R_1 \cap R_2$ (intersection of R_1 and R_2)
8.	First difference (3.39)	$x(n) - x(n - 1)$	$(1 - z^{-1})\, X(z)$	$R' = R \cap \{\|z\| > 0\}$
9.	Accumulation (3.40)	$\sum_{k=-\infty}^{n} x(k)$	$\frac{1}{1 - z^{-1}} X(z)$	$R' = R \cap \{\|z\| > 1\}$
10.	Differentiation in the z-domain (3.41)	$n\, x(n)$	$-z\frac{dX(z)}{dz}$	$R' = R$

Table 3.2 Some Additional Results in z-Transforms

1. **Initial value theorem (3.42):** For a causal sequence $x(n)$, $x(0) = \lim_{z\to\infty} X(z)$

2. **Final value theorem (3.44):** For a causal sequence $x(n)$, if its final value exists, then $x(\infty) = \lim_{z\to 1} (1-z^{-1})\,X(z)$

3. **Complex convolution (3.46):** If $y(n) = f(n) \cdot g(n)$, then

$$Y(Z) = \left.\begin{array}{l} \dfrac{1}{2\pi j}\oint_C F\left(\dfrac{z}{v}\right)\cdot G(v)\cdot v^{-1}dv \\ \dfrac{1}{2\pi j}\oint_C F(v)\cdot G\left(\dfrac{z}{v}\right)\cdot v^{-1}dv \end{array}\right\} \text{called complex convolution of } F(z) \text{ and } G(z)$$

4. **One sided z-transform (3.49) to (3.54):** When $x(n)$ is causal, one-sided (unilateral ZT) of $x(n)$ is defined as

$$\tilde{X}(z) = \sum_{n=0}^{\infty} x(n)\, z^{-n} \qquad \text{(definition)}$$

The properties of linearity, scaling in z-domain, differentiation in z-domain, Convolution: ($x_1(n) * x_2(n)$), first difference hold good as for two-sided (bilateral) ZT. But Time-shifting is a bit different

If $\tilde{Z}[x(n)] = \tilde{X}(z)$, then
$$\tilde{Z}[x(n-m)] = z^{-m}\left[\tilde{X}(z) + \sum_{k=1}^{m} x(-k)\, z^{k}\right],\ m \ge 0 \qquad ...(3.51)$$

$$\tilde{Z}[x(n+m)] = z^{m}\left[\tilde{X}(z) - \sum_{k=0}^{m-1} x(k)\, z^{-k}\right],\ m \ge 0$$

5. **Periodic sequence (3.55):** If $x_p(n)$ is a periodic discrete sequence with period N and $x(n) = x_p(n)$ for $n = 0$ to $N - 1$, with ZT, $X(z)$, then

$$X_p(z) = ZT[x_p(n)] = \frac{1}{1-z^{-N}}\, X(z), \qquad ...(3.55)$$

where $x(n) \xleftrightarrow{ZT} X(z)$, ROC : R, then ROC of $X_p(z) = R' = R$

3.8 DERIVATION OF z-TRANSFORMS OF STANDARD SIGNALS

We are now ready to find z-transforms of various signals. All the results are compiled in Table 3.3, given after the derivations.

3.8.1 *ZT* of *x*(*n*)

$$ZT[x(n)] = X(z) = \sum_{n=-\infty}^{\infty} x(n)\, z^{-n} \qquad \text{(by definition)}$$

3.8.2 ZT of $x(n) = \delta(n)$

$$\delta(n) \xleftrightarrow{ZT} \sum_{n=-\infty}^{\infty} \delta(n)\, z^{-n}$$

$$= 1 \cdot z^0 \qquad [\because \delta(n) = 1 \text{ only for } n = 0]$$

$$\therefore \quad ZT[\delta(n)] = 1, \text{ ROC: all } z \qquad \text{...(3.56)}$$

3.8.3 ZT of $x(n) = u(n)$

$$ZT[u(n)] = \sum_{n=-\infty}^{\infty} u(n)\, z^{-n}$$

$$= \sum_{n=0}^{\infty} z^{-n} \qquad [\because u(n) = 1 \text{ for } n \geq 0 \text{ and } u(n) = 0 \text{ for } n < 0]$$

$$= \frac{1}{1-z^{-1}} \qquad \text{Provided } |z^{-1}| < 1 \text{ i.e. } |z| > 1$$

$$\therefore \quad ZT[u(n)] = \frac{1}{1-z^{-1}}, \text{ ROC } |z| > 1 \qquad \text{...(3.57)}$$

3.8.4 ZT of $x(n) = u(n - m)$

$$ZT[u(n-m)] = \sum_{n=-\infty}^{\infty} u(n-m)\, z^{-n} \qquad \text{(by definition)}$$

Put $n - m = n'$ $\quad\therefore$ limits of summation become $n' = -\infty$ to ∞

$$\therefore \quad ZT[u(n-m)] = \sum_{n'=-\infty}^{\infty} u(n')\, z^{-(n'+m)}$$

$$= z^{-m} \sum_{n'=-\infty}^{\infty} u(n')\, z^{-n'}$$

$$= z^{-m}\, U(z) : \text{ROC that of } U(z) \text{ is } |z| > 1$$

$$= z^{-m} \frac{1}{1-z^{-1}}, \text{ ROC} : |z| > 1$$

$$\therefore \quad ZT[u(n-m)] = \frac{z^{-m}}{1-z^{-1}}, \text{ ROC} : |z| > 1 \qquad \text{...(3.58)}$$

Note. Since, $u(n) \xleftrightarrow{ZT} \dfrac{1}{1-z^{-1}}$, ROC : $|z|>1$

$$u(n-m) = \text{delay/shifting of } u(n) \text{ by } m$$

$\therefore$ By using time shifting property we could have get $ZT[u(n-m)]$ directly as $z^{-m}\dfrac{1}{1-z^{-1}}$, ROC, $R' = R$.

Delay/advance does not alter the ROC except it may add or delete the origin from the new ROC.

3.8.5 *ZT* of $x(n) = a^n u(n)$

$$ZT[a^n\,u(n)] = \sum_{n=-\infty}^{\infty}[a^n u(n)]\cdot z^{-n} \qquad \text{(by definition)}$$

$$= \sum_{n=0}^{\infty}\left(a\,z^{-1}\right)^n \qquad \because u(n) = 0 \text{ for } n \text{ –ve}$$

$$= \frac{1}{1-az^{-1}},\ \text{ROC} : |az^{-1}| < 1 \qquad \therefore \text{ROC } |a| < |z|$$

$$\therefore \quad \boxed{ZT[a^n\,u(n)] = \frac{1}{1-az^{-1}},\ \text{ROC} : |z| > |a|} \qquad ...(3.59)$$

3.8.6 *ZT* of $x(n) = a^{-n}u(n)$

$$ZT[a^{-n}\,u(n)] = \sum_{n=-\infty}^{\infty}[a^{-n}u(n)]\cdot z^{-n} \qquad \text{(by definition)}$$

$$= \sum_{n=0}^{\infty}(az)^{-n} \qquad \because u(n) = 0 \text{ for } n < 0$$

$$= \frac{1}{1-(az)^{-1}}$$

Provided $\left|(az)^{-1}\right| < 1$ *i.e.* $\left|\dfrac{1}{az}\right| < 1$

$$\therefore \quad \boxed{ZT[a^{-n}\,u(n)] = \frac{1}{1-(az)^{-1}},\ \text{ROC} : |z| > \left|\frac{1}{a}\right|} \qquad ...(3.60)$$

3.8.7 *ZT* of $x(n) = r(n) = nu(n)$

As $$u(n) \overset{ZT}{\longleftrightarrow} \frac{1}{1-z^{-1}}$$

$$\therefore \quad n\,u(n) \overset{ZT}{\longleftrightarrow} -z\frac{d}{dz}\left[\frac{1}{1-z^{-1}}\right] \qquad \text{(Differentiation in z-domain-property)}$$

$$= (-z)\frac{-(1/z^2)}{(1-z^{-1})^2} = \frac{z^{-1}}{(1-z^{-1})^2}$$

and ROC is the same as that of *ZT* of $u(n)$

Hence, $$ZT[r(n) = nu(n)] = \frac{z^{-1}}{(1-z^{-1})^2}, \quad \text{ROC}: |z|>1 \qquad ...(3.61)$$

3.8.8 *ZT* of $x(n) = \sin n\omega_0 \cdot u(n)$

$$ZT[\sin n\omega_0 \cdot u(n)] = \sum_{n=-\infty}^{\infty} [\sin n\omega_0 \cdot u(n)] z^{-n} \qquad \text{(by definition)}$$

$$= \sum_{n=0}^{\infty} \frac{1}{2j}\left(e^{jn\omega_0} - e^{-jn\omega_0}\right) z^{-n}$$

$$= \frac{1}{2j}\left[\frac{1}{1-e^{j\omega_0}z^{-1}} - \frac{1}{1-e^{-j\omega_0}z^{-1}}\right] \text{ROC}: \left|z^{-1}\right| < 1$$

After simplifying, we get

$$= \frac{(\sin\omega_0)z^{-1}}{1-2\cos\omega_0 z^{-1} + z^{-2}}, \text{ROC}: |z|>1$$

Hence, $$ZT[\sin n\omega_0 \cdot u(n)] = \frac{(\sin\omega_0)z^{-1}}{1-(2\cos\omega_0)z^{-1} + z^{-2}}, \text{ROC}: |z|>1 \qquad ...(3.62)$$

3.8.9 *ZT* of $x(n) = \cos n\omega_0 \cdot u(n)$

$$ZT[\cos n\omega_0 \cdot u(n)] = \sum_{n=-\infty}^{\infty} [\cos n\omega_0 \cdot u(n)] z^{-n} \qquad \text{(by definition)}$$

$$= \sum_{n=0}^{\infty} \frac{1}{2}\left(e^{jn\omega_0} + e^{-jn\omega_0}\right) \cdot z^{-n}$$

$$= \frac{1}{2}\left[\frac{1}{1-e^{j\omega_0}z^{-1}} + \frac{1}{1-e^{-j\omega_0}z^{-1}}\right], \text{ROC}: \left|z^{-1}\right| < 1$$

$$= \frac{1}{2}\left[\frac{\left(1-e^{-j\omega_0}z^{-1}\right) + \left(1-e^{j\omega_0}z^{-1}\right)}{\left(1-e^{j\omega_0}z^{-1}\right)\left(1-e^{-j\omega_0}z^{-1}\right)}\right]$$

$$= \frac{1-(\cos\omega_0)z^{-1}}{1-(2\cos\omega_0)z^{-1} + z^{-2}}$$

$$\therefore \quad ZT[\cos n\omega_0 \cdot u(n)] = \frac{1-(\cos\omega_0)z^{-1}}{1-(2\cos\omega_0)z^{-1} + z^{-2}}, \text{ROC}: |z|>1 \qquad ...(3.63)$$

3.8.10 *ZT* of $x(n) = r^n \sin n\omega_0 \cdot u(n)$

$$ZT[r^n \sin n\omega_0 \cdot u(n)] = \sum_{n=-\infty}^{\infty} \left[r^n \sin n\omega_0 \cdot u(n)\right] z^{-n} \qquad \text{(by definition)}$$

i.e., $$ZT[r^n \sin n\omega_0 \cdot u(n)] = \sum_{n=0}^{\infty} r^n \frac{e^{jn\omega_0} - e^{-jn\omega_0}}{2j} \cdot z^{-n}$$

$$= \frac{1}{2j}\left[\sum_{n=0}^{\infty}\left(r e^{j\omega_0} z^{-1}\right)^n - \sum_{n=0}^{\infty}\left(r e^{-j\omega_0} z^{-1}\right)^n\right]$$

$$= \frac{1}{2j}\left(\frac{1}{1 - re^{j\omega_0} z^{-1}} - \frac{1}{1 - re^{-j\omega_0} z^{-1}}\right), \quad \text{ROC}: \left|rz^{-1}\right| < 1 \text{ i.e. } |z| > r$$

$$= \frac{1}{2j} \frac{\left(1 - r e^{-j\omega_0} z^{-1}\right)\left(1 - r e^{j\omega_0} z^{-1}\right)}{\left(1 - re^{j\omega_0} z^{-1}\right)\left(1 - re^{-j\omega_0} z^{-1}\right)}$$

$$= \frac{1}{2j} \frac{r\left(e^{j\omega_0} - e^{-j\omega_0}\right) z^{-1}}{1 - r z^{-1}\left(e^{j\omega_0} + e^{-j\omega_0}\right) + r^2 z^{-2}}$$

$$\therefore \quad \boxed{ZT[r^n \sin n\omega_0 \, u(n)] = \frac{(r \sin \omega_0) z^{-1}}{1 - (2 r \cos\omega_0) z^{-1} + r^2 z^{-2}}, \text{ ROC } |z| > r} \quad \text{...(3.64)}$$

3.8.11 ZT of $x(n) = r^n \cos n\omega_0 \cdot u(n)$

$$ZT[r^n \cos n\omega_0 \cdot u(n)] = \sum_{n=0}^{\infty} r^n \left(\frac{e^{jn\omega_0} + e^{-jn\omega_0}}{2}\right) \cdot z^{-n}$$

$$= \frac{1}{2}\left[\sum_{n=0}^{\infty}\left(r e^{j\omega_0} z^{-1}\right)^n + \sum_{n=0}^{\infty}\left(r e^{-j\omega_0} z^{-1}\right)^n\right]$$

$$= \frac{1}{2}\left(\frac{1}{1 - re^{j\omega_0} z^{-1}} + \frac{1}{1 - re^{-j\omega_0} z^{-1}}\right), \text{ROC}: |z| > r$$

$$= \frac{1}{2}\left[\frac{\left(1 - r e^{-j\omega_0} z^{-1}\right) + \left(1 - r e^{j\omega_0} z^{-1}\right)}{\left(1 - re^{j\omega_0} z^{-1}\right)\left(1 - re^{-j\omega_0} z^{-1}\right)}\right]$$

$$= \frac{1}{2} \frac{2 - rz^{-1}\left(e^{j\omega_0} + e^{-j\omega_0}\right)}{1 - r\left(e^{j\omega_0} + e^{-j\omega_0}\right) z^{-1} + r^2 z^{-2}}$$

$$\therefore \quad \boxed{ZT[r^n \cos n\omega_0 \, u(n)] = \frac{1 - (r \cos \omega_0) z^{-1}}{1 - (2 r \cos\omega_0) z^{-1} + r^2 z^{-2}}, \text{ ROC } |z| > r} \quad \text{...(3.65)}$$

3.8.12 *ZT* of $x(n) = \frac{1}{2}\, n(n-1)\, u(n)$

To find $ZT\left[\frac{1}{2} n(n-1) u(n)\right]$, we proceed as follows:

We know that $u(n) \xrightarrow{ZT} \frac{1}{1-z^{-1}}$ and $nu(n) \xrightarrow{ZT} \frac{z^{-1}}{(1-z^{-1})^2}$ [see (3.57) and (3.61)]

$$\therefore \quad (n-1)\, u(n) = nu(n) - u(n) \xrightarrow{ZT} \frac{z^{-1}}{(1-z^{-1})^2} - \frac{1}{1-z^{-1}}$$

$$= \frac{z^{-1} - (1-z^{-1})}{(1-z^{-1})^2} = \frac{2z^{-1} - 1}{(1-z^{-1})^2}$$

$$\therefore \quad \frac{1}{2} n[(n-1)\, u(n)] \xrightarrow{ZT} \frac{1}{2}(-z)\frac{d}{dz}\left[\frac{2z^{-1}-1}{(1-z^{-1})^2}\right]$$

(differentiation in z-domain property)

$$= \frac{-z}{2}\left[(2z^{-1}-1)\frac{(-2z^{-2})}{(1-z^{-1})^3} + \frac{-2z^{-2}}{(1-z^{-1})^2}\right]$$

$$= \left(\frac{-z}{2}\right)\frac{-4z^{-3} + 2z^{-2} - 2z^{-2}(1-z^{-1})}{(1-z^{-1})^3}$$

$$= \left(\frac{z}{2}\right)\frac{2z^{-3}}{(1-z^{-1})^3}$$

$$\therefore \quad \frac{1}{2} n\,(n-1)\, u(n) = {}^{n}C_2\, u(n) \xrightarrow{ZT} \frac{z^{-2}}{(1-z^{-1})^3}, \quad \text{ROC} : |z| > 1 \qquad ...(3.66)$$

3.8.13 *ZT* of $x(n) = -u(-n-1)$

$$ZT[-u(-n-1)] = \sum_{n=-\infty}^{\infty} -u(-n-1)\, z^{-n} \qquad \text{(by definition)}$$

Put $-n-1 = n'$

$\therefore$ limits of n' for summation are $n' = \infty$ to $-\infty$ interchanging summation order, we get

$$ZT[-u(-n-1)] = -\sum_{n'=-\infty}^{\infty} u(n')\, z^{n'+1}$$

$$= -\sum_{n'=0}^{\infty} z^{n'+1} \qquad \because\ u(n)' = 0 \text{ for } n' < 0$$

$$= -z\sum_{n=0}^{\infty} z^{n}$$

$$= (-z)\cdot\frac{1}{1-z} \qquad \text{ROC}: |z| < 1$$

$$= \frac{1}{1-z^{-1}} \qquad \text{ROC}: |z| < 1$$

$$\therefore \quad \boxed{ZT[-u(-n-1)] = \frac{1}{1-z^{-1}} \qquad \text{ROC}: |z| < 1} \qquad ...(3.67)$$

3.8.14 *ZT* of $x(n) = -a^n\, u(-n-1)$

$$ZT[-a^n\, u(-n-1)] = \sum_{n=-\infty}^{\infty} (-a^n)\, u(-n-1)\, z^{-n}$$

Put $-n-1 = n'$, interchange summation order

$$= -\sum_{n'=-\infty}^{\infty} a^{-1-n'} \cdot u(n')\, z^{n'+1}$$

As $u(n') = 0$ for $n' < 0$, we get

$$\therefore \quad ZT[-a^n\, u(-n-1)] = (-a^{-1} z)\sum_{n'=0}^{\infty} a^{-n'} z^{n'}$$

$$= (-a^{-1} z)\frac{1}{1-a^{-1}z}, \text{ROC } |z| < |a|$$

$$= \frac{1}{1-az^{-1}}$$

$$\therefore \quad \boxed{ZT[-a^n\, u(-n-1)] = \frac{1}{1-az^{-1}},\ ROC: |z| < |a|} \qquad ...(3.68)$$

3.8.15 *ZT* of $x(n) = -n\, a^n\, u(-n-1)$

$ZT[-n\, a^n\, u(-n-1)]$ will be obtained from ZT of $-a^n\, u(-n-1)$

As $$ZT[-a^n\, u(-n-1)] = \frac{1}{1-az^{-1}},\ ROC: |z| < |a| \quad \text{[see result at (3.68)]}$$

$$\therefore \quad ZT\left[n\cdot\{-a^n\, u(-n-1)\}\right] = (-z)\frac{d}{dz}\frac{1}{(1-az^{-1})} \quad \text{(differentiation in } z\text{-domain)}$$

$$= (-z)\frac{az^{-2}}{(1-az^{-1})^2}$$

$$ZT[-n\,a^n\,u(-n-1)] = \frac{az^{-1}}{(1-az^{-1})^2},\ ROC: |z|<|a| \quad ...(3.69)$$

3.8.16 ZT of $x(n) = \begin{cases} a^n, 0 \le n \le N-1 \\ 0, \text{otherwise} \end{cases}$

$$ZT[x(n)] = \sum_{n=0}^{N-1} a^n z^{-n} \text{ for the given } x(n)$$

$$= \frac{1-a^N z^{-N}}{1-az^{-1}} \quad \text{(GP series of total } N \text{ terms)}$$

$$= \frac{1}{z^{N-1}}\left[\frac{z^N - a^N}{z-a}\right]$$

Note that there is a pole of $(N-1)$th order at $z = 0$ ∴ ROC is $|z| > 0$ (Note this argument)

$$\therefore \quad ZT\left[x(n) = \begin{cases} a^n, 0 \le n \le N-1 \\ 0, \text{otherwise} \end{cases}\right] = \frac{1-a^N z^{-N}}{1-az^{-1}},\ \text{ROC}: |z|>0 \quad ...(3.70)$$

3.8.17 To Show That

$${}^nC_r\,u(n) \xrightarrow{ZT} \frac{z^{-r}}{(1-z^{-1})^{r+1}} \quad ...(3.71)$$

SOLUTION: (Proof by Induction)

We know that $u(n) \xrightarrow{ZT} \frac{1}{1-z^{-1}},\ {}^nC_0 = 1$ ∴ here $r = 0$ see ...(3.57)

$n\,u(n) \xrightarrow{ZT} \frac{z^{-2}}{(1-z^{-1})^2},\ {}^nC_1 = n$ ∴ here $r = 1$ see ...(3.59)

$\frac{1}{2}n(n-1)\,u(n) \longrightarrow \frac{z^{-2}}{(1-z^{-1})^3},\ {}^nC_2 = \frac{1}{2}n(n-1)$ ∴ here $r = 2$ see ...(3.66)

Let $x_r(n) = {}^nC_r\,u(n) \xrightarrow{ZT} \frac{z^{-r}}{(1-z^{-1})^{r+1}}$, be true ...(A)

we wish to prove that $x_{r+1}(n) = {}^nC_{r+1}\,u(n)$ z-transforms to $\frac{z^{-(r+1)}}{(1-z^{-1})^{r+2}}$

(*i.e.* to show that if (*A*) is true, for some r, it is also true of next higher value $r+1$)

As $x_{r+1}(n) = \frac{n!}{(r+1)!(n-r-1)!}u(n) = \left(\frac{n-r}{r+1}\right)\frac{n!}{r!(n-r)!}u(n)$ (Note this step)

$$= \left(\frac{n-r}{r+1}\right)\cdot x_r(n)$$

$$= \frac{n}{r+1}x_r(n) - \frac{r}{r+1}x_r(n)$$

$$x_{r+1}(n) \xrightarrow{ZT} \frac{1}{r+1}\left((-z)\frac{d}{dz}X_r(z)\right) - \frac{r}{r+1}X_r(z)$$

$$= \frac{1}{r+1}(-z)\left[-(r+1)\frac{z^{-2}\cdot z^{-r}}{(1-z^{-1})^{r+2}} + \frac{(-r)z^{-r-1}}{(1-z^{-1})^{r+1}}\right] - \frac{r}{r+1}\frac{z^{-r}}{(1-z^{-1})^{r+1}}$$

[where $X_r(z)$ is RHS of (A)]

$$= \frac{(r+1)\,z^{-r-1} + r(1-z^{-1})\,z^{-r} - r(1-z^{-1})\,z^{-r}}{(r+1)(1-z^{-1})^{r+2}}$$

$$\therefore\ {}^{n}C_{r+1}\,u(n) \xleftrightarrow{ZT} \frac{z^{-(r+1)}}{(1-z^{-1})^{r+2}} \qquad ...(B)$$

i.e., if (A) is true for some r, it is also true for $r + 1$, due to (B). But (A) is true for $r = 1$ $\therefore$ it is true for $r = 2$ and hence for $r = 3$, ... thus, the result (A) is true for all values of $r = 0, 1, 2, ...$ **Q.E.D.**

3.8.18 To Show That

$$x(n) = \frac{r^n}{\sin\theta}\sin(n+1)\,\theta\,u(n) \xleftrightarrow{ZT} \frac{1}{1-(2r\cos\theta)\,z^{-1}+r^2z^{-2}} \quad \text{ROC} : |z| > r$$

and hence to deduce the value of summation $\sum_{n=0}^{\infty} x(n)$ ...(3.72)

SOLUTION:

$$X(z) = \sum_{n=-\infty}^{\infty} x(n)\,z^{-n} = \sum_{n=-\infty}^{\infty} \frac{r^n}{\sin\theta}\sin(n+1)\,\theta\,u(n)\cdot z^{-n} \qquad \text{(by definition)}$$

$$= \left(\sum_{n=0}^{\infty} r^n \sin(n+1)\,\theta\,z^{-n}\right)\frac{1}{\sin\theta}$$

$$= \frac{1}{\sin\theta}\left[\sum_{n=0}^{\infty}\frac{1}{2j}\left(e^{j(n+1)\theta} - e^{-j(n+1)\theta}\right)\left(\frac{z}{r}\right)^{-n}\right]$$

$$= \frac{1}{j\,2\sin\theta}\left[\sum_{n=0}^{\infty} e^{j\theta}\left(\frac{z}{re^{j\theta}}\right)^{-n} - e^{-j\theta}\left(\frac{z}{re^{-j\theta}}\right)^{-n}\right]$$

$$= \frac{1}{j\,2\sin\theta}\left[\frac{e^{j\theta}}{1-\left(\frac{z}{re^{j\theta}}\right)^{-1}} - \frac{e^{-j\theta}}{1-\left(\frac{z}{re^{-j\theta}}\right)^{-1}}\right] \qquad \text{ROC } |r| < |z| \ i.e., \ |z| > |r|$$

$$= \frac{1}{j\,2\sin\theta}\left[\frac{e^{j\theta}}{1-re^{j\theta}\,z^{-1}} - \frac{e^{-j\theta}}{1-re^{-j\theta}\,z^{-1}}\right]$$

$$= \frac{1}{j\,2\sin\theta}\left[\frac{e^{j\theta}(1-re^{-j\theta}z^{-1}) - e^{-j\theta}(1-re^{j\theta}\,z^{-1})}{1-2r\cos\theta\,z^{-1}+r^2z^{-2}}\right]$$

$$\therefore \quad X(z) = \frac{1}{1-2r\cos\theta\, z^{-1}+z^{-2}r^2}, \text{ ROC}|z|>|r|$$

To compute $\sum_{n=0}^{\infty} x(n)$, put $z^{-1} = 1$ in the above result

$$\therefore \quad \sum_{n=0}^{\infty} \frac{r^n}{\sin\theta}\sin(n+1)\theta = \frac{1}{1-2r\cos\theta+r^2}$$

3.8.19 To Show That

$$\sum_{n=-\infty}^{\infty} x_1(n)\cdot x_2^*(n) = \frac{1}{2\pi j}\oint_C X_1(v)\cdot X_2^*\left(\frac{1}{v^*}\right)v^{-1}\,dv \text{ Parseval's Relation} \qquad ...(3.73)$$

Proof.

$$\text{As} \quad \boxed{\sum_{n=-\infty}^{\infty} x_1(n)\cdot x_2^*(n) = \sum_{n=-\infty}^{\infty} x_2^*(n)\cdot x_1(n)} \qquad ...(A)$$

Replace $x_1(n)$ by the Inverse ZT of $X_1(z)$ using contour integral, on RHS of (A), we get

$$\text{RHS of (A)} = \sum_{n=-\infty}^{\infty} x_2^*(n)\left[\frac{1}{2\pi j}\oint_C X_1(v)\cdot v^{n-1}\,dv\right] \text{ (using (3.24), changing } z \text{ to } v)$$

$$= \frac{1}{2\pi j}\oint_C X_1(v)\sum_{n=-\infty}^{\infty} x_2^*(n)\cdot v^{n-1}\,dv$$

$$= \frac{1}{2\pi j}\oint_C X_1(v)\underbrace{\left[\sum_{n=-\infty}^{\infty} x_2(n)\left(\frac{1}{v^*}\right)^{-n}\right]^* . v^{-1}\,dv}_{=X_2^*\left(\frac{1}{v^*}\right)\times v^{-1}\cdot dv}$$

$$= \frac{1}{2\pi j}\oint_C X_1(v)\cdot X_2^*\left(\frac{1}{v^*}\right)v^{-1}\,dv$$

i.e.,

$$\sum_{n=-\infty}^{\infty} x_1(n)\cdot x_2^*(n) = \frac{1}{2\pi j}\oint_C X_1(v)\,X_2^*\left(\frac{1}{v^*}\right)v^{-1}\,dv$$

This is also called Parseval's relation in z-domain **Q.E.D.**

Table 3.3 Some Standard z-Transforms

S.N.	Function $x(n)$		$X(z)$	ROC
1	$x(n)$		$X(z) = \sum_{n=-\infty}^{\infty} x(n) z^{-n}$ (by definition)	
2	$\delta(n)$	(3.56)	1	All z
3	$u(n)$	(3.57)	$\frac{1}{1-z^{-1}}$	$\|z\| > 1$
4	$K\,u(n-m)$	(3.58)	$K \cdot Z^{-m} \frac{1}{1-z^{-1}}$	$\|z\| > 1$
5	$K\,a^n\,u(n)$	(3.59)	$K \cdot \frac{1}{1-az^{-1}}$	$\|z\| > \|a\|$
6	$K\,a^{-n}\,u(n)$	(3.60)	$K \cdot \frac{1}{1-a^{-1}z^{-1}}$	$\|z\| > \left\|\frac{1}{a}\right\|$
7	$r(n) = n\,u(n)$	(3.61)	$\frac{z^{-1}}{(1-z^{-1})^2}$	$\|z\| > 1$
8	$\sin n\omega_0 \cdot u(n)$	(3.62)	$\frac{(\sin\omega_0)\,z^{-1}}{1-(2\cos\omega)\,z^{-1}+z^{-2}}$	$\|z\| > 1$
9	$\cos n\omega_0 \cdot u(n)$	(3.63)	$\frac{1-(\cos\omega_0)\,z^{-1}}{1-(2\cos\omega)\,z^{-1}+z^{-2}}$	$\|z\| > 1$
10	$r^n \sin n\omega_0 \cdot u(n)$	(3.64)	$\frac{(r\sin\omega_0)\,z^{-1}}{1-(2r\cos\omega_0)\,z^{-1}+r^2 z^{-2}}$	$\|z\| > r$
11	$r^n \cos n\omega_0 \cdot u(n)$	(3.65)	$\frac{1-(r\cos\omega_0)\,z^{-1}}{1-(2r\cos\omega_0)\,z^{-1}+r^2 z^{-2}}$	$\|z\| > r$
12	$\frac{1}{2} n(n-1) \cdot u(n) = {}^nC_2 u(n)$	(3.66)	$\frac{z^{-2}}{(1-z^{-1})^3}$	$\|z\| > 1$
13	$-u(-n-1)$	(3.67)	$\frac{1}{1-z^{-1}}$	$\|z\| < 1$
14	$-a^n\,u(-n-1)$	(3.68)	$\frac{1}{1-az^{-1}}$	$\|z\| < \|a\|$
15	$-n\,a^n\,u(-n-1)$	(3.69)	$\frac{az^{-1}}{(1-az^{-1})^2}$	$\|z\| < \|a\|$
16	$\begin{cases} a^n, 0 \le n \le N-1 \\ 0, \text{otherwise} \end{cases}$	(3.70)	$\frac{1-a^N z^{-N}}{1-az^{-1}}$	$\|z\| > 0$
17	${}^nC_r\,u(n)$	(3.71)	$\frac{z^{-r}}{(1-z^{-1})^{r+1}}$	$\|z\| > 1$
18	$\frac{r^n}{\sin\theta} \sin(n+1)\,\theta\,u(n)$	(3.72)	$\frac{1}{1-(2r\cos\theta)\,z^{-1}+r^2 z^{-2}}$	$\|z\| > r$
19	$\sum_n x_1(n)\,x_2^*(n)$	(3.73)	$= \frac{1}{2\pi j} \oint_C X_1(v) \cdot X_2^*\left(\frac{1}{v^*}\right) v^{-1} dv$ Parseval's Relation	

EXAMPLE 3.6: *Find z-transforms for the functions: (a) d(n), (b) d(n – 1), (c) d(n + 1), (d)* $\left(\frac{1}{2}\right)^n [u(n)-u(n-10)]$.

SOLUTION: (a)

$$ZT[d(n)] = \sum_{n=-\infty}^{\infty} \delta(n)\, z^{-n}$$

$$= 1z^0 = 1 \text{ and it converges everywhere}$$ **Ans.**

(b)

$$ZT[\delta(n-1)] = \sum_{n=-\infty}^{\infty} \delta(n-1)\, z^{-n}$$

$$= 1z^{-1} = z^{-1} \qquad (\because\ \delta(n-1) = 1 \text{ for } n = 1)$$ **Ans.**

For ROC $|z^{-1}| < \infty \therefore |z| > 0$

(c)

$$ZT[\delta(n+1)] = \sum_{n=-\infty}^{\infty} \delta(n+1)\, z^{-n}$$

$$= z^{+1} \qquad (\because\ \delta(n+1) = 1 \text{ for } n = -1)$$ **Ans.**

For ROC $|z| < \infty \therefore 0 \le |z| < \infty$ is the ROC.

(d)

$$ZT\left(\frac{1}{2}\right)^n \left[(u(n)-u(n-10))\right] = \sum_{n=0}^{9} \left(\frac{1}{2}\right)^n z^{-n} \qquad (\because\ u(n)-u(n-10) = 0 \text{ for } n > 9)$$

$$= \sum_{n=0}^{9} \left(\frac{1}{2z}\right)^n = 1 + \left(\frac{1}{2z}\right)^1 + \left(\frac{1}{2z}\right)^2 + \ldots + \left(\frac{1}{2z}\right)^9 \quad \ldots(A)$$

$$= \frac{1-\left(\frac{1}{2z}\right)^{10}}{1-\left(\frac{1}{2z}\right)}$$

$$= \frac{1-(2z)^{-10}}{1-(2z)^{-1}}$$ **Ans.**

For ROC: $\left|\frac{1}{2z}\right| < \infty$ [see expansion (A)]

$\because$ $|z^{-1}| < \infty$

$\therefore$ $|z| > 0$, i.e. ROC is entire z-plane except $z = 0$

EXAMPLE 3.7: *Find the z-transform of the following discrete-time signals.*

SOLUTION: (a)

$$x(n) = \begin{cases} 1, & 0 \le n \le k \\ 0, & \text{otherwise} \end{cases} \qquad \text{(given signal)}$$

we can write $x(n) = u(n) - u(n-k-1)$ $\quad$ $\because$ $x(n)$ must have a value equalling unity for $n = 0$ to k

$$\therefore \quad X(z) = \frac{1}{1-z^{-1}} - \frac{z^{-(k+1)}}{1-z^{-1}}$$

$= [1 - z^{-(k+1)}]/(1 - z^{-1})$ ROC is entire z-plane except $z = 0$ **Ans.**

(*b*)
$$x(n) = \begin{cases} n, & 0 \le n \le 5 \\ 0, & \text{otherwise} \end{cases} \quad \text{(given signal)}$$

$$X(z) = \sum_{n=0}^{\infty} x(n)\, z^{-n} \quad \text{(by definition)}$$

$$= \sum_{n=0}^{5} n\, z^{-n}$$

$$= 0z^{-0} + 1z^{-1} + 2z^{-2} + 3z^{-3} + 4z^{-4} + 5z^{-5}$$

$$= z^{-1} + 2z^{-2} + 3z^{-3} + 4z^{-4} + 5z^{-5}$$ **Ans.**

ROC $|z^{-1}| \ne \infty$ *i.e.*, $|z| \ne 0$

i.e. ROC is entire z-plane except $z = 0$

(*c*)
$$x(n) = \begin{cases} 0, & n < 0 \\ 1, & 0 \le n \le 5 \\ 2, & 5 < n \le 10 \\ 3, & n > 10 \end{cases} \quad \text{(given signal)}$$

Here $x(n) = u(n) + u(n-6) + u(n-11)$ **(N.T.S.)**

$$\therefore \quad X(z) = \frac{1+z^{-6}+z^{-11}}{1-z^{-1}}, \text{ ROC } |z| > 1 \quad [\because x(n) \text{ is causal}]$$ **Ans.**

(*d*)
$$x(n) = \begin{cases} 0 & n < 0 \\ n & 0 \le n < 5 \\ n-5 & 5 \le n < 10 \\ n-10 & n \ge 10 \end{cases} \quad \text{(given signal)}$$

We can write
$$x(n) = \underbrace{\begin{cases} 0, & n < 0 \\ n, & 0 \le n < 5 \\ n, & 5 \le n < 10 \\ n, & n \ge 10 \end{cases}}_{\equiv n\,u(n)} + \underbrace{\begin{cases} 0 & n < 0 \\ 0 & 0 \le n < 5 \\ -5 & 5 \le n < 10 \\ -10 & n \ge 10 \end{cases}}_{\substack{\equiv -5[u(n-5)-u(n-10)] \\ -10\,u(n-10) \\ = -5\,u(n-5) - 5u(n-10)}} \quad \text{(Note this step)}$$

$$x(n) = n\,u(n) - 5[u(n-5) + u(n-10)]$$

$$X(z) = \frac{z^{-1}}{(1-z^{-1})^2} - 5\frac{z^{-5}+z^{-10}}{(1-z^{-1})}, \quad \text{ROC } |z| > 1$$

$$= \frac{z^{-1} - 5\left(z^{-5}+z^{-10}\right)\left(1-z^{-1}\right)}{\left(1-z^{-1}\right)^2}, \quad \text{ROC } |z| > 1$$

$$X(z) = \frac{z^{-1} - 5(z^{-5} - z^{-6} + z^{-10} - z^{-11})}{(1-z^{-1})^2}, \quad \text{ROC } |z| > 1 \; [\because x(n) \text{ is causal}]$$ **Ans.**

EXAMPLE 3.8: *Given $x(n) = a^n \sin\left(\frac{n\pi}{2}\right) . u(n)$, find the z-transform X(z). Assume a is real.*

SOLUTION:

$$x(n) = a^n\left(\sin\frac{n\pi}{2}\right)\cdot u(n)$$

$$\therefore \quad X(z) = \sum_{n=-\infty}^{\infty} a^n\left(\sin\frac{n\pi}{2}\right)\cdot u(n) . z^{-n}$$

$$= \sum_{n=0}^{\infty}\left(\sin\frac{n\pi}{2}\right)\cdot\left(a\,z^{-1}\right)^n \qquad \because u(n) = 0 \text{ for } n < 0$$

$$= 0 + a\,z^{-1} - a^3 z^{-3} + a^5 z^{-5} - \ldots$$

$$= a\,z^{-1}[1 - a^2 z^{-2} + a^4 z^{-4} - a^6 z^{-6} + \ldots]$$

$$= a z^{-1}\frac{1}{1-(a z^{-1})^2}, \quad \text{ROC: } |a\,z^{-1}| < 1 \;\therefore\; |z| > |a|$$

Thus,

$$X(z) = \frac{a z^{-1}}{1+(a z^{-1})^2}, \ \text{ROC}: |z| > |a| \qquad \textbf{Ans.}$$

EXAMPLE 3.9: *Find the z-transform for $x(n) = e^{-an} \sin \omega n. u(n)$*

SOLUTION:

$$X(z) = \sum_{n=0}^{\infty} e^{-an} \sin \omega n \cdot z^{-n}$$

$$= \frac{1}{2j}\left[\sum_{n=0}^{\infty} e^{-an}\cdot e^{j\omega n}\cdot z^{-n} - \sum_{n=0}^{\infty} e^{-an}\, e^{-j\omega n}\cdot z^{-n}\right]$$

$$= \frac{1}{2j}\left[\sum_{n=0}^{\infty}\left(e^{-a}\, e^{j\omega}\, z^{-1}\right)^n - \sum_{n=0}^{\infty}\left(e^{-a}\, e^{-j\omega}\, z^{-1}\right)^n\right]$$

$$= \frac{1}{2j}\left[\frac{1}{1-e^{-a}\, e^{j\omega}\, z^{-1}} - \frac{1}{1-e^{-a}\, e^{-j\omega}\, z^{-1}}\right], \ \text{ROC}: \left|e^{-a}\, z^{-1}\right|$$

$$= \frac{\left(1-e^{-a}\, e^{-j\omega}\, z^{-1}\right)-\left(1-e^{-a}\, e^{j\omega}\, z^{-1}\right)}{2j\left(1-e^{-a}\, z^{-1}(e^{j\omega}+e^{-j\omega})+e^{-2a}\, z^{-2}\right)}, \ \text{ROC}: |z| > e^{-a}$$

$$\therefore \quad X(z) = \frac{e^{-a}(\sin\omega)\, z^{-1}}{1-2\,e^{-a}(\cos\omega)\, z^{-1}+e^{-2a}\, z^{-2}}, \ \text{ROC}: |z| > e^{-a} \qquad \textbf{Ans.}$$

EXAMPLE 3.10: *Determine the z-transforms, indicating ROC for the signals.*

(a) $x_1(n) = \begin{cases}(1/3)^n, & n \geq 0\\ (1/2)^{-n}, & n < 0\end{cases}$

(b) $x_2(n) = \begin{cases}\left(\frac{1}{3}\right)^n - 2^n, & n \geq 0\\ 0, & n < 0\end{cases}$

(c) $x_3(n) = x_1(n + 4)$

(d) $x_4(n) = x_1(-n)$

SOLUTION: (*a*)

$$X_1(z) = \sum_{n=0}^{\infty}\left(\frac{1}{3}\right)^n z^{-n} + \sum_{n=-\infty}^{-1}\left(\frac{1}{2}\right)^{-n} z^{-n}$$

$$= \sum_{n=0}^{\infty}\left(\frac{1}{3}\right)^n z^{-n} + \sum_{n=-\infty}^{0}\left(\frac{1}{2}\right)^{-n} z^{-n} - 1$$

$$= \frac{1}{1-\frac{1}{3}z^{-1}} + \frac{1}{1-\frac{1}{2}z} - 1$$

$$= \frac{\left(1-\frac{1}{2}z\right)+\left(1-\frac{1}{3}z^{-1}\right)-\left(1+\frac{1}{6}-\frac{1}{2}z-\frac{1}{3}z^{-1}\right)}{\left(1-\frac{1}{3}z^{-1}\right)\left(1-\frac{1}{2}z\right)}$$

$$= \frac{5/6}{\left(1-\frac{1}{3}z^{-1}\right)\left(1-\frac{1}{2}z\right)}$$

ROC is $|z| > \frac{1}{3},\ |z| < \frac{1}{2}$

$\therefore$ ROC $\frac{1}{3} < |z| < \frac{1}{2}$ **Ans.**

(*b*)

$$X_2(z) = \sum_{n=0}^{\infty}\left(\frac{1}{3}\right)^n z^{-n} - \sum_{n=0}^{\infty} 2^n z^{-n}$$

$$= \frac{1}{1-\frac{1}{3}z^{-1}} - \frac{1}{1-2z^{-1}},\ \text{ROC: } |z| > 2$$

$$= \frac{-(5/3)\,z^{-1}}{\left(1-\frac{1}{3}z^{-1}\right)\left(1-2z^{-1}\right)},\ \text{ROC: } |z| > 2$$ **Ans.**

(*c*)

$$X_3(z) = \sum_{n=-\infty}^{\infty} x_1(n+4)\, z^{-n}$$

$$= [X_1(z)].\, z^4$$

$$= \frac{(5/6)\,z^4}{\left(1-\frac{1}{3}z^{-1}\right)\left(1-\frac{1}{2}z\right)},\ \text{ROC } \frac{1}{3} < |z| < \frac{1}{2}$$ [same as ROC for $X_1(z)$] **Ans.**

(*d*)

$$X_4(z) = \sum_{n=-\infty}^{\infty} x_1(-n)\, z^{-n}$$

$$= \sum_{m=-\infty}^{\infty} x_1(m)\, z^{m} = \sum_{m=-\infty}^{\infty} x_1(m)(z^{-1})^{-m}$$

$$= X_1(z^{-1})$$

$$= \frac{(5/6)}{\left(1-\frac{1}{3}z\right)\left(1-\frac{1}{2}z^{-1}\right)},$$

ROC: $|z^{-1}|$ lies between $\frac{1}{3}$ and 2 *i.e.*, ROC: $\frac{1}{2} < |z| < 3$ **Ans.**

EXAMPLE 3.11: *Determine the z-transform of each of the following sequences. Give ROC in each case.*

(a) $x_1(n) = \alpha^{|n|}, \quad 0 < |\alpha| < 1$

(b) $x_2(n) = Ar^n \cos(\omega_0 n + \phi)\, u(n), \quad 0 < r < 1$

SOLUTION: *(a)*

$$X_1(z) = \sum_{n=-\infty}^{\infty} x(n)\, z^{-n} \quad \text{(by definition)}$$

$$= \sum_{n=-\infty}^{\infty} \alpha^{|n|} z^{-n}$$

$$= \sum_{n=-\infty}^{-1} \alpha^{-n} z^{-n} + \alpha^0 z^0 + \sum_{n=1}^{\infty} \alpha^n z^{-n} \quad \text{(Note this step)}$$

$$= \sum_{n=1}^{\infty} \alpha^n z^n + \sum_{n=0}^{\infty} \alpha^n z^{-n}$$

$$= \frac{\alpha z}{1-\alpha z} + \frac{1}{1-\alpha z^{-1}}, \text{ provided } |\alpha z| < 1 \text{ i.e., } |z| < \frac{1}{|\alpha|},$$

and $|\alpha z^{-1}| < 1$ *i.e.*, $|z| > |\alpha|$

$$= \frac{\alpha z}{1-\alpha z} + \frac{z}{z-\alpha}$$

$$\therefore \quad X_1(z) = \frac{z(1-\alpha^2)}{(1-\alpha z)(z-\alpha)}, \quad \text{ROC}: |\alpha| < |z| < \frac{1}{|\alpha|} \quad \textbf{Ans.}$$

In drawing ROC, we have assumed that $|\alpha| < 1$ so that $\left|\frac{1}{\alpha}\right|$ is > 1.

Had we assumed $|\alpha| > 1$, then ROC would be given by equations will be

$$\left|\frac{1}{\alpha}\right| < |z| < |\alpha|$$

i.e., the unit circle is again included in the annular ring, as drawn.

$\therefore$ for ROC $|\alpha| < |z|$,

$|z| < \frac{1}{|\alpha|}$

$\therefore \quad |\alpha| < |z| < \frac{1}{|\alpha|}$

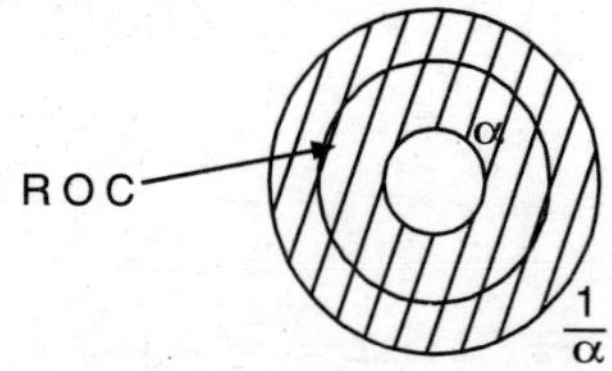

Fig. Ex. 3.11. Showing ROC-shaded area. This is an annular ring.

(b) $\quad x(n) = Ar^n \cos(\omega_0 n + \phi)\, u(n), \quad 0 < r < 1$

$$\therefore \quad X(z) = \sum_{n=0}^{\infty} Ar^n \cos(\omega_0 n + \phi)\, z^{-n}$$

$$= \frac{A}{2}\sum_{n=0}^{\infty} r^n \left(e^{j(\omega_0 n+\phi)} + e^{-j(\omega_0 n+\phi)}\right) z^{-n}$$

$$= \frac{A}{2}\left[e^{j\phi}\sum_{n=0}^{\infty}(r\,e^{j\omega_0})^n z^{-n} + e^{-j\phi}\sum_{n=0}^{\infty}(r\,e^{-j\omega_0})^n z^{-n}\right]$$

$$= \frac{A}{2}\left[e^{j\phi}\sum_{n=0}^{\infty}(r\,e^{j\omega_0}z^{-1})^n + e^{-j\phi}\sum_{n=0}^{\infty}(r\,e^{-j\omega_0}z^{-n})^n\right]$$

$$= \frac{A}{2}\left[e^{j\phi}\frac{1}{1-re^{j\omega_0}z^{-1}} + e^{-j\phi}\frac{1}{1-re^{-j\omega_0}z^{-1}}\right]$$

$| re^{j\omega_0}\, z^{-1} |, | re^{-j\omega_0}\, z^{-01} | < 1$ for convergence

i.e., $|rz^{-1}| < 1$ *i.e.,* $|z| > |r|$

$$= \frac{Az}{2}\left[\frac{e^{j\phi}}{z-re^{j\omega_0}} + \frac{e^{-j\phi}}{z-re^{-j\omega_0}}\right]$$

$$= \frac{Az}{2}\left[\frac{e^{j\phi}(z-re^{-j\omega_0}) + e^{-j\phi}(z-re^{j\omega_0})}{(z-re^{j\omega_0})(z-re^{-j\omega_0})}\right]$$

$$= \frac{Az}{2}\left[\frac{z(e^{j\phi}+e^{-j\phi}) - r(e^{j(\phi-\omega_0)}+e^{-j(\phi-\omega_0)})}{z^2 - rz(e^{j\omega_0}+e^{-j\omega_0}) + r^2}\right]$$

$$= Az\left[\frac{z\cos\phi - r\cos(\phi-\omega_0)}{z^2 - 2rz\cos\omega_0 + r^2}\right]$$ **Ans.**

Zero is at : $z \cos\phi = r\cos(\phi - \omega_0)$ *i.e.,* $z = \dfrac{\cos(\phi-\omega_0)}{\cos\phi}$

Poles at : $z = re^{\pm j\omega_0}$

EXAMPLE 3.12: *Find the z-transform of y(n) defined by*

$$y(n) = u(n)\cdot e^{-\alpha n}\sin n\omega$$

Use complex convolution method.

SOLUTION: As $y(n) = (u(n)\cdot e^{-an})\,[(\sin n\omega)\cdot u(n)]$ [form $f(n)\cdot g(n)$]

$$ZT[f(n)] = ZT\left[e^{-\alpha n}u(n)\right] = \frac{1}{1-e^{-\alpha}z^{-1}} = \frac{z}{z-e^{-\alpha}}$$ ROC: $|z| > e^{-\alpha}$

$$ZT[g(n)] = ZT[\sin n\omega\,.\,u(n)] = \frac{z^{-1}\sin\omega}{1-2\cos\omega z^{-1}+z^{-2}}$$

$$= \frac{z\sin\omega}{(z-e^{j\omega})(z-e^{-j\omega})}$$ ROC: $|z| > 1$

$$Y(z) = \frac{1}{2\pi j}\oint_C F\left(\frac{z}{v}\right)\cdot G(v)\,v^{-1}dv$$

$$= \frac{1}{2\pi j}\oint_C \left(\frac{z/v}{(z/v)-e^{-\alpha}}\right)\left(\frac{v\sin\omega}{(v-e^{j\omega})(v-e^{-j\omega})}\right)v^{-1}dv$$

$$= \frac{1}{2\pi j}\oint_C \frac{-z\,e^{\alpha}\sin\omega}{(v-ze^{\alpha})(v-e^{j\omega})(v-e^{-j\omega})}\,dv$$

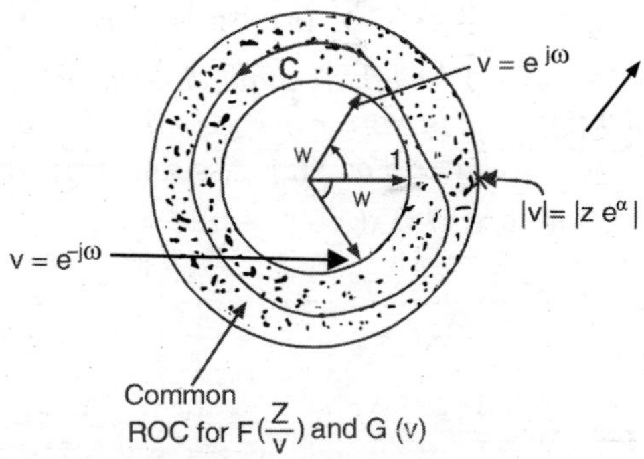

Fig. Ex. 3.12. Showing ROC of Y(z)

$$= (-ze^{\alpha}\sin\omega)\,.\sum \text{residues of}\left(\frac{1}{(v-ze^{\alpha})(v-e^{j\omega})(v-e^{-j\omega})}\right)$$

$v = ze^{\alpha}$ is outside C $\therefore$ disregard

$\left.\begin{array}{l} v = e^{j\omega} \\ v = e^{-j\omega}\end{array}\right\}$ inside common ROC $\therefore$ take residues here only

$$= (-ze^{\alpha}\sin\omega)\,.\sum \text{Residues of}\left(\frac{1}{(v-ze^{\alpha})(v-e^{j\omega})(v-e^{-j\omega})}\right)$$

Note that $\quad F(z) = \dfrac{1}{1-e^{-\alpha}z^{-1}}$ has ROC : $|z| > e^{-\alpha}$

$\therefore \quad F(z/v) = \dfrac{1}{1-e^{-\alpha}(z/v)^{-1}}$ has ROC : $\left|\dfrac{z}{v}\right| > e^{-\alpha}$ *i.e.*, $|v| < ze^{\alpha}$

and $\quad G(v) = \dfrac{v\sin\omega}{(v-e^{j\omega})(v-e^{-j\omega})}$ has ROC : $|v| > 1$

$\therefore$ Common ROC for $F(z/v)$ and $G(v)$ is $1 < |v| < ze^{\alpha}$ as shown by shaded area in Fig. Ex. 3.12. Since, the pole $v = ze^{\alpha}$ is not in the ROC, we disregard it for finding the residues of $F(z/v) \cdot G(v)$.

$$\therefore \quad Y(z) = (-ze^{\alpha}\sin\omega)\left[\left.\frac{1}{(v-ze^{\alpha})(e^{j\omega}-e^{-j\omega})}\right|_{v=e^{j\omega}} + \left.\frac{1}{(v-ze^{\alpha})(e^{-j\omega}-e^{j\omega})}\right|_{v=e^{-j\omega}}\right]$$

$$= (-ze^{\alpha}\sin\omega)\frac{1}{(e^{j\omega}-e^{-j\omega})}\left[\frac{1}{(e^{j\omega}-ze^{\alpha})} - \frac{1}{(e^{-j\omega}-ze^{\alpha})}\right]$$

$$= (-ze^{\alpha}\sin\omega)\left[\frac{(e^{-j\omega}-ze^{\alpha})-(e^{j\omega}-ze^{\alpha})}{1-ze^{\alpha}(e^{j\omega}+e^{-j\omega})+z^2e^{2\alpha}}\right]\frac{1}{(e^{j\omega}-e^{-j\omega})}$$

$$= \frac{+ze^{\alpha}\sin\omega}{1-2ze^{\alpha}\cos\omega+z^2e^{2\alpha}}$$

$$\therefore \qquad Y(z) = \frac{z^{-1}e^{-\alpha}\sin\omega}{1-2z^{-1}e^{-\alpha}\cos\omega+e^{-2\alpha}z^{-2}} \quad \textbf{Ans.}$$

ROC : $|z| > e^{-\alpha}$

EXAMPLE 3.13: *Let x(n), 0 £ n £ N – 1 be a finite-duration sequence, which is also real-valued. Show that the zeros of the polynomial X(z) occur in mirror-image pairs about the unit circle, that is, if z = re^{jq} is a zero of X(z) then z = (1/re^{jq}) is also a zero of X(z). Assume x(n) = x(N –1 – n).*

SOLUTION: The given condition is $x(n) = x(N-1-n)$.

Let N be odd

$$\therefore \qquad X(z) = \sum_{n=0}^{N-1} x(n)\, z^{-n}$$

$$= x(0)\,z^0 + x(1)\,z^{-1} + x(2)\,z^{-2} + \ldots + x\left(\frac{N-3}{2}\right)z^{-(N-3)/2} + x\left(\frac{N-1}{2}\right)z^{-(N-1)/2}$$

$$+ x\left(\frac{N+1}{2}\right)z^{-(N+1)/2} + \ldots + x(N-2)\,z^{-(N-2)} + x(N-1)\,z^{-(N-1)}$$

$$= z^{-(N-1)/2}\left[x(0)\,z^{(N-1)/2} + x(1)\,z^{(N-3)/2} + \ldots + x\left(\frac{N-3}{2}\right)z^{1}\right.$$

$$\left. + x\left(\frac{N+1}{2}\right)z^{-1} + x\left(\frac{N+3}{2}\right)z^{-2} + \ldots + x(N-2)\,z^{-(N-3)/2} + x(N-1)z^{-(N-1)/2}\right]$$

$$\nearrow x\left(\frac{N-3}{2}\right) \qquad \nearrow x\left(\frac{N-5}{2}\right) \qquad \nearrow x(1) \qquad \nearrow x(0)$$

(due to symmetry given)

$$= z^{-(N-1)/2}\left[x(0)\,z^{(N-1)/2} + x(1)\,z^{(N-3)/2} + \ldots + x\left(\frac{N-3}{2}\right)z^{1}\right.$$

$$\left. + x(0)\,z^{-(N-1)/2} + x(1)\,z^{-(N-3)/2} + \ldots + x\left(\frac{N-3}{2}\right)z^{-1} + x\left(\frac{N-1}{2}\right)\right]$$

$$\triangleq z^{-(N-1)/2}\left[P(z) + P(z^{-1}) + x\left(\frac{N-1}{2}\right)\right] \qquad \ldots(A)$$

$$\text{As} \qquad X(z) = z^{-(N-1)/2}\left[P(z) + P(z^{-1}) + x\left(\frac{N-1}{2}\right)\right]$$

↑ Not zero

$\therefore$ Zeros of $X(z)$ are the solutions of

$$P(z) + P(z^{-1}) + x\left(\frac{N-1}{2}\right) = 0 \qquad ...(B)$$

Clearly, if $z = z_1$ satisfies (B) then $z^{-1} = z_1$ also satisfies (B). Thus, if $X(z)$ has a zero at $z_1 = re^{j\theta}$ then it has also a zero at $1/(re^{j\theta})$ *i.e.*, the zeros occur in conjugate mirror symmetry.

If N is even

$$X(z) = \sum_{n=0}^{N-1} x(n)\, z^{-n} = \sum_{n=0}^{N/2-1} x(n)z^{-n} + \sum_{n=N/2}^{N-1} x(n)z^{-n} \qquad \textbf{N.T.S.}$$

In the second term on RHS, put $n' = N - 1 - n$ when $n = \frac{N}{2}$, $n' = \frac{N}{2} - 1$ when $n = N - 1$, $n' = 0$.

$$\therefore \quad X(z) = \sum_{n=0}^{N/2-1} x(n)\, z^{-n} + \sum_{n'=0}^{N/2-1} \underbrace{x\,(N-1-n')}_{=\,x(n')}\, z^{-(N-1-n')}$$

$$= z^{-(N-1)/2}\left[\sum_{n=0}^{N/2-1} x(n)\, z^{\frac{N-1}{2}-n} + \sum_{n=0}^{N/2-1} x(n)\, z^{-\left(\frac{N-1}{2}-n\right)}\right]$$

$$\triangleq z^{-(N-1)/2}\,[Q(z) + Q(z^{-1})]$$

Thus, zeros of $X(z)$ are given by

$$Q(z) + Q(z^{-1}) = 0$$

$\therefore$ A zero at $z = re^{j\theta}$ is also a zero for $z^{-1} = re^{j\theta}$. **Q.E.D.**

EXAMPLE 3.14: *A periodic sampled-data sequence is {0, 2, 1, 2, 0, 2, 1, 2, ...}. Derive the z-transform of this sequence.* *(DU, May 2003)*

SOLUTION: The sequence $x_p(n) = \{0, 2, 1, 2, 0, 2, 1, 2, ...\}$

has its one period $x(n) = \{0, 2, 1, 2\}$

$$X(z) = ZT\,[x(n)] = 0 + 2z^{-1} + z^{-2} + 2z^{-3}$$

Here the period $N = 4$

$$X_p(z) = X(z)\frac{1}{1-z^{-N}} \qquad \text{[See (3.55}a\text{)]}$$

$$= (2z^{-1} + z^{-2} + 2z^{-3})\,\frac{1}{1-z^{-4}}$$

$$\therefore \quad X_p(z) = \frac{z(2z^2 + z + 2)}{z^4 - 1} \qquad \textbf{Ans.}$$

3.9 INVERSE z-TRANSFORM (IZT)—METHODS

We shall be required to find the inverse z-transform of a given expression ($X(z)$ or $F(z)$) being the *ZT* of a sequence ($x(n)$ or $f(n)$). We shall resort to various approaches. The most common methods used are:

1. **By Partial Fraction:** Here, we split the given *ZT* into partial fractions, generally of first degree rational functions. Then comparing each of the partial fraction with standard z-transforms, we obtain the *IZT* of the given function $X(z)$.

2. **By Long Division:** Given $X(z) = \dfrac{N(z)}{D(z)}$, we divide $N(z)$ by $D(z)$ and get the quotient as a series in powers of (z^{-1}). We may write the quotient as a compact series, if possible, and try to obtain a form: $\sum_{n=-\infty}^{\infty} x(n) \cdot z^{-n}$, $x(n)$ being the coefficient sequence of various powers of (z^{-1}) in the quotient. Using this as the standard form, the *IZT* is obviously $x(n)$. In some cases, it will not be possible to put the complete quotient as a compact summation. In such cases, *IZT* of each term of the quotient, say, $a_0 + a_1z^{-1}, a_2z^{-2} + ...$ will give us time domain sequence $x(n) = \{\underset{\uparrow}{a_0}, a_1, a_2, ...,\}$.

3. **By Binomial Series Expansion:** In many cases, where $N(z)$ of given $X(z)$ is a constant, we can expand $\dfrac{k}{D(z)}$ as a binomial series. For example,

$$X(z) = \frac{k}{1 - az^{-1}} = k[1 + (az^{-1}) + (az^{-1})^2 + (az^{-1})^3...] \qquad ...(3.74)$$

We must take care here, that this expansion is valid only if $|az^{-1}|$ is less than 1. We may, at first, manipulate the given $X(z)$, where binomial expansion is feasible.

4. **By Contour Integration** (Using Residue Theorem)

We know that
$$x(n) = \frac{1}{2\pi j}\oint_C X(z)\, Z^{n-1} dz \qquad ...(3.75)$$
$$= \text{sum of Residues of } X(z)z^{n-1} \textit{ at poles contained inside the circle C.}$$

Here, we have to try for various values of n for finding complete $x(n)$. Here, the properties of ROC (see Section 3) will be very handy to decide whether the sequence $x(n)$ is causal, non-causal or mixed.

Use of Partial Fractions to Find Inverse *ZT*

EXAMPLE 3.15: *Find the inverse z-transform for*

(*a*) $X_1(z) = \dfrac{z}{\left(z-\frac{1}{2}\right)\left(z-\frac{1}{4}\right)}, \quad |z| > \dfrac{1}{2}$

(*b*) $X_2(z) = \dfrac{z}{z^2 + z + \frac{1}{2}}$

SOLUTION: Here we make use of standard results

(*a*)
$$X_1(z) = \frac{z}{\left(z-\frac{1}{2}\right)\left(z-\frac{1}{4}\right)} = \frac{1/2}{\left(z-\frac{1}{2}\right)\left(\frac{1}{2}-\frac{1}{4}\right)} + \frac{1/4}{\left(\frac{1}{4}-\frac{1}{2}\right)\left(z-\frac{1}{4}\right)}, \quad |z| > \frac{1}{2}$$
$$= \frac{2}{\left(z-\frac{1}{2}\right)} - \frac{1}{\left(z-\frac{1}{4}\right)} = \frac{2z^{-1}}{1-\frac{1}{2}z^{-1}} - \frac{z^{-1}}{1-\frac{1}{4}z^{-1}}, \quad |z| > \frac{1}{2}$$
$$\therefore \quad x_1(n) = 2\left(\frac{1}{2}\right)^n u(n)\Big|_{\text{change } n \text{ to } n-1} - \left(\frac{1}{4}\right)^n u(n)\Big|_{\text{change } n \text{ to } n-1}$$

$$= 2\left(\frac{1}{2}\right)^{n-1} u(n-1) - \left(\frac{1}{4}\right)^{n-1} u(n-1)$$

$$= 4\left[\left(\frac{1}{2}\right)^{n} - \left(\frac{1}{4}\right)^{n}\right] u(n-1)$$ **Ans.**

(b) $$X_2(z)/z = \frac{1}{z^2 + z + \frac{1}{2}} = \frac{A}{z - p_1} + \frac{B}{z - p_2}, \text{ say}$$

where $$p_1 = \frac{1}{\sqrt{2}} e^{j3\pi/4}, \ p_2 = \frac{1}{\sqrt{2}} e^{-j3\pi/4}$$

$$\therefore \quad A = \left.\frac{1}{z - p_2}\right|_{z = p_1} = \frac{1}{(p_1 - p_2)} = -j$$

$$B = \left.\frac{1}{z - p_1}\right|_{z = p_2} = \frac{1}{(p_2 - p_1)} = +j$$

$$\therefore \quad X_2(z) = \frac{jz}{z - p_1} - \frac{jz}{z - p_2} = \frac{-j}{1 - p_1 z^{-1}} + \frac{j}{1 - p_2 z^{-1}}$$

$$z^2 + z + \frac{1}{2} = 0$$

$$\therefore z_{1,2} = \frac{-1 \pm \sqrt{1-2}}{2} = \frac{-1}{2} \pm j\frac{1}{2} = \frac{1}{\sqrt{2}}\left(\frac{-1}{\sqrt{2}} \pm j\frac{1}{\sqrt{2}}\right) = \frac{1}{\sqrt{2}} e^{j\frac{3\pi}{4}}, \frac{1}{\sqrt{2}} e^{-j\frac{3\pi}{4}}$$

$$\therefore \quad x(n) = j\, u(n)\,[-p_1^n + p_2^n] = u(n)\, 2\left(\frac{1}{2}\right)^{n/2}\left[\frac{e^{j\frac{3n\pi}{4}} - e^{-j\frac{3n\pi}{4}}}{2j}\right] = 2\left(\frac{1}{2}\right)^{n/2} \sin\frac{3n\pi}{4}\, u(n)$$

Ans.

EXAMPLE 3.16: *Find x(n), if* $X(z) = \left(3 - \frac{5}{6} z^{-1}\right) \Big/ \left(1 - \frac{1}{4} z^{-1}\right)\left(1 - \frac{1}{3} z^{-1}\right)$ *with ROC:*

(*a*) $|z| > \frac{1}{3}$, (*b*) $\frac{1}{4} < |z| < \frac{1}{3}$, (*c*) $|z| < \frac{1}{4}$ *(different ROC's)*

SOLUTION:

$$X(z) = \frac{\left(3 - \frac{5}{6} z^{-1}\right)}{\left(1 - \frac{1}{4} z^{-1}\right)\left(1 - \frac{1}{3} z^{-1}\right)}$$

$$X(z) = \frac{1}{1 - \frac{1}{4} z^{-1}} + \frac{2}{\left(1 - \frac{1}{3} z^{-1}\right)}$$ (by partial fractions)

$$\triangleq X_1(z) + X_2(z) \text{ (say)}$$

$$x(n) = x_1(n) + x_2(n)$$

where $$x_1(n) = IZT\left[\frac{1}{1 - \frac{1}{4} z^{-1}}\right] \text{ and } x_2(n) = IZT\left[\frac{2}{1 - \frac{1}{3} z^{-1}}\right]$$

(*a*) For ROC: $|z| > \frac{1}{3}$,

$$x_1(n) = \left(\frac{1}{4}\right)^n u(n),$$

$$x_2(n) = 2\left(\frac{1}{3}\right)^n u(n); \quad \therefore \quad x(n) = \left[\left(\frac{1}{4}\right)^n + 2\left(\frac{1}{3}\right)^n\right] u(n)$$ **Ans.**

(*b*) For ROC: $\frac{1}{4} < |z| < \frac{1}{3}$,

$$x_1(n) = \left(\frac{1}{4}\right)^n u(n),$$

$$x_2(n) = -2\left(\frac{1}{3}\right)^n u(-n-1), \quad \therefore \quad x(n) = \left(\frac{1}{4}\right)^n u(n) - 2\left(\frac{1}{3}\right)^n u(-n-1)$$

Ans.

(*c*) For ROC: $|z| < \frac{1}{4}$,

$$x_1(n) = -\left(\frac{1}{4}\right)^n u(-n-1),$$

$$x_2(n) = -2\left(\frac{1}{3}\right)^n u(-n-1), \quad \therefore \quad x(n) = -\left[\left(\frac{1}{4}\right)^n + 2\left(\frac{1}{2}\right)^n\right] u(-n-1)$$

Ans.

Note that:

$$\frac{1}{1 - az^{-1}} \xrightarrow{IZT} a^n u(n) \text{ if } |z| > |a|$$

$$\frac{1}{1 - az^{-1}} \xrightarrow{IZT} -a^n u(-n-1) \text{ if } |z| < |a|$$

EXAMPLE 3.17: *Find, by partial fraction method, the Inverse Z-T for*

$$X(z) = \frac{1}{(1 - az^{-1})(1 - bz^{-1})} \qquad ROC: |z| > |a|, |b|$$

SOLUTION:

$$X(z) = \frac{A}{(1 - az^{-1})} + \frac{B}{(1 - bz^{-1})}$$

$$\therefore \quad A = \left.\frac{1}{1 - bz^{-1}}\right|_{z^{-1} = \frac{1}{a}} = \frac{1}{1 - \frac{b}{a}} = \frac{a}{a - b}$$

$$B = \left.\frac{1}{1 - az^{-1}}\right|_{Z^{-1} = \frac{1}{b}} = \frac{1}{1 - \frac{a}{b}} = \frac{b}{b - a}$$

$$\therefore \quad X(z) = \frac{1}{a - b}\left[\frac{a}{1 - az^{-1}} - \frac{b}{1 - bz^{-1}}\right]$$

$$\therefore \quad x(n) = \frac{a}{a - b} \cdot a^n u(n) - \frac{b}{a - b} b^n u(n)$$ **Ans.**

Note that this solution holds only if $|az^{-1}| < 1$ and also $|bz^{-1}| < 1$ *i.e.*

$$|z| > a \quad \text{and} \quad |z| > b$$

i.e., $|z| > \max(a, b)$

i.e., a contour (in Contour integral method) would include both the points $Z = a$ and $Z = b$.

EXAMPLE 3.18: *Find the inverse z-transform of X(z) by partial fraction method, where*

$$X(z) = \frac{1 - az^{-1}}{z^{-1} - a}, \quad ROC: |z| > \left|\frac{1}{a}\right| \qquad (DU\ 2004)$$

SOLUTION: To find *IZT* of $X(z) = \frac{1 - az^{-1}}{z^{-1} - a}$, $|z| > \left|\frac{1}{a}\right|$ by partial fraction

$$X(z) = \frac{1}{z^{-1} - a} - \frac{az^{-1}}{z^{-1} - a}$$

$$= -\frac{1}{a}\frac{1}{1 - \frac{1}{a}z^{-1}} + \frac{z^{-1}}{1 - \frac{1}{a}z^{-1}}$$

$$x(n) = \left(-\frac{1}{a}\right)\left(\frac{1}{a}\right)^n u(n) + \left(\frac{1}{a}\right)^{n-1} u(n-1)$$

$$x(0) = -1/a$$

$$x(n)\big|_{n>0} = -\left(\frac{1}{a}\right)^{n+1} + \left(\frac{1}{a}\right)^{n-1} = \frac{-1 + a^2}{a^{n+1}} = \frac{-(1 - a^2)}{a^{n+1}}$$

Hence,
$$x(n) = \begin{cases} -\frac{1}{a}, & n = 0 \\ -\frac{1 - a^2}{a^{n+1}}, & n > 0 \\ 0, & n < 0 \end{cases}$$ **Ans.**

We shall also solve this equation by Contour integration method and obtain the same answer (See solved Example 3.34).

EXAMPLE 3.19: *If* $X(z) = \frac{2 - (17/4)z^{-1}}{\left(1 - \frac{1}{4}z^{-1}\right)(1 - 4z^{-1})}$. *Take different ROC: (a)* $|z| > 4$, *(b)* $|z| < \frac{1}{4}$, *(c)* $\frac{1}{4} < |z| < 4$ *and determine x(n) in each case.* (*GGSIP Univ. 2007*)

SOLUTION: As
$$X(z) = \frac{2 - \frac{17}{4}z^{-1}}{\left(1 - \frac{1}{4}z^{-1}\right)(1 - 4z^{-1})}$$

$$= \frac{1}{\left(1 - \frac{1}{4}z^{-1}\right)} + \frac{1}{(1 - 4z^{-1})} \qquad \text{(by partial fractions)}$$

(a) Case ROC: $|z| > 4$ *(a causal sequence)*

Then
$$x(n) = \left(\frac{1}{4}\right)^n u(n) + (4)^n u(n)$$ **Ans.**

(b) Case ROC: $|z| < \frac{1}{4}$ *(an anticausal sequence)*

Then $$x(n) = -\left(\frac{1}{4}\right)^n u(-n-1) - (4)^n u(-n-1)$$ **Ans.**

(c) *Case ROC:* $\frac{1}{4} < |z| < 4$ *(a mixed sequence)*

Then $$x(n) = \left(\frac{1}{4}\right)^n u(n) - (4)^n u(-n-1)$$ **Ans.**

Remember that:

for $$X(z) = \frac{1}{1 - az^{-1}}$$

For ROC: $|z| > |a|$, $x(n) = a^n\, u(n)$
For ROC: $|z| < |a|$, $x(n) = -a^n\, u(-n-1)$

EXAMPLE 3.20: *Find Inverse z-transform of the function*

$$X(z) = \frac{2 - 14z + 32z^2}{1 - 6z + 8z^2}, \quad ROC: |z| > \frac{1}{2}$$ *(IP Univ. 2007)*

SOLUTION:
$$X(z) = \frac{4(1 - 6z + 8z^2) - 2 + 10z}{(1 - 6z + 8z^2)} = 4 + \frac{2(5z-1)}{(1-2z)(1-4z)}$$

$$= 4 + 2z^{-1}\frac{(5 - z^{-1})}{(z^{-1}-2)(z^{-1}-4)}$$

$$= 4 + \frac{2}{8}z^{-1}\frac{5 - z^{-1}}{\left(1 - \frac{1}{2}z^{-1}\right)\left(1 - \frac{1}{4}z^{-1}\right)}$$ (N.T.S.)

$$= 4 + \frac{1}{4}z^{-1}\left(\frac{6}{\left(1 - \frac{1}{2}z^{-1}\right)} - \frac{1}{\left(1 - \frac{1}{4}z^{-1}\right)}\right), \quad \text{ROC: } |z| > \frac{1}{2}$$

$$\therefore \quad x(n) = 4\delta(n) + \frac{1}{4}\left[6 \times \left(\frac{1}{2}\right)^{n-1} - \left(\frac{1}{4}\right)^{n-1}\right] u(n-1)$$ **Ans.**

EXAMPLE 3.21: *Determine the causal signal x(n) if its z-transform is*

$$X(z) = \frac{1}{4}\left[(1 + 6z^{-1} + z^{-2}) \,/\, (1 - 2z^{-1} + 2z^{-2})(1 - 0.5z^{-1})\right]$$ *(DU 1999)*

SOLUTION: Note that :

$$\frac{1 - r\cos\theta\, z^{-1}}{1 - 2r\cos\theta\, z^{-1} + r^2 z^{-2}} \overset{IZT}{\Rightarrow} r^n \,.\, \cos nq \,.\, u(n) \quad (3.65)$$

$$\frac{(r\sin\theta)\, z^{-1}}{1 - 2r\cos\theta\, z^{-1} + r^2 z^{-2}} \overset{IZT}{\Rightarrow} r^n \sin n\theta\, u(n) \quad (3.64)$$

Compare $1 - 2z^{-1} + 2z^{-2}$ to $1 - 2r\cos\theta\, z^{-1} + r^2 z^{-2}$ $\quad \therefore \quad r = \sqrt{2}$

$\cos\theta = 1/\sqrt{2}$

Let $$\frac{1}{4}\frac{1 + 6z^{-1} + z^{-2}}{(1 - 2z^{-1} + 2z^{-2})(1 - 0.5z^{-1})} = \frac{A(1 - z^{-1})}{1 - 2z^{-1} + 2z^{-2}} + \frac{Bz^{-1}}{1 - 2z^{-1} + 2z^{-2}} + \frac{C}{1 - 0.5z^{-1}}$$

(Note this step)

$$\therefore \quad 1 + 6z^{-1} + z^{-2} = 4\left[(A(1 - z^{-1}) + Bz^{-1})(1 - 0.5z^{-1}) + C(1 - 2z^{-1} + 2z^{-2})\right]$$

Compare constants ∴ $1 = 4[A + C]$ i.e., $A + C = 1/4$ (P)

Compare z^{-1} coefficient ∴ $6 = 4[B - A - 0.5A - 2C]$ i.e., $-6A + 4B - 8C = 6$ (Q)

Compare z^{-2} coefficient ∴ $1 = 4[(B - A)(-0.5) + 2C]$ i.e., $2A - 2B + 8C = 1$ (R)

Solving (P), (Q) and (R), we obtain $A = -3/5$, $B = 23/10$, $C = 17/20$.

Hence,
$$X(z) = \frac{(-3/5)(1 - z^{-1})}{1 - 2z^{-1} + 2z^{-2}} + \frac{(23/10)(z^{-1})}{1 - 2z^{-1} + 2z^{-2}} + \frac{(17/20)}{1 - 0.5z^{-1}}$$

$$\therefore \quad x(n) = \left[-\frac{3}{5}\left(\frac{1}{\sqrt{2}}\right)^n \cos\frac{\pi}{4}n + \frac{23}{10}\left(\frac{1}{\sqrt{2}}\right)^n \sin\frac{\pi}{4}n + \frac{17}{20}(0.5)^n\right] u(n) \quad \textbf{Ans.}$$

We have used (3.64) and (3.65) to find *IZT* for the first two terms, here $r = \sqrt{2}$, $\theta = \pi/4$,

EXAMPLE 3.22: *Find the inverse z-transform of the function*

(i) $X(z) = \dfrac{1}{2(z + 0.5)(z - 1)}$, ROC : $|z| > 1$

(ii) $F(z) = \dfrac{1}{\left(1 - \frac{1}{2}z^{-1}\right)\left(1 - \frac{1}{4}z^{-1}\right)}$ ROC: $|z| > \dfrac{1}{2}$ *(IP Univ. 2001)*

SOLUTION: (i)
$$X(z) = \frac{1}{2}\cdot\frac{1}{z^2}\left[\frac{1}{(1 + 0.5z^{-1})(1 - z^{-1})}\right] = \frac{\frac{1}{2}z^{-2}}{(1 + 0.5z^{-1})(1 - z^{-1})}, \quad \text{ROC: } |z| > 1$$

Let
$$X_1(z) = \frac{1}{(1 + 0.5z^{-1})(1 - z^{-1})} \quad \text{(N.T.S.)}$$

$$= \frac{1/3}{1 + 0.5z^{-1}} + \frac{2/3}{1 - z^{-1}}, \quad \text{ROC: } |z| > 1$$

$$\therefore \quad x_1(n) = \left[\frac{1}{3}(-0.5)^n + \frac{2}{3}\right] u(n)$$

$$x(n) = \frac{1}{2} \times x_1(n)\Big|_{\text{change } n \text{ to } n - 2}$$

$$\therefore \quad x(n) = \frac{1}{2}\left[\frac{1}{3}(-0.5)^{n-2} + \frac{2}{3}\right] u(n - 2) \quad \textbf{Ans.}$$

Note that $x(0) = 0$, $x(1) = 0$, $x(2) = \dfrac{1}{2}$, $x(3) = \dfrac{1}{4}$, ...,

(ii)
$$F(z) = \frac{1}{\left(1 - \frac{1}{2}z^{-1}\right)\left(1 - \frac{1}{4}z^{-1}\right)}, \quad \text{ROC: } |z| > \frac{1}{2}$$

$$= \frac{2}{1 - \frac{1}{2}z^{-1}} + \frac{-1}{1 - \frac{1}{4}z^{-1}} \quad \text{(by partial fraction)}$$

$$\therefore \quad f(n) = \left[2\left(\frac{1}{2}\right)^n - \left(\frac{1}{4}\right)^n\right] u(n)$$

$$= \left(\frac{1}{4}\right)^n [2(2)^n - 1]\, u(n)$$

$$= \left(\frac{1}{4}\right)^n [2^{n+1} - 1]\, u(n) \qquad \textbf{Ans.}$$

Note that $f(0) = 1, f(1) = \frac{3}{4}, f(2) = \frac{7}{16}, \ldots$

EXAMPLE 3.23: *Find the inverse z-transforms for causal functions $f_1(n)$ and $f_2(n)$ if*

(i) $F_1(z) = \dfrac{z}{z^2 - z + 1}$ (ii) $F_2(z) = \dfrac{z-1}{(z-a)^2}$ *(IP Univ. 2000)*

SOLUTION: (i) $F_1(z) = \dfrac{z}{z^2 - z + 1} = \dfrac{z}{(z - p_1)(z - p_2)}$, (say)

$$= \frac{p_1/(p_1 - p_2)}{(z - p_1)} + \frac{p_2/(p_2 - p_1)}{(z - p_2)}$$

(by partial fractions)

$$= \frac{\frac{1}{2\sqrt{3}}(\sqrt{3} - j)}{(z - p_1)} + \frac{\frac{1}{2\sqrt{3}}(\sqrt{3} + j)}{(z - p_2)}$$

$$= \frac{\sqrt{3} - j}{2\sqrt{3}} \cdot \frac{z^{-1}}{(1 - p_1 z^{-1})} + \frac{\sqrt{3} + j}{2\sqrt{3}} \cdot \frac{z^{-1}}{1 - p_2 z^{-1}}$$

$$\therefore \quad f_1(n) = \left[\frac{\sqrt{3} - j}{2\sqrt{3}} (p_1)^{n-1} + \frac{\sqrt{3} + j}{2\sqrt{3}} (p_2)^{n-1}\right] u(n-1) \quad \textbf{Ans.}$$

where $p_1 = \frac{1}{2}(1 + j\sqrt{3})$ and $p_2 = \frac{1}{2}(1 - j\sqrt{3})$,

(as shown in the RHS box)

$$z_{1,2} = \frac{1 \pm \sqrt{1-4}}{2}$$

$$p_{1,2} = \frac{1}{2} \pm j\frac{\sqrt{3}}{2}$$

where $p_1 = \frac{1}{2} + j\frac{\sqrt{3}}{2}$

$$p_2 = \frac{1}{2} - j\frac{\sqrt{3}}{2}$$

$$\therefore \; p_1 - p_2 = j\sqrt{3}$$

$$\frac{p_1}{(p_1 - p_2)} = \frac{\left(\frac{1}{2} + j\frac{\sqrt{3}}{2}\right)}{j\sqrt{3}} = \frac{1}{2} - j\frac{1}{2\sqrt{3}}$$

$$-\frac{p_2}{(p_1 - p_2)} = \frac{-\left(\frac{1}{2} - j\frac{\sqrt{3}}{2}\right)}{j\sqrt{3}} = \frac{1}{2\sqrt{3}}(\sqrt{3} + j)$$

(ii)
$$F_2(z) = \frac{z-1}{(z-a)^2}$$

$$= \frac{(z-a) - (1-a)}{(z-a)^2} = \frac{1}{z-a} + \frac{a-1}{(z-a)^2}$$

$$= \frac{z^{-1}}{1 - az^{-1}} + \left(\frac{a-1}{a}\right)(z^{-1}) \frac{az^{-1}}{(1 - az^{-1})^2}$$

$$\therefore \quad f_2(n) = a^n u(n)\Big|_{\text{change } n \text{ to } n-1} + \frac{a-1}{a} na^n u(n)\Big|_{\text{change } n \text{ to } n-1} \quad \text{assuming ROC: } |z| > |a|$$

$$= a^{n-1} u(n-1) + \frac{a-1}{a}(n-1)\, a^{n-1} u(n-1)$$

$$\because \; IZT\left[\frac{1}{(1 - az^{-1})^2} = na^n u(n)\right]$$

$$= \left[a^{n-1} + \frac{a-1}{a}(n-1)\,a^{n-1}\right]u(n-1) = a^{n-1}\left[1 + \frac{a-1}{a}(n-1)\right]u(n-1)$$

Ans.

Note that $f_2(0) = 0$, $f_2(1) = 1$, $f_2(2) = 2a - 1$ and so on.

EXAMPLE 3.24: *By using (i) long division, (ii) partial fraction, determine the inverse z-transform of* $X(z) = 1\Big/\left(1 - \frac{3}{2}z^{-1} + \frac{1}{2}z^{-2}\right)$ *when ROC* $|z| > 1$; *ROC* $|z| < \frac{1}{2}$.

SOLUTION:

(*i*) **By partial fractions**

$$X(z) = \frac{1}{1 - \frac{3}{2}z^{-1} + \frac{1}{2}z^{-2}} = \frac{1}{(1 - z^{-1})\left(1 - \frac{1}{2}z^{-1}\right)} = \frac{2}{(1 - z^{-1})} + \frac{-1}{\left(1 - \frac{1}{2}z^{-1}\right)} \quad \text{(Partial fractions)}$$

$\therefore$ for ROC : $|z| > 1$, $\quad x(n) = 2\,u(n) - \left(\frac{1}{2}\right)^n u(n)$ **Ans.** ...(*A*) RH sequence

for ROC : $|z| < \frac{1}{2}$ $\quad x(n) = \left[-2 + \left(\frac{1}{2}\right)^n\right]u(-n-1)$ **Ans.** ...(*B*) LH sequence

(*ii*) **By long division**

For ROC : $|z| > 1$, the function $x(n)$ is causal, hence, we have (to obtain $X(z)$ in power of z^{-k}, $k = 0, 1, ...$,

$$\begin{array}{r|l} & 1 + \frac{3}{2}z^{-1} + \frac{7}{4}z^{-2} + \frac{15}{8}z^{-3} \\ \hline 1 - \frac{3}{2}z^{-1} + \frac{1}{2}z^{-2} & 1 \\ & 1 - \frac{3}{2}z^{-1} + \frac{1}{2}z^{-2} \\ \hline & \frac{3}{2}z^{-1} - \frac{1}{2}z^{-2} \\ & \frac{3}{2}z^{-1} - \frac{9}{4}z^{-2} + \frac{3}{4}z^{-3} \\ \hline & \frac{7}{4}z^{-2} - \frac{3}{4}z^{-3} \\ & \frac{7}{4}z^{-2} - \frac{21}{8}z^{-3} + \frac{7}{8}z^{-4} \\ \hline & \frac{15}{8}z^{-3} - \frac{7}{8}z^{-4} \end{array}$$

$\therefore$ $X(z) = 1 + \frac{3}{2}z^{-1} + \frac{7}{4}z^{-2} + \frac{15}{8}z^{-3} + ..$ or $x(n) = \left\{\underset{\uparrow}{1}, \frac{3}{2}, \frac{7}{4}, \frac{15}{8}, ...\right\}$ we get the same values from (*A*)

For ROC : $|z| < \frac{1}{2}$, the function $x(n)$ is non-causal, hence (to obtain $X(z)$ in +ve power of z, and rearrange the divison terms (Note this step)

$$\begin{array}{r} 2z^2+6z^3+14z^4+30z^5 \\ \frac{1}{2}z^{-2}-\frac{3}{2}z^{-1}+1 \overline{) \; 1 \qquad\qquad\qquad\qquad} \\ \underline{1-3z+2z^2} \\ 3z-2z^2 \\ \underline{3z-9z^2+6z^3} \\ 7z^2-6z^3 \\ \underline{7z^2-21z^3+14z^4} \\ 15z^3-14z^4 \end{array}$$

$\therefore \quad X(z) = 2z^2 + 6z^3 + 14z^4 + 30z^5 + \ldots$ or $= 0 + 0z + 2z^2 + 6z^3 + 14z^4 + 30z^5 + \ldots$

$$x(n) = \left\{ \begin{matrix} \ldots 30, 14, 6, 2, 0, 0 \\ \uparrow \end{matrix} \right\}$$ **Ans.**

We get from (B), $x(0) = 0$, $x(-1) = 0$, $x(-2) = 2$, $x(-3) = 6$, $x(-4) = 14$ and so on $\therefore$ verified

Use of Binomial Expansion and Long Division to Find Inverse Z.T.

We give some examples to illustrate the determination of IZT by binomial expansion and long division.

EXAMPLE 3.25: *Find the inverse z-transform of*

$$X(z) = \frac{K}{z-\omega} \qquad ROC : |z| > |\omega|$$

SOLUTION: Assume $|z| > |\omega|$ *i.e.*, $|\omega z^{-1}| < 1$, then

$$X(z) = \frac{K}{z-\omega} = \frac{k}{z}\left(1-\omega z^{-1}\right)^{-1} \qquad \text{(Note this step)}$$

$$= \frac{K}{z}\left[1+\omega z^{-1}+\omega^2 z^{-2}+\omega^3 z^{-3}+\ldots\right]$$

$$= K\left[z^{-1}+\omega z^{-2}+\omega^2 z^{-3}+\omega^3 z^{-4}+\ldots\right]$$

$$= \sum_{n=1}^{\infty} K\omega^{n-1} z^{-n}$$

$$= \sum_{n=-\infty}^{\infty} K\omega^{n-1} z^{-n}\, u(n-1) \qquad \text{(Note this step)}$$

$$= K\sum_{n=-\infty}^{\infty} \left[\omega^{n-1} u(n-1)\right] z^{-n} \qquad \text{form } \sum_{n=-\infty}^{\infty} x(n) z^{-n}$$

By inspection $\quad x(n) = K\,\omega^{n-1} u(n-1)$ **Ans.**

EXAMPLE 3.26: *Find the inverse z-transform of X(z) given by*

$$X(z) = \frac{1}{1+\frac{1}{2}z^{-1}}, |z| > \frac{1}{2}$$

by (i) Binomial expansion, (ii) Long division method.

SOLUTION: ***(i)*** Binomial expansion of $\left(1+\frac{1}{2}z^{-1}\right)^{-1}$ is only possible if $\left|\frac{1}{2}z^{-1}\right| < 1$. Here as $|z| > \frac{1}{2}$, therefore, we can expand

$$\left(1+\frac{1}{2}z^{-1}\right) = 1-\left(\frac{1}{2}z^{-1}\right)+\left(\frac{1}{2}z^{-1}\right)^2-\left(\frac{1}{2}z^{-1}\right)^3+\ldots$$

$$= \sum_{n=0}^{\infty}(-1)^n\left(\frac{1}{2}z^{-1}\right)^n \quad \text{(putting in a series form)}$$

$$= \sum_{n=0}^{\infty}\left(-\frac{1}{2}\right)^n z^{-n} = \sum_{n=-\infty}^{\infty}\left(-\frac{1}{2}\right)^n u(n).z^{-n} \qquad \text{(Note this step)}$$

Hence, $\quad x(n) = \left(-\frac{1}{2}\right)^n u(n)$ **Ans.**

***(ii)* By long division**

$$\begin{array}{r|l}
 & 1-\frac{1}{2}z^{-1}+\frac{1}{4}z^{-2}-\ldots \\ \hline
1+\frac{1}{2}z^{-1} & 1 \\
 & \underline{1+\frac{1}{2}z^{-1}} \\
 & -\frac{1}{2}z^{-1} \\
 & \underline{-\frac{1}{2}z^{-1}-\frac{1}{4}z^{-2}} \\
 & \frac{1}{4}z^{-2} \\
 & \underline{\frac{1}{4}z^{-2}+\frac{1}{8}z^{-3}} \\
 & -\frac{1}{8}z^{-3} \\
 & \vdots
\end{array}$$

$\therefore$
$$X(z) = 1-\frac{1}{2}z^{-1}+\left(\frac{1}{2}\right)^2 z^{-2}-\left(\frac{1}{2}\right)^3 z^{-3}+\ldots$$

$$= \sum_{n=0}^{\infty}\left(-\frac{1}{2}\right)^n z^{-n} = \sum_{n=-\infty}^{\infty}\left(-\frac{1}{2}\right)^n u(n).z^{-n}$$

$\therefore \quad x(n) = \left(-\frac{1}{2}\right)^n u(n)$, as expected **Ans.**

EXAMPLE 3.27: *Find the discrete-time signal x(n) where ZT is given by* $X(z) = \log(1 + az^{-1})$, $|z| > |a|$.

SOLUTION: Let $X_1(z) = (-z)\frac{d}{dz}X(z)$ (N.T.S.)

$$= (-z)\frac{-az^{-2}}{1+az^{-1}}$$

$$= +(az^{-1})\frac{1}{1+az^{-1}} = a\frac{z^{-1}}{1-(-a)z^{-1}}$$

$$x_1(n) = a(-a)^{n-1}u(n-1)$$

But $\quad x_1(n) = n\,x(n) \quad \left(\because n\,x(n) \longrightarrow (-z)\frac{d}{dz}x(z)\right)$

$$x(n) = \frac{a}{n}(-a)^{n-1}\,u(n-1) = (-1)^{n-1}\frac{a^n}{n}\,u(n-1)$$ **Ans.**

Alternative Solution

We can also expand log $(1 + az^{-1})$ by using the series $\log(1+x) = x - \frac{x^2}{2} + \frac{x^3}{3} - \frac{x^4}{4} + \ldots$ if $|x| < 1$.

The solution by this approach is given in the next example.

EXAMPLE 3.28: *Obtain the Inverse z-transform for*

$$X(z) = \log_e(1 + az^{-1}) \quad \text{ROC} : |a| < |z|$$

SOLUTION: As $\log(1+x) = x - \frac{x^2}{2} + \frac{x^3}{3} - \frac{x^4}{4} + \ldots,\ x < 1$ (Standard expansion of $\log_e$).

$\therefore$
$$X(z) = \log_e(1 + az^{-1})$$
$$= az^{-1} - \frac{1}{2}(az^{-1}) + \frac{1}{3}(az^{-1})^3 - \frac{1}{4}(az^{-1})^4 + \ldots$$

Here, $|az^{-1}| = \left|\frac{a}{z}\right| < 1$ (given), hence log expansion is valid.

$\therefore$
$$X(z) = \sum_{n=1}^{\infty}(-1)^{n+1}\frac{1}{n}(az^{-})^n$$
$$= \sum_{n=-\infty}^{\infty}\left[(-1)^{n+1}\frac{a^n}{n}u(n-1)\right]z^{-n}, \text{ form } \sum_{n=-\infty}^{\infty}x(n)\,z^{-n}$$

$\therefore$ by inspection
$$x(n) = (-1)^{n+1}\frac{a^n}{n}u(n-1)$$ **Ans.**

or
$$x(n) = \begin{cases}(-1)^{n+1}\dfrac{a^n}{n}, & n \geq 1\\ 0, & n < 1\end{cases}$$ **Ans.**

EXAMPLE 3.29: *Find the inverse z-transform for*

$$X_1(z) = \frac{1-az^{-1}}{z^{-1}-a}, \quad ROC\ |z| < \left|\frac{1}{a}\right|$$ *(D.U. 1994, 1997)*

SOLUTION: Here $|az| < 1$

$$X_1(z) = \frac{1}{z^{-1}-a} - \frac{az^{-1}}{z^{-1}-a}$$
$$= \frac{z}{1-az} - \frac{a}{1-az}$$

Now $\frac{1}{1-az} = 1 + az + (az)^2 + (az)^3 + \ldots$ (since, $|az| < 1$, we can use Binomial expansion)

$$= \sum_{n=0}^{\infty} (az)^n$$

$$= \sum_{n=-\infty}^{0} (az)^{-n}$$

$$= \sum_{n=-\infty}^{\infty} a^{-n}u(-n)z^{-n} \qquad \because\ u(-n) = 0 \text{ for } n > 0$$

$$\therefore \qquad \frac{1}{1-az} \xrightarrow{IZT} = a^{-n}\, u(-n)$$

$$\frac{z}{1-az} - \frac{a}{1-az} \xrightarrow{IZT} a^{-(n+1)}\, u(-n-1) - a.a^{-n}\, u(-n)$$

$$X_1(z) \xrightarrow{IZT} a^{-(n+1)}\, u(-n-1) - a^{-(n-1)}\, u(-n)$$

i.e., $x_1(n) = a^{-(n+1)}\, u(-n-1) - a^{-(n-1)}\, u(-n)$

$x_1(0) = 0 - a$

Hence, $$x_1(n) = \begin{cases} -a, & n = 0 \\ a^{-(n+1)} - a^{-(n-1)}, & n \le -1 \\ 0, & n > 0 \end{cases}$$ **Ans.**

(Students should note the difference in Examples 3.18 and 3.29)

EXAMPLE 3.30: *Find the inverse z-transform of X(z), by long division method*

$$X(z) = \frac{1 - \frac{1}{2}z^{-1}}{1 + \frac{3}{4}z^{-1} + \frac{1}{8}z^{-2}}, \qquad ROC: |z| > \frac{1}{2}$$

SOLUTION: As the signal is causal and $X(z)$ has numerator degree of z^{-1} lower than that of the denominator, we proceed as follows for division

$$1 + \left(\frac{-3}{4} - \frac{1}{2}\right)z^{-1} + \left(-\frac{3}{16} + 1\right)z^{-2} + \ldots$$

$$1 + \frac{3}{4}z^{-1} + \frac{1}{8}z^{-2} \;\Big)\; 1 - \frac{1}{2}z^{-1}$$

$$1 + \frac{3}{4}z^{-1} + \frac{1}{8}z^{-2}$$

$$\left(\frac{-3}{4} - \frac{1}{2}\right)z^{-1} - \frac{1}{8}z^{-2}$$

$$\left(\frac{-3}{4} - \frac{1}{2}\right)z^{-1} + \frac{3}{4}\left(\frac{-3}{4} - \frac{1}{2}\right)z^{-2} + \frac{1}{8}\left(-\frac{3}{4} - \frac{1}{2}\right)z^{-3}$$

$$\left[-\frac{1}{8} + \frac{3}{4}\left(\frac{3}{4} + \frac{1}{2}\right)\right]z^{-2} + \frac{1}{8}\left(\frac{3}{4} + \frac{1}{2}\right)z^{-3}$$

$$\therefore \quad X(z) = 1 - \frac{1}{2}z^{-1} + 1z^{-2} - ...$$

$$- 3\left[\frac{1}{4}z^{-1} + \frac{1}{16}z^{-2} + ...\right] = (4 - 2z^{-1} + z^{-2} - ...) - 3\left(1 - \frac{1}{4}z^{-1} + \frac{1}{16}z^{-2}...\right)$$

$$= 4\sum_{n=0}^{+\infty}\left(\frac{-1}{2}\right)^n z^{-n} + \sum_{n=0}^{\infty}(-3)\left(\frac{-1}{4}\right)^n z^{-n}$$

Note that the method of arranging the quotient terms to elegent form may not always work.

$$\therefore \quad x(n) = 4\left(\frac{-1}{2}\right)^n u(n) - 3\left(\frac{-1}{4}\right)^n u(n)$$

$$= \left[\left(\frac{-1}{2}\right)^{n-2} - 3\left(\frac{-1}{4}\right)^n\right]u(n) \qquad \textbf{Ans.}$$

EXAMPLE 3.31: *Determine the inverse ZT for*

(i) $X_1(z) = \log(1 - 2Z),\ |z| < \frac{1}{2}$

(ii) $X_2(z) = \log\left(1 - \frac{1}{2}z^{-1}\right),\ |z| > \frac{1}{2}$ *(IP Univ. 2006)*

SOLUTION: We know that $\log(1 + x) = x - \frac{x^2}{2} + \frac{x^3}{3} - \frac{x^4}{4} + \frac{x^5}{5} - ...$ *if* $x < 1$

(i)

$$X_1(z) = \log(1 - 2z), \quad |z| < \frac{1}{2} \quad \therefore |2z| < 1.$$

$$= -\left[(2z) + \frac{1}{2}(2z)^2 + \frac{1}{3}(2z)^3 + \frac{1}{4}(2z)^4 + ...\right], \text{ valid expansion as } |2z| < 1$$

$$= -\sum_{n=1}^{\infty}(2z)^n \cdot \frac{1}{n}. \qquad \text{Put } n = -m$$

$$= -\sum_{m=-\infty}^{-1} 2^{-m} \cdot \left(\frac{-1}{m}\right) \cdot z^{-m}$$

$$= \sum_{m=-\infty}^{\infty}\left(\frac{2^{-m}}{m} \cdot z^{-m}\right)(u(-m-1))$$

$$= \sum_{n=-\infty}^{\infty}\left[+\frac{2^{-n}}{n}u(-n-1)\right] \cdot z^{-n} \qquad \text{(changing } m \text{ to } n\text{)}$$

$$x_1(n) = \frac{2^{-n}}{n}u(-n-1) = \frac{1}{n} \cdot \left(\frac{1}{2}\right)^n u(-n-1) \qquad \textbf{Ans.}$$

(ii)

$$X_2(z) = \log\left(1 - \frac{1}{2}z^{-1}\right), |z| > \frac{1}{2}$$

As $\left[\frac{1}{2}z^{-1}\right] < 1$, therefore, we have

$$X_2(z) = -\left[\frac{1}{2}z^{-1} + \frac{1}{2}\left(\frac{1}{2}z^{-1}\right)^2 + \frac{1}{3}\left(\frac{1}{2}z^{-1}\right)^3 + ...\right]$$

$$= -\sum_{n=1}^{\infty}\frac{1}{n}\left(\frac{1}{2}z^{-1}\right)^n$$

$$= -\sum_{n=-\infty}^{\infty}\left[\frac{1}{n}\left(\frac{1}{2}\right)^n . u(n-1)\right]z^{-n} \qquad (\because u(n-1) = 0 \text{ for } n < 1)$$

$$x_2(n) = -\frac{1}{n}\left(\frac{1}{2}\right)^n . u(n-1)$$ **Ans.**

EXAMPLE 3.32: *Find the inverse z-transform of*

(i) $F_1(z) = \dfrac{z(z^2+4z+1)}{(z-1)^4}, |z| > 1$

(ii) $F_2(z) = \dfrac{z(z^2+4z+1)}{(z-1)^4}, |z| < 1$

by long division method.

SOLUTION:

(i) Since, $|z| > 1$, we write the terms in denominator with |parameters| less than 1. Then we can divide (or even apply other methods)

$$F_1(z) = \frac{z(z^2+4z+1)}{(z-1)^4} = \frac{z^{-1}(1+4z^{-1}+z^{-2})}{(1-z^{-1})^4} \qquad \text{(Note this step, here } |z^{-1}| < 1)$$

$$= \frac{z^{-1}+4z^{-2}+z^{-3}}{1-4z^{-1}+6z^{-2}-4z^{-3}+z^{-4}}$$

arrange numerator and denominator such that these have decreasing values. Here, $|z^{-1}| < 1$, hence $|z^{-2}|$ is less than $|z^{-1}|$, and so on

$$\begin{array}{r l}
 & z^{-1}+8z^{-2}+27z^{-3}+64z^{-4}+125z^{-5}+216z^{-6}+... \\
1-4z^{-1}+6z^{-2}-4z^{-3}+z^{-4} \,\big) & z^{-1}+4z^{-2}+z^{-3} \\
 & z^{-1}-4z^{-2}+6z^{-3}-4z^{-4}+z^{-5} \\ \hline
 & 8z^{-2}-5z^{-3}+4z^{-4}-z^{-5} \\
 & 8z^{-2}-32z^{-3}+48z^{-4}-32z^{-5}+8z^{-6} \\ \hline
 & 27z^{-3}-44z^{-4}+31z^{-5}-8z^{-6} \\
 & 27z^{-3}-108z^{-4}+162z^{-5}-108z^{-6}+27z^{-7} \\ \hline
 & 64z^{-4}-131z^{-5}+100z^{-6}-27z^{-7} \\
 & 64z^{-4}-256z^{-5}+384z^{-6}-256z^{-7}+64z^{-8} \\ \hline
 & 125z^{-5}-284z^{-6}+229z^{-7}-64z^{-8} \\
 & 125z^{-5}-500z^{-6}+750z^{-7}... \\ \hline
 & 216z^{-6}-521z^{-7}...
\end{array}$$

Clearly, $$F_1(z) = \sum_{i=1}^{\infty} i^3 z^{-2}$$

$$= \sum_{n=-\infty}^{\infty} n^3 u(n) z^{-n}$$

$\therefore$ $$f_1(n) = n^3 u(n)$$ **Ans.**

(*ii*) $$F_2(z) = \frac{z(z^2+4z+1)}{(z-1)^4}, \quad \text{ROC: } |z| < 1$$

As ROC gives $|z| < 1$ $\therefore$ terms like $z^2, z^3...,$ have moduli, less than unity. Thus, we write

$$F_2(z) = \frac{z + 4z^2 + z^3}{1 - 4z + 6z^2 - 4z^3 + z^4}, \quad |z| > 1$$

$$\begin{array}{r|l}
 & z + 8z^2 + 27z^3 + 64z^4 + 125z^5 + 216z^6 + ... \\
\hline
1 - 4z + 6z^2 - 4z^3 + z^4 & z + 4z^2 + z^3 \\
 & z - 4z^2 + 6z^3 - 4z^4 + z^5 \\
\hline
 & 8z^2 - 5z^3 + 4z^4 - z^5 \\
 & 8z^2 - 32z^3 + 48z^4 - 32z^5 + 8z^6 \\
\hline
 & 27z^3 - 44z^4 + 31z^5 - 8z^6 \\
 & 27z^3 - 108z^4 + 162z^5 - 108z^6 + 27z^7 \\
\hline
 & 64z^4 - 131z^5 + 100z^6 - 27z^7 \\
 & 64z^4 - 256z^5 + 384z^6 - 256z^7 + 64z^8 \\
\hline
 & 125z^5 - 284z^6 + 229z^7 - 64z^8 \\
 & 125z^5 - 500z^6 + 750z^7 \\
\hline
 & 216z^6 - 521z^7 + ... \\
 & 216z^6 - ...
\end{array}$$

Clearly, $$F_2(z) = \sum_{i=1}^{\infty} i^3 z^i$$

$$= \sum_{n=-\infty}^{\infty} n^3 u(n-1) z^n$$

Change n to $-n'$ and dropping, dashes we have

$$F_2(z) = \sum_{n=-\infty}^{\infty} (-n)^3 u(-n-1) z^{-n} \qquad \therefore f_2(n) = (-n)^3 u(-n-1)$$ **Ans.**

EXAMPLE 3.33: *Find the inverse z-transform of the following by means of long division as well as by Residue method, given*

$$F(z) = \frac{z(z^2 + 4z + 1)}{(z-1)^4}, \quad |z| > 1$$

SOLUTION:
$$F(z) = \frac{z^3 + 4z^2 + z}{z^4 - 4z^3 + 6z^2 - 4z + z^0} = \frac{z^{-1} + 4z^{-2} + z^{-3}}{1 - 4z^{-1} + 6z^{-2} - 4z^{-3} + z^{-4}} \quad \text{(N.T.S)}$$

$$\begin{array}{r|l}
 & z^{-1} + 8z^{-2} + 27z^{-3} + 64z^{-4} + 125z^{-5} + \ldots \\
\hline
1 - 4z^{-1} + 6z^{-2} - 4z^{-3} + z^{-4} & z^{-1} + 4z^{-2} + z^{-3} \\
 & z^{-1} - 4z^{-2} + 6z^{-3} - 4z^{-4} + z^{-5} \\
\hline
 & 8z^{-2} - 5z^{-3} + 4z^{-4} - z^{-5} \\
 & 8z^{-2} - 32z^{-3} + 48z^{-4} - 32z^{-5} + 8z^{-6} \\
\hline
 & 27z^{-3} - 44z^{-4} + 31z^{-5} - 8z^{-6} \\
 & 27z^{-3} - 108z^{-4} + 162z^{-5} - 108z^{-6} + 27z^{-7} \\
\hline
 & 64z^{-4} - 131z^{-5} + 100z^{-6} - 27z^{-7} \\
 & 64z^{-4} - 256z^{-5} + 384z^{-6} - 256z^{-7} + 64z^{-8} \\
\hline
 & 125z^{-5} - 284z^{6}
\end{array}$$

Hence,
$$F(z) = z^{-1} + 8z^{-2} + 27z^{-3} + 64z^{-4} + 125z^{-5} + \ldots$$

$$= \sum_{n=0}^{\infty} n^3 z^{-n} = \sum_{n=-\infty}^{\infty} n^3 u(n) \cdot z^{-n}$$

$\therefore$
$$f(n) = n^3 u(n)$$
Ans.

An alternative method (Residue Method)

As
$$F(z) = \frac{z(z^2 + 4z + 1)}{(z-1)^4}$$

$$f(n) = \Sigma \text{ Residues of } F(z)\, z^{n-1}$$

$$= \text{Residue of } \left.\frac{z(z^2 + 4z + 1)\, z^{n-1}}{(z-1)^4}\right|_{z=1}$$

$$= \frac{1}{3!} + \frac{d^3}{dz^3}\left[z(z^2 + 4z + 1) z^{n-1}\right]\Big|_{z=1}$$

$$= \frac{1}{6}\frac{d^3}{dz^3}\left[z^{n+2} + 4z^{n+1} + z^n\right]\Big|_{z=1}$$

$$= \lim_{z \to 1} \frac{1}{6}\left[(n+2)(n+1)n \,.\, z^{n-1} + 4(n+1)\, n(n-1) z^{n-2} + n(n-1)(n-2)\, z^{n-3}\right]$$

$$= \frac{1}{6}\left[n\left\{n^2 + 3n + 2 + 4(n^2 - 1) + (n^2 - 3n + 2)\right\}\right]$$

$$= \frac{1}{6}\left[n\left\{6n^2 + 0 + 0\right\}\right]$$

$$= n^3$$

$$\therefore \quad f(n) = n^3 u(n)$$ **Ans.**

$n = -1$ $$F(z)\, z^{n-1} = \frac{z^2/+ 4z + 1}{(z-1)^4\, z}$$

$$\Sigma \text{ residues} = \underset{z=1}{\text{Residue}} + \underset{z=0}{\text{Residue}} = \frac{1}{6}\frac{d^3}{dz^3}\frac{z^2 + 4z + 1}{z}\Bigg|_{z=1} + \frac{z^4 + 4z + 1}{(z-1)}\Bigg|_{z=0}$$

$$= \frac{1}{6}\left[0 + 0 - \frac{6}{z^4}\right]\Bigg|_{z=1} + 1 = -1 + 1 = 0 \qquad \therefore x(-1) = 0$$

$n = -2$ $$F(z)\, z^{n-1} = \frac{z^2 + 4z + 1}{(z-1)^4\, z^2}$$

$$x(-2) = \Sigma \text{ residues of } F(z)z^{n-1} = \underset{z=1}{\text{Residue}}\ \frac{z^4 + 4z + 1}{(z-1)^4 z^2} + \underset{z=0}{\text{Residue}}\ \frac{z^4 + 4z + 1}{(z-1)^4\, z^2}$$

$$= \frac{1}{6}\frac{d^3}{dz^3}\left[\frac{z^4 + 4z + 1}{z^2}\right]\Bigg|_{z=1} + \frac{d}{dz}\frac{z^4 + 4z + 1}{(z-1)^4}\Bigg|_{z=0}$$

$$= \frac{1}{6}\left[0 - \frac{24}{z^4} - \frac{24}{z^5}\right]\Bigg|_{z=1} + \frac{(z-1)^4\,(4z^3 + 4) - 4(z-1)^3\,(z^4 + 4z + 1)}{(z-1)^8}\Bigg|_{z=0} = -8 + 8 = 0$$

We find that $x(n) = 0$ for n –ve, for all n.

Hence, $$x(n) = n^3 u(n)$$ **Ans.**

Inverse z-transform by Contour Integration/Residue Method

We give below some examples to illustrate the determination of *IZT* by the Contour Integration/ Residue method.

EXAMPLE 3.34: *Determine the inverse z-transform of X(z) by Contour Integration method, if*

$$X(z) = \frac{1 - az^{-1}}{z^{-1} - a}, \quad \text{ROC} : |z| > \left|\frac{1}{a}\right|$$

SOLUTION: Here $X(z) = \dfrac{1 - az^{-1}}{z^{-1} - a}$ $\quad |z| > |1/a|$

(*i*) By contour integration : $$x(n) = \frac{1}{2\pi j}\oint_C \frac{1 - az^{-1}}{z^{-1} - a}\, z^{n-1}\, dz$$

$$\therefore \quad x(n) = \frac{1}{2\pi j}\oint_C \frac{-(z-a)}{a\,(z - 1/a)}\, z^{n-1} dz,$$ C is a circle of radius > $1/a$

For $n > 0$, a single pole at $z = 1/a$ is enclosed by C.

$$x(n) = \left.\frac{-(z-a)z^{n-1}}{a\left(z-\frac{1}{a}\right)}\left(z-\frac{1}{a}\right)\right|_{z=\frac{1}{a}} = \frac{-\left(\frac{1}{a}-a\right)}{a}\left(\frac{1}{a}\right)^{n-1} = -\frac{1-a^{-2}}{a^{n+1}}, n > 0$$

For $n = 0$, the poles are at $z = 0$ $z = 1/a$.

Residue at for $n = 0$, at $z = 0$ is $\left.\frac{-(z-a)\,z^{n-1}}{za\left(z-\frac{1}{a}\right)} \times z\right|_{z=0} = \frac{a}{-1} = -a$

Residue for $n = 0$, at $z = \frac{1}{a}$ is $\left.\frac{-(z-a)}{z\,a\left(z-\frac{1}{a}\right)}\left(z-\frac{1}{a}\right)\right|_{z=\frac{1}{a}} = -\left(\frac{1}{a}-a\right) = a - \frac{1}{a}$

$\therefore$
$$x(0) = (-a) + \left(a - \frac{1}{a}\right) = -\frac{1}{a}$$

Thus,
$$x(n) = \begin{cases} \frac{-1}{a}, & n = 0 \\ -\frac{1-a^2}{a^{n+1}}, & n > 0 \\ 0, & n < 0 \end{cases} = -\frac{1}{a^{n+1}}\left[u(n) - a^2\,u(n-1)\right]$$

Ans.

(See also solved Example 3.18, solution by partial fraction method)

EXAMPLE 3.35: *Find inverse z-transform by Residue method/Contour method.*

SOLUTION: $X_2(z) = z(z+1)/(z-1)^3$, *ROC:* $|z| > 1$

As ROC is $|z| > 1$, it reveals that the sequence $x_2(n)$ is causal

$$x_2(n) = \frac{1}{2\pi j}\oint_C \frac{z(z+1)}{(z-1)^3} z^{n-1}\,dz$$

$$= \sum_{\substack{\text{residue} \\ \text{at pole } z=1}} \frac{z(z+1)\,z^{n-1}}{(z-1)^3}\,u(n)$$

$$= \text{Residue at } z = 1 \text{ for } [z^n(z+1)/(z-1)^3]\,u(n)$$

$$= \left.\frac{1}{2!}\frac{d^2}{dz^2}\left(z^n(z+1)\right)\right|_{z=1} u(n)$$

$$= \frac{1}{2}\left[(n+1)n + n(n-1)\right].\,u(n)$$

$\therefore$
$$x_2(n) = n^2 u(n)$$

Ans.

EXAMPLE 3.36: *Find inverse z-transform by (a) Partial fraction (b) Long division and (c) Contour integration method. Given* $X(z) = \dfrac{1-\frac{1}{2}z^{-1}}{1-\frac{1}{4}z^{-2}}, |z| > \frac{1}{2}$.

SOLUTION: (*a*) By partial fraction method

As
$$\frac{1-\frac{1}{2}z^{-1}}{1-\frac{1}{4}z^{-2}} = \frac{1}{1+\frac{1}{2}z^{-1}} = \frac{1}{1-\left(-\frac{1}{2}\right)z^{-1}}$$

$$\therefore \quad x(n) = \left(\frac{-1}{2}\right)^n u(n)$$ **Ans.**

(*b*) By long division method

$$\begin{array}{r|l} & 1 - \frac{1}{2}z^{-1} + \frac{1}{4}z^{-2} - \ldots \\ 1+\frac{1}{2}z^{-1} & 1 \\ & 1 + \frac{1}{2}z^{-1} \\ \hline & -\frac{1}{2}z^{-1} \\ & -\frac{1}{2}z^{-1} - \frac{1}{4}z^{-2} \\ \hline & +\frac{1}{4}z^{-2} \\ & +\frac{1}{4}z^{-2} + \frac{1}{8}z^{-3} \end{array}$$

$$\therefore \quad X(z) = 1 - \frac{1}{2}z^{-1} + \frac{1}{4}z^{-2} - \frac{1}{8}z^{-3} + \ldots$$

$$= \sum_{n=0}^{\infty}\left(-\frac{1}{2}\right)^n z^{-n} = \sum_{n=-\infty}^{\infty}\left[\left(-\frac{1}{2}\right)^n u(n)\right]z^{-n}$$

$$\therefore \quad x(n) = \left(\frac{-1}{2}\right)^n u(n)$$ **Ans.**

(*c*) By contour integration method

As
$$x(n) = \frac{1}{2\pi j}\oint_C X(z).z^{n-1}dz = \frac{1}{2\pi j}\oint_C \left(\frac{1}{1+\frac{1}{2}z^{-1}}\right)z^{n-1}dz, \text{ C: circle of radius } > \frac{1}{2}$$

$$= \text{Residue of } \frac{z^{n-1}}{1+\frac{1}{2}z^{-1}} = \text{Res } \frac{z^n}{z+\frac{1}{2}} \text{ at pole } z = -\frac{1}{2}$$

$$\therefore \quad x(n) = \left(-\frac{1}{2}\right)^n .u(n)$$ **Ans.** [we add $u(n)$ as $x(n)$ it is a right-sided sequence]

EXAMPLE 3.37: *Determine the inverse z-transform by (i) Contour integration, (ii) Partial fraction expansion for the function*

$$X(z) = \frac{1-\frac{1}{2}z^{-1}}{1+\frac{3}{4}z^{-1}+\frac{1}{8}z^{-2}}, \qquad |z| > \frac{1}{2}$$

SOLUTION:

(*i*) **By contour integration**

$$x(n) = \frac{1}{2\pi j}\oint_C \frac{\left(1-\frac{1}{2}z^{-1}\right)z^{n-1}}{\left(1+\frac{1}{4}z^{-1}\right)\left(1+\frac{1}{2}z^{-1}\right)}dz \quad \text{C is a circle of radius } r > \frac{1}{2}$$

The poles are at $z = -\frac{1}{4}, -\frac{1}{2}$ from $\frac{\left(1-\frac{1}{2}z^{-1}\right)z^{n-1}}{\left(1+\frac{1}{4}z^{-1}\right)\left(1+\frac{1}{2}z^{-1}\right)} = \frac{\left(1-\frac{1}{2}z^{-1}\right)z^{n+1}}{\left(z+\frac{1}{4}\right)\left(z+\frac{1}{2}\right)}$

$$\therefore \quad x(n) = \left.\frac{\left(1-\frac{1}{2}z^{-1}\right)z^{n+1}}{z+\frac{1}{2}}\right|_{z=-\frac{1}{4}} + \left.\frac{\left(1-\frac{1}{2}z^{-1}\right)z^{n+1}}{\left(z+\frac{1}{4}\right)}\right|_{z=-\frac{1}{2}}$$

$$= \frac{3\left(\frac{-1}{4}\right)^{n+1}}{1/4} + \frac{2\left(-\frac{1}{2}\right)^{n+1}}{-1/4}$$

$$= \left[-3\left(\frac{-1}{4}\right)^{n} + (-4)\times 2\left(\frac{-1}{2}\right)^{n+1}\right]u(n) \qquad [\because x(n) \text{ is right sided sequence}]$$

$$= \left[-3\left(\frac{-1}{4}\right)^{n} + \left(\frac{-1}{2}\right)^{n-2}\right]u(n)$$

Ans.

(*ii*) **By partial fraction expansion**

Let $$\frac{1-\frac{1}{2}z^{-1}}{\left(1+\frac{3}{4}z^{-1}+\frac{1}{8}z^{-2}\right)} = \frac{A}{1+\frac{1}{4}z^{-1}} + \frac{B}{1+\frac{1}{2}z^{-1}}$$

$$\therefore \quad A = \left.\frac{1-\frac{1}{2}z^{-1}}{1+\frac{1}{2}z^{-1}}\right|_{z^{-1}=-4} = \frac{1+2}{1-\frac{4}{2}} = -3$$

$$B = \left.\frac{1-\frac{1}{2}z^{-1}}{1+\frac{1}{4}z^{-1}}\right|_{z^{-1}=-2} = \frac{1+1}{1-\frac{1}{2}} = 4$$

$$\therefore \quad X(z) = \frac{-3}{1+\frac{1}{4}z^{-1}} + \frac{4}{1+\frac{1}{2}z^{-1}} = \frac{-3}{1-\left(\frac{-1}{4}\right)z^{-1}} + \frac{4}{1-\left(-\frac{1}{2}\right)z^{-1}}, \ |z| > \frac{1}{2}$$

$$\therefore \quad x(n) = \left[-3\left(\frac{-1}{4}\right)^n + 4\left(-\frac{1}{2}\right)^n\right]u(n) = \left[-3\left(\frac{-1}{4}\right)^n + \left(\frac{-1}{2}\right)^{n-2}\right]u(n) \qquad \textbf{Ans.}$$

EXAMPLE 3.38: *Find the inverse z-transform by* **Contour Integration** *method for* $X(z) = 1/(1 + 0.5z^{-1})$, *ROC:* $|z| < 1/2$.

SOLUTION:

$$x(n) = \frac{1}{2\pi j}\oint_C \frac{z^{n-1}}{1+0.5z^{-1}}dz, \qquad \text{ROC: } |z| < \frac{1}{2}$$

$$= \frac{1}{2\pi j}\oint_C \frac{2z^{n-1}}{z^{-1}+2}dz, \qquad \text{ROC: } |z| < \frac{1}{2}$$

Pole of $X(z)$ is at $z = -\frac{1}{2}$ and ROC is $|z| < \frac{1}{2}$. Therefore, any curve C drawn in ROC cannot contain the pole. In order to use the Contour Integration method, the contour curve C must enclose the pole.

$\therefore$ Here put $p = \frac{1}{z}$ *i.e.,* $z = \frac{1}{p}$ (Note this step)

$$\therefore \quad dz = -\frac{1}{p^2}dp$$

$$\therefore \quad x(n) = \frac{1}{2\pi j}\oint_{C'} \frac{2(p)^{-(n-1)}}{p+2}\left(\frac{-1}{p^2}\right)dp, \qquad \text{ROC } |p| > 2, C' \text{ is clockwise}$$

$$= \frac{1}{2\pi j}\oint_{C_1} \frac{2p^{-n-1}}{p+2}dp \qquad \therefore \text{ ROC } |p| > 2 \text{ i.e., } C_1 \text{ contour is anti-clockwise}$$

Now as ROC $|p| > 2$ can enclose the pole $p = -2$, the contour C_1 may be drawn in the ROC

$n = 0$ case

$$x(0) = x(n)|_{n=0} = \frac{1}{2\pi j}\oint_{C_1} \frac{2}{(p+2)p}dp$$

$$= \Sigma \text{ Residues at poles } p = -2,\ p = 0 \text{ for } \frac{2}{(p+2)p}$$

$$= 2\left[\frac{1}{-2} + \frac{1}{0+2}\right] = 0$$

$$\therefore \quad x(n) = 0, \text{ for } n = 0$$

$n > 0$ case

$$x(n) = \Sigma \text{ Residues of } \frac{2p^{-n-1}}{(p+2)}$$

$$= 2\Sigma \text{ Residues of } \frac{1}{(p+2)p^{n+1}}$$

poles being at $p = -2$, and at $p = 0$ of $(n + 1)^{th}$ order

$$= 2\left[\frac{1}{p^{n+1}}\bigg|_{p=-2} + \frac{1}{n!}(-1)^n\, n!\frac{1}{(p+2)^{n+1}}\bigg|_{p=0}\right]$$

$$= 2\left[\frac{1}{(-2)^{n+1}} - (-1)^{n+1}\frac{1}{2^{n+1}}\right] = 2\left[\frac{1}{(-2)^{n+1}} - \frac{1}{(-2)^{n+1}}\right] = 0$$

$n < 0$ case

Let $n = -n'$ where n' is +ve > 0

$$\therefore \quad x(n) = \Sigma \text{ Residues } \frac{2p^{n'-1}}{(p+2)}, \text{ pole is at } p = -2 \qquad \text{(see ** also)}$$

$$= 2(-2)^{n'-1} = 2(-2)^{-n-1}$$

****Important Note** It might look that we have also pole at $p = \infty$, of degree $n - 2$, but pole is allowed only for $p \le 2$ in the contour C_1. Hence, pole at ∞ is not considered.

Putting all the results together, we can write

$$x(n) = \begin{cases} 0, & n > 0 \\ 0, & n = 0 \\ 2(-2)^{-n-1}, & n < 0 \end{cases}$$

$$\therefore \quad x(n) = 2(-2)^{-n-1}\, u(-n-1) \qquad \textbf{Ans.}$$

Check As $X(z) = \dfrac{1}{1+0.5z^{-1}},\ |z| < \dfrac{1}{2}$

$$= \frac{z}{z+0.5} = 2z\frac{1}{1+2z}$$

$$= 2z\left[1-(2z)+(2z)^2-(2z)^3+\ldots\right]$$

$$= 2z\sum_{n=0}^{\infty}(-2)^n z^n$$

$$= 2z\sum_{n=0}^{\infty}(-2)^{-n} z^{-n} = 2z\sum_{n=-\infty}^{\infty}(-2)^{-n}\, u(-n), z^{-n}$$

$$\therefore \quad x(n) = 2(-2)^{-n}\, u(-n)\big|_{\text{change } n \text{ to } n+1} = 2(-2)^{-n-1}u(-n-1) \text{ as expected}$$

EXAMPLE 3.39: *Find the inverse z-transform of functions by Residue method*

(a) $$X_1(z) = \frac{(2z-1)z}{2(z-1)(z+0.5)},\ \text{ROC: } |z| > 1$$

(b) $$X_2(z) = \frac{(2z-1)}{2(z-1)(z+0.5)} = z^{-1}X_1(z)$$

SOLUTION:

(a) **For $n \geq 0$,** $x_1(n) = \underset{z=1}{Res}\left(X(z)z^{n-1}\right) + \underset{z=-0.5}{Res}\left(X(z).z^{n-1}\right)$, (as $|z|>1$ contains the poles $z = -0.5$ and $z = 1$)

$$= \left.\frac{(2z-1)z^n}{2(z+0.5)}\right|_{z=1} + \left.\frac{(2z-1)z^n}{2(z-1)}\right|_{z=-0.5}$$

$$= \frac{1}{3} + \frac{(-1-1)}{2\left(\frac{-3}{2}\right)}(-0.5)^n$$

$$= \frac{1}{3} + \frac{2}{3}\left(-\frac{1}{2}\right)^n$$

For $n < 0$, Let $n = -n'$ where n' is +ve

for $n = -1$ *i.e.,* $n' = +1$

$$x_1(n) = \sum Res \frac{(2z-1)z^n}{2(z-1)(z+0.5)} = \sum Res \frac{2z-1}{2z(z-1)(z+0.5)}, \text{ putting } n = -1$$

$$= \frac{1}{2}\left[\left.\frac{2z-1}{(z-1)(z+0.5)}\right|_{z=0} + \left.\frac{2z-1}{z(z+0.5)}\right|_{z=1} + \left.\frac{2z-1}{z(z-1)}\right|_{z=-0.5}\right]$$

$$= \frac{1}{2}\left[\frac{1}{0.5} + \frac{1}{3/2} + \frac{-2}{(-0.5)\left(-\frac{3}{2}\right)}\right] = \frac{1}{2}\left[\frac{2}{1} + \frac{2}{3} - \frac{8}{3}\right] = 0$$

In fact for all $n < 0$, $x_1(n) = 0$

Hence, $$Z^{-1}[X_1(z)] = x_1(n) = \frac{1}{3}\left[1 + 2\left(-\frac{1}{2}\right)^n\right]u(n) = \frac{1}{3}\left[1 - \left(-\frac{1}{2}\right)^{n-1}\right]u(n)$$ **Ans.**

(b) $$X_2(z) = 1\frac{(2z-1)}{2(z-1)(z+0.5)}$$

$$= z^{-1}\frac{z(2z-1)}{2(z-1)(z+0.5)} = z^{-1}X_1(z)$$

$$x_2(n) = x_1(n-1)$$

As $$x_1(n) = \frac{1}{3}\left[1 - \left(\frac{-1}{2}\right)^{n-1}\right]u(n)$$

Changing n to $(n-1)$, we obtain

$$x_2(n) = \frac{1}{3}\left[1 - \left(\frac{-1}{2}\right)^{n-2}\right]u(n-1)$$ **Ans.**

EXAMPLE 3.40: *Given that the sampling period is $T = 1$ second, determine $x(n)$ for*

$$X(z) = \frac{z(1-e^{-T})}{(z-1)(z-e^{-T})},$$

Use (i) Long division method, (ii) Partial fraction method, (iii) Contour method. Assume $x(n)$ causal.

SOLUTION:

(*i*) **By long division method**

Given $$X(z) = \frac{0.632\,z}{(z-1)(z-0.368)} = \frac{0.632\,z}{z^2 - 1.368z + 0.368} \quad \because\ 1 - e^{-T} = 0.632 \text{ for } T = 1$$

$$\begin{array}{r l} & 0.632z^{-1} + 0.865z^{-2} + 0.950z^{-3} + \ldots \\ z^2 - 1.368z + 0.368 \,\big) & 0.632z \\ & 0.632z - 0.865 + 0.233z^{-1} \\ \hline & 0.865 - 0.233z^{-1} \\ & 0.865 - 1.183z^{-1} + 0.318z^{-2} \\ \hline & 0.950z^{-1} - 0.318z^{-2} \end{array}$$

$\therefore$ $$X(z) = 0z^0 + 0.632z^{-1} + 0.865z^{-2} + 0.950z^{-3} + \ldots$$

Therefore, the values of $x(n)$ at the sampling instants (n = 0, 1, 2, 3, ...) are (0, 0.632, 0.865, 0.950, ...).

Note that the initial value zero can also be confirmed by applying the initial value theorem:

$$x(0) = \lim_{|z|\to\infty} X(z) = \lim_{|z|\to\infty} \frac{0.632\,z}{(z^2 - 1.368z + 0.368)} = 0 \text{ (as expected)}$$

The final value can be obtained by applying the final value theorem:

$$x(\infty) = \lim_{|z|\to 1} (1 - z^{-1})\, X(z) = \lim_{|z|\to 1} \frac{(z-1)\, 0.632z}{z\,(z-1)\,(z-0.368)} = 1$$

(*ii*) **By partial fraction expansion method**

As $$\frac{z\,(1-e^{-T})}{(z-1)(z-e^{-T})} = \frac{z}{z-1} - \frac{z}{z-e^{-T}}$$

$$= \frac{1}{1-z^{-1}} - \frac{1}{1-e^{-T}z^{-1}}$$

{Note that $X(z) = z\left[\dfrac{1-e^{-T}}{(z-1)(z-e^{-T})}\right]$ and we have made partial fractions of the function inside the bracket}

$\therefore$ $$x(n) = u(n) - e^{-nT}u(n)$$
$$= (1 - e^{-nT})\, u(n)$$ **Ans.**

Clearly $x(0) = 0$, $x(\infty) = 1$ (as expected)

(*ii*) **By residue method**

$$x(n) = \frac{1}{2\pi j}\oint_C X(z)\, z^{n-1} dz = \sum_{\substack{\text{all poles}\\ \text{of } X(z)}} \text{Residues of}\left[X(z)\, z^{n-1}\right]$$

As $$X(z)\, z^{n-1} = \frac{z\,(1-e^{-T})}{(z-1)(z-e^{-T})}\, z^{n-1}$$

Residue at $$z = 1 = \left.\frac{z\,(1-e^{-T})}{z-e^{T}}\, z^{n-1}\right|_{z=1} = 1$$

Residue at $$z = e^{-T} = \left.\frac{z\,(1-e^{-T})}{z-1}\, z^{n-1}\right|_{z=e^{-T}} = \frac{e^{T}(1-e^{-T})}{e^{-T}-1}\, e^{-T(n-1)} = -e^{-nT}$$

$\therefore \qquad x(n) = 1 - e^{-nT}, n \geq 0$

It will be seen that for n –ve, the sum of residues are all zero

$\therefore \qquad x(n) = (1 - e^{-nT})\, u(n)$ **Ans.**

$= (1 - e^{-nT})\, u(n-1) \qquad \therefore x(0) = 0$ here

Thus, we arrive at the same result by all the three methods.

EXAMPLE 3.41: *Use contour integration to determine the sequence x(n) where z-transform is given by*

(a) $X(z) = \dfrac{1}{1-\frac{1}{2}z^{-1}}, |z| > \dfrac{1}{2}$

(b) $X(z) = \dfrac{1}{1-\frac{1}{2}z^{-1}}, |z| < \dfrac{1}{2}$

SOLUTION:

(a) $$x(n) = \frac{1}{2\pi j}\oint_C \frac{z^{n-1}}{1-\frac{1}{2}z^{-1}}dz = \frac{1}{2\pi j}\oint_C \frac{z^n}{z-\frac{1}{2}}dz, \text{ ROC: is } |z| > \frac{1}{2}$$

For $n \geq 0$, $$x(n) = \sum_{\text{Residue}} \text{pole}\left(z = \frac{1}{2}\right)$$

$$= \left(\frac{1}{2}\right)^n u(n)$$

For $n = -1$, $$x(-1) = \frac{1}{2\pi j}\oint_C \frac{1}{z\left(z-\frac{1}{2}\right)}dz \quad \text{ROC is } |z| > \frac{1}{2}$$

$$= \left.\frac{1}{z-\frac{1}{2}}\right|_{z=0} + \left.\frac{1}{z}\right|_{z=\frac{1}{2}} \quad \text{as poles } z = 0, z = \frac{1}{2} \text{ are both the encircled by C}$$

$$= -2 + 2 = 0$$

$n = -2$, $$x(-2) = \frac{1}{2\pi j}\oint_C \frac{1}{z^2\left(z-\frac{1}{2}\right)}dz, \quad \text{ROC is } |z| > \frac{1}{2}$$

$$= \left.\frac{1}{z^2}\right|_{z=\frac{1}{2}} + \left.\frac{d}{dz}\left(\frac{1}{z-\frac{1}{2}}\right)\right|_{z=0} \quad \text{as poles } z = 0\ z = \frac{1}{2} \text{ are both the encircled by C}$$

$$= 4 + \left.\frac{-1}{\left(z-\frac{1}{2}\right)^2}\right|_{z=0}$$

$$= 4 - 4 = 0$$

Similarly, $x(n) = 0$ for $n < 0$

Hence, $x(n) = \left(\frac{1}{2}\right)^n u(n)$ **Ans.**

(b) $$x(n) = \frac{1}{2\pi j}\oint_C \frac{z^{n-1}}{1-\frac{1}{2}z^{-1}}dz, \quad |z| < \frac{1}{2}$$ *i.e., all poles are enclosed in a circle of radius* $< \frac{1}{2}$

$$= \frac{1}{2\pi j}\oint_C \frac{z^n}{z-\frac{1}{2}}dz \quad ...(A)$$

n = 0 :

$x(0)$ = Residues at pole $z = \frac{1}{2}$ is zero as the pole $z = \frac{1}{2}$ is outside the ROC *i.e.*, circle less than radius $< \frac{1}{2}$, hence not counted, therefore $x(0) = 0$ (No pole, no residue maxim.)

n = −1 : $$x(-1) = \frac{1}{2\pi j}\oint_C \frac{1}{z\left(z-\frac{1}{2}\right)}dz \quad \therefore \quad C \text{ is } |z| < \frac{1}{2}$$

$$= \left.\frac{1}{z-\frac{1}{2}}\right|_{z=0} = -2 \quad \text{(pole } z = 0 \text{ is enclosed by C)}$$

The pole at $z = \frac{1}{2}$ is not enclosed by C, hence, it has no residue. We have considered only pole at $z = 0$, which is enclosed by C.

n = −2 : $$x(-2) = \frac{1}{2\pi j}\oint_C \frac{1}{z^2\left(z-\frac{1}{2}\right)}dz, \quad \text{ROC is } |z| < \frac{1}{2}$$

= Residue at pole $z = 0$ only and Residue at pole $z = \frac{1}{2}$ not to be counted as it is not enclosed in the circle $|z| < \frac{1}{2}$

$$\therefore \quad x(-2) = \left.\frac{d}{dz}\left(\frac{1}{z-\frac{1}{2}}\right)\right|_{z=0} = \left.\frac{-1}{\left(z-\frac{1}{2}\right)^2}\right|_{z=0} = -4$$

n = − 3 : $$x(-3) = \frac{1}{2\pi j}\oint_C \frac{1}{z^3\left(z-\frac{1}{2}\right)}dz$$

$$= \left.\frac{1}{2!}\frac{d^2}{dz^2}\left(\frac{1}{z-\frac{1}{2}}\right)\right|_{z=0} \quad \text{(Residue at pole } z = 0 \text{ only)}$$

$$= \left.\frac{1}{2}.(-1)^2\frac{2}{\left(z-\frac{1}{2}\right)^3}\right|_{z=0} = -8$$

Continuing so, we get $x(n) = -(2)^{-n}u(-n-1)$ **Ans.**

EXAMPLE 3.42: *Determine the inverse z-transform of X(z) by (i) contour integrate (ii) partial fraction method, (iii) long division method, gives*

$$X(z) = \frac{1}{1+\frac{1}{2}z^{-1}}, |z| < \frac{1}{2}$$

SOLUTION: (*i*) Contour integration (see Example 3.38)

(*ii*) Partial fraction method, only one pole at $z = -\frac{1}{2}$

As $$X(z) = \frac{2z}{1+2z} = 2\frac{z}{1-(-2)z} \text{ compare with } a^n u(-n) \rightarrow \frac{1}{1-a^{-1}z}$$

$$\therefore \quad X(z) = 2 . \frac{z}{1-\left(\frac{-1}{2}\right)^{-1} z} \text{ has } x(n) = 2 . \left(\frac{-1}{2}\right)^n u(-n)\Big|_{\text{advance by 1}}$$

$$\therefore \quad x(n) = 2\left(-\frac{1}{2}\right)^{n+1} u(-n-1) = -(-2)^{-n} u(-n-1)$$ **Ans.**

(*iii*) Long division method

$$\begin{array}{r|l} & 2z^{+1} - 4z^{+2} + 8z^3 - 16z^4 + ... \\ \frac{1}{2}z^{-1}+1 & 1 \\ & \underline{1+2z^{+1}} \\ & -2z^{+1} \\ & \underline{-2z^{+1} - 4z^{+2}} \\ & +4z^2 \\ & \underline{4z^2 + 8z^3} \\ & -8z^3 \end{array}$$

$$\begin{aligned} \therefore \quad X(z) &= 2z - 4z^2 + 8z^3 - 16z^4 + ... \\ &= -\left[(-2z)^1 + (-2z)^2 + (-2z)^3 + ...\right] \\ &= -\sum_{n=-\infty}^{-1} (-2z)^{-n} = -\sum_{n=-\infty}^{-1} (-2)^{-n} z^{-n} \\ &= \sum_{n=-\infty}^{\infty} (-2)^{-n} u(-n-1) z^{-n} \end{aligned}$$

$$\therefore \quad x(n) = -(-2)^{-n} u(-n-1)$$ **Ans.**

Alternative method

$$X(z) = \frac{1}{1+\frac{1}{2}z^{-1}}, |z| < \frac{1}{2}$$

$$= \frac{2z}{1+2z} = 2z(1+2z)^{-1}, \; 2z < 1$$

$$= 2z - (2z)^2 + (2z)^3 - (2z)^4 + \ldots \qquad \text{(binomial expansion)}$$

$$= \sum_{n=1}^{\infty} (-1)^{n-1} (2z)^n$$

Put $\quad -n = n'$

$$= \sum_{n'=-1}^{-\infty} (-1)^{-n'-1} 2^{-n'} z^{-n'}$$

$$= \sum_{n=-\infty}^{\infty} -(-2)^{-n} z^{-n} u(-n-1)$$

$\therefore \quad x(n) = -(-2)^{-n} u(-n-1)$ **Ans.**

Comments: To use contour integration method. We find residues of $X(z)\,z^{n-1}$ for the poles enclosed inside the contour. Here ROC was $|z| < \frac{1}{2}$. *i.e.*, poles are located in the open region given by $|z| \geq \frac{1}{2}$. To enclose the poles, we change the variable $p = \frac{1}{z}$ such that in p-domain, the poles lie inside the contour C' of radius $|p| = \left|\frac{1}{z}\right| = 2$. Also, when we reverse the contour (C' is reverse of C), we must take a negative sign to redraw C' as C in anti-clockwise direction. The contour integration necessarily requires an anti-clockwise contour before we apply Residue theorem. The reader is advised to note the approach used in this question. See solved Example 3.38.

EXAMPLE 3.43: *Compute the convolution of the following sequences by means of the z-transform*

$$x_1(n) = \begin{cases} (1/3)^n, & n \geq 0 \\ (1/2)^{-n}, & n < 0 \end{cases} \quad \text{and } x_2(n) = \left(\frac{1}{2}\right)^n u(n)$$

SOLUTION:

$$X_1(z) = \underbrace{\sum_{n=0}^{\infty} \left(\frac{1}{3}\right)^n z^{-n}}_{\text{ROC } |z| > \frac{1}{3}} + \underbrace{\sum_{n=-\infty}^{-1} \left(\frac{1}{2}\right)^{-n} z^{-n}}_{\text{ROC } |z| < 2} = \sum_{n=0}^{\infty} \left(\frac{1}{3}\right)^n z^{-n} + \sum_{n'=0}^{\infty} \left(\frac{1}{2}\right)^{n'} z^{n'} - 1$$

$$= \frac{1}{1-\frac{1}{3}z^{-1}} + \frac{1}{1-\left(\frac{1}{2}\right)z} - 1 = \frac{+5/6}{\left(1-\frac{1}{3}z^{-1}\right)\left(1-\frac{1}{2}z\right)}, \quad \text{ROC for } X_1(z): \frac{1}{3} < |z| < 2$$

$$X_2(z) = \sum_{n=0}^{\infty} \left(\frac{1}{2}\right)^n z^{-n} = \frac{1}{1-\frac{1}{2}z^{-1}}, \; |z| > \frac{1}{2} \quad \text{ROC for } X_2(z): |z| > \frac{1}{2}$$

$$\therefore \quad X_1(z)\cdot X_2(z) = \frac{5/6}{\left(1-\frac{1}{3}z^{-1}\right)\left(1-\frac{1}{2}z\right)\left(1-\frac{1}{2}z^{-1}\right)} \quad \text{ROC } |z| > \frac{1}{3},\; |z| < 2,\; |z| > \frac{1}{2} \; \textit{i.e.,}$$

i.e., ROC : $\frac{1}{2} < |z| < 2$ for $X_1 \cdot X_2$

As $x_1(n) * x_2(n) \xrightarrow{ZT} X_1(z) \cdot X_2(z)$

$$\therefore \quad y(n) = x_1(n) * x_2(n) = IZT\,[X_1(z) \cdot X_2(z)]$$

$$= IZT\left[\frac{5/6}{\left(1-\frac{1}{3}z^{-1}\right)\left(1-\frac{1}{2}z\right)\left(1-\frac{1}{2}z^{-1}\right)}\right] \text{ ROC}: \frac{1}{2} < |z| < 2$$

$$= IZT\left[\frac{5/6\,(-2z^{-1})}{\left(1-\frac{1}{3}z^{-1}\right)(1-2z^{-1})\left(1-\frac{1}{2}z^{-1}\right)}\right]$$

$$= IZT\left[\frac{-2}{\left(1-\frac{1}{3}z^{-1}\right)} + \frac{10/3}{\left(1-\frac{1}{2}z^{-1}\right)} - \frac{4/3}{\left(1-2z^{-1}\right)}\right], \quad \frac{1}{2} < |z| < 2$$

$$\nearrow \qquad \nearrow \qquad \nearrow$$

Pole at $z = \frac{1}{3}$ Pole at $z = \frac{1}{2}$ Pole at $z = 2$

$$\therefore \quad y(n) = (-2).\left(\frac{1}{3}\right)^n u(n) + (10/3)\left(\frac{1}{2}\right)^n u(n) + \frac{4}{3}(2)^n\, u(-n-1)$$ **Ans.**

3.10 LINEAR CONSTANT COEFFICIENT DIFFERENCE EQUATIONS

By Convolution sum, we have the relation

$$y(n) = h(n) * x(n) = \sum_{k=-\infty}^{\infty} h(k) \cdot x(n-k) \qquad \text{...(3.76)}$$

As N^{th} order linear, constant coefficient, difference equation is of the form

$$\sum_{k=0}^{N} a_k\, y(n-k) = \sum_{r=0}^{M} b_r\, x(n-r) \qquad \text{...(3.77)}$$

a difference equation of Nth order

The first-order difference equation is of the form

$$y(n) - a\,y(n-1) = x(n) \qquad \text{...(3.78)}$$

The difference equation could represent causal/non-causal stable/unstable system. We can solve the difference equations very efficiently by the tool of z-transform, as will be shown here. We shall first solve the difference equation (DE) in time domain and then in z-domain to show the superiority of z-transform techniques. Let us take first the discrete system characterised by Eq. (3.78).

3.10.1 To Find the Solution of First Order Difference Equation

Assume that a discrete first order system is causal *i.e.*, we have impulse response $h(n) = 0$ for $n < 0$.

Let the system be characterized by the difference equation (3.78) *i.e.*,

$$y(n) = ay(n-1) + x(n)$$

Putting $\quad x(n) = \delta(n)$ and, therefore, $y(n) = h(n)$, we get

$$h(n) = a\,h(n-1) + \delta(n)$$

$$h(0) = a\,h(-1) + \delta(0) = a \times 0 + 1 = 1 \qquad \because h(-1) = 0 \text{ for causal system.}$$

$$h(1) = a\,h(0) + \delta(1) = a \times 1 + 0 = a$$

$$h(2) = a\,h(1) + \delta(2) = a\,(a) + 0 = a^2$$

$$\vdots$$

$$h(n) = a^n$$

Hence, $\quad h(n) = a^n u(n)$

The solution $\quad h(n) = y(n) = a^n u(n)$ for input $\delta(n)$. It represents a causal system, since, $y(n) = h(n)$, here for $x(n) = \delta(n)$ is zero for $n < 0$.

The system is stable if

$$\sum_n |a^n u(n)| < \infty \qquad \text{i.e., if } |a| < 1$$

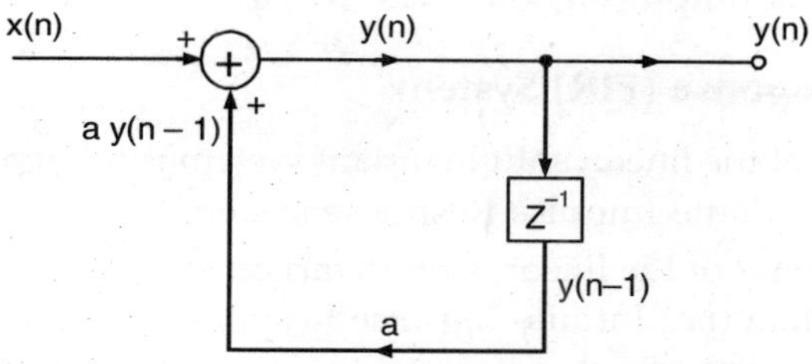

Fig. 3.7. The discrete system corresponding to DE : $y(n) = ay\,(n-1) + x\,(n)$

Figure 3.7 gives the realization for the system characterised by the difference equation (3.78). We have solved it in time domain to obtain the impulse response of the system as $h(n) = a^n u(n)$. It was an involved time-consuming iteration. Let us derive $h(n)$ via z-transform technique. As

$$y(n) = a\,y\,(n-1) + x\,(n) \qquad \text{...(3.79)}$$

Take *ZT* both the sides of (3.79), we obtain

$$Y(z) = az^{-1}\,Y(z) + X(z)$$

or $\quad Y(z)\,(1 - az^{-1}) = X(z)$

$$\therefore \quad H(z) = \frac{Y(z)}{X(z)} = \frac{1}{1 - az^{-1}} \qquad \text{...(3.80)}$$

Taking inverse *ZT* on both the sides of (3.80), we get for a causal system

$$h(n) = a^n u(n)$$

We have obtained the results in much less calculations.

3.10.2 Characterization by Difference Equations (DE)

Let the system be causal. Then a linear DE provides an explicit relationship between the input and the output.

As N^{th} order, linear, difference equation is of the form

$$\sum_{k=0}^{N} a_k\, y(n-k) = \sum_{r=0}^{M} b_r\, x(n-r) \qquad ...(3.81)$$

$$\therefore \quad a_0\, y(n) + \sum_{k=1}^{N} a_k\, y(n-k) = \sum_{r=0}^{M} b_r\, x(n-r)$$

$$\therefore \quad y(n) = -\sum_{k=1}^{N} \frac{a_k}{a_0}\, y(n-k) + \sum_{r=0}^{M} \frac{b_r}{a_0}\, x(n-r) \qquad ...(3.82)$$

n^{th} value of the O/P — N past values of O/P — M past values of Input and one present value of the input

$y(0)$ being the first O/P value

The solution implies that n^{th} value of the Output $y(n)$ can be computed from.

(*i*) n^{th} input value, $x(n)$

(*ii*) and N past values of output together with M past values of the input.

3.10.3 Finite Impulse Response (FIR) System

If the unit sample response of the linear, shift invariant system is of finite duration, then the system is called an FIR system (*i.e.*, Finite Impulse Response system).

If the unit sample response of the linear, shift invariant system is of infinite duration, then the system is called an IIR system (*i.e.*, Infinite Impulse Response system).

If $N = 0$ then we get from (3.82)

$$y(n) = \frac{1}{a_0}\left[\sum_{r=0}^{M} b_r\, x(n-r)\right] \qquad ...(3.83)$$

Comparing it with standard convolution $y(n) = h(n) * x(n)$, we have

$$y(n) = \sum_{k=-\infty}^{\infty} h(k)\, x(n-k) \qquad ...(3.84)$$

We can write from (3.83)

$$\text{for an FIR system : } h(n) = \begin{cases} \dfrac{b_n}{a_0}, & n = 0, 1, \ldots, M \\ 0, & \text{otherwise} \end{cases} \qquad ...(3.85)$$

Hence | for an FIR system, in Eq. (3.82) $N = 0$. It is non-recursive system
for an IIR system in Eq. (3.82) $N \neq 0$, but $N > 0$. It is recursive system. ...(3.86)

3.10.4 Discrete System Realizations Given $H(z)$

Consider the realization shown in Fig. 3.8. z^{-1} denotes a delay, and a_1, a_2 above the arrows show multipliers. Adder is shown by ⊕. Arrows show the direction of signal flow. Note the addition of $X(z)$, $a_1 z^{-1}\, Y(z)$, and $a_2 z^{-2}\, y(z)$ yields $Y(z)$. Hence, we can write.

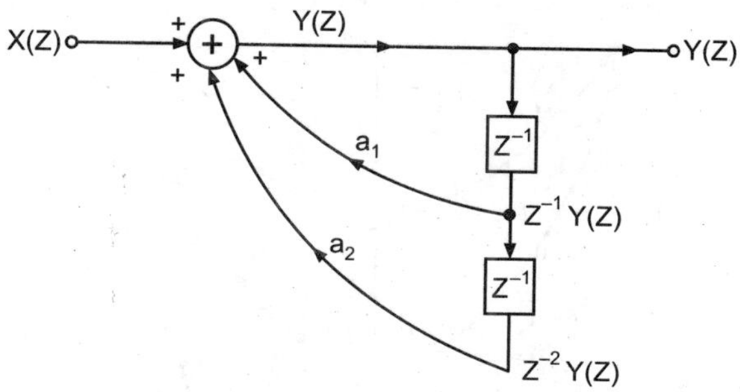

Fig. 3.8. Realization of $H(z) = \frac{1}{1-a_1z^{-1}-a_2z^{-2}}$

$$Y(z) = X(z) + a_1 z^{-1} Y(z) + a_2z^{-2}Y(z) \quad ...(3.87a)$$

$$\therefore \quad Y(z) [1 - a_1z^{-1} - a_2z^{-2}] = X(z) \quad ...(3.87b)$$

$$H(z) = \frac{Y(z)}{X(z)} = \frac{1}{1-a_1z^{-1}-a_2z^{-2}} \quad ...(3.87c)$$

If we take inverse ZT on both the sides of (3.87a), we get

$$y(n) = x(n) + a_1 y(n-1) + a_2 y(n-2)$$

Hence, if a difference equation characterizing a system is given, we can realize the system. We first convert the DE in z-domain and then realize the system.

We, in general, need not put a box $\boxed{z^{-1}}$ to show a delay. Also, the summer ⊕ can be replaced by a dot. Thus, Fig. 3.8 may be redrawn as a signal flow graph form. See Chapter 13 on signal flow graph for more details.

3.10.5 Other Commonly used Configurations

(a) Canonic Form

We can also realize more complicated system functions $H(z)$. One shown in Fig. 3.10 is called Canonical form. The coefficients b_0, b_1, b_2 on numerator of $H(z)$ appear with the same signs. b_0 is direct, b_1 from one delay z^{-1}, and b_2 connected to two delays point. The coefficients a_1, a_2...of the denominator of $H(z)$ appear with signs reversed.

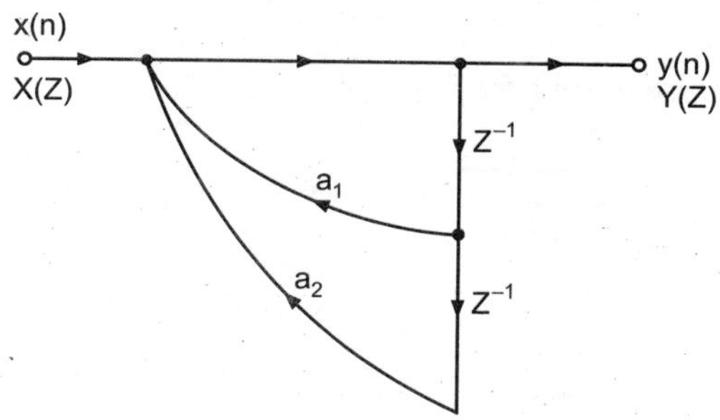

Fig. 3.9. Figure 3.8 redrawn as a signal flow representation

$$H(z) = \frac{1}{1-a_1z^{-1}-a_2z^{-2}}$$

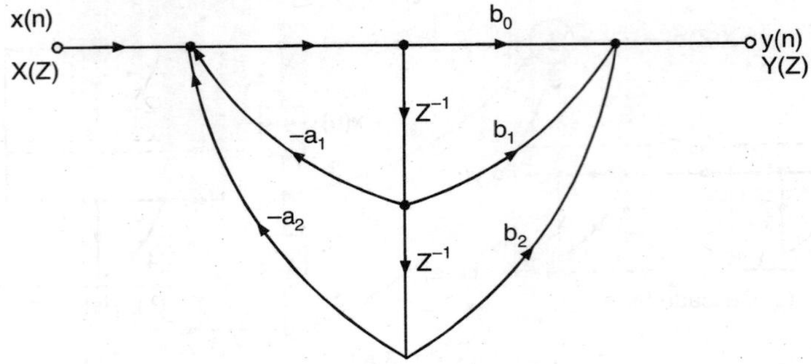

Fig. 3.10. Realization as canonical form for $H(z) = \dfrac{b_0 + b_1 z^{-1} + b_2 z^{-2}}{1 + a_1 z^{-1} + a_1 z^{-2}}$

(*b*) Cascade Form

If $H(z) = H_1(z) \cdot H_2(z)$ (see Fig. 3.11)

(*c*) Parallel Form

If $H(z) = H_1(z) + H_2(z)$ (done by partial fractions)

We realize it as shown in Fig. 3.12.

Realization in cascade form is shown in Fig. 3.11.

There are various other realizations of discrete systems such as Lattice form and Ladder form. The students will learn these when they study Chapter 4 on Realizations.

We shall now give more examples highlighting the utility of *z*-transform.

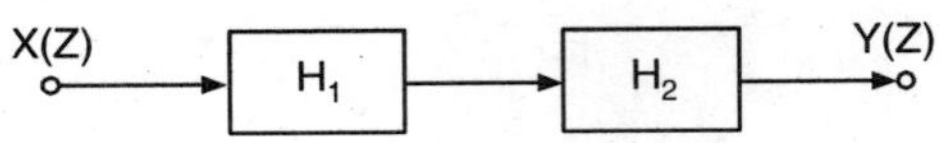

Fig. 3.11. Cascade realization $H(z) = H_1(z) \cdot H_2(z)$.

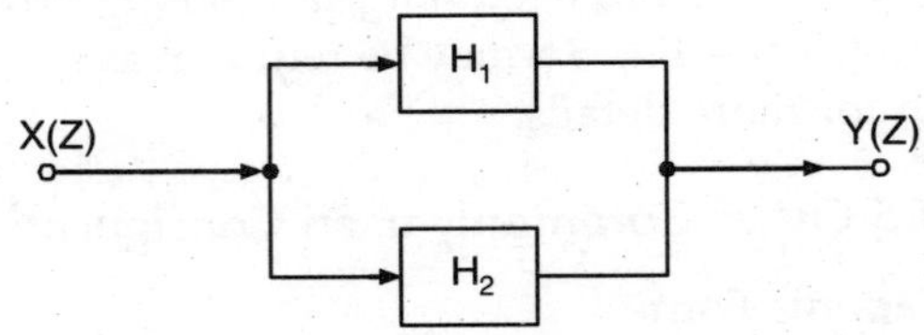

Fig. 3.12. Parallel realization $H(z) = H_1(z) + H_2(z)$.

3.10.6 Use of *z*-Transform to Solve Linear Difference Equations

The following examples illustrate how *z*-transform approach can be usefully exploited to solve the linear difference equations.

EXAMPLE 3.44: *Realize the system transfer function*

$$H(z) = \frac{1}{1 - \frac{3}{4} z^{-1} + \frac{1}{8} z^{-2}}$$

as a direct/canonic, cascade and parallel form.

SOLUTION:

$$H(z) = \frac{1}{1 - \frac{3}{4} z^{-1} + \frac{1}{8} z^{-2}}$$

$$= \frac{1}{\left(1 - \frac{1}{2} z^{-1}\right)\left(1 - \frac{1}{4} z^{-1}\right)} \triangleq H_1(z).\, H_2(z)$$

$$\frac{2}{\left(1 - \frac{1}{2} z^{-1}\right)} + \frac{-1}{\left(1 - \frac{1}{4} z^{-1}\right)} \triangleq H_3(z) + H_4(z)$$

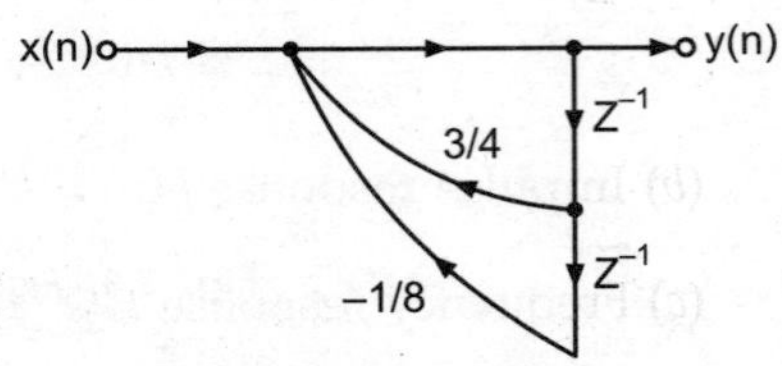

(a) Canonic/direct form II

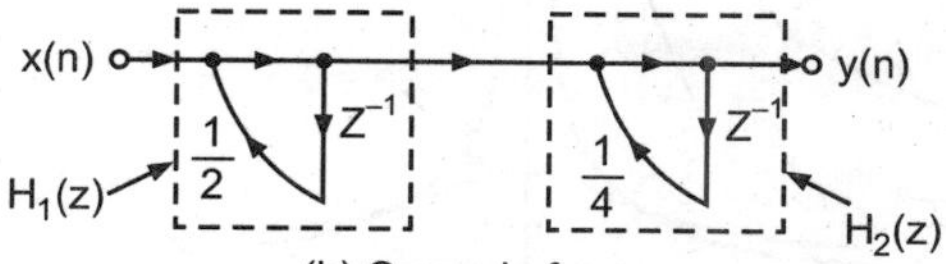

(b) Cascade form

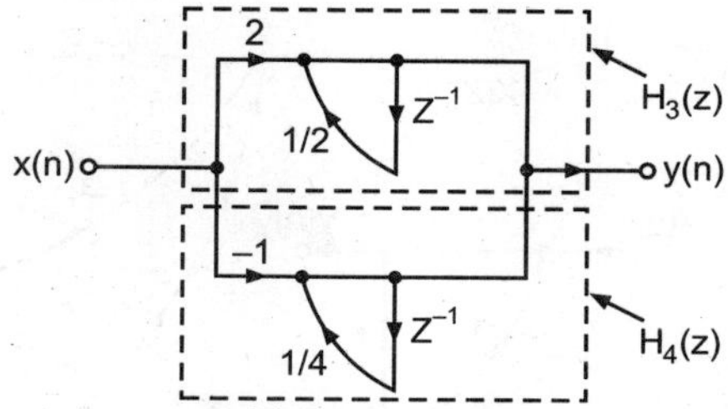

(c) Parallel form

Fig. Ex. 3.44.

EXAMPLE 3.45: *Find a linear, constant coefficient difference equation relating the input x(n) and the output y(n) for a system with impulse response*

$$h(n) = \left[\left(\frac{1}{2}\right)^n + \frac{1}{2}\left(\frac{1}{4}\right)^n\right] u(n)$$

SOLUTION: We can write

$$H(z) = \frac{1}{1-\frac{1}{2}z^{-1}} + \frac{1}{2}\frac{1}{1-\left(\frac{1}{4}\right)z^{-1}}$$

$$= \frac{2\left(1-\frac{1}{4}z^{-1}\right)+\left(1-\frac{1}{2}z^{-1}\right)}{2\left(1-\frac{1}{2}z^{-1}\right)\left(1-\frac{1}{4}z^{-1}\right)}$$

$$= \frac{3-z^{-1}}{2\left(1-\frac{3}{4}z^{-1}+\frac{1}{8}z^{-2}\right)}$$

$$\therefore \quad \frac{Y(z)}{X(z)} = \frac{3-z^{-1}}{2-\frac{3}{2}z^{-1}+\frac{1}{4}z^{-2}} \qquad \therefore Y(z)\left[2-\frac{3}{2}z^{-1}+\frac{1}{4}z^{-2}\right] = X(z)[3-z^{-1}]$$

The difference equation is obtained by taking *IZT* of the above equation, we get

$$2y(n) - \frac{3}{2}y(n-1) + \frac{1}{4}y(n-2) = 3x(n) - x(n-1) \qquad \textbf{Ans.}$$

EXAMPLE 3.46: *For the LTI-IIR system shown in the Figure, 0 < a < 1, (a) Find the system function, (b) Find impulse response h(n), (c) Draw the frequency response $H(e^{j\omega})$.*

SOLUTION: (*a*) From Fig. Ex. 3.46 (*a*), we get here

$$H(z) = \frac{1}{1-az^{-1}}, \ |a| < 1 \qquad \textbf{Ans.}$$

(*b*) Impulse response $h(n) = a^n\, u(n)$ (from standard ZTs) **Ans.**

(*c*) Frequency response $H(e^{j\omega}) = \dfrac{1}{1-ae^{-j\omega}} = \dfrac{1}{1-a\cos\omega + ja\sin\omega}$

$$\therefore \quad |H(e^{j\omega})|^2 = \frac{1}{(1-a\cos\omega)^2+(a\sin\omega)^2} = \frac{1}{1+a^2-2a\cos\omega}$$

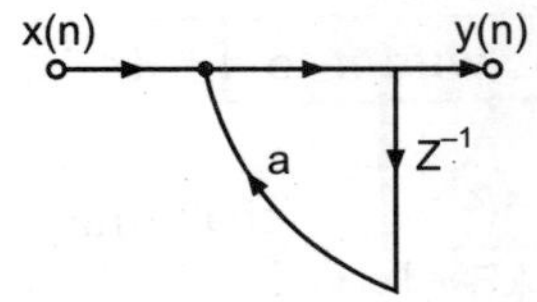

Fig. Ex. 3.46. (*a*) Given system.

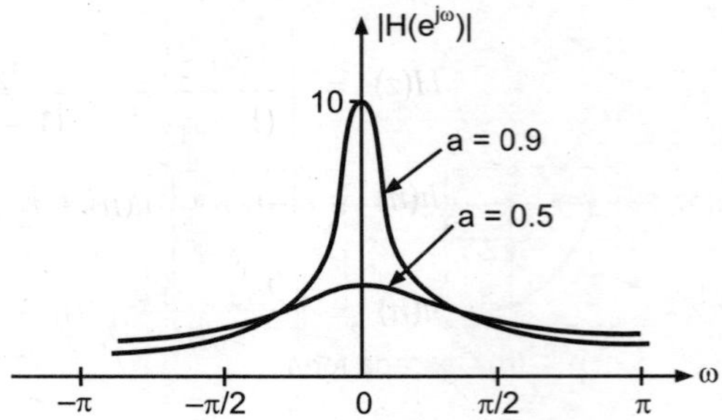

Fig. Ex. 3.46. (*b*) Frequency response.

$|H(e^{j\omega})|$ is shown in Figure (*b*) for $a = 0.9$ and $a = 0.5$.

It is a low pass filter – IIR filter.

EXAMPLE 3.47: *A causal linear shift-invariant system is described by the difference equation*

$$y(n) = y(n-1) + y(n-2) + x(n-1)$$

(*a*) *Find the system function* $H(z) = \dfrac{Y(z)}{X(z)}$ *for this system. Plot the poles and zeros of H(z) and indicate the region of convergence.*

(*b*) *Find the unit-sample response of this system.*

SOLUTION: (*a*) Clearly

$$Y(z) = z^{-1}\,Y(z) + z^{-2}\,Y(z) + z^{-1}\,X(z)$$

$$\therefore \qquad H(z) = \frac{Y(z)}{X(z)} = \frac{z^{-1}}{1 - z^{-1} - z^{-2}} = \frac{z}{z^2 - z - 1} = \frac{z}{(z-r_1)(z-r_2)}$$

where

$$r_1 = \frac{1-\sqrt{5}}{2}$$

$$r_2 = \frac{1+\sqrt{5}}{2}$$

$H(z)$ has poles at $z = r_1, r_2$

Zeros at $z = 0, \infty$

ROC of $H(z)$ is $|z| > \dfrac{1+\sqrt{5}}{2}$

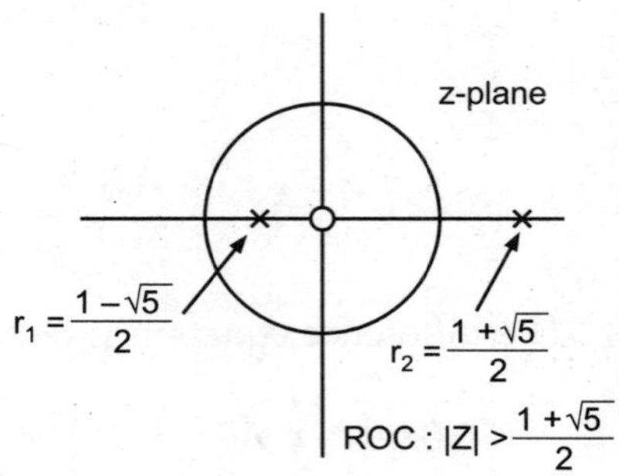

Fig. Ex. 3.47. Poles of H(*z*).

∴ In ROC, we do not have poles.

As one pole $z = r_2$ lies outside the unit circle $|z| = 1$, hence, the given $H(z)$ (causal case) is unstable.

(*b*) To find $h(n)$, $h(n)$ being causal

As

$$H(z) = \frac{z}{(z-r_1)(z-r_2)}$$

$$= \frac{r_1}{(z-r_1)(r_1-r_2)} + \frac{r_2}{(r_2-r_1)(z-r_2)} \qquad \text{(by partial fractions)}$$

As

$$r_2 - r_1 = (1+\sqrt{5})/2 - (1-\sqrt{5})/2 = \sqrt{5}$$

$$\therefore \quad H(z) = \left[\frac{-r_1 z^{-1}}{(1 - r_1 z^{-1})} + \frac{r_2 z^{-1}}{(1 - r_2 z^{-1})}\right] \cdot \frac{1}{\sqrt{5}}$$

$$\therefore \quad h(n) = [-r_1 \,.\, r_1^{\,n}\, u(n) + r_2 \,.\, r_2^{\,n}\, u(n)] / \sqrt{5}, \text{ with } n \text{ to } n-1$$

or
$$h(n) = \left(\frac{r_2^{\,n} - r_1^{\,n}}{\sqrt{5}}\right) u(n-1) \qquad \text{(changing } n \text{ to } n-1)$$

where
$$r_1 = \frac{1-\sqrt{5}}{2}, \qquad r_2 = \frac{1+\sqrt{5}}{2}$$

Ans.

EXAMPLE 3.48: *Determine the inverse z-transform for the function given below (by any method) and also realize the filter in parallel structure form*

$$H(z) = \frac{1}{\left(1 + \frac{1}{2} z^{-1}\right)(1 - 2z^{-1})(1 - 3z^{-1})} \qquad ROC: |z| > 3$$

SOLUTION:

$$H(z) = \frac{1}{\left(1 + \frac{1}{2} z^{-1}\right)(1 - 2z^{-1})(1 - 3z^{-1})} \qquad \text{ROC: } |z| > 3$$

$$= \frac{z^3}{\left(z + \frac{1}{2}\right)(z-2)(z-3)}$$

$$\therefore \quad \frac{H(z)}{z} = \frac{z^2}{\left(z + \frac{1}{2}\right)(z-2)(z-3)}$$

$$= \frac{A}{z + \frac{1}{2}} + \frac{B}{z-2} + \frac{C}{z-3}, \text{ say}$$

$$\therefore \quad A = \left.\frac{z^2}{(z-2)(z-3)}\right|_{z=-\frac{1}{2}} = \frac{1/4}{\left(-\frac{5}{2}\right)\left(-\frac{7}{2}\right)} = \frac{1}{35}$$

$$B = \left.\frac{z^2}{\left(z + \frac{1}{2}\right)(z-3)}\right|_{z=2} = \frac{4}{\left(\frac{5}{2}\right)(-1)} = -\frac{8}{5}$$

$$C = \left.\frac{z^2}{\left(z + \frac{1}{2}\right)(z-2)}\right|_{z=3} = \frac{9}{\left(\frac{7}{2}\right)(1)} = \frac{18}{7}$$

$$\therefore \quad \frac{H(z)}{z} = \frac{1}{35}\frac{1}{z + \frac{1}{2}} - \frac{8}{5}\frac{1}{z-2} + \frac{18}{7}\frac{1}{z-3}$$

or $$H(z) = \frac{1}{35}\frac{z}{z+\frac{1}{2}} - \frac{8}{5}\frac{z}{z-2} + \frac{18}{7}\frac{z}{z-3}$$

$$= \frac{1}{35}\frac{1}{1+\frac{1}{2}z^{-1}} - \frac{8}{5}\frac{1}{1-2z^{-1}} + \frac{18}{7}\frac{1}{1-3z^{-1}} \quad \text{ROC } |z| > 3$$

$\therefore$ $$h(n) = \left[\frac{1}{35}\left(-\frac{1}{2}\right)^n - \frac{8}{5}2^n + \frac{18}{7}(3)^n\right]u(n)$$

(using standard z-transforms) **Ans.**

Parallel Realization

As $$H(z) = \frac{1}{35}\frac{1}{1+\frac{1}{2}z^{-1}} + \left(\frac{-8}{5}\right)\frac{1}{1-2z^{-1}} + \frac{18}{7}\frac{1}{1-3z^{-1}}$$

each term is of the form $\frac{A}{1-\alpha z^{-1}}$. Then the overall structure in parallel form is as below:

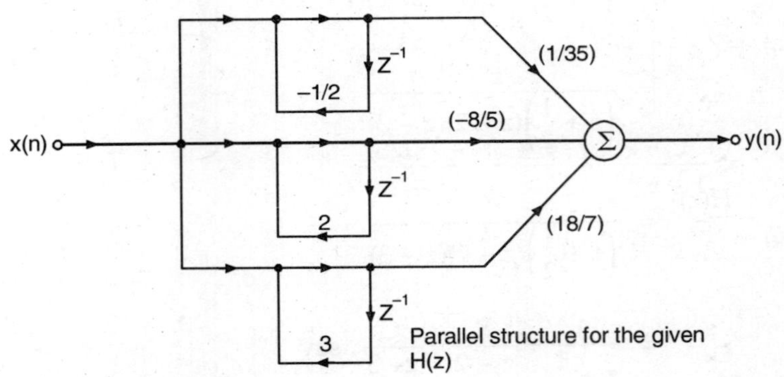

Parallel structure for the given H(z)

Ans.

As $$H(z) = \frac{1}{\left(1+\frac{1}{2}z^{-1}\right)(1-2z^{-1})(1-3z^{-1})}$$, its cascade form is as below:

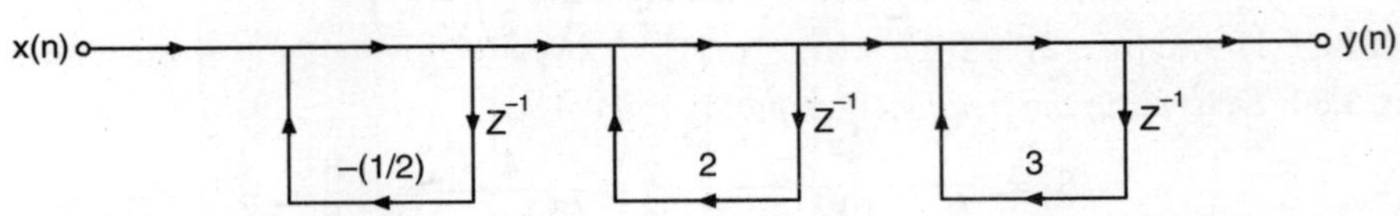

EXAMPLE 3.49: *Determine the response $y(n)$, $n \geq 0$ for the system described by the second order difference equation*

$$y(n) - 4y(n-1) + 4y(n-2) = x(n) - x(n-1)$$

Assume $x(n) = (-1)^n u(n)$ *and* $y(-1) = y(-2) = 0$

SOLUTION: Clearly, $$H(z) = \frac{1-z^{-1}}{1-4z^{-1}+4z^{-2}} = \frac{1-z^{-1}}{(1-2z^{-1})^2}$$

As $$x(n) = (-1)^n u(n) \quad \therefore \quad X(z) = \frac{1}{1+z^{-1}}$$

$\therefore \qquad Y(z) = X(z) \cdot H(z) = \dfrac{1-z^{-1}}{(1+z^{-1})(1-2z^{-1})^2} = \dfrac{-1}{4}\dfrac{z^{-1}-1}{(z^{-1}+1)\left(z^{-1}-\frac{1}{2}\right)^2}$

(To get partial fractions for $Y(z)$: for finding $y(n)$)

Let $$\frac{z^{-1}-1}{(z^{-1}+1)\left(z^{-1}-\frac{1}{2}\right)^2} = \frac{A}{(z^{-1}+1)} + \frac{B}{\left(z^{-1}-\frac{1}{2}\right)} + \frac{C}{\left(z^{-1}-\frac{1}{2}\right)^2}$$

$\therefore \qquad A = \dfrac{-2}{(-3/2)^2} = -8/9$

$$C = \frac{-1/2}{1+\frac{1}{2}} = \frac{-1}{3}$$

$$B = \frac{d}{dz^{-1}}\left(\frac{z^{-1}-1}{z^{-1}+1}\right)\Bigg|_{z^{-1}=\frac{1}{2}} = \frac{d}{dz^{-1}}\left[+1-\frac{2}{z^{-1}+1}\right]\Bigg|_{z^{-1}=\frac{1}{2}} = \frac{2}{(z^{-1}+1)^2}\Bigg|_{z^{-1}=\frac{1}{2}} = \frac{8}{9}$$

$\therefore \qquad Y(z) = -\dfrac{1}{4}\left[\dfrac{-8/9}{z^{-1}+1} + \dfrac{8/9}{z^{-1}-\frac{1}{2}} + \dfrac{-1/3}{\left(z^{-1}-\frac{1}{2}\right)^2}\right]$

$$= \frac{2/9}{1+z^{-1}} - \frac{4/9}{1-2z^{-1}} + \frac{1/3}{(1-2z^{-1})^2}(2z^{-1})\left(\frac{1}{2}z\right)$$

$\therefore \qquad y(n) = \dfrac{2}{9}(-1)^n u(n) - \dfrac{4}{9}2^n u(n) + \dfrac{1}{6}(n+1)\,2^{n+1}u(n+1)$

$$\left(\because \frac{az^{-1}}{(1-az^{-1})^2} \xrightarrow{IZT} na^n u(n)\right)$$

This gives $\qquad y(n) = \dfrac{1}{9}\{1, 2, 6, 14, 34, 78, \ldots\}$ (↑ under 1) **Ans.**

Note. If we calculate $y(n)$ from the difference equation $y(n) = 4y(n-1) - 4y(n-2) + (-1)^n u(n) - (-1)^{n-1} u(n-1)$, we get the same value of $y(n)$.

EXAMPLE 3.50: *Determine the frequency response of the system described by*

$$y(n) = (5/6)\, y(n-1) - \frac{1}{6}\, y(n-2) + x(n)$$ *(GGSIP Univ. 2007)*

SOLUTION: $\qquad y(n) = \left(\dfrac{5}{6}\right) y(n-1) - \dfrac{1}{6}\, y(n-2) + x(n)$

Taking *ZT* both sides, we readily obtain

$$H(z) = \frac{Y(z)}{X(z)} = \frac{1}{1-\frac{5}{6}z^{-1}+\frac{1}{6}z^{-2}} = \frac{6}{6-5z^{-1}+z^{-2}}$$

$$H(e^{j\omega}) = \frac{6}{(6-5e^{-j\omega}+e^{-j2\omega})} = \frac{6}{(e^{-j\omega}-2)(e^{-j\omega}-3)} \qquad \text{...(A)}$$

$$|H(e^{j\omega})|^2 = \frac{36}{((\cos\omega - 2)^2 + \sin^2\omega)((\cos\omega - 3)^2 + \sin^2\omega)}$$

$$= \frac{36}{(5 - 4\cos\omega)(10 - 6\cos\omega)} = \frac{36}{50 - 70\cos\omega + 24\cos^2\omega}$$

$$|H(e^{j\omega})|^2 = \frac{36}{50 - 70\cos\omega + 12(\cos 2\omega + 1)}$$

$$= \frac{36}{62 - 70\cos\omega + 12\cos 2\omega}$$

$$|H(e^{j\omega})| = \frac{3\sqrt{2}}{(31 - 35\cos\omega + 6\cos 2\omega)^{1/2}} \text{ amplitude response}$$

$$\text{Phase angle } \phi = -\left[\tan^{-1}\frac{-\sin\omega}{\cos\omega - 2} + \tan^{-1}\left(\frac{-\sin\omega}{\cos\omega - 3}\right)\right] \text{ [from (A)]}$$

$$\therefore \quad \phi(\omega) = \tan^{-1}\frac{\sin\omega}{\cos\omega - 2} + \tan^{-1}\frac{\sin\omega}{\cos\omega - 3}$$

EXAMPLE 3.51: *(a) Find h(n) of an LTI system described by the difference equation*

$$y(n) - \frac{3}{4}y(n-1) + \frac{1}{8}y(n-2) = 2x(n)$$

(b) Also, calculate the response y(n) to input $x(n) = \left(\frac{1}{4}\right)^n u(n)$

SOLUTION: *(a)* As

$$y(n) - \frac{3}{4}y(n-1) + \frac{1}{8}y(n-2) = 2x(n)$$

$$\therefore \quad H(z) = \frac{2}{1 - \frac{3}{4}z^{-1} + \frac{1}{8}z^{-2}} = \frac{2}{\left(1 - \frac{1}{2}z^{-1}\right)\left(1 - \frac{1}{4}z^{-1}\right)}$$

$$= \frac{4}{\left(1 - \frac{1}{2}z^{-1}\right)} + \frac{-2}{\left(1 - \frac{1}{4}z^{-1}\right)}$$

$$\therefore \quad h(n) = \left[4\left(\frac{1}{2}\right)^n - 2\left(\frac{1}{4}\right)^n\right]u(n) \quad \textbf{Ans.}$$

(b)

$$X(z) = ZT\left[\left(\frac{1}{4}\right)^n u(n)\right] = \frac{1}{1 - \frac{1}{4}z^{-1}}$$

$$Y(z) = X(z)\cdot H(z)$$

$$= \frac{2}{\left(1 - \frac{1}{4}z^{-1}\right)\left(1 - \frac{1}{2}z^{-1}\right)\left(1 - \frac{1}{4}z^{-1}\right)} = \frac{2}{\left(1 - \frac{1}{2}z^{-1}\right)\left(1 - \frac{1}{4}z^{-1}\right)^2}$$

$$= \frac{8}{1 - \frac{1}{2}z^{-1}} + \frac{-4}{1 - \frac{1}{4}z^{-1}} + \frac{-2}{\left(1 - \frac{1}{4}z^{-1}\right)^2} \quad \text{(By partial fractions **)}$$

$$= \frac{8}{1 - \frac{1}{2}z^{-1}} - \frac{4}{1 - \frac{1}{4}z^{-1}} - (8z)\frac{\frac{1}{4}z^{-1}}{\left(1 - \frac{1}{4}z^{-1}\right)^2}$$

**Let $$\frac{2}{\left(1-\frac{1}{2}z^{-1}\right)\left(1-\frac{1}{4}z^{-1}\right)^2} = \frac{A}{1-\frac{1}{2}z^{-1}} + \frac{B}{1-\frac{1}{4}z^{-1}} + \frac{C}{\left(1-\frac{1}{4}z^{-1}\right)^2}$$

$\therefore$ $$2 = A\left[\left(1-\frac{1}{4}z^{-1}\right)^2\right] + B\left[1-\frac{3}{4}z^{-1}+\frac{1}{8}z^{-2}\right] + D\left(1-\frac{1}{2}z^{-1}\right)$$

$Z^0 \Rightarrow 2 = A + B + C$

$Z^{-1} \Rightarrow 0 = -\frac{1}{2}A - \frac{3}{4}B - \frac{1}{2}C$

$Z^{-2} \Rightarrow 0 = \frac{1}{16}A + \frac{1}{8}B$

Solving these, we get $A = 8$, $B = -4$, $C = -2$

$$y(n) = 8\left(\frac{1}{2}\right)^n u(n) - 4\left(\frac{1}{4}\right)^n u(n) - 8\left[n\left(\frac{1}{4}\right)^n \cdot u(n)\Big|_{\text{change } n \text{ to } (n+1)}\right]$$

$$= \left[8\left(\frac{1}{2}\right)^n - 4\left(\frac{1}{4}\right)^n\right]u(n) - \left[8(n+1)\,.\left(\frac{1}{4}\right)^{n+1} u(n+1)\right]$$

$\therefore$ $$y(n) = 4\left[2\left(\frac{1}{2}\right)^n - \left(\frac{1}{4}\right)^n\right]u(n) - 2\left[(n+1)\left(\frac{1}{4}\right)^n u(n+1)\right] \quad \textbf{Ans.}$$

EXAMPLE 3.52: *Find the zero state and zero input responses of the system which is described by*

$$y(k+2) - \frac{5}{6}y(k+1) + \frac{1}{6}y(k) = 5f(k+1) - f(k)$$

given $y(-1) = 2$ and $y(-2) = 0$ and the input $f(k) = u(k)$. *(GGSIP Univ. 2005)*

SOLUTION: (*a*) **Zero state Response**

We get $$Y(z)\left[z^2 - \frac{5}{6}z + \frac{1}{6}\right] = F(z)\,[5z-1]$$

Put, $$F(z) = \frac{1}{1-z^{-1}} \quad \because\ f(k) = u(k) \text{ given}$$

$$Y(z) = \frac{5z-1}{1-z^{-1}} \times \frac{1}{z^2 - \frac{5}{6}z + \frac{1}{6}} = \frac{5z^{-1} - z^{-2}}{(1-z^{-1})\left(1-\frac{5}{6}z^{-1}+\frac{1}{6}z^{-2}\right)}$$

$$= \frac{5z^{-1}-z^{-2}}{(1-z^{-1})\left(1-\frac{1}{2}z^{-1}\right)\left(1-\frac{1}{3}z^{-1}\right)}$$

$$= \frac{12}{1-z^{-1}} + \frac{-18}{1-\frac{1}{2}z^{-1}} + \frac{+6}{1-\frac{1}{3}z^{-1}}$$

Hence, zero state response is

$$y(n) = \left[12 - 18\left(\frac{1}{2}\right)^n + 6\left(\frac{1}{3}\right)^n\right]u(n) \quad \textbf{Ans.}$$

(*b*) **Zero-input Response**

As $$y(k+2) - \frac{5}{6}\,y(k+1) + \frac{1}{6}\,y(k) = 5f(k+1) - f(k)$$

Put $$k + 2 = n$$

$$\therefore \quad y(n) - \frac{5}{6}\,y(n-1) + \frac{1}{6}\,y(n-2) = 5f(n-1) - f(n-2)$$

As input is zero $\therefore$ $f(n) = 0 \;\forall\; n$, and we get

$$y(n) - \frac{5}{6}\,y(n-1) + \frac{1}{6}\,y(n-2) = 0$$

Take unilateral *Z-T*

$$Y(z) - \frac{5}{6}\left[z^{-1}Y(z) + \underbrace{y(-1)}_{z^0 y(-1)\,=\,2}\right] + \frac{1}{6}\left[z^{-2}Y(z) + \underbrace{z^{-1}y(-1)}_{=\,2} + \underbrace{y(-2)}_{z^0 y(-2)\,=\,0\text{ (given)}}\right] = 0 \qquad \text{(Note this step)}$$

$$\therefore \; Y(z)\left[1 - \frac{5}{6}z^{-1} + \frac{1}{6}z^{-2}\right] = \left(\frac{5}{6}\times 2\right) - \frac{1}{6}\times 2\cdot z^{-1}$$

$$= \frac{5}{3} - \frac{1}{3}z^{-1}$$

$$Y(z) = \frac{5/3 - \frac{1}{2}z^{-1}}{\left(1 - \frac{1}{2}z^{-1}\right)\left(1 - \frac{1}{3}z^{-1}\right)} = \frac{3}{\left(1 - \frac{1}{2}z^{-1}\right)} + \frac{-4/3}{\left(1 - \frac{1}{3}z^{-1}\right)}$$

Hence, zero input response is

$$y(n) = \left[3\left(\frac{1}{2}\right)^n - \frac{4}{3}\left(\frac{1}{3}\right)^n\right]u(n) \qquad \textbf{Ans.}$$

EXAMPLE 3.53: *The following information about a discrete-time signal is given*

(i) x(n) is real and right handed

(ii) X(z) has exactly two poles,

(iii) X(z) has two zeros at origin

(iv) X(1) = 8/3 and

(v) X(z) has a pole at $z = \frac{1}{2}e^{j\pi/3}$

Find the value of x(n).

SOLUTION: Let $$X(z) = \frac{Az^2}{(z-a)(z-b)}$$

X(z) has two zeros at origin

X(z) has two poles

As $x[n]$ is real (and right handed), poles of $X(z)$ are either real or complex conjugate. The other pole is, therefore, at $z = \frac{1}{2}e^{-j\pi/3}$ (conjugate of $\frac{1}{2}e^{j\pi/3}$).

If $a = \frac{1}{2}e^{j\pi/3}$ then $b = \frac{1}{2}e^{-j\pi/3}$. Hence, X(z) reduces to

$$X(z) = \frac{Az^{-2}}{z^2 - (\cos \pi/3)\, z + \frac{1}{4}} = \frac{Az^2}{z^2 - \frac{1}{2}z + \frac{1}{4}}$$

Put $z = 1$ ∴

$$X(1) = \frac{A\,.\,(1)^2}{1 - \left(\frac{1}{2}\right).\,1 + \frac{1}{4}} = \frac{8}{3} \text{ given by condition } (iv)$$

∴

$$\frac{A}{3/4} = 8/3$$

or

$$A = 2$$

Hence,

$$X(z) = \frac{2z^2}{z^2 - \frac{1}{2}z + \frac{1}{4}} = \frac{2}{1 - \frac{1}{2}z^{-1} + \frac{1}{4}z^{-2}}$$

$$= \frac{2}{\left(1 - \frac{1}{2}e^{j\pi/3}z^{-1}\right)\left(1 - \frac{1}{2}e^{-j\pi/3}z^{-1}\right)}$$

$$= 2\left[\frac{\frac{1}{2\,j \sin \pi/3}\,.\,e^{j\pi/3}}{\left(1 - \frac{1}{2}e^{j\pi/3}z^{-1}\right)} + \frac{-\frac{1}{2\,j\sin \pi/3}\,e^{-j\pi/3}}{\left(1 - \frac{1}{2}e^{-j\pi/3}\,z^{-1}\right)}\right]$$

∴

$$x(n) = \left(\frac{1}{j \sin \frac{\pi}{3}}\right)\left[e^{j\pi/3}\left(\frac{1}{2}e^{j\pi/3}\right)^n - e^{-j\pi/3}\left(\frac{1}{2}e^{-j\pi/3}\right)^n\right]u(n)$$

$$= \frac{2\left(\frac{1}{2}\right)^n \sin\,(n+1)\,\pi/3}{\sin\,(\pi/3)}\,u(n)$$

Ans.

EXAMPLE 3.54: *Determine* $|H(\omega)|^2$ *for the system characterized by*

$$y(n) = -\,0.1y(n-1) + 0.2y(n-2) + x(n) + x(n-1) \qquad \text{(DU 2003)}$$

SOLUTION:

$$y(n) = -\frac{1}{10}\,y(n-1) + \frac{1}{5}\,y(n-2) + x(n) + x(n-1)$$

Take *ZT* on both sides and collect terms of $Y(z)$ on one side, we get

$$H(z) = \frac{Y(z)}{X(z)} = \frac{1 + z^{-1}}{1 + \frac{1}{10}z^{-1} - \frac{1}{5}z^{-2}}$$

$$= \frac{10(1 + z^{-1})}{10 + z^{-1} - 2z^{-2}}$$

Putting $Z = e^{j\omega}$, we obtain the Fourier Transform of $h(n)$ as

$$H(e^{j\omega}) = \frac{10(1 + e^{-j\omega})}{10 + e^{-j\omega} - 2e^{-j2\omega}}$$

$$= \frac{10(1 + \cos \omega - j \sin \omega)}{(10 + \cos \omega - 2\cos 2\omega) + j(-\sin \omega + 2\sin 2\omega)}$$

Hence, $$|H(e^{j\omega})|^2 = \frac{100[(1+\cos\omega)^2 + (\sin\omega)^2]}{(10+\cos\omega - 2\cos 2\omega)^2 + (-\sin\omega + 2\sin 2\omega)^2}$$

$$= \frac{100\,[1 + \overbrace{(\cos^2\omega + \sin^2\omega)}^{=1} + 2\cos\omega]}{100 + \underbrace{(\cos^2\omega + \sin^2\omega)}_{=1} + \underbrace{(4\cos^2 2\omega + 4\sin^2 2\omega)}_{=4} + 20\cos\omega - 4\cos\omega\cos 2\omega - 40\cos 2\omega \underbrace{-4\sin\omega\sin 2\omega}_{=-4\cos\omega}}$$

$$= \frac{100\,(2 + 2\cos\omega)}{105 + 16\cos\omega - 40\cos 2\omega}$$

$$= \frac{200(1+\cos\omega)}{105 + 16\cos\omega - 40\cos 2\omega}$$ **Ans.**

3.11 STABILITY TESTS OF THE DISCRETE-TIME SYSTEMS

We shall now learn various methods to determine the BIBO stability of the discrete-time systems.

3.11.1 Stability (BIBO Stability) in Time Domain

A digital filter is said to be stable if and only if any bounded excitation, $x(n)$, results in a bounded response, $y(n)$.

i.e., if $|x(n)| < \infty$ for all n

then a BIBO stable system yields

$$|y(n)| < \infty \text{ for all } n$$

For a LTI system, we have

$$y(n) = \sum_{k=0}^{\infty} h(k)\, x(n-k) \qquad \text{[a causal system has } h(n) = 0 \text{ for } n < 0]$$

$$|y(n)| \le \sum_{k=0}^{\infty} |h(k)|\,|x(n-k)| \qquad \text{...(A)}$$

$$\le M \sum_{k=0}^{\infty} |h(k)| \qquad \text{where } |x(n)| \le M < \infty\ \forall\ n$$

Thus, $|y(n)| < \infty$ *i.e.,* a bounded output iff $x(n)$ being bounded input

$$\sum_{k=0}^{\infty} |h(k)| < \infty : \text{Condition for BIBO stability}$$
Necessary and sufficient condition ...(3.88)

If $$x(n-k) = \begin{cases} M & \text{if } h(k) > 0 \\ -M & \text{if } h(k) < 0 \end{cases}$$

3.11.2 BIBO Stability Condition in z-domain

Let $H(z)$ be the ZT of $h(n)$ of the given system under BIBO test. Let $H(z)$ has N poles: $p_1, p_2, ..., p_N$ all being finite valued.

$$h(n) = IZT\,[H(z)] = \frac{1}{2\pi j} \oint_C H(z)\, z^{n-1}\, dz$$

For $n = 0$

$$h(0) = \operatorname*{Res}_{z=0} \frac{H(z)}{z} + \sum_{i=1}^{N} \operatorname*{Res}_{z=p_i} \left(\frac{H(z)}{z}\right) \quad (z \neq 0)$$

$$= H(0) + \sum_{i=1}^{N} \frac{1}{p_i} \underbrace{(\operatorname*{Res}_{z=p_i} H(z))}$$

$H(0)$: Finite since $H(z) = \infty$ only at poles p_i and no where else

$\frac{1}{p_i}$: Finite

$(\operatorname*{Res}_{z=p_i} H(z))$: Finite ($\because$ given $H(z)$ has finite valued poles p_i $\therefore$ must have finite valued residues)

$\therefore$ $h(0)$ is FINITE valued ...(A)

For $n > 0$ $(n = 1, 2, ...,)$

$$h(n) = \sum_{i=1}^{N} \left[\operatorname*{Res}_{z=p_i} H(z)\, z^{n-1}\right]$$

$$= \sum_{i=1}^{N} (\operatorname*{Res}_{z=p_i} H(z))\,.\, p_i^{n-1} \qquad ...(B)$$

Assume a generic pole, $p_i = r_i \,.\, e^{j\psi_i}$

Let $|p_i| \leq r_{max}$ for $i = 1, 2, ..., N$

also let $\left|\operatorname*{Res}_{z=p_i} H(z)\right| \leq R_{max}$ for $i = 1, 2, ..., N$

then (B) yields $|h(n)| \leq \sum_{i=1}^{N} \left|\operatorname*{Res}_{z=p_i} H(z)\right| \,.\, r_{max}^{n-1} \leq NR_{max}\, r_{max}^{n-1}$, $n = 1, 2, ...,$

Hence,

$$\sum_{n=0}^{\infty} |h(n)| = |\, h(0)\, | + \sum_{n=0}^{\infty} |h(n)|$$

$$\leq |\, h(0)\, | + \sum_{n=1}^{\infty} NR_{max}\, r_{max}^{n-1}$$

$$= |\, h(0)\, | + NR_{max} \sum_{n=1}^{\infty} r_{max}^{n-1} \qquad ...(C)$$

L.H.S. of (C) must be less than ∞ for BIBO stability.

∴ For BIBO stability, we must have

$$NR_{max} \sum_{n=1}^{\infty} r_{max}^{n-1} < \infty$$

i.e.,

$$\sum_{n=1}^{\infty} r_{max}^{n-1} < \infty$$

i.e., $r_{max} < 1$ for the series to converge

i.e., the pole length r_i which is less than or equal to r_{max} must be less than unity.

Hence, all poles must strictly lie inside the unit circle for BIBO stability ...(3.89)

For example:

Given $$H(z) = \frac{z^2 - z + 1}{z^2 - z + \frac{1}{2}} \triangleq \frac{z^2 - z + 1}{(z - p_1)(z - p_2)}$$

has poles $p_1, p_2 = \frac{1}{2} \pm j\frac{1}{2}$

as $|p_1| = |p_2| = \sqrt{\frac{1}{4} + \frac{1}{4}} = \sqrt{\frac{1}{2}} < 1.$

∴ The given filter is stable (BIBO stable)

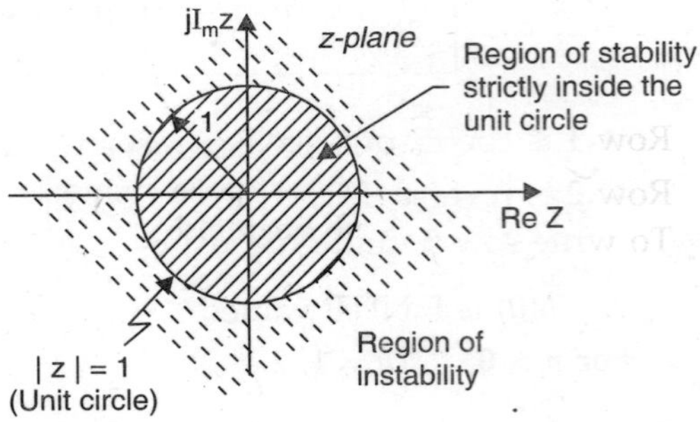

Fig. 3.13. Showing region of stability of $H(z)$.

3.11.3 Jury's Stability Criteria

This is a quicker method to test for stability of the digital systems. It is analogous to Routh-Hurwitz criteria in analog systems.

Let the given filter be characterized by

$$H(z) = \frac{N(z)}{D(z)} \quad ...(3.90)$$

where

$$D(z) = \sum_{i=0}^{N} b_i z^{N-i} \quad ...(3.91)$$

$$= b_0 z^N + b_1 z^{N-1} + b_2 z^{N-2} + ... + b_N,$$

then the stability criteria are (Jury's stability criteria)

With $b_0 > 0$ and $D(z)$ expanded in descending order of z

(*i*) $D(1) > 0$

(*ii*) $(-1)^N D(-1) > 0$

(*iii*) $|b_0| > |b_N|$. If all these conditions are satisfied, then $H(z)$ is a stable system.

$$\begin{aligned} |c_0| &> |c_{N-1}| \\ |d_0| &> |d_{N-2}| \\ &\vdots \\ |r_0| &> |r_2| \end{aligned} \quad ...(3.92)$$

How to form Jury's Array

Row	*Coefficients*						
1	b_0	b_1	b_2	...	b_{N-2}	b_{N-1}	b_N
2	b_N	b_{N-1}	b_{N-2}	...	b_2	b_1	b_0
3	c_0	c_1	c_2	...	c_{N-2}	c_{N-1}	
4	c_{N-1}	c_{N-2}	c_{N-3}	...	c_1	c_0	
5	d_0	d_1	d_2	...	d_{N-3}	d_{N-2}	
6	d_{N-2}	d_{N-3}	d_{N-4}	...	d_1	d_0	
$2N-3$	r_0	r_1	r_2				

Row 1 is coeffs. of $z^N, z^{N-1} \ldots, z^0$ in $D(z)$

Row 2 is reverse of row 1

To write row 3, find c_i by using:

$$c_i = \begin{vmatrix} b_i & b_N \\ b_{N-i} & b_0 \end{vmatrix}$$

Row 4 is reverse of row 3. To write row 5

$$d_i = \begin{vmatrix} c_i & c_{N-1} \\ c_{N-1-i} & c_0 \end{vmatrix}$$

Row 6 is reverse of row 5 and proceeding so on, the $(2N-3)^{\text{th}}$ row has only three elements *viz* r_0, r_1 and r_2.

3.11.4 Schür-Cohn Stability Test

It is well known that the stability of a system is determined by the position of the poles. For the system function

$$H(z) = \frac{B(z)}{A(z)} \qquad \ldots(3.93)$$

Where $$A(z) = 1 + a_1 z^{-1} + a_2 z^{-2} + \ldots + a_N z^{-N} \qquad \ldots(3.94)$$

If the system is causal, the roots of $A(z) = 0$ must lie inside the unti circle for the system $H(z)$ to be stable. Several stability criteria yield procedures to determine if any of the roots of $A(z)$ lies outside the unit circle. Schür-Cohn test procedure for the stability of a system characterized by the system function $H(z) = B(z)/A(z)$ is very simple. Let a polynomial of degree be denoted by

$$A_m(z) = \sum_{k=0}^{m} a_m(k)\, z^k \qquad \ldots(3.95)$$

where $a_m(0) = 1$, *i.e.*, the constant term is unity ...(3.96)

The reciprocal or reverse polynomial $B_m(z)$ of degree m is defined as:

$$B_m(z) \triangleq z^m A_m(z^{-1}) \qquad \text{...(3.97)}$$

$$= z^{-m} \sum_{k=0}^{m} a_m(k)\,(z^{-1})^{-k} = \sum_{k=0}^{m} a_m(k)\, z^{-(m-k)}$$

Put $m - k = k'$ $\quad \therefore$ when $k = 0$, $k' = m$

when $k = m$, $k' = 0$

$$\therefore \quad B_m(z) = \sum_{k'=m}^{0} a_m(m-k')\, z^{-k'}$$

$$= \sum_{k=0}^{m} a_m(m-k)\, z^{-k}$$ (dropping dashes and reversing the sequence of summation)

Thus, it is seen that the coefficients of $B_m(z)$ are the same as these of $A_m(z)$, but in reverse order.

In the Schür-Cohn stability test, to determine if the polynomial $A(z)$ has all its roots inside $|z| = 1$, we compute a set of reflection coefficients, k_m, $m = N, N-1, ..., 2, 1$ as follows:

$$K_N = a_N(N), \quad \text{where} \quad A_N(z) = A(z) \qquad \text{...(3.98)}$$

We compute the lower-degree polynomial $A(z)$, $m = N, N-1, N-2, ..., 2$ by the recursive equation

$$A_{m-1}(z) = \frac{A_m(z) - k_m B_m(z)}{1 - k_m^2} \qquad \text{...(3.99)}$$

where $k_m = a_m(m)$ ...(3.100)

i.e., k_m is the coefficient of z^m in the polynomial $A_m(z)$

> The Schür-Cohn stability test states that the polynomial $A(z) = \sum_{k=0}^{N} a_N(k)\, z^{-k}$ has all its roots inside the unit circle if and only if the coefficient k_m satisfy the condition $|k_m| < 1$ for all $m = N, N-1, N-2, ..., 1$ ...(3.101)

3.12 FREQUENCY DOMAIN ANALYSIS

It is also possible to determine the frequency response of the system $H(z)$ graphically. We proceed as follows:

Replacing $z = e^{j\omega}$ in $H(z)$, we get

$$H(e^{j\omega}) = H(z)|_{z=e^{j\omega}}$$

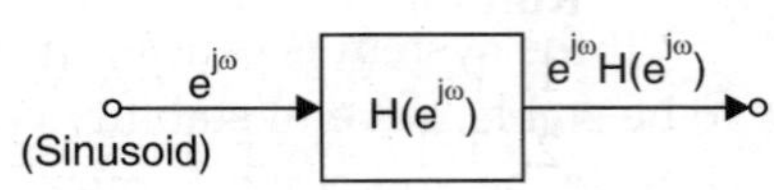

Note that $z = e^{j\omega}$ corresponds to a unit circle

Let

$$H(e^{j\omega}) = |H(e^{j\omega})|\, e^{j \arg H(e^{j\omega})} \triangleq \frac{H_0 \prod_{i=1}^{N} (e^{j\omega T} - z_i)}{\prod_{j=1}^{M} (e^{j\omega T} - p_i)}$$

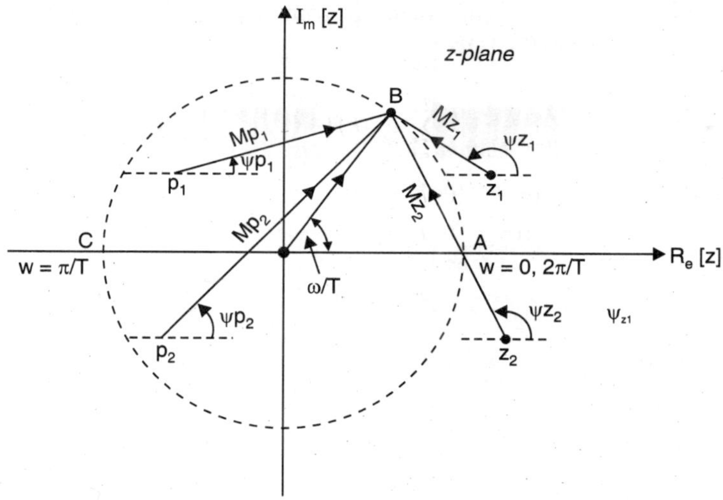

Fig. 3.14. Phasor diagram for 2nd order recursive filter

We let $e^{j\omega T} - z_i = Mz_i \; e^{j\psi_{zi}}$ corresponding to zeros of $H(e^{j\omega})$

$e^{j\omega T} - p_k = Mp_k \; e^{j\psi_{pk}}$ corresponding to poles of $H(e^{j\omega})$

In Fig. 3.12, drawn with two poles and two zeros, we have $| H(e^{j\omega}) | = M_{z1} \,.\, M_{z2}/(M_{p1}/M_{p2})$ and Arg $H(e^{j\omega}) = \psi_{z1} + \psi_{z2} - (\psi_{p1} + \psi_{p2})$. Extending this result for a generic case, we have

$$\underset{= M(\omega)}{|H(e^{j\omega})|} = \frac{H_0 \prod_{i=1}^{N} M_{zi}}{\prod_{k=1}^{M} M_{pk}}$$

$$\underset{= \theta(\omega)}{\text{Arg } H(e^{j\omega})} = \sum_{i=1}^{N} \psi_{zi} - \sum_{k=1}^{M} \psi_{pk}$$

Note that like in analog filter, in a digital filter too we can represent its effect on a sinusoidal excitation in frequency domain by an amplitude response $M(\omega)$ and the phase response $\theta(\omega)$. In analog filter, we evaluate the response $H(s)$ an imaginary axis $s = j\Omega$ and in digital filter we evaluate $H(z)$ on the unit circle $|z| = 1$ in z-plane.

Rule to determine $M(\omega)$ and $\theta(\omega)$, given zeros and poles of $H(z)$

1. Plot the given zeros and poles, z_i and p_i, respectively, in z-plane.
2. Take any point B on $| z | = 1$, say at angle ω/T. Draw vectors from z_i and p_i to B calling them M_{zi}, M_{pi} in lengths and denoting their angles by ψ_{zi} and ψ_{pi}, respectively.
3. Then $M(\omega) = \dfrac{\prod_{i=1}^{N} M_{zi}}{\prod_{i=1}^{M} M_{pi}}$; $\theta(\omega) = \sum_{i=1}^{N} \psi_{zi} - \sum_{i=1}^{M} \psi_{pi}$

4. Repeat above steps 2, 3 for various ω/T from 0 to π to compute the determine values of $M(\omega)$ and $\theta(\omega)$ for all ω/T, 0 to π.

Solved Examples on Stability

EXAMPLE 3.55: *Check if the filter shown is BIBO stable.*

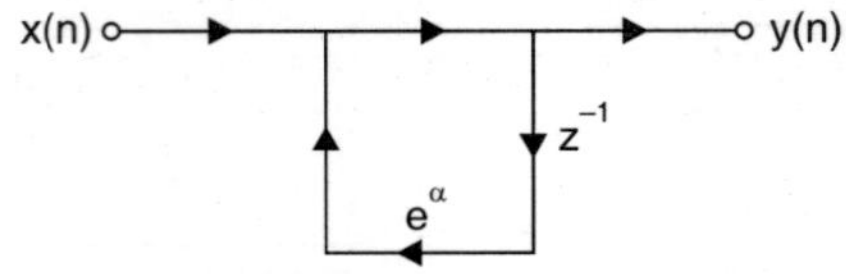

Fig. Ex. 3.55. The given IIR filter

SOLUTION: For the given filter, we have

$$H(z) = \frac{1}{1-e^{\alpha}z^{-1}}$$

$$\therefore \quad h(n) = e^{n\alpha}\,u(n)$$

$$\sum_{k=0}^{\infty}|h(k)| = \sum_{k=0}^{\infty}|e^{k\alpha}|$$

$$= 1 + |e^{\alpha}| + |e^{2\alpha}| + \ldots + |e^{k\alpha}| + \ldots$$

$$= \frac{1}{1-|e^{\alpha}|} \quad \text{the series converges iff } |e^{\alpha}| < 1$$

i.e., of $|e^{\alpha}| < 1$, the system is BIBO stable.

i.e., if $a < 0$, the system is BIBO stable. **Ans.**

EXAMPLE 3.56: *We want to design a causal discrete-time LTI system with the property that for input:*

$$x(n) = \left(\frac{1}{2}\right)^n u(n) - \frac{1}{4}\left(\frac{1}{2}\right)^{n-1} u(n-1) \text{ and the output is } y(n) = \left(\frac{1}{3}\right)^n u(n)$$

(a) Determine the impulse response h(n) and the system function H(z) of a system that satisfies the foregoing conditions.

(b) Find the difference equation that characterizes this system.

(c) Determine a realization of the system that requires the minimum possible amount of memory.

(d) Determine if the system is stable.

SOLUTION:

$$x(n) = \left(\frac{1}{2}\right)^n u(n) - \frac{1}{4}\left(\frac{1}{2}\right)^{n-1} u(n-1)$$

$$\therefore \quad X(z) = \frac{1}{1-\left(\frac{1}{2}\right)z^{-1}} - \frac{\left(\frac{1}{4}\right)z^{-1}}{1-\left(\frac{1}{2}\right)z^{-1}} = \frac{1-\frac{1}{4}z^{-1}}{1-\frac{1}{2}z^{-1}}$$

$$y(n) = \left(\frac{1}{3}\right)^n u(n)$$

(a)

$$Y(z) = \frac{1}{1-\left(\frac{1}{3}\right)z^{-1}}$$

$$H(z) = \frac{Y(z)}{X(z)} = \frac{1-\left(\frac{1}{2}\right)z^{-1}}{\left(1-\frac{1}{3}z^{-1}\right)\left(1-\frac{1}{4}z^{-1}\right)} = \frac{3}{\left(1-\frac{1}{4}z^{-1}\right)} - \frac{2}{\left(1-\frac{1}{3}z^{-1}\right)}$$

$$\therefore \quad h(n) = \left[3\left(\frac{1}{4}\right)^n - 2.\left(\frac{1}{3}\right)^n\right]u(n)$$

Ans.

(*b*) As
$$H(z) = \frac{1 - \frac{1}{2} z^{-1}}{\left(1 - \frac{1}{4} z^{-1}\right)\left(1 - \frac{1}{3} z^{-1}\right)}$$
$$= \frac{1 - \frac{1}{2} z^{-1}}{1 - \frac{7}{12} z^{-1} + \frac{1}{12} z^{-1}}$$

Hence, the difference equation becomes

$$y(n) = \frac{7}{12} y(n-1) - \frac{1}{12} y(n-2) + x(n) - \frac{1}{2} x(n-1)$$ **Ans.**

(*c*) The canonic realization (*i.e.*, with least delay or with least memory) is as shown

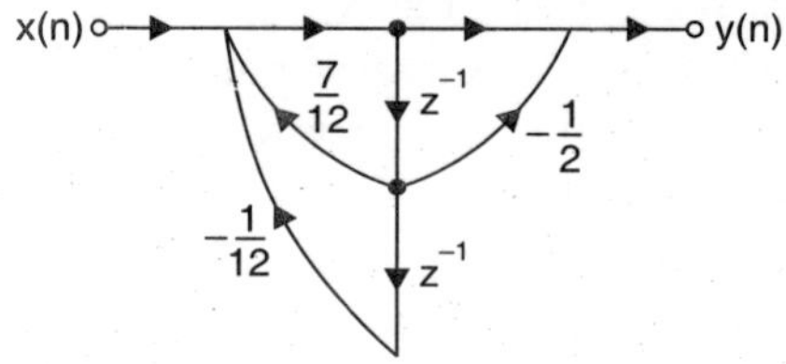

Fig. Ex. 3.56. The canonic realization of the system *H*(*z*)

(*d*) The poles of $H(z) = \frac{1 - \frac{1}{2} z^{-1}}{\left(1 - \frac{1}{4} z^{-1}\right)\left(1 - \frac{1}{3} z^{-1}\right)}$ are at $z = \frac{1}{4}, \frac{1}{3}$ and are inside the unit circle

Hence, the system is stable. **Ans.**

EXAMPLE 3.57: *A linear shift invariant system is characterised by its impulse response h(n), given by*

$$h(n) = 3\left(-\frac{1}{4}\right)^n u(n-1)$$

(i) Is the system causal? Why or why not?

(ii) Is the system BIBO stable? Why or why not?

(iii) Is the system an FIR or IIR? Why?

SOLUTION: (*i*) For causality, $h(n) = 0, \quad n < 0$

Here $h(n) = 0$ for all $n < 0$ due to the factor $u(n-1)$

∴ The system is causal **Ans.**

(*ii*)
$$\sum_{n=-\infty}^{\infty} |h(n)| = \sum_{n=1}^{\infty} \left| 3\left(-\frac{1}{4}\right)^n \right|$$
$$= 3 \sum_{n=1}^{\infty} \left| \left(-\frac{1}{4}\right)^n \right| = 3 \left| \frac{-\frac{1}{4}}{1 + \frac{1}{4}} \right| < \infty$$

∴ The system is BIBO stable **Ans.**

(*iii*) As $h(n) = 3\left(-\frac{1}{4}\right)^n u(n-1)$

i.e., $h(n)$ has an infinite impulses, hence, this $h(n)$ represents an IIR system. **Ans.**

EXAMPLE 3.58: *Determine whether the system characterized by H(z) is stable or not, where*

$$H(z) = \frac{1+z^{-1}+z^{-2}}{1-1.5z^{-1}+z^{-2}-0.5z^{-3}+0.5z^{-4}}$$

Realize the system in canonic form.

SOLUTION: We use **Jury's** test criteria

We have $H(z) = \frac{1+z^{-1}+z^{-2}}{1-1.5z^{-1}+z^{-2}-0.5z^{-3}+0.5z^{-4}} = \frac{2(z^4+z^3+z^2)}{2z^4-3z^3+2z^2-z+1} = \frac{N(z)}{D(z)}$

Here $D(z) = 2z^4 - 3z^3 + 2z^2 - z + 1$, degree $N = 4$

$D(1) = 2 - 3 + 2 - 1 + 1 = 1 > 0 \quad \therefore$ OK test passes

$(-1)^4 D(-1) = 2 + 3 + 2 + 1 + 1 = 9 > 0 \quad \therefore$ OK test passes

						Remarks
b_i	2	–3	2	–1	1	$\vert b_0 \vert > \vert b_4 \vert$
	1	–1	2	–3	2	*i.e.*, 2 > 1 ∴ test passes
c_i	3	–5	2	1		$\vert c_0 \vert > \vert c_3 \vert$
	1	2	–5	3		*i.e.*, 3 > 1 ∴ test passes
d_i	8	–17	11			$\vert d_0 \vert = 8$, $\vert d_2 \vert = 11$ As $\vert d_0 \vert \ngtr \vert d_2 \vert$ ∴ Jury's test fails

Hence, the system is NOT stable. Realization is as shown

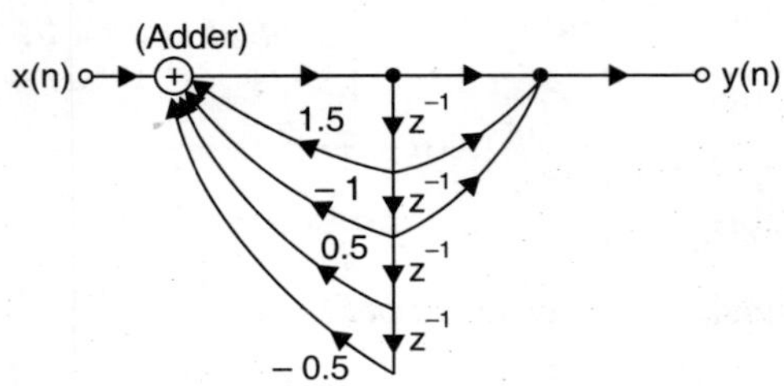

Fig. Ex. 3.58. Phasor diagram for 2nd order recursive filter

EXAMPLE 3.59: *A digital filter is characterized by* $H(z) = \frac{z^4}{4z^4+3z^3+2z^2+z+1}$. *Check the filter for stability by Jury's method.*

SOLUTION: (See solution by Schür-Cohn in Example 3.63)

Here,

$$D(z) = 4z^4 + 3z^2 + 2z^2 + z + 1 \quad \text{with } b_0 = 4 > 0$$
$$D(1) = 4 + 3 + 2 + 1 + 1 = 11 > 0, \quad \text{satisfied}$$
$$(-1)^4 D(-1) = 4 - 3 + 2 - 1 + 1 = 3 > 0, \quad \text{satisfied}$$
$$|b_0| > |b_N| \text{ as } |4| > |1|$$
$$|c_0| > |c_{N-1}| \text{ as } |15| > |1|$$
$$|r_0| > |r_2| \text{ as } |224| > |79|$$

[To find row 3, elements use determinants]

$$c_0 = \begin{vmatrix} 4 & 1 \\ 1 & 4 \end{vmatrix} = 15$$

$$c_1 = \begin{vmatrix} 3 & 1 \\ 1 & 4 \end{vmatrix} = 11$$

$$c_2 = \begin{vmatrix} 2 & 1 \\ 2 & 4 \end{vmatrix} = 6$$

$$c_3 = \begin{vmatrix} 1 & 1 \\ 3 & 4 \end{vmatrix} = 1$$ Thus, the system is stable **Ans.**

Row No	Array elements				
1	$4_{(b0)}$	$3_{(b1)}$	$2_{(b2)}$	$1_{(b3)}$	$1_{(b4)}$
2	1	1	2	3	4
3	$15_{(c0)}$	$11_{(c1)}$	$6_{(c2)}$	$1_{(c3)}$	
4	1	6	11	15	
5	$224_{(r0)}$	$159_{(r1)}$	$79_{(r2)}$		

EXAMPLE 3.60: *Check the stability of a digital filter characterized by* $H(z) = \dfrac{z^2 + 2z + 1}{z^4 + 6z^3 + 3z^2 + 4z + 5}$ *use Jury's test.*

SOLUTION: Here $D(z) = \sum_{i=0}^{N} b_i\, z^{N-1} = z^4 + 6z^3 + 3z^2 + 4z + 5$ with $b_0 = 1 > 0$

(*i*) $D(1) = 1 + 6 + 3 + 4 + 5 = 19 > 0$ ∴ test passes

(*ii*) $(-1)^4\, D(-1) = 1 - 6 + 3 - 4 + 5 = -1 \not> 0$ ∴ test fails

(*iii*) $|\, b_0 \,| > |\, b_N | \Rightarrow |\, 1 \,| > |\, 5 \,|$

∴ test fails

∴ the system is UNSTABLE **Ans.**

Had we formed the Jury's array, then we would get

$|\, c_0 \,| > |\, c_3 \,|$ ∴ fail

$|\, r_0 \,| > |\, r_2 |$ ∴ satisfied

Row No	Array elements				
1	$1_{(b0)}$	$6_{(b1)}$	$3_{(b2)}$	$4_{(b3)}$	$5_{(b4)}$
2	5	4	3	6	1
3	$-24_{(c0)}$	$-14_{(c1)}$	$-12_{(c2)}$	$-26_{(c3)}$	
4	−26	−12	−14	−24	
5	$-100_{(r0)}$	$24_{(r1)}$	$76_{(r2)}$		

As so many of the conditions are not satisfied, therefore, the system is unstable. Even if one condition is not satisfied, the system is unstable.

EXAMPLE 3.61: *Using Jury's test, check the stability of the system characterized by:* $H(z) = \dfrac{k}{\sum_{i=0}^{6} (-1)^i\, iz^i}$.

SOLUTION: Here

$$H(z) = k\,/[0 - z + 2z^2 - 3z^3 + 4z^4 - 5z^5 + 6z^6]$$

$$= (k\,.\,z^{-1})/[6z^5 - 5z^4 + 4z^3 - 3z^2 + 2z - 1] \triangleq \frac{N(z)}{D(z)}$$

∴ $D(z) = 6z^5 - 5z^4 + 4z^3 - 3z^2 + 2z - 1$ ∴ $N = 5$

$D(1) = 6 - 5 + 4 - 3 + 2 - 1 = 3 > 0$ ∴ test passes

$(-1)^5\, D(-1) = -[6 - 5 - 4 - 3 - 2 - 1] = 21 > 0$ ∴ test passes

$b_0 = 6,\ b_N = -1$, as $|\, b_0 \,| > |\, b_N \,|$ ∴ test passes

Jury's array is now formed as below:

							Remarks
b_i	6 ↗ b_0	–5	4	–3	2	–1 ↗ b_5	$\mid b_0 \mid > \mid b_5 \mid$
	–1	2	–3	4	–5	6	∴ test passes
c_i	35 ↗ c_0	–28	21	–14	7 ↗ c_4	×	$\mid c_0 \mid > \mid c_4 \mid$
	7	–14	21	–28	35	×	∴ test passes
d_i	1176 ↗ d_0	–882	588	–294 ↗ d_3	×	×	$\mid d_0 \mid > \mid d_3 \mid$
	–294	588	–882	1176	×	×	∴ test passes
e_i	1296540 ↗ e_0	–864360	432180 ↗ e_2	×	×	×	$\mid e_0 \mid > \mid e_2 \mid$ ∴ test passes

Hence, the given system is stable. **Ans.**

EXAMPLE 3.62: *Determine if the system having the system function* $H(z) = \dfrac{1}{\left(1-\frac{7}{4}z^{-1}-\frac{1}{2}z^{-2}\right)}$ *is stable. Apply Schür-Cohn method.*

SOLUTION: Here $A_2(z) = 1 - \frac{7}{4}z^{-1} - \frac{1}{2}z^{-2}$ (note the constant term is unity)

∴ $k_2 = -\frac{1}{2}$ (coeff. of z^{-2})

$$B_2(z) = -\frac{1}{2} - \frac{7}{4}z^{-1} + z^{-2}$$

$$A_2(z) = \frac{A_2(z) - k_2B_2(z)}{1-K_2^2}$$

$$= \frac{1}{1-\left(-\frac{1}{2}\right)^2}\left[1-\frac{7}{4}z^{-1}-\frac{1}{2}z^{-2}-\left(-\frac{1}{2}\right)\left(-\frac{1}{2}-\frac{7}{4}z^{-1}+z^{-2}\right)\right]$$

$$= 1 - \frac{7}{2}z^{-1}$$

As $A_1(z) = 1 - \frac{7}{2}z^{-1}$

∴ $k_1 = -\frac{7}{2}$ (the coeff. of z^{-1})

Since, $| k_1 | = \frac{7}{2} > 1$, hence, the system is unstable. **Ans.**

Check: $A(z) = 0$ gives $z^2 - \frac{7}{4}z^1 - \frac{1}{2} = 0$

$$\therefore \quad \left(z+\frac{1}{4}\right)(z-2) = 0$$

poles are at $z = -\frac{1}{4}$, $z = +2$ $\quad\therefore$ The system is unstable **Ans.**

EXAMPLE 3.63: *A digital filter is characterized by* $H(z) = \frac{z^4}{4z^4+3z^3+2z^2+z+1}$ *check its stability by using Schür-Cohn stability criteria.*

SOLUTION: (See solution by Jury's method, Example 3.59)

We can write:
$$H(z) = \frac{\frac{1}{4}}{1+\frac{3}{4}z^{-1}+\frac{1}{2}z^{-2}+\frac{1}{4}z^{-3}+\frac{1}{4}z^{-4}}$$

Here
$$A_4(z) = 1+\frac{3}{4}z^{-1}+\frac{1}{2}z^{-2}+\frac{1}{4}z^{-3}+\frac{1}{4}z^{-4} \qquad | k_4 | = \frac{1}{4} < 1 \quad \therefore \text{ OK}$$

$$B_4(z) = \frac{1}{4} + \frac{1}{4}z^{-1} + \frac{1}{2}z^{-2} + \frac{3}{4}z^{-3} + z^{-4} \qquad \text{(reversing the coefficients)}$$

$$A_3(z) = \frac{A_4(z)-k_4B_4(z)}{1-k_4^2}$$

$$= \frac{\left(1+\frac{3}{4}z^{-1}+\frac{1}{2}z^{-2}+\frac{1}{4}z^{-3}+\frac{1}{4}z^{-4}\right)-\frac{1}{4}\left(\frac{1}{4}+\frac{1}{4}z^{-1}+\frac{1}{2}z^{-2}+\frac{3}{4}z^{-3}+z^{-4}\right)}{1-\left(\frac{1}{4}\right)^2}$$

$$= \frac{16}{15}\left[\left(1-\frac{1}{16}\right)+z^{-1}\left(\frac{3}{4}-\frac{1}{16}\right)+z^{2}\left(\frac{1}{2}-\frac{1}{8}\right)+z^{-3}\left(\frac{1}{4}-\frac{3}{16}\right)+z^{-4}\left(\frac{1}{4}-\frac{1}{4}\right)\right]$$

$$\therefore \quad A_3(z) = 1+\frac{11}{15}z^{-1}+\frac{2}{5}z^{-2}+\frac{1}{15}z^{-3} \qquad | k_3 | = \frac{1}{15} < 1 \quad \therefore \text{ OK}$$

$$B_3(z) = \frac{1}{15}+\frac{2}{5}z^{-1}+\frac{11}{15}z^{-2}+z^{-3}$$

$$A_2(z) = \frac{A_3(z)-k_3B(z)}{1-k_3^2}$$

$$= \frac{\left(1+\frac{11}{15}z^{-1}+\frac{2}{5}z^{-2}+\frac{1}{15}z^{-3}\right)-\frac{1}{15}\left(\frac{1}{15}+\frac{2}{15}z^{-1}+\frac{11}{15}z^{2}+z^{-3}\right)}{1-\left(\frac{1}{15}\right)^2}$$

$\therefore \quad A_2(z) = 1 + \frac{159}{224}z^{-1} + \frac{79}{224}z^{-2} \qquad | k_2 | = \frac{79}{224} < 1 \quad \therefore$ OK

$$B_2(z) = \frac{79}{224} + \frac{159}{224}z^{-1} + \frac{79}{224}z^{-2}$$

$$A_1(z) = \frac{A_2(z) - k_2B_2(z)}{1 - K_2^2} = \frac{\left(1 + \frac{159}{224}z^{-1} + \frac{79}{224}z^{-2}\right) - \frac{79}{224}\left(\frac{79}{224} + \frac{159}{224}z^{-1} + \frac{79}{224}z^{-2}\right)}{1 - \left(\frac{79}{224}\right)^2}$$

$$= \frac{(224)^2}{43935}\left[\left(1 - \left(\frac{79}{224}\right)^2\right) + z^{-1}\left(\frac{159}{224} - \frac{79 \times 159}{(224)^2}\right)\right]$$

$= 1 + \frac{10335}{50176}z^{-1} \qquad | k_1 | = \frac{10335}{50176} < 1 \quad \therefore$ OK

As k_4, k_3, k_2, k_1 are all less than unity $\therefore$ the system is STABLE **Ans.**

EXAMPLE 3.64: *Use the Schür-Cohn stability test to derive the stability conditions*

$$|a(2)| < 1, \quad |a(1)| < 1 + a(2)$$

for the second-order filter, $H(z) = \dfrac{b(0)}{1 + a(1)z^{-1} + a(2)z^{-2}}$

SOLUTION: Here $\quad H_2(z) = 1 + a(1)z^{-1} + a(2)z^{-2} \qquad \boxed{\therefore\ k_2 = a(2)}$

$$H_1(z) = \frac{1}{1 - (a(2))^2}[1 + a(1)z^{-1} + a(2)z^{-2} - a(2)\{a(2) + a(1)z^{-1} + z^{-2}\}]$$

$$= 1 + \frac{1}{1 - a^2(2)}(a(1) - a(2) \cdot a(1))z^{-1}$$

$$= 1 + \left[\frac{1}{1 + a(2)}(a(1))\right]z^{-1}$$

$\therefore \quad H_1(z) = 1 + \frac{a(1)}{1 + a(2)}z^{-1} \qquad \boxed{\therefore\ k_1 = \frac{a(1)}{1 + a(2)}}$

For stability, $| k_2 | < 1$ and $| k_1 | < 1$

i.e., $| a(2) | < 1$, and $| k_1 | < 1$ gives us the condition

$$-1 < \frac{a(1)}{1 + a(2)} < 1$$

$\therefore \quad a(1) < 1 + a(2), \qquad$ ...(A)

and $\quad a(1) > -[1 + a(2)] \qquad$ ...(B)

(A) and (B) yields $| a(1) | < 1 + a(2)$

Hence, the given $H(z)$ is stable if $| a(2) | < 1$ and $| a(1) | < 1 + a(2)$ **Ans.**

EXAMPLE 3.65: *Determine whether the network characterised by* $H(z) = \dfrac{z^2}{36z^4 - 13z^2 + 1}$ *is stable or not. Determine the result by three different methods.*

SOLUTION: Method 1: (By determining the poles)

$$H(z) = \frac{1}{36}\frac{z^2}{z^4 - \frac{13}{36}z^2 + \frac{1}{36}} = \frac{1}{36}\frac{z^2}{\left(z^2 - \frac{8}{36}\right)\left(z^2 - \frac{4}{36}\right)}$$

$$= \frac{1}{36}\frac{z^2}{\left(z - \frac{1}{2}\right)\left(z + \frac{1}{2}\right)\left(z - \frac{1}{3}\right)\left(z + \frac{1}{3}\right)}$$

Clearly poles of $H(z)$ are at $z_{p_i} = \frac{1}{2}, -\frac{1}{2}, \frac{1}{3}, -\frac{1}{3}$

Since, each $|z_p|$ is less than unity, hence, all the poles lie inside the unit circle. Therefore, the network is BIBO stable. **Ans.**

Method 2: (By Jury's array)

Here
$$D(z) = 36z^4 + 0z^3 - 13z^2 + 0z^1 + 1$$
$$D(1) = 36 - 13 + 1 = 24 > 1 \text{ passes}$$
$$(-1)^4 D(-1) = 24 > 1 \text{ passes}$$
$$|b_0| > |b_4| \text{ passes}$$
$$|c_0| > |c_3| \text{ passes}$$

Row No	Array elements				
1	$36_{(b0)}$	0	– 13	0	$1_{(b4)}$
2	1	0	– 13	0	36
3	$1295_{(c0)}$	0	– 455	$0_{(c3)}$	
4	0	– 455	0	1295	
5	$16677025_{(d0)}$	0	$-589225_{(d2)}$		
6					

All the tests passed. Therefore, the given $H(z)$ represents a BIBO stable network. **Ans.**

Method 3: (By Schür-Cohn stability test)

Here
$$H(z) \triangleq \frac{B(z)}{A(z)} = \frac{(1/36)z^{-2}}{1 - \frac{13}{36}z^{-2} + \frac{1}{36}z^{-4}}$$

where
$$A_4(z) = 1 - \frac{13}{36}z^{-2} + \frac{1}{36}z^{-4}$$

$$k_4 = \frac{1}{36} \quad \text{(coeff. of } z^{-4}\text{)} \quad |k_4| = \frac{1}{36} < 1$$

$$B_4(z) = \frac{1}{36} - \frac{13}{36}z^{-2} + z^{-4} \quad \text{[mirror polynomial of } A_4(z)\text{]}$$

$$A_3(z) = \frac{A_4(z) - k_4 B_4(z)}{1 - k_4^2}$$

$$= \frac{\left(1 - \frac{13}{36}z^{-2} + \frac{1}{36}z^{-4}\right) - \frac{1}{36}\left(\frac{1}{36} - \frac{13}{36}z^{-2} + z^{-4}\right)}{1 - \left(\frac{1}{36}\right)^2}$$

$$= 1 - \frac{455}{1295}z^{-2} = 1 - \frac{13}{37}z^{2} + 0z^{-3}$$

$$k_3 = 0$$

$$A_2(z) = A_3(z) = 1 - \frac{13}{37}z^{-2} \qquad | k_3 | = 0 < 1$$

$$k_2 = -\frac{13}{37} \qquad | k_2 | = \frac{13}{37} < 1$$

$$B_2(z) = -\frac{13}{37} + z^{-2}$$

$$A_1(z) = \frac{A_2(z) - k_2 B_2(z)}{1 - k_2^2} = \frac{\left(1 - \frac{13}{37}z^{-2}\right) - \left(-\frac{13}{37}\right)\left(-\frac{13}{37} + z^{-2}\right)}{1 - \left(\frac{13}{37}\right)^2} = 1 + 0z^{-1}$$

$$k_1 = 0 \quad \text{(coeff. of } z^{-1}) \qquad | k_0 | = 0 < 1$$

As $| k_4 |$, $| k_3 |$, $| k_2 |$ and $| k_1 |$ are all less than 1, hence, $H(z)$ represents a stable system.

Ans.

EXAMPLE 3.66: *Determine the impulse response of the system characterise by the difference equation*

$$y(n) - y(n-1) - y(n-2) = x(n-1)$$

SOLUTION: Here, $H(z) = \frac{z^{-1}}{1 - z^{-1} - z^{-2}}$ Putting $x(n) = \delta(n)$ $\therefore$ $ZT\ x(n-1) = z^{-1}$

The poles are given by

$$z^2 - z - 1 = 0$$

i.e.,

$$p_{1,2} = \frac{1}{2}(1 \pm \sqrt{5}) \qquad \therefore \quad p_1 - p_2 = \sqrt{5}$$

The zeros of $H(z)$ are at $z = 0$ and $z = \infty$. We can write

$$H(z) = \frac{z^{-1}}{(1 - p_1 z^{-1})(1 - p_2 z^{-1})}$$

$$= \frac{1}{1 - p_1 z^{-1}} \cdot \frac{p_1^{-1}}{1 - p_2 p_1^{-1}} + \frac{1}{1 - p_2 z^{-1}} \cdot \frac{p_2^{-1}}{1 - p_1 p_2^{-1}}$$

$$= \frac{1}{(p_1 - p_2)}\left[\frac{1}{1 - p_1 z^{1}} - \frac{1}{1 - p_2 z^{-1}}\right]$$

$$\therefore \qquad h(n) = \frac{1}{p_1 - p_2}\left[(p_1)^n - (p_2)^n\right] u(n)$$

i.e., $$h(n) = \frac{1}{5^{1/2}}\left[\left(\frac{1+5^{1/2}}{2}\right) - \left(\frac{1-5^{1/2}}{2}\right)^n\right]u(n)$$ **Ans.**

Comment: The solution of given difference equation is called Fibonacci numbers.

EXAMPLE 3.67: *Find the unit step response of the filter shown*

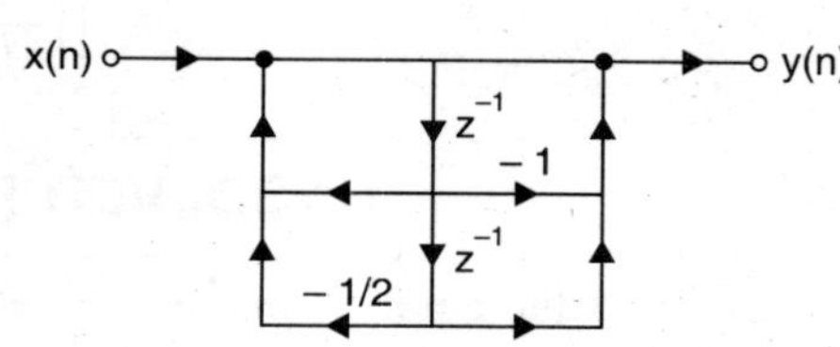

Fig. Ex. 3.67. The given filter

SOLUTION: Clearly, $$H(z) = \frac{1 - z^{-1} + z^{-2}}{1 - z^{-1} + \frac{1}{2}z^{-2}} = \frac{z^2 - z + 1}{z^2 - z + \frac{1}{2}}$$

$$X(z) = ZT\,[u(n)] = \frac{z}{z-1}$$

$$\therefore \quad Y(z) = X(z)\,.\,H(z) = \frac{z(z^2 - z + 1)}{\left(z^2 - z + \frac{1}{2}\right)(z-1)}$$

Let $$\frac{z(z^2 - z + 1)}{\left(z^2 - z + \frac{1}{2}\right)(z-1)} = \frac{A}{z - p_1} + \frac{B}{z - p_2} + \frac{C}{z-1}$$

where $$p_{1,2} = \frac{1 \pm \sqrt{1-2}}{2} = (1 \pm j)/2 \qquad \therefore \quad p_1 = (1 + j)/2,\ p_2 = (1 - j)/2$$

$$C = \left.\frac{z^2 - z + 1}{z^2 - z + \frac{1}{2}}\right|_{z=1} = 2 \qquad p_1 = \frac{1}{\sqrt{2}}\,e^{j\pi/4},\ p_2 = \frac{1}{\sqrt{2}}\,e^{-j\pi/4}$$

$$= \left(p_1^2 - p_1 + \frac{1}{2}\right) + \frac{1}{2} = 0 + \frac{1}{2}$$

$$A = \left.\frac{z^2 - z + 1}{(z - p_2)(z-1)}\right|_{z=p_1} = \frac{p_1^2 - p_1 + 1}{(p_1 - p_2)(p_1 - 1)} = \frac{1/2}{(j)\left(-\frac{1}{2} + j\frac{1}{2}\right)}$$

$$= \frac{\frac{1}{2}(-j)}{\sqrt{\frac{1}{2}}}\,e^{j3\pi/4} = \frac{1}{\sqrt{2}}\,e^{-j\pi/2}\,.\,e^{-j3\pi/4} = \frac{1}{\sqrt{2}}\,e^{-j5\pi/4}$$

$$\therefore \quad B = A^* = \frac{1}{\sqrt{2}}\,e^{j5\pi/4}$$

$$\therefore \quad Y(z) = z\left[\frac{1}{\sqrt{2}}e^{-j5\pi/4}\,\frac{1}{z - p_1} + \frac{1}{\sqrt{2}}e^{j5\pi/4}\,\frac{1}{z - p_2} + \frac{2}{z-1}\right]$$

$$\therefore \quad y(n) = \left(\frac{1}{\sqrt{2}} e^{-j5\pi/4}\, p_1^n + \frac{1}{\sqrt{2}} e^{j5\pi/4}\, p_2^n + 2\right) u(n)$$

$$= \left[\left(\frac{1}{\sqrt{2}}\right)^{n+1}\left(e^{j\left(n\frac{\pi}{4}-5\frac{\pi}{4}\right)} + e^{-j\left(n\frac{\pi}{4}-5\frac{\pi}{4}\right)}\right) + 2\right] u(n)$$

$$= \left[\left(\frac{1}{\sqrt{2}}\right)^{n-1} \cos(n-5)\frac{\pi}{4} + 2\right] u(n)$$ **Ans.**

UNSOLVED PROBLEMS WITH ANSWERS

3.1. Find the z-transforms for

(*a*) $x_1(n) = n^2 a^n\, u(n)$

(*b*) $x_2(n) = \cosh \alpha n \,.\, u(n)$

[Ans. (*a*) $X_1(z) = \dfrac{az(z+a)}{(z-a)^3}$, ROC : $|z| > |a|$

(*b*) $X_2(z) = \dfrac{z(z - \cos \alpha)}{1 - 2z \cosh \alpha + z^2}$, ROC : $|z| > e^{|\alpha|}$]

3.2. Find the z-transforms for

(*a*) $x_1(n) = [1 + (-1)^n] e^{-n}\, u(n)$

(*b*) $x_2(n) = ne^{-4n} \cdot u(n)$

(*c*) $x_3(n) = a^n\, u(n) + b^n\, u(-n-1)$, $|b| > |a|$

[Ans. (*a*) $X_1(z) = \dfrac{2z^2}{z^2 - e^{-2}}$, $|z| > e^{-1}$

(*b*) $X_2(z) = \dfrac{ze^{-4}}{(z-e^{-4})^2}$, $|z| > e^{-4}$

(*c*) $X_3(z) = \dfrac{(a-b)z^{-1}}{1-(a+b)z^{-1} + abz^{-2}}$. $|a| < |z| < |b|$]

3.3. Find the z-transform for

(*a*) $x_1(n) = \begin{cases} 1, & 0 \le n \le N-1 \\ 0, & \text{otherwise} \end{cases}$

(*b*) $x_2(n) = \begin{cases} n, & 0 \le n \le N \\ 2N - n, & N+1 \le n \le 2N \\ 0, & n > 2N, \text{ or } n < 0 \end{cases}$

[Ans. (*a*) $X_1(z) = \dfrac{z^N - 1}{z^{N-1}(z-1)}$, Poles at $z = 0$ of $(N-1)^{\text{th}}$ order zeros at $z^N = 1$, roots of 1 except $z =$ 1.

(*b*) $X_2(z) = \dfrac{1}{z^{2N-1}}\left[\dfrac{z^N - 1}{z-1}\right]^2$, ROC : $Z \ne 0$ or 1

Poles at $z = 0$ of $(2N-1)^{\text{th}}$ order zeros at $z^N - 1 = 0$ roots of 1 except 1 each zero of 2nd order.]

3.4. Find the z-transforms of the sequences given by

(a) $x_1(n) = \left(\frac{1}{5}\right)^n u(n-1)$, (b) $x_2(n) = \left(-\frac{1}{4}\right)^n u(n)$

(c) $x_3(n) = 2u(n) - 3u(n-5)$, (d) $x_4(n) = 5u(-n)$

[**Ans.** (a) $X_1(z) = \dfrac{(1/5)z^{-1}}{1-z^{-1}}, \; |z| > \dfrac{1}{5}$,

(b) $X_2(z) = \dfrac{1}{1+\frac{1}{4}z^{-1}}, \; |z| > \dfrac{1}{4}$

(c) $X_3(z) = \dfrac{2-3z^{-5}}{1-z^{-1}}, \; |z| > 1$

(d) $X_4(z) = \dfrac{5}{1-z}, \; |z| < 1$]

3.5. Find the inverse z-transform by partial fraction approach

$$H(z) = \frac{1}{1-(2r\cos\theta)z^{-1} + r^2z^{-2}}, \; |z| > |r|$$

[**Ans.** $h(n) = \dfrac{r^n}{\sin\theta}(\sin(n+1)\theta) \cdot u(n)$]

3.6. Find the inverse z-transforms by partial fraction method

(a) $X_1(z) = \dfrac{(z-1)^2}{z^2 - 0.1z - 0.56}, \; |z| > 0.8$

(b) $X_2(z) = \dfrac{4z^3}{(2z+1)(2z^3-2z+1)}, \; |z| > \dfrac{1}{2}$

[**Ans.** (a) $x_1(n) = \left(\dfrac{-1}{0.56}\right)\delta(n) + \dfrac{289}{85}(-0.7)^n u(n) + \dfrac{1}{30}(0.8)^n u(n)$

Hint: Put $X_1(z) = 1 + \dfrac{A}{z+0.7} + \dfrac{B}{z+0.8} = 1 - \dfrac{(289/150)z^{-1}}{1+0.7z^{-1}} + \dfrac{(2/75)z^{-1}}{(1-0.8z^{-1})}$

(b) $x_2(n) = \left[\dfrac{1}{5}\left(-\dfrac{1}{2}\right)^n + \dfrac{1}{\sqrt{5}}\left(\dfrac{1}{\sqrt{2}}\right)^{n-2} . \cos\left(\dfrac{n\pi}{4} - \tan^{-1}\dfrac{1}{2}\right)\right] . u(n)$

3.7. Given $X(z) = \dfrac{z-a}{1-az}, \quad \text{ROC} : |z| > \left|\dfrac{1}{a}\right|$

Find the inverse z-transform by contour integration method.

$$\left[\textbf{Ans. } x(n) = \begin{cases} 0, & n < 0 \\ -\dfrac{1}{a}, & n = 0 \\ \left(\dfrac{1}{a}\right)^{n+1}(a^2-1), & n > 0 \end{cases}\right]$$

3.8. For $X(z) = \dfrac{\left(1 - \frac{1}{4}z^{-1}\right)}{1 - \frac{1}{6}z^{-1} - \frac{1}{6}z^{-2}}, |z| > \frac{1}{2}$

Find inverse z-transform by (*i*) Partial fraction, (*ii*) Contour integration.

$\left[\textbf{Ans. } x(n) = \left[\frac{3}{10}\left(\frac{1}{2}\right)^n + \frac{7}{10}\left(-\frac{1}{3}\right)^n\right] u(n)\right]$

3.9. The step response $s(n)$ of a discrete-time *LTI* system is given by

$$s(n) = a^n u(n), \quad 0 < a < 1$$

Find the impulse response $h(n)$

(*a*) by using relationship between $s(n)$ and $h(n)$.

(*b*) by first finding $H(z)$, then its inverse z-transform.

[**Ans.** $h(n) = \delta(n) - (1 - a)\, a^{n-1}\, u(n-1)$]

3.10. A causal, linear, time-invariant system is described by the difference equation

$$y(n) - 5y(n-1) + 6y(n-2) = 2x(n-1)$$

(*a*) Determine its impulse response $h(n)$.

(*b*) Determine its step response $s(n)$.

(*c*) Is the system stable? Prove your answer.

(*d*) Find the frequency response of the system given by the above difference equation.

[**Ans.** (*a*) $h(n) = 2[3^n - 2^n]\, u(n-1)$, (*b*) $s(n) = (1 - 2^{n+2} + 3^{n+1})\, u(n)$

(*c*) the system is not stable, (*d*) $H(e^{j\omega}) = 2e^{j\omega}/[(e^{j\omega} - 2)(e^{j\omega} - 3)]$

3.11. Realize the *IIR* system characterized by the difference equation

$$y(n) = \frac{3}{4}y(n-1) - \frac{1}{8}y(n-2) + x(n) - \frac{1}{2}x(n-1) - \frac{1}{4}x(n-2)$$

Ans. A canonic realization is as shown

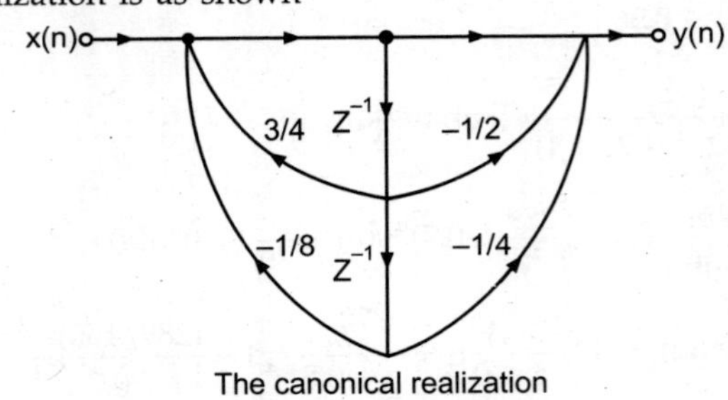

Fig. P. 3.11

3.12. For a system characterized by $y(n) = \frac{5}{2}y(n-1) - y(n-2) + x(n)$

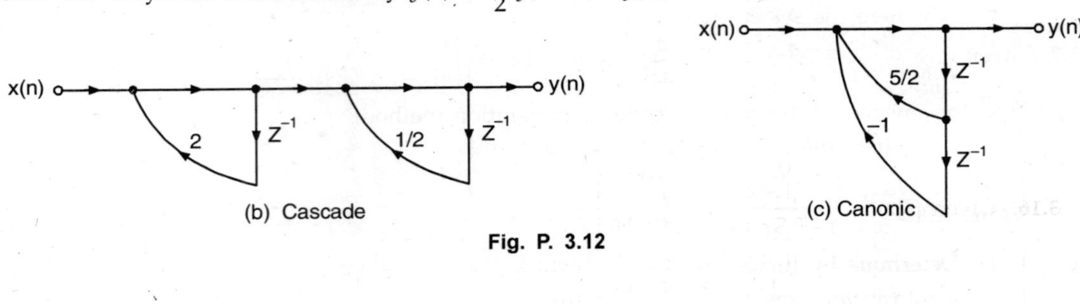

Fig. P. 3.12

(*a*) Find $H(z)$
(*b*) Cascade realization
(*c*) Canonic realization

$$\left[\textbf{Ans. } (a)\ H(z) = \frac{1}{(1-2z^{-1})\left(1-\frac{1}{2}z^{-1}\right)}\right]$$

3.13. Consider a discrete-time *LTI* system with unit sample response

$$h(n) = (n+1)\,a^n\,u(n),\ |a| < 1$$

show that the step response of the system is

$$s(n) = \left[\frac{1}{(a-1)^2} - \frac{a^{n+1}}{(a-1)^2} + \frac{(n+1)\,a^{n+1}}{(a-1)}\right]u(n)$$

$$\left[\textbf{Hint: } \text{Use the identity } \sum_{k=0}^{n}(k+1)a^k = \frac{d}{da}\sum_{k=0}^{n+1}a^k\right]$$

3.14. Show that the output of an LTI system can be expressed in terms of unit step response $s(n)$ as follows

$$y(n) = \sum_{k=-\infty}^{\infty}[s(k)-s(k-1)]\,.\,x(n-k)$$

$$= \sum_{k=-\infty}^{\infty}[x(k)-x(k-1)]\,.\,s(n-k)$$

3.15. A discrete-time LTI system is characterized by the transfer function

$$H(z) = \frac{z(3z-4)}{\left(z-\frac{1}{2}\right)(z-3)}$$

Specify the ROC of $H(z)$ and determine $h(n)$ for
(*i*) the system is stable
(*ii*) the system is causal
(*iii*) the system is anti-causal

[**Ans.** (*i*) $h(n) = \left(\frac{1}{2}\right)^n u(n) - 2(3)^n\,u(n-1)$ if ROC: $\frac{1}{2} < |z| < 3$

(*ii*) $h(n) = \left[\left(\frac{1}{2}\right)^n + 2(3)^n\right]u(n)$ if ROC: $|z| > 3$

here the system is causal but unstable

(*iii*) $h(n) = -\left(\frac{1}{2}\right)^n u(-n-1) - 2(3)^n\,u(-n-1)$ if ROC: $|z| < \frac{1}{2}$

here the system is anti-causal and unstable]

3.16. Given $H(z) = \dfrac{1+2z^{-1}+2z^{-2}+z^{-3}}{1-0.8z^{-1}+0.49z^{-2}-0.57z^{-3}}$

(*a*) Determine by Jury's test if the system is stable or not
(*b*) Confirm your result by using Schür-Cohn test
[**Ans.** The system is stable]

3.17. Check the stability of the system characterised by

$$H(z) = z^4 \Big/ \left[1 + \sum_{i=0}^{4} iz^i\right]$$

(*a*) By Jury's Array test
(*b*) By Schür-Cohn test
[**Ans.** The system is stable]

3.18. Check if the system characterised by

$$H(z) = (z-1)(z-2) \Big/ \left[\sum_{i=0}^{4} (-1)^i z^i\right] \text{ is stable or not}$$

[**Ans.** The system is unstable]

3.19. State the Jury's criteria of checking the stability of a discrete-time system with system function

$$H(z) = 7.2\, z^3/[5z^4 + 2z^2 + z + 1]$$

[**Ans.** The system is stable]

3.20. By using Schür-Cohn stability criteria, determine the stability of the system:

$$H(z) = \frac{2(z^2 + z + 1)}{2z^4 - 3z^3 + 2z^2 - z + 1}$$

Indicate the values of k_1, k_2, k_3, k_4

[**Ans.** The system is stable; $k_4 = \frac{1}{2}$, $k_3 = \frac{1}{3}$, $k_2 = \frac{11}{18}$, no need to find k_1]

3.21. Without factoring the denominator polynomial of $H(z) = \frac{N(z)}{D(z)}$, check the stability of $H(z)$, if $D(z)$

$$= 1 + 1.58z^{-1} + 1.638z^{-2} + 1.556z^{-3} + 0.4z^{-4}$$

[**Hint:** Use Schür-Cohn Test. $H(z)$ is an unstable system]

3.22. If $F(z) = F^*(1/z^*)$ then show that poles and zeros of $F(z)$ must occur in complex-conjugate reciprocal pairs.

[**Ans.** Let $F(z)$ be a rational function given by

$$F(z) = \frac{\prod_{i=1}^{M}(z - z_i)}{\prod_{j=1}^{N}(z - p_j)}$$

Where $z_1 > z_2 > \ldots > z_M$ are the zeros
$p_1 > p_2 > \ldots > p_N$ are the poles

If $F(z)$ represents a system function ($H(z)$) for a stable IIR digital system, then $F(z)$ cannot have poles at points $|\, z\,| \le 1$ *i.e.*, $N \le M$ here

Let $z_1 = \left(\frac{1}{z_M}\right)^*$, $z_2 = \left(\frac{1}{z_{M-1}}\right)^*$, ..., *i.e.*, $z_k = \left(\frac{1}{z_{M+1-k}}\right)^*$ and similarly, let $p_k = \left(\frac{1}{p_{N+1-k}}\right)^*$

Above assumptions ensure that $F(z)$ has its zeros occurring in complex conjugate reciprocal pairs and similarly its poles occur in complex-conjugate reciprocal pairs

$$F^*\left(\frac{1}{z^*}\right) = \frac{\left(\prod_{i=1}^{M}\left(\frac{1}{z^*} - z_i\right)\right)^*}{\left(\prod_{j=1}^{N}\left(\frac{1}{z^*} - p_j\right)\right)^*} = \frac{\prod_{i=1}^{M}\left(\frac{1}{z} - z_i^*\right)}{\prod_{j=1}^{N}\left(\frac{1}{z} - p_j^*\right)} = \frac{\prod_{i=1}^{M}\left(\frac{1}{z} - \frac{1}{z_{M+1-i}}\right)}{\prod_{j=1}^{N}\left(\frac{1}{z} - \frac{1}{p_{N+1-j}}\right)}$$

$$= \frac{(-1)^M \prod_{i=1}^{M} (z - z_{M+1-i})/z \,.\, z_{M+1-i}}{(-1)^N \prod_{j=1}^{N} (z - p_{N+1-j})/z \,.\, p_{N+1-j}}$$

$$= (-1)^{M-N} \,.\, z^{N-M} \,.\, \frac{\prod_{j=1}^{N} p_{N+1-j}}{\prod_{i=1}^{M} z_{M+1-i}} \,.\, \frac{\prod_{i=1}^{M} (z - z_i)}{\prod_{j=1}^{N} (z - p_j)}$$

$$= (-1)^{M-N} \,.\, \frac{\prod_{j=1}^{N} p_j}{\prod_{i=1}^{M} z_i} \,.\, \underbrace{\frac{\prod_{i=1}^{M} (z - z_i)}{\prod_{j=1}^{N} (z - p_j)}}_{= F(z)} \,.\, z^{N-M}$$

$$= K \,.\, F(z) \,.\, z^{N-M}$$

Where $$k = (-1)^{M-N} \frac{\prod_{j=1}^{N} p_j}{\prod_{i=1}^{M} z_i}$$

If $M = N$, then $F^*\left(\frac{1}{z^*}\right) = K_1 F(z)$, where $K_1 = \prod_{i=1}^{M} (p_i / z_i)$.

Thus, if $F(z)$ has its zeros and poles occurring in complex conjugate reciprocal pairs, then $F(z) = KF^*(1/z^*)$, where K is a constant.]

3.23. Given a linear shift invariant system specified by the following difference equation:

$$y(n) + \frac{1}{2}\, y(n-1) = x(n) - \frac{1}{2}\, x(n-1),\ n \geq 0$$

(*i*) Find the frequency response $H(e^{j\omega})$ for the system

(*ii*) Find the $|\, H(e^{j\omega}) \,|$

(*iii*) Find arg $H(e^{j\omega})$

(*iv*) Determine unit step response of the system.

[Ans. (*i*) As $y(n) + \frac{1}{2}\, y(n-1) = x(n) - \frac{1}{2}\, x(n-1)$

Take z-transform both the sides

$$\therefore \quad Y(z) + \frac{1}{2} z^{-1}\, Y(z) = X(z) - \frac{1}{2} z^{-1}\, X(z)$$

or $$Y(z) \left[1 + \frac{1}{2} z^{-1}\right] = Y(z) \left[1 - \frac{1}{2} z^{-1}\right]$$

$$\therefore \quad \frac{Y(z)}{X(z)} = \frac{1 - \frac{1}{2} z^{-1}}{1 + \frac{1}{2} z^{-1}}$$

or $$H(z) = \frac{1 - \frac{1}{2} z^{-1}}{1 + \frac{1}{2} z^{-1}}$$

$$\therefore \qquad H(e^{j\omega}) = \frac{1-\frac{1}{2}e^{-j\omega}}{1+\frac{1}{2}e^{-j\omega}} \qquad \textbf{Ans.}$$

(*ii*)

$$|H(e^{j\omega})| = \left|\frac{1-\frac{1}{2}(\cos\omega - j\sin\omega)}{1+\frac{1}{2}(\cos\omega - j\sin\omega)}\right|$$

$$= \left[\frac{\left(1-\frac{1}{2}\cos\omega\right)^2+\left(\frac{1}{2}\sin\omega\right)^2}{\left(1+\frac{1}{2}\cos\omega\right)^2+\left(\frac{1}{2}\sin\omega\right)^2}\right]^{1/2}$$

i.e.

$$|H(e^{j\omega})| = \left[\frac{1-\cos\omega+\frac{1}{4}\cos^2\omega+\frac{1}{4}\sin^2\omega}{1+\cos\omega+\frac{1}{4}\cos^2\omega+\frac{1}{4}\cos^2\omega}\right]$$

$$= \left[\frac{1-\cos\omega+\frac{1}{4}}{1+\cos\omega+\frac{1}{4}}\right]^{1/2}$$

$$= \left[\frac{\frac{5}{4}-\cos\omega}{\frac{5}{4}+\cos\omega}\right]^{1/2} = \left[\frac{5-4\cos\omega}{5+4\cos\omega}\right]^{1/2}$$

(*iii*)

$$\text{Arg } H(e^{j\omega}) = \text{Arg}\left[\frac{\left(1-\frac{1}{2}\cos\omega\right)+j\frac{1}{2}\sin\omega}{\left(1+\frac{1}{2}\cos\omega\right)-j\frac{1}{2}\sin\omega}\right]$$

$$= \tan^{-1}\frac{\frac{1}{2}\sin\omega}{1-\frac{1}{2}\cos\omega}+\tan^{-1}\frac{\frac{1}{2}\sin\omega}{1+\frac{1}{2}\cos\omega}$$

$$= \tan^{-1}\left[\frac{\frac{\sin\omega}{2-\cos\omega}+\frac{\sin\omega}{2+\cos\omega}}{1-\frac{\sin\omega}{2-\cos\omega}\cdot\frac{\sin\omega}{2+\cos\omega}}\right]$$

$$= \tan^{-1}\left(\frac{\sin\omega(2+\cos\omega+2-\cos\omega)}{(4-\cos^2\omega)-\sin^2\omega}\right)$$

$$= \tan^{-1}\left(\frac{4\sin\omega}{3}\right) \qquad \textbf{Ans.}$$

(iv) As the unit sample response is

$$H(z) = \frac{1-\frac{1}{2}z^{-1}}{1+\frac{1}{2}z^{-1}} = \frac{1}{1+\frac{1}{2}z^{-1}} - \frac{\frac{1}{2}z^{-1}}{1+\frac{1}{2}z^{-1}}$$

$$\Rightarrow \quad h(n) = \left(-\frac{1}{2}\right)^n u(n) - \frac{1}{2}\left(-\frac{1}{2}\right)^{n-1} u(n-1)$$

∴ Unit step response would be

$$H_1(z) = \frac{1-\frac{1}{2}z^{-1}}{1+\frac{1}{2}z^{-1}} \cdot \frac{1}{1-z^{-1}} = \frac{\frac{2}{3}}{1+\frac{1}{2}z^{-1}} + \frac{\frac{1}{3}}{1-z^{-1}}$$

$$\therefore \quad h_1(n) = \left(\frac{2}{3}\left(-\frac{1}{2}\right)^n + \frac{1}{3}\right)u(n)$$

Ans.

3.24. (a) Recursive filter is represented by

$$H(z) = \frac{z^6}{[6z^6+5z^5+4z^4+3z^3+2z^2+z+1]}$$

Check the filter for stability

(b) Repeat part (a) if

$$H(z) = \frac{(z+2)^2}{[6z^6+5z^5-4z^4+3z^3+2z^2+z+1]}$$

Ans. (a) Forming Jury's array we have

b_i	1	6	5	4	3	2	1	1
	2	1	1	2	3	4	5	6
c_i	3	35	29	22	15	8	1	
	4	1	8	15	22	29	35	
d_i	5	1224	1007	755	503	251		
	6	251	503	755	1007	1224		
e_i	7	1435175	1106315	734615	362915			
	8	362915	734615	1106315	1435175			
f_i	9	1.92×10^{12}	1.32×10^{12}	6.53×10^{11}				

Here $D(1) = 6 + 5 + 4 + 3 + 2 + 1 = 22 > 0$

$(-1)^6 D(-1) = 6 - 5 + 4 - 3 + 2 - 1 + 1 = 4 > 0$

$|b_0| > |b_6|, |c_0| > |c_5|, |d_0| > |d_4|, |e_0| > |e_3|, |f_0| > |f_2|$

∴ All the conditions are satisfied.

∴ The filter is stable. **Ans.**

(b) Here $H(z) = \dfrac{(z+2)^2}{6z^6+5z^5-4z^4+3z^3+2z^2+z+1}$

Here $D(1) = 6 + 5 - 4 + 3 + 2 + 1 + 1 = 14 > 0$

$(-1)^6 D(-1) = [6 - 5 - 4 - 3 + 2 - 1 + 1] = -4 < 0$

∴ Condition for stability is not satisfied. We need not proceed further to form Jury's array.

∴ The given filter is unstable. **Ans.**

CHAPTER 4

Realization of Digital Systems

4.0 INTRODUCTION

In this chapter, we focus on the realization of linear time-invariant (LTI) discrete-time systems. There are various structures for realization of any FIR as well as IIR discrete-time systems. Some structures are directly realizable given the system function $H(z)$. However, there are structures which have distinct advantages especially when quantization effects are taken into consideration. Some realizations of a filter are more robust than the others for the same filter. A robust realization means that the frequency response of the realized structure is almost same with that of the designed filter. It may be noted that when we design any filter (FIR or IIR), the computed design weights are not always binary friendly. We need to quantize these weight to fit them in binary form. The weights have to be rounded off or truncated in quantization process. Some structures are sensitive to changes in design weights (as a result of quantization). Some other structures, such as lattice and ladder type, are not so sensitive to changes in design coefficients. Some structures are computational efficient *i.e.*, involve less number of multiplications than the others for the same filter. We shall discuss the following structures in this chapter.

1. Direct Form-FIR system (Section 4.2)
2. Cascade Form-FIR system (Section 4.3)
3. Linear Phase-FIR system (section 4.4)
4. Frequency sampling-FIR system (Section 4.5)
5. Direct Form-IIR system (Section 4.6)
6. Cascade Form-IIR system (Section 4.7)
7. Parallel Form-IIR system (Section 4.8)
8. FIR Lattice Filters (Section 4.9.1)
9. IIR Lattice Filters (Sections 4.9.2 and 4.9.3)
10. Ladder structures (Section 4.10)
11. Complementary transfer functions (Section 4.11)
12. State variable realizations (Section 4.12)

4.1 A NOTE ON DIGITAL NETWORKS

A digital (discrete-time), linear, time-invariant system is described by a linear, constant coefficient difference equation of the form

$$y(n) = \sum_{k=0}^{M} b_k \, x(n-k) - \sum_{k=1}^{N} a_k \, y(n-k) \qquad \text{...(4.1)}$$

where a_k and b_k are constants. The system function corresponding to Eqn. (4.1) can be expressed, taking z-transform on both sides of (4.1), assuming $a_0 = 1$.

$$H(z) = \frac{Y(z)}{X(z)} = \frac{\sum_{k=0}^{M} b_k \, z^{-k}}{\sum_{k=0}^{N} a_k \, z^{-k}} \qquad \text{...(4.2)}$$

The basic computational elements needed to find the output $y(n)$, for input $x(n)$, at any time n are Adders, Multipliers, and Delays. It is convenient to use *block diagrams* to show how these basic elements are connected to implement a given system. The network is represented using a *signal flow graph*. These are directed graphs, using *directed branches* and connected to *nodes*. The nodes in a flowgraph correspond to either adder or branch points as shown in Fig. 4.1 (*a*), (*b*) and node k in Fig. 4.1 (*e*). An adder corresponds to a node with more than one incoming branches. The arrow on the top of a branch shows a multiplier, as shown in Fig. 4.1 (*c*). Moreover, a *Source Node* is a node having no incoming branch, see Fig. 4.1 (*f*), where node k is a source node. A *Sink Node* is a node that has no entering branch, and is used to represent output signal. In Fig. 4.1 (*f*), node p is a sink node.

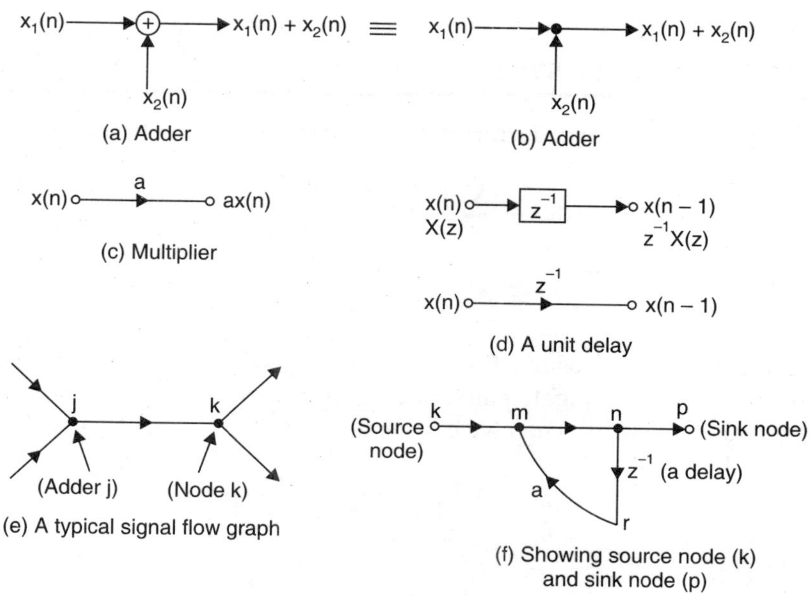

Fig. 4.1. Notations used for (*a*), (*b*): Adder, (*c*) Multiplier, (*d*) A unit delay, (*e*) A typical flowgraph (*f*) showing source node and sink node.

4.2 DIRECT FORM-FIR SYSTEM

A causal FIR filter has a system function of the form

$$H(z) = \sum_{n=0}^{N} h(n)\, z^{-n} \quad \ldots(4.3)$$

i.e., for input $x(n)$, the output $y(n)$ is given by

$$y(n) = \sum_{k=0}^{N} h(k) \,.\, x(n-k) \qquad \text{(convolution of } x(n) \text{ and } h(n))$$

$$= h(0)\, x(n) + h(1)\, x(n-1) + h(2)\, x(n-2) + \ldots + h(N)\, x(n-N) \quad \ldots(4.4)$$

System $H(z)$ requires $N + 1$ multiplications, N additions, and N delays. This system is of order N (*i.e.*, the highest delay is N). Realization of the FIR time-invariant system is shown in Fig. 4.2. In Fig. 4.2, there are $N + 1$ multiplications (*viz.* $h(0), h(1), \ldots, h(N)$), N delays (z^{-1}), and there are N adders indicated by nodes $a, b, c, \ldots, k$.

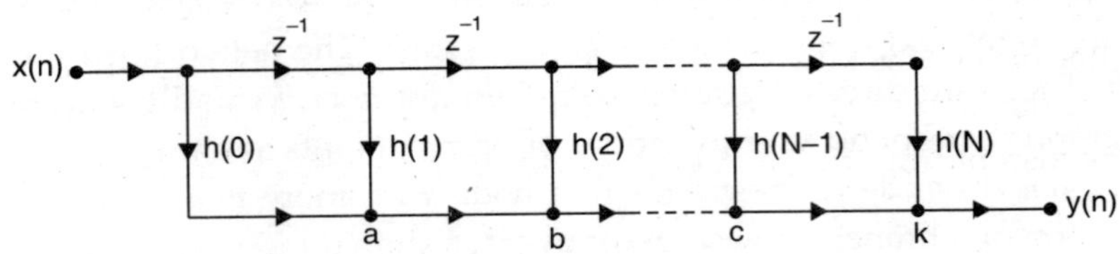

Fig. 4.2. Direct form realization of FIR system given by Eq. (4.3)

If the system $H(z)$ is a linear phase FIR filter, then the multiplications can be reduced to half, as shown in Section 4.4.

4.3 CASCADE FORM-FIR SYSTEM

For a causal FIR filter $H(z)$, we may factorize $H(z)$ as product of the first order factors *i.e.*,

$$H(z) = \sum_{n=0}^{N} h(n)\, z^{-n} \quad \ldots(4.5)$$

$$= A \prod_{k=1}^{N} (1 - \alpha_k\, z^{-1}) \quad \ldots(4.6)$$

where α_k, $k = 1, 2, \ldots, N$ are the zeros of $H(z)$. If $h(n)$ are all real coefficients then the complex roots of $H(z)$ will occur in complex conjugate pairs. Such complex roots (in pairs) can form the second-order factors with real coefficients. Then we can write, assuming degree N as even and $N_1 = N/2$,

$$H(z) = A \prod_{k=1}^{N_1} (1 + b_k(1)\, z^{-1} + b_k(2)\, z^{-2}) \quad \ldots(4.7a)$$

$$= \prod_{k=1}^{N_1} H_k(z) \quad \ldots(4.7b)$$

Equation (4.7) can be realized as shown in Fig. 4.3.

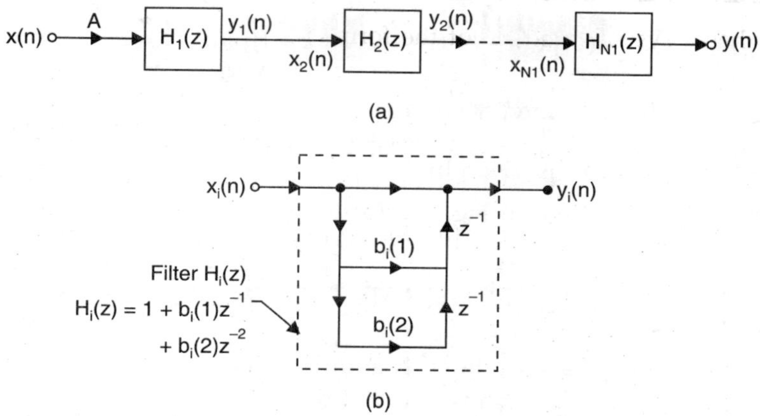

Fig. 4.3. (*a*) Cascade of N_1 FIR filters $H_1(z)$, $H_2(z)$, ..., $H_{N_1}(z)$ (*b*) Typical $H_i(z)$ filter, a second order FIR structure $i = 1, 2, ..., N_1$ in (*a*)

In case, the filter order N is odd, then $(N - 1)/2$ second order filter and one first order filter are in cascade for realization of $H(z)$. The constant A in (4.7*a*) may be put at input, as shown in Fig. 4.3(*a*). We may also put multiplier A at the output, at the end of last stage $H_{N_1}(z)$ to obtain $y(n)$.

4.4 LINEAR PHASE-FIR SYSTEM

A linear phase-FIR system $h(n)$ obeys the following conditions:

$$h(n) = h(N - 1 - n) \text{ (symmetric)} \qquad \ldots(4.8a)$$

or

$$h(n) = -h(N - 1 - n) \text{ (anti-symmetric)} \qquad \ldots(4.8b)$$

where $h(n)$ has length N (*i.e.*, $h(0), h(1), h(2), ..., h(N - 1 - n)$), and order $N - 1$. Let N be odd then assuming $(N - 1)/2$ as an integer (4.8*a*) may be written as

$$y(n) = \sum_{k=0}^{N-1} h(k)\, x(n-k), \; N \text{ odd}$$

$$= \sum_{k=0}^{(N-3)/2} h(k)\, x(n-k) + h\left(\frac{N-1}{2}\right) x\left(n - \frac{N-1}{2}\right) + \sum_{k=\frac{N+1}{2}}^{N-1} h(k)\,.\, x(n-k) \qquad \ldots(4.9)$$

Putting $k = N - 1 - l$ in last series of (4.9), we can write

$$\sum_{k=\frac{N+1}{2}}^{N-1} h(k)\, x(n-k) = \sum_{l=0}^{(N-3)/2} h(N-1-l)\,.\, x(n-N+l+1)$$

$$= \sum_{l=0}^{(N-3)/2} h(l)\,.\, x(n-N+l+1) \qquad \ldots(4.10)$$

$\because \; h(N - 1 - l) = h(l)$ due to (4.8*a*)

Combining RHS of (4.10) with first series of RHS in (4.9), we readily obtain

$$y(n) = \sum_{k=0}^{(N-3)/2} h(k)\,[x\,(n-k) + x(n-N+k+1)] + h\left(\frac{N-1}{2}\right)x\left(n - \frac{N-1}{2}\right) \quad \ldots(4.11)$$

For example, if $N = 7$ (odd), then from (4.11), we have

$$y(n) = h(0)[x(n) + x(n-6)] + h(1)[x(n-1) + x(n-5)] + h(2)[x(n-2) + x(n-4)] + h(3)\,.\,x(n-3) \quad \ldots(4.12)$$

We can realize (4.12) as shown in Fig. 4.4, for N odd.

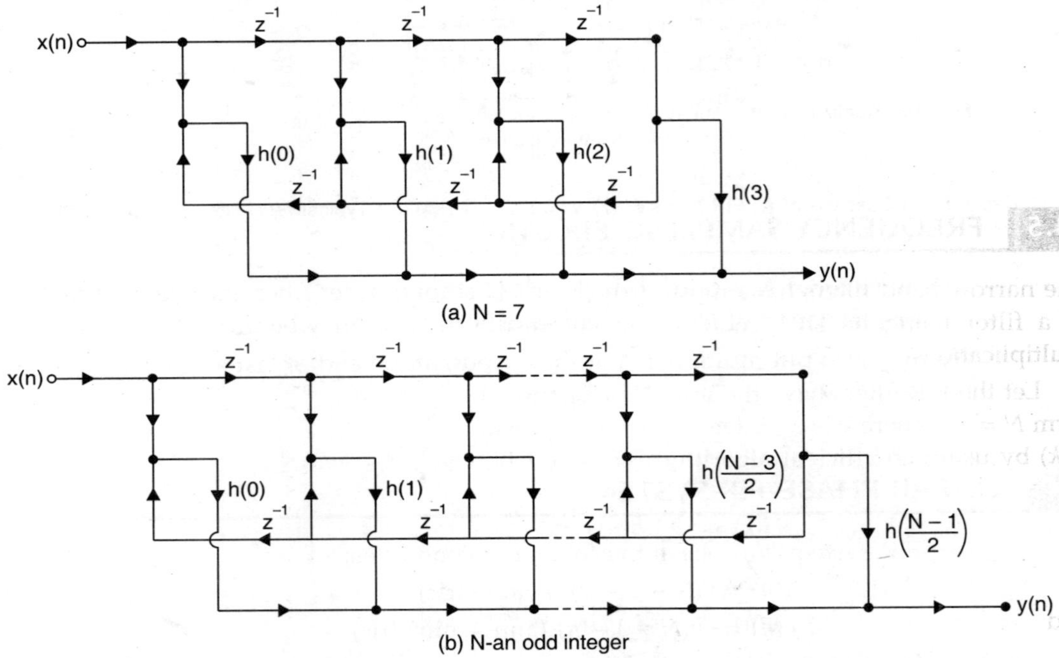

Fig. 4.4. Implementation for a Linear-phase FIR filter for filter length *N* odd

Note that the number of multiplications in Fig. 4.4(*a*) is 4 (*i.e.*, by $h(0)$, $h(1)$, $h(2)$ and $h(3)$), for $N = 7$. In Fig. 4.4(*b*), the number of multiplications is $\frac{(N+1)}{2}$. Thus, these realizations are efficient.

If *N* is even, then we can write

$$y(n) = \sum_{k=0}^{N-1} h(k)\,.\,x(n-k),\ N \text{ even} \quad \ldots(4.13)$$

i.e.,

$$y(n) = \sum_{k=0}^{N/2-1} h(k)\,x(n-k) + \sum_{k=N/2}^{N-1} h(k)\,.\,x(n-k) \quad \ldots(4.14)$$

If we put $k = N - 1 - l$ and replace $h(N - 1 - l)$ by $h(l)$ in the second series due to linear phase condition (4.8*a*), we shall arrive at

$$y(n) = \sum_{k=0}^{N/2-1} h(k)\,[x(n-k) + x(n-N+k+1)] \quad \ldots(4.15)$$

Realization of the linear-phase FIR filter for filter length N as even is shown in Fig. 4.5. Thus, if the FIR filter is linear-phase, the a aforementioned realizations have only half multipliers.

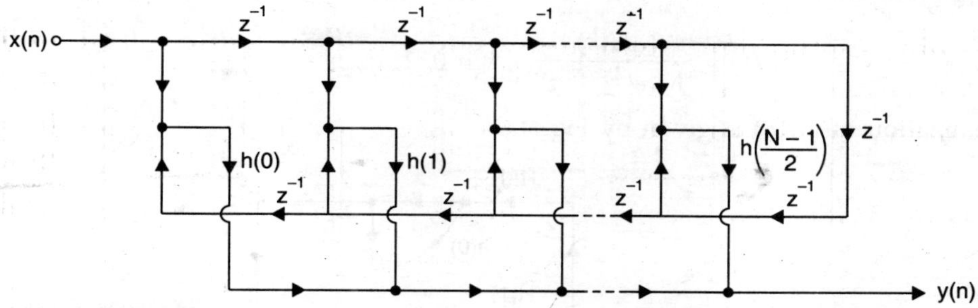

Fig. 4.5. Realization of a linear phase FIR filter with filter length N as even. Here, the number of multiplications is N/2.

4.5 FREQUENCY SAMPLING-FIR SYSTEM

The narrow band filters have most of their DFT coefficients, $H(k)$, equal to zero. The realization of a filter using its DFT coefficients will result in efficient structure due to reduction in multiplications.

Let the FIR filters have the impulse response $h(n)$, $n = 0, 1, 2, \ldots, N-1$. Generally, N is of the form $N = 2^v$, where v is an integer. Such a choice of N facilitates computation of DFT coefficients $H(k)$ by using an efficient algorithm FFT (see Chapter 6 on DFT). As

$$H(k) = \sum_{n=0}^{N-1} h(n)\, e^{-j2\pi kn/N}, \quad k = 0, 1, \ldots, N-1 \qquad \ldots(4.16)$$

and

$$h(n) = \frac{1}{N}\sum_{k=0}^{N-1} H(k)\, e^{j2\pi kn/N}, \quad n = 0, 1, \ldots, N-1 \qquad \ldots(4.17)$$

Taking z-transform on both sides of (4.17), we get

$$H(z) = \sum_{n=0}^{N-1} h(n)\, z^{-n}$$

$$= \sum_{n=0}^{N-1}\left(\frac{1}{N}\sum_{k=0}^{N-1} H(k)\, e^{j2\pi kn/N}\right) z^{-n} \qquad \ldots\text{Using (4.17)}$$

$$= \frac{1}{N}\sum_{k=0}^{N-1} H(k)\,.\sum_{n=0}^{N-1} e^{j2\pi kn/N}\, z^{-n}$$

i.e.,

$$H(z) = \frac{1}{N}\sum_{k=0}^{N-1} H(k)\,(1-e^{j2\pi Nk/N}\, z^{-N})/(1-e^{j2\pi k/N}\, z^{-1})$$

As $e^{j2\pi Nk/N} = 1$, we get

$$H(z) = \frac{(1-z^{-N})}{N}\sum_{k=0}^{N-1} H(k)/(1-e^{j2\pi k/N}\, z^{-1}) \qquad \ldots(4.18)$$

Equation (4.18) corresponds to a cascade of FIR filter $\frac{(1-z^{-N})}{N}$ with a parallel combination of IIR filters given by

$$H_k(z) = \frac{H(k)}{1 - e^{j2\pi k/N}\, z^{-1}}, \; k = 0, 1, ..., N-1 \qquad ...(4.19)$$

The realization of (4.18) is given by Fig. 4.6

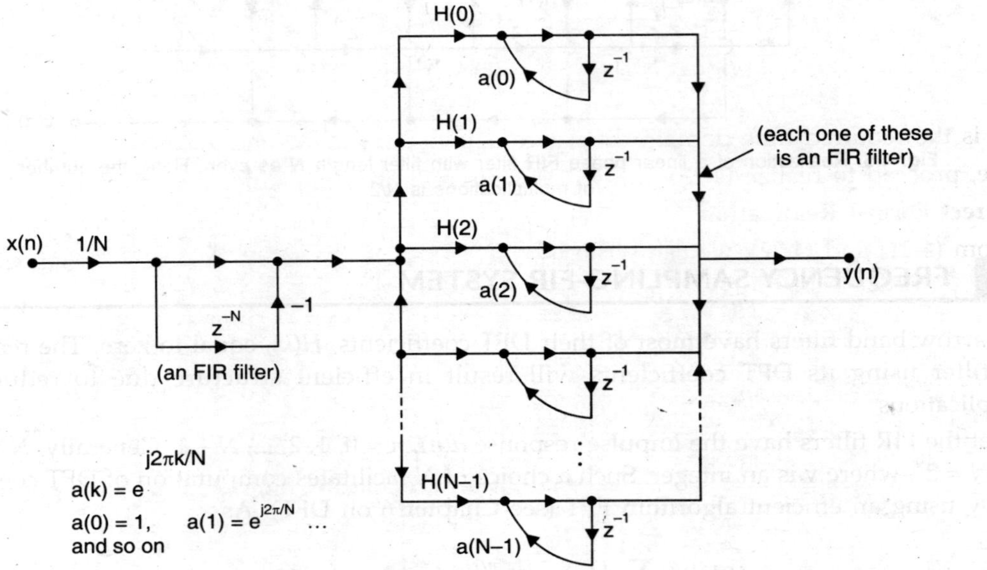

Fig. 4.6. Realization of FIR, *N* length filter using the frequency samples *H*(*k*), where *H*(*k*) = DFT of *h*(*n*)

4.6 DIRECT FORM-FIR IIR SYSTEM

The IIR filters have their system function, *H*(*z*), given by

$$H(z) = \frac{Y(z)}{X(z)} = \frac{\sum_{k=0}^{M} b(k)\, z^{-k}}{\sum_{k=0}^{N} a(k)\, z^{-k}} \qquad ...(4.20)$$

Assuming $a(0) = 1$, (4.20) reduces to

$$H(z) = \frac{\sum_{k=0}^{M} b(k)\, z^{-k}}{1 + \sum_{k=1}^{N} a(k)\, z^{-k}} \qquad ...(4.21)$$

$$\triangleq \frac{B(z)}{A(z)} \qquad ...(4.22)$$

From the rational function (4.21), to derive the equation in time domain, we first write, replacing $H(z)$ by $Y(z)/X(z)$ in (4.21)

$$Y(z) = \left[1+\sum_{k=1}^{N} a(k)\, z^{-k}\right] = X(z)\left[\sum_{k=0}^{M} b(k)\, z^{-k}\right]$$

or

$$Y(z) = \sum_{k=0}^{M} b(k) . X(z) . z^{-k} - \sum_{k=1}^{N} a(k) . Y(z) . z^{-k}$$

i.e.,

$$y(n) = \sum_{k=0}^{M} b(k) . x(n-k) - \sum_{k=1}^{N} a(k) . y(n-k) \qquad \ldots(4.23)$$

which is the required time domain difference equation corresponding to Eq. (4.21).

We, proceed to realize (4.23) *i.e.,* (4.21) as direct form-I and direct form-II.

Direct Form-I Realization

From (4.21) and (4.22), we can write

$$H(z) = \frac{B(z)}{A(z)} = B(z)\left[\frac{1}{A(z)}\right] \qquad \ldots(4.24)$$

where

$$B(z) = \sum_{k=0}^{M} b(k) . z^{-k}, \text{ an FIR filter}$$

and

$$\frac{1}{A(z)} = \frac{1}{\sum_{k=0}^{N} a(k) . z^{-k}} \text{ is an all-pole IIR filter.}$$

So, we can realize $H(z)$ as a cascade of $B(z)$ and $\frac{1}{A(z)}$ as shown in Fig. 4.7, as direct Form-I. Realization in Fig. 4.7 requires:

No. of multiplications = $M + N + 1$

No. of Additions = $M + N$

No. of Delays = $M + N$

for per output sample $y(n)$.

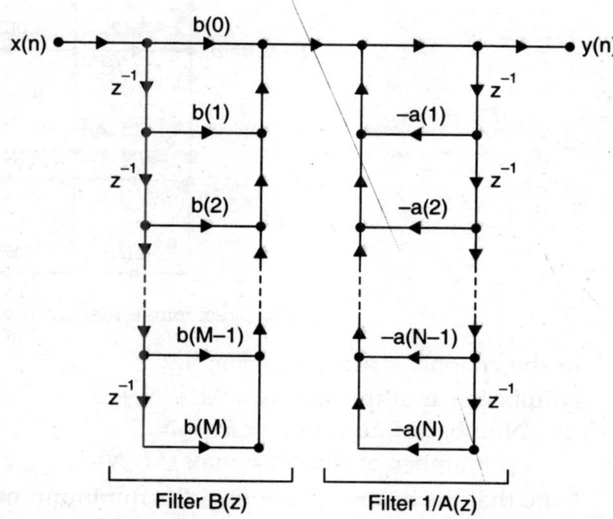

Fig. 4.7. Direct form-I realization of IIR filter $H(z)$ of Eq. (4.20)

Direct Form-II or Canonic form Realization

Direct form-I shown in Fig. 4.7 is highly inefficient and is rarely used in practice. To envolve direct form-II, we first interchange the cascade sequence of Fig. 4.7. Drawing $\frac{1}{A(z)}$ first followed by $B(z)$, we get Fig. 4.8.

Note that the node value at nodes Ⓐ and Ⓑ is $\omega(n-1)$. Similarly, the signals at nodes Ⓒ and Ⓓ are $\omega(n-2)$. Hence, we need not regenerate signal $\omega(n-1)$ at node Ⓑ, but use signal of node Ⓐ.

Similarly, ω(*n* – 2) available at node Ⓒ can be used instead of that at node Ⓓ. Thus, the structure of Fig. 4.8 can be simplified as shown in Fig. 4.9. This structure is called direct form-II or canonical form.

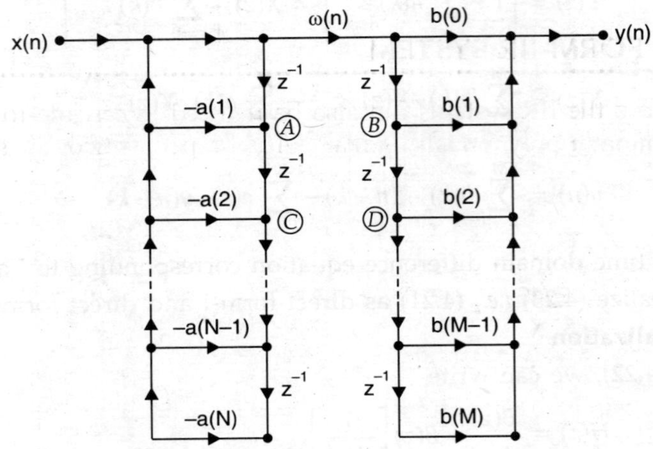

Fig. 4.8. Cascade order of Fig. 4.7 reversed

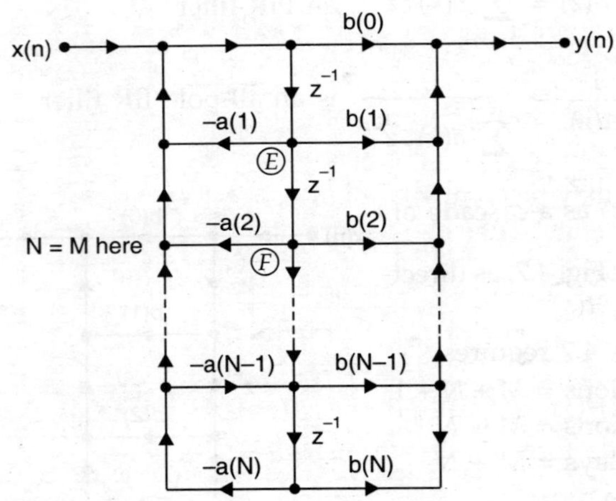

Fig. 4.9. Direct form-II realization of IIR filter (canonic form)

In the canonic structure of Fig. 4.9,

Number of multiplications = $M + N + 1$

Number of additions = $M + N$

Number of delays = max (M, N).

Note that the canonic form uses the minimum number of delays. *CANON* means *rule or law*. The number of delays equals the order of the filter $H(z)$, no more or no less, in the canonic form.

If $M \neq N$, as is the general case, the structure of Fig. 4.9. will have multipliers depending on values of N and M. Say, for example, $N = 7$ and $M = 3$, then we shall need 7 delays, besides $a(1)$, $a(2)$, ..., $a(7)$; $b(0)$, $b(1)$, $b(2)$ and $b(3)$ *i.e.*, 11 multipliers shown on LHS and RHS of the delay line in Fig. 4.9. In some cases, some of the coefficients $b(k)$, might be zero. For example, if $b(2) = 0$, then there would be no multiplier branch from Ⓕ, and so on.

Note: Some students confuse canonic with cannon. Canonic is derived from CANON, meaning rule or law. CANNON means guns. Surely, DSP obeys certain rules/methods and is no where near to guns. So dear students use canonic (single n) and be governed by prescribed rules of mathematics used in DSP.

4.7 CASCADE FORM-IIR SYSTEM

As in FIR cascade form, the IIR systems can also be realized in cascade form. We factorize the numerator and denominator polynomials, $B(z)$ and $A(z)$, respectively of the system function $H(z)$. Hence,

$$H(z) = \frac{B(z)}{A(z)} = \frac{\sum_{k=0}^{M} b(k)\, z^{-k}}{\sum_{k=0}^{N} a(k) \,.\, z^{-k}} \qquad \ldots(4.25)$$

is factorized as

$$H(z) = A\frac{\prod_{k=0}^{M} (1-\beta(k)\, z^{-1})}{\prod_{k=1}^{N} (1-\alpha(k)\, z^{-1})} \qquad \ldots(4.26)$$

where $\beta(k)$ are zeros of $B(z)$ and $\alpha(k)$ are zeros of $A(z)$. A is a constant equalling $\frac{b(0)}{a(0)}$. The coefficients $\alpha(k)$ and $\beta(k)$ may be complex. If $h(n)$ is real, then the roots of $H(z)$ will be either real or occur in complex conjugate. Then the factors of $B(z)$ and $A(z)$ may be combined in the form

$$H(z) = \frac{(1+\beta_1(1)\, z^{-1} + \beta_1(2)\, z^{-2})\,(1+\beta_2(1)\, z^{-1} + \beta_2(2)\, z^{-2})\ldots}{(1+\alpha_1(1)\, z^{-1} + \alpha_1(2)\, z^{-2})\,(1+\alpha_2(1)\, z^{-1} + \alpha_2(2)\, z^{-2})\ldots} \qquad \ldots(4.27)$$

We may put

$$H(z) = H_1(z) \,.\, H_2(z) \,.\, H_3(z) \ldots H_M(z) \qquad \ldots(4.28)$$

and realize $H(z)$ in cascade form as shown in Fig. 4.10.

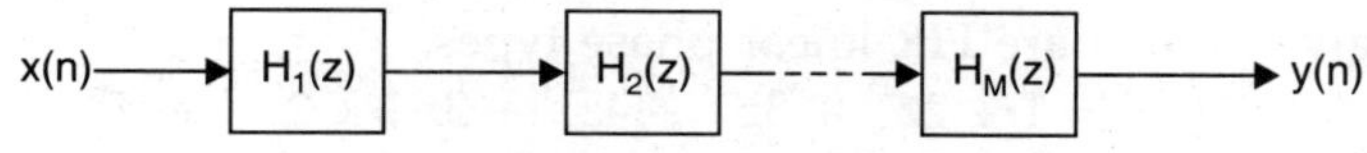

Fig. 4.10. Cascade form realization of $H(z)$

If each $H_1(z)$, $H_2(z)$, ..., $H_M(z)$ is of the second order, then $H(z)$ given by (4.28) and realized in Fig. 4.10 is of $2M$ order. The subfilters $H_i(z)$ may have order one or two in practical cases. Then the cascade of $H_i(z)$ will have overall order as the sum of orders of individual subfilters.

We may pair different numerator factor and denominator factor from (4.26) to choose different subfilters. This gives considerable flexibility in realization of IIR filters in cascade form. We may also use any sequence of cascading $H_1(z)$, $H_2(z)$, ..., $H_M(z)$. It will be shown in Chapter 10 on quantization that the sequence on placement of $H_1(z)$, $H_2(z)$, ..., $H_M(z)$ has an effect on quantization error.

4.8 PARALLEL FORM-IIR SYSTEM

An alternative way to split $H(z)$, given by (4.20), is by expanding in partial fractions. For example,

$$H(z) = \sum_{k=1}^{P} \frac{A_K}{(1 - \alpha(k)\, z^{-1})} \qquad \text{...(4.29)}$$

where $\alpha(k)$ are the zeros of $A(z)$. If $h(n)$ is real valued then the zeros of $A(z)$ or poles of $H(z)$ will occur in complex conjugate pairs. Hence, we may expand $H(z)$ as

$$H(z) = H_1(z) + H_2(z) + \ldots + H_P(z) \qquad \text{...(4.30)}$$

which may be realized in parallel form shown in Fig. 4.11.

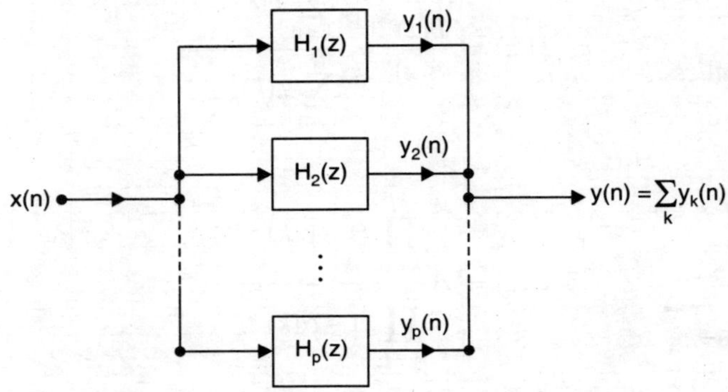

Fig. 4.11. Parallel structure $H(z) = \sum_k H_k(z)$

Solved Examples on FIR and IIR Structures

EXAMPLE 4.1: *Determine a direct form realization for the linear phase FIR filters.*

(a) $h_1(n) = \{\underset{\uparrow}{1}, 2, 3, 4, 3, 2, 1\}$ *i.e., filter length N = 7*

(b) $h_2(n) = \{\underset{\uparrow}{1}, 2, 3, 3, 2, 1\}$ *i.e., filter length N = 6.*

SOLUTION: The given filters are FIR linear phase types.

(a)
$$H_1(z) = 1 + 2z^{-1} + 3z^{-2} + 4z^{-3} + 3z^{-4} + 2z^{-5} + z^{-6}$$
$$= 1(1 + z^{-6}) + 2(z^{-1} + z^{-5}) + 3(z^{-2} + z^{-4}) + 4z^{-3}$$

Realization is shown in Fig. Ex. 4.1(*a*)

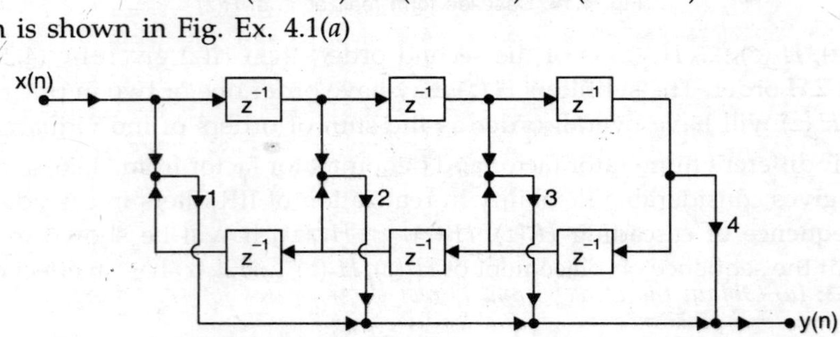

Fig. Ex. 4.1. (*a*) Realization of $H_1(z)$

(*b*) Here
$$H_2z = 1 + 2z^{-1} + 3z^{-2} + 3z^{-3} + 2z^{-4} + z^{-5}$$
$$= 1(1 + z^{-5}) + 2(z^{-1} + z^{-4}) + 3(z^{-2} + z^{-3})$$

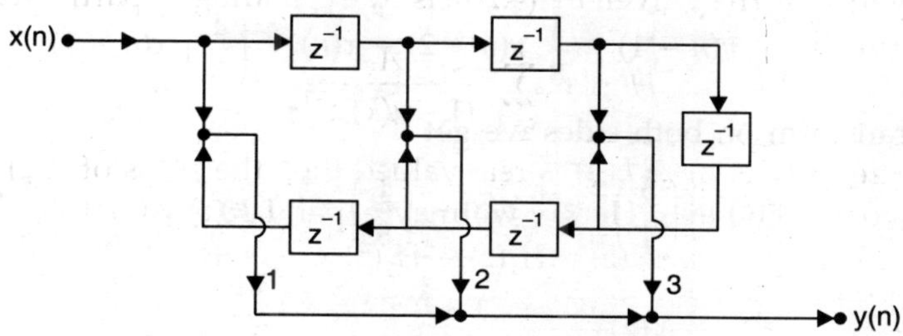

Fig. Ex. 4.1. (*b*) Realization of $H_2(z)$

EXAMPLE 4.2: *Realize the digital filter*

(*a*)
$$H_1(z) = \frac{1 + 2z^{-1} + z^{-2}}{1 - 0.75\, z^{-1} + 0.125\, z^{-2}} \text{ in canonic form}$$

(*b*)
$$H_2(z) = \frac{1}{(1 - 0.2\, z^{-1})\,(1 + 0.4\, z^{-1} - 0.21\, z^{-2})} \text{ in parallel form.}$$

SOLUTION: (*a*) $H_1(z)$ is realized as shown opposite. This is canonic or direct form-II realization.

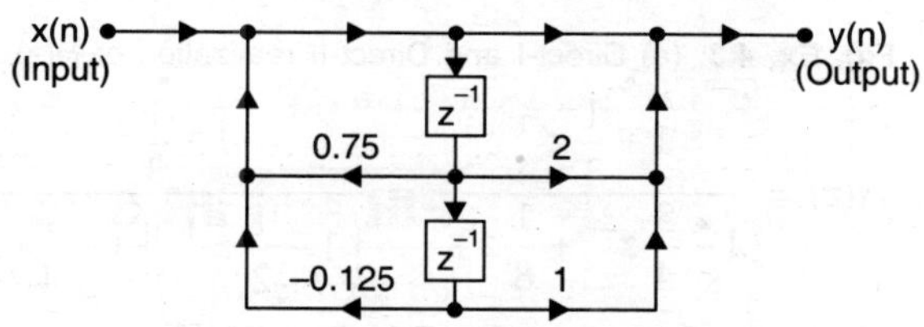

Fig. Ex. 4.2. (*a*) Canonic form structure of $H_1(z)$

(*b*)
$$H_2(z) = \frac{-4/9}{(1 - 0.2\, z^{-1})} + \frac{49/90}{(1 + 0.7\, z^{-1})} + \frac{9/10}{(1 - 0.3\, z^{-1})} \qquad \text{(by partial fractions)}$$

we realize it as a proper canonic form as shown in the figure.

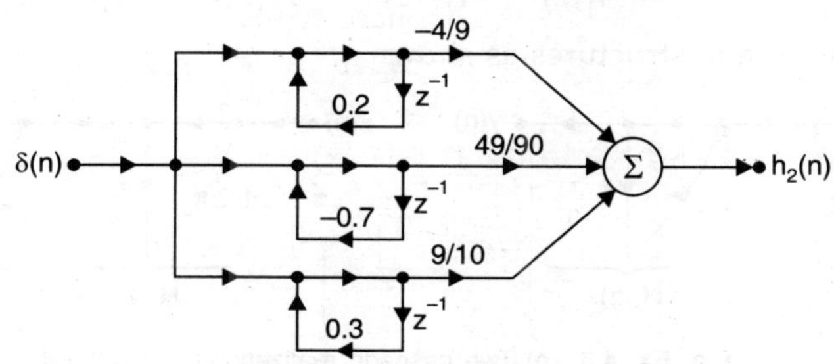

Fig. Ex. 4.2. (*b*) Parallel realization of $H_2(z)$

EXAMPLE 4.3: *(a) Obtain the Direct-I and Direct-II structures for the following system.*

$$y(n) = \frac{3}{4}\, y(n-1) - \frac{1}{8}\, y(n-2) + x(n) + \frac{1}{3}\, x(n-1)$$

(b) Realize the above system as cascade structures

(c) Realize the same system as a parallel structure.

SOLUTION: (*a*) $y(n) = \left(\frac{3}{4}\right) y(n-1) - \frac{1}{8} y(n-2) + x(n) + \left(\frac{1}{3}\right) x(n-1)$

$\therefore$ Taking z-transform on both sides we get

$$Y(z) = \left(\frac{3}{4}\right) . z^{-1} Y(z) - \left(\frac{1}{8}\right) z^{-2} Y(z) + X(z) + \left(\frac{1}{3}\right) z^{-1} X(z)$$

$$\therefore \qquad H(z) = \frac{Y(z)}{X(z)} = \frac{1+\frac{1}{3}z^{-1}}{1-\frac{3}{4}z^{-1}+\frac{1}{8}z^{-2}}$$

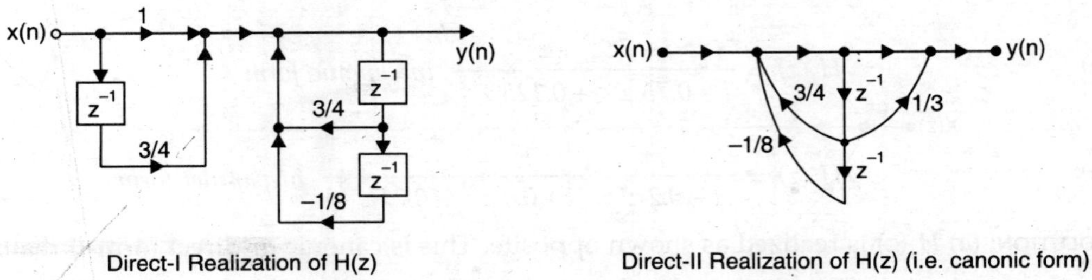

Fig. Ex. 4.3. (*a*) Direct-I and Direct-II realization of $H(z)$

(*b*) As $$H(z) = \frac{1+\frac{1}{3}z^{-1}}{1-\frac{3}{4}z^{-1}+\frac{1}{8}z^{-2}} = \frac{1+\frac{1}{3}z^{-1}}{\left(1-\frac{1}{2}z^{-1}\right)\left(1-\frac{1}{4}z^{-1}\right)}$$

Cascade structures for $H(z)$ is shown in the Fig. Ex. 4.3(*b*)

As $$H(z) = \underbrace{\frac{1+\frac{1}{3}z^{-1}}{1-\frac{1}{2}z^{-1}}}_{H_1(z)} . \underbrace{\frac{1}{1-\frac{1}{4}z^{-1}}}_{H_2(z)} = \underbrace{\frac{1}{1-\frac{1}{2}z^{-1}}}_{H_3(z)} . \underbrace{\frac{1+\frac{1}{3}z^{-1}}{1-\frac{1}{4}z^{-1}}}_{H_4(z)}$$

$\therefore$ We have two cascade structures as shown

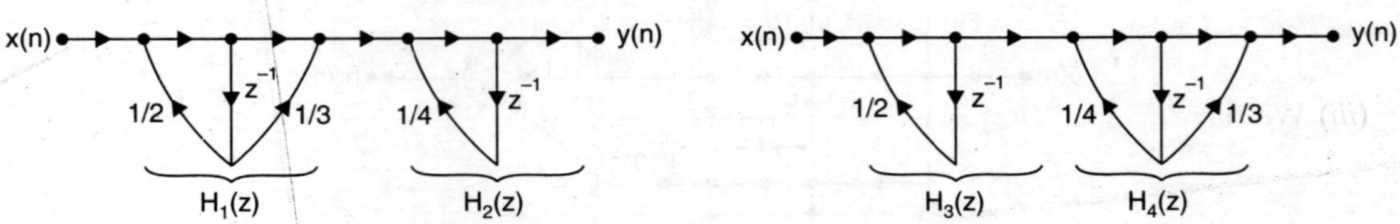

Fig. Ex. 4.3. (*b*) Two cascade realizations of $H(z)$

(*c*) To get a parallel realization, we first expand $H(z)$ as partial fractions

As $$H(z) = \frac{1+\frac{1}{3}z^{-1}}{\left(1-\frac{1}{2}z^{-1}\right)\left(1-\frac{1}{4}z^{-1}\right)} = \frac{\left(\frac{10}{3}\right)}{1-\frac{1}{2}z^{-1}} + \frac{-\left(\frac{7}{3}\right)}{1-\frac{1}{4}z^{-1}}$$

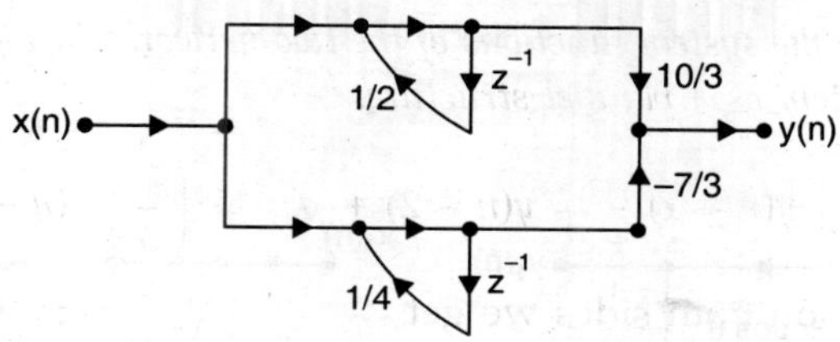

Fig. Ex. 4.3. (*c*) Parallel realization of *H*(*z*)

EXAMPLE 4.4: *Realize the system:*

$$H(z) = z^2/[(z-1)(z-2)(z-3)]$$

in (i) cascade form, (ii) parallel form, and (iii) canonic form.

SOLUTION: (*i*)

$$H(z) = \frac{z^{-1}}{(1-z^{-1})(1-2z^{-1})(1-3z^{-1})} = \underbrace{\frac{1}{1-z^{-1}}}_{H_1(z)} \cdot \underbrace{\frac{1}{1-2z^{-1}}}_{H_2(z)} \cdot \underbrace{\frac{z^{-1}}{1-3z^{-1}}}_{H_3(z)}$$

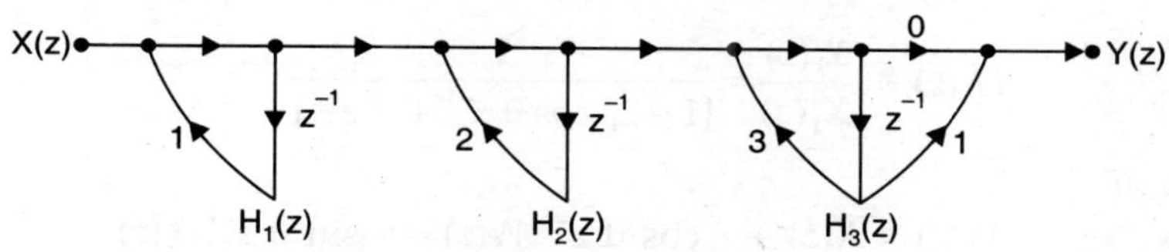

Fig. Ex 4.4 (*i*) Realization in cascade form

(*ii*) As

$$H(z) = \frac{\frac{1}{2}}{(1-z^{-1})} + \frac{-2}{(1-2z^{-1})} + \frac{\frac{3}{2}}{(1-3z^{-1})} \text{ (by partial fractions)}$$

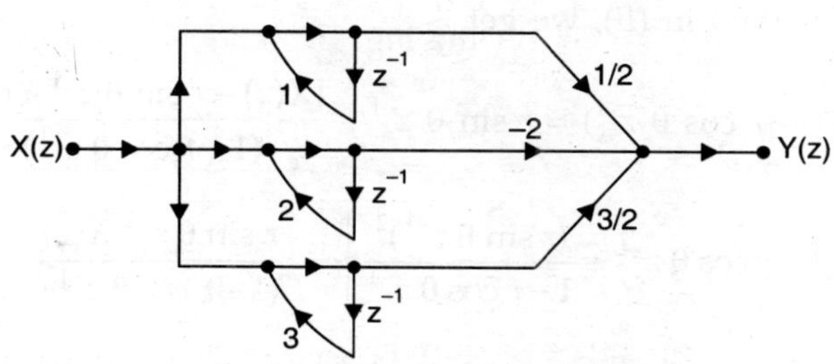

Fig. Ex 4.4 (*ii*) Realization as a parallel form

(*iii*) We have

$$H(z) = \frac{z^{-1}}{1-6z^{-1}+11z^{-2}-6z^{-3}}$$

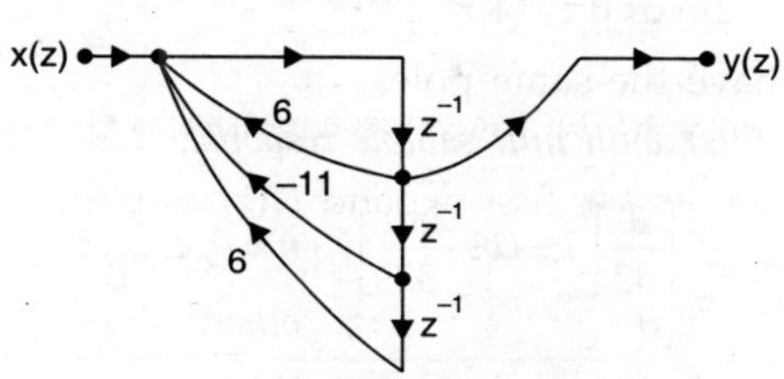

Fig. Ex 4.4 (*iii*) Canonic form realization

EXAMPLE 4.5: *Determine the system functions of the two networks in Fig. Ex. 4.5 and show that they have the same poles.*

SOLUTION:

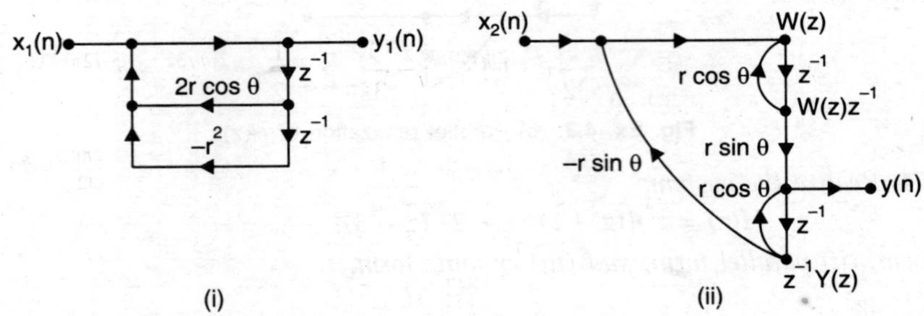

Fig. Ex. 4.5. The given two networks

For network (*i*)

$$Y_1(z) = 2r \cos \theta\, z^{-1}\, Y_1(z) - r^2 z^{-2}\, Y_1(z) + X_1(z)$$

$$\therefore \qquad H_1(z) \triangleq \frac{Y_1(z)}{X_1(z)} = \frac{1}{[1 - 2r\cos\theta\, z^{-1} + r^2 z^{-2}]}$$

For network (*ii*)

$$W(z) = X(z) + r \cos \theta\, z^{-1}\, W(z) - r \sin \theta\, z^{-1}\, Y(z) \qquad \ldots(A)$$

and

$$Y(z) = r \sin \theta\, z^{-1}\, W(z) + r \cos \theta\, z^{-1}\, Y(z) \qquad \ldots(B)$$

from (*A*) $W(z)[1 - r \cos \theta\, z^{-1}] = X(z) - r \sin \theta\, z^{-1}\, Y(z)$

i.e.

$$W(z) = \frac{[X(z) - r\sin\theta\, z^{-1}\, Y(z)]}{(1 - r\cos\theta\, z^{-1})}$$

Putting this value of $W(z)$ in (*B*), we get

$$Y(z)\,(1 - r\cos\theta\, z^{-1}) = r\sin\theta\, z^{-1}\,.\, \frac{[X(z) - r\sin\theta\, z^{-1}\, Y(z)]}{(1 - r\cos\theta\, z^{-1})}$$

$$\therefore \qquad Y(z)\left[1 - r\cos\theta\, z^{-1} + \frac{(r\sin\theta\, z^{-1})^2}{1 - r\cos\theta\, z^{-1}}\right] = \frac{r\sin\theta\, z^{-1}\, X(z)}{(1 - r\cos\theta\, z^{-1})}$$

or

$$Y(z)\left[\frac{(1 - r\cos\theta\, z^{-1})^2 + (r\sin\theta\, z^{-1})^2}{(1 - r\cos\theta\, z^{-1})}\right] = X(z)\frac{r\sin\theta\, z^{-1}}{1 - r\cos\theta\, z^{-1}}$$

$$\therefore \qquad H_2(z) \triangleq \frac{Y(z)}{X(z)} = \frac{r\sin\theta\, z^{-1}}{1 - 2r\cos\theta\, z^{-1} + r^2\, z^{-2}}.$$

Clearly $H_1(z)$ and $H_2(z)$ have the same poles.

EXAMPLE 4.6: *For the FIR filter with unit sample response*

$$h(n) = \begin{cases} \dfrac{1}{32}\left[1 - \cos\dfrac{2\pi n}{32}\right], & n = 0, 1, \ldots, 31 \\ 0, & \text{otherwise} \end{cases}$$

Draw the frequency sampling structure.

SOLUTION: Here $N = 32$

DFT $$H(k) = \sum_{n=0}^{N-1} h(n)\, e^{-j(2\pi/N)nk} = \sum_{n=0}^{31} \frac{1}{32}\left[1 - \cos\frac{2\pi n}{32}\right] e^{-j(2\pi/32)nk}$$

$$= \sum_{n=0}^{31} \frac{1}{32} e^{-j(2\pi/32)nk} - \frac{1}{32}\sum_{n=0}^{31} \frac{1}{2}\left(e^{j2\pi n/32} + e^{-j2\pi n/32}\right) e^{-j(2\pi/32)nk}$$

$$= \frac{1}{32}\sum_{n=0}^{31} e^{-j(2\pi/32)nk} - \frac{1}{64}\left[\sum_{n=0}^{31} e^{j\frac{2\pi n}{32}(1-k)} + e^{-j\frac{2\pi n}{32}(1+k)}\right]$$

$$= \frac{32}{32}\delta(k) - \frac{32}{64}[\delta(1-k) + \delta(1+k)]$$

$\therefore$ $$H(0) = 1$$

$$H(1) = -\frac{1}{2}$$

$$H(-1) = H(31) = -\frac{1}{2}$$ [$\because$ $H(k)$ is periodic with period N]

$\therefore$ $$H(z) = \frac{1}{N}(1 - z^{-N})\left[\sum_{k=0}^{N-1} \frac{H(k)}{1 - e^{j2\pi k/N} z^{-1}}\right]$$ from (4.18)

$$= \frac{1}{32}(1 - z^{-32})\left[\frac{1}{1 - z^{-1}} - \frac{(1/2)}{1 - e^{j2\pi/32} z^{-1}} - \frac{(1/2)}{1 - e^{-j2\pi/32} z^{-1}}\right],$$

$\because$ $k = 0, 1, -1$ only

$$= \frac{1}{32}(1 - z^{-32})\left[\frac{1}{1 - z^{-1}} - \frac{1 - \cos(2\pi/32)\, z^{-1}}{1 - 2\cos(2\pi/32)\, z^{-1} + z^{-2}}\right]$$

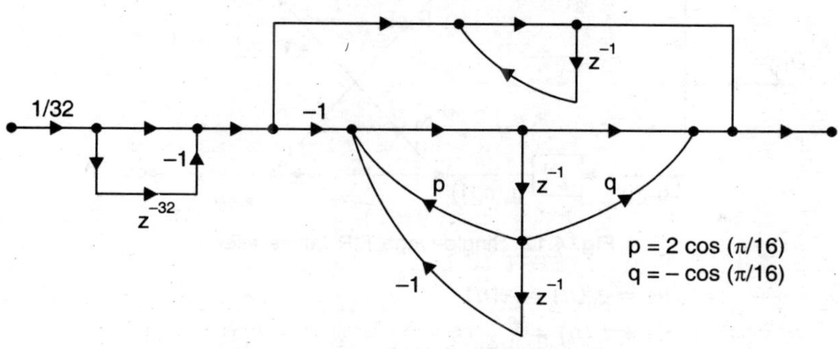

Fig. Ex. 4.6. Realization as frequency sampling structure

4.9 LATTICE STRUCTURE

We can also realize FIR as well as IIR filters as Lattice structures. Lattice filters are used extensively in digital speech processing and in implementation of adaptive filters. We shall first cover realization of FIR filters as lattice structure followed by IIR filters.

4.9.1 FIR Lattice Filters

Consider the system function

$$H_m(z) = A_m(z),\ m = 0, 1, ..., M - 1 \quad ...(4.31)$$

where $A_m(z)$ is the polynomial (assuming $\alpha_m(0) = 1$)

$$A_m(z) = 1 + \sum_{k=1}^{m} \alpha_m(k)\, z^{-k},\ m \geq 1 \quad ...(4.32a)$$

and $$A_0(z) = 1$$

The unit sample response of the m-th filter $A_m(z)$ is

$$h_m(k) = \begin{cases} 1, & k = 0 \\ \alpha_m(k), & k = 1, 2, ..., m \end{cases} \quad ...(4.32b)$$

The subscript m on the polynomial $A_m(z)$ denotes the degree of the polynomial. We take $\alpha_m(0) = 1$ for mathematical convenience.

If the input sequence to the system $H_m(z)$ is $x(n)$, then the output $y(n)$ is given by

$$y(n) = x(n) * h_m(n) \qquad (i.e., \text{ convolution})$$

$$= \sum_{k=0}^{m} \alpha_m(k) \,.\, x(n-k)$$

$$\therefore \qquad y(n) = x(n) + \sum_{k=1}^{m} \alpha_m(k) \,.\, x(n-k) \quad \because \quad \alpha_m(0) = 1 \quad ...(4.33)$$

Now suppose that $m = 1$, then taking $\alpha_1(0) = 1$, we have

$$y(n) = x(n) + \alpha_1(1)\, x(n-1) \quad ...(4.34)$$

The output $y(n)$ can be obtained from the structure shown in Fig. 4.12, which is the first-order lattice filter.

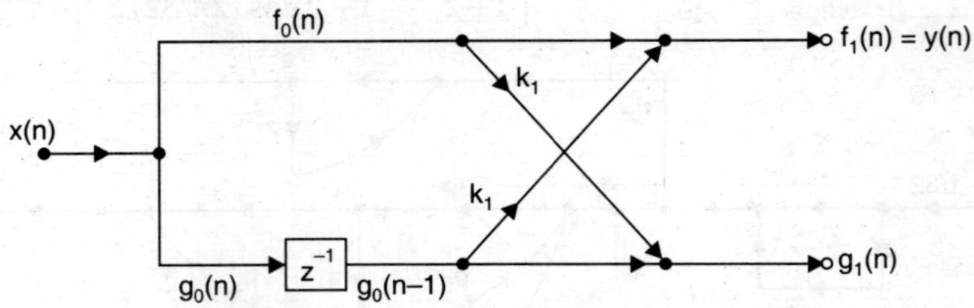

Fig. 4.12. Single-stage FIR lattice filter

$$f_0(n) = g_0(n) = x(n)$$
$$f_1(n) = f_0(n) + k_1 g_0(n-1) = x(n) + k_1 x(n-1)$$
$$g_1(n) = k_1 f_0(n) + g_0(n-1) = k_1 x(n) + x(n-1)$$

We excite the two branches at input of Fig. 4.12 by using the signal $x(n)$, and select the output from the top branch. If $k_1 = \alpha_1(1)$, then $y(n) = x(n) + \alpha_1(1)\, x(n-1)$, which is the same as (4.34). The parameters k_1 is called a *Reflection coefficient*, and it is identical to the reflection coefficient used in Schur-Cohn stability criteria described in Chapter 3.

Now consider an FIR filter with $m = 2$. In this case (and again $\alpha_2(0) = 1$), (4.33) gives us

$$y(n) = x(n) + \alpha_2(1)\, x(n-1) + \alpha_2(2)\, x(n-2) \quad ...(4.35)$$

By cascading two Lattice stages, as shown in Fig. 4.13, we obtain the same output as (4.35).

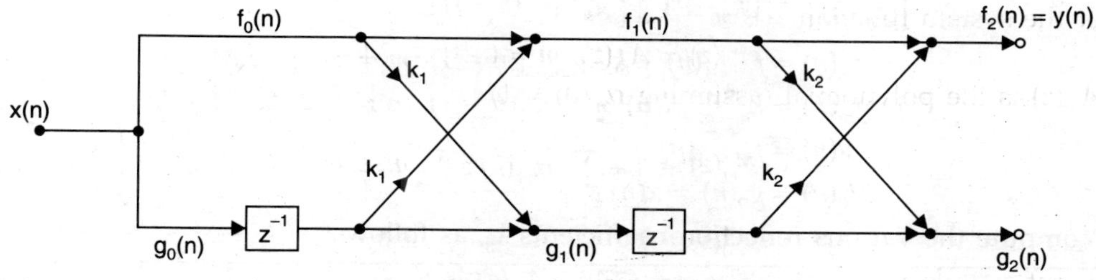

Fig. 4.13. A two-stage Lattice for second order FIR filter

Note that

$$\left.\begin{aligned} f_1(n) &= x(n) + k_1 x(n-1) \\ g_1(n) &= k_1 x(n) + x(n-1) \\ f_2(n) &= x(n) + k_1(1+k_2)\, x(n-1) + k_2 x(n-2) \\ g_2(n) &= k_2 x(n) + k_1(1+k_2)\, x(n-1) + x(n-2) \end{aligned}\right\} \quad \ldots(4.36)$$

Comparing (4.35) and (4.36), since, $f_2(n) = y(n)$, we get

$$\alpha_2(1) = k_1(1+k_2) \text{ and } \alpha_2(2) = k_2 \quad \ldots(4.37a)$$

or equivalently,

$$\boxed{k_2 = \alpha_2(2),\ k_1 = \frac{\alpha_2(1)}{1+\alpha_2(2)}} \quad \ldots(4.37b)$$

Hence, the reflection coefficients k_1 and k_2 of the lattice can be obtained from the coefficients $\{\alpha_m(k)\}$. Proceeding thus, we can realize a lattice structure for an FIR filter of order $M - 1$ as shown in Fig. 4.14.

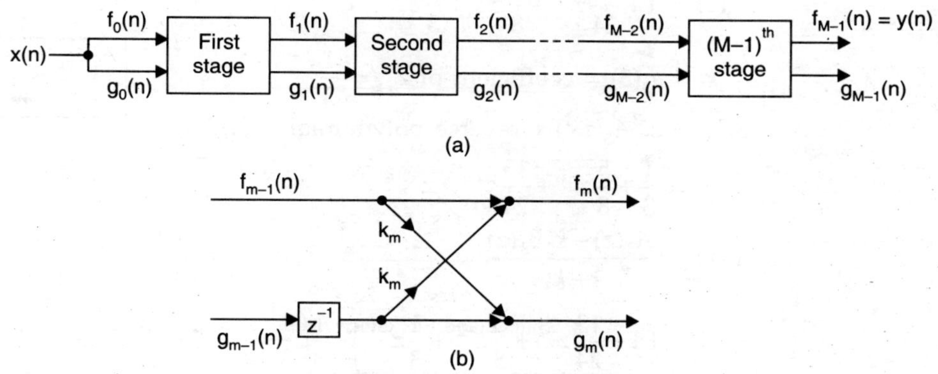

Fig. 4.14. (*a*) (*M* – 1) stage lattice filter for (*M* – 1) order FIR filter

(*b*) m^{th} stage parameters, *m* = 1, 2, ..., *M* – 1 and their relationships

The $(M - 1)$-stage filter's output on the top line in Fig. 4.14(*a*) *i.e.*, $f_{M-1}(n)$ gives the output. Fig. 4.14(*a*) is the $(M-1)$-stage block diagram of the lattice and Fig. 4.14(*b*) is to show typical stage computation. Various results are summarized as follows:

(a) $\begin{bmatrix} f_m(n) \\ g_m(n) \end{bmatrix} = \begin{bmatrix} 1 & k_m \\ k_m & 1 \end{bmatrix} \begin{bmatrix} f_{m-1} & (n) \\ g_{n-1} & (n-1) \end{bmatrix}$ matrix form for relations (b) and (c)

$$\left.\begin{aligned}
&(b) \quad f_m(n) = f_{m-1}(n) + k_m\, g_{m-1}(n-1),\ m = 1, 2, ..., M-1 \\
&(c) \quad g_m(n) = k_m\, f_{m-1}(n) + g_{m-1}(n-1),\ m = 1, 2, ..., M-1 \\
&(d) \quad y(n) = f_{M-1}(n) \\
&(e) \quad f_0(n) = g_0(n) = x(n)
\end{aligned}\right\} \quad ...(4.38)$$

We compute the various reflection coefficients k_m as follows:

Rule to compute k_m, given the FIR filter $A_{M-1}(z)$	
1.	Given $A_m(z) = 1 + \sum_{k=1}^{m} \alpha_m(k)\, z^{-k}$, $m \geq 1$
2.	$A_{m-1}(z) = \dfrac{A_m(z) - k_m B_m(z)}{1 - k_m^2}$, $m = M-1, M-2, ..., 1$
3.	$k_m = \alpha_m(m)$, $m = M-1, M-2, ..., 1$
4.	where $B_m(z)$ = reverse polynomial of $A_m(z) = z^{-m} A_m(z^{-1})$ This is called the *Step-down Recursion* (to find $k_1, k_2, ...$) ...(4.39)

EXAMPLE 4.7: *Determine the lattice coefficients corresponding to the FIR filter with system function*

$$H(z) = A_3(z) = 1 + \frac{13}{24}z^{-1} + \frac{5}{8}z^{-2} + \frac{1}{3}z^{-3}.$$

SOLUTION: We use the step-down recursion to find $k_1, k_2, ...,$

As
$$A_3(z) = 1 + \frac{13}{24}z^{-1} + \frac{5}{8}z^{-2} + \frac{1}{3}z^{-3}$$

$$k_3 = a_3(3) = \text{coefficient of } z^{-3} = \frac{1}{3} \qquad \boxed{k_3 = \frac{1}{3}}$$

$$B_3(z) = z^{-3}A_3(z^{-1}) \equiv \text{reverse polynomial } A_3(z)$$

$$= \frac{1}{3} + \frac{5}{8}z^{-1} + \frac{13}{24}z^{-2} + z^{-3}$$

$$A_2(z) = \frac{A_3(z) - k_3 B_3(z)}{1 - k_3^2}$$

$$= \frac{\left(1 + \frac{13}{24}z^{-1} + \frac{5}{8}z^{-2} + \frac{1}{3}z^{-3}\right) - \frac{1}{3}\left(\frac{1}{3} + \frac{5}{8}z^{-1} + \frac{13}{24}z^{-2} + z^{-3}\right)}{1 - \left(\frac{1}{3}\right)^2}$$

$$= \frac{\left(1 - \frac{1}{9}\right) + \left(\frac{13}{24} - \frac{5}{24}\right)z^{-1} + \left(\frac{5}{8} - \frac{13}{72}\right)z^{-2} + \left(\frac{1}{3} - \frac{1}{3}\right)z^{-3}}{\left(\frac{8}{9}\right)}$$

$$\therefore \quad A_2(z) = 1 + \frac{3}{8}z^{-1} + \frac{1}{2}z^{-2} \quad i.e.\ \alpha_2(2) = \frac{1}{2} \qquad \boxed{\therefore\ k_2 = \frac{1}{2}}$$

$$\therefore \quad B_2(z) = \frac{1}{2} + \frac{3}{8}z^{-1} + z^{-2} \qquad \text{[reverse polynomial of } A_2(z)]$$

$$A_1(z) = \frac{A_2(z) - k_2 B_2(z)}{1 - k_2^2}$$

$$= \frac{\left(1 + \frac{3}{8}z^{-1} + \frac{1}{2}z^{-2}\right) - \frac{1}{2}\left(\frac{1}{2} + \frac{3}{8}z^{-1} + z^{-2}\right)}{1 - \left(\frac{1}{2}\right)^2}$$

$$= \frac{\left(1 - \frac{1}{4}\right) + \left(\frac{3}{8} - \frac{3}{16}\right)z^{-1} + \left(\frac{1}{2} - \frac{1}{2}\right)z^{-2}}{\left(\frac{3}{4}\right)}$$

$\therefore$ $$A_1(z) = 1 + \frac{1}{4}z^{-1} \text{ i.e. } a_1(1) = \frac{1}{4}$$ $\boxed{\therefore\ k_1 = \frac{1}{4}}$

Hence, $k_1 = \frac{1}{4},\ k_2 = \frac{1}{2},\ k_3 = \frac{1}{3}$ **Ans.**

Conversion of Lattice Coefficients $\{K_i\}$ to Direct-form FIR Filter Coefficients $\{\alpha_m(k)\}$

We know that

$$A_0(z) = B_0(z) \quad \text{...(4.40a)}$$

$$A_m(z) = A_{m-1}(z) + K_m z^{-1} B_{m-1}(z),\ m = 1, 2, \ldots, M \quad \text{...(4.40b)}$$

$$B_m(z) = z^{-m} A_m(z^{-1}),\ m = 1, 2, \ldots, M \quad \text{...(4.40c)}$$

where $A_m(z) = \frac{F_m(z)}{X(z)} = \frac{F_m(z)}{F_0(z)}$ is the unit sample response of the mth filter

$$B_m(z) = \sum_{k=0}^{m} \alpha_m(m-k) z^{-k}$$

$$= z^{-m} \sum_{l=0}^{m} \alpha_m(l) z^{l} \quad \text{(putting } l = m - k \text{ in the above equation)}$$

$\therefore$ $$B_m(z) = z^{-m} A_m(z^{-1}),\ m = 1, 2, \ldots, M - 1 \quad \text{...(4.40d)}$$

$B_m(z)$ is also called the reciprocal or *reverse polynomial* of $A_m(z)$. To find $\alpha_{M-1}(k)$, given the reflection coefficients, we use the *Step-up Recursion*

(*i*) $A_m(z) = A_{m-1}(z) + K_m z^{-m} A_{m-1}(z^{-1})$, $m = 1, 2, \ldots, M$, Assume $A_0(z) = 1$ to start recursion.
or

(*ii*) (matrix form)

$$\begin{bmatrix} 1 \\ a_m(1) \\ a_m(2) \\ \vdots \\ a_m(m-1) \\ a_m(m) \end{bmatrix} = \begin{bmatrix} 1 \\ a_{m-1}(1) \\ a_{m-1}(2) \\ \vdots \\ a_{m-1}(m-1) \\ 0 \end{bmatrix} + K_m \begin{bmatrix} 0 \\ a_{m-1}(m-1) \\ a_{m-1}(m-2) \\ \vdots \\ a_{m-1}(1) \\ 1 \end{bmatrix}$$

To find $a_m(k)$, $k = 1, 2, \ldots, m$ given K_i
Vary m from $m = 1, 2, \ldots, M$ ...(4.41)

EXAMPLE 4.8: *Given 3 stage lattice coefficients as* $K_1 = \frac{1}{4}$, $K_2 = \frac{1}{2}$, $K_3 = \frac{1}{3}$, *determine the FIR filter coefficients for direct structure. (This is the reverse of Example 4.7).*

SOLUTION: We use Step-up Recursion. Given

$$K_1 = \frac{1}{4},\ K_2 = \frac{1}{2},\ K_3 = \frac{1}{3}$$

We know that

(Step-up Recursion)

$$A_m(z) = A_{m-1}(z) + K_m z^{-m} A_{m-1}(z^{-1}) \qquad \text{with } A_0(z) = 1$$

$$\therefore \quad A_1(z) = A_0(z) + K_1 z^{-1} A_0(z^{-1})$$

$$= 1 + \frac{1}{4}z^{-1}(1) = 1 + \frac{1}{4}z^{-1}$$

$$A_2(z) = A_1(z) + K_2 z^{-2} A_1(z^{-1}) \qquad \text{[putting } m = 2 \text{ in (4.41)]}$$

$$= \left(1 + \frac{1}{4}z^{-1}\right) + \frac{1}{2}z^{-2}\left(1 + \frac{1}{4}z^{+1}\right)$$

$$= 1 + \frac{3}{8}z^{-1} + \frac{1}{2}z^{-2}$$

$$A_3(z) = A_2(z) + K_3 z^{-3} A_2(z^{-1}) \qquad \text{[putting } m = 3 \text{ in (4.41)]}$$

$$= \left(1 + \frac{3}{8}z^{-1} + \frac{1}{2}z^{-2}\right) + \frac{1}{3}z^{-3}\left(1 + \frac{3}{8}z^{+1} + \frac{1}{2}z^{+2}\right)$$

$$= 1 + \left(\frac{3}{8} + \frac{1}{6}\right)z^{-1} + \left(\frac{1}{2} + \frac{1}{8}\right)z^{-2} + \frac{1}{3}z^{-3}$$

$$\therefore \quad A_3(z) = 1 + \frac{13}{24}z^{-1} + \frac{5}{8}z^{-2} + \frac{1}{3}z^{-3} \quad \textbf{Ans.}$$

Hence, the FIR filter with unit sample impulse response $\alpha_3(k) = \left\{\underset{\uparrow}{1}, \frac{13}{24}, \frac{5}{8}, \frac{1}{3}\right\}$ which is of order 3 will translate to a lattice filter with $K_i = \frac{1}{4}, \frac{1}{2}, \frac{1}{3}$.

4.9.2 Lattice Structure of IIR Filters (for All Pole Case)

Consider an all pole system with system function

$$H(z) = \frac{1}{1 + \sum_{k=1}^{N} a_N(k) z^{-k}} = \frac{1}{A_N(z)} \qquad \ldots(4.42)$$

The difference equation for this IIR system is

$$y(n) = -\sum_{k=1}^{N} a_N(k) y(n-k) + x(n) \qquad \ldots(4.43)$$

For an FIR system with system function $A_m(z)$, the input-output relation is given by

$$Y(z) = X(z) \cdot A_m(z) \quad \text{...(4.44)}$$

And for an IIR system with system function $H(z) = \dfrac{1}{A_N(z)}$ [as given in (4.42)], the input-output relation is given by

$$Y(z) = X(z) \cdot \frac{1}{A_N(z)}$$

$$\therefore \quad X(z) = Y(z) \cdot A_N(z) \quad \text{...(4.45)}$$

Equations (4.44) and (4.45) show that a lattice structure for an FIR filter can be adapted to a lattice structure for an all pole system function, if we interchange the roles of input and output [*i.e.* interchange $x(n)$ and $y(n)$ in (4.43)]. Hence, one system can be obtained from the other simply by interchanging the roles of input and output.

An N-order all pole filter is a cascade of N-stages with each stage being a 2-port network parametrized by its Reflection Coefficients K_m. An Nth order all pole lattice structure for an IIR filter is shown in Fig. 4.15.

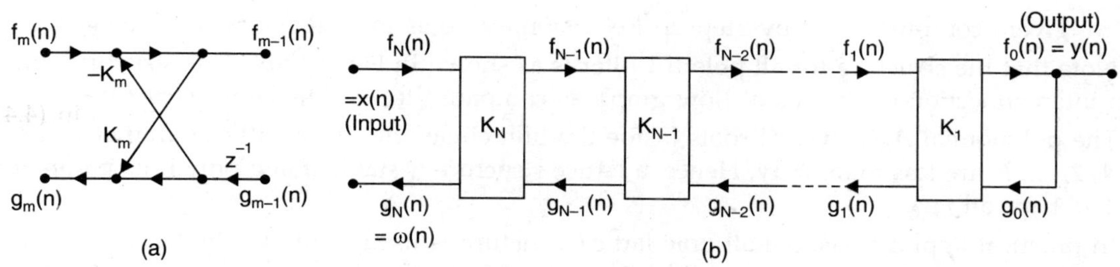

Fig. 4.15. An Nth order All pole Lattice Filter for an IIR filter, (*a*) Two-port Network for the mth stage of the All pole Lattice Filter (*b*) Cascaded N Lattice Stages of All pole Lattice Filter

Note that the signal flow directions are opposite in the top and the bottom signal flow lines. Also, the signs of K_m are opposite in two arms of the butterfly in Fig. 4.15(*a*). The two inputs $f_m(n)$ and $g_{m-1}(n)$ are related to two-outputs $f_{m-1}(n)$ and $g_m(n)$ of coupled difference equations. Various results holding true for all pole IIR lattice are given in (4.46).

The equations given by (4.46) can be readily seen to be the same as given by (*a*) and (*b*) of (4.38).

$$\left.\begin{aligned}
&(a)\ f_{m-1}(n) = f_m(n) - K_m g_{m-1}(n-1),\ m = N, N-1, \ldots, 1\\
&(b)\ g_m(n) = K_m f_{m-1}(n) + g_{m-1}(n-1),\ m = N, N-1, \ldots, 1\\
&(c)\ f_N(n) = x(n)\\
&(d)\ y(n) = f_0(n) = g_0(n)
\end{aligned}\right] \quad \text{...(4.46)}$$

To polynomial $A_N(z)$ is of order N, and can be generated by the recursion as follows:

$A_m(z) = A_{m-1}(z) + K_m z^{-m} A_{m-1}(z^{-1}),\ m = 1, 2, \ldots, N$
Start recursion by taking $A_0(z) = 1$
Step-up Recursion (to find $a_N(i)$, given K_i)

...(4.47)

System function relating the input $x(n)$ to the output $\omega(n)$, where $\omega(n) = g_N(n)$ is an all pass filter [Fig. 4.15(*b*)]

$$\therefore \quad \frac{W(z)}{X(z)} = \frac{z^{-N} A_N(z^{-1})}{A_N(z)} = H_{\text{all pass}}(z) \qquad \ldots(4.48)$$

Note that the system function of the Lattice structure, Fig. 4.15(*b*) is

$$\frac{F_0(z)}{X(z)} = \frac{1}{A_N(z)} \qquad \ldots(4.49)$$

It may be noted that the all zero (FIR system) and all pole lattice structure (for IIR system) are characterized by the same set of lattice parameters, namely, $K_1, K_2, \ldots, K_n$. Given $A_N(z)$ polynomial for all pole lattice filter: $H(z) = \dfrac{1}{A_N(z)}$, we proceed as follows, to determine $\{K_i\}$; and to obtain $H(z)$ from its lattice parameters $\{K_i\}$:

(*a*) Find reflection coefficients $K_1, K_2, \ldots, K_N$ by Step-down Recursion, same as for FIR filters case, see (4.39).

(*b*) Given a lattice structure for all pole system function $H(z) = \dfrac{1}{A_N(z)}$, *i.e.* $K_1, K_2, \ldots, K_N$ given, compute $A_N(z)$ by Step-up Recursion, same as for FIR filters case, see (4.47).

Note that the structure for all pole IIR filter is as shown in Fig. 4.15(*b*). This structure differs from interconnection of the signal flow graph as compared to the FIR lattice structure.

The polynomial $A_N(z)$ has its roots inside the unit circle only if the lattice parameters $|K_m|$, $m = 1, 2, \ldots, N$ are less than unity. Hence, a lattice structure is stable if and only if its parameters $|K_m| < 1$ for all m.

In practical applications, the all pole lattice structure is used to model the *human vocal tract* and *a stratified Earth* (*i.e.* earthquake-prone Earth). In such cases, the lattice parameters $\{K_m\}$ have the physical significance of being identical to the reflection coefficients in the physical media. This is precisely the reason that the lattice parameters $\{K_m\}$ are called the *reflection coefficients.* In such applications, a stable model of the concerned media requires that the reflection coefficients, obtained during the measurement on output signals from the medium be less than unity.

EXAMPLE 4.9: *Draw a lattice filter implementation for the all pole filter*

$$H(z) = \frac{1}{1 - 0.2z^{-1} + 0.4z^{-2} + 0.6z^{-3}},$$

and determine the number of multiplications, additions and delays required to implement the filter. Compare this structure to a direct realization of H(z) in terms of the number of multiplications, adders and delays.

SOLUTION: We first find the reflection coefficients K_3, K_2 and K_1 corresponding to the polynomial, by step-down recursion.

$$A_3(z) = 1 - 0.2z^{-1} + 0.4z^{-2} + 0.6z^{-3},\ a_3(3) = K_3 \qquad \boxed{\therefore\ K_3 = 0.6}$$

$$A_2(z) = \frac{1}{1 - K_3^2}[A_3(z) - K_3 z^{-3} A_3(z^{-1})]$$

$$= \underbrace{\frac{1}{1 - 0.6^2}}_{=0.64}[(1 - 0.2z^{-1} + 0.4z^{-2} + 0.6z^{-3}) - 0.6(0.6 + 0.4z^{-1} - 0.2z^{-2} + z^{-3})]$$

$$= 1 - 0.6875z^{-1} + 0.8125z^{-2},\ a_2(2) = K_2 \qquad \boxed{\therefore\ K_2 = 0.8125}$$

$$A_1(z) = \underbrace{\frac{1}{1-(0.8125)^2}}_{=0.3398} [1 - 0.6875z^{-1} + 0.8125z^{-2} - 0.8125\,(0.8125 - 0.6875z^{-1} + z^{-2})]$$

$$= 1 - 0.3793z^{-1},\ a_1(1) = K_1 \qquad \therefore \quad K_1 = -0.3793$$

The lattice structure is shown in Fig. Ex. 4.9

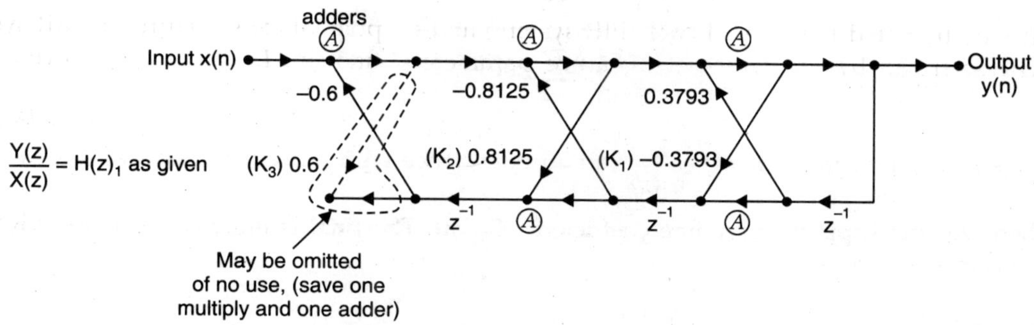

Fig. Ex. 4.9. Realization of $H(z)$

The lattice structure has 3 delays, 5 multiplications, and 5 additions (shown Ⓐ) to evaluate the output $y(n)$. A direct-form structure would require 3 delays, 3 multiplications and 3 additions. In general, the number of delays remains the same in lattice structure as in a canonic structure.

EXAMPLE 4.10: *An all pole IIR filter has reflection coefficients $K_1 = -0.3793$, $K_2 = 0.8125$, $K_3 = 0.6$. Determine the expression for H(z). (This example is reverse of Example 4.9).*

SOLUTION: We use Step-up Recursion

$$K_1 = -0.3739,\ K_2 = 0.8125,\ K_3 = 0.6$$

As

$$A_m(z) = A_{m-1}(z) + K_m z^{-m} A_{m-1}(z^{-1}),\ m = 1, 2, \ldots, N \qquad \text{[from (4.47)]}$$

$$A_0(z) = 1$$

$\therefore$

$$A_1(z) = A_0(z) + K_1 z^{-1} A_0(z^{-1})$$

$$= 1 + (-0.3739)z^{-1}(1) = 1 - 0.3739z^{-1}$$

$$A_2(z) = A_1(z) + K_2 z^{-2} A_1(z^{-1})$$

$$= (1 - 0.3793z^{-1}) + (0.8125)z^{-2} \cdot (1 - 0.3793z)$$

$$= (1 - 0.3793z^{-1}) + (0.8125z^{-2} - 0.3082z^{-1})$$

$$= 1 - 0.6875z^{-1} + 0.8125z^{-2}$$

$$A_3(z) = A_2(z) + K_3 z^{-3} A_2(z^{-1})$$

$$= (1 - 0.6875z^{-1} + 0.8125z^{-2}) + 0.6(0.8125z^{-1} - 0.6875z^{-2} + z^{-3})$$

$$= (1 - 0.6875z^{-1} + 0.8125z^{-2}) + (0.4875z^{-1} - 0.4125z^{-2} + 0.6z^{-3})$$

$$= 1 + z^{-1}(1 - 0.6875 + 0.4875) + z^{-2}(0.8125 - 0.4125) + 0.6z^{-3}$$

$$= 1 - 0.2z^{-1} + 0.4z^{-2} + 0.6z^{-3}$$

Hence,

$$H(z) = \frac{1}{A_N(z)} = \frac{1}{1 - 0.2z^{-1} + 0.4z^{-2} + 0.6z^{-3}} \qquad \textbf{Ans.}$$

4.9.3 Lattice-Ladder Structure for IIR Filters (Having Zeros and Poles)

The all pole lattice structure covered in Section 4.9.2 provides the building block for lattice-type structures that implement IIR systems having zeros and poles. Consider the IIR system with system function

$$H(z) = \frac{1+\sum_{i=1}^{M} b_M(i)z^{-i}}{1+\sum_{i=1}^{N} a_N(i)z^{-i}} \triangleq \frac{B_M(z)}{A_N(z)} \qquad \ldots(4.50)$$

with $M \le N$. We first implement $\frac{1}{A_N(z)}$, an all pole lattice with reflection coefficients $K_1, K_2, \ldots, K_N$. Then we add Tapped Delay line coefficients $C_M(m)$. The final realization assumes the form as shown in Fig. 4.16.

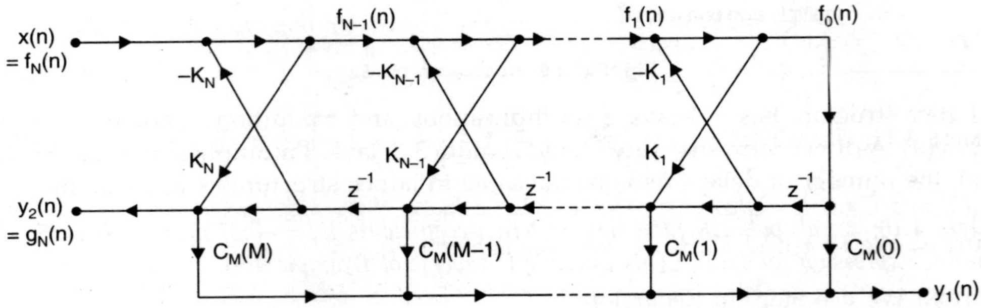

Fig. 4.16. An IIR Lattice Filter will *N* zeros and *N* poles

$$H(z) = \frac{Y_1(z)}{X(z)}, \ \frac{Y_2(z)}{X(z)} = \frac{z^{-N}A_N(z^{-1})}{A_N(z)} \text{ an all pass filter.}$$

The following procedure is followed to convert an IIR filter to an equivalent lattice-ladder structure and vice versa.

(*a*) Given

$$H(z) = \frac{1+\sum_{i=1}^{M} b_M(i)z^{-i}}{1+\sum_{i=1}^{N} a_N(i)z^{-i}} = \frac{B_M(z)}{A_N(z)} \qquad \ldots(4.51)$$

To find lattice coefficients (use *Step-down Recursion* for finding K_m)

$$\begin{cases} A_{m-1}(z) = \dfrac{A_m(z) - K_m z^{-m} A_m(z^{-1})}{1-K_m^2}, m = N, N-1, \ldots, 1 \\ K_m = a_m(m), \ m = 1, 2, \ldots, N \end{cases} \qquad \ldots(4.52a)$$

$$\begin{cases} C_M(k) = b_M(k) - \sum_{j=k+1}^{M} C_M(j)a_j(j-k), k = M-1, M-2, \ldots, 0 \\ C_M(M) = b_M(M) \end{cases} \qquad \ldots(4.52b)$$

(*b*) Given K_m, and $C_M(k)$, to find $A_N(z)$ and $B_M(z)$ *i.e.* $H(z) = \dfrac{B_M(z)}{A_N(z)}$ (use *Step-up Recursion* to find $A_N(z)$)

$$\begin{cases} A_m(z) = A_{m-1}(z) + K_m z^{-m} A_{m-1}(z^{-1}),\ m = 1, 2, \ldots, N \\ \text{start recursion by taking } A_0(z) = 1 \end{cases} \quad \ldots(4.53a)$$

$$\begin{cases} b_M(k) = \sum\limits_{j=k}^{M} C_M(j) a_j(j-k),\ k = M-1, M-2, \ldots, 0 \\ b_M(M) = C_M(M) \\ \text{assume } a_0(0) = 1 \end{cases} \quad \ldots(4.53b)$$

Note that: Above results refer to Fig. 4.16, where

$$\frac{Y_1(z)}{X(z)} = H(z);\ \frac{Y_2(z)}{X(z)} = \frac{z^{-N} A_N(z^{-1})}{A_N(z)} \text{ (an all pass filter)} \quad \ldots(4.53c)$$

EXAMPLE 4.11: *Given* $H(z) = \dfrac{1 + 2z^{-1} + 2z^{-2} + z^{-3}}{1 - 0.8z^{-1} + 0.49z^{-2} - 0.57z^{-3}}$. *Find the parameters* K_1, K_2, K_3, $C_3(0)$, $C_3(1)$, $C_3(2)$ *and* $C_3(3)$ *to realize this filter as a lattice-ladder structure.*

SOLUTION: We first find K_3, K_2, K_1 by *Step-down Recursion*

$$A_3(z) = 1 - 0.8z^{-1} + 0.49z^{-2} - 0.57z^{-3},\ a_3(3) = K_3 \qquad \boxed{\therefore\ K_3 = -0.57}$$

$$A_2(z) = \frac{1}{1 - K_3^2}(A_3(z) - K_3 z^{-3} A_3(z^{-1}))$$

$$= \underbrace{\frac{1}{1 - (-0.57)^2}}_{= 0.6751}[(1 - 0.8z^{-1} + 0.49z^{-2} - 0.57z^{-3}) - (-0.57)(-0.57 + 0.49z^{-1} - 0.8z^{-2} + z^{-3})]$$

$$\therefore \quad A_2(z) = 1 - 0.77z^{-1} + 0.05z^{-2},\ a_2(2) = K_2 \qquad \boxed{\therefore\ K_2 = 0.05}$$

$$A_1(z) = \frac{1}{1 - K_2^2}(A_2(z) - K_2 z^{-2} A_2(z^{-1}))$$

$$= \underbrace{\frac{1}{1 - (0.05)^2}}_{= 0.9975}[(1 - 0.77z^{-1} + 0.05z^{-2}) - (0.05)(0.05 - 0.77z^{-1} + z^{-2})]$$

$$\therefore \quad A_1(z) = 1 - 0.733z^{-1},\ a_1(1) = K_1 \qquad \boxed{\therefore\ K_1 = -0.733}$$

[To find $C_3(i)$], $i = 3, 2, 1, 0$

Given $\quad b_3(0) = 1,\ b_3(1) = 2,\ b_3(2) = 2,\ b_3(3) = 1$

$\quad a_3(0) = 1,\ a_3(1) = -0.8,\ a_3(2) = 0.49,\ a_3(3) = -0.57$

Take $\quad C_3(3) = b_3(3) = 1 \qquad \boxed{\therefore\ C_3(3) = 1}$

$$C_3(k) = b_3(k) - \sum_{j=k+1}^{3} C_3(j)a_j(j-k), \text{ putting } k = 2, \text{ we have}$$

$$\therefore \quad C_3(2) = b_3(2) - [C_3(3) \cdot a_3(1)]$$
$$= 2 - (1)(-0.8) = 2.8 \qquad \boxed{\therefore \; C_3(2) = 2.8}$$

$$C_3(1) = b_3(1) - \sum_{j=1+1}^{3} C_3(j)a_j(j-k), \text{ with } k = 1$$
$$= b_3(1) - [C_3(2) \cdot a_2(1) + C_3(3) \cdot a_3(2)]$$
$$= 2 - [(2.8)(-0.77) + (1)(0.49)]$$
$$= 3.666 \qquad \boxed{\therefore \; C_3(1) = 3.666}$$

$$C_3(0) = b_3(0) - \sum_{j=0+1}^{3} C_3(j)a_j(j-k), \text{ with } k = 0$$
$$= b_3(0) - [C_3(1)a_1(1) + C_3(2)a_2(2) + C_3(3)a_3(3)]$$
$$= 1 - [(3.666)(-0.733) + (2.8)(0.05) + (1)(-0.57)]$$
$$= 4.11 \qquad \boxed{\therefore \; C_3(0) = 4.11}$$

The lattice-ladder structure is as shown below:

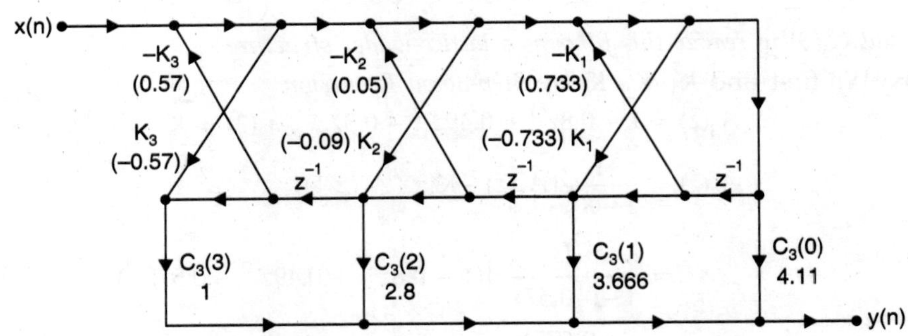

$$\frac{Y(z)}{X(z)} = H(z)$$

Fig. Ex. 4.11. Realization of the Lattice-ladder structure for the given $H(z)$

EXAMPLE 4.12: *Find the system function for the lattice filter shown below.*

SOLUTION:

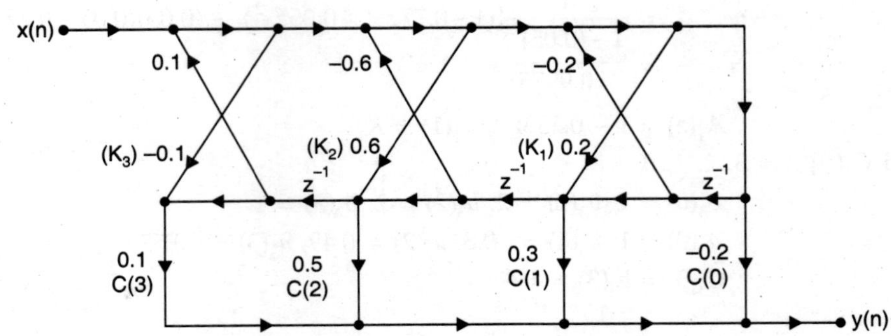

Fig. Ex. 4.12. The given Lattice structure

Given $K_1 = 0.2,\ K_2 = 0.6,\ K_3 = -0.1$

$C_3(0) = -0.2,\ C_3(1) = 0.3,\ C_3(2) = 0.5,\ C_3(3) = 0.1$

Let $H(z) = \frac{B_3(z)}{A_3(z)}$, here $M = N = 3$

We find $A_3(z)$ by using Step-up Recursion

$$A_0(z) = 1$$

$\therefore$ $A_1(z) = A_0(z) + K_1 z^{-1} A_0(z^{-1})$ [using $A_m(z) = A_{m-1}(z) + K_m z^{-m} A_{m-1}(z^{-1})$ *i.e.* (4.53*a*)

$\therefore$ $A_1(z) = 1 + 0.2z^{-1}(1) = 1 + 0.2z^{-1}$

$$A_2(z) = A_1(z) + K_2 z^{-2} A_1(z^{-1})$$
$$= (1 + 0.2z^{-1}) + (0.6)z^{-2}(1 + 0.2z)$$

$\therefore$ $A_2(z) = 1 + 0.32z^{-1} + 0.6z^{-2}$

$$A_3(z) = A_2(z) + K_3 z^{-3} A_2(z^{-1})$$
$$= (1 + 0.32z^{-1} + 0.6z^{-2}) + (-0.1)z^{-3}(1 + 0.32z + 0.6z^2)$$

$\therefore$ $A_3(z) = 1 + 0.26z^{-1} + 0.568z^{-2} - 0.1z^{-3}$

[To find the numerator $B_3(z)$ *i.e.* to compute $b_3(z)$, $b_3(2)$, $b_3(1)$ and $b_3(0)$].

We know that

$$\boxed{b_M(k) = \sum_{j=k}^{M} C_M a_j(j-k),\ k = M, M-1, \ldots, 0} \quad \text{from (4.53}b\text{)}$$

$\therefore$ $b_3(3) = \sum_{j=3}^{3} C_3 a_j(j-k)$ with $M = 3$ and $k = 3$

$$= C_3(3)a_3(0)$$
$$= (0.1)(1) = 0.1 \text{ (or directly } b_M(M) = C_M(M)) \qquad \boxed{\therefore\ b_3(3) = 0.1}$$

$$b_3(2) = \sum_{j=2}^{3} C_3(j)a_j(j-2)$$
$$= C_3(2)a_2(0) + C_3(3)a_3(1)$$
$$= (0.5)(1) + (0.1)(0.26) = 0.526 \qquad \boxed{\therefore\ b_3(2) = 0.526}$$

$$b_3(1) = \sum_{j=1}^{3} C_3(j)a_j(j-1)$$
$$= C_3(1)a_1(0) + C_3(2)a_2(1) + C_3(3)a_3(2)$$
$$= (0.3)(1) + (0.5)(0.32) + (0.1)(0.568)$$
$$= 0.3 + 0.16 + 0.0568 = 0.5168 \qquad \boxed{\therefore\ b_3(1) = 0.5168}$$

$$b_3(0) = \sum_{j=0}^{3} C_3(j)a_j(j-0)$$
$$= C_3(0)a_0(0) + C_3(1)a_1(1) + C_3(2)a_2(2) + C_3(3)a_3(3)$$
$$= (-0.2)(1) + (0.3)(0.2) + (0.5)(0.6) + (0.1)(-0.1)$$
$$= -0.2 + 0.06 + 0.3 - 0.01$$
$$= 0.15 \qquad \boxed{\therefore\ b_3(0) = 0.15}$$

Thus, $$H(z) = \frac{b_3(0) + b_3(1)z^{-1} + b_3(2)z^{-2} + b_3(3)z^{-3}}{a_3(0) + a_3(1)z^{-1} + a_3(2)z^{-2} + a_3(3)z^{-3}}$$

$$= \frac{0.15 + 0.5168z^{-1} + 0.526z^{-2} + 0.1z^{-3}}{1 + 0.26z^{-1} + 0.568z^{-2} - 0.1z^{-3}}$$ **Ans.**

Additional Solved Examples on Lattice Structures

EXAMPLE 4.13: *For the second-order FIR lattice filter with reflection coefficients $K_1 = \frac{1}{2}, K_2 = \frac{1}{4}$, find the FIR system. (Lattice FIR to normal FIR)*

SOLUTION: Given

$$K_1 = \frac{1}{2},\ K_2 = \frac{1}{4}$$

As $$A_m(z) = A_{m-1}(z) + K_m z^{-m} A_{m-1}(z^{-1})$$

and $$A_0(z) = 1 \quad \text{(initialize)}$$ } Step-up Recursion

∴ $$A_1(z) = A_0(z) + K_1 z^{-1} A_0(z^{-1})$$

$$= 1 + \frac{1}{2} \times z^{-1} \times 1$$

$$= 1 + \frac{1}{2} z^{-1} \qquad (\because\ A_0(z) = 1,\ \therefore\ A_0(z^{-1}) = 1)$$

Again $$A_2(z) = A_1(z) + K_2 z^{-2} A_1(z^{-1})$$

$$= \left(1 + \frac{1}{2}z^{-1}\right) + \frac{1}{4}z^{-2}\left(1 + \frac{1}{2}z\right) \qquad \left(\because\ A_1(z^{-1}) = A_1(z)|_{z \text{ to } z^{-1}} = 1 + \frac{1}{2}z\right)$$

$$= 1 + \frac{1}{2}z^{-1} + \frac{1}{4}z^{-2} + \frac{1}{8}z^{-1}$$

Hence, $$A_2(z) = 1 + \frac{5}{8}z^{-1} + \frac{1}{4}z^{-2}$$

Thus, $$A_2(z) = \sum_{i=0}^{2} a_2(i) z^{-i}$$

here $$a_2(0) = 1,\ a_2(1) = \frac{5}{8},\ a_2(2) = \frac{1}{4}$$ **Ans.**

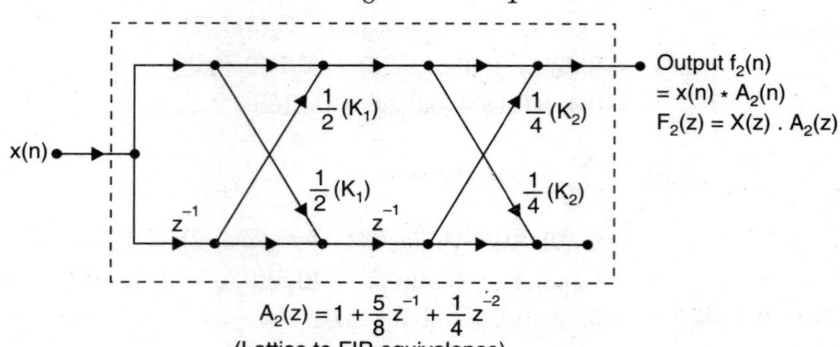

Fig. Ex. 4.13. The realization of Lattice structure (given) and its equivalent FIR system $A_2(z)$

EXAMPLE 4.14: *Obtain a lattice filter implementation of the FIR filters*

(a) $\tilde{H}_1(z) = 8 + 4z^{-1} + 2z^{-2} + z^{-3}$

(b) $\tilde{H}_2(z) = 6 + 3z^{-1} + 1.5z^{-2} + 0.75z^{-3}$.

SOLUTION:

(*a*) It is necessary to normalize $H(z)$ so that the first coefficient is unity.

$$\therefore \quad \tilde{H}(z) = (8)\left[1+\frac{1}{2}z^{-1}+\frac{1}{4}z^{-2}+\frac{1}{8}z^{-3}\right] \triangleq (8)\, H_3(z) \qquad \text{(Note this step)}$$

$$\therefore \quad H_3(z) = 1+\frac{1}{2}z^{-1}+\frac{1}{4}z^{-2}+\frac{1}{8}z^{-3},\ K_3 = a_3(3) \qquad \boxed{\therefore\ K_3 = \frac{1}{8} = 0.125}$$

We use Step-down Recursion to get lattice structure.

$$H_2(z) = \frac{1}{1-K_3^2}[H_3(z) - K_3 z^{-3} H_3(z^{-1})]$$

$$= \underbrace{\frac{1}{1-\left(\frac{1}{8}\right)^2}}_{=0.9844}\left[\left(1+\frac{1}{2}z^{-1}+\frac{1}{4}z^{-2}+\frac{1}{8}z^{-3}\right)-\frac{1}{8}\left(\frac{1}{8}+\frac{1}{4}z^{-1}+\frac{1}{2}z^{-2}+z^{-3}\right)\right]$$

$$\therefore \quad H_2(z) = 1 + 0.4762z^{-1} + 0.1905z^{-2},\ K_2 = a_2(2) \qquad \boxed{\therefore\ K_2 = 0.1905}$$

$$H_1(z) = \frac{1}{1-K_2^2}[H_2(z) - K_2 z^{-2} H_2(z^{-1})]$$

$$= \underbrace{\frac{1}{1-(0.1905)^2}}_{=0.9637}[(1 + 0.4762z^{-1} + 0.1905z^{-2}) - 0.1905(0.1905 + 0.4762z^{-1} + z^{-2})]$$

$$\therefore \quad H_1(z) = 1 + 0.4z^{-1},\ K_1 = a_1(1) \qquad \boxed{\therefore\ K_1 = 0.4}$$

The lattice structure is as shown in the Fig. Ex. 4.14(*a*)

$$\frac{Y(z)}{X(z)} = H(z), \text{ as given}$$

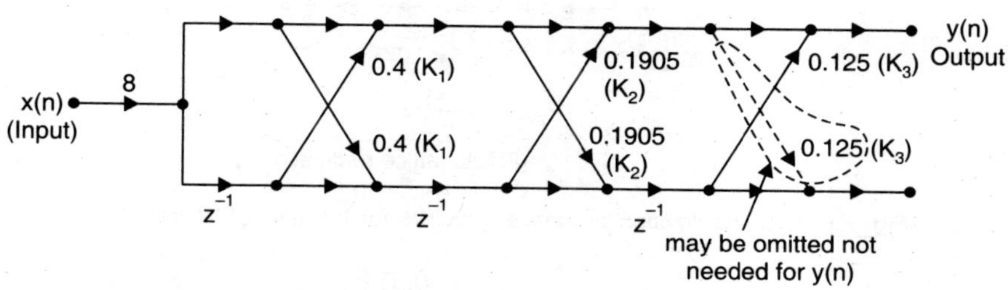

Fig. Ex. 4.14. (*a*) Realization

(*b*) As $\tilde{H}_2(z) = 6 + 3z^{-1} + 1.5z^{-2} + 0.75z^{-3} = 6\left(1+\frac{1}{2}z^{-1}+\frac{1}{4}z^{-4}+\frac{1}{8}z^{-3}\right) = (6)\,H_3(z)$

$\therefore$ Replace multiplier 8 by 6 in the above realization to obtain $\tilde{H}_2(z)$.

EXAMPLE 4.15: *Find the reflection coefficients corresponding to the second order FIR filter given by* $A_2(z) = 1-\frac{1}{2}z^{-2}$ *(Normal FIR to FIR lattice).*

SOLUTION:

$$A_2(z) = 1-\frac{1}{2}z^{-2} \equiv \underset{\nearrow=1}{a_2(0)} + \underset{\nearrow=0}{a_2(1)}z^{-1} + \underset{\nearrow=-\frac{1}{2}}{a_2(2)}z^{-2} \qquad \text{("Normal FIR" form)}$$

$\therefore$
$$K_2 = a_2(2) = -\frac{1}{2} \qquad \boxed{K_2 = -\frac{1}{2}}$$

As
$$A_{m-1}(z) = \frac{A_m(z) - K_m z^{-m} A_m(z^{-1})}{1-K_m^2} \qquad \text{(Step-down Recursion)}$$

$\therefore$
$$A_1(z) = \frac{\left(1-\frac{1}{2}z^{-2}\right)-\left(-\frac{1}{2}\right)z^{-2}\left(1-\frac{1}{2}z^{+2}\right)}{1-\left(-\frac{1}{2}\right)^2}$$

$$= \frac{4}{3}\left[\left(1-\frac{1}{2}z^{-2}\right)+\frac{1}{2}z^{-2}\left(1-\frac{1}{2}z^{2}\right)\right]$$

$$= \frac{4}{3}\left[1-\frac{1}{2}z^{-2}+\frac{1}{2}z^{-2}-\frac{1}{4}\right] = 1$$

$\therefore$
$$a_1(1) = 0 \quad \therefore \quad K_1 = 0 \qquad \boxed{\therefore \quad K_1 = 0}$$

Hence,
$$K_1 = 0,\ K_2 = -\frac{1}{2} \quad \textbf{Ans.}$$

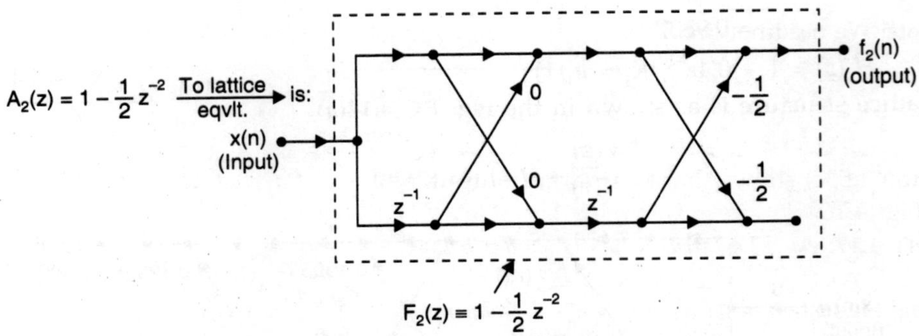

(FIR to lattice realization)

Fig. Ex. 4.15. Realization of Lattice structure for the given FIR filter $A_2(z)$

EXAMPLE 4.16: *Realize the all pass filter* $H_{ap}(z) = \dfrac{-0.512+0.64z^{-1}-0.8z^{-2}+z^{-3}}{1-0.8z^{-1}+0.64z^{-2}-0.512z^{-3}}$ *using lattice structure.*

SOLUTION: We use Step-down Recursion to find the reflection coefficients K_3, K_2, K_1.

As
$$A_3(z) = 1 - 0.8z^{-1} + 0.64z^{-2} - 0.512z^{-3},\ K_3 = a_3(3) \qquad \boxed{\therefore \quad K_3 = -0.512}$$

$$A_2(z) = \frac{1}{1-K_3^2}(A_3(z) - K_3 z^{-3} A_3(z^{-1}))$$

$$= \underbrace{\frac{1}{1-(-0.512)^2}}_{=0.7378}[1 - 0.8z^{-1} + 0.64z^{-2} - 0.512z^{-3}$$

$$- (-0.512)(-0.512 + 0.64z^{-1} - 0.8z^{-2} + z^{-3})]$$

$\therefore$
$$A_2(z) = 1 - 0.640z^{-1} + 0.3132z^{-2},\ K_2 = a_2(2) \qquad \boxed{\therefore\ K_2 = 0.3132}$$

$$A_1(z) = \frac{1}{1-K_2^2}(A_2(z) - K_2 z^{-2} A_2(z^{-1}))$$

$$= \underbrace{\frac{1}{1-(0.3132)^2}}_{=0.9025}[1 - 0.640z^{-1} + 0.3123z^{-2}$$

$$- (0.3123)(0.3123 - 0.640z^{-1} + z^{-2})]$$

$\therefore$
$$A_1(z) = 1 - 0.4877z^{-1},\ K_1 = a_1(1) \qquad \boxed{\therefore\ K_1 = -0.4877}$$

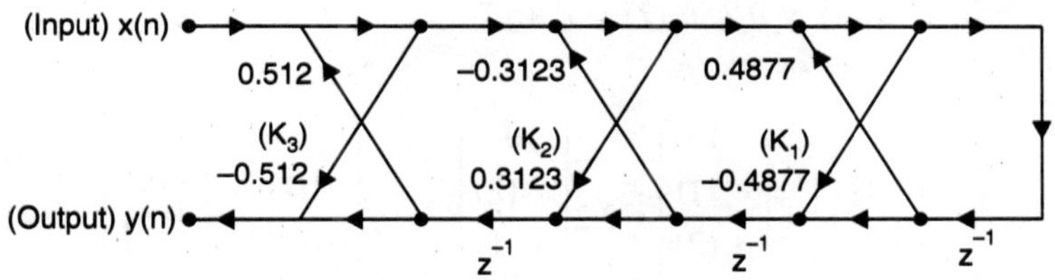

Fig. Ex. 4.16. Lattice implementation of all pass filter

Note: We need not find $C_3(0)$, $C_3(1)$, $C_3(2)$, $C_3(3)$, as

$$\boxed{\frac{Y(z)}{X(z)} = H_{ap}(z) = \frac{z^{-N}A_N(z^{-1})}{A_N(z)}}$$

Equation 4.53c) shows that the ratio of output $Y_2(z)$ to $X(z)$ is an all pass filter. Here $Y_2(z) = Y(z)$. See Fig. 4.16.

EXAMPLE 4.17: *An FIR lattice filter is shown below:*

(a) Find the system function $A(z) = \dfrac{F(z)}{X(z)}$ *relating the input x(n) to the output f(n). Does this system have minimum phase?*

(b) Repeat part (a) for the system function relating x(n) to g(n).

SOLUTION:

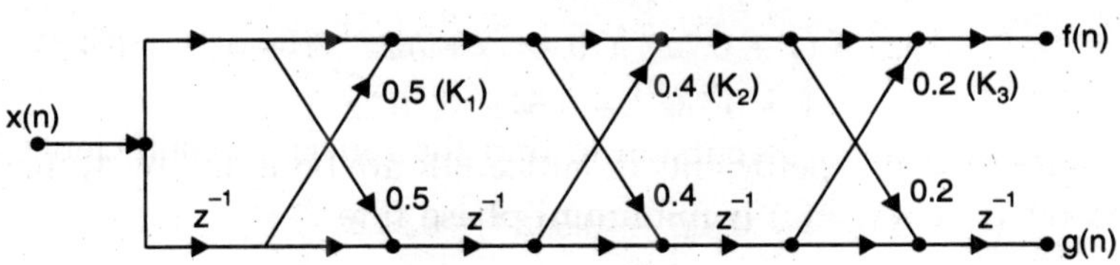

Fig. Ex. 4.17. The given filter

We use vector formula in lieu of step-up recursion.

(*a*) Clearly $K_1 = 0.5$, $K_2 = 0.4$, and $K_3 = 0.2$.

By using step-up recursion, we can find $A(z) = \sum_{i=1}^{3} a_3(i)z^{-i}$.

As
$$\begin{bmatrix} 1 \\ a_m(1) \\ a_m(2) \\ \vdots \\ a_m(m-1) \\ a_m(m) \end{bmatrix} = \begin{bmatrix} 1 \\ a_{m-1}(1) \\ a_{m-1}(2) \\ \vdots \\ a_{m-1}(m-1) \\ 0 \end{bmatrix} + K_m \begin{bmatrix} 1 \\ a_{m-1}(m-1) \\ a_{m-1}(m-2) \\ \vdots \\ a_{m-1}(1) \\ 0 \end{bmatrix}$$
and also $a_m(m) = K_m$, $m = 1, 2, \ldots,$. The vector formula used here is derived from formula (4.41).

$$\therefore \quad a_1(1) = K_1 = 0.5,\ A_0(z) = 1 \qquad \therefore \quad A_1(z) = 1 + 0.5z^{-1}$$

$$\begin{bmatrix} 1 \\ a_2(1) \\ a_2(2) \end{bmatrix} = \begin{bmatrix} 1 \\ a_1(1) \\ 0 \end{bmatrix} + K_2 \begin{bmatrix} 0 \\ a_1(1) \\ 1 \end{bmatrix} \quad \therefore \quad \begin{bmatrix} 1 \\ a_2(1) \\ a_2(2) \end{bmatrix} = \begin{bmatrix} 1 \\ 0.5 \\ 0 \end{bmatrix} + 0.4 \begin{bmatrix} 0 \\ 0.5 \\ 1 \end{bmatrix} = \begin{bmatrix} 1 \\ 0.7 \\ 0.4 \end{bmatrix}$$

$$\therefore \quad a_1(1) = 0.7,\ a_2(2) = 0.4.$$

Finally, with $K_3 = 0.2$, we have

$$\begin{bmatrix} 1 \\ a_3(1) \\ a_3(2) \\ a_3(3) \end{bmatrix} = \begin{bmatrix} 1 \\ a_2(1) \\ a_2(2) \\ 0 \end{bmatrix} + 0.2 \begin{bmatrix} 0 \\ a_2(2) \\ a_2(1) \\ 1 \end{bmatrix} \quad \therefore \quad \begin{bmatrix} 1 \\ a_3(1) \\ a_3(2) \\ a_3(3) \end{bmatrix} = \begin{bmatrix} 1 \\ 0.7 \\ 0.4 \\ 0 \end{bmatrix} + 0.2 \begin{bmatrix} 0 \\ 0.4 \\ 0.7 \\ 1 \end{bmatrix} = \begin{bmatrix} 1 \\ 0.78 \\ 0.54 \\ 0.2 \end{bmatrix}$$

$$\therefore \quad A(z) = 1 + 0.78z^{-1} + 0.54z^{-2} + 0.2z^{-3}$$ **Ans.**

[Alternative approach to find $A_3(z)$]

We know that

$$A_m(z) = A_{m-1}(z) + K_m z^{-m} A_{m-1}(z^{-1}) \text{ (Step-up Recursion)}$$

and
$$A_0(z) = 1 \text{ (Initialize, taking } A_0(z) = 1)$$

Given: $K_1 = 0.5$, $K_2 = 0.4$ and $K_3 = 0.2$ and $A_0(z) = 1$, we have

$$A_1(z) = A_0(z) + K_1 \cdot z^{-1} A_0(z^{-1})$$
$$= 1 + 0.5z^{-1} \qquad \because \ A_0(z) = A_0(z^{-1}) = 1$$
$$A_2(z) = A_1(z) + K_2 z^{-2} A_1(z^{-1})$$
$$= (1 + 0.5z^{-1}) + 0.4z^{-2}(1 + 0.5z)$$
$$= 1 + 0.7z^{-1} + 0.4z^{-2}$$
$$A_3(z) = A_2(z) + K_3 z^{-3} A_2(z^{-1})$$
$$\therefore \quad A_3(z) = (1 + 0.7z^{-1} + 0.4z^{-2}) + 0.2z^{-3}(1 + 0.7z + 0.4z^2)$$
$$= 1 + 0.78z^{-1} + 0.54z^{-2} + 0.2z^{-3}$$ **Ans.**

As K_1, K_2, K_3 the reflection coefficients of lattice FIR are bounded by 1, therefore, all zeros of $A(z)$ are bounded by 1, hence, $A(z)$ is minimum phase filter.

(*b*) The system function $A'(z) = \dfrac{G(z)}{X(z)}$ is related to $X(z)$ as

$$A'(z) = z^{-3} \cdot A(z^{-1}), \text{ since } \boxed{\frac{F(z)}{X(z)} = A_N(z) \text{ and } \frac{G(z)}{X(z)} = z^{-N}A_N(z^{-1})}$$

$$\therefore \quad A'(z) = z^{-3}(1 + 0.78z + 0.54z^2 + 0.2z^{+3})$$
$$= 0.2 + 0.54z^{-1} + 0.78z^{-2} + z^{-3}$$

As zeros of $A'(z)$ are formed by flipping the zeros of $A(z)$ about the unit circle, hence all zeros of $A'(z)$ are outside the unit circle. Hence, $A'(z)$ is maximum phase FIR filter.

EXAMPLE 4.18: *A third order low-pass IIR filter with cut off frequency, $\omega_c = 0.5\pi$ has a system function. Implement this filter using Lattice structure.*

SOLUTION:

$$H(z) = \frac{0.2759 + 0.5121z^{-1} + \overset{\swarrow b_3(2)}{0.5121z^{-2}} + \overset{\swarrow b_3(3)}{0.2759z^{-3}}}{1 - 0.0010z^{-1} + 0.6546z^{-2} - 0.0775z^{-3}}$$

$$\therefore \quad a_3(1) = -0.0010,\ a_3(2) = 0.6546,\ a_3(3) = -0.0775;$$
$$b_3(0) = 0.2759,\ b_3(1) = 0.5121,\ b_3(2) = 0.5121,\ b_3(3) = 0.2759$$

Here, $A_3(z) = 1 - 0.0010z^{-1} + 0.6546z^{-2} - 0.0775z^{-3}$

$$\therefore \quad K_3 = a_3(3) = -0.0775 \qquad \boxed{K_3 = -0.0775}$$

$$A_2(z) = \frac{A_3(z) - K_3z^{-3}A_3(z^{-1})}{1 - K_3^2} \quad \text{(Step-down Recursion)}$$

$$= \frac{(1 - 0.0010z^{-1} + 0.6546z^{-2} - 0.0775z^{-3}) - (-0.0755)(-0.0755 + 0.6546z^{-1} - 0.001z^{-2} + z^{-3})}{\underbrace{(1 - (-0.0775)^2)}_{0.99399}}$$

$$\therefore \quad A_2(z) = 1 + \underset{\nearrow a_2(1)}{0.0497z^{-1}} + \underset{\nearrow a_2(2)}{0.6536z^{-2}} \qquad \boxed{K_2 = 0.6536}$$

$$A_1(z) = \frac{(1 + 0.0497z^{-1} + 0.6536z^{-2}) - (0.6536)(0.6536 + 0.0497z^{-1} + z^{-3})}{\underbrace{(1 - (0.6536)^2)}_{0.5728}}$$

$$\therefore \quad A_1(z) = 1 + \underset{\nearrow a_1(1)}{0.301z^{-1}} \qquad \boxed{K_1 = 0.301}$$

[To find coefficients $C_3(k)$]

As $C_M(k) = b_M(k) - \sum_{j=k+1}^{M} C_M(j)a_j(j-k),\ k = M-1, M-2, \ldots, 0$ and $C_M(M) = b_M(M)$ from [4.52(*b*)]

$$\therefore \quad C_3(3) = b_3(3) = 0.2759$$

$$C_3(2) = b_3(2) - \sum_{j=3}^{3} C_3(j)a_j(j-2)$$
$$= b_3(2) - C_3(3)a_3(1) = 0.5121 - (0.2759)(-0.0010) = 0.512$$
$$C_3(1) = b_3(1) - \sum_{j=2}^{3} C_3(j)a_j(j-1)$$
$$= b_3(1) - C_3(2)a_2(1) - C_3(3)a_3(2)$$
$$= 0.5121 - (0.512)(0.0497) - (0.2759)(0.6546) = 0.3060$$
$$C_3(0) = b_3(0) - \sum_{j=1}^{3} C_3(j)a_j(j-0)$$
$$= b_3(0) - [C_3(1)a_1(1) + C_3(2)a_2(2) + C_3(3)a_3(3)]$$
$$= 0.2759 - [(0.3060)(0.301) + (0.512)(0.6536) + (0.2759)(-0.0775)]$$
$$= 0.2759 - (0.0921 + 0.3346 - 0.0214) = -0.1294$$

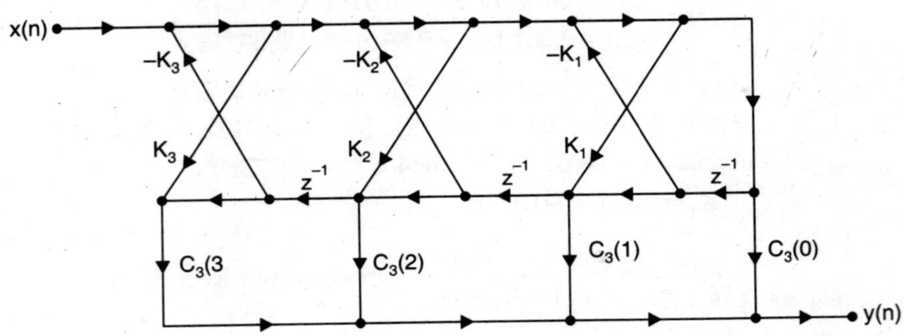

Fig. Ex. 4.18. Realization of the given filter as a Lattice structure

Here $K_3 = -0.0775;\ K_2 = 0.6536;\ K_1 = 0.301$

$C_3(3) = 0.2759,\ C_3(2) = 0.512,\ C_3(1) = 0.3060,\ C_3(0) = -0.1294.$

EXAMPLE 4.19: *Sketch a Lattice filter structure for each of the following system functions:*

(a) $H_1(z) = \dfrac{2 - z^{-1}}{1 + 0.7z^{-1} + 0.49z^{-2}}$. (b) $H_2(z) = \dfrac{1 + 1.3125z^{-1} + 0.75z^{-2}}{1 + 0.875z^{-1} + 0.75z^{-2}}$.

(c) $H_3(z) = \dfrac{0.75 + 0.875z^{-1} + z^{-2}}{1 + 0.875z^{-1} + 0.75z^{-2}}$.

SOLUTION: (a) $$H_1(z) = \frac{2 - z^{-1}}{1 + 0.7z^{-1} + 0.49z^{-2}}$$

[To find K_1, K_2, $C_1(0)$, $C_1(1)$]

$A_2(z) = 1 + 0.7z^{-1} + 0.49z^{-2},\ K_2 = a_2(1)$ $\therefore\ K_2 = 0.49$

$$A_1(z) = \underbrace{\frac{1}{1-(0.49)^2}}_{=0.7599}[(1 + 0.7z^{-1} + 0.49z^{-2}) - 0.49(0.49 + 0.7z^{-1} + z^{-2})]$$

$\therefore \qquad A_1(z) = 1 + 0.4698z^{-1},\ K_1 = a_1(1)$ $\qquad \boxed{\therefore\ K_1 = 0.4698}$

As $\qquad C_1(k) = b_1(k) - \sum_{j=k+1}^{1} C(j)a_j(j-k),\ k = 1, 0$

$\therefore \qquad C_1(1) = b_1(1) = -1$

$$C_1(0) = b_1(0) - \sum_{j=1}^{1} C_1(j)a_j(j)$$

$$= b_1(0) - [C_1(1)a_1(1)] = 2 - ((-1)(0.4698)) = 2.4698$$

The lattice-ladder is as shown below:

$$\frac{Y(z)}{X(z)} = H_1(z)$$

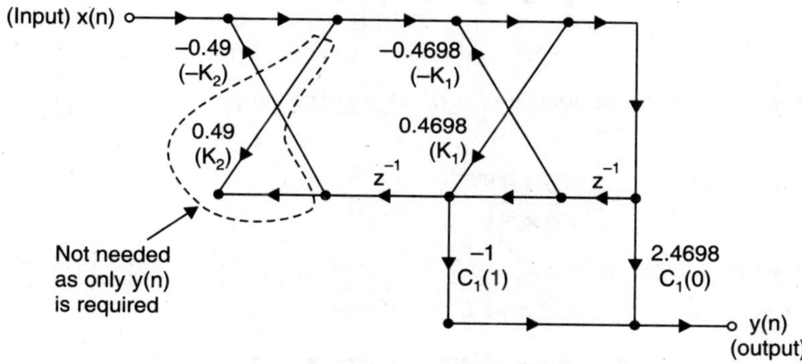

Fig. Ex. 4.19. (*a*) Realization of $H_1(z)$ as a Lattice structure. $H_1(z) = Y(z)/X(z)$

(*b*) $$H_2(z) = \frac{1 + 1.3125z^{-1} + 0.75z^{-2}}{1 + 0.875z^{-1} + 0.75z^{-2}}$$

[To find K_2, K_1, $C_2(2)$, $C_2(1)$ and $C_2(0)$]

$A_2(z) = 1 + 0.875z^{-1} + 0.75z^{-1}$ $\qquad K_2 = a_2(2)$ $\boxed{\therefore\ K_2 = 0.75}$

$$A_1(z) = \underbrace{\frac{1}{1-(0.75)^2}}_{=0.4375}[(1 + 0.875z^{-1} + 0.75z^{-2}) - (0.75)(0.75 + 0.875z^{-1} + z^{-2})]$$

$\therefore \qquad A_1(z) = 1 + 0.5z^{-1}$ $\qquad K_1 = a_1(1)$ $\boxed{\therefore\ K_1 = 0.5}$

$$C_2(k) = b_2(k) - \sum_{j=k+1}^{2} C_2(j)a_j(j-k)$$

$C_2(2) = b_2(2) = 0.75$ $\qquad \boxed{C_2(2) = 0.75}$

$$C_2(1) = b_2(1) - \sum_{j=2}^{2} C_2(j)a_j(j-1)$$

$= 1.3125 - (0.75)(0.875) = 0.65625$ $\qquad \boxed{C_2(1) = 0.65625}$

$$C_2(0) = b_2(0) - \sum_{j=0+1}^{2} C_2(j)a_j(j-0) = 1 - [C_2(1)a_1(1) + C_2(2)a_2(2)]$$

$= 1 - [(0.65625)(0.5) + (0.75)(0.75)] = 0.109375$ $\qquad \boxed{C_2(0) = 0.109375}$

Lattice-ladder is as shown in Fig. Ex. 4.19(*b*)

$$\frac{Y(z)}{X(z)} = H_2(z)$$

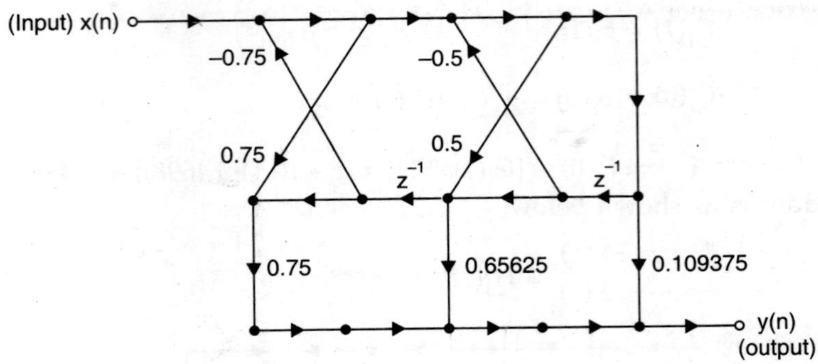

Fig. Ex. 4.19. (*b*) Realization of $H_2(z)$ as a Lattice structure. $H_2(z) = \frac{Y(z)}{X(z)}$

(*c*)
$$H_3(z) = \frac{0.75 + 0.875z^{-1} + z^{-2}}{1 + 0.875z^{-1} + 0.75z^{-2}}$$

$H_3(z)$ is an all pass filter. It has $K_1 = 0.5$, $K_2 = 0.75$ [from (*b*) above]. (Note this simplification) We need not find $C_2(0)$, $C_2(1)$ and $C_2(2)$. These would turn out to be zero.

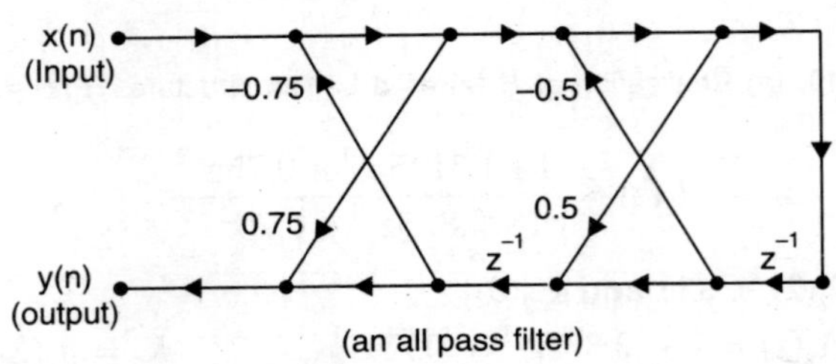

Fig. Ex. 4.19. (*c*) Realization of $H_3(z)$ as a Lattice structure. $H_3(z) = Y(z)/X(z)$

EXAMPLE 4.20: *Convert the following pole zero IIR filter into a Lattice-ladder structure:*

$$H(z) = \frac{1 + 2z^{-1} + 2z^{-2} + z^{-3}}{1 + (13/24)z^{-1} + (5/8)z^{-2} + (1/3)z^{-3}}.$$

SOLUTION:

As
$$H(z) = \frac{\sum_{m=0}^{M} b_M(m)z^{-m}}{1 + \sum_{m=0}^{N} a_N(m)z^{-m}} \triangleq \frac{B_M(z)}{A_N(z)}$$

Here
$$M = N = 3,\ b_M(0) = 1,\ b_M(1) = 2,\ b_M(2) = 2,\ b_M(3) = 1$$

$$a_N(0) = 1,\ a_N(1) = \frac{13}{24},\ a_N(2) = \frac{5}{8},\ a_N(3) = \frac{1}{3}$$

with $$A_N(z) = 1+\frac{13}{24}z^{-1}+\frac{5}{8}z^{-2}+\frac{1}{3}z^{-3} = A_3(z)$$

$$B_M(z) = 1 + 2z^{-1} + 2z^{-2} + z^{-3} = B_3(z)$$

[To find reflection coefficients K_1, K_2, K_3 for all pole function $1/A_3(z)$]

We know that

$$A_{m-1}(z) = \frac{A_m(z) - K_m \cdot z^{-m} A_{m-1}(z^{-1})}{1-K_m^2(m)} \quad \text{(Step-down Recursion)}$$

i.e. $$\boxed{a_{m-1}(k) = \frac{a_m(k) - K_m a_m(m-k)}{1-K_m^2}} \quad \boxed{\because \; K_m = a_m(m),\; i = 1, 2, \ldots, N}$$

$$\boxed{\therefore \; K_3 = \frac{1}{3}}$$

Put $m = 3$,

$\therefore$ for $k = 1$, $$a_2(1) = \frac{a_3(1) - K_3 a_3(2)}{1-K_3^2} = \frac{(13/24)-(1/3)(5/8)}{1-(1/3)^2}$$

$$= \frac{8/24}{8/9} = \frac{9}{24} = \frac{3}{8}$$

for $k = 2$, $$a_2(2) = \frac{a_3(2) - K_3 a_3(1)}{1-K_3^2} = \frac{(5/8)-1/3(13/24)}{1-(1/3)^2}$$

$$= \frac{32/72}{8/9} = \frac{1}{2}$$

$$\boxed{\therefore \; K_2 = \frac{1}{2}}$$

Put $m = 2$, $k = 1$,

$\therefore$ $$a_1(1) = \frac{a_2(1) - K_2 a_2(1)}{1-K_2^2} = \frac{(3/8)-1/2(3/8)}{1-(1/2)^2}$$

$$= \frac{3/16}{3/4} = \frac{1}{4}$$

$$\boxed{\therefore \; K_1 = \frac{1}{4}}$$

[To find coefficients C_i for Ladder structure]

We know that

$$C_m = b_m - \sum_{i=m+1}^{M} C_i a_i(i-m),\; m = M, M-1, \ldots, 0$$

Initial $\quad C_M = b_M$

$\therefore \quad C_3 = b_3 = 1$

Here $\quad M = 3$

$$\boxed{C_3 = 1}$$

$$C_2 = b_m - \sum_{i=3}^{m} C_i a_i(i-2) = b_2 - C_3 a_3(1)$$

$$= 2-(1)\left(\frac{13}{24}\right) = \frac{35}{24} = 1.4583$$

$$\boxed{C_2 = 1.4583}$$

$$C_1 = b_1 - \sum_{i=2}^{3} C_i a_i(i-1) = b_1 - [C_2 a_2(1) + C_3 a_3(2)]$$

$$= 2 - \left[(1.4583)\left(\frac{3}{8}\right) + (1)\frac{5}{8}\right]$$

$$= 2 - 1.1718 = 0.8281 \qquad \boxed{C_1 = 0.8281}$$

$$C_0 = b_0 - \sum_{i=1}^{3} C_i a_i(i) = b_0 - [C_1 a_1(1) + C_2 a_2(2) + C_3 a_3(3)]$$

$$= 1 - \left[(0.8281)\left(\frac{1}{4}\right) + (1.4583)\left(\frac{1}{2}\right) + (1)\left(\frac{1}{3}\right)\right]$$

$$= 1 - [0.2070 + 0.7291 + 0.3333]$$

$$= 1 - 1.2695 = -0.2695 \qquad \boxed{C_0 = -0.2695}$$

To final realization of the Lattice-ladder equivalent to given $H(z)$ is shown in Fig. Ex. 4.20.

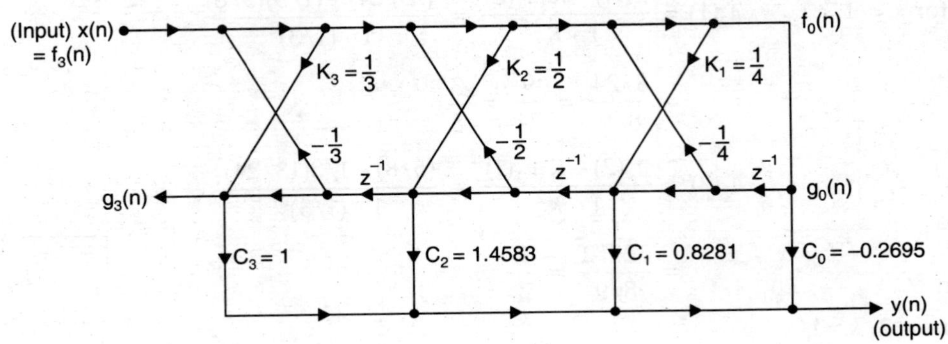

Fig. Ex. 4.20. Lattice-Ladder realization of $H(z) = Y(z)/X(z) = \dfrac{1+2z^{-1}+2z^{-2}+z^{-3}}{1+\frac{13}{24}z^{-1}+\frac{5}{8}z^{-2}+\frac{1}{3}z^{-3}}$.

4.10 LADDER STRUCTURES

It is well known that the analog filters realized using ladder structures have desirable coefficient sensitivity properties. In short, such filters are robust and less sensitive compared to many other realizations. Such good sensitivity properties are also true for digital filters. Various methods for developing ladder filters are available in the literature. However, we shall discuss only one method to obtain a Ladder filter in this section.

We assume that the system function, $H(z)$, which we wish to realize as a ladder structure *a* is given by

$$H(z) = \frac{a_N z^{-N} + a_{N-1}z^{-N+1} + \ldots + a_1 z^{-1} + a_0}{b_N z^{-N} + b_{N-1}z^{-N+1} + \ldots + b_1 z^{-1} + b_0} \qquad \ldots(4.54)$$

Note that (4.54) differs from the representation given by (4.2). The reason for this is that $H(z)$ of (4.54) will be required to form the *Routh Array* for determining the coefficients needed for ladder realization, as follows:

Continued-Fraction Expansion of $H(z)$

Let us expand $H(z)$ as a continued-fraction expansion (CFE) in the form

$$H(z) = \alpha_0 + \cfrac{1}{\beta_1 z^{-1} + \cfrac{1}{\alpha_1 + \cfrac{1}{\beta_2 z^{-1} + \ddots + \cfrac{1}{\alpha_N}}}} \quad \ldots(4.55)$$

We can determine the coefficients $\alpha_0, \beta_1, \alpha_1, \beta_2, \ldots, \alpha_N$ as shown in Table 4.1.

Table 4.1. Routh Array

z^{-N}	a_N	a_{N-1}	a_{N-2}	$\ldots a_1$	a_0
z^{-N}	b_N	b_{N-1}	b_{N-2}	$\ldots b_1$	b_0
z^{-N+1}	c_{N-1}	c_{N-2}	c_{N-3}	$\ldots c_0$	
z^{-N+1}	d_{N-1}	d_{N-2}	d_{N-3}	$\ldots d_0$	
z^{-N+2}	e_{N-2}	e_{N-3}	e_{N-4}		
z^{-N+2}	f_{N-2}	f_{N-3}	f_{N-4}		
$\vdots$					
1	g_0				
1	h_0				

Then $\alpha_0 = \dfrac{a_N}{b_N}$, $\beta_1 = \dfrac{b_N}{c_{N-1}}$, $\alpha_1 = \dfrac{c_{N-1}}{d_{N-1}}$, ..., $\alpha_N = \dfrac{g_0}{h_0}$

For example, for a system $H(z)$ given by

$$H(z) = \frac{2z^{-2} + 3z^{-1} + 1}{z^{-2} + z^{-1} + 1} \triangleq \frac{N(z)}{D(z)}$$

We determine the coefficients from the following array. Given $a_2 = 2$, $a_1 = 3$, $a_0 = 1$ and $b_2 = 1$, $b_2 = 1$, $b_1 = 1$, $b_0 = 1$ are the coefficients of $N(z)$ and $D(z)$.

$j \rightarrow$ / $\downarrow i$	1	2	3	4
1	z^{-2}	$a_2 = 2$	$a_1 = 3$	$a_0 = 1$
2	z^{-2}	$b_2 = 1$	$b_1 = 1$	$b_0 = 1$
3	z^{-1}	$c_1 = 1$	$c_0 = -1$	
4	z^{-1}	$d_1 = 2$	$d_0 = 1$	
5	1	$e_0 = -3/2$		
6	1	$f_0 = 1$		

$$c_1 = -\frac{1}{1}\begin{vmatrix} 2 & 3 \\ 1 & 1 \end{vmatrix} = 1$$

$$c_0 = -\frac{1}{1}\begin{vmatrix} 2 & 1 \\ 1 & 1 \end{vmatrix} = -1$$

$$d_1 = -\frac{1}{1}\begin{vmatrix} 1 & 1 \\ 1 & -1 \end{vmatrix} = 2$$

$$d_0 = -\frac{1}{1}\begin{vmatrix} 1 & 1 \\ 1 & 0 \end{vmatrix} = 1$$

$$e_0 = -\frac{1}{2}\begin{vmatrix} 1 & -1 \\ 2 & 1 \end{vmatrix} = -\frac{3}{2}$$

$$f_0 = -\frac{1}{-3/2}\begin{vmatrix} 2 & 1 \\ -3/2 & 0 \end{vmatrix} = 1$$

(See 4.56*a*) for formula to determine the various elements of the Routh Array)

$$\alpha_0 = \frac{a_2}{b_2} = \frac{2}{1} = 2$$

$$\beta_1 = \frac{b_2}{c_1} = \frac{1}{1} = 2$$

$$\alpha_1 = \frac{c_1}{d_1} = \frac{1}{2} = \frac{1}{2}$$

$$\beta_2 = \frac{d_1}{e_0} = \frac{2}{(-3/2)} = -\frac{4}{3}$$

$$\alpha_2 = \frac{e_0}{f_0} = \frac{(-3/2)}{1} = -\frac{3}{2}$$

Hence, the CFE for this $H(z)$, as given above, will be

$$H(z) = 2 + \cfrac{1}{1 \cdot z^{-1} + \cfrac{1}{\cfrac{1}{2} + \cfrac{1}{(-4/3)z^{-1} + \cfrac{1}{(-3/2)}}}}$$

We shall give the realization after finalizing the structure, as we progress.

Important Note: Note that for formulating the Routh Array in determining the stability of an analog system, we only require the denominator polynomial $D(s)$ of $H(s) = \dfrac{N(s)}{D(s)}$. The numerator polynomial $N(s)$, which gives zeros of $H(s)$, plays no part in determining the stability of $H(s)$. Only the poles of $H(s)$, given by $D(s) = 0$, are important to determine stability of the system. We call Table 4.1 as Routh Array in the sense that once having two rows of coefficients $a_N, a_{N-1}, \ldots, a_0$ and $b_N, b_{N-1}, \ldots, b_0$, we determine the remaining coefficients of the array using the formula

$$r_{i+1,\,j} = \frac{\det\begin{vmatrix} r_{i-1,1}, & r_{i-1,j+1} \\ r_{i,1}, & r_{i,j+1} \end{vmatrix}}{(-r_{i,1})} \qquad \ldots(4.56)$$

as given in Chapter covering stability. Formula (4.56) may be put as below for ease of memory.

$$\text{Element } r_{i+1,\,j} = \begin{vmatrix} \text{Elements of above two rows of } 1^{\text{st}} \text{ column } (i.e. \text{ rows } i-1 \text{ and } i) & \text{Elements of above two rows of next column } (i.e. \text{ column } j+1) \end{vmatrix} \Big/ (-\text{element } r_{i,1}) \qquad \ldots(4.56a)$$

For row $i + 1$, above two rows are i and $i - 1$

For column j, the next column is $j + 1$.

Realization of a Ladder structure: We can write

$$Y(z) = H(z) \cdot X(z) \qquad \ldots(4.57a)$$

$$= \left[\alpha_0 + \frac{1}{\beta z^{-1} + 1/T_1(z)}\right] X(z) \qquad \ldots(4.57b)$$

$$= \alpha_0 X(z) + H_1(z) X(z)$$

$$= [\alpha_0 + H_1(z)] X(z) \qquad \ldots(4.58)$$

where
$$H_1(z) = \frac{1}{\beta_1 z^{-1} + 1/T_1(z)} \qquad \ldots(4.59)$$

and
$$T_1(z) = \alpha_1 + \cfrac{1}{\beta_2 z^{-1} + \left(\alpha_2 + \cfrac{1}{\beta_3 z^{-1} + \ddots \cfrac{1}{\alpha_N}}\right)} \qquad \ldots(4.60)$$

To realize the equation (4.55) for $H(z)$, we realize Eqn. (4.58) in parallel form *i.e.* parallelling α_0 with $H_1(z)$, as shown in Fig. 4.17(*a*). Note that from Fig. 4.17(*b*), we can write

$$Y_1(z) = T_1(z)[X(z) - \beta_1 z^{-1} Y_1(z)] \qquad \ldots(4.61)$$

$$\therefore \qquad Y_1(z)[1 + \beta_1 z^{-1} T_1(z)] = T_1(z) \cdot X(z)$$

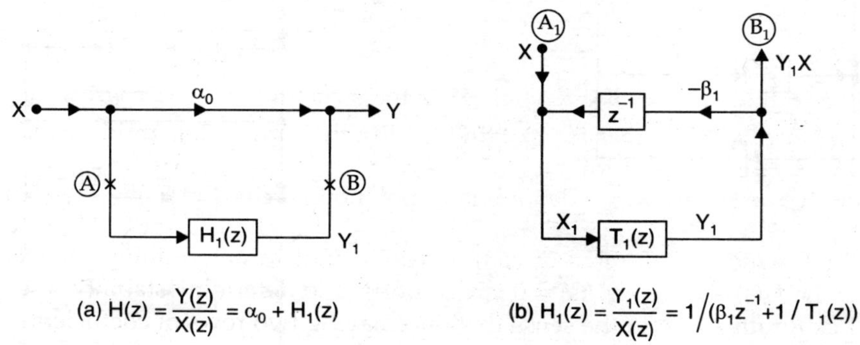

(a) $H(z) = \dfrac{Y(z)}{X(z)} = \alpha_0 + H_1(z)$ (b) $H_1(z) = \dfrac{Y_1(z)}{X(z)} = 1\Big/(\beta_1 z^{-1} + 1/T_1(z))$

Fig. 4.17. (*a*) A parallel-form realization of $H(z)$, (*b*) Realization of Eqn. (4.59) *i.e.* $H_1(z)$

i.e.
$$\frac{Y_1(z)}{X(z)} = \frac{T_1(z)}{1+\beta_1 z^{-1}T_1(z)}$$

or
$$H_1(z) = \frac{Y_1(z)}{X(z)} = \frac{1}{\beta_1 z^{-1} + [1/T_1(z)]} \qquad \text{...(4.62)}$$

Hence, Fig. 4.17(*b*) indeed realizes $H_1(z)$ given by (4.59).

As we connect Ⓐ to (A_1) and (*B*) to (B_1) from Fig. 4.17(*a*), (*b*), we get the realization, shown in Fig. 4.18, for *H*(*z*) in terms of $T_1(z)$.

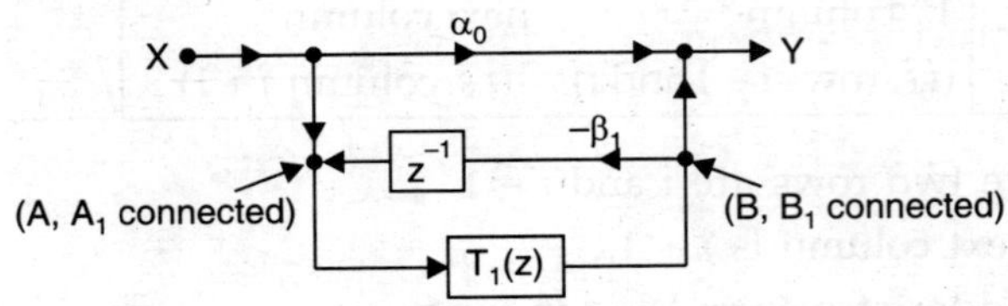

Fig. 4.18. Structure for $H(z) = \frac{\alpha_0 + 1}{[\beta_1 z^{-1} + (1/T_1(z)]}$

The next step in realization of *H*(*z*) is to replace $T_1(z)$ by

$$T_1(z) = \frac{Y_1(z)}{X_1(z)} = \alpha_1 + \frac{1}{\beta_2 z^{-1} + (1/T_2(z))} \qquad \text{...(4.63)}$$

from Eqn. (4.60). We compare (4.63) with (4.57) *i.e.*

$$H(z) = \alpha_0 + \frac{1}{\beta_1 z^{-1} + (1/T_1(z))} \qquad \text{...(4.64)}$$

It is readily seen that $T_1(z)$ can be obtained from the structure of *H*(*z*), shown in Fig. 4.18, if we replace α_0 by α_1, β_1 by β_2 and $T_1(z)$ by $T_2(z)$. The resulting structure is as shown in Fig. 4.19. Continuing this operation, we finally obtain structure shown in Fig. 4.20.

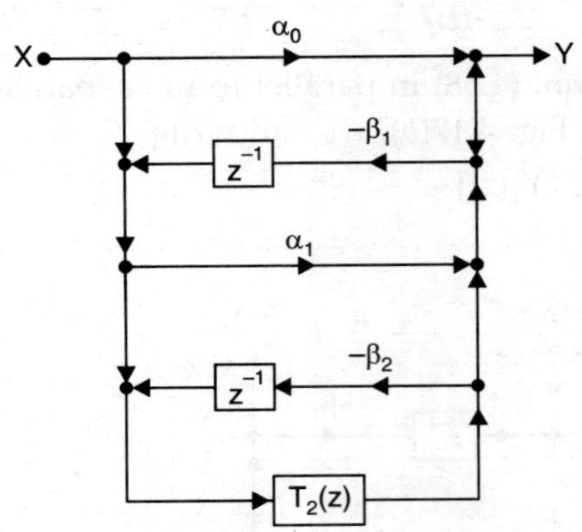

Fig. 4.19. Structure for Eqn. 4.57(*b*) and Eqn. (4.63)

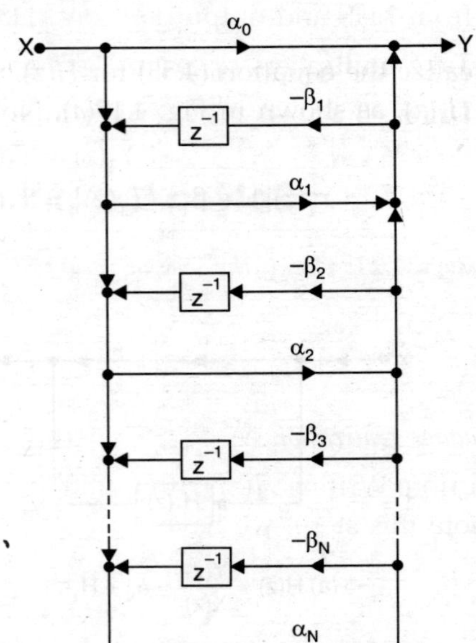

Fig. 4.20. CFE realization of *H*(*z*) of Eqn. (4.55)

Having finalized the structure of the ladder for $H(z)$, by using α_0, β_1, α_1, β_2, α_2, ..., as in Fig. 4.20, we can draw the structure for given $H(z)$ as

$$H(z) = \frac{2z^{-2} + 3z^{-1} + 1}{z^{-2} + z^{-1} + 1}$$

We have already computed the values

$$\alpha_0 = 2,\ \beta_1 = 1,\ \alpha_1 = \frac{1}{2},\ \beta_2 = -\frac{4}{3} \text{ and } \alpha_2 = -\frac{3}{2}$$

Hence, the ladder structure is as given in Fig. 4.21.

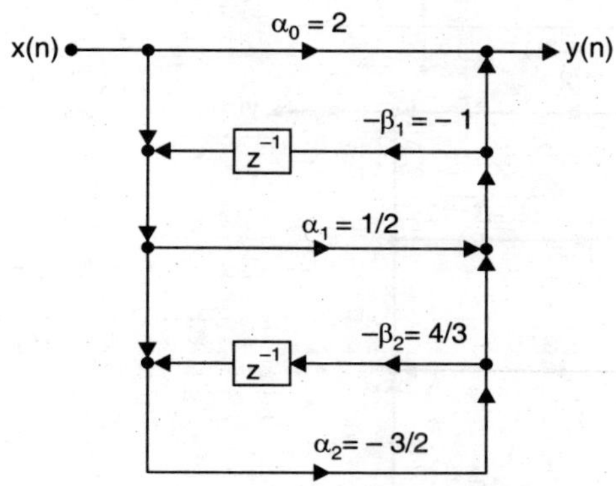

Fig. 4.21. Realization of $H(z) = \frac{(2z^{-2} + 3z^{-1} + 1)}{(z^{-2} + z^{-1} + 1)}$ as a ladder structure

Aid to Memory:

1. To draw the ladder structure, having computed α_0, α_1, α_2, ..., β_1, β_2, ..., assume $x(n)$ input from LHS and output $y(n)$ on RHS.
2. Take multipliers α_0, α_1, α_2, ... left to right on 1st, 3rd, 5th..., rungs.
3. Draw $-\beta_1 z^{-1}$, $-\beta_2 z^{-1}$, ..., right to left on 2nd, 4th, 6th, ... rungs.

Solved Examples on Ladder Structures

EXAMPLE 4.21: *Given the system function*

$$H(z) = \frac{2 + 8z^{-1} + 6z^{-2}}{1 + 8z^{-1} + 12z^{-2}}$$

obtain Ladder realization.

SOLUTION: Writing $H(z)$ with numerator and denominator polynomials in descending powers of z^{-1} (note this step), we have

$$H(z) = \frac{6z^{-2} + 8z^{-1} + 2}{12z^{-2} + 8z^{-1} + 1}$$

Make Routh Array

↓i	→ j	1	2	3
1	z^{-2}	$a_2 = 6,$	$a_1 = 8,$	$a_0 = 2$
2	z^{-2}	$b_2 = 12,$	$b_1 = 8,$	$b_0 = 1$
3	z^{-1}	$c_1 = 4,$	$c_0 = 3/2$	
4	z^{-1}	$d_1 = 3/2,$	$d_0 = 1$	
5	z^{0}	$e_0 = -7/6$		
6	z^{0}	$f_0 = 1$		

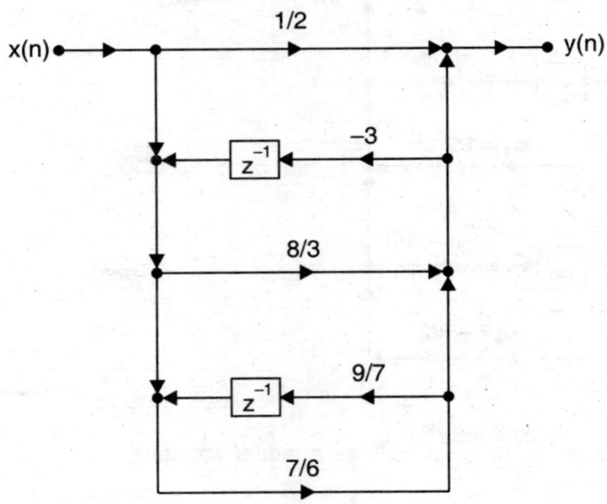

Fig. Ex. 4.21. Realization as a Ladder

Using formula (4.56), we compute

$$c_1 = -\frac{1}{12}\begin{vmatrix} 6 & 8 \\ 12 & 8 \end{vmatrix} = 4$$

$$c_0 = -\frac{1}{12}\begin{vmatrix} 6 & 2 \\ 12 & 1 \end{vmatrix} = \frac{3}{2}$$

$$d_1 = -\frac{1}{4}\begin{vmatrix} 12 & 8 \\ 4 & 3/2 \end{vmatrix} = \frac{3}{2}$$

$$d_0 = -\frac{1}{4}\begin{vmatrix} 12 & 1 \\ 4 & 0 \end{vmatrix} = 1$$

$$e_0 = -\frac{2}{3}\begin{vmatrix} 4 & 3/2 \\ 3/2 & 1 \end{vmatrix} = -\frac{7}{6}$$

$$f_0 = +\frac{6}{7}\begin{vmatrix} 3/2 & 1 \\ -7/6 & 0 \end{vmatrix} = 1$$

$$\alpha_0 = \frac{a_2}{b_2} = \frac{1}{2},\ \beta_1 = \frac{b_2}{c_1} = 3$$

$$\alpha_1 = \frac{c_1}{d_1} = \frac{8}{3},\ \beta_2 = \frac{d_1}{e_0} = -\frac{9}{7}$$

$$\alpha_2 = \frac{e_0}{f_0} = -\frac{7}{6}$$

EXAMPLE 4.22: *We may write H(z) as*

$$H(z) = \frac{a_N z^N + a_{N-1} z^{N-1} + \ldots + a_1 z + a_0}{b_N z^N + b_{N-1} z^{N-1} + \ldots + b_1 z + b_0}$$

and obtain the continued fraction expression as

$$H(z) = \alpha_0 + \cfrac{1}{\beta_1 z + \cfrac{1}{\alpha_1 + \cfrac{1}{\beta_2 z + \cfrac{1}{\ddots \cfrac{1}{\beta_N z + \cfrac{1}{\alpha_N}}}}}}$$

where the coefficients α_i and β_i are determined from the Routh Array, where rows are identified by the positive power of z^N, z^{N-1}, ...,. Obtain the CFE of $H(z) = \dfrac{z^2 + 3z + 2}{z^2 + z + 1}$.

SOLUTION:

z^2	$a_2 = 1,$	$a_1 = 3,$	$a_0 = 2$
z^2	$b_2 = 1,$	$b_1 = 1,$	$b_0 = 1$
z	$c_1 = 2,$	$c_0 = 1$	
z	$d_1 = 1/2,$	$d_0 = 1$	
z^0	$e_0 = 1$		
z^0	$f_0 = 1$		

$$c_1 = -\frac{1}{1}\begin{vmatrix} 1 & 3 \\ 1 & 1 \end{vmatrix} = 2,\ c_0 = \frac{-1}{1}\begin{vmatrix} 1 & 2 \\ 1 & 1 \end{vmatrix} = 1$$

$$d_1 = -\frac{1}{2}\begin{vmatrix} 1 & 1 \\ 2 & 1 \end{vmatrix} = \frac{1}{2},\ d_0 = -\frac{1}{2}\begin{vmatrix} 1 & 1 \\ 2 & 0 \end{vmatrix} = 1$$

$$e_0 = -2\begin{vmatrix} 2 & 1 \\ 1/2 & 0 \end{vmatrix} = 1,\ f_0 = \frac{1}{3}\begin{vmatrix} 1/2 & 1 \\ -3 & 0 \end{vmatrix} = 1$$

$$\alpha_0 = \frac{a_2}{b_2} = 1,\ \beta_1 = \frac{b_2}{c_1} = \frac{1}{2}$$

$$\alpha_1 = \frac{c_1}{d_1} = 4,\ \beta_2 = \frac{d_1}{e_0} = \frac{1}{2}$$

$$\alpha_2 = \frac{e_0}{f_0} = 1$$

$$H(z) = 1 + \cfrac{1}{\frac{1}{2}z + \cfrac{1}{4 + \cfrac{1}{\frac{1}{2}z + \frac{1}{1}}}}$$

is the required CFE on the form as required.

EXAMPLE 4.23: *Realize the system function*

$$H(z) = \frac{z^{-2} + 2z^{-1} + 2}{z^{-2} + z^{-1} + 3}$$

as a ladder structure.

SOLUTION:

Routh Array is

z^{-2}	$a_2 = 1$	$a_1 = 2$	$a_0 = 2$
z^{-2}	$b_2 = 1$	$b_1 = 1$	$b_0 = 3$
z^{-1}	$c_1 = 1$	$c_0 = -1$	
z^{-1}	$d_1 = 2$	$d_0 = 3$	
z^0	$e_0 = -5/2$		
z^0	$f_0 = 3$		

$$c_1 = -\frac{1}{1}\begin{vmatrix} 1 & 2 \\ 1 & 1 \end{vmatrix} = 1,\ c_0 = -\frac{1}{1}\begin{vmatrix} 1 & 2 \\ 1 & 3 \end{vmatrix} = -1$$

$$d_1 = -\frac{1}{1}\begin{vmatrix} 1 & 1 \\ 1 & -1 \end{vmatrix} = 2,\ d_0 = -\frac{1}{1}\begin{vmatrix} 1 & 3 \\ 1 & 0 \end{vmatrix} = 3$$

$$e_0 = -\frac{1}{2}\begin{vmatrix} 1 & -1 \\ 2 & 3 \end{vmatrix} = -\frac{5}{2},\ f_0 = \frac{2}{5}\begin{vmatrix} 2 & 3 \\ -5/2 & 0 \end{vmatrix} = 3$$

$$\therefore \quad \alpha_0 = \frac{a_2}{b_2} = 1,\ \beta_1 = \frac{b_2}{c_1} = 1$$

$$\alpha_1 = \frac{c_1}{d_1} = \frac{1}{2},\ \beta_2 = \frac{d_1}{e_0} = -\frac{4}{5}$$

$$\alpha_2 = \frac{e_0}{f_0} = -\frac{5}{6}$$

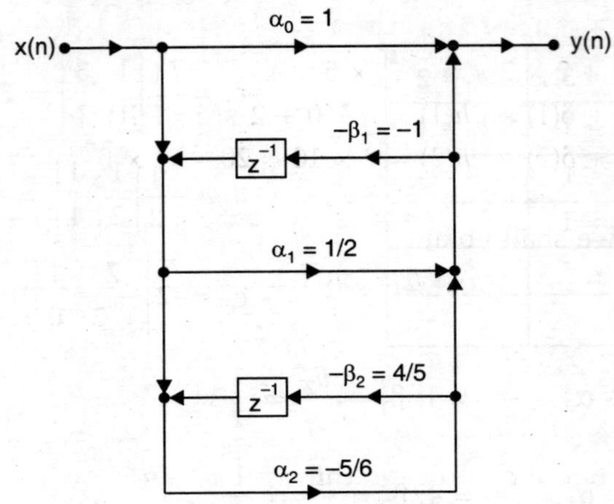

Fig. Ex. 4.23. Realization as a Ladder

EXAMPLE 4.24: *Show that the transfer functions*

(a) $H_1(z) = \dfrac{1}{\beta z + T(z)}$ *(b)* $H_2(z) = \dfrac{1}{\alpha + T(z)}$

can be realized as shown in the Fig. Ex. 4.24(a).

SOLUTION:

(a) $H_1(z) = \dfrac{Y(z)}{X(z)} = \dfrac{1}{\beta z + T(z)}$

$\therefore$ Cross multiplying, we have

$$(\beta z)Y(z) + (T(z)) \cdot Y(z) = X(z)$$

$\therefore$ $$Y(z) = \beta^{-1}z^{-1}[X(z) - T(z) \cdot Y(z)]$$

The realization of $H_1(z)$ as shown in Fig. Ex. 4.24(*a*).

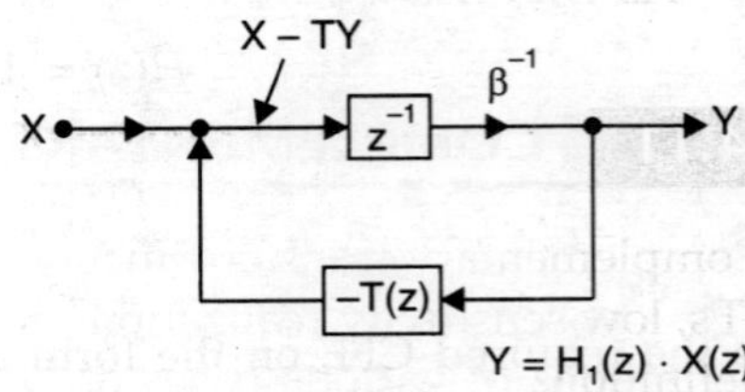

Fig. Ex. 4.24. (*a*) Realization of $H_1(z)$

(b) $H_2(z) = \dfrac{1}{\alpha + T(z)} = \dfrac{Y(z)}{X(z)}$

$\therefore$ Cross-multiplying, we have

$$\alpha Y(z) + T(z) \cdot Y(z) = X(z)$$

or $$\alpha Y(z) = X(z) - T(z) \cdot Y(z)$$

$\therefore$ $$Y(z) = \alpha^{-1}[X(z) - T(z)Y(z)]$$

The realization of $H_2(z)$ is shown in Fig. Ex. 4.24(*b*).

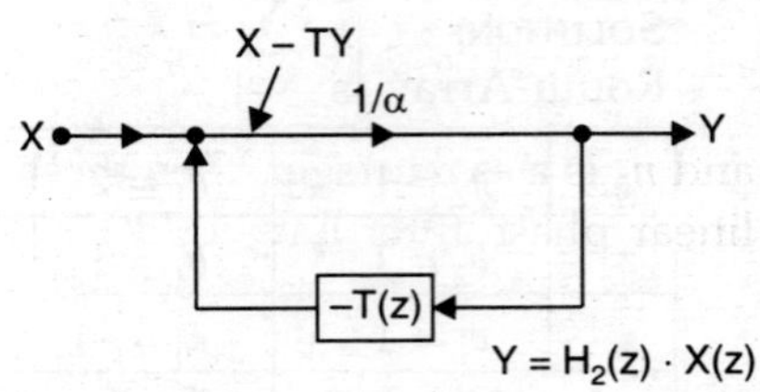

Fig. Ex. 4.24. (*b*) Realization of $H_2(z)$

EXAMPLE 4.25: *Check the filter given in Fig. Ex. 4.25 for probability.*

SOLUTION: $y(n) = 2x(n) + x(n-1) + 2y(n-1)$

Putting $x(n) = \delta(n)$ and therefore $y(n) = h(n)$, we get

$$h(n) = 2\delta(n) + \delta(n-1) + 2h(n-1)$$

$\therefore$ $$h(0) = 2\delta(0) + \delta(-1) + 2h(-1)$$

$\therefore$ $$h(0) = 2 + 0 + 0 = 2$$

[assuming causal system $\therefore$ $h(-1) = 0$]

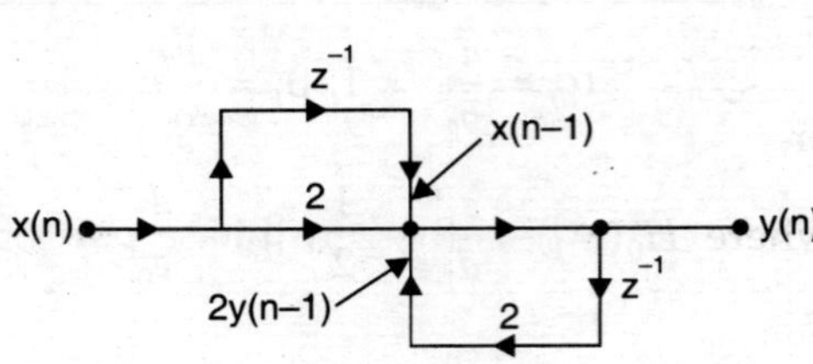

Fig. Ex. 4.25. The given structure

$$h(1) = 2\delta(1) + \delta(0) + 2h(0)$$
$$= 0 + 1 + 2 \times 2 = 5 = 2^0 \times 5$$
$$h(2) = 2\delta(2) + \delta(1) + 2h(1) = 0 + 0 + 2 \times 5 = 2 \times 5$$
$$h(3) = 2\delta(3) + \delta(2) + 2h(2) = 2 \times 10 = 20 = 2^2 \times 5$$
$$\vdots$$

Continuing similarly, we shall obtain

$$h(n) = 2^{n-1} \cdot 5$$

$$\therefore \qquad \lim_{n\to\infty} \sum_{k=0}^{n} |h(k)| = \lim_{n\to\infty} \sum_{k=0}^{n} 2^{k-1} \times 5 \to \infty$$

$\therefore$ The given system is unstable. **Ans.**

Check: Taking ZT on both sides of the given difference equation, we would get

$$H(z) = \frac{Y(z)}{X(z)} = \frac{2+z^{-1}}{1-2z^{-1}}.$$

As $H(z)$ has a pole outside the unit circle, hence, the system in unstable.

4.11 COMPLEMENTARY TRANSFER FUNCTIONS

Complementary transfer functions are often used in applications such as efficient realizations of TFs, low sensitivity realizations and filter banks design and implementations. We first discuss the definitions of various types of complementary transfer functions.

4.11.1 Delay-Complementary Transfer Functions

If a set of L TFs $[H_0(z), H_1(z), \ldots, H_{L-1}(z)]$ are such that:

$$\sum_{k=0}^{L-1} H_k(z) = \beta z^{-n_0} \quad (\beta \neq 0) \text{ delay complementary TFs} \qquad \ldots(4.65)$$

and n_0 is a +ve integer, then these filters are delay complementary. For example, let $H_0(z)$, an FIR, linear phase filter have odd length $M = 2K + 1$. $(\therefore \ \text{delay} = K)$

$$\therefore \qquad H_0(z)\Big|_{z=e^{j\omega}} = H_0(e^{j\omega}) = \underbrace{e^{-j\omega}}_{\text{delay part}} \ \underbrace{\tilde{H}_0(\omega)}_{\text{zero phase part}} \qquad \ldots(4.66)$$

Let $\beta = 1$, $n_0 = K$ in (4.65) then a delay complementary of $H_0(z)$ is $H_1(z)$, such that

$$H_0(e^{j\omega}) + H_1(e^{j\omega}) = 1 \cdot e^{-j\omega K}$$

or

$$H_1(e^{j\omega}) = e^{-j\omega K}(1 - \tilde{H}_0(e^{j\omega})) \quad \because \ H_0(e^{j\omega}) = e^{-jK\omega}\tilde{H}_0(\omega) \qquad \ldots(4.67)$$

where $\tilde{H}_0(e^{j\omega})$ is the zero phase part of $H_0(e^{j\omega})$.

Let $\tilde{H}_0(\omega)$ be such that

$$\tilde{H}_0(\omega) = \begin{cases} 1 \pm \delta_p & \text{in pass band} \\ \pm \delta_s & \text{in stop band} \end{cases} \qquad \ldots(4.68)$$

Then,

$$H_1(e^{j\omega}) = 1 - \tilde{H}_0(\omega) = \begin{cases} \pm \delta_p & \text{in pass band of } \tilde{H}_0(\omega) \\ 1 \pm \delta_s & \text{in stop band of } \tilde{H}_0(\omega) \end{cases} \qquad \ldots(4.69)$$

This means that if $\tilde{H}_0(\omega)$ or $\tilde{H}_0(z)$ is a LPF, then $1 - \tilde{H}_0(\omega)$ *i.e.* $H_1(z)$ is a HPF and vice versa.

If at ω_0, $\tilde{H}_0(\omega_0) = \tilde{H}_1(\omega_0) = 0.5$, then the gain responses of $H_0(z)$ and $H_1(z)$ are 6 dB below their maximum values. ω_0 is called 6 dB cross over frequency. As another example, consider a band stop filter given by

$$H_{BS}(z) = \frac{1}{64}(1 + z^{-2})^4(1 - 4z^{-2} + 5z^{-4} + 5z^{-8} - 4z^{-10} + z^{-12}),$$

we wish to find its delay complementary TF. Assume $H_{BS}(z)$ a linear phase filter. Note that $H_{BS}(z)$ is clearly a linear phase filter with order 20 ($\therefore$ Delay is = order/2 = 10)

$\therefore$ $H_{BP}(z) = z^{-10} - H_{BS}(z)$ (delay complementary of $H_{BS}(z)$)

$$= -\frac{1}{64}(1 - z^{-2})^4(1 + 4z^{-2} + 5z^{-4} + 5z^{-8} + 4z^{-10} + z^{-12})$$

Responses are as shown in Fig. 4.22.

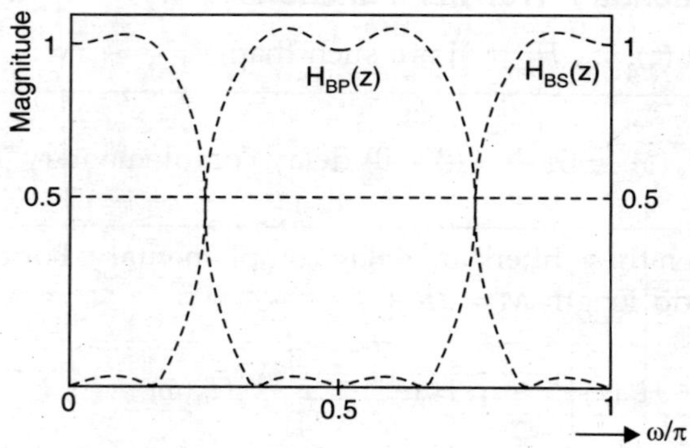

Fig. 4.22. Delay-complementary linear phase BS and BP filters responses

Applications of Delay-Complementary FIR Transfer Function pair: A useful application of Delay-complementary TF is in digital TV receives. It can be used for separation of luminance and chrominance (*i.e.* colour part) components from the incoming video signal.

The composite video signal tends to blur the luminance output of the comb filter $G_1(z)$.

The comb filters $G_0(z)$ and $G_1(z)$ can be generated from a single pass band or a single stop band filter, say $H(z)$ by replacing z in $H(z)$ by z^L. If magnitude response of $H(z)$ exhibits peak at $\omega_p = \frac{\pi}{2}$, then $|G(e^{j\omega})| = |H(e^{j\omega L})|$ exhibits peaks at $\frac{\pi}{2L}k$, $k = 1, 2, \ldots, L$. Similarly, if magnitude of $H(e^{j\omega})$ has a notch at $\omega = \frac{\pi}{2}$, then the magnitude of $|H(e^{j\omega L})|$ has L notches at $\omega = \frac{\pi k}{2L}$, $k = 1, 2, L$.

If $$G_0(z) = H_0(z^L) = \frac{1}{2}(1+z^{-L}) \text{ has } L \text{ peaks, } L \text{ notches}$$

$$G_1(z) = H_1(z^L) = \frac{1}{2}(1-z^{-L}) \text{ has } L \text{ peaks, } L \text{ notches at points where } G_0(z)$$

has notches and peaks, respectively.

If M is delay of one horizontal line scan, then $G_0(z)$ will give average luminance (*i.e.* the brightness), and $G_1(z)$ gives chrominance (*i.e.* the colours) signal out of input video signal. Generation of $G_0(z)$ and $G_1(z)$ is shown in Fig. 4.23.

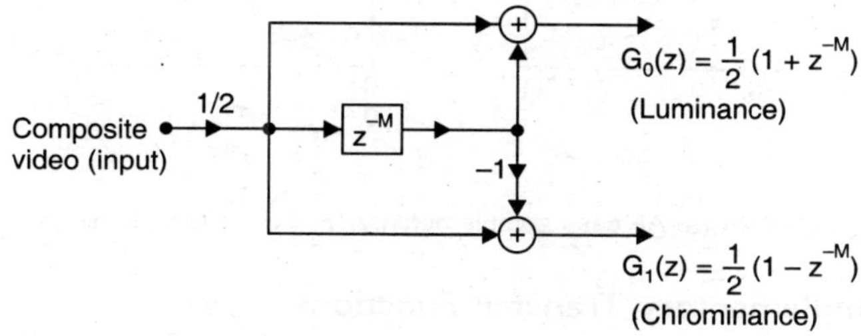

Fig. 4.23. Filter structure for separation of luminance and chrominance components of a composite video signal

Note that separation of luminance and chrominance components of the composite video signal tends to blur the luminance output resulting in loss of vertical details. However, the low frequency vertical details can be recovered from the output of the chrominance filter $G_1(z)$ by a LPF and adding the same to the luminance filter $G_0(z)$. The vertical details can be removed from the output of $G_1(z)$ by using a delay complementary to the low pass filter, as shown in Fig. 4.24.

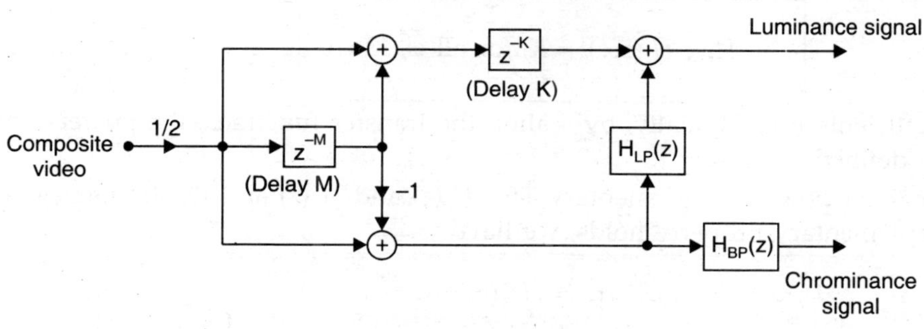

Fig. 4.24. Luminance and chrominance components separation filter structure with improved vertical details

$H_{LP}(z)$ employed is a low pass filter whose low frequency pass range coincides with the frequency range of the desired vertical details. $H_{BP}(z)$ is a band pass filter, it is delay complementary of $H_{LP}(z)$. Delay K on the top path is chosen to equalize the total delay in both the top and the bottom paths.

We can also design low-sensitivity FIR digital filters by using delay-complementary filters.

Delay-complementary are also used as cross over filters for separating the digital audio input signals into two or three sub-signals occupying different frequency bands, used for different loud-speakers to produce stereo effect.

4.11.2 All Pass Complementary Transfer Functions

A set of M digital TFs $\{H_i(z)\}$, $0 \le i \le M-1$ is defined to be all pass complementary of each other if

$$\sum_{i=0}^{M-1} H_i(z) = A(z), \text{ an all pass function} \quad \ldots(4.70)$$

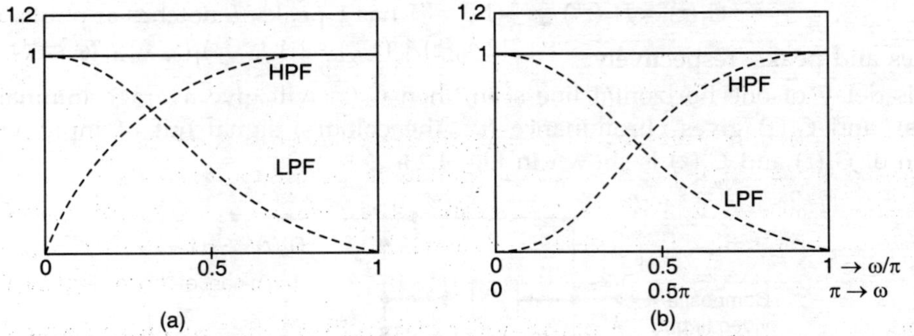

Fig. 4.25 (*a*) All pass complementary (*b*) Power complementary

4.11.3 Power Complementary Transfer Functions

A set of M digital TFs $\{H_i(z)\}$, $0 \le i \le M-1$ is defined to be power-complementary of each other if the sum of squares of their magnitude response is equal to a constant K, for all values of ω *i.e.*

$$\sum_{i=0}^{M-1} |H_i(e^{j\omega})|^2 = K \text{ for all } \omega,\ K > 0 \quad \ldots(4.71)$$

The above property is also equivalent to

$$\sum_{i=0}^{M-1} H_i(z)H_i(z^{-1}) = K, \text{ for all } \omega,\ K > 0 \quad \ldots(4.72)$$

for real-coefficients $H_i(z)$. Usually, by scaling the transfer functions, the power-complementary property is defined w.r.t. $K = 1$.

For a pair of power-complementary TFs, $H_0(z)$ and $H_1(z)$ and the frequency ω_0, where the power-complementary property holds, we have

$$|H_0(e^{j\omega_0})|^2 = |H_1(e^{j\omega_0})|^2 = \frac{1}{2}, \quad \ldots(4.73)$$

ω_0 is called cross over frequency or 3 dB cut off frequency.

Note that at $\omega = \omega_0$, $H_0(z)$ and $H_1(z)$ have each power gain response $= \frac{1}{2}$ *i.e.* $\omega = \omega_0$ gives half power point, hence called 3 dB frequency.

Consider two TFs $H_0(z)$ and $H_1(z)$ defined by

$$H_0(z) = \frac{1}{2}[A_0(z) + A_1(z)] \quad \ldots(4.74)$$

$$H_1(z) = \frac{1}{2}[A_0(z) - A_1(z)] \quad \ldots(4.75)$$

where $A_0(z)$ and $A_1(z)$ are stable all pass TFs. Then the sum $H_0(z) + H_1(z) = A_0(z)$ *i.e.* sum of $H_0(z)$ and $H_1(z)$ is an all pass filter. Hence, $H_0(z)$ and $H_1(z)$ are all pass complementary filters.

[To show that $H_0(z)$ and $H_1(z)$ are power complementary]

$$H_0(z)\cdot H_0(z^{-1}) + H_1(z)\cdot H_1(z^{-1}) = \frac{1}{4}[(A_0(z)+A_1(z))(A_0(z^{-1})+A_1(z^{-1})) + (A_0(z)-A_1(z))(A_0(z^{-1})-A_1(z^{-1}))]$$

$$= \frac{1}{4}[2A_0(z)A_0(z^{-1}) + 2A_1(z)\cdot A_1(z^{-1})] \quad \text{(see **)}$$

$$= \frac{1}{2}[A_0(z)\cdot A_0(z^{-1}) + A_1(z)A_1(z^{-1})]$$

$$\therefore \quad |H_0(e^{j\omega})|^2 + |H_1(e^{j\omega})|^2 = \frac{1}{2}[|A_0(e^{j\omega})|^2 + |A_1(e^{j\omega})|^2]$$

$$= \frac{1}{2}(1+1) = 1 \qquad (\because \ A_0(z) \text{ and } A_1(z) \text{ are APFs})$$

As $|H_0(e^{j\omega})|^2 + |H_1(e^{j\omega})|^2 = 1$, therefore, $H_0(z)$ and $H_1(z)$ are power complementary.

[To show that $H_0(z)$ and $H_1(z)$ are Bounded Real (BR) functions]

As

$$H_0(z)\cdot H_0(z^{-1}) = \frac{1}{4}[(A_0(z)+A_1(z))(A_0(z^{-1})+A_1(z^{-1}))]$$

$$= \frac{1}{4}[A_0(z)A_0(z^{-1}) + A_0(z)A_1(z^{-1}) + A_1(z)A_0(z^{-1}) + A_1(z)A_1(z^{-1})]$$

Put $z = e^{j\omega}$, $z^{-1} = e^{-j\omega}$

$$\therefore \quad |H_0(e^{j\omega})|^2 = \frac{1}{4}[A_0(e^{j\omega})\cdot A_0^*(e^{j\omega}) + A_0(e^{j\omega})A_1^*(e^{j\omega}) + A_1(e^{j\omega})A_0^*(e^{j\omega}) + A_1(e^{j\omega})A_1^*(e^{j\omega})]$$

Let $A_0(e^{j\omega}) = e^{j\phi_0(\omega)}$ and $A_1(e^{j\omega}) = e^{j\phi_1(\omega)}$ being all pass functions. Then we get

$$|H_0(e^{j\omega})|^2 = \frac{1}{4}[\underbrace{|A_0(e^{j\omega})|^2}_{=1} + e^{j(\phi_0-\phi_1)} + e^{j(\phi_1-\phi_2)} + \underbrace{|A_1(e^{j\omega})|^2}_{=1}]$$

$$= \frac{1}{4}[2 + e^{j(\phi_0-\phi_1)} + e^{-j(\phi_0-\phi_1)}]$$

≤ 1 since for $e^{j(\phi_0-\phi_1)}$ and $e^{-j(\phi_0-\phi_1)}$ their maximum values cannot exceed 1.

As $|H_0(e^{j\omega})|^2 \leq 1$ and also $H_0(z)$, being sum of two stable functions $A_0(z)$ and $A_1(z)$, is stable. Hence, $H_0(z)$ is a bounded real function. Similarly, $H_1(z)$ is a bounded real TF.

4.11.4 Doubly-Complementary Transfer Functions

A set of TFs satisfying both the all pass complementary property Eqn. (4.70) and the power-complementary property Eqn. (4.71) is known as doubly-complementary set. Note that a pair

** $(a + b)(c + d) + (a - b)(c - d) = (ac + \cancel{ad} + \cancel{bc} + bd) + (ac - \cancel{ad} - \cancel{bc} + bd) = 2ac + 2bd.$

doubly-complementary *IIR* TFs, $H_0(z)$ and $H_1(z)$ with a sum of all pass decomposition in the form of

$$H_0(z) = \frac{1}{2}[A_0(z) + A_1(z)] \quad \text{...(4.76)}$$

$$H_1(z) = \frac{1}{2}[A_0(z) - A_1(z)] \quad \text{...(4.77)}$$

can be realized by a parallel connection of the constituent all pass filters as shown in Fig. 4.26. It can be shown that such realizations also ensure low sensitivity in the pass band w.r.t. the multiplier coefficients. It can be shown that band pass TFs $H_{BP}(z)$ and band stop functions $H_{BS}(z)$ form doubly complementary pair, where

$$H_{BP}(z) = \frac{1-\alpha}{2} \cdot \frac{1-z^{-2}}{1-\beta(1+\alpha)z^{-1}+\alpha z^{-2}}$$

and

$$H_{BS}(z) = \frac{1+\alpha}{2} \cdot \frac{1-2\beta z^{-1}+z^{-2}}{1-\beta(1+\alpha)z^{-1}+\alpha z^{-2}} \quad \text{...(4.78)}$$

i.e. $H_{BP}(z)$ and $H_{BS}(z)$ given above form doubly complementary transfer functions.

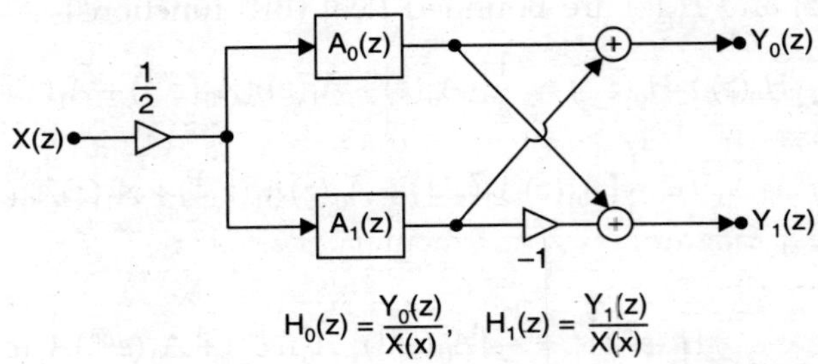

Fig. 4.26. Parallel all pass realization of doubly-complementary IIR TFs

4.11.5 Power-symmetric Filters and Conjugate Quadratic Filters

A real coefficient causal digital filter with TF $H(z)$ is said to be power-symmetric filter if it satisfies the condition

$$\boxed{H(z) \cdot H(z^{-1}) + H(-z) \cdot H(-z^{-1}) = K,\ K > 0, \text{ a constant}} \quad \text{...(4.79)}$$

It can be shown that the *gain function* $G(\omega)$ of the power symmetric TF *at* $\omega = \frac{\pi}{2}$ is given by

$$\boxed{10 \log_{10} K - 3 \text{ dB}} \quad \text{...(4.80)}$$

We define $G(z) = H(-z)$, then it follows that *$H(z)$ and $G(z)$ are power-complementary* since using (4.79) we have

$$H(z) \cdot H(z^{-1}) \cdot G(z) \cdot G(z^{-1}) = \text{a constant} \quad \text{...(4.81)}$$

If $H(z)$ of Eqn. (4.79) is the TF of an FIR digital filter of order N, then the FIR digital filter with transfer function

$$\boxed{G(z) = z^{-N}H(-z^{-1})} \quad \text{...(4.82)}$$

is called conjugate quadratic filter of $H(z)$ and vice versa.

It follows from Eqns. (4.79) and (4.82) that a pair of conjugate quadratic FIR filters $H(z)$ and $G(z)$ are also power-complementary as they satisfy Eqn. (4.81).

4.11.6 Magnitude-Complementary Filters

A set of M digital filters $\{G_i(z)\}$, $i = 0, 1, \ldots, M-1$, is defined to be magnitude-complementary of each other, if the sum of their magnitude responses is equal to a constant *i.e.*

$$\boxed{\sum_{i=0}^{M-1} |G_i(e^{j\omega})| = \beta, \text{ for all } \omega} \qquad \beta > 0, \text{ a constant} \qquad \ldots(4.83)$$

Consider two real-coefficient doubly-complementary TFs $H_0(z)$ and $H_1(z)$ such that

$$H_0(z) = \frac{1}{2}[A_0(z) + A_1(z)] \text{ where } A_0(z) \text{ and } A_1(z) \text{ are all pass TFs} \quad \ldots(4.84)$$

$$H_1(z) = \frac{1}{2}[A_0(z) - A_1(z)] \qquad \ldots(4.85)$$

Define

$$G_0(z) \triangleq H_0^2(z) = \frac{1}{4}[A_0(z) + A_1(z)]^2 \qquad \ldots(4.86)$$

$$G_1(z) \triangleq -H_1^2(z) = -\frac{1}{4}[A_0(z) - A_1(z)]^2 \qquad \ldots(4.87)$$

Then $G_0(z) + G_1(z) = A_0(z) \,.\, A_1(z)$, *i.e.* $G_0(z)$ and $G_1(z)$ are all pass complementary since $A_0(z) \cdot A_1(z)$ is an all pass TF. It can be shown that

$$|G_1(e^{j\omega})| + |G_1(e^{j\omega})| = |H_0(e^{j\omega})|^2 + |H_1(e^{j\omega})|^2 = 1 \qquad \ldots(4.88)$$

i.e. $G_0(z)$ and $G_1(z)$ are a magnitude-complementary pair of TFs.

4.12 STATE VARIABLE REALIZATIONS

A very important and efficient realization of IIR filters is by state variable approach, which we cover in this section.

4.12.1 Introduction of State Variable Analysis

We have studied several approaches for analysis and for design of electrical systems. We use Fourier transform and Laplace transform for analog systems, and Discrete-time Fourier transform and z-transform for analyzing/designing the discrete systems. These methods are used to determine the transfer function or the system function [$H(s)$ or $H(z)$] for the concerned system, where single-input single-output are there. When we try to extend the same techniques to analysis of multi-input, multi-output systems, they do work, but we are faced with the problem of having to write a large number of differential/difference equations and solving them. It makes the analysis of these systems very difficult and also increases the possibility of arriving at erroneous/incorrect results unless we adopt some very organized methods for dealing with these equations.

4.12.2 The State Variable (SV) Approach

To overcome the aforementioned problems and to have many other advantages, as given below, we adopt the state variable method, where multi-input multi-output (MIMO) signal processing is possible. We, therefore, first give the main advantages of SV approach.

Advantages of SV Method of System Analysis:

1. The state variable approach can be used for time-variant or time-invariant both types of systems.
2. The SV approach can be used for linear as well as for non-linear systems. Remember, the other conventional methods are suitable *only* for linear time invariant (LTI) systems.
3. The SV approach is most suitable for multi-input multi-output (MIMO) signal type systems, whereas the other conventional methods are not efficient for dealing, MIMO requirement.
4. The initial conditions of a system can be easily taken care of when the SV analysis is performed. This is a big advantage while adopting SV approach.
5. In the state variable approach, it is possible to confirm the state of the system parameters besides determining the input-output relations. This facility may be exploited to modify and optimize the system for best performance.

   The above mentioned advantages of SV analysis are the attractive features in spite of some disadvantages.

Disadvantages of SV Approach:

1. Complex techniques are required to realize the SV systems. In particular, to realize the building block: Integrator ($\boxed{s^{-1}}$) needed for analog SV systems, is not straightforward.

   The integrators and delays are necessarily needed to design SV systems besides the adders and multipliers.
2. Many computations are needed to realize the necessary parameters and intermediate signals needed to arrive at final output values.

4.12.3 Terminology used in State Variable Analysis

It is better to draw a block diagram of a SV system for understanding various parameters used in the system.

A typical state variable system with other parameters is shown in Fig. 4.27.

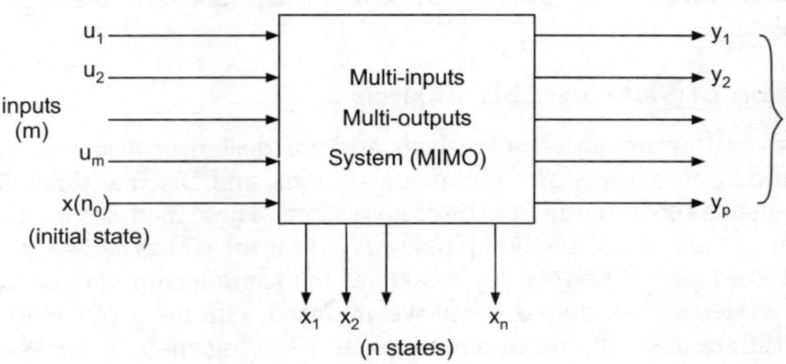

Fig. 4.27. Typical state model showing inputs, outputs and states

State: A compact and concise representation of the past history of the system is termed as state. For a dynamic system, the smallest number of variables (knowledge of these variables) at $n = n_0$ and for inputs at $n \geq n_0$, which can determine the behaviour of the system at $n \geq n_0$ is its state.

State Variables (SV): The smallest number of variables (generally orthogonal variables) that can determine the full state of the system are known as the state variables. There are n state variables, $x_1, x_2, \ldots, x_n$ that completely describe the behaviour of the SV system.

State Vector: The $n \times 1$ column vector with elements as $x_1, x_2, \ldots, x_n$ is called the state vector. The n-dimensional space whose coordinate axes are $x_1, x_2, \ldots, x_n$ is called state space.

We define some other parameters used for the SV analysis

$\underline{u}(k)$ is $m \times 1$ inputs vector.

$\underline{y}(k)$ is $p \times 1$ outputs vector.

$\underline{A}$ is $n \times n$ square matrix known as **Evolution matrix** or system matrix.

$\underline{B}$ is $n \times m$ matrix known as **Control matrix** or Input-coupling matrix. As the name implies, it gets multiplied with the inputs $\underline{u}(k)$ to produce part of signal $(\underline{B}\,\underline{u}(k))$ forming matrix $x(k+1)$.

$\underline{C}$ is $p \times n$ matrix called **Observation matrix** or also output-coupling matrix. By coupling with $\underline{x}(k)$ it generates $\underline{C}\,\underline{x}(k)$ which forms the part of output $\underline{y}(k)$, also called 'Homogeneous part' of the output.

$\underline{D}$ is $p \times m$ matrix called **Direct transmission matrix.** It converts the input $\underline{u}(k)$ into $\underline{D}\,\underline{u}(k)$ which also forms a part of output $\underline{y}(k)$, also known as 'Particular part' of the output. If $\underline{u}(k) = 0$, then this part is also zero.

The matrices $\underline{A}, \underline{B}, \underline{C}$ and $\underline{D}$ may be constant, (for time-invariant systems) or may be time-dependent (for time-variant systems). It is this property which enables the SV analysis to be adopted for wide range of practical systems.

Thus, we shall have, in matrix form, the various parameters as below:

Inputs: $$\underline{u}(k) = \begin{bmatrix} u_1(k) \\ u_2(k) \\ \vdots \\ u_m(k) \end{bmatrix}_{m\times 1} ; \quad \textbf{Outputs: } \underline{y}(k) = \begin{bmatrix} y_1(k) \\ y_2(k) \\ \vdots \\ y_p(k) \end{bmatrix}_{p\times 1} ;$$

State variables: $$\underline{x}(k) = \begin{bmatrix} x_1(k) \\ x_2(k) \\ \vdots \\ x_n(k) \end{bmatrix}_{n\times 1} ; \quad \underline{x}(k+1) = \begin{bmatrix} x_1(k+1) \\ x_2(k+1) \\ \vdots \\ x_n(k+1) \end{bmatrix}_{n\times 1}$$

$$\underline{A} = \begin{bmatrix} a_{11} & a_{12} & \cdots & a_{1n} \\ a_{21} & a_{22} & \cdots & a_{2n} \\ \vdots & \vdots & & \vdots \\ a_{n1} & a_{n2} & \cdots & a_{nn} \end{bmatrix}_{n\times n} ; \quad \underline{B} = \begin{bmatrix} b_{11} & b_{12} & \cdots & b_{1m} \\ b_{21} & b_{22} & \cdots & b_{2m} \\ \vdots & \vdots & & \vdots \\ b_{n1} & b_{n2} & \cdots & b_{nm} \end{bmatrix}_{n\times m} ;$$

$$\underline{C} = \begin{bmatrix} c_{11} & c_{12} & \cdots & c_{1n} \\ c_{21} & c_{22} & \cdots & c_{2n} \\ \vdots & \vdots & & \vdots \\ c_{p1} & c_{p2} & \cdots & c_{pn} \end{bmatrix}_{p\times n}; \quad \underline{D} = \begin{bmatrix} d_{11} & d_{12} & \cdots & d_{1m} \\ d_{21} & d_{22} & \cdots & d_{2m} \\ \vdots & \vdots & & \vdots \\ d_{p1} & d_{p2} & \cdots & d_{pm} \end{bmatrix}_{p\times m} \quad \ldots(4.89)$$

4.12.4 State Variable Equations (Discrete-time System)

If $\underline{u}(k)$ and $\underline{y}(k)$ are, respectively, the inputs and outputs and $\underline{A}, \underline{B}, \underline{C}$ and $\underline{D}$ are the state variables, the SV equations are defined as follows:

$$\underline{x}(k+1) = \underline{A}\,\underline{x}(k) + \underline{B}\,\underline{u}(k) \quad \ldots(4.90)$$

$$y(k) = \underline{C}\,\underline{x}(k) + \underline{D}\,\underline{u}(k) \quad \ldots(4.91)$$

We can always express the system function, $H(z)$, of the discrete system by SV equations, as will be shown by us in the following examples. Also, given the system's SV equations, we can compute $H(z)$.

We first derive the expressions of system function $H(z)$ from their SV equations.

4.12.5 Transfer Function Derivation from State Variable Model for Discrete-time System: *H(z)*

We know that the state variable equations are

$$\underline{x}(k+1) = \underline{A}\,\underline{x}(k) + \underline{B}\,\underline{u}(k) \quad \text{from (4.90) } (A)$$

$$y(k) = \underline{C}\,\underline{x}(k) + \underline{D}\,\underline{u}(k) \quad \text{from (4.91) } (B)$$

We wish to compute $H(z) = \dfrac{Y(z)}{U(z)}$

Taking zT of equation (A) and (B), we obtain

$$z(\underline{X}(z) - x(0)) = \underline{A}\,\underline{X}(z) + \underline{B}\,U(z) \quad \text{from } (A)$$

Assume $x(0) = 0$ (relaxed system)

$$(z\underline{I} - \underline{A})\,\underline{X}(z) = \underline{B}\,U(z)$$

$$\underline{X}(z) = (z\underline{I} - \underline{A})^{-1}\,\underline{B}\,U(z)$$

...($\underline{I}$ is identity matrix of $n \times n$ dimension) ...(C)

From (B), we get

$$Y(z) = \underline{C}\,\underline{X}(z) + \underline{D}\,U(z)$$

$$= \underline{C}\,[(z\underline{I} - \underline{A})^{-1}\,\underline{B}\,U(z)] + \underline{D}\,U(z) \quad \text{[due to (C)]}$$

$$= [\underline{C}\,(z\underline{I} - \underline{A})^{-1}\,\underline{B} + \underline{D}\,]\,U(z)$$

$$H(z) = \frac{Y(z)}{U(z)} = \underline{C}\,(z\underline{I} - \underline{A})^{-1}\,\underline{B} + \underline{D} \quad \ldots(4.92)$$

which is the expression of Transfer Function (*i.e.* system function) of discrete system analyzed by state variables.

4.12.6 SV Model of the First-order Discrete System

We shall evolve a method to analyse discrete and analog systems by using state variable approach. Let us consider a first-order discrete system, for example, given by the system function.

$$H(z) = \frac{z^{-1}}{1+4z^{-1}} \quad ...(A)$$

i.e. $$\frac{Y(z)}{U(z)} = \frac{z^{-1}}{1+4z^{-1}}$$ [Note that we have used input as $u(n)$ and not $x(n)$ as per the convention is SV approach] ...(B)

i.e. $$Y(z)\ (1 + 4z^{-1}) = z^{-1}\ U(z) \quad ...(C)$$

Take inverse zT on both the sides of (C), we get

$$y(k) + 4\ y(k-1) = u(k-1) \quad ...(D)$$

or $$y(k) = -4\ y(k-1) + u(k-1) \quad ...(E)$$

which is the difference equation characterizing the system function $H(z)$.

To realize $H(z)$, given by (A), we have the configuration given in Fig. 4.28. Here, we have shown multiplier (by −4) by a square block $\boxed{-4}$ and adder by the symbol ⊕. Normally, to simplify the drawing we use Fig. 4.29, which is the realization of the same *TF H*(*z*) as in Fig. 4.28, and is preferred in most of the books on digital signal processing (DSP). Figure 4.29 is reoriented and drawn as Fig. 4.30, as this way we can easily perform SV analysis, as will be seen when we solve the numerical examples.

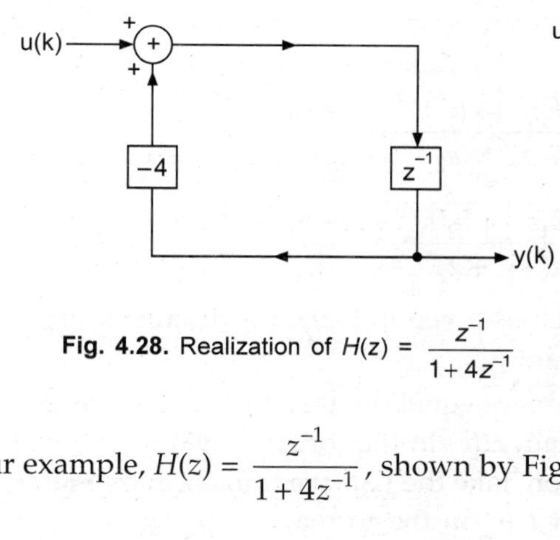

Fig. 4.28. Realization of $H(z) = \dfrac{z^{-1}}{1+4z^{-1}}$

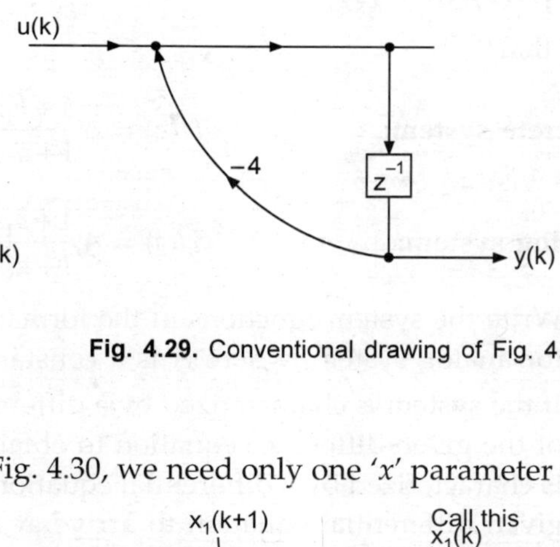

Fig. 4.29. Conventional drawing of Fig. 4.26

For our example, $H(z) = \dfrac{z^{-1}}{1+4z^{-1}}$, shown by Fig. 4.30, we need only one '*x*' parameter as $H(z)$ is of the first degree. The number of delays $\boxed{z^{-1}}$ used is always equal to the degree of the *TF H*(*z*). Similar will be the case in analog systems where the number of integrals $\boxed{s^{-1}}$ will be equal to the degree of *TF H*(*s*) for the analog system being analyzed.

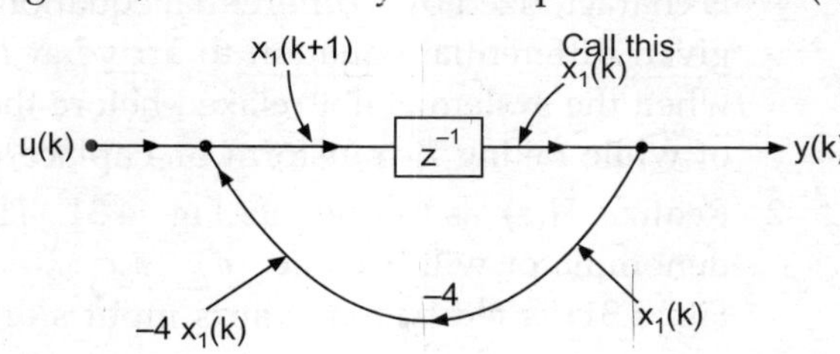

Fig. 4.30. Fig. 4.27 Reoriented being more explicit for SV analysis concept

We define $x_1(k)$, $x_2(k)$, ..., the *outputs of delays*. To start with we call output of the last delay as $x_1(k)$ and go on calling the outputs of delays on left by $x_2(k)$, $x_3(k)$ ... . Here, in the considered example, we have only one delay. We call the output of this delay as $x_1(k)$. This also happens to be the value of $y(k)$ as shown in Figs. 4.29 and 4.30. The signal input to the delay is $x_1(k+1)$. In Fig. 4.30, $x_1(k+1)$ is the result of addition of $u(k)$ and $-4x_1(k)$. Thus, we readily have the following equations, (see Fig. 4.30):

$$\left.\begin{aligned} x_1(k+1) &= -4x_1(k) + u(k) \\ y(k) &= x_1(k) + 0\, u(k) \end{aligned}\right\} \qquad \begin{aligned} &...(F) \\ &...(G) \end{aligned}$$

Comparing (*F*) with $\underset{\sim}{x}(k+1) = \underset{\sim}{A}\, \underset{\sim}{x}(k) + \underset{\sim}{B}\, \underset{\sim}{u}(k)$

we get $\underset{\sim}{A} = -4,\ \underset{\sim}{B} = 1$

Comparing (*G*) with $y(k) = \underset{\sim}{C}\, \underset{\sim}{x}(k) + \underset{\sim}{D}\, \underset{\sim}{u}(k)$

we get $\underset{\sim}{C} = 1,\ \ \underset{\sim}{D} = 0.$

Hence,

$$\underset{\sim}{A} = [-4]_{1\times1},\quad \underset{\sim}{B} = [1]_{1\times1},\quad \underset{\sim}{C} = [1]_{1\times1},\quad \underset{\sim}{D} = [0]_{1\times1}$$

i.e.,

$$\left.\begin{aligned} \underset{\sim}{x}(k+1) &= [-4]\,[x_1(k)] + [1]\,[u(k)] \\ y(k) &= [1]\,[x_1(k)] + [0]\,[u(k)] \end{aligned}\right\} \text{ are the SV equations of the given systems}$$

4.12.7 Steps to Compute the SV Matrices *A*, *B*, *C*, *D* for a given System Function [*H*(*z*) or *H*(*s*)]

Assume that

Discrete system:

$$H(z) = A\frac{1 + b_1 z^{-1} + b_2 z^{-2} + ... + b_M z^{-M}}{1 + a_1 z^{-1} + a_2 z^{-2} + ... + a_N z^{-N}} \qquad ...(4.93)$$

Analog system:

$$H(s) = A\frac{1 + b_1 s^{-1} + b_2 s^{-2} + ... + b_M s^{-M}}{1 + a_1 s^{-1} + a_2 s^{-2} + ... + a_N s^{-N}} \qquad ...(4.94)$$

1. Write the system functions in the format as given in (4.93) for discrete system and (4.94) for analog system, where *A* is a constant.
   If the system is characterized by a difference equation, take the *z*-transform on both sides of the given difference equation to obtain *H*(*z*) in the format (4.93). If the analog system is characterized by a differential equation, take the Laplace transform on both sides of the given differential equation to arrive at *H*(*s*) in the format (4.94). The initial conditions, when the system is not relaxed before the input *u*(*n*) or *u*(*t*) is applied, can be taken care of while taking *Z*-transform or Laplace transform of the characterizing equations.
2. Realize *H*(*z*) as shown in Fig. 4.31. The coefficients $a_1, a_2, ..., a_N$ appearing in the denominator will become $-a_1, -a_2, ..., -a_N$ when the signal from right hand side (in the Fig. 4.31) is fed back towards input side, on left hand side.
3. The coefficients $b_1, b_2, ..., b_M$ in the numerator will feed the output point *y*(*k*), without change of sign.
4. The constant *A*, if not unity, will be shown just after input *u*(*k*).

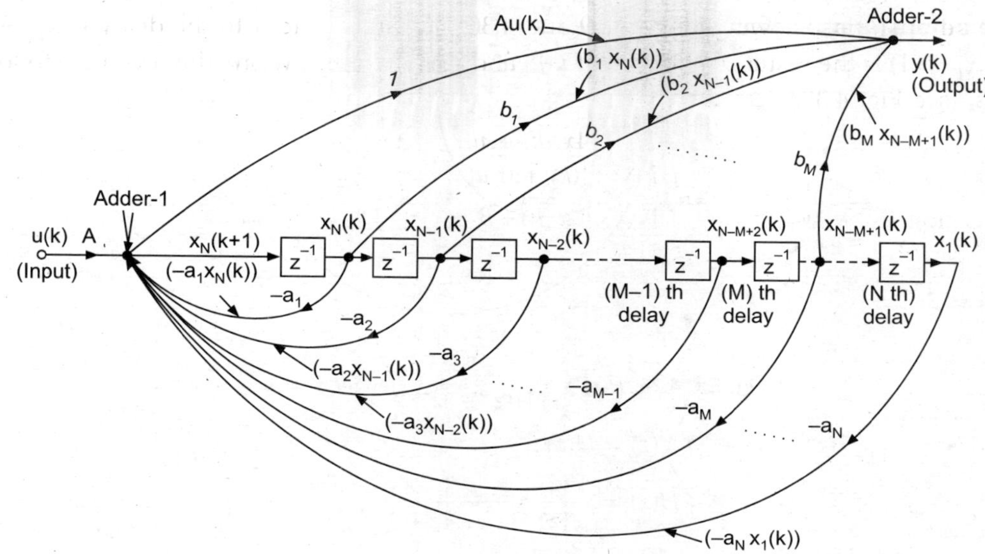

Fig. 4.31. Realization of $H(z)$ given by (4.93) for SV analysis

5. Designate parameters $x_1(k)$, $x_2(k)$, ..., $x_N(k)$ as the output from the delays. **$x_1(k)$ is the output from the last delay** (*i.e.* N^{th} delay, appearing on extreme RHS in the Fig. 4.31). $x_2(k)$ is the output of $(N-1)^{th}$ delay and so on, and finally $x_N(k)$ will be the output of the first delay.
6. With naming the signals, $x_1(k)$, $x_2(k)$, ..., $x_N(k)$, in this manner, it is clear that
$$x_i(k+1) = x_{i+1}(k), \quad i = 1, 2, ..., N-1 \qquad ...(4.95)$$
For example, $x_1(k + 1)$ is the same as $x_2(k)$, and $x_2(k + 1) = x_3(k)$ and so on.
7. Also, $\quad x_N(k+1) =$ Input to the first delay
$$= A\,u(k) - [a_1x_N(k) + a_2\,x_{N-1}(k) + ..., a_N\,x_1(k)] \qquad ...(4.96)$$
i.e. we write $x_N(k + 1)$ as the output of the Adder-1, where in the signals $A\,u(k)$, $-a_1\,x_N(k)$, $-a_2\,x_{N-1}(k)$, ..., $-a_N\,x_1(k)$ are fed.
8. Output of the Adder-2 is $y(k)$, given by
$$y(k) = A\,u(k) + [b_1\,x_N(k) + b_2\,x_{N-1}(k) + ... + b_M\,x_{N-M+1}(k)] \qquad ...(4.97)$$
9. Having obtained the equations for $x_i(k + 1)$ (*i.e.* 4.95) and $y(k)$ (*i.e.* 4.97) in terms of $x_1(k)$, $x_2(k)$, ..., $x_N(k)$, and $u(k)$ together with other constants such as A_1, a_i, b_i, thereafter, we can compare these two equations with the standard SV equations, and hence identify the matrices $\underline{A}, \underline{B}, \underline{C}$ and $\underline{D}$.

Note. For the analog systems, we replace z^{-1} by s^{-1} wherever it appears in Fig. 4.31. This substitution is also apparent if we compare equations (4.93) and (4.94) which define $H(z)$ and $H(s)$.

We elucidate the aforementioned procedure by a few examples as follows.

EXAMPLE 4.26: *A second order discrete system is characterized by the difference equation.*
$$y(k+2) + 4y(k+1) + 3y(k) = u(k)$$
Determine the $\underline{A}, \underline{B}, \underline{C}, \underline{D}$ *matrices for the state variable analysis.* *(IP Univ., 2007)*

SOLUTION: As $y(k + 2) + 4\, y(k + 1) + 3y(k) = u(k)$

Take z-transform on both sides

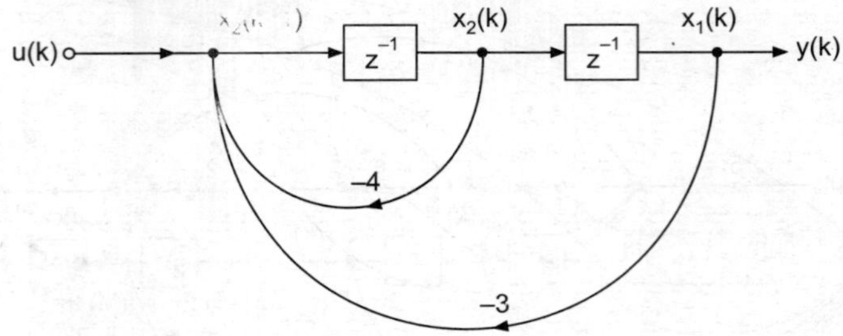

Fig. Ex. 4.26. $H(z) = \dfrac{z^{-2}}{1+4z^{-1}+3z^{-2}}$ for SV analysis

$$\therefore \qquad (z^2 + 4z + 3)\, Y(z) = U(z)$$

$$H(z) = \frac{Y(z)}{U(z)} = \frac{1}{z^2+4z+3}$$

$$H(z) = \frac{z^{-2}}{1+4z^{-1}+3z^{-2}} \qquad (\textit{i.e.}\text{ rational function in } z^{-1})$$

Realization of $H(z)$ is as shown in Fig. Ex. 4.26.

Name outputs of delays as $x_1(k)$ and $x_2(k)$ as shown

$$\therefore \qquad x_1(k + 1) = x_2(k) = 0\, x_1(k) + 1 \cdot x_2(k) + 0 \cdot u(k) \qquad ...(A)$$

$$x_2(k + 1) = -3x_1(k) - 4\, x_2(k) + 1 \cdot u(k)$$

$$y(k) = x_1(k) = x_1(k) + 0\, x_2\,(k) + 0\, u(k) \qquad ...(B)$$

(A) and (B) give us, in matrix form

$$\begin{bmatrix} x_1 & (k+1) \\ x_2 & (k+1) \end{bmatrix} = \begin{bmatrix} 0 & 1 \\ -3 & -4 \end{bmatrix} \begin{bmatrix} x_1\,(k) \\ x_2\,(k) \end{bmatrix} + \begin{bmatrix} 0 \\ 1 \end{bmatrix} u(k) \qquad \left[Cf.\, \underset{\sim}{x}\,(k+1) = \underset{\sim}{A}\, \underset{\sim}{x}\,(k) + \underset{\sim}{B}\, \underset{\sim}{u}\,(k) \right]$$

$$y(k) = [1 \quad 0] \begin{bmatrix} x_1\,(k) \\ x_2\,(k) \end{bmatrix} + [0]\, u(k) \qquad \left[Cf.\, y\,(k) = \underset{\sim}{C}\, \underset{\sim}{x}\,(k) + \underset{\sim}{D}\, \underset{\sim}{u}\,(k) \right]$$

$$\therefore \qquad \underset{\sim}{A} = \begin{bmatrix} 0 & 1 \\ -3 & -4 \end{bmatrix}\, \underset{\sim}{B} = \begin{bmatrix} 0 \\ 1 \end{bmatrix},\ \underset{\sim}{C} = [1 \quad 0],\ \underset{\sim}{D} = [0] \quad \textbf{Ans.}$$

EXAMPLE 4.27: *(a) Determine state matrices for* $H(s) = \dfrac{5\,(s+1)\,(s+2)}{(s+4)\,(s+5)}$

(b) Obtain H(s) back from the matrices $\underset{\sim}{A}, \underset{\sim}{B}, \underset{\sim}{C}, \underset{\sim}{D}$ *found in part (a).* *(IP Univ., 2006)*

SOLUTION: (*a*) Given $H(s) = 5 \times \dfrac{s^2+3s+2}{s^2+9s+20} = 5 \cdot \dfrac{1+3s^{-1}+2s^{-2}}{1+9s^{-1}+20s^{-2}}$

Realization of $H(s)$ is as shown in Fig. Ex. 4.27. x_1 is the output of last integrator: s^{-1} and x_2 is the output of the previous integrator s^{-1}. Hence, we can write

$$\dot{x}_1 = x_2$$

$$\dot{x}_2 = 5u - 20x_1 - 9x_2$$

$$y = 2x_1 + 3x_2 + \dot{x}_2 = 2x_1 + 3x_2 + (5u - 20x_1 - 9x_2)$$
$$= -18x_1 - 6x_2 + 5u$$

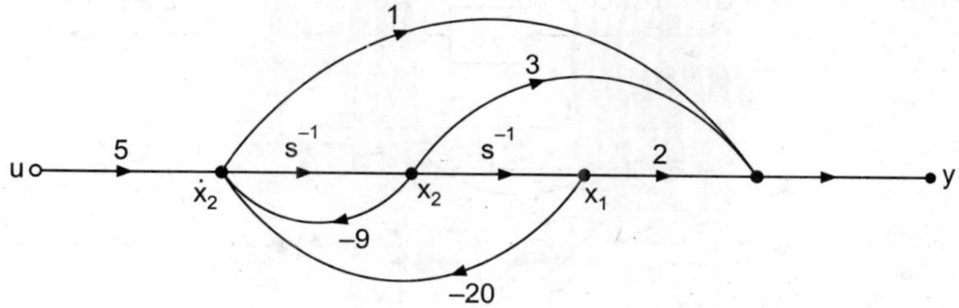

Fig. Ex. 4.27. $H(s) = \dfrac{5(1+3s^{-1}+2s^{-2})}{1+9s^{-1}+20s^{-2}}$ for SV analysis.

∴ We get

$$\begin{bmatrix} \dot{x}_1 \\ \dot{x}_2 \end{bmatrix} = \begin{bmatrix} 0 & 1 \\ -20 & -9 \end{bmatrix}\begin{bmatrix} x_1 \\ x_2 \end{bmatrix} + \begin{bmatrix} 0 \\ 5 \end{bmatrix} u$$

∴ $$\underline{A} = \begin{bmatrix} 0 & 1 \\ -20 & -9 \end{bmatrix}, \quad \underline{B} = \begin{bmatrix} 0 \\ 5 \end{bmatrix}$$

$$y = [-18 \ -6]\begin{bmatrix} x_1 \\ x_2 \end{bmatrix} + [5]u$$

$$\underline{C} = [-18, -6], \quad \underline{D} = [5]$$ **Ans.**

(*b*) [To find $H(s)$ from the $\underline{A}, \underline{B}, \underline{C}, \underline{D}$ found above]

$$\left[s\underline{I} - \underline{A}\right] = s\begin{bmatrix} 1 & 0 \\ 0 & 1 \end{bmatrix} - \begin{bmatrix} 0 & 1 \\ -20 & -9 \end{bmatrix} = \begin{bmatrix} s & -1 \\ 20 & s+9 \end{bmatrix}$$

$$\left|s\underline{I} - \underline{A}\right| = s(s+9) + 20 = s^2 + 9s + 20$$

∴ $$\left[s\underline{I} - \underline{A}\right]^{-1} = \frac{1}{s^2+9s+20}\begin{bmatrix} s+9 & 1 \\ -20 & s \end{bmatrix}$$

$$\left[s\underline{I} - \underline{A}\right]^{-1}\underline{B} = \frac{1}{s^2+9s+20}\begin{bmatrix} s+9 & 1 \\ -20 & s \end{bmatrix}\begin{bmatrix} 0 \\ 5 \end{bmatrix} = \frac{1}{s^2+9s+20}\begin{bmatrix} 5 \\ 5s \end{bmatrix}$$

$$\underline{C}\left[s\underline{I} - \underline{A}\right]^{-1}\underline{B} = \frac{1}{s^2+9s+20}[-18 \ -6]\begin{bmatrix} 5 \\ 5s \end{bmatrix} = \frac{-90-30s}{s^2+9s+20}$$

$$H(s) = \underline{C}\left[s\underline{I} - \underline{A}\right]^{-1}\underline{B} + \underline{D} = \frac{-90-30s}{s^2+9s+20} + 5 = \frac{5s^2+15s+10}{s^2+9s+20}$$

$$= 5 \times \frac{s^2+3s+2}{s^2+9s+20}$$

$$= 5 \times \frac{(s+1)(s+2)}{(s+4)(s+5)},$$ as expected.

EXAMPLE 4.28: *Find the A, B, C, D matrices/vectors for the system characterized by* $y(k) = -4y(k-1) - 5y(k-2) - 6y(k-3) + u(k-4)$ *(IP Univ., 2007)*

SOLUTION: From the given difference equation, we readily get, by taking z-transform on both sides

$$H(z) = \frac{Y(z)}{U(z)} = \frac{z^{-4}}{1+4z^{-1}+5z^{-2}+6z^{-3}} = \frac{z^{-4}}{1+4z^{-1}+5z^{-2}+6z^{-3}+0z^{-4}}$$

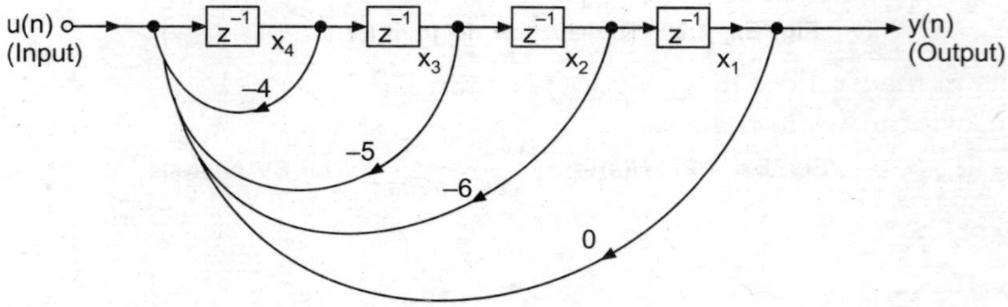

Fig. Ex. 4.28. The SV flow diagram (we require here, 4 delays)

We can write

$$x_1(n+1) = x_2(n)$$
$$x_2(n+1) = x_3(n)$$
$$x_3(n+1) = x_4(n)$$
$$x_4(n+1) = 0x_1(n) - 6x_2(n) - 5x_3(n) - 4x_4 + u(n)$$
$$y(n) = x_1(n)$$

$$\begin{bmatrix} x_1(n+1) \\ x_2(n+1) \\ x_3(n+1) \\ x_4(n+1) \end{bmatrix} = \underbrace{\begin{bmatrix} 0 & 1 & 0 & 0 \\ 0 & 0 & 1 & 0 \\ 0 & 0 & 0 & 1 \\ 0 & -6 & -5 & -4 \end{bmatrix}}_{\underset{\sim}{A}} \begin{bmatrix} x_1(n) \\ x_2(n) \\ x_3(n) \\ x_4(n) \end{bmatrix} + \underbrace{\begin{bmatrix} 0 \\ 0 \\ 0 \\ 1 \end{bmatrix}}_{\underset{\sim}{B}} [u(n)]$$

$$y(n) = \underbrace{[1,0,0,0]}_{\underset{\sim}{C}} \begin{bmatrix} x_1(n) \\ x_2(n) \\ x_3(n) \\ x_4(n) \end{bmatrix} + \underbrace{[0]}_{\underset{\sim}{D}} u(n)$$

Matrices/Vectors, A, B, C, D are as shown. **Ans.**

EXAMPLE 4.29: *Find the state variable model parameters* $\underset{\sim}{A}, \underset{\sim}{B}, \underset{\sim}{C}$ *and* $\underset{\sim}{D}$*, for a discrete system with system function as*

$$H(z) = \frac{Y(z)}{U(z)} = \frac{1}{z^4+4z^3+5z^2+6z+3}.$$

SOLUTION: We can write

$$H(z) = \frac{z^{-4}}{1+4z^{-1}+5z^{-2}+6z^{-3}+3z^{-4}}$$

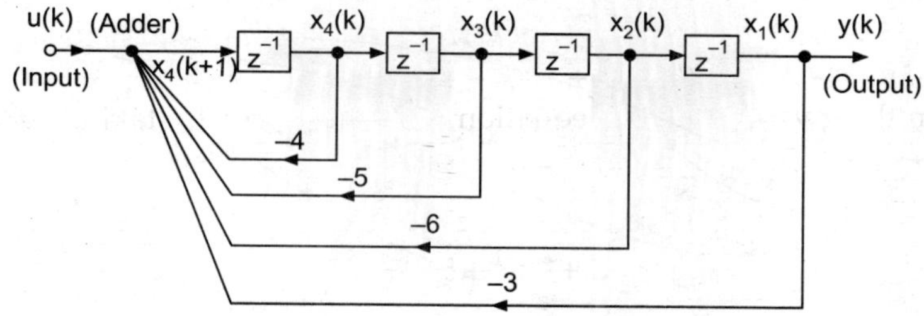

Fig. Ex. 4.29. The SV flow diagram for the given $H(z)$

This results in the SV flow diagram as shown in Fig. Ex. 4.29. Denoting $x_1(k)$, $x_2(k)$, $x_3(k)$ and $x_4(k)$ as shown, we can write the equations

$$x_1(k+1) = x_2(k)$$
$$x_2(k+1) = x_3(k)$$
$$x_3(k+1) = x_4(k)$$
$$x_4(k+1) = -3x_1(k) - 6x_2(k) - 5x_3(k) - 4x_4(k) + u(k)$$

Writing in matrix form, we get

$$\begin{bmatrix} x_1(k+1) \\ x_2(k+1) \\ x_3(k+1) \\ x_4(k+1) \end{bmatrix} = \underbrace{\begin{bmatrix} 0 & 1 & 0 & 0 \\ 0 & 0 & 1 & 0 \\ 0 & 0 & 0 & 1 \\ -3 & -6 & -5 & -4 \end{bmatrix}}_{\underline{A}} \begin{bmatrix} x_1(k) \\ x_2(k) \\ x_3(k) \\ x_4(k) \end{bmatrix} + \underbrace{\begin{bmatrix} 0 \\ 0 \\ 0 \\ 1 \end{bmatrix}}_{\underline{B}} u(k)$$

$$y(k) = x_1(k)$$

$\therefore$
$$y(k) = \underbrace{[1 \ \ 0 \ \ 0 \ \ 0]}_{C} \begin{bmatrix} x_1(k) \\ x_2(k) \\ x_3(k) \end{bmatrix} + \underbrace{[0]}_{D} u(k)$$ **Ans.**

EXAMPLE 4.30: *Find the state variable model of the system with transfer function*

$$H(z) = \frac{z^2 + 3z + 4}{z^3 + 7z^2 + 6z + 5}$$

(IP Univ., 2010)

SOLUTION: We can write

$$H(z) = \frac{0 + z^{-1} + 3z^{-2} + 4z^{-3}}{1 + 7z^{-1} + 6z^{-2} + 5z^{-3}}$$

(rational function in z^{-1})

Realization of $H(z)$ is shown in Fig. Ex. 4.30(a) (as a canonic form). It has been redrawn in Fig. Ex. 4.30(b) after reorienting for ease of understanding in SV analysis.

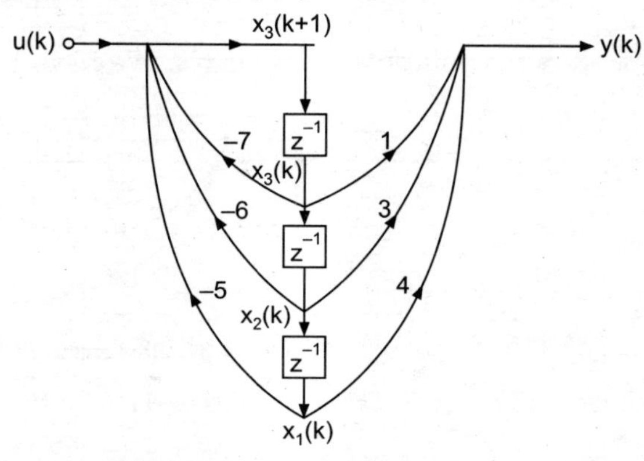

Fig. Ex. 4.30. (a) Realization of $H(z)$

Clearly,
$$x_1(k+1) = x_2(k)$$
$$x_2(k+1) = x_3(k)$$
$$x_3(k+1) = -5x_1(k) - 6x_2(k) - 7x_3(k) + u(k)$$

and
$$y(k) = 4x_1(k) + 3x_2(k) + x_3(k)$$

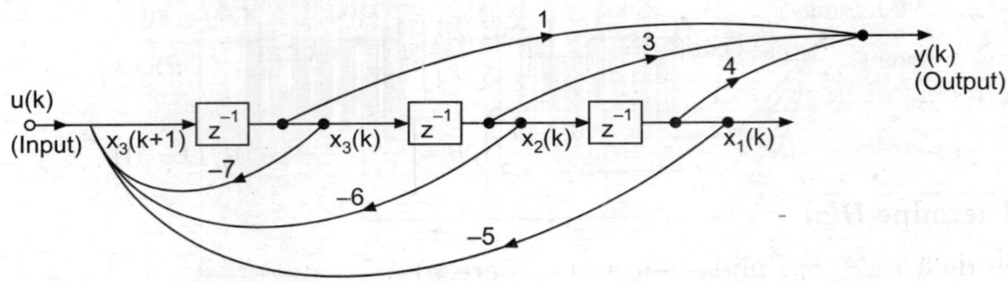

Fig. Ex. 4.30. (*b*) Conversion from Fig. Ex. 4.30 (*a*), the SV form

∴ We can write

$$\begin{bmatrix} x_1(k+1) \\ x_2(k+1) \\ x_3(k+1) \end{bmatrix} = \underbrace{\begin{bmatrix} 0 & 1 & 0 \\ 0 & 0 & 1 \\ -5 & -6 & -7 \end{bmatrix}}_{\underline{A}} \begin{bmatrix} x_1(k) \\ x_2(k) \\ x_3(k) \end{bmatrix} + \underbrace{\begin{bmatrix} 0 \\ 0 \\ 1 \end{bmatrix}}_{\underline{B}} u(k)$$

and $$y(k) = \underbrace{[4 \quad 3 \quad 1]}_{\underline{C}} \begin{bmatrix} x_1(k) \\ x_2(k) \\ x_3(k) \end{bmatrix} \qquad \underline{D} = 0 \text{ here.}$$ **Ans.**

EXAMPLE 4.31: (*a*) *Find SV model parameters* $\underline{A}, \underline{B}, \underline{C}$ *and* $\underline{D}$ *for the discrete system given its Transfer Function*

$$H(z) = \frac{1}{z^2 + 3z + 2}.$$

(*b*) *By* $\underline{A}, \underline{B}, \underline{C}$ *using and* $\underline{D}$ *found above, compute H(z).*

SOLUTION: (*a*) The realization of $H(z) = \dfrac{z^{-2}}{1 + 3z^{-1} + 2z^{-2}}$ is shown in Fig. Ex. 4.31. $x_1(k)$ and $x_2(k)$ are shown as outputs from delays. We have the relations

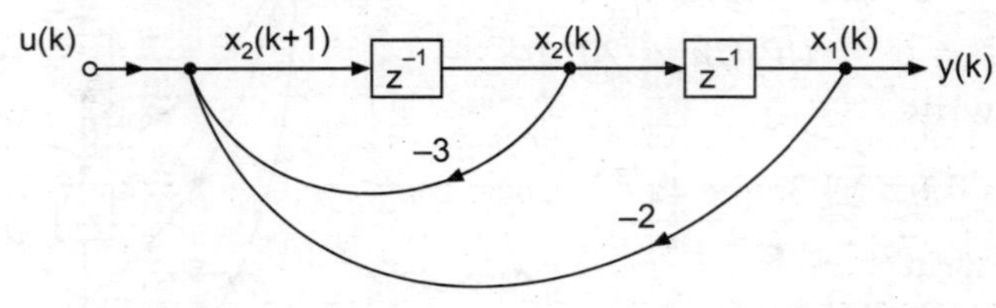

Fig. Ex. 4.31. Realization of *H*(*z*) to determine SV parameter

$$x_1(k+1) = 0x_1(k) + x_2(k)$$

$$x_2(k+1) = -2x_1(k) - 3x_2(k) + u(k) \qquad ...(A)$$

$$y(k) = x_1(k) \qquad ...(B)$$

Writing above equations in matrix form, we have

$$\begin{bmatrix} x_1(k+1) \\ x_2(k+1) \end{bmatrix} = \begin{bmatrix} 0 & 1 \\ -2 & -3 \end{bmatrix} \begin{bmatrix} x_1(k) \\ x_2(k) \end{bmatrix} + \begin{bmatrix} 0 \\ 1 \end{bmatrix} u(k) \qquad \text{from } (A)$$

$$y(k) = [1 \quad 0]\begin{bmatrix} x_1(k) \\ x_2(k) \end{bmatrix} + [0]\,u(k) \qquad \text{from } (B)$$

$$\therefore \quad \underline{A} = \begin{bmatrix} 0 & 1 \\ -2 & -3 \end{bmatrix}, \underline{B} = \begin{bmatrix} 0 \\ 1 \end{bmatrix}, \underline{C} = [1 \quad 0], \underline{D} = [0] \qquad \textbf{Ans.}$$

(*b*) **To determine *H*(*z*)**

The given data is $\underline{A}, \underline{B}, \underline{C}$ and $\underline{D}$ found in part (*a*). We know that

$$H(z) = \underline{C}\left[z\underline{I} - \underline{A}\right]^{-1}\underline{B} + \underline{D} \qquad \text{[see (4.92)]}$$

Now

$$z\underline{I} - \underline{A} = z\begin{bmatrix} 1 & 0 \\ 0 & 1 \end{bmatrix} - \begin{bmatrix} 0 & 1 \\ -2 & -3 \end{bmatrix} = \begin{bmatrix} z & -1 \\ 2 & z+3 \end{bmatrix}$$

$$\left|z\underline{I} - \underline{A}\right| = z(z + 3) + 2 = (z + 1)(z + 2)$$

$$\left[z\underline{I} - \underline{A}\right]^{-1} = \frac{1}{(z+1)(z+2)}\begin{bmatrix} (z+3) & 1 \\ -2 & z \end{bmatrix} \textbf{(see **)}$$

$$\underline{C}\left[z\underline{I} - \underline{A}\right]^{-1}\underline{B} + \underline{D} = [1 \quad 0]\frac{1}{(z+1)(z+2)}\begin{bmatrix} (z+3) & 1 \\ -2 & z \end{bmatrix}\begin{bmatrix} 0 \\ 1 \end{bmatrix} + [0]$$

$$= \frac{1}{(z+1)(z+2)}[1 \quad 0]\begin{bmatrix} 1 \\ z \end{bmatrix} + [0]$$

$$= \frac{1}{(z+1)(z+2)}$$

$$\therefore \quad H(z) = \frac{1}{z^2 + 3z + 2} \qquad \textbf{Ans.}$$

which was expected.

EXAMPLE 4.32: (*a*) *Find the SV model of the system having transfer function*

$$H(z) = \frac{z^3 + 3z^2 + z + 3}{z^3 + 4z^2 + 3z + 1}.$$

(*b*) *By using* $\underline{A}, \underline{B}, \underline{C}$ *and* $\underline{D}$ *found in (a) above, compute H(z).*

SOLUTION: We can write here

(*a*) $H(z) = \dfrac{1 + 3z^{-1} + z^{-2} + 3z^{-3}}{1 + 4z^{-1} + 3z^{-2} + z^{-3}}$

** **Note that**

Adj of (z) = (z + 3)

Adj of (–1) = –2

Adj of (2) = 1

Adj of (z + 3) = z

Realization of $H(z)$ is as shown in Fig. Ex. 4.32

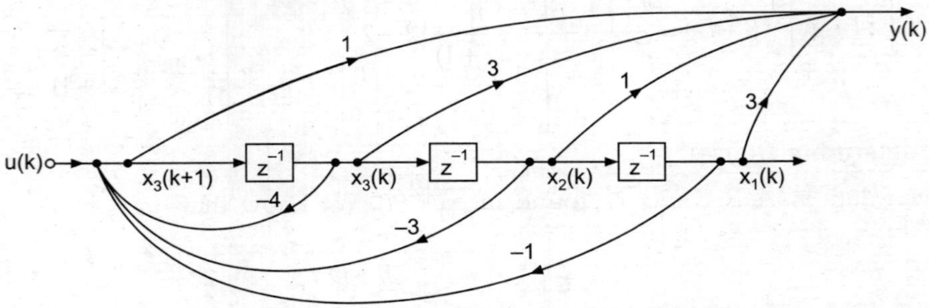

Fig. Ex. 4.32. Realization of $H(z)$ shown for SV analysis

$$\left.\begin{aligned} x_1(k+1) &= x_2(k) & (i)\\ x_2(k+1) &= x_3(k) & (ii)\\ x_3(k+1) &= -x_1(k) - 3x_2(k) - 4x_3(k) + u(k) & (iii)\end{aligned}\right\} \Rightarrow \begin{bmatrix} x_1(k+1)\\ x_2(k+1)\\ x_3(k+1)\end{bmatrix} \Rightarrow \underbrace{\begin{bmatrix} 0 & 1 & 0\\ 0 & 0 & 1\\ -1 & -3 & -4\end{bmatrix}}_{\underline{A}} \begin{bmatrix} x_1(k)\\ x_2(k)\\ x_3(k)\end{bmatrix} + \underbrace{\begin{bmatrix} 0\\ 0\\ 1\end{bmatrix}}_{\underline{B}} u(k)$$

Also
$$\begin{aligned} y(k) &= 3x_1(k) + x_2(k) + 3x_3(k) + x_3(k+1)\\ &= 3x_1(k) + x_2(k) + 3x_3(k) + [-x_1(k) - 3x_2(k) - 4x_3(k) + u(k)] \qquad \text{due to } (iii)\\ &= 2x_1(k) - 2x_2(k) - x_3(k) + u(k)\end{aligned}$$

$$\therefore \qquad y(k) = \underbrace{[2\ \ -2\ \ -1]}_{\underline{C}} \begin{bmatrix} x_1(k)\\ x_2(k)\\ x_3(k)\end{bmatrix} + \underbrace{[1]}_{\underline{D}} u(k)$$

Hence,
$$\underline{A} = \begin{bmatrix} 0 & 1 & 0\\ 0 & 0 & 1\\ -1 & -3 & -4\end{bmatrix},\ \underline{B} = \begin{bmatrix} 0\\ 0\\ 1\end{bmatrix},\ \underline{C} = [2\ \ -2\ \ -1] \text{ and } \underline{D} = [1]$$ **Ans.**

(*b*) Now we have to determine $H(z)$, given matrices $\underline{A}, \underline{B}, \underline{C}, \underline{D}$.

$$\underline{A} = \begin{bmatrix} 0 & 1 & 0\\ 0 & 0 & 1\\ -1 & -3 & -4\end{bmatrix},\ \underline{B} = \begin{bmatrix} 0\\ 0\\ 1\end{bmatrix},\ \underline{C} = [2\ \ -2\ \ -1],\ \underline{D} = [1]$$

$$[z\underline{I} - \underline{A}] = z\begin{bmatrix} 1 & 0 & 0\\ 0 & 1 & 0\\ 0 & 0 & 1\end{bmatrix} - \begin{bmatrix} 0 & 1 & 0\\ 0 & 0 & 1\\ -1 & -3 & -4\end{bmatrix} = \begin{bmatrix} z & -1 & 0\\ 0 & z & -1\\ 1 & 3 & z+4\end{bmatrix}$$

$$\text{Det } |z\underline{I} - \underline{A}| = z[z(z+4) + 3] + [1] = z^3 + 4z^2 + 3z + 1$$

$$\left[z\underline{I} - \underline{A}\right]^{-1} = \frac{1}{(z^3 + 4z^2 + 3z + 1)} \begin{bmatrix} z(z+4)+3 & (z+4) & 1\\ -1 & z(z+4) & z\\ -z & -(3z+1) & z^2\end{bmatrix}$$

$$C\left[z\underline{I}-\underline{A}\right]^{-1}\underline{B}+\underline{D} = \frac{1}{(z^3+4z^2+3z+1)}[2\ -2\ -1]\begin{bmatrix} z^2+4z+3 & (z+4) & 1 \\ -1 & z^2+4z & z \\ -z & -(3z+1) & z^2 \end{bmatrix}\begin{bmatrix} 0 \\ 0 \\ 1 \end{bmatrix}+[1]$$

$$= \frac{1}{(z^3+4z^2+3z+1)}[2-2-1]\begin{bmatrix} 1 \\ z \\ z^2 \end{bmatrix}+1$$

$$= \frac{1}{(z^3+4z^2+3z+1)}(2-2z-z^2)+1$$

$$= \frac{z^3+3z^2+z+3}{(z^3+4z^2+3z+1)}$$

$$\therefore \qquad H(z) = \frac{z^3+3z^2+z+3}{(z^3+4z^2+3z+1)}, \text{ (as expected)}$$

4.12.8 Other Realizations of $H(z)$ and $H(s)$ for SV Parametrization

The realization of $H(z)$ and $H(s)$ are not unique. There are other ways also to realize these TFs.

Parallel Realizations/Parallel Decomposition

$$\left.\begin{aligned} H(z) &= H_1(z) + H_2(z) + \ldots \\ H(s) &= H_1(s) + H_2(s) + \ldots \end{aligned}\right\} \text{Partial fraction expansions of } H(z) \text{ and } H(s)$$

Cascade Realizations/Cascade Decomposition

$$\left.\begin{aligned} H(z) &= H_1(z)\ .\ H_2(z)\ldots \\ H(s) &= H_1(s)\ .\ H_2(z)\ldots \end{aligned}\right\} \text{Factorization of } H(z) \text{ and } H(s)$$

Obviously, we shall obtain different expressions of matrices $\underline{A}, \underline{B}, \underline{C}$ and $\underline{D}$ in above cases of realizations. However, when we compute the value of $H(z)$ or $H(s)$ by using these $\underline{A}, \underline{B}, \underline{C}, \underline{D}$ and (4.92), we arrive at the same values of $H(z)$ and $H(s)$.

The reason for above observation is that the state space model is not unique, as we shall prove in Section 4.12.11. Some examples to realize $H(s)$ and $H(z)$ in parallel form will be given.

4.12.9 Parallel Decomposition Approach (Details) [Similar for $H(s)$ and $H(z)$]

Let

$$H(s) = \frac{Y(s)}{U(s)} = \frac{D(s)}{(s+a_1)(s+a_2)\ldots(s+a_n)}$$

$$\equiv \frac{d_1}{s+a_1}+\frac{d_2}{s+a_2}+\ldots+\frac{d_n}{s+a_n} \qquad \text{(by partial fraction)}$$

or

$$Y(s) = \frac{d_1}{s+a_1}U(s)+\frac{d_2}{s+a_2}U(s)+\ldots+\frac{d_n}{s+a_n}U(s)$$

$$\triangleq d_1Y_1(s) + d_2Y_2(s) + \ldots + d_nY_n(s)$$

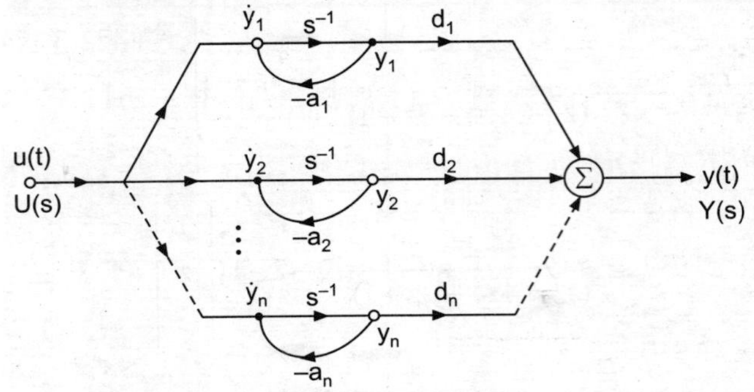

Fig. 4.32 (*a*) Parallel realization for *Y*(*s*)

We realize $y_1, y_2, ..., y_n$ and multiply these by $d_1, d_2, ..., d_n$ and add to obtain y

Hence,

$$\dot{y}_1 = -a_1 y_1 + u$$

$$\dot{y}_2 = -a_2 y_2 + u$$

$$\vdots$$

$$\dot{y}_n = -a_n y_n + u$$

and

$$y = a_1 y_1 + a_2 y_2 + ... + a_n y_n.$$

Hence, we can write

$$\begin{bmatrix} \dot{y}_1 \\ \dot{y}_2 \\ \vdots \\ \dot{y}_n \end{bmatrix} = \underbrace{\begin{bmatrix} -a_1 & 0 & \cdots & 0 \\ 0 & -a_2 & \cdots & 0 \\ \vdots & & & \\ 0 & \cdots & \cdots & -a_n \end{bmatrix}}_{\underline{A}} \begin{bmatrix} y_1 \\ y_2 \\ \vdots \\ y_n \end{bmatrix} + \underbrace{\begin{bmatrix} 1 \\ 1 \\ \vdots \\ 1 \end{bmatrix}}_{\underline{B}} [u]$$

and

$$y = \underbrace{[d_1 \;\; d_2 \;\; \cdots \;\; d_n]}_{\underline{C}} \begin{bmatrix} y_1 \\ y_2 \\ \vdots \\ y_n \end{bmatrix} + \underbrace{[0]}_{\underline{D}}[u]$$

Notes: That we always get $\underline{A}$ as a diagonal matrix in this case, if we get, first degree partial fractions.

It is possible to include, d_i's in y_i *i.e.*, to have

$$Y(s) = Y_1(s) + Y_2(s) + \ldots + \quad [\text{instead of } Y(s) = d_1Y_1(s) + d_2Y_2(s) + \ldots]$$

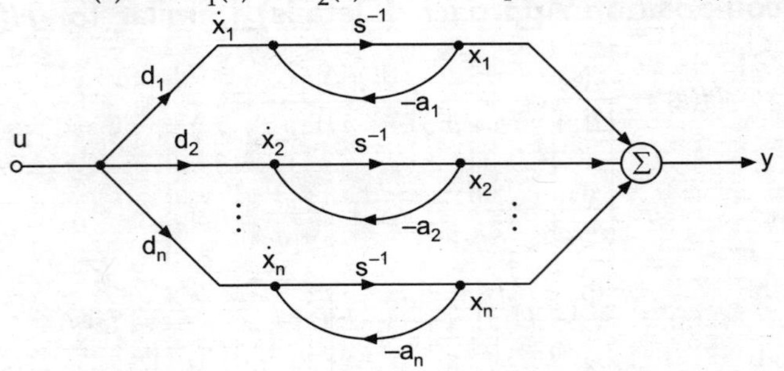

Fig. 4.32 (*b*) An alternative to realization for *Y*(*s*)

We multiply u by d_i

Here $\underline{C}$ becomes [1 1 ... 1] and $\underline{D}$ become $[d_1 \ d_2 \ \ldots \ d_n]^T$

EXAMPLE 4.33: *Find parallel decomposition of the transfer function given by*

$$\frac{Y(s)}{U(s)} = \frac{(s+1)}{(s+2)(s+3)(s+5)}, \text{ and find the SV matrices } \underline{A}, \underline{B}, \underline{C} \text{ and } \underline{D}.$$

SOLUTION:

$$\frac{Y(s)}{U(s)} = \frac{(s+1)}{(s+2)(s+3)(s+5)} = \frac{(-1/3)}{(s+2)} + \frac{(1)}{(s+3)} + \frac{(-2/3)}{(s+5)}$$

(by partial fraction)

or $Y(s) \equiv \left[(-1/3)Y_1(s) + Y_2(s) + \left(-\frac{2}{3}\right)Y_3(s)\right]U(s)$

$$y = \left(\frac{-1}{3}\right)y_1 + (1)\,y_2 + \left(-\frac{2}{3}\right)y_3$$

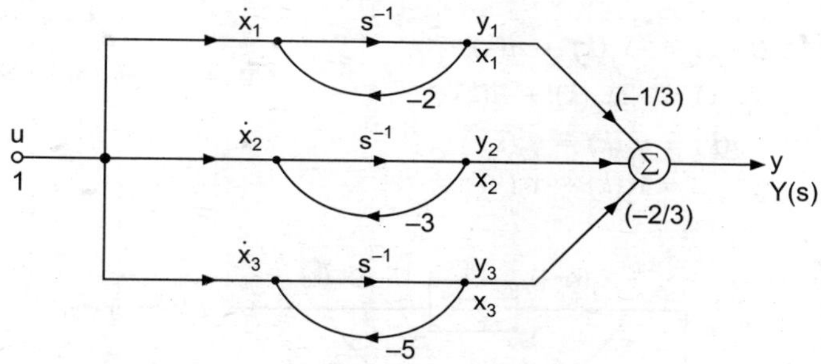

Fig. Ex. 4.33. Parallel realization of $H(s)$

$$\dot{x}_1 = -2x_1 + u$$
$$\dot{x}_2 = -3x_2 + u$$
$$\dot{x}_3 = -5x_3 + u$$

and $$y = \left(-\frac{1}{3}\right)x_1 + x_2 + \left(-\frac{2}{3}\right)x_3$$

Thus, $$\begin{bmatrix}\dot{x}_1\\ \dot{x}_2\\ \dot{x}_3\end{bmatrix} = \underbrace{\begin{bmatrix}-2 & 0 & 0\\ 0 & -3 & 0\\ 0 & 0 & -5\end{bmatrix}}_{\underline{A}}\begin{bmatrix}x_1\\ x_2\\ x_3\end{bmatrix} + \underbrace{\begin{bmatrix}1\\ 1\\ 1\end{bmatrix}}_{\underline{B}}[u]$$

$$y = \underbrace{\begin{bmatrix}-\frac{1}{3} & 1 & \frac{-2}{3}\end{bmatrix}}_{\underline{C}}\begin{bmatrix}x_1\\ x_2\\ x_3\end{bmatrix} + \underbrace{[0]}_{\underline{D}}[u]$$ **Ans.**

EXAMPLE 4.34: *Given the TF of a discrete system by*

$$H(z) = \frac{1}{z^2 + 3z + 2}$$

(a) Find $\underline{A}, \underline{B}, \underline{C}$ and $\underline{D}$ SV matrices by realizing as a parallel configuration.

(b) From the $\underline{A}, \underline{B}, \underline{C}$ and $\underline{D}$ so determined in part (a), compute H(z).

SOLUTION:

(*a*) As $$H(z) = \frac{1}{z^2+3z+2} = \frac{1}{(z+1)(z+2)} = \frac{1}{(z+1)} - \frac{1}{(z+2)} \quad \text{(by partial fractions)}$$

$$= \frac{z^{-1}}{1+z^{-1}} - \frac{z^{-1}}{1+2z^{-1}}$$

$$\triangleq H_1(z) - H_2(z)$$

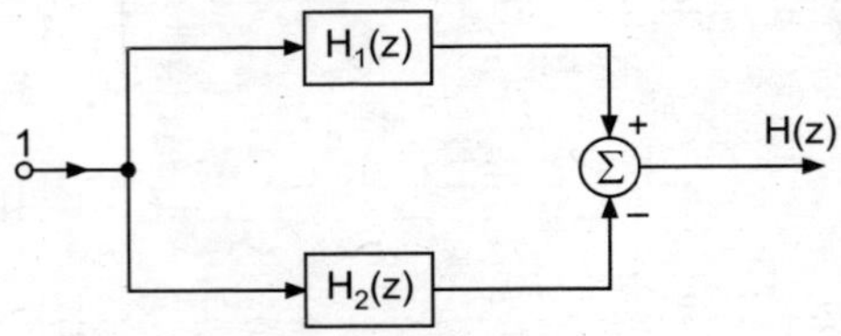

Fig. Ex. 4.34. (*a*) Parallel realization of *H*(*z*)

We realize *H*(*z*) as a parallel configuration shown in Fig. Ex. 4.34(*a*), and parametrize it as in Fig. 4.34(*b*). As

$$x_1(k+1) = -x_1(k) + u(k)$$
$$x_2(k+1) = -2x_2(k) + u(k)$$
$$y(k) = y_1(k) - y_2(k)$$
$$= x_1(k) - x_2(k)$$

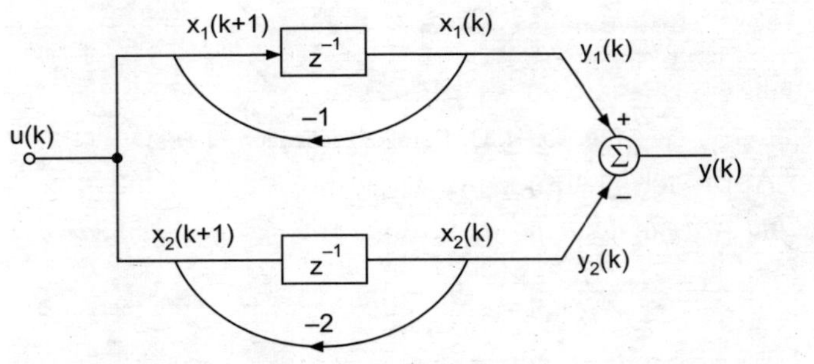

Fig. Ex. 4.34. (*b*) Realizations of $H_1(z)$ and $H_2(z)$ to compute SV matrices

Hence,

$$\begin{bmatrix} x_1(k+1) \\ x_2(k+1) \end{bmatrix} = \begin{bmatrix} -1 & 0 \\ 0 & -2 \end{bmatrix} \begin{bmatrix} x_1(k) \\ x_2(k) \end{bmatrix} + \begin{bmatrix} 1 \\ 1 \end{bmatrix} u(k)$$

$$y(k) = \begin{bmatrix} 1 & -1 \end{bmatrix} \begin{bmatrix} x_1(k) \\ x_2(k) \end{bmatrix} + [0]u(k)$$

Thus, we have determined

$$\underline{A} = \begin{bmatrix} -1 & 0 \\ 0 & -2 \end{bmatrix}, \underline{B} = \begin{bmatrix} 1 \\ 1 \end{bmatrix}, \underline{C} = [1 \quad -1], \underline{D} = [0]$$ **Ans.**

(b) To find $H(z)$, given above $\underline{A}, \underline{B}, \underline{C}$ and $\underline{D}$ matrices

$$\left[z\underline{I}-\underline{A}\right] = z\begin{bmatrix}1 & 0\\0 & 1\end{bmatrix}-\begin{bmatrix}-1 & 0\\0 & -2\end{bmatrix}=\begin{bmatrix}z+1 & 0\\0 & z+2\end{bmatrix}$$

$$\left|z\underline{I}-\underline{A}\right| = (z+1)(z+2)$$

$$\therefore \quad \left[z\underline{I}-\underline{A}\right]^{-1} = \frac{1}{(z+1)(z+2)}\begin{bmatrix}z+2 & 0\\0 & z+1\end{bmatrix}$$

$$\underline{C}\left[z\underline{I}-\underline{A}\right]^{-1}\underline{B}+\underline{D} = [1\ \ -1]\frac{1}{(z+1)(z+2)}\begin{bmatrix}z+2 & 0\\0 & z+1\end{bmatrix}\begin{bmatrix}1\\1\end{bmatrix}+[0]$$

$$= \frac{1}{(z+1)(z+2)}[1\ \ -1]\cdot\begin{bmatrix}z+2\\z+1\end{bmatrix}$$

$$= \frac{1}{(z+1)(z+2)}(z+2-z-1)=\frac{1}{(z+1)(z+2)}$$

$$\therefore \quad H(z) = \frac{1}{(z+1)(z+2)}=\frac{1}{z^2+3z+2} \qquad \text{(as expected)}$$

Note: The method of parallel realization of $H(z)$ is preferred only if we can easily split $H(z)$ in partial fractions. In general, the number of adders is more here than those in the composite canonical realization. However, there is no change in the number of delays needed here.

4.12.10 Cascade Decomposition Approach

In this approach, we express the system function (*TF*) in cascade form, as will be clear from the following example: Approach is similar for $H(s)$ and $H(z)$.

EXAMPLE 4.35: *Find cascade decomposition of the transfer function given by*

$$\frac{Y(s)}{X(s)} = \frac{5(s+1)(s+2)}{(s+4)(s+5)}. \qquad \textit{(I.P. Univ., 2006)}$$

SOLUTION:

Let

$$H(s) = 5\cdot\frac{s+1}{s+4}\cdot\frac{s+2}{s+5}$$

$$= 5\frac{1+s^{-1}}{1+4s^{-1}}\cdot\frac{1+2s^{-1}}{1+5s^{-1}}$$

$$\dot{x}_1 = x_2 + \dot{x}_2 - 5x_1 \qquad \text{...}(i)$$

$$\dot{x}_2 = -4x_2 + 5u \qquad \text{...}(ii)$$

$$\therefore \quad \dot{x}_1 = x_2 + [-4x_2 + 5u] - 5x_1$$

$$= -5x_1 - 3x_2 + 5u \qquad \text{...}(iii)$$

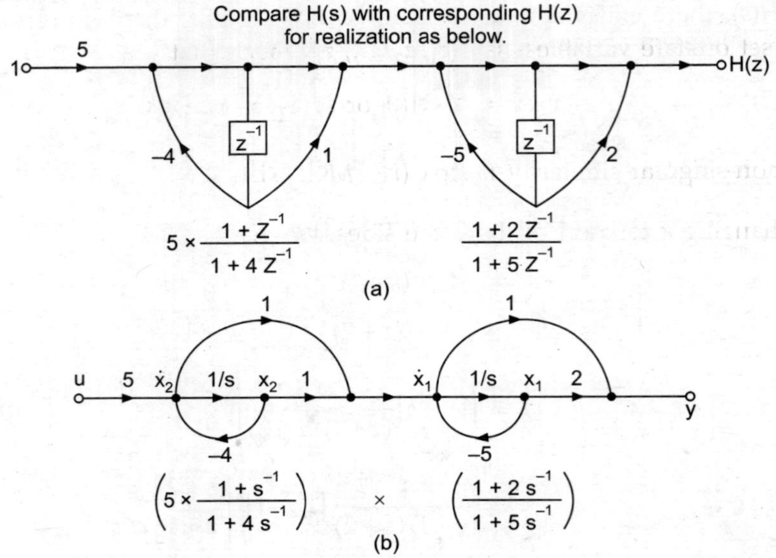

Fig. Ex. 4.35. (*a*) Realization of $H(z) = 5 \cdot \frac{1+z^{-1}}{1+4z^{-1}} \frac{1+2z^{-1}}{1+5z^{-1}}$ as a guidance.

(*b*) Replace z^{-1} by s^{-1} to get $H(s) = 5 \frac{1+s^{-1}}{1+4s^{-1}} \frac{1+2s^{-1}}{1+5s^{-1}}$ as required in this problem.

Also,

$$y = 2x_1 + \dot{x}_1 \qquad \text{[from Fig. Ex. 4.35}(b)\text{]}$$

$$= 2x_1 + [-5x_1 - 3x_2 + 5u] \qquad \text{[value of } x_1 \text{ was found above in } (iii)\text{]}$$

$$= -3x_1 - 3x_2 + 5u$$

Hence, we can write

$$\begin{bmatrix} \dot{x}_1 \\ \dot{x}_2 \end{bmatrix} = \underbrace{\begin{bmatrix} -5 & -3 \\ 0 & -4 \end{bmatrix}}_{\underline{A}} \begin{bmatrix} x_1 \\ x_2 \end{bmatrix} + \underbrace{\begin{bmatrix} 5 \\ 5 \end{bmatrix}}_{\underline{B}} u$$

$$y = \underbrace{\begin{bmatrix} -3 & -3 \end{bmatrix}}_{\underline{C}} \begin{bmatrix} x_1 \\ x_2 \end{bmatrix} + \underbrace{[5]}_{\underline{D}} u$$

Hence,

$$\underline{A} = \begin{bmatrix} -5 & -3 \\ 0 & -4 \end{bmatrix}, \underline{B} = \begin{bmatrix} 5 \\ 5 \end{bmatrix}, \underline{C} = [-3 \quad -3] \text{ and } \underline{D} = [5] \quad \textbf{Ans.}$$

4.12.11 Non-uniqueness of the State Variable Model (Linear or Similarity Transformation)

The choice of the state for a given system is not unique we can always have different state models, and therefore different matrices $\underline{A}, \underline{B}, \underline{C}$ and $\underline{D}$. The set of state variables $x_1, x_2, \ldots, x_n$ can analog system $H(s)$, there exists a state variable $[x_1, x_2, ..., x_n]^T$, then we can always obtain a linearly related set of state variables, say $(z_1, z_2, ..., z_n)^T$ such that

$$\underline{x}(k) = \underline{M} \cdot \underline{z}(k) \text{ or } \underline{z}(k) = \underline{M}^{-1} \underline{x}(k) \qquad ...(A)$$

where $\underline{M}$ is a non-singular similarity matrix (*i.e.* $\underline{M}^{-1}$ exists).

From (A), changing k to $k + 1$ on both the sides, we get

$$\underline{z}(k+1) = \underline{M}^{-1} \underline{z}(k+1)$$

$$= \underline{M}^{-1}[\underline{A}\,x(k) + \underline{B}\,u(k)] \qquad \text{using (4.90) for } \underline{x}(k+1)$$

$$= \underline{M}^{-1} \underline{A}\,\underline{x}(k) + \underline{M}^{-1} \underline{B}\,\underline{u}(k)$$

$$\therefore \quad \underline{z}(k+1) = (\underline{M}^{-1} \underline{A}\,\underline{M})\,\underline{z}(k) + (\underline{M}^{-1} \underline{B})\,\underline{u}(k) \qquad (\because \ \underline{x}(k) = \underline{M}\,\underline{z}(k))$$

or

$$\underline{z}(k+1) \triangleq \underline{\tilde{A}}\,\underline{z}(k) + \underline{\tilde{B}}\,\underline{u}(k) \qquad ...(4.98)$$

where $\underline{\tilde{A}} = \underline{M}^{-1} \underline{A}\,\underline{M}$, and $\underline{\tilde{B}} = \underline{M}^{-1} \underline{B}$.

As

$$\underline{y}(k) = \underline{C}\,\underline{x}(k) + \underline{D}\,\underline{u}(k) \qquad \text{[from (4.91)]}$$

$$= \underline{C}\,\underline{M}\,\underline{z}(k) + \underline{D}\,\underline{u}(k) \qquad [\text{Putting } x(k) = \underline{M}\,\underline{z}(k)]$$

or

$$\underline{y}(k) = \underline{\tilde{C}}\,\underline{z}(k) + \underline{\tilde{D}}\,\underline{u}(k) \qquad ...(4.99)$$

where $\underline{\tilde{C}} = \underline{C}\,\underline{M}$, and $\underline{\tilde{D}} = \underline{D}$.

Thus, in this transformation, we have the matrix relations between $\underline{A}, \underline{B}, \underline{C}, \underline{D}$ and $\underline{\tilde{A}}, \underline{\tilde{B}}, \underline{\tilde{C}}, \underline{\tilde{D}}$ as given below:

$$\boxed{\begin{aligned} \underline{\tilde{A}} &= \underline{M}^{-1} \underline{A}\,\underline{M} \\ \underline{\tilde{B}} &= \underline{M}^{-1} \underline{B} \\ \underline{\tilde{C}} &= \underline{C}\,\underline{M} \\ \underline{\tilde{D}} &= \underline{D} \end{aligned}} \qquad ...(4.100)$$

Though we have derived these relations for discrete-time systems, the above transformations (4.100) also hold good for continuous-time systems. These relations are called *Similarity Transformation relations.*

Equations (4.98) and (4.99) are the new SV equations of the given system $H(z)$, and are similar to the ones earlier defined in equations (4.90) and (4.91).

> **Note:** That we have derived the new SV equation as (4.98) and (4.99) by using the earlier SV equations (4.90) and (4.91), representing the *SAME* system $H(z)$. Hence, we must be able to obtain the expression of the same $H(z)$ from both the sets of SV equations. We first give the results which we shall prove soon after.

(*i*) Matrices $\underline{A}$ and $\underline{\tilde{A}}$ have the same characteristic equation *i.e.* the eigen values of matrices $\underline{A}$ and $\underline{\tilde{A}}$ are invariant to the similarity transformation given in (4.100).

(*ii*) The transfer function $H(z)$ is also invariant to the similarity transformation.

We now prove the above two results.

4.12.12 Invariance of Eigen Values in Similarity Transformation

The characteristic polynomials $\left|z\underline{I}-\underline{A}\right|$ and $\left|z\underline{I}-\underline{\tilde{A}}\right|$ must be identical, if they are to yield the same eigen values, under similarity transformation, *i.e.* we must show that

$$\left|z\underline{I}-\underline{\tilde{A}}\right| = \left|z\underline{I}-\underline{A}\right| \qquad \text{...(4.101)}$$

where $|x|$ means determinant of x.

Proof. We can write

$$\left|z\underline{I}-\underline{\tilde{A}}\right| = \left|z\underline{M}^{-1}\underline{M}-\underline{M}^{-1}\underline{A}\underline{M}\right| \qquad \text{...(4.102)}$$

because $\qquad \underline{I}$ = identity matrix = $\underline{M}^{-1}\underline{M}$ $\qquad$ (matrix algebra)

and $\qquad \underline{\tilde{A}} = \underline{M}^{-1}\underline{A}\underline{M}$ $\qquad$ due to (4.100)

Replacing $\underline{M}$ by $\underline{I}\,\underline{M}$ in (4.102). we get

$$\left|z\underline{I}-\underline{\tilde{A}}\right| = \left|\underline{M}^{-1}z\underline{I}\,\underline{M}-\underline{M}^{-1}\underline{A}\underline{M}\right| \qquad \text{(Note this step)}$$

$$= \left|\underline{M}^{-1}(z\underline{I}-\underline{A})\underline{M}\right|$$

$$= \left|\underline{M}^{-1}\right|\left|\underline{M}\right|\left|z\underline{I}-\underline{A}\right| \qquad \text{...(4.103)}$$

As $\qquad \left|\underline{M}^{-1}\right|\left|\underline{M}\right| = \left|\underline{M}^{-1}\underline{M}\right| = 1$ $\quad$ (product of determinant and its inverse is unity)

∴ Equation (4.103) gives us

$$\boxed{\left|z\underline{I}-\underline{\tilde{A}}\right| = \left|z\underline{I}-\underline{A}\right|} \qquad \text{...(4.104)}$$

Hence, the eigen values of matrices $\underline{A}$ and $\underline{\tilde{A}}$ are invariant under the similarity transformation.

4.12.13 Some Important Properties of Eigen Values

1. If all the elements $\{a_{ij}\}$ of an $n \times n$ matrix $\underline{A}$ are real, then its eigen values λ_i, $i = 1, 2, ..., n$ are either real or are in conjugate pairs.
2. If λ_i, $i = 1, 2, ..., n$ are the eigen values of matrix $\underline{A}$ (an $n \times n$ matrix), then the eigen values of matrix $\underline{\tilde{A}} = \underline{M}^{-1}\underline{A}\underline{M}$ are also the same λ_i, $i = 1, 2, ..., n$.

3. The matrix $\tilde{A} = M^{-1} A M$ is a diagonal matrix where M is a non-singular similarity transform matrix.
4. If matrix A is a non-singular matrix with eigen values λ_i, $i = 1, 2, \ldots, n$, then the matrix A^{-1} is also a non-singular matrix and has its eigen value as $\frac{1}{\lambda_i}$, $i = 1, 2, \ldots, n$.

4.12.14 Invariance of Transfer Functions (*H*(*s*)) or *H*(*z*)) in Similarity Transform

We want to prove that $H(s)$ obtained from A, B, C, D is the same as that obtained from $\tilde{A}, \tilde{B}, \tilde{C}, \tilde{D}$ *i.e.*, we want to show that:

$$H(s) = C\left[sI - A\right]^{-1} B + D = \tilde{C}\left[sI - \tilde{A}\right]^{-1} \tilde{B} + \tilde{D} \qquad \ldots(4.105)$$

i.e. $H(s)$ can be calculated either from the SV equation

$$\left.\begin{aligned} \dot{x}(t) &= A\,x(t) + B\,u(t) \\ y(t) &= C\,x(t) + D\,u(t) \end{aligned}\right\}$$

or from the SV equations

$$\dot{x}(t) = \tilde{A}\,x(t) + \tilde{B}\,u(t)$$

$$y(t) = \tilde{C}\,x(t) + \tilde{D}\,u(t)$$

where the relations between A, B, C, D and $\tilde{A}, \tilde{B}, \tilde{C}, \tilde{D}$ are given by (4.100).

Proof.

$$\tilde{C}\left[sI - \tilde{A}\right]^{-1} \tilde{B} + \tilde{D} = C\,M\left[s\,M^{-1} M - M^{-1} A\,M\right]^{-1} M^{-1} B + D \qquad \ldots(4.106)$$

We have used the relations from (4.100) and replaced I by $M^{-1} M$ in (4.106).

$$\text{RHS of (4.106)} = C\,M\left[M^{-1}(sI - A)\,M\right]^{-1} M^{-1} B + D \qquad \ldots(A)$$

We know from matrix algebra that

$$\begin{aligned} (A \cdot B)^{-1} &= B^{-1} A^{-1} \\ M\,M^{-1} &= M^{-1} M = I \end{aligned} \qquad \ldots(4.107)$$

Hence, using above results in (*A*), we obtain

$$\begin{aligned} \tilde{C}\left[sI - \tilde{A}\right]^{-1} \tilde{B} + \tilde{D} &= C\,M \cdot M^{-1}\left[M^{-1}(sI - A)\right]^{-1} M^{-1} B + D \\ &= C\left[(sI - A)^{-1}\right] M \cdot M^{-1} B + D \\ &= C\left[sI - A\right]^{-1} B + D = H(s) \end{aligned}$$

Hence

$$\underset{\sim}{\tilde{C}}\left[s\underset{\sim}{I}-\underset{\sim}{\tilde{A}}\right]^{-1}\underset{\sim}{\tilde{B}}+\underset{\sim}{\tilde{D}} = \underset{\sim}{C}\left[s\underset{\sim}{I}-\underset{\sim}{A}\right]^{-1}\underset{\sim}{B}+\underset{\sim}{D}=H(s)$$

Similarly, for discrete-time systems, we get the results

$$\underset{\sim}{\tilde{C}}\left[z\underset{\sim}{I}-\underset{\sim}{\tilde{A}}\right]^{-1}\cdot\underset{\sim}{\tilde{B}}+\underset{\sim}{\tilde{D}} = \underset{\sim}{C}\left[z\underset{\sim}{I}-\underset{\sim}{A}\right]^{-1}\cdot\underset{\sim}{B}+\underset{\sim}{D}=H(z) \quad \text{...(4.108)}$$

Unsolved Problems with Answers (Realizations)

4.1. Realize the system function

$$H(z) = 1+\frac{3}{4}z^{-1}+\frac{17}{8}z^{-2}+\frac{3}{4}z^{-3}+z^{-4}$$

[**Ans.** (*a*) General direct form
(*b*) Linear phase form]

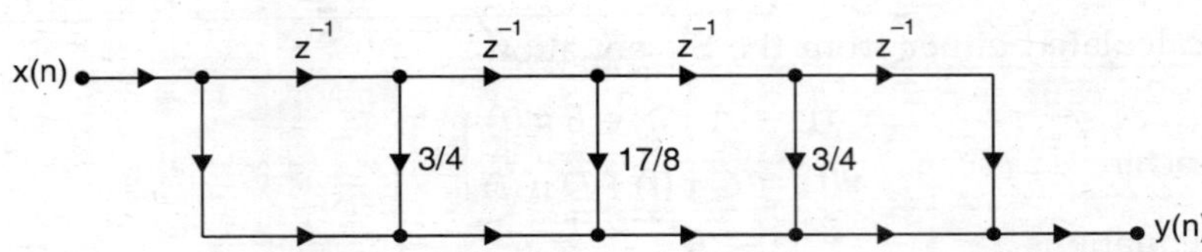

Fig. Prob. 4.1. (*a*) Realization of *H*(*z*) as direct form

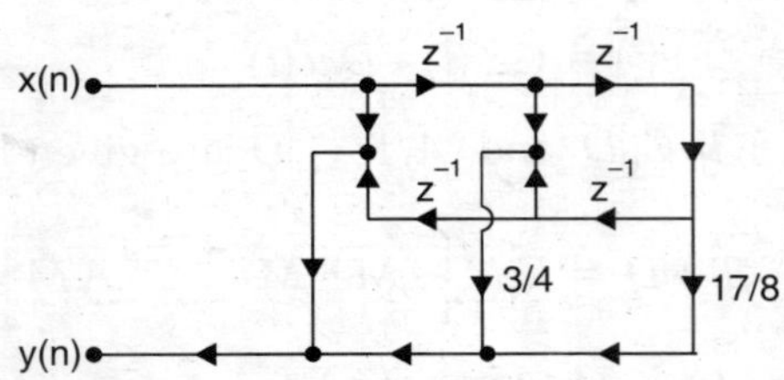

Fig. Prob. 4.1. (*b*) Realization of *H*(*z*) as linear-phase form

4.2. Obtain the cascade of *H*(*z*) given is above problem, using the minimum number of multipliers.

$\left[\textbf{Ans.} \text{ Note that } H(z) = \left(1+\frac{1}{2}z^{-1}+z^{-2}\right)\left(1+\frac{1}{4}z^{-1}+z^{-2}\right)\right]$

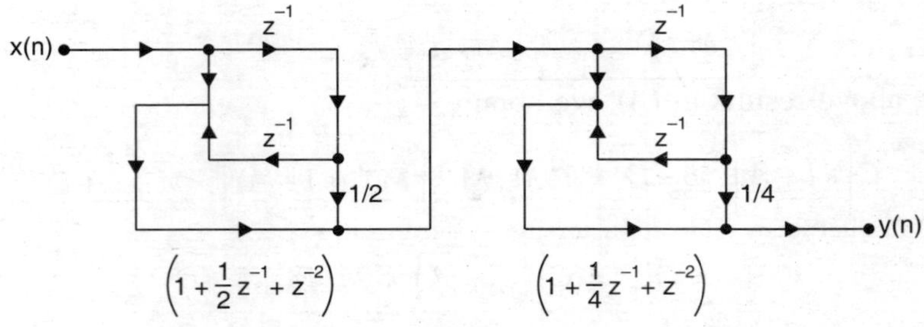

Fig. Prob. 4.2. Realization as cascade form for *H*(*z*)

4.3. What is the system function corresponding to the following structures:

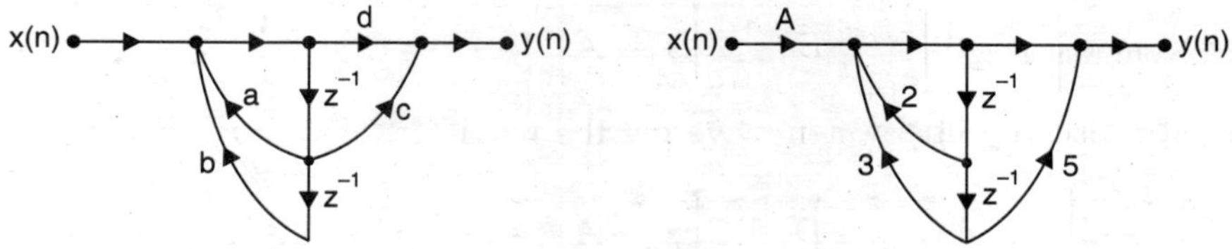

(a) (b)

$$\left[\textbf{Ans. } (a)\ H(z) = \frac{d + cz^{-1}}{1 - az^{-1} - bz^{-2}} \qquad (b)\ H(z) = \frac{A(1+5z^{-2})}{(1-2z^{-1}-3z^{-2})}\right]$$

4.4. Determine the numerator polynomial $N(z)$, so that $H(z) = \dfrac{N(z)}{1 + az^{-1} + bz^{-2}}$ is an all pass filter.

[**Ans.** $N(z) = b + az^{-1} + z^{-2}$]

4.5. Draw canonic structure (Direct form-II) to realize

$$H(z) = \frac{1}{1 - 2r\cos\theta z^{-1} + r^2 z^{-2}}$$ where are the poles of $H(z)$.

[**Ans.** Structure is as shown in Fig. Prob. 4.5. Poles of $H(z)$ are

$$z = re^{+j\theta}$$
$$a = 2r\cos\theta$$
$$b = -r^2]$$

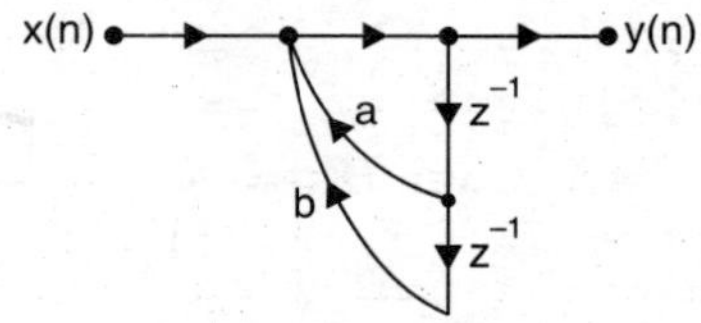

Fig. Prob. 4.5.

4.6. Using the first order sections, obtain a parallel-form realization for

$$H_1(z) = \frac{\left(1 + \frac{1}{2}z^{-1}\right)\left(1 + \frac{1}{4}z^{-1}\right)}{\left(1 - \frac{1}{2}z^{-1}\right)\left(1 - \frac{1}{4}z^{-1}\right)\left(1 - \frac{1}{8}z^{-1}\right)}.$$

[**Ans.** The parallel realization is as shown in Fig. Prob. 4.6].

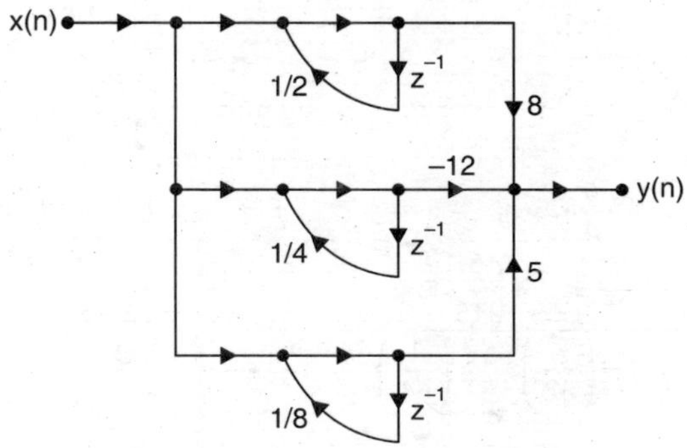

Fig. Prob. 4.6. Realization of $H_1(z)$ in parallel form

4.7. Obtain a parallel-form realization for the system function

$$H_2(z) = \frac{2 + z^{-1} + \left(\frac{1}{4}\right)z^{-2}}{\left(1 + \frac{1}{2}z^{-1}\right)\left(1 + z^{-1} + \frac{1}{2}z^{-2}\right)}.$$

$$\left[\textbf{Ans. } \text{Note that } H_2(z) = \frac{1}{1+\frac{1}{2}z^{-1}} + \frac{1-\frac{1}{2}z^{-1}}{1+z^{-1}+\frac{1}{2}z^{-2}}\right]$$

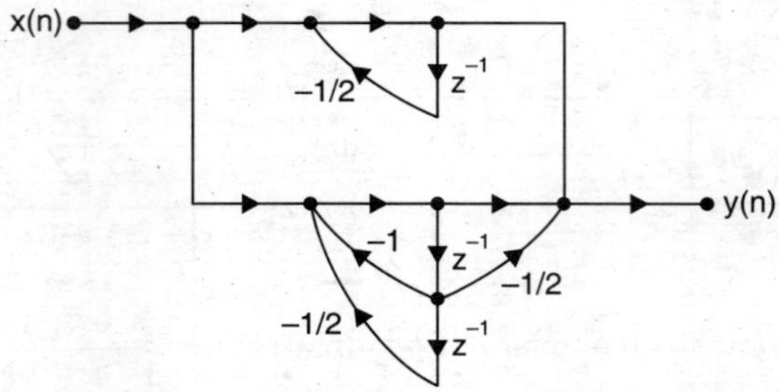

Fig. Prob. 4.7. Realization of $H_2(z)$ in parallel form

4.8. Given $H(z) = \dfrac{14-\left(\frac{37}{4}\right)z^{-1}+\left(\frac{21}{16}\right)z^{-2}}{\left(1-\frac{1}{2}z^{-1}\right)\left(1-\frac{1}{4}z^{-1}\right)\left(1-\frac{1}{8}z^{-1}\right)}$

Realize $H(z)$ as (*a*) parallel structure (*b*) Cascade structure (*c*) Canonic (Direct-II) structure

Ans.

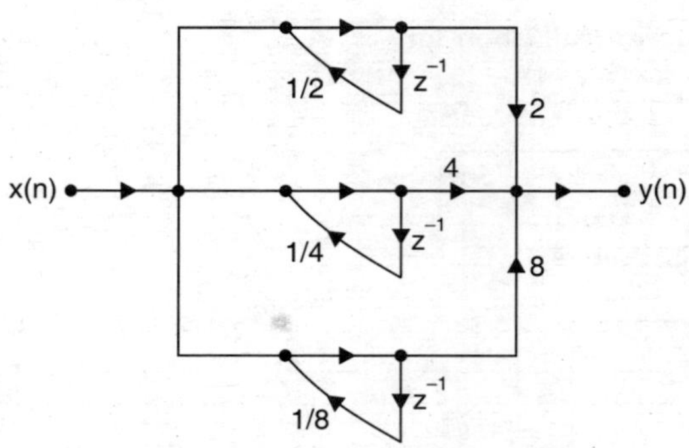

(a) Parallel structure

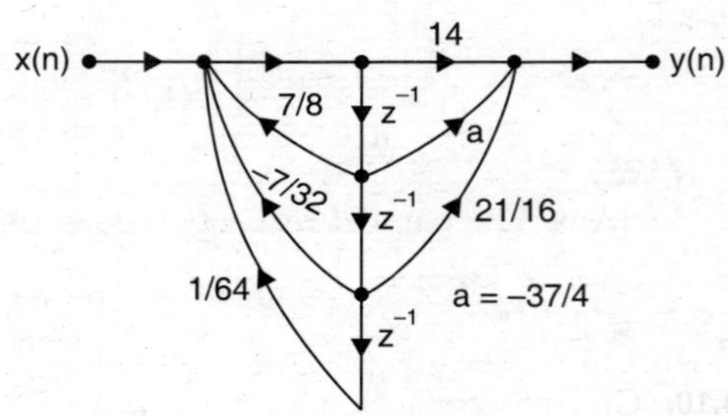

(b) Canonic structure

$$H(z) = \frac{14-\left(\frac{37}{4}\right)z^{-1}+\left(\frac{21}{16}\right)z^{-2}}{1-\left(\frac{7}{8}\right)z^{-1}+\left(\frac{7}{32}\right)z^{-2}-\left(\frac{1}{64}\right)z^{-3}}$$

$$= \frac{2}{1-\frac{1}{2}z^{-1}} + \frac{4}{1-\frac{1}{4}z^{-1}} + \frac{8}{1-\frac{1}{8}z^{-1}}$$

$$= \left(\frac{1}{16}\right)\frac{(1-0.454\,z^{-1})(1-0.206\,z^{-1})}{\left(1-\frac{1}{2}z^{-1}\right)\left(1-\frac{1}{4}z^{-1}\right)\left(1-\frac{1}{8}z^{-1}\right)}$$

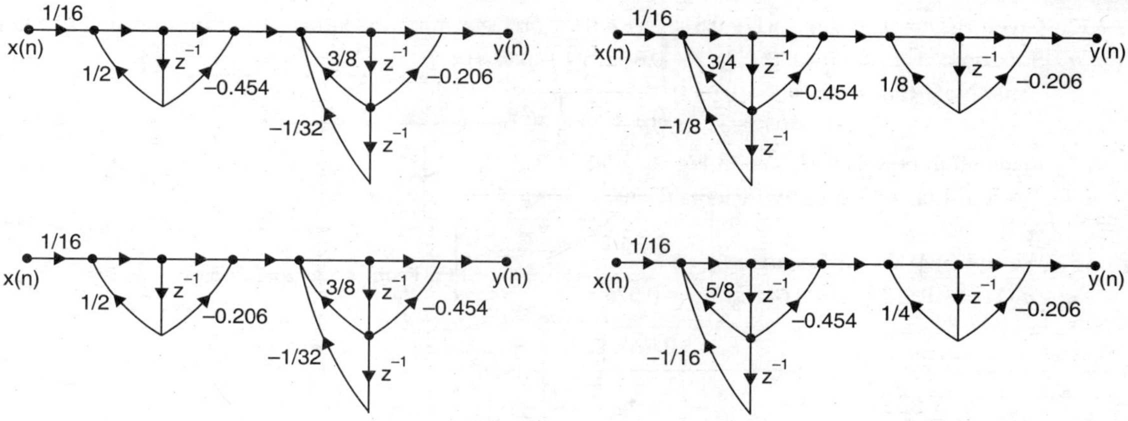

(c) A few cascade realizations of H(z). There are in all 14 different configurations.

Fig. Prob. 4.8. A few possible parallel realizations

4.9. Realize the system $h(n) = \sin\left(\frac{\pi}{2}\right)[u(n) - u(n-4)]$ as a frequency sampling FIR configuration.

[**Hint.** $h(n) = \{0, 1, 0, -1\}$
$H(0) = 0$, $H(1) = -j2$, $H(2) = 0$, $H(3) = j2$. Here $N = 4$]

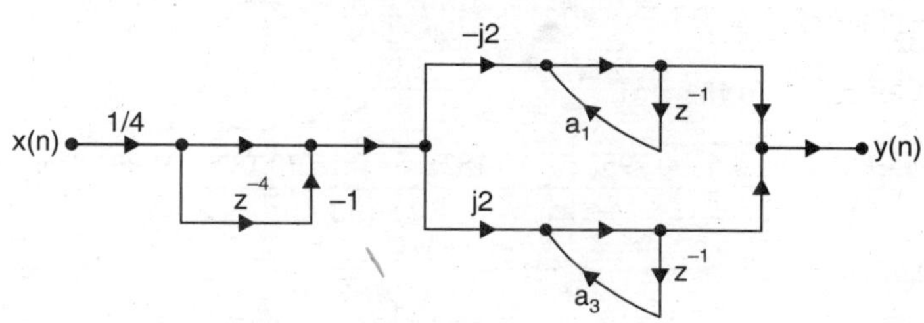

$a_1 = e^{j\pi/2} = j$, $a_3 = e^{j3\pi/2} = -j$

Fig. Prob. 4.9. Realization of $H(z)$

4.10. Given the reflection coefficients for an FIR Lattice filter, $k_1 = \frac{1}{3}$, $k_2 = \frac{1}{3}$ and $k_3 = 1$. Determine FIR filter $A(z)$.

$$\left[\textbf{Ans. } A(z) = 1 + \left(\frac{7}{9}\right)z^{-1} + \left(\frac{7}{9}\right)z^{-2} + z^{-3}\right]$$

4.11. Realize the FIR transfer function
$H(z) = 1 + 1.2z^{-1} + 1.12z^{-2} + 0.12z^{-2} - 0.08z^{-4}$ as a Lattice realization.

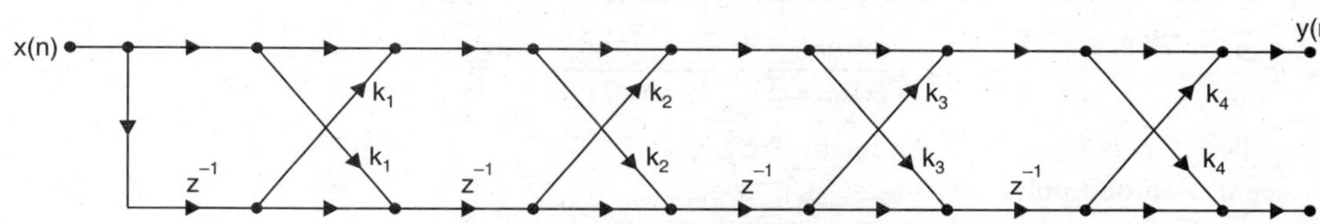

$k_1 = 0.5$, $k_2 = 1.0$, $k_3 = 0.2174$, $k_4 = -0.08$

Fig. Prob. 4.11. Realization of $H(z)$ in Lattice form

4.12. Given $A(z) = (1 - 0.8\,jz^{-1})(1 + 0.8\,jz^{-1})(1 - 0.9\,z^{-1})$. Determine the lattice structure for this FIR filter.

SOLUTION: $A_3(z) = (1 - 0.8\,jz^{-1})(1 + 0.8\,jz^{-1})(1 - 0.9z^{-1})$

$= (1 + 0.64z^{-2})(1 - 0.9z^{-1})$

$= 1 - 0.9z^{-1} + 0.64z^{-2} - 0.576z^{-3}$

Realization of $A(z)$ is shown in Fig. 4.12 (*a*)

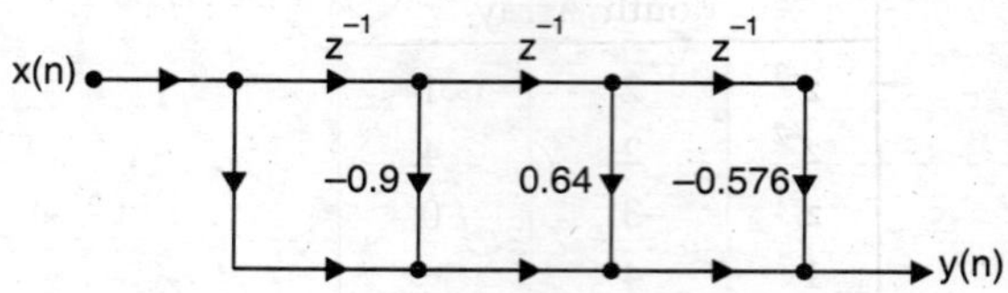

Fig. Prob. 4.12. (*a*) The given FIR filter

[To find the reflection coefficients k_i, $i = 3, 2, 1$]

We use Step down Recursion

$a_3(1) = -0.9,\ a_3(2) = 0.64,\ a_3(3) = -0.576$

$$\therefore\ k_3 = -0.576$$

$$A_2(z) = \frac{A_3(z) - k_3B_3(z)}{1-k_3^2}$$

$$= \frac{(1-0.9z^{-1}+0.64z^{-2}-0.576z^{-3})-(-0.576)(-0.576+0.64\,z^{-1}-0.9\,z^{-2}+z^{-3})}{1-(-0.576)^2}$$

$$= \frac{1}{(1-0.3318)}[1 - 0.9z^{-1} + 0.64z^{-2} - 0.576z^{-3} - (0.3318 - 0.3686z^{-1} + 0.5184z^{-2} - 0.576z^{-3})]$$

$$= \frac{1}{0.6682}(0.6682 - 0.5314z^{-1} + 0.1216z^{-2})$$

$$= 1 - 0.7952\,z^{-1} + 0.182\,z^{-2}$$

$$\therefore\ k_2 = 0.182$$

$$A_1(z) = \frac{A_2(z) - k_2B_2(z)}{1-k_2^2} = \frac{1-0.7952z^{-1}+0.182z^{-2}-0.182(0.182-0.7952z^{-1}+z^{-2})}{1-(0.182)^2}$$

$$= 1 - 0.673z^{-1}$$

$$\therefore\ k_1 = -0.673$$

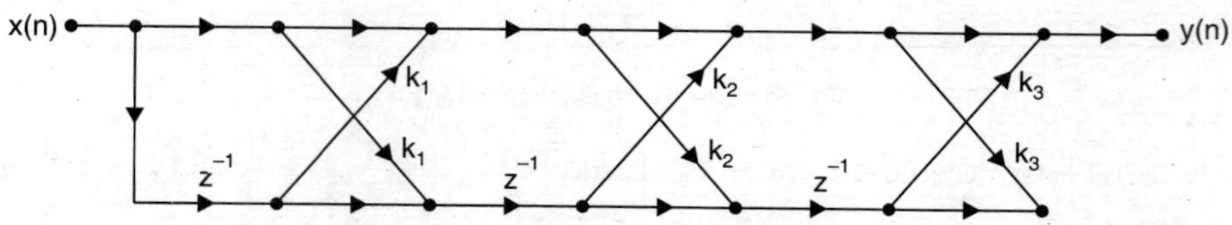

Fig. Prob. 4.12. (*b*) Realization of *A*(*z*) as a Lattice structure

4.13(*a*) Obtain a Ladder realization for $H(z) = \dfrac{4}{2z^{-3}+2z^{-2}+z^{-1}+4}$.

SOLUTION: Here, numerator is a constant equalling 4. We form

$$H(z) = \frac{a_0}{P(z)+Q(z)} = \frac{a_0/P(z)}{1+Q(z)/P(z)}.$$

where $P(z)$ is an even polynomial $= 2\,z^{-2} + 4$

$Q(z)$ is an odd polynomial $= 2z^{-3} + z^{-1}$

$$\frac{Q(z)}{P(z)} = \frac{2z^{-3}+z^{-1}}{2z^{-2}+4} \triangleq T(z).$$

To realize α_0, α_1, α_2 for $T(z)$

Routh Array is

Routh Array		
z^{-3}	2	1
z^{-2}	2	4
z^{-1}	–3	0
1	4	

$$\therefore \quad \alpha_0 = \frac{2}{2} = 1$$

$$\alpha_1 = \frac{2}{-3} = -\frac{2}{3}$$

$$\alpha_2 = \frac{-3}{4} = -\frac{3}{4}$$

Realization of $H(z)$ is shown in Fig. Prob. 4.12.

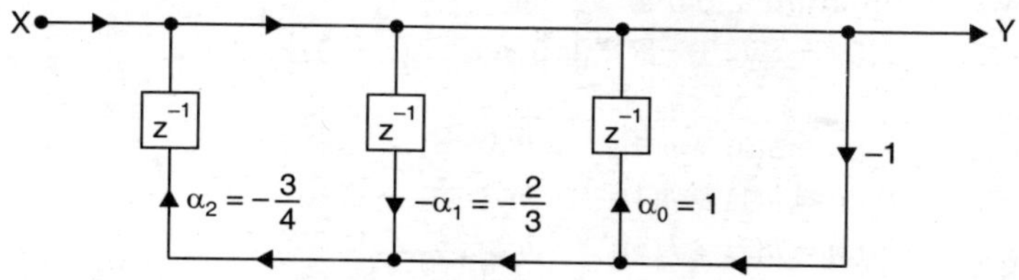

Fig. Prob. 4.13 (*a*) The Ladder realization

4.13(*b*) Obtain Ladder realization of $H(z) = \dfrac{4}{z^{-4} + 2z^{-3} + 2z^{-2} - z^{-1} + 4}$

SOLUTION:

Routh Array			
z^{-4}	1	2	4
z^{-3}	2	–1	
z^{-2}	5/2	4	
z^{-1}	21/5		
1	4		

$$\alpha_0 = \frac{1}{2},\ \alpha_1 = \frac{2}{(5/2)} = \frac{4}{5},$$

$$\alpha_2 = \frac{(5/2)}{(21/5)} = \frac{25}{42},\ \alpha_3 = \frac{(21/5)}{4} = \frac{21}{20}$$

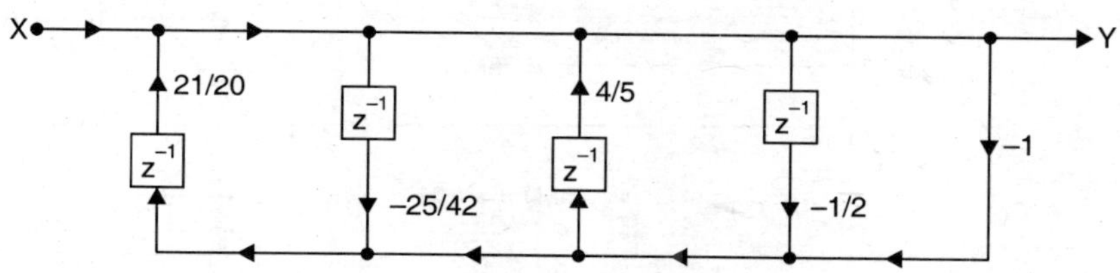

Fig. Prob. 4.13 (*b*) The Ladder realization

4.14. Show that the Ladder realization shown in the figure realizes the system function

$$H(z) = \frac{z^2 + 3z + 2}{z^2 + z + 1}.$$

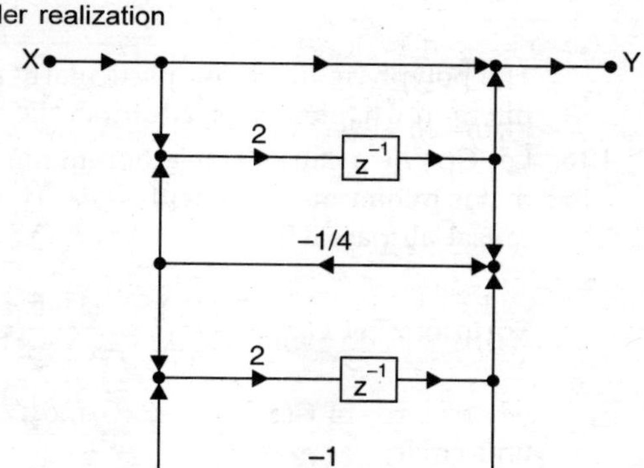

Fig. Prob. 4.14 The Ladder

4.15. Consider an FIR filter $H(z) = \sum_{i=0}^{8} h(i)z^{-i}$. Realize $H(z)$ as Polyphase realizations for two branch, three branch, L-branch.

SOLUTION:

$$H(z) = (h(0) + h(2)z^{-2} + h(4)z^{-4} + h(6)z^{-6} + h(8)z^{-8}) + (h(1)z^{-1} + h(3)z^{-3} + h(5)z^{-5} + h(7)z^{-7})$$

$$= [h(0) + h(2)z^{-2} + h(4)z^{-4} + h(6)z^{-6} + h(8)z^{-8}] + z^{-1}[h(1) + h(3)z^{-2} + h(5)z^{-4} + h(7)z^{-6}]$$

$$H(z) \triangleq E_0(z^2) + z^{-1}E_1(z^2)$$

where $E_0(z) = h(0) + h(2)z^{-1} + h(4)z^{-2} + h(6)z^{-3} + h(8)z^{-4}$

and $E_1(z) = h(1) + h(3)z^{-1} + h(5)z^{-2} + h(7)z^{-3}$

$E_1(z)$ and $E_2(z)$ are two branch polyphase filters, shown in Fig. Prob. 4.15(*a*).

Similarly, if we group in three parts, we get

$$H(z) = E_0(z^3) + z^{-1}E_1(z^3) + z^{-2}E_2(z^3)$$

where now

$$E_0(z) = h(0) + h(3)z^{-1} + h(6)z^{-2}$$
$$E_1(z) = h(1) + h(4)z^{-1} + h(7)z^{-2}$$
$$E_2(z) = h(2) + h(5)z^{-1} + h(8)z^{-2}$$

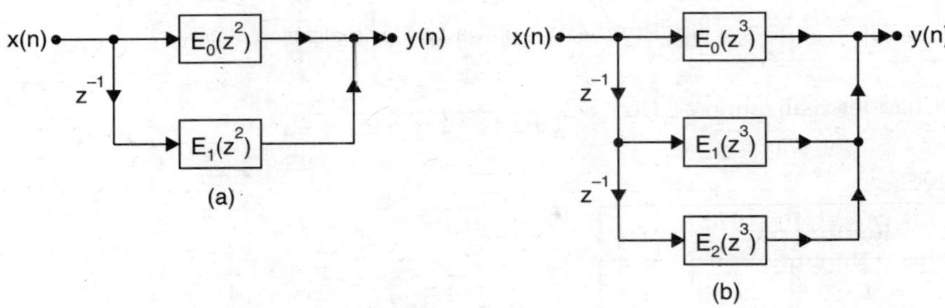

Fig. Prob. 4.15. Polyphase realizations, (*a*) two-branch in parallel, (*b*) three-branch in parallel

For L-branch polyphase decomposition, we have

$$H(z) = \sum_{m=0}^{L-1} z^{-m}E_m(z^L)$$

where

$$E_m(z) = \sum_{n=0}^{\lfloor (N+1)/L \rfloor} h[Ln+m]z^{-n}, \quad 0 \le m \le L-1$$

where $\lfloor x \rfloor$ mean integral part of x, N = filter order.

The polyphase filters are particularly used in Multirate DSP networks. We shall come across such filters in Chapter 12 on Multirate DSP.

4.16. Let $G(z)$ be a causal stable non-minimum-phase TF and let $H(z)$ denotes another causal stable TF that is minimum-phase with $|G(e^{j\omega})| = |H(e^{j\omega})|$. Show that $G(z) = H(z) \cdot A(z)$, where $A(z)$ is a stable causal all pass TF.

SOLUTION: Let $G(z) = \dfrac{N(z)}{D(z)} = \dfrac{(1-\alpha_1 z^{-1})(1-\alpha_2 z^{-1})\ldots(1-\alpha_N z^{-1})(1-\beta_1 z^{-1})(1-\beta_2 z^{-1})\ldots(1-\beta_M z^{-1})}{D(z)}$

where zeros of $G(z)$ are at $z = \alpha_1, \alpha_2, \ldots, \alpha_N$ inside the unit circle and $z = \beta_1, \beta_2, \ldots, \beta_M$ outside the unit circle.

Consider the function

$$G(z) = \frac{[(1-\alpha_1 z^{-1})(1-\alpha_2 z^{-1})] \ldots (1-\alpha_N z^{-1})][(1-\beta_1^* z^{-1})(\beta_2^* - z^{-1}) \ldots (\beta_M^* - z^{-1})]}{D(z)} \times A(z)$$

where $A(z) = \dfrac{\prod_{i=1}^{M}(1-\beta_i z^{-1})}{\prod_{i=1}^{M}(\beta_i^* - z^{-1})}$ is an all pass filter, since, its zeros β_i and poles $\dfrac{1}{\beta_i^*}$ are mirror image symmetry.

Also,
$$G(z) \triangleq H(z) \cdot A(z)$$

where
$$H(z) = \frac{\prod_{i=1}^{N}(1-\alpha_N z^{-1}) \cdot \prod_{i=1}^{M}(\beta_i^* - z^{-1})}{D(z)}$$

and $|G(e^{j\omega})| = |H(e^{j\omega})| \because$ by replacing a few zeros by their mirror image zeros, the magnitude response remains the same.

$A(z)$ has its poles at $z = \dfrac{1}{\beta_i^*}$, as $|\beta_i| < 1 \therefore \left|\dfrac{1}{\beta_i^*}\right| < 1$ *i.e.* $A(z)$ is stable.

If $G(z)$ is causal, then $H(z)$ and $A(z)$, both are causal. Q.E.D.

4.17. If $H(z)$ is a minimum-phase system with a Fourier transform magnitude given by $|H(e^{j\omega})|^2 = \dfrac{17}{16} - \dfrac{1}{2}\cos\omega$. Find $H(z)$ of the minimum-phase system.

SOLUTION:
$$|H(e^{j\omega})|^2 = \frac{17}{16} - \frac{1}{2}\cos\omega$$

$$\therefore \quad H(z) \cdot H(z^{-1}) = \frac{17}{16} - \frac{1}{4}(z + z^{-1}) \qquad \text{putting } e^{j\omega} = z$$

$$= -\frac{1}{4}z\left(z^{-2} - \frac{17}{4}z^{-1} + 1\right)$$

$$= -\frac{1}{4}z\left(z^{-1} - \frac{1}{4}\right)(z^{-1} - 4)$$

$$= \left(1 - \frac{1}{4}z\right)\left(1 - \frac{1}{4}z^{-1}\right)$$

zero at $z = \dfrac{1}{4}$

$\therefore$ The minimum phase system is $H(z) = \left(1 - \dfrac{1}{4}z^{-1}\right)$ **Ans.**

4.18. A minimum-phase filter with frequency response $H(e^{j\omega})$ has $|H(e^{j\omega})|^2 = \dfrac{5}{4} - \cos\omega$. Find $H(z)$ of the minimum phase filter.

SOLUTION: We have $H(z) \cdot H(z^{-1}) = \frac{5}{4} - \frac{1}{2}(z + z^{-1})$

$$= -\frac{1}{2}z\left(z^{-2} - \frac{5}{2}z^{-1} + 1\right)$$

$$= -\frac{1}{2}z\left[\left(z^{-1} - \frac{1}{2}\right)(z^{-1} - 2)\right]$$

$$= -\frac{1}{2}\left(1 - \frac{1}{2}z\right)(z^{-1} - 2)$$

$$H(z)\ (Hz^{-1}) = \left(1 - \frac{1}{2}z\right)\left(1 - \frac{1}{2}z^{-1}\right)$$

zero at $z = 2$ (first factor); zero at $z = \frac{1}{2}$ (second factor)

Minimum phase filter $\therefore$ $H(z) = \left(1 - \frac{1}{2}z^{-1}\right)$ **Ans.**

4.19. Check the validity of the following statements:

(*a*) The convolution of two minimum-phase sequences is always a minimum-phase sequence.

(*b*) The sum of two minimum-phase sequences is always minimum-phase.

SOLUTION: (*a*) Correct. When we convolve two sequences, say $x_1(n)$ and $x_2(n)$ which are minimum phase and hence zeros of $X_1(z)$ and $X_2(z)$ are inside the unit circle, then $x_1(n) * x_2(n) \xrightarrow{zT} X_1(z) \cdot X_2(z)$. Thus, zeros of $X_1(z)X_2(z)$ are the combination of zeros of $X_1(z)$ and $X_1(z)$. Hence, $X_1(z) \cdot X_1(z)$ is also a minimum phase function.

(*b*) Incorrect. For example, consider two minimum phase functions

$$H_1(z) = \frac{1 - \frac{1}{2}z^{-1}}{1 - \frac{1}{3}z^{-1}}, \quad H_2(z) = \frac{-2\left(1 + \frac{1}{3}z^{-1}\right)}{1 - \frac{1}{3}z^{-1}}$$

zeros at $z = \frac{1}{2}$ (for H_1); zeros at $z = -\frac{1}{3}$ (for H_2)

If we add them *i.e.*,

$$H_1(z) + H_2(z) = \frac{\left(1 - \frac{1}{2}z^{-1}\right) - 2\left(1 + \frac{1}{3}z^{-1}\right)}{1 - \frac{1}{3}z^{-1}}$$

$$= \frac{-1 - \left(\frac{7}{8}\right)z^{-1}}{1 - \frac{1}{3}z^{-1}}$$

has zero at $z = -\frac{8}{7}$ and $\therefore$ not minimum phase.

4.20. Let $G(z)$ be a causal stable, non-minimum-phase transfer function and let $H(z)$ denotes another causals stable transfer function that is minimum-phase with $|G(e^{j\omega})| = |H(e^{j\omega})|$. Show that $G(z) = H(z) \cdot A(z)$, where $A(z)$ is a stable causal all pass transfer function. (Minimum phase TF).

SOLUTION: Since, $G(z)$ is non-minimum phase but causal TF, it will have some zeros outside the unit circle.

Let $z = \alpha$ be one such zero. We can then write

$$G(z) = P(z) \cdot (1 - \alpha z^{-1})$$

$$= P(z)(-\alpha^* + z^{-1})\left[\frac{1-\alpha z^{-1}}{-\alpha^* + z^{-1}}\right]$$

As $\left(\frac{1-\alpha z^{-1}}{-\alpha^* + z^{-1}}\right)$ is a stable first order all pass function, since, its pole is at $z = \frac{1}{\alpha^*}$ and zero at $z = \alpha$. As $|\alpha| > 1$, $\therefore$ $\left|\frac{1}{\alpha^*}\right| < 1$ *i.e.* pole is inside the unit circle, and pole and zero are mirror symmetric. We can carry at this operation to all zeros of $G(z)$ which are outside the unit circle. We finally write

$$G(z) = H(z) \cdot A(z)$$

$H(z)$ will have all zeros inside the unit circle and is hence minimum phase. $A(z)$ will be a product of the first order all pass functions, and hence an all pass function.

4.21. Determine the minimum-phase system whose squared magnitude is given by:

(*a*) $|H(\omega)|^2 = \dfrac{\frac{5}{4} - \cos\omega}{\frac{10}{9} - \frac{2}{3}\cos\omega}$, (*b*) $|H(\omega)|^2 = \dfrac{2(1-a^2)}{(1+a^2) - 2a\cos\omega}$, $|a| < 1$.

SOLUTION: (*a*) We know that $|H(\omega)|^2 = H(z)\cdot H(z^{-1})\big|_{z=e^{j\omega}}$

$$\text{As } |H(\omega)|^2\Big|_{e^{j\omega}=2} = \frac{\frac{5}{4} - \frac{1}{2}(z+z^{-1})}{\frac{10}{9} - \frac{1}{3}(z+z^{-1})}$$

$$= \frac{-\frac{1}{2}z^{-1}\left[z^2 - \frac{5}{2}z + 1\right]}{-\frac{1}{3}z^{-1}\left[z^2 -- \frac{10}{3} + 1\right]}$$

$$= \frac{3}{2}\cdot\frac{\left(z - \frac{1}{2}\right)(z-2)}{\left(z - \frac{1}{3}\right)(z-3)}$$

$$= \frac{3}{2}\,\frac{\left(1 - \frac{1}{2}z^{-1}\right)(1 - 2z^{-1})}{\underbrace{\left(1 - \frac{1}{3}z^{-1}\right)}_{\text{Minimum phase}}(1 - 3z^{-1})}$$

$$\therefore \quad H(z)\cdot H(z^{-1}) = \left(\sqrt{\frac{3}{2}}\,\frac{1-\frac{1}{z^{-1}}}{\frac{z^{-1}}{3}}\right)\left(\sqrt{\frac{3}{2}}\,\frac{1-2z^{-1}}{1-3z^{-1}}\right) \quad \text{(Note this step)}$$

$$\therefore \quad H(z) = \sqrt{\frac{3}{2}}\,\frac{1-\frac{1}{2}z^{-1}}{1-\frac{1}{3}z^{-1}}, \text{ which is stable, minimum-phase system} \qquad \textbf{Ans.}$$

(*b*) Here,

$$H(z)H(z^{-1}) = 2(1-a^2)\left[\frac{1}{(1+a^2)-a(z+z^{-1})}\right], \ |a| < 1$$

$$= \frac{2(1-a^2)}{-az}\left[\frac{1}{z^{-2}-\frac{1+a^2}{a}z^{-1}+1}\right] \qquad \text{...}(A)$$

$$\therefore \quad z^{-1} = \frac{\frac{1+a^2}{a} \pm \sqrt{\left(\frac{1+a^2}{a}\right)^2 - 4}}{2}$$

$$= \frac{(1+a^2)\pm(1-a^2)}{2a}$$

$$= \frac{1}{a}, a$$

As

$$H(z)\,.\,H(z^{-1}) = \frac{2(1-a^2)}{-az}\,\frac{1}{(z^{-1}-a)\left(z^{-1}-\frac{1}{a}\right)} \quad \text{from } (A)$$

$$= 2(1-a^2)\frac{1}{(-az)\frac{1}{a}}\,\frac{1}{(z^{-1}-a)(az^{-1}-1)}$$

$$= 2(1-a^2)\frac{1}{(1-az^{-1})(1-az)}$$

Pole at $z = a \therefore$ stable; Pole at $z = \frac{1}{a} \therefore$ unstable

$$\therefore \quad H(z) = \sqrt{2(1-a^2)}\,\frac{1}{1-az^{-1}} \text{ is TF for stable minimum phase system.}$$

and

$$H(z^{-1}) = 2\sqrt{(1-a^2)}\cdot\frac{1}{1-az} \quad \left(\text{not stable} \because \text{ pole at } z = \frac{1}{a}\right)$$

4.22. Let $A_0(z)$ and $A_1(z)$ be two causal stable all pass TFs. Define two causal stable IIR TFs as follows:

$$H_0(z) = A_0(z) + A_1(z),\ H_1(z) = A_0(z) - A_1(z)$$

Show that the numerators of $H_0(z)$ and $H_1(z)$ are, respectively a symmetric and antisymmetric polynomial.

SOLUTION: Let $A_0(z)$ and $A_1(z)$ be all pass functions of order M and N, respectively, with no common factors. Hence, the orders of $H_0(z)$ and $H_1(z)$ as defined in the problem are $M + N$. We can also write

$$A_0(z) = \frac{z^{-M}D_0(z^{-1})}{D_0(z)} \text{ and } A_1(z) = \frac{z^{-N}D_1(z^{-1})}{D_1(z)}$$

$$\therefore \quad H_0(z) = \frac{P(z)}{D(z)} = \frac{z^{-M}D_0(z^{-1})}{D_0(z)} + \frac{z^{-N}D_1(z^{-1})}{D_1(z)} = \frac{z^{-M}D_0(z^{-1})D_1(z) + z^{-N}D_1(z^{-1})D_0(z)}{D_0(z)\cdot D_1(z)}$$

$$H_1(z) = \frac{Q(z)}{D(z)} = \frac{z^{-M}D_0(z^{-1})}{D_0(z)} - \frac{z^{-N}D_1(z^{-1})}{D_1(z)} = \frac{z^{-M}D_0(z^{-1})D_1(z) - z^{-N}D_1(z^{-1})D_0(z)}{D_0(z)\,D_1(z)}$$

$P(z)$ is of degree $M + N$. Similarly, $Q(z)$ is also of degree $M + N$.

Note that $\quad P(z) = z^{-M}D_0(z^{-1})D_1(z) + z^{-N}D_0(z^{-1})D_0(z)$

$$\therefore \quad z^{-(M+N)} \cdot P(z^{-1}) = z^{-(M+N)}[z^{M}D_0(z)D_1(z^{-1}) + z^{N}D_1(z)D_0(z^{-1})]$$

$$= z^{-N}D_0(z)D_1(z^{-1}) + z^{-M}D_0(z^{-1})D_1(z) = P(z)$$

As $\quad z^{-(M+N)}P(z^{-1}) = P(z)$, hence $P(z)$ is symmetric polynomial.

Now $\quad z^{-(M+N)}Q(z^{-1}) = z^{-(M+N)}[z^{+M}D_0(z^{+1})D_1(z^{-1}) - z^{+N}D_1(z^{+1})D_0(z^{-1})]$

$$= z^{-N}D_0(z)D_1(z^{-1}) - z^{-M}D_0(z^{-1})D_1(z) = -Q(z)$$

As $\quad z^{-M+N}Q(z^{-1}) = -Q(z)$, hence $Q(z)$ is anti-symmetric polynomial.

4.23. Verify the relation

$$|G_0(e^{j\omega})| + |G_1(e^{j\omega})| = |H_0(e^{j\omega})|^2 + |H_1(e^{j\omega})|^2 = 1$$

where G_0, G_1 are magnitude complementary given below:

SOLUTION: Given

$$\left.\begin{aligned} G_0(z) &= \frac{1}{4}[A_0(z) + A_1(z)]^2 \\ G_1(z) &= -\frac{1}{4}[A_0(z) - A_1(z)]^2 \end{aligned}\right\} \text{ (given)}$$

$$\therefore \quad |G_0(e^{j\omega})| + |G_1(e^{j\omega})| = \frac{1}{4}[|A_0(e^{j\omega}) + A_1(e^{j\omega})|^2 + |A_0(e^{j\omega}) - A_1(e^{j\omega})|^2]$$

i.e. replacing z by $e^{j\omega}$ and taking mod values, therefore, $-\frac{1}{4}$ in $G_1(z)$ becomes $-\frac{1}{4}$ in mod value.

(Note this step)

$$\therefore \quad |G_0(e^{j\omega})| + |G_1(e^{j\omega})| = \frac{1}{4}[(A_0(e^{j\omega}) + A_1(e^{j\omega}))(A_0^*(e^{j\omega}) + A_1^*(e^{j\omega}))$$

$$+ (A_0(e^{j\omega}) - A_1(e^{j\omega}))(A_0^*(e^{j\omega}) - A_1^*(e^{j\omega}))]$$

$$= \frac{1}{4}[\{A_0(e^{j\omega}) \cdot A_0^*(e^{j\omega}) + \cancel{A_0(e^{j\omega})A_1^*(e^{j\omega})} + \cancel{A_1(e^{j\omega})A_0^*(e^{j\omega})}$$

$$+ A_1(e^{j\omega}) \cdot A_1^*(e^{j\omega})\} + \{A_0(e^{j\omega})A_0^*(e^{j\omega})$$

$$- \cancel{A_0(e^{j\omega})A_1^*(e^{j\omega})} - \cancel{A_1(e^{j\omega})A_0^*(e^{j\omega})} + A_1(e^{j\omega})A_1^*(e^{j\omega})\}]$$

$$= \frac{1}{4}[2|A_0(e^{j\omega})|^2 + 2|A_1(e^{j\omega})|^2]$$

$$= \frac{1}{4}[2\times 1 + 2\times 1] = 1 \qquad \because \; A_0(e^{j\omega}) \text{ and } A_0(e^{j\omega}) \text{ are LPFs}$$

$$\therefore \quad |A_0(e^{j\omega})| = |A_1(e^{j\omega})| = 1$$

$$\therefore \quad |G_0(e^{j\omega})| + |G_0(e^{j\omega})| = 1$$

Q.E.D.

4.24. Show that $H(z) = 1 - 2z^{-1} + 6z^{-2} + 3z^{-3}$ in power-symmetric transfer functions.

SOLUTION: Given $H(z) = 1 - 2z^{-1} + 6z^{-2} + 3z^{-3}$

$$\therefore \quad H(z)\cdot H(z^{-1}) + H(-z)\cdot H(-z^{-1}) = (1 - 2z^{-1} + 6z^{-2} + 3z^{-3})(1 - 2z + 6z^2 + 3z^3) + (1 + 2z^{-1} + 6z^{-2} - 3z^{-3})(1 + 2z + 6z^2 - 3z^3)$$

$$= \Big(\underbrace{(1+6z^{-2})}_{a} - \underbrace{(2z^{-1} - 3z^{-3})}_{b}\Big)\Big(\underbrace{(1+6z^2)}_{c} - \underbrace{(2z - 3z^3)}_{d}\Big) + \Big[\underbrace{(1+6z^{-2})}_{a} + \underbrace{(2z^{-1} - 3z^{-3})}_{b}\Big]\Big[\underbrace{(1+6z^2)}_{c} + \underbrace{(2z - 3z^3)}_{d}\Big]$$

$$= 2[(1 + 6z^{-2})(1 + 6z^2) + (2z^{-1} - 3z^{-3})(2z - 3z^3)] \text{ (see *)}$$

$$= 2[(1 + \cancel{6z^2} + \cancel{6z^{-2}} + 36) + (4 - \cancel{6z^2} - \cancel{6z^{-2}} + 9)]$$

$$= 2[1 + 36 + 4 + 9] = 2(50) = 100$$

$\therefore$ $H(z)$ is a power-symmetry transfer function. Q.E.D.

4.25. Consider the real-coefficient stable IIR transfer function:
$H(z) = A_0(z^2) + z^{-1}A_1(z^2)$, where $A_0(z)$ and $A_1(z)$ are stable all pass transfer functions. Show that $H(z)$ is power-symmetric transfer function.

SOLUTION: Given $H(z) = A_0(z^2) + z^{-1}A_1(z^2)$

$$\therefore \quad H(z)\cdot H(z^{-1}) + H(-z)\cdot H(-z^{-1}) = [A_0(z^2) + z^{-1}A_1(z^2)][A_0(z^{-2}) + zA_1(z^{-2})] + [A_0(z^2) - z^{-1}A_1(z^2)][A_0(z^{-2}) - zA_1(z^{-2})]$$

$$= A_0(z^2)A_0(z^{-2}) + \cancel{zA_0(z^2)\cdot A_1(z^{-2})} + \cancel{z^{-1}A_0(z^{-2})A_1(z^{-2})} + A_1(z^2)\cdot A_1(z^{-2})$$

$$+ A_0(z^2)\cdot A_0(z^{-2}) - \cancel{zA_0(z^2)A_1(z^{-2})} - \cancel{z^{-1}A_0(z^{-2})A_1(z^2)} + A_1(z^2)A_1(z^{-2})$$

$$= 2A_0(z^2)A_0(z^{-2}) + 2A_1(z^2)A_1(z^{-2})$$

But $\quad A_0(z^2)\cdot A_0(z^{-2}) = A_1(z^2)A_1(z^{-2}) = 1$ (see **)

$\therefore \quad H(z)\cdot H(z^{-1}) + H(-z)\cdot H(-z^{-1}) = 4$ a constant.

$\therefore$ $H(z)$ is power-symmetric transfer function.

4.26. For the first order LPF $H_{LP}(z)$ as given, determine its power-complementary HP transfer function $H_{HP}(z)$.

SOLUTION: Given
$$H_{LP}(z) = \frac{1}{2}\frac{1-\alpha+z^{-1}-\alpha z^{-1}}{1-\alpha z^{-1}}$$

This may be put in the form

$$H_{LP}(z) = \frac{1}{2}\left[1+\frac{-\alpha+z^{-1}}{1-\alpha z^{-1}}\right] = \frac{1}{2}[A_0(z) + A_1(z)]$$

---

* $(a - b)(c - d) + (a + b)(c + d) = (ac - \cancel{ad} - \cancel{bc} + bd) + (ac + \cancel{ad} + \cancel{bc} + bd) = 2(ac + bd)$

** $H(z)$ is a real coefficient TF, hence $A_0(z^2)$ and $A_1(z^2)$ and, therefore, $A_0(z)$ and $A_1(z)$ are also real coefficient stable all pass TFs.

$$A_0^*(e^{j\omega}) = A_0(e^{-j\omega}) \text{ also } |A_0(e^{j\omega})|^2 = 1 \text{ being all pass filter } \forall\, \omega$$

$$\therefore \quad A_0(e^{j2\omega})\cdot A_0(e^{-j2\omega}) = |A(e^{j2\omega})|^2 = 1 \text{ or } A_0(z^2)\cdot A_0(z^{-2}) = 1$$

Similarly, $A_1(z^2)A_1(z^{-2}) = 1$.

where $A_0(z)$ and $A_1(z)$ are all pass TFs, given by

$$A_0(z) = 1,\ A_1(z) = \frac{-\alpha + z^{-1}}{1 - \alpha z^{-1}}$$

Compare $H_{LP}(z)$ with $H_0(z) = \frac{1}{2}[A_0(z) + A_1(z)]$

Hence, its power-complementary HP function is given by

$$H_{HP}(z) = \frac{1}{2}[A_0(z) + A_1(z)] = \frac{1}{2}\left[1 - \frac{-\alpha + z^{-1}}{1 - \alpha z^{-1}}\right] = \frac{1}{2}\left[\frac{1 - \alpha z^{-1} + \alpha - z^{-1}}{1 - \alpha z^{-1}}\right]$$

$$= \frac{1}{2}\frac{(1+\alpha)(1 - z^{-1})}{1 - \alpha z^{-1}} = \frac{1+\alpha}{2}\cdot\frac{1 - z^{-1}}{1 - \alpha z^{-1}}$$ which is the first order high pass TF. **Ans.**

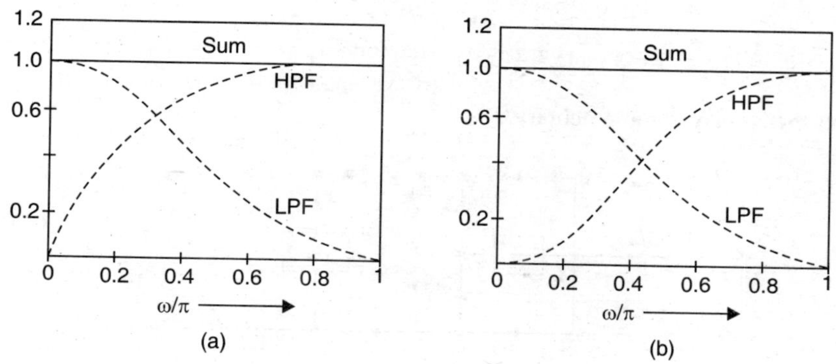

Fig. Prob. 4.26. Complementary properties of the first order LP and HP transfer functions with $\alpha = 0.3$ (*a*) All pass complementary (*b*) Power-complementary

4.27. Show that the value of the gain function $G(\omega)$ of a power-symmetric TF defined by $H(z) \cdot H(z^{-1}) + H(-z) \cdot H(-z^{-1}) = K$ at $\omega = \frac{\pi}{2}$ is $10 \log_{10} K - 3$ dB.

SOLUTION: As $H(z) \cdot H(z^{-1}) + H(-z) \cdot H(-z^{-1}) = K$ (given)
with $z = e^{j\omega}$, we have $H(e^{j\omega}) \cdot H(e^{-j\omega}) + H(-e^{j\omega}) \cdot H(-e^{-j\omega}) = K$
i.e. $|H(e^{j\omega})|^2 + |H(-e^{j\omega})|^2 = K$ (if $H(z)$ is a real coefficient transfer function

$\because$ then "$H^*(e^{j\omega}) = H(e^{-j\omega})$")

But $$|H(-e^{j\omega})|^2 = |H(e^{j(\pi+\omega)})|^2. \quad ...(A)$$

Thus, for $\omega = \frac{\pi}{2}$, (*A*) reduces to

$$\left|H(e^{j\omega})\right|^2_{\omega=\pi/2} + \left|H(e^{j(\pi+\omega)})\right|^2_{\omega=\pi/2} = \left|H(e^{j\pi/2})\right|^2 + \left|H(e^{j(\pi+\pi/2)})\right|^2 = K$$

$$\therefore \quad \left|H(e^{j\pi/2})\right|^2 + \left|H(e^{-j\pi/2)})\right|^2 = K \quad ...(B)$$

But $|H(e^{j\omega})| = |H(e^{-j\omega})|$ for real coefficient $H(z)$, hence, $\left|H(e^{-j\pi/2})\right|$ can be replaced by $\left|H(e^{j\pi/2})\right|$.
With this (*B*) reduces to

$$2\left|H(e^{j\pi/2})\right|^2 = K \quad ...(C)$$

Taking $\log_{10}$ on both sides of (C), we get

$$\log_{10} 2 + 2\log_{10} |H(e^{j\omega})| = \log K$$

or $$20\log_{10} |H(e^{j\omega})| = 10\log_{10} K - 10\log_{10} 2 \quad (=3)$$

or $$G(\omega)|_{\omega=\pi/2} \text{ in dB} = 10\log_{10} K - 3$$ **Ans.**

4.28. The following band stop FIR TFs $H_{BS}(z)$ have also been proposed for the recovery of vertical details in the structure of Figure (shown below) employed for the separation of the luminance and the chrominance components (delay complementary TFs)

(a) $H_{BS}(z) = \dfrac{1}{4}(1+z^{-2})^2$

(b) $H_{BS}(z) = \dfrac{1}{16}(1+z^{-2})^2(-1+6z^{-2}-z^{-4})$

(c) $H_{BS}(z) = \dfrac{1}{32}(1+z^{-2})^2(-3+14z^{-2}-3z^{-4})$

Develop their delay-complementary.

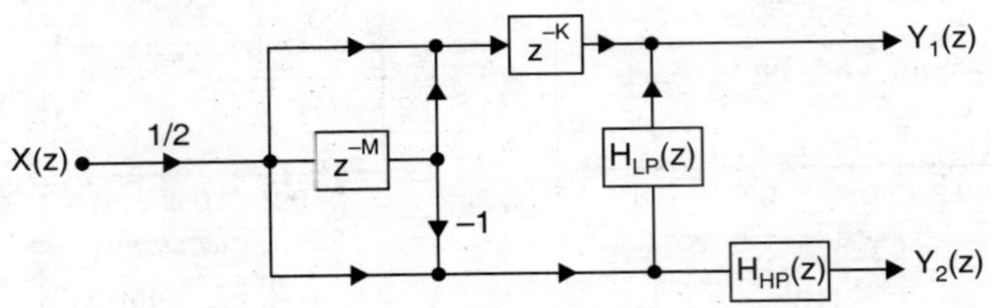

X(z) = Composite video signal
Y_1(z) = Luminance signal
Y_2(z) = Chrominance signal

Fig. Prob. 4.28. The given structure

SOLUTION: (a) $H_{BS}(z) = \dfrac{1}{4}(1+z^{-2})^2$. This is of order 4 and delay is 2

$$\therefore \quad H_{BP}(z) = z^{-2} - H_{BS}(z) = z^{-2} - \frac{1}{4}(1+z^{-2})^2 = \frac{1}{4}[4z^{-2} - (1+2z^{-2}+z^{-4})] = -\frac{1}{4}(1-z^{-2})^2$$ **Ans.**

(b) $H_{BS}(z) = \dfrac{1}{16}(1+z^{-2})^2(-1+6z^{-2}-z^{-4})$ is of order 8 and hence delay is 4.

$$\therefore \quad H_{BP}(z) = z^{-4} - \frac{1}{16}(1+z^{-2})^2(-1+6z^{-2}-z^{-4}) = \frac{1}{16}[16z^{-4} - (1+2z^{-2}+z^{-4})(-1+6z^{-2}-z^{-4})]$$

$$= \frac{1}{16}[16z^{-4} - (-1+4z^{-2}+10z^{-4}+4z^{-4}-z^{-8})]$$

$$= \frac{1}{16}[1-4z^{-2}+6z^{-4}-4z^{-6}+z^{-8}]$$

$$= \frac{1}{16}(1-z^{-2})^4$$ **Ans.**

(c) $H_{BS}(z) = \frac{1}{32}(1+z^{-2})^2(-3+14z^{-2}-3z^{-4})$ is of order 8, therefore, delay = 4.

$$\therefore \quad H_{BP}(z) = z^{-4} - \frac{1}{32}(1+z^{-2})^2(-3+14z^{-2}-3z^{-4})$$

$$= z^{-4} - \frac{1}{32}(1+2z^{-2}+z^{-4})(-3+14z^{-2}-3z^{-4})$$

$$= \frac{1}{32}[32z^{-4} - (-3+8z^{-2}+22z^{-4}+8z^{-6}-3z^{-8})]$$

$$= \frac{1}{32}[3-8z^{-2}+10z^{-4}-8z^{-6}+3z^{-8}]$$

Ans.

4.29. For a SV model of a discrete system. If $\underline{A}, \underline{B}, \underline{C}, \underline{D}$, matrices are given as

$$\underline{A} = \begin{bmatrix} 0 & 1 \\ -2 & -3 \end{bmatrix}, \underline{B} = \begin{bmatrix} 0 \\ 1 \end{bmatrix}, \underline{C} = [-2 \quad -1], \underline{D} = [1]$$

Find the system function $H(z)$. *(IP Univ., 2008)*

[**Ans.** $H(z) = \frac{1+2z^{-1}}{1-3z^{-1}+2z^{-2}}$]

4.30. Obtain the state variable model of the network shown.

[**Ans.** Hint Take, $x_1 = v_C$ and $x_2 = i_L$

$$\begin{bmatrix} \dot{v}_C \\ i_L \end{bmatrix} = \begin{bmatrix} 0 & -\frac{1}{C} \\ \frac{1}{L} & \frac{-R}{L} \end{bmatrix} \begin{bmatrix} v_C \\ i_L \end{bmatrix} + \begin{bmatrix} \frac{1}{C} \\ 0 \end{bmatrix} [i]$$

$$v_R = [0 \quad R] \begin{bmatrix} v_C \\ i_L \end{bmatrix} + [0][i]$$

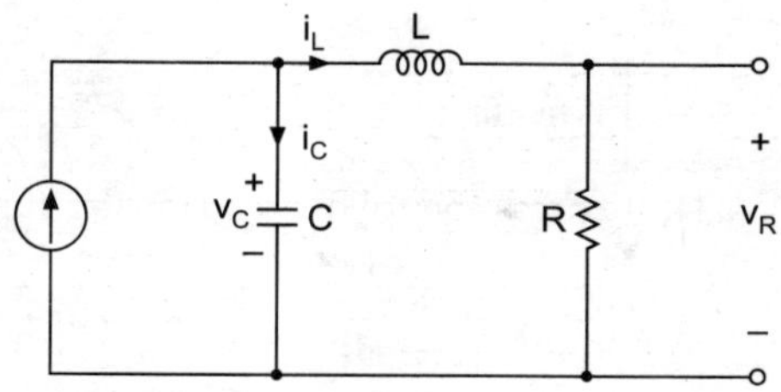

Fig. Prob. 4.30. The given network

4.31. Show that the $\underline{A}, \underline{B}, \underline{C}, \underline{D}$ matrices given by

$$\underline{A} = \begin{bmatrix} 0 & 0 & -3/2 \\ 1 & 0 & -3 \\ 0 & 1 & -2 \end{bmatrix}, \underline{B} = \begin{bmatrix} 2 \\ 0 \\ 0 \end{bmatrix}, \underline{C} = [0 \quad 0 \quad 1], \underline{D} = [0]$$

represent the analog system; $H(s) = \frac{4}{2s^3+4s^2+6s+3}$.

4.32. Obtain the state variable model for the given RLC parallel network shown in the figure.

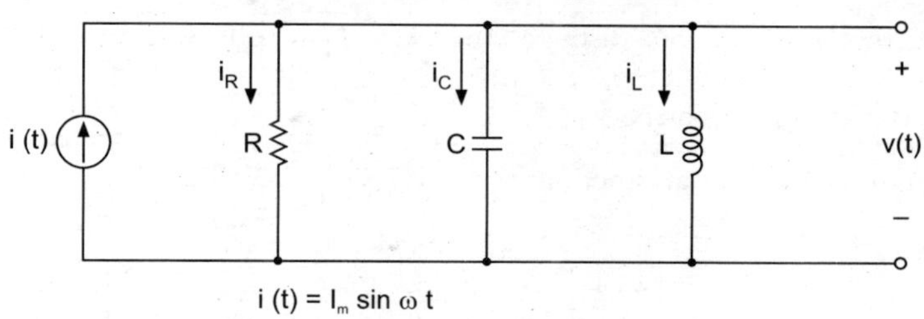

Fig. Prob. 4.32. The given RLC network

[**Ans.** $$\begin{bmatrix} \dot{x}_1(t) \\ \dot{x}_2(t) \end{bmatrix} = \begin{bmatrix} 0 & 1 \\ \frac{-1}{LC} & \frac{-1}{RC} \end{bmatrix} \begin{bmatrix} x_1(t) \\ x_2(t) \end{bmatrix} + \begin{bmatrix} 0 \\ \frac{\omega}{C}\cot\omega t \end{bmatrix} [I_m \sin\omega t]$$

$$v(t) = [1 \quad 0]\begin{bmatrix} x_1(t) \\ x_2(t) \end{bmatrix} + [0][u]$$

Hint. $$i(t) = \frac{v(t)}{R} + C\frac{dv(t)}{dt} + \frac{1}{L}\int v(t)\,dt = I_m \sin\omega t$$

$$\therefore \quad \frac{d^2 v(t)}{dt^2} + \frac{1}{RC}\frac{dv(t)}{dt} + \frac{1}{LC}v(t) = \frac{\omega I_m}{C}\cos\omega t$$

Take $x_1(t) = v(t)$, $x_2(t) = \dfrac{dv(t)}{dt}$ and so on]

4.33. Find the system function $H(s)$ if SV matrices are

(a) $$\underline{A} = \begin{bmatrix} 0 & 1 \\ -20 & -9 \end{bmatrix}, \underline{B} = \begin{bmatrix} 0 \\ 5 \end{bmatrix}, \underline{C} = [-18 \quad -6], \underline{D} = [5]$$

(b) $$\underline{A} = \begin{bmatrix} 0 & 1 & 0 \\ 0 & 0 & 1 \\ -5 & -12 & -5 \end{bmatrix}, \underline{B} = \begin{bmatrix} 0 \\ 0 \\ 1 \end{bmatrix}, \underline{C} = [7 \quad 2 \quad 3], \underline{D} = [0]$$ *(IP Univ., 2006)*

[**Ans.** *(a)* $H(s) = \dfrac{5(s^2+3s+2)}{s^2+9s+20}$ *(b)* $H(s) = \dfrac{3s^2+2s+7}{s^3+5s^2+12s+5}$]

4.34. Express the following Transfer function in terms of SV model for an analog system described by

$$2\frac{d^3 y(t)}{dt^3} + 4\frac{d^2 y(t)}{dt^2} + 6\frac{dy(t)}{dt} + 3y\frac{\pi}{3} = 4\, u(t)$$

where $u(t)$ is the input signal.

[**Ans.** $$\underline{A} = \begin{bmatrix} 0 & 0 & -3/2 \\ 1 & 0 & -3 \\ 0 & 1 & -2 \end{bmatrix}, \underline{B} = \begin{bmatrix} 2 \\ 0 \\ 0 \end{bmatrix}, \underline{C} = [0 \quad 0 \quad 1], \underline{D} = [0]$$]

4.35. Find the state equations for the discrete-time system characterized by the difference equation $y(k) - \frac{3}{4}y(k-1) + \frac{1}{8}y(k-2) = x(k) + \frac{1}{2}x(k+1)$ where $y(k)$ is the output and $x(k)$ is the input.

[**Ans.** $\underline{A} = \begin{bmatrix} 0 & 1 \\ -1/8 & 3/4 \end{bmatrix}, \underline{B} = \begin{bmatrix} 0 \\ 1 \end{bmatrix}, \underline{C} = \left[-\frac{1}{8}, \frac{5}{4}\right], \underline{D} = [1]$]

4.36. Find the state representation of a discrete-time LTI system with system function $H(z) = \dfrac{z}{2z^2 - 3z + 1}$ such that A is a diagonal matrix.

[**Hint.** Split $H(z)$ by partial fractions *i.e.* $H(z) = \dfrac{1}{1-z^{-1}} - \dfrac{1}{1-\frac{1}{2}z^{-1}}$, use parallel realization

$$\underline{A} = \begin{bmatrix} 1 & 0 \\ 0 & \frac{1}{2} \end{bmatrix}, \underline{B} = \begin{bmatrix} 1 \\ -1 \end{bmatrix}, \underline{C} = \left[1 \quad \frac{1}{2}\right], \underline{D} = [0]$$]

CHAPTER 5

Response of Pole-Zero Systems with Non-Zero Initial Conditions

5.0 INTRODUCTION

In this chapter, we cover the procedure to determine response of practical digital as well as analog systems with non-zero initial conditions.

5.1 DIFFERENCE EQUATIONS

Let $x(n)$ signal be applied to the Pole-Zero system as shown in the Fig. 5.1. If $x(n)$ is applied at $n = 0$, then $x(n)$ can be assumed to be causal. The effect of all the previous input signals to the system may be assumed as the initial conditions: $y(-1)$, $y(-2)$, ..., $y(-N)$ etc. As the input $x(n)$ is causal, we determine the output $y(n)$ for $n \geq 0$, hence, we may use one-sided z-transform, which allows us to deal with the initial conditions. Consider the system described by linear constant-coefficient difference equation of the form

$$y(n) = -\sum_{k=1}^{N} a_k y(n-k) + \sum_{k=0}^{M} b_k x(n-k) \qquad ...(5.1)$$

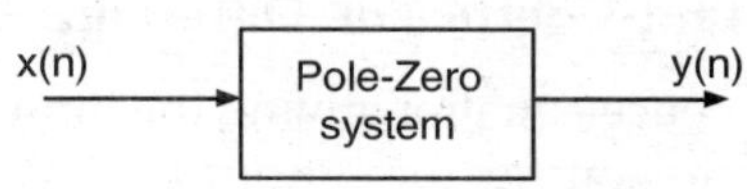

Fig. 5.1. A Pole-Zero system, input $x(n)$ and output $y(n)$

Taking one-sided z-transform of (5.1), we have

$$Y^{+}(z) = -\sum_{k=1}^{N} a_k z^{-k}\left[Y^{+}(z) + \sum_{n=1}^{k} y(-n)z^{n}\right] + \sum_{k=0}^{M} b_k z^{-k} X^{+}(z) \qquad ...(5.2)$$

As $x(n)$ is causal, we can set $X^{+}(z) = X(z)$. [+ sign above $Y(z)$ or $X(z)$ indicates one-sided ZT]

Hence, Eq. (5.2) becomes

$$Y^+(z) = \frac{\sum_{k=0}^{M} b_k z^{-k}}{1+\sum_{k=1}^{N} a_k z^{-k}} X(z) - \frac{\sum_{k=1}^{N} a_k z^{-k}\left(\sum_{n=1}^{k} y(-n)z^n\right)}{1+\sum_{k=1}^{N} a_k z^{-k}} \qquad ...(5.3)$$

$$\therefore \quad Y^+(z) = H(z)\cdot X(z) + \frac{N_0(z)}{A(z)} \qquad (a)$$

where
$$N_0(z) = -\sum_{k=1}^{N} a_k z^{-k}\left(\sum_{n=1}^{k} y(-n)z^n\right) \qquad (b) \qquad ...(5.4)$$

and
$$A(z) = 1+\sum_{k=1}^{N} a_k z^{-k} \qquad (c)$$

Equation (5.4*a*) may be written in the form

$$Y^+(z) = H(z)\cdot X(z) \qquad \text{(output for zero state response)}$$

$$+\frac{N_0(z)}{A(z)} \qquad \text{(output part due to non-zero initial conditions)}$$

or
$$Y_{zs}(z) = H(z)\cdot X(z) \text{ (zero state, and } x(n) \text{ as the input, response)} \qquad ...(5.5a)$$

$$Y^+_{zi} = \frac{N_0(z)}{A(z)} \qquad \text{(zero input response with } x(n) = 0 \text{ and response due to only initial conditions)} \qquad ...(5.5b)$$

$$\therefore \quad Y^+(z) = Y_{zs}(z) + Y_{zi}(z) \qquad ...(5.5c)$$

or
$$y(n) = y_{zs}(n) + y_{zi}(n) \qquad [\text{Cf. } y(n) = y_p(n) + y_h(n)]$$

Note that the initial conditions alter the natural response, and there are no new poles introduced due to the non-zero initial conditions. Also, there is no effect on the forced response of the system.

5.1.1 Solution of Linear Constant-Coefficient Difference Equations

If a linear constant-coefficient difference equation giving the input-output relationship is available, we can determine an explicit expression for the output $y(n)$. We can use *direct method* (without using any transform) or we can use *indirect method* (by using z-transform). The complete solution $y(n)$ is given by

$$y(n) = y_h(n) + y_p(n) \qquad ...(5.6)$$

$y_h(n)$ is known as the *homogeneous* or *complementary* part of $y(n)$, and $y_p(n)$ is called the *particular solution.*

$y_h(n)$ is the solution $y(n)$ with $x(n) = 0$. We always apply the input signal at $n \geq 0$ and assume $x(n) = 0$ for $n < 0$. Thus, the homogeneous difference equation is

$$\sum_{k=0}^{N} a_k y(n-k) = 0, \qquad a_0 = 1 \qquad ...(5.7)$$

The procedure to solve linear constant-coefficient difference equation is very similar to the procedure for solving a linear constant-coefficient differential equation. We assume that the solution $y_h(n)$ is in the form of an exponential given by:

$$y_h(n) = \lambda^n \quad ...(5.8)$$

The subscript h on $y(n)$ refers to homogeneous solution. Putting $y(n) = \lambda^n$ in Eq. (5.7), we get

$$\sum_{k=0}^{N} a_k \lambda^{n-k} = 0 \quad ...(5.9)$$

i.e., $$\lambda^{n-N}(\lambda^N + a_1\lambda^{N-1} + a_2\lambda^{N-2} + ... + a_{N-1}\lambda + a_N) = 0 \quad ...(5.10)$$

We have assumed $a_0 = 1$. If $a_0 \neq 1$, then even the above equation is in the same form. Equation (5.10) is called the *characteristic polynomial.* It has N roots. If all a_k are real, the complex valued roots will occur in complex-conjugate pairs. We may finally determine N roots of Eq. (5.10) and write

$$y_h(n) = c_1\lambda_1^n + c_2\lambda_2^n + ... + c_N\lambda_N^n \quad ...(5.11)$$

The constants $c_1, c_2, ..., c_N$ are found from the initial specified conditions. Note that $y_h(n) \neq y_{zi}(n)$, though in most of the cases $y_h(n)$ may be equal to $y_{zi}(n)$.

The particular solution $y_p(n)$ satisfies the difference equation

$$\sum_{k=0}^{N} a_k y_p(n-k) = \sum_{k=0}^{M} b_k x(n-k), \qquad a_0 = 1 \quad ...(5.12)$$

Here we assume zero state (relaxed state) of the system at $n = 0$.

Note that $y_p(n) \neq y_{zs}(n)$. However, $y_{zs}(n)$ may contain both $y_p(n)$ and $y_h(n)$.

5.1.2 Rule to Solve a Difference Equation by Classical Method

Let the given difference equation be

$$\sum_{k=0}^{N} a_k y(n-k) = \sum_{k=0}^{M} b_k x(n-k) \quad ...(5.13)$$

and initial conditions $y(0^+), y(-1), y(-2), ...$ are given

Input $x(n)$ is also defined

1. Find the roots of the characteristic equation

   $$\lambda^N + a_1\lambda^{N-1} + a_2\lambda^{N-2} + ... + a_N = 0 \qquad [\text{we assume } y_h(n) = \lambda^N \text{ and } x(n) = 0]$$

   Let the roots be $\lambda_1, \lambda_2, ..., \lambda_N$

   (*a*) Then $y_h(n) = c_1(\lambda_1)^n + c_2(\lambda_2)^n + ... + c_N(\lambda_N)^n$ for all roots distinct *i.e.,* $y_h(n) = \sum_i c_i(\lambda_i)^n$

   (*b*) If roots are equal, say $\lambda_1 = \lambda_2 = \lambda_3$, the rest being distinct, then

   $$y_h(n) = c_1(1 + n + n^2)(\lambda_1)^n + c_4(\lambda_4)^n + ... + c_N(\lambda_N)^n$$

   (*c*) If $\lambda = a \pm jb$, then $y_h(n) = r^n\,[A_1 \cos n\theta + A_2 \sin \theta]$

   Take $r = \sqrt{a^2+b^2}$, and $\theta = \tan^{-1}(b/a)$

2. Find the particular solution $y_p(n)$, which depends on $x(n)$

   Take $y_p(n)$ as given in the Table 5.1 for various inputs $x(n)$

Find the constant in the solution $y_p(n)$ by making $y_p(n)$ to satisfy the given difference equation (5.13). Take $y_p(n)$ for that value of n such that no term vanishes.

3. Take $y(n) = y_h(n) + y_p(n)$ ...(5.14)

Determine the constants $c_1, c_2, ..., c_N$ by satisfying Eq. (5.14) by initial conditions.

Table 5.1. General Form of the Particular Solution for Various Types of Input Signal *x*(*n*)

S.No.	Input Signal $x(n)$	Particular Solution $y_p(n)$
1.	A (a constant)	$K\ u(n)$
2.	$A\delta(n)$	0, since input is zero for $n > 0$
3.	$A\ u(n)$	$KA^n u(n)$
4.	AM^n	KM^n
5.	An^M	$(K_0\ n^M + K_1\ n^{M-1} + ... + K_M) = \sum_{i=0}^{M} K_i n^{M-i}$
6.	$A^n n^M$	$A^n(K_0 n^M + K_1 n^{M-1} + ... + K_M) = A^n \sum_{i=0}^{M} K_i n^{M-i}$
7.	$A \cos \omega_0 n$	$K_1 \cos \omega_0 n + K_2 \sin \omega_0 n$
8.	$A \sin \omega_0 n$	
9.	$a^n\ u(n)$ and one root of characteristic equation is also $\lambda_1 = a$	$K \cdot n \cdot a^n\ u(n)$

EXAMPLE 5.1: *Determine the unit step response of the system described by the difference equation*

$$y(n) = 0.9y(n-1) - 0.81\ y(n-2) + x(n)$$

under the initial conditions (*a*) $y(-1) = y(-2) = 0$ (*b*) $y(-1) = y(-2) = 1$.

SOLUTION: As $y(n) = 0.9y(n-1) - 0.81\ y(n-2) + x(n)$

$$\therefore \quad H(z) = \frac{1}{1-0.9z^{-1}+0.81z^{-2}}$$

The poles are found by putting $1 - 0.9z^{-1} + 0.81z^{-2} = 0$

i.e. $$z^2 - 0.9z + 0.81 = 0$$

$$\therefore \quad z = \frac{0.9 \pm \sqrt{0.81 - 4\times 0.81}}{2} = 0.9\,[1 \pm j\sqrt{3}]/2$$

$$= 0.9e^{\pm j\pi/3}$$

as $x(n) = u(n)$ $\therefore$ $X(z) = \dfrac{1}{1-z^{-1}}$

(*a*) With initial conditions zero *i.e.*, zero state response is given by

$$Y_{zs}(z) = H(z) \cdot X(z) \qquad \text{From (5.5}a\text{)}$$

$$= \frac{1}{(1-0.9e^{j\pi/3}z^{-1})(1-0.9e^{-j\pi/3}z^{-1})(1-z^{-1})}$$

$$= \frac{0.542 - j0.049}{1-0.9e^{j\pi/3}z^{-1}} + \frac{0.542 + j0.049}{1-0.9e^{-j\pi/3}z^{-1}} + \frac{1.099}{1-z^{-1}} \quad \text{(by partial fractions)}$$

$$\left(\because \quad \frac{1}{1-0.9e^{j\pi/3}} \times \frac{1}{1-0.9e^{-j\pi/3}} = \frac{1}{1-0.9\times 2\cos\pi/3+0.81} = \frac{1}{1-0.9+0.81} = \frac{1}{0.91} = 1.099\right.$$

and so on. Similarly, we find the coefficients of other two partial fraction terms $\Big)$

$$\therefore \quad y_{zs}(n) = 1.099u(n) + (0.542 - j0.049)\,(0.9e^{j\pi/3n})u(n) + (0.542 + j0.049)(0.9e^{-j\pi/3n})u(n)$$

$$= 1.099u(n) + (0.9)^n\left[\sqrt{0.296}\,e^{j(\pi/3n-5.2^\circ)} + \sqrt{0.296}\,e^{-j(\pi/3-5.2^\circ)}\right]u(n)$$

$$\therefore \quad y(n) = 1.099u(n) + (1.088)(0.9)^n \cos\left(\frac{\pi}{3}n - 5.2^\circ\right)u(n) \qquad \textbf{Ans.}$$

(*b*) For non-zero initial condition $y(-1) = y(-2) = 1$

$$Y_{zi}(z) = \frac{N_0(z)}{A(z)} = \frac{-\sum_{k=1}^{N} a_k z^{-k}\left(\sum_{n=1}^{k} y(-n)z^n\right)}{A(z)} \qquad \text{...From (5.5}b\text{)}$$

$N = 2$ here $a_1 = -0.9$, $a_2 = 0.81$

$$\therefore \quad N_0(z) = -\left[\sum_{k=1}^{z} a_k z^{-k}\left(\sum_{n=1}^{k} y(-n)z^n\right)\right]$$

$$= -[a_1 z^{-1} y(-1)z^1] + a_2 z^{-2}\, y(-1)z^1 + y(-2)z^2)]$$

$$= -[-0.9 + 0.81(z^{-1} + 1)] \qquad \because\; y(-1) = y(-2) = 1$$

$$= 0.9 - 0.81z^{-1}$$

Hence,

$$Y_{zi}(z) = \frac{0.9-0.81z^{-1}}{1-0.9z^{-1}+0.81z^{-2}} \qquad \text{putting value of } A(z) \text{ from } (a)$$

$$= \frac{0.026-j0.4936}{1-0.9e^{j\pi/3}z^{-1}} + \frac{0.026-j0.4936}{1-0.9e^{-j\pi/3}z^{-1}}$$

$$y_{zi}(n) = [(0.026 + j0.4936)(0.9)^n e^{j\pi/3n}) + (0.026 - j0.4936)(0.9)^n e^{j\pi/3n}]u(n)$$

$$= 0.988(0.9)^n \cos\left(\frac{\pi}{3}n + 87^\circ\right)u(n)$$

In this case, the total response will be

$$Y(z) = Y_{zs}(z) + Y_{zi}(z) \qquad \text{...[From (5.5}c\text{)]}$$

$$= \left[\frac{(0.542-j0.049)+(0.026+j0.4936)}{1-0.9e^{j\pi/3}z^{-1}} + \frac{(0.542-j0.049)+(0.026-j0.4936)}{1-0.9e^{-j\pi/3}z^{-1}} + \frac{1.099}{1-z^{-1}}\right]$$

$$= \frac{0.568+j0.445}{1-0.9e^{j\pi/3}z^{-1}} + \frac{0.568-j0.445}{1-0.9e^{-j\pi/3}z^{-1}} + \frac{1.099}{1-z^{-1}}$$

$$\therefore \quad y(n) = 1.099u(n) + 1.44(0.9)^n \cos\left(\frac{\pi}{3}n + 38^\circ\right)u(n) \qquad \textbf{Ans.}$$

EXAMPLE 5.2: *Determine the particular solution of the first order difference equation*

$$y(n) + a_1 y(n-1) = x(n), \quad |a_1| < 1$$

Assume $x(n) = u(n)$.

SOLUTION: Here, $y(n) + a_1 y(n-1) = u(n), \quad |a_1| < 1$ ...(A)

Input $x(n)$ *is also sometimes called forcing function.* As $x(n) = u(n)$ is constant for $n \geq 0$, the form of the solution is also constant for $n \geq 0$. **(Note this argument)**. Hence, we may write

$$y_p(n) = Ku(n) \text{ (serial 1 of Table 5.1)} \quad ...(B)$$

Putting $y(n) = y_p(n) = Ku(n)$ in (A), we get

$$Ku(n) + a_1 Ku(n-1) = u(n) \quad ...(C)$$

Put $n = 1$ in (C) ($n \geq 1$, so that none of the terms is zero),

$$\therefore \quad K + a_1 K = 1 \quad \therefore \quad K = \frac{1}{1+a_1}$$

Hence, $y_p(n) = \dfrac{1}{1+a_1} u(n)$ is the particular solution **Ans.**

Note. If we take z-transform on both sides of (A), we get

$$Y(z)[1 + a_1 z^{-1}] = \frac{1}{1-z^{-1}}$$

or

$$Y(z) = \frac{1}{1+a_1 z^{-1}} \cdot \frac{1}{1-z^{-1}} = \frac{a_1/(1+a_1)}{1+a_1 z^{-1}} + \frac{1(1+a_1)}{1-z^{-1}}$$

This gives $y(n) = \left[\dfrac{a_1}{1+a_1}(-a_1)^n + \dfrac{1}{1+a_1}\right] u(n)$ which is not correct. Can you guess why? (see Ex. 5.15)

EXAMPLE 5.3: *Determine the particular solution of the difference equation*

$$y(n) = \frac{5}{6} y(n-1) - \frac{1}{6} y(n-2) + x(n)$$

Take $x(n) = 2^n u(n)$.

SOLUTION: $y(n) = \dfrac{5}{6} y(n-1) - \dfrac{1}{6} y(n-2) + x(n)$ ...(A)

Since, $x(n) = 2^n u(n)$ 'Form AM^n'

$\therefore$ take the particular solution as

$$y_p(n) = K2^n, \quad n \geq 0 \quad \text{i.e. } y_p(n) = K2^n u(n) \text{ (see serial 2 of Table 5.1)}$$

Putting $y(n) = K2^n u(n)$ in (A), we get

$$K2^n u(n) = \frac{5}{6} K2^{n-1} u(n-1) - \frac{1}{6} K2^{n-2} u(n-2) + 2^n u(n) \quad ...(B)$$

To determine K, we put $n \geq 2$, so that none of the terms in (B) get cancelled. We get with $n = 2$ (Note this step)

$$K2^2 = \frac{5}{6} K2^1 - \frac{1}{6} K2^0 + 2^2$$

$$\therefore \quad K\left(4 - \frac{5}{3} + \frac{1}{6}\right) = 4$$

$$\therefore \qquad 2.5K = 4 \quad \text{or} \quad K = \frac{8}{5}$$

Hence, the particular solution is

$$y_p(n) = \frac{8}{5} \cdot 2^n, \qquad n \geq 0$$ **Ans.**

EXAMPLE 5.4: *Find out the response y(n) of the system described by*

$$y(n) = \frac{1}{2} y(n-1) + \frac{1}{2} y(n-2) + \left(\frac{1}{2}\right)^n, \qquad n \geq 0$$

Assume initial conditions y(–1), y(–2) = 0.

SOLUTION: Here, $y(n) - \frac{1}{2}\, y(n-1) - \frac{1}{2}\, y(n-2) = \left(\frac{1}{2}\right)^n \cdot u(n), \qquad n \geq 0$ ...(A)

[Homogeneous solution: $y_h(n)$]

Let $\qquad y_h(n) = \lambda^n$

Putting $y(n) = \lambda^n$ in the given equation (A) with input $\left(\frac{1}{2}\right)^n u(n) = 0$

$$\therefore \quad \lambda^n - \frac{1}{2}\lambda^{n-1} - \frac{1}{2} \cdot y^{n-2} = 0$$

or $$\lambda^2 - \frac{1}{2}\lambda - \frac{1}{2} = 0$$ (This is the characteristic equation)

$$\therefore \qquad \lambda_1 = 1, \quad \lambda_2 = -\frac{1}{2}$$ (distinct roots)

The general form of homogeneous solution is

$$y_h(n) = c_1(1)^n + c_2\left(-\frac{1}{2}\right)^n$$ ...(B)

[Particular solution $y_p(n)$]

> Distinct roots λ_i
>
> $\therefore \quad y_h(n) = \sum_i c_i(\lambda_i)^n$

As the input $\qquad x(n) = \left(\frac{1}{2}\right)^n u(n)$

$$\therefore \qquad y_p(n) = K\left(\frac{1}{2}\right)^n u(n)$$

Putting $y(n) = y_p(n)$ in (A), we get

$$K\left(\frac{1}{2}\right)^n u(n) - \frac{1}{2}K\left(\frac{1}{2}\right)^{n-1} u(n-1) - \frac{1}{2}K\left(\frac{1}{2}\right)^{n-2} \cdot u(n-2) = \left(\frac{1}{2}\right)^n u(n)$$ ...(C)

To find K, put $n = 2$ when no term in (C) becomes zero (Note this step)

$$\therefore \qquad K\left(\frac{1}{2}\right)^2 u(n+2) - \frac{1}{2}K\left(\frac{1}{2}\right)^1 u(1) - \frac{1}{2}K\left(\frac{1}{2}\right)^0 = \left(\frac{1}{2}\right)^2 u(2)$$

or $$\frac{1}{4}K - \frac{1}{4}K - \frac{1}{2}K = \frac{1}{4} \qquad \therefore \quad K = -\frac{1}{2}$$

$$\therefore \qquad y_p(h) = \left(-\frac{1}{2}\right)\left(\frac{1}{2}\right)^n u(n)$$

The total response is given by

$$y(n) = y_h(n) + y_p(n)$$

$$\therefore \quad y(n) = c_1(1)^n + c_2\left(-\frac{1}{2}\right)^n - \frac{1}{2}\left(\frac{1}{2}\right)^n, \quad n \geq 0 \quad \text{...(D)}$$

[To find c_1 and c_2 using initial conditions]

From (D)

$$\left.\begin{aligned} y(0) &= c_1 + c_2 - \frac{1}{2} \\ y(1) &= c_1 - c_2 - \frac{1}{4} \end{aligned}\right\} \quad \text{...(E)}$$

But from the given difference equation (A)

$$y(0) = \frac{1}{2}y(-1) + \frac{1}{2}y(-2) + 1$$

$$= \frac{1}{2}(1) + \frac{1}{2}(0) + 1 = \frac{3}{2} \qquad \because\ y(-1) = 1,\ y(-2) = 0 \text{ (given)}$$

$$y(1) = \frac{1}{2}y(0) + \frac{1}{2}y(-1) + \frac{1}{2}$$

$$= \frac{1}{2}\left(\frac{3}{2}\right) + \frac{1}{2}(1) + \frac{1}{2} = \frac{7}{4}$$

Using the values of $y(0)$ and $y(1)$ found above in (E), we get

$$c_1 + c_2 - \frac{1}{2} = \frac{3}{2}$$

$$c_1 - c_2 - \frac{1}{4} = \frac{7}{4}$$

or

$$c_1 + c_2 = 1$$

$$c_1 - c_2 = 2$$

Solving these we get $c_1 = 2$, $c_2 = 0$. Hence, finally, we get from (D)

$$y(n) = 2u(n) - \frac{1}{2}\left(\frac{1}{2}\right)^n u(n) \qquad \textbf{Ans.}$$

EXAMPLE 5.5: *Find the response $y(n)$ for the discrete-time system described by*

$$y(n) - 3y(n-1) - 4y(n-2) = x(n) + 2x(n-1)$$

if the input is $x(n) = 4^n u(n)$. Assume relaxed initial state.

SOLUTION: $y(n) - 3y(n-1) - 4y(n-2) = x(n) + 2x(n-1)$ ...(A)

[To find $y_h(n)$]

Here, put input $x(n) = 0$. We therefore, put $y(n) = y_h(n) = \lambda^n$

Putting $y(n) = \lambda^n$ and making $x(n)$, $x(n-1)$ zero in (A), we get

$$\lambda^n - 3\lambda^{n-1} - 4\lambda^{n-2} = 0$$

$\therefore$ The characteristic equation is $\lambda^2 - 3\lambda - 4 = 0$

$$\therefore \quad \lambda_1 = 4, \quad \lambda_2 = -1$$

The general form of the homogeneous solution is

$$y_h(n) = c_1(\lambda_1)^n + c_2(\lambda_2)^n$$

or
$$y_h(n) = c_1(4)^n + c_2(-1)^n \quad ...(B)$$

[To find $y_p(n)$]

As $x(n) = 4^n u(n)$ and the particular solution should be of the form

$$y_p(n) = K4^n u(n)$$

But this particular solution has the same term as in the $y_h(n)$. Hence, we modify $y_p(n)$ to

> If $x(n) = a^n u(n)$
> and one λ root is also $\lambda_1 = a$
> Take $y_p(n) = Kna^n u(n)$

$$y_p(n) = K \cdot n4^n u(n) \quad ...(C)$$ (Note this step)

Hence, $y_p(n) - 3y_p(n-1) - 4y_p(n-2) = x(n) + 2x(n-1)$ (see serial 9 of Table 5.1)

reduces to

$$Kn4^n u(n) - 3K(n-1)4^{n-1} u(n-1) - 4K(n-2)\, 4^{n-2} u(n-2) = 4^n u(n) + 2.4^{n-1} u(n-1) \quad ...(D)$$

Put $n = 2$ in (D), so that no term like $u(n)$, $u(n-1)$, vanishes, we get

$$K \times 2.4^2 u(2) - 3K(1)\, 4^1 u(1) - 4K(0)\, 4^o u(0) = 4^2 u(2) + 2.4^1 u(1)$$ (Note this step)

or
$$32K - 12K + 0 = 16 + 8 \quad \therefore \quad 20K = 24 \quad \text{or} \quad K = 6/5$$

$\therefore$
$$y(n) = y_h(n) + y_p(n) \text{ gives us}$$

$$y(n) = c_1(4)^n u(n) + c_2(-1)^n u(n) + \frac{6n}{5}(4)^n u(n) \quad ...(E)$$

[To find c_1 and c_2]

From (E),
$$\left.\begin{aligned} y(0) &= c_1 + c_2 \\ y(1) &= 4c_1 - c_2 + \frac{24}{5} \end{aligned}\right\} \quad ...(F)$$

From (A), $y(0) - 3y(-1) - 4y(-2) = x(0) + 2x(-1)$ [Note that $x(n) = 4^n u(n)$

or $y(0) - 0 - 0 = 1 \quad \therefore \quad y(0) = 1$ $\quad \therefore \quad x(0) = 1, x(-1) = 0$]

[assuming $y(-1) = y(-2) = 0$]

From (A), $y(1) - 3y(0) - 4y(-1) = x(1) + 2x(0)$

$\therefore$ $y(1) - 3(1) - 0 = 4 + 2$ or $y(1) = 9$ [$\because$ $x(1) = 4$, $x(0) = 2$]

Thus, from (F), putting the values of $y(0)$ and $y(1)$ found above, we get for $n = 0, 1$ in $4^n\, u(n)$

$$1 = c_1 + c_2$$

$$9 = 4c_1 - c_2 + \frac{24}{5}$$

which given $c_1 = 26/25$, $c_2 = -1/25$.

Finally, we have

$$y(n) = \frac{26}{25}(4)^n u(n) - \frac{1}{25}(-1)^n u(n) + \frac{6n}{5}(4)^n u(n)$$ **Ans.**

EXAMPLE 5.6: *Determine the Impulse Response of the system*

$$y(n) + 2y(n-1) + 2y(n-2) = x(n).$$

Given that $y(-1) = y(-2) = 0$. *(a relaxed system)*

SOLUTION: Taking $y_h(n) = \lambda^n$, with $x(n) = 0$, we obtain

$$\lambda^n + 2\lambda^{n-1} + 2\lambda^{n-2} = 0 \quad i.e., \quad \lambda^2 + 2\lambda + 2 = 0$$

This is the characteristic equation, solving for λ, we get

$$\lambda_1 = -1 + j, \quad \lambda_2 = -1 - j \quad (i.e.\ a \pm jb = -1 \pm j1)$$

$$\therefore \quad y_h(n) = r^n[A_1 \cos n\theta + A_2 \sin n\theta]$$

where $$r = \sqrt{(-1)^2 + (1)^2} = \sqrt{2}$$

$$\theta = \tan^{-1}\frac{-1}{1} = \tan^{-1}(-1) = \frac{3\pi}{4},$$

$\theta = \frac{3\pi}{4}$ satisfies $\tan^{-1}\frac{b}{a}$ here $a = -1$, $b = 1$

$$\therefore \quad y_h(n) = (2)^{n/2}\left[A_1 \cos\frac{3n\pi}{4} + A_2 \sin\frac{3n\pi}{4}\right] \quad \text{...(A)}$$

Here $x(n) = \delta(n) \quad \therefore \quad y_p(n) = 0$ (Note this step)

$$\therefore \quad y(n) = y_h(n) = y_p(n)$$

or $$y(n) = 2^{n/2}\left[A_1 \cos\frac{3n\pi}{4} + A_2 \sin\frac{3n\pi}{4}\right] \quad \text{...(B)}$$

[To find A_1, A_2]

From the given difference equation

$$y(n) = -2y(n-1) - 2y(n-2) + \delta(n)$$

$$\left.\begin{aligned} y(0) &= -2y(-1) + 2y(-2) + \delta(0) = 1 \\ y(1) &= -2y(0) + 2y(-1) + \delta(1) = -2 + 0 + 0 = -2 \end{aligned}\right\} \quad \text{...(C)}$$

From (*B*), we get

$$y(0) = 2^0[A_1 \cos 0 + A_2 \sin 0]$$

$$\therefore \quad y(0) = A_1 \quad \text{...(D-1)}$$

$$y(1) = 2^{1/2}\left[A_1 \cos\frac{3\pi}{4} + A_2 \sin\frac{3\pi}{4}\right]$$

$$= 2^{1/2}\left[-A_1\frac{1}{\sqrt{2}} + A_2\frac{1}{\sqrt{2}}\right]$$

$$\therefore \quad y(1) = -A_1 + A_2 \quad \text{...(D-2)}$$

Using (*C*) and (*D*-1), (*D*-2), we can write

$$-A_1 + A_2 = -2$$

$$A_1 = 1$$

$$\therefore \quad A_1 = 1, \quad A_2 = -1$$

Hence, $$y(n) = 2^{n/2}\left[\cos\frac{3n\pi}{4} - \sin\frac{3n\pi}{4}\right]$$

$$= \sqrt{2}\, 2^{n/2}\left[\frac{1}{\sqrt{2}}\cos\frac{3n\pi}{4} - \frac{1}{\sqrt{2}}\sin\frac{3n\pi}{4}\right]$$

$$= 2^{(n+1/2)}\cos(3n+1)\frac{\pi}{4} \qquad \left(\because \frac{1}{\sqrt{2}} = \cos\frac{\pi}{4} = \sin\frac{\pi}{4}\right)$$ **Ans.**

When	$\lambda = a \pm jb$ is the solution of characteristic equation	
Take	$y_h(n) = r^n[A_1 \cos n\theta + A_2 \sin n\theta]$	[due to 1(*c*) of 5.13]
where	$r = \sqrt{a^2 + b^2}$	
	$\theta = \tan^{-1}\frac{b}{a}$ Complex conjugate roots λ_i	

5.2 RULE TO SOLVE A DIFFERENTIAL EQUATION BY CLASSICAL METHOD

Let the given differential equation (*DE*) be

$$\sum_{i=0}^{N} a_k \frac{d^k y(t)}{dt^k} = \sum_{i=0}^{M} b_k \frac{d^k x(t)}{dt^k} \qquad ...(5.15)$$

With the initial conditions *i.e.*, values of $y(0^+)$, $y(-1)$, $y(-2)$ ... given and the input signal $x(t)$ is also given.

1. Find homogeneous solution $y_h(t)$, using the characteristic equation

$$\sum_{i=0}^{N} a_k \lambda^k = 0 \qquad \text{(we assumed } y_h(t) = Ke^{\lambda t}\text{)}$$

Let roots of the characteristic equation be $\lambda_1, \lambda_2, ..., \lambda_N$

If λ_i are distinct, $y_h(t) = c_1 e^{\lambda_1 t} + c_2 e^{\lambda_2 t} + ... + c_N e^{\lambda_N t}$

If roots are equal, say $\lambda_1 = \lambda_2 = \lambda_3$, the rest being distinct, then

$$y_h(t) = c_1(1 + t + t^2)\, e^{\lambda_3 t} + c_4 e^{\lambda_4 t} + c_5 e^{\lambda_5 t} + ... + c_N e^{\lambda_N t}$$

2. Find the particular solution $y_p(t)$ using the Table 5.2

Table 5.2. Particular solution for different Inputs *x*(*t*)

S.No.	Input $x(t)$	Particular solution
1.	$\delta(t)$	0
2.	K, *a* constant	A, *a* constant
3.	e^{at}, $a \neq \lambda_i$	Ae^{at}
4.	If $a = \lambda_1$ say	$At\, e^{at}$
5.	$\cos(\omega t + \theta)$	$A \cos(\omega t + \theta)$

3. Find constant A by $y_p(t)$ satisfying the given *DE*

4. $y(t) = y_h(t) + y_p(t)$

Find $c_1, c_2, ..., c_N$ using initial conditions for $y(t)$ to be satisfied.

EXAMPLE 5.7: *By using the classical method, solve*

$$\frac{d^2y(t)}{dt^2} + 4\frac{dy(t)}{dt} + 4y(t) = \frac{dx(t)}{dt} + x(t)$$

If the initial conditions are: $y(0^+) = \frac{9}{4} \cdot \frac{dy(0^+)}{dt} = 5$, *and if the input* $x(t) = e^{-3t}u(t)$.

(*GGSIP Univ., 2009*)

SOLUTION: We obtain the characteristic equation by putting $y_h(t) = ce^{\lambda t}$ and $x(t) = 0$ in the given differential equation. Hence

$$c \cdot \lambda^2 e^{\lambda t} + 4c\lambda e^{\lambda t} + 4ce^{\lambda t} = 0$$

or $$\lambda^2 + 4\lambda + 4 = 0$$

$\therefore$ $(\lambda + 2)^2 = 0$ *i.e.*, two roots of λ are equal $= \lambda_1 = \lambda_2 = -2$

$\therefore$ $$y_h(t) = (c_1 + tc_2)e^{-2t} \quad \text{(Note this step)} \quad ...(A)$$

This is the homogeneous solution.

For input $x(t) = e^{-3t}u(t)$, the particular solution will be of the form (see Serial No. 3 in Table 5.2)

$$y_p(t) = Ke^{-3t}$$

Putting $y(t) = y_p(t) = Ke^{-3t}$ in the given differential equation, we get

$$\frac{d^2y_p(t)}{dt^2} + 4\frac{dy_p(t)}{dt} + 4y_p(t) = \frac{dx(t)}{dt} + x(t)$$

$\therefore$ $$K(-3)^2e^{-3t} + K(-12)e^{-3t} + 4Ke^{-3t} = -3e^{-3t} + e^{-3t} \quad [\because x(t) = e^{-3t}, y_p(t) = Ke^{-3t}]$$

i.e., $$9K - 12K + 4K = -2$$

$\therefore$ $$K = -2$$

Hence, $$y_p(t) = Ke^{-3t}u(t) = -2e^{-3t}u(t) \quad ...(B)$$

The total response is given by

$$y(t) = y_h(t) + y_p(t) \quad \text{[adding (A) and (B)]}$$

$$= (c_1 + tc_2)\, e^{-2t} - 2e^{-3t}; \quad t > 0 \quad ...(C)$$

[To find c_1 and c_2]

From (C), we have

$$y(0^+) = (c_1 + 0c_2) \times 1 - 2 \times 1 = c_1 - 2 \quad ...(D)$$

$$\left.\frac{dy(t)}{dt}\right|_{t=0^+} = \frac{dy(0^+)}{dt} = [-2c_1e^{-2t} + c_2(1 \cdot e^{-2t} - 2te^{-2t}) + 6e^{-3t}]_{t=0}$$

$$= -2c_1 + c_2 + 6 \quad ...(E)$$

Given initial conditions are

$$y(0^+) = \frac{9}{4} \quad ...(F)$$

$$\frac{dy(0^+)}{dt} = 5 \quad ...(G)$$

Equating RHS of (D) and (F), and RHS of (E) and (G), we get

$$c_1 - 2 = \frac{9}{4} \qquad \text{i.e.,} \quad c_1 = \frac{17}{4}$$

$$-2c_1 + c_2 + 6 = 5 \qquad \text{i.e.,} \quad -\frac{17}{2} + c_2 = -1$$

$$\therefore \quad c_2 = \frac{15}{2}$$

Hence, $$y(t) = \left(\frac{17}{4} + \frac{15}{2}t\right)e^{-2t} - 2e^{-3t}$$ **Ans.**

Check: $$y(0^+) = \frac{17}{4} - 2 = \frac{9}{4}$$

$$\frac{dy(0^+)}{dt} = (-2)\frac{17}{4} + \frac{15}{2} + 6 = 5, \text{ as expected.}$$

EXAMPLE 5.8: *A continuous-time LTI system is characterized by*

$$\frac{d^2y(t)}{dt^2} + 5\frac{dy(t)}{dt} + 6y(t) = \frac{dx(t)}{dt} + 4x(t)$$

The input $x(t) = e^{-t}u(t)$. *Assume* $y(0^+) = 3$, $\frac{dy(0^+)}{dt} = 0$. *Find total response.*

SOLUTION: As $$\frac{d^2y(t)}{dt^2} + 5\frac{dy(t)}{dt} + 6y(t) = \frac{dx(t)}{dt} + 4x(t) \qquad ...(A)$$

[To find $y_h(t)$]

Take $y(t) = y_h(t) = Ke^{\lambda t}$ with $x(t)$ as zero. Putting in (A), we get the characteristic equation

$$\lambda^2 + 5\lambda + 6 = 0$$

$$\therefore \quad \lambda_1 = -2, \ \lambda_2 = -3$$

$$\therefore \quad y_h(t) = c_1e^{-2t} + c_2e^{-3t}$$

$$\therefore \quad y_h(0^+) = c_1 + c_2 = 3 \text{ given, as initial condition}$$

$$\frac{dy_h(0^+)}{dt} = -2c_1 - 3c_2 = 0 \text{ given, as initial condition}$$

we solve for c_1 and c_2 and get $c_1 = 9$, $c_2 = -6$

$$\therefore \quad y_h(t) = 9e^{-2t} - 6e^{-3t} \qquad ...(B)$$

[To find $y_p(t)$]

As $x(t) = e^{-t}u(t)$ $\therefore$ take $y_p(t) = Ke^{-t}$ (From serial 3 of Table 5.2)

Putting $y(t) = y_p(t) = Ke^{-t}$ in (A), we have

$$\frac{d^2y_p(t)}{dt^2} + 5\frac{dy_p(t)}{dt} + 6y_p(t) = \frac{dx(t)}{dt} + 4x(t)$$

$$\therefore \quad Ke^{-t} - 5Ke^{-t} + 6Ke^{-t} = -e^{-t} + 4e^{-t}$$

or $$K = 3/2$$

$$\therefore \quad y_p(t) = \frac{3}{2}e^{-t}$$

The natural response is the homogeneous response as given by

$$y_n(t) = y_h(t) = 9e^{-2t} - 6e^{-3t} \quad ...(C)$$

The forced response is the sum of homogeneous solution and the particular solution *i.e.*,

$$y_{\text{forced}}(t) = y_h(t) + y_p(t)$$

i.e.,
$$y_f(t) = (c_1e^{-2t} + c_2e^{-3t}) + \frac{3}{2}e^{-t} \quad ...(D)$$

We shall find c_1 and c_2 for the forced response $y_f(t)$ after adding $y_h(t)$ and $y_p(t)$ and using initial conditions on $y_f(t)$

$$y(0) = c_1 + c_2 + \frac{3}{2} = 3 \qquad \text{(given)}$$

$$\therefore \quad c_1 + c_2 = \frac{3}{2} \quad ...(E)$$

$$\left.\frac{dy(t)}{dt}\right|_{t=0} = \left(-2c_1e^{-2t} - 3c_2e^{-3t} - \frac{3}{2}e^{-t}\right)\Bigg|_{t=0}$$

$$= -2c_1 - 3c_2 - \frac{3}{2} = 0 \quad \text{(given)}$$

$$\therefore \quad 2c_1 + 3c_2 = -\frac{3}{2} \quad ...(F)$$

Solving (*E*) and (*F*) for, we obtain $c_1 = 6$, $c_2 = -9/2$

Putting these values of c_1 and c_2, we get

$$y(t) = 6e^{-2t} - 4.5e^{-3t} + 1.5e^{-t} \quad \textbf{Ans.}$$

EXAMPLE 5.9: *Consider a continuous-time system with input x(t) and output y(t), related by*

$$\frac{dy(t)}{dt} + ay(t) = x(t)$$

where 'a' is a constant. (a) Find y(t) with the auxiliary condition $y(0) = y_0$, *and* $x(t) = Ke^{-bt}u(t)$.
(b) Express y(t) in terms of the zero-input and zero-state responses.

SOLUTION: (*a*) Let $y(t) = y_p(t) + y_h(t)$ ...(A)

where $y_p(t)$ is the particular solution satisfying

$$\frac{dy(t)}{dt} + ay(t) = x(t) \quad ...(B)$$

and $y_h(t)$ is the homogeneous solution which satisfies

$$\frac{dy_h(t)}{dt} + ay_h(t) = 0 \quad ...(C)$$

Assume $\quad y_p(t) = Ae^{-bt} \qquad (\because\ x(t) = Ke^{-bt})$

Putting $y(t) = y_p(t) = Ae^{-bt}$ in (*B*), we have

$$-bAe^{-bt} + aAe^{-bt} = Ke^{-bt}$$

$$A(-b + a) = K \quad \text{or} \quad A = K/(a - b)$$

$$\therefore \quad y_p(t) = \frac{K}{a-b}e^{-bt}$$

To obtain $y_h(t)$, assume

$$y_h(t) = Be^{\lambda t}$$

Putting $y(t) = y_h(t)$ in (C), we get

$$B\lambda e^{\lambda t} + aBe^{\lambda t} = 0$$

or

$$(\lambda + a) = 0 \quad \therefore \quad \lambda = -a$$

Hence,

$$y_h(t) = Be^{-at}$$

Combining $y_p(t)$ and $y_h(t)$, we get

$$y(t) = y_p(t) + y_h(t)$$

$$= \frac{K}{a-b}e^{-bt} + Be^{-at}, \qquad t > 0 \qquad ...(D)$$

$$y(0) = \frac{K}{a-b} + B = y_0 \qquad \text{(given)}$$

$$\therefore \quad B = y_0 - \frac{K}{a-b}$$

Hence,

$$y(t) = \frac{K}{a-b}e^{-bt} + \left(y_0 - \frac{K}{a-b}\right)e^{-at}, \qquad t > 0 \quad \textbf{Ans.} \qquad ...(E)$$

For $t < 0$, we have $x(t) = 0$, Equation (*B*) and (*C*) are the same

$$\therefore \quad y(t) = y_h(t) = Be^{-at}, \qquad t < 0 \quad \textbf{Ans.} \qquad ...(F)$$

(*b*) Combining (*E*) and (*F*), we can express $y(t)$ in terms of y_{zi} (zero-input response) and y_{zs} (zero-state response) as follows:

$$y(t) = y_0e^{-at} + \frac{K}{a-b}(e^{-bt} - e^{-at})\,u(t)$$

$$\triangleq y_{zi}(t) + y_{zs}(t)$$

where

$$y_{zi}(t) = y_0e^{-at}$$

$$y_{zs}(t) = \frac{K}{a-b}(e^{-bt} - e^{-at})\,u(t) \qquad \textbf{Ans.}$$

EXAMPLE 5.10: *Find the forced response for the system*

$$y(n) - y(n-1) = \cos 2n.$$

SOLUTION: As $\cos 2n = e^{j2n} + e^{-j2n}$

$$\therefore \quad y_p(n) = A\cos 2n + B\sin 2n \text{ (see serial 7 of Table 5.1)}$$

Putting this value of $y_p(n)$ to satisfy the given difference equation, we have

$$(A\cos 2n + B\sin 2n) - [A\cos 2(n-1) + B\sin 2(n-1)] = \cos 2n$$

$$\therefore \quad (A\cos 2n + B\sin 2n) - A(\cos 2n\cos 2 + \sin 2n\sin 2) - B(\sin 2n\cos 2 - \cos 2n\sin 2) = \cos 2n$$

or

$$[A(1-\cos 2) + B\sin 2]\cos 2n + [-A\sin 2 + B(1-\cos 2)]\sin 2n = \cos 2n$$

Since, $\cos 2n$ and $\sin 2n$ are linearly independent (Note this argument)

$$\therefore \quad A(1-\cos 2) + B\sin 2 = 1 \qquad ...(A)$$

$$-A\sin 2 + B(1-\cos 2) = 0 \qquad ...(B)$$

Solving (A) and (B), we get $A = \frac{1}{2}$

$$B = \frac{\sin 2}{2(1-\cos 2)} = \frac{1}{2}\cot 1$$

Hence,

$$y_p(n) = \frac{1}{2}\cos 2n + \frac{1}{2}(\cot 1)\sin 2n$$

$$= \frac{1}{2\sin 1}[\cos 2n \sin 1 + \cos 1 \sin 2n]$$

$$= \frac{\sin(2n+1)}{2\sin 1}$$ **Ans.**

EXAMPLE 5.11: *Find the forced response for the causal system*

$$y(n) + 2y(n-1) + y(n-2) = 9(2^n) - 8n + 4.$$

SOLUTION: The characteristic equation is

$$\lambda^2 + 2\lambda + 1 = 0$$

$\therefore$ $\lambda = -1, -1$ *i.e.* equal roots

Assume $y_p(n) = A(2^n) + Bn + C$ (using serials 4, 6 and 1, respectively)

Using this value of $y(n)$ in the given difference equation,

$$(A2^n + Bn + C) + 2[A2^{n-1} + B(n-1) + C] + [A2^{n-2} + B(n-2) + C] = 9 \times 2^n - 8n + 4$$

Compare coefficients of 2^n: $A\left(1+1+\frac{1}{4}\right) = 9 \quad \therefore A = 4$

Compare coefficients of n: $B(1 + 2 + 1) = -8 \quad \therefore B = -2$

Compare constants: $C(1 + 2 + 1) + B(-2 - 2) = 4$

i.e. $4C - 4B = 4$

$$C = \frac{(4+4B)}{4} = \frac{4-8}{4} = -1$$

Hence, $y_p(n) = 4(2^n) - 2n - 1$ **Ans.**

EXAMPLE 5.12: *Determine the zero-input response of the system described by the second-order difference equation*

$$3y(n-1) + 4y(n-2) = x(n).$$

SOLUTION: Putting $x(n) = 0$, we obtain

$$3y(n-1) + 4y(n-2) = 0$$

i.e.

$$y(n-1) + \frac{4}{3}y(n-2) = 0$$

Putting $n = 0, 1, 2, \ldots$, we obtain

$n = 0$: $y(-1) = -\frac{4}{3}y(-2)$

n = 1: $$y(0) = -\frac{4}{3}y(-1) = \left(-\frac{4}{3}\right)^2 y(-2)$$

n = 2: $$y(1) = -\frac{4}{3}y(-2) = \left(-\frac{4}{3}\right)^3 y(n-2)$$

$$\vdots$$

n = k + 1: $$y(k) = \left(-\frac{4}{3}\right)^{k+2} y(n-2)$$ **Ans.**

EXAMPLE 5.13: *Compute the zero-state response of the system described by the difference equation*

$$y(n) + \frac{1}{2}y(n-1) = x(n) + 2x(n-2)$$

$$x(n) = \{1, 2, \underset{\uparrow}{3}, 4, 2, 1\}.$$

SOLUTION: As $$y(n) = -\frac{1}{2}y(n-1) + x(n) + 2x(n-2)$$

Put $n = -2, -1, 0, 1, \ldots$ etc. in above relation

n = –2: $$y(-2) = -\frac{1}{2}y(-3) + x(-2) + 2x(-4)$$

$$= 0 + 1 + 0 = 1$$

$\because$ $y(-3) = 0$ (unknown)
$x(-2) = 1$ (given)
$x(-4) = 0$

n = –1: $$y(-1) = -\frac{1}{2}y(-2) + x(-1) + 2x(-3)$$

$$= -\frac{1}{2}(1) + 2 + 0 = \frac{3}{2}$$

n = 0: $$y(0) = -\frac{1}{2}y(-1) + x(0) + 2x(-2)$$

$$= -\frac{1}{2}\left(\frac{3}{2}\right) + 3 + 2(1) = \frac{17}{4}$$

n = 1: $$y(1) = -\frac{1}{2}y(0) + x(1) + 2x(-1)$$

$$= -\frac{1}{2}\left(\frac{17}{4}\right) + 4 + 2(2) = \frac{47}{8}$$ and so on.

$\therefore$ $$y(n) = \left\{1, \frac{3}{2}, \underset{\uparrow}{\frac{17}{4}}, \frac{47}{8}, \ldots\right\}$$ **Ans.**

EXAMPLE 5.14: *Determine (i) homogeneous solution $y_h(n)$ and (ii) zero-input response $y_{zi}(n)$ for the system given by*

$$y(n) + a_1 y(n-1) = x(n).$$

SOLUTION: (*i*) Assume the solution, obtained by setting $x(n) = 0$ in the given difference equation, as

$$y_h(n) = \lambda^n \qquad \text{due to (5.8)}$$

Putting the value in the given difference equation, with $x(n) = 0$, we get

$$\lambda^n + a_1 \lambda^{n-1} = 0$$

$$\lambda^{n-1}(\lambda + a_1) = 0$$

$\therefore$ $$\lambda = -a_1$$

$\therefore$ The solution to the homogeneous difference equation is

$$y_h(n) = K\lambda^n$$

Hence, $$y_h(n) = K(-a_1)^n$$ **Ans.**

(*ii*) **To find $y_{zi}(n)$**

As $y(n) = -a_1 y(n-1)$ [given equation with $x(n) = 0$]

$\therefore$ $$y(0) = -a_1 y(-1)$$

But $$y_h(0) = K \qquad [\because \; y_h(n) = K(-a_1)^n]$$

Putting $y(0) = y_h(0)$ gives us

$$K = -a_1 y(-1)$$

Putting this value of K in $y_h(n) = K(-a_1)^n$, we get

$$y_{zi}(n) = y_h(n) \text{ with } K \text{ substituted by } -a_1 y(-1)$$

$$= [-a_1 y(-1)]\,(-a_1)^n, \; n \geq 0$$

$$= (-a_1)^{n+1} y(-1), \qquad n \geq 0$$

Hence, for this example

$$\left.\begin{aligned} y_h(n) &= K(-a_1)^n \\ y_{zi}(n) &= (-a_1)^{n+1} y(-1), \; n \geq 0 \end{aligned}\right\}$$ **Ans.**

EXAMPLE 5.15: *Determine the total solution $y(n)$, $n \geq 0$ to the difference equation*

$$y(n) + a_1 y(n-1) = x(n)$$

when $x(n)$ is a unit step sequence $x(n) = u(n)$ and $y(-1)$ is the initial condition.

SOLUTION: From example 5.14, we have found the homogeneous solution

$$y_h(n) = K(-a_1)^n \qquad \ldots(A)$$

From example 5.2, we found the particular solution [$x(n)$ was $u(n)$ there too]

$$y_p(n) = \frac{1}{1+a_1} \qquad \ldots(B)$$

Hence, the total solution is

$$y(n) = y_h(n) + y_p(n)$$

$\therefore$ $$y(n) = K(-a_1)^n + \frac{1}{1+a_1}, \quad n \geq 0 \qquad \ldots(C)$$

[To find K]

(*i*) If $y(-1) = 0$, say, then from

$$y(n) = a_1 y(n-1) + u(n) \quad \ldots(D)$$

$$y(n) = K(-a_1)^n + \frac{1}{1+a_1} \quad \ldots(E)$$

Putting $n = 0$, $y(-1) = 0$, we obtain

$$y(0) = 1 \quad \text{from } (D) \ldots(F)$$

$$y(0) = K + \frac{1}{1+a_1} \quad \text{from } (E) \ldots(G)$$

From (*F*) and (*G*),

$$K + \frac{1}{1+a_1} = 1$$

$$\therefore \quad K = 1 - \frac{1}{1+a_1} = \frac{a_1}{1+a_1}$$

Putting this value of K in (*C*), the total solution becomes,

$$y(n) = \frac{a_1}{1+a_1}(-a_1)^n + \frac{1}{1+a_1}, \quad n \geq 0$$

$$\therefore \quad y(n) = \frac{1-(-a_1)^{n+1}}{1+a_1}, \quad n \geq 0 \qquad \textbf{Ans.}$$

(*ii*) If $y(-1) \neq 0$, to find the value of K

Putting $n = 0$ in (*D*), we get

$$y(0) = -a_1 y(-1) + 1 \quad \ldots(H)$$

Putting $n = 0$ in (*E*), we get

$$y(0) = K + \frac{1}{1+a_1} \quad \ldots(I)$$

Equating RHS of (*H*) and (*I*), we have

$$K + \frac{1}{1+a_1} = -a_1 y(-1) + 1$$

or

$$K = -a_1 y(-1) + 1 - \frac{1}{1+a_1}$$

$$= -a_1 y(-1) + \frac{a_1}{1+a_1}$$

Finally, putting this value of K in (*C*), the total solution becomes

$$y(n) = \left(-a_1 y(-1) + \frac{a_1}{1+a_1}\right)(-a_1)^n + \frac{1}{1+a_1}, \quad n \geq 0$$

$$= (-a_1)^{n+1}\, y(-1) + \frac{1-(a_1)^{n+1}}{1+a_1}, \quad n \geq 0$$

$\therefore$ $$y(n) = y_{zi}(n) + y_{zs}(n)$$ **Ans.**

UNSOLVED PROBLEMS WITH ANSWERS

5.1. Find the zero-state and zero-input responses of the discrete-time system described by

$$y(k+2) - \frac{5}{6}y(k+1) + \frac{1}{6}y(k) = 5x(k+1) - x(k)$$

given $y(-1) = 2$ and $y(-2) = 0$ and input $x(k) = u(k)$.

[Hint. For zero-state response, solve the difference equation

$$Y(z)\left[z^2 - \frac{5}{6}z + \frac{1}{6}\right] = X(z)[5z - 1] \text{ with } X(z) = \frac{1}{1-z^{-1}}$$

We get $y(n) = \left[12 - 18\left(\frac{1}{2}\right)^n + 6\left(\frac{1}{3}\right)^n\right]u(n)$ which is the zero-state response. We assume $y(n) = 0$ for $n < 1$.

For zero-input response, solve the difference equation

$$y(k+2) - \frac{5}{6}y(k+1) + \frac{1}{6}y(k) = 0. \text{ Put } k + 2 = n$$

Take unilateral ZT for the difference equation

$$y(n) - \frac{5}{6}y(n-1) + \frac{1}{6}y(n-2) = 0$$

and solve for $y(n)$ $\therefore$ $$y(n) = \left[3\left(\frac{1}{2}\right)^n - \frac{4}{3}\left(\frac{1}{3}\right)^n u(n)\right]$$ **Ans.**

5.2. For the discrete-time system

$$y(n) - ay(n-1) = u(n),\ a \neq 1$$

and $y(-1) = 0$, determine the values of $y_p(n)$ and $y_h(n)$.

[**Ans.** $y_p(n) = \frac{1}{1-a}$, $y_p(n) = -\left(\frac{a}{1-a}a^n\right)u(n)$

The complete response $y(n) = y_p(n) + y_h(n) = \frac{1-a^{n+1}}{1-a}u(n)$]

5.3. Find the forced response for the system

$y(n) - 2y(n-1) = (-1)^n$.

[**Ans.** $y_p(n) = \frac{1}{3}(-1)^n$]

5.4. Find the forced response for the system

$$y(n) - ay(n-1) = a^n u(n)$$

[**Hint.** Here, $y_p(n) = A\, n\, a^n$ (see serial 9 of Table 5.1)

$\therefore \quad A\, n\, a^n - aA(n-1)a^{n-1} = a^n, \therefore\ A = 1$

Hence, $\quad y_p(n) = na^n$] **Ans.**

5.5. Find the zero-input response of the system described by the homogeneous second-order difference equation

$$y(n) - 3y(n-1) - 4y(n-2) = 0.$$

[**Ans.** $y_{zi}(n) = (-1)^{n+1} + (4)^{n+2},\ n \geq 0$]

5.6. Determine the total solution to the system described by the difference equation

$$y(n) = \frac{5}{6}y(n-1) - \frac{1}{6}y(n-2) + x(n)$$

for $x(n) = 2^n u(n)$, $y(-1) = y(-2) = 0$

$$\left[\textbf{Ans. } y(n) = \frac{8}{5}(2)^n - \left(\frac{1}{2}\right)^n + \frac{2}{5}\left(\frac{1}{3}\right)^n u(n)\right]$$

The Discrete Fourier Transform (DFT): Properties and Applications

CHAPTER 6

6.0 INTRODUCTION

Frequency analysis of a discrete-time signal is most efficiently carried out by a digital signal processor. The practical digital processor may be a general/purpose digital computer or a special purpose (dedicated) digital hardware, which converts the signal $x(n)$ into an equivalent frequency-domain representation.

The discrete-time Fourier transform (DTFT) converts the sequence $x(n)$ into $X(e^{j\omega})$ or $X(\omega)$. However, $X(\omega)$ is a continuous function of frequency ω, and therefore, not convenient to store in a digital computer. If we have finite number of samples of $X(\omega)$, we can store these finite samples in the digital computer. Such representation of $X(\omega)$ is called discrete Fourier transform (DFT). Also, DFT of a signal $x(n)$ can be computed by a very efficient algorithm, called Fast Fourier Transform (FFT). FFT is a powerful computational tool for performing frequency analysis of discrete-time signals.

Discrete Fourier Transform (DFT) is an important mathematical tool in software implementation of digital filters. It is closely related to z-transform on the one hand and Continuous Fourier Transform (CFT) on the other hand.

6.1 DEFINITION OF DFT: $X(k)$

Let $x(n)$ be a finite time duration real valued time signal. We form a periodic signal $x_p(n)$ by repeating $x(n)$ with period N, *i.e.*,

$$x_p(n) \triangleq \sum_{r=-\infty}^{\infty} x(n+rN)$$
$$r = 0, \pm 1, \pm 2, \pm 3, \ldots \qquad \ldots(6.1)$$

Note that we can obtain $x(n)$ from $x_p(n)$ by the relation

$$x(n) = x_p(n)\,[u(n) - u(n-N)] \qquad \ldots(6.2)$$

where $x(n)$ is defined for $n = 0, 1, \ldots, N-1$.

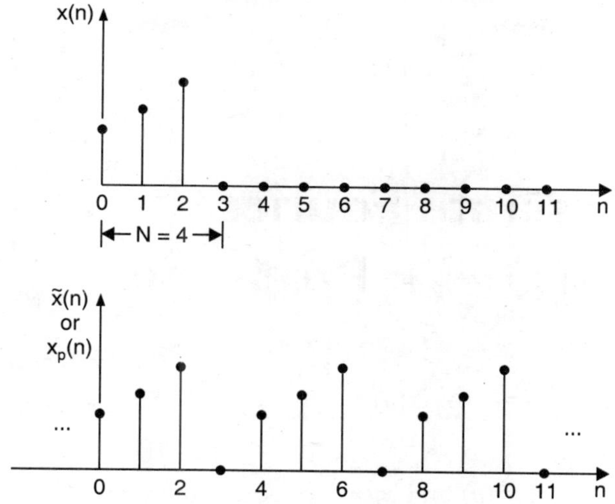

Fig. 6.1. $x(n)$ and $\tilde{x}(n)$

DFT of $x_p(n)$ is defined as

$$\text{DFT}\,[x_p(n)] = X(k) \triangleq \sum_{n=0}^{N-1} x_p(n)\, W_N^{nk}, \; k = 0, 1, ..., N-1 \quad ...(6.3)$$

where $W_N \triangleq e^{-j2\pi/N}$ ...[6.3(a)]

In general, $X(k)$ is a complex quantity and can be put in the form

$$X(k) = |X(k)|\, e^{j\,\text{Arg}\,X(k)} \quad ...(6.4)$$

$|X(k)|$ is called, Amplitude spectrum and Arg $[X(k)]$ is called the Phase spectrum of $X(k)$.

Note 1: Note that we cannot get z-transform of $x_p(n)$ as it is a repetitive signal and NOT FINITE duration. Since, a *repetitive signal does not converge, thus such signals cannot have z-transforms.* However, the Fourier transform of $x_p(n)$ can be found as a sum of sine and cosine functions. Fundamental frequency of such a F.T. would be $2\pi/N$ radian and the other frequencies would be integral multiples of the fundamental $(2\pi/N)$ frequency. Also,

$$\sin\left(\frac{2\pi}{N} + 2\pi r\right) = \sin\frac{2\pi}{N}$$

i.e.,

$$\sin\left((N+1)\frac{2\pi}{N}\right) = \sin\frac{2\pi}{N}$$

Thus, the maximum number of different frequencies contained in the F.T. of $x_p(n)$ would be N *viz.*

$$\frac{2\pi}{N}, \frac{2\pi}{N}.2, \frac{2\pi}{N}.3, ..., \frac{2\pi}{N}(N-1), \frac{2\pi}{N}N \; (\textit{viz. dc})$$

Note 2: If we evaluate $Z.T.$ of $x(n)$ on the unit circle, we get DFT of $x_p(n)$ if the points of evaluation are discrete $\frac{2\pi}{N}k$.

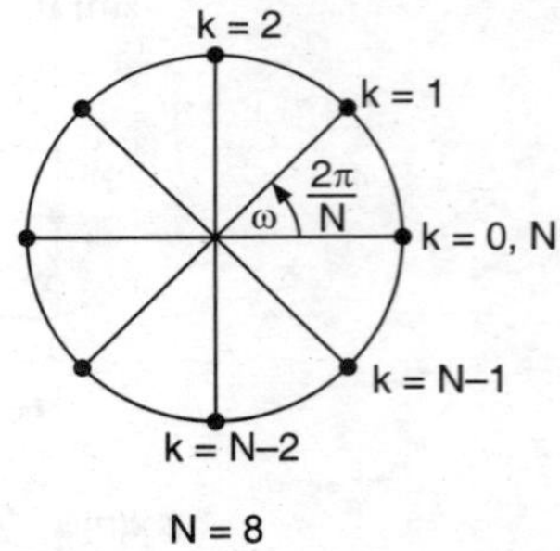

Fig. 6.2. N frequencies $\omega = \frac{2\pi}{N}k$ equally spaced, $k = 0, 1, 2, ..., N-1$

Proof:

$$ZT\,[x(n)] = \sum_{n=0}^{N-1} x(n)\, z^{-n}$$

$$ZT\,[x(n)]\Big|_{z=e^{j\omega}} = \sum_{n=0}^{N-1} x(n)\, e^{-j\omega n}$$

Put

$$\omega = \frac{2\pi}{N} k$$

$$\therefore \quad ZT\,[x(n)]\Big|_{z=e^{j\omega},\ \omega=\frac{2\pi}{N}k} = \sum_{n=0}^{N-1} x(n)\, e^{-j\frac{2\pi kn}{N}}$$

In the range $0 \le n \le N-1$, $x(n)$ and $x_p(n)$ are equal, therefore, replace $x(n)$ by $x_p(n)$ in (*A*)

$$\therefore \quad ZT\,[x(n)]\Big|_{\substack{\text{discrete pts}\\ \text{on unit circle}}} = \sum_{n=0}^{N-1} x_p(n)\, e^{-j\frac{2\pi kn}{N}}$$

$$= X(k).$$

Some Important Results

We give here some important results which will be used later on.

(*a*)
$$\sum_{n=0}^{N-1} W_N^{nk} = N\,\delta((k))_N\,,\ W_N = e^{-j\,2\pi/N}$$

(*b*)
$$\sum_{n=n_0}^{N-1+n_0} x(n)\, W_N^{nk} = \sum_{n=0}^{N-1} x(n)\, W_N^{nk}\,,\ W_N = e^{-j2\pi/N}.$$

Proof:

(*a*)
$$\sum_{n=0}^{N-1} W_N^{nk} = \frac{1-W_N^{Nk}}{1-W_N^{k}} = \frac{1-e^{-j\,2\pi k}}{1-e^{-j\,2\pi k/N}}$$

$$= 0 \text{ if } k \ne N \quad \text{or} \quad k \ne 0 \textit{ i.e.}, ((k))_N \ne 0$$

If $k = 0$, then $\lim\limits_{k\to 0} \dfrac{1-e^{-j\,2\pi k}}{1-e^{-j\,2\pi k/N}}$

$$= \lim_{k\to 0} \frac{0 + j\,2\pi\, e^{-j\,2\pi k}}{0 + j\dfrac{2\pi}{N}\, e^{-j\,2\pi k/N}} = N \quad \text{(Using L' Hospital Rule)}$$

$$\therefore \quad \boxed{\sum_{n=0}^{N-1} W_N^{nk} = N\,\delta((k))_N} \qquad ...(6.5)$$

(b)
$$\sum_{n=n_0}^{N-1+n_0} x(n)\, W_N^{nk} = \underset{(A)}{\sum_{n=0}^{N-1} x(n)\, W_N^{nk}} + \underset{(B)}{\sum_{n=N}^{N-1+n_0} x(n)\, W_N^{nk}} - \underset{(C)}{\sum_{n=0}^{n_0-1} x(n)\, W_N^{nk}}$$

Put $n = m + N$, $\therefore$ when $n = N, m = 0$
when $n = N - 1 + n_0$, $\quad m = n_0 - 1$

$$\therefore \qquad (B) = \sum_{n=N}^{N-1+n_0} x(n)\, W_N^{nk} = \sum_{m=0}^{n_0-1} x(m+N)\, W_N^{(m+N)k}$$

$$= \sum_{m=0}^{n_0-1} x(m)\, W_N^{mk} = (C) \because \quad x(m+N) = x(m) \text{ due to periodicity of } x(n).$$

$\therefore$ Terms (*B*) and (*C*) cancel.

Hence,
$$\boxed{\sum_{n=n_0}^{N-1+n_0} x(n)\, W_N^{nk} = \sum_{n=0}^{N-1} x(n)\, W_N^{nk}} \qquad ...(6.6)$$

Thus, we can shift the limits of

$n = n_0$ to $N - 1 + n_0$ span N *i.e.* $n = < N >$

as $\quad n = 0$ to $N - 1$ span N *i.e.* $n = < N>$

This is an extremely useful result, used for proving various properties in DFT.

6.1.1 Inverse DTF [to find $x_p(n)$, given $X(k)$]

Consider the expression $\dfrac{1}{N}\sum_{k=0}^{N-1} X(k)\, e^{j\frac{2\pi}{N}kn}$ ...(6.7)

Putting $X(k) = \sum_{m=0}^{N-1} x_p(m)\, e^{-j2\pi mk/N}$ in (6.7), we have

$$\frac{1}{N}\sum_{k=0}^{N-1} X(k)\, e^{j\frac{2\pi}{N}kn} = \frac{1}{N}\sum_{k=0}^{N-1}\left(\sum_{m=0}^{N-1} x_p(m)\, e^{-j2\pi mk/N}\right) e^{j2\pi kn/N}$$

$$= \frac{1}{N}\sum_{m=0}^{N-1} x_p(m) \sum_{k=0}^{N-1} e^{-j2\pi k(n-m)/N}$$

$$= \frac{1}{N}\sum_{m=0}^{N-1} .\, x_p(m)\, .\, N\,\delta(n-m) \qquad \text{[Due to (6.5)]}$$

$$= x_p(n)$$

Hence,

$$x_p(n) = \frac{1}{N}\sum_{k=0}^{N-1} X(k)\, W_N^{-nk} = \frac{1}{N}\sum_{k=0}^{N-1} X(k)\, e^{j2\pi nk/N} \qquad \ldots(6.8)$$

6.1.2 Inter-relationship between DFT and the z-Transform

$$X_p(k) = \sum_{n=0}^{N-1} x_p(n)\, W_N^{kn}, \text{ where } W_N = e^{-j2\pi/N}$$

$$= \sum_{n=0}^{N-1}\left(\sum_{r=-\infty}^{\infty} x(n+rN)\right) W_N^{kn} = \sum_{r=-\infty}^{\infty}\sum_{n=0}^{N-1} x(n+kN)\,.\, W_N^{kn}$$

Put $n + rN = m$ $\quad\therefore$ when $n = 0$, $m = rN$

when $n = N - 1$, $\quad m = rN + N - 1$

$$\therefore \quad X_p(k) = \sum_{r=-\infty}^{\infty}\sum_{m=rN}^{rN+N-1} x(m)\, W_N^{k(m-rN)}$$

$$= + \ldots + \underbrace{\sum_{m=-N}^{-1} x(m)\, W_N^{km}}_{\text{For } r=-1} + \underbrace{\sum_{m=0}^{N-1} x(m)\, W_N^{km}}_{\text{For } r=0} + \underbrace{\sum_{m=N}^{2N-1} x(m)\, W_N^{km}}_{\text{For } r=+1} + \ldots$$

$$= \sum_{m=-\infty}^{\infty} x(m)\, W_N^{km}$$

$$\therefore \quad X_p(k) = \sum_{m=-\infty}^{\infty} x(m)\, e^{-j2\pi km/N}$$

$$= \sum_{m=-\infty}^{\infty} x(m)\, z^{-m}\Big|_{z=e^{j2\pi k/N}}$$

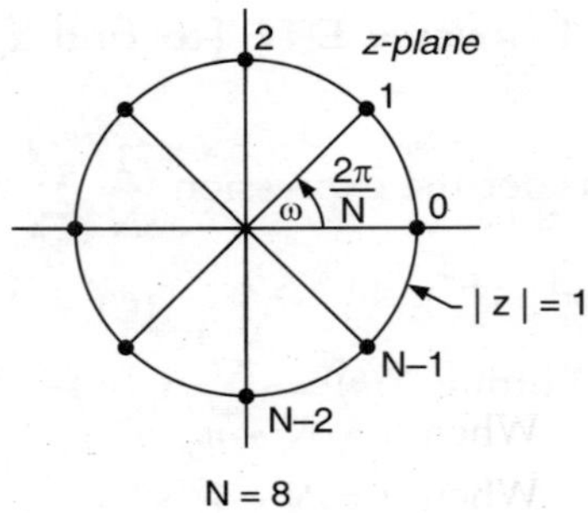

Fig. 6.3. Evaluation of $X(z)$ on unit circle at $\omega = 2\pi k/N$

Thus, $\quad X_p(k) = Z.T[x(n)]\,\big|_{z=e^{j2\pi k/N}} \qquad \ldots(6.9)$

i.e., DFT of $x_p(n)$ numerically equals the discrete Fourier frequency function obtained by sampling $X(z)$ on the unit circle, at angles $\omega = 2\pi k/N$. $k = 0, 1, \ldots, N-1$, as shown in Fig. 6.3.

6.2 PROPERTIES OF DISCRETE FOURIER TRANSFORM (DFT)

6.2.1 Linearity

$$a_1x_1(n) + x_2(n) \xrightarrow{\text{DFT}} a_1X_1(k) + a_2X_2(k) \qquad \text{...(6.10)}$$

Proof trivial

6.2.2 Time Shifting

$$x((n - n_0))_N \xrightarrow{\text{DFT}} W_N^{kn_0} X(k) \qquad \text{...(6.11)}$$

Proof: DFT $[x((n - n_0))_N] = \sum_{n=0}^{N-1} x((n-n_0))_N \cdot W_N^{nk}$, $x(n)$ is a periodic sequence with period N

Put $n - n_0 = n'$, $\therefore\ n = n' + n_0$

$$\therefore \quad \text{DFT}[x((n - n_0))_N] = \sum_{n'=-n_0}^{N-1-n_0} x(n')\, W_N^{(n'+n_0)k}$$

$$= W_N^{kn_0} \sum_{n'=-n_0}^{N-1-n_0} x(n') \cdot W_N^{n'k}$$

$$= W_N^{kn_0} \left[\underset{(A)}{\sum_{n'=0}^{N-1} x(n') \cdot W_N^{n'k}} + \underset{(B)}{\sum_{n'=-n_0}^{-1} x(n')\, W_N^{n'k}} - \underset{(C)}{\sum_{n'=N-n_0}^{N-1} x(n')\, W_N^{n'k}} \right]$$

$$(A) = X(k)$$

$$(C) = \sum_{n=N-n_0}^{N-1} x(n)\, W_N^{nk} \quad \text{Put } n'' = n - N$$

$\therefore$ When $n = N - n_0$, $n'' = -n_0$
When $n = N - 1$, $n'' = -1$

$$\therefore \quad (C) = \sum_{n''=-n_0}^{-1} x(n''+N)\, W_N^{(n''+N)k} = \sum_{n=-n_0}^{-1} x(n)\, W_N^{nk}$$

$\because\ x(n) = x(n + N)$ and $W_N^{Nk} = 1$

$$\therefore \quad (B) - (C) = 0$$

$$\therefore \quad \text{DFT}[x((n - n_0))_N] = W_N^{kn_0} \cdot X(k)$$

Q.E.D.

6.2.3 Frequency Shifting

$$W_N^{-k_0 n}\, x(n) \xrightarrow{\text{DFT}} X((k - k_0))_N \qquad \text{...(6.12)}$$

Proof:

$$\text{DFT}\,[W_N^{-k_0 n}\ x(n)] = \sum_{n=0}^{N-1} (x(n)\,W_N^{-k_0 n}) . W_N^{kn}$$

$$= \sum_{n=0}^{N-1} x(n) . W_N^{(k-k_0)n}$$

$$= X(k-k_0) = X((k-k_0))_N$$

$\because$ $X(k)$ is periodic in k with period N.

6.2.4 Conjugation

$$\boxed{x^*(n) \xrightarrow{\text{DFT}} X^*(-k)} \qquad \ldots(6.13)$$

Proof:

$$\text{DFT}\,[x^*(n)] = \sum_{n=0}^{N-1} x^*(n)\,W_N^{kn} = \sum_{n=0}^{N-1} x^*(n) . e^{-jkn\,2\pi/N}$$

$$= \left(\sum_{n=0}^{N-1} x(n) . e^{+j\frac{2\pi}{N}kn}\right)^* = \left(\sum_{n=0}^{N-1} x(n)\,W_N^{n(-k)}\right)^*, \text{ assuming } x(n) \text{ real}$$

$$= X^*(-k)$$

6.2.5 Time Reversal

$$\boxed{x((-n))_N \xrightarrow{\text{DFT}} X((-k))_N} \qquad \ldots(6.14)$$

Proof:

$$\text{DFT}\,[x((-n))_N] = \sum_{n=0}^{N-1} x((-n))_N\ W_N^{nk} = \sum_{n=0}^{N-1} x(N-n)\,W_N^{nk}$$

Put $N - n = n'$

$$= \sum_{n'=1}^{N} x(n')\,W_N^{(N-n')k} = \sum_{n'=0}^{N-1} x(n')\,W_N^{-n'k} + \underbrace{x(N)\,W_N^{-Nk} - x(0)W_N^{0k}}_{=0\ \because x(N)=x(0)}$$

$$= \sum_{n=0}^{N-1} x(n)\,W_N^{n(-k)} = X((-k))_N$$

6.2.6 Duality

$$\boxed{\text{If } x(n) \xrightarrow{\text{DFT}} X(-k), \text{ then } X(n) \xrightarrow{\text{DFT}} Nx((-k))_N} \qquad \ldots(6.15)$$

Proof: As

$$X(k) = \sum_{n=0}^{N-1} x(n)\,W_N^{nk}$$

Change k to n and n to k. (Note this step)

$$\therefore \quad X(n) = \sum_{k=0}^{N-1} x(k)\, W_N^{nk} \qquad \ldots(A)$$

$$\text{DFT of } X(n) = \sum_{n=0}^{N-1} X(n) \,.\, W_N^{nk}$$

$$= \sum_{n=0}^{N-1} \left(\sum_{k'=0}^{N-1} x(k') \,.\, W_N^{nk'} \right) W_N^{nk}$$ [Using value of $X(n)$ from (A) dummy k in (A) changed to k']

$$= \sum_{k'=0}^{N-1} x(k') \,.\, \underbrace{\sum_{n=0}^{N-1} W_N^{n(k+k')}}_{\substack{= N\delta(k+k') \\ = N\delta((k+k'))_N}}$$

$$= \sum_{k'=0}^{N-1} x(k') \,.\, N\delta\, [(k+k')]_N$$

$$= N\, x(k') \big|_{k' = [(-k)]_N}$$ [$\because$ If $k + k'$ is multiple of N then $((k + k'))_N = 0$ and $k' = ((-k))_N$]

$$= Nx[(-k)]_N$$

$$\therefore \quad X(n) \xrightarrow{\text{DFT}} Nx[(-k)]_N$$ Q.E.D.

6.2.7 Circular Convolution

If $x_1(n);\, x_2(n) \xrightarrow{\text{DFT}} X_1(k);\, X_2(k)$ then $x_1(n)$ Ⓝ $x_2(n) \xrightarrow{\text{DFT}} X_1(k) \,.\, X_2(k)$

...(6.16)

Proof:

$$X_1(k) = \sum_{n=0}^{N-1} x_1(n)\, W_N^{nk}, \text{ and } X_2(k) = \sum_{n=0}^{N-1} x_2(n)\, W_N^{nk}$$

$$\therefore \quad \text{IDFT}\, [X_1(k) \,.\, X_2(k)] = \frac{1}{N} \sum_{k=0}^{N-1} [X_1(k) \,.\, X_2(k)] \,.\, W_N^{-nk}$$

$$= \frac{1}{N} \sum_{k=0}^{N-1} \left(\sum_{m=0}^{N-1} x_1(m)\, W_N^{mk} \right) \left(\sum_{l=0}^{N-1} x_1(l)\, W_N^{lk} \right) .\, W_N^{-nk}$$

$$\therefore \quad \text{IDFT}\, [X_1(k) \,.\, X_2(k)] = \frac{1}{N} \sum_{m=0}^{N-1} x_1(m) \,.\, \sum_{l=0}^{N-1} x_2(l) \,.\, \underbrace{\sum_{k=0}^{N-1} W_N^{(m+l-n)k}}_{\substack{= N\delta(m+l-n) \\ = N\delta((m+l-n))_N}}$$

$$= \frac{1}{N}\sum_{m=0}^{N-1} x_1(m) \sum_{l=0}^{N-1} x_2(l)\, N\delta((m+l-n))_N$$

i.e., $(m + l - n)$ is a multiple of N

$$= \sum_{m=0}^{N-1} x_1(m) \sum_{l=0}^{N-1} x_2(l) . \underbrace{\delta((l-(m-n))_N}_{\therefore\ l=((m-n))_N}$$

$$= \sum_{m=0}^{N-1} x_1(m) . x_2((m-n))_N$$

$$= x_1(n) \textcircled{N} x_2(n) \qquad \text{(by definition of circular convolution)}$$

i.e., $x_1(n) \textcircled{N} x_2(n) \xrightarrow{\text{DFT}} X_1(k) . X_2(k)$ Q.E.D.

Alternatively: DFT $[x_1(n) \textcircled{N} x_2(n)] = \sum_{n=<N>} [x_1(n) \textcircled{N} x_2(n)]\, W_N^{nk}$

$$= \sum_{n=<N>} \left[\sum_{m=<N>} x_1(m) . x_2((n-m))_N\right] W_N^{nk}$$

$$= \sum_{m=<N>} x_1(m) \sum_{n=<N>} x_2((n-m))\, W_N^{nk}$$

↖ Put $n - m = l$

$$= \sum_{m=<N>} x_1(m) \sum_{l=<N>} x_2(l)\, W_N^{(l+m)k}$$

$$= \sum_{m=<N>} x_1(m) . W_N^{mk} \sum_{l=<N>} x_2(l)\, W_N^{lk}$$

$$= \sum_{m=<N>} x_1(m) . W_N^{mk}\, X_2(k)$$

$$= X_1(k) . X_2(k)$$

Q.E.D.

6.2.8 Multiplication

If $x_1(n); x_2(n) \xrightarrow{\text{DFT}} X_1(k); X_2(k)$ then $x_1(n) . x_2(n) \xrightarrow{\text{DFT}} \frac{1}{N} X_1(k) \textcircled{N} X_2(k)$

...(6.17)

Proof: DFT $[x_1(n) . x_2(n)] = \sum_{n=0}^{N-1} x_1(n) . x_2(n)\, W_N^{nk}$

$$= \sum_{n=0}^{N-1} \left(\frac{1}{N}\sum_{k_1=0}^{N-1} X_1(k_1)\, W_N^{-nk_1}\right)\left(\frac{1}{N}\sum_{k_2=0}^{N-1} X_2(k_2)\, W_N^{-nk_2}\right) . W_N^{nk}$$

$$= \frac{1}{N^2} \sum_{k_1=0}^{N-1} X_1(k_1) . \sum_{k_2=0}^{N-1} X_2(k_2) . \underbrace{\sum_{n=0}^{N-1} W_N^{n(k-k_1-k_2)}}_{\substack{= N\delta(k-k_1-k_2) \\ = N\delta((k-k_1-k_2))_N}}$$

$$= \frac{1}{N^2} \sum_{k_1=0}^{N-1} X_1(k_1) . \sum_{k_2=0}^{N-1} X_2(k_2) . N\delta((k-k_1-k_2))_N$$

$$k_2 = \delta((k - k_1))_N$$

$$= \frac{1}{N} \sum_{k_1=0}^{N-1} X_1(k_1) . X_2((k-k_1))_N$$

$\therefore$ $$\text{DFT } [x_1(n) \, . \, x_2(n)] = \frac{1}{N} X_1(k) \, Ⓝ \, X_2(k)$$

i.e., $$x_1(n) \, . \, x_2(n) \xrightarrow{\text{DFT}} \frac{1}{N} X_1(k) \, Ⓝ \, X_2(k)$$ Q.E.D.

Alternatively:

$$\text{DFT } [x_1(n) \, . \, x_2(n)] = \sum_{n=<N>} x_1(n) . x_2(n) \, W_N^{nk}$$

$$= \sum_{n=<N>} x_1(n) \left[\sum_{k'=<N>} \frac{1}{N} X_2(k') \, W_N^{-nk'} \right] W_N^{nk}$$

$$= \sum_{k'=<N>} \frac{1}{N} . X_2(k') \sum_{n=<N>} x_1(n) \, W_N^{n(k-k')}$$

$$= \frac{1}{N} \sum_{k'=<N>} X_2(k') \cdot X_1((k-k'))_N \qquad \because \; W_N^{n(k-k')} = W_N^{n((k-k'))_N}$$

$$= \frac{1}{N} X_1(k) \, Ⓝ \, X_2(k)$$ Q.E.D.

6.2.9 Real Sequence

If $x(n)$ is a real sequence, then $X^*(k) = X(-k)$ ...(6.18*a*)

i.e., $| X(k) | = | X(-k) |$ and $\text{Arg } [X(k)] = -\text{Arg } [X(-k)]$ ...(6.18*b*)

Proof: Is $x(n)$ is real, therefore $x(n) = x^*(n)$

$$X(k) = \sum_{n=0}^{N-1} x(n) \, W_N^{nk}$$ (By definition)

$$= \sum_{n=0}^{N-1} x^*(n)\, W_N^{nk} \qquad [\because \; x(n) = x^*(n)]$$

$$= \left(\sum_{n=0}^{N-1} x(n)\, W_N^{-nk} \right)^*$$

$$= X^*(-k)$$

$\therefore$ $$X^*(k) = X(-k) = X(N-k) = X[(-k)]_N$$

Note that $$X(k) = X^*(-k)$$

$\therefore$ $$|\, X(k) \,| = |\, X(-k) \,| \qquad \because \text{ amplitude is an even function of } k$$

We know that $$X(k) = \text{Re } X(k) + j\, I_m\, X(k)$$

$$X(-k) = \text{Re } X(-k) + j\, I_m\, X(-k)$$

If $$X^*(k) = X(-k)$$

then $$\text{Re } X(k) - j\, I_m\, X(k) = \text{Re } X(-k) + j\, I_m\, X(-k) \qquad \ldots(A)$$

Equating real and imaginary parts on both sides of (A), we have

$$\text{Re } X(k) = \text{Re } X(-k) \quad \text{and} \quad I_m\, X(k) = -I_m\, X(-k)$$

$\therefore$ $$X^2(k) = \text{Re}^2 X(k) + I_m^2\, X(k) = \text{Re}^2\, X(-k) + I_m^2\, X(-k)$$

i.e., $$|\, X(k) \,|^2 = |\, X(-k) \,|^2 \; i.e., \; |\, X(k) \,| = |\, X(-k) \,|$$

Also, $$\frac{I_m\, X(k)}{\text{Re } X(k)} = \frac{-I_m\, X(-k)}{\text{Re } X(-k)} \qquad \because \; \text{Arg } [X(k)] = -\text{Arg } [X(-k)] \qquad \text{Q.E.D.}$$

6.2.10,11 Even Component and Odd Component

> If $x(n)$ is real and
> $$x(n) = x_e(n) + x_0(n)$$
> then $$X_e(k) = \text{Re}[X(k)] \text{ and } X_0(k) = j\, I_m[X(k)]$$

Proof: $x_e(n)$ is real $\quad \therefore\; x^*_e(n) = x_e(n)$

$x_e(n)$ is even $\quad \because\; x_e(n) = x_e(-n) = x_e\,(N-n)$, as $x(n)$ is periodic with period N

$$X_e(k) = \sum_{n=0}^{N-1} x_e(n)\, W_N^{nk} = \sum_{n=0}^{N-1} x_e(-n)\, W_N^{nk}$$

$$= \sum_{n=0}^{N-1} x_e(N-n)\, W_N^{nk} \qquad \text{Put } N - n = m$$

when $n = 0,\, m = N$

when $n = N-1,\, m = 1$

$$\therefore \quad X_e(k) = \sum_{m=1}^{N} x_e(m)\, W_N^{(N-m)k}$$

$$= \sum_{m=0}^{N-1} x_e(m)\, W_N^{-mk} + \underbrace{x_e(N)\, W_N^{-Nk} - x_e(0)\, W_N^{0k}}_{=0} \quad [\because \; x_e(N) = x_e(0)]$$

$$= \left(\sum_{m=0}^{N-1} x_e(m)\, W_N^{mk} \right)^* \qquad [\because \; x_e(m) = x_e^*(m),\; x_e(m) \text{ being real}]$$

$$\therefore \quad X_e(k) = X_e^*(k) \qquad \text{i.e., } X_e(k) \text{ is purely real}$$

or

$$\boxed{X_e(k) = \text{Re}\,[X(k)]} \qquad \ldots(6.19)$$

If $x_0(n)$ is odd real then $x_0(n) = x_0(-n)$ and $x_0(n) = x_0^*(n)$

$$X_0(k) = \sum_{n=0}^{N-1} x_0(n)\, W_N^{nk} = -\sum_{n=0}^{N-1} x_0(-n)\, W_N^{nk} = -\sum_{n=0}^{N-1} \underbrace{x_0(N-n)}_{\text{Put } N-n=m} W_N^{nk}$$

$$= -\sum_{m=0}^{N-1} x_0(m)\, W_N^{-mk}$$

$$= -\left(\sum_{m=0}^{N-1} x_0(m)\, W_N^{nk} \right)^* = -X_0^*(k) \text{ i.e., } X_0(k) \text{ is purely imaginary}$$

As $\quad X_0(k) = -X_0^*(k), \quad \therefore \boxed{X_0(k) = j\, I_m\,[X(k)]} \qquad \ldots(6.20)$

As $\quad x(n) = x_e(n) + x_0(n) \quad \therefore \quad X(k) = X_e(k) + X_0(k)$

$\therefore \quad X(k) = \text{Re}[X(k)] + j\, I_m[X(k)] \qquad$ [Due to (A) and (B)] Q.E.D.

6.2.12 Parseval's Relation

$$\boxed{\sum_{n=0}^{N-1} |\,x(n)\,|^2 = \frac{1}{N} \sum_{k=0}^{N-1} |\,X(k)\,|^2} \qquad \ldots(6.21)$$

Proof:

$$\sum_{n=0}^{N-1} |\,x(n)\,|^2 = \sum_{n=0}^{N-1} x^*(n)\, x(n)$$

$$= \sum_{n=0}^{N-1} x^*(n) \,.\, \frac{1}{N} \sum_{k=0}^{N-1} X(k)\, W_N^{-nk}$$

$$= \frac{1}{N} \sum_{k=0}^{N-1} X(k) \,.\, \sum_{n=0}^{N-1} x^*(n)\, W_N^{-nk} \quad \text{(interchanging summation order)}$$

$$= \frac{1}{N} \sum_{k=0}^{N-1} X(k) \,.\left(\sum_{n=0}^{N-1} x(n) \,.\, W_N^{nk} \right)^* = \frac{1}{N} \sum_{k=0}^{N-1} X(k) \,.\, X^*(k)$$

$$\therefore \quad \sum_{n=0}^{N-1} |x(n)|^2 = \frac{1}{N}\sum_{k=0}^{N-1} |X(k)|^2 \qquad \text{Q.E.D.}$$

This relation expresses the energy of finite duration sequence $x(n)$ in terms of the discrete frequency components $X(k)$.

6.2.13 DFT of Circular Correlation

To prove that $\boxed{\text{DFT}\,[r_{xy}(l)] = X(k)\,.\,Y^*(k)}$ ...(6.22)

$$\text{As} \quad r_{xy}(l) = \sum_{n=0}^{N-1} x(n)\,.\,y^*[(n-l)]_N \quad \text{[Circular correlation of } x(n) \text{ and } y(n)]$$

$$\text{DFT of } r_{xy}(l) = \sum_{l=0}^{N-1} r_{xy}(l)\,.\,W_N^{kl} = \sum_{l=0}^{N-1}\left(\sum_{n=0}^{N-1} x(n)\,.\,y^*[(n-l)]_N\right).\,W_N^{lk}$$

$$= \sum_{n=0}^{N-1} x(n) \sum_{l=0}^{N-1} \underbrace{y^*[(n-l)]_N}_{\text{Put } n-l=m-N}\,.\,W_N^{lk} \qquad \therefore \text{ when } l=0,\ m=N+n$$

$$\text{when } l = N-1,\ m = n+1$$

$$= \sum_{n=0}^{N-1} x(n) \sum_{m=n+1}^{N+n} y^*[(m-N)]_N\,.\,W_N^{(N+n-m)k}$$

$$= \sum_{n=0}^{N-1} x(n)\,.\,W_N^{nk}\,.\sum_{m=n+1}^{N+n} y^*[(m)]_N\,.\,W_N^{-mk}$$

$$[\because \ y[(m-N)]_N = y[(m)]_N]$$

$$= \sum_{n=0}^{N-1} x(n)\,.\,W_N^{nk}\left[\sum_{m=0}^{N-1} y^*[(m)]_N\,.\,W_N^{-mk} + \sum_{m=N}^{N+n} y^*[(m)]W_N^{-mk} - \sum_{m=0}^{n} y^*[(m)]_N\,W_N^{-mk}\right]$$

Put $m = m' + N$ ↗

$$= \sum_{n=0}^{N-1} x(n)\,.\,W_N^{nk}\left[\sum_{m=0}^{N-1} y^*[(m)]_N\,.\,W_N^{-mk} + \underbrace{\left(\sum_{m'=0}^{n} y^*[(m')]_N\,.\,W_N^{-(m'+N)k} - \sum_{m=0}^{n} y[(m)]_N\,.\,W_N^{-mk}\right)}_{=0}\right]$$

$$W_N^{-(m'+N)k} = W_N^{-m'k}$$

$$\therefore \quad \text{DFT}\,[r_{xy}(l)] = \sum_{n=0}^{N-1} x(n)\,W_N^{nk}\left(\sum_{m=0}^{N-1} y[(m)]_N\,.\,W_N^{mk}\right)^*$$

$$= X(k)\,.\,Y^*(k) \quad \text{(Hence proved)}$$

Various properties derived for DFT are shown in Table 6.1 for ready reference.

Table 6.1. Discrete Fourier Transform-Properties (DFT)

Definition: For $x_p(n)$ a periodic signal with $x_p(n) = \sum_{r=-\infty}^{\infty} x(n+rN)$ or with $x(n) = 0$ outside the range $0 \le n \le N-1$, we have:

$$(a)\ X(k) = \sum_{n=0}^{N-1} x(n)\, W_N^{nk},\ k = 0, 1, ..., N-1,\ W_N = e^{-j(2\pi/N)}$$

$$(b)\ x(n) = \frac{1}{N}\sum_{k=0}^{N-1} X(k) . W_N^{-nk},\ n = 0, 1, ..., N-1$$

	Sequence		DFT	
1.	**Linearity:**	$a_1x_1(n) + a_2x_2(n)$	$a_1X_1(k) + a_2X_2(k)$	(6.10)
2.	**Time Shifting:**	$x((n-n_0))_N$	$W_N^{kn_0} X(k),\ W_N = e^{-j(2\pi/N)}$	(6.11)
3.	**Frequency Shifting:**	$W_N^{-k_0 n} x(n)$	$X((k-k_0))_N$	(6.12)
4.	**Conjugation:**	$x^*(n)$	$X^*((-k))_N$	(6.13)
5.	**Time Reversal:**	$x((-n))_N$	$X((-k))_N$	(6.14)
6.	**Duality:**	$X(n)$	$Nx((-k))_N$	(6.15)
7.	**Circular Convolution:**	$x_1(n)\ Ⓝ\ x_2(n)$	$X_1(k) . X_2(k)$	(6.16)
8.	**Multiplication:**	$x_1(n) . x_2(n)$	$\frac{1}{N} X_1(k)\ Ⓝ\ X_2(k)$	(6.17)
9.	**Real Sequence:**	$x(n) = x_e(n) + x_0(n)$	$X(k) = X^*(-k)$ $\lvert X(k) \rvert = \lvert X(-k) \rvert$ $\text{Arg}[X(k)] = -\text{Arg}[X(-k)]$	(6.18)
10.	**Even Component:**	$x(n) = x_e(n) + x_0(n)$	$\text{Re}[X(k)] = X_e(k)$	(6.19)
11.	**Odd Component:**	$x(n)$ real	$jI_m[X(k)] = X_0(k)$	(6.20)
12.	**Parseval's Relation:**	$\sum_{n=0}^{N-1} \lvert x(n) \rvert^2$	$\frac{1}{N}\sum_{k=0}^{N-1} \lvert X(k) \rvert^2$	(6.21)
13.	**Circular Correlation:**	$R_{xy}(l) = \sum_{n=0}^{N-1} x(n)\, y^*((n-l))_N$	$X(k) . Y^*(k)$	(6.22)

6.3 FREQUENCY DOMAIN SAMPLING THEOREM

This theorem is analogcus to the time-domain sampling theorem. It states that, "If $x(n)$ is a time-limited digital sequence: between $n = 0$ to $n = N-1$, then it can be uniquely determined from its frequency domain samples $X(e^{j\omega})$ for $\omega = 2\pi k/N$". Equivalently, $X(z)$, the *ZT* of $x(n)$, can be uniquely determined from N frequency domain samples of $X(e^{j\omega})$ *i.e.*, from the DFT of $x_p(n)$.

6.3.1 To Determine X(z) Given the DFT X(k)

Proof: $$x(n) = x_p(n)\,[u(n) - u(n-N)]$$

$$\therefore \qquad ZT \text{ of } x(n) = X(z) = ZT\,.\left(u(n) - u(n-N)].\overbrace{\frac{1}{N}\sum_{k=0}^{N-1} X(k)\, W_N^{-nk}}^{x_p(n)} \right)$$

$$= \frac{1}{N}\sum_{k=0}^{N-1} X(k)\,.\,ZT\,[(u(n) - u(n-N))\,W_N^{-nk}]$$

But $\quad ZT\,[u(n)W_N^{-nk}] = 1/(1 - W_N^{-k}\, z^{-1})$

and $\quad ZT\,[u(n-N)W_N^{-nk}] = ZT\,[u(n-N)W_N^{-(n-N)k}]\,.\,W_N^{-Nk} \leftarrow = +1$

$$= z^{-N}/(1 - W_N^{-k}\, z^{-1})$$

$$\therefore \qquad X(z) = \frac{1}{N}\sum_{k=0}^{N-1} X(k)\left(\frac{1 - z^{-N}}{1 - W_N^{k}\, z^{-1}}\right)$$

i.e.,

$$ZT \text{ of } x(n) = X(z) = \frac{1 - z^{-N}}{N}\sum_{k=0}^{N-1} X_p(k)\,\frac{1}{1 - W_N^{-k}\, z^{-1}}\,, \quad W_N = e^{-j2\pi/N}$$

(DFT of $x_p(n)$) ...(6.23)

Realization: Consider the realization of $H_r(z)$ as shown. This forms one terms of the above series. We realize the complete $X(z)$ by putting in parallel such N filters for $r = 0$ to $N - 1$ and a multiplier as shown. The multiplier $(1 - z^{-N})/N$ may also be shifted after the summation on R.H.S.

To summarise: If $x(n)$ is time limited sequence.

(*i*) $x_p(n)$ can be obtained from $x(n)$ by repeating $x(n)$.

(*ii*) DFT $X_p(k)$ of $x_p(n)$ is the same as sampling $X(z)$ on the unit circle at $W_k = 2\pi k/N$, $k = 0$, 1, ..., $N - 1$.

(*iii*) $x(n)$ is one period sequence of $x_p(n)$.

(*iv*) $X(z) = ZT\,[x(n)]$ can be realized from $X_p(k)$ as in above Fig. 6.4.

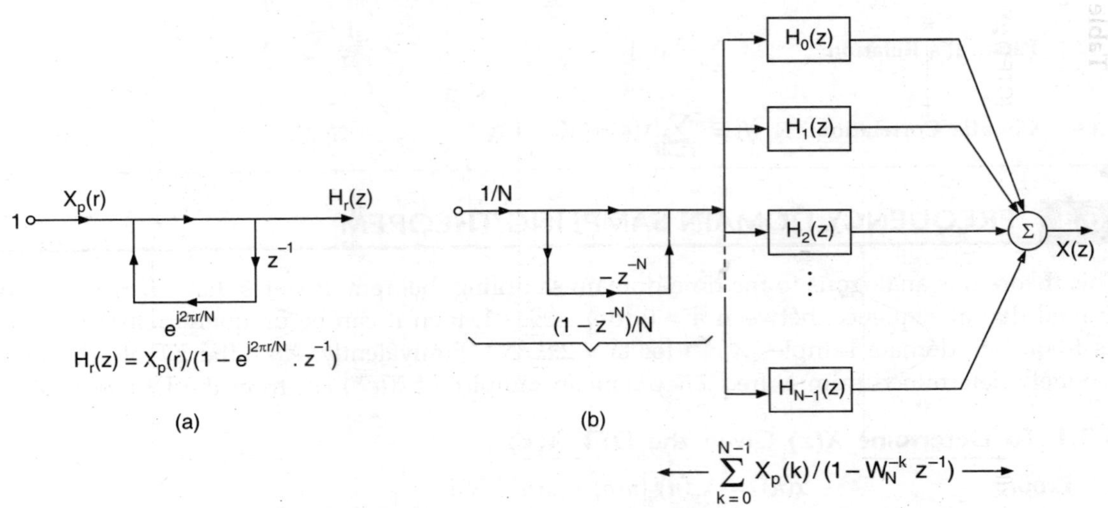

Fig. 6.4. (*a*) Realization of a typical filter $H_r(z)$, (*b*) Realization of $X(z)$ from $X_p(k)$

Table 6.2. Inter-relationships between Various Transforms

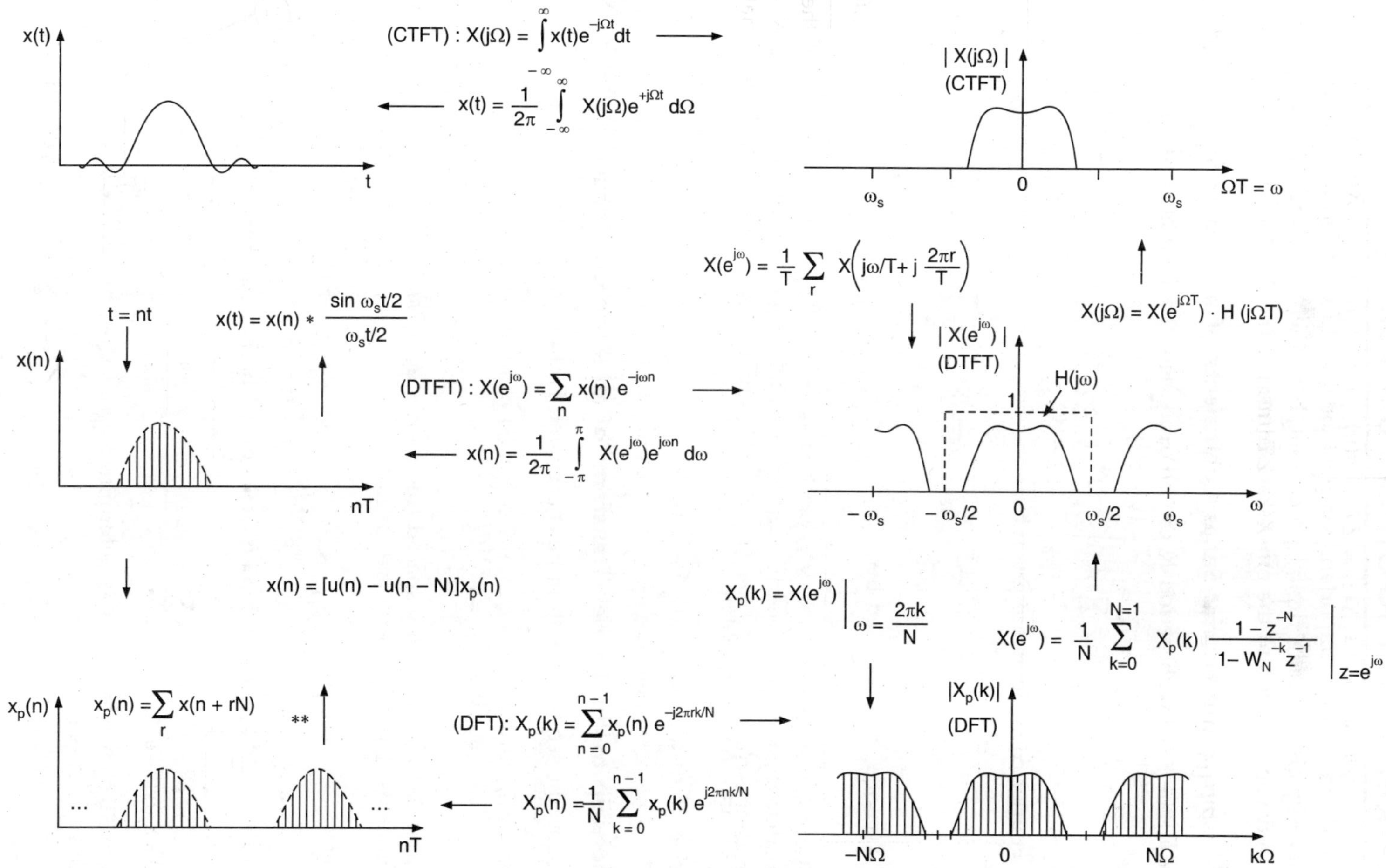

** Not possible when there is time-domains aliasing

6.4 RELATIONS OF DFT TO OTHER TRANSFORMS

We have learnt that DFT is an important computational tool for performing frequency analysis of discrete-time signals by using digital processors. It is, therefore, important to establish the relationships between the DFT to the other transforms.

6.4.1 Relationship to the Fourier Series Coefficients of a Periodic Sequence $x_p(n)$

A periodic sequence $x_p(n)$ with period N can be expressed in a Fourier series form

$$x_p(n) = \sum_{k=0}^{N-1} a_k\, e^{j2\pi nk/N} \qquad \text{...(6.24)}$$

where a_k the Fourier coefficients are given by

$$a_k = \frac{1}{N}\sum_{n=0}^{N-1} x_p(n)\, e^{-j2\pi nk/N} \qquad \text{...(6.25)}$$

But DFT $X(k)$ of $x_p(n)$ is defined by

$$X(k) = \sum_{n=0}^{N-1} x_p(n)\, e^{-j2\pi nk/N} \qquad \text{...(6.26)}$$

Using (6.25) and (6.26), we obtain

$$\boxed{X(k) = Na_k} \qquad \text{...(6.27)}$$

6.4.2 Relationship to the Fourier Transform of an Aperiodic Sequence $x(n)$

If $x(n)$ is an aperiodic sequence with finite energy and Fourier transform $X(e^{j\omega})$ or $X(\omega)$, we have

$$X(\omega) = \sum_{n=-\infty}^{\infty} x(n)\, e^{-j\omega n} \qquad \text{...(6.28)}$$

If we sample $X(\omega)$ at N equally spaced frequencies $\omega_k = 2\pi k/N$, $k = 0, 1, ..., N-1$, then the spectral components defined as $X(k)$ are given by

$$X(k) = X(\omega)\big|_{\omega=2\pi k/N} = \sum_{n=-\infty}^{\infty} x(n)\,.\,e^{-j2\pi nk/N} \qquad \text{...(6.29)}$$

$X(k)$ given by (6.29) are the DFT coefficients of the periodic sequence of period N, given by

$$x_p(n) = \sum_{l=-\infty}^{\infty} x(n-lN) \qquad \text{...(6.30)}$$

Equation (6.30) shows that $x_p(n)$ is determined by aliasing the aperiodic sequence $\{x(n)\}$ over the interval $0 \le n \le N-1$.

Note that definite-duration sequence defined by

$$\hat{x}(n) \triangleq \begin{cases} x_p(n), & 0 \le n \le N-1 \\ 0, & \text{otherwise} \end{cases} \qquad \ldots(6.31)$$

does not resemble the original aperiodic sequence $\{x(n)\}$, unless $x(n)$ has finite duration and has length $L \le N$. In such a case

$$x(n) = \hat{x}(n), \; 0 \le n \le N-1 \qquad \ldots(6.32)$$

Only in this case (*i.e.*, $L \le N$ case), the IDFT of frequency samples $X(k)$, given by (6.29), will yield the original sequence $x(n)$.

6.4.3 Relationship to the *z*-transform

Let a sequence $x(n)$ have z-transform

$$X(z) = \sum_{n=-\infty}^{\infty} x(n)\, z^{-n} \qquad \ldots(6.32a)$$

Let ROC of $X(z)$ include the unit circle $|z| = 1$. If $X(z)$ is sampled at N equally spaced points on the unit circle *i.e.*, $z_k = e^{j2\pi k/N}$, $k = 0, 1, \ldots, N-1$, we obtain

$$X(z)\big|_{z=e^{j2\pi k/N}} \triangleq X(k), \; k = 0, 1, \ldots, N-1$$

$$= \sum_{n=-\infty}^{\infty} x(n)\, e^{-j2\pi nk/N} \qquad \ldots(6.33)$$

Expression (6.33) is identical to the Fourier transform $X(\omega)$ evaluated at N equally spaced frequencies $\omega_k = 2\pi k/N$, $k = 0, 1, \ldots, N-1$, as found in Eqn. (6.29). Hence, if the sequence duration: $L \le N$, then we can uniquely determine $x(n)$ from N points of its ZT, evaluated over the unit circle $|z| = 1$. In other words, $X(z)$ can be expressed as a function of the DFT components $\{X(k)\}$, shown as follows:

As $$X(z) = \sum_{n=0}^{N-1} x(n)\, z^{-n} \qquad \text{[Assuming } x(n) \text{ has length } N]$$

$$= \sum_{n=0}^{N-1} \left[\frac{1}{N} \sum_{k=0}^{N-1} X(k)\, e^{j2\pi nk/N} \right] z^{-n}$$

$$= \frac{1}{N} \sum_{k=0}^{N-1} X(k) \sum_{n=0}^{N-1} (e^{j2\pi k/N} z^{-1})^n \qquad \ldots(6.34)$$

$$= \frac{1}{N} \sum_{k=0}^{N-1} X(k) . \left(\frac{1 - e^{j2\pi k}\, z^{-N}}{1 - e^{j2\pi k/N}\, z^{-1}} \right)$$

$$= \frac{1 - z^{-N}}{N} \sum_{k=0}^{N-1} \frac{X(k)}{1 - e^{j2\pi k/N}\, z^{-1}} \qquad \ldots(6.35)$$

Equation $X(z)$ given by (6.35) can be realized by using *N-IIR* filters in parallel, as shown in Fig. 6.4(*b*).

Evaluation of $X(z)$, determined by Eq. (6.35), at unit circle yields the Fourier transform $X(\omega)$ in terms of DFT components $X(k)$ *i.e.*, putting $z = e^{j\omega}$ in (6.35), we get

$$X(\omega) = \frac{1-e^{-j\omega N}}{N}\sum_{k=0}^{N-1}\frac{X(k)}{1-e^{-j(\omega-2\pi k/N)}} \quad \text{...(6.36)}$$

This expression of the Fourier transform is a polynomial (Lagrange's polynomial) interpolation formula of $X(\omega)$ expressed in terms of the values $\{X(k)\}$ of the polynomial at a net of equally spaced discrete frequencies $\omega_k = 2\pi k/N$, $k = 0, 1, ..., N-1$.

6.4.4 Relationship to the Fourier Series Coefficients of a Continuous-time Signal

As the Fourier series expansion holds for a periodic continuous signal, let

$x_a(t)$ be a continuous-time periodic signal with time period T. Hence, we can write

$$x_a(t) = \sum_{k=-\infty}^{\infty} c_k\, e^{jk\omega_0 t}, \text{ where } \omega_0 = 2\pi/T \quad \text{...(6.37)}$$

where c_k are the Fourier coefficients for $x_a(t)$, given by

$$c_k = \frac{1}{T}\int_T x_a(t)\, e^{-jk\omega_0 t}\, dt \quad \text{...(6.38)}$$

Let us sample $x_a(t)$ at $t = nT_s$, where T_s is the inter-sample time interval, such that $T_s = T/N$, therefore, from (6.37) we obtain

$$x(n) \triangleq x_a(nT_s) = \sum_{k=-\infty}^{\infty} c_k \,.\, e^{jk\omega_0 nT_s} \quad \text{...(6.39)}$$

Now $\omega_0 T_s = (2\pi/T).\,(T/N) = 2\pi/N$. Hence, (6.39) reduces to

$$x(n) = \sum_{k=-\infty}^{\infty} c_k\, e^{j2\pi nk/N} \quad \text{...(6.40)}$$

Since, $e^{j2\pi nk/N} = 1$ for $k = 0, \pm N, \pm 2N$ ..., therefore

We can write (6.40) as

$$x(n) = \sum_{k=0}^{N-1}\left[\sum_{m=-\infty}^{\infty} c_{k-mN}\right] e^{j2\pi nk/N} \text{ (Note this step)} \quad \text{...(6.41)}$$

If we compare (6.41) with IDFT formula, (6.42) where

$$x(n) = \frac{1}{N}\sum_{k=0}^{N-1} X(k)\, e^{j2\pi nk/N} \quad \text{...(6.42)}$$

We can write

$$X(k) = N\sum_{m=-\infty}^{\infty} c_{k-mN} \triangleq N\tilde{c}_k \quad \text{...(6.43)}$$

and $$\tilde{c}_k = \sum_{m=-\infty}^{\infty} c_{k-mN} \quad \text{...(6.44)}$$

Then, $\{\tilde{c}_k\}$ sequence is an aliased version of the Fourier series coefficients $\{c_k\}$.

6.5 THE GOERTZEL ALGORITHM

The Goertzel algorithm exploits the periodicity of the phase function W_N^k, and it allows us to express the computation of DFT of a sequence $x(n)$, as a linear operation. Note that $W_N^{-kN} = 1$. Hence, we can multiply the DFT by a factor W_N^{-kN}. Thus,

$$X(k) = \sum_{m=0}^{N-1} x(m) . W_N^{km} = W_N^{-kN} \sum_{m=0}^{N-1} x(m)\, W_N^{km}$$

$$= \sum_{m=0}^{N-1} x(m) . W_N^{-(N-m)k} \quad \text{...(6.45)}$$

Equation (6.45) is the form of a convolution. If we define

$$y_k(n) = x(n) * [W_N^{-kn}\, u(n)]$$

$$= \sum_{m=0}^{N-1} x(m) . W_N^{-k(n-m)} \quad \text{...(6.46)}$$

i.e., $y_k(n)$ defined in (6.46) is a convolution of the finite-duration input sequence $x(n)$ of length N and the filter that has an impulse response given by

$$h_k(n) = W_N^{-kn}\, u(n) \quad \text{...(6.47)}$$

Note that

$$y_k(n)\big|_{n=N} = \sum_{m=0}^{N-1} x(m) . W_N^{-k(N-m)}$$

$$= \sum_{m=0}^{N-1} x(m)\, W_N^{km}$$

$\therefore$ $$y_k(n)\big|_{n=N} = X(k) \text{ is the DFT of } x(n) \quad \text{...(6.48)}$$

The filter (6.47) has the system function

$$H_k(z) = \frac{1}{1 - W_N^{-k}\, z^{-1}} \quad \text{...(6.49)}$$

Clearly, $H_k(z)$ has a pole at $z = W_N^{-k}$ *i.e.*, at frequency $W_k = 2\pi k/N$ ($\because\ W_N^{-k} = e^{j2\pi k/N}$). This means that the entire DFT, (at all frequencies ω_k, $k = 0, 1, ..., N-1$) can be computed by passing the block of input data into a parallel bank of N filters ($h_0(n)$, $h_1(n)$, ..., $h_{N-1}(n)$) each having a single-pole. Such filters, with single pole at a frequency ω_k, $k = 0, 1, ..., N-1$ are called resonators.

From (6.49), we can write

$$\frac{Y_k(z)}{X(z)} = \frac{1}{1 - W_N^{-k} z^{-1}} \quad \text{...(6.50)}$$

by cross multiplying and taking *IZT* in (6.50) we get

$$y_k(n) - W_N^{-k} y_k(n-1) = x(n)$$

or

$$y_k(n) = W_N^{-k} y_k(n-1) + x(n) \quad \text{...(6.51)}$$

Hence, we can use the difference equation (6.51) to perform the function of the filter given by (6.50), and realize $y_k(n)$ recursively, assuming $y_k(-1) = 0$. The desired output is

$$X(k) = y_k(N),\ k = 0, 1, ..., N-1 \quad \text{...(6.52)}$$

The expression for $H_k(z)$, given by (6.49) has complex multiplications and additions due to the phase factor $W_N^{-k} = e^{j2\pi k/N}$. We can avoid the complex multiplications and addition, as follows:

$$H_k(z) = \frac{1}{1 - e^{j2\pi k/N} z^{-1}} \times \frac{1 - e^{-j2\pi k/N} z^{-1}}{1 - e^{-j2\pi k/N} z^{-1}}$$

$$\therefore \quad H_k(z) = \frac{1 - W_N^k z^{-1}}{1 - 2\cos(2\pi k/N) z^{-1} + z^{-2}} \quad \text{...(6.53)}$$

Realization of $H_k(z)$ is shown in Fig. 6.5. Note that

$$v_k(n) = 2\cos(2\pi k/N) \cdot v_k(n-1) - v_k(n-2) + x(n) \quad \text{...(6.54a)}$$

and

$$y_k(n) = v_k(n) - W_N^k v_k(n-1) \quad \text{...(6.54b)}$$

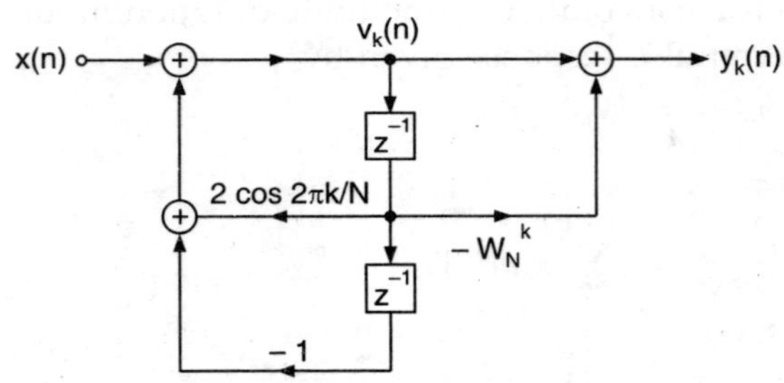

Fig. 6.5. Canonic (Direct form II) realization of two-pole resonator for computing the DFT

and we use the initial conditions $v_k(-1) = v_k(-2) = 0$ to compute the values of $v_k(n)$ and $y_k(n)$ given by Eq. (6.54). The recursive relation in (6.54*a*) is iterated for $n = 0, 1, ..., N$, but the equation (6.54*b*) is computed at $n = N$. Each iteration requires one real multiplication (by $2\cos 2\pi k/N$) and two additions. Consequently, for real input sequence $x(n)$, this algorithm requires $N + 1$ real multiplications to yield $X(k)$. We also obtain, due to symmetry, the value of $X(N-k)$ at no extra cost. This method of computing $X(k)$ is called Goertzel algorithm.

The Goertzel algorithm is particularly useful when DFT is to be computed at a relatively small number M of values, where $M \leq \log_2 N$. Otherwise, the FFT algorithm is more efficient method.

6.6 THE CHIRP-Z TRANSFORM ALGORITHM

We know that the DFT of an N-point data sequence $x(n)$, is the z-transform of $x(n)$ evaluated at N equally spaced points on the unit circle *i.e.*, at frequencies $\omega_k = 2\pi k/N$, $k = 0, 1, ..., N-1$. In other words, DFT $X(k)$ may be viewed as N equally spaced samples of the Fourier transform $X(\omega)$ of $x(n)$. We now view the evaluation of ZT, $X(z)$, of $x(n)$ on other points in the z-plane, besides the unit circle.

Suppose that we wish to compute the values of the z-transform at a set of points $\{z_k\}$. Then we can write

$$X(z_k) = \sum_{n=0}^{N-1} x(n)\, z_k^{-n}, \; k = 0, 1, ..., N-1 \qquad \text{...(6.55)}$$

If the contour in z-plane is a circle of radius r, and z_k are equally spaced points, then

$$z_k = re^{j2\pi k/N}, \; k = 0, 1, ..., N-1 \qquad \text{...(6.56)}$$

and hence

$$X(z_k) = \sum_{n=0}^{N-1} x(n)\,(re^{j2\pi k/N})^{-n} \qquad \text{...(6.57)}$$

i.e.,

$$X(z_k) = \sum_{n=0}^{N-1} [x(n)\, r^{-n}]\, e^{-j2\pi kn/N}, \; k = 0, 1, ..., N-1 \qquad \text{...(6.58)}$$

Hence, in this case, the DFT algorithm may be applied on the modified sequence $(x(n) \,.\, r^{-n})$, to obtain $X(z_k)$ as given by Eq. (6.58).

More generally, suppose that the points z_k in the z-plane lie on an arc which begins at some point

$$z_0 = r_0 e^{j\theta_0} \qquad \text{...(6.59)}$$

The spiral on which z_k lie may be closing towards the origin $z = 0$ or may spread out away from the origin. In these cases, the points $\{z_k\}$ are defined as

$$z_k = r_0 e^{j\theta_0} (R_0 e^{j\phi_0})^k, \; k = 0, 1, ..., L-1 \qquad \text{...(6.60)}$$

If $R_0 < 1$, the points z_k fall on the contour that spirals towards the origin. If $R_0 > 1$, the contour spirals away from the origin. If $R_0 = 1$ the contour is a circular arc of radius r_0. If $r_0 = 1$ and $R_0 = 1$, the arc contour is the unit circle. For the case of $r_0 = R_0 = 1$ allows us to compute the frequency content of the sequence $x(n)$ at a dense set of L frequencies in the range covered by the arc of z_k points. We have assumed $L > N$ here.

If $r_0 = R_0 = 1$, $\theta_0 = 0$, $\phi_0 = 2\pi/N$, and $L = N$, the contour of z_k is the entire unit circle and the frequencies are those of DFT *i.e.,* $\omega_k = 2\pi k/N$, $k = 0, 1, ..., N-1$.
The points $\{z_k\}$ of (6.60) are shown in Fig. 6.6 for various contours.

Putting $z_k = r_0 e^{j\theta_0} (R_0 e^{j\phi_0})$ in the expression for the z-transform of $x(n)$, we get

$$X(z_k) = \sum_{n=0}^{N-1} x(n)\, z_k^{-n}$$

$$= \sum_{n=0}^{N-1} x(n) \,.\, (r_0 e^{j\theta_0})^{-n} \,.\, V^{-nk} \qquad \text{...(6.61)}$$

where

$$V = R_0\, e^{j\phi_0} \qquad \text{...(6.62)}$$

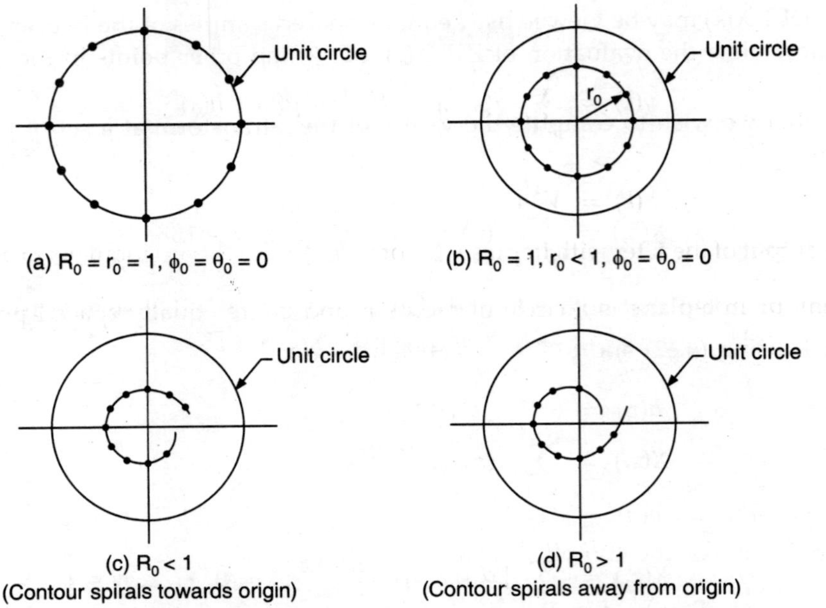

Fig. 6.6. Examples of contours on which we let z_k take positions for taking *z*-transform

We use the identity

$$nk = \frac{1}{2}[n^2 + k^2 - (k-n)^2] \text{ (Note this step)} \quad \ldots(6.63)$$

∴ (6.61) yields

$$X(z_k) = \sum_{n=0}^{N-1} x(n).(r_0 e^{j\theta_0})^{-n}.V^{-\frac{1}{2}[n^2+k^2-(k-n)^2]} \quad \ldots(6.64)$$

$$= V^{-k^2/2}\sum_{n=0}^{N-1}[x(n).(r_0e^{j\theta_0})^{-n}.V^{-n^2/2}]V^{(k-n)^2/2}$$

$$\therefore \quad X(z_k) = V^{-k^2/2}\sum_{n=0}^{N-1} g(n).V^{(k-n)^2/2} \quad \ldots(6.65)$$

where $\quad g(n) \triangleq x(n)\ (r_0e^{j\theta_0})^{-n}\ V^{-n^2/2} \quad \ldots(6.66)$

Equation (6.65) shows that the expression under the summation is equivalent to

$$g(k) * V^{k^2/2} \quad \ldots(6.67)$$

i.e., convolution of $g(n)$ and $V^{n^2/2}$. Call $V^{n^2/2} = h(n)$. Hence, (6.65) may be expressed as

$$X(z_k) = V^{-k^2/2}.y(k) \quad \ldots(6.68)$$

$$= y(k)/h(k) \quad \text{...(6.69)}$$

where
$$y(k) = \sum_{n=0}^{N-1} g(n).V^{(k-n)^2/2} = g(k) * h(k) \quad \text{...(6.70)}$$

$$h(k) = V^{k^2/2} \quad \text{...(6.71)}$$

i.e., $y(k)$ is the output of the filter with impulse response $h(n) = V^{n^2/2}$ and input $g(n) = x(n) . (r_0 e^{j\theta_0})^{-n}$. $V^{-n^2/2}$. It may be noted that both $h(n)$ and $g(n)$ are complex valued sequences.

For $R_0 = 1$, using (6.62) and (6.71), we can write

$$h(n) = (e^{j\phi_0})^{n^2/2}$$

$$= e^{jn^2\phi_0/2}$$

Phase response of $h(n) = \text{Arg}\,[h(n)] = n^2\phi_0/2.$

Hence, frequency of the complex exponential signal $h(n)$ is given by $(n^2\phi_0/2)/n$ [Note that frequency = phase/time]. Hence, the frequency $n\phi_0/2$ increases linearly with time n.
Such signals are used in radar systems to minimise uncertainty. Such signals are called **Chirp Signals**. Hence, the z-transform evaluated in (6.65) is called **Chirp-z-Transform**.

6.7 COMPUTATION OF DFT BY FFT ALGORITHM

The discrete Fourier transform (DFT) plays an important role in many applications of DSP including linear filtering, correlation analysis and spectrum analysis. A major reason for the importance of DFT is the availability of an efficient algorithm, called Fast Fourier transform (FFT), to compute the DFT coefficients $X(k)$.

We shall learn in this section that DFT of size N, where N is a composite number, is reduced to the computation of smaller DFTs from which the larger DFT is computed. In particular, when N is a power of 2 (*i.e.*, $N = 2^v$, v an integer) or when N is a power of 4 (*i.e.*, $N = 4^m$, m an integer), the use of FFT is highly useful. We have already discussed the use of Goertzel algorithm and the Chirp-z-transform algorithm for computing the DFT *via.* linear filtering of the data sequence.

6.7.1 Need of FFT

The discrete Fourier transform, $X(k)$ of a periodic sequence $x(n)$ of period N is defined as

$$X(k) = \sum_{n=0}^{N-1} x(n).W_N^{kn}, \; k = 0, 1, ..., N-1 \quad \text{...(6.72)}$$

where
$$W_N = e^{-j2\pi/N} \quad \text{...(6.73)}$$

The inverse discrete Fourier transform (IDFT) is given by

$$x(n) = \frac{1}{N}\sum_{k=0}^{N-1} X(k)\,W_N^{-kn}, \; n = 0, 1, ..., N-1 \quad \text{...(6.74)}$$

In general, $x(n)$ and $X(k)$ may be complex. As the Eqns. (6.72) and (6.74) are similar, and (6.74) differs from (6.72) for sign of W_N and a scale factor $1/N$, FFT procedure to get $X(k)$ can be directly applied to obtain $x(n)$ from its DFT $X(k)$ with very slight modification. If $x(n)$ is complex, we can write

$$X(k) = \sum_{n=0}^{N-1} \Big\{\big(\text{Re}[x(n)].\text{Re}[W_N^{kn}] - I_m[x(n)].I_m[W_N^{kn}]\big)$$

$$+ j\big(\text{Re}[x(n)].I_m[W_N^{kn}] + I_m[x(n)].\text{Re}[W_N^{kn}]\big)\Big\} \quad \ldots(6.75)$$

Note that computation of $X(k)$, for one typical value of k, in (6.75) requires

(4N – 2) real additions and (4N) real multiplications

...(6.76)

Explanation: Let $X(k) = X_k'(0) + X_k'(1) + \ldots + X_k'(N-1)$, where dashes show sub-additions. For $n = 0$, we compute $X_k'(0)$ and that requires two additions and four multiplications. For $n = 1$, we compute $X_k'(1)$ which also requires two additions and four multiplications. Adding $X_k'(1)$ to $X_k'(0)$ requires two more additions. Totally, we have made 6 additions and 8 multiplications to obtain the partial sum $X_k'(0) + X_k'(1)$. For obtaining the partial sum $X_k'(0) + X_k'(1) + X_k'(2)$, we shall require totally 12 multiplications and 10 additions. Continuing this way we obtain $X(k)$ for one typical value of k. It would require $(4N - 2)$ real additions and $4N$ real multiplications. In general, N is fairly large. Therefore, complete $X(k)$, (for N different values of k), the direct computation of DFT by using (6.75) will require

$N(4N - 2) \approx 4N^2$ real additions and $4N^2$ real multiplications

...(6.77)

We know that $\quad W_N^{kn} = W_N^{n(k+N)}$ and $W_N^{k(N-n)} = (W_N^{kn})^*$ $\quad \ldots(6.78)$

By using the properties (6.78), we can write (6.75), by regrouping as

$$\text{Re}[x(n)]\,.\,\text{Re}[W_N^{kn}] + \text{Re}[x(N-n)]\,.\,\text{Re}\,[W_N^{k(N-n)}]$$
$$= (\text{Re}[x(n)] + \text{Re}[x(N-n)])\,.\,\text{Re}[W_N^{kn}] \quad \ldots(6.79)$$
$$(\because \ \text{Re}[W_N^{kn}] = \text{Re}[W_N^{k(N-n)}])$$

Similarly,
$$-(I_m[x(n)]\,.\,I_m[W_N^{kn}] + I_m[x(N-n)])\,.I_m[W_N^{k(N-n)}])$$
$$= -(I_m[x(n)] - I_m[x(N-n)])\,.\,I_m[W_N^{kn}] \quad \ldots(6.80)$$
$$(\because \ I_m[W_N^{kn}] = -I_m[W_N^{k(N-n)}])$$

Similar groupings can be found for other terms in (6.75) too. By doing so, we can reduce the number of multiplications by a factor of 2 approximately. But the fact remains that $X(k)$ computation requires $4N^2$ real multiplications and $4N^2$ real additions. Take the practical example of a system capacity of performing 10^6 multiplications/sec, then

for $N = 10^6$, $4N^2 = 4 \times 10^{12}$ multiplications would take 46 days

for $N = 10^5$, $4N^2 = 4 \times 10^{10}$ multiplications would take 11.2 hours.

Thus, computation of $X(k)$ by using (6.75) series is quite a time consuming process. FFT Algorithm is very efficient for computation of $X(k)$, as will be shown what follows.

* J.W. Cooley and J.W. Tukey. An algorithm for the machine calculation of complex Fourier series. Math. Computation Vol. 19, pp. 297-301, 1965.

6.7.2 Decimation-in-time FFT Algorithm (DIT-FFT)*

We decompose the computation of the DFT into successively smaller DFT computations. **We exploit the symmetry and the periodicity of the complex exponential** *i.e.*, of

$$W_N^{kn} \triangleq e^{-j(2\pi/N)kn} \quad \text{...(6.81)}$$

Algorithm in which the decomposition is based on decomposing the sequence $x(n)$, into successively smaller sub-sequences is called decimation-in-time (DIT). Let the value of N be such that

$$N = 2^v, \; v \text{ an integer} \quad \text{...(6.82)}$$

As N is an even integer, we compute $X(k)$ by separating $x(n)$ into two $N/2$ sequences *i.e.*,

$$X(k) = \sum_{n=0}^{N-1} x(n)\, W_N^{nk}, \; k = 0, 1, 2, ..., N-1 \quad \text{...(6.83)}$$

(By definition of DFT)

$$= \sum_{\substack{n \text{ even} \\ i.e.,\, n=0,2,4,..., \\ N-2}}^{N-1} x(n)\, W_N^{nk} + \sum_{\substack{n \text{ odd} \\ i.e.,\, n=1,3,5,..., \\ N-1}}^{N-1} x(n)\, W_N^{nk}$$

Put $n = 2r$ for n even and $n = 2r + 1$ for n odd (*i.e.*, the second series above)

$$\therefore \quad X(k) = \sum_{r=0}^{N/2-1} x(2r)\, W_N^{2rk} + \sum_{r=0}^{N/2-1} x(2r+1)\, W_N^{(2r+1)k} \quad \text{...(6.84)}$$

But $\quad W_N^2 = W_{N/2}$

$$\because \quad W_N^2 = e^{-j\frac{2\pi}{N}\times 2} = e^{-j\frac{2\pi}{N/2}} = W_{N/2}^1 \text{ (in general, } W_K^l = W_{N/l})$$

$\therefore$ Equation (6.84) can be written as

$$X(k) = \sum_{r=0}^{(N/2)-1} \underbrace{x(2r)}_{\triangleq g(r)} W_{N/2}^{rk} + W_N^k \sum_{r=0}^{(N/2)-1} \underbrace{x(2r+1)}_{\triangleq h(r)} W_{N/2}^{rk} \quad \text{...(6.85)}$$

$$\therefore \quad \boxed{X(k) \triangleq G(k) + W_N^k H(k), \; k = 0, 1, 2, ..., (N-1)} \quad \text{...(6.85a)}$$

i.e., each sum in (6.85) is an $N/2$-point DFT. $G(k)$ being $N/2$-point DFT of the samples $x(n)$ for n even of the original sequence, and $H(k)$ is $N/2$-point DFT of the samples at odd-numbers points of the original sequence $x(n)$. Although the index k ranges over N values ($k = 0, 1, ..., N-1$), each of the sums (*i.e.*, $G(k)$ and $H(k)$) need only be computed for k between 0 and $N/2 - 1$, **since $G(k)$ and $H(k)$ each are periodic in k with period $N/2$.** After computing $G(k)$ and $H(k)$, the overall $X(k)$ can be computed as per (6.86). For $N = 8$, thus, we get the following signal flow graph, shown in Fig. 6.7.

Thus,

$$X(0) = G(0) + W_N^0 H(0)$$
$$X(1) = G(1) + W_N^1 H(1)$$
$$X(2) = G(2) + W_N^2 H(2)$$
$$X(3) = G(3) + W_N^3 H(3)$$

* J.W. Cooley, P.A.W. Lewis and P.D. Welch, 'Historical notes on the Fast Fourier Transform.' IEEE Tr Audio Electroacoust., Vol. AU-15, pp. 76-79, June, 1967.

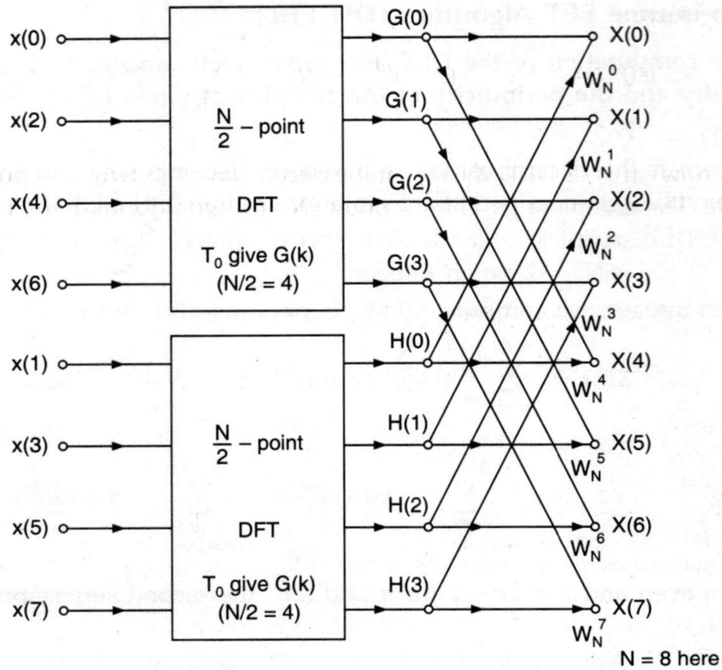

Fig. 6.7. Flow graph of the decimation-in-time decomposition of an *N*-point DFT computation into two *N*/2-point DFT computation (*N* = 8)

$$\left.\begin{aligned} X(4) &= G(4) + W_N^4\, H(4) = G(0) + W_N^4\, H(0) \\ X(5) &= G(5) + W_N^5\, H(5) = G(1) + W_N^5\, H(1) \\ X(6) &= G(6) + W_N^6\, H(6) = G(2) + W_N^6\, H(2) \\ X(7) &= G(7) + W_N^7\, H(7) = G(3) + W_N^7\, H(3) \end{aligned}\right\} \because G(k) \text{ and } H(k) \text{ are periodic with period } 8/2 = 4 \text{ here.}$$

and

We can further break $N/2$ point DFTs $G(k)$ and $H(k)$ in $N/4$ points DFTs as $N/2$, $N/4$, ..., always remains even (since $N = 2^v$) till we reach 1.

Breaking each sum of (6.85) into two $N/4$ point DFT's, which would then be combined to $N/2$ point DFT's for $G(k)$ and $H(k)$, *i.e.*

$$G(k) = \sum_{r=0}^{(N/2-1)} g(r)\, W_{N/2}^{rk},$$

where $g(r) = x(2r)$ = even numbered samples of $x(n)$

$$= \sum_{l=0}^{(N/4-1)} g(2l)\, W_{N/2}^{2lk} + \sum_{l=0}^{(N/4-1)} g(2l+1)\, W_{N/2}^{(2l+1)k}$$

$$= \sum_{l=0}^{(N/4-1)} g(2l)\, W_{N/4}^{lk} + \left(\sum_{l=0}^{(N/4-1)} g(2l+1)\, W_{N/4}^{2lk} \right) W_{N/2}^{k}$$

Similarly, we may have

$$H(k) = \sum_{l=0}^{(N/4-1)} h(2l)\, W_{N/4}^{lk} + W_{N/2}^{k} \sum_{l=0}^{(N/4-1)} h(2l+1)\, W_{N/4}^{lk}$$

where $h(l) = x(2l + 1)$.

Figure 6.8 shows how an $N/2$ DFT of $G(k)$ can be decomposed to two $N/4$ point DFTs. Here, $N = 8$, in our example. The complete DFT, for 8 point ($N = 8$) would look like Fig. 6.10. We note that, $N/4 = 2$ point DFT for samples $x(0)$ and $x(4)$ reduces to just multiplication by + 1 or – 1 and addition.

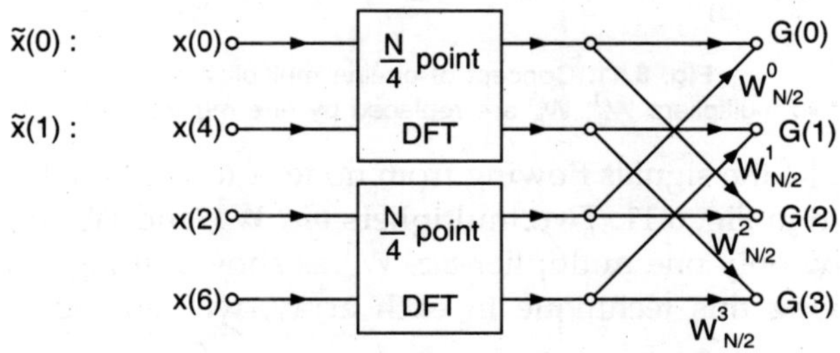

Fig. 6.8. Flow graph of the decimation-in-time decomposition of an *N*/4 point DFT computations

A 2-point DFT of, say, two samples $x(0)$ and $x(4)$ defined as $\tilde{x}(0)$, $\tilde{x}(1)$ is

$$\tilde{X}(0) = \sum_{i=0}^{1} \tilde{x}(i)\, W_2^{i.0} = x(0) + x(4)$$

$$\tilde{X}(1) = \sum_{i=0}^{1} \tilde{x}(i)\,.\, W_2^{i.1}$$

$$= x(0) + x(4)\,.\,W_2^{\,1}$$

$$= x(0) + x(4)\, e^{j2\pi.1/2}$$

$$= x(0) - x(4)$$

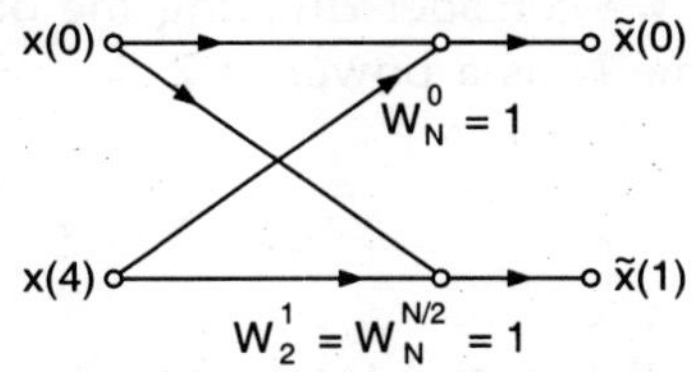

Fig. 6.9. Flow graph of a two-point DFT

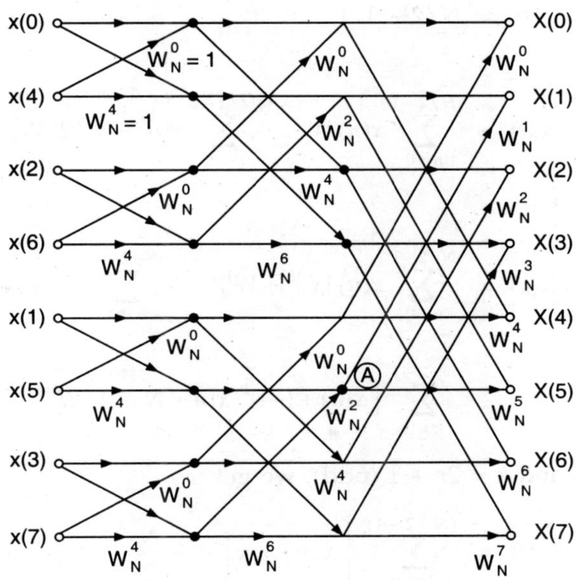

Fig. 6.10. Flow graph of complete decimation-in-time decomposition of an eight-point DFT computation (without on-line multiplication)

For the more general case with N as a power of 2, with $N = 2^v$, v an integer greater than 3, we go on decomposing the DFT into $N/2, N/4, N/8, \ldots$ point DFTs, till we arrive at a two point DFTs, till we arrive at a two point DFT. A 2-point DFT is shown in Fig. 6.9.

In Fig. 6.10, each stage has 8 (*i.e.*, N) multiplications. This can be reduce to half as follows:

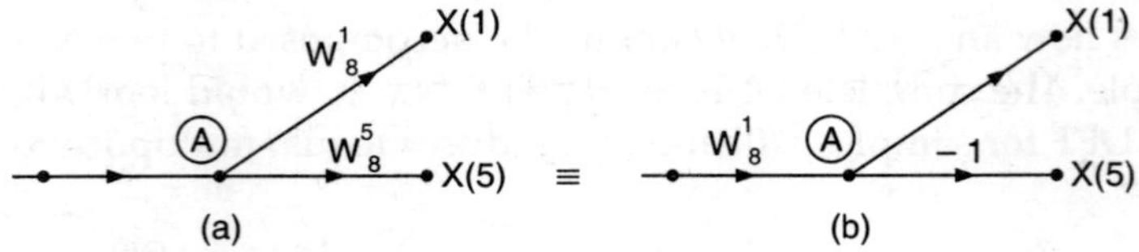

Fig. 6.11. Concept of on-line multiplication.
In Fig. (*a*), two multipliers W_8^1, W_8^5 are replaced by one multiplier of W_8^1, in Fig. (*b*).

Consider, for example, the signals flowing from node A towards $X(1)$ and $X(5)$ output nodes, in Fig. 6.10, and redrawn in Fig. 6.11. Two multipliers *viz.* W_8^1, and W_5^1 are needed in Fig. 6.11(*a*). These can be replaced by only one multiplier *viz.* W_8^1 as shown in Fig. 6.11(*b*), without affecting the function. By following this technique in each array, we can reduce the total number of multipliers from $N \,.\, v$ to $\dfrac{N}{2} \,.\, v$ to compute DFT and FFT algorithm.

6.7.3 Decimation-in Frequency FFT Algorithm (DIF-FFT)

Here, we consider dividing the output sequence, $X(k)$, into smaller and smaller subsequences. Assume N as a power of 2.

$$X(k) = \sum_{n=0}^{(N/2)-1} x(n)\, W_N^{nk} + \sum_{n=N/2}^{N-1} x(n)\, W_N^{nk} \qquad \ldots(6.85b)$$

In the second term, put $n = n' + N/2$ *i.e.*, put $n' = n - N/2$

$\therefore$ when $n = N/2$, $n' = 0$

when $n = N - 1$, $n' = N/2 - 1$

$\therefore$ we get:

$$X(k) = \sum_{n=0}^{N/2-1} x(n)\, W_N^{nk} + \sum_{n'=0}^{N/2-1} x(n' + N/2)\, W_N^{(n'+N/2)k} \qquad \ldots(6.86)$$

Dropping dashes we have:

$$X(k) = \sum_{n=0}^{N/2-1} x(n)\, W_N^{nk} + W_N^{(N/2)k} \sum_{n=0}^{N/2-1} x(n + N/2)\, W_N^{nk} \qquad \ldots(6.87)$$

$$= \sum_{n=0}^{N/2-1} \left[x(n) + (-1)^k\, x(n + N/2) \right] W_N^{nk} \quad (\because \;\; {W_N}^{N/2} = -1) \ldots(6.88)$$

Taking $k = 2r$ (even) and $k = 2r + 1$ (odd), we get

$$X(2r) = \sum_{n=0}^{(N/2-1)} \left[x(n) + x\left(n + \frac{N}{2} \right) \right] W_N^{2rn}, \text{ when } k = 2r$$

$$= \underbrace{\sum_{n=0}^{(N/2-1)} \left[x(n) + x\left(n + \frac{N}{2}\right) \right]}_{\triangleq g(n)} W_{N/2}^{rn} \qquad \ldots(6.89)$$

$$X(2r+1) = \sum_{n=0}^{N/2-1} \left[x(n) - x\left(n + \frac{N}{2}\right) \right] W_N^n \, W_N^{2rn}, \text{ when } k = 2r+1$$

$$= \underbrace{\sum_{n=0}^{N/2-1} \left[x(n) - x\left(n + \frac{N}{2}\right) \right]}_{\substack{\triangleq h(n) \\ r = 0, 1, 2, \ldots, (N/2-1)}} W_{N/2}^{rn} \cdot \underbrace{W_N^n} \qquad \ldots(6.90)$$

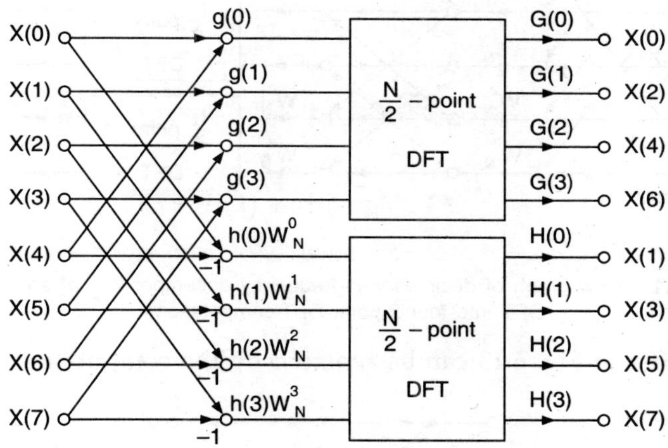

Fig. 6.12. Flow graph of the decimation-in-frequency decomposition of an *N*-point DFT computation into two *N*/2-point DFT computations (*N* = 8).

Equations (6.89) and (6.90) are clearly $N/2$-point DFT's. In the case of (6.89), the input sequence is the sum of the first half and the second half *viz.* $x(n) + x\left(n + \frac{N}{2}\right)$. In the case of (6.90), the input sequence is the product of W_N^n and the difference of the first half and the second half *viz.* $\left[x(n) - x\left(n + \frac{N}{2}\right) \right] W_N{}^n$. Thus, we first compute the sequences

$$g(n) \triangleq x(n) + x\left(n + \frac{N}{2}\right) \qquad \ldots(6.91)$$

and

$$h(n) \triangleq x(n) - x\left(n + \frac{N}{2}\right) \qquad \ldots(6.92)$$

The DFT is then obtained as shown in the above Fig. 6.12.

Since, $N = 2^v$, we can go on dividing N by 2. *i.e.*, it is feasible to compute the $N/2$-point DFT's by two $N/4$-point DFT's, where one $N/4$-point DFT would compute the even numbered and the other $N/4$-point DFT would compute the odd-numbered output points of the $N/2$ DFT.

The flow chart for 8-point DFT, when 2-$N/2$ point DFT's are realized by 4-$N/4$ point DFT's is as shown in Fig. 6.13.

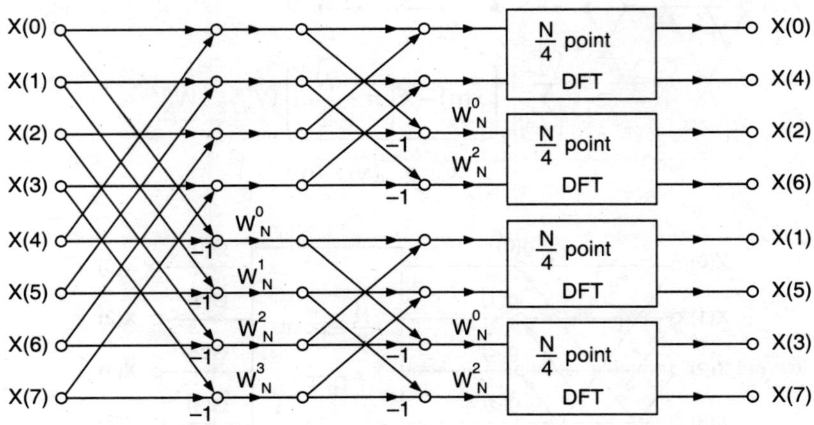

Fig. 6.13. Flow graph of decimation-in-frequency decomposition of an 8-point DFT into four 2-point DFT-computations.

The two-point DFT's in Fig. 6.13 can be replaced by the computation shown in Fig. 6.14.

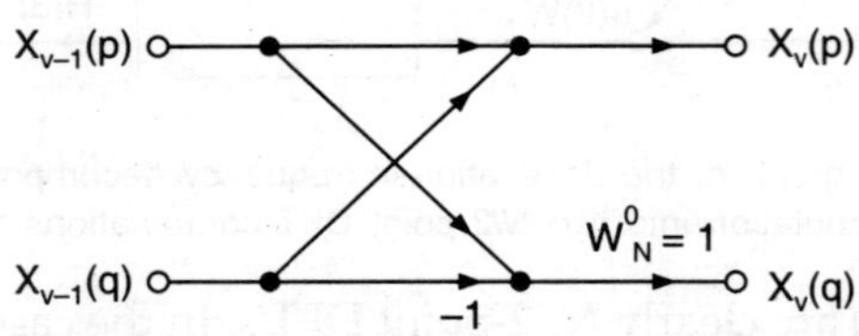

Fig. 6.14. Flow graph of a typical two-point DFT as required in the last stage of decimation-in-frequency decomposition.

Figure 6.15 shows the overall flow graph of complete DIF decomposition of an 8-point DFT computation. It is relevant to add that Fig. 6.15 (DIF-FFT) can be obtained by transposition of Fig. 6.10 (DIT-FFT) and vice versa.

Saving in Computation time for computing the DFT by FFT Algorithm

As $N = 2^v$, there are v number of array stages in FFT algorithm, both in DIT-FFT and DIF-FFT. Hence, there are $v \cdot N/2$ total complex multiplications compared to N^2 as given in (6.77). A comparison, as follows will convince about the superiority and efficiency of FFT algorithm.

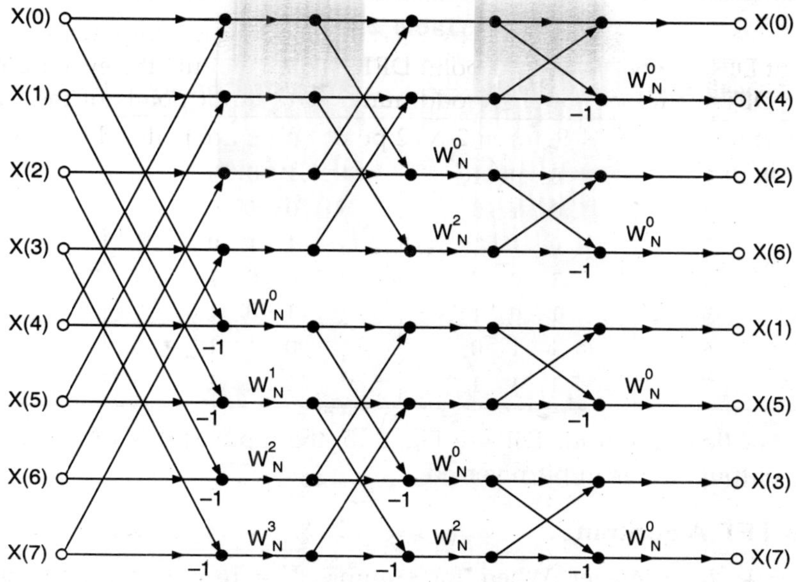

Fig. 6.15. Flow graph of complete decimation-in-frequency decomposition of an 8-point DFT computation (N = 8, v = 3 arrays)

Assuming a computer system performing 10^6 multiplications per second, computation times are as in Table 6.3.

Table 6.3. Computation Comparison

S.No.	*Operation*	*Direct Method*	*FFT Algorithm*	*Time Taken*		
				N	*Direct*	*By FFT*
1.	Real Multiplications	$4N^2$	$2N \log_2 N$	$N = 10^5$ $N = 10^6$	11.2 hrs 46 days	3.3 seconds 40 seconds
2.	Real Additions	$N(4N - 2)$ $\approx 4N^2$	$4N \log_2 N$			

It will be seen that FFT algorithm is far superior and efficient for computation of DFT coefficients $X(k)$ when N is large.

To perform the computations for various butterflies used in the FFTs, the shuffling of input sequence $x(n)$ takes place in decimation-in-time. In Fig. 6.10, note that the input $x(n)$ to the first array is $x(0)$, $x(4)$, $x(2)$, $x(6)$, $x(1)$, $x(5)$, $x(3)$ and $x(7)$ from top node to the bottom node. However, the outputs $X(k)$ appear in proper order *viz.* $X(0)$, $X(1)$, $X(2)$, $X(3)$, $X(4)$, $X(5)$, $X(6)$ and $X(7)$. The ordering that results in the input $x(n)$ results corresponding to a bit-reversed indexing of the input sequence. In other words, if the index n is written in binary form, the order in which the input sequence $x(n)$ is accessed is found by reading the binary representation for n in reverse order as shown in Table 6.4.

Table 6.4.

Number (n)	*Binary*	*Bit-reversed Binary*	*n′*
0	0 0 0	0 0 0	0
1	0 0 1	1 0 0	4
2	0 1 0	0 1 0	2
3	0 1 1	1 1 0	6
4	1 0 0	0 0 1	1
5	1 0 1	1 0 1	5
6	1 1 0	0 1 1	3
7	1 1 1	1 1 1	7

For the case of flow graph for DIF-see Fig. 6.15, the input $x(n)$ is in normal sequence $x(0)$, $x(1)$, ..., but the output $X(k)$ is in bit reversed.

6.7.4 Radix 4 FFT Algorithm

In this FFT, $N = 4^L$, L an integer. When, for example, $N = 16 = 4^2$, the given sequence $x(n)$ is decimated into four sequences of length $N/4$ each.

Example: $x(n) = \{\underset{\uparrow}{0}, 1, 0, 1, 0, 1, 0, 1, 0, 1, 0, 1, 0, 1, 0, 1\}$

$$X(k) = \sum_{n=0}^{3} x(4n)\, W_{16}^{4nk} + \sum_{n=0}^{3} x(4n+1)\, W_{16}^{(4n+1)k} + \sum_{n=0}^{3} x(4n+2)\, W_{16}^{(4n+2)k} + \sum_{n=0}^{3} x(4n+3)\, W_{16}^{(4n+3)k}$$

$$= \underbrace{\sum_{n=0}^{3} x(4n)\, W_{16}^{4nk}}_{X_1(k)} + W_{16}^{k} \underbrace{\sum_{n=0}^{3} x(4n+1)\, W_{16}^{4nk}}_{X_2(k)} + W_{16}^{2k} \underbrace{\sum_{n=0}^{3} x(4n+2)\, W_{16}^{4nk}}_{X_3(k)} + W_{16}^{3k} \underbrace{\sum_{n=0}^{3} x(4n+3)\, W_{16}^{4nk}}_{X_4(k)}$$

$$\boxed{X(k) \triangleq X_1(k) + W_{16}^{k}\, X_2(k) + W_{16}^{2k}\, X_3(k) + W_{16}^{3k}\, X_4(k)} \qquad \ldots(6.93)$$

where $$X_1(k) = \sum_{n=0}^{3} x(4n)\, W_{16}^{4nk} = x(0) + x(4)\, W_{16}^{4k} + x(8)\, W_{16}^{8k} + x(12)\, W_{16}^{12k}$$

$$X_2(k) = \sum_{n=0}^{3} x(4n+1)\, W_{16}^{4nk} = x(1) + x(5)\, W_{16}^{4k} + x(9)\, W_{16}^{8k} + x(13)\, W_{16}^{12k}$$

$$X_3(k) = \sum_{n=0}^{3} x(4n+2)\, W_{16}^{4nk} = x(2) + x(6)\, W_{16}^{4k} + x(10)\, W_{16}^{8k} + x(14)\, W_{16}^{12k}$$

and $$X_4(k) = \sum_{n=0}^{3} x(4n+3)\, W_{16}^{4nk} = x(3) + x(7)\, W_{16}^{4k} + x(11)\, W_{16}^{8k} + x(15)\, W_{16}^{12k}$$

Also, note that $X_i(k)$ is periodic in k with period $\frac{N}{4}$, (being 4 here, as $N = 16$)

$$\therefore \quad X(0) = X_1(0) + X_2(0) + X_3(0) + X_4(0)$$
$$X(1) = X_1(1) + W_{16}^1 X_2(1) + W_{16}^2 X_3(1) + W_{16}^3 X_4(1)$$
$$X(2) = X_1(2) + W_{16}^2 X_2(2) + W_{16}^4 X_3(2) + W_{16}^6 X_4(2)$$
$$X(3) = X_1(3) + W_{16}^3 X_2(3) + W_{16}^6 X_3(3) + W_{16}^9 X_4(3)$$
$$X(4) = X_1(4) + W_{16}^4 X_2(4) + W_{16}^8 X_3(4) + W_{16}^{12} X_4(4)$$
$$= X_1(0) + W_{16}^4 X_2(0) + W_{16}^8 X_3(0) + W_{16}^{12} X_4(0) \qquad (\because \; X_i(4) = X_i(0))$$
$$X(5) = X_1(5) + W_{16}^5 X_2(5) + W_{16}^{10} X_3(5) + W_{16}^{15} X_4(5)$$
$$= X_1(1) + W_{16}^5 X_2(1) + W_{16}^{10} X_3(1) + W_{16}^{15} X_4(1)$$

Similarly,

$$X(6) = X_1(2) + W_{16}^6 X_2(2) + W_{16}^{12} X_3(2) + W_{16}^{18} X_4(2)$$
$$X(7) = X_1(3) + W_{16}^7 X_2(3) + W_{16}^{14} X_3(3) + W_{16}^{21} X_4(3)$$
$$X(8) = X_1(0) + W_{16}^8 X_2(0) + W_{16}^{16} X_3(0) + W_{16}^{24} X_4(0) \qquad (\because \; X_i(8) = X_i(0))$$
$$X(9) = X_1(1) + W_{16}^9 X_2(1) + W_{16}^{18} X_3(1) + W_{16}^{27} X_4(1)$$
$$X(10) = X_1(2) + W_{16}^{10} X_2(2) + W_{16}^{20} X_3(2) + W_{16}^{30} X_4(2)$$
$$X(11) = X_1(3) + W_{16}^{11} X_2(3) + W_{16}^{22} X_3(3) + W_{16}^{33} X_4(3)$$
$$X(12) = X_1(0) + W_{16}^{12} X_2(0) + W_{16}^{24} X_3(0) + W_{16}^{36} X_4(0)$$
$$X(13) = X_1(1) + W_{16}^{13} X_2(1) + W_{16}^{26} X_3(1) + W_{16}^{39} X_4(1)$$
$$X(14) = X_1(2) + W_{16}^{14} X_2(2) + W_{16}^{28} X_3(2) + W_{16}^{42} X_4(2)$$
$$X(15) = X_1(3) + W_{16}^{15} X_2(3) + W_{16}^{30} X_3(3) + W_{16}^{45} X_4(3)$$

As

$$X_1(k) = \sum_{n=0}^{3} x(4n)\, W_{16}^{4nk} = x(0) + x(4)W_{16}^{4k} + x(8)W_{16}^{8k} + x(12)W_{16}^{12}$$

$$\therefore \quad X_1(0) = x(0) + x(4) + x(8) + x(12)$$
$$X_1(1) = x(0) + x(4)W_{16}^{4} + x(8)W_{16}^{8} + x(12)W_{16}^{12}$$
$$X_1(2) = x(0) + x(4)W_{16}^{8} + x(8)W_{16}^{16} + x(12)W_{16}^{24}$$
$$X_1(3) = x(0) + x(4)W_{16}^{12} + x(8)W_{16}^{24} + x(12)W_{16}^{36}$$

The resulting flow graph, drawn partially, to illustrate the concept, of radix 4, $N = 16$ point FFT is shown in Fig. 6.16. Computation of $X(0)$, $X(4)$, $X(8)$ and $X(12)$ is shown in the flow graph. The digits on the branch lines correspond to W_{16} index power. For example, $12 \equiv W_{16}^{12}$ and $0 \equiv W_{16}^{0}$ and so on.

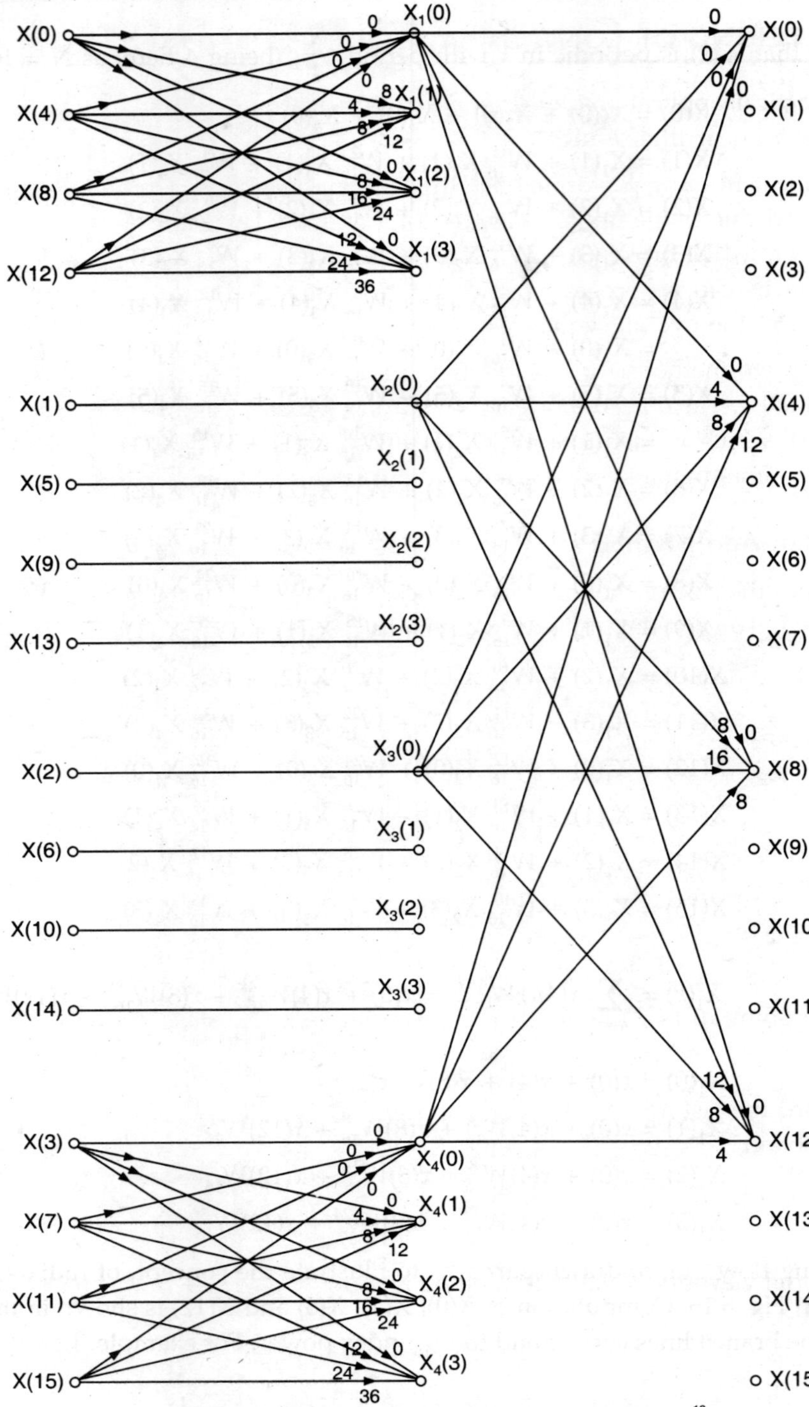

The digits online correspond to (W_{16}) index power. Thus $12 \equiv W_{16}^{12}$

Fig. 6.16. Flow graph for DIT-FFT for radix 4, N = 16

6.8 FILTERING OF LONG DATA SEQUENCES

In many practical applications, we come across very long data sequences, which need to be processed by a linear filter $h(n)$.

As the linear filtering performed *via.* the DFT involves operations on a block of data, which must be limited due to the limited memory of a digital computer, therefore, a long input signal sequence $x(n)$ must be broken to fixed-size blocks prior to processing. As the filtering is linear, successive blocks can be processed one at a time (*via.* DFT) and the output blocks are fixed together to form the overall sequence $y(n)$.

There are two methods for linear filtering a long sequence on a block-by-block basis using the DFT and IDFT. The output blocks $y_1(n)$, $y_2(n)$, ..., are fitted together to form an overall output sequence $y(n)$, which is identical (same) to the sequence obtained if the long block had been processed *via.* time-domain convolution without partitioning $x(n)$ into blocks.

6.8.1 Overlap-Add Method

In this method, the size of the input data block $x(n)$ is L points, the size of the DFT and IDFT is $N = L + M - 1$. To each data block we append $M - 1$ zeros and compute N-point DFT.

Hence,
$$x_1(n) = \left\{x(0), x(1), ..., x(L-1), \underbrace{0, 0, ..., 0}_{M-1 \text{ Zeros}}\right\} \quad ...(6.94)$$

$$x_2(n) = \left\{x(L), x(L+1), ..., x(2L-1), \underbrace{0, 0, ..., 0}_{M-1 \text{ Zeros}}\right\} \quad ...(6.95)$$

$$x_3(n) = \left\{x(2L), x(2L+1), ..., x(3L-1), \underbrace{0, 0, ..., 0}_{M-1 \text{ Zeros}}\right\} \quad ...(6.96)$$

and so on. N-point DFTs $H(k)$ and $X_m(k)$ are multiplied, and by IDFT, we compute

$$y_m(n) = \{y_m(0), y_m(1), ..., y_m(N-1)\} \quad ...(6.97)$$

We discard the last $M - 1$ points of $y_m(n)$ and add these to the first $M - 1$ points of $y_{m+1}(n)$. Finally, we obtain

$$y(n) = \{y_1(0), y_1(1), ... y_1(L-1), (y_1(L) + y_2(0)), (y_1(L+1) + y_2(1)), ..., (y_1(N-1) + y_2(M-1)), ...\} \quad ...(6.98)$$

The pictorial view of overlap-add method is shown in Fig. 6.17 followed by a solved example on this method.

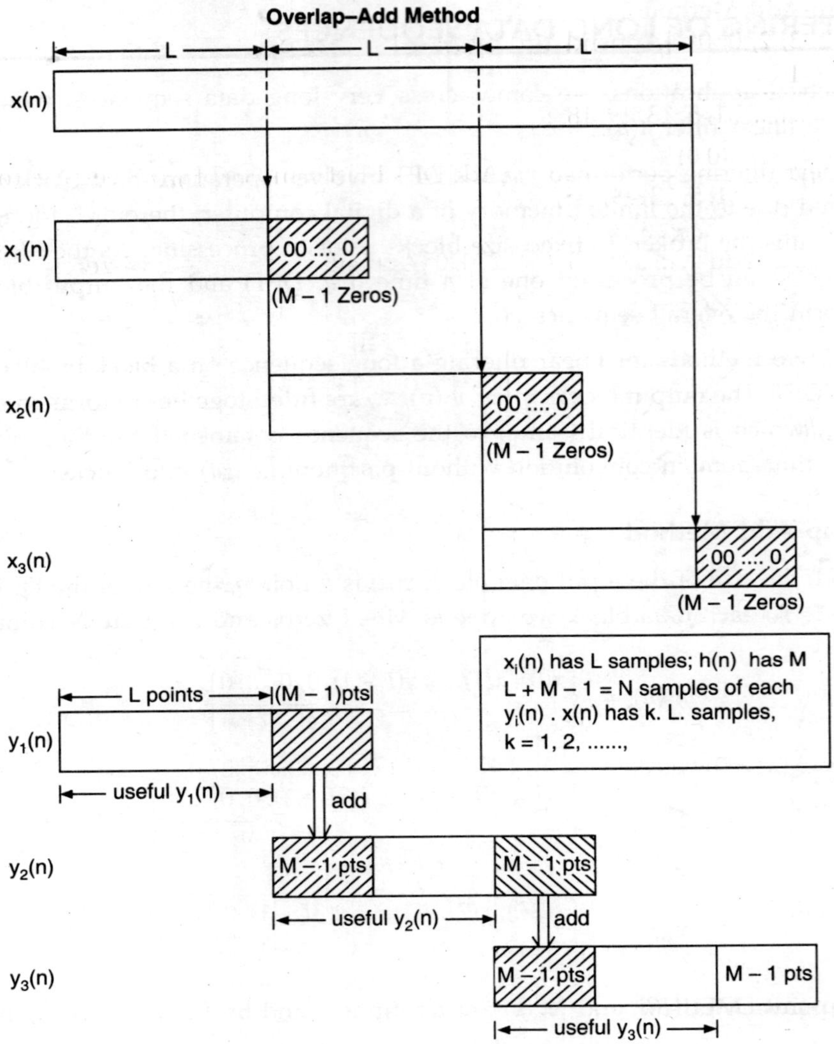

Rule: $x_i(n) = L$ samples of $x(n)$ followed by $(M - 1)$ Zeros

$y_i(n) = x_i(n) * h(n) \equiv L + M - 1$ samples

"useful $y_i(n)$" = add **last (M – 1) points** of $y_{i-1}(n)$ to first $(M - 1)$ points of $y_i(n)$. This is "useful $y_i(n)$". Retain first L samples of "useful $y_i(n)$" and discard its last $M - 1$ samples.

Fig. 6.17. Linear FIR filtering by overlap-add method

EXAMPLE: *Compute convolution of sequence x(n) and h(n) by Overlap-Add method.*

SOLUTION: Given $x(n) = \{\overbrace{1, 2, 3, 2}^{L=4}, \overbrace{3, 4, 1, 2}^{L=4}, \overbrace{0, 1, 2, 2}^{L=4}\}$ = 12 samples

$h(n) = \{1, 3, 4\}$ = 3 samples

Choose $L = 4$ and here $M = 3$

By ordinary method: $x(n) = 1, 2, 3, 2, 3, 4, 1, 2, 0, 1, 2, 2$

$h(-n) = 4, 3, 1$

$$x(n) * h(n) = \underbrace{1, 5, 13, 19}_{\text{OK}-1}, \underbrace{21, 21, 25, 21}_{\text{OK}-2}, \underbrace{10, 9, 5, 12}_{\text{OK}-3}, \underbrace{14, 8}_{\substack{=14 \text{ samples} \\ \text{OK}-4}} \quad \ldots(A)$$

By Overlap-Add Method

$x_1(n) = 1, 2, 3, 2, 0, 0$ [Append $x(n)$ by $M - 1 = 2$ zeros]

$h(-n) = 4, 3, 1$

$y_1(n) = \ldots\ldots 1, 5, 13, 19, 18, 8$

"Useful $y_1(n)$" ...... (0 0) [Add $M - 1$ last samples of $y_0(n)$, being zero here]

$\underbrace{1, 5, 13, 19}_{\text{OK}-1}, (18, 8)$

$x_2(n) = \ldots\ldots$ add $\ldots\ldots$ 3, 4, 1, 2, 0, 0 [Append $x(n)$ by $M - 1 = 2$ zeros]

$h(-n) = \ldots\ldots$ 4, 3, 1

$y_2(n) = \ldots\ldots$ 3, 13, 25, 21, 10, 8

"Useful $y_2(n)$" ...... (18, 8) [Add $M - 1$ last samples of $y_1(n)$]

$\underbrace{21, 21, 25, 21}_{\text{OK}-2}, (10, 8)$

$x_3(n)$ ...... 0, 1, 2, 2, 0, 0 (Add $M - 1 = 2$ zeros at end)

$h(-n)$ ...... add 4, 3, 1

$x_3(n) * h(n) = y_3(n) = \ldots\ldots 0, 1, 5, 12, 14, 8$

(10, 8) [Add $M - 1$ last samples of $y_2(n)$]

"Useful $y_3(n)$" ...... $\underbrace{10, 9, 5, 12}_{\text{OK}-3}, (14, 8)$

$y_4(n)$ (since $x_4(n) = 0$) has all zeros add 0, 0, 0, 0, 0, 0

"Useful $y_4(n)$" (14, 8)

$\underbrace{(14, 8)}_{\text{OK}-4}$

Taking all OK – 1 to OK – 4, we get

$$y(n) = \{1, 5, 13, 19, 21, 21, 25, 21, 10, 9, 5, 12, 14, 8\} \text{ as in } (A)$$

6.8.2 Overlap-save Method

Let
$$h(n) = \{h(0), h(1), ..., h(M - 1)\} \text{ i.e., of length } M$$
$$x(n) = \{x(0), x(1), ...\} \text{ has } k \,.\, L \text{ samples}$$

Define
$$N = L + M - 1$$

We compute N point DFT of each block (after overlap) of data $x_1(n)$, $x_2(n)$, ... Compute $H(k) \,.\, X_m(k)$

Call
$$\hat{Y}_m(k) = H(k) \,.\, X_m(k),\ k = 0, 1, ..., N - 1$$
$$\text{IDFT} = [\hat{Y}_m(k)] = \hat{y}_m(n) = \{\hat{y}_m(0),\ \hat{y}_m(1),\ \ldots\ \hat{y}(N-1)\} \quad \ldots(6.99)$$

and discard first $M - 1$ points of each $\hat{y}_m(n)$ and retain last L points of $\hat{y}_m(n)$. Formulate $x_m(n)$ as follows:

$$x_1(n) = \left\{\underbrace{0, 0, ..., 0}_{M-1 \text{ points}}, \underbrace{x(0), x(1), ..., x(L-1)}_{L \text{ first data points}}\right\} \quad \ldots(6.100)$$

$$x_2(n) = \left\{\underbrace{x(L-M+1), ..., x(L-1)}_{M-1 \text{ data points from } x_1(n)}, \underbrace{x(L), ...\ x(2L-1)}_{L \text{ new data points}}\right\} \quad \ldots(6.101)$$

$$x_3(n) = \{\underbrace{x(2L-M+1), ..., x(2L-1)}_{M-1 \text{ data points from } x_2(n)}, \underbrace{x(2L), ...\, x(3L-1)}_{L \text{ new data points}}\} \quad ...(6.102)$$

and so forth till last (k^{th}) block of $L - 1$ data points of $x(n)$ are covered. The pictorial view is shown in Fig. 6.18, followed by a solved example on this method.

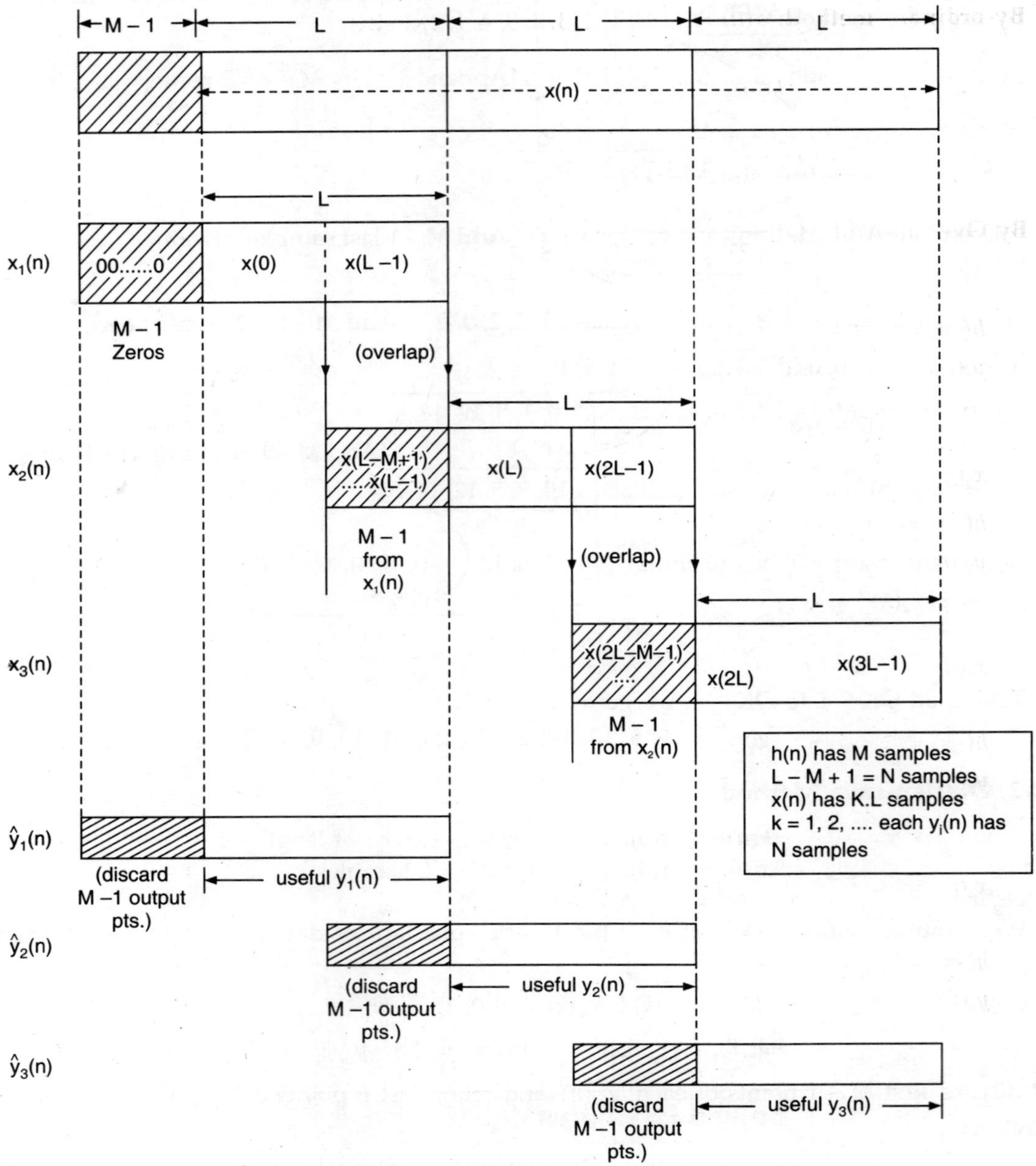

Rule: For $x_i(n)$ = last $M - 1$ samples of $x_{i-1}(n)$ followed by L samples of $x(n)$

$y_i(n)$ = convolution of $x_i(n)$ and filter's impulse response $h(n)$ equalling $x_i(n) * h(n)$

"useful" $y_i(n)$ = Discard first $M - 1$ output points of each $y_i(n)$ and retain its remaining L points.

Fig. 6.18. Linear FIR filtering by overlap-save method

EXAMPLE: *Compute convolution of sequence x(n) and h(n) by overlap-save method.*

SOLUTION: Given $x(n) = \{\overbrace{1, 2, 3, 2}^{L=4}, \overbrace{3, 4, 1, 2}^{L=4}, \overbrace{0, 1, 2, 2}^{L=4}\}$ = 12 samples

$h(n) = \{1, 3, 4\}$ = 3 samples ("M" samples)

Choose $L = 4$, and here $M = 3$

By ordinary method: $x(n) = 1, 2, 3, 2, 3, 4, 1, 2, 2 1 2 2$
↑

$h(-n) = 4, 3, 1$
↗

$x(n) * h(n) = \underbrace{1, 5, 13, 19}, \underbrace{21, 21, 25, 21}, \underbrace{10, 9, 5, 12}, 14, 8$ = 14 samples

By Overlap-Add Method: Here, $L = 4$, $M = 3$, $N = L + M - 1 = 6$

$x_1(n) = 0, 0, 1, 2, 3, 2$ [Add $(M-1)$ zeros before $x(n)$ to get $x_1(n)$]

$h(-n) = 4, 3, 1$ Overlap

$y_1(n) = 0, 0, 1, 5, 13, 19$ Compute only N outputs $= L + M - 1 = N = 6$
[Discard first $M - 1 = 2$ samples of $y_1(n)$]

↗ Discard

$x_2(n) = 3, 2, 3, 4, 1, 2$ [Overlap $M - 1) = 2$ of $x_1(n)$ to get $x_2(n)$]

$h(-n) = 4, 3, 1$ Overlap

$y_2(n) = 3, 11, 21, 21, 25, 21$ (Discard first $M - 1$ samples of $y_2(n)$]

↗ Discard

Overlap

$x_3(n) = 1, 2, 0, 1, 2, 2$ [Overlap $M - 1 = 2$ samples of $x_2(n)$ to get $x_3(n)$]

$h(-n) = 4, 3, 1$

$y_3(n) = 1, 5, 10, 9, 5, 12$ [Discard first $M - 1$ samples of $y_3(n)$]

↗ Discard

$x_4(n) = 2, 2, 0, 0, 0, 0$ [Overlap $M - 1 = 2$ samples of $x_3(n)$ to get $x_4(n)$]

$h(-n) = 4, 3, 1$

$y_4(n) = 2, 8, 14, 8, 0, 0$ [Discard first $M - 1$ samples of $y_4(n)$]

↗ Discard

Solved Examples on DFT, IDFT, FFT

EXAMPLE 6.1: *Find the DFT of $x_p(n)$ defined as*

$$x_p(n) = \begin{cases} 1, & 2 \le n \le 6 \\ 0, & n = 0, 1, 7, 8, 9 \end{cases}$$

Assume N = 10.

SOLUTION:

$$X(k) = \sum_{n=0}^{N-1} x_p(n)\, e^{-j2\pi nk/N}$$

$$= \sum_{n=0}^{9} x_p(n)\, e^{-j2\pi nk/10} = \sum_{n=2}^{6} 1 \,.\, e^{-j2\pi nk/10}$$

$$= \frac{e^{-j2\pi 2k/10}\,(1 - e^{-j2\pi 5k/10})}{(1 - e^{-j2\pi k/10})}$$

$$= e^{j\pi 4k/10} \,.\, e^{-j\pi 5k/10}\,(e^{+j\pi 5k/10} - e^{-j\pi 5k/10}) / e^{-j\pi k/10}\,(e^{j\pi k/10} - e^{-j\pi k/10})$$

$$= e^{-j\pi k\,(4+5-1)/10} \,.\, \left(\sin \frac{\pi k}{2}\right) \Big/ \left(\sin \frac{\pi k}{10}\right)$$

$$= e^{-j\frac{4}{5}k\pi} \,.\, \frac{\sin (k\pi/2)}{\sin (k\pi/10)}$$

$\therefore$ $$\theta(k) = -\frac{4}{5}k\pi \;:\; \text{(Phase spectrum)}$$

$$A(k) = |X(k)| = \frac{\sin(k\pi/2)}{\sin(k\pi/10)} \;:\; \text{(Magnitude spectrum)} \quad \textbf{Ans.}$$

EXAMPLE 6.2: *Determine the circular convolution of the sequences*

$$x_1(n) = \{\underset{\uparrow}{1}, \underbrace{2, 3, 1}\},\; x_2(n) = \{\underset{\uparrow}{4}, \underbrace{3, 2, 2}\}.$$

SOLUTION: Here $N = 4$.

We know that in circular convolution

$$y(n) = x_1(n) \, ⓝ \, x_2(n) = x_1(n) \, ④ \, x_2(n), \text{ here } N = 4$$

$$= \sum_{m=0}^{3} x_1(m) \,.\, x_2\,[(n-m)]_N \quad N = 4 \text{ here}$$

$\therefore$ $$y(0) = \sum_{m=0}^{3} x_1(m)\; x_2\,[(0-m)]_4 \qquad [\because x_2[(-1)]_4 = x_2(3),\; x_2[(-2)]_4 = x_2(2),\; x_2[(-3)]_4 = x_2(1)]$$

$$= x_1(0) \,.\, x_2(0) + x_1(1) \,.\, x_2(3) + x_1(2) \,.\, x_2(2) + x_1(3) \,.\, x_2(1)$$

$$= 1 \times 4 + 2 \times 2 + 3 \times 2 + 1 \times 3 = 4 + 4 + 6 + 3 = 17$$

$$y(1) = \sum_{m=0}^{3} x_1(m)\, x_2[(1-m)]_4 \qquad [\because x_2[(-1)]_4 = x_2(3) \text{ and } x_2[(-2)]_4 = x_2(2)]$$

$$= x_1(0) \,.\, x_2(1) + x_1(1)\, x_2(0) + x_1(2)\, x_2(3) + x_1(3) \,.\, x_2(2)$$

$$= 1 \times 3 + 2 \times 4 + 3 \times 2 + 1 \times 2 = 3 + 8 + 6 + 2 = 19$$

$$y(2) = \sum_{m=0}^{3} x_1(m)\, x_2((2-m))_4$$

$$= x_1(0)\,.\,x_2(2) + x_1(1)\, x_2(1) + x_1(2)\, x_2(0) + x_1(3)\, x_2(3)$$
$$= 1 \times 2 + 2 \times 3 + 3 \times 4 + 1 \times 2 = 2 + 6 + 12 + 2 = 22$$

$$y(3) = \sum_{m=0}^{3} x_1(m)\,.\,x_2((3-m))_4$$

$$= x_1(0)\, x_2(3) + x_1(1)\, x_2(2) + x_1(2)\, x_2(1) + x_1(3)\, x_2(0)$$
$$= 1 \times 2 + 2 \times 2 + 3 \times 3 + 1 \times 4 = 2 + 4 + 9 + 4 = 19$$

$\therefore$ $\underset{\text{Circular}}{y(n)} = \{\underset{\uparrow}{17}, 19, 22, 19\}$ **Ans.**

Note: $x_1(n) * x_2(n) \neq x_1(n) \; Ⓝ \; x_2(n)$

Here $x_1(n) * x_2(n) = \sum_{m=0}^{3} x_1(m)\, x_2(n-m)$ $\overset{n \to 0\;1\;2\;3\;|\;4\;5\;6}{\{\underset{\uparrow}{4}, 11, 20, 19, | 13, 8, 2\}}$ $\neq y(n)$ found above.**

EXAMPLE 6.3: *Compute (a) linear convolution of two given sequences by matrix representation (b) also, find circular convolution (c) deduce circular convolution from linear convolution.*

SOLUTION: Given $x_1(n) = \{\underset{\uparrow}{1}, 1, 2, 2\}$, $x_2 = \{\underset{\uparrow}{1}, 2, 3, 4\}$

(*a*) Write $x_1(n)$ as a row and $x_2(n)$ as a column
Row 1 is $x_1(n) \times x_1(0)$
Row 2 is $x_1(n) \times x_2(1)$
Row 3 is $x_1(n) \times x_2(2)$
Row 4 is $x_1(n) \times x_2(3)$
Draw diagonal lines as shown.
Add elements in diagonal linear, we get:

	$x_2(n)$ \ $x_1(n)$	1	1	2	2
row 1	$x_2(0) = 1$	1	1	2	2
row 2	$x_2(1) = 2$	2	2	4	4
row 3	$x_2(2) = 3$	3	3	6	6
row 4	$x_2(3) = 4$	4	4	8	8

$x_3(n) = x_1(n) * x_2(n) = \{1, 3, 7, 13, 14, 14, 8\}$ **Ans.**

(*b*) $x_1(n) \; Ⓝ \; x_2\,(n) = \sum_{k=0}^{3} x_1(k)\, x_2((n-k))_4 \triangleq x_4(n)$

$\therefore$
$$x_4(0) = x_1(0)\, x_2(0) + x_1(1)\, x_2(3) + x_1(2)\, x_2(2) + x_1(3)\, x_2(1)$$
$$= 1 \times 1 + 1 \times 4 + 2 \times 3 + 2 \times 2 = 15$$
$$x_4(1) = x_1(0)\,.\,x_2(1) + x_1(1)\, x_2(0) + x_1\,(2)\, x_2(3) + x_1(3)\, x_2(2)$$
$$= 1 \times 2 + 1 \times 1 + 2 \times 4 + 2 \times 3 = 17$$
$$x_4(2) = x_1(0)\, x_2(2) + x_1(1)\, x_2(1) + x_1(2)\, x_2(0) + x_1(3)\, x_2(3)$$
$$= 1 \times 3 + 1 \times 2 + 2 \times 1 + 2 \times 4 = 15$$

**Note that: to get circular convolution from linear convolution, proceed as follows:
Add $y((n))_N$ terms of linear convolution $y(n)$ to get circular convolution. Here $y((4))_4 = y(0)$
$\therefore$ add 13 to 4 = 17. Similarly, 8 + 11 = 19; 2 + 20 = 22.

$$x_4(3) = x_1(0)\,x_2(3) + x_1(1)\,x_2(2) + x_1(2)\,x_2(1) + x_1(3)\,x_2(0)$$
$$= 1 \times 4 + 1 \times 3 + 2 \times 2 + 2 \times 1 = 13$$

$\therefore$ $x_4(n) = \{15, 17, 15, 13\}$ is the circular convolution.

(c) As $x_3(n) = \{1, 3, 7, 13, | 14, 14, 8\}$ $\Rightarrow$ $\{15, 17, 15, 13\}$ the circular convolution $x_3(n)$ **Ans.**

add add add

EXAMPLE 6.4: *(i) Find the linear convolution $x_1(n) * x_2(n)$ if*

$$x_1(n) = \{1, -1, -2, 3, -1\}, \text{ and } x_2(n) = \{1, 2, 3\}.$$

(ii) Deduce circular convolution from the linear convolution found above.

SOLUTION: *Linear convolution is determined by matrix*

$x_2(n)$ ↓ \ $x_1(n)$ →	1	−1	−2	3	−1
1	1	−1	−2	3	−1
2	2	−2	−4	6	−2
3	3	−3	−6	9	−3

$$x_1(n) * x_2(n) = \{1, 1, -1, -4, -1, 7, -3\}$$ **Ans.**

To find $x_1(n)$ ⑤ $x_2(n) = \{1, 1, -1, -4, -1, | 7, -3\} = \{8, -2, -1, -4, -1\}$ **Ans.**

Check: $x_1(n)$ Ⓝ $x_2(n)$

Let $x_2'(n) = \{1, 2, 3, 0, 0\}$ make 5 samples by zero padding

$$\begin{array}{c} x_1((-n))_5 \rightarrow \\ x_1(n) \downarrow \end{array} \begin{bmatrix} 1 & -1 & 3 & -2 & -1 \\ -1 & 1 & -1 & 3 & -2 \\ -2 & -1 & 1 & -1 & 3 \\ 3 & -2 & -1 & 1 & -1 \\ -1 & 3 & -2 & -1 & 1 \end{bmatrix} \times \overset{x'_2(n)}{\begin{bmatrix} 1 \\ 2 \\ 3 \\ 0 \\ 0 \end{bmatrix}} = \begin{bmatrix} 8 \\ -2 \\ -1 \\ -4 \\ -1 \end{bmatrix} \equiv \{8, -2, -1, -4, -1\}$$ **Ans.**

(Confirmed)

EXAMPLE 6.5: *Given $x_1(n) = \{1, 2, 2, 1\}$, $x_2(n) = \{1, 2, 3, 4\}$.*

Determine (i) $x_1(n) * x_2(n)$ (linear convolution)

(ii) $x_1(n)$ ④ $x_2(n)$ (circular convolution).

SOLUTION: (*i*) To find $x_1(n) * x_2(n)$

	1	2	3	4
1	1	2	3	4
2	2	4	6	8
2	2	4	6	8
1	1	2	3	4

$\therefore \quad x_1(n) * x_2(n) = \{1, 4, 9, 15, 16, 11, 4\}$ **Ans.**

(ii) $x_1(n)$ ④ $x_2(n) = \{1, 4, 9, 15, 16, 11, 4\}$

$= \{17, 15, 13, 15\}$ **Ans.**

Alternatively:

$$x_1((-n))_4 \rightarrow$$

$$x_1(n)\downarrow\begin{bmatrix} 1 & 1 & 2 & 2 \\ 2 & 1 & 1 & 2 \\ 2 & 2 & 1 & 1 \\ 1 & 2 & 2 & 1 \end{bmatrix} \times \begin{bmatrix} 1 \\ 2 \\ 3 \\ 4 \end{bmatrix} = \begin{bmatrix} 17 \\ 15 \\ 13 \\ 15 \end{bmatrix}$$

We have used: $x_1[(0)]_4 = x_1(0) = 1$
$x_1[(-1)]_4 = x_1(3) = 1$
$x_1[(-2)]_4 = x_1(2) = 2$
$x_1[(-3)]_4 = x_1(1) = 2$

$\therefore \quad x_1(n)$ ④ $x_2(n) = \{17, 15, 13, 15\}$ **Ans.**

EXAMPLE 6.6: *Determine the linear convolution $y(n) = x(n) * h(n)$ for $x(n) = \{1, 2, 3, 1\}$, and $h(n) = \{4, 3, 2, 2\}$ using circular convolution.*

SOLUTION: Linear convolution (by array) by direct method

x(n) \ h(n)	4	3	2	2
1	4	3	2	2
2	8	6	4	4
3	12	9	6	6
1	4	3	2	2

$$\Rightarrow \therefore \quad y(n) = x(n) * h(n) = \{\underset{\uparrow}{4}, 11, 20, 19, 13, 8, 2\}$$

[Linear convolution *via.* circular convolution.]

As $x(n)$ and $h(n)$ each is of length 4, therefore, $y(n)$ will be of length $4 + 4 - 1 = 7$. We add zeros to $x(n)$ and $h(n)$ to make each sequence equal to length 7.

$$x'(0) = \{\overset{x'(0)}{1} \quad \overset{x'(1)}{2} \quad \overset{x'(2)}{3} \quad \overset{x'(3)}{1} \quad \overset{x'(4)}{0} \quad \overset{x'(5)}{0} \quad \overset{x'(6)}{0}\},$$

and

$$h'(n) = \{\overset{h'(0)}{4}, \overset{h'(1)}{3}, \overset{h'(2)}{2}, \overset{h'(3)}{2}, \overset{h'(4)}{0}, \overset{h'(5)}{0}, \overset{h'(6)}{0}]$$

Then $\quad x'(n)$ ⑦ $h'(n) = x(n) * h(n)$

$$\rightarrow x'[(-n)]_7$$

$$\downarrow x'(n) \begin{bmatrix} 1 & 0 & 0 & 0 & 1 & 3 & 2 \\ 2 & 1 & 0 & 0 & 0 & 1 & 3 \\ 3 & 2 & 1 & 0 & 0 & 0 & 1 \\ 1 & 3 & 2 & 1 & 0 & 0 & 0 \\ 0 & 1 & 3 & 2 & 1 & 0 & 0 \\ 0 & 0 & 1 & 3 & 2 & 1 & 0 \\ 0 & 0 & 0 & 1 & 3 & 2 & 1 \end{bmatrix} \cdot \begin{bmatrix} 4 \\ 3 \\ 2 \\ 2 \\ 0 \\ 0 \\ 0 \end{bmatrix} = \begin{bmatrix} 4 \\ 11 \\ 20 \\ 19 \\ 13 \\ 8 \\ 2 \end{bmatrix}$$

$\therefore \quad y(n) = x(n) * h(n) = \{\underset{\uparrow}{4}, 11, 20, 19, 13, 8, 2\}$ as expected **Ans.**

Note $\quad x(n)$ ④ $h(n) = \{17, 19, 22, 19\}$ as obtained from $x(n) * h(n)$

EXAMPLE 6.7: *(a) Compute linear convolution of sequences $x_1(n)$ and $x_2(n)$ via circular convolution. Given* $x_1(n) = \{\underset{\uparrow}{1}, 2, 4\}$, $x_2(n) = \{\underset{\uparrow}{1}, 2, 3\}$.

(b) Compute circular convolution of $x_1(n)$ and $x_2(n)$ via. linear convolution.

SOLUTION: *(a)* Direct Linear Convolution

$x_1(n) \downarrow$ \ $x_2(n) \rightarrow$	1	2	3
1	1	2	3
2	2	4	6
4	4	8	12

$\equiv \{\underset{\uparrow}{1}, 4, 11, 14, 12\} = x_1(n) * x_2(n)$

Another Method to fixed $x_1(n) * x_2(n)$

$$
\begin{aligned}
ZT\,[x_1(n) * x_2(n)] &= X_1(z)\,.\,X_2(z) \\
&= [1 + 2z^{-1} + 4Z^{-2}]\,[1 + 2z^{-1} + 3z^{-2}] \\
&= [1 + 4z^{-1} + 11z^{-2} + 14z^{-3} + 12z].
\end{aligned}
$$

$\therefore \quad y(n) = \{\underset{\uparrow}{1}, 4, 11, 14, 12\}$ **Ans.**

(b) Direct Circular Convolution

$\rightarrow x_1((-n))_N$

$$
\begin{array}{c} \\ \downarrow \\ x_1(n) \end{array}
\begin{array}{ccc} x_1[(0)]_3 & x_1[(-1)]_3 & x_1[(-2)]_3 \\ \end{array}
\quad x_2[(n)]_3 \downarrow
$$

$$
\begin{bmatrix} 1 & 4 & 2 \\ 2 & 1 & 4 \\ 4 & 2 & 1 \end{bmatrix}
\begin{bmatrix} 1 \\ 2 \\ 3 \end{bmatrix}
=
\begin{bmatrix} 15 \\ 16 \\ 11 \end{bmatrix}
$$

$$
x_1(n) = \{\underset{\uparrow}{1}, 2, 4\} \quad (x_1(0)\;x_1(1)\;x_1(2)), \quad x_2 = \{\underset{\uparrow}{1}, 2, 3\}
$$

$N = 3$ here

$\therefore \quad x_1(n)$ ③ $x_2(n) = \{\underset{\uparrow}{15}, 16, 11\}$

Note that

$$
\begin{aligned}
x_1[(-n)]_N &= x_1(0) \text{ for } n = 0 \\
x_1[(-n)]_N &= x[(-1)]_3 \quad \text{for} \quad -n = -1 \\
&= x(2)
\end{aligned}
$$

$$x_1[(-n)]_N = x_1[(-2)]_3 \quad \text{for} \quad -n = -2$$
$$= x_1(1).$$

(c) Circular through linear Convolution

As $\quad x_1(n) * x_2(n) = \{1, 4, 11, 14, 12\}$

$\therefore \quad x_1(n) ③ x_2(n) = \{\underset{\uparrow}{15}, 16, 11\}$ **Ans.**

(d) Linear Convolution through Circular Convolution: Add zeros to make each sequence $= N_1 + N_2 - 1$

$$x_1(n) * x_2(n) = x_1'(n) ⑤ x_2'(n) \text{ where } x_1'(n) = \{\underset{\uparrow}{1}, 2, 4, 0, 0\},\ x'_2(n) = \{\underset{\uparrow}{1}, 2, 3, 0, 0\}$$

$\rightarrow x'_1((-n))_{N'}$

$$\therefore \quad x_1'(n) ⑤ x_2'(n) = \begin{array}{c} \\ \downarrow \\ x_1'(n) \end{array} \begin{bmatrix} x'_1((0))_5 & x'_1((-1))_5 & x'_1((-2))_5 & x'_1((-3))_5 & x'_1((-4))_5 \\ 1 & 0 & 0 & 4 & 2 \\ 2 & 1 & 0 & 0 & 4 \\ 4 & 2 & 1 & 0 & 0 \\ 0 & 4 & 2 & 1 & 0 \\ 0 & 0 & 4 & 2 & 1 \end{bmatrix} \times \begin{bmatrix} x_2'(n) \\ 1 \\ 2 \\ 3 \\ 0 \\ 0 \end{bmatrix}$$

$$= \begin{bmatrix} 1 \\ 4 \\ 11 \\ 14 \\ 12 \end{bmatrix} = \{\underset{\uparrow}{1}, 4, 11, 14, 12\}$$ **Ans.**

EXAMPLE 6.8: *(a) Find (i) linear convolution, (ii) circular convolution of two sequences*

$$x_1 = \{\underset{\uparrow}{1}, 2, 4\} \text{ and } x_2(n) = \{\underset{\uparrow}{1}, 2\}$$

(b) Find linear convolution of $x_1(n)$ and $x_2(n)$ via. circular convolution.

SOLUTION: (a) (i) Using matrix form

$$x_1(n) * x_2(n) = \{\underset{\uparrow}{1}, 4, 8, 8\}$$ **Ans.**

$$\text{length} = N_1 + N_2 - 1 = 3 + 2 - 1 = 4$$

$x_2(n)$ \ $x_1(n)$	1	2	3
1	1	2	4
2	2	4	8

$$\therefore \quad x_1(n) * x_2(n) = \{\underset{\uparrow}{1}, 4, 8, 8\}$$

(ii) If we assume $x_1(n) = \{\underset{\uparrow}{1}, 2, 4\}$ and $x_2'(n) = \{\underset{\uparrow}{1}, 2, 0\}$ Make $N_1 = N_2$ by zero padding

Then $\quad x_1(n) ③ x'_2(n) = \{(1 + 8), 4, 8\} = \{\underset{\uparrow}{9}, 4, 8\}$

(b) Linear Convolution *via.* Circular Convolution

As $N_1 + N_2 - 1 = 3 + 2 - 1 = 4$. We zero pad $x_1(n)$ and $x_2(n)$ to have total 4 samples (note this step). Hence revised $x_1(n)$ and $x_2(n)$ are as below

$$x_1(n) = \{\underset{\uparrow}{1}, 2, 4, 0\}\ ;\ x_2(n) = \{\underset{\uparrow}{1}, 2, 0, 0\}$$

Using above $x_1(n)$ and $x_2(n)$ to get circular convolution

$$y(n) = \sum_{m=0}^{3} x_1(m) \,.\, x_2\,[(n-m)]_4$$

$$\begin{aligned} y(0) &= x_1(0)\, x_2(0) + x_1(1)\, x_2(3) + x_1(2)\, x_2(2) + x_1(3)\, x_2(1) \\ &= 1 \times 1 + 2 \times 0 + 4 \times 0 + 0 \times 1 = 1 \\ y(1) &= x_1(0)\, x_2(1) + x_1(1)\, x_2(0) + x_1(2)\, x_2(3) + x_1(3)\, x_2(2) \\ &= 1 \times 2 + 2 \times 1 + 0 + 0 = 4 \\ y(2) &= x_1(0)\, x_2(2) + x_1(1)\, x_2(1) + x_1(2)\, x_2(0) + x_1(3)\, x_2(3) \\ &= 1 \times 0 + 2 \times 2 + 4 \times 1 + 0 \times 0 = 8 \\ y(3) &= x_1(0)\, x_2(3) + x_1(1)\, x_2(2) + x_1(2)\, x_2(1) + x_1(3)\, x_2(0) \\ &= 1 \times 0 + 2 \times 0 + 4 \times 2 + 0 \times 1 = 8 \end{aligned}$$

$$\therefore \quad y(n) = \{\underset{\uparrow}{1}, 4, 8, 8\}. \text{ Thus } x_1(n) \text{ (N) } x_2(n) = x_1(n) * x_2(n) \text{ here}$$

> **Important Note:**
> Thus to find linear convolution *via.* FFT algorithm, we make sequences $x_1(n)$ and $x_2(n)$ each of length $N_1 + N_2 - 1$, and find the circular convolution of and $x_1'(n)$ and $x_2'(n)$ *via.* FFT.

EXAMPLE 6.9: *Find the circular convolution of the given data sequences using matrix multiplication*

$$x(n) = \{\underset{\uparrow}{1}, 3, 5, 7\}\,,\ h(n) = \{\underset{\uparrow}{2}, 4, 6, 8\}.$$

SOLUTION:

$$h(n) = \{\underset{\uparrow}{2}, 4, 6, 8\}\,,\ x(n) = \{\underset{\uparrow}{1}, 3, 6, 8\}$$

We first find circular convolution by conventional approach

$$y(n) = h(n) \text{ (N) } x(n) = \sum_{n=0}^{3} h(m)\, x[(n-m)]_4$$

$$\begin{aligned} y(0) &= h(0)\, x(0) + h(1)\, x(3) + h(2)\, x(2) + h(3)\, x(1) \\ &= (2)\,(1) + (4)\,(7) + (6)\,(5) + (8)\,(3) = 2 + 28 + 30 + 24 = 84 \\ y(1) &= h(0)\, x(1) + h(1)\, x(0) + h(2)\, x(3) + h(3)\, x(2) \\ &= (2)\,(3) + (4)\,(1) + (6)\,(7) + (8)\,(5) = 6 + 4 + 42 + 40 = 92 \\ y(2) &= h(0)\, x(2) + h(1)\, x(1) + h(2)\, x(0) + h(3)\, x(3) \\ &= (2)\,(5) + (4)\,(3) + (6)\,(1) + (8)\,(7) = 10 + 12 + 6 + 56 = 84 \\ y(3) &= h(0)\, x(3) + h(1)\, x(2) + h(2)\, x(1) + h(3)\, x(0) \\ &= (2)\,(7) + (4)\,(5) + (6)\,(3) + (8)\,(1) = 14 + 20 + 18 + 8 = 60 \end{aligned}$$

$$y(n) = \begin{bmatrix} x(0) & x(3) & x(2) & x(1) \\ x(1) & x(0) & x(3) & x(2) \\ x(2) & x(1) & x(0) & x(3) \\ x(3) & x(2) & x(1) & x(0) \end{bmatrix} \begin{bmatrix} h(0) \\ h(1) \\ h(2) \\ h(3) \end{bmatrix}$$

(columns: $x(0)_4$, $x(-1)_4$, $x(-2)_4$, $x(-3)_4$)

$$\equiv \begin{bmatrix} 1 & 7 & 5 & 3 \\ 3 & 1 & 7 & 5 \\ 5 & 3 & 1 & 7 \\ 7 & 5 & 3 & 1 \end{bmatrix} \begin{bmatrix} 2 \\ 4 \\ 6 \\ 8 \end{bmatrix} = \begin{bmatrix} 84 \\ 92 \\ 84 \\ 60 \end{bmatrix}$$ **Ans.**

$$\therefore \quad x(n) \circledast_4 y(n) = \{\underset{\uparrow}{84}, 92, 84, 60\}$$ **Ans.**

Top row is $x[(-n)]_N$. Remaining rows one shifted circularly first column is $x(n)$.

[Linear convolution *via.* Circular convolution]

If we with to find linear convolution of

$x(n) = \{1, 3, 5, 7\}$ and $h(n) = \{2, 4, 6, 8\}$, we must add zeros for each to make length equal to $4 + 4 - 1 = 7$. Thus, we get

$$x'(n) = \{\underset{x'(0)}{1}, \underset{x'(1)}{3}, \underset{x'(2)}{5}, \underset{x'(3)}{7}, \underset{x'(4)}{0}, \underset{x'(5)}{0}, \underset{x'(6)}{0}\} \quad \text{and} \quad h'(n) = \{\underset{\uparrow}{2}, 4, 6, 8, 0, 0, 0\}$$

$$\begin{bmatrix} 1 & 0 & 0 & 0 & 7 & 5 & 3 \\ 3 & 1 & 0 & 0 & 0 & 7 & 5 \\ 5 & 3 & 1 & 0 & 0 & 0 & 7 \\ 7 & 5 & 3 & 1 & 0 & 0 & 0 \\ 0 & 7 & 5 & 3 & 1 & 0 & 0 \\ 0 & 0 & 7 & 5 & 3 & 1 & 0 \\ 0 & 0 & 0 & 7 & 5 & 3 & 1 \end{bmatrix} \times \begin{bmatrix} 2 \\ 4 \\ 6 \\ 8 \\ 0 \\ 0 \\ 0 \end{bmatrix}$$

(columns: $x[(0)]_7$, $x(-1)_7$, $x[(-2)]_7$, $x[(-3)]_7$, $x[(-4)]_7$, $x[(-5)]_7$, $x[(-6)]_7$; $h'(n)$)

$$x(n) * h(n) = \begin{bmatrix} 2 \\ 10 \\ 28 \\ 60 \\ 82 \\ 82 \\ 56 \end{bmatrix}$$

$\therefore \quad x(n) * h(n) = \{2, 10, 28, 60, 82, 82, 56\}$ linear convolution by matrix method.

Check: $x(n)$ ④ $h(n) = \{84, 92, 84, 60\}$ as expected... circular convolution by matrix method.

The first column is $x'(n)$. The first rows $x'((-n))_N$. $N = 7$ here the $x'(n)$ matrix is formed by shifting by one the elements of the previous to get the need row.

EXAMPLE 6.10: *Determine the periodic (or circular) convolution of the sequences*

$$g(n) = \sin(n\pi/2)\,[u(n) - u(n-4)]$$
$$h(n) = 2^n[u(n) - u(n-4)]$$

by any method. Also, verify the result obtained by another method.

SOLUTION: Clearly $g(n) = \{0, 1, 0, -1\}$ and $h(n) = \{1, 2, 4, 8\}$ (↑ at the first element of each)

$$y(n) = g((n))_4 * h((n))_4. \text{ Here } N = 4$$

$$= \sum_{m=0}^{3} g((m))_4 \,.\, h((n-m))_4$$

$$\therefore \quad y(n) = \underset{\nearrow = 1}{g(1)}\; h((n-1))_4 + \underset{\nearrow = -1}{g(3)}\; h((n-3))_4 \quad \because g(0) = g(2) = 0$$

$$y(0) = h((0-1))_4 - h((-3))_4 = h(3) - h(1) = 8 - 2 = 6$$
$$y(1) = h(0) - h((-2))_4 = h(0) - h(2) = 1 - 4 = -3$$
$$y(2) = h(+1) - h((-1))_4 = h(1) - h(3) = 2 - 8 = -6$$
$$y(3) = h(2) - h(0) = 4 - 1 = 3$$
$$\therefore \quad y(n) = g((n))_4 * h((n))_4 = \{6, -3, -6, 3\}$$

[Verification by another method]

We should prove that DFT of $y(n)$ = DFT $[g(n)]$. DFT $[h(n)]$

$$Y(k) = \sum_{n=0}^{3} y(n)\, e^{-j\frac{2\pi}{4}nk} = \sum_{n=0}^{3} y(n)\, e^{-j\frac{\pi nk}{2}}$$

$$= 6e^{-j\frac{\pi \times 0k}{2}} - 3e^{-j\frac{\pi k}{2}} - 6e^{-j\pi k} + 3e^{-j\frac{3\pi k}{2}}$$

$$\therefore \quad Y(0) = 6 - 3 - 6 + 3 = 0$$
$$Y(1) = 6 - 3(-j) - 6(-1) + 3(+j) = 12 + j6$$
$$Y(2) = 6 - 3(-1) - 6(1) + 3(-1) = 0$$
$$Y(3) = 6 - 3(+j) - 6(-1) + 3(-j) = 12 - j6$$
$$\therefore \quad Y(k) = \{0, (12 + j6), 0, (12 - j6)\}$$

[To find DFT's $G(k)$ and $H(k)$]

$$G(k) = \sum_{n=0}^{3} g(n)\, e^{-j\frac{2\pi}{4}nk} = \sum_{n=0}^{3} g(n)\, e^{-j\frac{\pi nk}{2}}$$

$$= e^{-j\frac{\pi k}{2}} - e^{-j\frac{3\pi k}{2}} \qquad \because g(0) = g(2) = 0,\ g(1) = 1,\ g(3) = -1$$

$$\therefore \quad G(0) = 1 - 1 = 0$$
$$G(1) = -j - j = -j2$$
$$G(2) = -1 - (-1) = 0$$

$$G(3) = j - (-j) = 2j \quad \therefore \quad G(k) = \{0, -j2, 0, j2\}$$
$$\uparrow$$

$$H(k) = \sum_{n=0}^{3} h(n)\, e^{-j\frac{\pi nk}{2}} = e^0 + 2e^{-j\frac{\pi k}{2}} + 4e^{-j\pi k} + 8e^{-j\frac{3\pi k}{2}}$$

$\therefore$
$$H(0) = 1 + 2 + 4 + 8 = 15$$
$$H(1) = 1 + 2(-j) + 4(-1) + 8(+j) = -3 + j6$$
$$H(2) = 1 + 2(-1) + 4(1) + 8(-1) = -5$$
$$H(3) = 1 + 2(+j) + 4(-1) + 8(-j) = -3 - 6j$$

$\therefore$
$$H(k) = \{15, (-3 + j6), -5, (-3 - j6)\}$$
$$\uparrow$$

Now
$$\begin{aligned} G(k)\,.\,H(k) &= \{0, -j2, 0, j2\} \times \{15, (-3 + j6), -5, (-3 - j6)\} \\ &= \{0, -j2(-3 + j6), 0, j2(-3 - j6)\} \\ &= \{0, (12 + j6), 0, (12 - j6)\} \\ &= Y(k) \end{aligned}$$

Hence, $y(0)$ computed earlier is verified.

EXAMPLE 6.11: *Determine a sequence $x(n)$ satisfying the three conditions:*
Condition 1: The Fourier transform of $x(n)$ is $X(e^{j\omega}) = 1 + A_1 \cos \omega + A_2 \cos 2\omega$, A, B constants
Condition 2: The sequence $x(n) * \delta(n - 3)$ evaluated at $n = 2$ is 5
Condition 3: The 8-point circular convolution of $\omega(n)$, given as shown, and $x(n - 3)$ at $n = 2$ is 11

i.e.
$$\left. \sum_{m=0}^{7} \omega(m)\, x((n - 3 - m))_8 \right|_{n=2} = 11.$$

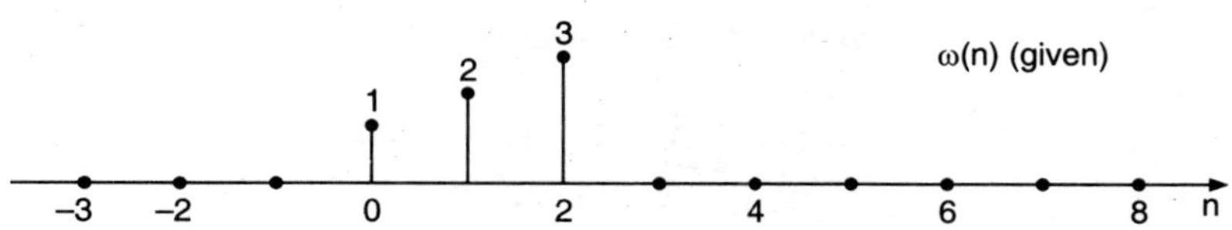

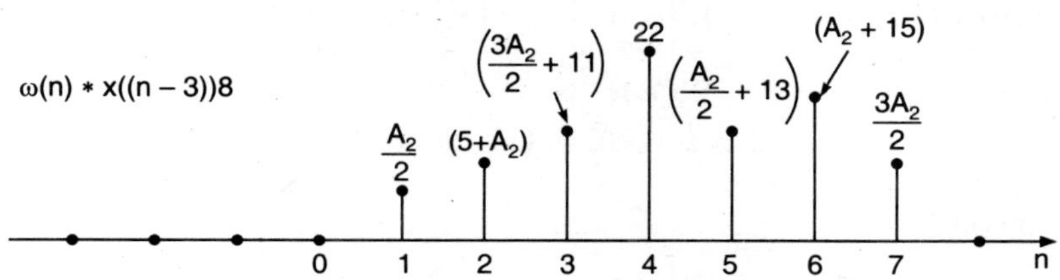

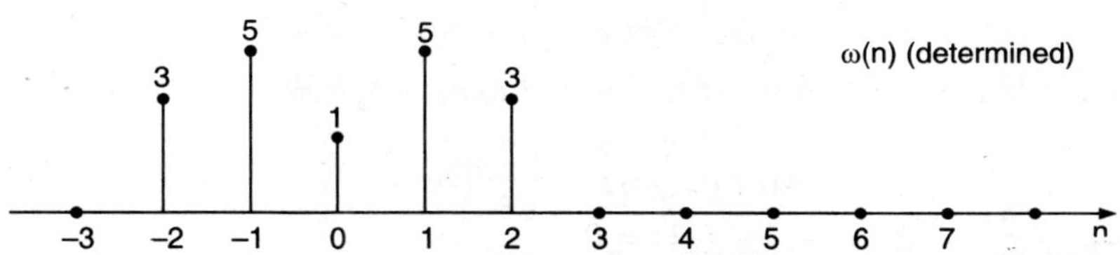

SOLUTION: Condition 1:

As $$X(e^{j\omega}) = 1 + A_1 \cos \omega + A_2 \cos 2\omega \qquad \text{(given)}$$

i.e. $$X(e^{j\omega}) = 1 + \frac{A_1}{2}(e^{j\omega} + e^{-j\omega}) + \frac{A_2}{2}(e^{j2\omega} + e^{-j2\omega})$$

$\therefore$ $$x(n) = \delta(n) + \frac{A_1}{2}\,(\delta(n+1) + \delta(n-1)) + \frac{A_2}{2}\,(\delta(n+2) + \delta(n-2)) \qquad ...(1)$$

$\therefore$ $x(n)$ has only 5 samples.

Condition 2: As $x(n) * \delta(n-3) = x(n-3)$

$$x(n-3)\big|_{n=2} = x(-1) = \frac{A_1}{2} \text{ (from (1))} \quad \therefore \quad \frac{A_1}{2} = 5 \quad \therefore \quad A_1 = 10.$$

Condition 3: Let $$y(n) = \sum_{m=0}^{1} \omega(m)\, x((n-3-m))_8$$

$$= \sum_{m=0}^{2} \omega(m)\, x((n-3-m))_8 \qquad (\because \ \omega(m) = 0 \text{ for } m > 2)$$

$\therefore$ $$y(0) = \sum_{m=0}^{2} \omega(m)\, x((-3-m))_8$$

$$= \omega(0)\, \underbrace{x((-3))_8}_{= x(5) = 0} + \omega(1)\, \underbrace{x((-4))_8}_{= x(4) = 0} + \omega(2)\, \underbrace{x((-5))_8}_{= x(3) = 0} = 0$$

$$y(1) = \sum_{m=0}^{2} \omega(m)\, x((-2-m))_8$$

$$= \underbrace{\omega(6)}_{=1}\ \underbrace{x((-2))_8}_{=\frac{A_2}{2}} + \omega(1)\ \underbrace{x((-3))_8}_{=0} + \omega(2)\ \underbrace{x((-4))_8}_{=0} = \frac{A_2}{2}$$

$$y(2) = \sum_{m=0}^{2} \omega(n)\, x((-1-m))_8 = \underbrace{\omega(0)}_{=1}\, \underbrace{x((-1))_8}_{=\frac{A_1}{2}=5} + \underbrace{\omega(1)}_{=2}\, \underbrace{x((-2))_8}_{=\frac{A_2}{2}} + \omega(2)\, \underbrace{x((-3)_8}_{=0} = 5 + \frac{A_2}{2}\cdot 2$$

As $y(2) = 1$ (given)

$\therefore$ $$5 + \frac{2A_2}{2} = 11 \quad \therefore \quad A_2 = 6$$

Hence, $$x(n) = \delta(n) + 5[\delta(n+1) + \delta(n-1)] + 3[\delta(n+2) + \delta(n-2)] \quad \textbf{Ans.}$$

EXAMPLE 6.12: *If $h(n)$ is an N-point sequence and $\omega(n)$ is the Hanning window given by*

$$\omega(n) = \frac{1}{2} + \frac{1}{2}\cos\left[\frac{2\pi}{N}\left(n - \frac{N}{2}\right)\right], \; n = 0, 1, \ldots, N-1$$

Find the DFT of the windowed sequence $h(n) \cdot \omega(n)$.

SOLUTION: Given

$$\omega(n) = \frac{1}{2} + \frac{1}{2}\cos\left[\frac{2\pi}{N}\left(n - \frac{N}{2}\right)\right]$$

$$= \frac{1}{2} + \frac{1}{4}\left[e^{j\frac{2\pi}{N}\left(n-\frac{N}{2}\right)} + e^{-j\frac{2\pi}{N}\left(n-\frac{N}{2}\right)}\right]$$

$$= \frac{1}{2} + \frac{1}{4}e^{-j\pi}e^{j2\pi n/N} + \frac{1}{4}e^{j\pi}e^{-j2\pi n/N}$$

$$= \frac{1}{2} - \frac{1}{4}e^{j2\pi n/N} - \frac{1}{4}e^{-j2\pi n/N} \qquad (\because \; e^{\pm j\pi} = -1)$$

$$\therefore \quad h(n)\cdot\omega(n) = \frac{1}{2}h(n) - \frac{1}{4}h(n)\cdot e^{j2\pi n/N} - \frac{1}{4}e^{-j2\pi n/N}\cdot h(n)$$

$$\therefore \quad \text{DFT}\;[h(n)\cdot\omega(n)] = \frac{1}{2}H(k) - \frac{1}{4}[(k-1)] - \frac{1}{4}H[(k+1)],\; k = 0, 1, \ldots, N-1$$

Ans.

EXAMPLE 6.13: *Compute DFT for the sequences*
(a) $x_1(n) = \delta(n)$, *(b)* $x_2(n) = \delta(n - m)$ *for* $0 < m < N$
(c) $x_3(n) = a^n$, $0 \le n \le N - 1$
(d) $x_4(n) = u(n) - u(n - n_0)$, $0 < n_0 \le N - 1$.

SOLUTION:

(a)
$$X_1(k) = \sum_{n=0}^{N-1} x_1(n)W_N^{nk},\; k = 0, 1, \ldots, N-1$$

$$= \sum_{n=0}^{N-1} \delta(n)\cdot W_N^{nk} = 1$$

Ans.

(b)
$$X_2(k) = X_2(z) \text{ for } z = e^{j2\pi k/N} = W_N^{-k} \quad \because \quad W_N = e^{-j2\pi/N}$$

As
$$X_2(z) = \sum_{n=-\infty}^{\infty} \delta(n-m)z^{-n} = z^{-m}$$

$$\therefore \quad X_2(k) = W_N^{mk},\; k = 0, 1, \ldots, N-1$$

Ans.

(c)
$$X_3(k) = \sum_{n=0}^{N-1} x_3(n)W_N^{nk} = \sum_{n=0}^{N-1} a^n W_N^{nk}$$

$$\therefore \quad X_3(k) = \frac{1-(aW_N^k)^N}{1-aW_N^k},\; k = 0, 1, \ldots, N-1$$

$$= \frac{1-a^N}{1-aW_N^k},\; k = 0, 1, \ldots, N-1$$

Ans.

(d)
$$X_4(k) = \sum_{n=0}^{N-1} x_4(n)\,W_H^{nk}$$

$$= \sum_{n=0}^{N-1} [u(n) - u(n-n_0)]W_N^{nk} = \sum_{n=0}^{n_0-1} W_N^{nk}$$

$$\therefore \quad X_4(k) = \frac{1-W_N^{n_0k}}{1-W_N^k} = \frac{W_N^{n_0k/2}\,(W_N^{-n_0k/2} - W_N^{n_0k/2})}{W_N^{k/2}(W^{-k/2} - W_N^{k/2})}$$

$$= W_N^{k(n_0-1)/2}\,\frac{e^{jn_0k2\pi/2N} - e^{-jn_0k2\pi/2N}}{e^{jk2\pi/2N} - e^{-jk2\pi/2N}}$$

$$= e^{-j2\pi k(n_0-1)/2N} \cdot \frac{\sin\left(\dfrac{n_0k\pi}{N}\right)}{\sin\left(\dfrac{k\pi}{N}\right)}, \; k = 0, 1, \ldots, N-1$$

$$= (e^{-j\pi k(n_0-1)/N}) \cdot \frac{\sin\left(\dfrac{n_0k\pi}{N}\right)}{\sin\left(\dfrac{k\pi}{N}\right)} \qquad \textbf{Ans.}$$

EXAMPLE 6.14: *For the sequence*

$$x(n) = \delta(n) + 2\delta(n-2) + \delta(n-3)$$

(a) Find 4-point DFT X(k)

(b) If $y(n) = x(n)$ ④ $x(n)$, find y(n) and Y(k)

(c) If $h(n) = \delta(n) + \delta(n-1) + 2\delta(n-3)$ find 4-point circular convolution of x(n) and h(n).

SOLUTION:

(*a*) Using $\quad \delta(n) \xrightarrow{\text{DFT}} 1, \; x(n-n_0) \xrightarrow{\text{DFT}} X(k)W_N^{n_0k}$

we obtain $\quad X(k) = 1 + 2W_4^{2k} + W_4^{3k}$ **Ans.**

(*b*)

$$Y(k) = \text{DFT}\,[x(n) \text{ ④ } x(n)] = X(k) \cdot X(k)$$

$$= (1 + 2W_4^{2k} + W_4^{3k})^2$$

$$= 1 + 4W_4^{2k} + 2W_4^{3k} + 4W_4^{4k} + 4W_4^{5k} + W_4^{6k}$$

$$= 1 + 4W_4^{2k} + 2W_4^{3k} + 4 + 4W_4^{k} + W_4^{2k}$$

$$= 5 + 4W_4^{k} + 5W_4^{2k} + 2W_4^{3k}$$

$$\therefore \quad y(n) = \text{IDFT}\,[Y(k)] = 5\delta(n) + 4\delta(n-1) + 5\delta(n-2) + 2\delta(n-3)$$

Ans.

(*c*) We first find linear convolution of $x(n)$ and $h(n)$ and then deduce circular convolution $x(n)$ ④ $h(x)$.

$x(n)$ ↓ \ $h(n)$ →	1	1	0	2
1	1	1	0	2
0	0	0	0	0
2	2	2	0	4
1	1	1	0	2

$\equiv \{\underset{\uparrow}{1}, 1, 2, 5, 1, 4, 2\}$ is $x(n) * h(n)$

$$\therefore \quad x(n) \text{ ④ } h(n) = \{2, 5, 4, 5\}$$

$$\therefore \quad = 2\delta(n) + 5\delta(n-1) + 4\delta(n-2) + 5\delta(n-3) \qquad \textbf{Ans.}$$

EXAMPLE 6.15: *Find $X_1(k)$, $X_2(k)$ for $x_1(n) = \{\underset{\uparrow}{2}, 1, 2, 1\}$, $x_2(n) = \{\underset{\uparrow}{1}, 2, 3, 4\}$. Also find $X_3(k)$ for $x_3(n) = x_1(n)$ Ⓝ $x_2(n)$. Confirm that $X_3(k) = X_1(k) \cdot X_2(k)$.*

SOLUTION:

$$X_1(k) = \sum_{n=0}^{3} x_1(n)e^{-j2\pi kn/4},\ k = 0, 1, 2, 3 \text{ and } x_1(n) = \{2, 1, 2, 1\}$$

$$= 2 + e^{-j\pi k/2} + 2e^{-j\pi k} + e^{-j3\pi k/2}$$

$\therefore$ $$X_1(0) = 6,\ X_1(1) = 0,\ X_1(2) = 2,\ X_1(3) = 0$$

$$X_2(k) = \sum_{n=0}^{3} x_2(n)e^{-j2\pi kn/4},\ k = 0, 1, 2, 3 \text{ and } x_2(n) = \{1, 2, 3, 4\}$$

$$= 1 + 2e^{-j\pi k/2} + 3e^{-j\pi k} + 4e^{-j3\pi k/2}$$

$\therefore$ $$X_2(0) = 10,\ X_2(1) = -2 + j2,\ X_2(2) = -2,\ X_2(3) = -2 - j2$$

Now, $$x_3(n) = x_1(n) \text{ Ⓝ } x_2(n) = \sum_{m=0}^{N-1} x_1(m) \cdot x_2[(n-m)]_4$$

$$x_3(0) = \sum_{m=0}^{3} x_1(m)\, x_2[(-m)]_4$$

$$= x_1(0)\, x_2(0) + x_1(1)\, x_2(3) + x_1(2)\, x_2(2) + x_1(3)\, x_2(1)$$

$$= (2)(1) + (1)(4) + (2)(3) + (1)(2) = 14$$

$$x_3(1) = \sum_{m=0}^{3} x_1(m)\, x_2[(1-m)]_4$$

$$= x_1(0)\, x_2(1) + x_1(1)\, x_2(0) + x_1(2)\, x_2(3) + x_1(3)\, x_2(2)$$

$$= (2)(2) + (1)(1) + (2)(4) + (1)(3) = 16$$

$$x_3(2) = \sum_{m=0}^{3} x_1(m)\, x_2[(2-m)]_4$$

$$= x_1(0)\, x_2(2) + x_1(1)\, x_2(1) + x_1(2)\, x_2(0) + x_1(3)\, x_2(3)$$

$$= (2)(3) + (1)(2) + (2)(1) + (1)(4) = 14$$

$$x_3(3) = \sum_{m=0}^{3} x_1(m)\, x_2[(3-m)]_4$$

$$= x_1(0)\, x_2(3) + x_1(1)\, x_2(2) + x_1(2)\, x_2(1) + x_1(3)\, x_2(0)$$

$$= (2)(4) + (1)(3) + (2)(2) + (1)(1) = 16$$

$$X_3(k) = \sum_{n=0}^{3} x_3(n)e^{-j2\pi kn/4}$$

$$= 14 + 16e^{-jk\pi/2} + 14e^{-j\pi k} + 16e^{-j3\pi k/2}$$

$$X_3(0) = 60,\ X_3(1) = 0,\ X_3(2) = -4,\ X_3(3) = 0$$

Check: $$X_1(k)\ X_2(k) \equiv \{\underset{\uparrow}{60}, 0, -4, 0\}$$

Thus, $X_3(k) = X_1(k) \cdot X_2(k) =$ DFT of $x_1(n)$ Ⓝ $x_2(n)$ Q.E.D.

EXAMPLE 6.16: *Determine the N-point DFT for*

$$x(n) = \cos(n\omega_0),\ 0 \le n \le N-1.$$

SOLUTION:

As $$x(n) = \frac{1}{2}[e^{jn\omega_0} + e^{-jn\omega_0}]$$

$\therefore$ $$X(k) = \sum_{n=0}^{N-1} x(n)\cdot e^{-j2\pi kn/N}$$

$$= \frac{1}{2}\sum_{n=0}^{N-1} e^{jn\omega_0}.e^{-j2\pi kn/N} + \frac{1}{2}\sum_{n=0}^{N-1} e^{-jn\omega_0}.e^{-j2\pi kn/N}$$

$$= \frac{1}{2}\sum_{n=0}^{N-1} e^{-jn\left(\frac{2\pi k}{N}-\omega_0\right)} + \frac{1}{2}\sum_{n=0}^{N-1} e^{-jn\left(\frac{2\pi k}{N}+\omega_0\right)}$$

Assume $\omega_0 = 2\pi k_0/N$

$\therefore$ $$X(k) = \frac{1}{2}\sum_{n=0}^{N-1} e^{-jn\frac{2\pi}{N}(k-k_0)} + \frac{1}{2}\sum_{n=0}^{\infty} e^{-j\frac{2\pi}{N}(k+k_0)}$$

$$= \frac{1}{2}[N\delta(k-k_0)] + \frac{1}{2}[N\delta(N-k_0)]$$

$\therefore$ $$X(k) = \begin{cases} N/2 & \text{for } k = k_0 \text{ and } k = N-k_0 \\ 0, & \text{otherwise} \end{cases}$$ **Ans.**

EXAMPLE 6.17: *If we express $\underline{X} = \underline{W}_N\,\underline{x}$, where $\underline{X} = [X(0), X(1), \ldots, X(N-1)]^T$, $\underline{x} = [x(0), x(1), \ldots, x(N-1)]^T$ and*

$$\underline{W}_N = \begin{bmatrix} 1 & 1 & 1 & \ldots & 1 \\ 1 & W_N & W_N^2 & \ldots & W_N^{N-1} \\ 1 & W_N^2 & W_N^4 & \ldots & W_N^{2(N-1)} \\ \vdots & & & & \\ 1 & W_N^{N-1} & W_N^{2(N-1)} & \ldots & W_N^{(N-1)(N-1)} \end{bmatrix}$$

(DFT matrix, an N × N matrix)

(a) Show that $\underline{W}_N^{-1} = \frac{1}{N}\underline{W}_N^*$

(b) Find $\underline{W}_4$ and $\underline{W}_4^{-1}$ explicitly.

SOLUTION: (*a*) Note that $\underline{W}_N^T = \underline{W}_N$ as $\underline{W}_N$ is a symmetrical matrix and $\underline{W}_N^*$ is the conjugate and $\underline{W}_N^{-1}$ inverse of matrix $\underline{W}_N$.

As $$\underline{X} = \underline{W}_N\,\underline{x} \quad \ldots(A)$$

$\therefore$ $$\underline{x} = \underline{W}_N^{-1}\,\underline{X}$$ (Pre multiply both sides of (*A*) by $\underline{W}_N^{-1}$)

As IDFT : $$x(n) = \frac{1}{N}\sum_{k=0}^{N-1} X(k)(W_N^{nk})^*$$

$\therefore \qquad \underline{x}(n) = \frac{1}{N}\underline{W}_N^* \cdot \underline{X}(k)$ ...(B)

Comparing (A) and (B), we get $\boxed{\underline{W}_N^{-1} = \frac{1}{N}\underline{W}_{-N}^*}$ Q.E.D.

(b) Here, $N = 4$ $\quad\therefore\quad W_4^{jnk} = e^{(-j2\pi/4)nk} = (-j)^{nk}$

$$\begin{array}{c} \\ n=0 \\ n=1 \\ n=2 \\ n=3 \end{array}\begin{array}{c} k=0 \;\; k=1 \;\; k=2 \;\; k=3 \\ \begin{bmatrix} 1 & 1 & 1 & 1 \\ 1 & -j & -1 & j \\ 1 & -1 & 1 & -1 \\ 1 & j & -1 & -j \end{bmatrix}\end{array} \text{ and } \underline{W}_4^{-1} = \frac{1}{4}\begin{bmatrix} 1 & 1 & 1 & 1 \\ 1 & +j & -1 & -j \\ 1 & -1 & 1 & -1 \\ 1 & -j & -1 & +j \end{bmatrix} \quad \textbf{Ans.}$$

EXAMPLE 6.18: *(a) Find the DFT X[k] of x(n) = {0, 1, 2, 3}.*
(b) Find the IDFT from X(k) obtained in part (a).

SOLUTION: Here $N = 4$.

(a) Hence $\underline{W}_4$, the DFT matrix becomes $e^{\left(-j\frac{2\pi}{4}\right)nk} = (-j)^{nk}$

$$\underbrace{\begin{bmatrix} X(0) \\ X(1) \\ X(2) \\ X(3) \end{bmatrix}}_{\underline{X}(k)} = \underbrace{\begin{bmatrix} 1 & 1 & 1 & 1 \\ 1 & -j & -1 & j \\ 1 & -1 & 1 & -1 \\ 1 & j & -1 & -j \end{bmatrix}}_{\underline{W}_N} \underbrace{\begin{bmatrix} 0 \\ 1 \\ 2 \\ 3 \end{bmatrix}}_{\underline{x}(n)} = \begin{bmatrix} 6 \\ -2+j2 \\ -2 \\ -2-j2 \end{bmatrix} \quad \textbf{Ans.}$$

(b)
$$\underbrace{\begin{bmatrix} x(0) \\ x(1) \\ x(2) \\ x(3) \end{bmatrix}}_{\underline{x}(k)} = \frac{1}{4}\underbrace{\begin{bmatrix} 1 & 1 & 1 & 1 \\ 1 & +j & -1 & -j \\ 1 & -1 & 1 & -1 \\ 1 & -j & -1 & +j \end{bmatrix}}_{\underline{W}_N^*} \underbrace{\begin{bmatrix} 6 \\ -2+j2 \\ -2 \\ -2-j2 \end{bmatrix}}_{\underline{X}(n)} = \begin{bmatrix} 0 \\ 1 \\ 2 \\ 3 \end{bmatrix} \quad \textbf{Ans.}$$

EXAMPLE 6.19: *Consider the unit sample response*

$$h(n) = \left(\frac{1}{4}\right)^n u(n)$$

The frequency response $H(e^{j\omega})$ of this filter is sampled at $\omega_k = 2\pi k/N$, $k = 0, 1, \ldots, N-1$ and $N = 16$. The resulting samples are $G(k) = H(e^{j\omega})|_{\omega = 2\pi k/16}$, $k = 0, 1, \ldots, N-1$.

Find the IDFT g(n) of G(k).

SOLUTION: We use the frequency sampling theorem, which states that if the DTFT of a sequence $x(n)$ is sampled at N equally spaced frequencies between 0 and 2π then the IDFT of such samples, $g(n)$, is the time aliased sequence

$$g(n) = \left\{\sum_{k=-\infty}^{\infty} h(n-kN)\right\},\ n = 0, 1, \ldots, N-1.$$

$\therefore$ Here
$$g(n) = \left\{\sum_{k=-\infty}^{\infty} \left(\frac{1}{4}\right)^{n-kN} \cdot u(n-kN)\right\},\ n = 0, 1, \ldots, N-1$$

For k + ve, $u(n - kN) = 0$ for $0 \le n \le N - 1$. Hence

$$g(n) = \sum_{k=\infty}^{\infty} \left(\frac{1}{4}\right)^{n-kN} = \left(\frac{1}{4}\right)^{n} \sum_{k=-\infty}^{0} \left(\frac{1}{4}\right)^{-kN}$$

$$= \left(\frac{1}{4}\right)^{n} \sum_{k=0}^{\infty} \left(\frac{1}{4}\right)^{kN}$$

$$= \left(\frac{1}{4}\right)^{n} \cdot \frac{1}{1-\left(\frac{1}{4}\right)^{N}} \qquad \because \left(\frac{1}{4}\right)^{N} < 1$$

$$\therefore \qquad g(n) = \left(\frac{1}{4}\right)^{n} \cdot \frac{1}{1-\left(\frac{1}{4}\right)^{N}}, \; n = 0, 1, \ldots, N-1 \quad \textbf{Ans.}$$

EXAMPLE 6.20: *Let X(k) denotes the N-point DFT of the N-point sequence x(n), (a) Show that if x(n) satisfies the relation*

$$x(n) = -x(N-1-n)$$

then

$$X(0) = 0.$$

(b) Show that with N even and if

$$x(n) = x(N-1-n)$$

then

$$X\left(\frac{N}{2}\right) = 0.$$

SOLUTION: As $X(k) = \sum_{n=0}^{N-1} x(n)\, W_N^{kn}$, where $W_N \triangleq e^{-j\frac{2\pi}{N}}$

$$\therefore \qquad X(0) = \sum_{n=0}^{N-1} x(n) \underbrace{W_N^{0.n}}_{=1}$$

$$= \sum_{n=0}^{N-1} x(n)$$

$$= x(0) + x(2) + x(3) + \ldots + x(N-3) + x(N-2) + x(N-1) \quad \text{(total } N \text{ terms)} \quad \ldots(A)$$

If N is odd, then $x(n) = -x(N-1-n)$ implies that

$$\left.\begin{aligned} x(0) &= -x(N-1) \\ x(1) &= -x(N-2) \\ x(2) &= -x(N-3) \\ &\vdots \\ x\left(\frac{N-3}{2}\right) &= -x\left(\frac{N+1}{2}\right) \\ x\left(\frac{N-1}{2}\right) &= x\left(\frac{N-1}{2}\right) = 0 \end{aligned}\right\}$$

This means if we group terms (as shown in different tick marks) in (*A*), then each group has a zero sum. An alone term $x\left(\frac{N-1}{2}\right)$ is left, which is incidently zero if the relation $x(n) = -x(N-1-n)$ is to be obeyed. Thus for N odd, $X(0) = 0$.

If *N* is even, then we have, with $x(n) = -x(N-1-n)$

$$\left.\begin{aligned} x(0) &= -x(N-1) \\ x(1) &= -x(N-2) \\ x(2) &= -x(N-3) \\ x\left(\frac{N}{2}-2\right) &= -x\left(\frac{N}{2}+1\right) \\ x\left(\frac{N}{2}-1\right) &= -x\left(\frac{N}{2}\right) \end{aligned}\right\}$$

all terms covered

Thus, we have in all N (an even value) terms and $\frac{N}{2}$ groups are formed in (*A*). Each group has, clearly zero sum. Hence, here also $X(0) = 0$.

Thus, for any value of N (even or odd), $X(0) = 0$ **Ans.** Q.E.D.

(*b*) As $$X(k) = \sum_{n=0}^{N-1} x(n) W_N^{kn}, \quad W_N \triangleq e^{-j\frac{2\pi}{N}}$$

$$\therefore \quad X\left(\frac{N}{2}\right) = \sum_{n=0}^{N-1} x(n) W_N^{\frac{N}{2}n}$$

$$= \sum_{n=0}^{N-1} x(n) e^{-j\pi n} \quad \because \quad W_N^{\frac{N}{2}n} = e^{\left(-j\frac{2\pi}{N}\right)\frac{Nn}{2}} = e^{-j\pi n}$$

$$\therefore \quad X\left(\frac{N}{2}\right) = x(0) - x(1) + x(2) - + \ldots + x(N-2) - x(N-1) \quad \ldots(B)$$

$\because$ $N-1$ is odd here.

The condition $x(n) = x(N-1-n)$ implies

$$\left.\begin{aligned} x(0) &= x(N-1) \\ x(1) &= x(N-2) \\ x(2) &= x(N-3) \\ &\vdots \\ x\left(\frac{N}{2}-1\right) &= x\left(\frac{N}{2}\right) \end{aligned}\right\}$$

using these results in (*B*), we can form $\frac{N}{2}$ groups. Each group has zero sum. Hence, we obtain

$$X\left(\frac{N}{2}\right) = 0$$

Thus, $$X\left(\frac{N}{2}\right) = 0$$ Q.E.D.

Short cut for (*a*)

$$X(k) = \sum_{n=0}^{N-1} x(n) W_N^{nk} \quad \therefore \quad X(0) = \sum_{n=0}^{N-1} x(n) \quad ...(A)$$

Put $$n = N - 1 - n'$$

$\therefore$ $$X(k) = \sum_{n'=0}^{N-1} x(N-1-n') W_N^{(N-1-n')k}$$

$$= \sum_{n \le 0}^{N-1} -x(n') W_N^{(N-1-n')k} \quad \because \quad x(N-1-n) = -x(n) \text{ (given)}$$

$\therefore$ $$X(0) = -\sum_{n'=0}^{N-1} x(n') \quad ...(B)$$

add (*A*) and (*B*) $\therefore$ $$X(0) = 0$$ **Ans.**

Short cut for (*b*)

$$X(k) = \sum_{n=0}^{N-1} x(n)\, W_N^{nk} \quad \therefore \quad X\left(\frac{N}{2}\right) = \sum_{n=0}^{N-1} x(n) \cdot (-1)^n \quad ...(C)$$

$$= \sum_{n=0}^{N-1} x(N-1-n) W_N^{nk} \quad \because \quad x(n) = x(N-1-n) \text{ (given)}$$

Put $N - 1 - n = m$

$$= \sum_{m=0}^{N-1} x(m) W_N^{(N-1-m)k}$$

$$X\left(\frac{N}{2}\right) = \sum_{m=0}^{N-1} x(m)(-1)^{m+1} = -\sum_{n=0}^{N-1} x(n)(-1)^n \quad ...(D)$$

add (*C*) and (*D*) $\therefore$ $X\left(\frac{N}{2}\right) = 0$ **Ans.**

EXAMPLE 6.21: *Let X(k) denotes the N-point DFT of an N-point sequence x(n). X(k) is an N-point sequence. If the DFT of X(k) is computed to obtain a sequence $x_1(n)$, determine $x_1(n)$ in terms of x(n).*

SOLUTION: We know that

$$X(k) = \sum_{n=0}^{N-1} x(n) \cdot W_N^{kn}, \; W_n \triangleq e^{-j2\pi/N}$$

$$\text{DFT of } X(k) = \sum_{k=0}^{N-1} X(k) \cdot W_N^{kn}$$

$$\therefore \quad x_1(n) = \sum_{k=0}^{N-1} \left(\sum_{l=0}^{N-1} x(l)\, W_N^{kl} \right) W_N^{kn}$$

$$= \sum_{l=0}^{N-1} x(l) \sum_{k=0}^{N-1} W_N^{k(l+n)} \quad \text{interchanging order of summation}$$

$$= \sum_{l=0}^{N-1} x(l) \cdot \frac{1-(W_N^{l+n})^N}{1-W_N^{l+n}}$$

$$= \sum_{l=0}^{N-1} x(l) \cdot N\delta(l+n) \quad \text{where } \delta(k) = \begin{cases} 1, & k=0 \\ 0, & k \neq 0 \end{cases}$$

$$= x(-n) \cdot N$$

$$= Nx(-n)$$

Thus DFT of $X(k) = Nx(-n)$

or $x_1(n) = Nx(-n)$ **Ans.** (see also S. No. in Table 6.1)

EXAMPLE 6.22: *Analog signal $x_a(t)$ which is band limited to 10 kHz, is sampled at Nyquist rate to obtain x(n). An N = 1000 pt. DFT X(k) is obtained for x(n).*

(a) What is the analog frequency of X(k) for k = 150, and k = 700?

(b) What is the spacing between the spectral samples of X(k)?

SOLUTION: Here, $X(k) = \sum_{n=0}^{N-1} x(n) e^{-j2\pi nk/N}$, with $N = 1000$

The Nyquist rate = 2 × maximum frequency of $x_a(t)$

$$= 2 \times 10k = 20k = 20{,}000/\text{s} \triangleq f_s$$

$$\omega = \frac{\Omega}{f_s} \qquad (\because \ \omega \text{ is analog frequency normalised by } f_s)$$

(*a*) For $k = 150$, $\omega_k = \dfrac{2\pi}{N} \cdot k$ radians

$$\therefore \quad f_k = \frac{k}{N} = \frac{150}{10000} \equiv 150\, f_s \text{ of analog frequency}$$

$$= \frac{150}{1000} \times 20{,}000 = 3000 = 3 \text{ kHz} \qquad \textbf{Ans.}$$

For $k = 700$. It is equivalent to

$$\equiv k - N = 700 - 1000 = -300 \qquad \because \ X(e^{j\omega}) = X(e^{j(\omega+2\pi)})$$

$$\therefore \quad f_k = -\frac{300}{1000} \times 20{,}000 = -6000 = -6 \text{ kHz} \qquad \textbf{Ans.}$$

(*b*) Spectral spacing $= \frac{f_s}{N} = \frac{20{,}000}{1000} = 20$ Hz **Ans.**

EXAMPLE 6.23: *If $x_1(n)$ and $x_2(n)$ are N-point sequences with DFTs $X_1(k)$ and $X_2(k)$, respectively, show that*

$$\sum_{n=0}^{N-1} x_1(n)\cdot x_2^*(n) = \frac{1}{N}\sum_{k=0}^{N-1} X_1(k)\cdot X_2^*(k).$$

SOLUTION: Let $x(n) = x_1(n) \cdot x_2^*(n)$

$$\therefore \qquad \text{DFT}[x(n)] = X(k) = \sum_{n=0}^{N-1} [x_1(n)\cdot x_2^*(n)]W_N^{nk}$$

For $k = 0$,
$$X(0) = \sum_{n=0}^{N-1} x_1(n)\cdot x_2^*(n) \qquad \ldots(A)$$

We know that $\quad x_1(n) \xrightarrow{\text{DFT}} X_1(k)$

and $\quad x_2^*(n) \xrightarrow{\text{DFT}} X_2^*(-k)$

$$\therefore \qquad \text{DFT }[x_1(n)\cdot x_2^*(n)] = \frac{1}{N}\text{ circular convolution of } X(k) \text{ and } X_2^*(-k)$$

$$= \frac{1}{N}\sum_{l=0}^{N-1} X_1(l)\cdot X_2^*(-(k-l))$$

$$\therefore \qquad X(k) = \frac{1}{N}\sum_{l=0}^{N-1} X_1(l)\cdot X_2^*(l-k) \qquad \ldots(B)$$

Taking $k = 0$ in (*B*) and using (*A*), we have

$$\sum_{n=0}^{N-1} x_1(n)\cdot x_2^*(n) = X(0) = \frac{1}{N}\sum_{l=0}^{N-1} X_1(l)\cdot X_2^*(l)$$

$$\therefore \qquad \sum_{n=0}^{N-1} x_1(n)\cdot x_2^*(n) = \frac{1}{N}\sum_{k=0}^{N-1} X_1(k)\cdot X_2^*(k) \qquad \text{Q.E.D.}$$

EXAMPLE 6.24: *If x(n) has its DTFT $X(e^{j\omega})$, and y(n) is a finite length, N, sequence such that*

$$Y(k) = X(e^{j\omega})\,|_{\omega=2\pi k/N},\ k = 0, 1, \ldots, N-1.$$

Show that y(n) is formed by aliasing x(n) in time.

SOLUTION: We know that $\quad X(e^{j\omega}) = \sum_{n=-\infty}^{\infty} x(n)e^{-j\omega n}$ (DTFT of $x(n)$)

$$\therefore \qquad Y(k) = X(e^{j\omega})\,|_{\omega=2\pi k/N} = \sum_{n=-\infty}^{\infty} x(n)e^{-j2\pi kn/N} \qquad \ldots(A)$$

$$\therefore \qquad y(n) = \frac{1}{N}\sum_{k=0}^{N-1} Y(k)e^{j2\pi kn/N} \quad \text{(definition of IDFT)}$$

$$= \frac{1}{N}\sum_{k=0}^{N-1}\left\{\sum_{l=-\infty}^{\infty} x(l)\cdot e^{-j2\pi kl/N}\right\}e^{j2\pi kn/N} \quad \text{due to (4)}$$

$$y(n) = \frac{1}{N}\sum_{l=-\infty}^{\infty} x(l)\left\{\sum_{k=0}^{N-1} e^{j2\pi(n-l)k/N}\right\} \quad \ldots(B)$$

But $$\sum_{k=0}^{N-1} e^{j2\pi(n-l)k/N} = \begin{cases} N & \text{for } l = n + mN \\ 0, & \text{otherwise} \end{cases}$$

∴ $$y(n) = \sum_{m=-\infty}^{\infty} x(n+mN)$$

or $$y(n) = \sum_{m=-\infty}^{\infty} x(n-mN) \text{ i.e. } y(n) \text{ is formed by aliasing } x(n) \quad \text{Q.E.D.}$$

EXAMPLE 6.25: *Consider the finite-length complex exponential sequence:*

$$x(n) = \begin{cases} e^{j\omega_0 n}, & 0 \le n \le N-1 \\ 0, & otherwise \end{cases}.$$

(a) Find the Fourier transform $X(e^{j\omega})$ of $x(n)$
(b) Find the N-point DFT $X(k)$ of $x(n)$

SOLUTION: (*a*) $$X(e^{j\omega}) = \sum_{n=-\infty}^{\infty} x(n)\, e^{-j\omega n} \quad \text{(by definition of DTFT)}$$

$$= \sum_{n=0}^{N-1} (e^{+j\omega_0 n})(e^{-j\omega n})$$

$$= \sum_{n=0}^{N-1} e^{-j(\omega-\omega_0)n}$$

$$= \frac{1-e^{-j(\omega-\omega_0)N}}{1-e^{-j(\omega-\omega_0)}} = \frac{e^{-j(\omega-\omega_0)N/2}\left(e^{+j(\omega-\omega_0)N/2} - e^{-j(\omega-\omega_0)N/2}\right)}{e^{-j(\omega-\omega_0)/2}\left(e^{j(\omega-\omega_0)/2} - e^{-j(\omega-\omega_0)/2}\right)}$$

$$= e^{j(\omega-\omega_0)(N-1)/2}\cdot\frac{\sin[(\omega-\omega_0)N/2)]}{\sin[(\omega-\omega_0)/2)]} \quad \textbf{Ans.}$$

(*b*) $$X(k) = X(e^{j\omega})\Big|_{\omega=\frac{2\pi}{N}k}$$

$$= e^{j\left(\left(\frac{2\pi k}{N}\right)-\omega_0\right)\frac{(N-1)}{2}}\frac{\sin[(2\pi k/N-\omega_0)N/2)]}{\sin[(2\pi k/N-\omega_0)1/2)]} \quad \textbf{Ans.}$$

EXAMPLE 6.26: *Find the inverse DFT of X(k) = {1, 2, 3, 4}.*

SOLUTION: We know that $x(n) = \frac{1}{N}\sum_{k=0}^{N-1} X(k)e^{j\frac{2\pi}{N}nk}$, $n = 0, 1, 2, \ldots, N-1$.

Here $N = 4$

$$\therefore \quad x(n) = \frac{1}{4}\sum_{k=0}^{3} X(k)e^{j\frac{\pi}{2}nk}$$

When $n = 0$,

$$x(0) = \frac{1}{4}\sum_{k=0}^{3} X(k)\cdot 1 = (X(0)+X(1)+X(2)+X(3))\frac{1}{4}$$

$$= \frac{1}{4}(1+2+3+4) = \frac{5}{2}$$

When $n = 1$,

$$x(1) = \frac{1}{4}\sum_{k=0}^{3} X(k)e^{j\frac{\pi}{2}k}$$

$$= \frac{1}{4}\left[1.e^{j\frac{\pi}{2}\times 0} + 2.e^{j\frac{\pi}{2}\times 1} + 3.e^{j\frac{\pi}{2}\times 2} + 4.e^{j\frac{\pi}{2}\times 3}\right]$$

$$= \frac{1}{4}[1 + 2(j) + 3(-1) + 4(-j)] = -\frac{1}{2} - j\frac{1}{2}$$

When $n = 2$,

$$x(2) = \frac{1}{4}\sum_{k=0}^{3} X(k)e^{j\pi k}$$

$$= \frac{1}{4}[1(1)+2(-1)+3(1)+4(-1)] = -\frac{1}{2}$$

When $n = 3$,

$$x(3) = \frac{1}{4}\sum_{k=0}^{3} X(k)e^{j\frac{3\pi}{2}k}$$

$$= \frac{1}{4}[1(1)+2(-j)+3(-1)+4(+j)]$$

$$= \frac{1}{4}[-2+j2] = -\frac{1}{2}+j\frac{1}{2}$$

Hence,

$$x(n) = \left\{\frac{5}{2}, \left(-\frac{1}{2}-j\frac{1}{2}\right), -\frac{1}{2}, \left(-\frac{1}{2}+j\frac{1}{2}\right)\right\}$$ **Ans.**

EXAMPLE 6.27: *Prove the statement "Multiplication of two DFT's $X_1(k)$ and $X_2(k)$ are related to circular convolution of $x_1(n)$ and $x_2(n)$".*

SOLUTION: Consider two N length sequences $x_1(n)$ and $x_2(n)$. Therefore,

$$X_1(k) = \sum_{n=0}^{N-1} x_1(n)e^{-j2\pi nk/N}, \ k = 0, 1, 2, \ldots, N-1 \quad \ldots(A)$$

and

$$X_2(k) = \sum_{n=0}^{N-1} x_2(n)e^{-j2\pi nk/N}, \ k = 0, 1, 2, \ldots, N-1 \quad \ldots(B)$$

Let $X_3(k) = X_1(k) \cdot X_2(k)$ (multiplication of two DFT's)

We now determine IDFT of $X_3(k)$ *i.e.* IDFT of $(X_1(k) \cdot X_2(k))$

$$x_3(n) = \frac{1}{N}\sum_{k=0}^{N-1} X_3(k)e^{j2\pi nk/N}$$

$$= \frac{1}{N}\sum_{k=0}^{N-1} X_1(k)X_2(k)e^{j2\pi nk/N}, \; n = 0, 1, ..., N-1 \qquad ...(C)$$

$$= \frac{1}{N}\sum_{k=0}^{N-1}\left(\sum_{m=0}^{N-1} x_1(m)e^{-j2\pi mk/N}\right)\left(\sum_{l=0}^{N-1} x_2(l)e^{-j2\pi lk/N}\right)\cdot e^{j2\pi nk/N}$$

$$= \frac{1}{N}\sum_{m=0}^{N-1} x_1(m)\sum_{l=0}^{N-1} x_2(l)\cdot\sum_{k=0}^{N-1} e^{j2\pi k(n-m-l)/N}, \; n = 0, 1, ..., N-1 \; ...(D)$$

Note that: $\sum_{k=0}^{N-1} e^{j2\pi kp/N} = \begin{cases} N, & p = 0 \text{ or } p = \text{multiple of } N \\ 0, & p \neq \text{a multiple of } N \end{cases}$

Hence, in (D) $\sum_{k=0}^{N-1} e^{j2\pi k(n-m-l)/N} = N$ only when $n - m - l$ = a multiple of N

$\therefore \quad l = ((n-m))_N = 0$ (Note this step)

$\therefore$ (D) reduces to $x_3(n) = \frac{1}{N}\sum_{m=0}^{N-1} x_1(m)Nx_2(l)\Big|_{l=((n-m))_N}$,

$$\therefore \quad \boxed{\text{IDFT}\,[X_1(k)\cdot X_2(k)] = \sum_{m=0}^{N-1} x_1(m)x_2((n-m))_N, \; n = 0, 1, ..., N-1}$$

(Also, see S. No. in Table 6.1)

= circular convolution of $x_1(n)$ and $x_2(n)$.

EXAMPLE 6.28: *Let x(n) be a real finite-length sequence for $0 \le n \le N-1$ (of length N), and let X(k) denote the N-point DFT of x(n)*

(a) Is Re[X(k)] = DFT of $\left[x_e(n) \triangleq \frac{1}{2}(x(n) + x(-n))\right]$?

(b) What is IDFT of Re[X(k)]?

SOLUTION: (*a*) As $x(n)$ exists for $0 \le n \le N-1 \; \therefore \; x_e(n) = \frac{1}{2}[x(n) + x(-n)]$ is $(2N - 1)$ long sequence

$$\therefore \quad x_e(n) = \begin{cases} \frac{1}{2}[x(n) + x(-n)], & -N+1 \le n \le N-1 \\ 0, & \text{Otherwise} \end{cases}, \qquad \text{(Note this step)}$$

i.e.
$$X_e(k) = \sum_{n=-N+1}^{N-1} x_e(n)e^{-jnk2\pi/(2N-1)}$$

$$= \sum_{n=-N+1}^{N-1} \frac{1}{2}[x(n)]e^{-j2\pi nk/(2N-1)} + \sum_{n=-N+1}^{N-1} \frac{1}{2}x(-n)e^{-j2\pi nk/(2N-1)}$$

↗ zero for $n < 0$ ↗ zero for $n > 0$

$$= \sum_{n=0}^{N-1} \frac{1}{2} x(n) e^{-j2\pi nk/(2N-1)} + \sum_{n=-N+1}^{0} \frac{1}{2} x(-n) e^{-j2\pi nk/(2N-1)}$$

Put $n = -n'$

$$= \sum_{n=0}^{N-1} \frac{1}{2} x(n)[e^{-j2\pi nk/(2N-1)} + e^{+j2\pi nk/(2N-1)}]$$

$$= \sum_{n=0}^{N-1} x(n) \cos\left(\frac{2\pi nk}{(2N-1)}\right)$$

$$\neq \underbrace{\text{Re} \sum_{n=0}^{N-1} x(n) e^{-j2\pi nk/N}}_{\text{the } X(k) \text{ i.e. } N-\text{point DFT of } x(n)}, \quad k = 0, 1, \ldots, N-1$$

$\therefore$ DFT of $[x_e(n)] = X_e(k) \neq \text{Re}[X(k)]$ (Also, see serial 10 on Table 6.1. Note that there $x_e(n)$ was periodic. Here $x_e(n)$ is not periodic)

(*b*)

$$\text{Re}[X(k)] = \frac{1}{2}[X(k) + X^*(k)]$$

$$= \frac{1}{2} \sum_{n=0}^{N-1} x(n) . e^{-j2\pi nk/N} + \frac{1}{2} \sum_{n=0}^{N-1} x(n) . e^{+j2\pi nk/N}$$

Put $n = -n' + N$

$$= \frac{1}{2} \text{DFT of } x(n) + \frac{1}{2}\left[\sum_{n'=1}^{N} x(N-n') + e^{j2\pi k(N-n')/N}\right]$$

$$= \frac{1}{2} X(k) + \frac{1}{2}\left[\sum_{n'=0}^{N-1} x(N-n') e^{-j2\pi n'k/N}\right]$$

$\therefore$ $$\text{Re}[X(k)] = \frac{1}{2}[\text{DFT of } x(n) + \text{DFT of } x(N-n)]$$ **Ans.**

EXAMPLE 6.29: *For the following signal flow diagram, compute the outputs X(0), X(1), X(2) and X(3). Take* $x(n) = \sin\frac{n\pi}{2}$.

SOLUTION:

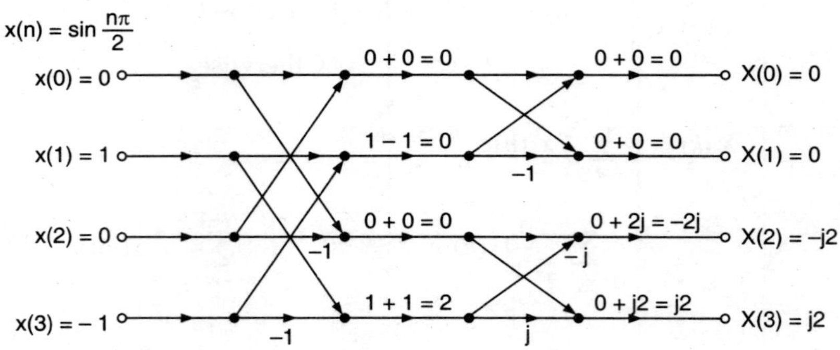

The values of signal on each line is shown above. Hence,

$X(0) = 0$, $X(1) = 0$, $X(2) = -j2$ and $X(3) = j2$ **Ans.**

EXAMPLE 6.30: *Assuming an 8-point sequence*

$$1,\ \frac{j}{\sqrt{2}},\ -1,\ \frac{1+j}{\sqrt{2}},\ 0,\ -j\sqrt{2},\ 1,\ \sqrt{2}$$

compute DFT by using decimation-in-time FFT flow-graph. Indicate the values of signal at each line.

SOLUTION:

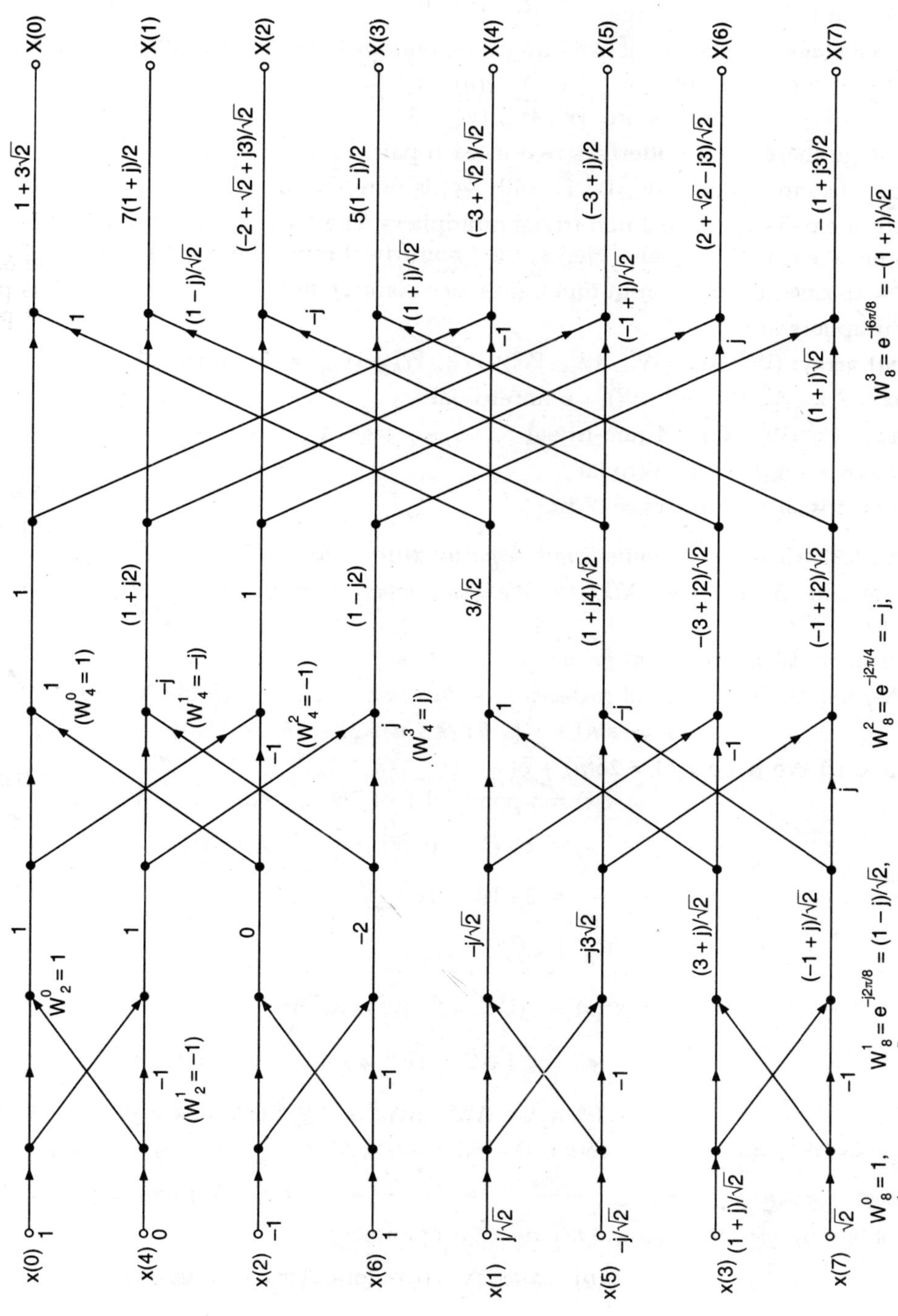

EXAMPLE 6.31: *Find the absolute minimum possible number of non-trivial multipliers required in a decimation-in-time, N-point FFT for (i) N = 8, (ii) N = 16.*

SOLUTION:

(*i*) **N = 8 case** (Decimation-in-time) (in-place computations)

Here $2^v = 8 \therefore v = 3$

There are three array stages

In the last stage (3rd stage) out of 4 butterflies, bottom 4 lines have multipliers of $W_8^0, W_8^1, W_8^2, W_8^3$ for in place computations.

Here non-trivial multipliers are: W_8^1, W_8^2, W_8^3 = **3.**

In **2nd stage** there are 4 butterflies two in each pair.

Each pair has multipliers W_4^0, W_4^1 *i.e.* only W_4^1 is non-trivial.

For both the pairs we have **2** non-trivial multipliers. The 1st stage has again 4 butterflies and four multipliers, each W_8^0 (trivials). Hence, total non-trivial multipliers = 3 + (1 × 2) + 0 = 5 **Ans.**

(*ii*) **N = 16 case** (decimation-in-time), (in-place computations)

The multipliers are

4th (last) array: $(W_{16}^0, W_{16}^1, W_{16}^2, W_{16}^3, W_{16}^4, W_{16}^5, W_{16}^6, W_{16}^7)$ = 7 non-trivial

3rd array: $2 \times (W_8^0, W_8^1, W_8^2, W_8^3)$ = 6 non-trivial

2nd array: $4 \times (W_4^0, W_4^1)$ = 4 non-trivial

1st array: $8 \times (W_4^0)$ = 0 non-trivial

Total non-trivial multipliers = 17 hr.

EXAMPLE 6.32: *Consider the finite-length sequence x(n) = 2δ(n) + δ(n – 1) + δ(n – 2).*

(i) We compute 5-point DFT X(k), (ii) We also compute 5-point IDFT of $Y(k) \triangleq X^2(k)$ to obtain sequence y(n).

(a) Determine the sequence y(n) for n = 0, 1, 2, 3, 4.

(b) If N-point DFTs are used in two-step procedure, how should we choose N so that

$$y(n) = x(n) * x(n) \text{ for } 0 \le n \le N-1?$$

SOLUTION: (*i*) We have $x(n) = 2\delta(n) + \delta(n-1) + \delta(n-2)$

$$X(k) = \text{5-point DFT of } 2\delta(n) + \delta(n-1) + \delta(n-2)$$

$$= 2 + (X(k) \text{ of } \delta(n)) \cdot W_5^k + (X(k) \text{ of } \delta(n)) \cdot W_5^{2k}$$

$$= 2 + W_5^k + W_5^{2k},\ 0 \le k \le 5$$

where $$W_5^k = e^{-j2\pi k/5}$$

(*ii*) $$X^2(k) = Y(k) = (2 + W_5^k + W_5^{2k})^2$$

$$= 4 + W_5^{2k} + W_5^{4k} + 4W_5^k + 2W_5^{3k} + 4W_5^{2k}$$

$\therefore$ $$Y(k) = 4 + 4W_5^k + 5W_5^{2k} + 2W_5^{3k} + W_5^{4k},\ k = 0, 1, \ldots, 4.$$

By inverse DFT, $y(n) = 4\delta(n) + 4\delta(n-1) + 5\delta(n-2) + 2\delta(n-3) + \delta(n-4),\ n = 0, 1, \ldots, 4$ **Ans.**

(*b*) As $y(n) = x(n)$ Ⓝ $x(n)$ $\quad$ ($\because$ $Y(k)$ was $X^2(k) = X(k) \cdot X(k)$)

Thus obtaining $y(n)$ by taking IDFT of $X^2(k)$ amounts to

$$y(n) = x(n) \text{ Ⓝ } x(n) \quad \text{(circular convolution)}$$

The IDFT and DFT suggests us that the convolution is circular. Hence, to ensure there is no aliasing, the size of DFT must be $N \geq 2M - 1$, where M is the length of $x(n)$. In this question $M = 3$, N is $\geq 2 \times 3 - 1$ *i.e.* $N \geq 5$, *i.e.* why $y(n)$ obtained thro 5-point IDFT of $X^2(k)$ is the same as $x(n)$ ⑤ $x(n)$.

Note: As IDFT $[X^2(k)] = x(n)$ Ⓝ $n(n) = \sum_{m=0}^{2} x(m)\, x((n-m))_N$ we obtain $x(0) = 4$, $x(1) = 4$, $x(2) = 5$, $x(3) = 2$, and $x(4) = 1$ (as expected).

EXAMPLE 6.33: *The discrete Hartley transform (DHT) is defined by*

$$DHT\{x(n)\} = H(k) \triangleq \sum_{n=0}^{N-1} x(n)\, cas\left(\frac{2\pi kn}{N}\right),\ k = 0, 1, 2, \ldots, N-1$$

where

$$cas\ \theta \triangleq \cos\theta + \sin\theta$$

(a) Show that

$$cas\ \theta_1 \cdot cus\ \theta_2 = \cos(\theta_1 - \theta_2) + \sin(\theta_1 + \theta_2)$$

(b) Show that

$$\sum_{n=0}^{N-1} cas\left(\frac{2\pi kn}{N}\right) \cdot cas\left(\frac{2\pi km}{N}\right) = N\delta_{n,m},\ 0 \leq n, m \leq N-1$$

(c) Obtain the relation for the inverse discrete Hartley transform (IDHT)

$$x(n) = IDHT\{H(k)\} = \frac{1}{N}\sum_{k=0}^{N-1} X(k)\, cas\left(\frac{2\pi kn}{N}\right),$$

$$n = 0, 1, 2, \ldots, N-1.$$

SOLUTION: (*a*)

$$\begin{aligned} \text{cas}\ \theta_1 \cdot \text{cas}\ \theta_2 &= (\cos\theta_1 + \sin\theta_1)(\cos\theta_2 + \sin\theta_2) \\ &= (\cos\theta_1\cos\theta_2 + \sin\theta_1\sin\theta_2) + (\sin\theta_1\cos\theta_2 + \cos\theta_1\sin\theta_2) \\ &= \cos(\theta_1 - \theta_2) + \sin(\theta_1 + \theta_2) \quad \textbf{Ans.} \end{aligned}$$

$$\boxed{\text{cas}\ \theta_1 . \text{cas}\ \theta_2 = \cos(\theta_1 - \theta_2) + \sin(\theta_1 + \theta_2)} \qquad \ldots(A)$$

(*b*)

$$\sum_{k=0}^{N-1} \text{cas}\left(\frac{2\pi kn}{N}\right) \cdot \text{cas}\left(\frac{2\pi km}{N}\right)$$

$$= \sum_{k=0}^{N-1}\left[\cos\left(\frac{2\pi k}{N}(n-m)\right) + \sin\left(\frac{2\pi k}{N}(n+m)\right)\right] \qquad \ldots[\text{using } (A)]$$

$$= \text{Re}\sum_{k=0}^{N-1} e^{j\frac{2\pi k}{N}(n-m)} + I_m \sum_{k=0}^{N-1} e^{j\frac{2\pi k}{N}(n+m)}$$

$$= \text{Re}\left[\frac{e^{j\frac{2\pi}{N}(n-m)\cdot N} - 1}{e^{j\frac{2\pi}{N}(n-m)} - 1}\right] + I_m\left[\frac{e^{j\frac{2\pi}{N}(n+m)N} - 1}{e^{j\frac{2\pi}{N}(n+m)} - 1}\right]$$

$$= \text{Re}\left[\frac{e^{j2\pi(n-m)} - 1}{e^{j\frac{2\pi}{N}(n-m)} - 1}\right] + I_m\underbrace{\left[\frac{e^{j2\pi(n+m)} - 1}{e^{j\frac{2\pi}{N}(n+m)} - 1}\right]}_{= N\delta(n+m)}$$

$$= \text{Re}[N \cdot \delta(n - m)] + I_m[0] \quad \because \quad e^{j2\pi(n + m)} = 1$$

$I_m[N\delta(n + m)] = 0$ as n, m are +ve integers

Since, when $n - m = 0$, then $\dfrac{e^{j2\pi(n-m)} - 1}{e^{j\frac{2\pi}{N}(n-m)} - 1} = \dfrac{0}{0}$ form

$= N$ by l' Hospital's Rule

Thus, we have

$$\boxed{\sum_{k=0}^{N-1} \text{cas}\left(\frac{2\pi kn}{N}\right) \cdot \text{cas}\left(\frac{2\pi km}{N}\right) = N\delta_{n,m} = N\delta(n - m),\ n, m = 0, 1, 2, \ldots, N - 1}$$

(*c*) Consider the function

$$\sum_{k=0}^{N-1} X(k) \cdot \text{cas}\frac{2\pi kn}{N},\ n = 0, 1, 2, \ldots, N - 1$$

$$= \sum_{k=0}^{N-1} \left[\sum_{m=0}^{N-1} x(m)\,\text{cas}\frac{2\pi km}{N}\right] \cdot \text{cas}\frac{2\pi kn}{N}$$

$$\because \quad X(k) \triangleq \sum_{n=0}^{N-1} x(n)\,\text{cas}\frac{2\pi kn}{N}$$

we have used m in lieu of n, being a dummy variable, to avoid confusion with n already appearing in the next term

$$= \sum_{m=0}^{N-1} x(m) \sum_{k=0}^{N-1} \text{cas}\left(\frac{2\pi km}{N}\right) \cdot \text{cas}\left(\frac{2\pi kn}{N}\right)$$

by interchanging the order of summation

$$= \sum_{m=0}^{N-1} x(m) \cdot N\delta_{n,m} \quad \text{using the result of part } (b)$$

$$= Nx(n)$$

Thus

$$\boxed{x(n) = \frac{1}{N}\sum_{k=0}^{N-1} X(k) \cdot \text{cas}\frac{2\pi kn}{N},\ n = 0, 1, 2, \ldots, N - 1.}$$

EXAMPLE 6.34: *Derive the following relation between the discrete Hartley transform DHT and the discrete Fourier transform DFT:*

$$DHT\,\{x(n)\} = Re\ DFT\,\{x(n)\} - I_m\ DFT\,\{x(n)\}.$$

SOLUTION: By definition

$$\text{DHT}\,\{x(n)\} = \sum_{n=0}^{N-1} x(n) \cdot \text{cas}\frac{2\pi kn}{N}$$

$$= \sum_{n=0}^{N-1} x(n)\left[\cos\frac{2\pi kn}{N} + \sin\frac{2\pi kn}{N}\right]$$

$$= \sum_{n=0}^{N-1} x(n)\left[\text{Re}\, e^{-j\frac{2\pi kn}{N}} - I_m e^{-j\frac{2\pi kn}{N}}\right]$$

Assuming $x(n)$ as real valued sequence

$$\text{DHT}\,\{x(n)\} = \text{Re}\sum_{n=0}^{N-1} x(n)\cdot e^{-j\frac{2\pi kn}{N}} - I_m \sum_{n=0}^{N-1} x(n)\cdot e^{-j\frac{2\pi kn}{N}} \qquad \text{Q.E.D.}$$

$$= \text{Re DFT}\,\{x(n)\} - I_m \text{ DFT}\,\{x(n)\}$$

$\left[\because \text{ by definition DFT } \{x(n)\} \text{ is defined as DFT } \{x(n)\} = \sum_{n=0}^{N-1} x(n)\, W_N^{nk} = \sum_{n=0}^{N-1} x(n)\cdot e^{-j\frac{2\pi nk}{N}}\right]$

UNSOLVED PROBLEMS ON DFT WITH ANSWERS

6.1. For the sequence $x(n) = \cos n\omega_0$, $0 \le n \le N-1$ find the DFT. Assume $\omega_0 \ne 2\pi k_0/N$.

$\left[\textbf{Hint. } x(n) = \frac{1}{2}(e^{jn\omega_0} + e^{-jn\omega_0})\right.$

$$\therefore \qquad X(k) = \frac{1}{2}\left[\sum_{n=0}^{N-1} (e^{jn\omega_0} + e^{-jn\omega_0})\, e^{-j2\pi nk/N}\right]$$

$$= \frac{1}{2}\left[\frac{1-e^{-jN\left(\frac{2\pi k}{N}-\omega_0\right)}}{1-e^{-j\left(\frac{2\pi k}{N}-\omega_0\right)}} + \frac{1-e^{-jN\left(\frac{2\pi k}{N}+\omega_0\right)}}{1-e^{-j\left(\frac{2\pi k}{N}+\omega_0\right)}}\right]$$

$$= \frac{1}{2}e^{-j\left(\frac{N-1}{2}\right)\left(\frac{2\pi k}{N}-\omega_0\right)}\cdot\frac{\sin(\pi k - N\omega_0/2)}{\sin(\pi k/N - \omega_0/2)}$$

$$\left.+\frac{1}{2}e^{-j\left(\frac{N-1}{2}\right)\left(\frac{2\pi k}{N}+\omega_0\right)}\cdot\frac{\sin(\pi k + N\omega_0/2)}{\sin(\pi k/N + \omega_0/2)} \qquad \textbf{Ans.}\right]$$

6.2. Find the N-point DFT for the sequence

$$x(n) = 4 + \cos^2\left(\frac{2\pi n}{N}\right)$$

$\left[\textbf{Hint. } \text{Replace } \cos^2\left(\frac{2\pi n}{N}\right) = \frac{1}{2}\left(\cos\frac{4\pi n}{N} + 1\right)\right.$

$$\therefore \qquad x(n) = 4 + \frac{1}{2} + \frac{1}{4}(e^{j4\pi n/N} + e^{-j4\pi n/N})$$

$$= \frac{9}{2} + \frac{1}{4}(e^{j2\pi/N(2n)} + e^{j2\pi/N(-2n)})$$

$$= \frac{9}{2} + \frac{1}{4}(e^{j2\pi/N(2n)} + e^{j2\pi/N(N-2)n})$$

$$\therefore \qquad X(k) = \begin{cases} \frac{9}{2}N, & k=0 \\ \frac{1}{4}N, & k=2, k=N-2 \\ 0, & \text{otherwise} \end{cases} \quad \textbf{Ans.}$$

6.3. For $x(n) = 2\delta(n) + \delta(n-1) + \delta(n-3)$

(a) Find 5 point DFT $X(k)$

(b) Find $y(n) = \text{IDFT}\,[X^2(k)]$

$$\left[X(k) = 2 + W_5^k + W_5^{3k}\right.$$

$$\left. y(n) = 4\delta(n) + 5\delta(n-1) + \delta(n-2) + 4\delta(n-3) + 2\delta(n-4) \quad \textbf{Ans.}\right]$$

6.4. If $x(n) = x_1(n) + jx_2(n)$, and DFT of $x(n) = X(k)$. Find the values of DFTs $X_1(k)$ and $X_2(k)$ of $x_1(n)$ and $x_2(n)$, respectively, in terms of $X(k)$

$$\left[X_1(k) = \frac{1}{2}[X(k) + X^*(-k)] \text{ i.e. conjugate symmetric part of } X(k)\right.$$

$$\left. X_2(k) = \frac{1}{2}[X(k) - X^*(-k)] \text{ i.e. conjugate anti-symmetric part of } X(k) \quad \textbf{Ans.}\right]$$

6.5. Given $x_1(n) = \cos\left(\frac{2\pi n k_1}{N}\right)$ and $x_2(n) = \cos\left(\frac{2\pi n k_2}{N}\right)$ evaluate the sum $S = \sum_{n=0}^{N-1} x_1(n)\, x_2^*(n)$.

[**Hint.** Use the result

$$\sum_{n=0}^{N-1} x_1(n)\, x_2^*(n) = \frac{1}{N}\sum_{k=0}^{N-1} X_1(k)\cdot X_2^*(k) \quad \text{(by Parseval's Relation)}$$

$$X_1(k) = \begin{cases} N/2, & k=k_1, k=N-k_1 \\ 0, & \text{otherwise} \end{cases}, \quad X_2(k) = \begin{cases} N/2, & k=k_2, k=N-k_2 \\ 0, & \text{otherwise} \end{cases}$$

$\therefore$ Sum $S = N/2$ for $k_1 = k_2$ or $k_1 = N - k_2$, and otherwise $S = 0$ **Ans.**]

6.6. Compute N-point DFT for the sequence

(i) $x_1(n) = \cos\dfrac{2\pi k_0 n}{N}$

(ii) $x_2(n) = a^n$, $0 \le n \le N-1$.

[**Hint.** (i) $X_1(k) = \sum_{n=0}^{N-1} x_1(n)\, W_N^{nk} = \sum_{n=0}^{N-1} \cos\dfrac{2\pi k_0 n}{N} W_N^{nk}$, $k = 0, 1, \ldots, N-1$ where $W_N \triangleq e^{-j2\pi/N}$

$$= \frac{1}{2}\sum_{n=0}^{N-1} \left(e^{j2\pi k_0 n/N} + e^{-j2\pi k_0 n/N}\right) e^{-j2\pi k n/N}$$

$$= \frac{1}{2}\sum_{n=0}^{N-1} \left(e^{j\frac{2\pi n}{N}(k_0-k)} + e^{-j\frac{2\pi}{N}n(k_0+k)}\right)$$

$$= \frac{1}{2}\left[\frac{1-e^{j2\pi(k_0-k)}}{1-e^{j2\pi(k_0-k)/N}} + \frac{1-e^{-j2\pi(k_0+k)}}{1-e^{-j2\pi(k_0+k)/N}}\right]$$

But $$\frac{1-e^{j2\pi l}}{1-e^{j2\pi l/N}} = \begin{cases} 0, & l \neq 0 \\ N, & l = 0 \end{cases} = N\delta(l)$$

∴ Using this result, we get

$$X_1(k) = \frac{1}{2}[N\delta(k_0 - k) + N\delta(k_0 + k)]$$

$$= \frac{N}{2}[\delta(k_0 - k) + \delta(k_0 + k)], \; k = 0, 1, 2, \ldots, N-1 \quad \textbf{Ans.}$$

(*ii*) $$X_2(k) = \sum_{n=0}^{N-1} x_2(n) W_N^{nk}, \; k = 0, 1, 2, \ldots, N-1$$

$$= \sum_{n=0}^{N-1} a^n e^{-j2\pi nk/N} = \sum_{n=0}^{N-1} (ae^{-j2\pi k/N})^n$$

$$= \frac{1-(ae^{-j2\pi k/N})^N}{[1-ae^{-j2\pi k/N}]}$$

$$= \frac{1-a^N e^{-j2\pi k}}{1-ae^{-j2\pi k/N}} \qquad \text{but } e^{-j2\pi k} = 1$$

$$= \frac{(1-a^N)}{(1-ae^{-j2\pi k/N})}$$

∴ $$X_2(k) = \frac{1-a^N}{1-ae^{-j2\pi k/N}}, \; k = 0, 1, 2, \ldots, N-1 \quad \textbf{Ans.]}$$

6.7. Show that if $x(n)$ is real, then DFT $X(k)$ satisfies the relation: $X(N-k) = X^*(k)$, where $*$ denotes the complex conjugation.

[Hint: As $$X(k) = \sum_{n=0}^{N-1} x(n) W_N^{nk}$$

∴ $$X(N-k) = \sum_{n=0}^{N-1} x(n) W_N^{n(N-k)}$$

$$= \sum_{n=0}^{N-1} x(n) W_N^{-nk} \qquad \because \; W_N^{Nn} = 1$$

$$= \left(\sum_{n=0}^{N-1} x(n) W_N^{nk}\right)^* \qquad x(n) = x^*(n) \text{ being real}$$

$$= X^*(k)$$

∴ $$X(N-k) = X^*(k)$$ Q.E.D.]

6.8. Show that: $x(n) = \text{IDFT}\,[X(k)] = \frac{1}{N}[DFT\,\{X^*(k)\}]^*$.

[Hint: We can write

$$x(n) = \frac{1}{N}\sum_{k=0}^{N-1} X(k)\,.\,e^{+j\frac{2\pi}{N}nk} \quad \text{(IDFT formula)}$$

$$= \frac{1}{N}\underbrace{\left(\sum_{k=0}^{N-1} X^*(k)\,e^{-j\frac{2\pi}{N}nk}\right)^*}_{\text{"DFT of } X^*(k)\text{"}} \quad \text{answer being a function of } n$$

$$\therefore \quad x(n) = \frac{1}{N}\,(\text{DFT of } X^*(k))^*] \qquad \text{Q.E.D.}$$

6.9. (*a*) Perform circular convolution for the sequences

$$x_1(n) = \{2, 1, 2, 1\},\; x_2(n) = \{1, 2, 3, 4\}$$

(*b*) Find $y(n) = x_1(n)$ ④ $x_2(n)$ by using DFT's of $x_1(n)$ and $x_2(n)$.

[Hint: (*a*) Here each sequence is of length $N = 4$

$$y(n) = x_1(n) \text{ Ⓝ } x_2(n) = x_1(n) \text{ ④ } x_2(n) = \sum_{m=0}^{3} x_1(m)\,.\,x_2\,((n-m))_4$$

$$\therefore \quad y(0) = \sum_{m=0}^{3} x_1(m)\,x_2\,((-m))_4$$

$$= x_1(0)\,x_2(0) + x_1(1)\,x_2(3) + x_1(2)\,x_2(2) + x_1(3)\,x_2(1)$$

$$= 2 \times 1 + 1 \times 4 + 2 \times 3 + 1 \times 2 = 2 + 4 + 6 + 2 = 14$$

$$y(1) = \sum_{m=0}^{3} x_1(m)\,x_2\,((1-m))_4$$

$$= x_1(0)\,x_2(1) + x_1(1)\,x_2(0) + x_1(2)\,x_2(3) + x_1(3)\,x_2(2)$$

$$= 2 \times 2 + 1 \times 1 + 2 \times 4 + 1 \times 3 = 4 + 1 + 8 + 3 = 16$$

$$y(2) = \sum_{m=0}^{3} x_1(m)\,x_2\,((2-m))_4$$

$$= x_1(0)\,x_2(2) + x_1(1)\,x_2(1) + x_1(2)\,x_2(0) + x_1(3)\,x_2(3)$$

$$= 2 \times 3 + 1 \times 2 + 2 \times 1 + 1 \times 4 = 6 + 2 + 2 + 4 = 14$$

$$y(3) = \sum_{m=0}^{3} x_1(m)\,x_2\,((3-m))_4$$

$$= x_1(0)\,x_2(3) + x_1(1)\,x_2(2) + x_1(2)\,x_2(1) + x_1(3)\,x_2(0)$$

$$= 2 \times 4 + 1 \times 3 + 2 \times 2 + 1 \times 1 = 8 + 3 + 4 + 1 = 16$$

$$\therefore \quad y(n) = x_1(n) \text{ ④ } x_2(n) = \{\underset{\uparrow}{14}, 16, 14, 16\} \quad \textbf{Ans.}$$

(*b*) As $Y(k) = X_1(k) \cdot X_2(k)$

We first find DFT's $X_1(k)$ and $X_2(k)$. Multiply $X_1(k)$ and $X_2(k)$ and find $y(n)$ = IDFT of $X_1(k) \cdot X_2(k)$. We shall get the same answer as found above.]

6.10. For a linear, shift-invariant system characterized by

$$y(n) = \sum_{k=1}^{p} a(k)\, y(n-k) + \sum_{k=0}^{q} b(k)\, x(n-k).$$

Find the DFT of the equivalent system function $H(z)$

[**Ans.** $$H(k) = \frac{B(k)}{A(k)}$$

where $$A(k) = 1 - \sum_{k=1}^{p} a(k)\, W_N^{nk},\ k = 0, 1, \ldots, N-1$$

$$B(k) = \sum_{k=0}^{q} b(k)\, W_N^{nk},\ k = 0, 1, \ldots, N-1$$]

6.11. If $X(k)$ is the N-point DFT of $x(n)$ what would be the DFT of windowed sequence $y(n) = x(n) \cdot \omega(n)$, if Blackman window is used.

[**Hint:** Use Blackman window

$$\omega(n) = 0.42 - 0.5 \cos\left(\frac{2\pi n}{N-1}\right) + 0.08 \cos \frac{4\pi n}{N-1},\ 0 \le n \le N-1$$

$$Y(k) = 0.42\, X(k) - 0.25\, [X(k-1) + X(k+1)] + 0.04\, [X(k-2) + X(k+2)].$$

$k = 0, 1, \ldots, N-1$ **Ans.**]

6.12. Given

$$h(n) = \{\underset{\uparrow}{1}, 2, 3\} \text{ and } x(n) = \{\underset{\uparrow}{1}, 2, 2, 1\}$$

(*a*) Find 4-point DFTs for $h(n)$ and $x(n)$

(*b*) Find the value of $x(n) * h(n)$ (*i.e.* linear convolution)

(*c*) Find the value of $x(n)$ ④ $h(n)$ (*i.e.* 4-point circular convolution)

[**Ans.** (*a*) $X(k) = \{6, (-1 - j), 0, (-1 + j)\}$

$H(k) = \{6, (-2 - j2), 2, (-2 + j2)\}$

(*b*) $x(n) * h(n) = \{1, \underset{\uparrow}{4}, 9, 11, 8, 3\}$

(*c*) $x(n)$ ④ $h(n) = \{9, \underset{\uparrow}{7}, 9, 11\}$]

6.13. If $x(n)$ is a sequence that is zero outside the interval $[0, N-1]$ and has z-transform $X(z)$. Find the DFT of the following sequences, each of length $2N$ in terms of $X(z)$.

(*a*) $$y_1(n) = \begin{cases} x(n), & 0 \le n < N \\ 0, & N \le n \le 2N-1 \end{cases}$$

(*b*) $y_2(n) = x(n) + x(n - N)$

(c) $y_3(n) = \begin{cases} x(n/2), & n \text{ even} \\ 0, & n \text{ odd} \end{cases}$

[**Ans.** (a) $Y_1(k) = X(z)\big|_{z=e^{j2\pi k/2N}} = X(e^{j\pi k/N})$

(b) $Y_2(k) = (1 - z^{-N})\ X(z)\big|_{z=e^{j2\pi k/2N}} = \begin{cases} 2X(e^{j\pi k/N}), & k \text{ even} \\ 0 \quad , & k \text{ odd} \end{cases}$

(c) $Y_3(k) = X(z^2)\big|_{z=e^{j2\pi k/2N}} = X(e^{j2\pi k/N}),\ k = 0, 1, .., 2N - 1$].

6.14. BY means of the DFT and IDFT, determine the response of the FIR filter with impulse response $h(n) = \{\underset{\uparrow}{1}, 2, 3\}$ and input $x(n) = \{\underset{\uparrow}{1}, 2, 2, 1\}$

[**Hint.** As $h(n)$ is of length 3 and $x(n)$ of length 4, therefore, $x(n) * h(n)$ (*i.e.* the linear convolution) is of length 3 + 4 – 1 = 6.

We must pad zeros to $h(n)$ and $x(n)$ to make each sequence of length 6. We make each length as 8 for ease of calculation.

$\therefore \quad h'(n) = \{1, 2, 3, 0, 0, 0, 0, 0\}$ and $x'(n) = \{1, 2, 2, 1, 0, 0, 0, 0\}$

$$\therefore \quad H(k) = \sum_{n=0}^{1} h'(n)\, W_8^{nk} = \sum_{n=0}^{1} h'(n)\, e^{-j\frac{2\pi}{8}nk},\ k = 0, 1, 2, .., 7$$

$$= 1 + 2\, .\, e^{-j\pi k/4} + 3e^{-j\pi k/2}$$

$$\therefore \quad H(0) = 1 + 2 + 3 = 6$$

$$H(1) = 1 + 2\left(\frac{1}{\sqrt{2}} - j\frac{1}{\sqrt{2}}\right) + 3(0 - j) = 1 + \sqrt{2} - j(3 + \sqrt{2})$$

$$H(2) = 1 + 2(-j) + 3(-1 + j0) = -2 - j\sqrt{2}$$

$$H(3) = 1 + 2\left(-\frac{1}{\sqrt{2}} - j\frac{1}{\sqrt{2}}\right) + 3(0 + j1) = (1 - \sqrt{2}) + j(3 - \sqrt{2})$$

$$H(4) = 1 + 2(-1 + j0) + 3(1 + j0) = 2$$

$$H(5) = 1 + 2\left(-\frac{1}{\sqrt{2}} + j\frac{1}{\sqrt{2}}\right) + 3(0 - j1) = (1 - \sqrt{2}) - j(3 - \sqrt{2})$$

$$H(6) = 1 + 2(0 + j2) + 3(-1 + j0) = -2 + j2$$

$$H(7) = 1 + 2\left(\frac{1}{\sqrt{2}} + j\frac{1}{\sqrt{2}}\right) + 3(0 + j) = (1 + \sqrt{2}) + j(3 + \sqrt{2})$$

Next we find DFT values of $X(k)$

$$h'(n) = \{\underset{\uparrow}{1}, 2, 2, 1, 0, 0, 0, 0\}$$

$$X(k) \sum_{n=0}^{7} x'(n)\, W_8^{nk} = \sum_{n=0}^{7} x'(n)\, e^{-j\frac{2\pi}{8}nk},\ k = 0, 1, ..., 7$$

$$= 1 + 2e^{-j\pi k/4} + 2\, e^{-j\pi k/2} + 1\, .\, e^{-j3\pi k/4}$$

$\therefore$ $X(0) = 1 + 2 + 2 + 1 = 6$

$$X(1) = 1 + 2\left(\frac{1}{\sqrt{2}} - j\frac{1}{\sqrt{2}}\right) + 2\ (0 - j1) + \left(-\frac{1}{\sqrt{2}} - j\frac{1}{\sqrt{2}}\right) = \frac{2+\sqrt{2}}{2} - j\frac{4+3\sqrt{2}}{2}$$

$$X(2) = 1 + 2(0 - j1) + 2(-1 + j0) + 1(0 + j1) = -1 - j$$

$$X(3) = 1 + 2\left(-\frac{1}{\sqrt{2}} - j\frac{1}{\sqrt{2}}\right) + 2\ (0 + j1) + 1\ \left(+\frac{1}{\sqrt{2}} - j\frac{1}{\sqrt{2}}\right) = \frac{2-\sqrt{2}}{2} + j\frac{4-3\sqrt{2}}{2}$$

$$X(4) = 1 + 2\ (-1 + j0) + 2(1 + j0) + 1(-1 + j0) = 0$$

$$X(5) = 1 + 2\left(-\frac{1}{\sqrt{2}} - j\frac{1}{\sqrt{2}}\right) + 2(0 - j1) + 1\left(\frac{1}{\sqrt{2}} - j\frac{1}{\sqrt{2}}\right) = \frac{2-\sqrt{2}}{2} - j\frac{4-3\sqrt{2}}{2}$$

$$X(6) = 1 + 2(0 + j1) + 2(-1 + j0) + 1(0 - j1) = -1 + j$$

$$X(7) = 1 + 2\left(\frac{-1}{\sqrt{2}} + j\frac{1}{\sqrt{2}}\right) + 2(0 - j1) + 1\left(-\frac{1}{\sqrt{2}} + j\frac{1}{\sqrt{2}}\right) = \frac{2+\sqrt{2}}{2} + j\frac{4+3\sqrt{2}}{2}$$

Product of two DFT's *i.e.* $Y(k) = H(k)\ .\ X(k)$, gives us

$Y(0) = 36$, $Y(1) = -14.07$, $Y(2) = 14$, $Y(3) = 0.07 + j\ 0.515$, $Y(4) = 0$,

$Y(5) = 0.07 - j0.515$, $Y(6) = -j4$, $Y(7) = -14.07 + j\ 17.48$

Now we take IDFT of $Y(k)$ *i.e.*

$$y(n) = \sum_{k=0}^{7} Y(k)\, e^{+j\frac{2\pi}{8}nk}\ ,\ n = 0, 1, 2, ..., 7$$

We obtain $y(n) = \{\underset{\uparrow}{1}, 4, 9, 11, 8, 3, 0, 0\}$

$\underbrace{\qquad\qquad}_{\text{the desired outpect } = h(n) * x(n)}$

$\therefore$ $h(n) * x(n) = \{1, 4, 9, 11, 8, 3\}$ **Ans.**

Check: $h(n) * x(n) = 1, 2, 2, 1, 3, 2, 1 = \{1, 4, 9, 11, 8, 3\}$ as expected.]

6.15. Define circular correlation of two sequences $x(n)$ and $y(n)$, denoted by $r_{xy}(l)$. Find DFT of $r_{xy}(l)$ in terms of $X(k)$ and $Y(k)$. *(I.P. Univ. 2008)*

SOLUTION: We define circular correlation of $x(n)$ and $y(n)$ as

$$\boxed{r_{xy}(l) = \sum_{n=0}^{N-1} x(n)\, y^*((n-l))_N} \quad \text{Circular coordination definition}$$

As
$$r_{xy}(l) = \sum_{n=0}^{N-1} x(n)\, .\, y*((n-l))_N$$

$$= \sum_{m=0}^{N-1} x(m)\, y^*((m-l))_N = \sum_{m=0}^{N-1} x(m)\, .\, y^*((-(l-m)))_N \quad \text{(Note this step)}$$

$\therefore$
$$\boxed{r_{xy}\ (l) = x(n) \ \textcircled{N}\ y*\ (-\ l)}$$

As DFT of $r_{xy}(l) = \text{DFT}\ [x(n)]\ .\ \text{DFT}\ [y*\ (-\ l)]$

[To find DFT of $y*(-\ l)$]

$$\text{DFT}\,[y^*(-l)] = \sum_{l=0}^{N-1} y^*(-l)\, W_N^{lk}$$

$$= \left(\sum_{l=0}^{N-1} \underbrace{y(N-l)}_{\text{Put } N-l=m} W_N^{-lk}\right)^* \qquad \because\ y(l) \text{ is periodic } \therefore\ y(-l) = y(N-l)$$

$$\left(\sum_{m=1}^{N} y(m)\, W_N^{-(N-m)k}\right)^* = \left(\sum_{m=0}^{N-1} y(m)\, W_N^{mk}\right)^* \quad **$$

$$\therefore \qquad [y^*(-l)] \xrightarrow{\text{DFT}} Y^*(k)$$

Hence,
$$\boxed{r_{xy}(l) = \sum_{n=0}^{N-1} x(n)\,.\,y^*[(n-l)]_N \xrightarrow{\text{DFT}} X(k)\,.\,Y^*(k)}$$ **Ans.**

6.16. Show that

(*i*) DFT [Real part of $x_p(n)$] = Conjugate symmetric part of $X_p(k)$

(*ii*) DFT $[x^*_p(-n)] = X^*_p(k)$

where $X_p(k)$ is the DFT of $x_p(n)$.

Ans. (*i*) DFT of $x^*_p(-n) = \sum_{n=0}^{N-1} x_p^*(-n)\, e^{-j\frac{2\pi}{N}kn}$, $k = 0, 1, ..., N-1.$

$$= \left[\sum_{n=0}^{N-1} x_p(-n)\, e^{+j\frac{2\pi}{N}kn}\right]^*$$

$$= \left[\sum_{n=0}^{N-1} x_p(N-n)\, e^{j\frac{2\pi kn}{N}}\right]^*$$

$$\because\ x_p(n) \text{ is periodic with period } N \ \therefore\ x_p(-n) = x_p(-n+N)$$

Put $N - n = n' \therefore$ when $n = 0,\ n' = N$

when $n = N-1,\ n' = 1$

$$\text{DFT of } x^*_p(-n) = \left[\sum_{n'=1}^{N} x_p(n')\, e^{j\frac{2\pi k'}{N}(N-n')}\right]^*$$

$$= \left(\sum_{n'=1}^{N} x_1(x')\, e^{-j\frac{2\pi kn'}{N}}\right)^*$$

Drop dashes. Also $x_p(N)\, e^{-j\frac{2\pi kN}{N}} = x_p(0)\, e^0$ becomes the first term

$$\therefore \qquad \text{DFT}\,[x_p^*(-n)] = \left(\sum_{n=0}^{N-1} x_p(n)\,.\,e^{-j\frac{2\pi kn}{N}}\right)^* = X_p^*(k)$$ Q.E.D.

** How this step $\Rightarrow \sum_{m=1}^{N} y(m)\, W_N^{mk} = \sum_{m=0}^{N-1} y(m)\, W_N^{mk} + \underbrace{y(N)\, W_N^{Nk} - y(0)\, W_N^{0k}}_{\substack{\text{as } y(N) = y(0) = 0 \\ W_N^{Nk} = W_N^{ok}}}$

(ii) DFT [Real part of $x_p(n)$] = DFT of $\left[\frac{1}{2}(x_p(n)+x_p^*(n))\right]$ ...(A)

But DFT of $\quad x_p(n) \;=\; X_p(k)$

and $\quad \text{DFT}\,[x_p^*(n)] \;=\; \sum_{n=0}^{N-1} x_p^*(n)\,W_N^{nk} \;=\; \left(\sum_{n=0}^{N-1} x_p(n)\,e^{j\frac{2\pi}{N}nk}\right)^*$

$$= X^*_p(-k)$$

$\therefore$ DFT of Real part of $x_p(n) = \frac{1}{2}[X_p(k)+X_p^*(-k)]$

= **Conjugate symmetric** part of $X_p(k)$ Q.E.D.

6.17. Define the sequence

$$y_k(n) \triangleq \sum_{r=0}^{N-1} x(r)\,W_n^{-k(n-r)}$$

Show that $X(k) = y_k(n)\big|_{n=N}$. Taking the impulse response as $h(n) = W_N^{-kn}$, with k a parameter, construct a black diagram or signal-flow graph for the system having $y_k(n)$ as the output, and $x(n)$ as the input. Show that the system function can be written as

$$H_k(z) = \frac{1-W_N^k z^{-1}}{1-2\cos(2\pi k/N)\,z^{-1}+z^{-2}}$$

Construct s signal-flow graph for this system function.

Ans. As $\quad y_k(n) = \sum_{r=0}^{N-1} x(r)\,W_N^{-k(n-r)} \quad$ where $\quad W_N \triangleq e^{-j2\pi/N}$ ...(A)

$$\therefore \quad y_k(n)\big|_{n=N} = \sum_{r=0}^{N-1} x(r)\,.\,W_N^{-k(N-r)}$$

$$= \sum_{r=0}^{N-1} x(r)\,W_N^{kr}\,.\,\underbrace{W_N^{-kN}}_{=1} \qquad \because (e^{-j2\pi/N})^{-kN} = e^{j2\pi k} = 1$$

$$= \sum_{r=0}^{N-1} x(r)\,W_N^{kr}$$

$= X(k)$ (by definition of DFT of $x(n)$)

(A) shows that $y_k(n) = x(n) * W_N^{-kn}$

i.e. $y_k(n)$ is the output of a system having input as $x(n)$ and system unit sample response $h(n)$ as

$$h(n) = W_N^{-kn}$$

i.e.,

$$H(z) = \sum_{n=0}^{\infty} W_N^{-kn}\,z^{-n}$$

$$= \frac{1}{1 - W_N^{-k} z^{-1}}$$

$$= \frac{1}{1 - W_N^{-k} z^{-1}} \times \frac{1 - W_N^{k} z^{-1}}{1 - W_N^{k} z^{-1}} \qquad \text{(Note this step)}$$

$$= \frac{1 - W_N^{k} z^{-1}}{1 - (W_N^{-k} + W_N^{k}) z^{-1} + z^{-2}}$$

$$= \frac{1 - W_N^{k} z^{-1}}{1 - 2[\cos\{2\pi k(N)\}] z^{-1} + z^{-2}} \qquad ...(B)$$

Realization of $H(z)$, given in (B) is shown below.

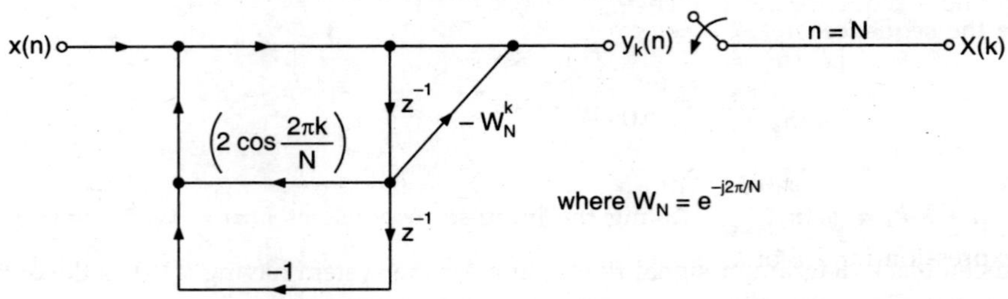

Fig. Goertzel algorithm—Realization of DFT

6.18. (*a*) Compute the Fourior transform $X(\omega)$ of the signal

$$x(n) = \{1, 2, \underset{\uparrow}{3}, 2, 1, 0\}$$

(*b*) Compute the 6-point DFT $V(k)$ of the signal

(*c*) Is there any relation between $X(\omega)$ and $V(k)$? Explain.

Ans. (*a*)

$$FT\ X(\omega) = \sum_{n=-\infty}^{\infty} x(n)\, e^{-j\omega n} = \sum_{n=-2}^{3} x(n)\, e^{-j\omega n}$$

$$= 1.e^{j2\omega} + 2.e^{j\omega} + 3.e^{j0\omega} + 2e^{-j\omega} + 1e^{-j2\omega} + 0.e^{-j3\omega}$$

$$= 3 + 2\cos 2\omega + 4\cos\omega \quad \textbf{Ans.} \qquad ...(A)$$

(*b*)

$$V(k) = \sum_{n=0}^{N-1} x(n)\, e^{-j2\pi nk/N}$$

$$= \sum_{n=0}^{5} x(n)\, e^{-j2\pi nk/6} = \sum_{n=0}^{5} x(n)\, e^{-j\pi nk/3}$$

$$\underset{\substack{\nearrow\\3}}{x(0)\,e^{-j0}} + \underset{\substack{\nearrow\\2}}{x(1)\,e^{-j\pi k/3}} + \underset{\substack{\nearrow\\1}}{x(2)\,e^{-j2\pi k/3}} + \underset{\substack{\nearrow\\0}}{x(3)\,e^{-j3\pi k/3}} + \underset{\substack{\nearrow\\= x(-2) = 1}}{x(4)\,e^{-j\frac{4\pi k}{3}}} + \underset{\substack{\nearrow\\= x(-1) = 2}}{x(5)\,e^{-j\frac{5\pi k}{3}}}$$

due to periodicity $N = 6$ here

$$3e^{0j} + 2e^{-j\pi k/3} + 1\,.\,e^{-j2\pi k/3} + 0 + 1.e^{-j\frac{4\pi k}{3}} + 2.e^{-j\frac{5\pi k}{3}}$$

$$3 + 2e^{-j\pi k/3} + e^{-j2\pi k/3} + e^{+j2\pi k/3} + 2e^{+j\frac{\pi k}{3}} \qquad \left(\because\ e^{-j\frac{5\pi k}{3}} = e^{j\frac{\pi k}{3}}\right)$$

$$= 3 + 4\cos\frac{\pi k}{3} + 2\cos\frac{2\pi k}{3} \qquad ..(B)$$

(c) If we put $\omega = \frac{2\pi k}{6}$ i.e., $\omega = \frac{\pi k}{3}$ in (A) we get (B).

Hence, $V(k) = X(\omega)\big|_{\omega=\frac{2\pi k}{6}=\frac{\pi k}{3}}$ as expected.

6.19. Given the sequences

$$x_1(n) = \{0, 1, 2, 3, 4\} \text{ and } x_2(n) = \{0, 1, 0, 0, 0\}$$

Determine a sequence $x_3(n)$, such that $X_3(k) = X_1(k) \,.\, X_2(k)$

$$[x_3(n) = \{\underset{\uparrow}{4}, 0, 1, 2, 3\} \quad \textbf{Ans.}$$

[**Hint:** $x_3(n) = x_1(n) \circledS x_2(n) = \sum_{m=0}^{4} x_1(m)\, x_2((n-m))_5$]

6.20. The expression for ZT of $h(n)$, $H(z)$ in terms of its DFT values $H(k)$ is given by [(see (6.23)]:

$$H(z) = \frac{1}{N}(1 - z^{-N})\sum_{k=0}^{N-1}\frac{H(k)}{1-(W_N^k Z)^{-1}}, \text{ where } W_N = e^{-2\pi/N}$$

when N is odd, show that

$$H(z) = \frac{1}{N}(1 - z^{-N})\left[\frac{H(0)}{1-z^{-1}} + \sum_{k=1}^{(N-1)/2}\frac{A(k) - B(k)z^{-1}}{1 - 2\cos(2\pi k/N)z^{-1} + z^{-2}}\right]$$

where

$$A(k) = H(k) + H(N-k)$$

$$B(k) = H(k) \,.\, W_N^k + H(N-k)W_N^{-k}$$

CHAPTER 7

Sampling and Reconstruction of Band-limited Signals (Sampling Theorem)

7.0 INTRODUCTION

Most of the signals that we use in practice are continuous-time signals such as speech signals, the seismic signals and the image signals. When these signals are to be transmitted over a distance, or stored, or are to be processed in some manner, a lot of advantages are possible if these signals are first converted into discrete/digital signals for the various operations. Converting an analog signal into its digital form is called Analog to Digital (A/D) conversion. A to D conversion involves three steps *viz.* sampling, quantizing and encoding. The reverse process of converting a digital signal into analog form is called Digital to Analog (D/A) conversion. We shall study the sampling and signal reconstruction techniques in this chapter. In fact, the vast field of digital communication, the operation of modern computers, the networking, the cellophone systems and remote sensing/remote control etc. all invariably use digital signals. The sampling principle is, therefore, a very important topic.

7.1 ANALOG-TO-DIGITAL CONVERSION (ADC)

An A/D converter transforms an analog signal (*i.e.*, a continuous-time signal) to a digital sequence. The components of an A/D converter are shown in Fig. 7.1.

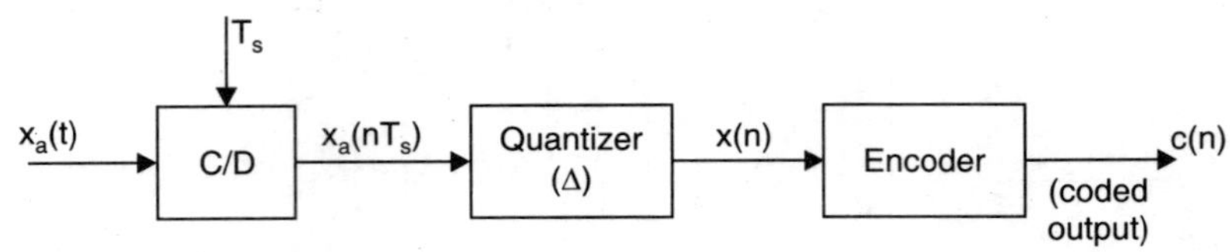

Fig. 7.1. The components of an Analog-to-Digital converter (*ADC*). *C/D* block represents Continuous-to-Discrete sampler.

We assume $x_a(t)$ as real-valued function of continuous variable t. In most of the cases, t represents time, though t can also be any other variable. At each value of t, the function $x_a(t)$ may be any real number. The continuous-to-discrete (C/D) converter is the sampler and it converts $x_a(t)$ into $x_a(nT_s)$ by multiplying $x_a(t)$ by train of pulses $p_a(t)$, also called periodic sequences of impulses given by

$$p_a(t) = \sum_{n=-\infty}^{\infty} \delta(t - nT_s) \quad \ldots(7.1)$$

Output of C/D back in $x_a(nT_s)$, given by

$$x_p(t) = x_a(t) \cdot p_a(t)$$

$$= x_a(t) \cdot \sum_{n=-\infty}^{\infty} \delta(t - nT_s)$$

$$\therefore \quad x_p(t) = \sum_{n=-\infty}^{\infty} x_a(nT_s) \cdot \delta(t - nT_s) \quad \ldots(7.2)$$

$x_p(t)$ is still an analog signal, though at discretized time nT_s. In general, $x_p(t)$ can have any possible amplitude. The second block in Fig. 7.1 is called Quantizer, denoted by symbol Δ. Quantizer is also indicated by the notation $Q[\cdot]$. The quantizer maps $x_p(t)$ into a discrete set of amplitudes. Depending on the number of bits, b, in the computer processor, there are finite values of levels equaling 2^b into which $x_p(t)$ can fit. For example, if $b = 3$, then possible levels are 0, 1, 2, 3, 4, 5, 6, 7. So, a signal $x_p(t) = 2.3$ will be rounded to 2.0. Similarly, $x_p(t) = 3.7$ is mapped to 4.0. In the process of quantization $x_p(t)$ are mapped to appropriate discrete magnitudes to obtain $x(n)$. In Chapter 10, we shall discuss in detail the effect of quantization. The last block in Fig. 7.1 is Encoder. It takes the digital signal $x(n)$ and converts it into a sequence of binary sequence as the coded word, for further use by the computer.

Figure 7.2 gives the stages of waveform $x_a(t)$ to conversion of digital signal $x(n)$. As $x_a(t)$ [Fig. 7.2(*a*)] and $p_a(t)$ [Fig. 7.2(*b*)] are both analog signals, therefore, $x_p(t) = x_a(t) \cdot p_a(t)$ is also an analog signal in the form of impulses of various values $x_a(nT_s)$, shown in Fig. 7.2(*c*). After quantization, $x_a(nT_s)$ gets converted into $x(n)$, and are shown in Fig. 7.2(*d*). Note that $x(n)$ consists of samples of various heights depending on values of $x_a(nT_s)$. Figure 7.2(*e*) gives the representation of generating $x_p(t)$ from $x_a(t)$.

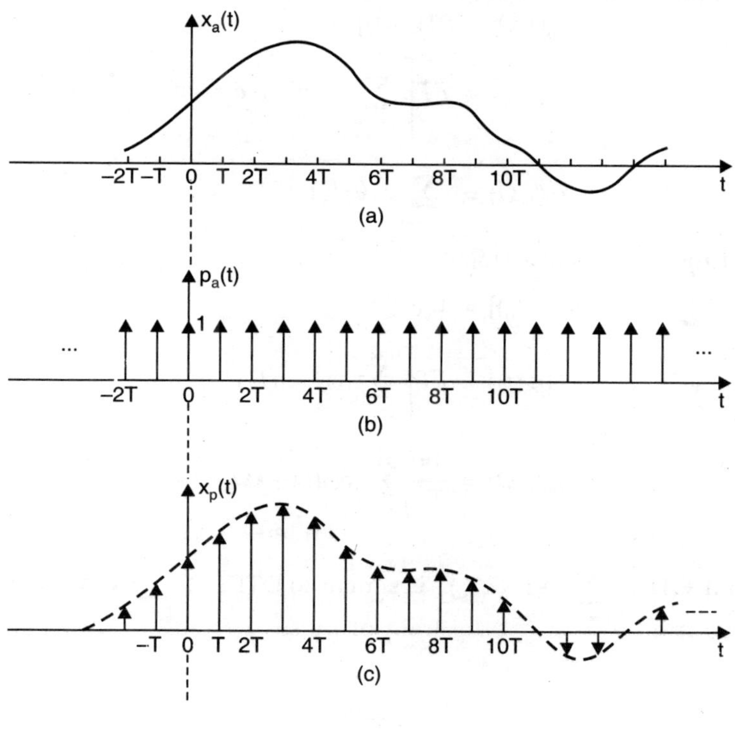

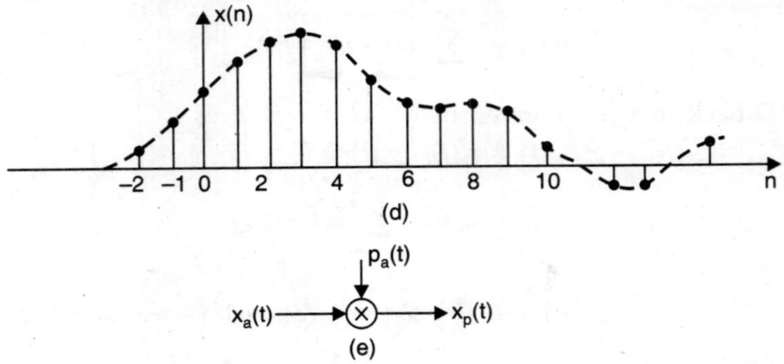

Fig. 7.2. The waveforms at various stages for generation of $x(n)$: (*a*) The given analog signal $x_a(t)$, (*b*) Sampling pulses $p_a(t)$, (*c*) $x_a(nT_s) = x_p(t) = x_a(t) \cdot p_a(t)$, (*d*) After quantization: $x(n) = Q[x_p(t)]$, (*e*) Representation of impulse train sampling.

7.2 PERIODIC SAMPLING AND SPECTRUM OF $x(n)$

We shall now analyze the effect of sampling $x_a(t)$ to $x(n)$. It is assumed in our discussion that the quantization error is zero, and that

$$x(n) = x_a(nT_s) \qquad \text{...(7.3)}$$

The sampling spacing T_s is the sampling period and

$$f_s = \frac{1}{T_s}, \ (T_s \text{ in seconds}) \qquad \text{...(7.4)}$$

is the sampling frequency in samples per second. To obtain $x(n)$, we first form $x_p(t)$, by multiplying $x_a(t)$ by $p_a(t)$ as given in (7.2). The effect of *A* to *D* (assuming ideal *A* to *D* converter) may be analyzed in the frequency domain. Let the Fourier transform of $x_p(t)$ be given by

$$X_p(j\,\Omega) = FT[x_p(t)]$$

$$= FT\left[\sum_{n=-\infty}^{\infty} x_a(nT_s)\cdot\delta(t-nT_s)\right]$$

$$\therefore \qquad X_p(j\,\Omega) = \sum_{n=-\infty}^{\infty} x_a(nT_s)\cdot e^{-jn\Omega T_s} \qquad \text{...(7.5)}$$

We have used the result that $FT[\delta(t)] = 1$

and $$FT[\delta(t - t_0)] = 1\cdot e^{-jt_0\Omega}$$

Also, $$FT[p_a(t)] = FT\left[\sum_{n=-\infty}^{\infty}\delta(t-nT_s)\right]$$

$$\therefore \qquad p_a(j\,\Omega) = \frac{2\pi}{T_s}\sum_{k=-\infty}^{\infty}\delta(j(\Omega-k\Omega_s)) \qquad \text{...(7.6)}$$

where $\Omega_s = \dfrac{2\pi}{T_s}$, and CTFT$\left[\sum_{k=-\infty}^{\infty}\delta(t-nT_s)\right]$ is similar to DTFT of $\sum_{k=-\infty}^{\infty}\delta(n-kN)$. See result (2.103).

As $$x_p(t) = x_a(t) \cdot p_a(t)$$

$\therefore$ $$X_p(j\,\Omega) = \frac{1}{2\pi} X_a(j\,\Omega) * P_a(j\,\Omega) \qquad \text{...(7.7)}$$

$$= \frac{1}{2\pi} X_a(j\,\Omega) * \frac{2\pi}{T_s} \sum_{k=-\infty}^{\infty} \delta(j(\Omega - k\Omega_s))$$

$$= \frac{1}{T_s} \sum_{k=-\infty}^{\infty} X_a(j\,\Omega) * \delta(j(\Omega - k\Omega_s))$$

$\therefore$ $$X_p(j\,\Omega) = \frac{1}{T_s} \sum_{k=-\infty}^{\infty} X_a(j\,\Omega - jk\Omega_s) \qquad \text{...(7.8)}$$

As DTFT $[x(n)]$ is given by

$$X(e^{j\omega}) = \sum_{n=-\infty}^{\infty} x(n) e^{-j\omega n} \qquad \text{(Definition of DTFT)}$$

$$= \sum_{n=-\infty}^{\infty} x_a(nT_s) e^{-j\omega n} \qquad \because\ x(n) = x_a(nT_s) \text{ due to (7.3)}$$

$$= X_p(j\,\Omega)\Big|_{\Omega=\omega/T_s} \qquad \text{(Due to (7.5))}$$

$$= \frac{1}{T_s} \sum_{k=-\infty}^{\infty} X_a(j\,\Omega - jk\Omega_s),\ \Omega = \frac{\omega}{T_s}$$

The final result is, putting $\Omega = \dfrac{\omega}{T_s}$ in above equation,

$$\boxed{\begin{aligned} X(e^{j\omega}) &= \frac{1}{T_s} \sum_{k=-\infty}^{\infty} X_a\left(j\frac{\omega}{T_s} - j\frac{2\pi k}{T_s}\right) \\ X_p(j\omega) &\triangleq X(e^{j\omega});\ \omega = \Omega T_s \end{aligned}} \qquad \text{...(7.9)}$$

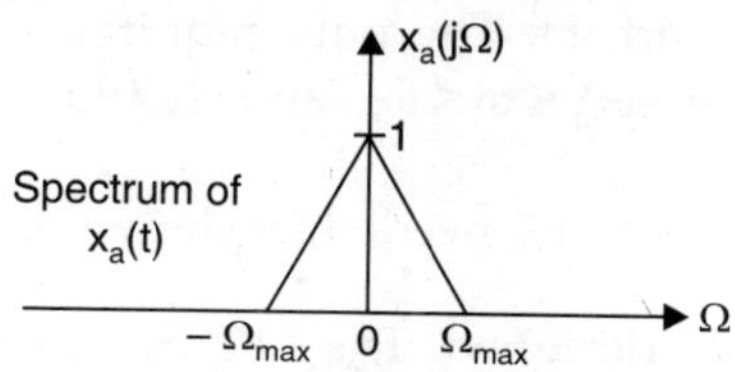

(a)

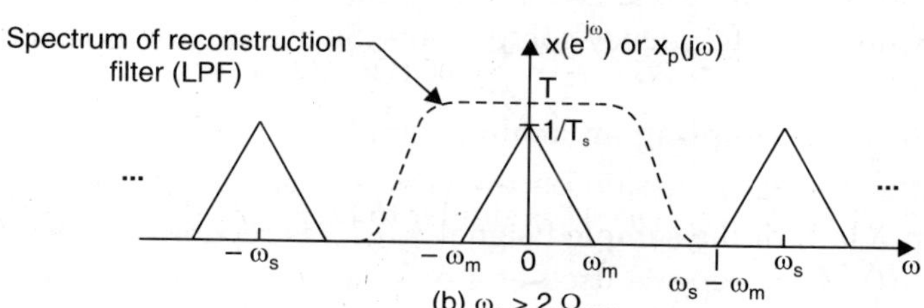

(b) $\omega_s > 2\,\Omega_{max}$

(No aliasing, guard band available)

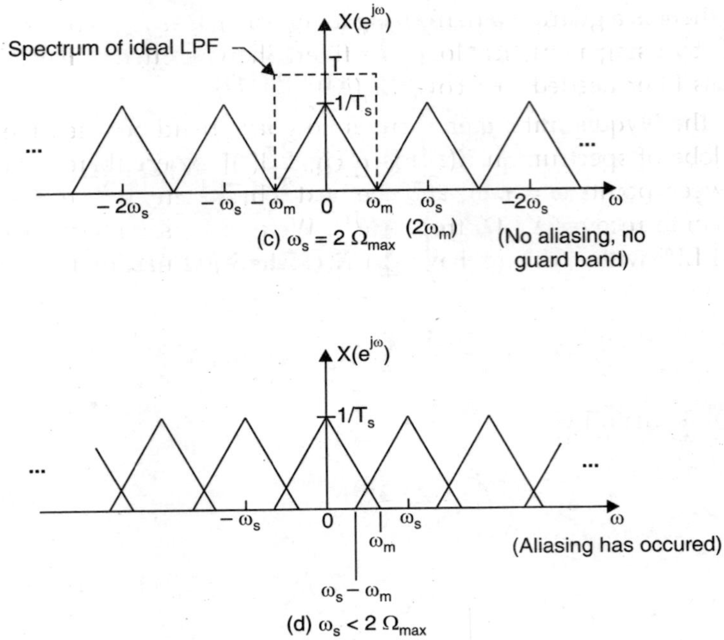

Fig. 7.3. (*a*) Spectrum of $x_a(t)$ *i.e.* $X_a(j\ \Omega)$, band limited to Ω_{max}, (*b*) spectrum of $X(e^{j\omega})$, when $x(n) = x_a(nT_s)$ for $\omega_s = \dfrac{2\pi}{T_s} > 2\Omega_{max}$; $\Omega T_s = \omega$ spectrum of $X(e^{j\omega})$ for: (*c*) $\omega_s = 2\Omega_{max}$, (*d*) $\omega_s < 2\Omega_{max}$.

Figure 7.3(*a*) gives the spectrum $X_a(j\ \Omega)$ of the analog signal $x_a(t)$. Assume that $X_a(j\ \Omega)$ is band-limited with highest frequency of $\Omega_{max} = 2\pi f_{max}$. Figure 7.3(*b*) shows the spectrum $X(e^{j\omega})$ of the discrete-time signal $x(n)$, where $x(n) = x_a(nT_s)$. $X(e^{j\omega})$ is periodic in ω, with period ω_s where $\omega_s = 2\pi f_s = \dfrac{2\pi}{T_s}$. Figure 7.3(*c*) is the spectrum of $X(e^{j\omega})$ if $\omega_s = 2\Omega_{max}$ and Fig. 7.3(*d*) is the spectrum of $X(e^{j\omega})$, for $\omega_s < 2\Omega_{max}$.

To recover $X_a(j\ \Omega)$, and hence $x_a(t)$, we use low-pass filter having spectrum as shown by dotted curves in Figs. 7.3(*b*) and (*c*). The only requirement of the LPF is that it should have constant magnitude $H_{LP}(j\omega)$ for $-\omega_m \le \omega \le \omega_m$, and should decay to zero response for $|\omega_m| < |\omega| < \left|\dfrac{\omega_s}{2}\right|$. A typical response of the LPF needed, is shown in Fig. 7.3(*b*), which has no sharp (brick shape) edges and can be easily designed. The LPF as shown in Fig. 7.3(*c*) has sharp edges, and it cannot be designed. In fact theoretically, such a sharp-edged (brick-shape) response requires an infinite length and hence cannot be realized. In Fig. 7.3(*d*), we cannot recover $X_a(j\ \Omega)$ by any filter, due to mixing of low and high frequency components. Such a mixing is called *Aliasing* and is not desirable.

Summary of effects of sampling an analog signal

We summarise the above discussion on the effects of sampling rate as follows:

(*a*) The spectrum $X(e^{j\omega})$ of the sampled signal $x_a(nT_s)$ is repetitive of the baseband spectrum $X_a(j\Omega)$ of the signal $x(t)$. $X(e^{j\omega})$ repeats itself at a regular interval of ω_s, where $\omega_s = 2\pi f_s$ and f_s is the sampling frequency.

(*b*) If $f_s > 2f_m$, there is a guard band from ω_m to $(\omega_s - \omega_m)$, [see Fig. 9.3 (*b*)]. It is easy to separate $X_a(j\Omega)$ from $X(e^{j\omega})$ by using a practical low pass filter. Shown dotted in Fig. 7.3(*b*) is the spectrum of such a low pass filter needed to recover $X_a(j\Omega)$.

(*c*) If $f_s = 2f_m$, the Nyquist rate, then there is no guard band between the point $\omega = \omega_m$ and the start of next lobe of spectrum in $X(e^{j\omega})$ [see Fig. 7.3(c)], where there is no separation (so, no guard band) between points $\omega = \pm\, \omega_m$ and the next lobes. Here, we need an ideal LPF, shown dotted in Fig. 7.3(*c*) to recover $X_a(j\Omega)$ from $X(e^{j\omega})$. We also must remember that it is impossible to design an ideal LPF with spectrum having a brick shape, as needed for signal recovery in this case.

(*d*) **If $f_s < 2f_m$, then aliasing takes place.** Aliasing means high frequency components mix with low frequency component.

In this case, it is not possible to recover $X_a(j\Omega)$ from $X(e^{j\omega})$ *i.e.*, we cannot recover $x_a(t)$ from $x(n)$. In Fig. 7.3(*d*), we have drawn $X(e^{j\omega})$ for the case $f_s < 2f_m$. Note that from $\omega = \omega_s - \omega_m$ to ω_m, there is mixing of high and low frequency amplitudes.

To avoid aliasing, we must ensure that (*i*) $x(t)$ is strictly band limited to f_m (*ii*) f_s is greater than $2f_m$	...(7.10)

7.2.1 Use of Anti-aliasing Filter

We have assumed that the signal which we sample is band limited $-\Omega_m < \Omega < \Omega_m$ *i.e.* $X_a(j\Omega) = 0$ for $|\Omega| > |\Omega_m|$. Theoretically, a signal must extend from $-\infty \le t \le \infty$ to be a band limited one. Practically, no signal is extending in time up to infinity, rather each useful signal has duration for finite time. This implies that all practically useful signals will have non-band limited spectrum. In such cases, therefore, *we must first band limit the given signal before sampling.*

An anti-aliasing filter is basically a low pass filter (LPF) of constant magnitude response. Here, we pass the signal $x_a(t)$, with spectrum $X_a(j\Omega)$, through an anti-aliasing filter to obtain a band limited spectrum.

In Fig. 7.4, the spectrum $X_a(j\Omega)$ after hashed portions are removed, will be a band limited $-\Omega_m \le \Omega \le \Omega_m$. Now we can sample the resulting signal using $f_s \ge 2f_m$ without any fear of aliasing.

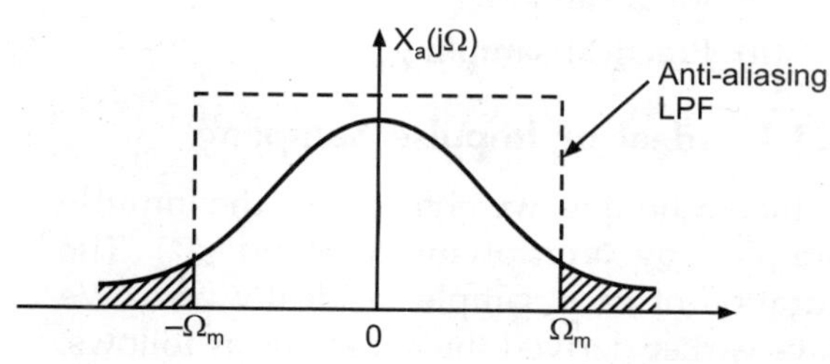

Fig. 7.4. Band limiting the spectrum $X_a(j\Omega)$ before sampling. Hashed part is removed by the anti-aliasing LPF.

The choice of Ω_m depends on the application. For example, speech signals can have frequencies up to even 15 kHz, if it is a female voice. But for digital telephone it is first band limited, using anti-aliasing filter, to 3.4 kHz. Then we use $f_s = 8$ kHz for sampling. Note that $f_s > 2 \times 3.4$ kHz, and there will be no aliasing. Signal reconstruction will not be a problem at the receiving end. Similarly, for high fidelity (HI-FI) music, we use $\Omega_m = 20$ kHz and $f_s = 44.1$ kHz which is more than twice the Ω_m value here (here, $f_s = 2.2$ times Ω_m).

7.2.2 Statement of the Sampling Theorem

Let a signal $x(t)$ be strictly band limited with Fourior spectrums

$$\boxed{X(j\Omega) = 0 \text{ for } |\Omega| > |\Omega_m|} \qquad ...(7.11)$$

i.e. the highest frequency content of $X(j\omega)$ is $f_m = \frac{\Omega_m}{2\pi}$ Hz.

If $x(t)$ is sampled at the rate of f_s samples per second such that

$$\boxed{f_s \geq 2f_m} \qquad ...(7.12)$$

then the original signal $x(t)$ can be completely recovered from its samples $x_p(t) = x(nT_s)$ without loss of information.

The minimum sampling frequency

$$f_s = 2f_m$$

is called an **Nyquist sampling rate.** The sampling interval

$$\boxed{T_s = \frac{1}{f_s}} \qquad ...(7.13)$$

is called the **Nyquist interval.**

For practical considerations, we always choose f_s more than $2f_m$.

This facilitates ease in recovering $x(t)$ from $x_p(t)$ as we can use non-ideal low pass filter (LPF) for signal reconstruction. A perfect, ideal (square pulse shape response) LPF theoretically cannot be designed. So, choice of f_s greater than $2f_m$ is a necessity for practical considerations.

7.3 SAMPLING TECHNIQUES

The sampling techniques can be categorised as

(*i*) Ideal sampling

(*ii*) Practical sampling.

7.3.1 Ideal or Impulse Sampling

In this technique, we obtain $x_p(t)$, the impulse samples, by multiplying $x(t)$ and $p(t)$. The duration of each sample in ideally zero. We have earlier derived the equations as follows:

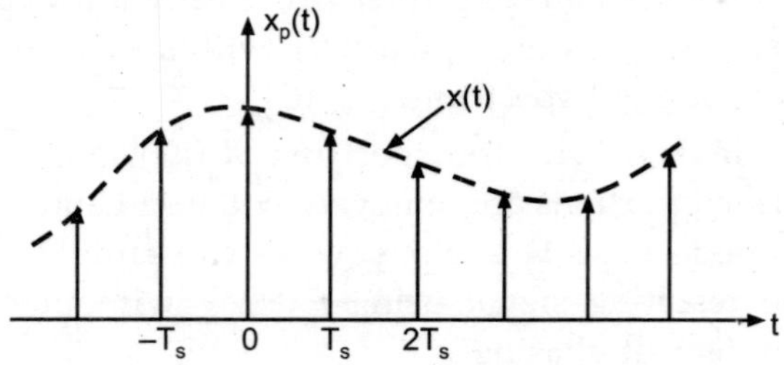

Fig. 7.5. Ideally sampled sequence $x_p(t)$. Width of each sample is zero.

$$p(t) = \sum_{k=-\infty}^{\infty} \delta(t - kT_s) \qquad \text{[from (7.1)]}$$

$$x_p(t) = x(t).\sum_{k=-\infty}^{\infty} \delta(t - kT_s) = \sum_{k=-\infty}^{\infty} x(kT_s).\delta(t - kT_s) \qquad \text{[from (7.2)]} \qquad ...(7.14)$$

$$X(e^{j\omega}) = \frac{1}{T_s}\sum_{k=-\infty}^{\infty} X\left(j\frac{\omega}{T_s} - j\frac{2\pi k}{T_s}\right), \Omega_s = \frac{2\pi}{T_s} \qquad \text{[from (7.9)]}$$

The spectrum of ideally sampled signal $x_p(t)$ consists of original spectrum $X_a\left(j\frac{\omega}{T_s}\right)$ and its replicas centred at $\pm\ \Omega_s \pm 2\Omega_s \pm 3\Omega_s$ ...etc.

The ideal samples have zero width *i.e.* zero energy and, therefore, cannot be transmitted. Also, zero width type samples $x_p(kT_s)$ cannot be practically produced. So we adopt practical sampling as covered next.

7.3.2 Practical Sampling (Flat-top Sampling)

As sampling by pulse function

$$p(t) = \sum_{k=-\infty}^{\infty} \delta(t - kT_s)$$

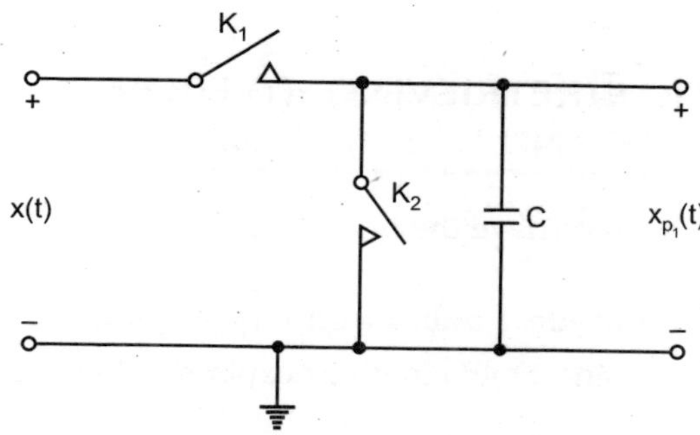

Fig. 7.6. Schematic of a sample and Hold (SH) Circuit.

will theoretically produce impulse type (*i.e. width zero*) samples $x(kT_s)$, which is practically neither feasible nor desirable. We cannot transmit narrow width (nearly zero width) large amplitude pulses. The practical sampling is to produce the samples by either of the following approaches.

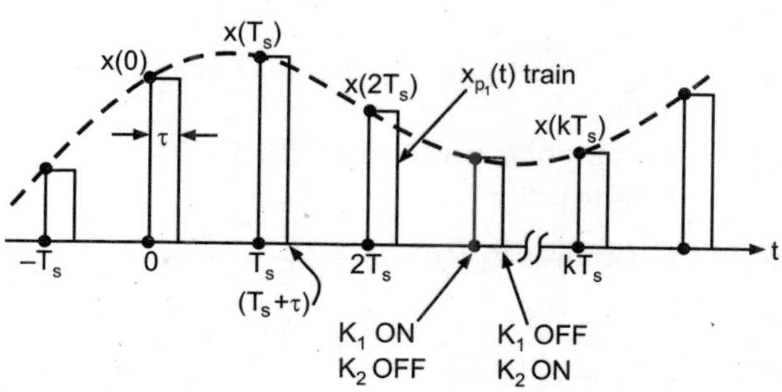

Fig. 7.7. Signal $x(t)$ and output $x_{p_1}(t)$ Sample and Hold Circuit.

(*i*) Sample and Hold type narrow width pulse (width τ) at the sampling instants kT_s. See Fig. 7.7. This is a preferred approach.

(*ii*) Narrow pulses with pulse top following the contour of $x(t)$, not a preferred one.

We shall describe the Sample and Hold type of practical sampling technique. Figure 7.7 shows a circuit with input $x(t)$ and output $x_{p_1}(t)$. The circuit consists of two switches K_1 and K_2 and a capacitor C. The opening and closing of switches K_1 and K_2 follows the cycle (*a*), (*b*), (*c*), and so on. These cycles are as follows:

(a) First, K_1 is closed and K_2 opened. When K_2 is opened, K_1 is closed, for a very short period at each sampling instant 0, T_s, $2T_s$, ... kT_s. With K_1 closed (and K_2 open) the capacitor C gets charged to value $x(kT_s)$ *i.e.* equal to the input signal $x(t)$ at time $t = kT_s$. K_1 opens immediately after closing for a very small time. During the period K_1 was ON, capacitor has got charged to voltage $x(kT_s)$, assuming charging time of the capacitor C as extremely small.

(b) Then, K_1 and K_2 are both opened. The capacitor had assumed voltage $x(kT_s)$, and this voltage is available across the capacitor C as long as K_2 is also open. At the end of time τ after the instance kT_s, switch K_2 closes, making output zero. Thus, the singal value at $t = kT_s$ remains available for τ seconds from $t = kT_s$ to $t = kT_s + \tau$.

(c) Finally, K_1 is opened and K_2 closed. Since K_2 is ON *i.e.*, closed, the capacitor C gets discharged to zero and the output is zero.

Thereafter, K_1 will close and K_2 opens at $t = (k + 1)\ T_s$ and the cycle repeats as above. Note that K_1 and K_2 are never closed together, since, this would short circuits the signal source.

7.4 RECONSTRUCTION/RETRIEVING $x(t)$ FROM PRACTICALLY SAMPLED (SAMPLE AND HOLD) SIGNAL $x_{p_1}(t)$

We have earlier discussed how to retrieve the original baseband singal $x(t)$ from ideally sampled signal $x_p(t)$.

There, $p(t)$ was a sequence of ideal train of impulses. Now, we have the signal's train of pulses $x_{p_1}(t)$ obtained by Sample and Hold circuit as explained in the previous sections. We wish to recover $x(t)$ from the samples $x_{p_1}(t)$.

From Fig. 7.7, it is clear that the sampled version of $x(t)$ is $x_{p_1}(t)$ and it consists of sequence of rectangular pulses each of width τ, the leading edge of the kth pulse in $x_{p_1}(t)$ being at $t = kT_s$ and the amplitude of the pulse is the value of $x(t)$ at $t = kT_s$ *i.e.* $x(kT_s)$. Hence, we can write

$$x_{p_1}(t) = \sum_{k=-\infty}^{\infty} x(kT_s)\cdot p_1(t - kT_s) \quad ...(7.15)$$

where $p_1(t)$ = Rectangular pulse of width τ and height unity

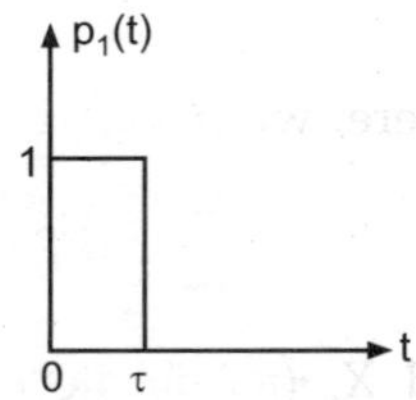

Fig. 7.8. The pulse $p_1(t)$

Figure 7.7 shows the train of pulses $x_{p_1}(t)$.

The pulse, $p_1(t)$ is shown in Fig. 7.8.

The Fourier transform of $p_1(t)$ is

$$P_1(j\omega) = (e^{-j\omega\tau/2})\left(\tau\frac{\sin(\omega\tau/2)}{(\omega\tau/2)}\right) \quad ...(7.16)$$

The spectra of $x(t)$ (= $X(j\Omega)$), of ideally sampled $x(t)$ [= $X(e^{j\omega})$], and that of S ple and Hold sampled [= $X_{p_1}(j\omega)$] are shown in **Fig. 7.9.**

As $p_1(t - kT_s) = p_1(t) * \delta(t - kT_s)$ (Note this step)

Putting this value of $p_1(t - kT_s)$ in (7.15), we get

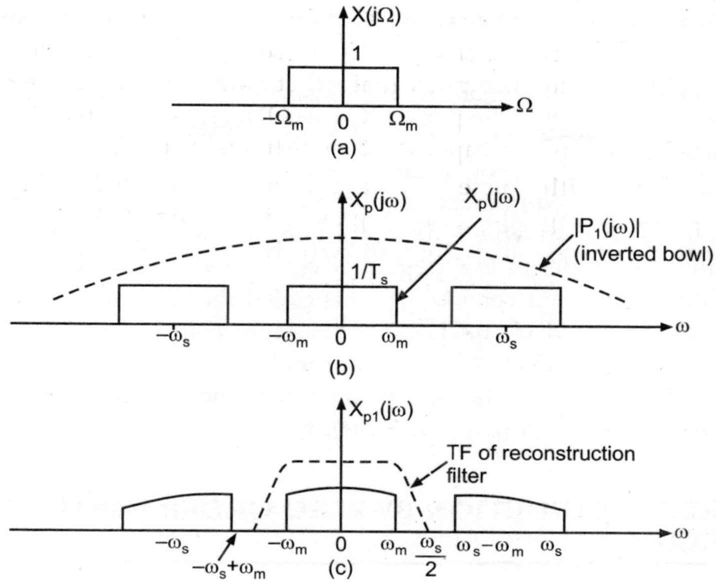

Fig. 7.9. The spectra (*a*) $X(j\Omega)$, (*b*) Ideally sampled $X_p(j\omega)$, and $P_1(j\omega)$ (dotted curve), (*c*) $X_{p_1}(j\omega) = X_p(j\omega).\ P_1(j\omega)$. (Note that $\omega = \Omega T_s$)

$$x_{p_1}(t) = \sum_{k=-\infty}^{\infty} x(kT_s)\,[p_1(t) * \delta(t-kT_s)]$$

or

$$x_{p_1}(t) = p_1(t) * \sum_{k=-\infty}^{\infty} x(kT_s).\,\delta(t-kT_s) \qquad ...(7.17)$$

Taking Fourier transform on both sides of (7.17), we get

$$\boxed{X_{p_1}(j\omega) = P_1(j\omega)\ .\ X_p(j\omega)} \qquad ...(7.18)$$

where, we have used the relation from (7.14) *i.e.,*

$$\sum_{k=-\infty}^{\infty} x(kT_s).\,\delta(t-kT_s) = x_p(t) \xrightarrow{FT} X_p(j\omega)$$

and $X_p(j\omega)$ is the *FT* of ideally sampled (by impulses $\delta(t - kT_s)$) signal $x(kT_s)$. Note that the response $X_{p1}(j\omega)$ degenerates to ideally sampled case when $\tau \to 0$. With $\lim_{\tau\to 0} p_1(t) = \delta(t)$ and $P_1(j\omega) \to 1$ for $\tau \to 0$. Hence, for $\tau \to 0$, we readily get

$$\begin{aligned}\lim_{\tau\to 0} X_{p_1}(j\omega) &= \lim_{\tau\to 0} [P_1(j\omega).\,X_p(j\omega)] \\ &= \left(\lim_{\tau\to 0} P_1(j\omega)\right) X_p(j\omega) \\ &= 1 \times X_p(j\omega) \\ &= X_p(j\omega) \text{ (as expected)}\end{aligned}$$

Assuming $X_p(j\omega)$ as shown in Fig. 7.9(*b*) and $P_1(j\omega)$ also shown in Fig. 7.9(*b*) (dotted curve), when we multiply $X_p(j\omega)$ and $P_1(j\omega)$ (due to Eq. (7.18)), we obtain $X_{p_1}(j\omega)$ as shown in Fig. 7.9 (*c*).

As $P_1(j\omega)$ is not constant, it is infact, an inverted bowl shape, the resultant $X_{p_1}(j\omega)$ will not be exact replica of $X(j\Omega)$. However, when τ is very small ($\tau << T_s$), then $P_1(j\omega)$ has nearest zeros at $f = \pm \frac{1}{\tau}$, which are far away from $\pm \omega_s$. Very small value of width τ makes response $P_1(j\omega)$ almost flat.

We reconstruct the baseband signal $x(t)$ by passing $X_{p_1}(j\omega)$ through a low pass filter, as shown in Fig. 7.9(*c*) (dotted curve). However, the output of the filter will not be exactly $x(t)$, it will be a distorted version of $x(t)$. It is distorted, because, the magnitudes of the high-frequency components are relatively reduced because of multiplication of $X_p(j\omega)$ by an inverted bowl type response, $P_1(j\omega)$. Such a distortion, where the amplitudes of the high-frequency components are reduced relative to the amplitudes of low frequency components, in the reconstructed singal $x(t)$ obtained from the flat-top sampled version of $x(t)$ is called the **Aperture Effect**. Hence, the time τ for which the sample-and-hold circuit holds the sample value, should be made as small as possible to reduce the aperture effect. As we cannot make $\tau = 0$, we try to keep the pulse width reasonably small and try to reduce the distortion within the message frequency by using an Equaliser with Transfer function: $H_e(j\omega) = 1/P_1(j\omega)$, $|\omega| < \omega_m$.

7.5 SIGNAL RECONSTRUCTION BY ZERO ORDER HOLD CIRCUIT (ZOH CIRCUIT)

In order to obtain the analog signal $x(t)$ back from the samples $x_p(t)$ with spectrum $X_p(j\omega)$ given by Fig. 7.3, we use Zero-Order-Hold (ZOH) circuit followed by a low-pass filter $h_r(t)$. We first extend each sample of $x_p(t)$ to T_s second long by ZOH and remove the unwanted high frequency components by LPF having spectrum $|\omega| \leq \frac{\omega_s}{2}$.

The block diagram of a ZOH system is shown in Fig. 7.10(*a*). The ZOH circuit is fed by the samples $x_p(t)$ and its output is $x_0(t)$. Fig 7.10(*c*) shows the impulse response $h_0(t)$ of the ZOH system. $h_0(t)$ is defined by:

$$h_0(t) = \begin{cases} 1, & 0 \leq t \leq T_s \\ 0, & \text{otherwise} \end{cases} \qquad \ldots(7.19)$$

as drawn in Fig. 7.10(*c*). This can be shown as follows:

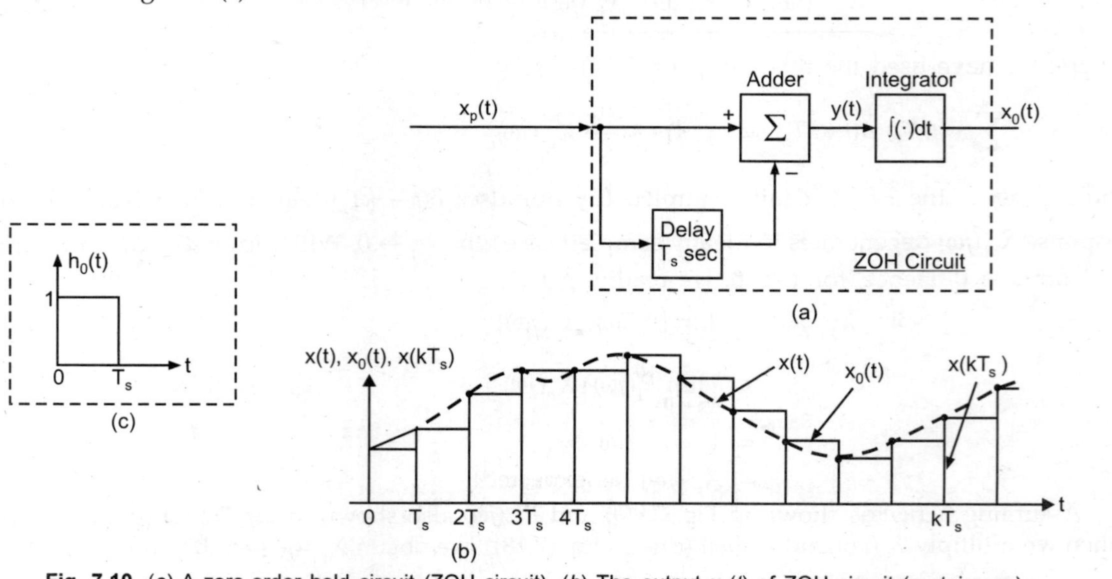

Fig. 7.10. (*a*) A zero-order hold circuit (ZOH circuit), (*b*) The output $x_0(t)$ of ZOH circuit (a staircase), (*c*) The impulse response of system inside the dashed boundary of (*a*) – called ZOH system.

To find impulse response of ZOH circuit [See circuit of Fig. 7.10(*a*)]

To find the impulse response, say $h_0(t)$ of ZOH, let us input $\delta(t)$ to the ZOH circuit. Then the output of ZOH circuit will be its impulse response. Due to input $\delta(t)$ and delayed input $\delta(t - T_s)$ the output of the adder is

$$y(t) = \delta(t) - \delta(t - T_s) \qquad ...(7.20)$$

After integration, output of integrator is $h_0(t)$, given by

$$h_0(t) = \int [\delta(t) - \delta(t - T_s)]\, dt$$

$$= u(t) - u(t - T_s) \qquad [\because \text{ Integration of } \delta(t) \text{ is } u(t)]$$

$$= \text{A square pulse of width } T_s \qquad [\text{see Fig. 7.10 } (c)]$$

We may now redraw Fig. 7.10 as Fig. 7.11 for better understanding the system.

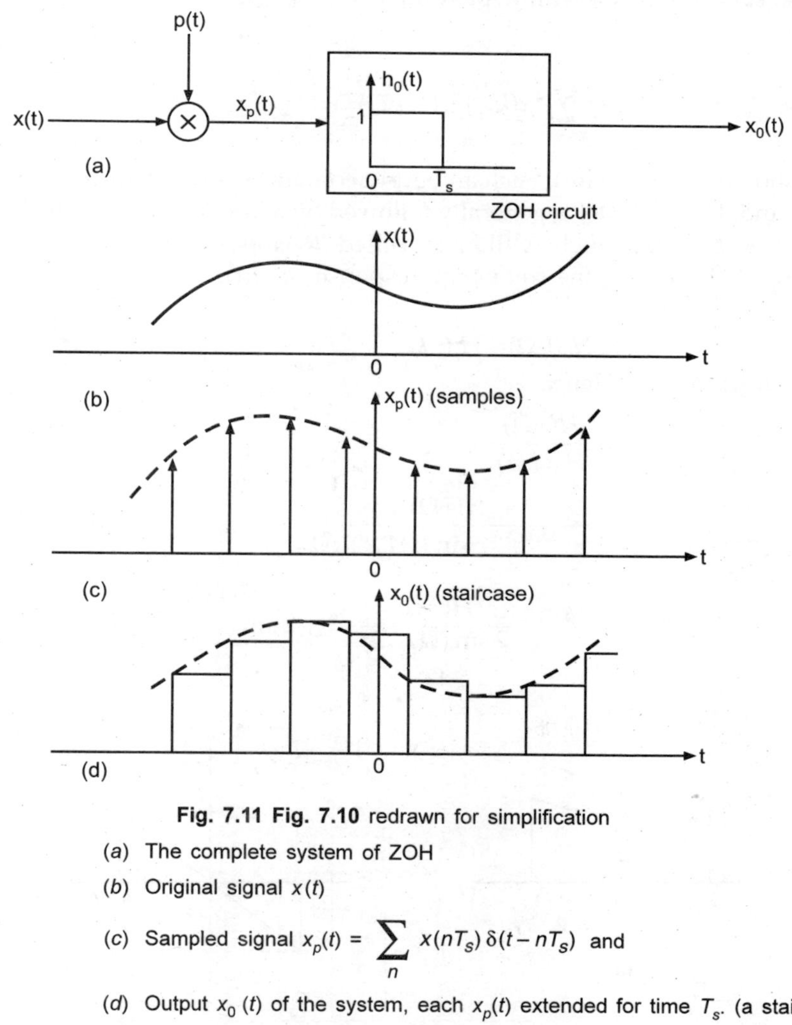

Fig. 7.11 Fig. 7.10 redrawn for simplification

(*a*) The complete system of ZOH

(*b*) Original signal $x(t)$

(*c*) Sampled signal $x_p(t) = \sum_n x(nT_s)\,\delta(t - nT_s)$ and

(*d*) Output $x_0(t)$ of the system, each $x_p(t)$ extended for time T_s. (a staircase)

[To find frequency response $H_0(j\ \Omega)$ of the ZOH circuit]

$$H_0(j\ \Omega) = \int_{-\infty}^{\infty} h_0(t) e^{-j\Omega t}\, dt$$

$$= \int_0^{T_s} 1 \cdot e^{-j\Omega t}\, dt = \frac{-1}{j\,\Omega}[e^{-j\Omega t}]_0^{T_s}$$

$$= \frac{-1}{j\,\Omega}[e^{-j\Omega T_s} - 1] = \frac{e^{-j\Omega T_s/2}}{j\,\Omega}(e^{j\Omega T_s/2} - e^{-j\Omega T_s/2})$$

$$\therefore \quad \boxed{H_0(j\ \Omega) = e^{-j\Omega T_s/2} \cdot T_s \cdot \sin(\Omega T_s/2)/(\Omega T_s/2)} \qquad \ldots(7.21)$$

Note that $H_0(j\ \Omega)$ is not a perfect low-pass filter. The output of the ZOH circuit for input $x_p(t)$ given by (7.14), *i.e.*,

$$x_p(t) = \sum_{k=-\infty}^{\infty} x(kT_s)\delta(t - kT_s)$$

is a stair case as shown in Fig. 7.11(*d*). Such an output contains several high-frequency components outside the baseband. Hence, ZOH is generally followed by a low-pass filter with cut-off frequency Ω_m radians/sec (*i.e.* f_m kHz). Such a filter is called ***Reconstruction Filter***, denoted by $h_r(t)$ (or $H_r(j\ \Omega)$) in Fig. 7.13. To find the frequency response of $h_r(t)$, denoted by $H_r(j\ \Omega)$, we use the relation

$$H(j\ \Omega) = H_0(j\ \Omega) \cdot H_r(j\ \Omega) \qquad \ldots(7.22)$$

where $H(j\ \Omega)$ is an ideal LPF. Hence,

$$H_r(j\ \Omega) = \frac{H(j\,\Omega)}{H_0(j\,\Omega)}$$

$$= \frac{H(j\,\Omega)}{e^{-j\Omega T_s/2} \cdot 2\sin(\Omega T_s/2)/\Omega}$$

$$= e^{j\Omega T_s/2}\frac{H(j\,\Omega)}{\frac{2\sin(\Omega T_s/2)}{\Omega}} \triangleq \left|\frac{H(j\,\Omega)}{\frac{2\sin(\Omega T_s/2)}{\Omega}}\right| \measuredangle\, \theta_r(\Omega) \qquad \ldots(7.23)$$

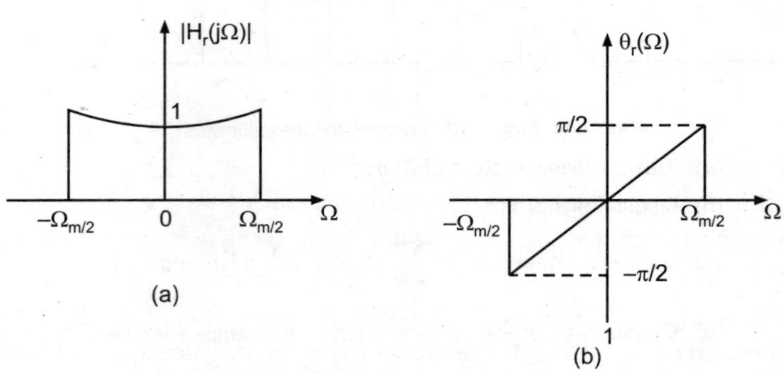

Fig. 7.12. (*a*) Magnitude $H_r(j\Omega)$ and (*b*) Phase $\theta_r(\Omega)$ of reconstruction filter.

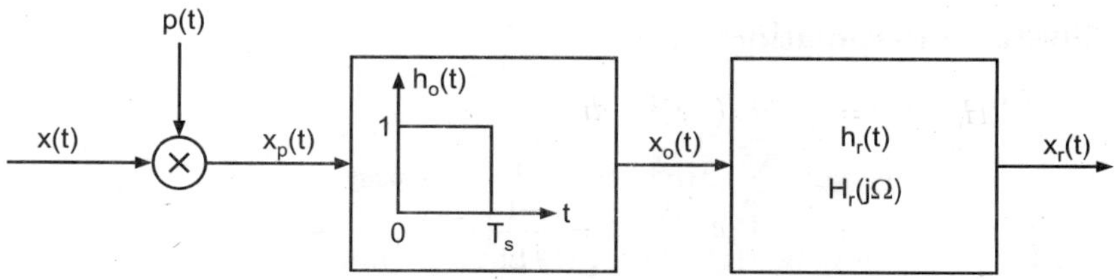

Fig. 7.13. Final system used for ZOH, by cascading $H_r(j\ \Omega)$ with system given in 7.11(*a*).

Typical magnitude and phase response given by (7.23) is shown in Fig. 7.13. With the addition of reconstruction filter, the overall cascade combination of zero-order-hold system becomes as shown in Fig. 7.13. It is desirable that $H(j\Omega)$ should be as close to an ideal LPF as feasible.

7.6 SIGNAL RECONSTRUCTION—OTHER METHODS

To retrieve the baseband signal $x(t)$ from its samples $x_p(t)$ is termed as "signal reconstruction". There are various ways to obtain $x(t)$ *i.e.*, $X(j\Omega)$ from $X_p(j\omega)$. One of the methods is by sampling with zero order hold (ZOH) as discussed in Section 7.5. The output $x_r(t)$ available after the reconstruction filter $H_r(j\Omega)$ is very close to $x(t)$, provided the cascade combination of $h_o(t)$ and $h_r(t)$ is the ideal low-pass filter $H(j\Omega)$. In many situations, the output of the zero-order hold is considered an adequate approximation of the original signal $x(t)$, without any additional low pass filtering, and in essence, $x_r(t)$, see Fig. 7.13, represents a possible very coarse interpolation between the sample values. In some other applications, we may wish to perform some better interpolation between the sample values $x_p(t)$. We explain, in more details, the general concept and interpretation of reconstruction of signal $x(t)$ from its samples $x_p(t)$, in the following sections.

7.6.1 Use of Interpolation to Reconstruct the Signal $x(t)$

As the interpolation implies the fitting of a continuous signal to a set of sample values, there could be various options. One simple interpolation procedure is the **linear interpolation.** Here,

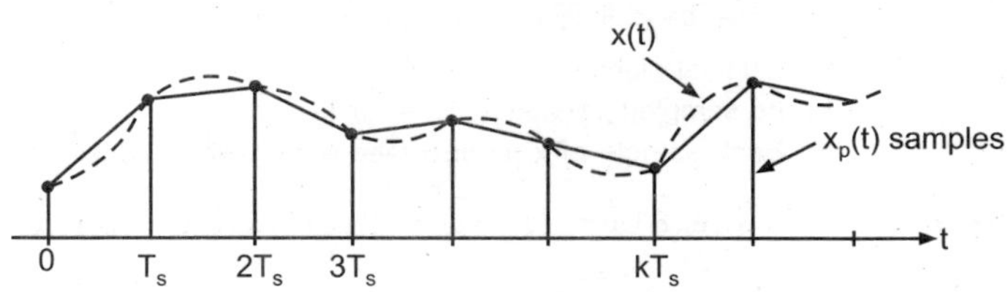

Fig. 7.14. Linear interpolation between sample point:
The dashed curve is the original signal $x(t)$,
and the solid curve is the one obtained by linear interpolation.

the adjacent sample points are connected by a straight line, as shown in Fig. 7.14. In more complicated interpolation (non-linear one), the sample points may be connected by higher order polynomials or other mathematical functions such as **Lagrange's** interpolation polynomial or **Bernstein** polynomial etc.

We have proved in sampling theorem that a band-limited signal, if the sampling rate $f_s \geq 2 f_{max}$, can be reconstructed exactly (*i.e.* without any error) from its samples $x_p(t)$. This was evident when we considered the effect on baseband $X(j\Omega)$ after $x(t)$ is sampled, see Fig. 7.3.

7.6.2 Band Limited Interpolation

We have proved earlier that

$$x_p(t) = \sum_{n=-\infty}^{\infty} x(nT)\,\delta(t-nT) \qquad \text{[see (7.14)]}$$

Let the ideal LPF for retrieving $x(t)$ from $x_p(t)$ have its impulse response $h(t)$ and frequency response $H(j\Omega)$. Note that $H(j\Omega) = T$, for $|\Omega| \leq |\Omega_m|$

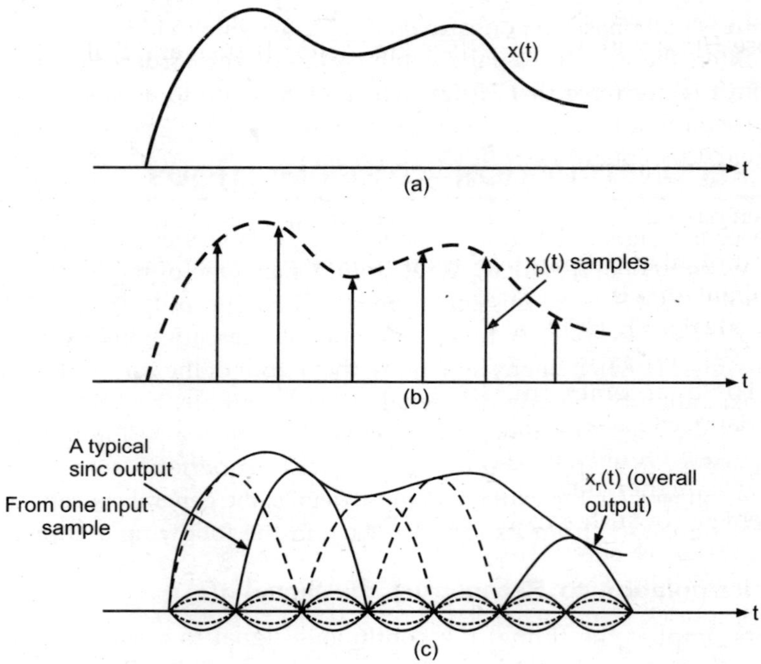

Fig. 7.15. Ideal band limited interpolation using sinc function:
(*a*) Original signal x(t),
(*b*) Its sampled version $x_p(t)$, = x(nT)
(*c*) Each sample of $x_p(t)$ becomes a sinc when passes through an ideal LPF.

The impulse response of the ideal LPF: $H(j\,\Omega) = T$ for $|\Omega| \leq |\Omega_c|$, is given by

$$h(t) = \left(\frac{\Omega_c}{\pi}\cdot\frac{\sin(\Omega_c t)}{(\Omega_c t)}\right)\cdot T \qquad \text{...(7.24)}$$

where Ω_c is the cut-off frequency of the LPF. For our case, $\Omega_m = \Omega_c$ as the signal $x(t)$ to be reconstructed from the samples $x_p(t)$ *i.e.* $x(n)$ is band-limited to Ω_m [see Fig. 7.3(*a*)].

The recovered signal $x_r(t)$ is given by

$$x_r(t) = x_p(t) * h(t) \qquad \text{...(7.25)}$$

$$= \left[\sum_{n=-\infty}^{\infty} x(nT)\,\delta(t-nT)\right] * \frac{(\Omega_c T)\sin(\Omega_c t)}{\pi\Omega_c t}$$

$$= \sum_{n=-\infty}^{\infty} x(nT) \cdot \frac{\Omega_c T \sin(\Omega_c(t-nT))}{\pi\Omega_c(t-nT)}$$

Hence, the reconstructed signal $x_r(t)$ is given by

$$x_r(t) = \sum_{n=-\infty}^{\infty} x(nT) \frac{T \sin(\Omega_c(t-nT))}{\pi(t-nT)} \quad \ldots(7.26)$$

For perfect reconstruction, we know that the LPF used for reconstruction must have constant frequency response $H(j\Omega)$ with $\Omega_c = \frac{\Omega_s}{2}$ [see Fig. 7.3(*c*)]. If such an ideal LPF is used for signal reconstruction from $x_p(t)$ (or from $x(n)$), then such an interpolation process is called *Band-Limited-Interpolation*. If the sampling rate f_s is in accordance with the sampling theorem (*i.e.* $f_s \geq 2f_m$), then the recovered signal $x_r(t)$ equals $x(t)$ with zero error. Fig. 7.15 shows $x(t)$, $x_p(t)$ and $x_r(t)$. Each sample $x_p(nT)$ when passed through the LPF, $H(j\Omega)$, produces a sinc type output: $x(nT)\,\frac{\sin(\omega_s t/2)}{(\omega_s/2)t}$ at $t = nT$. Addition of all such sincs by various samples gives output as shown in Fig. 7.15 (*c*). Their overall resultant $x_r(t)$ is exact $x(t)$.

Note that an ideal LPF $H(j\Omega)$ as shown in Fig. 7.3 is rather an impossibility. To overcome this problem, we invariably choose $f_s > 2f_m$, and never $f_s = 2f_m$. As a thumb rule in DSP, we take f_s 10% higher than $2f_m$ theoretical requirement. In such a case the spectrum $X_p(j\Omega)$ is as shown in Fig. 7.16 [same as Fig. 7.3(*b*)]. Here, the LPF required is not a brick shape. The necessary requirement is that $X(j\Omega)$ is constant from $-\omega_m$ to ω_m. Thereafter $H(j\Omega)$ falls to zero at $\omega = \pm\, \omega_s/2$. Such a filter can be relatively easily realized.

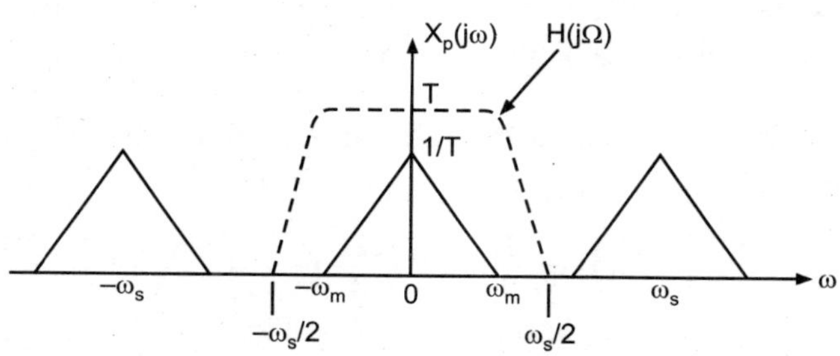

Fig. 7.16. Spectrum $X_p(j\omega)$ and LPF $H(j\Omega)$ for the case $f_s > 2f_m$

7.6.3 Zero Order Hold Circuit as Interpolation Filter (A Simpler Circuit)

In many cases, it is preferable to use less accurate, but simpler filter or a simple interpolating function than the ideal function given by (7.24) which is a *sinc function*. A zero-order hold can be also viewed as a form of interpolation between the sample values $x_p(t)$, in which interpolating function $h(t)$ is the impulse response $h_0(t)$. Such a system is shown in Fig. 7.17(*b*). The output $H_0(j\Omega)$ is as in Fig. 7.17(*a*).

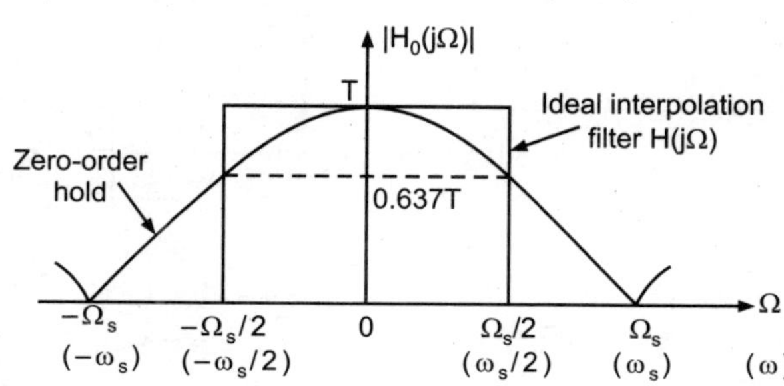

Fig. 7.17. (*a*) Transfer function for the zero-order hold (ZOH) and the ideal interpolation filter (LPF)

In this case, $x_0(t)$ corresponds to the approximation of $x(t)$, and $h_0(t)$ represents approximation to $h(t)$ given by (7.24). Figure 7.17(*a*) shows the response of ideal LPF interpolation filter $H(j\Omega)$ and that of zero-order hold filter $H_0(j\Omega)$. It may be noted that interpolation used by band limited LPF and that by ZOH circuit only differ from type of filter used. We also note that ZOH differs from ideal filter in two ways *viz*.

(i) ZOH alters the signals much before $\omega_s/2$. It changes T to $0.637T$ from $\Omega = 0$ to $\Omega = \Omega_s/2$ (where as desired was constant T from $\Omega = 0$ to $\Omega = \Omega_s/2$).

(ii) ZOH allows high frequency components.

We accept above degradation to achieve simplicity–see circuit of ZOH in Fig. 7.10(a).

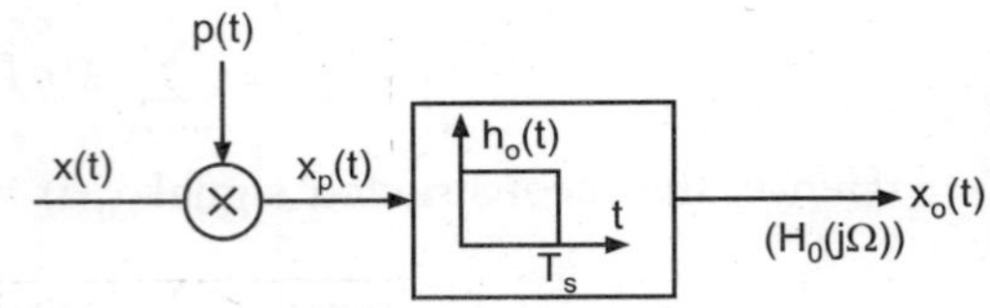

Fig. 7.17. (b) Zero-order hold circuit as interpolation filter

7.6.4 Higher Order Holds Interpolation (First Order Hold)

In case the approximate interpolation available by zero-order hold (ZOH) is not acceptable, we may use other interpolation approaches. Note that the output produced by ZOH has discontinuities at each multiple of T_s. See Fig. 7.10(b), where the output $x_0(t)$ changes abruptly at T_s, $2T_s$, ..., kT_s. In contrast, the linear interpolation has also discontinuities in the form of change of slopes between two samples $x_p(t)$ and $x_p(t \pm T_s)$, see Fig. 7.14. A linear interpolation, called first-order hold, can also be viewed as interpolation in the form of another impulse response $h_1(t)$ instead $h_0(t)$ (which was for zero-order hold) as shown in Fig 7.18. Note that $h_1(t)$ looks like a triangular signal.

[To find the Transfer Function $H_1(j\Omega)$ for $h_1(t)$]

We know that a triangle signal denoted by $\Delta\left(\frac{t}{T}\right)$, as shown in Fig. 7.18, has Fourier transform

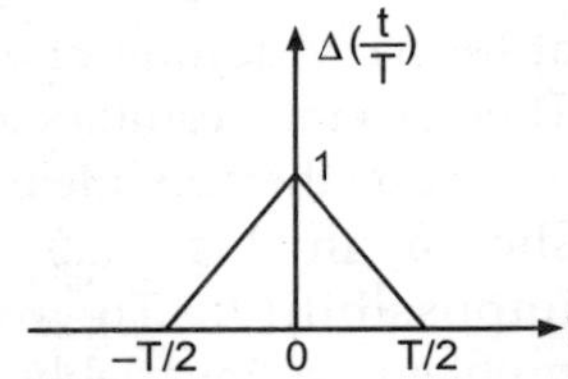

Fig. 7.18. A typical triangle pulse for base width = T

$$FT\left[\Delta\left(\frac{t}{T}\right)\right] = \frac{T}{2}\,\text{sinc}^2\left(\frac{\Omega T}{4}\right) \qquad ...(7.27)$$

For the triangle pulse shown in Fig. 7.19(d), the width is $2T$. Replacing T by $2T$ in (7.27) we get

$$H_1(j\Omega) = T\,\text{sinc}^2\left(\frac{\Omega T}{2}\right) = \frac{1}{T}\left[\frac{\sin(\Omega T/2)}{\Omega/2}\right]^2 \qquad ...(7.28)$$

Figure 7.19 shows, in detail, the various features of the First-Order Hold Interpolation. In this case, the recovered signal $x_r(t)$ is closer to the original singal $x(t)$ than that we obtained by ZOH method of singal reconstruction from its samples $x_p(t)$.

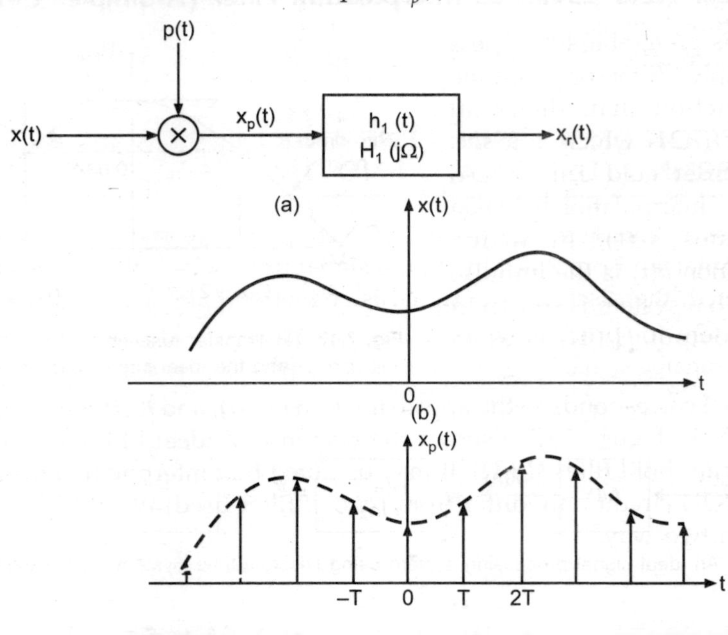

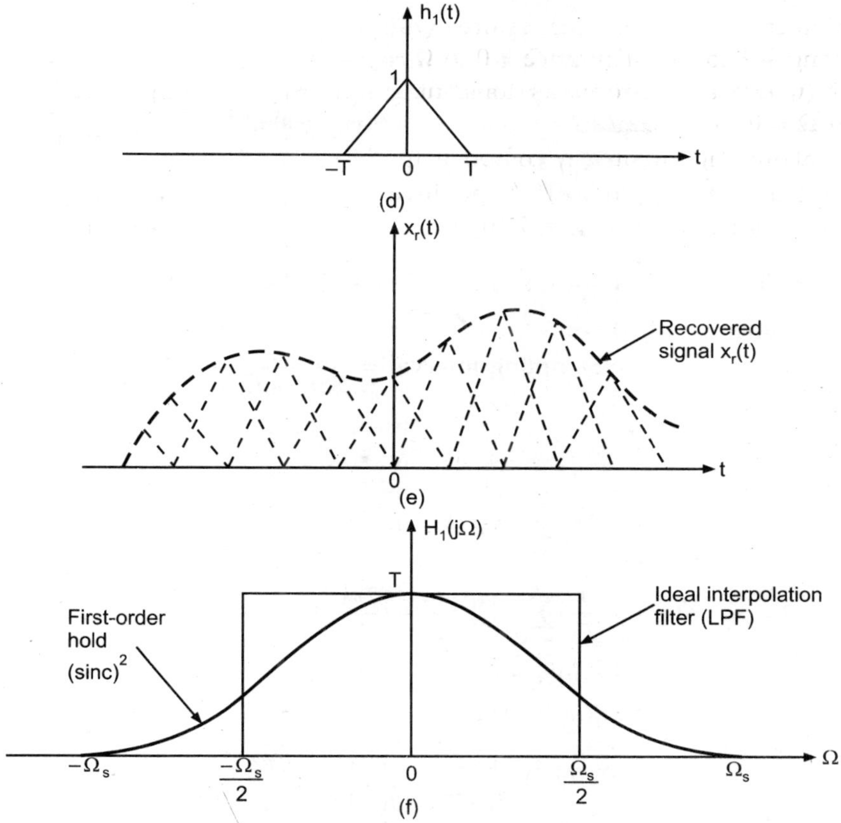

Fig. 7.19. (*a*) The 1st order Hold reconstruction,
(*b*), (*c*), (*d*) give $x(t)$, $x_p(t)$ and $h_1(t)$, respectively,
(*e*) Recovered signal $x_r(t)$ and
(*f*) Frequency response of ideal LPF and $H_1(j\Omega)$ used here.

In case of still higher accuracy in signal recovery we may use second and higher order hold circuits. A second-order hold circuits yields an interpolation of sample values that is continuous and has no discontinuities in the first and the second order derivatives.

7.7 A NOTE ON PROCESSING THE ANALOG SIGNALS BY DISCRETE-TIME PROCESSING (USE OF *A/D* AND *D/A* CONVERTORS)

In order to process an analog signal, using DSP techniques, we first convert an analog signal into a discrete-time signal, and process it by digital signal processing techniques. After the processing has been completed, the discrete-time signal is converted back into analog domain.

A typical system for processing an analog signal using a discrete-time system is shown in Fig. 7.20. Here, the analog signal $x_a(t)$ is converted into discrete-time signal $x(n)$ by A/D convertor. The

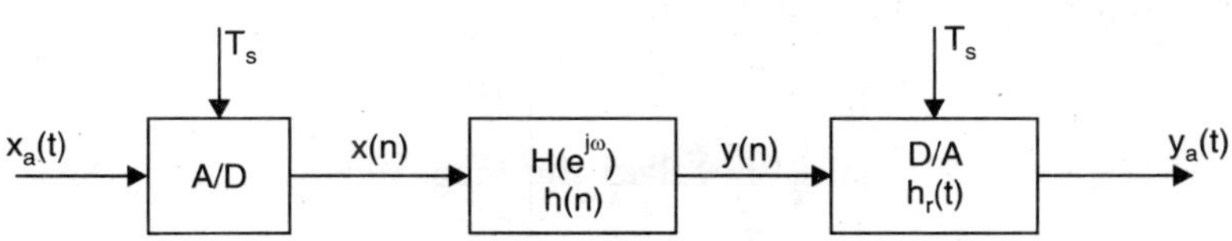

Fig. 7.20. An ideal signal processing system using Discrete-time System. T_s = sampling interval.

signal $x(n)$ is processed by the digital system with impulse response $h(n)$ to give output $y(n) = x(n) * h(n)$. Thereafter, $y(n)$ is inputted to D/A convertor (ideally, a low-pass filter) for signal reconstruction to $y_a(t)$. As the input $x_a(t)$ and the output $y_a(t)$ are both analog signals, therefore, the overall system is equivalent to a "continuous-time system."

Let

$$FT \text{ of } x_a(t) = X_a(j\,\Omega) \qquad \text{...(7.29)}$$

$$DFT \text{ of } x(n) = X(e^{j\omega}) \qquad \text{...(7.30)}$$

$$DFT \text{ of } y(n) = Y(e^{j\omega}) \qquad \text{...(7.31)}$$

$$T_s = \frac{1}{f_s}$$

$$= \text{Sampling interval} = \frac{1}{\text{Sampling frequency}} \qquad \text{...(7.32)}$$

$$\Omega T_s = \omega \qquad \text{...(7.33)}$$

As

$$X(e^{j\omega}) = \frac{1}{T_s}\sum_{k=-\infty}^{\infty} X_a(j\,\Omega - j\omega_s k)$$

$$\therefore \quad X(e^{j\omega}) = \frac{1}{T_s}\sum_{k=-\infty}^{\infty} X_a\left(j\frac{\omega}{T_s} - j\frac{2\pi k}{T_s}\right) \qquad \text{...(7.34)}$$

We know that

$$y(n) = x(n) * h(n) \qquad \text{...(7.35)}$$

$$\therefore \quad Y(e^{j\omega}) = X(e^{j\omega}) \cdot H(e^{j\omega}) \qquad \text{...(7.36)}$$

$$= H(e^{j\omega})\cdot\frac{1}{T_s}\sum_{k=-\infty}^{\infty} X_a\left(j\frac{\omega}{T_s} - j\frac{2\pi k}{T_s}\right) \qquad \text{...(7.37)}$$

(Using 7.34 for $X(e^{j\omega})$)

Finally, the D/A convertor produces the analog signal $y_a(t)$ from the samples $y(n)$ as follows:

$$y_a(t) = \sum_{n=-\infty}^{\infty} y(n)\cdot\frac{\sin \pi(t - nT_s)/T_s}{\pi(t - nT_s)/T_s} = \sum_{n=-\infty}^{\infty} y(n) * \left(\sin\frac{\pi T}{T_s}\Big/\frac{\pi t}{T_s}\right) \qquad \text{...(7.38)}$$

The readers may go through the Appendix to this chapter for proofs of Eqns. (7.34) to (7.39) used above.

By taking Fourier transforms on both sides, the Eqn. (7.38) reduces to

$$Y_a(j\,\Omega) = H_r(j\,\Omega)\; Y(e^{j\Omega T}) \qquad \text{...(7.39)}$$

$$= H_r(j\,\Omega)\cdot H(e^{j\Omega T_s})\cdot X(e^{j\Omega T_s})$$

$$= H_r(j\,\Omega) H(e^{j\Omega T_s})\cdot\frac{1}{T_s}\sum_{k=-\infty}^{\infty} X_a\left(j\,\Omega - j\frac{2\pi k}{T_s}\right) \qquad \text{...(7.40)}$$

Note that we have FT of

$$\left[\frac{\left(\sin\dfrac{\pi t}{T_s}\right)}{\left(\dfrac{\pi t}{T_s}\right)}\right] = H_r(j\,\Omega) \qquad \text{...(7.41)}$$

$h_r(t)$ is the impulse response of ideal LPF, called the ideal reconstruction filter, shown as D/A in Fig. 7.20. As $x_a(t)$ is band limited to $\frac{f_s}{2}$, therefore,

$$X_a(j\,\Omega) = 0 \text{ for } |\Omega| > \frac{\Omega_s}{2}, \qquad \ldots(7.42)$$

where $$\Omega_s = 2\pi f_s = \frac{2\pi}{T_s}$$

The LPF $H_r(j\,\Omega)$ eliminates all the terms in the sum given in (7.40), and we get

$$Y_a(j\,\Omega) = \begin{cases} H(e^{j\Omega T_s}) \cdot X_a(j\,\Omega), & |\Omega| \le \pi/T_s \\ 0 &, \text{ otherwise} \end{cases} \qquad \ldots(7.43)$$

We may write (7.43) as

$$Y_a(j\,\Omega) = H_a(j\,\Omega) \cdot X_a(j\,\Omega) \qquad \ldots(7.44)$$

where $$H_a(j\,\Omega) = \begin{cases} H(e^{j\Omega T_s}), & |\Omega| \le \pi/T_s \\ 0 &, \text{ otherwise} \end{cases} \qquad \ldots(7.45)$$

This implies that the overall system shown in Fig. 7.20 behaves as an LTI system with effective frequency response given by (7.45) *i.e.* $H_a(j\,\Omega) = H(e^{j\Omega T_s})$.

As a dual system to that of Fig. 7.20, it is also possible to implement a discrete-time system in terms of a continuous-time system, shown in Fig. 7.21.

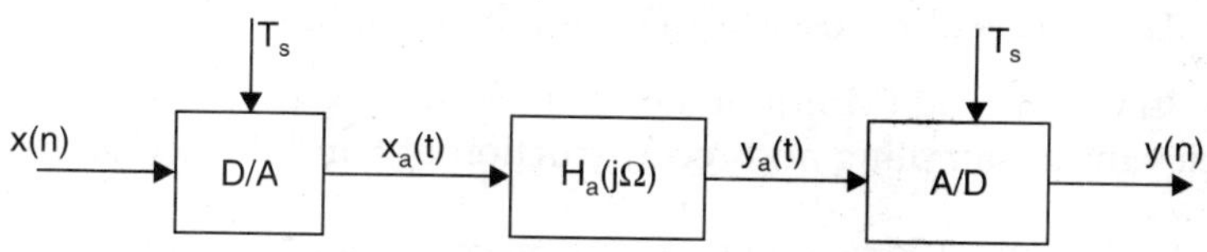

Fig. 7.21. An ideal signal processing system using a continuous-time system (Dual to Fig. 7.20).

The results obtained above in Eq. (7.38) onwards may be derived proceeding similarly. The signal $x_a(t)$ is related to the sequence $x(n)$ by relation

$$x_a(t) = \sum_{n=-\infty}^{\infty} x(n) \cdot \frac{\sin \pi(t - nT_s)/T_s}{\pi(t - nT_s)/T_s} \qquad \ldots(7.46)$$

(Compare (7.46) with (7.38). We obtained $y_a(t)$ from $y(n)$ in (7.38), and we obtain $x_a(t)$ from $x(n)$ in (7.46)).

The equation connecting *FT* of $x_a(t)$ *i.e.* $X_a(j\,\Omega)$ and DTFT of $x(n)$ *i.e.* $X(e^{j\omega})$ or $X(e^{j\Omega T_s})$ is

$$X_a(j\,\Omega) = \begin{cases} T_s\, X(e^{j\Omega T_s}), & |\Omega| < \dfrac{\pi}{T_s} \\ 0 &, \text{ otherwise} \end{cases} \qquad \ldots(7.47)$$

[Equation (7.47) is similar to (7.34) if we take only one term in the summation series, R.H.S. of (7.34)].

The relationship between Fourier transforms of $x_a(t)$ and $y_a(t)$ is

$$Y_a(j\,\Omega) = \begin{cases} H_a(j\,\Omega)\, X_a(j\,\Omega), & |\Omega| < \dfrac{\pi}{T_s} \\ 0 &, \text{ otherwise} \end{cases} \qquad \ldots(7.48)$$

Hence,

$$Y(e^{j\omega}) = \frac{1}{T_s} Y_a\left(\frac{j\omega}{T_s}\right), \ |\omega| < \pi \qquad \text{...(7.49)}$$

and the frequency response of equivalent discrete-time system is

$$H(e^{j\omega}) = H_a\left(\frac{j\omega}{T_s}\right), \ |\omega| < \pi \qquad \text{...(7.50)}$$

7.8 SAMPLING OF DISCRETE-TIME SIGNALS (DECIMATION AND INTERPOLATION)

In many situations, we are required to change the sampling rate of a discrete-time signal $x(n)$. We call it sample rate conversion. If we decrease the sampling rate f_s of $x(n)$ to a lower sampling rate, say, $\frac{f_s}{M}$, and call the new signal $x_d(n)$ (d in the subscript means decreased sampling rate), the process is called *Decimation.* If we increase the sampling rate of $x(n)$ from f_s to $L \cdot f_s$, and call the new signal $x_i(n)$ (i in the subscript means increase of sampling rate), such a process is called Up-sampling or *Interpolation.* It is also possible to revise the sampling rate f_s to $\frac{L}{M} f_s$. These cases are discussed in detail in Chapter 12 (Multirate DSP). In this chapter, we shall cover basics of sample rate conversion relevant to sampling and reconstruction of band limited signals. We first explain Decimation $\left(f_s \text{ becomes } \frac{1}{M} f_s\right)$, followed by Interpolation (f_s becomes Lf_s) and finally give method to convert the sampling rate f_s to $\frac{L}{M} f_s$.

7.8.1 Sample Rate Reduction: f_s to $\frac{1}{M} f_s$ (Decimation)

We wish to reduce the sampling rate f_s of $x(n)$ to a new sampling rate $\frac{1}{M} f_s$, where M is an integer. We shall call new sampling period $T_s' = MT_s$, the resampled signal, denoted by $x_d(n)$ is

$$x_d(n) = x_a(nT_s') = x_a(nMT_s) = x(nM) \qquad \text{...(7.51)}$$

We reduce the sampling rate by a down sampler shown by symbol given in Fig. 7.22(a).

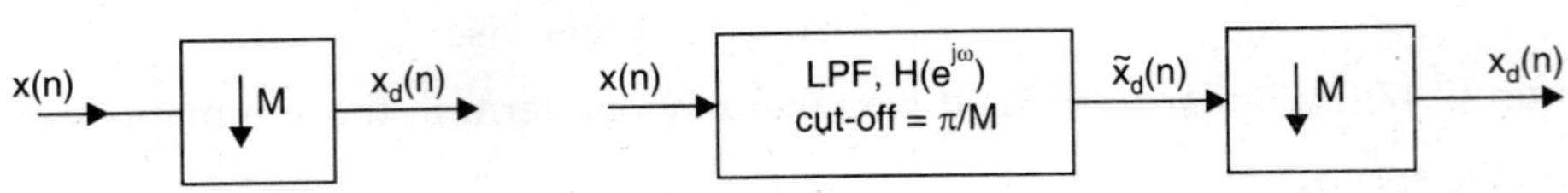

(a) (b)

Fig. 7.22. (a) Down-sampler by an integer M down sampler (b) Decimator by a factor M. $H(e^{j\omega})$ is a low-pass filter, with gain unity and cut off-$\omega_c = \frac{\pi}{M}$.

Reduced sampling rate $\frac{f_s}{M}$ can cause aliasing unless the signal to be down sampled has bandwidth $\frac{\pi}{M}$. Hence, a LPF of gain unity and cut-off $\frac{\pi}{M}$ is cascaded to input signal $x(n)$, and obtain $\tilde{x}_d(n)$. Note that $x(n)$ and $\tilde{x}_d(n)$, both have sampling rate f_s. We know that $x(n) = x_a(nT_s)$. DTFT of $x(n)$ is related is $X_a(j\,\Omega)$ by

$$X(e^{j\omega}) = \frac{1}{T_s}\sum_{k=-\infty}^{\infty} X_a\left(j\frac{\omega}{T_s} - j\frac{2\pi k}{T_s}\right),\ \omega = \Omega T_s \quad \text{...(7.52)}$$

Similarly, DTFT of $x_d(n) = x(nM) = x_a(nMT_s)$ is

$$X_d(e^{j\omega}) = \frac{1}{MT_s}\sum_{r=-\infty}^{\infty} X_a\left(j\frac{\omega}{MT_s} - j\frac{2\pi r}{MT_s}\right) \quad \text{...(7.53)}$$

We may express the summation index r above as

$$r = i + kM \quad \text{(Note this step)}$$

where $-\infty < k < \infty$ and $0 \le i \le M - 1$. Hence (7.53) reduces to

$$X_d(e^{j\omega}) = \frac{1}{MT_s}\sum_{i=0}^{M-1}\sum_{k=-\infty}^{\infty} X_a\left(j\frac{\omega}{MT_s} - j\frac{2\pi}{MT_s}(i+kM)\right)$$

$$= \frac{1}{M}\sum_{i=0}^{M-1}\left[\frac{1}{T_s}\sum_{k=-\infty}^{\infty} X_a\left(j\frac{\omega-2\pi i}{MT_s} - j\frac{2\pi k}{T_s}\right)\right] \quad \text{...(7.54)}$$

From (7.52), we have

$$X(e^{j(\omega-2\pi i)/M}) = \frac{1}{T_s}\sum_{k=-\infty}^{\infty} X_a\left(j\frac{\omega-2\pi i}{MT_s} - j\frac{2\pi k}{T_s}\right) \quad \text{...(7.55)}$$

$\therefore$ (7.54) gives us, using RHS of (7.55) in the square bracket of (7.54),

$$X_d(e^{j\omega}) = \frac{1}{M}\sum_{i=0}^{M-1} X(e^{j(\omega-2\pi i)/M})$$

or

$$X_d(e^{j\omega}) = \frac{1}{M}\sum_{k=0}^{M-1} X(e^{j(\omega-2\pi k)/M}) \quad \text{...(7.56)}$$

Equation (7.56) shows that the decimated version $x_d(n)$ has its spectrum $X_d(e^{j\omega})$ as an expanded version of spectrum $X(e^{j\omega})$ because, if $k = 0$ in (7.56), we get

$$X_d(e^{j\omega}) = \frac{1}{M}X(e^{j\omega/M}) \quad \text{...(7.57)}$$

Hence, the spectrum $X(e^{j\omega})$ of $x(n)$ must be reduced to $\frac{\pi}{M}$ before down sampling. So we have used a low-pass filter with cut-off equalling $\frac{\pi}{M}$ before down sampling by M, as shown in Fig. 7.22(b).

7.8.2 Sample Rate Increase: f_s to Lf_s (Interpolation)

If we like to increase the sampling rate of $x(n)$ from f_s to Lf_s (L an integer), it amounts to decrease the inter sample time from T_s to $\frac{T_s}{L}$. As $x_a(t)$ is sampled with a sampling frequency $f_s = \frac{1}{T_s}$, then we have

$$x(n) = x_a(nT_s) \qquad ...(7.58)$$

If $x_a(t)$ is sampled by a sampling frequency $Lf_s = \frac{1}{LT_s}$, then we get

$$x_i(n) = x_a\left(\frac{nT_s}{L}\right) \qquad ...(7.59)$$

The samples $x_i(n)$ for argument n when n is multiple of L can be obtained from $x(n)$ by using the relation

$$x_i(nL) = x(n) \qquad ...(7.60)$$

Figure 7.23(a) shows an upsampler that produces the sequence

$$\tilde{x}_i(n) = \begin{cases} x(n/L), & n = 0, \pm L, \pm 2L, \ldots, \\ 0 \quad , & \text{otherwise} \end{cases} \qquad ...(7.61)$$

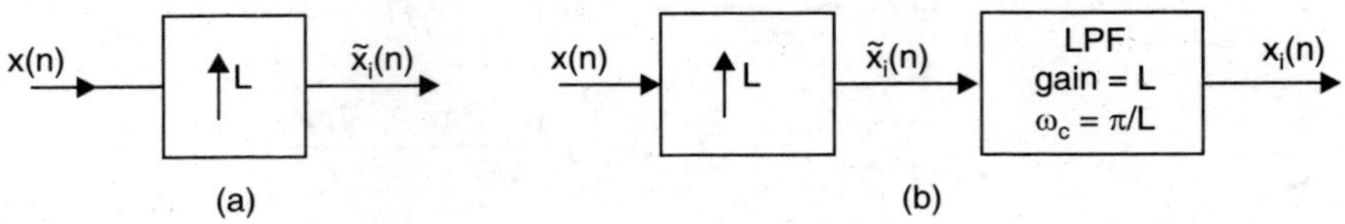

Fig. 7.23. (a) An upsampler by an integer factor L, (b) Interpolator by a factor of L.

The upsampler [Fig. 7.23(a)] expands the time scale by a factor L, and inserts $L - 1$ zeros between each sample of $x(n)$. The upsampling is described in frequency domain by

$$\tilde{X}_i(e^{j\omega}) = \sum_{n=-\infty}^{\infty} \tilde{x}_i(n)e^{-jn\omega}$$

$$= \sum_{\substack{n=-\infty \\ n \text{ integer of } L}}^{\infty} x(n/L)e^{-jn\omega} \qquad ...(7.62)$$

Put $\frac{n}{L} = m$, $\therefore$ $m = -\infty$ to ∞ for the summation of (7.62)

$$\therefore \qquad \tilde{X}_i(e^{j\omega}) = \sum_{m=-\infty}^{\infty} x(m)e^{-jmL\omega}$$

i.e.,

$$\tilde{X}_i(e^{j\omega}) = X(e^{jL\omega}) \qquad ...(7.63)$$

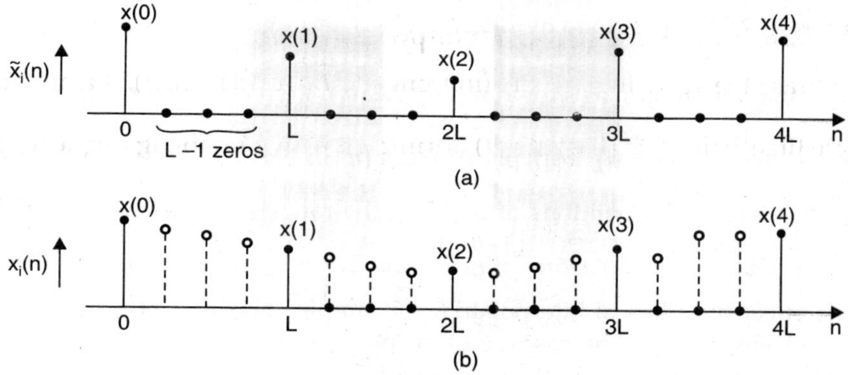

Fig. 7.24. (*a*) The output $\tilde{x}_i(n)$ of the upsampler, (*b*) After interpolation, adding $L - 1$ samples between each sample of $x(n)$ by LPF, the overall sequence $x_i(n)$ $L = 4$ here.

Equation (7.63) shows that $\widetilde{X}_i(e^{j\omega})$ is obtained by scaling the frequency of $X(e^{j\omega})$. After up-sampling, it is necessary to remove the frequency scaled images of $X_a(j\ \Omega)$, except those that are

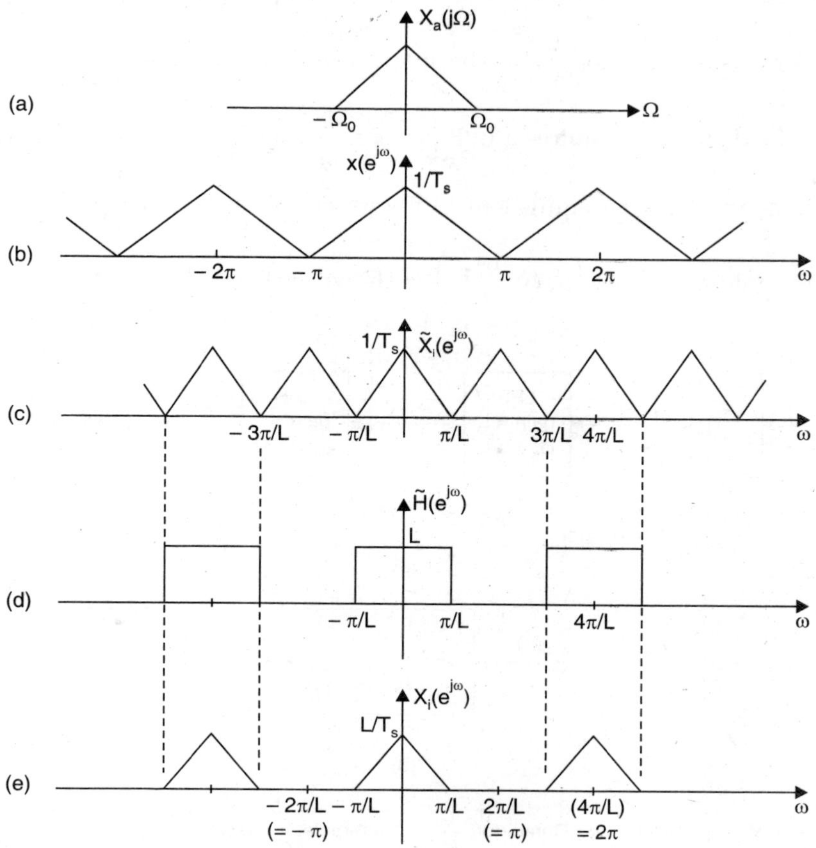

Fig. 7.25. Illustration in frequency domain, of the Interpolation process (we have assumed $L = 2$ here). (*a*) The Fourier transform of $x_a(t) = X_a(j\ \Omega)$, (*b*) DTFT of $x(n) = X(e^{j\omega})$, hence periodic with period 2π (*c*) DTFT of $\tilde{x}_i(n)$ *i.e.*, the upsampler output = $\widetilde{X}_i(e^{j\omega})$, (*d*) The ideal LPF, cut-off $\frac{\pi}{L}$, gain = L (*e*) The DTFT of the interpolated signal $x_i(n) = X_i(e^{j\omega})$.

integer multiples of 2π. This is done by filtering $\tilde{x}_i(n)$ through a low-pass filter that has cut-off frequency of $\frac{\pi}{L}$, and a gain of L, as shown in Fig. 7.23(b). We have shown the frequency domain illustration of various signals $x_a(t)$, $x(n)$, $\tilde{x}_i(n)$ and $x_i(n)$ in Fig. 7.25. We note that the frequency response $\tilde{X}_i(e^{j\omega})$ contains L repetitions of $X(e^{j\omega})$ in the range $-\pi$ to π. The low-pass filter $H(e^{j\omega})$ suppresses $L - 1$ lobes of $X(e^{j\omega})$ from $\tilde{X}_i(e^{j\omega})$ and results the spectrum $X_i(e^{j\omega})$ as shown in Fig. 7.25(e). The effect of LPF is to interpolate $L - 1$ samples between $x(0)$, $x(L)$, $x(2L)$ ... and the result is shown in Fig. 7.24(b). The cascade of an upsampler with a low-pass filter is called an *interpolator*.

7.8.3 Sample Rate Conversion by a Rational Factor $\left(\textit{i.e. } f_s \text{ to } \frac{L}{M} f_s\right)$

The cascade of an interpolator (f_s to Lf_s) and a decimator $\left(f_s \text{ to } \frac{1}{M} f_s\right)$ will result in an overall sampling rate conversion of f_s to $\frac{L}{M} f_s$. The interpolator requires a LPF $\left(\text{cut-off } \frac{\pi}{L}\right)$ after the upsampler, and the decimator requires a LPF $\left(\text{cut-off } \frac{\pi}{m}\right)$ before the down sampler. We cascade the two LPF filters and have an equivalent LPF with cut-off $\omega_c = \min\left\{\frac{\pi}{M}, \frac{\pi}{L}\right\}$ ...(7.64)

The sampling rate convertor $\left(f_s \text{ to } \frac{L}{M} f_s\right)$ is shown in Fig. 7.26.

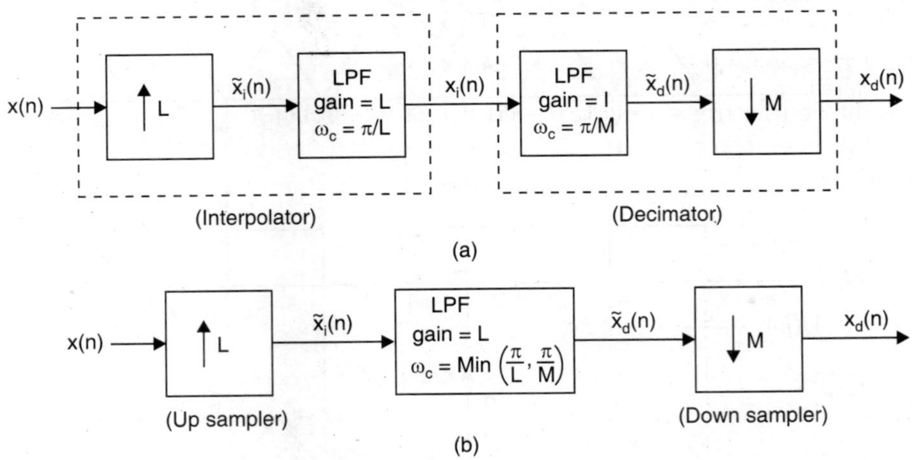

Fig. 7.26. Realization of a Sampling Rate Convertor $\frac{L}{M}$. (a) Interpolator cascaded with decimator using two low-pass filters with cut-offs $\frac{\pi}{L}$ and $\frac{\pi}{M}$, (b) Efficient realization of system (a) by combining low-pass filters to a single LPF with gain = L and cut-off $\omega_c = \min\left\{\frac{\pi}{L}, \frac{\pi}{M}\right\}$

For example if we wish to convert $x(n)$ having sampling rate $f_{s_1} = 8$ kHz to a new signal $x_d(n)$ having sampling rate $f_{s_2} = 10$ kHz, we need ratio $\frac{L}{M} = \frac{10}{8} = \frac{5}{4}$. Hence, in Fig. 7.26, L would be 5 and M would be 4. The composite LPF will have cut-off $\omega_c = \min\left\{\frac{\pi}{5}, \frac{\pi}{4}\right\} = \frac{\pi}{5}$, and a gain of 5.

7.9 SAMPLING OF BANDPASS SIGNALS

In this section, we consider sampling of a Bandpass signal. In communication, bandpass signals are often used for efficient communication and processing, by using samples. Before we appreciate the fact that a bandpass signal appearing in the band $B_1 < F < B_2$, and thus having a bandwidth of $B = B_2 - B_1$, is required to be sampled at sampling rate $2B$ and not $2B_2$, we need some background as follows.

7.9.1 Representation of Bandpass Signals

Consider a real-valued signal $x(t)$ with a narrow-band spectrum as shown in Fig. 7.27. Note that $|X(F)|$ is an even function, and the phase function Arg $[X(F)]$ is an odd function of F. We wish to develop a mathematical representation of such signals. Let $X_+(F)$ represent only the positive frequencies of $X(F)$. Let

$$X_+(F) = 2V(F) \cdot X(F) \qquad \ldots(7.65)$$

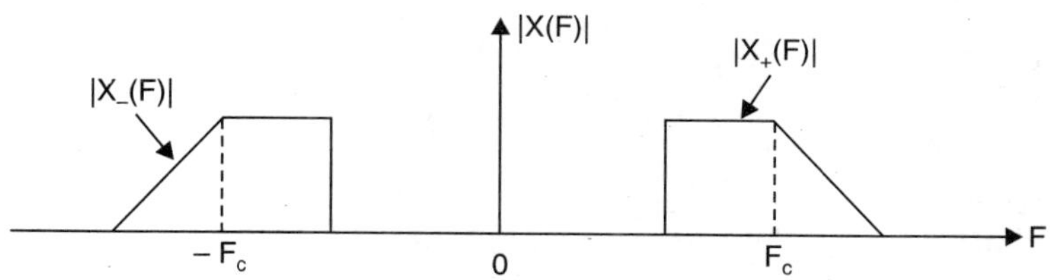

Fig. 7.27. Spectrum $|X(F)|$ of a typical band-pass signal $x(t)$. Here, $x(t)$ is a real-valued signal.

where $X(F)$ is the Fourier transform of $x(t)$ and $V(F)$ is the unit step function in frequency domain *i.e.* it is $U(F)$. We have taken a factor of 2 on RHS of (7.65), to arrive at elegant results. Reader may note that

$$u(t) \xrightarrow{FT} \pi\delta(\omega) + \frac{1}{j\omega}$$

$$\therefore \quad U(j\omega) \xrightarrow{IFT} \frac{1}{2\pi}\left[\pi\delta(-t) + \frac{1}{j(-t)}\right] \qquad \text{(By Duality theorem)}$$

$$= \frac{1}{2}\delta(t) + \frac{j}{2\pi t}$$

i.e.

$$V(F) \xrightarrow{IFT} \frac{1}{2}\left[\delta(t) + \frac{j}{\pi t}\right] \qquad \ldots(7.66)$$

We have used the notation $V(F)$ for Fourier transformation $U(j\omega)$. Taking *IFT* on both sides of (7.65) and using con volution theorem, we have

$$x_+(t) = 2 \cdot \text{IFT}[V(F)] * \text{IFT}[X(F)]$$

$$= \left[\delta(t) + \frac{j}{\pi t}\right] * x(t)$$

$$= x(t) + \frac{j}{\pi t} * x(t) \qquad \text{...(7.67)}$$

Define $\hat{x}(t)$ by

$$\hat{x}(t) \triangleq \frac{1}{\pi t} * x(t)$$

$$= \frac{1}{\pi}\int_{-\infty}^{\infty} \frac{x(\tau)}{t-\tau}\, d\tau \qquad \text{...(7.68)}$$

Thus, $\hat{x}(t)$ can be viewed as the output of the filter with impulse response

$$h(t) = \frac{1}{\pi t}, \; -\infty < t < \infty \qquad \text{...(7.69)}$$

when excited by the input signal $x(t)$. A filter with impulse response $h(t)$ given by (7.69) is called a *Hilbert transformer*. The frequency response of this filter is given by

$$H(F) = \int_{-\infty}^{\infty} h(t)\, e^{-j2\pi Ft}\, dt$$

$$= \frac{1}{\pi}\int_{-\infty}^{\infty} \frac{1}{t} e^{-j2\pi Ft}\, dt$$

$$\therefore \quad \underset{\text{(Hilbert transformer)}}{H(F)} = \begin{cases} -j, & F > 0 \\ 0, & F = 0 \\ j, & F < 0 \end{cases} \qquad \text{...(7.70a)}$$

We may note that

$$|H(F)| = 1, \quad \text{Arg}[H(F)] = \begin{cases} -\pi/2, & F > 0 \\ \pi/2, & F < 0 \end{cases} \qquad \text{...(7.70b)}$$

So, the filter $h(t)$ is basically a 90° phase shifter for all frequencies to the input signals. These properties are similar to the discrete-time Hilbert transformer.

The signal

$$x_+(t) = x(t) + j\hat{x}(t) \qquad \text{...(7.71)}$$

is called the *analytic signal*. Note that $x(t)$ as well as $\hat{x}(t)$ are both real valued analog signals. $\hat{x}(t)$ is the Hilbert transform of $x(t)$. Equation (7.65) shows that $X_+(F)$ gives the positive frequencies of $X(F)$. Since $X(F)$ is a band pass signal as shown in Fig. 7.27, therefore $X_+(F)$ represents band on positive side of the frequency axis. If we want to translate $X_+(F)$ to a low pass signal, we must shift $X_+(F)$ to left on F-axis by F_c. Calling this a low pass signal $X_l(F)$, we can write

$$X_l(F) = X_+(F + F_c) \qquad \text{...(7.72)}$$

i.e. in time domain, the relation is

$$x_l(t) = x_+(t) \cdot e^{-j2\pi F_c t}$$

$$= [x(t) + j\hat{x}(t)]\, e^{-j2\pi F_c t} \qquad \ldots(7.73)$$

or equivalently $$x(t) + j\hat{x}(t) = x_l(t)\, e^{j2\pi F_c t} \qquad \ldots(7.74)$$

As $x_l(t)$ is a complex-valued, we can express $x_l(t)$ as

$$x_l(t) = u_c(t) + ju_s(t) \qquad \ldots(7.75)$$

Putting the value of $x_l(t)$ in (7.74), we get

$$x(t) + j\hat{x}(t) = (u_c(t) + ju_s(t))\,(\cos 2\pi F_c t + j \sin 2\pi F_c t)$$

Equating real and imaginary parts on both sides, we get

$$\boxed{x(t) = u_c(t) \cos 2\pi F_c t - u_s(t) \sin 2\pi F_c t} \qquad \ldots(7.76)$$

$$\boxed{\hat{x}(t) = u_c(t) \sin 2\pi F_c t + u_s(t) \cos 2\pi F_c t} \qquad \ldots(7.77)$$

The expression (7.76) is the desired form of a band-pass signal $x(t)$ in terms of low-frequency signal components $u_c(t)$ and $u_s(t)$. The low-frequency components $u_c(t)$ and $u_s(t)$ can be viewed as amplitude modulations impressed by the carrier components $\cos 2\pi F_c t$ and $\sin 2\pi F_c t$, respectively. As these carrier components are in phase quadrature, $u_c(t)$ and $u_s(t)$ are called the *Quadrature Components*.

$x(t)$ given by (7.76) can also be expressed by

$$x(t) = \text{Re}\,[u_c(t) + ju_s(t)]\, e^{j2\pi F_c t}$$

$\therefore$ $$\boxed{x(t) = \text{Re}\,[x_l(t) \cdot e^{j2\pi F_c t}]} \qquad \ldots(7.78)$$

The low-pass signal $x_l(t)$ is called the Complex Envelope of the real band-pass signal $x(t)$. Note that $x_l(t)$ is basically the equivalent low pass signal corresponding to the band-pass signal $x(t)$.

From (7.75), we can also write

$$x_l(t) = a(t) \cdot e^{j\theta(t)} \qquad \ldots(7.79)$$

where $$a(t) = \sqrt{u_c^2(t) + u_s^2(t)} \qquad \ldots(7.80)$$

$$\theta(t) = \tan^{-1} \frac{u_s(t)}{u_c(t)} \qquad \ldots(7.81)$$

Then $$x(t) = \text{Re}\,[x_l(t) \cdot e^{j2\pi F_c t}] \qquad \text{from (7.78)}$$

$$= \text{Re}\,[a(t) \cdot e^{j[2\pi F_c t + \theta(t)]}] \qquad \text{using (7.79)}$$

$\therefore$ $$\boxed{x(t) = a(t) \cdot \cos\,[2\pi F_c t + \theta(t)]} \qquad \ldots(7.82)$$

The signal $a(t)$ is called the *Envelope of $x(t)$* and $\theta(t)$ is called the *phase of $x(t)$*. Hence, (7.76), (7.78) and (7.82) are the three equivalent representations of a band-pass signal $x(t)$.

We shall use the results (7.76), (7.78) and (7.82) to derive relationships between $x_l(t)$ and $x(t)$ *i.e.* between $X_l(F)$ and $X(F)$.

As $$X(F) = \int_{-\infty}^{\infty} x(t) e^{-j2\pi F t}\, dt$$

$$= \int_{-\infty}^{\infty} (\text{Re}\,[x_l(t) \cdot e^{j2\pi F_c t}])e^{-j2\pi Ft}\,dt \text{ (using (7.78))} \quad \ldots(7.83)$$

We use the identity

$$\text{Re}\,[y] = \frac{1}{2}[y + y^*] \quad \ldots(7.84)$$

$$\therefore \quad X(F) = \frac{1}{2}\int_{-\infty}^{\infty} [x_l(t)e^{j2\pi F_c t} + x_l^*(t)e^{-j2\pi F_c t}] \cdot e^{-j2\pi Ft}\,dt$$

$$= \frac{1}{2}\int_{-\infty}^{\infty} x_l(t) \cdot e^{-j2\pi(F-F_c)t}\,dt + \left(\frac{1}{2}\int_{-\infty}^{\infty} x_l(t)e^{-j2\pi(-F-F_c)t}\,dt\right)^*$$

$$\therefore \quad X(F) = \frac{1}{2}[X_l(F - F_c) + X_l^*(-F - F_c)] \quad \ldots(7.85)$$

where $X_l(F)$ is the Fourier transform of $x_l(t)$. Equation (7.85) is the basic relationship between the spectra of the real bandpass signal $x(t)$ and that of the equivalent low-pass signal $x_l(t)$.

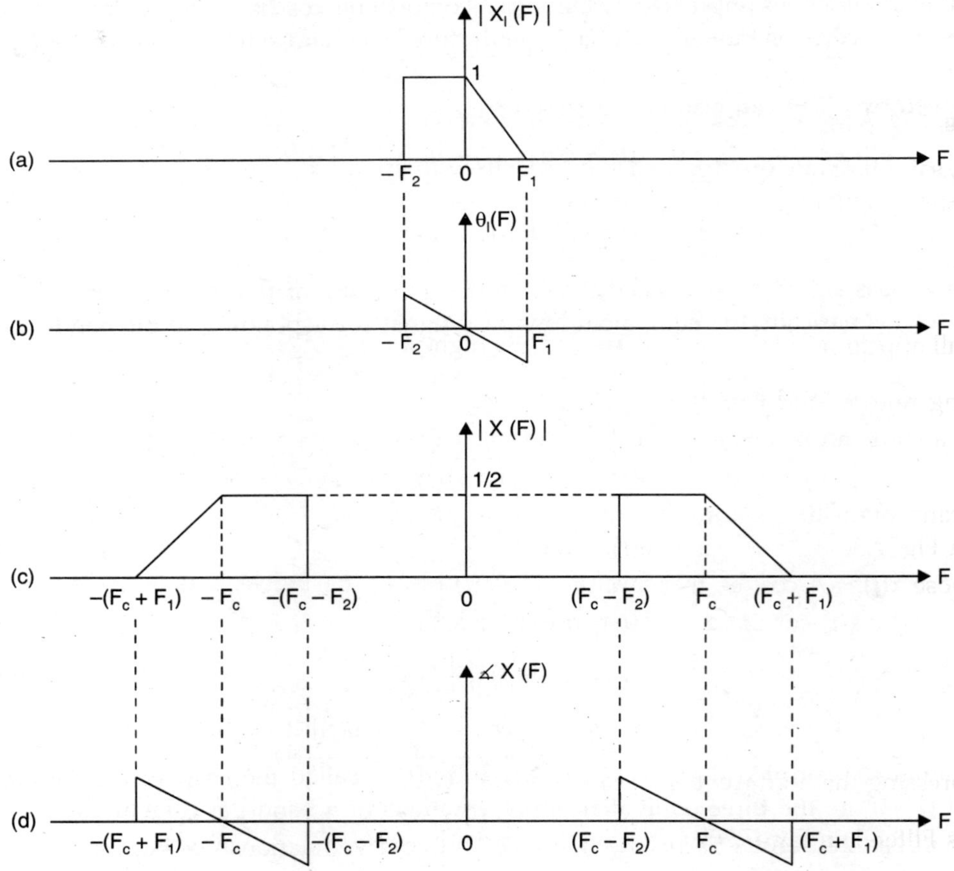

Fig. 7.28. (*a*) Spectrum $|X_l(F)|$ and (*b*) Phase $\theta_l(F)$ of the low-pass signal $x_l(t)$ (*c*) Spectrum $|X(F)|$ and (*d*) phase $\measuredangle X(F)$ of the band-pass signal

Equation (7.85) can be used to construct the spectrum $X(F)$ of bandpass signal $x(t)$ from the spectrum $X_l(F)$ of the low-pass filter $X_l(t)$. Given $X_l(F)$, see Fig. 7.28, we get $x_l(F - F_c)$ by shifting $X_l(F)$ right by F_c. To obtain $X_l^*(-F - F_c)$, fold $X_l(F)$ around $F = 0$ to obtain $X_l(-F)$, take conjugate to get $X_l^*(-F)$ and shift left by F_c to get $X_l^*(-F - F_c)$. Scale $X_l(F - F_c)$ and $X_l^*(-F - F_c)$ by $\frac{1}{2}$. Finally, we get $X(F)$ as shown in Fig. 7.28(*c*). Corresponding phases $\theta_l(F)$ and Arg $[X(F)]$ are shown in Figs. 7.28(*b*) and (*d*), respectively. Note that $|X(F)|$ is an even function of F and Arg $[X(F)]$ is an odd function of F. It was also expected so, because $x(t)$ is a real valued signal.

7.9.2 Sampling of Bandpass Signals

As per the sampling theorem, a continuous-time signal with highest frequency B can be uniquely represented by its samples taken at $2B$ samples per second. Now consider a signal with a bandpass spectrum as shown in Fig. 7.29.

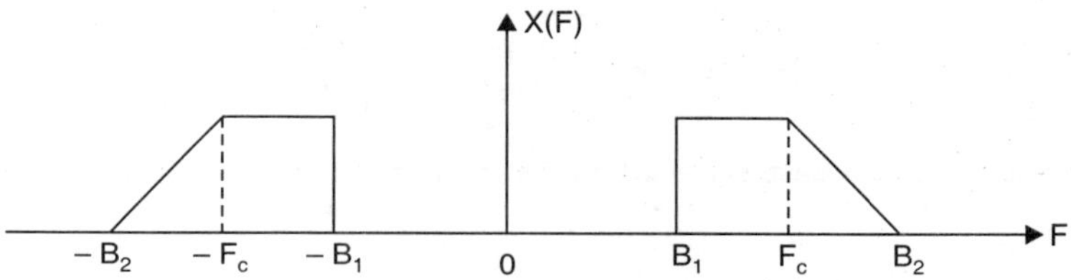

Fig. 7.29. A typical bandpass spectrum $X(F)$ of continuous-time signal $x(t)$. Band width $B = B_2 = B_1$.

Here, sampling rate of $2B_2$ can of course be used to uniquely represent $x(t)$. But if we can shift the band-pass signal by an amount

$$F_c = \frac{B_1 + B_2}{2} \qquad \ldots(7.86)$$

then it will appear as a low pass signal, with its highest frequency $B_2 - F_c = \frac{(B_2 - B_1)}{2} = \frac{B}{2}$. Then a sampling rate needed will be much less than $2B_2$.

Such a shift can be achieved by first putting $x(t)$ in the form, as shown in (7.76),

$$x(t) = u_c(t) \cos 2\pi F_c(t) - u_s(t) \sin 2\pi F_c t \qquad \ldots(7.87)$$

We can obtain the quadrature components $u_c(t)$ and $u_s(t)$, which are low pass signals, as shown in Fig. 7.30.

Suppose $x(t) = A \cos \omega t$, then multiplying $x(t)$ by $\cos 2\pi F_c t$ gives us

$$x(t) \cos 2\pi F_c t = A \cos \cos \omega t \cdot \cos 2\pi F_c t$$

$$= \frac{A}{2}[\cos(\omega - 2\pi F_c)t + \cos(\omega + 2\pi F_c)t] \qquad \ldots(7.88)$$

Suppressing the high frequency component $\frac{A}{2}\cos(\omega - 2\pi F_c)t$ by a low-pass filter (shown as: Low-pass Filter-1 in Fig. 7.30).

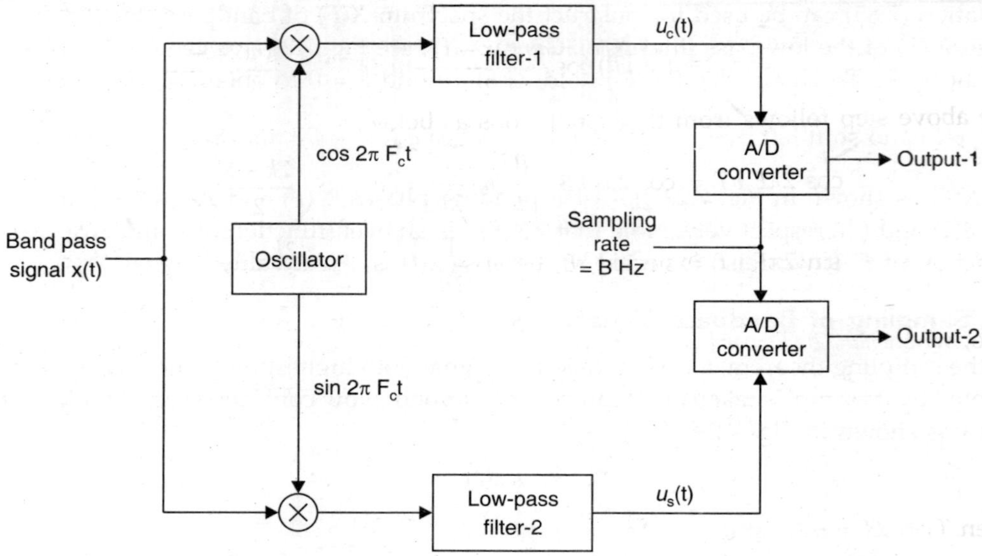

Fig. 7.30. Sampling of a bandpass signal $x(t)$ by first converting to an equivalent low-pass filter $x_l(t)$.

We obtain

$$\frac{A}{2}\cos(\omega - 2\pi F_c)t \triangleq u_c(t) \qquad \ldots(7.89)$$

Similarly, by multiplying $x(t)$ by $\sin 2\pi F_c t$ and passing this signal through low-pass filter-2, shown in Fig. 7.30, we obtain

$$\frac{A}{2}\sin(\omega - 2\pi F_c)t \triangleq u_s(t) \qquad \ldots(7.90)$$

The outputs 1 and 2 in Fig. 7.30, together constitute the complex-valued low-pass signal

$$x_l(t) = u_c(t) + ju_s(t) \qquad \ldots(7.91)$$

as given by Eq. (7.75).

The frequency conversion from ω to $\omega - \omega_{c_1}$ where $\omega_c = 2\pi F_c$, as demonstrated above, is similar to removing carrier frequency from an incoming received radio signal using a mixer to convert the incoming signal to *IF* range.

In view of the fact that frequency conversion to low pass allows us to reduce the sampling rate from $2B_2$ to $2B$ (and $B \ll B_2$) per second, thus it is possible to sample a bandpass signal at a lower rate. We follow it by a mathematical proof to this statement.

Suppose for the bandpass spectrum shown in Fig. 7.29, the upper frequency $F_c + \frac{B}{2}$ is a multiple of $B\left(\text{i.e. } F_c + \frac{B}{2} = kB\right)$. This implies that a k number of spectra B_1 to B_2 can be accommodated in frequency range: 0 to B_2.

If we sample $x(t)$ at the rate $2B = \frac{1}{T}$ samples per sample, then (7.87) gives us (putting $t = nT$ on both sides)

$$x(nT) = u_c(nT)\cos 2\pi F_c nT - u_s(nT)\sin 2\pi F_c nT$$

$$= u_c(nT)\cos\frac{\pi n(2k-1)}{2} - u_s(nT)\sin\frac{\pi n(2k-1)}{2} \quad \text{...(7.92)}$$

The above step follows from the calculations as below.

$$\cos 2\pi F_c nT = \cos 2\pi\left(kB - \frac{B}{2}\right)n\cdot\frac{1}{2B} = \cos \pi n\left(\frac{2k-1}{2}\right)$$

$$\sin 2\pi F_c nT = \sin 2\pi\left(kB - \frac{B}{2}\right)n\cdot\frac{1}{2B} = \sin \pi n\left(\frac{2k-1}{2}\right)$$

Also, when $n = 2mT = mT_1$, where $T_1 = 2T = \frac{1}{B}$, then

$$\cos \pi n\left(\frac{2k-1}{2}\right) = \cos \pi\cdot 2m\left(\frac{2k-1}{2}\right) = \cos \pi m\ (2k-1)$$

$$= (-1)^m \quad \text{...(7.93a)}$$

when $T_1 = 2T = \frac{1}{B}$, and $n = 2m - 1$, then

$$\sin \pi n\left(\frac{2k-1}{2}\right) = \sin \pi(2m-1)\left(\frac{2k-1}{2}\right)$$

$$= \sin\frac{\pi}{2}(4mk - 2m - 2k + 1)$$

$$= \sin\frac{\pi}{2}(-2m - 2k + 1) = \cos \pi\ (m + k)$$

$$= (-1)^{m+k+1} \quad \text{...(7.93b)}$$

Hence, when n is even *i.e.* $n = 2m$, then the second term in (7.92) becomes zero and using (7.93*a*) in (7.92), we get

$$x(2mT) \triangleq x(mT_1) = (-1)^m\ u_c(mT_1) \quad \text{...(7.94)}$$

When n is odd *i.e.* $n = 2m - 1$, then the first term in (7.92) becomes zero, and using (7.93*b*) in (7.92), we arrive at

$$x(2mT - T) \triangleq x\left(mT_1 - \frac{\pi}{2}\right) = (1)^{m+k+1} u_s\left(mT_1 - \frac{\pi}{2}\right) \quad \text{...(7.95)}$$

Hence, even-numbered samples of $x(t)$ *i.e.* $x(2mT)$ which occur at a rate $\frac{1}{2T} = \frac{1}{T_1} = B$. Samples per second produce the samples of the low-pass signal component $u_c(t)$, as given by (7.94). Similarly, the odd-numbered samples of $x(t)$ *i.e.* $x((2m - 1)T)$ *i.e.* $x\left(mT_1 - \frac{T_1}{2}\right)$, which also occur at the rate $\frac{1}{2T} = \frac{1}{T_1} = B$ samples per second produce samples of the low-pass signal component $u_s(t)$.

We can use the samples $u_c(mT_1)$ and $u_s\left(mT_1 - \frac{T_1}{2}\right)$ to reconstruct the equivalent low-pass signal components, *viz.* $u_c(t)$ and $u_s(t)$. According to the sampling theorem, we can write

$$u_c(t) = \sum_{m=-\infty}^{\infty} u_c(mT_1) \frac{\sin\left(\frac{\pi}{T_1}\right)(t - mT_1)}{\left(\frac{\pi}{T_1}\right)(t - mT_1)} \quad \ldots(7.96)$$

$$u_s(t) = \sum_{m=-\infty}^{\infty} u_s\left(mT_1 - \frac{T_1}{2}\right) \cdot \frac{\sin\left(\frac{\pi}{T_1}\right)\left(t - mT_1 + \frac{T_1}{2}\right)}{\left(\frac{\pi}{T_1}\right)\left(t - mT_1 + \frac{T_1}{2}\right)} \quad \ldots(7.97)$$

We know that

$$x(t) = u_c(t) \cos 2\pi F_c t - u_s(t) \sin 2\pi F_c t \quad \ldots(7.98)$$

Putting the values of $u_c(t)$ and $u_s(t)$ from (7.96) and (7.97) in (7.98), and replacing $u_c(t)$ and $u_s(t)$ in terms of $x(2mT)$ and $x(2mT - T)$ from (7.94) and (7.95), we get

$$x(t) = \sum_{m=-\infty}^{\infty} \left\{ (-1)^m x(2mT) \frac{\sin\left(\frac{\pi}{2T}\right)(t - 2mT)}{\left(\frac{\pi}{2T}\right)(t - 2mT)} \cdot \cos 2\pi F_c t \right.$$

$$\left. + (-1)^{m+k} x((2m-1)T) \frac{\sin\left(\frac{\pi}{2T}\right)(t - 2mT + T)}{\left(\frac{\pi}{2T}\right)(t - 2mT + T)} \sin 2\pi F_c t \right\} \quad \ldots(7.99)$$

But $\qquad (-1)^m \cos 2\pi F_c t = \cos 2\pi F_c (t - 2mT)$

and $\qquad (-1)^{m+k} \sin 2\pi F_c t = \cos 2\pi F_c (t - 2mT + T)$

with these substitutions in (7.99), we get

$$x(t) = \sum_{m=-\infty}^{\infty} x(2mT) \frac{\sin\left(\frac{\pi}{2T}\right)(t - 2mT)}{\left(\frac{\pi}{2T}\right)(t - 2mT)} \cos 2\pi F_c (t - 2mT)$$

$$+ \sum_{m=-\infty}^{\infty} x(2mT - T) \frac{\sin\left(\frac{\pi}{2T}\right)(t - 2mT + T)}{\left(\frac{\pi}{2T}\right)(t - 2mT + T)} \cos 2\pi F_c (t - 2mT + T) \quad \ldots(7.100)$$

Putting $2m = m'$ is first summation of (7.100), m' varies from $- \ldots -4, -2, 0, 2, 4, \ldots$ *i.e.* all even values. Putting $2m - 1 = m''$ in the second summation of (7.100), m'' varies from $-3, -1, 1, 3, \ldots$ *i.e.* all odd values. Thus, we can combine both summation terms in one as follows

$$x(t) = \sum_{m=-\infty}^{\infty} x(mT) \frac{\sin\left(\frac{\pi}{2T}\right)(t - mT)}{\left(\frac{\pi}{2T}\right)(t - mT)} \cos 2\pi F_c (t - mT) \quad \ldots(7.101)$$

where $T = \dfrac{1}{2B}$. Thus, $x(t)$ can be reconstructed from its samples $x(nT)$. Note that B is the bandwidth of the bandpass signal $x(t)$. Though the spectrum of $x(t)$ lies between B_1 to B_2, where B_2 is much greater than B we need not take the sampling rate $2B_2$ (as required by the sampling theorem). The theory covered above has been evolved by converting $x(t)$ to quadrature low-pass components $u_c(t)$ and $u_s(t)$.

Finally, we have come to the conclusion that the bandwidth B of $X(j\,\Omega)$ is important to choose the sampling rate (equalling $2B$) and not the highest frequency of $X(j\,\Omega)$ component B_2.

The reconstruction formula is as given by (7.101). It has an additional factor $\cos 2\pi F_c(t - mT)$.

We have assumed in the foregoing mathematical proof that B_2 (the upper edge of the spectrum) is such that $B_2 = kB$, *i.e.* k spectrum lobes (B_1 to B_2) can fit up to B_2. However, in more general cases, it may not be so. In Fig. 7.31(a), the bandpass spectrum B_1 to B_2 with $B = B_2 - B_1$ is such that an integer number k of B can fit in the range 0 to B_2. In Fig. 7.31(b) exact multiple of B cannot fit in the range. In such cases, we assume an integer

$$r = \left\lfloor \frac{B_2}{B} \right\rfloor$$

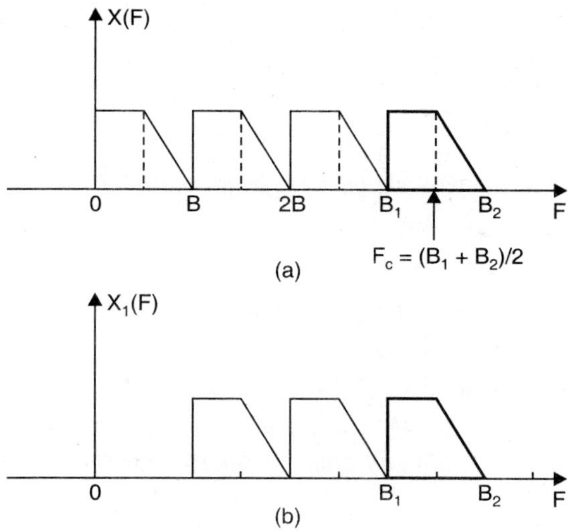

Fig. 7.31. (a) 0 to $B_2 = k \cdot B$, $k = 4$, (b) 0 to B_2 does not contain an integral number of B

where $\lfloor p \rfloor$ means integral part of p. Then we assume

$$\left.\begin{aligned} &\text{new band width} \qquad B' = \frac{B_2}{r},\ B_1 = B_2 - B' \\ &\text{new} \qquad F_c' = B_2 - \frac{B'}{2} \\ &\text{new sampling rate} = 2B' \\ &T' = \frac{1}{2B'} \end{aligned}\right\} \qquad \ldots(7.102)$$

and proceed as if $x(t)$ has band width B' instead of B.

Solved Examples on Sampling and Reconstruction of Bandlimited Signals

EXAMPLE 7.1: *Consider a sequence x(n) with Fourier-transform such that*

$$X(e^{j\omega}) = 0 \text{ for } 2\pi/9 \leq |\omega| \leq \pi.$$

Determine the lowest rate at which x(n) may be sampled without the possibility of aliasing.

SOLUTION: We must find the largest value of N, such that

$$\frac{2\pi}{N} \geq 2(\omega_m)$$

i.e. $$\frac{2\pi}{N} \geq 2\left(\frac{2\pi}{9}\right) \qquad \left(\because \text{the given signal has its spectrum non-zero form } \frac{-2\pi}{9} < \omega < \frac{2\pi}{9}\right)$$

$\therefore$ $$N \leq 9/2$$

But N must be as integer, $\therefore N_{max} = 4$ and $\omega_s = \frac{2\pi}{4} = \frac{\pi}{2}$ rad/s

and $$f_s = \frac{2\pi}{\omega_s} < \frac{2\pi}{\pi/2} = 4 \text{ samples/s}$$ **Ans.**

EXAMPLE 7.2: *Let x(t) be a low-pass signal with band width W Hz. Compute the Nyquist rate for*

(i) $x(t) + x(t-1)$ *(ii)* $x^2(t)$. *(I.P. Univ. 2007)*

SOLUTION:

(i) For $x(t)$ as well as for $x(t-1)$, $f_{max} = W$ Hz

$\therefore$ $$f_s = 2W \text{ Hz}$$ **Ans.**

(ii) For $x^2(t)$, maximum frequency will be $2.W$ Hz

$\therefore$ $$f_s = 2(2W) = 4W \text{ Hz}$$ **Ans.**

EXAMPLE 7.3: *Find the Nyquist rate and Nyquist interval for the signals: (a) to (f) as given.*

SOLUTION:

(a) $x_1(t) = 1 + \cos(2000\,\pi t) + \sin(4000\,\pi t)$ (Given signal)

Maximum $\omega_m = 4000\pi$ rad/s $\therefore \omega_s = 2\omega_m = 8000\pi$ rad/s **Ans.**

$\therefore$ Nyquist interval: $T_s = \frac{2\pi}{\omega_s} = \frac{\pi}{\omega_m} = \frac{1}{4000}$ s **Ans.**

(b) $x_2(t) = \frac{1}{\pi t}(\sin(4000\,\pi\, t))$ (Given signal)

$\omega_m = 4000\pi \quad \therefore \quad \omega_s = 8000\pi, \quad T_s = \frac{2\pi}{\omega_s} = \frac{\pi}{\omega_m} = \frac{1}{4000}$ s **Ans.**

(c) $x_3(t) = \text{sinc}\,(100\,\pi t)$ (Given signal)

Clearly $\omega_m = 100\pi$, $\therefore \omega_s = 200\pi$ and $T_s = \frac{1}{100}$ s **Ans.**

(d) $x_4(t) = \text{sinc}\,(100\pi t) + \text{sinc}\,(50\pi t)$ (Given signal)

$\omega_m = 100\pi$, $\therefore \omega_s = 200\pi$ and $T_s = \frac{1}{100}$ s **Ans.**

(e) $x_5(t) = \left[\frac{\sin(200\pi)t}{\pi t}\right]^2$ (Given signal)

$$x_5(t) = \frac{1}{\pi^2 t^2}\left[\frac{1}{2}(1-\cos(400\pi t))\right]$$

$\therefore\ \omega_m = 400\pi \quad \therefore\ \omega_s = 800\pi$ and $\therefore\ T_s = \frac{1}{400}$ s **Ans.**

(*f*) $x_6(t) = \underbrace{\cos 2\pi t.\frac{\sin \pi t}{\pi t}}_{} + 3\sin 6\pi t.\underbrace{\frac{\sin 2\pi t}{\pi t}}_{}$ (Given signal)

$$= \frac{1}{2\pi t}[\sin(3\pi t) - \sin \pi t] \qquad = \frac{3}{2\pi t}[\cos 4\pi t - \cos 8\pi t]$$

$\therefore\ \omega_m = 8\pi, \quad \therefore\ \omega_s = 16\pi$ and $T_s = \frac{1}{8}$ s **Ans.**

EXAMPLE 7.4: *Find the Nyquist interval T_s for the following signals: (a) to (d).*

SOLUTION:

(*a*) $x_1(t) = 3\cos(50\pi t) + 5\sin(300\pi t) - \cos(200\pi t)$. (Given signal)

$\omega_{m1} = 300\pi \quad \therefore\ \omega_{s1} = 600\pi, \quad T_s = \frac{1}{300}$ s **Ans.**

(*b*) $x_2(t) = 1 + \cos(20\pi t) + 3\sin(30\pi t)$ (Given signal)

$\omega_{m2} = 30\pi \quad \therefore\ \omega_{s2} = 60\pi, \quad T_s = \frac{1}{30}$ s **Ans.**

(*c*) $x_3(t) = [\text{sinc } 50\pi t]^2$ (Given signal)

$\omega_{m3} = 2 \times 50\pi = 100\pi \quad \therefore\ \omega_{s3} = 200\pi$ and $T_s = \frac{1}{100}$ **Ans.**

(*d*) $x_4(t) = \text{sinc}(200\pi t).\cos(300\pi t)$ (Given signal)

$\omega_{m4} = 500\pi \quad \therefore\ \omega_{s4} = 1000\pi, \quad T_s = \frac{1}{500}$ s **Ans.**

EXAMPLE 7.5: *The signal y(t) is (a) convolution, (b) multiplication, (c) addition of $x_1(t)$ and $x_2(t)$, where $x_1(t)$ and $x_2(t)$ are band limited such that $X_1(j\omega) = 0$, $|\omega| > 1000\pi$ and $X_2(j\omega) = 0$, $|\omega| > 2000\pi$. Determine Nyquist sampling frequencies and Nyquist interval T_s in each cases.*

(*DU, 1998*)

SOLUTION: Here $\omega_{\max 1} = 1000\pi$ for $x_1(t)$, and $\omega_{\max 2} = 2000\pi$ for $x^2(t)$

(*a*) Convolution: $x_1(t) * x_2(t) \xrightarrow{FT} X_1(j\omega).X_2(j\omega)$

$\therefore\ \omega_m = 1000\pi$ (lower of the two LPFs) (Note this step)

$\therefore\ \omega_s = 2000\pi$ and $T_s = \frac{1}{1000}$ s **Ans.**

(*b*) Multiplication: $x_1(t) . x_2(t)$ yield frequencies $\omega_1 \pm \omega_2$

$\omega_m = 1000\pi + 2000\pi = 3000\pi$ rad/s

$\therefore\ \omega_s = 6000\pi$ rad or $f_s = 3000$ Hz

$\therefore\ T_s = \frac{1}{f_s} = \frac{1}{3000}$ s **Ans.**

(*c*) Addition: $\omega_m = 2000\pi$ *i.e.*, higher of ω_{m_1} and ω_{m_2}

$\therefore \quad \omega_s = 4000\pi$ and $T_s = \frac{1}{2000}$ s

EXAMPLE 7.6: *How many minimum number of samples are required to exactly describe the signal?*

$$x(t) = 10 \cos(6\pi t) + 4 \sin(8\pi t).$$

SOLUTION: $x(t) = 10 \cos(6\pi t) + 4 \sin(8\pi t)$

[To find period of $x(t)$]

Period of $10 \cos 6\pi t = T_1 = \frac{2\pi}{6\pi} = \frac{1}{3}$ second

Period of $4 \sin 8\pi t = T_2 = \frac{2\pi}{8\pi} = \frac{1}{4}$ second

$\frac{T_1}{T_2}$ is a rational number. Hence, $x(t)$ is periodic with period T, such that

$$T = \text{LCM}\left(\frac{1}{3}, \frac{1}{4}\right) = 1 \text{ s}$$

As maximum frequency present in $x(t)$ is 4 Hz due to 4 sin (8 πt) component, therefore,

$$f_s = 8 \text{ sample per second} \quad (\because f_s = 2f_m)$$

Number of sample of $x(t)$ in one period (T = 1 s) is therefore 8. **Ans.**

EXAMPLE 7.7: *A signal $x(t) = 12 \cos(800\pi t)$. $\cos^2(1800\pi t)$ is ideally sampled at 4600 samples per second. What is the minimum allowable sampling frequency? What is range of permissible cut off frequencies for the low-pass filter to be used for reconstructing the signal?*

SOLUTION:

We can write

$$x(t) = 12 \cos(800\pi t)\left[\frac{1}{2}(1 + \cos 3600\pi t)\right]$$

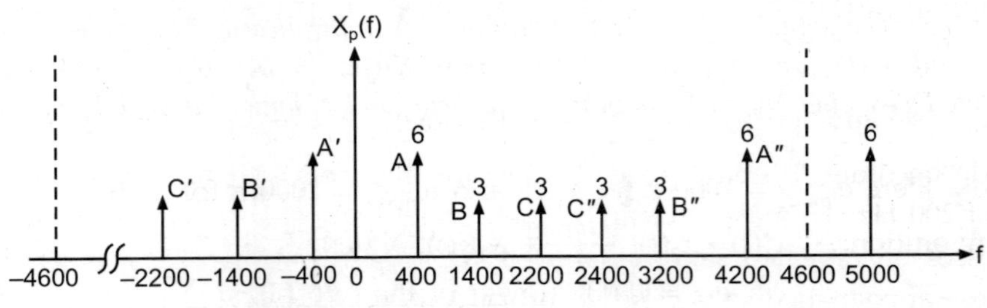

Fig. Ex. 7.7 Spectrum of ideally sampled version of $x(t)$
(A, B, C, A', B', C' is one spectrum. A" is obtained by shifting A' to right by 4600. Similarly, for B", and C").

$$\therefore \quad x(t) = 6 \cos 800\pi t + 6(\cos 800\pi t)(\cos 3600\pi t)$$

$$= 6 \cos 800\pi t + 3 \cos 2800\pi t + 3 \cos 4400\pi t$$

The highest frequency in $x(t)$ is 2200 Hz, so the minimum allowable samples rate (Nyquist criteria) is 2 × 2200 = 4400 samples per second. The spectrum of $x(t)$ is shown in the Figure.

If we wish to recover, say 400, 1400 and 2200 Hz only, then the ideal LPF needed should have cut-off above 2200 Hz but less than 2400 Hz to reject frequencies of 2400 and above. **Ans.**

EXAMPLE 7.8: *A signal $x(t) = 6 \cos 120\pi t$ is ideally sampled at a frequency f_s = 200 samples per second. Sketch the spectrum of sampled signal $x_p(t)$?* (DU, 2000)

SOLUTION:

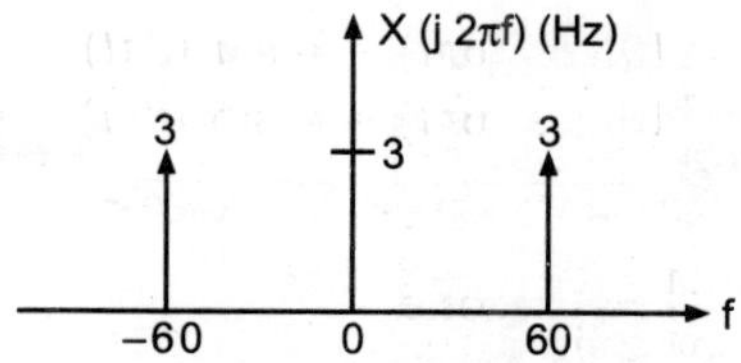

(a)

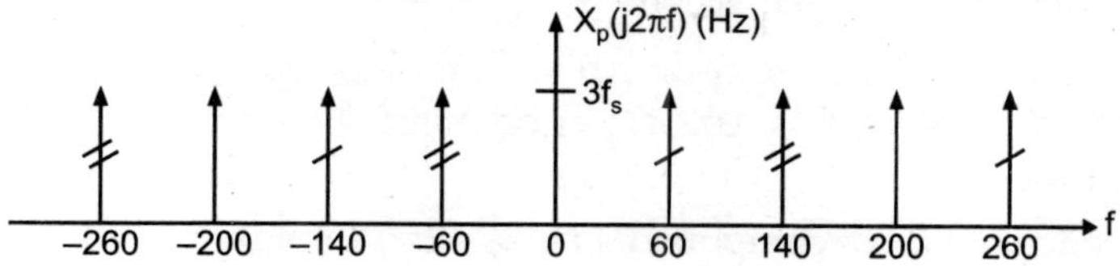

(b)

Fig. Ex. 7.8 (*a*) Spectrum of 6 cos 120 πt (*i.e.*, f_0 = 60 Hz)

(*b*) Spectrum of sampled *x*(*t*) *i.e.*, $X_p(j2\pi f)$

We know that

$$\cos \omega_0 t \xleftrightarrow{FT} \pi[\delta(\omega - \omega_0) + \delta(\omega + \omega_0)]$$

with vertical scale in radians/s.

or
$$\cos(2\pi f_0 t) \xleftrightarrow{FT} \frac{1}{2}\left[\delta(f - f_0) + \delta(f + f_0)\right]$$

with vertical scale in Hz. This is shown in Fig. Ex. 7.8.

After sampling $x(t)$ by f_s = 200 samples/s, the resulting spectrum $X_p(j2\pi f)$ is drawn as follows. See Fig. (*b*).

Draw the baseband spectrum *i.e.* same as that of Fig. Ex. 7.8(*a*) but scaled by $\frac{1}{T_s}$ or by f_s. So the amplitude becomes $3f_s$. Baseband samples are then repeated both sides of vertical axis at periodicity of 200 Hz. To make it clear we have shown one cross on repeated samples of 60 Hz and two crosses on repeated samples of – 60 Hz. Clearly, we can recover baseband signal of 60 Hz, as these appear distinctly around vertical axis f = 0. Here f_s was 200 which is more than twice of 60 Hz.

EXAMPLE 7.9: *A signal* $x(t) = 6 \cos 120\ \pi t$ *is ideally sampled at a sampling frequency* f_s = *100 samples per second. Draw the spectrum of sampled signal* $x_p(t)$?

SOLUTION:

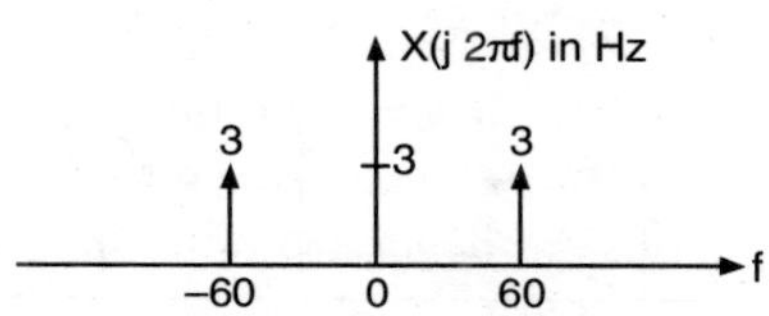

(a)

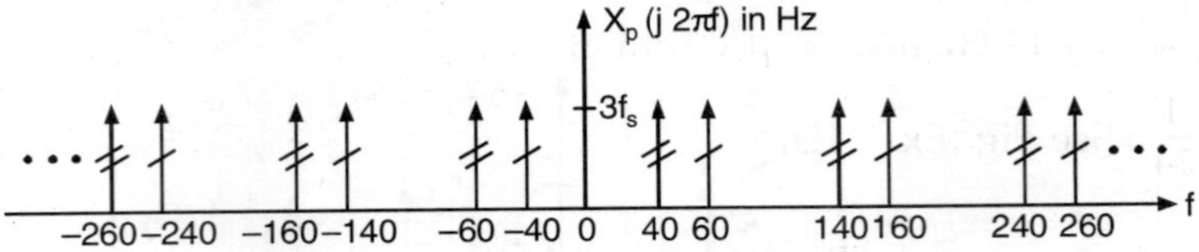

(b)

Fig. Ex. 7.9 (*a*) Spectrum of 6 cos 120π*t* = *X*(*j*ω) = *X*(*j*2π*f*)

(*b*) Spectrum of $X_p(j\omega) = X_p(j2\pi f)$

As in the last example, spectrum of $x(t) = X(j\omega)$ has $\delta(f - 60)$ and $\delta(f + 60)$ of height 3, as shown in Fig. Ex. 7.9(*a*). $X_p(j\,2\pi f)$ is $X(j2\pi f)$ periodic in f with period $f_s = 100$, as shown in Fig. Ex. 7.9(*b*), with amplitudes $3f_s$.

Note the presence of 40 Hz components in $X_p(j\,2\pi f)$ though $X(j2\pi f)$ contains only 60 Hz. This is due to choice of f_s less than 2×60, and hence aliasing.

EXAMPLE 7.10: (*a*) *Sketch the spectrum of the analog signal* $x(t) = 6\cos 10\pi(t)$.

(*b*) *Let* $x(t)$ *be sampled at the rate of 7 Hz. Sketch the spectrum of the sampled signal in the range –12 Hz to + 12 Hz.*

(*c*) *Let* $x(t)$ *be sampled at the rate 14 Hz. Sketch the spectrum of the sampled signal in the range – 33 Hz to + 33 Hz.*

(*d*) *If the original signal is to be recovered from the sampled signal of part* (*b*) *what should be cut-off frequency of the ideal low-pass filter?*

(*e*) *If the original signal is to be recovered from the sampled signal of part* (*c*), *what should be the cut-off frequency of the ideal low-pass filter?* (*GGSIP Univ.*, *2005*)

SOLUTION: (*a*) $x(t) = 6\cos 10\,\pi t \quad \therefore\ \omega_0 = 10\pi$

$$X(j\omega) = 6[\pi\delta(\omega - 10\pi) + \pi\,\delta(\omega + 10\pi)]$$

Spectrum of $x(t)$ is shown in Fig. (*a*)

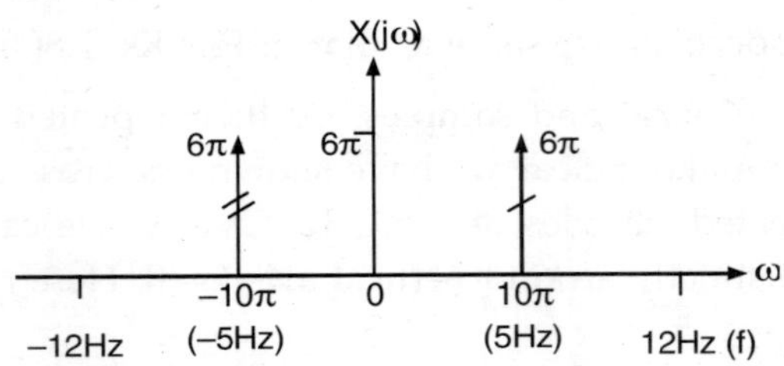

(a) Spectrum of x(t) = 6 cos 10πt

(*b*) Sampling $x(t)$ by 7 Hz makes spectrum of unsampled $x(t)$ *i.e.* $X(j\omega)$ periodic with period $f_s = 7$ Hz see Fig. Ex. 7.10(*b*). $T_s = \dfrac{1}{7}$

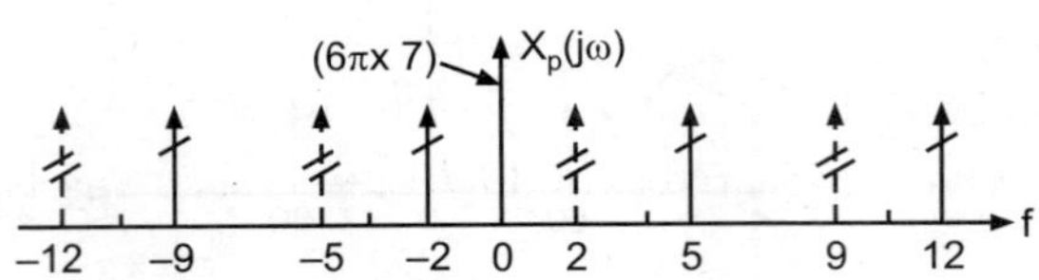

(b) Spectrum of $x_p(t)$, f_s = 7 Hz, T_s = 1/7

(*c*) Sampling $x(t)$ by 14 Hz makes spectrum of $x(t)$, *i.e.*, $X(j\omega)$ periodic with period $f_s = 14$ Hz. Here $T_s = \frac{1}{f_s} = \frac{1}{14}$. See Fig. Ex. 7.10(*c*)

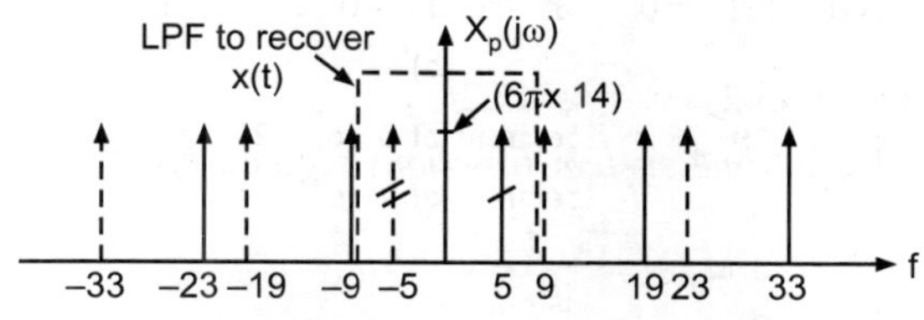

(c) Spectrum of $x_p(t)$, f_s = 14 Hz ∴ T_s = 1/14

Fig. Ex. 7.10 Showing (*a*) Spectrum $X(j\omega)$

(*b*) Spectrum $X_p(j\omega)$ of $x_p(t)$, f_s = 7 Hz

(*c*) Spectrum $X_p(j\omega)$ of $X_p(t)$, f_s = 14 Hz

(*d*) As f_m = 5 Hz, f_5 = 7 Hz ($\neq 2f_m$) ∴ we cannot recover $x(t)$ from Fig. (*b*).

(*e*) To recover $x(t)$ from $X_p(j\omega)$, the ideal LPF should have cut-off frequency $5 < f_c < 9$ as shown in Fig. Ex. 7.10 (*c*).

EXAMPLE 7.11: *The first order low pass filter with 3 dB cut-off frequency f_c is given by*

$$H(f) = \frac{1}{1 + j(f / f_c)}$$

and is used as anti-aliasing filter. The analog signal $x(t)$ is sampled at a frequency f_s. What is the minimum value of f_s if the response to the aliased component at the edge of the passband i.e. at f_c is to be at least 30 dB below the response at f_c?

SOLUTION:

Response at

$$f_c = \left| \frac{1}{1 + jf / fc} \right|_{f = f_c}$$

$$= \left| \frac{1}{1 + j} \right| = \frac{1}{\sqrt{2}}$$

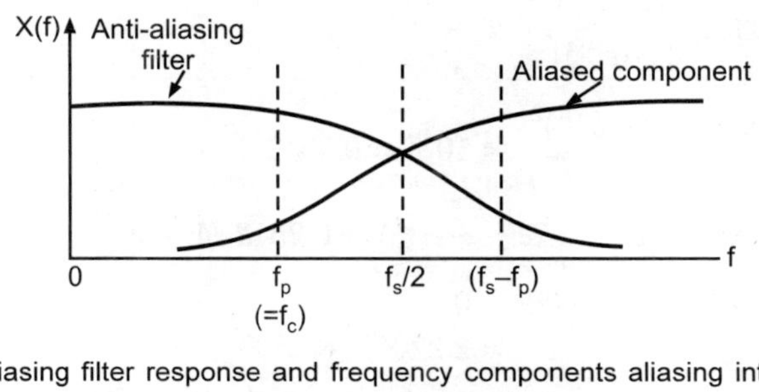

Fig. Ex. 7.11 Anti-aliasing filter response and frequency components aliasing into the baseband

In our case the pass band frequency $f_p = f_c$ of the given filter.

Response at $(f_s - f_c)$ which appears beyond $f_s/2$ due to aliasing is required to be 30 dB below the response at f_c.

$$\therefore \quad 20 \log_{10} \frac{\text{Response at } f_c}{\text{Response at } (f_s - f_c)} \geq 30 \text{ dB is required.}$$

i.e., $$20\log\frac{1\sqrt{2}}{\left[\dfrac{1}{1+\left(\dfrac{f_s-f_c}{f_c}\right)^2}\right]^{1/2}} = 30\text{ dB} \quad \text{or} \quad \frac{1+(x-1)^2}{2} \geq 10^3 \quad \text{where } x = \frac{f_s}{f_c}$$

Solving for x, we get $x \geq 45.2 \quad \therefore f_s \geq 45.2 f_c$ **Ans.**

EXAMPLE 7.12: *A continuous-time system function is given by*

$$H_a(s) = \frac{1}{s+1}$$

The corresponding impulse response $h_a(t)$ is sampled to form a discrete-time unit sample $h(n) = h_a(nT)$.

Find the value of sampling interval T so that $H(e^{j\omega})$ at $\omega = \frac{\pi}{2}$ is 6 dB down from its value at $\omega = 0$.

SOLUTION: $h_a(t)$ = Inverse Laplace Transform of $\dfrac{1}{s+1}$

$$= e^{-t}u(t)$$

$$\therefore \quad h(n) = h_a(nT) = e^{-nT}u(nT)$$

$$H(e^{j\omega}) = \sum_{n=-\infty}^{\infty} h(n)e^{-j\omega n}$$

$$= \sum_{n=-\infty}^{\infty} e^{-nT}\, e^{-j\omega n} = \frac{1}{1-e^{-T}e^{-j\omega}}$$

$$|H(e^{j\omega})|_{\omega=0} = \frac{1}{1-e^{-T}}$$

$$|H(e^{j\omega})|^2_{\omega=\pi/2} = \left|\frac{1}{1-e^{-T}e^{-j\pi/2}}\right|^2 = \left|\frac{1}{1+je^{-T}}\right|^2 = \frac{1}{1+e^{-2T}}$$

As $$10\log\frac{|H(e^{j\pi/2})|^2}{|H(e^{j0})|^2} = -6$$

$$\therefore \quad \frac{(1-e^{-T})^2}{(1+e^{-2T})} = 10^{+6} = 0.2512$$

Cross multiplying, we get $(1 - 2e^{-T} + e^{-2T}) = 0.2512\,(1 + e^{-2T})$

or $$0.7488e^{-2T} - 2e^{-T} + 0.7488 = 0$$

$$\therefore \quad e^{-T} = 2.2206, -0.4503$$

Taking +ve value of e^{-T}, we get $T = \log_e\left(\dfrac{1}{2.206}\right) = 0.7978$ **Ans.**

EXAMPLE 7.13: *Find two different continuous-time signals that will produce the sequence*

$$x(n) = \cos(0.15\, n\pi)$$

when sampled with a sampling frequency f_s = 8 kHz.

SOLUTION: Let the continuous-time signal be

$$x_a(t) = \cos(2\pi f_0 t)$$

$$\therefore \quad x(n) = x_a(nT_s) = \cos(0.15\, n\pi) \qquad \ldots(A)$$

$$\therefore \quad 2\pi f_0 \times nT_s = 0.15\, n\pi$$

or

$$f_0 = \frac{0.15\, n\pi}{2\pi n T_s} = \frac{0.15}{2} \times 8 \times 10^3 \qquad \left(\because \frac{1}{T_s} = 8 \times 10^3\right)$$

$$= 0.15 \times 4 \times 10^3$$

$$= 600 \text{ Hz}$$

$$\therefore \quad x_{a_1}(t) = \cos(2 \times 600\, \pi t) = \cos(1200\, \pi t) \qquad \textbf{Ans.}$$

From (A), $\cos(0.15\, n\pi) = \cos(0.15\, n\pi + 2\, n\pi)$ (Note this step)

$$= \cos\left[nT_s\left(\frac{0.15\pi}{T_s} + \frac{2\pi}{T_s}\right)\right]$$

As

$$\frac{2\pi}{T_s} = \pi \times 2 \times 8 \times 10^3 = \pi \times 16000$$

and

$$\frac{0.15\pi}{T_s} = \pi \times 0.15 \times 8 \times 10^3 = \pi \times 1200$$

Hence

$$x_{a_2}(t) = \cos((16000 + 1200)\, \pi t)$$

$$= \cos(17200\, \pi t) \qquad \textbf{Ans.}$$

Thus, the two continuous-time signals are $x_{a_1}(t) = \cos(1200\, \pi t)$, $x_{a_2}(t) = \cos(17200\, \pi t)$ **Ans.**

EXAMPLE 7.14: *For the following processing system*

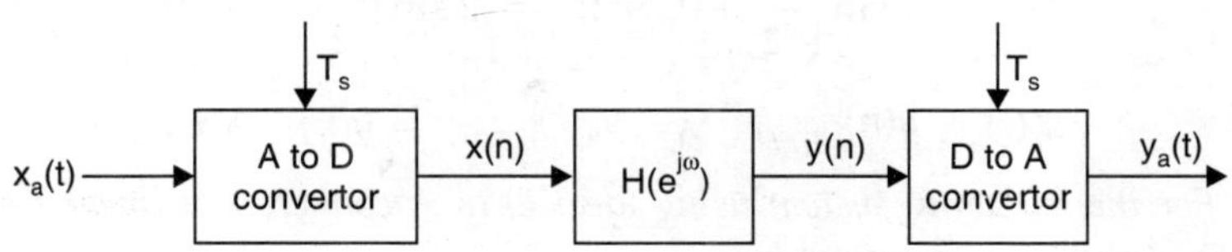

Given $H(e^{j\omega}) = \dfrac{2\left(\frac{1}{3} - e^{j\omega}\right)}{\left(1 - \frac{1}{3}e^{-j\omega}\right)}$, $f_s = 2$ *kHz, and* $x_a(t) = \sin(1000\, \pi t)$, *find the output* $y_a(t)$.

SOLUTION: $x(n) = x_a(nT_s) = \sin(1000\, \pi \cdot nT_s) = \sin\left(1000\, \pi n \dfrac{1}{2000}\right) = \sin\dfrac{n\pi}{2}$

As $x(n)$ is a sinusoid, hence $y(n)$ is of the form (Note this argument)

$$y(n) = A \sin\left(\frac{n\pi}{2} + \phi\right)$$

As $$|H(e^{j\omega})|^2 = 4\left|\frac{\frac{1}{3}-e^{-j\omega}}{1-\frac{1}{3}e^{-j\omega}}\right|^2 = 4 \quad \because H(e^{j\omega}) \text{ is an all pass filter}$$

As $$H(e^{j\omega}) = 2\frac{\left(\frac{1}{3}-e^{-j\omega}\right)}{\left(1-\frac{1}{3}e^{-j\omega}\right)}\times\frac{1-\frac{1}{3}e^{+j\omega}}{1-\frac{1}{3}e^{+j\omega}}$$

$$= 2\frac{\frac{2}{3}-\frac{1}{9}e^{j\omega}-e^{-j\omega}}{\left|1-\frac{1}{3}e^{-j\omega}\right|^2}$$

$$= 2\frac{\frac{2}{3}-\frac{10}{9}\cos\omega+j\frac{8}{9}\sin\omega}{\left|1-\frac{1}{3}e^{-j\omega}\right|^2}$$

$\therefore$ $$\phi_h(\omega) = \tan^{-1}\frac{\left(\frac{8}{9}\sin\omega\right)}{\left(\frac{2}{3}-\frac{10}{9}\cos\omega\right)}$$

at $$\omega = \frac{\pi}{2},\ \phi_h(\omega) = \tan^{-1}\frac{\frac{8}{9}}{\frac{2}{3}} = \tan^{-1}\frac{4}{3} = 0.295\pi$$

Hence, $$y(n) = 2\sin\left(\frac{n\pi}{2}+0.295\pi\right) = 2\sin\left(\frac{\pi}{2}(n+0.59)\right)$$

$\therefore$ $$y_a(t) = y(n)\big|_{n=t/T_s} \quad \because \quad y_a(t)\big|_{t=nT_s} = y(n) \quad \textbf{Ans.}$$

EXAMPLE 7.15: *For the following system using ideal D to A converter, a linear-time-invariant filter, and an ideal A to D converter is inputted by*

$$x(n) = \left[\frac{(\sin n\pi/2)}{(n\pi/2)}\right]^2$$

and the LTI filter has frequency response

$$H_a(f) = \begin{cases} 1 & |f| \le 10\,kHz \\ 0, & otherwise \end{cases}$$

(a) If $T_1 = T_2 = 10^{-4}$, find the expression relating the output y(n) to the input x(n)

(b) If $T_1 = \frac{1}{4}\times 10^{-4}$, and $T_2 = 10^{-4}$, find y(n).

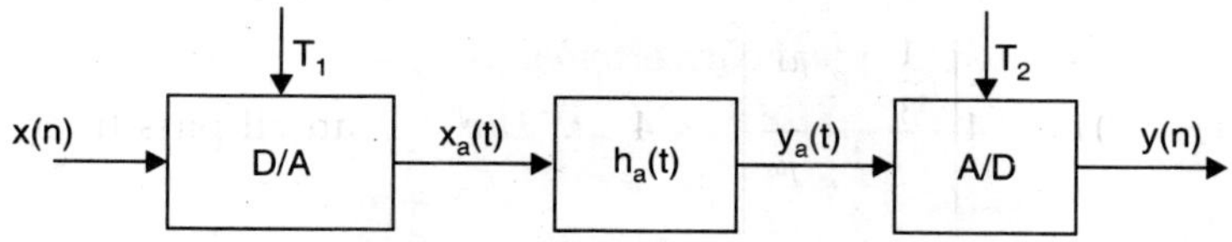

The given system

SOLUTION: We know that $\sin\frac{(n\omega_c)}{(n\pi)}$ has DTFT a LPF with cut-off ω_c as shown in Fig. (*a*)

i.e., $\text{DTFT}\left[\frac{\omega_c}{\pi}\cdot\frac{\sin n\omega_c}{n\omega_c}\right]$ is as in Fig. (*a*).

Putting $$\omega_c = \frac{\pi}{2}$$

DTFT of $\frac{1}{2}\frac{\sin\frac{n\pi}{2}}{\frac{n\pi}{2}}$ is a LPF with magnitude unity.

$\therefore$ DTFT $\frac{\sin\frac{n\pi}{2}}{\frac{n\pi}{2}}$ is a LPF with magnitude 2.

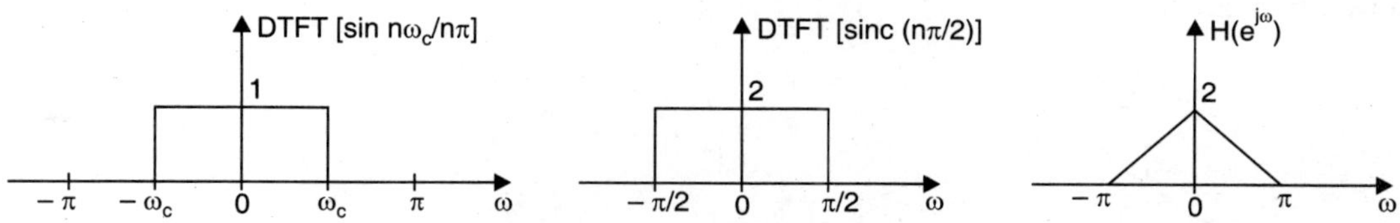

(*a*) (*b*) (*c*)

Now $$\text{DTFT}\left[\left\{\frac{\sin\left(\frac{n\pi}{2}\right)}{\left(\frac{n\pi}{2}\right)}\right\}^2\right] = \frac{1}{2\pi}\left[\left\{\text{DTFT}\left(\text{sinc}\,\frac{n\pi}{2}\right)\right\} * \left\{\text{DTFT}\sin\left(\frac{n\pi}{2}\right)\right\}\right]$$

$\therefore$ $$\text{DTFT of } x(n) = \left[\frac{\sin(n\pi/2)}{n\pi/2}\right]^2$$ is an shown in Fig. (*c*).

(*a*) When $T_1 = T_2$, the given system behaves like a shift-invariant discrete-time linear system. We have assumed ideal *D* to *A* and *A* to *D* converters.

As $$T_1 = T_2 = 10^{-4}$$

$\therefore$ $$f_{s_1} = f_{s_2} = 10\ K$$

As $H_a(f)$ is an ideal LPF, with passband of 10 kHz (given), therefore, output of $\frac{D}{A}$, which is band limited to $\frac{10}{2}$ = 5 kHz fully passes through $H_a(f)$, and $y_a(t) = x_a(t)$. Now $x_a(t)$ is passed through $\frac{A}{D}$ convertor, (assumed an ideal convertor) and $T_2 = T_1 = 10^{-4}$ *i.e.* $f_{s_2} = 10\ K$, hence, $y(n) = x_a(nT_{s_1})$

$$= x(n) \qquad \text{[As } x_a(t) \text{ was obtained from } x(n) \text{ using } f_{s_1} = 10\ K]$$

Thus, $\quad y(n) = x(n)$ **Ans.**

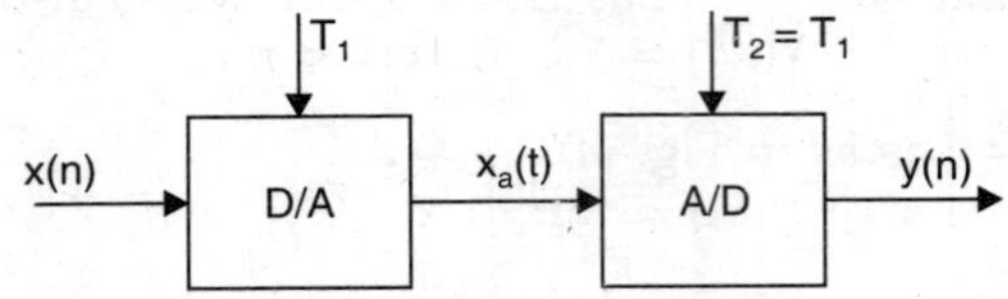

Fig. (*d*) When $T_1 = T_2$, $y(n) = x(n)$

Note that an ideal *D* to *A* converter followed by an ideal *A* to *D* converter is an identity system. That is why Fig. (*d*) resulted $y(n) = x(n)$.

(*b*) When $T_1 \neq T_2$, the system, in general, is not *LTI* one but is a linear time-variant system. It is easy to analyze the system in frequency domain.

The DTFT of $x(n)$, *i.e.*, $X(e^{j\omega})$ is shown in Fig. (*d*). As $T_1 = \frac{1}{4}10^{-4}$, therefore, $f_{s_1} = 40\ K$. The signal $x(n)$ is band limited to 20 kHz. Hence, $x(n)$ gets converted to $x_a(t)$ with $x_a(f)$ shown in Fig. (*e*).

The analog LPF $H_a(f)$ removes frequencies above 10 kHz to produce $y_a(t)$ with spectrum $Y_a(f)$ is shown in Fig. (*f*).

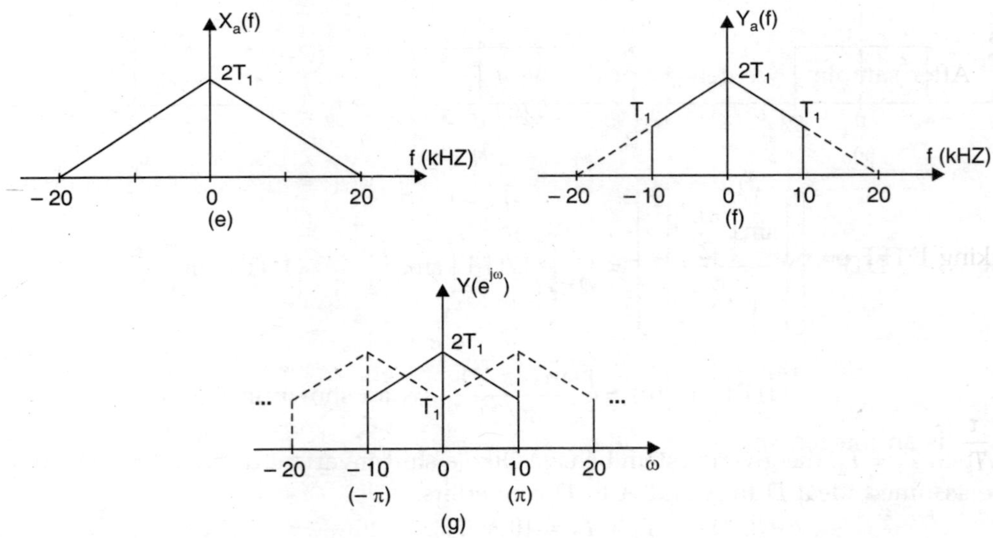

Fig. Ex. 7.15. Aliasing of $Y(e^{j\omega})$ as f_{s2} is half the required Nyquistrate.

As $y_a(t)$ has the highest frequency of 10 kHz, and $f_{s_2} = \frac{1}{T_2} = 10\ K$. Hence, $y_a(t)$ will be aliased.

The DTFT of $y(n)$ is related to $Y_a(j\ \Omega)$ as

$$Y(e^{j\omega}) = \frac{1}{T_2}\sum_{k=-\infty}^{\infty} Y_a\left(\frac{j\omega}{T_2} - j\frac{2\pi k}{T_2}\right)$$

From 0 to π and 0 to $-\pi$, we get

$$Y(e^{j\omega}) = \frac{1}{T_2}(2T_1 + T_1) = 3\frac{T_1}{T_2}$$

$\therefore$ $$Y(e^{j\omega}) = 3\times\frac{1}{4},\ |\omega| < \pi$$

$\therefore$ $$y(n) = \frac{3}{4}\delta(n)$$ **Ans.**

EXAMPLE 7.16: *A continuous-time signal $x_a(t)$ with band width B and its echo $x_a(t - \tau)$ arrives simultaneously at a TV receiver. The received signal*

$$r_a(t) = x_a(t) + ax_a(t - \tau),\ |a| < 1$$

is processed as shown in Fig. Ex. 7.16. Is it possible to specify F_s and $H(z)$ so that $y_a(t) = x_a(t)$, so as to remove the ghost $x_a(t - \tau)$ from the received signal?

SOLUTION:

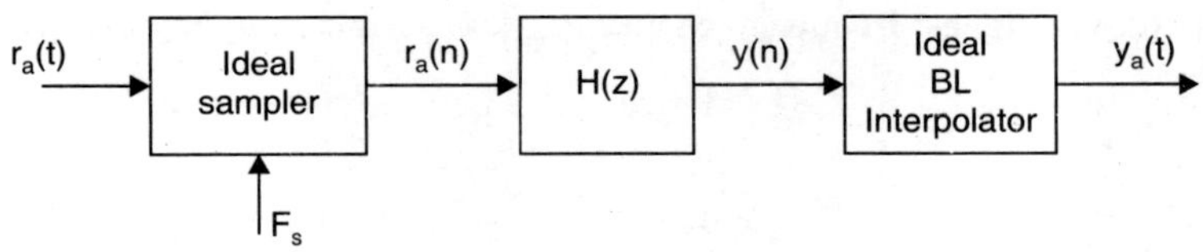

Fig. Ex. 7.16

As $$r_a(t) = x_a(t) + ax_a(t - \tau),\ |a| < 1$$

$\therefore$ After sampling we get, replacing t by nT_s

$$r_a(nT_s) = x_a(nT_s) + ax_a(nT_s - \tau)$$

or $$r(n) = x(n) + ax\left(n - \frac{\tau}{T_s}\right)$$ (Dividing each argument by T_s)

Taking DTFT on both sides, we get

$$R(e^{j\omega}) = X(e^{j\omega})[1 + ae^{-j(\tau/T_s)\omega}]$$

$\therefore$ $$R(e^{j\omega})/X(e^{j\omega}) = 1 + ae^{-j(\tau/T_s)\omega}$$

If $\frac{\tau}{T_s}$ is an integer, say $\frac{\tau}{T_s} = L$, then $H(z) = \frac{1}{1 + az^{-L}}$

i.e., $$H(e^{j\omega}) = \frac{1}{1 + a^{-jL\omega}}$$ yields: $Y(e^{j\omega}) = R(e^{j\omega}) \times H(e^{j\omega}) = X(e^{j\omega})$

Hence, $$y_a(t) = x_a(t)$$ **Ans.**

UNSOLVED PROBLEMS WITH ANSWERS

7.1. Determine the minimum sampling frequency to be used to sample the singal $x(t) = 100 \text{ sinc}^2 (100 \pi t)$, if the signal is to be recovered from the samples without any distortion.

[**Ans.** 200 samples per sec]

7.2. Let $X_1(j\omega)$ and $X_2(j\omega)$ be the Fourier transforms of signals $x_1(t)$ and $x_2(t)$, respectively. If $X_1(j\omega)$ and $X_2(j\omega)$ are low-pass spectra such that.

$$X_1 (j\omega) = 0, \ |\omega| \geq \omega_1$$
$$X_2 (j\omega) = 0, \ |\omega| \geq \omega_2$$

compute the Nyquist sampling rate for $y_1(t) = x_1(t). \ x_2(t)$ and $y_2(t) = x_1(t) * x_2(t)$ *(IP Univ., 2007)*

[**Ans.** for $y_1(t)$, $f_s = \dfrac{\omega_1 + \omega_2}{\pi}$ samples per second

for $y_2(t)$, $f_s = \dfrac{\omega_1}{\pi}$ if $\omega_1 < \omega_2$

$f_s = \dfrac{\omega_2}{\pi}$ if $\omega_2 < \omega_1$]

[**Hint.** When two LPF spectra multiply, the resultant spectra is the lower of the two spectra.]

7.3. The signal $x(t)$ has highest frequency content ω_{max}. Determine the Nyquist rate (is radians/s) for the signals

(a) $x_1(t) = x^2(t)$, *(b)* $x_2(t) = \dfrac{d}{dt}[x^2(t)]$

(c) $x_3(t) = x(t) + \dfrac{d}{dt} x(t)$, *(d)* $x_4(t) = \int_0^t x(t) \, dt$, *(e)* $x_5(t) = x(t) \cos (\Omega_0 t)$

[**Ans.** *(a)* $4\omega_{max}$, *(b)* $4\omega_{max}$, *(c)* $2\omega_{max}$ *(d)* $2\omega_{max}$, *(e)* $2(\omega_{max} + \Omega_0)$]

7.4. The Nyquist rate of a signal $x(t)$ is ω_0 radians/s. Determine the sampling frequency for no aliasing for the signals

(a) $x_1(t) = x(t) + \cos \omega_0 t$, *(b)* $x_2(t) = x(t) \, . \cos \omega_0 t$

(c) $x_3(t) = x(t) \, . \sin \omega_c t$ *(d)* $x_4(t) = x^2(t) \, . \sin \omega_c t$

[**Ans.** *(a)* ω_0 *(b)* $3\omega_0$ *(c)* $\omega_0 + 2\omega_c$ *(d)* $2(\omega_0 + \omega_c)$]

7.5. Find the Nyquist rate as per sampling theorem for the signals

(a) $x_1(t) = \cos 20\pi t + \sin 80\pi t$ *(b)* $x_2(t) = \left(\dfrac{\sin 60\pi t}{\pi t}\right)^2$.

[**Ans.** *(a)* 160π *(b)* 240π rads/s]

7.6. If a continuous time signal $x_a(t) = \cos (1000\pi t)$ is sampled at the sampling frequency $f_s = 10$ Hz, find the expression for the sampled signal.

[**Ans.** $x(n) = x_a(nT_s) = \cos 100\pi n$. In the given signal, replace t by T_s]

7.7. Let $x(t)$ be a real valued band limited signal with

$$X(j\omega) = 0, \ |\omega| > \omega_m$$

Show that $x(t)$ can be expressed as

$$x(t) = \sum_{k=-\infty}^{\infty} x(kT_s) \text{ sinc } [\omega_m(t - kT_s)]$$

where $T_s = \pi/\omega_m$.

7.8. If two discrete-time LTI systems have frequency responses.

$$H_1(e^{j\omega}) = \left(1+\frac{1}{2}e^{-j\omega}\right)\Big/\left(1+\frac{1}{4}e^{-j\omega}\right)$$

and
$$H_2(e^{j\omega}) = \left(\frac{1}{2}+e^{-j\omega}\right)\Big/\left(1+\frac{1}{4}e^{-j\omega}\right)$$

Show that

(a) $|H_1(e^{j\omega})| = |H_2(e^{j\omega})|$

(b) $\measuredangle H_2(e^{j\omega}) > \measuredangle H_1(e^{j\omega})$ for $\omega > 0$.

7.9. If $x_p(n)$ is impulse train sample of sequence $x(n)$, given $X(e^{j\omega})$ has $\omega_{max} = 3\pi/7$, find N_{max} to avoid aliasing.

$\left[\textbf{Ans. } N_{max} = 2. \text{ Note that } N_{max} \le \dfrac{2\pi}{2\omega_{max}}\right]$

7.10. A discrete-time sequence

$$x(n) = \cos\left(\frac{n\pi}{8}\right)$$

is required to be produced by sampling a continuous-time signal $x_a(t) = \cos(2\pi f_0 t)$ by $f_s = 10$ kHz. Find two different continuous-time signals which will produce $x(n)$.

[**Ans.** Let $x_a(t) = \cos(2\pi f_0 t)$

$$\therefore \quad x(n) = x_a(2\pi f_0 \cdot nT_s),\ T_s = \frac{1}{f_s}$$
$$= \cos(2\pi f_0 \cdot nT_s)$$
$$= \cos\left(2\pi\frac{f_0}{f_s}n\right)$$
$$= \cos\left(2\pi\frac{f_0}{f_s}\left(n+k\frac{f_s}{f_0}\right)\right),\ k \text{ an integer}$$
$$= \cos\left(2\pi\frac{f_0+kf_s}{f_s}\cdot n\right)$$

Hence, any sinusoid with frequency

$$f = f_0 + kf_s$$

will produce the same sequence, when sampled with a sampling frequency f_s.

As
$$x(n) = \cos\left(2\pi\frac{1}{16}n\right) \equiv \cos\left(2\pi\frac{f_0}{f_s}n\right)$$

$$\therefore \quad \frac{f_0}{f_s} = \frac{1}{16} \text{ or } f_0 = \frac{10{,}000}{16} = 625$$

$$f = 625 \text{ or } 625 + 10{,}000 \text{ will produce } \cos\left(\frac{n\pi}{8}\right)$$

$$\therefore \quad x_{a_1}(t) = \cos(2\pi \times 625\, t) = \cos(1250\,\pi t)$$

and
$$x_{a_2}(t) = \cos(2\pi \times 10{,}625\, t) = \cos(21250\, t)$$

Ans.

7.11. If the Nyquist rate for $x_a(t)$ is f_s find the Nyquist rate for

(*a*) $x^2(2t)$, (*b*) $x\left(\frac{t}{3}\right)$, (*c*) $x(t) * x(t)$.

Ans. (*a*) $4f_s$, (*b*) $\frac{f_s}{3}$, (*c*) f_s Note that the highest frequency of $FT[x(t) * x(t)]$ is the same as that of $FT[x(t)]$

7.12. If $x_a(t)$ is band limited to 10 kHz.

(*a*) What is the Nyquist rate for $x_a(t)$?

(*b*) What is the Nyquist rate for $x_a(t) \cdot \cos(2\pi \cdot 1000\, t)$?

[**Ans.** (*a*) 20 kHz, (*b*) 22 kHz]

7.13. Let $x_a(t) = \cos(650\,\pi t) + 2\sin(800\,\pi t)$

(*a*) What is the Nyquist rate for $x_a(t)$?

(*b*) If $x(n) = x_a(nT_s)$ and $f_s = \frac{1}{T_s}$ 1600, what are the frequencies of the sinusoids in $x(n)$?

$$\left[\textbf{Ans. } (a)\ 800\ \text{Hz}\ (b)\ \frac{325}{800}\pi = \frac{17}{32}\pi,\ \frac{400}{800}\pi = \frac{\pi}{2}\right]$$

7.14. If a continuous-time signal $x_a(t)$ is sampled at sampling frequency f_s to get $x(n) = x_a(nT_s)$, what will be the cut-off frequency of $x(n)$ and $x\left(\frac{n}{2}\right)$?

[**Ans.** π, $\pi/2$]

7.15. An analog waveform is sampled at sampling frequency $f_s = 12$ kHz. We wish to eliminate information up to 60 Hz in the original $x_a(t)$, by cascading $x_a(nT_s)$ by a high-pass filter (HPF) $H_{HP}(e^{j\omega})$. What should be the lowest cut-off frequency ω_c of $H_{HP}(e^{j\omega})$?

$$\left[\textbf{Ans. } \omega_c = \frac{60}{12\times10^3}\times 2\pi = 0.01\pi \text{ radians}\right]$$

7.16. For the band limited input signals, the system shown as follows is a *LTI* continuous-time system

$$y(n) = \frac{1}{2}y(n-1) + x(n)$$

Find the frequency response of the equivalent continuous-time system.

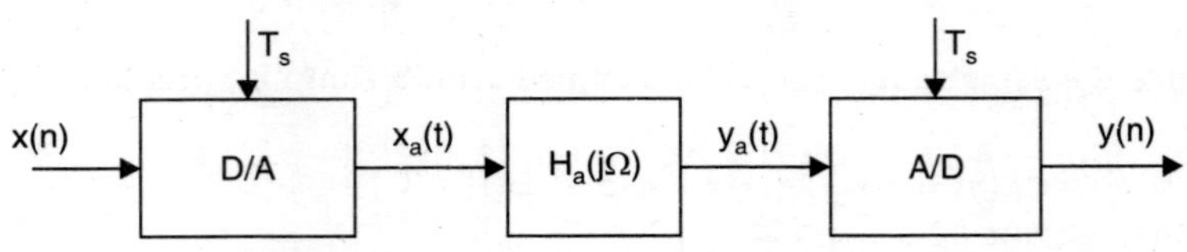

Fig. Prob. 7.16. The given system for processing a discrete-time signal using a continuous-time system

Hint.

$$H(z) = \frac{1}{1-\frac{1}{2}z^{-1}} \quad \therefore\ H(e^{j\omega}) = \frac{1}{1-\frac{1}{2}e^{-j\omega}}$$

$$H_a\left(\frac{j\omega}{T_s}\right) = H(e^{j\omega}),\ |\omega| < \pi,\ \Omega T_s = \omega$$

$$\therefore \quad H_a(j\,\Omega) = \frac{1}{1-\frac{1}{2}e^{-j\Omega T_s}},\ |\Omega| < \frac{\pi}{T_s} \quad \textbf{Ans.}$$

7.17. A discrete-time sequence is band limited such that

$$X(e^{j\omega}) = 0,\ 0.3\pi < |\omega| < \pi$$

$x(n)$ is sampled to form a new sequence $y(n) = x(nN)$, where N is an integer. Find the largest value of N so that $x(n)$ may be uniquely recovered from $y(n)$.

[Hint.

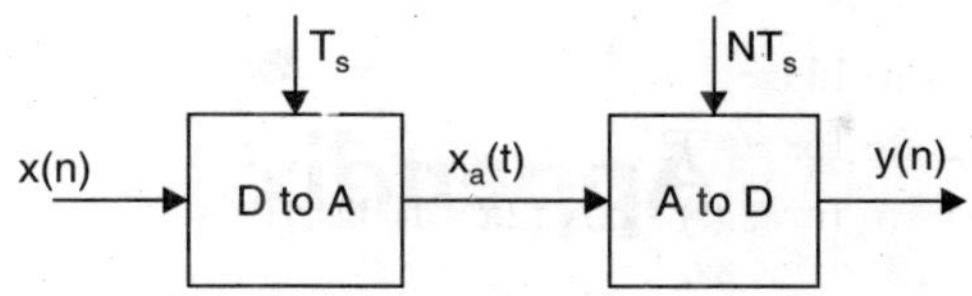

Assume the system as shown in the figure.

If D to A is ideal then $T_s = \frac{1}{f_s}$ must be such that $x_a(t)$ is band limited to $f_0 = 0.3 \times \frac{f_s}{2}$. (because $x_a(t)$ sampled by f_s is such that π radians of $X(e^{j\omega})$ corresponds to $\frac{f_s}{2}$ Hz of $x_a(t)$. Therefore, 0.3π radian of $X(e^{j\omega})$ means $x_a(t)$ had maximum frequency, $f_0 = 0.3 \cdot \frac{f_s}{2}$).

To avoid aliasing

$$f_s' \geq 2f_0$$

or $$T_s' \leq \frac{1}{2f_0} = \frac{1}{0.3f_s} = 3.33T_s$$

$\therefore$ $$T_s' = 3T_s$$

$$y(n) = x_a(nT_s') = x_a(3nT_s) = x(3n)$$

Hence, $N = 3$ for $x(n)$ to be uniquely recovered from $y(n)$] **Ans.**

7.18. A sequence $x(n)$ is obtained from a band-limited continuous-time signal using a sampling frequency of 12 kHz. However, the sequence should have been sampled using a sampling frequency $f_s = 15$ kHz. Design a system for digitally changing the sampling rate.

[**Ans.** To convert f_{s_1} of 12 kHz to $f_{s_2} = 15$ kHz. We need sampling rate conversion of $\frac{15}{12} = \frac{5}{4}$.

Hence, use $L = 5$ for upsampler, followed by a LPF with $\omega_c = \frac{\pi}{5}$, and cascade it by a downsampler using $M = 4$]

7.19. Show that the two analog signals

$$x_{a_1}(t) = A\cos\left[\left(\frac{2\pi}{T}\right)(k+\alpha)t\right]$$

and $$x_{a_2}(t) = A\cos\left(\left(\frac{2\pi}{T}\right)\cdot \alpha t\right)$$

when sampled at $f_s = \frac{1}{T}$ produce the same discrete-time signal.

[**Hint.** Put $t = nT$ in $x_{a_1}(t)$ and $x_{a_2}(t)$. We get, in both the cases, $x_{a_1}(nT) = x_{a_2}(nT) = A\cos(2\pi\alpha nT)$ which we may call $x(n) = A\cos(2\pi\alpha n)$.]

Appendix

DISCRETE-TIME SIGNALS OBTAINED BY SAMPLING

We, here, give an alternative approach to obtain the spectrum of sampled signal $x_a(nT)$ is terms of spectrum of $x_a(t)$.

Let analog signal be $x_a(t)$ and its Fourier transform be $X_a(j\,\Omega)$

$$\therefore \qquad X_a(j\,\Omega) = FT[x_a(t)] = \int_{-\infty}^{\infty} x_a(t)e^{-j\Omega t}\,dt \qquad \text{...(A-1)}$$

and

$$x_a(t) = IFT[X_a(j\,\Omega)] = \frac{1}{2\pi}\int_{-\infty}^{\infty} x_a(j\,\Omega)e^{j\Omega t}\,d\Omega \qquad \text{...(A-2)}$$

We obtain a discrete-time signal $\boldsymbol{x(n) = x_a(nT)}$ by sampling the analog signal once every T seconds, where

$$T = \text{Sampling period}$$

$$f_s = \frac{1}{T}, \text{ [The sampling frequency (or sampling rate)]}$$

$$\therefore \qquad x(n) \triangleq x_a(nT)$$

$$= \frac{1}{2\pi}\int_{-\infty}^{\infty} X_a(j\,\Omega)e^{j\Omega nT}\,d\Omega \qquad \text{[Due to (A-2)]} \qquad \text{...(A-3)}$$

We also know that

$$X(e^{j\omega}) = FT[x(n)] = \sum_{n=-\infty}^{\infty} x(n)e^{-j\omega n} \qquad \text{...(A-4)}$$

and

$$x\,(n) = \frac{1}{2\pi}\int_{-\pi}^{\pi} X(e^{j\omega})e^{j\omega n}\,d\omega \qquad \text{...(A-5)}$$

We can write (*A*-3) by breaking the limits of integration to, $\ldots -\frac{3\pi}{T}$ to $-\frac{\pi}{T}$, $-\frac{\pi}{T}$ to $\frac{\pi}{T}$, $\frac{\pi}{T}$ to $\frac{3\pi}{T}$, ..., as

$$x(n) = \frac{1}{2\pi}\sum_{k=-\infty}^{\infty}\int_{(2k-1)\pi/T}^{(2k+1)\pi/T} X_a(j\,\Omega)e^{j\Omega nT}\,d\Omega \quad \text{(Note this step)} \qquad \ldots(A\text{-}6)$$

Put $\quad \Omega - \frac{2\pi k}{T} = \Omega'$

$\therefore \quad d\Omega = d\Omega'$

When $\quad \Omega = \frac{(2k-1)\pi}{T}$, then $\Omega' = \frac{(2k-1)\pi}{T} - \frac{2\pi k}{T} = \frac{-\pi}{T}$

When $\quad \Omega = \frac{(2k+1)\pi}{T}$, then $\Omega' = \frac{(2k+1)\pi}{T} - \frac{2\pi k}{T} = \frac{+\pi}{T}$

$\therefore$ (*A*-6) reduces to

$$x(n) = \frac{1}{2\pi}\sum_{k=-\infty}^{\infty}\int_{-\pi/T}^{\pi/T} X_a\left(j\left(\Omega' + \frac{2\pi k}{T}\right)\right)e^{j(\Omega' + 2\pi k/T)nT}\,d\Omega'$$

$$= \frac{1}{2\pi}\sum_{k=-\infty}^{\infty}\int_{-\pi/T}^{\pi/T} X_a\left(j\left(\Omega' + \frac{2\pi k}{T}\right)\right)e^{j\Omega' nT}\underbrace{e^{j2nk\pi}}_{=1}\,d\Omega'$$

Dropping dashes, above equation reduces to

$$x(n) = \frac{1}{2\pi}\sum_{k=-\infty}^{\infty}\int_{\Omega=-\pi/T}^{\Omega=\pi/T} X_a\left(j\left(\Omega + \frac{2\pi k}{T}\right)\right)e^{j\Omega nT}\,d\Omega \qquad \ldots(A\text{-}7)$$

Put $\boxed{\Omega T = \omega}$

Ω is in radians/s

ω is in radians

$\therefore \quad d\Omega = \frac{1}{T}d\omega$, when $\Omega = -\pi/T$, $\omega = -\pi$

when $\Omega = +\pi/T$, $\omega = +\pi$

Hence equation (*A*-7) reduces to

$$x(n) = \frac{1}{2\pi}\sum_{k=-\infty}^{\infty}\frac{1}{T}\int_{\omega=-\pi}^{\omega=\pi} X_a\left(j\left(\frac{\omega}{T} + \frac{2\pi k}{T}\right)\right)e^{jn\omega}\,d\omega$$

$$= \frac{1}{2\pi}\int_{-\pi}^{\pi}\underbrace{\frac{1}{T}\sum_{k=-\infty}^{\infty} X_a\left(j\frac{\omega}{T} + j\frac{2\pi k}{T}\right)}_{X(e^{j\omega})}e^{jn\omega}\,d\omega \qquad \ldots(A\text{-}8)$$

Comparing (*A-5*) and (*A-8*), we have

$$X(e^{j\omega}) = \frac{1}{T}\sum_{k=-\infty}^{\infty} X_a\left(j\frac{\omega}{T} + j\frac{2\pi k}{T}\right) \qquad \text{...(A-9)}$$

or, in terms of analog frequency Ω, we get, putting $\omega = \Omega T$:

$$X(e^{j\Omega T}) = \frac{1}{T}\sum_{k=-\infty}^{\infty} X_a\left(j\Omega + j\frac{2\pi k}{T}\right) \qquad \text{...(A-10)}$$

↗ a scaling factor (for $\frac{1}{T}$)

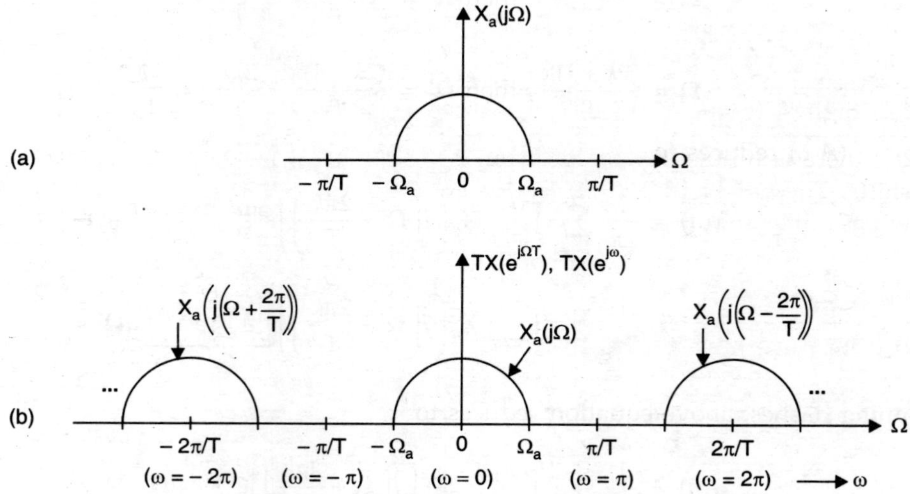

Fig. (*A-1*) (*a*) Graph of $X_a(j\,\Omega)$: spectrum of $x_a(t)$
(*b*) Graph of $X(e^{j\Omega T})$: spectrum of the sampled signal $x(n)$

i.e. $X(e^{j\Omega T}) = \frac{1}{T}X_a(j\,\Omega)$, $\frac{-\pi}{T} \le \Omega \le \frac{\pi}{T}$.

Also $\qquad \Omega T = \omega$

Thus, we obtain the frequency response $X(e^{j\omega})$ by superimposing the shifted components of $X_a(j\,\Omega)$, where the shifts are multiples of $2\pi/T$ both to the left and to the right. As

$$X(e^{j\omega}) = \sum_{n=-\infty}^{\infty} x(n)e^{-j\omega n} \qquad \text{(By definition of DTFT)}$$

Putting $\Omega T = \omega$ in (*A-10*), we can write

$$\therefore \quad \sum_{n=-\infty}^{\infty} x(n)e^{-j\omega n} = \frac{1}{T}\sum_{k=-\infty}^{\infty} X_a\left(j\frac{\omega}{T} + j\frac{2\pi k}{T}\right)$$

Substitute $x(n) = x_a(nT)$ and $\omega = \Omega T$, $\therefore$ we obtain

$$\sum_{n=-\infty}^{\infty} x_a(nT)e^{-jn\Omega T} = \frac{1}{T}\sum_{k=-\infty}^{\infty} X_a\left(j\Omega + j\frac{2\pi k}{T}\right) \quad \ldots(A\text{-}11)$$

Poisson's formula

Let the highest frequency in the (band limited) signal be f_m

i.e. $\Omega_m = 2\pi f_m$

To avoid aliasing, we must have $2\Omega_m \le \dfrac{2\pi}{T}$

i.e. $\Omega_m \le \dfrac{\pi}{T}$

i.e. $2\pi f_m \le \pi f_s$

$\therefore$ $f_s \ge 2f_m$ or

$f_s \ge 2$ (highest frequency of the analog signal) ...(A-12a)

If $f_s \ge 2f_m$, there is no overlap of spectrum $X_a(j\,\Omega)$ when repeated at intervals $2\pi/T$ (or its multiples) shifts. The baseband $X_a(j\,\Omega)$ can be completely recovered from $X(e^{j\omega})$ *i.e.* $X(e^{j\Omega T})$ by using a low-pass filter that blocks all frequencies above π/T.

When $\Omega_m > \dfrac{\pi}{T}$, *i.e.*, $2\pi f_m > \pi f_s$ or if $f_s < 2f_m$, then aliasing results. We cannot hope to recover back $X_a(j\,\Omega)$ from $X(e^{j\Omega T})$, by any means.

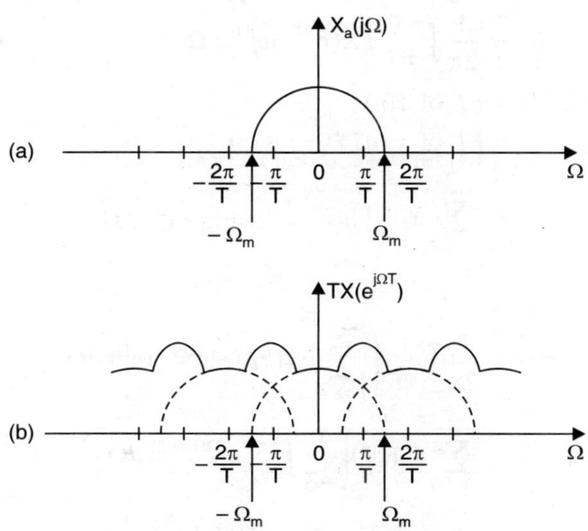

Fig. (A-2) (*a*) $X_a(j\,\Omega)$ and

(*b*) $X(e^{j\Omega T})$ when aliasing is there

Recovery of the Analog Signal from its Sampled version:

Let the band limited signal have the highest radian frequency = $\Omega_m = 2\pi f_m$

Let the sampling frequency, $f_s \geq 2f_m$

i.e., $\Omega_s = 2\pi f_s \geq 2\Omega_m$

Then f_s(or Ω_s) is called the Nyquist sampling frequency, and there would be no aliasing if $f_s \geq 2f_m$. Then we have

$$X(e^{j\Omega T}) = \frac{1}{T}X_a(j\,\Omega),\ -\frac{\pi}{T} \leq \Omega \leq \frac{\pi}{T} \qquad \text{...(A-12b)}$$

Putting $\omega = \Omega T$,

$$X(e^{j\omega}) = \frac{1}{T}X_a(j\omega/T)\ -\pi \leq \omega \leq \pi \qquad \text{...(A-12c)}$$

As $X_a(j\,\Omega)$ is zero outside the interval $-\frac{\pi}{T} \leq \Omega \leq \frac{\pi}{T}$, we can write

$$x_a(t) = \text{Inverse } FT \text{ of } X_a(j\,\Omega)$$

$$= \frac{1}{2\pi}\int_{-\infty}^{\infty} X_a(j\,\Omega)e^{j\Omega t}\,d\Omega \quad \text{(By definition of } IFT \text{ in analog signals)}$$

$$= \frac{1}{2\pi}\int_{-\pi/T}^{\pi/T} X_a(j\,\Omega)e^{j\Omega t}\,d\Omega \qquad \text{...(A-13)}$$

$\because$ $X_a(j\,\Omega)$ is zero for $|\Omega| > |\pi/T|$.

Using (*A*-11) and (*A*-13), we get

$$x_a(t) = \frac{1}{2\pi}\int_{-\pi/T}^{\pi/T} TX(e^{j\Omega T})e^{j\Omega t}\,d\Omega \qquad \text{...(A-14)}$$

but

$$X(e^{j\Omega T}) = FT \text{ of } x(n)$$

$$= FT \text{ of } x_a(nT) \qquad \because\ x(n) = x_a(nT)$$

$$= \sum_{k=-\infty}^{\infty} x_a(kT)e^{-j\Omega kT} \quad \text{using } \omega = \Omega T \qquad \text{...(A-15)}$$

$\therefore$ (*A*-14) becomes

$$x_a(t) = \frac{T}{2\pi}\int_{-\pi/T}^{\pi/T}\left(\sum_{k=-\infty}^{\infty} x_a(kT)e^{-j\Omega kT}\right)e^{j\Omega t}\,d\Omega$$

$$= \sum_{k=-\infty}^{\infty} x_a(kT)\left[\frac{T}{2\pi}\int_{-\pi/T}^{\pi/T} e^{j\Omega(t-kT)}\,d\Omega\right]$$

$$= \sum_{k=-\infty}^{\infty} x_a(kT)\cdot\frac{T}{2\pi}\left[\frac{e^{j\Omega(t-kT)}}{j(t-kT)}\right]_{\Omega=-\pi/T}^{\Omega=\pi/T}$$

$$= \sum_{k=-\infty}^{\infty} x_a(kT)\frac{T}{\pi}\left(\frac{e^{j(\pi/T)(t-kT)} - e^{-j(\pi/T)(t-kT)}}{2j(t-kT)}\right)$$

$$= \sum_{k=-\infty}^{\infty} x_a(kT) \frac{\sin(\pi/T)(t-kT)}{(\pi/T)(t-kT)}$$

$$\therefore \quad \boxed{x_a(t) = \sum_{k=-\infty}^{\infty} x_a(kT) \cdot \text{sinc}\left[\left(\frac{1}{T}\right)(t-kT)\right]} \qquad \text{...(A-16a)}$$

$$\text{where} \quad \text{sinc}\ \mu \triangleq \frac{\sin \pi\mu}{\pi\mu} \qquad \text{...(A-16b)}$$

or $\quad x_a(t) =$ '$x_a(nT)$ * sinc (t/T)'

The function $\left(\dfrac{\sin[(\pi/T)(t-kT)]}{(\pi/T)(t-kT)}\right)$ is called the *interpolating function.*

$\therefore$ We can completely, recover the analog signal $x_a(t)$ from the samples $x_a(nT)$ by passing the samples through a filter with impulse response

$$h(t) = \text{sinc}\left(\frac{1}{T}\right)t = \sin\frac{(\pi t/T)}{(\pi t/T)} \qquad \text{...(A-17)}$$

$h(t)$ represents a low-pass filter with its spectrum $H_{LP}(j\Omega)$ as shown in Fig. *A*-3.

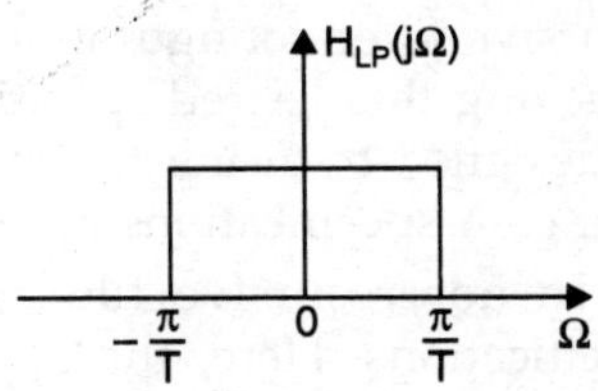

Fig. A-3. *LPF* to give *h*(*t*) given by (*A*-17)

The Sampling Theorem: If a signal $x_a(t)$ has a band limited frequency response $X_a(j\,\Omega)$ such that $X_a(j\,\Omega) = 0$ for $|\Omega| \geq |\Omega_m|$, then $x_a(t)$ can be uniquely reconstructed from equally spaced samples $x_a(nT)$, $-\infty < n < \infty$, if $\dfrac{1}{T} = f_s \geq 2f_m$, where $f_m = \Omega_m/2\pi$. That is, the sampling frequency f_s should be at least twice the highest frequency content of the signal $x_a(t)$. A sampling rate greater than $2f_m$ is preferred. However, a sampling rate less than $2f_m$ will cause aliasing, and we cannot recover $x_a(t)$ back from $x(n)$ in this case.

Design of Non-recursive Filters (FIR Filters)

CHAPTER 8

8.1 INTRODUCTION

The frequency selective filters such as LPF, HPF, BPF, BSF, etc., can be easily designed by using recursive filter configurations. However, it is, in general, difficult to get constant delay besides achieving the desired specifications in recursive filters. Note that constant-delay filters can also be designed by using the invariant-impulse method, but the constant delay and the prescribed loss/gain specifications are difficult to achive simultaneously.

In non-recursive filters, we can readily obtain constant delay and the prescribed loss specifications. Here, the approximation problem is usually solved by using Fourier series or numerical-analysis formula or alternatively by using Discrete Fourier transform.

8.1.1 Necessity of Linear-phase (*i.e.*, Constant Delay) Property

Consider a composite signal $x(n)$ such as a piece of Music having low frequency $\omega_1 = 1$ kHz (say, that of the table), $\omega_2 = 3$ kHz (say that of the singer) and $\omega_3 = 15$ kHz (say that of the harmonium). The essential requirement of this signal (music) is a perfect synchronism between its constituent frequencies ω_1, ω_2 and ω_3. If $x(n)$ signal is inputted to a filter, say, for getting higher volume, the output $y(n)$ must maintain the synchronism among ω_1, ω_2 and ω_3. This requires that each frequency component is delayed by the same amount, say τ. This will cause the phase delays of $\theta_1(\omega) = \omega_1\tau$ for ω_1, $\theta_2(\omega) = \omega_2\tau$ for ω_2 and $\theta_3(\omega) = \omega_3\tau$ for ω_3. In general, if the phase delay caused due to the filter is $\theta(\omega) = \omega\tau$, we call it linear phase shift, (or constant time delay, here τ), then each frequency component is delayed by the same time. This will ensure no relative time shift between the constituent frequencies of the input signal, and this ensures the signal quality for $y(n)$ as was for $x(n)$.

8.2 PROPERTIES OF NON-RECURSIVE FILTERS

We, now discuss some of the important properties of the non-recursive filters.

8.2.1 Constant delay Filters

A non-recursive (*NR*) filter is characterised by the transfer function

$$H(z) = \sum_{n=0}^{N-1} h(n)\, z^{-n} \qquad \ldots(8.1)$$

and its frequency response is given by

$$H(e^{j\omega}) = \sum_{n=0}^{N-1} h(n)\, e^{-j\omega n} \qquad \text{...(8.2)}$$

$$\triangleq M(\omega)\,.\, e^{j\theta(\omega)}$$

where

$$M(\omega) = |H(e^{j\omega})| \qquad \text{...(8.3a)}$$

$$\theta(\omega) = \arg H(e^{j\omega}) \qquad \text{...(8.3b)}$$

We define the phase delay and group delay by

$$\text{Phase delay, } \tau_p \triangleq -\frac{\theta(\omega)}{\omega} \qquad \text{...(8.4a)}$$

$$\text{Group delay, } \tau_g \triangleq -\frac{d\,\theta(\omega)}{d\omega} \qquad \text{...(8.4b)}$$

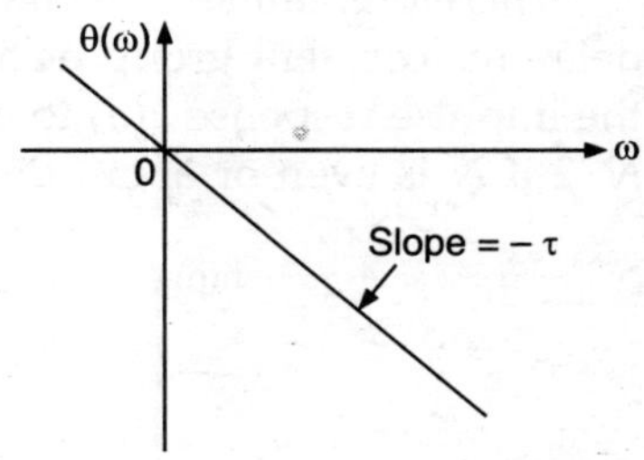

Fig. 8.1. Plot of $\theta(\omega) = -\tau\omega$

For τ_p and τ_g both to be constant, we must have

$$\boxed{\theta(\omega) = -\tau\omega} \qquad \text{...(8.5)}$$

Then $\tau_p = \tau_g = \tau =$ constant.

From (8.2), we have

$$H(e^{j\omega}) = \sum_{n=0}^{N-1} [h(n)\cos(\omega n) - j\,h(n)\sin(\omega n)] \qquad \text{...(8.6)}$$

By using (8.5) and finding $\theta(\omega)$ from (8.6), we get

$$\theta(\omega) = -\tau\omega = -\tan^{-1}\frac{\sum_{n=0}^{N-1} h(n)\sin(\omega n)}{\sum_{n=0}^{N-1} h(n)\cos(\omega n)} \qquad \text{(for constant delay case)}$$

i.e.,

$$\frac{\left[\sum_{n=0}^{N-1} h(n)\sin(\omega n)\right]}{\left[\sum_{n=0}^{N-1} h(n)\cos(\omega n)\right]} = \tan\omega\tau \qquad \text{...(8.7)}$$

Putting $\tan\omega\tau = \sin\omega\tau/\cos\omega\tau$ in (8.7), cross-multiplying and rearranging we readily obtain

$$\sum_{n=0}^{N-1} h(n)\,[\cos(\omega n)\sin(\omega\tau) - \sin(\omega n)\cos(\omega\tau)] = 0$$

i.e.,

$$\sum_{n=0}^{N-1} h(n)\sin(\omega\tau - \omega n) = 0 \qquad \text{...(8.8)}$$

The solution of the above equation can be shown to be

$$\tau = \frac{N-1}{2} \quad \ldots(8.9)$$

$$h(n) = h(N-1-n) \text{ for } 0 \le n \le N-1 \quad \ldots(8.10)$$

i.e., the impulse response is symmetric
for $\theta(\omega) = -\tau\omega$ (constant phase and constant group delays)

Therefore, unlike a recursive filter, a non-recursive filter can be realized for a constant phase delay (or constant group delay) requirements over the entire baseband. It is only necessary for the impulse response $h(n)$ to be symmetrical about the midpoint between samples $(N-2)/2$ and $N/2$ if N is even or about the sample $h((N-1)/2)$ if N is odd, as explained below;

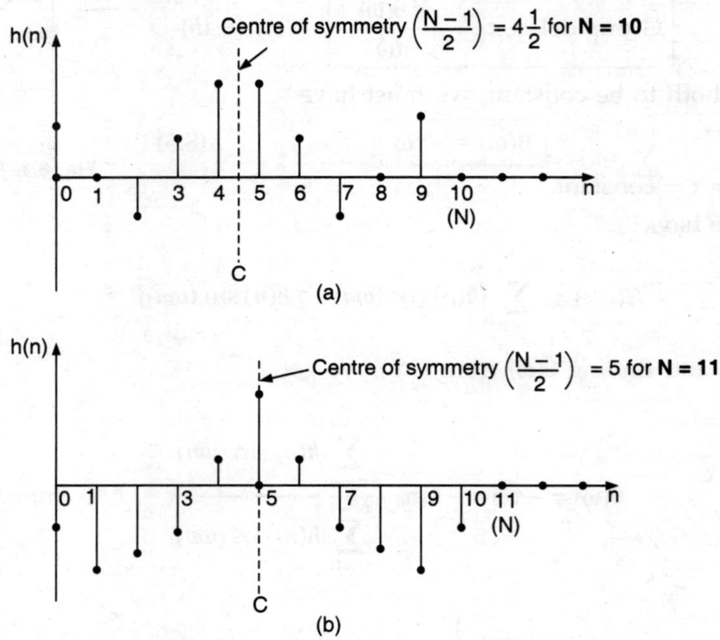

Fig. 8.2. Impulse response for constant group and phase delays (*a*) $N = 10$, (*b*) $N = 11$

When N is even, as in Fig. 8.2(*a*), the centre of symmetry, *i.e.*, point C is between the time $\frac{N-2}{2}$ and $\frac{N}{2}$, *i.e.*, for $N = 10$, the symmetry point lies between $n = 4$ and $n = 5$.

Note that $\tau = \frac{(N-1)}{2}$ is not an integer here. But we require half a delay to arrive at a point C, where $n = \frac{N-1}{2}$. This is not a desirable feature in many large systems.

When N is odd, the centre of symmetry C is at $n = (N-1)/2$ and is an integer. Point C is at a samplable point. Thus,

Centre of symmetry is for $\theta(\omega) = -\tau\omega$

N even between $\frac{N-2}{2}$ and $\frac{N}{2}$ ...(8.11)

N odd about $(N-1)/2$

8.2.2 Group Delay Constant Case (Phase delay may not be constant)

Here we can have $\tau_g = -\,d\theta(\omega)/d\omega$

Hence, $\theta(\omega) = \theta_0 - \tau_g(\omega)$ ...(8.12)

Proceeding as in the previous case, we get here

$$\tan(\theta_0 - \tau_g\omega) = \frac{\sum_{n=0}^{N-1} h(n)\sin(\omega n)}{\sum_{n=0}^{N-1} h(n)\cos(\omega n)} \quad ...(8.13)$$

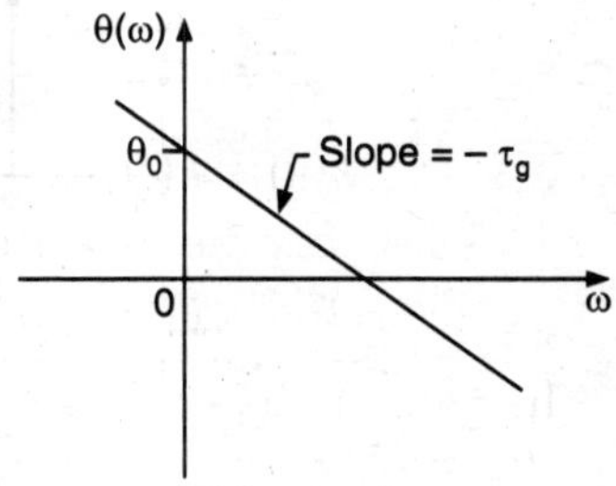

Fig. 8.3. Plot for $\theta(\omega) = \theta_0 - \tau\omega$ case

i.e.,

$$\sum_{n=0}^{N-1} \sin(\theta_0 - \tau_g\omega)\,.\,h(n)\cos\omega n - \sum_{n=0}^{N-1} \cos(\theta_0 - \tau_g\omega)\,.\,h(n)\sin(\omega n) = 0$$

or

$$\sum_{n=0}^{N-1} h(n)\sin(\omega n - \tau_g\omega + \theta_0) = 0 \quad ...(8.14)$$

If $\theta_0 = \pm\,\pi/2$ (as is the usual case in many situations), then (8.14) reduces to

$$\sum_{n=0}^{N-1} \pm\, h(n)\cos(\omega n - \tau_g\omega) = 0$$

i.e.,

$$\sum_{n=0}^{N-1} h(n)\cos(\omega n - \tau_g\omega) = 0 \quad ...(8.15)$$

Solution of (8.15) can be shown to be

$\tau_g = (N-1)/2$	constant group delay	...(8.16*a*)
$h(n) = -h(N-1-n)$,	antisymmetric	
for $0 \le n \le N-1$	if $\theta(\omega) = \pm\frac{\pi}{2} - \tau_g\omega$	...(8.16*b*)

Here, the impulse response takes the form as shown in Fig. 8.4, for N even and odd cases. Note that for N even, the centre of antisymmetric C is between $(N-2)/2$ and $N/2$. For N odd, the centre of anti-symmetric C is at $h((N-1)/2)$. Hence, we must have:

$$h((N-1)/2) = 0 \text{ here} \qquad \left[\because\; h\left(\frac{N-1}{2}\right) = -h\left(\frac{N-1}{2}\right)\right]$$

or the value of $h(n) = 0$ at the centre of anti-symmetric. To summarize, we have the following results:

Centre of symmetry if $\theta(\omega) = \pm\,\pi/2 - \tau_g\omega$	(constant group delay τ_g)	
N even, C is between $\frac{N-2}{2}$ and $\frac{N}{2}$		...(8.17*a*)
N odd, C is at $n = (N-1)/2$		...(8.17*b*)
Here $h(n) = -h(N-1-n)$, $n = 0, 1, 2, ..., N-1$	(anti-symmetric)	

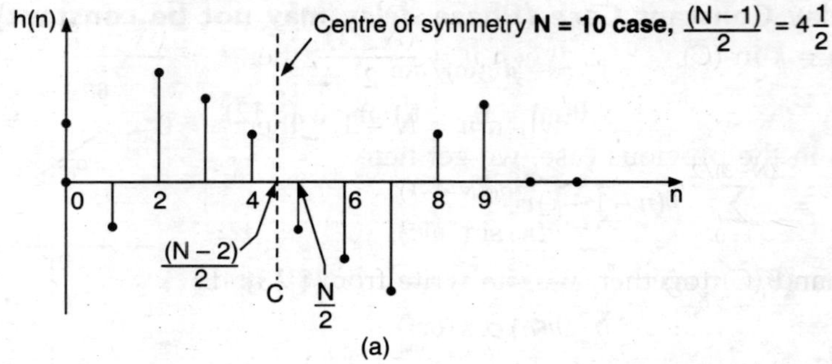

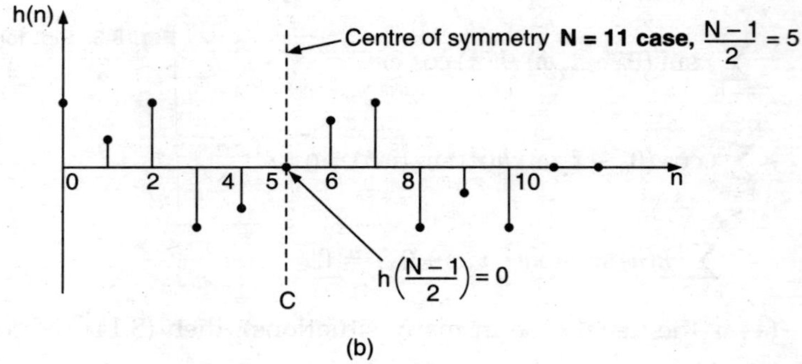

Fig. 8.4. Impulse response for constant group delay (*a*) *N* even, (*b*) *N* odd

Thus, in linear phase filters as discussed above, $h(n) = \pm\, h(N - 1 - n)$. The filter length is N and the filter order is $N - 1$. The mandatory delay is $(N - 1)/2$ samples. (Delay in time $= (N - 1)/2$ multiplied by T_s seconds, where T_s = intersample time interval). If N is odd, the delay is achieved at a point C (see Fig. 8.2 and Fig. 8.4) *i.e.*, a clock point and hence the filter output can be read at C and onwards. If N is even, the delay $(N - 1)/2$ point C is not a clock point. Hence, we invariably prefer N as odd, in our FIR filter designs.

8.3 FREQUENCY RESPONSE OF FOUR CASES—NON-RECURSIVE FILTERS

We have four cases *viz.* N even or odd, and $h(n)$ symmetric (8.10) or $h(n)$ anti-symmetric (8.16*b*) for the linear phase non-recursive filters. We shall determine the frequency responses for these cases.

Case A: *N* odd and symmetrical *h(n)* *i.e.*, $h(n) = h(N - 1 - n)$

We know that

$$H(e^{j\omega}) = \sum_{n=0}^{N-1} h(n)\, e^{-j\omega n}$$

$$= \sum_{n=0}^{(N-3)/2} h(n)\, e^{-j\omega n} + h\left(\frac{N-1}{2}\right) e^{-j\omega\frac{N-1}{2}} + \sum_{n=(N+1)/2}^{N-1} h(n)\, e^{-j\omega n} \quad \ldots(1)$$

(*A*) (*B*) (C) (Note this step)

$$(C) = \sum_{n=(N+1)/2}^{N-1} h(n) e^{-j\omega n}$$

Put $N-1-n=k$ in (C), $\therefore$ when $n = \dfrac{(N+1)}{2}$, then $k = \dfrac{(N-3)}{2}$

when $n = N-1$, then $k = 0$

$$= \sum_{k=0}^{(N-3)/2} h(n-1-k)e^{-j\omega(N-1-k)} \qquad \ldots(2)$$

Clubbing (A) and (C) together, we can write from (1) and (2)

$$H(e^{j\omega}) = \sum_{n=0}^{(N-3)/2} [h(n)e^{-j\omega n} + h(N-1-n)e^{-j\omega(N-1-n)}] + h\left(\frac{N-1}{2}\right)e^{-j\omega\frac{N-1}{2}}$$

$$= \sum_{n=0}^{(N-3)/2} h(n)[e^{-j\omega n} + e^{-j\omega(N-1-n)}] + h\left(\frac{N-1}{2}\right)e^{-j\omega\frac{N-1}{2}}$$

(using $N-1-n = h(n)$)

$$= e^{-j\omega(N-1)/2} \sum_{n=0}^{(N-3)/2} h(n)\left[e^{j\omega\left(\frac{N-1}{2}-n\right)} + e^{-j\omega\left(\frac{N-1}{2}-n\right)}\right]$$

$$+ h\left(\frac{N-1}{2}\right)e^{-j\omega(N-1)/2}$$

$$\therefore \quad H(e^{j\omega}) = e^{-j\omega(N-1)/2}\left[\sum_{n=0}^{(N-3)/2} 2h(n)\cos\left(\frac{N-1}{2}-n\right)\omega + h\left(\frac{N-1}{2}\right)\right] \qquad \ldots(3)$$

Put $\dfrac{N-1}{2} - n = k$ $\quad\therefore$ when $n = 0$, $k = \dfrac{(N-1)}{2}$

when $n = \dfrac{(N-3)}{2}$, $k = 1$

Thus, (3) gives

$$H(e^{j\omega}) = e^{-j\omega(N-1)/2}\left[\sum_{k=1}^{(N-1)/2} 2h\left(\frac{N-1}{2}-k\right)\cos k\omega + h\left(\frac{N-1}{2}\right)\cdot\cos o\omega\right] \quad \text{(Note this step)}$$

$$\boxed{H(e^{j\omega}) = e^{-j\omega(N-1)/2} \sum_{k=0}^{(N-1)/2} a_k \cos k\omega,\ N \text{ odd}} \qquad \ldots(8.18a)$$

where

$$\boxed{a_k = \begin{cases} h((N-1)/2), & k=0 \\ 2h((N-1)/2-k), & k=1,2,\ldots,(N-1)/2 \end{cases}} \qquad \ldots(8.18b)$$

Case B: N odd and $h(n)$ anti-symmetrical *i.e.*, $h(n) = -h(N-1-n)$

Proceeding as in case A, here above (C) would be with –ve sign, *i.e.*,

$$H(e^{j\omega}) = (A) + (B) + (C)$$

where $\quad (B) = h\left(\dfrac{(N-1)}{2}\right)e^{-j(N-1)/2} = 0$ as $h\left(\dfrac{(N-1)}{2}\right) = 0$

and
$$(C) = \sum_{k=0}^{(N-3)/2} h(N-1-k)e^{-j\omega(N-1-k)}$$

$$= -\sum_{k=0}^{(N-3)/2} h(k)e^{-j\omega(N-1-k)} \qquad (\because \; h(N-1-k) = -h(k))$$

$$\therefore \quad H(e^{j\omega}) = \sum_{n=0}^{(N-3)/2} e^{-j\omega(N-1)/2}[h(n)e^{j\omega((N-1)/2-n)} - h(n)e^{-j\omega(N-1/2-n)}]$$

$$= e^{-j\omega(N-1)/2} \sum_{n=0}^{(N-3)/2} 2jh(n)\sin\left(\frac{(N-1)}{2} - n\right)\omega$$

Put
$$\frac{N-1}{2} - n = k$$

$$\therefore \quad H(e^{j\omega}) = \sum_{k=1}^{(N-1)/2} 2je^{-j\omega(N-1)/2}\, h\left(\frac{N-1}{2} - k\right)\sin k\omega$$

Hence,
$$\boxed{H(e^{j\omega}) \triangleq e^{-j\omega(N-1)/2}\, e^{j\pi/2} \sum_{k=1}^{(N-1)/2} a_k \sin k\omega,\; N \text{ odd}} \qquad ...(8.19)$$

Case C: N even and $h(n)$ symmetrical *i.e.*, $h(n) = +\,h(N-1-n)$

Given N even and $h(n) = +\,h(N-1-n)$

$$H(e^{j\omega}) = \sum_{n=0}^{N-1} h(n)e^{-j\omega n}$$

$$= \underbrace{\sum_{n=0}^{N/2-1} h(n)e^{-j\omega n}}_{(A)} + \underbrace{\sum_{n=N/2}^{N-1} h(n)e^{-j\omega n}}_{(B)} \qquad ...(1)$$

(Note this step)

$$(B) = \sum_{n=N/2}^{N-1} h(n)e^{-j\omega n}$$

Put $N-1-n = k$ in (B) $\therefore$ when $n = \frac{N}{2}$, $k = \frac{N}{2} - 1$

when $n = N-1$, $k = 0$

$$\therefore \quad (B) = \sum_{k=0}^{N/2-1} h(N-1-k)e^{-j\omega(N-1-k)}$$

$$= \sum_{k=0}^{N/2-1} h(k)e^{-j\omega(N-1-k)} \qquad (\because \; h(N-1-k) = h(k)) \qquad ...(2)$$

Combining (A) and (B), using (1) and (2), we get

$$\therefore \quad H(e^{j\omega}) = (A) + (B) = \sum_{n=0}^{N/2-1} h(n)[e^{-j\omega n} + e^{-j\omega(N-1-n)}] \qquad ...(3)$$

$$= e^{-j\omega\left(\frac{N-1}{2}\right)} \sum_{n=0}^{N/2-1} h(n)\left[e^{j\omega\left(\frac{N-1}{2}-n\right)} + e^{-j\omega\left(\frac{N-1}{2}-n\right)}\right]$$

$$= e^{-j\omega\frac{N-1}{2}} \sum_{n=0}^{N/2-1} 2h(n)\cos\left(\frac{N-1}{2}-n\right)\omega \qquad \ldots(4)$$

Put $\frac{N}{2}-n = k$ in (4) $\therefore$ when $n = 0$, $k = \frac{N}{2}$

when $n = \frac{N}{2}-1$, $k = 1$

Hence, we obtain

$$\therefore \quad H(e^{j\omega}) = e^{-j\omega(N-1)/2} \sum_{k=1}^{N/2} \underbrace{2h\left(\frac{N}{2}-k\right)}_{\triangleq b_k} \cdot \cos\left(k-\frac{1}{2}\right)\omega \qquad \ldots(5)$$

Hence, we can write

$$\therefore \quad H(e^{j\omega}) = e^{-j\omega\left(\frac{N-1}{2}\right)} \sum_{k=1}^{N/2} b_k \cos\left(\left(k-\frac{1}{2}\right)\omega\right),\ N \text{ even} \qquad \ldots(8.20a)$$

$$\text{where} \quad b_k = 2h\left(\frac{N}{2}-k\right) \text{ and } h(n) = +h(N-1-n) \qquad \ldots(8.20b)$$

Case D: N even and $h(n)$ anti-symmetrical *i.e.*, $h(n) = -h(N-1-n)$

Proceeding as in case C, here the term (B) would be with –ve sign

$$\therefore \quad H(e^{j\omega}) = (A) + (B) = \sum_{n=0}^{N/2-1} h(n)[e^{-j\omega n} - e^{-j\omega(N-1-n)}] \quad \text{[using (3) of Case } C]$$

$$= e^{-j\omega(N-1)/2} \sum_{n=0}^{N/2-1} 2jh(n)\sin\left(\frac{N-1}{2}-n\right) \qquad \ldots(1)$$

Put $\frac{N}{2}-n = k$ in (1), $\therefore$ when $n = 0$, $k = \frac{N}{2}$

when $n = \frac{N}{2}-1$, $k = 1$

$$\therefore \quad H(e^{j\omega}) = e^{-j\omega(N-1)/2} \sum_{k=1}^{N/2} \underbrace{j2h\left(\frac{N}{2}-k\right)}_{b_k}\sin\left(k-\frac{1}{2}\right)\omega$$

$$= e^{-j\omega(N-1)/2}\, e^{j\pi/2} \sum_{k=1}^{N/2} b_k \sin\left(k-\frac{1}{2}\right)\omega$$

i.e.,

$$H(e^{j\omega}) = e^{-j\omega(N-1)/2}\, e^{j\pi/2} \sum_{k=1}^{N/2} b_k \sin\left(\left(k-\frac{1}{2}\right)\omega\right),\ N \text{ even} \qquad \ldots(8.21a)$$

$$\text{where} \quad b_k = 2h\left(\frac{N}{2}-k\right),\ N \text{ even and } h(n) = -h(N-1-n) \qquad \ldots(8.21b)$$

We give the results of four cases discussed above in Table 8.1 for ready reference.

Table 8.1. Summary of Frequency Responses in Linear Phase FIR Filters

$h(n)$	N	$H(e^{j\omega})$	
$h(n)$ Symmetrical	odd	$e^{-j\omega(N-1)/2} \sum_{k=0}^{(N-1)/2} a_k \cos k\omega$, N odd	(8.18)
$h(n) = h(N-1-n)$	even	$e^{-j\omega(N-1)/2} \sum_{k=1}^{N/2} b_k \cos\left(\left(k-\frac{1}{2}\right)\omega\right)$, N even	(8.20)
$h(n)$ Antisymmetrical	odd	$e^{-j\omega(N-1)/2} \cdot e^{j\pi/2} \sum_{k=1}^{(N-1)/2} a_k \sin k\omega$, N odd	(8.19)
$h(n) = -h(N-1-n)$	even	$e^{-j\omega(N-1)/2} \cdot e^{j\pi/2} \sum_{k=1}^{N/2} b_k \sin\left(\left(k-\frac{1}{2}\right)\omega\right)$, N even	(8.21)
where: $a_0 = h\left(\frac{N-1}{2}\right)$; $a_k = 2h\left(\frac{N-1}{2}-k\right)$; $k \neq 0$, $k = 1, 2, \ldots, \frac{N-1}{2}$ $b_k = 2h\left(\frac{N}{2}-k\right)$ $k = 1, 2, \ldots, \frac{N}{2}$			

Aid to Memory

1. In all the cases, the delay is $\frac{(N-1)}{2}$ samples.
2. For antisymmetrical $h(n)$, extra phase of $\frac{\pi}{2}$ radian is there and, therefore, factor $e^{j\pi/2}$ appears in such cases.
3. Symmetric cases have cos (·) and antisymmetric cases have sin (·) in summation series.
4. Summation is upto $\frac{(N-1)}{2}$ for **N** odd and upto $\frac{N}{2}$ for N even cases. Also, for N even fractional frequencies appear *i.e.*, $\left(\frac{k-1}{2}\right)\omega$ as the angle for sine and cosine term.

8.4 LOCATION OF ZEROS IN LINEAR PHASE FIR (NON-RECURSIVE) FILTERS

Poles: FIR Filters have all poles at $z = 0$.

$$\text{As} \qquad H(z) = \sum_{n=0}^{N-1} h(n)z^{-n} = h(0) + h(1)z^{-1} + h(2)z^{-2} + h(3)z^{-3} + \ldots + h(N-1)z^{-(N-1)}$$

assuming $|h(n)| < \infty\ \forall n$, clearly $H(z) = \infty$ only for $z = 0$ and nowhere else. Thus, a causal FIR filter has all its poles at $z = 0$, *i.e.*, inside the unit circle $|z| = 1$. Therefore, all such filters are stable. An FIR filter of length N (therefore, order $N-1$) has $N-1$ poles at $z = 0$ is **unconditionally STABLE.** This is a very attractive feature of FIR filters.

Zeros: Assume N to be odd and symmetrical $h(n)$ (*i.e.*, constant phase and group delay case)

$$\therefore \qquad h(n) = h(N-1-n)$$

But $$H(z) = \sum_{n=0}^{N-1} h(n)z^{-n}$$

$$= \underset{(A)}{\sum_{n=0}^{(N-3)/2} h(n)z^{-n}} + \underset{(B)}{h\left(\frac{N-1}{2}\right)z^{-(N-1)/2}} + \underset{(C)}{\sum_{n=(N+1)/2}^{N-1} h(n)z^{-n}} \quad \ldots(1)$$

In (C), put $N - 1 - n = m$ $\therefore$ when $n = \dfrac{(N+1)}{2}$, $m = \dfrac{(N-3)}{2}$

when $n = N - 1$, $m = 0$

$$\therefore\ H(z) = \sum_{n=0}^{(N-3)/2} h(n)[z^{-n} + z^{-(N-1-n)}] + h\left(\frac{N-1}{2}\right)z^{-(N-1)/2}$$

$$= z^{-(N-1)/2}\left\{\sum_{n=0}^{(N-3)/2} h(n)\left[z^{\frac{N-1}{2}-n} + z^{-\left(\frac{N-1}{2}-n\right)}\right] + h\left(\frac{N-1}{2}\right)z^{0}\right\}$$

$$= z^{-(N-1)/2}\left\{\sum_{n=0}^{(N-3)/2} h(n)\left[z^{\frac{(N-1)}{2}-n} + z^{-\left(\frac{N-1}{2}-n\right)}\right] + \frac{1}{2}h\left(\frac{N-1}{2}\right)(z^{0} + z^{-0})\right\} \quad \ldots(2)$$

(Note this step)

To put this expression in elegant form, we put

$\dfrac{N-1}{2} - n = k$ $\therefore$ when $n = 0$, $k = \dfrac{(N-1)}{2}$,

when $n = \dfrac{N-3}{2}$, $k = 1$. Hence, (2) gives us

$$\therefore\quad H(z) = z^{-(N-1)/2}\left\{\sum_{k=(N-1)/2}^{1} h\left(\frac{N-1}{2} - k\right)[z^{k} + z^{-k}] + \frac{1}{2}h\left(\frac{N-1}{2}\right)(z^{0} + z^{-1})\right\}$$

$$= z^{-(N-1)/2}\left\{\sum_{k=0}^{(N-1)/2} \frac{1}{2}a_k\,(z^{k} + z^{-k})\right\} \quad \ldots(3)$$

where $$a_k = \begin{cases} h\left(\dfrac{N-1}{2}\right), & k = 0 \\ 2h\left(\dfrac{N-1}{2} - k\right), & k = 1, 2, \ldots, \dfrac{(N-1)}{2} \end{cases}$$ [as defined earlier, in (8.18*b*)]

$$H(z) \triangleq \frac{N(z)}{D(z)} = \frac{\displaystyle\sum_{k=0}^{(N-1)/2} \frac{1}{2}a_k(z^{k} + z^{-k})}{z^{(N-1)/2}} \quad \ldots(4)$$

The zeros of $H(z)$ are the roots of $N(z)$ *i.e.* zeros of $H(z)$ are given by

$$N(z) = \sum_{k=0}^{(N-1)/2} \frac{1}{2} a_k (z^k + z^{-k}) = 0 \qquad \text{[Putting } N(z) = 0] \qquad \ldots(5)$$

Note that $N(z)$ is an **Image Polynomial**. Here, the powers of z and that of z^{-1} are equal as $N(z^{-1}) = N(z)$. This implies that whatever roots *viz.* $z = z_1, z_2, \ldots, z_{(N-1)/2}$ are valid for $N(z) = 0$, the same roots are also valid for $N(z^{-1}) = 0$. This is only feasible of the roots $z_1, z_2, \ldots, z_{(N-1)/2}$ have combinations $z_1, z_1^{-1}, z_2, z_2^{-1}$; and so on.

We have considered the symmetric impulse response: $h(n) = +h(N - 1 - n)$ to arrive at above equation, given in (5). Had we taken the anti-symmetric impulse response, $h(n) = -h(N - 1 - n)$, we would have obtained, for getting the zeros of $H(z)$, an equation

$$\sum_{k=0}^{(N-1)/2} \frac{1}{2} a_k (z^k - z^{-k}) = 0 \qquad \text{“}N(z) = 0\text{”} \qquad \ldots(6)$$

Here also $N(z) = N(z^{-1})$ holds

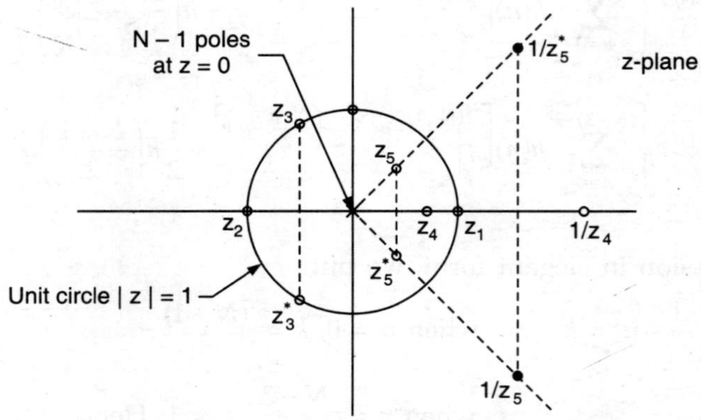

Fig. 8.5. Typical zero-pole plot of a linear phase FIR filter

We note that

(*i*) Any number of zeros can be located at $z_i = \pm 1$, since, $z_i^{-1} = \pm 1$, here see points z_1 and z_2. Zeros at only z_1 or at only z_2 can exist in singles.

(*ii*) An arbitrary number of complex conjugate zeros can be located on the unit circle. Zeros at z_3 and z_3^* (on the unit circle) can exist in duals.

(*iii*) Real zeros, off the unit circle, such as $z_4, \dfrac{1}{z_4}$ also occur in duals.

(*iv*) Complex zeros such as z_5, occur in **quadrangle symmetry** *i.e.* $z_5, z_5^*, \dfrac{1}{z_5}, \dfrac{1}{z_5^*}$ occur in fours. This is called (Mirror imaging) Polynomials with above properties are called Mirror Image Polynomials.

8.5 DESIGN TECHNIQUES FOR FIR FILTERS

The linear-phase FIR filters are designed by using the following methods:

1. Design using Fourier series
2. Design using Windows
3. Design using Frequency-sampling Method
4. Design of Optimum Equiripple FIR Filters.

For designing frequency-selective filters, the desired filter specifications are given in terms of the desired magnitude and phase response. Since, FIR filters can be easily designed as linear-phase, we invariably use such design methods those yield linear-phase FIR filter approximations. The first three approaches are based on exact mathematical techniques. The optimum equiripple design is based on Parks and McClellan Algorithm, using Alternation Theorem and Remez Exchange approach. Optimum equiripple designs are Clebyshev approximations and most popular.

8.5.1 Design Using the Fourier Series

The frequency response of a non-recursive filter is a periodic function of ω, with period 2π. (Note that $\omega = \frac{2\pi F}{F_s} = 2\pi f$ where f is the normalised frequency in cycles/samples and ω is in radians. Thus, we can write

$$H(e^{j\omega}) = \sum_{n=-\infty}^{\infty} h(n)e^{-j\omega n} \quad \text{[DTFT of } h(n)] \qquad \ldots(8.22)$$

and by taking inverse DTFT

$$h(n) = \frac{1}{2\pi}\int_{-\pi}^{\pi} H(e^{j\omega})\, e^{j\omega n}\, d\omega,\ n = 0, \pm 1, \pm 2, \ldots \qquad \ldots(8.23)$$

It may be seen that (8.22) gives an infinite Fourier's series of $H(e^{j\omega})$ where the Fourier's constants, $h(n)$, are given by (8.23). Changing $e^{j\omega}$ to z in (8.22), we get

$$H(z) = \sum_{n=-\infty}^{\infty} h(n)z^{-n} \qquad \ldots(8.24)$$

Thus, given a desired frequency response *viz.* (8.22), a corresponding transfer function $H(z)$ can be readily derived by letting $e^{j\omega} = z$ in the given frequency response.

$H(z)$ found in (8.24) in non-causal and of infinite order.

To get a 'definite order', $H(z)$ we must truncate (8.24) by taking

$$h(n) = 0 \text{ for } |n| > \frac{(N-1)}{2} \qquad \ldots(8.25)$$

Note that we have assumed N as odd for obtaining integral delay in the designed filter. Thus,

$$H(z)\,|_{\text{truncated}} = \sum_{n=-N-1/2}^{N-1/2} h(n)z^{-n},\ N \text{ odd}$$

$$= h(0) + \sum_{n=1}^{(N-1)/2} [h(-n)z^{n} + h(n)z^{-n}] \qquad \ldots(8.26)$$

The above $H(z)$ is yet not causal and has the highest 'advancement' of $z^{(N-1)/2}$. To make (8.26) causal let us multiply R.H.S. by a delay $z^{-(N-1)/2}$, doing so we get

$$\boxed{\begin{aligned} H(z) &= z^{-(N-1)/2}\, H(z)|_{\text{truncated}} \\ &= z^{-(N-1)/2}\left\{h(0) + \sum_{n=1}^{(N-1)/2}[h(-n)z^{n} + h(n)z^{-n}]\right\} \end{aligned}} \qquad \ldots(8.27)$$

Such a modification will not affect the frequency response. Only the phase delay will get increased by $\left(\frac{N-1}{2}\right)T_s$ seconds. However, such an $H(z)$ is both finite and causal and hence realizable.

EXAMPLE 8.1: *Design a low-pass filter with a frequency response*

$$H(e^{j\omega}) = \begin{cases} 1, & |\omega| \le \omega_c \\ 0, & \omega_c \le |\omega| \le \pi \end{cases}.$$

SOLUTION:

$$h(n) = \frac{1}{2\pi}\int_{-\pi}^{\pi} H(e^{j\omega})\, e^{j\omega n}\, d\omega$$

$$= \frac{1}{2\pi}\int_{-\omega_c}^{\omega_c} 1\cdot e^{j\omega n}\, d\omega$$

$$= \frac{1}{2\pi}\cdot\left[\frac{e^{j\omega n}}{jn}\right]_{\omega=-\omega_c}^{\omega_c}$$

$$= \frac{1}{2\pi}\cdot\frac{1}{jn}(e^{j\omega_c n} - e^{-j\omega_c n}) = \frac{1}{\pi n}\sin\omega_c n$$

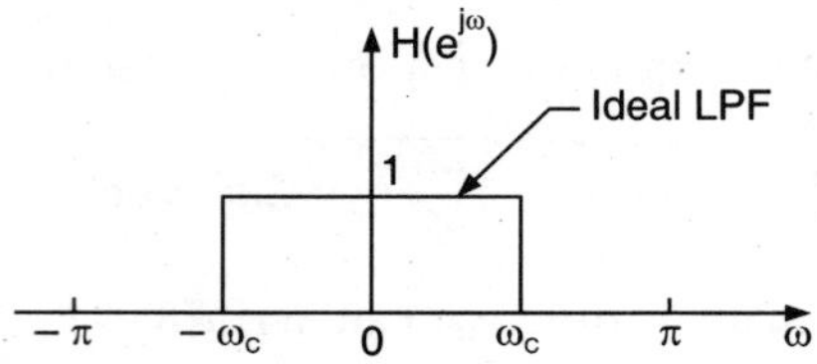

Fig. Ex. 8.1. The frequency response of the desired low-pass filter.

$$\therefore \qquad \boxed{h(n) = \frac{\sin\omega_c n}{n\pi}} \qquad \ldots(8.28)$$

Note that $h(n)$ is an even function of n, *i.e.*, $h(n) = h(-n)$. Also the value of $h(0) = \frac{\omega_c}{\pi}$ and is the maximum value. $h(n)$ has infinite terms which are the design weights. However, a practical filter must have finite design weights $h(n)$. So, we truncate $h(n)$ to have range: $\frac{-(N-1)}{2} \le n \le \frac{(N-1)}{2}$, *i.e.* total N weights. We invariably choose N as odd so that the designed causal filter has a delay of $\frac{(N-1)}{2}$ samples, being an integer. However, the truncation of $h(n)$ from ∞ terms to N terms will not yield perfect desired frequency response, such as desired in Fig. Ex. 8.1. The truncation is a necessity for practical realizability of $H(z)$. The Gibb's phenomenon, as discussed in the next section, is caused by the truncation.

8.5.2 Gibb's Phenomenon

by taking different values of N, say, equalling 11, 21, 31 here the oscillations are decaying and their frequency increases as N increases. **However, for all N, the last ripple in the passband and the first ripple in the stopband remains unchanged.**

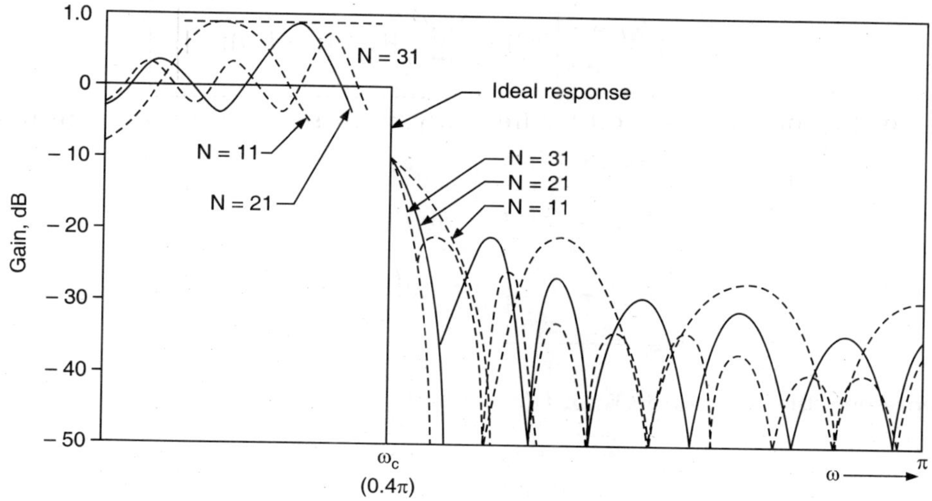

Fig. 8.6. Amplitude response of a low-pass filter

Such a performance, however, is not desirable. We must be able to decrease all the ripples including the last in the passband and the first in the stopband as we increase N. The property that the last ripple in the passband and the first ripple in the stopband not decreasing due increase of N, is call^d the Gibb's phenomenon. Of course, these ripples (or oscillations) are undesirable. Ripple free designs are prefered.

To minimise the Gibb's oscillations, we should avoid sharp discontinuities in the desired frequency response. A low-pass filter may have the following response to minimise Gibb's oscillations.

$$H(e^{j\omega}) = \begin{cases} 1, & |\omega| \le \omega_p \\ -\dfrac{\omega - \omega_a}{\omega_a - \omega_p}, & \omega_p \le |\omega| < \omega_c \\ 0, & \text{otherwise} \end{cases} \qquad \ldots(8.29)$$

Such as frequency response would look like as given in Fig. 8.7:

So, we should find $h(n)$ of modified $H(e^{j\omega})$, as shown in Fig. 8.7. Such a $h(n)$ will have much low Gibb's oscillations. An alternative to reduce the Gibb's oscillations is to use window functions, as discussed in the next section.

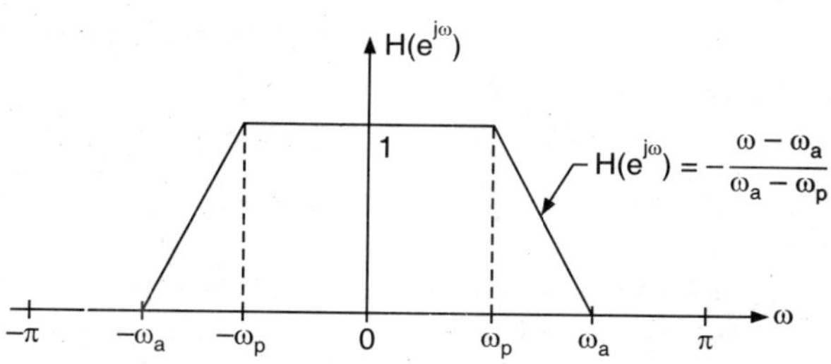

Fig. 8.7. The suggested frequency response to decrease Gibb's oscillations

8.5.3 Use of Window Functions

An alternative and easy-to-apply technique for the reduction of Gibb's oscillations is to precondition $h(n)$ obtained by

$$h(n) = \frac{1}{2\pi}\int_{-\pi}^{\pi} H(e^{j\omega})e^{j\omega n}\, d\omega \text{ (ideal)} \quad ...(8.30)$$

using a time domain function called Window, $\omega(n)$

Let

$$H(z) = ZT[h(n)] = \sum_{n=-\infty}^{\infty} h(n)z^{-n} \quad ...(8.31)$$

$$W(z) = ZT[\omega(n)] = \sum_{n=-\infty}^{\infty} \omega(n)z^{-n} \quad ...(8.32)$$

$$H_\omega(z) = ZT[\omega(n) \cdot h(n)] \quad ...(8.33)$$

$$\therefore \quad \boxed{H_\omega(z) = \frac{1}{2\pi j}\oint_\Gamma H(v)W\left(\frac{z}{v}\right)v^{-1}\, dv} \text{ (the complex convolution)} \quad ...(8.34)$$

where Γ represents the common ROC of $H(v)$ with $W\left(\frac{z}{v}\right)$ by putting

$$v = e^{j\Omega}, \text{ and } z = e^{j\omega}$$

$$\therefore \quad dv = jv\, d\Omega$$

and if $H(v)$ and $W\left(\frac{z}{v}\right)$ converge on the unit circle then $H(v)$ as well as $W\left(\frac{z}{v}\right)$ converge on the unit circle $|v| = 1$ of the v-plane. Expression (8.34) reduces to

$$\therefore \quad H_\omega(e^{j\omega}) = \frac{1}{2\pi j}\int_0^{2\pi} H(e^{j\Omega})W(e^{j(\omega-\Omega)})\, v^{-1}(jv\, d\Omega)$$

$$\therefore \quad \boxed{H_\omega(e^{j\omega}) = \frac{1}{2\pi}\int_0^{2\pi} H(e^{j\Omega})\, W(e^{j(\omega-\Omega)})\, d\Omega} \quad ...(8.35)$$

Clearly, $H_\omega(e^{j\omega})$ is the convolution of $H(e^{j\omega})$ and $W(e^{j\omega})$.

For example, let

$$H(e^{j\Omega}) = \begin{cases} 1, & 0 \le |\Omega| \le \omega_c \\ 0, & \omega_c \le |\Omega| \le \pi \end{cases} \quad \textit{i.e.} \text{ ideal LPF}$$

and also let $W(e^{j\Omega})$ be real with the form shown in Fig. 8.8(*b*) with

$$W(e^{j\Omega}) = 0, \text{ for } \omega_m \le |\Omega| \le \pi \quad ...(8.36)$$

Then to obtain

$$H_\omega(e^{j\omega}) = \frac{1}{2\pi}\int_0^{2\pi} H(e^{j\Omega})W(e^{j(\omega-\Omega)})\, d\Omega \quad ...(8.37)$$

We proceed as follows: (the convolution procedure)

1. Shift $W(e^{j\Omega})$ to right side by ω as in Fig. 8.8(*c*)
2. Multiply $H(e^{j\Omega})$ by $W(e^{j(\omega-\Omega)})$ as in Fig. 8.8(*d*)

Note that $W(e^{j\Omega}) = W(e^{-j\Omega})$ shifting right $W(e^{-j\Omega})$ by ω gives us $W(e^{-j(\Omega-\omega)}) = W(e^{j(\omega-\Omega)})$ as shown in the Fig. 8.8.

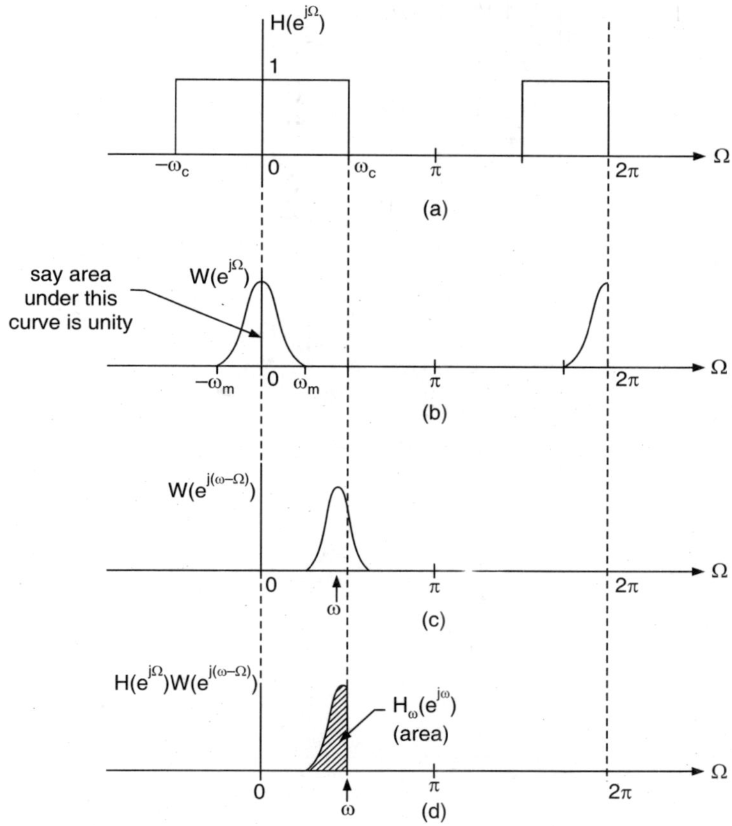

Fig. 8.8. Complex convolution steps. (*a*) The given $H(e^{j\omega})$ drawn by changing ω to Ω. (*b*) The given $W(e^{j\omega})$ drawn by changing ω to Ω. (*c*) Shifting $W(e^{-j\Omega})$ by ω to get $W(e^{-j(\Omega-\omega)}) = W(e^{j(\omega-\Omega)})$. (*d*) Multiplication of curves (*b*) and (*c*) to get $H(e^{j\Omega}) \cdot W(e^{j(\omega-\Omega)})$

Assume that the area under the curve $W(e^{j\Omega})$ is unity. Then the function $H_\omega(e^{j\omega})$ will have maximum height of unity, provided $W(e^{j\Omega})$ has $\omega << \omega_c$ and the approximation $H_\omega(e^{j\omega})$ is very close to $H(e^{j\omega})$ and will be also free from Gibb's oscillations.

To summarize, if we use the window $\omega(n)$, we first obtain $h_\omega(n) = h(n) \cdot \omega(n)$. The frequency response of $h_\omega(n)$ is convolution of $H(e^{j\omega})$ and $W(e^{j\omega})$ we may use $h_\omega(n)$ as the windowed impulse response of the designed FIR filter.

The filter

$$H(z) = \sum_{n=-\infty}^{\infty} h(n)z^{-n} \qquad \text{...(8.38)}$$

represents an infinite delay filter (unrealizable) whereas the filter

$$H_\omega(z) = \sum_{n=-(N-1)/2}^{(N-1)/2} [h(n) \cdot \omega(n)]z^{-n} \qquad \text{...(8.39)}$$

is a finite order filter, with order $N - 1$ and lengths N. $H_\omega(z)$ is realizable as it has N terms.

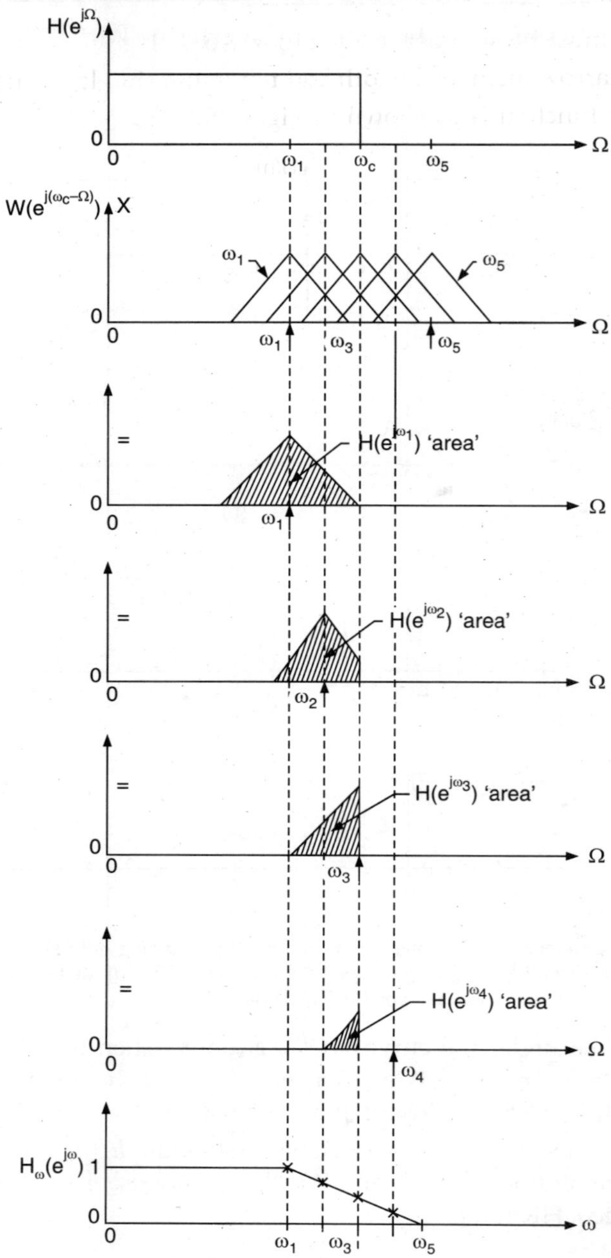

Fig. 8.9. The effect of a window function

8.5.4 Time-domain Properties of Windows

A window function $\omega(n)$ must have the following properties.

(*i*) It must be zero for $|n| > \dfrac{(N-1)}{2}$

(*ii*) For odd N, it must be symmetrical about $n = 0$

(*iii*) Should have narrow main lobe width and minimum side-lobes in its frequency spectrum.

A typical window function is as shown in Fig. 8.10.

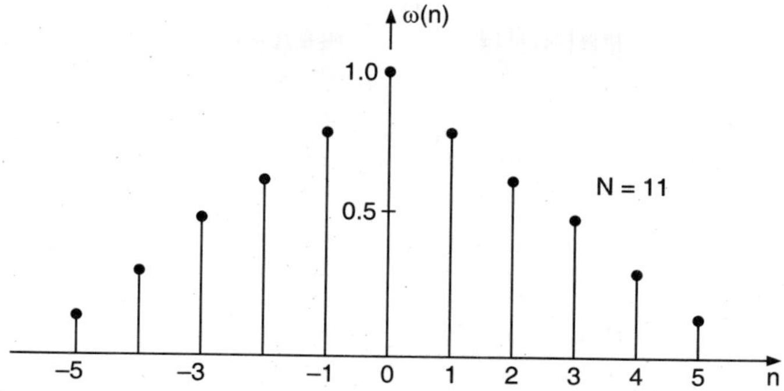

Fig. 8.10. Typical window function ω(n)

Such a window has main lobe width $= k\dfrac{2\pi}{N} = k\dfrac{\omega_s}{N}$

where k is a constant and $\omega_s = 2\pi$. A typical window has also side lobes. Due to broad main lobe, the ideal frequency response cannot be obtained and that $H_W(e^{j\omega})$ has greater transition width than that of $H(e^{j\omega})$. The sidebands of $W(e^{j\omega})$ cause frequency response $H_W(e^{j\omega})$ non-zero even in stopbands.

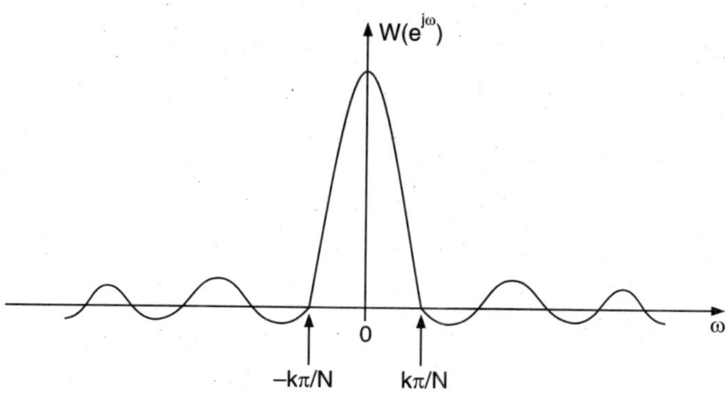

Fig. 8.11. Typical spectrum of a window function

Moreover, the sidebands of $W(e^{j\omega})$ also cause the Gibb's oscillations in the amplitude response of the designed filter. Therefore, it is desirable to have

(*i*) Sharpest possible main lobe width for $W(e^{j\omega})$

(*ii*) Least side band lobes of $W(e^{j\omega})$

(*iii*) For high selectivity, N and hence the order of the filter should be large and k should be small; then the main lobe width which depends on $\dfrac{k}{N}$ will be small. We shall learn that the value of integer k depends on the type of window.

8.6 THE WINDOW FUNCTIONS

Some of the popular windows are as follows:

1. Rectangular window : $\omega_R(n)$
2. Hann (or Hanning) window : $\omega_{\text{Han}}(n)$, $\omega_H(n)$
3. Hamming window : $\omega_{\text{Ham}}(n)$, $\omega_H(n)$
4. Blackman window : $\omega_B(n)$
5. Kaiser window : $\omega_K(n)$
6. Bartlett (triangular) window : $\omega_{BA}(n)$
7. Lanczos window : $\omega_L(n)$
8. Tukey window : $\omega_T(n)$
9. Dolph-Chebyshev window : $\omega_{DC}(n)$
10. Papoulis window : $\omega_P(n)$.

We shall discuss the first six windows in this chapter for our FIR filter designs. We shall use the desired impulse response $h_d(n)$ and the window function $\omega(n)$ to obtain windowed (and truncated) impulse response $h_d(n) \cdot \omega(n)$ to compute the final design weights. To make it a causal design, we shall delay the design weights by $\frac{(N-1)}{2}$. Such an approach requires almost half the calculations.

8.6.1 Rectangular Window

The rectangular window is given by**

$$\boxed{\omega_R(n) = \begin{cases} 1, & |n| \le \dfrac{(N-1)}{2} \\ 0, & \text{otherwise} \end{cases}} \qquad \ldots(8.40)$$

This corresponds to the direct truncation of the Fourier series. The Fourier transform of $\omega_R(n)$ is given by

$$W_R(e^{j\omega}) = \sum_{n=-(N-1)/2}^{(N-1)/2} 1 \cdot e^{-j\omega n}$$

which is a G.P. with 'r' $= e^{-j\omega}$ and number of terms $= N$

$$\therefore \qquad W_R(e^{j\omega}) = \frac{e^{j\omega(N-1)/2}(1-e^{-j\omega N})}{1-e^{-j\omega}}$$

$$= \frac{e^{j\omega(N-1)/2} - e^{-(N+1)/2}}{e^{-j\omega/2}(e^{j\omega/2} - e^{-j\omega/2})}$$

$$= \frac{e^{j\omega N/2} - e^{-j\omega N/2}}{e^{j\omega/2} - e^{-j\omega/2}} = \frac{\sin(N\omega/2)}{\sin(\omega/2)}$$

** Some books define

$$\omega_R(n) = \begin{cases} 1, & 0 \le n \le N-1 \\ 0, & \text{Otherwise} \end{cases} \qquad \ldots(8.40a)$$

This is the case of causal window function. We shall, however, not use causal $h(n)$ and $\omega(n)$, as explained above.

$\therefore$ Frequency response of a rectangular window is given by

$$\boxed{W_R(e^{j\omega}) = \frac{\sin(N\omega/2)}{\sin(\omega/2)}} \quad \ldots(8.41)$$

For $\omega = \frac{2\pi m}{N}$, $m = \pm 1, \pm 2, \ldots, \pm(N-1)$, we get

$$W_R(e^{j\omega}) = \frac{\sin\left(\frac{2\pi m}{N}\cdot\frac{N}{2}\right)}{\sin\frac{2\pi m}{2N}}$$

$$= \frac{\sin(\pi m)}{\sin\left(\frac{\pi m}{N}\right)} = 0$$

$\therefore W_R(e^{j\omega}) = 0$ at $m = \pm 1, \pm 2, \ldots, \pm(N-1)$

$$\text{Main lobe width} = \frac{4\pi}{N} \quad \ldots(8.42)$$

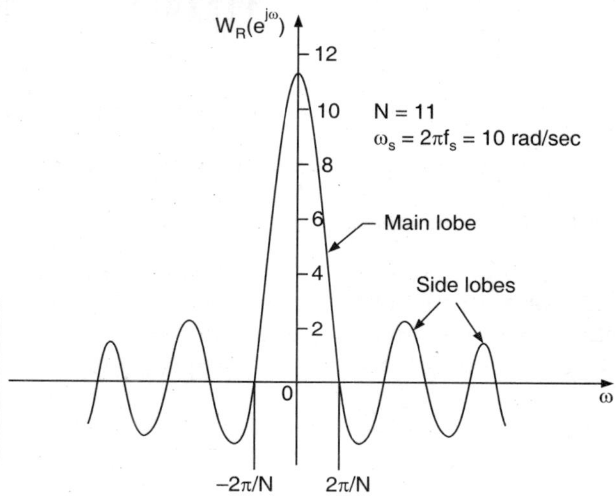

Fig. 8.12. Spectrum of a rectangular window $\omega_R(n)$

There are also side lobes besides the main lobe of $W_R(e^{j\omega})$. We define a new parameter, Ripple Ratio, to assess the performance of a window.

$$\boxed{\text{Ripple Ratio, RR} \triangleq \frac{\text{Maximum side-lobe amplitude}}{\text{Main lobe amplitude}} \times 100} \quad \ldots(8.43)$$

For rectangular window $W_R(e^{j\omega})$, RR is 22.3% for $N = 11$ and decreases as N increases. This is of very high value and is not acceptable in many cases. So, we discuss the other windows as follows.

8.6.2 Hann and Hamming Windows

The Hann and Hamming windows are defined by

$$\omega_H(n) = \begin{cases} \alpha + (1-\alpha)\cos\left(\frac{2\pi n}{N-1}\right), & |n| \le \frac{N-1}{2} \\ 0, & \text{Otherwise} \end{cases} \quad \ldots(8.44)$$

where

$$\alpha = 0.50 \text{ for Hann window} \quad \ldots(8.45a)$$

$$\alpha = 0.54 \text{ for Hamming window} \quad \ldots(8.45b)$$

We can obtain the spectra of Hann and Hamming windows by the first letting

$$\omega_H(n) = \omega_R(n)\left[\alpha + (1-\alpha)\cos\left(\frac{2\pi n}{N-1}\right)\right]$$

$$= \alpha\omega_R(n) + \frac{1-\alpha}{2}\omega_R(n)[e^{j2\pi n/(N-1)} + e^{-j2\pi n/(N-1)}] \qquad \text{(Note this step)}$$

$$\therefore \qquad W_H(e^{j\omega}) = FT\left[\alpha\omega_R(n) + \left(\frac{1-\alpha}{2}\right)\omega_R(n)(e^{j2\pi n/(N-1)} + e^{-j2\pi n/(N-1)})\right]$$

$$= \alpha W_R(e^{j\omega}) + \left(\frac{1-\alpha}{2}\right)\left[W_R\left(e^{j\left(\omega-\frac{2\pi}{N-1}\right)}\right) + W_R\left(e^{j\left(\omega+\frac{2\pi}{N-1}\right)}\right)\right]$$

$$= \alpha\frac{\sin\frac{\omega N}{2}}{\sin\frac{\omega}{2}} + \frac{1-\alpha}{2}\left[\frac{\sin\frac{N}{2}\left(\omega-\frac{2\pi}{N-1}\right)}{\sin\left(\omega-\frac{2\pi}{N-1}\right)\Big/2} + \frac{\sin\frac{N}{2}\left(\omega+\frac{2\pi}{N-1}\right)}{\sin\frac{1}{2}\left(\omega+\frac{2\pi}{N-1}\right)}\right] \qquad \ldots(8.46)$$

Consequently, the spectra for Hann and Hamming windows can be formed by shifting $W_R(e^{j\omega})$ first to the right and also to the left by $\frac{2\pi}{(N-1)}$ which gives 2nd and 3rd terms in equation (8.46). See Fig. 8.13, it is seen that **the second and the third terms tend to cancel the right and the left side lobes in $\alpha W_R(e^{j\omega})$,** and as a result both the Hann and the Hamming windows have **reduced side lobes** compared to the Rectangular window. For $N = 11$, $\omega_s = 2\pi f_s = 10$, the RR for the two windows are 2.67% and 0.93%, respectively.

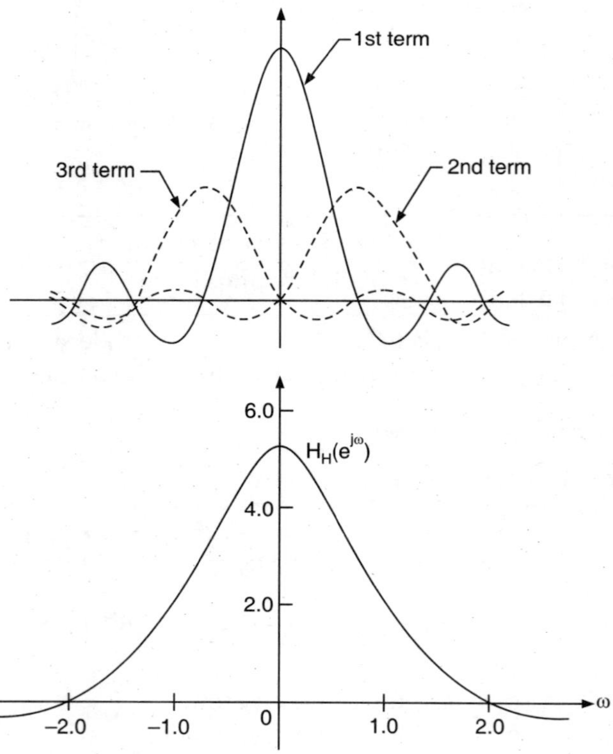

Fig. 8.13. Spectrum of Hann or Hamming window

The first term in (8.46) is zero at

$$\omega = \frac{2\pi m}{N}$$

and the 2nd and 3rd terms are zero at

$$\omega = \left(m + \frac{N}{N-1}\right)\frac{2\pi}{N} \text{ and } \omega = \left(m - \frac{N}{N-1}\right)\frac{2\pi}{N}.$$

For $N \gg 1$, (8.46) has their first common zero at $|\omega| \approx \frac{4\pi}{N}$. Hence, the main lobe width for $W_H(e^{j\omega})$ is approximately $\frac{8\pi}{N}$.

8.6.3 Blackman Window

The Blackman window is defined by

$$\omega_B(n) = \begin{cases} 0.42 + 0.5\cos\frac{2\pi n}{N-1} + 0.08\cos\frac{4\pi n}{N-1}, & |n| \le \frac{N-1}{2} \\ 0, & \text{otherwise} \end{cases} \qquad \text{...(8.47)}$$

The additional cosine term leads to a further reduction in the amplitude of Gibb's oscillations. The main lobe width is, however, increased to about $\frac{12\pi}{N}$.

(**Aid to Memory:** In the Hann window change 0.5 to 0.42 and add a new term $0.08\cos\frac{4\pi n}{(N-1)}$ as if 0.08 sliced away from 0.50 appears as a 2nd harmonic.)

8.6.4 Bartlett Window (Triangular Window)

This is an important window and is particularly used in parameter estimation. It is defined as (see footnote for causal Bartlett window**)

$$\omega_{BA}(n) = \begin{cases} 1 - \frac{2|n|}{N-1}, & |n| \le \frac{N-1}{2} \\ 0, & \text{otherwise} \end{cases} \qquad \text{...(8.48)}$$

It can be shown that the spectrum of Bartlett window $\omega_{BA}(n)$ is

$$W_{BA}(e^{j\omega}) = \frac{1}{M}\left(\frac{\sin\frac{M\omega}{2}}{\sin\frac{\omega}{2}}\right)^2, \; M = \frac{(N-1)}{2} \qquad \text{...(8.49)}$$

** The causal case Bartlett window is defined by

$$\omega_{BA}(n) = \begin{cases} 2n/(N-1), & 0 \le n \le (N-1)/2 \\ 2 - 2n/(N-1), & (N-1)/2 \le n \le N-1 \end{cases} \qquad \text{...(8.50)}$$

Table 8.2. Summary of Window Parameters

Type of window		*Main-lobe width*	*Ripple Rates, %*		
			N = 11,	*N = 21,*	*N = 31*
Rectangular	$\omega_R(n)$	$\frac{4\pi}{N}$	22.34	21.89	21.80
Hann	$\omega_{Hann}(n)$	$\frac{8\pi}{N}$	2.62	2.67	2.67
Hamming	$\omega_{Ham}(n)$	$\frac{8\pi}{N}$	1.47	0.93	0.82
Blackman	$\omega_B(n)$	$\frac{12\pi}{N}$	0.08	0.12	0.12
Bartlett	$\omega_{BA}(n)$	$\frac{8\pi}{N}$	4.50		

Summary of Ripple Ratios of some windows and the main lobe widths are given in Table 8.2. Note that the Hamming window and the Blackman window have broad main lobe widths though their ripple ratios are the smallest.

8.6.5 Kaiser Window

In the window functions mentioned earlier, a trade-off exists between ripple ratio and the main-lobe width; *i.e.* as the RR is decreased from window to window, the main-lobe width gets increased (see Table 8.2). The main-lobe width $\left(\text{of the form: } k\frac{2\pi}{N}\right)$ can be adjusted by varying *N*. The RR, however, is approximately constant for a given window *i.e.* by increasing *N* (in order to decrease the main-lobe width), the ripple ratio does not vary to that extent (*i.e.* RR remains almost constant for different *N*). As the known windows are limited and hence the possible ripple ratios are limited **we cannot obtain any desired RR whereas any desired main-lobe width is feasible by varying *N*.** A designer should first select a window with an appropriate RR and then choose *N* to achieve the prescribed transition width (by selecting the main-lobe width).

The designer may often have to accept for a window with an unnecessarily low ripple ratio which will of course have an unnecessarily high main-lobe width. Subsequently, to achieve the desired width, the value *N*, (and hence the filter order) will have to be increased to an unnecessarily high value. Kaiser window overcomes such problems. The window is defined by

$$\omega_K(n) = \begin{cases} \dfrac{I_0(\beta)}{I_0(\alpha)}, & |n| \le \dfrac{N-1}{2} \\ 0, & \text{otherwise} \end{cases} \qquad \text{...(8.51}a\text{)}$$

Kaiser window:

where

$$\beta = \alpha\sqrt{1-\left(\frac{2n}{N-1}\right)^2} \qquad \text{...(8.51}b\text{)}$$

$I_0(x)$ is the **zeroth-order** Bessel function of **first kind** $I_0(x)$ can be evaluated to any desired degree of accuracy by using the rapidly converging series given by

$$I_0(x) = 1+\sum_{k=1}^{\infty}\left[\frac{1}{k!}\left(\frac{x}{2}\right)^k\right]^2$$

$$= \sum_{k=0}^{\infty}\left[\frac{1}{k!}\left(\frac{x}{2}\right)^k\right]^2 \quad \text{...(8.52)}$$

Note that

$$I_0(0) = 1 \quad \text{...(8.53a)}$$

$$\left.\frac{I_0(\beta)}{I_0(\alpha)}\right|_{\alpha=\beta=0} = 1 \quad \text{...(8.53b)}$$

$$\omega_K(-n) = \omega_K(n) \quad \text{...(8.53c)}$$

It can be easily seen that since $\omega_K(n) = \omega_K(-n)$, the spectrum of $\omega_K(n)$ as defined in (8.51*a*) is

$$W_K(e^{j\omega}) = \omega_K(0)+2\sum_{n=1}^{(N-1)/2}\omega_K(n)\cos n\omega \quad \text{...(8.54)}$$

Continuous counter-part of Kaiser Window

$$\omega_K(t) = \begin{cases}\dfrac{I_0(\beta)}{I_0(\alpha)}, & |t|\le\tau \\ 0\ , & \text{Otherwise}\end{cases} \quad \text{...(8.55a)}$$

where

$$\beta = \alpha\sqrt{1-\left(\frac{t}{\tau}\right)^2}\ ,\ \tau = \frac{N-1}{2}T \quad \text{...(8.55b)}$$

The spectrum of $\omega_K(t)$ can be shown as

$$W_K(j\,\Omega) = \frac{2}{I_0(\alpha)}\frac{\sin\left(\tau\sqrt{\Omega^2-\Omega_a^2}\right)}{\sqrt{\Omega^2-\Omega_a^2}} \quad \text{...(8.56)}$$

where $\Omega_a = \dfrac{\alpha}{\tau}$.

If $W_K(j\,\Omega) \approx 0$ for $|\Omega| \ge \dfrac{2\pi f_s}{2} = \dfrac{\Omega_s}{2}$, then $W_K(j\,\Omega)$ is a bandlimited Kaiser window spectrum. Hence, the spectrum of a sampled version of signal $\omega_K(t)$ or equivalently the spectrum of discrete $\omega_K(n)$ can be expressed as:

$$W_K(j\,\Omega) = W_K(e^{j\Omega T}) \approx \frac{1}{T}W_K(j\,\Omega)\,,\ 0\le|\Omega|\le\frac{\Omega_s}{2}$$

$$\Omega_s = 2\pi f_s \text{ and } T = \frac{1}{f_s} \quad \text{...(8.57)}$$

The above result follows from: (using the results of Sampling Theorem)

$$X(j\,\Omega) = X_D(e^{j\Omega T}) = \frac{1}{T}\sum_{k=-\infty}^{\infty} X(j\,\Omega + jk\Omega_s) \qquad \text{...(8.58}a\text{)}$$

or

$$X_D(e^{j\omega}) = \frac{1}{T}\sum_{k=-\infty}^{\infty} X\left(j\frac{\omega}{T} + jk\omega_s\right) \qquad \text{...(8.58}b\text{)}$$

where $x_D(n)$ is sampled version of $x(t)$.

From (8.56) and (8.57), a closed-form but approximate expression for $W_K(e^{j\omega})$ can be deduced as

$$W_K(e^{j\omega}) \approx \frac{N-1}{\alpha I_0(\alpha)}\cdot\frac{\sin\left[\alpha\sqrt{(\omega/\omega_a)^2 - 1}\right]}{\sqrt{(\omega/\omega_a)^2 - 1}} \qquad \text{...(8.59)}$$

Advantages of Kaiser Window:

1. In Kaiser window, the ripple ratio (RR) can be varied continuously from the low value as in Blackman window to a high value as in the Rectangular window by simply varying the parameter α.
2. Main lobe width can be varied continuously by varying N, as in other windows.

In short, Kaiser window is a versatile one which can be adjusted to suit almost any set of prescribed filter specifications.

We now give the design method using Kaiser window.

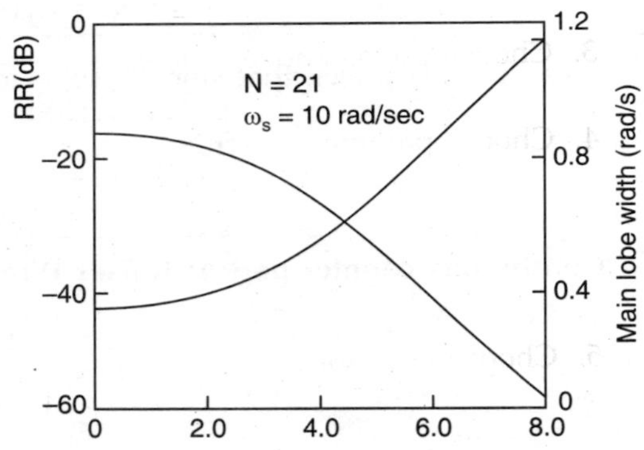

Fig. 8.14. Kaiser window: typical curves

Rule to design an FIR (linear phase) Filter by using the Kaiser window

Considering a low-pass filter, LPF let

$$A_p = 20\log\frac{1+\delta_1}{1-\delta_1} \qquad \text{...(8.60)}$$

$$A_a = -20\log\delta_2 \qquad \text{...(8.61)}$$

where A_p and A_a are positive quantities. Define transition width B_t by

$$B_t = \begin{cases} \omega_a - \omega_p \text{ for LPF} \\ \omega_p - \omega_a \text{ for HPF} \end{cases} \qquad \text{...(8.62)}$$

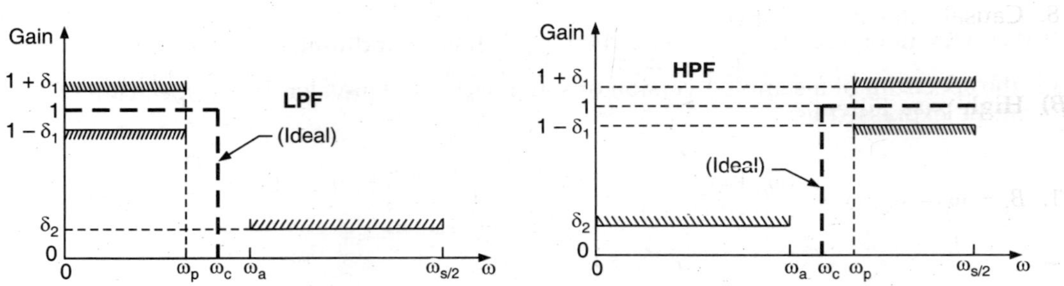

(a) (b)

(A) Low-pass Filters

1. (*i*) Determine $h(n)$, assuming the idealised frequency response: taking $\omega_c = \dfrac{(\omega_p + \omega_a)}{2}$

   (*ii*) $H(e^{j\omega}) = \begin{cases} 1, & |\omega| \le \omega_c \\ 0, & \text{otherwise} \end{cases}$

   (*iii*) Find $h(n)$ by inverse DTFT of $H(e^{j\omega})$

   (*iv*) $B_t = \omega_a - \omega_p$ is the transition bandwidth.

2. Find δ_1 and δ_2, choose $\delta = \min(\delta_1, \delta_2)$

   when
   $$\delta_1 = \frac{(10^{0.05A_p} - 1)}{(10^{0.05A_p} + 1)}$$
   $$\delta_2 = 10^{-0.05A_a}$$

3. Choosing δ as above, calculate the revised value of A_a using
   $$A_a = -20 \log \delta$$

4. Choose parameter α from
   $$\alpha = \begin{cases} 0, & A_a \le 21 \\ 0.5842(A_a - 21)^{0.4} + 0.07886(A_a - 21), & 21 < A_a \le 50 \\ 0.1102(A_a - 8.7), & A_a > 50 \end{cases}$$

5. Choose D as follows
   $$D = \begin{cases} 0.9222, & A_a \le 21 \\ \dfrac{A_a - 7.95}{14.36}, & A_a > 21 \end{cases}$$

6. Select the lowest odd value of N satisfying the inequality
   $$N \ge \frac{\omega_s D}{B_t} + 1$$

7. Form $\omega_K(n)$ using
   $$\omega_K(n) = \begin{cases} \dfrac{I_0(\beta)}{I_0(\alpha)}, & |n| \le \dfrac{N-1}{2} \\ 0, & \text{otherwise} \end{cases}$$

8. Causal filter is given by
   $$H_W'(z) = z^{-(N-1)/2} H_W(z), \text{ where } H_W(z) = ZT[\omega_K(n)\, h(n)]$$

(B) High-pass Filters

1. $B_t = \omega_p - \omega_a$, $\omega_c = \dfrac{(\omega_p + \omega_a)}{2}$, $H(e^{j\omega}) = \begin{cases} 0, & |\omega| \le \omega_c \\ 1, & \omega_c \le |\omega| \le \dfrac{\omega_s}{2} \end{cases}$

(C) Band-pass Filters

1.
$$B_t = \min[(\omega_{p_1} - \omega_{a_1}), (\omega_{a_2} - \omega_{p_2})]$$

$$\omega_{c_1} = \omega_{p_1} - \frac{B_t}{2}; \ \omega_{c_2} = \omega_{p_2} + \frac{B_t}{2}$$

$$H(e^{j\omega}) = \begin{cases} 0, & 0 \le |\omega| \le \omega_{c_1}; \omega_{c_2} \le |\omega| \le \dfrac{\omega_s}{2} \\ 1, & \omega_{c_1} \le |\omega| \le \omega_{c_2} \end{cases}$$

2-8 same steps as for low-pass filters.

(D) Band-stop Filters

1.
$$B_t = \min[(\omega_{a_1} - \omega_{p_1}), (\omega_{p_2} - \omega_{a_2})]$$

$$\omega_{c_1} = \omega_{p_1} - \frac{B_t}{2}; \ \omega_{c_2} = \omega_{p_2} + \frac{B_t}{2}$$

$H(e^{j\omega}) = 1$ for 0 to ω_{c_1}; ω_{c_2} to $\dfrac{\omega_s}{2}$ and zero otherwise

steps 2 to 8, same as for LPF.

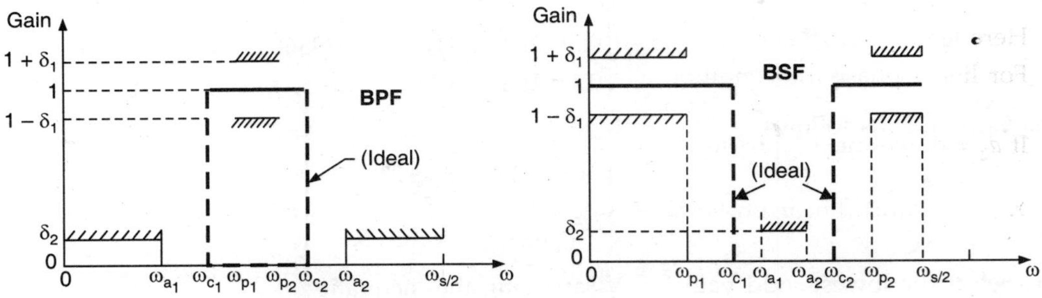

Fig. 8.16. Idealised frequency responses for BPF and BSF.

Design Examples based on Windows

EXAMPLE 8.2: *(a) A non-recursive filter is characterized by the Transfer Function*

$$H(z) = \frac{1}{z^6}(1 + 2z + 3z^2 + 4z^3 + 3z^4 + 2z^5 + z^6)$$

Find the group delay of the filter.

(b) Repeat part (a) if $H(z) = \dfrac{1}{z^6}(1 - 2z + 3z^2 - 4z^3 + 3z^4 - 2z^5 + z^6)$.

SOLUTION:

(a)
$$H(z) = z^{-3}(z^{-3} + 2z^{-2} + 3z^{-1} + 4 + 3z + 2z^2 + z^3)$$

$\therefore$
$$H(e^{j\omega}) = e^{-j3\omega}(e^{-j3\omega} + 2e^{-j2\omega} + 3e^{-j\omega} + 4 + 3e^{j\omega} + 2e^{j2\omega} + e^{j3\omega})$$
$$= e^{-j3\omega}[2\cos 3\omega + 4\cos 2\omega + 6\cos\omega + 4] \triangleq e^{-j3\omega}C(\omega), \text{ say} \quad \ldots(A)$$

Phase angle $\theta(\omega) = -3\omega + \theta_0$

where
$$\theta_0 = \begin{cases} 0, & \text{if } C(\omega) \ge 0 \\ \pi, & \text{if } C(\omega) < 0' \end{cases}$$

$$\therefore \qquad \tau_g = -\frac{d\theta(\omega)}{d\omega} = +3 \text{ or delay} = 3T_s \text{ where } T_s = \text{intersample}$$

interval.

(*b*) Here $H(e^{j\omega}) = e^{-j3\omega}(e^{-j3\omega} - 2e^{-j2\omega} + 3e^{-j\omega} - 4 + 3e^{j\omega} - 2e^{j2\omega} + e^{j3\omega})$

$$= e^{-j3\omega}[2 \cos 3\omega - 4 \cos 2\omega + 6 \cos \omega - 4]$$

$$= e^{-j3\omega} \cdot B(\omega), \text{ say}$$

$$\theta(\omega) = -3\omega + \theta_1$$

where
$$\theta_1 = \begin{cases} 0, & \text{if } B(\omega) \geq 0 \\ \pi, & \text{if } B(\omega) < 0 \end{cases}$$

Hence, $\tau_g = -\dfrac{d\theta(\omega)}{d\omega} = +3$ or delay $= 3T_s$ as above in part (*a*) **Ans.**

EXAMPLE 8.3: *Express the transfer function $H(z) = 1 + a_1z^{-1} + a_2z^{-2} + a_3z^{-3} + a_4z^{-4}$ as the sum of a linear phase transfer function $H_1(z)$ of length 5 and a non-linear phase transfer $H_2(z)$ and obtain a canonic realization of $H(z)$ in terms of $H_1(z)$ and $H_2(z)$.*

SOLUTION:

$$H(z) = 1 + a_1z^{-1} + a_2z^{-2} + a_3z^{-3} + a_4z^{-4} \qquad \ldots(A)$$

$$\therefore \qquad h(n) = \left\{\begin{matrix} 1, a_1, a_2, a_3, a_4 \\ \uparrow \end{matrix}\right\} \text{ taking } IZT \text{ of } (A)$$

Here length $N = 5$ and order of $H(z) = N - 1 = 4$.

For linear phase the condition is

$$h(n) = \pm h(N - 1 - n)$$

If $a_2 \neq 0$, we must have $h(n) = +h(N - 1 - n) = h(5 - 1 - n) = h(4 - n)$

$$\therefore \qquad h_1(n) \text{ (linear phase filter)} = \left\{\begin{matrix} a_4, a_3, a_2, a_3, a_4 \\ \uparrow \end{matrix}\right\} \quad \because \quad h_1(n) = h_1(4 - n)$$

$$h_2(n) = h(n) - h_1(n) \text{ (non-linear phase filter)}$$

$$= \left\{\begin{matrix} (1 - a_4), (a_1 - a_3), 0, 0, 0 \\ \uparrow \end{matrix}\right\}$$

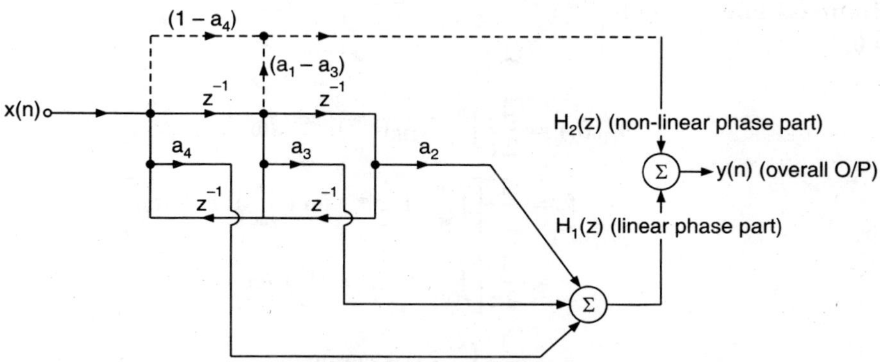

Canonic realization: $H(z) = H_1(z) + H_2(z)$

Total delays = 4

Total multiplications = 5

Fig. Ex. 8.3. Realization of $H(z)$ as $H(z) = H_1(z) + H_2(z)$

EXAMPLE 8.4: *Determine the unit sample responses for ideal LPF, HPF, BPF and BSF cases when T ≠ 1 i.e. take non-normalised frequencies.*

SOLUTION:

Ideal Lowpass Filter (LPF)

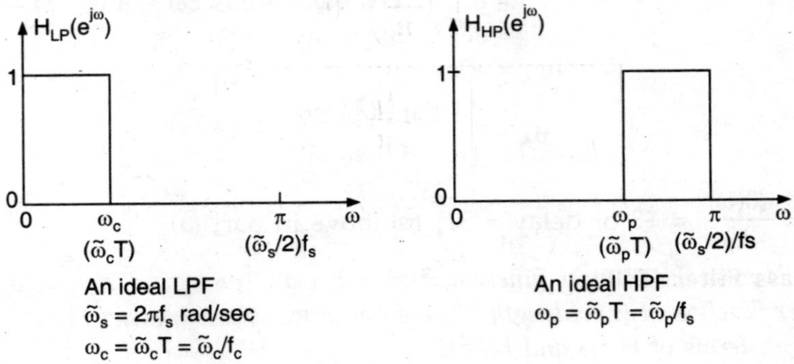

Fig. Ex. 8.4. (*a*) Ideal LPF, (*b*) An ideal HPF

Assume

$$\tilde{\omega} = \omega f_s \text{ where } \omega \text{ is in radians and } \tilde{\omega} \text{ is in rad/sec}$$
$$\therefore \omega = \tilde{\omega}/f_s = \tilde{\omega} T$$

$$h_{LP}(n) = \frac{1}{2\pi}\int_{-\pi}^{\pi} H_{LP}(e^{j\omega})e^{j\omega n}\, d\omega$$

$$= \frac{1}{2\pi}\int_{-\omega_c}^{\omega_c} e^{j\omega n}\, d\omega$$

$$= \frac{1}{2\pi}\left[\frac{e^{j\omega n}}{jn}\right]_{-\omega_c}^{\omega_c} = \frac{\sin n\omega_c}{\pi n}$$

$$\therefore \quad h_{LP}(nT) = \frac{\sin n\omega_c}{n\pi} = \frac{\sin n\tilde{\omega}_c T}{n\pi}$$

Ideal Highpass Filter (HPF)

For *n* ≠ 0,

$$h_{HP}(n) = \frac{1}{2\pi}\int_{-\pi}^{\pi} H_{HF}(e^{j\omega})e^{j\omega n}\, d\omega$$

$$= \frac{1}{2\pi}\left[\int_{-\pi}^{-\omega_p} 1\cdot e^{j\omega n}\, d\omega + \int_{\omega_p}^{\pi} 1\cdot e^{j\omega n}\, d\omega\right]$$

$$= \frac{1}{2\pi}\left[\int_{\omega_p}^{\pi} (e^{j\omega n} + e^{-j\omega n})\, d\omega\right] \quad \ldots(A)$$

$$= \frac{1}{2\pi}\int_{\omega_p}^{\pi} 2\cos n\omega\, d\omega$$

$$= \frac{1}{n\pi}[\sin n\omega]_{\omega_p}^{\pi} = \frac{-1}{n\pi}\sin n\omega_p,\ n \neq 0$$

For $n = 0$,

$$h(n) = \frac{1}{\pi}\int_{\omega_p}^{\pi} 1 \cdot d\omega \qquad \text{(due to (A))}$$

$$= \left(1 - \frac{\omega_p}{\pi}\right) \cdot \delta(n)$$

$$h_{HP}(n) = \begin{cases} 1 - \dfrac{\omega_p}{\pi}, & n = 0 \\ \dfrac{-\sin n\omega_p}{n\pi}, & n \neq 0 \end{cases}$$

Ideal Bandpass Filter (BPF)

$$h_{BP}(n) = \frac{1}{2\pi}\int_{-\pi}^{\pi} H_{BP}(e^{j\omega})e^{j\omega n}\, d\omega$$

$$= \frac{1}{2\pi}\left[\int_{-\omega_{c_2}}^{-\omega_{c_1}} e^{j\omega n}\, d\omega + \int_{\omega_{c_1}}^{\omega_{c2}} e^{j\omega n}\, d\omega\right]$$

$$= \frac{1}{2\pi}\left[\int_{\omega_{c_1}}^{\omega_{c2}} (e^{j\omega n} + e^{-j\omega n})\, d\omega\right]$$

$$= \frac{1}{2\pi} \cdot \int_{\omega_{c_1}}^{\omega_{c_2}} 2\cos n\omega\, d\omega$$

$$= \frac{1}{\pi n}[\sin n\omega]_{\omega_{c_1}}^{\omega_{c2}}$$

$$= \frac{\sin n\omega_{c_2} - \sin n\omega_{c_1}}{\pi n}$$

$$\therefore \quad h_{BP}(nT) = \frac{\sin n\omega_{c_2} - \sin n\omega_{c_1}}{n\pi} = \frac{\sin n\tilde{\omega}_{c_2}T - \sin n\tilde{\omega}_{c_1}T}{n\pi}$$

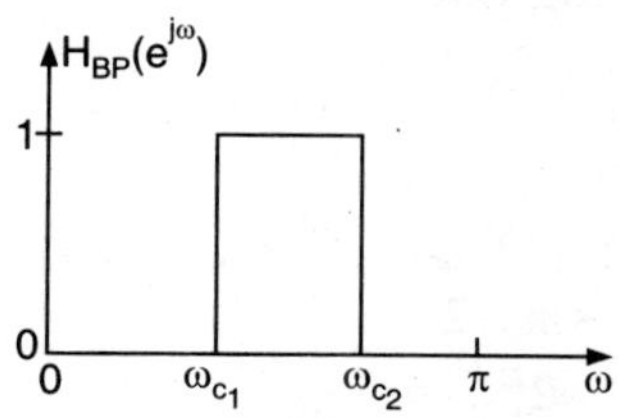

An ideal BPF
$\tilde{\omega}_s = 2\pi f_s$ rad/sec
$\omega_{c_1} = \tilde{\omega}_{c_1}T$; $\omega_{c_2} = \tilde{\omega}_{c_1}T$

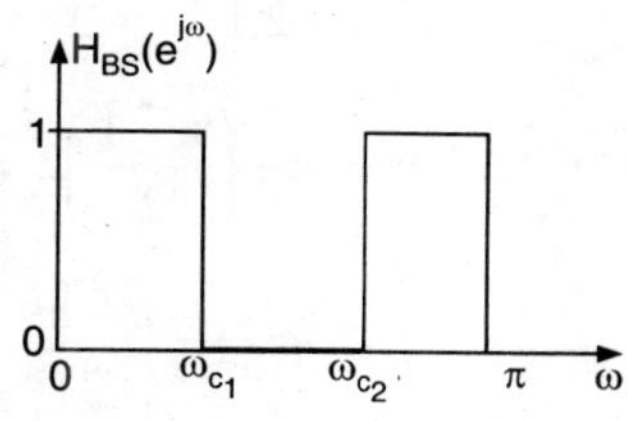

An ideal BSF
$\tilde{\omega}_s = 2\pi f_s$ rad/sec
$\omega_{c_1} = \tilde{\omega}_{c_1}T$; $\omega_{c_2} = \tilde{\omega}_{c_2}T$

Fig. Ex. 8.4. (*c*) An Ideal BPF (*d*) An ideal BSF

Ideal Bandstop Filter (BSF)

$$h_{BS}(n) = \frac{1}{2\pi}\int_{-\pi}^{\pi} H_{BS}(e^{j\omega})\, e^{j\omega n}\, d\omega$$

$$= \frac{1}{2\pi}\left[\int_{-\pi}^{-\omega_{c2}} e^{j\omega n}\, d\omega + \int_{-\omega_{c_1}}^{\omega_{c1}} e^{j\omega n}\, d\omega + \int_{\omega_{c_2}}^{\pi} e^{j\omega n}\, d\omega\right]$$

$$= \frac{1}{2\pi}\left[\int_{\omega_{c_2}}^{\pi} 2\cos\omega n\, d\omega + \int_{-\omega_{c1}}^{\omega_{c_1}} e^{j\omega n}\, d\omega\right]$$ (combining first and the last term from above)

$$= \frac{1}{2\pi}\left[2\left(\frac{\sin n\omega}{n}\right)_{\omega_{c_2}}^{\pi} + \frac{1}{jn}\left(e^{j\omega n}\right)_{-\omega_{c_1}}^{\omega_{c_1}}\right] = -\frac{\sin n\omega_{c_2}}{n\pi} + \frac{\sin n\omega_{c_1}}{n\pi}$$

$$\therefore \quad \boxed{h_{BS}(nT) = \frac{-[\sin n\omega_{c_2} - \sin n\omega_{c_1}]}{n\pi} = \frac{-[\sin n\tilde{\omega}_{c_2}T - \sin n\tilde{\omega}_{c_1}T]}{n\pi}.}$$

EXAMPLE 8.5: *Given the identity*

$$\cos n\omega = \frac{n}{2}\sum_{k=0}^{\lfloor n/2\rfloor} \frac{(-1)^k\,(n-k-1)!\,2^{n-2k}}{k!\,(n-2k)!}(\cos\omega)^{n-2k} \tag{6.102}$$

$$\triangleq \sum_{m=0}^{n} a_{mn}(\cos\omega)^m$$

Determine the value of a_{mn} for n odd; n even cases. Note that $\lfloor x \rfloor$ means the largest less than or equal to integral part of x.

SOLUTION: Given $\cos n\omega = \dfrac{n}{2}\displaystyle\sum_{k=0}^{\lfloor n/2\rfloor} \frac{(-1)^k\,(n-k-1)!\,2^{n-2k}}{k!(n-2k)!}(\cos\omega)^{n-2k}$ ...(1)

Let n be odd

Put $n - 2k = m$, when $k = 0$, $m = n$

when $$k = \left\lfloor\frac{n}{2}\right\rfloor = \frac{n-1}{2} \quad n \text{ being odd}$$

then $$m = n - \left(\frac{n-1}{2}\right)2 = 1$$

$$n - k - 1 = n - 1 - \frac{n-m}{2} = \frac{n+m-2}{2}$$

Clearly, $m = n - 2k$ is odd varying from 1, 3, 5, ..., n.

Hence, (1) yields

$$\cos n\omega = \frac{n}{2}\sum_{\substack{m=1\\ m\text{ odd}}}^{n} \frac{(-1)^{(n-m)/2}\left(\frac{n+m-2}{2}\right)!\,2^m}{\left(\frac{n-m}{2}\right)!\,m!}(\cos\omega)^n, \; n \text{ odd}$$

$$\therefore \qquad a_{mn}\big|_{n \text{ odd}} = \left(\frac{n}{2}\right)\frac{(-1)^{(n-m)/2}\,\dfrac{(n+m-2)}{2}!\,2^m}{m!\left(\dfrac{n-m}{2}\right)!}, \quad m, n \text{ odd} \quad \textbf{Ans.}$$

Let *n* be even

As
$$\cos n\omega = \left(\frac{n}{2}\right)\sum_{k=0}^{\lfloor n/2 \rfloor} \frac{(-1)^k\,(n-k-1)!\,2^{n-2k}}{k!\,(n-2k)!}(\cos\omega)^{n-2k} \qquad \ldots(2)$$

Put $n - 2k = m$, when $k = 0$, $m = n$

$$\text{when } k = \left\lfloor \frac{n}{2} \right\rfloor = \frac{n}{2} \quad (n \text{ being even})$$

then
$$m = n - 2\frac{n}{2} = 0$$

Also, $n - 2k = m$ gives m as even, from 0, 2, 4, ..., n

$$n - k - 1 = n - 1 - \frac{n-m}{2} = \frac{n+m-2}{2}$$

Then (2) reduces to

$$\cos n\omega = \left(\frac{n}{2}\right)\sum_{\substack{m=0 \\ m \text{ even}}}^{n} \frac{(-1)^{(n-m)/2}\left(\dfrac{n+m-2}{2}\right)!\,2^m}{\left(\dfrac{n-m}{2}\right)!\,m!}(\cos\omega)^m$$

Thus,

$$a_{mn} = \left(\frac{n}{2}\right)\frac{(-1)^{(n-m)/2}\left(\dfrac{n+m-2}{2}\right)!\,2^m}{m!\left(\dfrac{n-m}{2}\right)!}, \quad n, m \text{ even} \quad \textbf{Ans.}$$

Thus,

$$\cos n\omega = \sum_{\substack{m=0 \\ m\,\text{even}}\Big/\substack{m=1 \\ m\,\text{odd}}}^{n} a_{mn}(\cos\omega)^m \qquad \text{If } n \text{ is even, } m = 0, 2, \ldots, n$$

If n is odd, $m = 1, 3, \ldots, n$

$$a_{mn} = \left(\frac{n}{2}\right)\frac{(-1)^{(n-m)/2}\left(\dfrac{n+m-2}{2}\right)!\,2^m}{m!\left(\dfrac{n-m}{2}\right)!} \qquad m, n \text{ both odd or even}$$

$$= (-1)^{(n-m)/2}\left(\frac{n}{n+m}\right)\cdot 2^m \binom{(n+m)/2}{m}$$

EXAMPLE 8.6: *If $h(n) = h(N-1-n)$, then*

$$H(e^{j\omega}) = e^{-j\omega(N-1)/2}\, H_1(\omega)$$

where $$H_1(\omega) = Q(\omega) \cdot P(\omega)$$

Determine the values of $Q(\omega)$ and $P(\omega)$ for N odd and N even cases i.e. show that

N	$Q(\omega)$	$P(\omega)$
Odd	1	$\sum_{n=0}^{(N-1)/2} a(n)\cos n\omega$
Even	$\cos\left(\frac{\omega}{2}\right)$	$\sum_{n=0}^{(N/2)-1} \tilde{b}(n)\cos n\omega$

Determine the relationship between $a(n)$, $h(n)$ and $\tilde{b}(n)$.

SOLUTION: (*a*) Let N be odd and also $h(n) = h(N-1-n)$

$$\therefore \quad H(e^{j\omega}) = \sum_{n=0}^{N-1} h(n)e^{-j\omega n} \quad \text{(definition of Fourier Transform)}$$

$$= \underbrace{\sum_{n=0}^{(N-3)/2} h(n)e^{-j\omega n}}_{(A)} + \underbrace{h\left(\frac{N-1}{2}\right)e^{-j\omega(N-1)/2}}_{(B)} + \underbrace{\sum_{n=\frac{N+1}{2}}^{N-1} h(n)e^{-j\omega n}}_{(C)} \qquad \ldots(1)$$

But $$(C) = \sum_{n=\frac{N+1}{2}}^{N-1} h(n)e^{-j\omega n}$$

$$= \sum_{n=\frac{N-1}{2}}^{N-1} h(N-1-n)e^{-j\omega n} \qquad \text{symmetry property of } h(n) \text{ (given)}$$

Put $N-1-n = k$ $\quad \therefore$ when $n = \frac{N-1}{2}$, $k = \frac{N-3}{2}$

when $n = N-1$, $k = 0$

$$\therefore \quad (C) = \sum_{k=0}^{(N-3)/2} h(k)e^{-j\omega(N-1-k)} \qquad \ldots(2)$$

From (1) and (2),

$$H(e^{j\omega}) = h\left(\frac{N-1}{2}\right)e^{-j\omega(N-1)/2} + \sum_{n=0}^{(N-3)/2} h(n)[e^{-j\omega n} + e^{-j\omega(N-1-n)}]$$

$$= e^{-j\omega(N-1)/2}\left[h\left(\frac{N-1}{2}\right) + \sum_{n=0}^{(N-3)/2} h(n)\left(e^{-j\omega\left(n-\frac{N-1}{2}\right)} + e^{+j\omega\left(n-\frac{N-1}{2}\right)}\right)\right]$$

$$= e^{-j\omega(N-1)/2}\left[h\left(\frac{N-1}{2}\right) + \sum_{n=0}^{(N-3)/2} 2h(n)\cos\underbrace{\left(n-\frac{N-1}{2}\right)\omega}_{=\cos\left(\frac{N-1}{2}-n\right)\omega}\right] \qquad \ldots(3)$$

Put $\dfrac{N-1}{2} - n = k$

$\therefore$ when $n = 0,\quad k = \dfrac{N-1}{2}$

when $n = \dfrac{N-3}{2}, k = 1$

$\therefore$ (3) yields

$$H(e^{j\omega}) = e^{-j\omega(N-1)/2}\left[h\left(\frac{N-1}{2}\right) + \sum_{k=1}^{N-1/2} 2h\left(\frac{N-1}{2} - k\right)\cos k\omega\right]$$

$$= e^{-j\omega(N-1)/2} \sum_{k=0}^{(N-1)/2} (2 - \delta_{k,0})\, h\left(\frac{N-1}{2} - k\right)\cos k\omega$$

$$= e^{-j\omega(N-1)/2} \sum_{n=0}^{(N-1)/2} (2 - \delta_{n,0})\, h\left(\frac{N-1}{2} - n\right)\cos n\omega$$

$$\triangleq \underbrace{e^{-j\omega(N-1)/2}}_{\text{Phase}} \underbrace{\sum_{n=0}^{(N-1)/2} a(n)\cos n\omega}_{H_1(\omega) \triangleq Q(\omega)\cdot P(\omega)}$$

where
$$Q(n) = \begin{cases} h\left(\dfrac{N-1}{2}\right), & n = 0 \\ 2h\left(\dfrac{N-1}{2} - n\right), & n = 1, 2, 3, \ldots, \dfrac{N-1}{2} \end{cases}$$

$$Q(\omega) = 1,\ P(\omega) = \sum_{n=0}^{(N-1)/2} a(n)\cos n\omega \quad \textbf{Ans.}$$

(*b*) Let N be an even integer and also $h(n) = h(N-1-n)$

$$H(e^{j\omega}) = \sum_{n=0}^{N/2-1} h(n)e^{-j\omega n} + \sum_{n=N/2}^{N-1} h(n)e^{-j\omega n}$$

$$= \underbrace{\sum_{n=0}^{N/2-1} h(n)e^{-j\omega n}}_{(A)} + \underbrace{\sum_{n=N/2}^{N-1} h(N-1-n)e^{-j\omega n}}_{(B)}$$

[Symmetry property of $h(n)$] ...(1)

But
$$(B) = \sum_{n=N/2}^{N-1} h(N-1-n)e^{-j\omega n}$$

Put $N - 1 - n = k \quad \therefore$ when $n = \dfrac{N}{2},\quad k = \dfrac{N}{2} - 1$

when $n = N - 1,\ k = 0$

$\therefore$
$$(B) = \sum_{k=0}^{N/2-1} h(k)e^{-j\omega(N-1-k)} \qquad \text{...(2)}$$

From (1) and (2), we get

$$H(e^{j\omega}) = \sum_{n=0}^{N/2-1} h(n)\,[e^{-j\omega n} + e^{-j\omega(N-1-n)}]$$

$$= e^{-j\omega(N-1)/2} \sum_{n=0}^{N/2-1} h(n)\left[e^{-j\omega\left(n-\frac{N-1}{2}\right)} + e^{+j\omega\left(n-\frac{N-1}{2}\right)}\right]$$

$$= \underbrace{e^{-j\omega(N-1)/2}}_{\text{Phase part}} \underbrace{\sum_{n=0}^{N/2-1} 2h(n)\cos\left(\frac{N-1}{2}-n\right)\omega}_{H_1(\omega)\triangleq Q(\omega)\cdot P(\omega)} \qquad \ldots(3)$$

Put $\frac{N}{2}-n = k$ in $H_1(\omega)$

when $n = 0,\ k = \frac{N}{2}$

when $n = \frac{N}{2}-1\ \ k = 1$

$$\therefore \quad H_1(\omega) = \sum_{k=1}^{N/2} 2h\left(\frac{N}{2}-k\right)\cdot\cos\left(k-\frac{1}{2}\right)\omega \qquad \ldots(4)$$

i.e.

$$H_1(\omega) = \sum_{k=1}^{N/2} 2h\left(\frac{N}{2}-k\right)\cos\left(k-\frac{1}{2}\right)\omega$$

$$\triangleq \sum_{n=1}^{N/2} b(n)\cos\left(n-\frac{1}{2}\right)\omega, \text{ where } b(n) = 2h\left(\frac{N}{2}-n\right),$$

$$n = 1, 2, \ldots, \frac{N}{2}$$

[To convert "$b(n)\cos\left(n-\frac{1}{2}\right)\omega$" in the form of "$\hat{b}(n)\cos n\omega$"]

Note that

$$\sum_{n=0}^{N/2-1} \hat{b}(n)\cos n\omega = \frac{1}{2}\left[\sum_{n=0}^{N/2-1} \hat{b}(n)\left(2\cos n\omega\cos\frac{\omega}{2}\right)\Big/\cos\frac{\omega}{2}\right] \qquad \text{(Note this step)}$$

$$\therefore \quad \sum_{n=0}^{N/2-1} \hat{b}(n)\cos n\omega\cdot\cos\frac{\omega}{2} = \frac{1}{2}\left[\underbrace{\sum_{n=0}^{N/2-1} \hat{b}(n)\cos\left(n+\frac{1}{2}\right)\omega}_{(A)} + \underbrace{\sum_{n=0}^{N/2-1} \hat{b}(n)\cos\left(n-\frac{1}{2}\right)\omega}_{(B)}\right] \qquad \ldots(5)$$

In (A), put $n' = n + 1$

$$\therefore \quad (A) = \sum_{n'=1}^{N/2} \hat{b}(n'-1)\cos\left(n'-\frac{1}{2}\right)\omega$$

$$\therefore \quad \sum_{n=0}^{N/2-1} \hat{b}(n)\cos n\omega \cdot \cos\frac{\omega}{2} = \frac{1}{2}\left[\sum_{n'=1}^{N/2-1} \hat{b}(n'-1)\cos\left(n'-\frac{1}{2}\right)\omega + \hat{b}\left(\frac{N}{2}-1\right)\cos\frac{N-1}{2}\omega \right.$$

$$\left. + \hat{b}(0)\cos\frac{\omega}{2} + \sum_{n=1}^{N/2-1} \hat{b}(n)\cos\left(n-\frac{1}{2}\right)\omega\right]$$

$$= \frac{1}{2}\left[\sum_{n=1}^{N/2-1} (\hat{b}(n-1)+\hat{b}(n))\cos\left(n-\frac{1}{2}\right)\omega \right.$$

$$\left. + \hat{b}(0)\cos\frac{\omega}{2} + \hat{b}\left(\frac{N}{2}-1\right)\cos\frac{N-1}{2}\omega\right]$$

$$\therefore \quad \cos\frac{\omega}{2}\sum_{n=0}^{N/2-1} \hat{b}(n)\cos n\omega \triangleq \sum_{n=1}^{N/2} b(n)\cos\left(n-\frac{1}{2}\right)\omega, \text{ where } b(n) = h\left(\frac{N}{2}-n\right).$$

Compare coefficient of $\cos\frac{\omega}{2}$, $\cos\frac{N-1}{2}\omega$ and of $\cos\left(n-\frac{1}{2}\right)$ in the identity

$$\sum_{n=1}^{N/2} b(n)\cos\left(n-\frac{1}{2}\right)\omega \equiv \frac{1}{2}\left[\hat{b}(0)\cos\frac{\omega}{2} + \hat{b}\left(\frac{N}{2}-1\right)\cos\frac{N-1}{2}\omega \right.$$

$$\left. + \sum_{n=1}^{N/2-1} (\hat{b}(n-1)+\hat{b}(n))\cos\left(n-\frac{1}{2}\right)\omega\right]$$

$$\left.\begin{aligned}
\cos\frac{\omega}{2}:\ b(1) &= \frac{1}{2}[\hat{b}(0)+(\hat{b}(0)+\hat{b}(1)] & \therefore\ \hat{b}(0) &= b(1)-\frac{1}{2}\hat{b}(1)\\
\cos\frac{N-1}{2}\omega:\ b\left(\frac{N}{2}\right) &= \frac{1}{2}\left[\hat{b}\left(\frac{N}{2}-1\right)+0\right] & \therefore\ \hat{b}\left(\frac{N}{2}-1\right) &= 2b\left(\frac{N}{2}\right)\\
\cos\left(n-\frac{1}{2}\right)\omega:\ b(n) &= \frac{1}{2}[\hat{b}(n-1)+\hat{b}(n)] & \therefore\ \hat{b}(n-1) &= 2b(n)-\hat{b}(n)
\end{aligned}\right\} \textbf{Ans.}$$

EXAMPLE 8.7: *An FIR digital filter is required to approximate the ideal low-pass filter:*

$$H_d(e^{j\omega}) = \begin{cases} e^{-j6\omega}, & -\dfrac{\pi}{8} \le \omega \le \dfrac{\pi}{8} \\ 0, & \text{otherwise} \end{cases}$$

Determine the filter coefficients $h_d(n)$. If we use a Hann window in the design, determine the windowed coefficients $h(n)$.

SOLUTION: By inspection, the filter length $N = 13$ $(\because 6 = (N-1)/2)$

As $$h_d(n) = \frac{\sin(\omega_c n)}{\pi n} \quad \text{(non-causal case)}$$

For Hann window, we have

$$\omega_{\text{Hann}}(n) = \begin{cases} \dfrac{1}{2}\left(1+\cos\dfrac{2n\pi}{N-1}\right), & |n| \le \dfrac{N-1}{2} \\ 0, & \text{otherwise} \end{cases} \quad \text{(non-causal version)}$$

$$= \begin{cases} \cos^2 \dfrac{n\pi}{N-1}, & |n| \le \dfrac{N-1}{2} \\ 0 \quad , & \text{otherwise} \end{cases}$$

$$= \begin{cases} \cos^2 \dfrac{n\pi}{12}, & |n| \le \dfrac{N-1}{2} \\ 0 \quad , & \text{otherwise} \end{cases} \qquad \because \; N = 13$$

n	$h_d(n) = \dfrac{\sin \dfrac{\pi n}{8}}{\pi n}$	$\omega_{\text{Hann}}(n) = \cos^2 \dfrac{n\pi}{12}$	$h(n) = h_d(n) \cdot \omega(n)$
0	$h_d(0) = \dfrac{1}{8} = 0.1250$	$\omega(0) = 1$	$h(0) = \dfrac{1}{8} \times 1 = 0.1250$
1	$h_d(1) = \dfrac{\sin\left(\dfrac{\pi}{8}\right)}{\pi} = 0.1218119$	$\omega(1) = \cos^2 \dfrac{\pi}{12} = 0.9330$	$h(1) = 0.11365$
2	$h_d(2) = \dfrac{\sin\left(\dfrac{\pi}{4}\right)}{2\pi} = 0.1125395$	$\omega(2) = \cos^2 \dfrac{\pi}{6} = 0.7500$	$h(2) = 0.0844$
3	$h_d(3) = \dfrac{\sin\left(\dfrac{3\pi}{8}\right)}{3\pi} = 0.0980266$	$\omega(3) = \cos^2 \dfrac{\pi}{4} = 0.5000$	$h(3) = 0.04901$
4	$h_d(4) = \dfrac{\sin\left(\dfrac{\pi}{2}\right)}{4\pi} = 0.079577$	$\omega(4) = \cos^2 \dfrac{\pi}{3} = 0.25$	$h(4) = 0.0397885$
5	$h_d(5) = \dfrac{\sin\left(\dfrac{5\pi}{8}\right)}{5\pi} = 0.0588159$	$\omega(5) = \cos^2 \dfrac{5\pi}{12} = 0.0669$	$h(5) = 0.0039399$
6	$h_d(6) = \dfrac{\sin\left(\dfrac{3\pi}{4}\right)}{6\pi} = 0.037513179$	$\omega(6) = \cos^2 \dfrac{\pi}{2} = 0$	$h(6) = 0.00000$

Hence, the frequency response is given by

$$H(e^{j\omega}) = \sum_{n=-6}^{6} h(n)\, e^{-j\omega n}$$

$$= h(0) + 2(h(1) \cos \omega + h(2) \cos 2\omega + h(3) \cos 3\omega + h(4) \cos 4\omega + h(5) \cos 5\omega + h(6) \cos 6\omega)$$

$$= 0.1250 + 2[0.11365 \cos \omega + 0.0844 \cos 2\omega + 0.04901 \cos 3\omega + 0.03978 \cos 4\omega + 0.0039399 \cos 5\omega]$$

Check at $\omega = 0$,

$$H(e^{j\omega})|_{\omega=0} = 0.1250 + 2(0.11365 + 0.0844 + 0.04901 + 0.03978 + 0.0039399)$$
$$= 0.7065768 \approx 0.707$$

at $\omega = \pi$, $H(e^{j\omega})|_{\omega=\pi}$

$$= 0.1250 + 2(-0.11365 + 0.0844 - 0.04901 + 0.03978 - 0.0039399)$$
$$= 0.04016 \equiv -25 \text{ dB below } H(e^{j\omega})$$

We need a delay of 6 samples for the realization of the filter.

EXAMPLE 8.8: *(a) Derive the frequency response of linear phase, FIR digital filter for symmetrical impulse response with order N as odds*

(b) The desired frequency response of a low pass filter is given by

$$H_d(e^{j\omega}) = \begin{cases} e^{-j3\omega}, & -\pi/4 \le \omega \le \pi/4 \\ 0, & \pi/4 \le |\omega| \le \pi \end{cases}$$

Design a filter using Hann window with N = 7.

SOLUTION:

(*a*) As $H(z) = \sum_{n=0}^{N-1} h(n)z^{-n}$ for a causal, FIR filter

$\therefore$
$$H(e^{j\omega}) \triangleq M(\omega) \cdot e^{j\theta(\omega)}$$
$$= \sum_{n=0}^{N-1} h(n)e^{-j\omega n} \quad \text{Putting } z = e^{j\omega} \qquad \ldots(1)$$

where $M(\omega) = |H(e^{j\omega})|$, the magnitude response
and $\theta(\omega) = \arg H(e^{j\omega})$, the phase response.

Also
$$\tau_p = \text{phase delay} = -\frac{\theta(\omega)}{\omega} \qquad \ldots(2)$$

and
$$\tau_g = \text{group delay} = -\frac{d\theta(\omega)}{d\omega} \qquad \ldots(3)$$

From (1),
$$\theta(\omega) = \tan^{-1}\left[-\sum_{n=0}^{N-1} h(n)\sin n\omega \Big/ \sum_{n=0}^{N-1} h(n)\cos n\omega\right]$$

$\therefore$
$$\tan\theta(\omega) = \tan(-\omega\tau_p) \text{ for linear phase due to (2)} \qquad \ldots(4)$$

Combining (3) and (4), we get

$$\frac{\sin\omega\tau_p}{\cos\omega\tau_p} = \frac{\sum_{n=0}^{N-1} h(n)\sin n\omega}{\sum_{n=0}^{N-1} h(n)\cos n\omega}$$

or
$$\sum_{n=0}^{N-1} h(n)[\sin\omega\tau_p \,.\, \cos n\omega - \cos\omega\tau_p \sin n\omega] = 0$$

$$\therefore \qquad \sum_{n=0}^{N-1} h(n) \sin(\omega\tau_p - n\omega) = 0 \qquad \text{...(5)}$$

Equation (5) can be shown to be true if

$$\boxed{\begin{aligned} \tau_p &= \frac{(N-1)}{2} \\ h(n) &= h(N-1-n) \end{aligned}}$$

and condition for linear phase FIR filter.

If $\theta(\omega) = \theta_0 - \tau_g\omega$ giving constant group delay

If we use $\theta_0 = \pm\frac{\pi}{2}$, the solution turns out to be

$$\boxed{\begin{aligned} \tau_g &= \frac{(N-1)}{2} \\ h(n) &= -h(N-1-n) \end{aligned}} \quad \text{with } \theta(\omega) = \pm\frac{\pi}{2} - \tau_g(\omega)$$

Thus, for constant phase delay ($\theta(\omega) = -\omega\tau_p$), the impulse response is symmetrical about the mid point between samples $\frac{(N-2)}{2}$ and $\frac{N}{2}$ for even N or about sample $\frac{(N-1)}{2}$ for odd N.

For constant group delay ($\theta(\omega) = -\omega\tau_s + \pi/2$), the impulse response is anti-symmetric about the mid point between $\frac{(N-2)}{2}$ and $\frac{N}{2}$ for even N or about the sample $\frac{(N-1)}{2}$ for odd N.

Frequency response for symmetric $h(n)$ and odd N

As $$H(e^{j\omega}) = \sum_{n=0}^{(N-1)} h(n)e^{-j\omega n} \quad (h(n) \text{ is causal here})$$

$$= \underbrace{\sum_{n=0}^{(N-3)/2} h(n)e^{-j\omega n}}_{(I)} + \underbrace{h\left(\frac{N-1}{2}\right)e^{-j\omega(N-1)/2}}_{(II)} + \underbrace{\sum_{n=(N+1)/2}^{N-1} h(n)e^{-j\omega n}}_{(III)}$$

Now $$(III) = \sum_{n=(N+1)/2}^{N-1} h(n)e^{-j\omega n}$$

$$= \sum_{n=(N+1)/2}^{N-1} h(N-1-n)e^{-j\omega n} \qquad [\because\ h(n) = h(N-1-n) \text{ for linear phase FIR condition}]$$

Put $N-1-n = m$

when $n = \frac{(N+1)}{2}$, $\quad m = \frac{(N-3)}{2}$

when $n = N-1$, $\quad m = 0$

$\therefore$ $$(III) = \sum_{m=(N-3)/2}^{0} h(m) \cdot e^{-j\omega(N-1-m)}$$

$$= \sum_{n=0}^{N-3/2} h(n) \cdot e^{-j\omega(N-1-n)}$$

Thus, $$H(e^{j\omega}) = (I) + (II) + (III)$$

$$= h\left(\frac{N-1}{2}\right)e^{-j\omega\frac{N-1}{2}} + \sum_{n=0}^{N-3/2} h(n)[e^{-j\omega n} + e^{-j\omega n(N-1-n)}]$$

$$= e^{-j\omega\frac{N-1}{2}}\left[h\left(\frac{N-1}{2}\right) + \sum_{n=0}^{(N-3)/2} 2h(n)\cos\underbrace{\left(\frac{N-1}{2}-n\right)}_{\text{Put } \frac{N-1}{2}-n=k}\right]$$

$$= e^{-j\omega\frac{N-1}{2}}\left[h\left(\frac{N-1}{2}\right) + \sum_{k=N-1/2}^{1} 2h\left(\frac{N-1}{2}-k\right)\cos\omega k\right]$$

$$\triangleq e^{-j\omega\frac{N-1}{2}} \sum_{k=0}^{N-1/2} a_k \cos\omega k$$

where $a_0 = h\left(\frac{N-1}{2}\right)$

$$a_k = 2h\left(\frac{N-1}{2}-k\right),\ k = 1, 2, \ldots, \frac{N-1}{2}$$ **Ans.**

(*b*) $$H_d(e^{j\omega}) = \begin{cases} e^{-j3\omega}, & -\pi/4 \le \omega \le \pi/4 \\ 0, & \pi/4 \le |\omega| \le \pi \end{cases}$$

This is a low-pass filter with $\omega_c = \pi/4$ radians

$$h_d(n) = \frac{1}{2\pi}\int_{-\pi}^{\pi} H_d(e^{j\omega})\, e^{j\omega n}\, d\omega$$

$$= \frac{1}{2\pi}\int_{-\pi/4}^{\pi/4} e^{-j3\omega} \cdot e^{+j\omega n}\, d\omega$$

$$= \frac{1}{2\pi}\int_{-\pi/4}^{\pi/4} e^{j\omega(n-3)}\, d\omega$$

$$= \frac{1}{2\pi}\left[\frac{e^{j\omega(n-3)}}{j(n-3)}\right]_{-\pi/4}^{\pi/4}$$

$$= \frac{1}{2\pi}\left[\frac{1}{j(n-3)}\left\{e^{j\frac{\pi}{4}(n-3)} - e^{-j\frac{\pi}{4}(n-3)}\right\}\right]$$

$\therefore$ $$h_d(n) = \frac{1}{\pi(n-3)}\sin\left(\frac{\pi}{4}(n-3)\right)$$ a non-casual case

$$N = 7 \text{ here } \because 3 = \frac{N-1}{2} \quad **$$

A Hann window is

$$\underset{\text{(causal case)}}{\omega_h(n)} = \begin{cases} \frac{1}{2}\left[1 - \cos\frac{2\pi n}{N-1}\right], & n = 0, 1, 2, \ldots, (N-1) \\ 0, & \text{otherwise} \end{cases} \quad \text{(Causal version)}$$

The above values of $\omega_h(n)$ are for causal case.

For undelayed (non-causal) case, as we have

$$\omega_{\text{hann}}(n) = \begin{cases} \frac{1}{2}\left(1 + \cos\frac{2n\pi}{N-1}\right), & |n| \le \frac{N-1}{2} \\ 0 &, \text{otherwise} \end{cases}$$

$$= \begin{cases} \cos^2\frac{n\pi}{N-1}, & |n| \le \frac{N-1}{2} \\ 0 &, \text{otherwise} \end{cases}$$

$$= \begin{cases} \cos^2\frac{n\pi}{6}, & |n| \le 3 \\ 0 &, \text{otherwise} \end{cases} \quad \text{putting } N = 7$$

$$\therefore \quad \omega_{\text{hann}}(0) = 1$$

$$\omega_{\text{hann}}(1) = \cos^2\frac{\pi}{6} = \left(\frac{\sqrt{3}}{2}\right)^2 = 0.75 = \omega_{\text{hann}}(-1)$$

$$\omega_{\text{hann}}(2) = \cos^2\frac{2\pi}{6} = \left(\frac{1}{2}\right)^2 = 0.25 = \omega_{\text{hann}}(-2)$$

$$\omega_{\text{hann}}(3) = \cos^2\frac{3\pi}{6} = 0 = \omega_{\text{hann}}(-3)$$

Also, $$h(n)\big|_{\text{undelayed case}} = \frac{\sin\frac{\pi}{4}n}{n\pi}$$

$$\therefore \quad h(0) = \frac{\sin\frac{\pi n}{4}}{4 \cdot \frac{\pi n}{4}} = \frac{1}{4} = 0.25$$

$$h(1) = h(-1) = \frac{\sin\frac{\pi}{4}}{\pi} = 0.2251$$

****Or directly**

Here $$h(n) = \frac{\sin n\omega_c}{n\pi}$$

For the given numerical, $\omega_c = \pi/4$

$$\therefore \quad h(n) = \frac{\sin n\pi/4}{n\pi}$$

If delay is 3 $\because e^{-j3\omega}$ factor

we obtain $$h_d(n) = h(n-3) = \frac{\sin\frac{\pi}{4}(n-3)}{\pi(n-3)}.$$

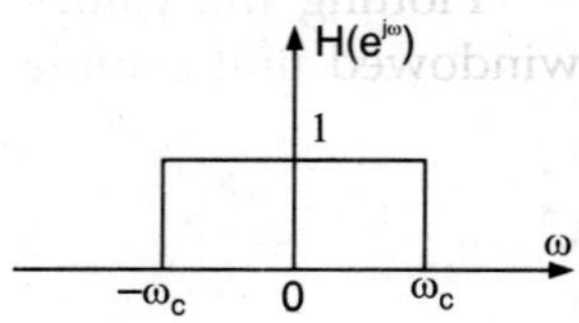

$$h(2) = h(-2) = \frac{\sin\frac{2\pi}{4}}{(2\pi)} = 0.1592$$

$$h(3) = h(-3) = \frac{\sin\frac{3\pi}{4}}{(3\pi)} = 0.0750$$

We need not compute beyond $|n| \leq 3$, since, $N = 7$ in our case.

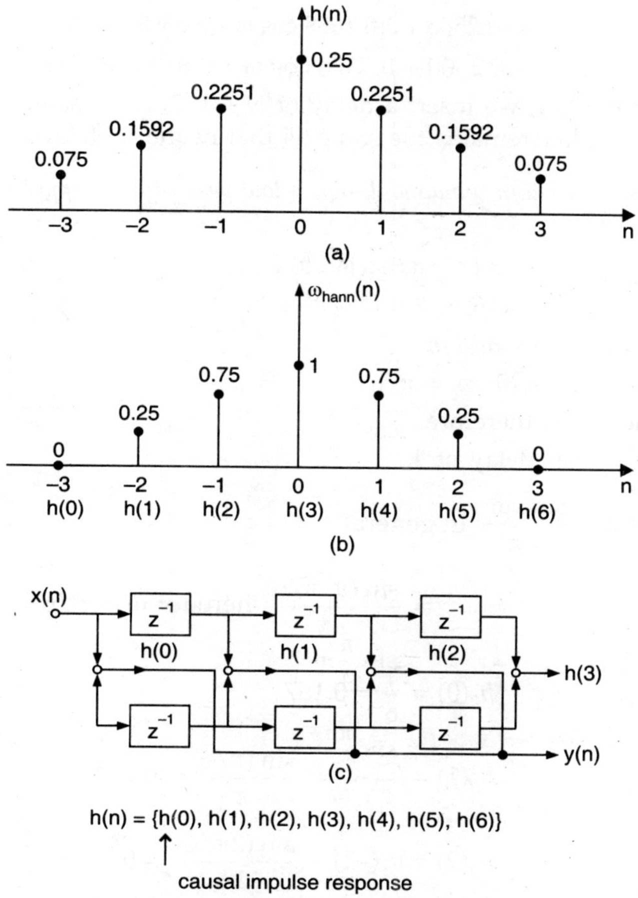

Fig. Ex. 8.8. Design weights and realization of the LPF filter

Plotting the values of $h(n)$ and $\omega_{hann}(n)$ with no delay, $h(n)$ and $\omega_{hann}(n)$ as shown. The windowed unit sample response is

$$\tilde{h}(n) = h(n) \cdot \omega_{hann}(n)$$

$$\tilde{h}(0) = 0.25 \times 1 = 0.25 \times 1 = 0.2500$$

$$\tilde{h}(1) = \tilde{h}(-1) = 0.2251 \times 0.75 = 0.1688$$

$$\tilde{h}(2) = \tilde{h}(-2) = 0.1592 \times 0.25 = 0.0398$$

$$\tilde{h}(3) = \tilde{h}(-3) = 0.075 \times 0 = 0.000$$

Hence, the frequency response of undelayed (non-causal) windowed filter is

$$H(e^{j\omega}) = \sum_{n=-3}^{3} \tilde{h}(n)e^{-j\omega n}$$

from $(e^{j\omega} + e^{-j\omega})$ ↙ from $(e^{j2\omega} + e^{-j2\omega})$ ↙

$$= 0.2500 + 2[0.1688 \cos\omega + 0.0398 \cos 2\omega + 0 \cos 3\omega]$$

$$\therefore \quad H(e^{j\omega}) = 0.2500 + 0.3376 \cos\omega + 0.0796 \cos 2\omega$$ **Ans.**

If we want a **causal filter,** we insert a delay of $N - 1/2$, *i.e.*, 3 sample time. The frequency response of the delayed filter remains the same as that of the undelayed (non-causal) filter.

EXAMPLE 8.9: *By using a Hann window, design a low pass filter to approximate the ideal response given by*

$$H_d(e^{j\omega})|_{ideal} = \begin{cases} 1, & -\pi/6 \le \omega \le \pi/6 \\ 0, & Otherwise \end{cases}$$

use the filter length N = 9 in your design.

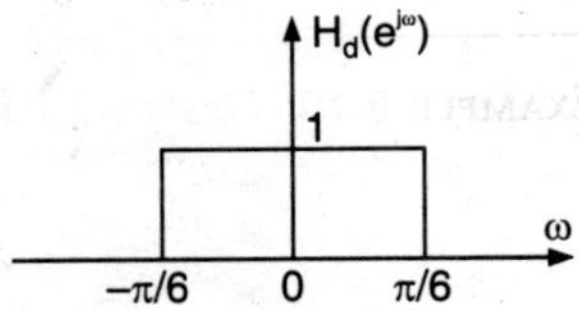

Fig. Ex. 8.9. The given ideal frequency response

SOLUTION: This is a LPF with $\omega_c = \pi/6$

We have N = 9 here and therefore

$e^{-j\omega(N-1)/2}, = e^{-j4\omega}$, *i.e.*, delay of 4.

We know that $h_d(n) = \dfrac{\sin n\omega_c}{n\pi}$ in general

$$= \frac{\sin(n \cdot \pi/6)}{n\pi} \text{ here for } \omega_c = \pi/6$$

$$\therefore \quad h_d(0) = \frac{1}{6} = 0.167$$

$$h_d(1) = h_d(-1) = \frac{\sin(\pi/6)}{\pi} = 0.159$$

$$h_d(2) = h_d(-2) = \frac{\sin(2\pi/6)}{2\pi} = 0.1378$$

$$h_d(3) = h_d(-3) = \frac{\sin(3\pi/6)}{3\pi} = 0.1061$$

$$h_d(4) = h_d(-4) = \frac{\sin(4\pi/6)}{4\pi} = 0.0689$$

For Hann window, $\omega_H(n) = \omega_H(-n) = \cos^2 \dfrac{\pi n}{N-1} = \cos^2 \dfrac{\pi n}{8}$ as here for $N = 9$

$$\boldsymbol{h_\omega(n) = h_d(n) \cdot \omega(n)}$$

$\therefore$

$$\omega_H(0) = \cos^2 0 = 1;\ h_\omega(0) = 0.167 \times 1 = 0.1670$$

$$\omega_H(1) = \omega_H(-1)\cos^2\frac{\pi}{8} = 0.8535;\ h_\omega(1) = h_\omega(-1)$$

$$= 0.159 \times 0.8535 = 0.1357$$

$$\omega_H(2) = \omega_H(-2)\cos^2\frac{\pi}{4} = 0.5;\ h_\omega(2) = h_\omega(-2) = 0.1378 \times 0.5 = 0.0689$$

$$\omega_H(3) = \omega_H(-3)\cos^2\frac{3\pi}{8} = 0.1464;\ h_\omega(3) = h_\omega(-3)$$

$$= 0.1061 \times 0.1464 = 0.0155$$

$$\omega_H(4) = \omega_H(-4)\cos^2\frac{\pi}{2} = 0;\ h_\omega(4) = h_\omega(-4)$$

$$= 0.0689 \times 0 = 0.0000$$

Ans.

> **Note:** $\omega_c = \dfrac{2\pi f_c}{f_s}$ *e.g.*, if $f_c = 100$ Hz, and $f_s = 1200$ Hz, then $\omega_c = \dfrac{2\pi \times 100}{1200} = \dfrac{\pi}{6}$, as here.

EXAMPLE 8.10: *Design an FIR linear-phase high-pass filter for the specifications.*

$$H_d(e^{j\omega}) = \begin{cases} e^{-j4\omega}, & \pi/6 \le |\omega| \le \pi \\ 0, & otherwise \end{cases}$$

Use Hann window for the design.

SOLUTION:

Here, $\quad N = 2 \times 4 + 1 = 9$

Here $\quad h_d(n) = \int_{-\pi}^{-\pi/6} 1 . e^{j\omega n}\, d\omega + \int_{\pi/6}^{\pi} 1 . e^{j\omega n}\, d\omega$

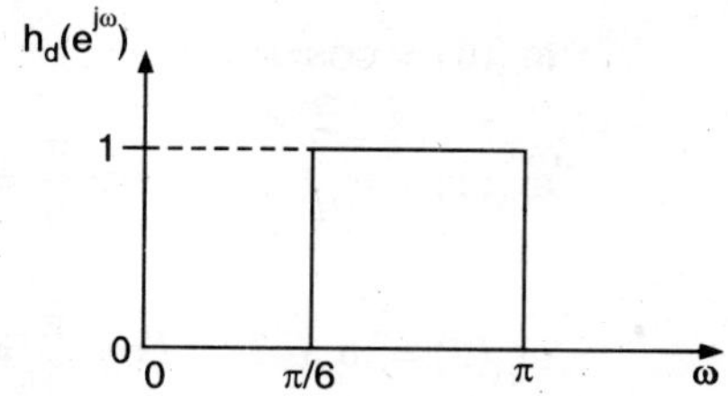

Fig. Ex. 8.10. Desired HPF

$\swarrow \omega_c$

$$= \frac{\sin \pi n}{\pi n} - \frac{\sin \frac{\pi}{6} n}{\pi n}$$

Clearly, $\quad h_d(0) = \left(1 - \dfrac{\omega_c}{\pi}\right),\ h_d(n)\Big|_{n \ne 0} = -\dfrac{\sin \omega_c n}{n\pi}$

$$\boxed{h_d(n) = \left(1 - \frac{\omega_c}{\pi}\right)\delta(n) - \frac{\sin \omega_c n}{n\pi} u(n-1)}$$

i.e.,

$$h_d(n) = \begin{cases} 1 - \dfrac{\omega_c}{\pi}, & n = 0 \\ -\dfrac{\sin n\omega_c}{n\pi}, & n = 1, 2, \ldots \end{cases}$$

as also derived in Example 8.4

$$h_d(n) = \underbrace{\left(1-\frac{1}{6}\right)}_{h_d(0)}, -\frac{\sin\frac{\pi}{6}n}{\pi n} \text{ for } n = 1, 2, ...,$$

$$h_d(0) = 1 - 1/6 = 1 - 0.167 = 0.833$$

$$h_d(1) = h_d(-1) = -\frac{\sin\left(\frac{\pi}{6}\right)}{\pi} = -\frac{0.5}{\pi} = -0.159$$

$$h_d(2) = h_d(-2) = -\frac{\sin\left(\frac{\pi}{3}\right)}{2\pi} = -\frac{0.86}{2\pi} = -0.1378$$

$$h_d(3) = h_d(-3) = -\frac{\sin\left(\frac{\pi}{2}\right)}{3\pi} = -\frac{1}{3\pi} = -0.1061$$

$$h_d(4) = h_d(-4) = -\frac{\sin\left(\frac{2\pi}{3}\right)}{4\pi} = -\frac{0.866}{4\pi} = -0.0689$$

For Hann window $\omega_H(n) = \omega_H(-n) = \cos^2\frac{\pi n}{N-1} = \cos^2\frac{\pi n}{8}$ ($\because$ $N = 9$ here)

$\omega_H(0) = \cos^2 0 = 1$	$h_\omega(0) = 0.833 \times 1 = 0.833$
$\omega_H(1) = \omega_H(-1) = \cos^2\frac{\pi}{8} = 0.8535$	$h_\omega(1) = h_\omega(-1) = (-0.159) \times (0.8535) = -0.1357$
$\omega_H(2) = \omega_H(-2) = \cos^2\frac{\pi}{4} = 0.5$	$h_\omega(2) = h_\omega(-2) = (-0.1378) \times (0.5) = -0.0689$
$\omega_H(3) = \omega_H(-3) = \cos^2\frac{3\pi}{8} = 0.1464$	$h_\omega(3) = h_\omega(-3) = (-0.1061) \times (0.1464) = -0.0155$
$\omega_H(4) = \omega_H(-4) = \cos^2\frac{4\pi}{8} = 0.0$	$h_\omega(4) = h_\omega(-4) = (-0.0689) \times (0.0)\ \underbrace{0.000}$

Check: At $\omega = 0$, $H(e^{j0})$ $= h(0) + 2(h(1) + h(2) + h(3) + h(4))$
$= 0.833 - 2(0.1357 + 0.0689 + 0.0155)$ **Ans.**
$= 0.833 - 2(0.2201) = 0.3928$

At $\omega = \frac{\pi}{6}$, $H(e^{j\pi/6})$ $= h(0) + 2\left(h(1)\cos\frac{\pi}{6} + h(2)\cos\frac{\pi}{3} + h(3)\cos\frac{\pi}{2} + h(4)\cos\frac{5\pi}{6}\right)$
$= 0.833 + 2[(-0.1357)(0.866) + (-0.0689)(0.5) + 0 + 0]$
$= 0.833 - 2 \times 0.152 = 0.529$

At $\omega = \pi$, $H(e^{j\pi})$

$$\begin{aligned} H(e^{j\pi}) &= h(0) + 2(-h(1) + h(2) - h(3) + h(4)) \\ &= 0.833 + 2(0.1357 - 0.0689 + 0.0155 + 0) \\ &= 0.833 + 2(0.0823) = 0.9976 \approx 1 \text{ (expected)} \end{aligned}$$

EXAMPLE 8.11: *The desired frequency response of a high pass filter is*

$$H_d(e^{j\omega}) = \begin{cases} 0, & |\omega| \le \frac{3}{4}\pi \\ 1, & \frac{3\pi}{4} \le |\omega| \le \pi \end{cases}$$

Design an FIR filter by using Hann window with N = 9. How would you ensure the filter to be causal?

SOLUTION: Here, $\omega_p = \dfrac{3\pi}{4}$ rad. We first find $h_d(n)$

$$\therefore \quad h_d(n) = \frac{1}{2\pi}\int_{-\pi}^{\pi} H_d(e^{j\omega})\, e^{+j\omega n}\, d\omega$$

$$= \frac{1}{2\pi}\left[\int_{-\pi}^{-3\pi/4} \underbrace{.1\, e^{j\omega n}}_{\text{Put } \omega = -\omega'}\, d\omega + \int_{3\pi/4}^{\pi} 1.\, e^{j\omega n}\, d\omega\right]$$

$$= \frac{1}{2\pi}\left[\int_{3\pi/4}^{\pi} e^{-j\omega' n}\, d\omega' + \int_{3\pi/4}^{\pi} e^{j\omega n}\, d\omega\right]$$

$$= \frac{1}{2\pi}\int_{3\pi/4}^{\pi} \underbrace{(e^{j\omega n} + e^{-j\omega n})}_{= 2\cos\omega n}\, d\omega = \frac{1}{\pi}\left[\frac{\sin \omega n}{n}\right]_{3\pi/4}^{\pi}$$

$$= \frac{\sin \pi n}{\pi n} - \frac{\sin\left(\frac{3\pi}{4}n\right)}{\pi n}$$

Hence, we get

$h_d(n) = \left(1 - \dfrac{\omega_p}{\pi}\right)\delta(n) - \dfrac{1}{n\pi}\sin\left(\dfrac{3\pi}{4}n\right)$	$h_d(n) = h_d(-n)$

$\therefore$ Symmetric about $n = 0$

$$h(0) = \delta(n)\left(1 - \frac{\omega_p}{\pi}\right) = 1\left(1 - \frac{3\pi/4}{4}\right) = \frac{1}{4}$$

$$h(1) = h(-1) = -\frac{1}{\pi}\sin\frac{3\pi}{4} = -0.225079$$

$$h(2) = h(-2) = -\frac{1}{2\pi}\sin\frac{6\pi}{4} = 0.1592$$

$$h(3) = h(-3) = -\frac{1}{3\pi}\sin\frac{9\pi}{4} = -0.075$$

$$h(4) = h(-4) = -\frac{1}{4\pi}\sin 3\pi = 0.$$

Now Hann window is $\omega_H(n) = \begin{cases} 0.5 + 0.5\cos\dfrac{2\pi n}{N-1}, & |n| \le \dfrac{N-1}{2} \\ 0, & \text{otherwise} \end{cases}$

$$= \begin{cases} 0.5\left(1 + \cos\dfrac{2\pi n}{8}\right), & |n| \le 4 \\ 0, & \text{otherwise} \end{cases}$$

Thus, $\omega_H(n) = \omega_H(-n) = \cos^2\dfrac{\pi n}{8}$

$\therefore$ $\omega_H(0) = 1$

$$\omega_H(1) = \omega_H(-1) = \cos^2\frac{\pi}{8} = 0.8535$$

$$\omega_H(2) = \omega_H(-2) = \cos^2\frac{2\pi}{8} = \cos^2\frac{\pi}{4} = 0.5$$

$$\omega_H(3) = \omega_H(-3) = \cos^2\frac{3\pi}{8} = 0.1464$$

$$\omega_H(4) = \omega_H(-4) = \cos^2\frac{4\pi}{8} = 0$$

The windowed response is $h_\omega(n) = h(n) \, . \, \omega_H(n)$

$\therefore$ $h_\omega(0) = h(0)\,\omega_H(0) = \left(1 - \dfrac{3}{4}\right) \times 1 = 1 - \dfrac{3}{4} = \dfrac{1}{4}$

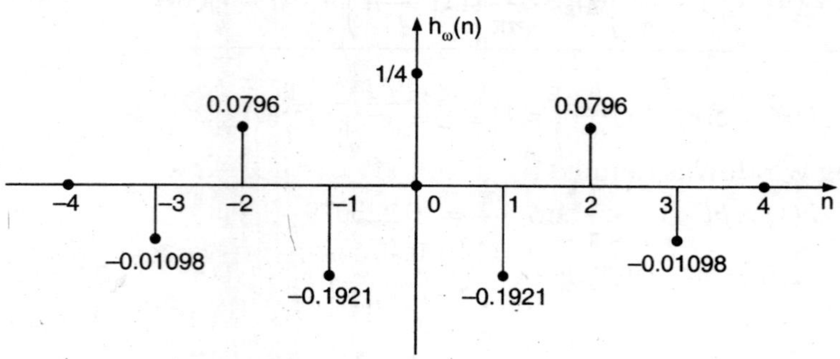

Fig. Ex. 8.11. Non-causal, windowed response

$$h_\omega(1) = h_\omega(-1) = (-0.225079)\,(0.8535) = -0.1921$$
$$h_\omega(2) = h_\omega(-2) = h_\omega(2)\,.\,\omega_H(2) = (-0.1592)\,(0.5) = 0.0796$$
$$h_\omega(3) = h_\omega(-3) = h_\omega(3)\,.\,\omega_H(3) = (-0.075)\,(0.1464) = -0.01098$$
$$h_\omega(4) = h_\omega(-4) = h_\omega(4)\,.\,\omega_H(4) = (0)\,(0) = 0$$

To make the filter causal, we insert a delay of $\frac{N-1}{2} = 4$ samples **Ans.**

EXAMPLE 8.12: *Design an FIR linear phase, low pass filter approximating the ideal frequency response*

$$H_d(\omega) = \begin{cases} 1, & |\omega| \le \pi/6 \\ 0, & \pi/6 \le |\omega| \le \pi \end{cases} \qquad \textit{(LPF, Hamming window)}$$

Determine the weights for the filter ***for 11 taps*** *based on the Hamming window.*

SOLUTION: As we have 11 taps,

$\therefore \quad N = 11$

and $\qquad e^{-j(N-1)/2\,.\,\omega} = e^{-j5\omega}$

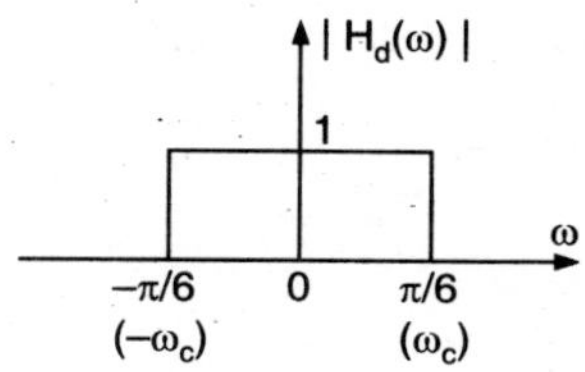

Fig. Ex. 8.12. Ideal frequency response $|H_d(\omega)|$

As $\qquad h_d(n) = \dfrac{\sin n\omega_c}{n\pi}$ in general

$$= \frac{\sin n\pi/6}{n\pi}, \text{ here } \omega_c = \pi/6$$

$\therefore \qquad h(0) = \dfrac{1}{6} = 0.167$

$$h(1) = h(-1) = \frac{\sin(\pi/6)}{\pi} = 0.159$$

$$h(2) = h(-2) = \frac{\sin(2\pi/6)}{2\pi} = 0.1378$$

$$h(3) = h(-3) = \frac{\sin(3\pi/6)}{3\pi} = 0.1061$$

$$h(4) = h(-4) = \frac{\sin(4\pi/6)}{4\pi} = 0.0689$$

$$h(5) = h(-5) = \frac{\sin(5\pi/6)}{5\pi} = 0.0318$$

The Hamming window is defined by

$$\omega_{\text{Ham}}^{(n)} = \begin{cases} 0.54 + 0.46\cos\dfrac{2n\pi}{N-1}, & |n| \le \dfrac{N-1}{2} \\ 0, & \text{otherwise} \end{cases} \quad \textit{i.e.,}\ |n| \le 5 \text{ here}$$

Thus, we have $\qquad w_{\text{Hann}}^{(n)} = 0.54 + 0.46\cos\dfrac{2n\pi}{10}$

$$\therefore \quad \omega(0) = \omega(\pm 0) = 1.0$$

$$\omega(1) = \omega(-1) = 0.54 + 0.46 \cos \frac{2\pi}{10} = 0.912$$

$$\omega(2) = \omega(-2) = 0.54 + 0.46 \cos \frac{2\pi}{5} = 0.682$$

$$\omega(3) = \omega(-3) = 0.54 + 0.46 \cos \frac{3\pi}{5} = 0.397$$

$$\omega(4) = \omega(-4) = 0.54 + 0.46 \cos \frac{4\pi}{5} = 0.168$$

$$\omega(5) = \omega(-5) = 0.54 + 0.46 \cos \frac{5\pi}{5} = 0.080$$

$$\therefore \quad h_\omega(0) = h(0) \,.\, \omega(0) = 0.167 \times 1 = 0.167$$

$$h_\omega(1) = h(1) \,.\, \omega(1) = 0.159 \times 0.912 = 0.145$$

$$h_\omega(2) = h(2) \,.\, \omega(2) = 0.1378 \times 0.682 = 0.094$$

$$h_\omega(3) = h(3) \,.\, \omega(3) = 0.1061 \times 0.397 = 0.042$$

$$h_\omega(4) = h(4) \,.\, \omega(4) = 0.0689 \times 0.168 = 0.0116$$

$$h_\omega(5) \cdot \omega(5) = 0.0318 \times 0.080 = 0.0025$$

The causal filter is, therefore

$$H_{LP}(z) = z^{-5} \sum_{n=-5}^{5} h_\omega(n)\, z^{-n}$$

$$= z^{-5} [0.167 + 0.145(z + z^{-1}) + 0.094(z + z^{-2}) + 0.042(z^3 + z^{-3}) + 0.0116\,(z^4 + z^{-4}) + 0.0025\,(z^5 + z^{-5})]$$

$$H_{LP}(e^{j\omega}) = e^{-j5\omega}[0.167 + 0.29 \cos \omega + 0.188 \cos 2\omega + 0.084 \cos 3\omega + 0.0232 \cos 4\omega + 0.005 \cos 5\omega]$$ **Ans.**

Check: $H_{LP}(e^{j0}) = 0.7772$

This is due to the fact that we have used only 11 taps. With $N > 100$, say $H_{LP}(e^{0j}) \to 1$.

EXAMPLE 8.13: *The desired frequency response of a low pass filter is given by*

$$H_d(e^{j\omega}) = \begin{cases} e^{-j4\omega}, & |\omega| \le \pi/4 \\ 0, & otherwise \end{cases} \qquad \text{(LPF, Bartlett Window)}$$

The window to be used has the response given by

$$\omega(n) = \begin{cases} 1 - 2|n|/(N-1), & |n| \le (N-1)/2 \\ 0 \quad , & otherwise \end{cases}$$

Choosing a suitable value of N, design and FIR, causal filter.

SOLUTION: The expression $e^{-j4\omega}$ shows that the delay required to make the causal filter is 4 *i.e.*, $N = 4 \times 2 + 1 = 9$. Ignoring the requirement of delay required, for the moment, we need

$$H_d(\omega) = \begin{cases} 1, & |\omega| \le \pi/4 \\ 0, & \text{otherwise} \end{cases} \qquad \text{(non-causal version)}$$

$\therefore$ $$h_d(n) = \frac{1}{2\pi}\int_{-\pi}^{\pi} H_d(e^{j\omega})\, e^{j\omega n}\, d\omega$$

$$= \frac{1}{2\pi}\int_{-\pi/4}^{\pi/4} 1 \,.\, e^{j\omega n}\, d\omega$$

$$= \frac{\sin n\frac{\pi}{4}}{n\pi} \qquad \left(h_d(n) = \frac{\sin n\omega_c}{n\pi} \right)$$

Clearly, $h_d(n) = h_d(-n)$ and this would lead to non-causal design

$$h(0) = \frac{1}{4}\left.\frac{\sin n\pi/4}{n\pi/4}\right|_{n=0} = \frac{1}{4} = 0.25000$$

$$h(1) = h(-1) = \frac{1}{\pi}\sin\frac{\pi}{4} = \frac{1}{\pi}\cdot\frac{1}{\sqrt{2}} = 0.22508$$

$$h(2) = h(-2) = \frac{1}{2\pi}\sin\frac{2\pi}{4} = \frac{1}{2\pi} = 0.15915$$

$$h(3) = h(-3) = \frac{1}{3\pi}\sin\frac{3\pi}{4} = \frac{1}{3\pi}\times\frac{1}{\sqrt{2}} = 0.07503$$

and $h(4) = h(-4) = 0.$

The given window function

$$\omega(n) = \begin{cases} 1 - 2|n|/(N-1), & |n| \le \dfrac{(N-1)}{2} \\ 0 \qquad , & \text{otherwise} \end{cases} \quad \text{(a Bartlett window)}$$

given, for $N = 9$

$$\omega(0) = 1$$

$$\omega(1) = \omega(-1) = 1 - \frac{2}{8} = \frac{3}{4}$$

$$\omega(2) = \omega(-2) = 1 - \frac{4}{8} = \frac{1}{2}$$

$$\omega(3) = \omega(-3) = 1 - \frac{6}{8} = \frac{1}{4}$$

$$\omega(4) = \omega(-4) = 1 - \frac{8}{8} = 0$$

Thus, the windowed impulse response is given by

$$h_\omega(n) = h_d(n)\,.\,\omega(n)$$

$\therefore$ $$h_\omega(0) = 0.25 \times 1 = 0.25$$

$$h_\omega(1) = h_\omega(-1) = 0.22508 \times \frac{3}{4} = 0.16881$$

$$h_\omega(2) = h_\omega(-2) = 0.15915 \times \frac{1}{2} = 0.07958$$

$$h_\omega(3) = h_\omega(-3) = 0.07503 \times \frac{1}{4} = 0.01876$$

$$h_\omega(4) = h_\omega(-4) = 0 \times 0 = 0$$

Thus, non-causal filter $H(z) = \sum_{n=-4}^{4} h_\omega(n)\, z^{-n}$

$$\therefore \quad H(z) = 0(z^4 + z^{-4}) + 0.01876(z^3 + z^{-3}) + 0.07958(z^2 + z^{-2}) + 0.16881(z + z^{-1}) + 0.25$$

$$= 0.25 + 0.01876z^3 + 0.07958z^2 + 0.1688z + 0.16881z^{-1} + 0.07958z^{-2} + 0.01876z^{-3}$$

Causal filter (FIR) would be $z^{-4} . H(z)$

$$\therefore \quad \tilde{H}(z) = z^{-4}H(z) = z^{-4}[0.01876z^3 + 0.07958z^2 + 0.16881z + 0.25 + 0.16881z^{-1} + 0.07958z^{-2} + 0.01876z^{-3}]$$ **Ans.**

Note: In this question, a delay of z^{-3} could also work to make the filter a causal.

EXAMPLE 8.14: *The desired frequency response of a low-pass filter is*

$$H_d(e^{j\omega}) = \begin{cases} e^{-j4\omega}, & |\omega| \le \pi/6 \\ 0, & otherwise \end{cases}$$ *(LPF, Bartlett Window)*

By using a window function defined by

$$W(n) = \begin{cases} 1 - 2|n|/(N-1), & |n| \le (N-1)/2 \\ 0, & otherwise \end{cases}$$

and choosing a suitable value of N, design and FIR, causal filter.

SOLUTION: The expression $e^{-j4\omega}$ shows that the delay is 4 *i.e.*, $(N - 1)/2 = 4 \quad \therefore \quad N = 9$ and we have

$$H_d(e^{j\omega}) = \begin{cases} 1, & |\omega| \le \pi/6 \\ 0, & \text{otherwise} \end{cases}$$

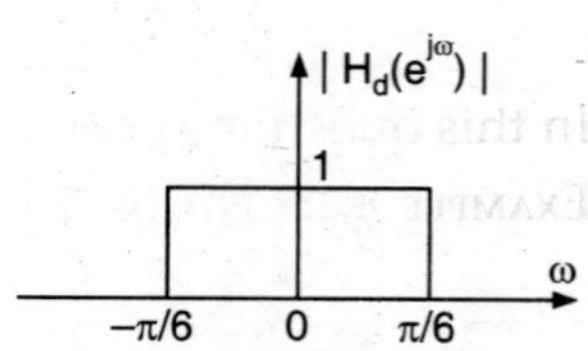

Fig. Ex. 8.14. The desired frequency response

Here $\omega_c = \pi/6$

$$h_d(n) = \frac{\sin n\omega_c}{n\pi}$$

$$= \frac{\sin n\pi/6}{n\pi}$$

$$\therefore \quad h(0) = \frac{1}{6} = 0.167$$

$$h(1) = h(-1) = \frac{\sin(\pi/6)}{\pi} = 0.159$$

$$h(2) = h(-2) = \frac{\sin(2\pi/6)}{2\pi} = 0.1378$$

$$h(3) = h(-3) = \frac{\sin(3\pi/6)}{3\pi} = \frac{1}{3\pi} = 0.1061$$

$$h(4) = h(-4) = \frac{\sin(4\pi/6)}{4\pi} = 0.0689$$

The window (Bartlett window) gives us

$$\omega(0) = 1 - 0 = 1$$

$$\omega(1) = \omega(-1) = 1 - 2 \times 1/8 = 1 - \frac{1}{4} = 0.75$$

$$\omega(2) = \omega(-2) = 1 - 2 \times 2/8 = 0.5$$

$$\omega(3) = \omega(-3) = 1 - 2 \times 3/8 = 0.25$$

$$\omega(4) = \omega(-4) = 1 - 2 \times 4/8 = 0$$

Thus, the windowed impulse response is given by

$$h_\omega(n) = h_d(n) \,.\, \omega(n)$$

$\therefore$

$$h_\omega(0) = 0.167 \times 1 = 0.167$$

$$h_\omega(1) = h_\omega(-1) = 0.159 \times 0.75 = 0.11925$$

$$h_\omega(2) = h_\omega(-2) = 0.1378 \times 0.5 = 0.0689$$

$$h_\omega(3) = h_\omega(-3) = 0.1061 \times 0.25 = 0.0265$$

$$h_\omega(4) = h_\omega(-4) = 0.0689 \times 0 = 0$$

The non-causal filter

$$H(z) = \sum_{n=-4}^{4} h_\omega(n)\, z^{-n}$$

$$= 0(z^4 + z^{-4}) + 0.0265(z^3 + z^{-3}) + 0.0689(z^2 + z^{-2}) + 0.11925(z^1 + z^{-1}) + 0.167$$

$\therefore$ Causal filter is

$$z^{-4} \,.\, H(z) = z^{-4}[0.0265(z^3 + z^{-3}) + 0.0689(z^2 + z^{-2}) + 0.11925(z + z^{-1}) + 0.167] \quad \textbf{Ans.}$$

In this questions even a delay z^{-3} (instead of z^{-4}) would suffice.

EXAMPLE 8.15: *For the Bartlett window defined by*

$$\omega_{BAR}(n) = \begin{cases} 1 - \dfrac{2|n|}{N-1}, & |n| \le \dfrac{(N-1)}{2} \\ 0, & \text{otherwise} \end{cases}$$

find the frequency response.

SOLUTION: Define

$$\frac{N-1}{2} = M$$

∴ The window is characterized by

$$\omega_{BAR}(n) = \begin{cases} 1 - \dfrac{|n|}{M}, & |n| \le M \\ 0, & \text{otherwise} \end{cases}$$

$\left(i.e., \text{ for each increase of } n \text{ by 1, } \omega_{BAR}(n) \text{ varies by } \dfrac{1}{M} \right)$

$$= \begin{cases} 1 - \dfrac{|n|}{M}, & |n| \le M-1 \\ 0, & \text{otherwise} \end{cases}$$

(*i.e.*, total $2M - 1$ non-zero samples)

∵ For $|n| = M$, $\omega_{BAR}(n) = 0$ (A)

Note that $\omega_{BAR}(n)\Big|_{n=0, \frac{M-1}{2}, M-1} = 1, \dfrac{M+1}{2}, \dfrac{1}{M}$

Method-1: Since, the Bartlett window's impulse response is a triangular form as shown, therefore, it can be represented as a convolution of two rectangular windows of half its length, as below:

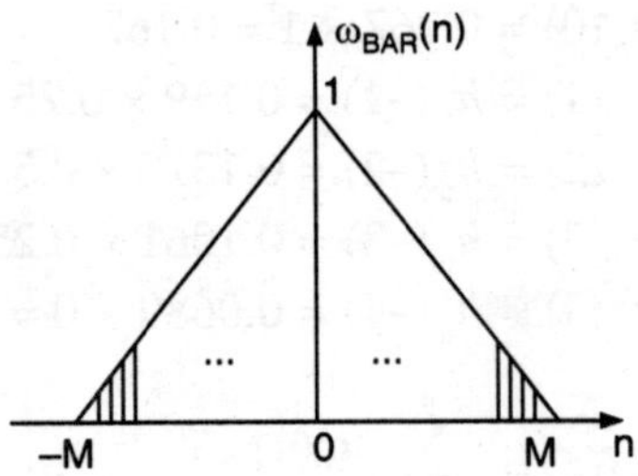

(a)

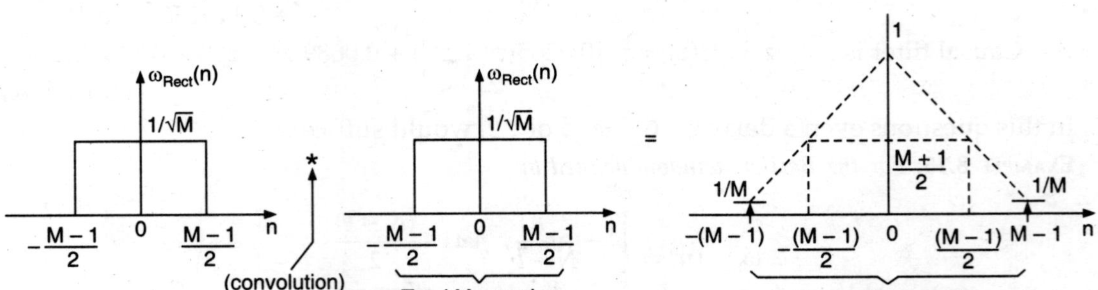

(b) (c)

Fig. Ex. 8.15. (*a*) The window $\omega_{BAR}(n)$, (*b*) convolving $\omega_{RECT}(n)$ with $\omega_{RECT}(n)$, (*c*) Convolution in (*b*) yields a Bartlett sequence *i.e.* $\omega_{REC}(n) * \omega_{REC}(n) = \omega_{BAR}(n)$

where $$\omega_{REC}(n) = \begin{cases} 1/\sqrt{M}, & |n| \le \dfrac{M-1}{2} \\ 0, & \text{otherwise} \end{cases}$$

$$\omega_{BAR}(n) = \begin{cases} 1-\dfrac{|n|}{M}, & |n| \le M-1 \\ 0, & \text{otherwise} \end{cases}$$

As $$\omega_{REC}(n) * \omega_{REC}(n) = \omega_{BAR}(n) \qquad \ldots(B)$$

Taking Fourier transform on both sides of (*B*)

$$FT[\omega_{BAR}(n)] = FT([\omega_{REC}(n)] * [\omega_{REC}(n)])$$

$$= \{FT[\omega_{REC}(n)]\}^2$$

$$= \left\{\frac{1}{\sqrt{M}} \cdot \frac{\sin\dfrac{M\omega}{2}}{\sin\dfrac{\omega}{2}}\right\}^2$$

$$= \frac{1}{M} \frac{\sin^2 \dfrac{M\omega}{2}}{\sin^2 \dfrac{\omega}{2}}$$

$$\therefore \quad W_{BAR}(e^{j\omega}) = \frac{1}{M}\left(\frac{\sin\left(\dfrac{M\omega}{2}\right)}{\sin\left(\dfrac{\omega}{2}\right)}\right)^2, \text{ where } M = \frac{N-1}{2} \text{ i.e., } N = 2M+1 \quad \textbf{Ans.}$$

Method-2:

$$W_{BAR}(e^{j\omega}) = \sum_{n=-M}^{M} \left(1 - \frac{|n|}{M}\right) e^{-j\omega n}$$

$$= \sum_{n=-M}^{M} e^{-j\omega n} - \frac{1}{M}\left[\sum_{n=-M}^{-1} (-n)\, e^{-j\omega n} + \sum_{n=0}^{M} n\, e^{-j\omega n}\right]$$

$$= \sum_{n=-M}^{M} e^{-j\omega n} - \frac{1}{M}\left[\sum_{n=0}^{M} n\, e^{j\omega n} + \sum_{n=0}^{M} n\, e^{-j\omega n}\right]$$

$$\triangleq A(\omega) - \frac{1}{M}[B(\omega) + C(\omega)]$$

$$= A(\omega) - \frac{1}{M}[B(\omega) + B(-\omega)] \qquad \because \; C(\omega) = B(-\omega)$$

where $$A(\omega) = \sum_{n=-M}^{M} e^{-j\omega n} \text{ and } B(\omega) = \sum_{n=0}^{M} n e^{j\omega n} \quad \text{(Note this step)}$$

Now $$A(\omega) = \sum_{n=-M}^{M} e^{-j\omega n} \text{ is } FT \text{ of rectangular window.}$$

We know that

$$\sum_{n=-\left(\frac{N-1}{2}\right)}^{(N-1)/2} e^{-j\omega n} = \frac{\sin\frac{N\omega}{2}}{\sin\frac{\omega}{2}}$$

Putting $N = 2M + 1$, we get

$$A(\omega) = \sum_{n=-M}^{M} e^{-j\omega n} = \frac{\sin\frac{2M+1}{2}\omega}{\sin\frac{\omega}{2}}$$

We also know that

Arithmetic-Geometrical Progression

$$a + (a+d)r + (a+2d)r^2 + \ldots + (a+(P-1)d)r^{P-1} = \sum_{i=0}^{P-1} (a+id)\, r^i$$

↑ P terms

$$= \frac{a}{1-r} - \frac{[a+(P-1)\,d]r^P}{1-r} + \frac{dr\,(1-r^{P-1})}{(1-r)^2}$$

As $$B(\omega) = \sum_{i=0}^{M} (0+i)\, e^{+j\omega i}$$

Comparing with Arithmetic-Geometrical Progression $\sum_{i=0}^{P-1} (a+id)\, r^i$

we have $a = 0, d = 1, r = e^{+j\omega}, P = M + 1$

$$\therefore \quad B(\omega) = \frac{0}{1-e^{+j\omega}} - \frac{(0+M)\, e^{j\omega(M+1)}}{(1-e^{j\omega})} + \frac{e^{j\omega}\,(1-e^{j\omega M})}{(1-e^{j\omega})^2}$$

$$= \frac{1}{(1-e^{j\omega})^2}[-(1-e^{j\omega})\, Me^{j\omega(M+1)} + e^{j\omega}(1-e^{j\omega M})]$$

$$= \frac{1}{e^{j\omega}\left(2j\sin\frac{\omega}{2}\right)^2}\,[e^{j\omega}\{-Me^{j\omega M} + Me^{j\omega(M+1)} + 1 - e^{j\omega M}\}]$$

$$= \frac{-1}{4\sin^2\frac{\omega}{2}}\,[1-(M+1)e^{j\omega M} + Me^{j\omega(M+1)}]$$

$$\therefore A(\omega) - \frac{1}{M}[B(-\omega) + B(-\omega)] = \frac{1}{M}\Big[M \sin\frac{\omega}{2} . \sin\frac{2M+1}{2}\omega + \frac{1}{4}\{2-(M+1)$$

$$(e^{j\omega M} + e^{-j\omega M}) + M(e^{j\omega(M+1)} + e^{-j\omega(M+1)})\}\Big]\Big/\sin^2\frac{\omega}{2}$$

$$\therefore \quad W_{BAR}(e^{j\omega}) = \frac{1}{M\sin^2\frac{\omega}{2}}\Big[M\sin\frac{\omega}{2}\sin\frac{2M+1}{2}\omega + \frac{1}{4}\{2-2(M+1)\cos\omega M$$

$$+ 2M\cos(M+1)\omega\}\Big]$$

$$= \frac{1}{M\sin^2\frac{\omega}{2}}\Big[M\sin\frac{\omega}{2}\sin\omega\frac{2M+1}{2} + \frac{1}{4}\Big\{4\sin^2\frac{\omega M}{2}$$

$$-2M(\cos\omega M - \cos(M+1)\omega)\Big\}\Big]$$

$$= \frac{1}{M\sin^2\frac{\omega}{2}}\Big[M\sin\frac{\omega}{2}\sin\frac{2M+1}{2}\omega + \frac{1}{4}\Big(4\sin^2\frac{\omega M}{2}$$

$$-4M\sin\frac{\omega}{2}\sin\frac{2M+1}{2}\omega\Big)\Big]$$

$$= \frac{\sin^2\frac{M\omega}{2}}{M\sin^2\frac{\omega}{2}} = \frac{1}{M}\left(\frac{\sin\frac{M\omega}{2}}{\sin\frac{\omega}{2}}\right)^2 \qquad \textbf{Ans.}$$

EXAMPLE 8.16: *Show that the Kaiser window includes the rectangular window as a special case.*

SOLUTION: The Kaiser window is defined as

$$\omega_K(n) = \begin{cases} \frac{I_0(\beta)}{I_0(\alpha)}, & |n| \le \frac{N-1}{2} \\ 0, & \text{otherwise} \end{cases}$$

and the rectangular window is defined as

$$\omega_R(n) = \begin{cases} 1, & |n| \le \frac{N-1}{2} \\ 0, & \text{otherwise} \end{cases}$$

Thus, for the Kaiser window to function as a rectangular window, we must have

$$\frac{I_0(\beta)}{I_0(\alpha)} = 1 \text{ for all } n$$

i.e.,
$$\alpha = \beta \text{ for all } n$$

But
$$\beta = \alpha\sqrt{1-\left(\frac{2n}{N-1}\right)^2}$$

$$\therefore \quad \alpha = \alpha\sqrt{1-\left(\frac{2n}{N-1}\right)^2} \text{ for all values of } n \qquad (\text{putting } \beta = \alpha)$$

i.e., $\alpha = \beta = 0$ must hold for all values of n

$\because$ then $$\frac{I_0(\beta)}{I_0(\alpha)} = \frac{I_0(0)}{I_0(0)} = \frac{1}{1} = 1 \text{ for all } n$$

Thus, for $\alpha = \beta = 0$, the Kaiser window becomes a rectangular window.

> **Note:** One possibility seems to be
>
> $$\sqrt{1\left(\frac{2n}{N-1}\right)^2} = 2 \text{ i.e., } 1-\left(\frac{2n}{N-1}\right)^2 = 1$$
>
> $\therefore$ *i.e.* $n = 0$. But it is not a generic result for all n. *Hence,* $n = 0$ is not the answer.

EXAMPLE 8.17: *Design a low-pass filter satisfying the following specifications:*
Passband ripple in the frequency range 0 to 1.5 rad/s ≤ 0.1 dB.
Minimum stop band attenuation in the frequency range 2.5 to 5.0 rad/s ≥ 40 dB.
Sampling frequency 10 rad/s.

SOLUTION:

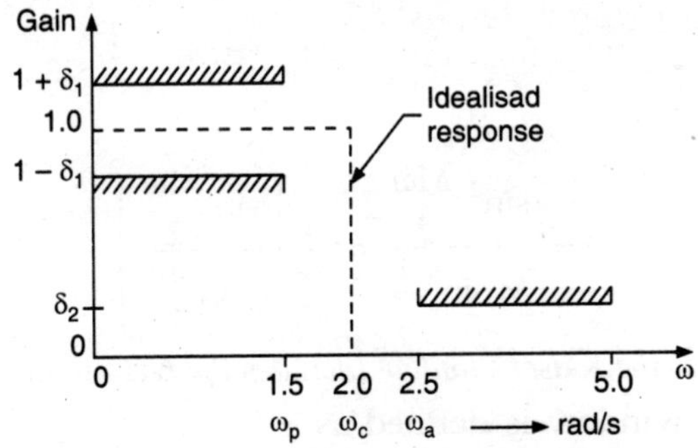

Fig. Ex. 8.17. (*a*) The specified LPF

Step 1: Here, $$\omega_s = 10 \text{ rad/s}$$

$\therefore$ $$T = \frac{1}{f_s} = \frac{2\pi}{10} = \frac{\pi}{5} = 0.682 \text{ s.}$$

(*i*) $$\omega_c = \frac{1}{2}(\omega_p + \omega_a) = \frac{1}{2}(1.5 + 2.5) = 2 \text{ rad/s}$$

(*ii*) $$H(e^{j\omega}) = \begin{cases} 1, & |\omega| \le 2 \\ 0, & \text{otherwise} \end{cases}$$

(*iii*) $$h(n) = \frac{1}{2\pi}\int_{-\omega_c T}^{\omega_c T} 1 \,.\, e^{j\omega n}\, d\omega^{**}$$

$$= \frac{\sin \omega_c T n}{n\pi} = \frac{\sin 2nT}{n\pi} = \frac{\sin\left(\frac{2\pi}{5}\right)n}{n\pi}$$

**The formula $h(n) = \frac{1}{2\pi}\int_{-\pi}^{\pi} H(e^{j\omega}) . e^{j\omega n}\, d\omega = \frac{1}{2\pi}\int_{-\omega_c}^{\omega_c} 1 . e^{j\omega n}\, d\omega$ holds good for normalized ω's. Here normalized ω_c = actual ω_c/f_s = (actual ω_c) $T = 2T$.

(*iv*) $B_t = \omega_a - \omega_p = 2.5 - 1.5 = 1$ rad/s.

Step 2: As $\boxed{A_p = 20 \log \frac{1+\delta_1}{1-\delta_1}}$ $\therefore \quad \frac{1+\delta_1}{1-\delta_1} = 10^{A_p/20}$

Hence,
$$\delta_1 = \frac{(10^{0.05A_p} - 1)}{(10^{0.05A_p} + 1)}$$

$$\delta_1 = \frac{(10^{0.05A_p} - 1)}{(10^{0.05A_p} + 1)} = \frac{(10^{0.05(0.1)} - 1)}{(10^{0.05(0.1)} + 1)}$$
$$= 0.0057564 = 5.7564 \times 10^{-3}$$
$$\delta_2 = 10^{-0.05A_a} = 10^{-0.05(40)} = 0.01 = 10.00 \times 10^{-3}$$
$$\boxed{A_a \triangleq -20 \log_{10} \delta_2}$$

Choose
$$\delta = \min(\delta_1, \delta_2)$$
$$= \min(5.7564 \times 10^{-3}, 10.00 \times 10^{-3})$$
$$= 5.7564 \times 10^{-3}$$

Step 3: Choosing δ of step 2, recalculate A_a as
$$A_a = -20 \log \delta = -20 \log (5.7564 \times 10^{-3}) = 44.797 \text{ dB}.$$

Step 4: Choose parameter α from:
$$\alpha = \begin{cases} 0 & , \quad A_a < 21 \text{ dB} \\ 0.5842(A_a - 21)^{0.4} + 0.07886\,(A_a - 21), & 21 < A_a \le 50 \\ 0.1102\,(A_a - 8.7) & , \quad A_a > 50 \text{ dB} \end{cases}$$

$\therefore$ Here
$$\alpha = 0.5842\,(44.797 - 21)^{0.4} + 0.07886\,(44.797 - 21)$$
$$= 3.9524.$$

Step 5: Choose D from:
$$D = \begin{cases} 0.9222, & A_a \le 21 \\ \dfrac{A_a - 7.95}{14.36}, & A_a > 21 \end{cases}$$

$\therefore$
$$D = (44.797 - 7.95)/14.36 = 2.5659.$$

Step 6: Select the lowest odd value of N satisfying the inequality
$$N \ge \frac{\omega_s D}{B_t} + 1$$

$\therefore$
$$N \ge \frac{10(2.5659)}{1.0} + 1 \quad i.e., N \ge 26.659 \quad \because \quad \text{Choose } N = 27.$$

Step 7: From
$$\omega_K(n) = \begin{cases} \dfrac{I_0(\beta)}{I_0(\alpha)}, & |n| \le \dfrac{(N-1)}{2} \\ 0 \quad , & \text{otherwise} \end{cases}$$

We require Bessel's function curves to compute $\omega_K(n)$.

Step 8: The causal filter is given by $H'_W(z) = z^{-(N-1)/2} \cdot ZT[\omega_K(n) \cdot h(n)]$

Calculation of $h(nT)$ *i.e.,* $h(n)$

We know that the 'normalised ω_c'' = (ω_c in rad/s)/f_s.

Here, ω_c in rad/s =2.0 and $f_s = \dfrac{5}{\pi}$ Hz

$$\therefore \qquad \text{Normalised } \omega_c = \frac{2.0}{(5/\pi)} = \frac{2\pi}{5} \text{ rad}$$

Hence,
$$h(n) = h(nT) = \frac{\sin \omega_c n}{n\pi} = \frac{\sin \dfrac{2\pi n}{5}}{n\pi}$$

$$'h(0)' = \lim_{n\to 0} \frac{\sin \dfrac{2\pi n}{5}}{n\pi} = \lim_{n\to 0} \frac{\sin \dfrac{2\pi n}{5}}{\dfrac{2\pi n}{5}} \times \frac{2}{5} = 0.4$$

$$h(1) = \frac{\sin\left(\dfrac{2\pi}{5}\right)}{(1\,.\,\pi)} = 0.302731$$

$$h(2) = \frac{\sin\left(\dfrac{4\pi}{5}\right)}{(2\,.\,\pi)} = 0.0935489$$

Similarly, we find '$h(3)$' to '$h(13)$'. $h(nT)$ and $h_\omega(nT)$ are given below:

n	$h(nT)$	$\omega_K(nT) \cdot h(nT)$
0	4.00000×10^{-1}	4.00000×10^{-1}
1	3.02731×10^{-1}	2.99692×10^{-1}
2	9.35489×10^{-2}	8.98359×10^{-2}
3	-6.23660×10^{-2}	-5.69018×10^{-2}
4	-7.56827×10^{-2}	-6.42052×10^{-2}
5	0.0	0.0
6	5.04551×10^{-2}	3.45003×10^{-2}
7	2.67283×10^{-2}	1.57769×10^{-2}
8	-2.33872×10^{-2}	-1.15598×10^{-2}
9	-3.36367×10^{-2}	1.34373×10^{-2}
10	0.0	0.0
11	2.75210×10^{-2}	6.23505×10^{-3}
12	1.55915×10^{-2}	2.39574×10^{-3}
13	-1.43921×10^{-2}	-1.32685×10^{-3}

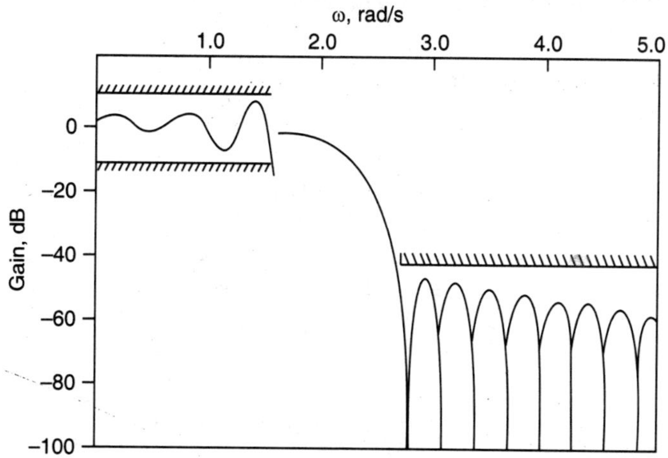

Fig. Ex. 8.17. (*b*) The amplitude response of low-pass filter designed by using Kaiser window

EXAMPLE 8.18: *Design a bandpass filter satisfying the specifications:*
Minimum attenuation for $0 \le \omega \le 200$: *45 dB*
Passband ripple for $400 < \omega < 600$: *0.2 dB*
Minimum attenuation for $700 \le \omega < 1000$: *45 dB*
Sampling frequency: 2000 rad/s.

SOLUTION:

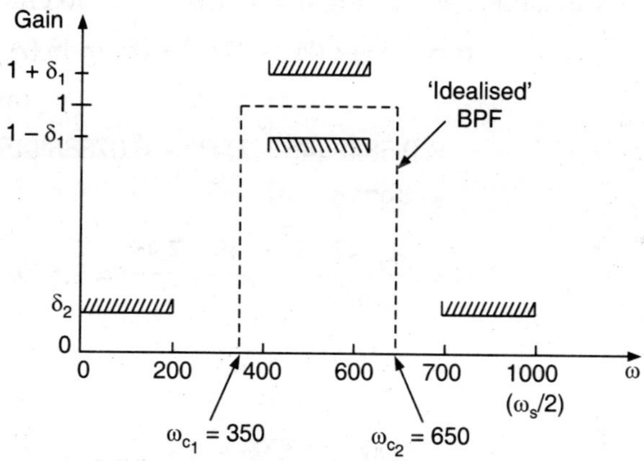

Fig. Ex. 8.18. (*a*) The specified BPF

Step 1: $\omega_s = 2000 \text{ rad/s}$

$\therefore$ $$T = \frac{2\pi}{\omega_s} = \frac{2\pi}{2000} = \frac{\pi}{1000}$$

(*i*) $$B_t = \min[(400 - 200), (700 - 600)] = 100 \text{ rad/s}$$

(*ii*) $$\omega_{c_1} = \omega_{p_1} - B_t/2 = 400 - \frac{100}{2} = 350 \text{ rad/s}$$

$$\omega_{c_2} = \omega_{p_2} + B_t/2 = 600 + \frac{100}{2} = 650 \text{ rad/s}$$

(iii) $$H(e^{j\omega}) = \begin{cases} 0, & 0 \le |\omega| \le \omega_{c_1} \\ 1, & \omega_{c_1} \le |\omega| \le \omega_{c_2} \\ 0, & \omega_{c_2} \le |\omega| \le \omega_{s/2} \end{cases}$$

(iv) $$h(n) = \frac{1}{\omega_s} \int_{-\omega_s/2}^{\omega_s/2} H(e^{j\omega})\, e^{j\omega nT}\, d\omega$$

$$= \frac{1}{\omega_s} \int_{0}^{w_s/2} H(e^{j\omega})\,[e^{j\omega nT} + e^{-j\omega nT}]\, d\omega$$

$$\because \quad H(e^{-j\omega}) = H(e^{j\omega})$$

$$= \frac{1}{\omega_s} \int_{\omega_{c_1}}^{\omega_{c_2}} 1 . 2 \cos \omega nT \, d\omega$$

$$= \frac{1}{\pi n} (\sin \omega_{c_2} nT - \sin \omega_{c_1} nT).$$ (** see footnote)

Step 2: $$\delta_1 = \frac{(10^{0.05(0.2)} - 1)}{(10^{0.05(0.2)} + 1)} = 1.1512 \times 10^{-2}$$

$$\delta_2 = 10^{-0.05(45)} = 5.6234 \times 10^{-3}$$

$$\delta = \min(\delta_1, \delta_2) = 5.6234 \times 10^{-3}.$$

Step 3: Revised $A_a = -20 \log \delta = 45$ dB (No change)

Step 4: $$\alpha = 0.5842\,(A_a - 21)^{0.4} + 0.07886\,(A_a - 21)$$

(as A_a lies 21 to 50 range)

$$= 0.5842\,(45 - 21)^{0.4} + 0.07886\,(45 - 21)$$

$$= 3.9754.$$

Step 5: $$D = \frac{A_a - 7.95}{14.36} = \frac{45 - 7.95}{14.36} = 2.5793.$$

Step 6: $$N \ge \frac{\omega_s D}{B_t} + 1, N \text{ odd}$$

$$= \frac{2000 \times 2.5793}{100} + 1 = 52.586$$

$\therefore$ $N = 53$ (nearest odd)

** **Note:** The above expression for $h(n)$ can also be used

for LPF: by putting $\omega_{c_1} = 0$

$\omega_{c_2} = \omega_c$

for HPF: by putting $\omega_{c_1} = \omega_c$

$\omega_{c_2} = \omega_s/2$

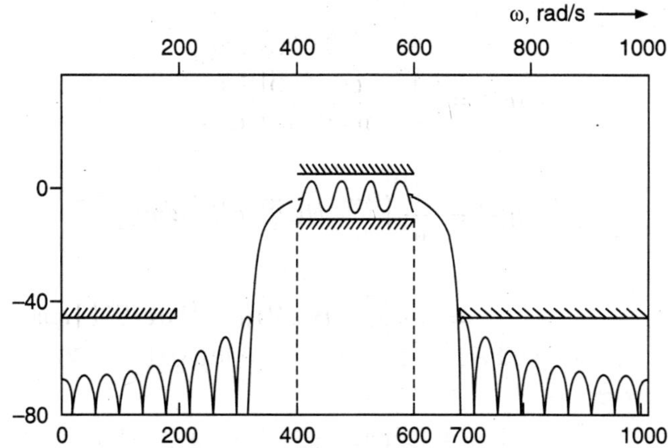

Fig. Ex. 8.18. (*b*) The amplitude response of the filter designed, by using Kaiser window

EXAMPLE 8.19: *Find the order of the FIR bandpass filter required to meet the following specifications*

$$A_p \le 0.2\ dB,\ A_a \ge 40\ dB$$

$$\omega_{p_1} = 2000\ rads/s,\ \omega_{p_2} = 3000\ rads/s$$

$$\omega_{a_1} = 1000\ rads/s,\ \omega_{a_2} = 4000\ rads/s,\ \omega_s = 10{,}000\ rad/s.$$

Use Kaiser window in your design.

SOLUTION:

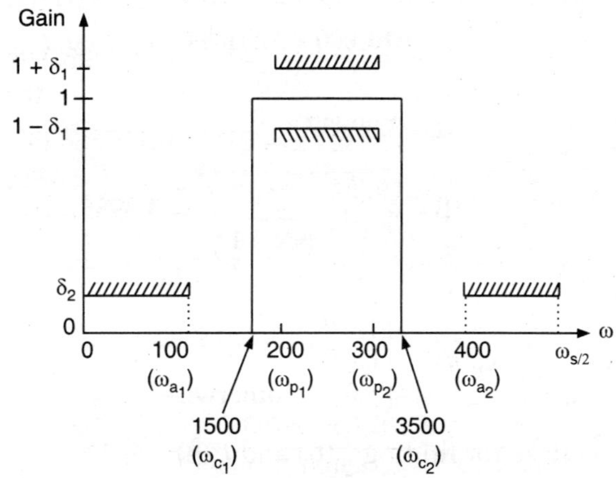

Fig. Ex. 8.19. The specified and the idealised BPF's

Step 1: (*i*)

$$B_t = \min\,[(2000 - 1000),\ (4000 - 3000)]$$
$$= 1000\ \text{rad/s}$$

(*ii*)

$$\omega_{c_1} = \omega_{p_1} - B_t/2 = 2000 - \frac{1000}{2}$$
$$= 1500\ \text{rad/s}$$

$$\omega_{c_2} = \omega_{p_2} + B_t/2 = 3500\ \text{rad/s}$$

(*iii*)
$$H(e^{j\omega}) = \begin{cases} 1, & 1500 \le |\omega| \le 3500 \\ 0, & 0 \le |\omega| \le 1500 \\ 0, & 3500 \le |\omega| \le 5000 \end{cases}$$

Step 2:
$$\delta_1 = \frac{(10^{0.05(0.2)} - 1)}{(10^{0.05(0.2)} + 1)} = \frac{1.023293 - 1}{1.023293 + 1} = 0.0115124$$

$$\delta_2 = 10^{-0.05(40)} = 0.01$$

$$\delta = \min(\delta_1, \delta_2) = \min(0.0115124, 0.01) = 0.01$$

Step 3: Revised $A_a = -20 \log \delta = -20 \log 0.01 = +40$

Step 4: Choose α from

$$\alpha = 0.5852\,(A_a - 21)^{0.4} + 0.07886\,(A_a - 21)$$

(A_a is between 21 and 50)

$$= 0.5852\,(40 - 21)^{0.4} + 0.07886\,(40 - 21) = 3.39857$$

Step 5: Choose D from

$$D = \frac{A_a - 7.95}{14.36} = \frac{40 - 7.95}{14.36} = 2.2318941$$

Step 6: Select N from

$$N \ge \frac{\omega_s D}{B_t} + 1$$

$$\ge \frac{10{,}000 \times 2.2318941}{1000} + 1 \ge 23.318941 = 25 \text{ (N being odd)}$$

Thus,
$$\alpha = 3.39857$$

$$\beta = \alpha \sqrt{1 - \left(\frac{2n}{N-1}\right)^2} = 3.39857\,\sqrt{1 - (12n)^2} \qquad (\because N = 25)$$

Take Kaiser window
$$\omega_K(n) = \begin{cases} \dfrac{I_0(\beta)}{I_0(\alpha)}, & |n| \le 12 \\ 0\;, & \text{otherwise} \end{cases}$$

We need the Bessel's curve for finding $I_0(\alpha)$ and $I_0(\beta)$.

8.7 FREQUENCY-SAMPLING TECHNIQUE TO DESIGN FIR FILTERS

Here, a set of samples is determined from the desired frequency response and this set is taken as a discrete Fourier transform (DFT). The filter coefficients are then determined as the IDFT of this set of samples.

The set of frequency samples can be obtained by sampling a desired frequency response, $H_d(e^{j\omega})$, at N equally spaced points ω_k, $k = 0, 1, ..., N - 1$, over the unit circle.

Type I Design

Here

$$\omega_k = \frac{2\pi k}{N}, k = 0, 1, 2, ..., N-1 \qquad ...(8.63)$$

Sampling the desired frequency response $H_d(e^{j\omega})$ at ω_k, we get

$$\tilde{H}(k) \triangleq H_d(e^{j\omega})\Big|_{\omega=\omega_k}, k = 0, 1, 2, ..., N-1$$

$$= H_d(e^{j2\pi k/N}) \qquad ...(8.64)$$

From DFT points $\tilde{H}(k)$, so obtained, we can use IDFT to compute the coefficients $h(n)$ *i.e.*,

$$h(n) = \frac{1}{N}\sum_{k=0}^{N-1} \tilde{H}(k)\, e^{j2\pi nk/N}, n = 0, 1, ..., N-1 \qquad ...(8.65)$$

We wish to obtain real valued coefficients $h(n)$. This is possible if $\tilde{H}(0)$ is real as well as $\tilde{H}(N-k) = \tilde{H}^*(k)$, and a few more conditions as follows.

If N is odd and $\tilde{H}(0)$ is real, then we note that

$$\tilde{H}(N-k)\; e^{j2\pi n(N-k)/N} = \tilde{H}(N-k)\; .\, e^{-j2\pi nk/N}$$

If additionally,

$$\tilde{H}(N-k) = \tilde{H}^*(k), k = 1, 2, ..., \frac{(N-1)}{2}$$

then

$$\tilde{H}(N-k)\, e^{\frac{j2\pi n(N-k)}{N}} = \tilde{H}^*(k)\; .\, e^{-j2\pi nk/N}$$

$$= [\tilde{H}(k)\, .\, e^{-j2\pi nk/N}]^*, k = 1, 2, ..., \frac{(N-1)}{2}$$

Thus,

$$h(n) = \frac{1}{N}\left[\tilde{H}(0) + \sum_{k=1}^{N-1} \tilde{H}(k)\, e^{j2\pi nk/N}\right]$$

$$= \frac{1}{N}\left\{\tilde{H}(0) + \sum_{k=1}^{(N-1)/2} [(\tilde{H}(k)\, e^{j2\pi nk/N}) + (\tilde{H}(k)\, e^{j2\pi nk/N})^*]\right\}$$

$$k = 1, 2, ..., \frac{(N-1)}{2}$$

$$= \frac{1}{N}\left[\tilde{H}(0) + 2\sum_{k=1}^{(N-1)/2} \text{Re}\, [\tilde{H}(k)\, e^{j2\pi nk/N}\right], \; N \text{ odd.}$$

Hence, For N odd, $\tilde{H}(0)$ = a real quantity and $\tilde{H}(N-k) = \tilde{H}^*(k)$

$$h(n) = \frac{1}{N}\left[\tilde{H}(0) + 2\sum_{k=1}^{(N-1)/2} \text{Re}\,[\tilde{H}(k)\, e^{j2\pi nk/N}\right], N \text{ odd} \qquad \ldots(8.66)$$

gives the real values of the coefficients $h(n)$.

Similarly,

For N even, $\tilde{H}(0)$ = real quantity and $\tilde{H}(N-k) = \tilde{H}^*(k)$; $\tilde{H}(N/2) = 0$

$$h(n) = \frac{1}{N}\left[\tilde{H}(0) + 2\sum_{k=1}^{N/2-1} \text{Re}\,[\tilde{H}(k)\, e^{j2\pi nk/N}\right], N \text{ even} \qquad \ldots(8.67)$$

gives the real values of the coefficients $h(n)$. It may be noted that if $\tilde{H}(0)$ is included and N is even, then $\tilde{H}(N/2)$ will lie at $\omega = \pi$, and $\tilde{H}(N/2)$ will zero for LPF and BPFs. For HPF $\tilde{H}(N/2)$ will not be zero so for HPFs, we must take N odd if $\tilde{H}(0)$ is an included sample of $\tilde{H}(k)$.

The $h(n)$ as derived above will yield exact $H_d(e^{j\omega})$ at $\omega_k = \frac{2\pi k}{N}$. However, the response $H(e^{j\omega}) = \sum_{n=1}^{N-1} h(n)\, e^{-j\omega n}$ will not yield exact $H_d(e^{j\omega})$ at other frequencies except at $\omega_k = \frac{2\pi k}{N}$.

Type-II Design

(A sample at $\omega = 0$ not included)

Here,

$$\omega_k = \frac{2\pi(2k+1)}{2N}, k = 0, 1, 2, \ldots, N-1 \qquad \ldots(8.68)$$

$$= \frac{2\pi\left(k+\frac{1}{2}\right)}{N}, k = 0, 1, 2, \ldots, N-1 \qquad \ldots(8.69)$$

i.e., we take DFT coefficient samples as:

$$\tilde{H}(k) = H_d(e^{j\omega k})$$
$$= H_d(e^{j\pi(2k+1)N}) \,.\, k = 0, 1, 2, \ldots, N-1 \qquad \ldots(8.70)$$

(*i*) If N is odd

$$\left.\begin{aligned} \tilde{H}(N-k-1) &= \tilde{H}^*(k), k = 0, 1, \ldots, N-1 \\ \tilde{H}\left(\frac{N-1}{2}\right) &= 0 \text{ (as in LPF, BPF)} \end{aligned}\right\} \qquad \ldots(8.71)$$

Points for N odd are shown in Fig. 8.17 (*a*). For type I, $k = 0$ starts from $\omega = 0$. For type II, $k = 0$ starts from $\omega = \dfrac{\pi}{N}$.

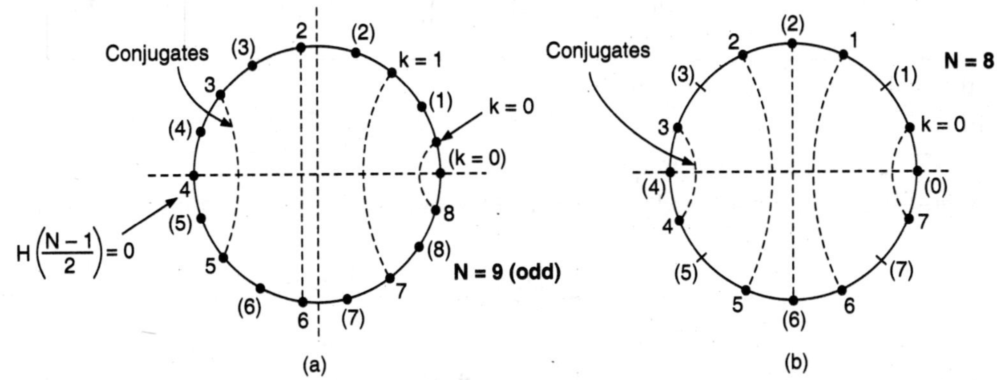

Fig. 8.17. (*a*) Location of $\tilde{H}(k)$ points for N odd (*a*) Points shown in brackets *i.e.*, (k = (0), (1), (2) ..., (8)) are for type I. and points k = 0, 1, 2, ..., 8 are for type II. (*b*) Location of $\tilde{H}(k)$ points for N even.

(*ii*) If *N* is even

$$\tilde{H}(N-k-1) = \tilde{H}^*(k),\ k = 0, 1, 2, ..., \left(\frac{N}{2}-1\right) \qquad ...(8.72)$$

After choosing $\tilde{H}(k)$ samples as above, we obtain

$$h(n) = \frac{2}{N} \sum_{k=0}^{(N-3)/2} \text{Re}\,[\tilde{H}(k) \,.\, e^{j\pi n(2k+1)N}],\ N \text{ odd} \qquad ...(8.73)$$

$$\nearrow \tilde{H}\left(\frac{N-1}{2}\right) = 0 \text{ in } (8.71)$$

$$n = 0, 1, ..., N-1$$

$$h(n) = \frac{2}{N} \sum_{k=0}^{N/2-1} \text{Re}\,[\tilde{H}(k)\, e^{j\pi n(2k+1)N}],\ N \text{ even} \qquad ...(8.74)$$

$$n = 0, 1, ..., N-1$$

Aid to memory

To draw Type-I sampling circle, start for $k = 0$ at $\omega = 0$. Then go on joining new sample points by progressing anti-clockwise by $\dfrac{2\pi}{N}$ radians. See points shown in brackets in Fig. 8.17 (*b*) *i.e.*, (k = 0), (1), (2), ..., (8).

To draw Type-II, the first sample ($k = 0$) is at $\frac{2\pi}{2N}$ *i.e.,* $\frac{\pi}{N}$ radians. Then go on joining new sample points by progressing anti-clockwise by $\frac{2\pi}{N}$ radians. See points $k = 0, 1, 2, ..., 8$ in Fig. (*a*), for type-II designs.

The numbering $k = 0, 1, ..., N - 1$, for type-II is $\frac{\pi}{N}$ radians ahead (anti-clockwise) of the respective *k*'s of type-I sampling frequencies.

Once $h(n)$ has been determined, the system function of the designed filter is given by

$$H(z) = \sum_{n=0}^{N-1} h(n)\, z^{-n}$$

Note that

$$\begin{aligned} H(z)\Big|_{z=e^{j2\pi k/N}} &= \sum_{n=0}^{N-1} h(n)\, e^{-j2\pi nk/N} \\ &= \text{DFT of } h(n) \\ &= \tilde{H}(k) \\ &= H_d(e^{j2\pi k/N}) \end{aligned}$$

Thus, the values of $H(e^{j\omega})$ and $H_\alpha(e^{j\omega})$ coincide when $\omega = \omega_k = 2\pi k/N$. At other values of ω, we can think of $H(e^{j\omega})$ as an interpolation of the sampled desired frequency response.

If the frequency response $H(e^{j\omega})$ is not suitable, then we might increase N and/or vary $H_d(e^{j\omega})$.

It is also possible to improve the approximation $H(e^{j\omega})$ if some of the samples of $\tilde{H}(k)$ are taken not those given by $H_d(e^{j\omega})$ but their values are determined so as to optimize the frequency response $H(e^{j\omega})$.

EXAMPLE 8.20: *(FIR filter by frequency sampling)*

Design a linear phase, FIR filter by frequency-sampling technique, to approximate an ideal low-pass filter with $\omega_c = \frac{\pi}{2}$.

SOLUTION: The ideal frequency response is given by

$$H_d(e^{j\omega}) = \begin{cases} e^{-j(N-1)\omega/2}, & 0 \le \omega \le \frac{\pi}{2} \\ 0, & \text{otherwise} \end{cases} \qquad (A)$$

The given response is for a causal, linear-phase FIR filter.

Assume N = 17

The ideal magnitude and phase responses are as shown in figure 8.20 for $N = 17$. (We have added π rads to the phase response at $\omega = \frac{\pi}{2}$, we could have subtracted π rads just as well). The samples, obtained from $H_d(e^{j\omega})$ for $N = 17$ are:

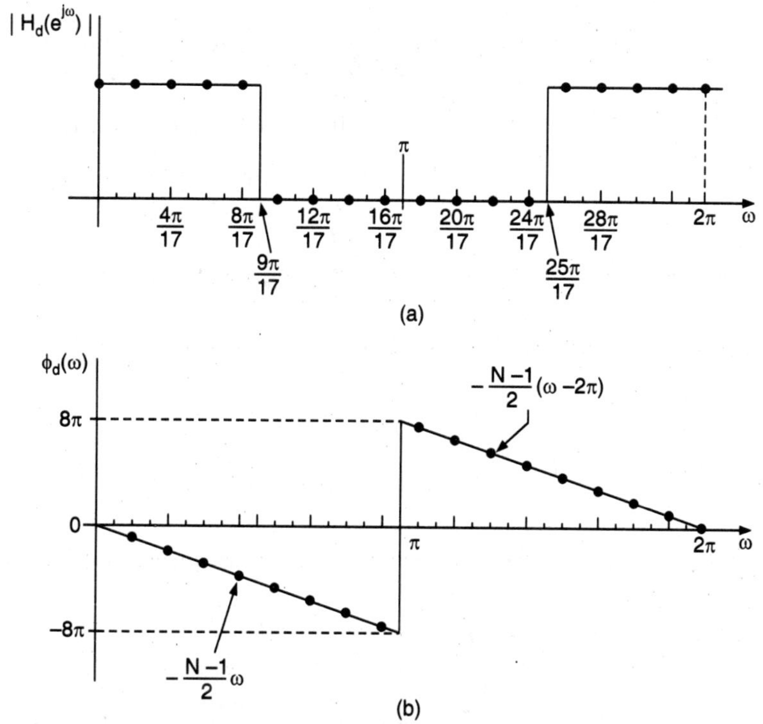

Fig. Ex. 8.20. Magnitude and phase responses for $H_d(e^{j\omega})$ given in (*A*)

$$\tilde{H}(k) = H_d(e^{j2\pi k/17})$$

$$= \begin{cases} e^{-j16\pi k/17}, & 0 \le k \le 4 \\ 0, & 5 \le k \le 12 \\ e^{-j16\pi(k-17)/17}, & 13 \le k \le 16 \end{cases} \qquad \left.\begin{array}{r}\text{putting } N = 17 \\ \text{and } \omega = \dfrac{2\pi}{17}k\end{array}\right\} \text{ in } (A)$$

Note that $\tilde{H}(0) = 1$, a real quantity

$$\tilde{H}(16) = e^{-j16\pi(-1)/17}$$

$$= e^{j16\pi/17} = \tilde{H}^*(1) \text{ and so on.}$$

Thus, here $\tilde{H}(N-k) = \tilde{H}^*(k)$ is obeyed. Hence, we have

$$h(n) = \frac{1}{N}\left[\tilde{H}(0) + 2\sum_{k=1}^{(N-1)/2} \text{Re}\,\{\tilde{H}(k)\,e^{j2\pi nk/N}\}\right], n = 0, 1, ..., N-1$$

$$= \frac{1}{17}\left[1 + 2\sum_{k=1}^{8} \text{Re}\,\{e^{-j16\pi k/17}\,.\,e^{j2\pi nk/17}\}\right]$$

$$= \frac{1}{17}\left[1 + 2\sum_{k=1}^{4} \text{Re}\{e^{-j2\pi k(8-n)/17}\}\right]$$

$$= \frac{1}{17}\left[1 + 2\sum_{k=1}^{4} \cos\frac{2\pi k(8-n)}{17}\right]$$

The values of all the weights $h(0), h(1), ..., h(16)$ can be easily computed from expression for $h(n)$.

EXAMPLE 8.21: *A low-pass filter has the desired frequency response*

$$H_d(e^{j\omega}) = \begin{cases} e^{-j3\omega}, & 0 \le |\omega| < \frac{\pi}{2} \\ 0, & \frac{\pi}{2} \le |\omega| \le \pi \end{cases}$$

Determine the filter coefficients h(n) for N = 7, using type-I frequency sampling technique.

SOLUTION: We replace ω by $\omega_k = \frac{2\pi k}{N} = \frac{2\pi k}{7}, k = 0, 1, ..., 6$

Given $N = 7$ and a sample at $\omega = 0$ is included. $\omega_k = \frac{2\pi k}{7}, k = 0, 1, ..., 6$

The samples would be as follows:

$$H(k) = \begin{cases} e^{-j3(2\pi k/7)} & , k = 0, 1 \\ 0 & , k = 2, 3, 4, 5 \\ e^{-j3(2\pi 6/7)} = e^{-j36\pi k/7)} & , k = 6 \end{cases}$$

i.e., $H(k)$ are non-zero only for $k = 0, 1, 6$ within the passband. The filter coefficients are given by

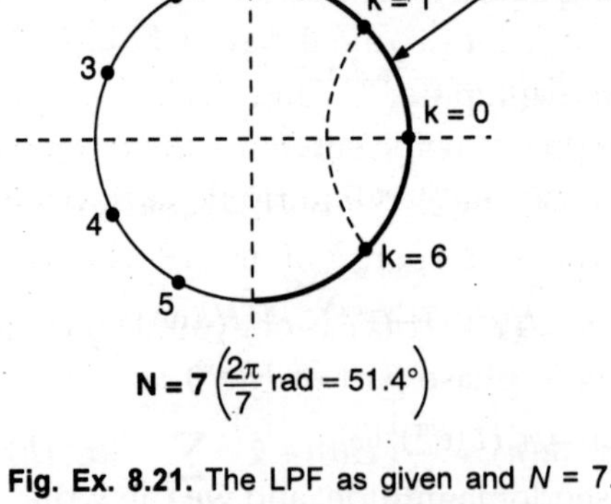

Fig. Ex. 8.21. The LPF as given and $N = 7$.
Only $k = 0, 1, 6$ falls in passband range.

$$h(n) = \frac{1}{N}\left[\sum_{k=0}^{6} H(k)\, e^{j2\pi kn/7}\right], n = 0, 1, 2, ..., 6$$

Replace $H_d(e^{j\omega})$ by its discrete samples $e^{-j3\frac{2\pi}{7}k}$, $k = 0, 1, ..., 6$ and then compute $h(n)$

$$\therefore \quad h(n) = \frac{1}{7}\left[\left(\sum_{k=0}^{1} \underset{\nearrow H(k)}{(e^{-j6\pi k/7})} . e^{j2\pi kn/7}\right) + \underset{\nearrow H(6)}{e^{-j36\pi/7}} . e^{j2\pi kn/7}\Big|_{k=6}\right]$$

$$= \frac{1}{7}\left[1 + e^{(-j6\pi/7 + j2\pi n/7)} + e^{j12\pi(n-3)/7}\right]$$

$$= \frac{1}{7}[1 + e^{j2\pi(n-3)/7} + e^{j2\pi(n-3)/7}]$$

$$= \frac{1}{7}\left[1 + 2\cos\left(2\pi\frac{(n-3)}{7}\right)\right]$$

$$h(n) = 0.1429 + \frac{2}{7}\cos\left(\frac{2\pi}{7}(n-3)\right) \quad \textbf{Ans.}$$

8.8 DESIGN OF OPTIMUM EQUIRIPPLE FIR FILTERS

It is well-known that the optimal analog filters are those which are equiripple in both the passband and the stopband. This is also true for linear-phase FIR digital filters. The design approach for these filters is based on minimax or Chebyshev-type approximation. This procedure is based on computer optimisation technique. The technique involves determination of a weighted error function based on the desired magnitude of the filter, since, ideal filter are impossible to realize, we always specify the tolerances in the passband and the stopband of the practical filters. The ripples in the passband having equal magnitudes, say, $\pm\ \delta_1$ are termed as equiripple passband. Similarly, the ripples in the stopband, if equal, say, $\pm\ \delta_2$ are called equiripple stopband. If $\delta_1 = \delta_2$, then the time taken by the computer to find design weights is relatively less. The design weight (also called impulse response coefficients $h(n)$) are so computed by the computing algorithm such that the frequency response $H(e^{j\omega})$ is equiripple as specified.

We know that the linear phase response of an FIR filter is of the form

$$H(e^{j\omega}) = e^{-j\omega(N-1)/2}\, H_1(\omega) \qquad ...(8.75)$$

where $H_1(\omega)$ is the value of zero phase part of $H(e^{j\omega})$ *i.e.*,

$$H_1(\omega) = |\, H(e^{j\omega})\, |.$$

$H_1(\omega)$ is also called the pseudomagnitude, and we can write

$$H_1(\omega) = Q(\omega) . P(\omega) \qquad ...(8.76)$$

where $P(\omega)$ and $Q(\omega)$ are given by (see solved example 8.6)

Table 8.3

N	$Q(\omega)$	$P(\omega)$
odd	1	$\sum_{n=0}^{(N-1)/2} a(n) \cos n\omega$
even	$\cos\left(\frac{\omega}{2}\right)$	$\sum_{n=0}^{(N/2)-1} \tilde{b}(n) \cos n\omega$

Note: The upper limit of summation for $P(\omega)$ is denoted by N_0.

In the case of a low-pass filter, the desired (ideal) function to be approximated optimally is

$$\tilde{H}_1(\omega) = \begin{cases} 1, & 0 \le \omega \le \omega_p \\ 0, & \omega_s \le \omega \le \pi \end{cases} \qquad ...(8.77)$$

where $0 \le \omega \le \omega_p$ is the passband, and $\omega_s \le \omega \le \pi$ is the stopband. The weighted error function is defined by

$$E(\omega) = W(\omega)\,[\tilde{H}_1(\omega) - H_1(\omega)] \qquad ...(8.78)$$

where function (called the error weighting function). $E(\omega)$ is defined as

$$W(\omega) = \begin{cases} 1/k, & 0 \le \omega \le \omega_p \\ 1, & \omega_s \le \omega \le \pi \end{cases} \qquad ...(8.79)$$

According to the theory of approximation (minimax approximation), the minimum of the maximum absolute error $|E(\omega)|$ over the passband and stopbands, $0 \le \omega \le \omega_p$ and $\omega_s \le \omega \le \pi$, respectively, is achieved when $E(\omega)$ exhibits at best $N_0 + 2$ alternations. By denoting E_{max} as the maximum error value of $|E(\omega)|$ over the passbands and stopbands, above statement means that there is at least $N_0 + 2$ frequencies in the range such that

$$E(\omega_i) = -E(\omega_{i-1}) + \pm E_{max},\ i = 1, 2, ..., N_0 + 1 \qquad ...(8.80)$$

where $\omega_0 < \omega_1 < ... < \omega_{N_0+1}$. The value of N_0 is equal to the upper limit on summation giving $P(\omega)$ as given in Table 8.3. Thus, when N is odd, then $N_0 = \frac{(N-1)}{2}$ and when N is even, then $N_0 = \frac{N}{2-1}$.

From (8.78), we can write

$$H_1(\omega) = \tilde{H}_1(\omega) - E(\omega)/W(\omega) \text{ in the passband} \qquad ...(8.81)$$

$$H_1(\omega) = \tilde{H}_1(\omega) - K.\, E(\omega) \text{ in the passband,} \qquad ...(8.82)$$

Let $\delta_2 > \delta_1$ *i.e.* the maximum value of $E(\omega)$ is δ_2. Also, let

$$K = \frac{\delta_1}{\delta_2} = \frac{\delta_1}{E(\omega)} \text{ in (8.82), doing so we obtain}$$

$$H_1(\omega) = \tilde{H}_1(\omega) - \delta_1 \text{ in the passband} \quad ...(8.83)$$

Let (8.83) hold good at frequency ω_i *i.e.* we have taking $\tilde{H}_1(\omega) = 1$,

$$H_1(\omega_i) = 1 - \delta_1 \quad ...(8.84)$$

For $\omega_{i+1} > \omega_i$ in the range $0 \le \omega_{i+1} \le \omega_p$, we know that $E(\omega_{i+1}) = -\delta_2$. Consequently we can write

$$H_1(\omega_{i+1}) = 1 + \delta_1 \quad ...(8.85)$$

Since, ω_i and ω_{i+1} are typical consecutive frequencies at which the error $E(\omega)$ alternates in the passband, we can see that $H_1(\omega)$ varies between $1 - \delta_1$ and $1 + \delta_2$ in the passband. Such variations of $H_1(\omega)$ are shown in Fig. 8.18.

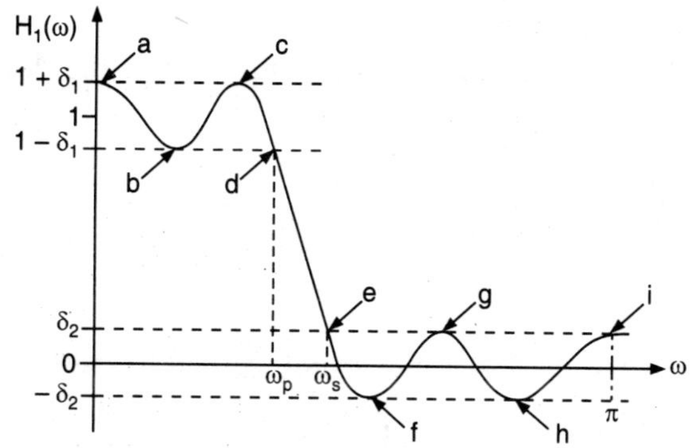

Fig. 8.18. Equiripple approximation of $H_1(\omega)$ (an extraripple filter)

Passband extrema points are at *a, b, c, i.e.* $N_p = 3$

Stopband extrema points are at *f, g, h, i, i.e.* $N_s = 4$

Passband alternations are at *a, b, c, d* = 4 points

Stopband alternations are at *e, f, g, h, i* = 5 points

If we let ω_i and ω_{i+1} as the consecutive external frequencies of the error $E(\omega)$ in the stopband, $\omega_s \le \omega \le \pi$, then we have

$$\left.\begin{aligned} H_1(\omega_i) &= -E(\omega_i) = -\delta_2 \quad ...(8.86) \\ H_1(\omega_{i+1}) &= -E(\omega_{i+1}) = +\delta_2 \quad ...(8.87) \end{aligned}\right\} \text{ in stopband}$$

We note that in the stopband, $\omega_s \le \omega \le \pi$, $H_1(\omega)$ varies from $-\delta_2$ to $+\delta_2$ as shown in the Fig. 8.18.

It is apparent that the Chebyshev approximation as described above results in an equiripple approximation for $H_1(\omega)$. This filter $H_1(\omega)$ has response similar to the response of an elliptic filter. The maximum deviation from the ideal filter response is δ_1 in the passband and δ_2 in the stopband. In many designs δ_1 and δ_2 are equal.

The number of relative extrema in the passband is denoted by N_p. (see points *a, b,* and *c* in Fig. 8.18. Here, $N_p = 3$). The number of relative extrema in the stopband is denoted by N_s. (see points *f, g, h,* and *i*, in Fig. 8.18. Here, $N_s = 4$). The total number of relative extrema is denoted by N_e. Thus, $N_e = N_p + N_s$. In Fig 8.18, $N_e = 3 + 4 = 7$. Also, we define the points of alternations in the response curve as the points where the value of $H_1(\omega)$ is $1 + \delta_1$, $1 - \delta_1$, δ_2 or $-\delta_2$. In Fig. 8.18, the alternation points in the passband are *a, b, c* and *d* (*i.e.*, 4 points), and the alternation points in the stopband are *e, f, g, h* and *i* (*i.e.*, 5 points).

The relation $N_e = N_p + N_s$ shows that N_p and N_s parameters are arbitrary except the sum of N_p and N_s always equals to the value of N_e. Also, the value N_e is fixed by the relation

$$N_e \le \frac{N+1}{2} = N_0 + 1, N \text{ odd} \quad \text{...(8.88a)}$$

$$N_e \le \frac{N}{2} + 1 = N_0 + 1, N \text{ even} \quad \text{...(8.88b)}$$

EXAMPLE 8.22: *For linear-phase FIR digital filter designed as optimal/Chebyshev/filters, show that the number of relative extrema points N_e is given by the relation*

$$N_e \le \begin{cases} (N+1)/2, & N \text{ odd} \\ N/2 & N \text{ even} \end{cases}$$

where N is the number of design weights of the filter.

SOLUTION: We know that the zero-phase magnitude part of the designed filter is given by

$$H_1(\omega) = Q(\omega) \,.\, P(\omega) \quad \text{...(A)}$$

where $Q(\omega)$ and $P(\omega)$ are given in table as follows.

N	$Q(\omega)$	$P(\omega)$
Odd	1	$\sum_{n=0}^{(N-1)/2} a(n) \,.\, \cos(n\omega)$
Even	$\cos \omega/2$	$\sum_{n=0}^{(N/2)-1} \tilde{b}(n) \cos(n\omega)$

Case N odd

Here
$$H_1(\omega) = \sum_{n=0}^{(N-1)/2} a(n) \cos(n\omega) \quad \text{...(B)}$$

we can always express cos $n\omega$ is terms powers of cos ω (see Example 8.5). Hence, $H_1(\omega)$ given in (B) reduces to

$$H_1(\omega) = \sum_{n=0}^{(N-1)/2} a(n) \left[\sum_{m=0}^{n} a_{mn} \cos^m \omega \right] \quad \text{...(C)}$$

where a_{mn} is related to Chebyshev polynomials of degree m and value of n. We may write (C) as

$$H_1(\omega) = \sum_{n=0}^{(N-1)/2} A(n) \cos^n \omega \quad \text{...(D)}$$

where $A(n)$ are related to $a(n)$ and a_{mn}. To obtain the extrema (*i.e.*, maxima and minima) of $H_1(\omega)$, we put $\frac{dH_1(\omega)}{d\omega} = 0$. As

$$\frac{dH_1(\omega)}{d\omega} = \sum_{n=0}^{(N-1)/2} A(n) \,.\, n(-\sin \omega) \,.\, \cos^{n-1} \omega$$

$$= -\sin \omega \sum_{n=1}^{(N-1)/2} nA(n) \cos^{n-1} \omega \quad \text{...(E)}$$

The zeros of $\frac{dH_1(\omega)}{d\omega}$, given by (*E*) occur in the interval $0 \leq \omega \leq \pi$ where

$$\sin \omega = 0 \qquad ...(F)$$

or

$$\sum_{n=1}^{(N-1)/2} nA(n) \cos^{n-1} \omega = 0 \qquad ...(G)$$

From (*F*), $\omega = 0$ or $\omega = \pi$. The expression in (*G*) is a polynomial in cos ω with degree $\frac{(N-3)}{2}$.

Consequently it has at the most $\frac{(N-3)}{2}$ values of ω in $0 \leq \omega \leq \pi$. Hence, (*E*) has at the most $\frac{(N-3)}{2} + 2 = \frac{(N+1)}{2}$ relative extrema of $H_1(\omega)$ in the range $0 \leq \omega \leq \pi$. The number of these relative extrema N_e can be at the most $(N + 1)/2$, *i.e.*, we can write

$$N_e \leq \frac{N+1}{2} = N_0 + 1, N \text{ odd} \qquad ...(H)$$

where $N_0 = \frac{N-1}{2}$, as defined in Table 8.3.

Case *N* even

Here

$$H_1(\omega) = Q(\omega) \,.\, P(\omega)$$

$$= \cos(\omega/2) \sum_{n=0}^{N/2-1} \tilde{b}(n) \cos n\,\omega \quad \text{(from Table 8.3)} \qquad ...(I)$$

$$= \cos(\omega/2) \sum_{n=0}^{N/2-1} \tilde{b}(n) \left[\sum_{m=0}^{n} a_{mn} \cos^n \omega \right] \text{ as in (C)} \qquad ...(J)$$

We may write (*J*) as

$$H_1(\omega) = \cos(\omega/2) \sum_{n=0}^{N/2-1} B(n) \,.\, \cos^n \omega \qquad ...(K)$$

where $B(n)$ are related to $\tilde{b}(n)$ and a_{mn}. To determine extrema frequencies, we let $\frac{dH_1(\omega)}{d\omega} = 0$.

From (*K*), we have

$$\frac{dH_1(\omega)}{d\omega} = \left(-\frac{1}{2} \sin \frac{\omega}{2}\right) \sum_{n=0}^{N/2-1} B(n) \,.\, \cos^{n-1} \omega$$

$$+ (\cos \omega/2) \sum_{n=0}^{N/2-1} B(n) (-n \sin \omega) \cos^{n-1} \omega$$

$$= \left(-\frac{1}{2} \sin \frac{\omega}{2}\right) \sum_{n=0}^{N/2-1} B(n) \,.\, \cos^{n-1} \omega \left[\cos \omega + 2n \cos^2 \frac{\omega}{2} \right]$$

$$= \left(-\frac{1}{2}\sin\frac{\omega}{2}\right)\sum_{n=0}^{N/2-1} B(n).\cos^{n-1}(\omega)\left[\cos\omega + n(\cos\omega - 1)\right]$$

$$= \left(-\frac{1}{2}\sin\frac{\omega}{2}\right)\sum_{n=0}^{N/2-1} B(n)\{(n+1)\cos^{n}(\omega) - n\cos^{n-1}\omega\} \quad ...(L)$$

In the range $0 \le \omega \le \pi$, $\frac{dH_1(\omega)}{d\omega} = 0$ implies

$$\sin\frac{\omega}{2} = 0, \qquad i.e., \omega = 0 \quad ...(M)$$

$$\sum_{n=0}^{N/2-1} B(n)\{(n+1)\cos^{n}\omega - n\cos^{n-1}\omega\} = 0 \quad ...(N)$$

(*N*) has $\frac{N}{2} - 1$ roots as it has a polynomial in cos ω of degree $\frac{N}{2} - 1$.

Hence, the number of relative extrema N_e can be at the most $\left(\frac{N}{2} - 1\right) + 1$

i.e.,

$$N_e \le \frac{N}{2} = N_0 + 1, N \text{ even} \quad ...(O)$$

where $\frac{N}{2} - 1$ equals N_0, as defined in Table 8.3.

Extraripple Case of Approximation $H_1(\omega)$

It has been shown in solved Example 8.22, that the number of relative extrema N_e holds the inequality

$$N_e \le N_0 + 1 \quad ...(8.89)$$

where $N_0 = \frac{(N-1)}{2}$ when *N* is odd and $N_0 = \frac{N}{2} - 1$ when *N* is even. Hence, the maximum possible alternations can be $(N_0 + 1)$ extrema and one each at ω_p and ω_s, *i.e.* totalling $N_0 + 3$ alternations. Note that out of $N_0 + 1$ extrema N_e, there is one at $\omega = 0$ and also one at $\omega = \pi$. Note that there is ALWAYS an alternation at ω_p as well as at ω_s. But there may not be an alternation at $\omega = 0$ or at $\omega = \pi$. This would be the case when there is no extrema at $\omega = 0$ or at $\omega = \pi$.

For an optimal filter design, we must have at least $N_0 + 2$ alternations. In this case, there would be an alternation at $\omega = 0$ or at $\omega = \pi$, but not at both these frequencies.

The filters having $N_0 + 3$ alternations are called Extraripple Filters. Obviously, an extraripple filter will always have an alternation at $\omega = 0$ as well as at $\omega = \pi$. The filter response $H_1(\omega)$ shown in Fig. 8.18 is that of an extraripple design, since, there are extrema *i.e.,* alternations at $\omega = 0$ as well as at $\omega = \pi$.

It may be noted that $N_e = N_p + N_s$ allows us to have various choices. In Fig. 8.19, each response has $N_e = 4$ and $N_p = 1, 2, 3$, respectively, in Figs. *a, b, c* of Fig. 8.19. The value of N_s is always, $N_e - N_p$ *i.e.,* $N_s = 4 - N_p$, here as indicated. Since, all these filters have as extrema at $\omega = 0$ as well as at $\omega = \pi$, the number of alternations for each case is 6, and all these filters are extraripple type. It can be readily guessed that $N_0 = 3$ and $N_e = N_0 + 1 = 4$ in designs shown in Fig. 8.19. Value of $N_0 = 3$ implies that $N = 7$ if N is odd or $N = 8$, if N is even in the equiripple design.

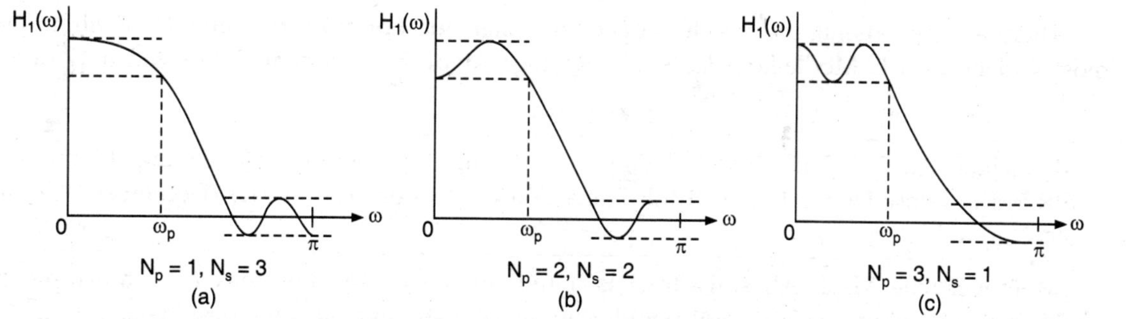

Fig. 8.19. Response of extraripple low-pass filter

Alternation Theorem

Let an equiripple approximation of a linear-phase, FIR filter be $H_1(\omega)$, given by

$$H_1(\omega) = Q(\omega) \cdot P(\omega) \qquad ...(8.90)$$

where $Q(\omega)$ is as given is Table 8.3. In all the cases, we can write (see solved Example 8.22):

$$H_1(\omega) = \sum_{n=0}^{N_0} A(n) \cos^n \omega \qquad ...(8.91)$$

where $N_0 = \frac{(N-1)}{2}$ where N is odd and $N_0 = \frac{N}{2} - 1$ where N is even.

A necessary and sufficient condition for $H_1(\omega)$ to be a unique, best weighted equiripple (*i.e.* Chebyshev) approximation is that the error function $E(\omega)$ given by

$$E(\omega) = W(\omega) = [\tilde{H}(\omega) - H_1(\omega)] \qquad ...(8.92)$$

must have $N_0 + 2$ alternations. $\tilde{H}_1(\omega)$ is the ideal filter and $W(\omega)$ is the weighting function. This implies that

$$| E(\omega_i) | = \delta, i = 1, 2, ..., N_0 + 2 \qquad ...(8.93)$$

where δ is the maximum error and there are $N_0 + 2$ discrete frequencies. The alternation frequencies are the points of $H_1(\omega)$, where $H_1(\omega)$ has values $1 + \delta$, $1 - \delta$, $+\delta$, $-\delta$. It has been assumed that $\delta_1 = \delta_2 = \delta$ and, therefore, $W(\omega_i) = 1$ for $i = 1, 2, ..., N_0 + 2$.

The optimal, equiripple design is achieved using Remez Exchange algorithm which arrives at $N_0 + 2$ equiripple alternations, thus resulting in a unique equiripple design of $H_1(\omega)$.

Computer Design Approach

In order to obtain an equiripple, linear phase, FIR digital filters, the parameters that we specify to describe $H_1(\omega)$ are: δ_1 (passband maximum error), δ_2 (stopband maximum error) K (= $\frac{\delta_1}{\delta_2}$, if $\delta_1 = \delta_2$, then $K = 1$), ω_p (passband frequency), ω_s (stopband frequency), N(filter length), N_p

(passband extrema), N_s (stopband extrema). Also, we know that $(N_p + N_s) \le N_0 + 1$, where $N_0 = \frac{(N-1)}{2}$ when N is odd and $N_0 = \frac{N}{2} - 1$ when N is even.

There are various algorithms developed to design the optimum (minimax) FIR filter. The most widely used is McClellan, Parks and Rabiner Algorithm. Students interested may down load.

Mc Clellan, J.H., T.W. Parks, and L.R. Rabiner, 'A Computer Program for Designing Optimum FIR Linear Phase Digital Filters', IEEE Trans. Audio Electroacoust. AU-21 (December 1973): 506-526.

Moreover, the MATLAB software has a tool to design the minimax (*i.e.* equiripple or Chebyshev) FIR filters. This is very popular among the students and the designers.

A wide variety of optimal FIR filters such as low-pass, high-pass, band pass, band-reject as well as differentiators, Hilbert transformers and also-multi-band filters can be designed by aforementioned algorithm. A typical design example for optimal linear-phase filter is as follows.

EXAMPLE 8.23: *Design an optimal, linear-phase FIR low-pass filter for the specifications, N = 35 and*

$$H_{\text{ideal}}(\omega) = \begin{cases} 1, & 0 \le f \le 0.08 \\ 1, & 0.16 \le f \le 0.5 \end{cases}$$

Take weighting function

$$W(\omega) = \begin{cases} 1, & 0 \le f \le 0.08 \\ 1, & 0.16 \le f \le 0.5 \end{cases}$$

where f is the frequency in Hz and $\omega = 2\pi f$.

SOLUTION: Note that ω-axis is from 0 to 0.5 *i.e.* the normalized frequency f = actual frequency (Hz)/sampling frequency (samples/s). Since, we have specified N as 35, the values of deviations $\delta_1 = \delta_2$ will be determined by the program. The printout will be typically

$h(1) = h(35) = 0.1298 \times 10^{-2}$, $h(2) = h(34) = -0.1647 \times 10^{-2}$

$h(3) = h(33) = -0.3889 \times 10^{-2}$, $h(4) = h(32) = -0.5133 \times 10^{-2}$

$h(5) = h(31) = -0.2935 \times 10^{-2}$, $h(6) = h(30) = 0.3480 \times 10^{-2}$

$h(7) = h(29) = 0.1158 \times 10^{-1}$, $h(8) = h(28) = 0.1577 \times 10^{-1}$

$h(9) = h(27) = 0.1030 \times 10^{-1}$, $h(10) = h(26) = -0.6329 \times 10^{-2}$

$h(11) = h(25) = -0.2804 \times 10^{-1}$, $h(12) = h(24) = -0.4167 \times 10^{-1}$

$h(13) = h(23) = -0.3229 \times 10^{-1}$, $h(14) = h(22) = 0.8723 \times 10^{-2}$

$h(15) = h(21) = 0.7715 \times 10^{-1}$, $h(16) = h(20) = 0.1550$

$h(17) = h(19) = 0.2168$ $h(18) = h(18) = 0.2403$

	Band 1	Band 2
Lower Band Edge	0.0000	0.1600 (f_c)
Upper Band Edge	0.0799 (f_p)	0.5000 ($f_5/2$)
Desired Value ($H_d(\omega)$)	1.0000	0.0000
Weighting ($W(\omega)$)	1.0000	1.0000
Deviation (δ_1, δ_2)	0.0032 (δ_1)	0.0032 (δ_2)
Deviation in dB	0.0278	–49.8549.

Extremal Frequencies (N_0 = $(N - 1)/2$ = 17. Hence, N_e = 17 + 2 = 19)

0.0000,	0.0277,	0.0520,	0.0729,	0.8000
0.1600,	0.1669,	0.1860,	0.2120,	0.2381
0.2659,	0.2954,	0.3231,	0.3527,	0.3822
0.4117,	0.4412,	0.4707,	0.5000	

CHAPTER 9

Design of IIR Filters

9.0 INTRODUCTION

The infinite impulse response (IIR) digital filters form an important subset of digital filters used in various practical systems. Linear time-invariant systems must be considered where the IIR filter has to be used. Designing the IIR digital filters involves the determination of a transfer function in z^{-1} that meets certain performance specifications. After obtaining the transfer function, the next step in the design procedure is to realize the system using finite-precision arithmetic. The techniques used for IIR filter design are based on converting an analog filter into a digital filter. As the analog design techniques are well developed, so we convert the specifications of the desired digital filter into an equivalent analog domain. After designing the analog filter, we convert the design into the digital domain.

9.1 SOME ELEMENTARY PROPERTIES OF IIR FILTERS

Magnitude-Squared response, phase response and group delay

In IIR filters design techniques, we often analyse three most important parameters given below:

(*i*) Magnitude-squared response

(*ii*) Phase response

(*iii*) Group delay of the filter.

It is so as the general approximation problem of filter's system function, $H(z)$, involves a complex transfer function in ω ($\because \quad z = e^{j\omega}$). Thus, both the magnitude and the phase response must be examined to determine the nature of the resulting filter approximation.

Since, the phase function is generally highly non-linear in IIR designs, the filter group delay response is often used as a measure of how much dispersal a typical input will undergo when being processed by the filter.

9.1.1 Magnitude-Squared Response

When an IIR filter is determined strictly in terms of a magnitude approximation, disregarding the phase completely, we consider

$$| H(e^{j\omega}) |^2 = | H(z) . H(z^{-1}) |_{z = e^{j\omega}} \quad ...(9.1)$$

The poles and zeros of $H(z) . H(z^{-1})$ are appearing with mirror image symmetry w.r.t. $| z | = 1$ (the unit circle) in z-plane. Then the poles of $H(z)$ are uniquely determined from the poles of $| H(z) H(z^{-1}) |$ function as those lying inside the unit circle. This ensures stability of $H(z)$.

The zeros of $H(z)$ may lie anywhere, in general, except in the important case where all the zeros of $H(z)$ are to lie on the unit circle. In most cases, the zeros of $H(z)$ are also picked up from the zeros of $(H(z) . H(z^{-1}))$ those lying inside or on the unit cirle. In such a choice, the resulting $H(z)$ will be a minimum phase filter. (The maximum phase filters have all their zeros outside the unit circle ($| z | = 1$). As

$$H(z) = \sum_n h(n) z^{-n} \qquad \therefore \quad H(e^{j\omega}) = \sum_n h(n) e^{j\omega n}$$

$$H(z^{-1}) = \sum_n h(n) z^n \qquad \therefore \quad H(z^{-1})\Big|_{z=e^{j\omega}} = \sum_n h(n) e^{j\omega n}$$

$$= \left(\sum_n h^*(n) e^{-j\omega n}\right)^* = H^*(e^{j\omega}), \text{ if } h(n) = h^*(n)$$

$\therefore$ for $h(n)$ real $| H(e^{j\omega}) |^2 = H(e^{j\omega}) . H^*(e^{j\omega}) = \left|H(z) . H(z^{-1})\right|_{z=e^{j\omega}}$. This proves (9.1)

9.1.2 Phase Response

The transfer function of an IIR filter, in general, is a complex function of ω *i.e.*,

$$H(e^{j\omega}) = \text{Re}\,[H(e^{j\omega})] + jI_m[H(e^{j\omega})]$$

$$\therefore \quad \beta(e^{j\omega}) = \tan^{-1}\left(\frac{I_m\,[H(e^{j\omega})]}{\text{Re}[H(e^{j\omega})]}\right)$$

$$\therefore \quad \boxed{\beta(e^{j\omega}) = \tan^{-1}\left(\frac{I_m\,[H(z)]}{\text{Re}[H(z)]}\right)\Bigg|_{z=e^{j\omega}}} \quad ...(9.2)$$

Proof: As
$$\tan^{-1} x = \frac{1}{2j} \log_e \frac{1+jx}{1-jx} \quad ...(9.3)$$

(from trigonometry)

Taking $x = \dfrac{I_m\,[H(z)]}{\text{Re}\,[H(z)]}$ in (9.2) and using (9.3), we get

$$\beta(e^{j\omega}) = \frac{1}{2j} \ln \frac{(1 + jI_m[H(z)]/\text{Re}\,H(z))}{(1 - jI_m[H(z)]/\text{Re}\,H(z))}\Bigg|_{z=e^{j\omega}}$$

$$= \frac{1}{2j} \ln\left(\frac{\text{Re}\,H(z) + jI_mH(z)}{\text{Re}\,H(z) - jI_mH(z)}\right)\Bigg|_{z=e^{j\omega}}$$

$$\therefore \qquad \boxed{\beta(e^{j\omega}) = \frac{1}{2j}\ln\frac{H(z)}{H(z^{-1})}\bigg|_{z=e^{j\omega}}} \qquad \text{...[9.3(a)]}$$

Also note that

$$H(z) = |H(z)|\,e^{j\beta(z)}$$
$$H(z^{-1}) = |H(z^{-1})|\,e^{-j\beta(z)} \qquad \text{...(9.4)}$$

9.1.3 Group Delay

The group delay τ_g is defined by

$$\boxed{\begin{aligned}\tau_g(e^{j\omega}) &\triangleq -\frac{d\beta(e^{j\omega})}{d\omega}\\ &= -jz\frac{d\beta(z)}{d\omega}\bigg|_{z=e^{j\omega}}\end{aligned}} \qquad \text{...(9.5)}$$

A constant value of τ_g over the band of ω is desirable for a good design.

$$\because \qquad \frac{d\beta}{d\omega} = \frac{d\beta(e^{j\omega})}{de^{j\omega}}\cdot\frac{de^{j\omega}}{d\omega}$$
$$= \frac{d\beta(e^{j\omega})}{de^{j\omega}} \times je^{j\omega}$$
$$= \frac{d\beta(z)}{dz}(jz)\bigg|_{z=e^{j\omega}}$$

$$\text{As} \qquad \tau_g(e^{j\omega}) = -je^{j\omega}\,\frac{d\beta(e^{jw})}{de^{jw}}$$

$$= -je^{j\omega}\frac{d}{de^{j\omega}}\left(\frac{1}{2j}\ln\frac{H(e^{j\omega})}{H^*(e^{j\omega})}\right), \text{ where } H^*(e^{j\omega}) \text{ is complex conjugate of } H(e^{j\omega})$$

$$= -\frac{1}{2}\,e^{j\omega}\,\frac{d}{de^{j\omega}}\left(\ln\frac{H(e^{j\omega})}{H^*(e^{j\omega})}\right)$$

$$= -\frac{1}{2}\,e^{j\omega}\left[\frac{H^*(e^{j\omega})}{H(e^{j\omega})}\,\frac{H^*(e^{j\omega})\dfrac{dH(e^{j\omega})}{de^{j\omega}} - H(e^{j\omega})\,.\,\dfrac{dH^*(e^{j\omega})}{de^{j\omega}}}{(H^*(e^{j\omega}))^2}\right]$$

$$= -\frac{1}{2}\,e^{j\omega}\left[\frac{1}{H(e^{j\omega})}\frac{dH(e^{j\omega})}{de^{j\omega}} - \frac{1}{H^*(e^{j\omega})}\cdot\frac{dH^*(e^{j\omega})}{de^{j\omega}}\right]$$

$$= -\frac{1}{2}\,e^{j\omega}\left[\frac{1}{H(e^{j\omega})}\cdot\frac{dH(e^{j\omega})}{de^{j\omega}} - \frac{1}{H^*(e^{j\omega})}\,\frac{dH^*(e^{j\omega})}{de^{-j\omega}}\cdot\frac{de^{-j\omega}}{de^{j\omega}}\right]$$

$$= -\frac{1}{2}\left[\frac{e^{j\omega}}{H(e^{j\omega})}\frac{dH(e^{j\omega})}{de^{j\omega}} + \frac{e^{-j\omega}}{H^*(e^{j\omega})}\frac{dH^*(e^{j\omega})}{de^{-j\omega}}\right] \qquad \left(\because \frac{de^{-j\omega}}{de^{j\omega}} = -e^{-2j\omega}\right)$$

$$= -\frac{1}{2}\left[\frac{e^{j\omega}}{H(e^{j\omega})}\cdot\frac{dH(e^{j\omega})}{de^{j\omega}} + \left(\frac{e^{j\omega}}{H(e^{j\omega})}\frac{dH(e^{j\omega})}{de^{j\omega}}\right)^*\right]$$

$$= -\text{Re}\left[\frac{e^{j\omega}}{H(e^{j\omega})}\frac{dH(e^{j\omega})}{de^{j\omega}}\right]$$

$$\therefore \quad \tau_g(e^{j\omega}) = -\text{Re}\left\{\frac{z}{H(z)}\frac{dH(z)}{dz}\right\}_{z=e^{j\omega}}$$

$$= -\text{Re}\left\{z\frac{d}{d(z)}\ln H(z)\right\}_{z=e^{j\omega}} \qquad \text{...(9.6)}$$

Alternative Proof of (9.6)

We know that

Phase delay, $\tau_p(\omega) \triangleq -\dfrac{\theta(\omega)}{\omega}$ ...(9.7)

Group delay, $\tau_g(\omega) \triangleq -\dfrac{d\theta(\omega)}{d\omega}$, also denoted as $\tau_g(e^{j\omega})$

[Here $\theta(\omega)$ is the same parameter as $\beta(e^{j\omega})$ used in (9.5)]

Let $\quad H(z)\big|_{z=e^{j\omega}} = |\, H(e^{j\omega})\,|\, e^{j\theta(\omega)} \triangleq M(\omega)\, e^{j\theta(\omega)}$ ...(9.8)

Taking log to the base e on both sides, we get

$$\ln H(z)\big|_{z=e^{j\omega}} = \ln M(\omega) + j\theta(\omega) \qquad \text{...(9.9)}$$

Take derivative w.r.t. z on both sides of (9.9)

$$\therefore \quad \frac{d}{dz}[\ln H(z)]\bigg|_{z=e^{j\omega}} = \frac{d}{dz}[\ln . M(\omega) + j\theta(\omega)]$$

$$= \frac{d}{d\omega}[\ln . M(\omega) + j\theta(\omega)] . \frac{d\omega}{dz} \qquad \text{...(9.10)}$$

As $\quad z = e^{j\omega}$

$$\therefore \quad \frac{dz}{d\omega} = je^{j\omega}$$

$$= jz \text{ or } \frac{d\omega}{dz} = \frac{1}{jz} \qquad \text{...(9.11)}$$

From (9.10) and (9.11), we have

$$\frac{d}{dz}[\ln H(z)]\bigg|_{z=e^{j\omega}} = \left(\frac{d}{d\omega}\ln M(\omega) + j\frac{d\theta(\omega)}{d\omega}\right)\cdot\frac{1}{jz}$$

$$\therefore \quad \left(-z\frac{d}{dz}\ln H(z)\right)\Bigg|_{z=e^{j\omega}} = -\left(-j\frac{d}{d\omega}\ln M(\omega)+\frac{d\theta(\omega)}{d\omega}\right)$$

$$= j\frac{d}{d\omega}\ln M(\omega)-\frac{d\theta(\omega)}{d\omega}$$

As $M(\omega)$ and $\theta(\omega)$ are real quantities $\therefore$ $j\frac{d}{d\omega}\ln M(\omega)$ is imaginary and $\frac{d\theta(\omega)}{d\omega}$ is real quantity.

Thus, Real part of $\left(-z\frac{d}{dz}\ln H(z)\right)\Bigg|_{z=e^{j\omega}} = -\frac{d\theta(\omega)}{d\omega} = \tau_g(e^{j\omega})$ Q.E.D.

which is same as (9.6).

9.2 BILINEAR TRANSFORMATION (INTEGRAL METHOD)

We now derive the expression for bilinear transformation which will be used in the design of IIR filters.

Here, we integrate the differential equations of analog filter and then use numerical approximation to the integral. Let

$$c_1 y_a'(t) + c_0 y_a(t) = d_0 x_a(t) \qquad \ldots(9.12)$$

be the first order analog filter. Taking Laplace transform on both sides of (9.12), we get

$$c_1 s Y_a(s) + c_0 Y_a(s) = d_0 X_a(s)$$

$$\therefore \quad H_a(s) = \frac{Y_a(s)}{X_a(s)} = \frac{d_0}{c_0 + c_1 s} \qquad \ldots(9.13)$$

We can write

$$y_a(t) = y_a(t) - y_a(t_0) + y_a(t_0) \qquad \text{(Note this step)}$$

$$= \int_{t_0}^{t} y_a'(t)\,dt + y_a(t_0)$$

Let $t_0 = (n-1)t,\ t = nT$

$$\therefore \quad y_a(t)\big|_{t=nT} = \int_{(n-1)T}^{nT} y_a'(t)\,dt + y_a((n-1)T)$$

i.e., $$y_a(nT) = \underbrace{\frac{T}{2}[y_a'(nT) + y_a'((n-1)T)]}_{\text{by Trapezoidal Rule of integration}} + y_a((n-1)T) \qquad \ldots(9.14)$$

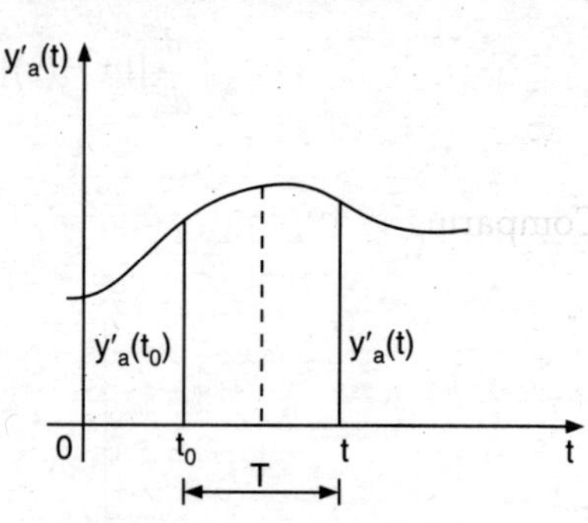

Fig. 9.1. Explaining trapezoidal rule of integration

We can write from (9.12), putting $t = nT$ there,

$$y_a'(nT) = -\frac{c_0}{c_1} y_a(nT) + \frac{d_0}{c_1} x_a(nT) \qquad \ldots(9.15)$$

$$\therefore \quad y'_a[(n-1)\,T] = -\frac{c_0}{c_1} y_a[(n-1)T] + \frac{d_0}{c_1} x_a[(n-1)T] \quad \text{(Changing } n \text{ to } n-1 \text{ in (9.15))}$$

Using these values of $y'_a(nT)$ and $y'_a[(n-1)\,T]$ in (9.14), we have

$$y_a(nT) = \frac{T}{2}\left[-\frac{c_0}{c_1}\{y_a(nT) + y_a[(n-1)T]\}\right.$$

$$\left. + \frac{d_0}{c_1}\{x_a(nT) + x_a[(n-1)T]\}\right] + y_a[(n-1)T] \quad \ldots(9.16)$$

Defining $y_a(nT) \triangleq y(n)$ and $x_a(nT) \triangleq x(n)$ (9.16) yields

$$y(n) - y(n-1) = \frac{T}{2}\left[-\frac{c_0}{c_1}\{y(n) + y(n-1)\} + \frac{d_0}{c_1}\{x(n) + x(n-1)\}\right]$$

Taking z-transform on both sides, we get

$$Y(z)\,[1 - z^{-1}] = \frac{T}{2}\left[-\frac{c_0}{c_1}\{Y(z)\,(1+z^{-1})\} + \frac{d_0}{c_1} X(z)\,x(1+z^{-1})\right]$$

$$\text{or} \quad Y(z)\left[(1-z^{-1}) + \frac{T}{2}\frac{c_0}{c_1}(1+z^{-1})\right] = X(z)\frac{T}{2}\frac{c_0}{c_1}(1+z^{-1})$$

$$\therefore \quad H(z) \triangleq \frac{Y(z)}{X(z)} = \frac{\frac{T}{2}\frac{d_0}{c_1}(1+z^{-1})}{(1-z^{-1}) + \frac{T}{2}\frac{c_0}{c_1}(1+z^{-1})} \quad \ldots(9.17)$$

Dividing the numerator and denominator of R.H.S. of (9.17), by $\frac{T(1+z^{-1})}{2c_1}$, we get

$$H(z) = \frac{d_0}{c_1\left(\frac{2}{T}\frac{1-z^{-1}}{1+z^{-1}}\right) + c_0} \quad \ldots(9.18)$$

Comparing (9.18) with $H_a(s) = \dfrac{d_0}{c_0 + c_1 s}$, we find that

$$s = \frac{2}{T}\frac{1-z^{-1}}{1+z^{-1}}$$

$$z^{-1} = \frac{1 - \frac{T}{2}s}{1 + \frac{T}{2}s} \quad \text{Bilinear transformation} \quad \ldots(9.19a)$$

This is the Bilinear transformation *i.e.*, in the given $H_a(s)$, if we replace s by $\frac{2}{T}\frac{(1-z^{-1})}{(1+z^{-1})}$, we obtain $H(z)$. Hence,

$$H(z) = H_a(s)\Big|_{s=\frac{2}{T}\frac{(1-z^{-1})}{(1+z^{-1})}} \quad \text{...(9.19b)}$$

Important Note:

Though we have derived the Bilinear transformation formula based on the first order differential equation, $c_1 y_a'(t) + c_0 y_a(t) = d_0 x_a(t)$, the result thus obtained holds good also for N-th differential equation of the generic form

$$\sum_{k=0}^{N} c_k\, y_a^{(k)}(t) = \sum_{k=0}^{M} d_k\, x^{(k)}(t) \quad \text{...(9.20)}$$

where the function $f_{(t)}^{(k)}$ implies $\frac{d^k f(t)}{dt^k}$. This is so because the above equation can be written as a set of N first order linear equations of the form:

$$c_1 y_a'(t) + c_0 y_a(t) = d_0\, x_a(t)$$

In short, the transformation $s = \frac{2}{T}\frac{(1-z^{-1})}{(1+z^{-1})}$ or $z = \frac{\left(1+\frac{T}{2}s\right)}{\left(1-\frac{T}{2}s\right)}$ can be used for all order differential equations.

Also, it is well known that bilinear transformation is conformal. This important property ensures that the 'shape' of the response $H(s)$ will be similar to the shape of the response $H(z)$, if we use *BLT* (bilinear transformation).

9.2.1 Mapping of *s*-Plane to *z*-Plane in Bilinear Transformation

As $s = \sigma + j\Omega$ and the bilinear transformation is

$$z = \frac{\left(1+\frac{T}{2}s\right)}{\left(1-\frac{T}{2}s\right)} \quad \text{...(9.21)}$$

$j\Omega$ Axis Mapping (*i.e.*, $s = j\Omega$)

Put $s = j\Omega$ in (9.21)

$$\therefore \quad z = \frac{\left(1+\frac{T}{2}j\Omega\right)}{\left(1-\frac{T}{2}j\Omega\right)}$$

$$= \left[\frac{1+\left(\frac{T}{2}\Omega\right)^2}{1+\left(\frac{T}{2}\Omega\right)^2}\right]^{1/2} \angle 2\tan^{-1}\left(\frac{\Omega T}{2}\right)$$

$$\therefore \qquad e^{j\omega} = e^{j2\tan^{-1}(\Omega T/2)}$$

or

$$\omega = 2\tan^{-1}\left(\frac{\Omega T}{2}\right)$$

or

$$\boxed{\frac{\Omega T}{2} = \tan\frac{\omega}{2}} \qquad \ldots(9.22)$$

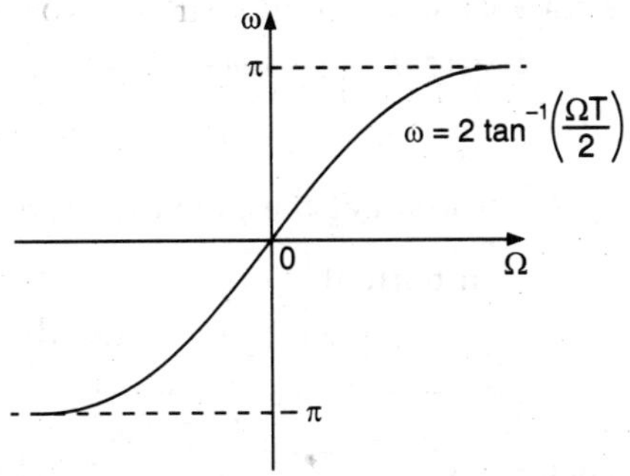

Fig. 9.2. Mapping of analog frequency Ω on to the unit circle using Bilinear transformation

Putting $s = j\Omega$ in (9.21), we get $|z| = 1$ for all values of Ω. Thus, $j\Omega$ axis maps to the unit circle $|z|$ in z-plane. Also, from (9.22) when Ω is +ve, ω is +ve and for Ω –ve, ω is –ve. Hence +ve and –ve parts of $j\Omega$ axis map to upper and lower halves, respectively, on the z-plane unit circle $|z| = 1$. In fact, $j\Omega = -\infty$ to $+\infty$ maps the unit circle $|z| = 1$ ONLY ONCE, as is apparent from Fig. 9.2.

Mapping of LHP and RHP of *s* Plane

Put

$$s = \sigma + j\Omega \text{ in } z = \frac{\left(1+\frac{Ts}{2}\right)}{\left(1-\frac{Ts}{2}\right)}$$

$$\therefore \qquad z = \frac{1+\frac{T}{2}(\sigma + j\Omega)}{1-\frac{T}{2}(\sigma + j\Omega)}$$

$$|z|^2 = \frac{\left(1+\frac{T\sigma}{2}\right)^2 + \left(\frac{T\Omega}{2}\right)^2}{\left(1-\frac{T\sigma}{2}\right)^2 + \left(\frac{T\Omega}{2}\right)^2}$$

Clearly, for

$$\sigma < 0, \ |z|^2 < 1 \qquad \ldots(9.23a)$$

$$\sigma > 0, \ |z|^2 > 1 \qquad \ldots(9.23b)$$

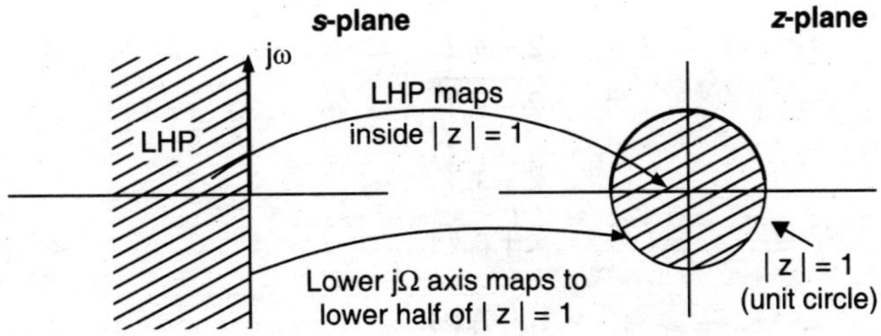

Fig. 9.3. Mapping of s-plane to z-plane in Bilinear transformation

Hence, LHP s-plane maps to inside the unit circle $|z| = 1$ and RHP s-plane maps to outside the unit circle $|z| = 1$. The stable analog filter $H_a(s)$ yields a stable digital filter $H(z)$, because, if $H_a(s)$ has all its poles on left half of s-plane, and these poles of stable $H_a(s)$ map inside the unit circle to gives stable $H(z)$.

Also, the entire $j\Omega$ axis, from $-\infty$ to $+\infty$, maps to ONE TRACING of the unit circle. Thus, there is no aliasing.

EXAMPLE 9.1: *An analog filter $H_a(s)$ has a pair of poles at $s = \pm s_p$. What would be the transformed pole pair z_{p_1}, z_{p_2} if we use bilinear transformation to obtain $H(z)$ from $H_a(s)$?*

SOLUTION: Let the given function be

$$H_a(s) = \frac{K.N(s)}{(s - s_p)(s + s_p)}$$

$$\vdots$$

where $N^0(s) \le 1$ [$N^0(s)$ means degree of $N(s)$].

The bilinear transformation is $s = \frac{2}{T}\frac{1-z^{-1}}{1+z^{-1}}$ we can take $T = 1$ for simplicity. However, we assume $T \ne 1$ to deal with the most generic case here.

$$\therefore \quad H(z) = H_a(s)\Big|_{s=\frac{2}{T}\frac{1-z^{-1}}{1+z^{-1}}}$$

$$= KN\left(\frac{2}{T}\frac{1-z^{-1}}{1+z^{-1}}\right) \Big/ \left[\left(\frac{2}{T}\frac{1-z^{-1}}{1+z^{-1}} - s_p\right) \times \left(\frac{2}{T}\frac{1-z^{-1}}{1+z^{-1}} + s_p\right)\right]$$

$$\therefore \quad H(z) = \frac{KN\left(\frac{2}{T}\frac{1-z^{-1}}{1+z^{-1}}\right) T^2(1+z^{-1})^2}{[2(1-z^{-1}) - s_pT(1+z^{-1})][2(1-z^{-1})] + s_pT(1+z^{-1})]}$$

Poles of $H(z)$ are given by

$$[2(1-z^{-1}) - s_pT(1+z^{-1})][2(1-z^{-1}) - s_pT(1+z^{-1})] = 0$$

i.e.,
$$[z^{-1}(2 + s_pT) - (2 - s_pT)][z^{-1}(2 - s_pT) - (2 + z^{-1})] = 0$$

i.e.,
$$\left[z^{-1} - \frac{2 - s_pT}{2 + s_pT}\right]\left[z^{-1} - \frac{2 + s_pT}{2 - s_pT}\right] = 0$$

$\therefore$ The poles are
$$z_{p_1} = \frac{2 + s_pT}{2 - s_pT}$$

$$z_{p_2} = \frac{2 - s_pT}{2 + s_pT}$$

We note that $z_{p_1} \,.\, z_{p_2} = 1$. **Ans.**

EXAMPLE 9.2: *Show that in a Bilinear Transformation*

$$s = \frac{2}{T}\frac{1-z^{-1}}{1+z^{-1}}$$

the pole pair $s = s_p$, $s = -s_p$ of $H_a(s)$ transform to the pole pair z_p and z_p^{-1} in z-domain.

SOLUTION: Let $H_a(s)$ have the pole pair $s \pm s_p$

$$\therefore \quad H_a(s) = \frac{1}{(s - s_p)(s + s_p)} \text{ (a typical case)}$$

Put $$s = \frac{2}{T}\frac{1 - z^{-1}}{1 + z^{-1}} \text{ to transform } H_a(s) \text{ to } H(z) \text{ i.e.,}$$

$$H(z) = \left.\frac{1}{(s^2 - s_p^2)}\right|_{s = \frac{2}{T}\frac{1-z^{-1}}{1+z^{-1}}}$$

$$= \frac{1}{\left(\frac{2}{T}\frac{1 - z^{-1}}{1 + z^{-1}}\right)^2 - s_{p^2}} = \frac{\left(\frac{T}{2}\right)^2 (1 + z^{-1})^2}{(1 - z^{-1})^2 - \left(\frac{T}{2}(1 + z^{-1})\, s_p\right)^2}$$

$$= \frac{\left(\frac{T}{2}\right)^2 (1 + z^{-1})^2}{\left[1 - z^{-1} + \frac{T}{2} s_p (1 + z^{-1})\right]\left[1 - z^{-1} - \frac{T}{2} s_p (1 + z^{-1})\right]}$$

$$= \frac{\left(\frac{T}{2}\right)^2 (1 + z^{-1})^2}{\left[z^{-1}\left(\frac{T}{2} s_p - 1\right) + \left(1 + \frac{T}{2} s_p\right)\right]\left[z^{-1}\left(-\frac{T}{2} s_p - 1\right) + \left(1 - \frac{T}{2} s_p\right)\right]}$$

$$= \frac{\left(\frac{T}{2}\right)^2 (1 + z^{-1})^2 \left(\dfrac{1}{1 - \frac{T^2}{4} s_{p^2}}\right)}{\left(z^{-1} - \dfrac{1 + \frac{T}{2} s_p}{1 - \frac{T}{2} s_p}\right)\left(z^{-1} - \dfrac{1 - \frac{T}{2} s_p}{1 + \frac{T}{2} s_p}\right)}$$

$$\nearrow z_p^{-1} \qquad\qquad \nearrow z_p$$

Clearly, the poles are of the form z_p and z_p^{-1}.

Note that the results obtained here are the same as in Example 9.1, where we found $z_{p_1} = (z_{p_2})^{-1}$.

9.3 TYPICAL STANDARD FILTERS

We shall now explain the basic properties and parameters of some of the analog filters used for designing the IIR digital filters.

The most important typical filters are:

(i) **Butterworth Filter:** Is monotonic in passband as well as in stopband.

(ii) **Chebyshev Filter:** An equiripple characteristic in the pass band and monotonic in stopband.

(iii) **Elliptical Filter:** Is equiripple in both the passband as well as in stopband.

During the bilinear transformation, the above properties are preserved. However, **the linear phaseness is lost** *i.e.*, if we are interested in a digital lowpass filter with linear-phase characteristic, we cannot obtain such a filter by applying bilinear transformation to analog low-pass filter having linear phase characteristics.

Note: Chebyshev filters can be further classified as the following:

(*a*) **Type I. Chebyshev filters** are all pole filters that are equiripple in the passband and monotonic characteristic in the stopband.

(*b*) **Type II. Chebyshev filters** contain both poles and zeros and exhibit a monotonic behaviour in the passband and an equiripple behaviour in the stopband. The zeros of this class of filters lie on the imaginary axis in the *s*-plane.

9.3.1 Digital Butterworth Filters

Properties:

(*i*) Butterworth filters are defined by the property that the magnitude response is maximally flat in the passband.

(*ii*) For an Nth-order low-pass filter, the first $2N - 1$ derivatives of $|H_a(j\Omega)|^2$ are zero at $\Omega = 0$.

(*iii*) The approximation is monotonic in the passband as well as in the stopband.

If $H_a(j\Omega)$ is the frequency response of the Butterworth filter then

$$|H_a(j\Omega)|^2 = \frac{1}{1+\left(\frac{j\Omega}{j\Omega_c}\right)^{2N}}$$

N^{th}-order Butterworth low-pass filter, in analog domain ...(9.24)

As N increases, the filter characteristics become sharper, as shown in Fig. 9.4. They remain closer to unity over more of the passband and become close to zero more rapidly in the stop band.

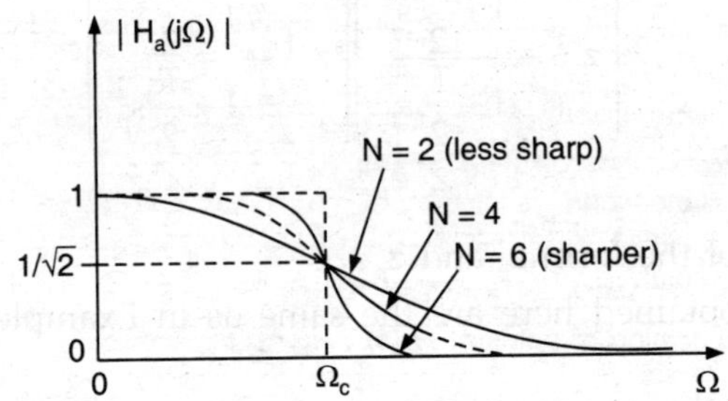

Fig. 9.4. Magnitude response of a Butterworth filter

The magnitude function at $\Omega = \Omega_c$ is always $\frac{1}{\sqrt{2}}$.

Note: We can also have

$$|H_a(j\Omega)|^2 = \frac{1}{1+\varepsilon^2\left(\frac{j\Omega}{j\Omega_c}\right)^{2N}} \quad ...(9.25)$$

Here, the magnitude $|H_a(j\Omega)| = \left(\dfrac{1}{1+\varepsilon^2}\right)^{1/2}$ at $\Omega = \Omega_c$ for all order N. If we put $\varepsilon = 1$ in (9.25), we obtain (9.24). So (9.25) is the expression of a generic Butterworth LPF.

To find poles of $|H_a(s)|^2$: Putting $j\Omega = s$ in (9.24), we have

$$H_a(s) \cdot H_a(-s) = \frac{1}{1+\left(\dfrac{s}{j\Omega_c}\right)^{2N}} \quad \because \quad |H_a(j\Omega)|^2_{j\Omega = s} = H_a(s)\,H_a(-s)$$

The poles of $(H_a(s) \cdot H_a(-s))$ are given by

$$1 + \left(\frac{s}{j\Omega_c}\right)^{2N} = 0$$

$$\therefore \qquad \frac{s}{(j\Omega_c)} = (-1)^{1/2N}$$

$$s_p \text{ (the pole)} = (j\Omega_c)\, e^{j(\pi + 2k\pi)/2N},\ k = 0, \pm 1, \ldots, \pm (N-1), N$$

i.e.,

$$s_p = \Omega_c\, e^{j\left[\frac{\pi}{2} + (2k+1)\frac{\pi}{2N}\right]},\ k = 0, \pm 1, \ldots, \pm (N-1), + N \text{ or } k = 0, 1, 2, \ldots, 2N-1 \qquad \ldots(9.26)$$

Thus, the $2N$ poles of $|H_a(s)|^2_{s = j\Omega}$ have the properties as follows:

(*i*) There are $2N$ poles in all for $|H_a(j\Omega)|^2$.

(*ii*) All the poles lie on the Butterworth circle of radius Ω_c.

(*iii*) The poles are symmetrically placed w.r.t. the imaginary axis

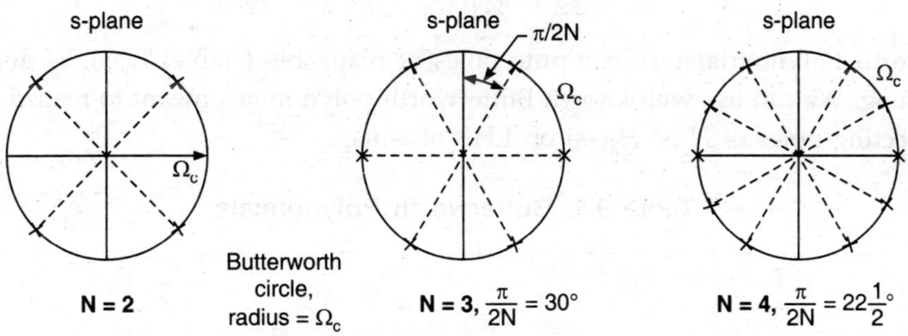

Fig. 9.5. Location of poles of $H_a(s) \cdot H_a(-s)$ for $N = 2$, 3, and 4

(*iv*) A pole never falls on the imaginary axis.

(*v*) For N odd, a pole can occur on the real axis but a pole cannot occur on real axis for N even.

(*vi*) Angular spacing between the poles is π/N radians.

(*vii*) Poles on LHP of s-plane occur in conjugates.

Typically the pole positions for $N = 2, 3, 4$ are shown in Fig. 9.5. Note that

$N = 3$: $\qquad \dfrac{\pi}{N} = \dfrac{\pi}{3} = 60° \quad \therefore$ poles are 60° apart

$\therefore$ Poles are at $\qquad \theta = \dfrac{\pi}{2} + \dfrac{\pi}{6}(1, 3, 5, 7, 9, 11) \quad \theta = \dfrac{\pi}{2} + \dfrac{\pi}{2N}(1+2k),\ k = 0, 1, \ldots, (2N-1)$

$$\therefore \qquad \theta = \underbrace{120°, 180°, 240°}_{\text{LHP poles}}, 300°, 360°, 60°$$

$$N = 4: \qquad \frac{\pi}{N} = \frac{\pi}{4} = 45° \quad \therefore \quad \text{poles are } 45° \text{ apart}$$

$$\therefore \quad \text{Poles are at} \qquad \theta = \frac{\pi}{2} + \frac{\pi}{8}(1, 3, 5, 7, 9, 11, 13, 15)$$

$$\therefore \qquad \theta = 90° + 22\frac{1}{2}°(1, 3, 5, 7, 9, 11, 13, 15)$$

$$= \underbrace{112\frac{1}{2}°, 157\frac{1}{2}°, 202\frac{1}{2}°, 247\frac{1}{2}°}_{\text{LHP poles}}, 292\frac{1}{2}°, 337\frac{1}{2}°, 22\frac{1}{2}°, 67\frac{1}{2}°$$

$$22\frac{1}{2}°, 67\frac{1}{2}°,$$

To realize a stable $H_a(s)$, we choose LHP poles in the s-plane from above poles.

$$\therefore \text{For } N = 3, \qquad H_a(s)\big|_{N=3} = (s - e^{j2\pi/3})\,(s - e^{j\pi})\,(s - e^{j4\pi/3})$$

$$= \left[s - \left(\cos\frac{2\pi}{3} + j\sin\frac{2\pi}{3}\right)\right][s+1]\left[s - \left(\cos\frac{4\pi}{3} + j\sin\frac{4\pi}{3}\right)\right]$$

$$= \left[s + \frac{1}{2} - j\frac{\sqrt{3}}{2}\right][s+1]\left[s + \frac{1}{2} + j\frac{\sqrt{3}}{2}\right] = (s+1)\,(s^2 + s + 1). \quad \text{...(9.23)}$$

Butterworth Polynomials: To compute poles of realizable (stable) $H_a(s)$, as done above, is time consuming. We can use well-known Butterworth polynomials meant to realize Butterworth filter *i.e.*, selecting poles of $H_a(s)\,H_a(-s)$ on LHP of s-plane.

Table 9.1. Butterworth Polynomials

N	*Factor form of $H_a(s)$*	*$\Omega_c = 1$ here*
1.	$s + 1$	
2.	$s^2 + \sqrt{2}\,s + 1$	$= s^2 + 1.414s + 1$
3.	$(s + 1)\,(s^2 + s + 1)$	$= s^3 + 2s^2 + 2s + 1$
4.	$(s^2 + 0.765s + 1)\,(s^2 + 1.848s + 1)$	$= s^4 + 2.613s^3 + 3.414s^2 + 2.613s + 1$
5.	$(s + 1)\,(s^2 + 0.618s + 1)(s^2 + 1.618s + 1)$	
6.	$(s^2 + 0.518s + 1)\,(s^2 + \sqrt{2}\,s + 1)\,(s^2 + 1.932s + 1)$	
7.	$(s + 1)\,(s^2 + 0.44s + 1)\,(s^2 + 1.247s + 1)\,(s^2 + 1.802s + 1)$	
8.	$(s^2 + 0.39s + 1)\,(s^2 + 1.111s + 1)\,(s^2 + 1.166s + 1)$ $(s^2 + 1.962s + 1)$	

For any Ω_c: Above values are for $\Omega_c = 1$. For generic value $\Omega_c \neq 1$, we modify the polynomial, say, $N = 3$.

Replace $s^3 + 2s^2 + 2s + 1$ by $s^3 + 2s^2\Omega_c^1 + 2s\Omega_c^2 + 1\Omega_c^3$ and so on. Similarly, for $N = 4$, we shall obtain

$$H_a(s) = (s^2 + 0.765s\Omega_c + \Omega_c^2)\,(s^2 + 1.848s\Omega_c + \Omega_c^2).$$

This manipulation amounts to replacing s by s/Ω_c in the polynomials given in Table 9.1

Properties of Bilinear Transformation from Analog to Digital Butterworth Filter

The Butterworth filter has

$$|\,H_a(s)\,|^2 = \frac{1}{1+(s/j\Omega_c)^{2N}} \qquad \text{(bilinear transformation)}$$

Putting

$$s = \frac{2}{T}\frac{1-z^{-1}}{1+z^{-1}}$$

we obtain

$$|\,H(z)\,|^2 = \frac{1}{1+\left[\left(\frac{2}{T}\frac{1-z^{-1}}{1+z^{-1}}\right)\Big/ j\Omega_c\right]^{2N}}$$

$$= \frac{[j\Omega_c(1+z^{-1})]^{2N}}{((1+z^{-1})\,j\Omega_c)^{2N} + (2\,(1-z^{-1}))^{2N}} \qquad \text{(letting } T = 1) \quad \ldots(9.28)$$

1. $|\,H(z)\,|^2$ has $2N$ zeros at $1 + z^{-1}$ *i.e.*, at $z = -1$ *i.e.*, at $\omega = \pi$.
2. Also, the Butterworth circle in s-plane maps to a circle in z-plane, since, the bilinear transformation is conformal.

To find the centre of Butterworth circle mapped in z-plane we put the values of transformation as follows:

Transformation of the Butterworth Circle Forms to z Domain

In s-phase the Butterworth circle is given by

$$s = \Omega_c e^{j\,\arg s} \qquad \ldots(9.29)$$

i.e.,

$$|\,s\,|^2 = \Omega_c^2 \qquad \ldots(9.30)$$

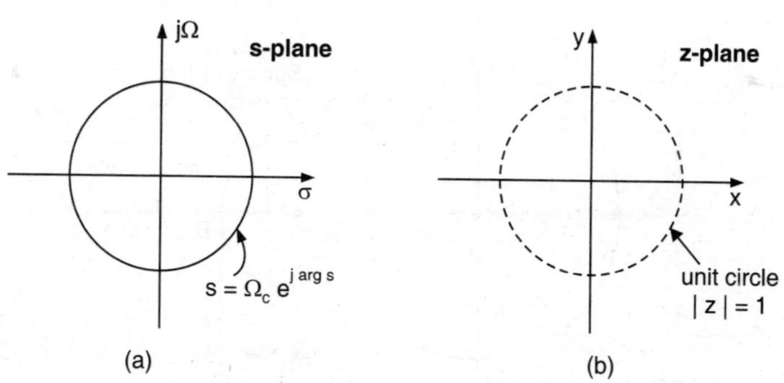

Fig. 9.6. (*a*) Showing a circle of radius Ω_c in *s*-plane, (*b*) Showing a unit circle in *z*-plane

Putting

$$s = \frac{2}{T}\frac{1-z^{-1}}{1+z^{-1}} = \frac{2}{T}\frac{z-1}{z+1}, \text{ we have}$$

$$\left|\frac{2}{T}\frac{z-1}{z+1}\right|^2 = \Omega_c^2$$

Let $z = x + jy$ in the z plane

$$\therefore \quad \left|\frac{x+jy-1}{x+jy+1}\right|^2 = \left(\frac{\Omega_c T}{2}\right)^2 \swarrow \text{ put } \frac{\Omega_{cT}}{2} = K$$

$$\therefore \quad (x-1)^2 + y^2 = K^2[(x+1)^2 + y^2] \qquad \text{...(9.31)}$$

$$x^2[1 - K^2] + y^2[1 - K^2] - 2x(1 + K^2) = K^2 - 1$$

$$x^2 - 2x\,\frac{1+K^2}{1-K^2} + y^2 = -1$$

$$\left(x - \frac{1+K^2}{1-K^2}\right)^2 + y^2 = -1 + \left(\frac{1+K^2}{1-K^2}\right)^2$$

or
$$\left(x - \frac{1+K^2}{1-K^2}\right)^2 + y^2 = \frac{4K^2}{(1-K^2)^2} \qquad \text{form } (x - x_0)^2 + y^2 = a^2$$

This is a circle with radius

$$'a' = \frac{2K}{1-K^2} = \frac{2\left(\frac{\Omega_c T}{2}\right)}{1-\left(\frac{\Omega_c T}{2}\right)^2} = \frac{\Omega_c T}{1-\left(\frac{\Omega_c T}{2}\right)^2} \qquad \text{...(9.32}a\text{)}$$

The centre is at $C(x_0, 0)$

where
$$x_0 = \frac{1+K^2}{1-K^2} = \frac{1+\left(\frac{\Omega_c T}{2}\right)^2}{1-\left(\frac{\Omega_c T}{2}\right)^2} \qquad \text{...(9.32}b\text{)}$$

Extremities of the circle are

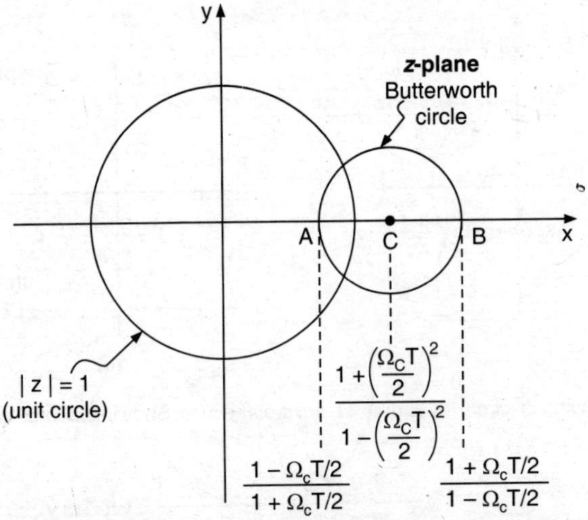

Fig. 9.7. Butterworth circle $s = \Omega_c e^{j \arg s}$ transformed by bilinear transformation

Point A: x_0 – radius

$$= \frac{1+K^2}{1-K^2} - \frac{2K}{1-K^2} = \frac{(1-K)^2}{1-K^2} = \frac{1-K}{1+K} = \frac{1-\left(\frac{\Omega_c T}{2}\right)}{1+\left(\frac{\Omega_c T}{2}\right)} \quad \ldots(9.32c)$$

Point B: x_0 + radius

$$= \frac{1+K^2}{1-K^2} + \frac{2K}{1-K^2} = \frac{1+K}{1-K} = \frac{1+\left(\frac{\Omega_c T}{2}\right)}{1-\left(\frac{\Omega_c T}{2}\right)} \quad \ldots(9.32d)$$

Hence, the Butterworth circle $s = \Omega_c e^{j \arg s}$ in s domain transforms to another "Butterworth" circle in z domain by Bilinear transformation with its

$$\text{Centre } C = \left(\frac{1+K^2}{1-K^2}, 0\right)$$

$$\text{Radius} = \frac{2K}{1-K^2} \quad \ldots(9.33)$$

$$\text{Point } A \left(\frac{1+K}{1-K}, 0\right) \qquad \text{Point } B \left(\frac{1+K}{1-K}, 0\right)$$

where $K = \dfrac{\Omega_c T}{2}$.

EXAMPLE 9.3: *Show that the transfer function of the Butterworth filter which has order n is given by*

$$H(s) = \frac{1}{\prod_{k=1}^{n/2} (s^2 + 2s\cos\theta_k + 1)}, \ \theta_k = \frac{2k-1}{2n}\pi, \ n \text{ even}$$

and

$$H(s) = \frac{1}{\left[(s+1) \prod_{k=1}^{(N-1)/2} (s^2 + 2s\cos\theta_k + 1)\right]}, \ \theta_k = \frac{\pi k}{n}, \ n \text{ odd.}$$

SOLUTION: Let n be even [see Fig. Ex. 9.3(a)]

Here, there is no pole at $\theta = \pi$ and the poles are $\theta_i = [n + (2i - 1)] \dfrac{\pi}{2n}$, $i = 1, 2, \ldots, n$.

Consider the poles at θ_r and θ_{n+1-r}, $r = 1, 2, \ldots, \dfrac{n}{2}$ LHP poles for n even

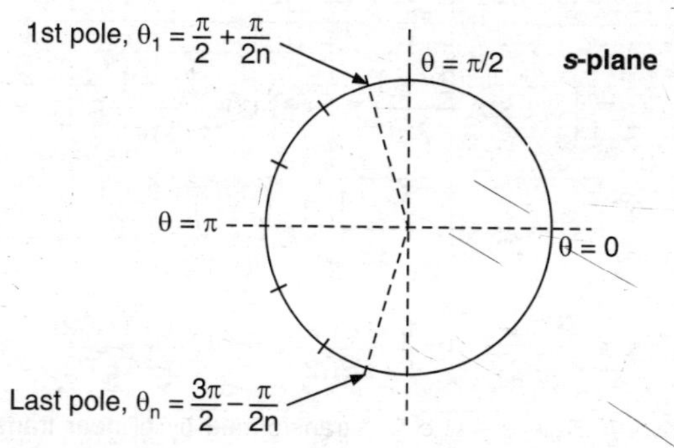

Fig. Ex. 9.3. (a) Location of poles when n is even

$$\therefore \quad (s - e^{j\theta_r})(s - e^{j\theta_{n+1-r}}) = (s - e^{j(n+2r-1)\frac{\pi}{2n}})(s - e^{j(3n-2r+1)\frac{\pi}{2n}})$$

$$= (s - e^{j(n+2r-1)\frac{\pi}{2n}})(s - e^{j(-n-2r+1)\frac{\pi}{2n}})$$

$$= (s - je^{j(2r-1)\frac{\pi}{2n}})(s + je^{-j(2r-1)\frac{\pi}{2n}})$$

$$= \left(s + \sin(2r-1)\frac{\pi}{2n}\right)^2 + \left(\cos(2r-1)\frac{\pi}{2n}\right)^2$$

$$= s^2 + 2s\sin\frac{(2r-1)\pi}{2n} + 1, \; r = 1, 2, ..., \frac{n}{2}$$

Put $\quad k = \frac{n}{2} - r + 1 \quad \therefore \quad 2r - 1 = n - 2k + 1$

when $r = 1, \; k = \frac{n}{2}$, when $r = \frac{n}{2}, k = 1$

$\therefore$ all terms yield

$$= \prod_{k=1}^{n/2}\left(s^2 + 2s\sin\frac{n-2k+1}{2n}\pi + 1\right), \; n \text{ even}$$

$$= \prod_{k=1}^{n/2}\left[s^2 + 2s\cos\left(\frac{2k-1}{2n}\right)\cdot\pi + 1\right]$$

$\therefore$ This is the result for n even, where $\theta_k = \frac{2k-1}{2n}\pi$.

Let n be odd [see Fig. Ex. 9.3(*b*)]

$$\theta_i = [n + (2i-1)]\frac{\pi}{2n}$$

Consider the pole pair at

$$\theta_r \text{ and } \theta_{n+1-r}, \quad r = 1, 2, ..., \frac{n-1}{2}$$

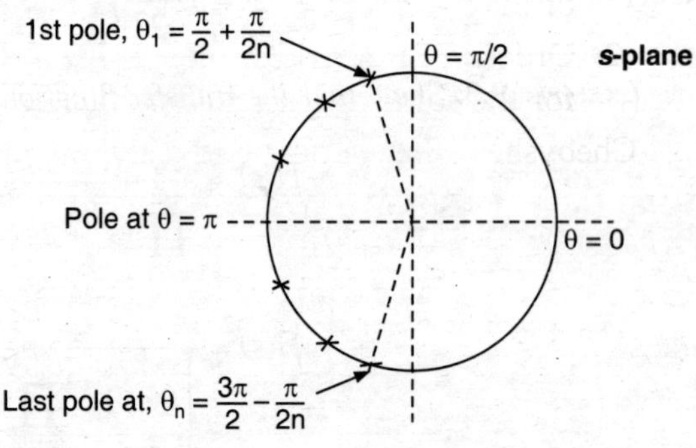

Fig. Ex. 9.3. (*b*) Location of poles when *n* is odd

$$(s - e^{j\theta_r})(s - e^{j\theta_{n+1-r}}) = (s - e^{(n+(2r-1))\frac{\pi}{2n}})(s - e^{j(3n-2r+1)\frac{\pi}{2n}}), \quad r = 1, 2, ..., \frac{n-1}{2}$$

$$= (s - je^{j(2r-1)\frac{\pi}{2n}})(s + je^{-j(2r-1)\frac{\pi}{2n}})$$

$$= \left(s + \sin\frac{2r-1}{2n}\pi\right)^2 + \left(\cos\frac{2r-1}{2n}\pi\right)^2$$

$$= s^2 + 2s\sin\frac{2r-1}{2n}\pi + 1, \quad r = 1, 2, ..., \frac{n-1}{2}$$

Put $\quad k = \frac{n-1}{2} - r + 1 \quad \therefore \quad 2r - 1 = n - 2k$

$$\therefore \quad \text{when } r = 1,\ k = \frac{n-1}{2},$$

$$\text{when } r = \frac{n-1}{2},\ k = 1.$$

Taking all the poles including at $s = -1$, we have the denominator as

$$(s+1)\prod_{k=1}^{(n-1)/2}\left(s^2 + 2s\sin\frac{n-2k}{2n}\pi + 1\right)$$

$$= (s+1)\prod_{k=1}^{(n-1)/2}\left(s^2 + 2s\cos\frac{k}{n}\pi + 1\right)$$

$$= (s+1)\prod_{k=1}^{(n-1)/2}(s^2 + 2s\cos\theta_k + 1),\quad n \text{ odd},\quad \theta_k = \frac{k\pi}{n} \qquad \text{Q.E.D.}$$

9.3.2 Digital Chebyshev Filters

In filter designs, the Chebyshev filters (also called equiripple filters) are the most popular ones due to their equiripple (in the passband for type I) response. Drawbacks of Butterworth filters are:

1. It is monotonic both in passband as well as in stopband. If, say, an LPF (low-pass filter) is defined by maximum passband approximation and we use Butterworth filter, then such a designed filter would adversely exceed the specifications on lower frequency end of the passband, *i.e.*, it would be better at $\omega = 0$ but worst at $\omega = \omega_c$.
2. Order of Butterworth filter is usually higher than that of other types of filters available for the same specifications.

Chebyshev filter is defined by the magnitude square response given by

$$|H_a(j\Omega)|^2 \triangleq \frac{1}{1+\varepsilon^2 V_N^2\left(\dfrac{\Omega}{\Omega_c}\right)},\ \text{Chebyshev filters}$$

where $V_N(x) = \cos(N\cos^{-1}x)$, **Chebyshev polynomial** ...(9.34)

If $N = 0$, $\quad V_N(x) = \cos(0\,.\,\cos^{-1}x) = 1\ \forall x$

For $x < 1$, $\cos^{-1} x$ will be a real function and $\cos(N\cos^{-1}x)$ varies between 0 and 1

At $\Omega = 0$ (*i.e.*, dc),

$$V_N\left(\frac{\Omega}{\Omega_c}\right) = \cos\left(N\cos^{-1}\frac{\Omega}{\Omega_c}\right) = 1,\ V_N(0) = \begin{cases} 0, & N \text{ odd} \\ \pm 1, & N \text{ even}\end{cases}$$

$$\therefore \quad |H_a(j\Omega)|^2\Big|_{\Omega=0} = \frac{1}{1+\varepsilon^2}$$

The variation of $V_N(x)$ is as shown in Fig. 9.8. We, therefore, prefer the design for x upto 1 *i.e.*,

$$\Omega = \Omega_c$$

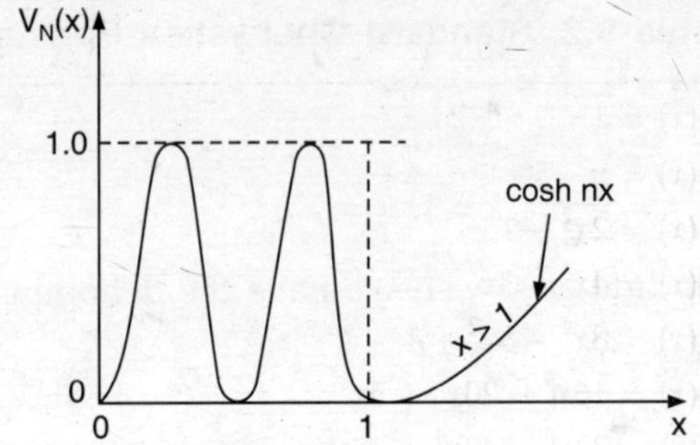

Fig. 9.8. $V_N(x)$ versus x

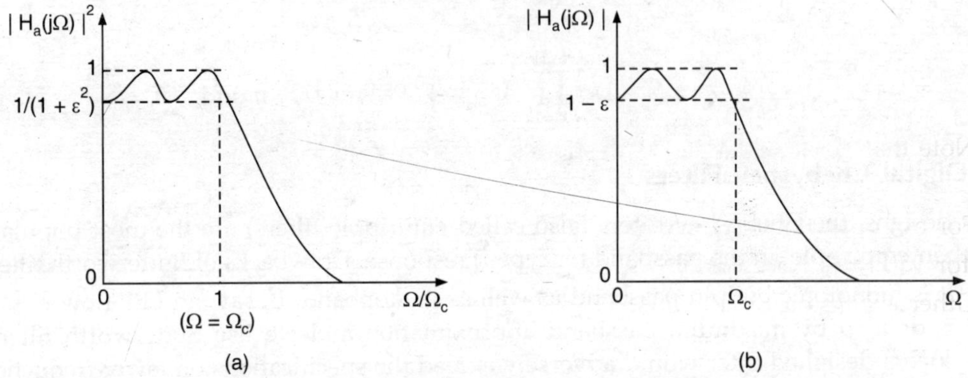

Fig. 9.9. (*a*) Response square of a Chebyshev LPF (*b*) Frequency response of a Chebyshev low-pass filter

Properties of Chebyshev Filters

1. It is equiripple in passband and monotonic in stopband or it is monotonic in passband and equiripple in stopband, *i.e.*, it is equiripple in one band (pass or stop) and monotonic in the other band.
2. We get a better (lower) transition band width by using these designs.
3. It has lower order than the Butterworth filters for the same passband widths and attenuations.

Recursive relation for derivation of $V_N(x)$

We define

$$V_N(x) = \cos(N \cos^{-1} x) \quad \text{(also called Chebyshev of first kind)}$$

Let $\cos^{-1} x = y \quad \therefore \quad x = \cos y$

$\therefore \quad V_N(x) = \cos N y$

Note that

$$\cos[(N+1)\,y] + \cos[(N-1)y] = 2 \cos N y \,.\, \cos y$$

$$\therefore \quad V_{N+1}(x) + V_{N-1}(x) = 2\, V_N(x) \,.\, x$$

$$\therefore \quad \boxed{V_{N+1}(x) = 2x V_N(x) - V_{N-1}(x)} \qquad \ldots(9.35)$$

[Note that $V_N(x) = \sin\,(N \cos^{-1} x)$ is called the Chebyshev of second kind. We shall not use this type of Chebyshev function].

Table 9.2. Standard Chebyshev Polynomials

$V_0(x) = 1$
$V_1(x) = x$
$V_2(x) = 2x^2 - 1$
$V_3(x) = 4x^3 - 3x$
$V_4(x) = 8x^4 - 8x^2 + 1$
$V_5(x) = 16x^5 - 20x^3 + 5x$
$V_6(x) = 32x^6 - 48x^4 + 18x^2 - 1$
$V_7(x) = 64x^7 - 112x^5 + 56x^3 - 7x$
$V_8(x) = 128x^8 - 256x^6 + 160x^4 - 32x^2 + 1$
$V_9(x) = 256x^9 - 576x^7 + 432x^5 - 120x^3 + 9x$
$V_{10}(x) = 512x^{10} - 1280x^8 + 1120x^6 - 400x^4 + 50x^2 - 1$

Note that expansion $V_N(x)$ corresponds to $\cos(Nx) = \sum_{i=0}^{N} d_i (\cos x)^i$

For example, for $V_2(x)$, we have $\cos 2x = 2\cos^2 x - 1$ and for $V_3(x)$, we have $\cos 3x = 4\cos^3 x - 3\cos x$ etc.

Other expansion for $V_N(x)$ is

$$V_N(x) = \sum_{k=0}^{\lfloor N/2 \rfloor} \frac{(-1)^k (n-k-1)!(2x)^{n-2k}}{k!(n-2k)!} \qquad \ldots(9.36)$$

Some Useful Results for Chebyshev Filters

1. $|H_a(j\Omega)|^2$ ripples between 1 and $\frac{1}{1+\varepsilon^2}$ in passband.
2. $|H_a(j\Omega)|$ ripples between 1 and $1 - \varepsilon$ in passband.
3. Chebyshov polynomial of two different orders has the recursive relation [proved in (9.35)]
$$V_{N+1}(x) = 2xV_N(x) - V_{N-1}(x).$$
4. For $x < 1$, $V_N^2(x)$ varies between 0 and 1.
5. For $x > 1$, $V_N(x)$ increases exponentially *i.e.*, $V_N(x)$ behaves as hyperbolic cosine for $x > 1$.
6. For $\frac{\Omega}{\Omega_c} \le 1$, $|H_a(j\Omega)|^2$ ripples between 1 and $\frac{1}{1+\varepsilon^2}$.

   For $\frac{\Omega}{\Omega_c} > 1$, $|H_a(j\Omega)|^2$ decreases monotonically.
7. Three parameters are required to specify the Chebyshev filter, *viz.* Ω_c, N and ε . ε is usually specified by allowable passband ripples and Ω_c is specified by the desired cut off frequency. The order N is then chosen (derived) to meet the stopband specifications. For larger N, ε decreases.

8. Poles of Chebyshev filters lie on an ellipse in *s*-plane.

The ellipse is

$$\text{Minor axis} = a\Omega_c = \frac{1}{2}\,\Omega_c(\alpha^{1/N} - \alpha^{-1/N})$$

$$\text{Major axis} = b\Omega_c = \frac{1}{2}\,\Omega_c(\alpha^{1/N} + \alpha^{-1/N}) \quad \ldots(9.37)$$

$$\text{where } \alpha = \varepsilon^{-1} + \sqrt{1+\varepsilon^2}\,.$$

Rule to Locate Poles of Chebyshev Filters

1. Let N be the order of the filter. Draw $\frac{\pi}{N}$ angles spaced equally around $j\Omega$ axis symmetrically as in a Butterworth circle.
2. Draw minor circle (radius, $a\Omega_c$) and the major circle radius $b\Omega_c$ (see the circles, in Fig. 9.10).
3. The poles of Chebyshev filter will have abscissa as segment on minor circle and ordinate as the segment on major circle where the equispaced angular lines intersect these circles. Thus, P_1, P_2 are so plotted.
4. All poles on LH of *s*-plane are chosen for $H_a(s)$ for the Chebyshev filter [to ensure stability of $H_a(s)$].

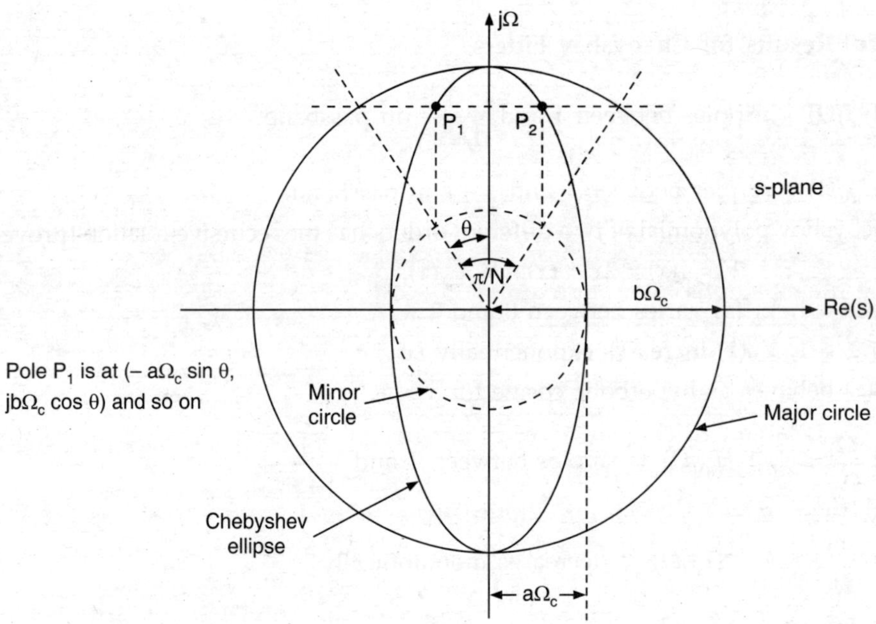

Fig. 9.10. Showing location of poles of a Chebyshev filter for order *N*

9.3.3 Elliptic Filters (or Cauer Filters)

(*i*) We recollect that a Butterworth filter is monotonic in both passband as well as in stopband.

(*ii*) A Chebyshev filter is equiripple in one band and monotonic in the other.

Now the most efficient, lowest order design is feasible with Elliptic filters. An elliptic filter is equiripple both in passband as well as in the stopband.

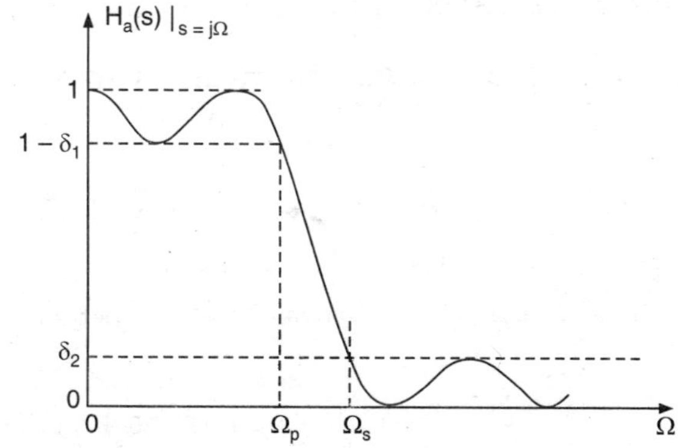

Fig. 9.11. An equiripple approximation in both the passband and stopband

Salient Features of Elliptic Filters

1. The elliptic filter has both the poles and zeros.
2. Zeros of this filter lie on $j\Omega$ axis of s-plane where $H_a(j\Omega) = 0$.
3. This method of approximation leads to the best amplitude response. Digital filters derived from elliptic filters by bilinear transformation (with pre-warping Ω_p and Ω_s) are also optimum *viz.* they have the smallest transition bandwidth $(\Omega_s - \Omega_p)$ for given values of N, Ω_p, δ_1 and δ_2.
4. Impulse invariant transformation technique would destroy the optimality of this filter.
5. Elliptic filter yields lowest-order (*i.e.*, lowest N) that meets the specifications, compared to the Butterworth or Chebyshev filters.
6. We need four parameters (δ_1, δ_2, δ_p and δ_s) to define the elliptic filters.
7. These filters are equiripple in pass and stopband, both.

For analog filters, elliptic filter approximation is obtained as

$$|H_a(j\Omega)|^2 = \frac{1}{1+\varepsilon^2 U_N^2(\Omega)}, \ N \text{ is filter order} \quad \ldots(9.38)$$

where $U_N(\Omega)$ is a **Jacobian elliptic function**. To obtain equiripple error in both the passband and stopband, elliptic filters must have both the poles and zeros.

In general, the design approach for elliptic filter is quite involved, as it requires the use of Jacobian elliptic function $U_N(x)$ requiring the use of tables. Computer programs are also available for designing the elliptic filters.

9.4 IMPULSE INVARIANT (IIR) METHOD

The invariant impulse response (IIR) is another transformation method which is particularly useful for designing low-pass filters.

In this method, the design starts from the specifications of analog filter. We have to replace the analog filter $H_a(s)$ by a digital filter $H(z)$, provided the frequency response of $H(z)$ resembles that of $H_a(s)$. If the impulse response $h_a(t)$ of $H_a(s)$ and the impulse response $h(n)$ that of $H(z)$ are invariant *i.e.*, if

$$h(n) = h_a(nT) \quad \text{...(9.39)}$$

then $H(e^{j\omega})$ and $H_a(j\Omega)$ have similar responses.

9.4.1 The Transformation of $H_a(s)$ of $H(z)$ for Invariant Impulse Response

Let

$$H_a(s) = \sum_{i=1}^{N} \frac{A_i}{s - p_i} \quad \text{...(9.40)}$$

where p_1 are the poles of $H_a(s)$ and A_i are the partial fraction coefficients, if

$$H_a(s) = \frac{N(s)}{(s-p_1)(s-p_2)\dots(s-p_N)} \quad \text{...(9.41)}$$

Taking inverse Laplace transform of (9.40), we obtain

$$h_a(t) = \sum_{i=1}^{N} A_i \, e^{p_i t} \quad \text{...(9.42)}$$

$$h_a(nT) = h(n) = \sum_{i=1}^{N} A_i \, e^{p_i nT} \quad \text{[replacing } t \text{ by } nT \text{ in ...(9.42)]}$$

Taking *z*-transform on both the sides of (9.42), we get

$$H(z) = \sum_{n=-\infty}^{\infty} h(n) \, z^{-n} \quad \text{(by definition)}$$

$$= \sum_{n=0}^{\infty} \left(\sum_{i=1}^{N} A_i \, e^{p_i nT} \right) z^{-n} \quad \text{for casual } h(n)$$

$$= \sum_{i=1}^{N} \sum_{n=0}^{\infty} A_i \, e^{p_i nT} \, z^{-n}$$

$$\therefore \quad H(z) = \sum_{i=1}^{N} \frac{A_i}{1 - e^{p_i T} z^{-1}} \quad \text{...(9.43)}$$

which is the required digital filter $H(z)$ obtained from $H_a(s)$.

9.4.2 Mapping of Poles, Relationship of *s*-plane to *z*-plane

Thus, $\dfrac{1}{s - p_i}$ maps to $\dfrac{1}{1 - e^{p_i T} z^{-1}}$

i.e., a pole $s = p_i$ of $H_a(s)$ maps to a pole $z = e^{p_i T}$ of $H(z)$.

In other words,

$$\boxed{z = e^{sT}} \quad \text{...(9.44)}$$

Let $s = \sigma + j\Omega$ and $z = re^{j\omega}$, r real

$\therefore$ $$re^{j\omega} = e^{(\sigma + j\Omega)T}$$

or $$re^{j\omega} = e^{\sigma T} \cdot e^{j\Omega T}$$

$\therefore$ $$\boxed{\begin{aligned} r &= e^{\sigma T}, \\ \omega &= \Omega T \end{aligned}} \quad \text{...(9.45)}$$

If σ is +ve, $r = e^{\sigma T} > 1$

If σ is –ve, $r = e^{\sigma T} < 1$

If $\sigma = 0$, $r = e^0 = 1$.

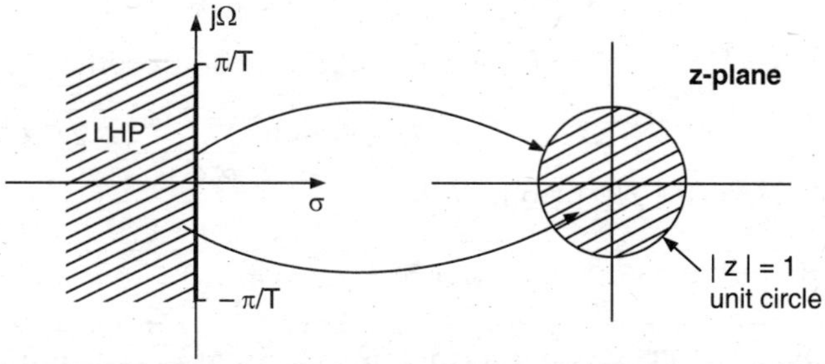

Fig. 9.12. Mapping in invariant impulse response transformation.

Hence, L.H.S. of s-plane maps inside the unit circle *i.e.*, a stable analog filter $H_a(s)$ results in a stable digitals circle $H(z)$.

R.H.S. of s-plane maps outside the unit circle $|z| = 1$. The $j\Omega$ axis maps on the circumference of the unit circle.

As $$\omega = \Omega T$$

$\therefore$ $$\Omega = -\frac{\pi}{T} \text{ to } +\frac{\pi}{T} \text{ maps to } \omega = -\pi \text{ to } +\pi$$

$$\Omega = \frac{\pi}{T} \text{ to } \frac{3\pi}{T} \text{(say) maps to } \omega = \pi \text{ to } 3\pi \text{ i.e., } \omega = -\pi \text{ to } \pi$$

(as $e^{j\omega}$ is periodic with period 2π)

This implies that when $|\Omega|$ exceeds $\frac{\pi}{T}$, then these frequencies overlap in frequencies mapped by $|\Omega| \le \frac{\pi}{T}$. This causes ALIASING.

9.4.3 Drawbacks of Impulse Invariance Method

1. Analog frequency $-\frac{\pi}{T} \le \Omega \le \frac{\pi}{T}$ covers $e^{j\omega}$ from $-\pi$ to π ($\therefore \ \omega = \Omega T$). Mapping of $-(i+1)\frac{\pi}{T}$ to $(i+1)\frac{\pi}{T}$ maps many times, $(i + 1)$ times, in $e^{j\omega}$ domains. Thus, the mapping from analog frequency Ω to digital frequency ω is one to many or many to one. The mapping is not one to one.

2. Due to aliasing, only limited frequency band $-\frac{\pi}{T} \leq \Omega \leq \frac{\pi}{T}$ filter can be transferred without aliasing in z domain.
3. The change in value of sampling time T has no effect to remove aliasing.

Rule to Design a Digital Filter Using Impulse Invariance Method

1. With given specifications of digital filter $H(z)$, obtain expression of $H_a(s)$ here $\omega = \Omega T$. Frequency transformation is linear as ω is proportional to Ω.
2. Express $H_a(s)$ in partial fractions (in first or record degree terms)
3. Obtain $H(z)$ from above partial fractions using standard expressions *viz.*

$$\frac{1}{s-p} \longrightarrow \frac{1}{1-e^{pT}z^{-1}}; \quad \frac{s+a}{(s+a)^2+b^2} \longrightarrow \frac{1-e^{-\alpha T}(\cos bT)\,z^{-1}}{1-2e^{-\alpha T}(\cos bT)\,z^{-1}+e^{-2\alpha T}z^{-2}};$$

$$\frac{b}{(s+a)^2+b^2} \longrightarrow \frac{e^{-\alpha T}(\sin bT)\,z^{-1}}{1-2e^{-aT}(\cos bT)\,z^{-1}+e^{-2aT}z^{-2}}$$

4. We have, thus, obtained $H(z)$ from $H_a(s)$.

Note that $|\ \Omega\ |$ should be $\leq \frac{\pi}{T}$ to avoid in z-domain.

Standard Expressions for Invariant Impulse Response Transformation

$$\boxed{\frac{1}{s-p} \longrightarrow \frac{1}{1-e^{pT}z^{-1}}} \quad \text{...(9.46)}$$

To show that

$$\frac{s+a}{(s+a)^2+b^2} \overset{\text{IIR}}{\longleftrightarrow} \frac{1-e^{-aT}(\cos bT)\,z^{-1}}{1-2e^{-aT}(\cos bT)\,z^{-1}+e^{-2aT}z^{-2}}$$

Proof:

Poles of $\frac{s+a}{(s+a)^2+b^2}$ are at $p_1 = -a + jb$, $p_2 = -a - jb$

$$\therefore \quad \frac{s+a}{(s+a)^2+b^2} = \frac{s+a}{(s-p_1)+(s-p_2)} = \frac{p_1+a}{(s-p_1)+(p_1-p_2)} + \frac{p_2+a}{(s-p_2)+(p_2-p_1)}$$

$$= \frac{1}{p_1-p_2}\left[\frac{p_1+a}{s-p_1} - \frac{p_2+a}{s-p_2}\right] = \frac{1}{2jb}\left[\frac{jb}{s-p_1} - \frac{-jb}{s-p_2}\right]$$

$$= \frac{1}{2}\left[\frac{1}{s-p_1} + \frac{1}{s-p_2}\right]$$

L.H.S. Transforms to $\frac{1}{2}\left(\frac{1}{1-e^{p_1T}z^{-1}} + \frac{1}{1-e^{p_2T}z^{-1}}\right)$

$$= \frac{1}{2}\left(\frac{1}{1-e^{(-a+jb)T}z^{-1}} + \frac{1}{1-e^{(-a-jb)T}z^{-1}}\right)$$

$$= \frac{1}{2}\,\frac{2 - z^{-1}\,e^{-aT}\,(e^{jbT} + e^{-jbT})}{1 - z^{-1}(e^{-aT}(e^{jbT} + e^{-jbT})) + z^{-2}\,e^{-2aT}}$$

$$= \frac{1}{2}\,\frac{2 - e^{-aT}\,(2\cos bT)\,z^{-1}}{1 - e^{-aT}(2\cos bT)\,z^{-1}\,e^{-2aT}\,z^{-2}}$$

$$\therefore \quad \boxed{\frac{s+a}{(s+a)^2 + b^2} \xleftrightarrow{\text{IIR}} \frac{1 - e^{-aT}(\cos bT)\,z^{-1}}{1 - 2e^{-aT}(\cos bT)\,z^{-1} + e^{-2aT}z^{-2}}} \qquad \ldots(9.47)$$

To find IIR transformation for $\dfrac{b}{(s+a)^2 + b^2}$

Proof:

Poles of $\dfrac{b}{(s+a)^2 + b^2}$ are $p_1 = -a + jb$

$p_2 = -a - jb$

$$\therefore \quad \frac{b}{(s+a)^2 + b^2} = b\,\frac{1}{(s-p_1)(s-p_2)}$$

$$= b\left[\frac{1}{(s-p_1)(p_1-p_2)} + \frac{1}{(s-p_2)(p_2-p_1)}\right]$$

$$= \left(\frac{b}{p_1 - p_2}\right)\left[\frac{1}{s-p_1} - \frac{1}{s-p_2}\right]$$

Hence, L.H.S. transforms to:

$$H(z) = \frac{b}{p_1 - p_2}\left[\frac{1}{1 - e^{p_1T}z^{-1}} - \frac{1}{1 - e^{p_2T}z^{-1}}\right]$$

$$= \frac{b}{2jb}\left(\frac{1}{1 - e^{(-a+jb)T}z^{-1}} - \frac{1}{1 - e^{(-a-jb)T}z^{-1}}\right)$$

$$= \frac{1}{2j}\left(\frac{\cancel{1} - e^{-aT}\,e^{-jbT}\,z^{-1} - (\cancel{1} - e^{-aT}\,e^{jbT}\,z^{-1}}{1 - e^{-aT}\,(e^{jbT} + e^{-jbT})\,z^{-1} + e^{-2aT}\,z^{-2}}\right)$$

$$= \frac{1}{2j}\,\frac{e^{-aT}\,(e^{jbT} - e^{jbT})\,z^{-1}}{1 - 2e^{-aT}\,(\cos bT)\,z^{-1} + e^{-2aT}\,z^{-2}}$$

$$\therefore \quad \boxed{\frac{b}{(s+a)^2 + b^2} \xleftrightarrow{\text{IIR}} \frac{e^{-\alpha T}(\sin bT)\,z^{-1}}{1 - 2e^{-\alpha T}(\cos bT)\,z^{-1} + e^{-2\alpha T}z^{-2}}} \qquad \ldots(9.48)$$

EXAMPLE 9.4: *If $H_a(s) = \dfrac{1}{(s+1)(s+2)}$, find the corresponding H(z) using impulse invariant method for sampling frequency 5 samples/s.*

SOLUTION: Here $f_s = 5$ samples/s $\quad \therefore \quad T = \dfrac{1}{f_s} = \dfrac{1}{5} = 0.2$ s

As $$H_a(s) = \frac{1}{(s+1)(s+2)} = \frac{1}{(s+1)} - \frac{1}{s+2}$$

Here, $$p_1 = -1, p_2 = -2$$

$\therefore$ $$H(z) = \frac{1}{1 - e^{p_1 T} z^{-1}} - \frac{1}{1 - e^{p_2 T} z^{-1}}$$

$$= \frac{1}{1 - e^{-1(0.2)} z^{-1}} - \frac{1}{1 - e^{-2(0.2)} z^{-1}}$$

$$= \frac{1}{1 - e^{-0.2} z^{-1}} - \frac{1}{1 - e^{-0.4} z^{-1}}$$

$$= \frac{1 - e^{-0.4}\ z^{-1} - (1 - e^{-0.2}\ z^{-1})}{1 - z^{-1}\ (e^{-0.2} + e^{-0.4}) + e^{-0.6}\ z^{-2}}$$

$$= \frac{(-0.67 + 0.818)\ z^{-1}}{1 - z^{-1}\ (0.818 + 0.67) + 0.548\ z^{-2}}$$

$$= \frac{0.148\ z^{-1}}{1 - 1.488\ z^{-1} + 0.548\ z^{-2}} \quad \textbf{Ans.}$$

EXAMPLE 9.5: *The system function of an analog filter is given by*

$$H_a(s) = \frac{s + 0.2}{(s + 0.2)^2 + 9}$$

Convert this analog filter into a digital filter using impulse invariant technique, assuming T = 1 sec.

SOLUTION: Given

$$H_a(s) = \frac{s + 0.2}{(s + 0.2)^2 + 9} \quad \text{'form } \frac{s + a}{(s + a)^2 + b^2}\text{'}$$

Here, $$a = 0.2, b = 3, T = 1$$

$\therefore$ $$H(z) = \frac{1 - e^{-aT} (\cos bT) . z^{-1}}{1 - 2e^{-aT} (\cos bT)\ z^{-1} + e^{-2aT}\ z^{-2}} \quad \text{[see (9.47)]}$$

$$= \left. \frac{1 - e^{-0.2} \cos (3T)\ z^{-1}}{1 - 2e^{-0.2T} \cos (3T)\ z^{-1} + e^{-0.4T}\ z^{-2}} \right|_{T=1}$$

$$= \frac{1 - e^{-0.2} \cos (3) . z^{-1}}{1 - 2e^{-0.2} \cos (3) . z^{-1} + e^{-0.4}\ z^{-2}}$$

$$= \frac{1-(0.8187)(-0.9899)\, z^{-1}}{1-2\,(0.8187)(-0.9899)\, z^{-1}+0.6703\, z^{-2}}$$

$$= \frac{1+(0.8104)\, z^{-1}}{1+1.6208\, z^{-1}+0.6703\, z^{-2}} \quad \textbf{Ans.}$$

EXAMPLE 9.6: *Given an analog system*

$$H_a(s) = \frac{1}{(s+0.5)(s^2+0.5+2)}$$

Obtain a digital filter by using impulse invariant response (IIR) transforms. Assume T = 1.

SOLUTION: As $\quad H_a(s) = \dfrac{1}{(s+0.5)((-0.5)^2+0.5(-0.5)+2)} + \dfrac{As+B}{(s^2+0.5s+2)}$

$$= \frac{0.5}{(s+0.5)} + \frac{As+B}{(s^2+0.5s+2)}$$

To find A, B

As $\quad 1 = 0.5(s^2 + 0.5s + 2) + (As + B)(s + 0.5)$

Compare s^0 $\quad \therefore \; 1 = 1 + 0.5B \quad \therefore \; B = 0$

Compare s^2 $\quad \therefore \; 0 = 0.5 + A \quad \therefore \; A = -0.5$

Hence, $\quad H_a(s) = \underset{(I)}{\left[\dfrac{0.5}{s+0.5}\right]} + \underset{(II)}{\left[\dfrac{-0.5s}{s^2+0.5s+2}\right]}$

(I) $\quad \xrightarrow{\text{IIR}} = \dfrac{0.5}{1-e^{-0.5}\, z^{-1}} = \dfrac{0.5}{1-0.6065\, z^{-1}}$

(II) $\quad = \dfrac{-0.5\,[s+0.25]+0.125}{(s+0.25)^2+(2-0.0625)}$ $\quad \nearrow = (1.3919)^2$

$$= -(0.5)\frac{s+0.25}{(s+0.25)^2+(1.3919)^2} + \left(\frac{0.125}{1.3919}\right)\frac{1.3919}{(s+0.25)^2+(1.3919)^2}$$

$$\xrightarrow{\text{IIR}} -(0.5)\frac{1-e^{-0.25T}\,[\cos(1.3919\,T)]\, z^{-1}}{1-2e^{-0.25T}\cos(1.3919T)z^{-1}+e^{-0.5T}\, z^{-2}}$$

$$+ (0.898)\frac{e^{-0.25}\sin(1.3919\,T)\, z^{-1}}{1-2e^{-0.25T}\cos(1.3919T)z^{-1}+e^{-0.5T}\, z^{-2}}$$

$$\therefore \quad H(z) = I + II = \frac{0.5}{1-0.6065z^{-1}} + \frac{(-0.5)\,[1-0.1385\, z^{-1}]+(0.898)\,[0.7663\, z^{-1}]}{1-0.277\, z^{-1}+0.606\, z^{-2}}$$

Ans.

EXAMPLE 9.7: *The system function of an analog filter is given as*

$$H_a(s) = \frac{s+0.1}{(s+0.1)^2+3^2}$$

Obtain the system function of the IIR digital filter by using invariant impulse response method.

SOLUTION: $H_a(s) = \frac{s+0.1}{(s+0.1)^2+3^2}$ form $H_a(s) = \frac{s+a}{(s+a)+b^2}$

Here $a = 0.1, b = 3$

$$\therefore \quad H(z) = \frac{1+e^{-aT}(\cos bT)\, z^{-1}}{1-2e^{-aT}(\cos bT)\, z^{-1}+e^{-2aT}\, z^{-2}}$$

$$= \frac{1+e^{-0.1T}(\cos(3T))\, z^{-1}}{1-2e^{-0.1T}\cos(3T)\, z^{-1}+e^{-0.2T}\, z^{-2}} \quad \textbf{Ans.}$$

If $T = 1$, for example, then

$$H(z) = \frac{1-e^{-0.1}(\cos 3T)\, z^{-1}}{1-2e^{-0.1}(\cos 3)\, z^{-1}+e^{-0.2}\, z^{-2}}$$

$$= \frac{1-(0.9048)(-0.9899)\, z^{-1}}{1-2(0.9048)(-0.9899)\, z^{-1}+(0.8187)\, z^{-2}}$$

$$= \frac{1+0.8956\, z^{-1}}{1-2(0.8956)\, z^{-1}+0.8187\, z^{-2}}$$

$$= \frac{1+0.8956\, z^{-1}}{1-1.7913\, z^{-1}+0.8187\, z^{-2}} \quad \textbf{Ans.}$$

EXAMPLE 9.8: *The system function of an analog filter is given by*

$$H_a(s) = \frac{s+2.3}{(s+0.3)^2+16}$$

Obtain the system function of IIR digital filter by using invariant impulse response method.

SOLUTION: We can write $H_a(s)$ as

$$H_a(s) = \frac{(s+0.3)+2}{(s+0.3)+4^2} = \frac{s+0.3}{(s+0.3)^2+4^2} + \frac{1}{2}\frac{s+4}{(s+0.3)^2+4^2}$$

$$\text{Form } \frac{s+a}{(s+a)^2+b^2} \nearrow \qquad \text{Form } \frac{b}{(s+a)^2+b^2} \nearrow$$

Here $a = 0.3, b = 4$

$$H(z) = \frac{1-e^{-aT}(\cos bT)\,.\, z^{-1}}{1-2\,e^{-aT}(\cos bT)\, z^{-1}+e^{-2aT}\, z^{-2}} + \frac{1}{2}\frac{e^{-aT}(\sin bT)\, z^{-1}}{1-2\,e^{-aT}(\cos bT)\, z^{-1}+e^{-2aT}\, z^{-2}}$$

Assume $T = 1$, use $a = 0.3$ and $b = 4$

$$\therefore \qquad H(z) = \frac{1 + e^{-0.3}\left(-\cos 4 + \frac{1}{2}\sin 4\right)z^{-1}}{1 - 2e^{-0.3}(\cos 4)\,z^{-1} + e^{-0.6}\,z^{-2}}$$

$$= \frac{1 + 0.7408\,(-(-0.6536) + 0.5\,(-0.7568))\,z^{-1}}{1 - 2\,(0.7408)\,(-0.6536)\,z^{-1} + 0.5488\,z^{-2}}$$

$$= \frac{1 + 0.7408\,(0.2752)\,z^{-1}}{1 + 0.9683\,z^{-1} + 0.5488\,z^{-2}}$$

$$= \frac{1 + 0.2038\,z^{-1}}{1 + 0.9683\,z^{-1} + 0.5488\,z^{-2}} \qquad \textbf{Ans.}$$

EXAMPLE 9.9: *Design a Butterworth low-pass digital filter, assuming passband magnitude constant within 1 dB for 0 to 0.2 π stopband magnitude (attenuation) is ≤ 15 dB from 0.3 π to π use impulse invariance transformation.*

SOLUTION:

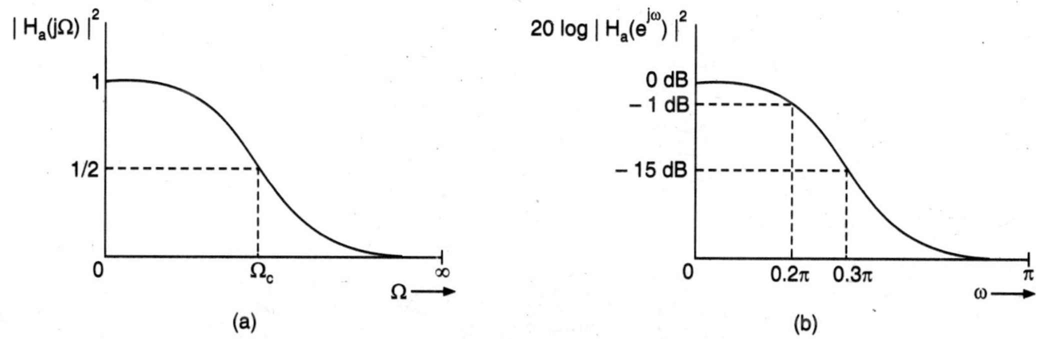

Fig. Ex. 9.9. (*a*) Analog Butterworths filters (typical), (*b*) Specified digital LPF filter

The given data is

$$20 \log_{10} |H(e^{j\omega})| \geq -1 \text{ dB for } |\omega| \leq 0.2\pi$$

$$20 \log_{10} |H(e^{j\omega})| \leq -15 \text{ dB for } 0.3\pi \leq |\omega| \leq \pi$$

In impulse invariance method of transformation,

(*i*) Frequency is mapped linearly

(*ii*) There is aliasing problem

To start with, we assume negligible effect of aliasing, and check such a performance after the design

As, here $\boxed{z = e^{sT}, \omega = \Omega T}$ $\qquad e^{j\omega} = e^{j\Omega T} \qquad \therefore\ z = e^{sT},\ \because\ j\Omega = s$

$$\therefore \qquad H_a(s) \Rightarrow H_a(s)\big|_{e^{sT} = z} = H(z)$$

Thus,
$$H(z) = H_a(s)\big|_{e^{sT} = z}$$

As in a Butterworth filter we have

$$|H_a(j\Omega)|^2 = \frac{1}{1 + \left(\dfrac{j\Omega}{j\Omega_c}\right)^{2N}}$$

Here $\omega = \Omega T$

Taking $T = 1$ gives us

$$\omega = \Omega$$

$\omega_1 = 0.2\,\pi$ gives $\Omega_1 = 0.2\,\pi$ for 1 dB attenuation

$\omega_2 = 0.3\,\pi$ gives $\Omega_2 = 0.3\,\pi$ for 15 dB attenuation

i.e.,

$$20 \log \mid H_a(j\,0.2\,\pi) \mid = -1 \text{ dB}$$

and

$$20 \log \mid H_a(j\,0.3\,\pi) \mid = -15 \text{ dB}$$

$$\therefore \quad 10 \log \left[1 + \left(\frac{j\,0.2\,\pi}{j\Omega_c}\right)^{2N}\right] = 1$$

$$10 \log \left[1 + \left(\frac{j\,0.3\,\pi}{j\Omega_c}\right)^{2N}\right] = 15$$

i.e.,

$$\left(\frac{0.2\,\pi}{\Omega_c}\right)^{2N} = 10^{0.1} - 1 = 0.2589 \qquad \ldots(A)$$

$$\left(\frac{0.2\,\pi}{\Omega_c}\right)^{2N} = 10^{1.5} - 1 = 30.6227 \qquad \ldots(B)$$

Dividing (*B*) by (*A*) gives

$$\left(\frac{0.3\,\pi}{0.2\,\pi}\right)^{2N} = \frac{30.6227}{0.2589} = 118.28$$

$$\therefore \quad (1.5)^{2N} = 118.28$$

$$2\,N \underbrace{\log 1.5}_{\nearrow = 0.176} = \log 118.28 = 2.0729$$

$$\therefore \quad N = \frac{2.0729}{2 \times 0.176} = 5.88$$

$$\boxed{\text{Choose } N = 6}$$

Putting $N = 6$ in (*B*) yields

$$\left(\frac{\Omega_c}{0.3\,\pi}\right)^{2N} = \frac{1}{30.6227}$$

$$\underbrace{2N}_{\nearrow = 12} \log \left(\frac{\Omega_c}{0.3\,\pi}\right) = -\log 30.6227 = -1.4860$$

$$\therefore \quad \frac{\Omega_c}{0.3\,\pi} = 10^{-1.4860/12} = 0.7519$$

$\therefore \quad \Omega_c = 0.3\,\pi \times 0.7519 = 0.7086 \quad \therefore \quad \Omega_c = 0.7086$

Given $\quad N = 6, \Omega_c = 0.7086$, we have

$$H_a(s) = \frac{\Omega_c^6}{(s^2 + 0.518\, s\Omega_c + 1\Omega_c^2)(s^2 + \sqrt{2}\, s\Omega_c + 1\Omega_c^2)(s^2 + 1.932\, s\Omega_c + 1\Omega_c^2)}$$

$$= \frac{0.12659}{(s^2 + 0.3670\, s + 0.502)(s^2 + 1.002\, s + 0.502)(s^2 + 1.369\, s + 0.502)} \quad \left(\because \Omega_c^6 = (0.7086)^6 = 0.12659\right)$$

To obtain $H(z)$, we must put $H_a(s)$ in the form

$$H_a(s) = \sum_{k=1}^{N} \frac{A_k}{s - s_k} \qquad \because \text{ poles are } s = s_k$$

and then

$$H(z) = \sum_{k=1}^{N} \frac{T \cdot A_k}{1 - e^{s_k T} - z^{-1}} \qquad \text{Here } T = 1 \quad N = 6$$

$$\because \text{ poles are } z = e^{s_k T}$$

We finally get

$$H(z) = \frac{0.2871 - 0.4466\, z^{-1}}{1 - 0.1297\, z^{-1} + 0.6949\, z^{-2}} + \frac{-2.1428 + 1.1454\, z^{-1}}{1 - 1.0691\, z^{-1} + 0.3699\, z^{-2}} + \frac{1.8558 - 0.6304\, z^{-1}}{1 - 0.9972\, z^{-1} + 0.2570\, z^{-2}}$$

Ans.

The above $H(z)$ can be realized by parallel form, each arm with 2nd order. This filter meets exactly the specifications at passband and exceeds specifications in the stopband. If the designed filter fails to meet the specifications, we can try again worth higher order filter.

EXAMPLE 9.10: *By using bilinear transformation method, design an IIR digital filter with maximum flatness at* $\omega = 0$ *and*

$$0.8 \le |H(e^{j\omega})| \le 1, \quad 0 \le \omega \le 0.2\,\pi$$
$$|H(e^{j\omega})| \le 0.2, \quad 0.6\pi \le \omega \le \pi$$

Find out the system response H(z) of the designed filter.

SOLUTION: This is a Butterworth filter case. If we use bilinear transformation, then

$$\boxed{\Omega = \frac{2}{T} \tan \frac{\omega}{2}}$$

Assume $\quad T = 1$

$$\therefore \quad \Omega_1 = 2 \tan \frac{0.2\,\pi}{2} = 0.6498$$

$$\Omega_2 = 2 \tan \frac{0.6\,\pi}{2} = 2.7527$$

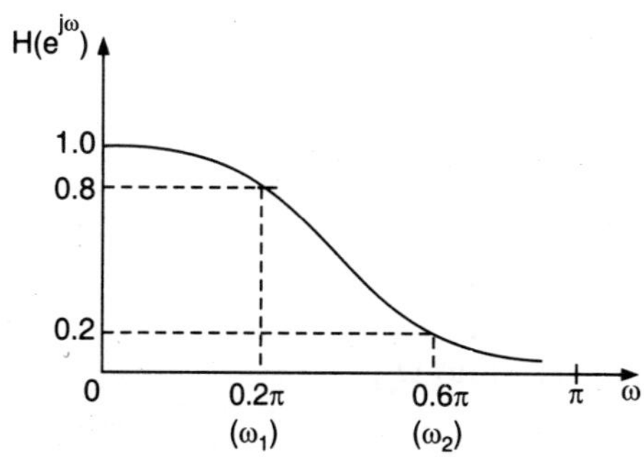

Fig. Ex. 9.10. The desired digital filter

As

$$|H_a(j\Omega)|^2 = \frac{1}{1 + \left(\dfrac{\Omega}{\Omega_c}\right)^{2N}} \qquad \text{[for an analog Butterworth filter]}$$

$$\therefore \quad \frac{1}{1+\left(\frac{\Omega_1}{\Omega_c}\right)^{2N}} \geq (0.8)^2$$

$$\frac{1}{1+\left(\frac{\Omega_2}{\Omega_c}\right)^{2N}} \leq (0.2)^2$$

or taking equality signs, we can write

$$1+\left(\frac{\Omega_1}{\Omega_c}\right)^{2N} = \frac{1}{(0.8)^2} = \frac{25}{16}$$

$$1+\left(\frac{\Omega_2}{\Omega_c}\right)^{2N} = \left(\frac{1}{0.2}\right)^2 = 25$$

$$\therefore \quad \left(\frac{\Omega_1}{\Omega_c}\right)^{2N} = \frac{25}{16} - 1 = \frac{9}{16} \qquad \ldots(1)$$

$$\left(\frac{\Omega_2}{\Omega_c}\right)^{2N} = 25 - 1 = 24 \qquad \ldots(2)$$

[To find N, Ω_c]
Dividing (1) by (2)

$$\left(\frac{\Omega_1}{\Omega_2}\right)^{2N} = \frac{9}{16 \times 24} = \frac{3}{128}$$

$$\therefore \quad \left(\frac{0.6498}{2.7527}\right)^{2N} = \frac{3}{128}$$

$$2N \log \frac{0.6498}{2.7527} = \log \frac{3}{128}$$

$$\therefore \quad N = \frac{1}{2} \frac{\log\left(\frac{3}{128}\right)}{\log \frac{0.6498}{2.7527}} = \frac{1}{2} \frac{-1.63008}{-0.62697} = 1.29$$

Choose $N = 2$ (an integer) $\boxed{N = 2}$

[To find Ω_c]

Let $|H_a(j\Omega_1)|^2 = (0.8)^2$ at $\Omega = \Omega_1$ with $N = 2$

$$\therefore \quad 1 + \left(\frac{\Omega_1}{\Omega_c}\right)^{2N} = \left(\frac{1}{0.8}\right)^2 = \frac{100}{64}$$

or

$$\left(\frac{\Omega_c}{\Omega_1}\right)^{2\times 2} = \frac{1}{\frac{100}{64} - 1} = \frac{64}{36} = \frac{16}{9}$$

$$\therefore \quad \Omega_c = \Omega_1 \left(\frac{16}{9}\right)^{1/4} = \Omega_1 \times 1.1547$$

$$= 0.6498 \times 1.1547 = 0.7503, \text{ say, } 0.75 \qquad \boxed{\Omega_c = 0.75}$$

For $N = 2$ and $\Omega_c = 0.75$, we can write

$$H_a(s) = \frac{\Omega_c^2}{s^2 + \sqrt{2}s\,.\,\Omega_c + \Omega_c^2} \qquad \text{for a Butterworth filter}$$

$$= \frac{(0.75)^2}{s^2 + \sqrt{2}\,(0.75)s + (0.75)^2}$$

$$= \frac{0.5625}{s^2 + 1.0607s + 0.5625}$$

Put $$s = \frac{2}{T}\left(\frac{1-z^{-1}}{1+z^{-1}}\right) = 2\,\frac{1-z^{-1}}{1+z^{-1}}, \text{ taking } T = 1, \text{ here}$$

$$\therefore \quad H(z) = \frac{0.5625}{\left[2^2\left(\frac{1-z^{-1}}{1+z^{-1}}\right)^2 + 1.0607 \times 2\,.\left(\frac{1-z^{-1}}{1+z^{-1}}\right) + 0.5625\right]}$$

$$= \frac{0.5625\,(1+z^{-1})^2}{\left[4\,(1-z^{-1})^2 + 1.1214\,(1-z^{-1})\,(1+z^{-1}) + 0.5625\,(1+z^{-1})^2\right]}$$

$$= \frac{0.5625\,(1+z^{-1})^2}{[(4 + 1.1214 + 0.5625) + z^{-1}(-8 + 2 \times 0.5625) + z^{-2}\,(4 - 1.1214 + 05625)]}$$

$$= \frac{0.5625\,(1+z^{-1})^2}{(6.6839 - 6.875z^{-1} + 2.441\,z^{-2})}$$

$$\therefore \quad H(z) = \frac{0.0842\,(1+z^{-1})^2}{1 - 1.0286\,z^{-1} + 0.3652\,z^{-2}}$$ **Ans.**

Check: $$H(z)\big|_{z=1} = \frac{0.0842\,(1+1)^2}{1 - 1.0286 + 0.3652}$$

$$= \frac{0.3368}{1.3652 - 1.0286}$$

$$= \frac{0.3368}{0.3366} \approx 1 \text{ as expected}$$

$\therefore$ dc response is of value of 1, for this low-pass filter.

EXAMPLE 9.11: *By using bilinear transformation method, design an IIR digital filter with maximum flatness at* $\omega = \pi$ *with the specifications: (HPF)*

$$0.8 \le | H(e^{j\omega}) | \le 1, \quad 0.6\pi \le | \omega | \le \pi$$

$$| H(e^{j\omega}) | \le 0.2, \quad 0 \le | \omega | \le 0.2\pi$$

Determine the order N, and H(z) of the filter.

SOLUTION:

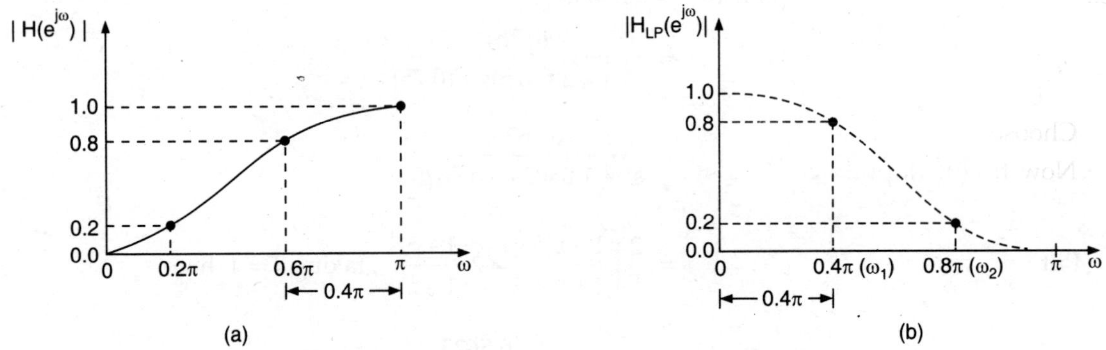

Fig. Ex. 9.11. (*a*) The desired HPF, (*b*) We aim at such LPF

Formulate the problem of an equivalent, LPF with

$$0.8 \le | H_{LP}(e^{j\omega}) | \le 1 \text{ for } 0 \le | \omega | \le 0.4\pi$$

$$| H_{LP}(e^{j\omega}) | \le 0.2 \text{ for } 0.8\pi \le | \omega | \le \pi$$

By bilinear transformation, going to analog domain requires, taking $T = 1$

$$\Omega = 2 \tan \frac{\omega}{2}$$

$$\therefore \quad \Omega_1 = 2 \tan \frac{\omega_1}{2} = 2 \tan (0.2\pi) = 1.45308$$

$$\Omega_2 = 2 \tan \frac{\omega_2}{2} = 2 \tan (0.4\pi) = 6.15536$$

By using Butterworth filter, we get

$$| H(j\Omega) |^2 = \frac{1}{1 + \left(\frac{\Omega}{\Omega_c}\right)^{2N}}$$

At $\Omega_1 = 1.45308$, $1 + \left(\frac{1.45308}{\Omega_c}\right)^{2N} = \left(\frac{1}{0.8}\right)^2 = \frac{100}{64}$

$$\therefore \quad \left(\frac{1.45308}{\Omega_c}\right)^{2N} = \frac{36}{64} \qquad \ldots(A)$$

At $\Omega_2 = 6.15536$, $1 + \left(\frac{6.15536}{\Omega_c}\right)^{2N} = \left(\frac{1}{0.2}\right)^2 = 25$

$$\therefore \qquad \left(\frac{6.15536}{\Omega_c}\right)^{2N} = 24 \qquad \ldots(B)$$

Dividing (*B*) by (*A*), we have

$$\left(\frac{6.15536}{1.45308}\right)^{2N} = \frac{24 \times 64}{36} = 42.6666$$

i.e.,

$$(4.236)^{2N} = 42.6666$$

$$\therefore \qquad N = \frac{1}{2}\frac{\log 42.6666}{\log 4.236} = \frac{1}{2}\frac{1.63008}{0.6269} = 1.3$$

Choose $N = 2$ $\boxed{N = 2}$

Now from (*A*), putting $N = 2$, we obtain

$$\left(\frac{1.45308}{\Omega_c}\right)^{2\times 2} = \frac{36}{64}$$

$$\therefore \qquad \left(\frac{1.45308}{\Omega_c}\right) = \left(\frac{36}{64}\right)^{1/4} = 0.866025$$

$$\therefore \qquad \Omega_c = \frac{1.45308}{0.866025} = 1.6778 \qquad \boxed{\Omega_c = 1.6778}$$

For $N = 2$, $\Omega_c = 1.6778$, the Butterworth LPF is given by

$$\tilde{H}_{LP}(s) = \frac{\Omega_c^2}{s^2 + \sqrt{2} + \Omega_c s + (\Omega_c)^2} = \frac{2.815}{s^2 + 2.3728s + 2.815}$$

To transform $\tilde{H}_{LP}(s)$ to digital LPF $H_{LP}(z)$, put $s = \frac{2}{T}\frac{1-z^{-1}}{1+z^{-1}}$ in $\tilde{H}_{LP}(s)$. Assuming $T = 1$, we have

$$H_{LP}(z) = \tilde{H}_{LP}(s)\Big|_{s=\frac{2(1-z^{-1})}{1+z^{-1}}} = \frac{2.815}{\left(\frac{2(1-z^{-1})^2}{1+z^{-1}}\right)^2 + 2.3728 \,.\, \frac{2(1-z^{-1})}{1+z^{-1}} + 2.815}$$

$$= \frac{2.815\,(1+z^{-1})^2}{4(1-z^{-1})^2 + 4.7456\,(1-z^{-2}) + 2.815\,(1+z^{-1})^2}$$

$$= \frac{2.815\,(1+z^{-1})^2}{z^{-2}(4-4.7456+2.815) + z^{-1}(-8+2\times 2.815) + (4+4.7456+2.815)}$$

$$= \frac{2.815\,(1+z^{-1})^2}{2.0694\,z^{-2} - 2.37\,z^{-1} + 11.5606}$$

$$= \frac{1.3603\,(1+z^{-1})^2}{z^{-2} - 1.1452\,z^{-1} + 5.5864}$$

$$\boxed{H_{HP}(z) = H_{LP}(z)\,|_{z \text{ changed to } -z}}$$

$$= \frac{1.3603\,(1+z^{-1})^2}{z^{-2}+1.1452\,z^{-1}+5.5864}$$

Check: $H_{HP}(z)\big|_{z=e^{j\pi}=-1} = \frac{1.3603\,(1+1)^2}{(1)^2+1.1452\,(-1)+5.5864} = 1.0$, as expected

$H_{HP}(z)\big|_{z=e^{j0}=1} = 0$, as expected

$$H_{HP}(z)\Big|^2_{\substack{z=e^{j0.6\pi}=-0.309+j0.951\\ \therefore z^{-1}=-0.309-j0.951\\ z^{-2}=-0.809+j0.588}} = \left|\frac{1.3603\,(1+0.309+j\,0.951)^2}{(-0.809+j0.588)+1.1452\,(-0.309-j0.951)+5.5864}\right|^2$$

$$\Rightarrow \frac{12.686}{19.818} = 0.6401 \geq 0.8^2 \quad \therefore \quad \text{OK}$$

Check at ω = 0.2π

$$|H_{HP}(z)|^2_{\substack{\text{at } z=e^{j0.2\pi}\\ \text{i.e. } z^{-1}\, e^{-j0.2\pi}=0.809-j0.5878\\ z^{-2}=e^{-j0.4\pi}=0.309-j0.951}} = \left|\frac{1.3603\,(1-0.809+j0.5878)^2}{(0.309-j0.951)-1.1452\,(0.809-j0.5878)+5.5864}\right|^2$$

$$= \frac{0.270}{(4.9689)^2+(-0.2779)^2} = 0.0109 = (0.104)^2 \leq (0.2)^2$$

Thus, the designed *IIR*, Butterworth filter has

$\mid H(e^{j\omega})\mid$	**Specified**	**Achieved**
at ω = 0	0.0	0.0
ω = π	1.0	1.0
ω = 0.2π	≤ 0.2	0.104
ω = 0.6π	≥ 0.8	0.80006

Hence, the design meets the specifications in a better way

Thus, $H_{HP}(z) = \frac{1.3603\,(1-z^{-1})^2}{z^{-2}+1.1452\,z^{-1}+5.5864}$ **Ans.**

EXAMPLE 9.12: *Design an IIR, low-pass filter with specifications:*
Passband 0 to 0.25π radians, magnitude within 0.75 dB
Stopband 0.4π to π radians, attenuation at least 20 dB
Use bilinear transformation and design a maximally flat filter in the Butterworth sense. Use
For $N = 5,\ (s+1)(s^2+1.618\,s+1)\,(s^2+0.618\,s+1)$
$N = 6,\ (s^2+1.932\,s+1)\,(s^2+1.414s+1)\,(s^2+0.518\,s+1)$.

SOLUTION: The given specifications are:

$$20\log_{10}|H(e^{j0.25\pi})| \geq -0.75 \text{ dB}$$
$$20\log_{10}|H(e^{j0.4\pi})| \leq -20 \text{ dB}$$

In bilinear transformation case, above specifications correspond to (pre-warping)

$$\because \Omega = \frac{2}{T}\tan\frac{\omega}{2}$$

$$20\log_{10}\left|H_a\left(j\,2\tan\left(\frac{0.25\pi}{2}\right)\right)\right| \geq -0.75 \text{ dB} \quad \left(\frac{\Omega T}{2} = \tan\frac{\omega}{2}.\ \text{Take } T=1 \because \Omega = 2\tan\frac{\omega}{2}\right)$$

$$20 \log_{10} \left| H_a\left(j\,2 \tan\left(\frac{0.40\pi}{2}\right)\right) \right| \le -20 \text{ dB}$$

Using Butterworth design, therefore, we have

$$| H_a (j\Omega) |^2 = \frac{1}{1 + (j\Omega / j\Omega_c)^{2N}}$$

Taking equality signs, we have:

$$20 \log_{10} \left[1 + \left(\frac{j2 \tan 0.125\pi}{j\Omega_c} \right)^{2N} \right]^{1/2} = 0.75$$

i.e.

$$\log_{10} \left[1 + \left(\frac{2 \tan 0.125\pi}{\Omega_c} \right)^{2N} \right] = \frac{0.75}{10} \qquad \text{...(A)}$$

Similarly,

$$\log_{10} \left[1 + \left(\frac{2 \tan 0.20\,\pi}{\Omega_c} \right)^{2N} \right] = \frac{20}{10} \qquad \text{...(B)}$$

[To solve (A) and (B) for N and Ω_c]

From (A), we have

$$\left(\frac{2 \tan 0.125\,\pi}{\Omega_c} \right)^{2N} = 10^{0.075} - 1 = 0.1885 \qquad \text{...(C)}$$

From (B), we have

$$\left(\frac{2 \tan 0.2\,\pi}{\Omega_c} \right)^{2N} = 10^{2} - 1 = 99.000 \qquad \text{...(D)}$$

i.e.,

$$\left(\frac{\overbrace{\tan 0.2\,\pi}^{=0.7265}}{\underbrace{\tan 0.125\,\pi}_{=0.4142}} \right)^{2N} = \frac{99.0000}{0.1885} = 525.1989$$

$\therefore$

$$2N \underbrace{\left(\log \frac{0.7265}{0.4142} \right)}_{=0.244} = (\log 525.1989) = 2.72032$$

$$N = \frac{2.72032}{(2 \times 0.244)}$$

$$N = 5.57$$

Choose $N = 6$ $\boxed{N = 6}$

Putting $N = 6$ in (C), we have

$$\left(\frac{2 \tan 0.125\,\pi}{\Omega_c} \right)^{2 \times 6} = 0.1885$$

i.e.,
$$\frac{2\times 0.4142}{\Omega_c} = (0.1885)^{1/12} = 0.87018$$

$$\therefore \quad \Omega_c = \frac{2\times 0.4142}{0.87018} = 0.95198, \text{ say } 0.952 \qquad \boxed{\Omega_c = 0.952}$$

For $N = 6$, Butterworth polynomial for $\Omega_c = 1$

$$B_6 = (s^2 + 1.932\,s + 1)(s^2 + 1.414\,s + 1)(s^2 + 0.518\,s + 1)$$

Hence,
$$H_a(j\Omega) = \frac{\Omega_c^6}{(s^2+1.932s\Omega_c+\Omega_c^2)(s^2+1.414s\Omega_c+\Omega_c^2)(s^2+0.518s\Omega_c+\Omega_c^2)}$$
$$\nearrow$$
$$j\Omega = s$$

Putting $\Omega_c = 0.952$, we get

$$H_a(j\Omega) = \frac{0.7444}{(s^2+1.839s+0.906)(s^2+1.346\,s+0.906)(s^2+0.493s+0.906)}$$
$$\nearrow$$
$$H_a(s)$$

To transform in digital domain, put $s = \dfrac{2}{T}\dfrac{1-z^{-1}}{1+z^{-1}}$

Using $T = 1$ for simplicity, $s = \dfrac{2(1-z^{-1})}{[(1+z^{-1})]}$

$$\therefore H(z) = H_a(s)\Big|_{s=\frac{2(1-z^{-1})}{(1+z^{-1})}}$$

$$= \frac{0.7444}{\left[\left(\frac{(1-z^{-1})\times 2}{(1+z^{-1})}\right)^2 + 1.839\frac{(1-z^{-1})\times 2}{1+z^{-1}} + 0.906\right]\left[\left(\frac{(1-z^{-1})\times 2}{(1+z^{-1})}\right)^2 + 1.346\frac{(1-z^{-1})\times 2}{(1+z^{-1})} + 0.906\right] \times \left[\left(\frac{(1-z^{-1})\times 2}{(1+z^{-1})}\right)^2 + 0.4938\frac{(1-z^{-1})\times 2}{1-z^{-1}} + 0.906\right]}$$

$$\therefore H(z) = \frac{0.7444\,(1+z^{-1})^6}{[4(1-z^{-1})^2+3.678\,(1-z^{-2})+0.906\,(1-z^{-1})^2][4(1-z^{-1})^2+2.692\,(1-z^{-2}) + 0.906\,(1+z^{-1})^2][4(1-z^{-1})^2+0.9876\,(1-z^{-2})+0.906\,(1+z^{-1})^2]}$$

$$= \frac{0.7444\,(1+z^{-1})^6}{(1.228\,z^{-2}-6.188\,z^{-1}+8.584)(2.214\,z^{-2}-6.188\,z^{-1}+7.598)(3.9184\,z^{-2}-6.1882\,z^{-1}+5.8936)}$$

$$\therefore \quad H(z) = \frac{0.06988\,(1+z^{-1})^6}{(z^{-2}-5.039\,z^{-1}+6.990)(z^{-2}-2.795\,z^{-1}+3.432)(z^{-2}-1.579.2^{-1}+1.504)}$$ **Ans.**

Check at $\omega = 0$ *i.e.* $z = 1$, we have

$$H(z)\,|_{z=1} = \frac{0.6988\,(2)^6}{(2.951)\,(1.6369)\,(0.923)} = 1.0031 \quad \text{very close to 1.0 as expected.}$$

EXAMPLE 9.13: *By using bilinear transformation method, design an IIR digital high-pass filter with maximum flatness at $\omega = \pi$ given specifications (HPF)*

Passband: $0.8 \le |\,H(e^{j\omega})\,| \le 1.0$ for $0.7\,\pi \le |\,\omega\,| \le \pi$

Stopband: $|\,H(e^{j\omega}) \le 0.2$ for $0 \le |\,\omega\,| \le 0.2\pi$

Determine N and H(z) of the approximated filter.

SOLUTION: We first formulate the problem to an LPF with specification

$0.8 \le |\,H_{LP}(e^{j\omega})\,| \le 1.0$ for $0 \le |\,\omega\,| \le 0.3\,\pi$

$|\,H_{LP}(e^{j\omega})\,| \le 0.2$ for $0.8\,\pi \le |\,\omega\,| \le \pi$.

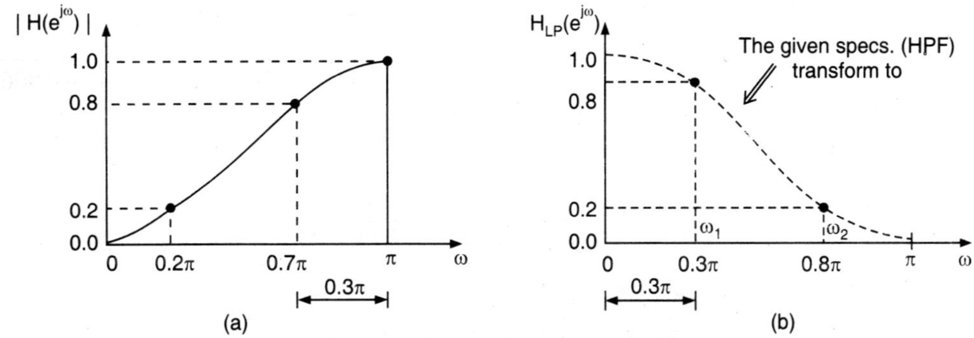

Fig. Ex. 9.13. (*a*) The given specification (HPF), (*b*) The transformed LPF

Design of $H_{LP}(e^{j\omega})$: By bilinear transformation, we have

$$\Omega = 2\tan\frac{\omega}{2}$$

$$\therefore \qquad \Omega_1 = 2\tan\frac{\omega_1}{2} = 2\tan 0.15\,\pi = 1.01905$$

$$\Omega_2 = 2\tan\frac{\omega_2}{2} = 2\tan 0.4\,\pi = 6.15536$$

By using Butterworth filter, we get

$$|\,H(j\Omega)\,|^2 = \frac{1}{1+(\Omega/\Omega_c)^{2N}}$$

At $\Omega_1 = 1.01905$, $\quad 1+\left(\dfrac{1.01905}{\Omega_c}\right)^{2N} = \left(\dfrac{1}{0.8}\right)^2 = \dfrac{100}{64}$

$$\therefore \qquad \left(\frac{1.01905}{\Omega_c}\right)^{2N} = \frac{36}{64} \qquad \text{...}(A)$$

At $\Omega_2 = 6.15536$, $\quad 1+\left(\dfrac{6.15536}{\Omega_c}\right)^{2N} = \left(\dfrac{1}{0.2}\right)^2 = 25$

$$\therefore \qquad \left(\frac{6.15536}{\Omega_c}\right)^{2N} = 24 \qquad \text{...}(B)$$

Dividing (*B*) by (*A*), we have

$$\left(\frac{6.15536}{1.01905}\right)^{2N} = \frac{24 \times 64}{36} \quad \therefore \quad (6.04029)^{2N} = 42.666$$

This gives us $$N = \frac{1}{2}\frac{\log 42.666}{\log 6.04029} = \frac{1}{2}\frac{1.630081929}{0.78105779} = 1.0435$$

$\therefore$ Choose $N = 2$ $\boxed{N = 2}$

Put $N = 2$ in (*A*) $\therefore \; \Omega_c^2 = (1.01905)^2 \times \frac{8}{6} \quad \therefore \; \boxed{\Omega_c = 1.1767}$

For $N = 2$, $\Omega_c = 1.1767$, the Butterworth LPF is given by

$$\tilde{H}_{LP}(s) = \frac{\Omega_c^2}{s^2 + \sqrt{2}\,\Omega_c s + (\Omega_c)^2} = \frac{1.3846}{s^2 + 1.6641\,s + 1.3846}$$

$$H_{LP}(z) = \tilde{H}_{LP}(s)\Big|_{s = \frac{2(1-z^{-1})}{(1+z^{-1})}} = \frac{1.3846}{\frac{4(1-z^{-1})^2}{(1+z^{-1})^2} + 1.6641 . \frac{2(1-z^{-1})}{1+z^{-1}} + 1.3846}$$

$$= \frac{1.3846\,(1+z^{-1})^2}{z^{-2}(4 - 3.3282 + 1.3846) + z^{-1}(-8 + 2 \times 1.3846) + (4 + 3.3282 + 1.3846)}$$

$$= \frac{1.3846\,(1+z^{-1})^2}{2.0564\,z^{-2} - 5.2308\,z^{-1} + 8.7128}$$

$$\therefore \quad H_{LP}(z) = \frac{0.67331\,(1+z^{-1})^2}{z^{-2} - 2.5437\,z^{-1} + 4.2369}$$

Desired $$\boxed{H_{HP}(z) = H_{LP}(z)\,|_{\text{change } z \text{ to } -z}} = \frac{0.6733\,(1-z^{-1})^2}{z^{-2} + 2.5437\,z^{-1} + 4.2369}$$ **Ans.**

Check: $H_{HP}(z)\,|_{z=1} = 0$

$H_{HP}(z)\,|_{z=-1} = 1$

It can be easily verified that $H_{HP}(z)\,|_{\omega = 0.7\pi} = 0.8$ so the design is OK.

$$e^{-j\,0.7\pi} = -0.58778 - j0.809; \; e^{-j1.4\pi} = -0.309 + j\,0.9511$$

$$H(z)\,|_{\omega = 0.7\,\pi} = \frac{0.6733\,[1 - 2(-0.58778 - j\,0.809) + (-0.309 + j\,0.9511)}{(-0.309 + j\,0.9511) + 2.5437\,(-0.58778 - j\,0.809) + 4.2369}$$

$$= \frac{0.6733\,(1.86656 + j\,2.5691)}{2.43276 + j(-1.1067533)} = 0.79999 \text{ in magnitude}$$

EXAMPLE 9.14: *By using bilinear transformation method, design an IIR digital low-pass filter with maximum flatness at* $\omega = 0$, *and meeting the specifications (LPF)*

Passband: $0.9 \le |\,H(e^{j\omega})\,| \le 1, \qquad 0 \le |\,\omega\,| \le 0.3\pi$

Stopband: $|\,H(e^{j\omega})\,| \le 0.2, \qquad 0.4\pi \le |\,\omega\,| \le \pi$

Determine the value of order (N), Butterworth circle radius (Ω_c), *and system function H(z) of the digital filter.*

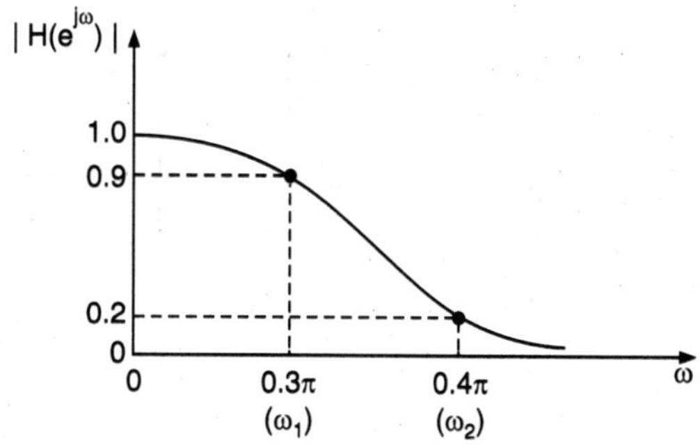

Fig. Ex. 9.14. The desired specifications of LPF

SOLUTION: Since, we use bilinear transformation here to design a Butterworth filter, we first determine mapped analog filter's parameters. As $H(e^{j\omega})$ has passband till ω_1 and stopband beyond ω_2, the corresponding values of Ω_1 and Ω_2 are given by

$$\Omega_1 = 2\tan^{-1}\frac{\omega_1}{2} = 2\tan^{-1}\left(\frac{0.3\pi}{2}\right)$$

$$= 1.0190 \text{ rad/sec}$$

$$\Omega_2 = 2\tan^{-1}\frac{\omega_2}{2} = 2\tan^{-1}\frac{0.4\pi}{2}$$

$$= 1.453 \text{ rad/sec}$$

We have the equations

$$(0.9)^2 = \frac{1}{1+\left(\dfrac{1.019}{\Omega_c}\right)^{2N}} \quad \therefore \quad 1+\left(\frac{1.019}{\Omega_c}\right)^{2N} = \frac{100}{81} \qquad \ldots(A)$$

$$(0.2)^2 = \frac{1}{1+\left(\dfrac{1.453}{\Omega_c}\right)^{2N}} \quad \therefore \quad 1+\left(\frac{1.453}{\Omega_c}\right)^{2N} = \frac{100}{4} \qquad \ldots(B)$$

From (A) and (B), we get $\dfrac{(1.019)^{2N}}{(1.453)^{2N}} = \dfrac{\left(\dfrac{100}{81}-1\right)}{\left(\dfrac{100}{4}-1\right)} = \dfrac{\dfrac{19}{81}}{24}$

$$\therefore \quad (1.425)^{2N} = \frac{24\times 81}{19} = 10.23 \qquad \therefore \quad N = 6.522 \text{ say } \boxed{N=7}$$

Putting $N = 7$ in (A), we have

$$\left(\frac{1.019}{\Omega_c}\right)^{2\times 7} = \frac{19}{81} = 0.23456$$

$$\therefore \quad (\Omega_c)^{14} = 5.548 \quad i.e., \quad \boxed{\Omega_c = 1.13}$$

Butterworth polynomial of 7th degree is given by

$$B_7(s) = 1 + 4.494s + 10.0978s^2 + 14.5918s^3 + 14.5918s^4 + 10.0978s^5 + 4.4940s^6 + s^7$$

$$\therefore \quad H_7(s) = \left.\frac{1}{B_7(s)}\right|, \text{ putting } (\Omega_c)^{7-n} \text{ along with } s^n \text{ powers}$$

$$= \frac{1}{(\Omega_c^7 + 4.494s\Omega_c^6 + 10.0978s^2\Omega_c^5 + 14.5918s^3\Omega_c^4 + 14.5918s^4\Omega_c^3 + 10.0978s^5\Omega_c^2 + 4.4940s^6\Omega_c + s^7)}$$

$$H(z) = H_7(s)\Big|_{s=\frac{2}{T_s}\left(\frac{1-z^{-1}}{1+z^{-1}}\right)}, \text{ Take } T_s = 1$$

Hence, the digital Butterworth filter of 7th order can be determined by replacing s by $\dfrac{2(1-z^{-1})}{(1+z^{-1})}$ in $H_7(s) = \dfrac{1}{B_7(s)}$ found above. The value of Ω_c is 1.13 as found earlier.

EXAMPLE 9.15: *By using bilinear transformation method, design an IIR digital high-pass filter with maximal flatness at $\omega = \pi$, with the given specifications:*

Passband: $0.8 \le |H(e^{j\omega})| \le 1, \quad 0.7\pi \le |\omega| \le \pi$

Stopband: $|H(e^{j\omega})| \le 0.2, \quad 0 \le |\omega| \le 0.2\pi$

Determine the filter order N, and H(z) of the approximated filter.

SOLUTION:

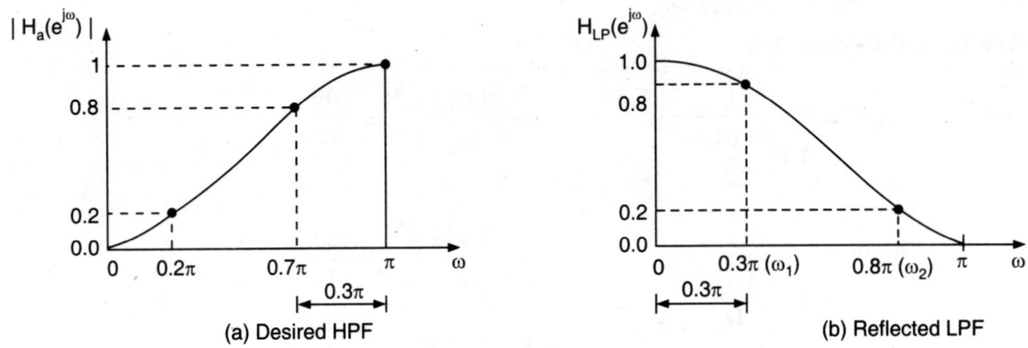

Fig. Ex. 9.15. (*a*) Desired HPF, (*b*) Reflected LPF

We design a reflected LPF as shown i.e.,

$$0.8 \le |H_{LP}(e^{j\omega})| \le 1, \qquad \text{for } 0 \le |\omega| \le 0.3\pi$$

$$|H_{LP}(e^{j\omega})| \le 0.2, \qquad \text{for } 0.8\pi \le |\omega| \le \pi.$$

Design of $H_{LP}(e^{j\omega})$

By bilinear transformation, we have

$$\Omega = 2\tan\frac{\omega}{2}$$

$$\Omega_1 = 2\tan\frac{\omega_1}{2} = 2\tan\frac{0.3\pi}{2} = 2\tan 0.15\pi = 1.01905$$

$$\Omega_2 = 2\tan\frac{\omega_2}{2} = 2\tan\frac{0.8\pi}{2} = 2\tan 0.4\pi = 6.15536$$

By using Butterworth filter design eqn.

$$|H(j\Omega)|^2 = \frac{1}{1+\left(\dfrac{\Omega}{\Omega_c}\right)^{2N}}$$

$\therefore$ At $\Omega = \Omega_1$, $\quad (0.8)^2 = \dfrac{1}{1+\left(\dfrac{1.01905}{\Omega_c}\right)^{2N}} \qquad \therefore \quad \left(\dfrac{1.01905}{\Omega_c}\right)^{2N} = \dfrac{36}{64} \qquad \text{...}(A)$

At $\Omega = \Omega_2$, $\quad (0.2)^2 = \dfrac{1}{1+\left(\dfrac{6.15536}{\Omega_c}\right)^{2N}} \quad \therefore \quad \left(\dfrac{6.15536}{\Omega_c}\right)^{2N} = 24 \qquad \ldots(B)$

Dividing (*B*) by (*A*), we get $\left(\dfrac{6.15536}{1.01905}\right)^{2N} = \dfrac{24 \times 64}{36}$

$\therefore \quad N = 1.0435 \qquad \boxed{\text{Assume } N = 2}$

Put $N = 2$ in (*A*) $\therefore \quad \left(\dfrac{\Omega_c}{1.01905}\right)^{2\times 2} = \dfrac{64}{36}$

$\therefore \quad \Omega_c = 1.1767 \qquad \boxed{\Omega_c = 1.1767}$

$$\therefore \quad H_{LP}(s) = \frac{\Omega_c^2}{s^2 + \sqrt{2}\,.\,\Omega_c s + \Omega_c^2} = \frac{1.3846}{s^2 + 1.6641s + 1.3846}$$

$$H_{LP}(z) = H_{LP}(s)\Big|_{s=2\frac{1-z^{-1}}{1+z^{-1}}} = \frac{1.3846}{2^2\left(\dfrac{1-z^{-1}}{1+z^{-1}}\right)^2 + 1.6641 \times 2\left(\dfrac{1-z^{-1}}{1+z^{-1}}\right) + 1.3846}$$

$$= \frac{0.67331(1+z^{-1})^2}{z^2 - 2.5437z^{-1} + 4.2369}$$

$$\therefore \quad H_{HP}(z) = H_{LP}(z)\Big|_{\text{Change } z \text{ to } -z}$$

$$\therefore \quad H_{HP}(z) = \frac{0.67331(1+z^{-1})^2}{z^2 + 2.5437z^{-1} + 4.2369} \quad \textbf{Ans.}$$

Check at $\quad \omega = \pi$ *i.e.*, $z^{-1} = -1 \quad H_{HP}(z) = 1$ as expected.

It can be shown that for

$$\omega = 0.7\pi$$

i.e., $\quad e^{-j\omega} = e^{-j0.7\pi} = \cos 0.7\pi - j \sin 0.7\pi = -0.58778 - j\,0.809$

the response of $H_{HP}(z)\Big|_{\text{at } \omega = .0.7\pi} = 0.7999 = 0.8,$ as expected.

EXAMPLE 9.16: *(Chebyshev Filter) Given the specifications*

$20 \log_{10} |H(e^{j0.20\pi})| \le -1$ dB $\quad \therefore$ *passband 0 to 0.20π rad*

$20 \log_{10} |H(e^{j0.30\pi})| \le -15$ dB $\quad \therefore$ *stopband 0.30π to π rad.*

Design a Chebyshev approximation of the afore specified LPF by using (a) Impulse invariant design, (b) Bilinear transformation.

SOLUTION:

(*a*) By Impulse invariant design method

A Chebyshev filter is defined by

$$|H_a(j\Omega)|^2 = \frac{1}{1+\varepsilon^2 V_N^2\left(\dfrac{\Omega}{\Omega_c}\right)}$$

[To find Ω_c, ε, N]

We can design the filter to exactly meet the requirement in the passband 0 – 0.20π with frequency response to be equiripple between 0 to 0.20π radian.

Thus, $\Omega_c = 0.20\pi$

(Note this step)

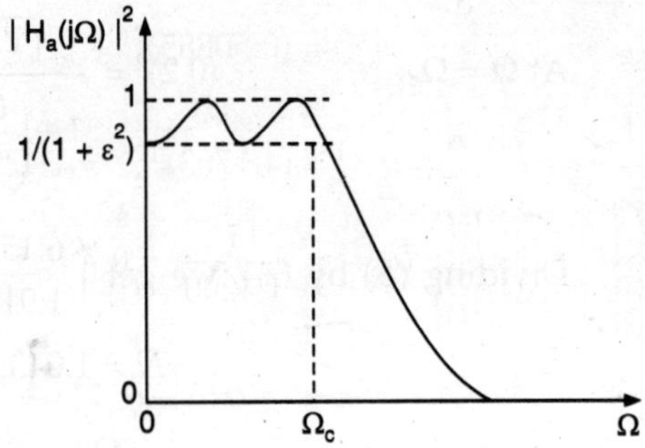

Fig. Ex. 9.16. (*a*) The typical response

At $\Omega = \Omega_c$, $V_N\left(\dfrac{\Omega}{\Omega_c}\right) = V_N(1) = \cos(N \cos^{-1} 1)$

$$= \cos(N \times 0) = \cos 0 = 1$$

$$\therefore \quad |H_a(j\Omega)|^2\Big|_{\Omega=\Omega_c} = \frac{1}{1+\varepsilon^2}$$

$$\therefore \quad 10 \log |H_a(j\Omega_c)|^2 = 10 \log \frac{1}{1+\varepsilon^2} = -1 \text{ dB} \qquad \text{(given)}$$

We obtain, therefore, $\varepsilon = 0.50885$

Having found Ω_c (= 0.20π) and ε(= 0.50885), we have to determine N **by hit and trial** (*i.e.*, by iteration)

At $\Omega = 0.30\pi$, $20 \log_{10} |H_a(j\Omega)| \leq -15$ dB (given)

Put N = 3

$$\therefore \quad 20 \log |H_a(j0.30\pi)| = 10 \log \left(\frac{1}{1+\varepsilon^2 V_N^2\left(\dfrac{\Omega}{\Omega_c}\right)}\right)\Bigg|_{\Omega=0.30\pi}$$

As $V_N = 3\left(\dfrac{0.3\pi}{0.2\pi}\right) = \cos\left(3 \cos^{-1} \dfrac{0.3\pi}{0.2\pi}\right) = \cos(3 \cos^{-1} 1.5)$

By using tables for V_N, it is found that for $N = 3$, $20 \log_{10} |H_a(j0.3\pi)|$ yields –13.418, which is less than the prescribed specification (of ≤ –15 dB). We, therefore, discard $N = 3$.

Put N = 4: Here we would get

$$10 \log \frac{1}{1+\varepsilon^2 V_4^2\left(\dfrac{0.3\pi}{0.2\pi}\right)} = -21.5834 \text{ (from Table of } V_N(x))$$

This exceeds the specifications. Hence, choose $N = 4$

Thus, for $\Omega_c = 0.2\pi$, $N = 4$, $\varepsilon = 0.50885$

$$\alpha = \varepsilon^{-1} + \sqrt{1+\varepsilon^2}$$

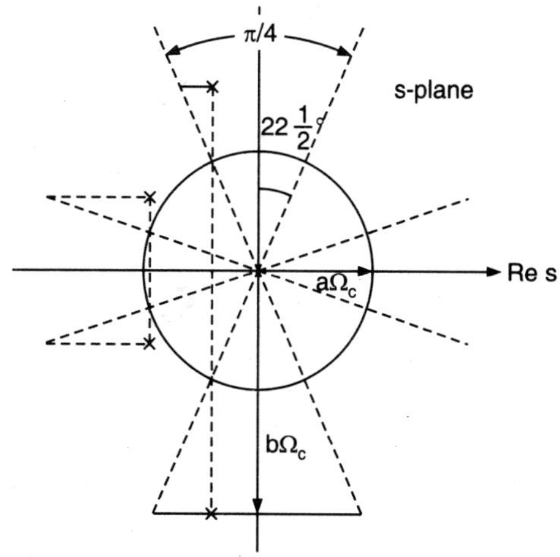

Fig. Ex. 9.16. (*b*) For *N* = 4, pole plot for $H_a(s)$ – Chebyshev filter

$$= (0.50885)^{-1} + \sqrt{1 + (0.50885)^2}$$

$$= 4.1703$$

$$\alpha^{1/4} = (4.1703)^{0.25} = 1.4290$$

$$\alpha^{-1/4} = \frac{1}{1.4290} = 0.7$$

$$a = \frac{1}{2}(\alpha^{1/4} - \alpha^{-1/4}) = \frac{1}{2}(1.4290 - 0.7)$$

$$= 0.3646$$

$$b = \frac{1}{2}(\alpha^{1/4} + \alpha^{-1/4}) = \frac{1}{2}(1.4290 + 0.7)$$

$$= 1.0644$$

$$a\Omega_c = 0.3646\ (0.20\pi) = 0.2290$$

$$b\Omega_c = 1.0644\ (0.20\pi) = 0.6687$$

Poles on LH *s*-plane are given by:

$$\left(-a\Omega_c \sin 22\frac{1°}{2} \pm jb\Omega_c \cos 22\frac{1°}{2}\right);\ \left(-a\Omega_c \sin 67\frac{1°}{2} \pm jb\Omega_c \cos 67\frac{1°}{2}\right)$$

$$= (-a\Omega_c \times 0.3826 \pm jb\Omega_c \times 0.9238); (-a\Omega_c \times 0.9238 \pm jb\Omega_c \times 0.3826)$$

$$= (-0.21155 \pm j0.2558); (-0.0876 \pm j0.6177)$$

$$H_a(s) = \frac{1}{[(s + 0.21155)^2 + (0.2558)^2]\,[(s + 0.0876)^2 + (0.1677)^2]}$$

$$= \frac{1}{(s^2 + 0.4231s + 0.1118) + (s^2 + 0.1752s + 0.3892)}$$

As
$$|H_a(s)|^2_{s=0} = \frac{1}{1+\varepsilon^2} = \frac{1}{1.258925}$$

∴ To normalize the expansion, we multiply by

$$\sqrt{\frac{1}{1+\varepsilon^2}(0.1103)^2\,(0.3894)^2} = 0.038286$$

$$H_a(s) = \frac{1 \times 0.038286}{(s^2 + 0.4233s + 0.1103)\,(s^2 + 0.1753s + 0.3894)}$$

The T.F. $H(z)$ by using invariant impulse method is

$$H(z) = \frac{0.08327 + 0.0239\,z^{-1}}{1 - 1.5658z^{-1} + 0.6549z^{-2}} - \frac{0.08327 + 0.0246\,z^{-1}}{1 - 1.4934\,z^{-1} + 0.8392\,z^{-2}}$$

Note that due to aliasing, the attenuation at the stop edge $\Omega_s = 0.3\pi$ is slightly worse than for the analog filter. However, since, the analog design provided *N* (more than required) as an integer, the resulting filter meets the specifications.

(b) Design using Bilinear transformation

The given specifications are

$$20 \log_{10} \left| H_a\left(j\,2 \tan\left(\frac{0.2\pi}{2}\right)\right)\right| \le -1 \text{ dB} \qquad \because \quad \Omega = 2 \tan\frac{\omega}{2} \text{ for } T = 1$$

$$20 \log_{10} \left| H_a\left(j \tan\left(\frac{0.3\pi}{2}\right)\right)\right| \le -15 \text{ dB}$$

For equiripple in the passband, we have

$$\frac{\Omega}{\Omega_c} = 1, \quad \therefore \quad \text{for } \Omega_{\text{pass}} = 2 \tan \frac{0.2\pi}{2} = 0.6498 \text{ rads/sec}$$

i.e.,

$$\Omega_c = 0.6498 \text{ rad/sec} \qquad \boxed{\Omega_c = 0.6498}$$

At stopband, $\Omega_{\text{stop}} = 2 \tan \dfrac{0.3\pi}{2} = 1.0191 \text{ rad/sec}$

Thus, we have the relations

$$|H_a(j\Omega)|^2 = \frac{1}{1+\varepsilon^2 V_N^2\left(\frac{\Omega}{\Omega_c}\right)} \qquad \text{('Chebyshev filter relation')}$$

Put $\Omega = \Omega_c$

$$\therefore \quad |H_a(j\Omega)|^2\Big|_{\Omega=\Omega_c} = \frac{1}{1+\varepsilon^2 V_N^2\left(\frac{\Omega}{\Omega_c}\right)}$$

$$= \frac{1}{1+\varepsilon^2 V_N^2(1)} = \frac{1}{1+\varepsilon^2} \qquad V_N(1) = 1$$

$$10 \log |H_a(j\Omega_c)|^2 = -10 \log (1 + \varepsilon^2) \qquad \therefore \quad V_N^2(1) = 1$$

$$= -1 \text{ dB} \qquad \text{(given)}$$

The relation $10 \log (1 + \varepsilon^2) = 1$ gives us $\boxed{\varepsilon = 0.50885}$

At $\Omega = \Omega_{\text{stop}}$ $\quad 2 \tan \dfrac{0.3\pi}{2} = 1.0191 \text{ rad/sec}$

$$\therefore \quad \frac{\Omega_{\text{stop}}}{\Omega_c} = \frac{1.0191}{0.6498} = 1.5683 \qquad \boxed{\frac{\Omega_{\text{stop}}}{\Omega_c} = 1.5683}$$

To choose N (by hit and trial iteration)

Let *N* be 3

Then $\quad |H_a(j\Omega)|^2\Big|_{\Omega=\Omega_c} = \dfrac{1}{1+\varepsilon^2 V_N^2(1)} = \dfrac{1}{1+\varepsilon^2 \times 1} = \dfrac{1}{1+\varepsilon^2}$

For $\varepsilon = 0.50885$, $20 \log |H_a(j\Omega_c)| = -1$ dB

$\therefore$ satisfied at $\quad \Omega = \Omega_c$

Now $\quad |H_a(j\Omega_{\text{stop}})|^2 = \dfrac{1}{1+\varepsilon^2 V_3^2\left(\frac{\Omega_{\text{stop}}}{\Omega_c}\right)}$

$$= \frac{1}{1+\varepsilon^2 V_3^2(1.5683)}$$

As $$V_3(x) = 4x^3 - 3x$$

$$V_3^2(x)\Big|_{x=1.5683} = [4 \times (1.5683)^3 - 3(1.5683)]^2 = (10.7244)^2$$

$$|H_a(j\Omega_{stop})|^2 = \frac{1}{1+\underset{\nearrow \varepsilon}{(0.50885)^2} \,.\, \underset{\nearrow V_N(x)}{(10.7244)^2}}$$

$$20 \log (H_a(j\Omega_{stop})) = 10 \log \frac{1}{30.78029}$$

$$= -14.88 > -15 \text{ dB}$$

The attenuation at $\Omega = \Omega_{stop}$ is higher than the given value of 15 dB. Therefore, $N = 3$ is a low order not meeting the given specifications. We, therefore, try now $N = 4$.

Let $N = 4$

As $$V_4(x) = 8x^4 - 8x^2 + 1$$

$\therefore$ $$V_4(1.5683) = 8(1.5683)^4 - 8(1.5683)^2 + 1 = 29.7191$$

$$|H_a(j\Omega_{stop})|^2 = \frac{1}{1+\underset{\nearrow \varepsilon}{(0.50885)^2} \,.\, \underset{\nearrow V_4(x)}{(29.7191)^2}} = \frac{1}{1+228.6919}$$

$$20 \log (H_a(j\Omega_{stop})) = -10 \log (229.6919)$$

$$= -23.61 < -15 \text{ dB (the given specification)}$$

Hence, $N = 4$ meets (overmeets) the given specification

For $N = 4$, we have**

$$H_a(s) = \frac{0.04381}{(s^2 + 0.1814s + 0.4166)(s^2 + 0.4378s + 0.1180)}$$

By bilinear transformation, using $s = \frac{2}{T}\frac{1-z^{-1}}{1+z^{-1}}$ for $T = 1$, the corresponding digital filter is given by

---

** Having found ε, Ω_c, N, we obtain

$$\alpha = \varepsilon^{-1} + \sqrt{1+\varepsilon^2} = (0.50885)^{-1} + \sqrt{1+(0.50885)^2} = 3.0872$$

$\therefore$ $$\alpha^{1/4} = 1.3255$$

$$\alpha^{-1/4} = 0.7544$$

$\therefore$ $$a = \frac{1}{2}(\alpha^{1/4} - \alpha^{-1/4}) = \frac{1}{2}(1.3255 - 0.7544) = 0.28555$$

$$b = \frac{1}{2}(\alpha^{1/4} + \alpha^{-1/4}) = \frac{1}{2}(1.3255 + 0.7544) = 1.03995.$$

Thereafter we obtain poles on the ellipse.

$$H(z) = \frac{0.001836(1+z^{-1})^4}{(1-1.4996z^{-1}+0.8482z^{-2})(1-1.5548z^{-1}+0.6493z^{-2})} \quad \textbf{Ans.}$$

Note that in Butterworth filter, N was 6. Thus, here in Chebyshev design $N = 4$ (and $N \neq 6$), and this filter is more economical.

EXAMPLE 9.17: *(Elliptic Filter) Design an elliptic approximation of a lowpass digital filter for specification*

$20 \log_{10} |H(e^{j0.20\pi})| \leq -1$ dB

i.e., passband $\omega_p = 0$ *to* 0.20π *rad*

$20 \log_{10} |H(e^{j0.30\pi})| \leq -15$ dB

i.e., stopband 0.30π *to* π *rads.*

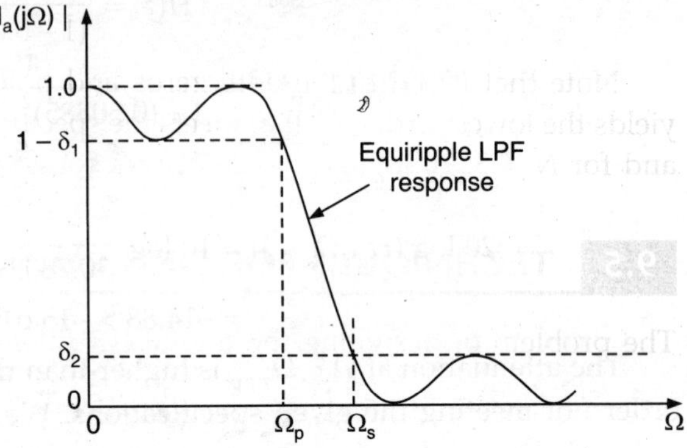

Fig. Ex. 9.17. The given specifications

SOLUTION: Given data is

$$\omega_p = 0.20\pi \text{ rads}$$
$$\omega_s = 0.30\pi \text{ rads}$$

[To find δ_1 and δ_2]

At $\omega = \omega_p = 0.20\pi$,

$$20 \log_{10} |H(e^{j0.20\pi})| = -1 \text{ dB}$$

i.e., $$20 \log (1-\delta_1) = -1 \text{ dB}$$

$\therefore$ $$1-\delta_1 = 10^{-0.05} \quad \text{or} \quad \delta_1 = 0.1088$$

At $\omega = \omega_s = 0.30\pi$, $20 \log_{10} |H(e^{j0.30\pi})| = -15$ dB

$\therefore$ $$20 \log \delta_2 = -15 \text{ dB}$$

$\therefore$ $$\delta_1 = 10^{-15/20} \qquad \therefore \delta_2 = 0.1778$$

[To find Ω_p, Ω_s]

In bilinear transformation, $$\Omega = 2 \tan\left(\frac{\omega}{2}\right)$$

$\therefore$ $$\Omega_p = 2 \tan\left(\frac{0.20\pi}{2}\right) = 0.6498$$

$$\Omega_s = 2 \tan\left(\frac{0.30\pi}{2}\right) = 1.01905$$

If we fix δ_1, ω_p and ω_s, it turns out that $N = 3$, $20 \log_{10}(\delta_2) = -26.71$ dB, thus, exceeding the specifications. Pre-warping the critical frequencies so that

$$\Omega_p = 2 \tan\left(\frac{0.20\pi}{2}\right)$$

and $$\Omega_s = 2 \tan\left(\frac{0.30\pi}{2}\right),$$ we obtain the system function

$$H_a(s) = \frac{0.12460(s^2+1.3040)}{(0.6498s+0.2448)(s^2+0.2521s+0.4313)}$$

By using the bilinear transformation

$$s = \frac{2}{T}\frac{1-z^{-1}}{1+z^{-1}}, \text{ take } T = 1,$$

the above system function transforms to

$$H(z) = \frac{0.05634(1+z^{-1})(1-1.0166z^{-1}+z^{-2})}{(1-0.6830z^{-1})(1-1.4461z^{-1}+0.7957z^{-2})}$$

Note that $H(z)$ has the both zeros and poles. Also, $H(z)$ found here by elliptic filter design yields the lowest-order, N, that meets the specifications. We found N here by hit and trial (iteration) and for $N = 3$, $20 \log_{10} \delta_2 = -26.71$ was found by using tables of Elliptic design.

9.5 TECHNIQUES FOR DETERMINING IIR FILTER COEFFICIENTS

The problem of designing the digital IIR filters is one of finding the coefficients a_i's and b_i's in

$$H(z) = \frac{\sum_{i=0}^{M} b_i z^{-i}}{1+\sum_{i=1}^{N} a_i z^{-i}} = \sum_{n=0}^{\infty} h(n) z^{-n} \qquad \ldots(9.49)$$

in such a way that some aspects of the filter's response (*i.e.*, time response, frequency response, group delay etc.) are met optimally. Various optimality criteria may be used such as minimum mean square error or minimax error. Thus, we can use mathematical tools used for approximation and optimization techniques etc. If the approximation problem is solved in z domain (s-domain), the resulting filter is a digital (analog) one. Other possible filter classes are optical filters, and transmission line filters. The commonality for all design is the mathematics of functions with filter-like properties.

Thus, the design of IIR filter depends on the knowledge that is available in the literature for designing other filters. In order to redevelop the theory for digital filters, it is convenient to transform the digital filters to analog domain or in any other filter's domain, design in that domain (by using the techniques available in those domains) and finally re-transform the designed filter to the digital domain. This techniques of designing an appropriate continuous time filter, $H_a(s)$, say, and then digitizing the resulting design is commonly used to design standard filters such as low-pass, bandpass, bandstop and high-pass filters.

A Second Approach: Of designing an IIR filters is a direct closed form design in z-domain. Given the specified response of the filter, one can often decide where to place poles and zeros to approximate the specified response.

A Third Way: To design IIR filters is by using optimization procedure, to place poles and zeros at appropriate positions in z-plane, meeting the condition of optimality. However, this method requires iterations and also it does not yield closed form expressions for the filter coefficients. We shall give here a Pade' approximation which is commonly used for IIR filter designs.

9.5.1 Padé Approximation Method

Except for the impulse-invariant method, the design techniques for IIR filters involves the conversion of an analog filter into a digital filter by some mapping from s-plane to the z-plane. It is also feasible to design an IIR filters directly without reference to the analog domain.

In Pade' approximation method and in the least-squares design method, the specifications are given in the time domain and the design of IIR filters is directly carried in time domain. It is also feasible to directly design an IIR filter, if the specifications are given in frequency domain, least-squares technique is applied.

Pade' approximation method is a direct design method for IIR filters when the specifications are given in time-domain. Let the desired impulse response be $h_d(n)$ be specified for $n \geq 0$. Let us approximate $h_d(n)$ by $h(n)$. Then

$$H(z) = \sum_{k=0}^{\infty} h(k)\, z^{-k} \qquad \text{...(9.50)}$$

$$\triangleq \frac{\sum_{k=0}^{M} b_k\, z^{-k}}{1 + \sum_{k=1}^{N} a_k\, z^{-k}} \qquad \text{...(9.51)}$$

The approximated system function $H(z)$ has $L = M + N + 1$ parameters *viz.* $\{a_k\}$ and $\{b_k\}$, to be determined with some optimality criteria.

Here, we choose the optimality criteria of minimization of the sum of squared errors *viz.* defining the $(\text{error})^2$, ξ, as

$$\xi = \sum_{n=0}^{U} [h_d(n) - h(n)]^2 \qquad \text{...(9.52)}$$

We minimize ξ w.r.t. the filter parameters $\{a_k\}$ and $\{b_k\}$, where U is some upper limit for the summation in (9.52). In general, $h(n)$ is a non-linear function of the filter parameters a_k's and b_k's. However, if we choose $U = L - 1$, then (9.52) gives us L equations to solve for L unknowns, $(M + N + 1)$, needed in (9.51) then it would be possible to match $h(n)$ perfectly with the prescribed $h_d(n)$ for $n = 0$ to $M + N$ *i.e.*, $M + N + 1$ values of $h_d(n)$. We proceed as follows:

From (9.51), the difference equation is

$$y(n) = \sum_{k=0}^{M} b_k\, x(n-k) - \sum_{k=1}^{N} a_k\, y(n-k) \qquad \text{...(9.53)}$$

By putting $x(n) = \delta(n)$ and, therefore, $y(n) = h(n)$, we have from above

$$h(n) = b_0\delta(n) + b_1\delta(n-1) + \ldots + b_M\delta(n-M) - [a_1 h(n-1) + a_2 h(n-2) + \ldots + a_N h(n-N)] \qquad \text{...(9.54)}$$

But $\delta(n - k) = 0$ except for $n = k$ where $\delta(n - k) = 1$. Therefore, (9.54) reduces to:

$$h(n) = \begin{cases} b_n - [a_1\, h(n-1) + a_2\, h(n-2) + \ldots + a_N h(n-N)], & 0 \leq n \leq M \quad \text{...(9.55)} \\ -[a_1\, h(n-1) + a_2\, h(n-2) + \ldots + a_N\, h(n-N)], & n > M \quad \text{...(9.56)} \end{cases}$$

[To determine a_k's], $k = 1, 2, 3, \ldots, N$.

Set $h(n) = h_d(n)$ and take $n = M + 1, M + 2, \ldots, M + N$ in (9.56) *i.e.*, use

$$h_d(n) = -a_1\, h_d(n-1) - a_2\, h_d(n-2) - \ldots - a_N\, h_d(n-N),\ n > M$$

and determine $a_1, a_2, a_3, \ldots, a_N$.

[To determine b_k's], $k = 0, 1, 2, M$

Set $h(n) = h_d(n)$ and use $\{a_k\}$ found above, in (9.56), and take $n = 0, 1, 2, \ldots, M$, *i.e.*, use

$$h_d(n) = b_n - a_1\, h_d(n-1) - a_2\, h_d(n-2) - \ldots - a_N\, h_d(n-N),\ n = 0, 1, \ldots, M$$

Thus, we obtain a perfect match between $h(n)$ and $h_d(n)$ for first L (= $M + N + 1$) values of the impulse response in this Pade' approximation procedure.

Padés approximation matches only L number of filter parameters $h_d(n)$ *i.e.*, for $n = 0, 1, ..., M + N$, thus higher the value of L, better is the approximation *viz.* for better and better approximation, the design filter $H(z)$ must have a large number of poles and zeros. For this reason, the Pade' approximation method is of limited use in practical applications.

When the desired system function $H_d(z)$ is a rational function, of the form $\frac{N(z)}{D(z)}$, and we have prior knowledge of the number of poles and zeros in $H_d(z)$, Pade' approximation results in a perfect match *i.e.*, $H(z) = H_d(z)$. However, in general, $H_d(z)$ may not be a rational function, since, $h_d(n)$, the given desired unit sample response, is determined from some desired frequency response specifications $H_d(e^{j\omega})$. In such cases, Padé approximation is tried for different M (*i.e.*, number of zeros) and N (*i.e.*, number of poles) and it renders the technique cumbersome.

EXAMPLE 9.18: *Given the desired unit sample response*

$$h_d(n) = 2 \,.\, \left(\frac{1}{2}\right)^n u(n)$$

Determine the parameters of the filter with system function

$$H(z) = \frac{b_0 + b_1 z^{-1}}{1 + a_1 z^{-1}}$$

by using Pade' approximation technique.

SOLUTION: Directly (without Padés technique)

$$H_d(z) = \sum_{n=-\infty}^{\infty} h(d)\, z^{-n} = \sum_{n=-\infty}^{\infty} 2 \,.\left(\frac{1}{2}\right)^n u(n)\, z^{-n} = 2\, \frac{1}{1 - \frac{1}{2} z^{-1}}$$

Compare $\frac{b_0 + b_1 z^{-1}}{1 + a_1 z^{-1}}$ and $\frac{2}{1 + \left(-\frac{1}{2}\right) z^{-1}}$

Clearly $b_0 = 2,\ b_1 = 0,\ a_1 = -\frac{1}{2}$ and we have perfect match.

By Padés Approach:

$$h(n) = -a_1\, h(n-1) + b_0\, \delta(n) + b_1\, \delta(n-1)$$

For $n > 1$, $\delta(n)$ and $\delta(n - 1)$ are both zeros

$\therefore \quad h(n) = -a_1\, h(n-1), \quad n > 1$

Equivalently

$$h_d(n) = -a_1\, h_d(n-1), \quad n > 1$$

Put $\quad n = 2 \quad \therefore \quad h_d(2) = -a_1\, h_d(1)$

$$\therefore \quad a_1 = -\frac{h_d(2)}{h_d(1)} = -\frac{1/2}{1} = -\frac{1}{2}$$

as $h_d(n) = 2\left(\frac{1}{2}\right)^n \mu(n)$

$\because \quad h_d(0) = 2$

$h_d(1) = 1$

$h_d(2) = \frac{1}{2}$

$h_d(3) = \frac{1}{4}$

$\vdots$

$\because \quad a_1 = -\frac{1}{2}$

[To solve for b_0 and b_1]

As $$h(n) = -a_1 h(n-1) + b_0\,\delta(n) + b_1\,\delta(n-1)$$

Put $$h(n) = h_d(n),\ a_1 = -\frac{1}{2} \text{ (just found)}$$

$$\therefore \quad h_d(n) = \frac{1}{2}\,h_d(n-1) + b_0\,\delta(n) + b_1\,\delta(n-1) \qquad \ldots(B)$$

Put $n = 0$ in (B) $\therefore$ $h_d(0) = 0 + b_0 + 0$

i.e., $2 = b_0$ $\boxed{b_0 = 2}$

Put $n = 1$ in (B) $\therefore$ $h_d(1) = \frac{1}{2}\,h_d(0) + 0 + b_1$

$\therefore$ $1 = \frac{1}{2}\,.\,2 + b_1$

$\therefore$ $b_1 = 0$ $\boxed{b_1 = 0}$

Hence, by Padés approximation is given by

$$H(z) = \frac{2}{1 + \frac{1}{2}\,z^{-1}}$$

Here we have, by chance, $H(z) = H_d(z)$, a perfect match. **Ans.**

EXAMPLE 9.19: *A fourth-order Butterworth filter has the system function:*

$$H_d(z) = \frac{4.8334 \times 10^{-13}\,(z+1)^4}{(z^2 - 1.3205\,z + 0.6326)\,(z^2 - 1.0482\,z + 0.2959)}$$

The unit sample response corresponding to $H_d(z)$ is illustrated in the Fig. 9.19(a). Use Pade' approximation method to approximate $H_d(z)$.

SOLUTION: We observe here that the desired filter has $M = 4$, $N = 4$ *i.e.*, number of poles = number of zeros = 4. Padé approximation matches perfectly if we choose in $H(z)$ $M \geq 4$ and $N \geq 4$. The frequency response of such cases for $N = 4$, $M = 4$ and $N = 5$, $M = 4$ is continuous curve in Fig. Ex. 9.19(*b*) [curve (*a*)].

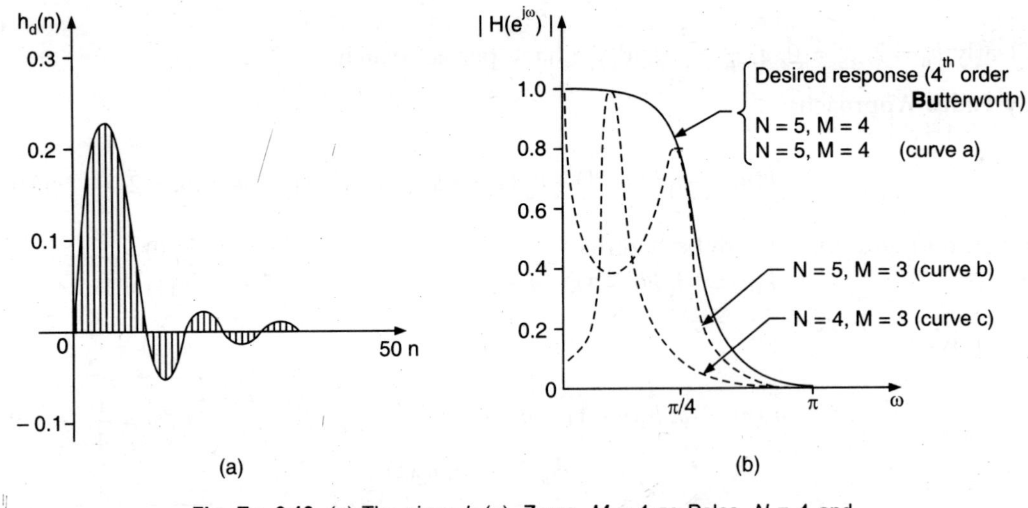

Fig. Ex. 9.19. (*a*) The given $h_d(n)$. Zeros, $M = 4$ as Poles, $N = 4$ and (*b*) Filter designs based on Padé approximation

If we taken $M = 3$ (zeros) and $N = 4$ (poles) we have very poor response [curve *c*]. However, if $M = 3$ (zeros), $N = 5$ (poles) *i.e.*, one pole more than the desired in $H_d(z)$ there is improvement in curve *c* to curve *b*.

Thus, in Pade' approximation, the proper choice of zeros (M) and poles (N) is an important feature for correct approximate.

EXAMPLE 9.20: *A three-pole and three zero type II low-pass Chebyshev digital filter has the system function*

$$H_d(z) = \frac{0.3060\,(1+z^{-1})\,(0.2652-0.09\,z^{-1}+0.2652\,z^{-2})}{(1-0.3880\,z^{-1})\,(1-1.1318\,z^{-1}+0.5387\,z^{-2})}$$

Its unit sample response is shown in Fig. 9.20. Use Padé approximation method to approximation $H_d(z)$.

SOLUTION: As in Example 9.19, we determine Padé approximation for $(M, N) = (2, 3), (3, 3), (2, 4)$ and $(3, 4)$. The frequency responses are in Fig. Ex. 9.20(*b*).

If we underestimate the zeros (M) say to 2, (curves *a*, *b* in Fig. Ex. 9.20(*b*)), the frequency responses degrade. For $(M, N) = (3, 3), (3, 4)$, we obtain perfect match since $H_d(z)$ has $M = 3$ and $N = 3$, curves *c* and *d* in Fig. Ex. 9.20(*b*).

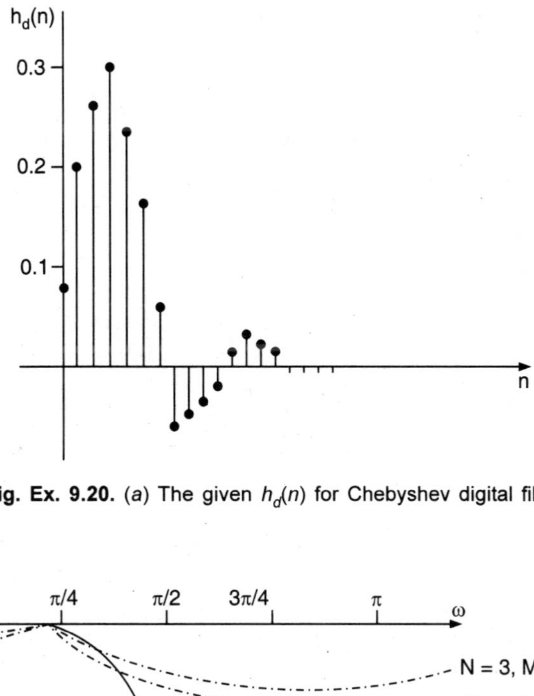

Fig. Ex. 9.20. (*a*) The given $h_d(n)$ for Chebyshev digital filter

Fig. Ex. 9.20. (*b*) Filter design based an Padé approximation method Curves *c* and *d* almost overlap

9.6 MINIMUM-PHASE, MAXIMUM-PHASE, AND MIXED-PHASE SYSTEMS

The invertability of a linear time-invariant system is related to the characteristics of the phase-spectral function [*i.e.*, $\theta(\omega)$] of the system. Consider two FIR characteristics.

$$H_1(z) = \left(1 + \frac{1}{2}z^{-1}\right) = z^{-1}\left(z + \frac{1}{2}\right) \quad \ldots(9.57)$$

$$H_2(z) = \left(\frac{1}{2} + z^{-1}\right) = z^{-1}\left(\frac{1}{2} + z + 1\right) \quad \ldots(9.58)$$

The system $H_1(z)$ has a zero at $z = -\dfrac{1}{2}$ and $H_2(z)$ has a zero at $z = -2$. The impulse responses are:

$$h_1(n) = \left\{\underset{\uparrow}{1}, \frac{1}{2}\right\} \text{ and } h_1(n) = \left\{\underset{\uparrow}{\frac{1}{2}}, 1\right\}$$

Note that $h_1(n)$ is reverse of $h_2(n)$. This is due to reciprocal relationship between the zeros of $H_1(z)$ and $H_2(z)$. Note that

$$|H_1(\omega)|^2 = \left(1 + \frac{1}{2}\cos\omega\right)^2 + \left(\frac{1}{2}\sin\omega\right)^2 = \frac{5}{4} + \cos\omega$$

$$|H_2(\omega)|^2 = \left(\frac{1}{2} + \cos\omega\right)^2 + (\sin\omega)^2 = \frac{5}{4} + \cos\omega$$

$$\theta_1(\omega) = \text{Arg of}\left[e^{-j\omega}\left(e^{j\omega} + \frac{1}{2}\right)\right] = -\omega + \tan^{-1}\frac{\sin\omega}{\frac{1}{2} + \cos\omega} \quad \ldots(9.59)$$

$$\theta_2(\omega) = \text{Arg of}\left[e^{-j\omega}\left(\frac{1}{2}e^{j\omega} + 1\right)\right] = -\omega + \tan^{-1}\frac{\sin\omega}{2 + \cos\omega} \quad \ldots(9.60)$$

Note that

$$\theta_1(\omega) = -\omega + \tan^{-1}\frac{\sin\omega}{\frac{1}{2} + \cos\omega}$$

$$\theta_1(\omega)\big|_{\omega=0} = 0$$

$$\theta_1(\omega)\big|_{\omega=\pi/2} = -\frac{\pi}{2} + \underbrace{\tan^{-1}2}_{=1.1071} = -0.4636 \text{ rads}$$

$$\theta_1(\omega)\Big|_{\omega=\frac{2}{3}\pi} = -\frac{2}{3}\pi + \tan^{-1}\frac{0.866}{\frac{1}{2} + (-0.5)}$$

$$= -\frac{2}{3}\pi + \frac{\pi}{2} = -0.5235 \text{ rads}$$

$$\theta_1(\omega)\Big|_{\omega=\pi} = -\pi + \tan^{-1}\frac{0}{\frac{1}{2} - 1} = -\pi - \pi \equiv 0 \text{ rad}$$

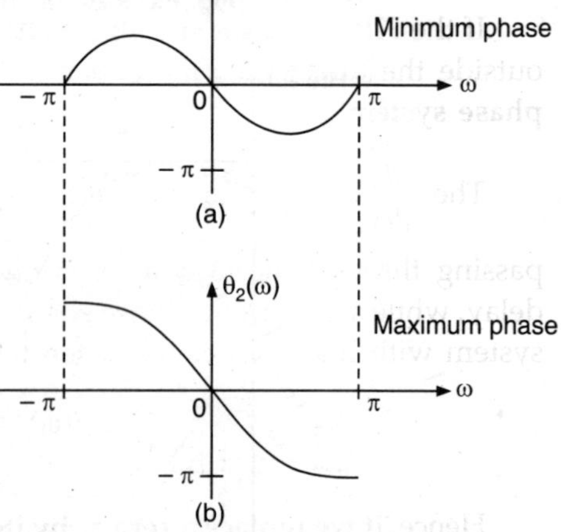

Fig. 9.13. Phase spectra $\theta_1(\omega)$ and $\theta_2(\omega)$ for the systems $H_1(z)$ and $H_2(z)$, respectively

$\theta_1(\omega)$ is shown in Fig. 9.13(*a*)

For
$$\theta_2(\omega) = -\omega + \tan^{-1}\frac{\sin\omega}{2+\cos\omega}$$

$$\theta_2(\omega)\big|_{\omega=0} = 0$$

$$\theta_2(\omega)\big|_{\omega=\pi/2} = -\frac{\pi}{2} + \tan^{-1}\frac{1}{2} = -\frac{\pi}{2} + 0.4636 = -1.1071 \text{ rads}$$

$$\theta_2(\omega)\Big|_{\omega=\frac{2}{3}\pi} = -2\frac{\pi}{3} + \tan^{-1}\frac{0.866}{2-0.5} = -\frac{2\pi}{3} + 0.5235 = -1.5709 \text{ rads}$$

$$\theta_2(\omega)\big|_{\omega=\pi} = -\pi + \tan^{-1}\frac{0}{2-1} = -\pi + 0 = -\pi \text{ rads}$$

$\theta_2(\omega)$ is shown in Fig. 9.13(*b*).

We note that
$$\boxed{\begin{array}{ll}\theta_1(\pi) - \theta_1(0) = 0 & \text{For minimum phase system} \\ \theta_2(\pi) - \theta_2(0) = -\pi & \text{For maximum phase system}\end{array}} \qquad \ldots(9.61)$$

If $H_{\min}(\omega) \triangleq b_0(1 - z_1 e^{-j\omega})(1 - z_2 e^{-j\omega}) \ldots (1 - z_M e^{-j\omega})$, where the zeros $|z_i| < 1$

then
$$\measuredangle H_{\min}(\pi) - \measuredangle H_{\min}(0) = 0 + 0 + 0 + \ldots 0 = 0 \qquad \ldots(9.62a)$$

For $H_{\max}(\omega) \triangleq c_0(1 - z_1' e^{-j\omega})(1 - z_2' e^{-j\omega}) \ldots (1 - z_M' e^{-j\omega})$, where the zeros $|z_i'| > 1$

then
$$\measuredangle H_{\max}(\pi) - \measuredangle H_{\max}(0) = -M\pi \qquad \ldots(9.62b)$$

In
$$H_{\min}(\omega) = b_0(1 - z_1 e^{-j\omega})(1 - z_2 e^{-j\omega}) \ldots |z_i| < 1$$

if there is a pair of complex conjugate zeros, their net phase contribution is zero.

In
$$H_{\max}(\omega) = c_0(1 - z_1' e^{-j\omega})(1 - z_2' e^{-j\omega}) \ldots (1 - z_M' e^{-j\omega}),\ |z_i'| > 1$$

if there is a pair of complex conjugate zeros, then this pair contributes a total of zero phase and in that case, we have $H_{\max}(\pi) - H_{\max}(0) \neq -M\pi$ but $-(M-2)\pi$ radians. Similarly, each pair of conjugate zeros decreases the total $M\pi$ by 2π radians. It is also clear that:

$$\boxed{|\measuredangle H_{\max}(\pi)| \geq |\measuredangle H_{\min}(\pi)|} \qquad \ldots(9.63)$$

If the FIR system with M zeros has some of its zeros inside the unit circle and the remaining outside the unit circle, then such a system is called a **mixed-phase system** or **non-minimum phase system.**

The $\frac{d}{d\omega}[\theta(\omega)]$ is a measure of time delay that signal frequency components undergo in passing through the system, a minimum-phase delay characteristic implies a minimum time delay, while a maximum-phase characteristic implies a maximum delay. Suppose we have an FIR system with real coefficients. Then the (magnitude)^2 value of frequency response is given by

$$|H(\omega)|^2 = H(z).H(z^{-1})\big|_{z=e^{j\omega}} \qquad \ldots(9.64)$$

Hence, **if we replace a zero z_k by its inverse $\frac{1}{z_k}$, then $|H(\omega)|^2$ remains unchanged.** Magnitude $|H(\omega)|$ does not change if any zero is replaced by its reciprocal value. If $H(\omega)$ has M zeros, there are 2^M possible configurations all having the same value of $|H(\omega)|^2$. Out of these 2^M configurations are configuration will correspond to all zeros inside the unit circle (*i.e.*, a minimum phase configuration) and one configuration will correspond to all zeros outside the unit circle (*i.e.*, a maximum phase configuration). A complex conjugate pair of zeros (z_1, z_1^*) can either be both inside the unit circle (giving a minimum phase) or can be both outside the unit circle (giving a maximum phase). Thus, two complex conjugate zeros can give only two different configurations (and not $2^2 = 4$), whereas a pair of real zeros (z_1, z_2) can give $2^2 = 4$ possible different configurations, two mixed ones and one each a minimum and a maximum phase.

Consider the following systems:

$$H_1(z) = 6 + z^{-1} - z^{-2} \rightarrow \text{zeros at } z = -\frac{1}{2}, \frac{1}{3} \quad \therefore \text{ Minimum phase}$$

$$H_2(z) = 1 - z^{-1} - 6z^{-2} \rightarrow \text{zeros at } z = -2, 3 \quad \therefore \text{ Maximum phase}$$

$$H_3(z) = 1 - \frac{5}{2}z^{-1} - \frac{3}{2}z^{-2} \rightarrow \text{zeros at } z = -\frac{1}{2}, 3 \quad \therefore \text{ Mixed phase}$$

$$H_4(z) = 1 + \frac{5}{3}z^{-1} - \frac{2}{3}z^{-2} \rightarrow \text{zeros at } z = -2, \frac{1}{3} \quad \therefore \text{ Mixed phase}$$

Each system has the same $|H(\omega)|$, since, the zeros are reciprocal of one another. But phase characteristic of each $H_i(z)$ is different for different $i = 1, 2, 3, 4$.

9.6.1 Maximum/Minimum Phase IIR Filters

The minimum-phase property of FIR systems carries over to IIR system also. A system

$$H(z) = \frac{N(z)}{D(z)} \qquad \ldots(9.65)$$

is minimum-phase if all zeros and poles are inside $|z| = 1$
is maximum-phase if all zeros are outside $|z| = 1$
is mixed-phase if some, but not all zeros are outside $|z| = 1$

Note that for a stable, causal system, the poles must be inside the unit circle. Hence, in all above three cases, we assume all poles inside $|z| = 1$.

Thus, a stable, minimum-phase system $H(z)$ has its inverse $\frac{1}{H(z)}$ also a stable and minimum phase *i.e.*, if $\frac{N(z)}{D(z)}$ has all its zeros and poles inside $|z| = 1$, then $\frac{D(z)}{N(z)}$ has also its zeros and poles inside unit circle $|z| = 1$.

9.6.2 Decomposition of a Non-minimum-phase Pole-zero System

Let
$$H(z) = \frac{N(z)}{D(z)} = \frac{N_1(z) \cdot N_2(z)}{D(z)} \qquad \ldots(9.66)$$

where $D(z)$ has all zeros inside $|z| = 1$ *i.e.*, $H(z)$ is stable and causal

$N_1(z)$ has all its zeros inside $|z| = 1$

$N_2(z)$ has all its zeros outside $|z| = 1$

$\therefore$ $N_2(z^{-1})$ will have all its zeros inside $|z| = 1$.

Consider $$H(z) = \left(\frac{N_1(z)\,N_2(z^{-1})}{D(z)}\right)\left(\frac{N_2(z)}{N_2(z^{-1})}\right)$$

The TF $\frac{N_1(z)\,N_2(z^{-1})}{D(z)}$ has all its zeros inside the unit circle. Hence, it represents a minimum phase function $H_{\min}(z)$. The TF $\frac{N_2(z)}{N_2(z^{-1})}$ has its poles and zeros inversed, hence, it represents an all pass function $H_{\text{all pass}}(z)$. Hence, we can write

$$\therefore \qquad \boxed{H_{\text{mix}}(z) = H_{\min}(z)\,.\,H_{\text{all pass}}(z)} \qquad \ldots(9.67)$$

9.6.3 Group Delay of a Non-minimum-phase System

$$\tau_g(\omega)\,|_{\text{mix}} = \tau_g(\omega)\,|_{\text{of min}} + \tau_g(\omega)\,|_{\text{of all pass}} \qquad \ldots(9.68)$$

as all $\tau_g(\omega)$ are +ve hence $\tau_g(\omega)\,|_{\text{mix}} \geq \tau_g(\omega)\,|_{\text{of min}}$.

i.e., among all pole-zero systems having the same $|H(\omega)|$ response, **the minimum-phase system has the smallest group delay**.

The partial energy of a causal system, $h(n)$, is defined by:

$$E(n) = \sum_{k=0}^{n} |h(k)|^2 \qquad \ldots(9.69)$$

Then the minimum-phase system has the largest partial energy $E(n)$. This can be mathematically proved.

EXAMPLE 9.21: *Under what conditions will the filter H(z) be an all pass filter, where*

$$H(z) = \frac{a_0 + a_1 z + a_2 z^2}{b_0 + b_1 z + b_2 z^2}.$$

SOLUTION: We can write, replacing z by $e^{j\omega}$,

$$H(e^{j\omega}) = \frac{a_0 + a_1 e^{j\omega} + a_2 e^{j2\omega}}{b_0 + b_1 e^{j\omega} + b_2 e^{j2\omega}}$$

$$= e^{j2\omega}\,\frac{(a_0 e^{-j2\omega} + a_1 e^{-j\omega} + a_2)}{b_2 e^{j2\omega} + b_1 e^{j\omega} + b_0}$$

$$\triangleq e^{j2\omega}\,\frac{N(e^{j\omega})}{D(e^{j\omega})}$$

If $$D(e^{j\omega}) = N^*(e^{j\omega}), \text{ then } |N(e^{j\omega})| = |D(e^{j\omega})|$$
and also $|e^{j2\omega}| = 1$, it will result in $|H(e^{j\omega})| = 1$, and all pass filter.

Thus, $H(z)$ will be an all pass filter if

$$b_2 = a_0^*,\ b_1 = a_1^* \text{ and } b_0 = a_2^*$$

With this assumption $D(e^{j\omega})$ will be equal to $N^*(e^{j\omega})$ **Ans.**

EXAMPLE 9.22: *Convert H(z) into H(z) = $H_{min}(z)\,.\,H_{all\ pass}(z)$, where*

$$H(z) = \frac{\left(1 - \frac{1}{3}z^{-1}\right)(1 - 5\,z^{-1})}{\left(1 - \frac{1}{2}z^{-1}\right)\left(1 - \frac{1}{4}z^{-1}\right)}.$$

SOLUTION: Clearly $H(z)$ has zeros at $z = \frac{1}{3}$, 5, and poles at $z = \frac{1}{2}, \frac{1}{4}$ [hence $H(z)$ is stable]

A minimum phase filter has all zeros inside the unit circle $|z| = 1$. Also, if we replace a zero by its inverse, the magnitude of its frequency response remains unchanged.

Let

$$H(z) = \frac{\left(1-\frac{1}{3}z^{-1}\right)\left(1-\frac{1}{5}z^{-1}\right)}{\left(1-\frac{1}{2}z^{-1}\right)\left(1-\frac{1}{4}z^{-1}\right)} \times \frac{(1-5z^{-1})}{\left(1-\frac{1}{5}z^{-1}\right)}$$

$$\triangleq H_{min}(z) \,.\, H_{allpass}(z)$$

where

$$H_{min}(z) = \frac{\left(1-\frac{1}{3}z^{-1}\right)\left(1-\frac{1}{5}z^{-1}\right)}{\left(1-\frac{1}{2}z^{-1}\right)\left(1-\frac{1}{4}z^{-1}\right)} \quad \begin{array}{l}\text{has zeros at } z = \frac{1}{3}, \frac{1}{5} \\ \text{has poles at } z = \frac{1}{2}, \frac{1}{4}\end{array}$$

Hence, $H_{min}(z)$ is a minimum-phase, stable IIR filter

and

$$H_{all\ pass}(z) = \frac{1-5z^{-1}}{1-\frac{1}{5}z^{-1}}, \quad \begin{array}{l}\text{has zeros at } z = 5 \\ \text{has poles at } z = \frac{1}{5}\end{array}$$

$\therefore$ $H_{all\ pass}(z)$ is a stable, all pass filter. **Ans.**

9.7 NOTCH FILTERS

A notch filter is a filter that contains one or more deep notches (ideally perfect null/zero) at its notch frequency. A typical notch filter's frequency response is shown in Fig. 9.14, here notches are at $\omega = \omega_0, \omega_1$. The Notch filters are useful in many applications where specific frequency component must be eliminated. For example, instrumentation and recording systems require the power-line frequency of 60 Hz and its harmonics to be eliminated.

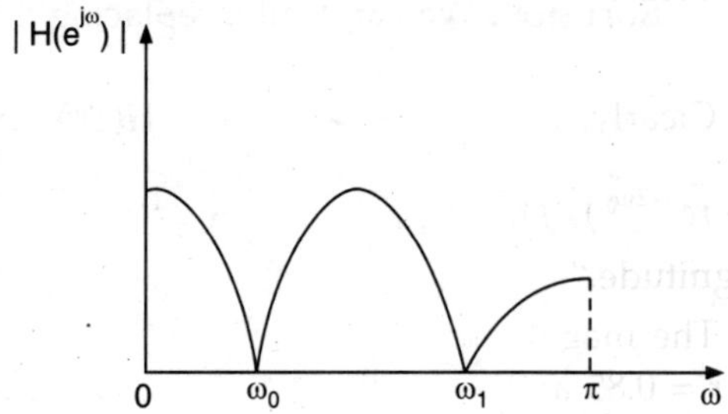

Fig. 9.14. Frequency response characteristic of a Notch filter, notches at $\omega = \omega_0, \omega_1$

To create a null in the frequency response at ω_0, say, we introduce a pair of complex-conjugate zeros on the unit circle at an angle ω_0 *i.e.*,

$$z_1 = e^{j\omega_0}, z_2 = e^{-j\omega_0} \qquad \ldots(9.70)$$

The system function of an FIR notch filters is simply

$$H(z) = b_0(1 - e^{-j\omega_0} z^{-1})(1 - e^{j\omega_0} z^{-1}) \qquad \ldots(9.71a)$$

$$= b_0[1 - 2\cos\omega_0 z^{-1} + z^{-2}] \qquad \ldots(9.71b)$$

It has zeros at $z = e^{j\omega_0}$, and $z = e^{-j\omega_0}$.

Figure. 9.15 gives the magnitude response for a notch having a null at $\omega = \frac{\pi}{4}$.

But **an FIR notch filter** has a relatively large **band width** *i.e.,* the frequency components around ω_0 are severely attenuated.

To reduce the band width of the null we may resort to a more sophisticated, longer FIR. Alternatively, we can attempt to improve the freqeuency response by introducing poles in the system function. If we place a pair of complex-conjugate poles at

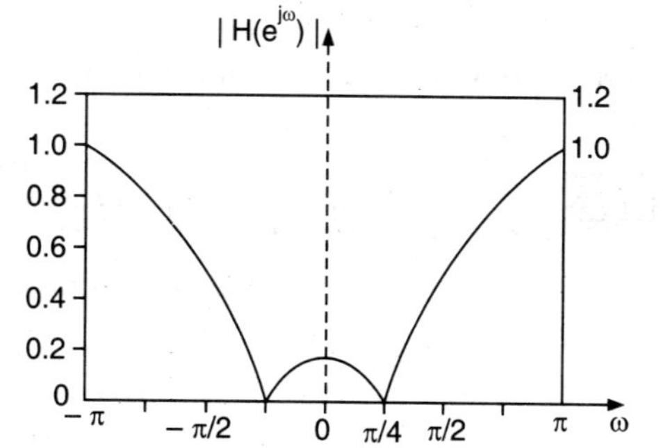

Fig. 9.15. Frequency response of a Notch filter with a notch at $\omega = \pi/4$, $H(z) = (1 - 2\cos\omega_0\, z^{-1} + z^{-2})$

$$p_{1,2} = re^{\pm j\omega_0} \quad \text{...(9.72)}$$

then

$$H(z) = (b_0)\,\frac{[(1 - e^{j\omega_0}\, z^{-1})\,(1 - e^{-j\omega_0}\, z^{-1})]}{[(1 - re^{j\omega_0}\, z^{-1})\,(1 - re^{-j\omega_0}\, z^{-1})]} \quad \text{...(9.73)}$$

The effect of the poles is to introduce resonance in the vicinity of the null and thus reduce the band width (or make the notch sharper). The resulting system function is given by:

$$H(z) = \frac{(b_0)\,[1 - 2\cos\omega_0\, z^{-1} + z^{-2}]}{1 - 2r\cos\omega_0\, z^{-1} + r^2\, z^{-2}} \quad \text{...(9.74)}$$

$$= (b_0)\,\frac{(1 - e^{-j\omega_0}\, z^{-1})\,(1 - e^{j\omega_0}\, z^{-1})}{(1 - re^{-j\omega_0}\, z^{-1})\,(1 - re^{j\omega_0}\, z^{-1})}$$

Clearly,

$$H(e^{j\omega}) = (b_0)\,\frac{(1 - e^{-j(\omega_0 + \omega)})\,(1 - e^{-j(\omega_0 - \omega)})}{(1 - re^{-j(\omega_0 + \omega)})\,(1 - re^{j(\omega_0 - \omega)})}$$

Clearly, at $\omega = \omega_0$ or at $\omega = -\omega_0$, $H(e^{j\omega})|_{\omega = \pm\omega_0} = 0$, (as expected) "at $\omega = \omega_0$, poles are: $(1 - re^{-j2\omega_0})$, $(1 - r) = (1 + r^2 - 2r\cos 2\,\omega_0)^{1/2}$, $(1 - r)$ in magnitude."

The magnitude response $|H(e^{j\omega})|$ is shown in Fig. 9.16 for $r = 0.85$ and $r = 0.95$.

The effect of the pole is to reduce the band width of the notch.

In addition to reducing the band width of the notch, the introduction of a **pole in the vicinity** of the null may result in a small **ripple in the passband** of the filter due to the resonances created by the pole. The effect of the ripple can be reduced by introducing additional poles and/or zeros in the system function of the notch filter. The major problem with this approach is that it is basically an *ad hoc*, trial-and-error method.

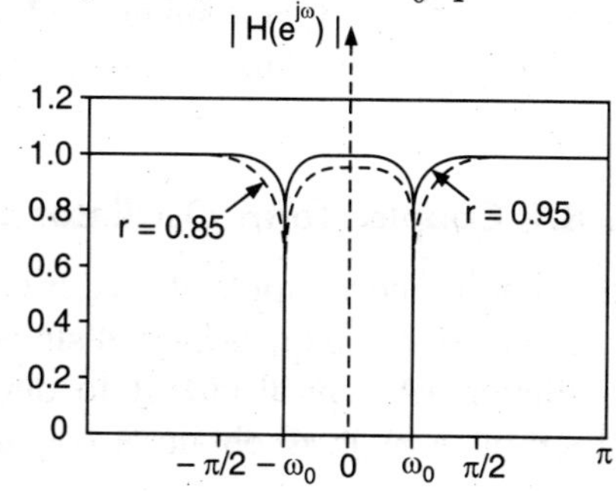

Fig. 9.16. Frequency response of notch filters

$$H(z) = \frac{b_0\,(1 - 2\cos\omega_0\, z^{-1} + z^{-2})}{1 - 2\,r\cos\omega_0\, z^{-1} + r^2\, z^{-2}}$$

It is also possible to obtain extremely narrow band width notch filters by using amplitude change functions, see Section 9.9.

9.8 DIGITAL SINUSOID OSCILLATORS

We are often required to realize a sinusoid function, as for an oscillator, such as $A \sin n\omega_0$. We can realize it as follows.

Consider the system function

$$H(z) = \frac{b_0}{1 - 2r \cos \omega_0 \, z^{-1} + r^2 \, z^{-2}} \equiv \frac{1}{1 + a_1 z^{-1} + a_2 z^{-2}} \qquad \ldots(9.75)$$

Its inverse z-transform is given by

$$\therefore \qquad h(n) = (b_0) \frac{r^n}{\sin \omega_0} \sin (n+1)\omega_0 \, . \, u(n) \qquad \ldots(9.76)$$

Thus, if excitation is $\delta(n)$ *i.e.*, only one impulse, and thereafter the output is $h(n)$. If $b_0 = A \sin \omega_0$, then (9.76) gives us

$$h(n) = Ar^n \sin (n+1)\, \omega_0 \, u(n) \qquad \ldots(9.77a)$$

$$\therefore \qquad h(n) = A \sin (n+1)\, \omega_0 \, u(n), \text{ if } r = 1 \qquad \ldots(9.77b)$$

Hence, the output is $\{A \sin \omega_0, A \sin 2\omega_0, A \sin 3\omega_0, \ldots\}$
$\uparrow$

$$\equiv A \sin nT\omega_0 = A \sin \omega_0 t \,|_{t = nT} \qquad \ldots(9.78)$$

Note that the difference equation for $y(n)$ given in Fig. 9.17 is

$$y(n) = -a_1 y(n-1) - a_2 y(n-2) + b_0 \, \delta(n) \qquad \ldots(9.79)$$

where $a_1 = 2r \cos \omega_0$
$a_2 = -r^2$
$b_0 = A \sin \omega_0$

Then the IIR filter given in Fig. 9.17 gives the output $A \sin n\omega_0$.

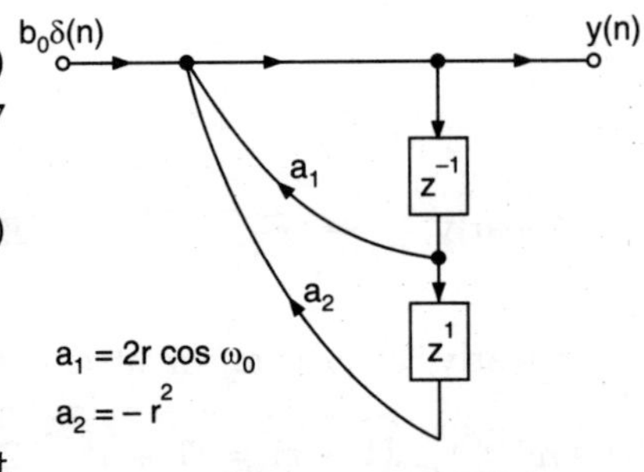

Fig. 9.17. Digital sinusoid Generator

9.8.1 Coupled-form Oscillator to Realize sin $\omega_0 n$ and cos $\omega_0 n$

In some practical applications, involving modulation of two sinusoidal carrier signals in phase quadrature, we require both $A \sin \omega_0 n$ and $A_0 \cos \omega_0 n$. These can be generated by a coupled-form oscillator. (A typical circuit to demodulate an amplitude modulated, single side band signal $A \sin (\omega_c + \omega_m)t$, to obtain $A \cos \omega_m t$ (modulating signal) is shown in Fig. 9.18). Consider

$$\cos (n\omega_0) = \cos ((n-1)+1)\omega_0 = \cos (n-1)\omega_0 \cos \omega_0 - \sin (n-1)\omega_0 \sin \omega_0 \qquad \ldots(9.80)$$

$$\sin (n\omega_0) = \sin ((n-1)+1)\omega_0 = \sin (n-1)\omega_0 \cos \omega_0 + \cos (n-1)\omega_0 \sin \omega_0 \qquad \ldots(9.81)$$

Define $\cos n\omega_0 = y_c(n)$ and $\sin n\omega_0 = y_s(n)$ (Note this step)

$\therefore$ Equations (9.80), and (9.81) reduced to

$$y_c(n) = y_c(n-1) \cos \omega_0 - y_s(n-1) \sin \omega_0 \qquad \ldots(9.82)$$

$$y_s(n) = y_s(n-1) \cos \omega_0 + y_c(n-1) \sin \omega_0$$
$$= y_c(n-1) \, . \, \sin \omega_0 + y_s(n-1) \cos \omega_0 \qquad \ldots(9.83)$$

Or in the matrix form, we can write

$$\begin{bmatrix} y_c(n) \\ y_s(n) \end{bmatrix} = \begin{bmatrix} \cos\omega_0 & -\sin\omega_0 \\ \sin\omega_0 & \cos\omega_0 \end{bmatrix} \cdot \begin{bmatrix} y_c(n-1) \\ y_s(n-1) \end{bmatrix} \qquad \ldots(9.84)$$

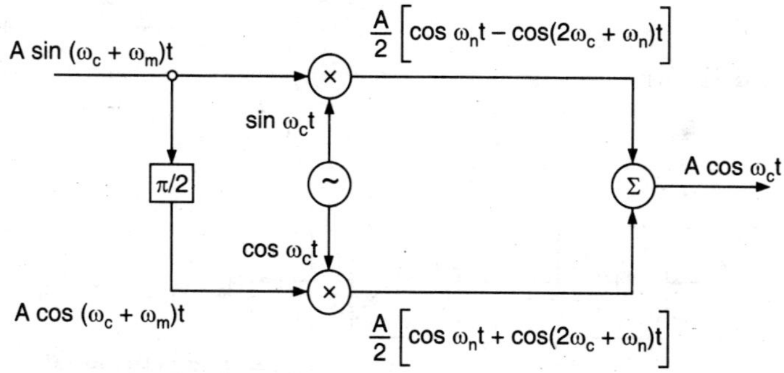

Fig. 9.18. Recovery of modulating signal $A \cos \omega_m t$ from a *SSB-AM* signal $A \sin(\omega_c + \omega_m)t$

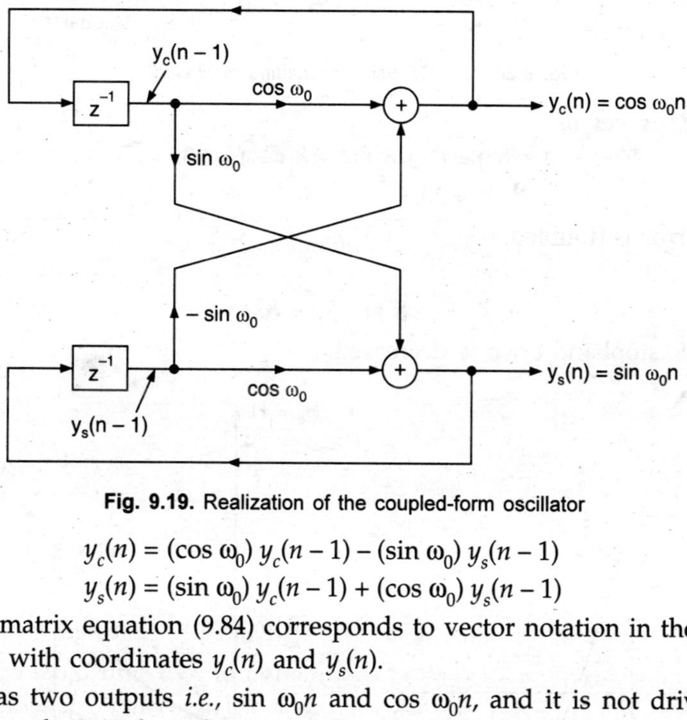

Fig. 9.19. Realization of the coupled-form oscillator

Clearly,

$$y_c(n) = (\cos\omega_0)\, y_c(n-1) - (\sin\omega_0)\, y_s(n-1)$$
$$y_s(n) = (\sin\omega_0)\, y_c(n-1) + (\cos\omega_0)\, y_s(n-1)$$

Note that the matrix equation (9.84) corresponds to vector notation in the two-dimensional coordinate system with coordinates $y_c(n)$ and $y_s(n)$.

The system has two outputs *i.e.*, $\sin \omega_0 n$ and $\cos \omega_0 n$, and it is not driven by any input. However, it requires the initial conditions, $y_c(-1) = A \cos \omega_0 n$, and $y_s(-1) = -A \sin \omega_0$ in order to begin its self-sustaining oscillations.

Fig. 9.19 shows a commonly used realization, to obtain $\sin \omega_0 n$ and $\cos \omega_0 n$.

9.9 AMPLITUDE CHANGE FUNCTIONS (ACF)

Sharpening the Response of Non-recursive Filters

(J.F. Kaiser, and R.W. Hamming, 'Sharping the response of a symmetric non-recursive filter by multiple use of the same filter,' IEEE Tr. ASSP-25, pp. 415-422, No.5, October,-1977).

It is often necessary to improve the performance of the filter either by increasing the stopband loss (δ_2) rejection or by decreasing the error in the passband. It can be done by processing the data by repeated passes through the same filter. Each pass either increases δ_1 and decreases δ_2 or vice versa.

9.9.1 Cascading

This is shown in Fig. 9.20. (*a*)

Here, $$H_0 = H \cdot H \quad \ldots(9.85)$$

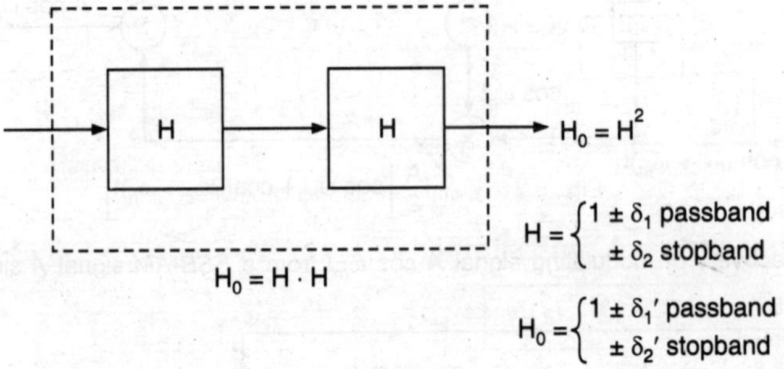

Fig. 9.20. (*a*) ACF using cascading of *H* with *H*

For passband, H_0 gives us

$$(1 \pm \delta'_1) = (1 \pm \delta_1)\,(1 \pm \delta_1) = 1 \pm 2\delta_1 + \delta_1^2$$

$$\delta'_1 \approx 2\delta_1$$

∴ Passband error is doubled

For stopband

$$\pm\,\delta'_2 = (\pm\,\delta_2)\,(\pm\,\delta_2) = \delta_2^2$$

∴ $\delta'_2 << \delta_2$, *i.e.*, stopband error is decreased.

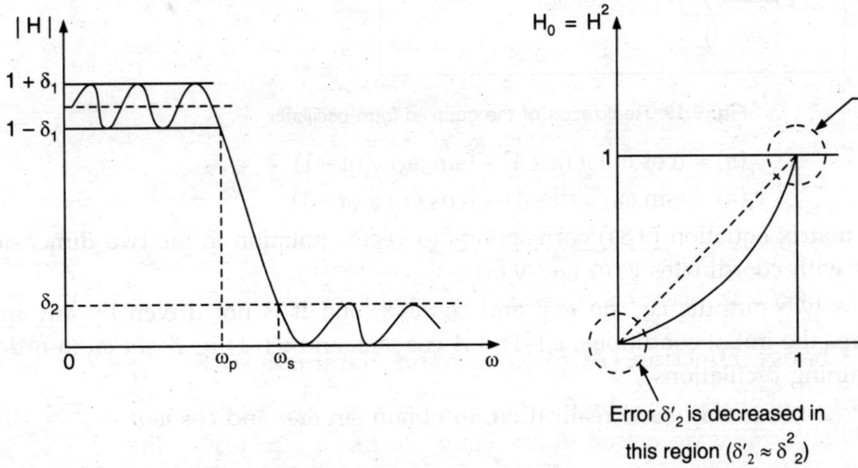

Fig. 9.20. (*b*) Showing the variation of error of H^2 in cascading

This is not an ideal sharpening outcome, as the stopband error is decreased but the passband error is doubled. This is shown in Fig. 9.20(*b*).

9.9.2 Twicing (Turkey's Scheme)

Another realization of an ACF, called twicing is shown in Fig. 9.21.

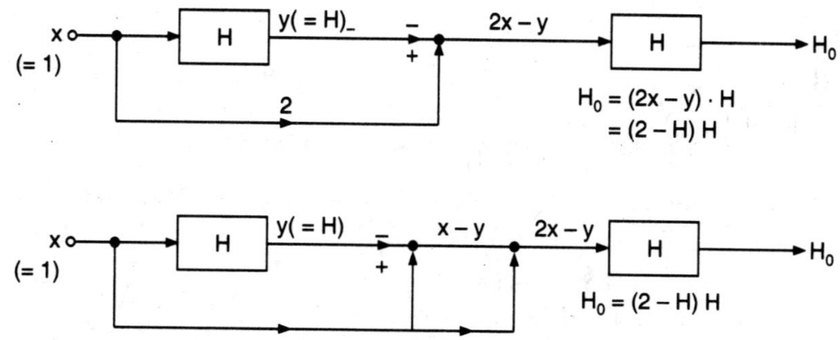

Fig. 9.21. Twicing scheme of ACF.

In the above scheme, if $x = 1$ (unit sample's $ZT = 1$), then $y = H(z)$

Clearly, $$\boxed{H_0 = (2 - H)H} \quad \text{...(9.86)}$$

In the passband, we have

$$1 \pm \delta_1' = [2 - (1 \pm \delta_1)]\,(1 \pm \delta_1) = (1 \mp \delta_1)\,(1 \pm \delta_1)$$
$$= 1 - \delta_1^2 \quad \therefore \quad \delta_1' = \delta_1^2$$

In the stopband

$$\pm \delta_2' = [2 - (1 \pm \delta_2)]\,(1 \pm \delta_2) = \pm 2\delta_1 - \delta_2^2 \approx \pm 2\delta_2$$

Thus, here error (δ_1') in the passband is decreased and error in the stopband (δ_2') is increased. This case is the opposite of cascading case discussed earlier. Figure 9.22 gives the relative performance of two schemes discussed.

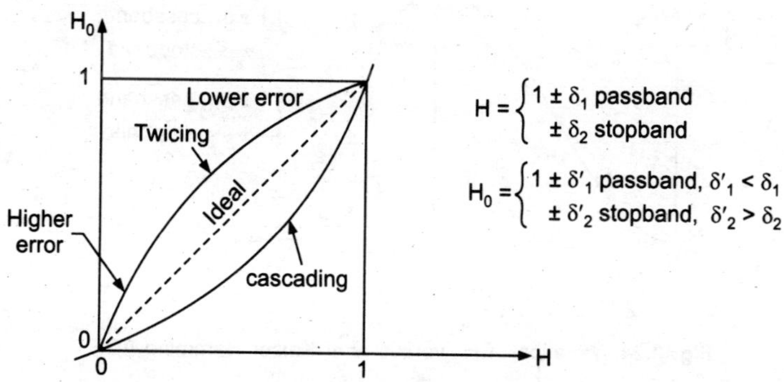

Fig. 9.22. Variation of H_0 versus H for different ACF schemes

9.9.3 Amplitude Change Function (ACF)-Kaiser and Hamming ACF

In the earlier, two cases of sharpening (by Cascading or by Twicing), H_0 reason H curves, called ACF curves, show that error is decreased in one band but increased in the other.

Now consider the polynomial (assume $H[e^{j\omega}) = x$ and $H_0(e^{j\omega}) = P(x)]$

$$P(x) = 3x^2 - 2x^3 = x^2(3 - 2x) \quad \text{...(9.87)}$$

$$\frac{dP}{dx} = 6x - 6x^2 = 6x\,(1 - x)$$

$$\therefore \quad \frac{dP}{dx} = 0 \text{ at } x = 0, x = 1$$

This means that an output H_0, if chosen as $P(x)$ with $H = x$, the resultant filter H_0 would have minimum error both at $H = 0$ and $H = 1$. For an ideal LPF, $H = 0$ in stopband and $H = 1$ in passband.

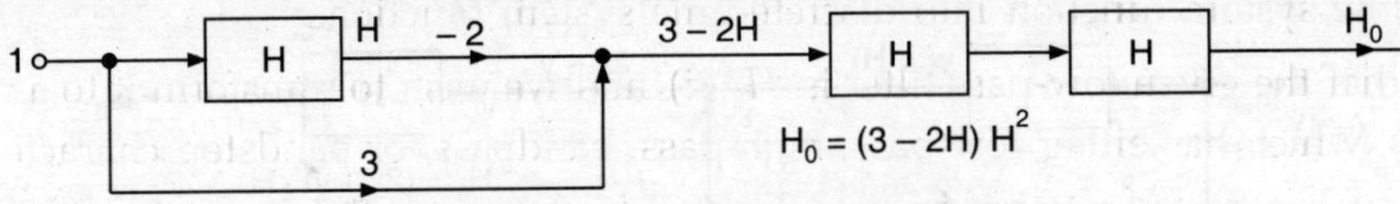

Fig. 9.23. Realization of Kaiser and Hamming ACF

Consider a LPF $H(e^{j\omega})$ an specified in Fig. 9.24. In the Passband, we have

$$1 \pm \delta_1' = [3 - 2(1 \pm \delta_1)]\,(1 \pm \delta_1)^2 \qquad [\because\ H_0 = (3 - 2H)H_2]$$

$$= (1 \pm 2\delta_1)\,(1 \pm 2\delta_1) \qquad \because\ (1 \pm \delta_1)^2 \approx 1 \pm 2\delta_1$$

$$= 1 - 4\delta_1^2$$

$$\therefore \qquad \delta_1' = 4\delta_1^2 \qquad i.e.\ \boxed{\delta_1' \ll \delta_1} \qquad \ldots(9.88a)$$

In the stopband, we have

$$\pm\delta_2' = [3 - 2(\pm\delta_2)]\,[\pm\delta_2]^2 = [3 \pm 2\delta_2)]\delta_2^2$$

$$= 3\delta_2^2 \pm 2\delta_2^3 \approx 3\delta_2^2$$

$$\text{Again} \qquad \boxed{\delta_2' \ll \delta_2} \qquad \ldots(9.88b)$$

The error is decreased both in the passband as well as in the stopband.

Some other ACF of higher orders are available. Students may refer Kaiser and Hamming paper of 1977.

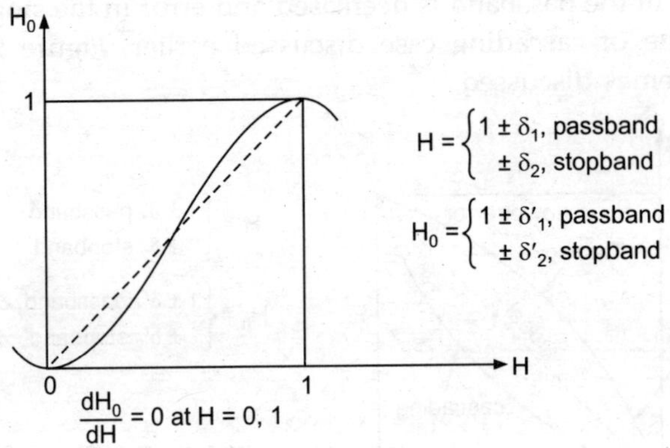

Fig. 9.24. Variation of H_0 versus H in Kaiser Hamming ACF

9.10 FREQUENCY TRANSFORMATIONS OF IIR FILTERS (CONSTANTINIDES TRANSFORMATIONS)

To get any selective filter *viz.*, LPF, HPF, BPF, BSF, etc., we first design a low-pass filter with frequency normalised prototype. Then by algebraic transformations, we derive the desired LPF, HPF, ..., etc. filters. One may think that we can directly design any type of analog filter (true) but if we then resort to invariant impulse transform to obtain the corresponding digital filter, it does not work. This is so as there is aliasing in invariant impulse transformation from analog to the digital filter. Perhaps, for bilinear transformation, this procedure would be acceptable. The sure method is to always design a LPF (analog), convert it to digital filter LPF (using any transformation), and convert such a digital (LPF) to a desired digital filter of any type LPF, HPF, ...,. Such a process would be equivalent to 'Bilinear Transformation', used to transform a continuous-time system function into discrete-time system function.

Assume that the given low-pass filter is $H_{lp}(\tilde{z})$ and we wish to transform it to a new system function $H(z)$, which has either low-pass, high-pass, bandpass, or bandstop characteristic when evaluated on the unit circle. We have associated capital $\tilde{z}$ with the given domain and small z with the transformed domain. We, therefore, define the mapping as

$$\tilde{z}^{-1} = G(z^{-1}) \quad \text{...(9.89)}$$

such that

$$\underset{\text{(new filter)}}{H(z)} = \underset{\text{(given filter)}}{H_{lp}(\tilde{z})|_{\tilde{z}^{-1}=G(z^{-1})}} \quad \text{...(9.90)}$$

Thus, we simply replace $\tilde{z}^{-1}$ in the given LPF $H_{lp}(\tilde{z})$ by $G(z^{-1})$.

The desirable conditions are:

(*i*) $G(z^{-1})$ must be a rational function of z^{-1}.

(*ii*) The inside of the unit circle of $\tilde{z}$ plane (and hence the poles of the given stable filter) must map to the inside of the unit circle of the z-plane. This would ensure a stable filter mapping to a stable new filter.

(*iii*) The unit circle of the $\tilde{z}$ plane must map onto the unit circle of the z-plane.

(*iv*) If $H_{lp}(\tilde{z})$ is causal, $H(z)$ must also be causal.

Let $\tilde{z} = e^{j\theta}$ the given domain *i.e.* for $H_{lp}(\tilde{z})$

$z = e^{j\omega}$ the transformed domain *i.e.* for $H(z)$

then the condition (*iii*) above holds if

$$\tilde{z}^{-1} = G(z^{-1})$$

yields

$$e^{-j\theta} = |G(e^{-j\omega})|\, e^{j\arg G(e^{-j\omega})} \quad \text{...(9.91)}$$

and $|G(e^{-j\omega})| = 1$ (*i.e.* unit circle $|\tilde{z}| = 1$ maps to the unit circle $|z| = 1$) and that $G(z^{-1})$ is an all pass filter. ...(9.92)

Hence, the relationship between the frequency variables is

$$-\theta = \arg G(e^{-j\omega}) \quad \text{...(9.93)}$$

It has been shown by Constantinides that the most general form of the function $G(z^{-1})$ that satisfies all the above requirements is

$$\tilde{z}^{-1} = G(z^{-1}) = \pm\prod_{k=1}^{N} \frac{z^{-1}-\alpha_k}{1-\alpha_k z^{-1}} \; ** \quad \text{...(9.94)}$$

$|\alpha_k| < 1$ for stability

** **Check:** $|G(z^{-1})|^2 = \left|\dfrac{e^{-j\omega}-\alpha_k}{1-\alpha_k e^{-j\omega}}\right|^2 = \dfrac{(\cos\omega-\alpha_k)^2+\sin^2\omega}{(1-\alpha_k\cos\omega)^2+(\alpha_k\sin\omega)^2} = \dfrac{1-2\alpha_k\cos\omega+\alpha_k^2}{1-2\alpha_k\cos\omega+\alpha_k^2} = 1$ ...(9.94*a*)

Thus, $G(e^{-j\omega})$ is an all pass filter.

By choosing appropriate values for N and the constants α_k, a variety of mapping can be obtained.

9.10.1 Low-pass to Low-pass Transformation

We wish to transform a LPF (in $\tilde{z}$ domain) to a new LPF (in z domain)

Here $$\boxed{\tilde{z}^{-1} = G(z^{-1}) = \frac{z^{-1} - \alpha}{1 - \alpha z^{-1}}} \quad ...(9.95)$$

Put $$\tilde{z} = e^{j\theta},\ z = e^{j\omega}$$

$$\therefore \quad e^{-j\omega} = \frac{e^{-j\omega} - \alpha}{1 - \alpha e^{-j\omega}} \quad ...(9.96)$$

$$\therefore \quad e^{-j\theta}(1 - \alpha e^{-j\omega}) = e^{-j\omega} - \alpha \quad ...(A)$$

$$\therefore \quad \alpha[1 - e^{-j(\theta+\omega)}] = e^{-j\omega} - e^{-j\theta}$$

$$\alpha = \frac{(e^{-j\omega} - e^{-j\theta})}{(1 - e^{-j(\theta+\omega)})} = \frac{e^{-j\left(\frac{\theta+\omega}{2}\right)}\left(e^{j\left(\frac{\theta-\omega}{2}\right)} - e^{-j\left(\frac{\theta-\omega}{2}\right)}\right)}{e^{-j(\theta-\omega)/2}\left(2j\sin\frac{\theta+\omega}{2}\right)} = \frac{\sin\left(\frac{\theta-\omega}{2}\right)}{\sin\left(\frac{\theta+\omega}{2}\right)}$$

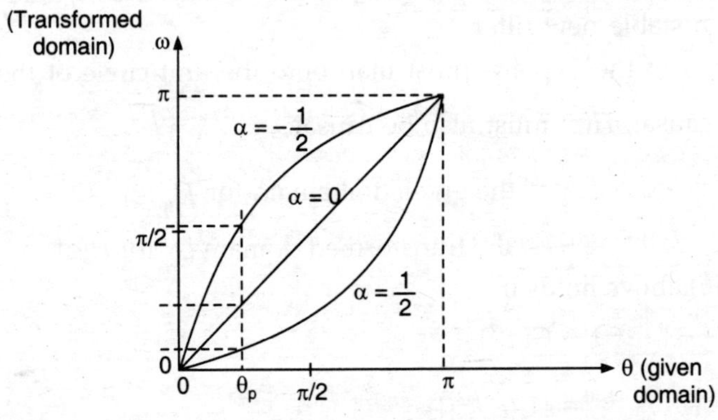

Fig. 9.25. Warping of the frequency scale low-pass of low-pass transform

Let θ_p map to ω_p

$$\therefore \quad \boxed{\alpha = \frac{\sin[(\theta_p - \omega_p)/2]}{\sin[(\theta_p + \omega_p)/2]}} \quad ...(9.97)$$

Also, from (A), we have $e^{-j\omega}(1 + \alpha e^{-j\theta}) = \alpha + e^{-j\theta}$

$$\therefore \quad e^{j\omega} = \frac{1 + \alpha e^{-j\theta}}{\alpha + e^{-j\theta}} = \frac{(1 + \alpha\cos\theta) - j\alpha\sin\theta}{(\alpha + \cos\theta) - j\sin\theta}$$

$$\therefore \quad \omega = \tan^{-1}\frac{\sin\theta}{\alpha + \cos\theta} - \tan^{-1}\frac{\alpha\sin\theta}{1 + \alpha\cos\theta} = \tan^{-1}\left(\frac{\frac{\sin\theta}{\alpha + \cos\theta} - \frac{\alpha\sin\theta}{1 + \alpha\cos\theta}}{1 + \frac{\alpha\sin^2\theta}{(\alpha + \cos\theta)(1 + \alpha\cos\theta)}}\right)$$

$$= \tan^{-1}\frac{\sin\theta + \alpha\sin\theta\cos\theta - \alpha^2\sin\theta - \alpha\sin\theta\cos\theta}{\alpha + \alpha^2\cos\theta + \cos\theta + \alpha\cos^2\theta + \alpha\sin^2\theta} = \tan^{-1}\left(\frac{(1-\alpha^2)\sin\theta}{2\alpha + (1+\alpha^2)\cos\theta}\right)$$

The frequency relation, as below

$$\omega = \tan^{-1}\left(\frac{(1-\alpha^2)\sin\theta}{2\alpha + (1+\alpha^2)\cos\theta}\right) \quad \text{...(9.98)}$$

shows the warping of the frequency scale (except in the case $\alpha = 0$, which corresponds to $\tilde{z}^{-1} = z^{-1}$, a trivial transformation), as shown in Fig. 9.25.

Let A and $\tilde{z}$ domain map to A' in z domain. Hence, $\tilde{z} = 1$ and $z = 1$ must satisfy (9.95). Putting $\tilde{z} = 1$ and $z = 1$ in (9.95), we get

$$1 = \frac{1-\alpha}{1-\alpha}$$

which is true. Hence, point A maps to point A'.

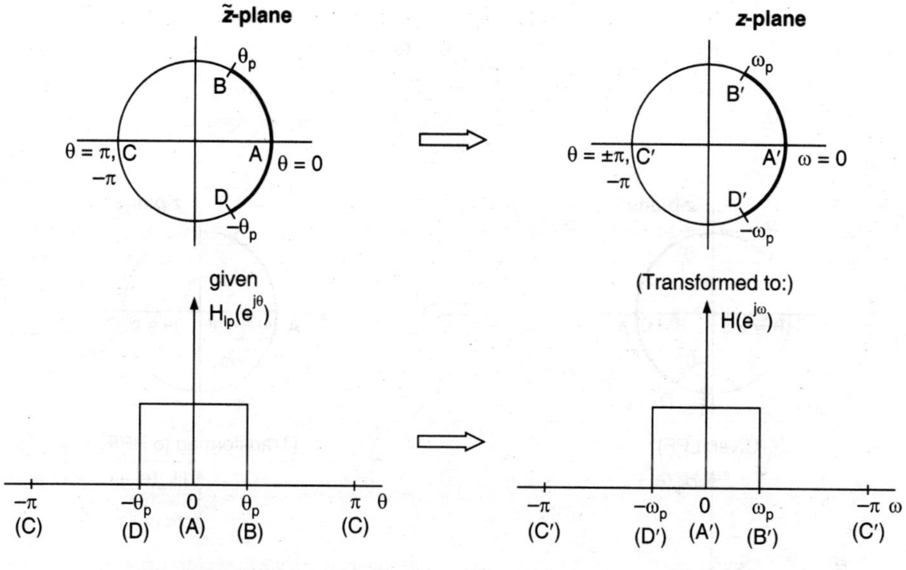

Fig. 9.26. Mapping of various points in LPF to LPF transformation

The pictorial view may be seen from above figures, how each point in $e^{j\theta}$ circle maps to $e^{j\omega}$ is low-pass $(0-\theta_p)$ to a new low-pass $(0-\omega_p)$ filter transformation. Thus, in this case, we replace each delay $\tilde{z}^{-1}$ by $\dfrac{z^{-1}-\alpha}{1-\alpha z^{-1}}$, *i.e.*,

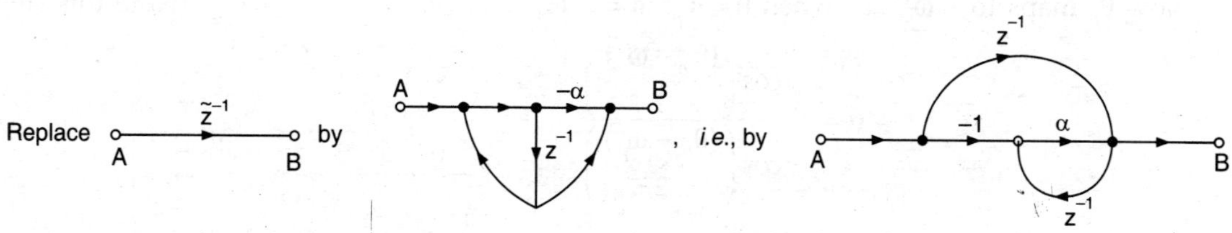

Fig. 9.27. For LP to LP transformation, we replace $\tilde{z}^{-1}$ by shown structure

9.10.2 Low-pass to High-pass Transformation

To transform $H_{lp}(e^{j\theta})$ to $H_{hp}(e^{j\omega})$. Here, the transformation is

$$\boxed{\tilde{z}^{-1} = -\frac{z^{-1}+\alpha}{1+\alpha z^{-1}}}^{*} \qquad \text{...(9.99)}$$

Put $\tilde{z} = e^{j\theta}, z = e^{j\omega}$

$$\therefore \quad e^{-j\theta}(1+\alpha\, e^{-j\omega}) = -[e^{j\omega}+\alpha] \qquad (A)$$

$$\alpha\,[e^{-j(\theta+\omega)}+1] = -(e^{-j\omega}+e^{-j\theta})$$

$$\therefore \quad \alpha = -\frac{e^{-j\omega}+e^{-j\theta}}{1+e^{-j(\theta+\omega)}} = -\frac{e^{-j\left(\frac{\omega+\theta}{2}\right)}\left[e^{j\left(\frac{\theta-\omega}{2}\right)} e^{-j\left(\frac{\theta-\omega}{2}\right)}\right]}{e^{-j\frac{(\theta+\omega)}{2}}\left[2\cos\frac{\theta+\omega}{2}\right]}$$

$$= -\frac{\cos\left(\frac{\theta-\omega}{2}\right)}{\cos\left(\frac{\theta+\omega}{2}\right)}$$

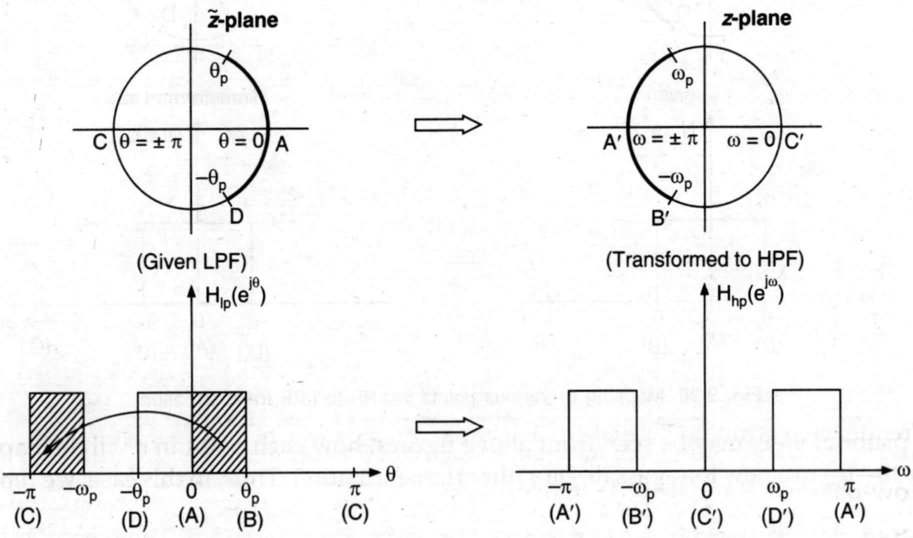

Fig. 9.28. Mapping of various points in LPF to HPF transform

Now θ_p maps to $-\omega_p$, *i.e.*, when $\theta = \theta_p$, $\omega = -\omega_p$ (Note this step)

$$\therefore \quad \alpha = -\frac{\cos\left(\frac{(\theta_p-\omega_p)}{2}\right)}{\cos\left(\frac{(\theta_p+\omega_p)}{2}\right)}$$

Thus, here
$$\alpha = -\frac{\cos\left(\frac{\theta_p + \omega_p}{2}\right)}{\cos\left(\frac{\theta_p - \omega_p}{2}\right)}, \text{ where } \omega_p = \text{desired cut-off frequency} \qquad ...(9.100)$$

***Note:** at $\tilde{z}$-plane A, $\tilde{z}^{-1} = +1$

$\therefore$ Transformation leads to $1 = -\frac{z^{-1}+\alpha}{1+\alpha z^{-1}}$ *i.e.* $(1 + \alpha z^{-1}) = -(z^{-1} + \alpha)$

$\therefore$ $z^{-1} = -1$ $\therefore$ A of $\tilde{z}$ plane does transform to A' of z plane as shown.

Also, from (A), we get $e^{-j\omega}(1 + \alpha e^{-j\theta}) = -(\alpha + e^{-j\theta})$

$$\therefore \quad e^{j\omega} = -\frac{1+\alpha e^{-j\theta}}{\alpha + e^{-j\theta}} = -\frac{(1+\alpha\cos\theta) - j\alpha\sin\theta}{(\alpha+\cos\theta) - j\sin\theta}$$

$$\nearrow$$
$$= -e^{j(\pi+\omega)}$$

$$\therefore \quad \pi + \omega = \tan^{-1}\frac{\sin\theta}{\alpha+\cos\theta} - \tan^{-1}\frac{\alpha\sin\theta}{1+\alpha\cos\theta}$$

$$= \tan^{-1}\left[\frac{\dfrac{\sin\theta}{\alpha+\cos\theta} - \dfrac{\alpha\sin\theta}{1+\alpha\cos\theta}}{1+\dfrac{\alpha\sin^2\theta}{(\alpha+\cos\theta)(1+\alpha\cos\theta)}}\right]$$

$$= \tan^{-1}\left[\frac{\sin\theta + \cancel{\alpha\sin\theta\cos\theta} - \alpha^2\sin\theta - \cancel{\alpha\sin\theta\cos\theta}}{\alpha + \alpha^2\cos\theta + \cos\theta + \alpha\cos^2\theta + \alpha\sin^2\theta}\right]$$

$$\therefore \quad \boxed{\omega = -\pi + \tan^{-1}\left(\frac{(1-\alpha^2)\sin\theta}{2\alpha + (1+\alpha^2)\cos\theta}\right)}$$

$\therefore$ Frequency warping is similar to LP to LP case. ...(9.101)

9.10.3 Low-pass to Bandstop Transformation

Given the LPF, $H_{LP}(e^{j\theta})$ and we are to derive $H_{BS}(e^{j\omega})$ *i.e.* a bandstop filter. The points A, B, C and D of given $\tilde{z}$ domain map twice (retrace) and z domain, as shown *i.e.* we go around $|\tilde{z}| = 1$ circle twice to obtain once-going around $|z| = 1$ circle. Let the transformation be

$$\boxed{\tilde{z}^{-1} = \frac{z^{-2} - \frac{2\alpha}{1+k}z^{-1} + \frac{1-k}{1+k}}{\frac{1-k}{1+k}z^{-2} - \frac{2\alpha}{1+k}z^{-1} + 1}} \quad \text{or} \quad \tilde{z}^{-1} = \frac{z^{-2} + \beta z^{-1} + \gamma}{\gamma z^{-2} + \beta z^{-1} + 1} \qquad ...(9.102)$$

$$\beta = \frac{-2\alpha}{1+k};\ \gamma = \frac{1-k}{1+k}, \text{ where } \alpha \text{ and } k \text{ are functions of } \theta_p, \omega_{p_1}, \omega_{p_2}$$

To make it more generic, add a scaling factor and an elegant expression for transformation is

$$\tilde{z}^{-1} = e^{j\xi\pi} \frac{z^{-2} + \beta z^{-1} + \gamma}{\gamma z^{-2} + \beta z^{-1} + 1} \quad ...(1)$$

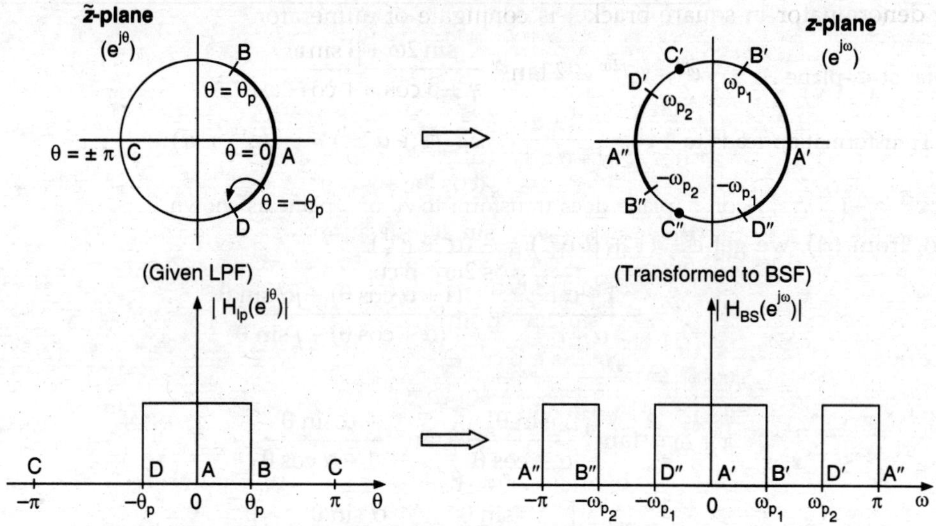

Fig. 9.29. Mapping of various points in LPF to BSF transformation

[To determine the value of ξ] (A must map to A')

At $\quad A, \theta = 0 \quad \therefore \quad \tilde{z} = 1$ and $\therefore \quad \tilde{z}^{-1} = 1$

At $\quad A', \omega = 0, \quad \therefore \quad z = 1$ and $\therefore \quad z^{-1} = 1$

Putting $\tilde{z}^{-1} = z^{-1} = 1$ as (1), we have

$$1 = e^{j\xi\pi} \frac{1+\beta+\gamma}{\gamma+\beta+1} \quad \therefore \quad \xi = 0$$

(A must also map to A'')

Taking $\xi = 0$, we have ensured that A maps to A'

Check at A, $\tilde{z}^{-1}$ and at A'' in z plane

At $\quad A_1, \tilde{z}^{-1} = 1$, at A'' $z^{-1} = -1$ and $\therefore \quad z^{-2} = +1$

Putting those values of $\tilde{z}^{-1}, z^{-1}, z^{-2}$ in (1) with $\xi = 0$, we have

$$1 = (1) \frac{+1-\beta+\gamma}{+\gamma-\beta+1} \text{ which is satisfied.}$$

Hence A maps to A' and also at A'' in z plane

[To determine the values of β and γ]

Put $\tilde{z} = e^{j\theta}$ and $z = e^{j\omega}$ in (1) with $\xi = 0$; we get

$$e^{-j\theta} = \frac{e^{-j2\omega} + \beta e^{-j\omega} + \gamma}{\gamma e^{-j2\omega} + \beta e^{-j\omega} + 1} = \frac{1 + \beta e^{j\omega} + \gamma e^{j2\omega}}{\gamma + \beta e^{j\omega} + e^{j2\omega}} \quad ...(2)$$

i.e.,

$$e^{j\theta} = \frac{\gamma + \beta\, e^{j\omega} + e^{j2\omega}}{1 + \beta\, e^{j\omega} + \gamma\, e^{j2\omega}}$$

$$= \frac{(\cos 2\omega + \beta \cos \omega + \gamma) + j\,(\sin 2\omega + \beta \sin \omega)}{e^{j2\omega}\,[e^{-j2\omega} + \beta\, e^{-j\omega} + \gamma]} \qquad \text{(Note this step)}$$

The denominator in square bracket is conjugate of numerator

$$\therefore \qquad e^{j\theta} = e^{-j2\omega} \angle\, 2 \tan^{-1} \frac{\sin 2\omega + \beta \sin\omega}{\gamma + \beta \cos\omega + \cos 2\omega}$$

$$\therefore \qquad \theta = -2\omega + 2 \tan^{-1} \frac{(\sin 2\omega + \beta \sin\omega)}{(\cos 2\omega + \beta \cos\omega + \gamma)}$$

$$\tan \frac{\theta}{2} = \tan\left[\tan^{-1} \frac{\sin 2\omega + \beta \sin\omega}{\cos 2\omega + \beta \cos \omega + \gamma} - \omega\right]$$

$$= \frac{\dfrac{\sin 2\omega + \beta \sin\omega}{\cos 2\omega + \beta \cos \omega + \gamma} - \tan\omega}{1 + \tan\omega \,.\, \dfrac{\sin 2\omega + \beta \sin\omega}{\cos 2\omega + \beta \cos\omega + \gamma}}$$

$$= \frac{\cos\omega\,(\sin 2\omega + \beta \sin\omega) - \sin\omega\,(\cos 2\omega + \beta \cos\omega + \gamma)}{\cos\omega\,(\cos 2\omega + \beta \cos\omega + \gamma) + \sin\omega\,(\sin 2\omega + \beta \sin\omega)}$$

$$= \frac{\overbrace{(\sin 2\omega \cos\omega - \cos 2\omega \sin\omega)}^{=\,\sin\omega} - \gamma \sin\omega}{\beta + \gamma \cos\omega + \underbrace{(\cos 2\omega \cos\omega + \sin 2\omega \sin\omega)}_{=\,\cos\omega}} = \frac{(1-\gamma)\sin\omega}{(1+\gamma)\cos\omega + \beta}$$

As

$$\tan \frac{\theta}{2} = \frac{(1-\gamma)\sin\omega}{(1+\gamma)\cos\omega + \beta} \qquad \text{...(3)}$$

[To find the value of β, γ]

The mapping conditions are

At B, $\theta = \theta_p$ and at B', $\omega = +\,\omega_{p_1}$

At D, $\theta = -\theta_p$ and at D', $\omega = +\,\omega_{p_2}$

Substituting conditions of points (B, B') and (D, D') in (3), we have

$$\tan \frac{\theta_p}{2} = \frac{(1-\gamma)\sin\omega_{p_1}}{(1+\gamma)\cos\omega_{p_1} + \beta} \qquad \text{...(4)}$$

$$-\tan \frac{\theta_p}{2} = \frac{(1-\gamma)\sin\omega_{p_2}}{(1+\gamma)\cos\omega_{p_2} + \beta} \qquad \text{...(5)}$$

(4) and (5) yield, respectively:

$$\beta + (1+\gamma)\cos\omega_{p_1} - \cot\frac{\theta_p}{2}\,(1-\gamma)\sin\omega_{p_1} = 0 \qquad \text{...(6)}$$

$$\beta + (1+\gamma)\cos\omega_{p_2} + \cot\frac{\theta_p}{2}\,(1-\gamma)\sin\omega_{p_2} = 0 \qquad \text{...(7)}$$

Subtracting (7) from (6) yields, after dividing both sides by $(1-\gamma)$

$$\frac{1+\gamma}{1-\gamma} = \frac{\cot\frac{\theta_p}{2}(\sin\omega_{p_1} + \sin\omega_{p_2})}{(\cos\omega_{p_1} - \cos\omega_{p_2})}$$

By componendo and dividendo

$$\gamma = \frac{\cot\frac{\theta_p}{2}(\sin\omega_{p_1} + \sin\omega_{p_2}) - (\cos\omega_{p_1} - \cos\omega_{p_2})}{\cot\frac{\theta_p}{2}(\sin\omega_{p_1} + \sin\omega_{p_2}) + (\cos\omega_{p_1} - \cos\omega_{p_2})}$$

$$= \frac{1 - \tan\frac{\theta_p}{2}(\cos\omega_{p_1} - \cos\omega_{p_2})/(\sin\omega_{p_1} + \sin\omega_{p_2})}{1 + \tan\frac{\theta_p}{2}(\cos\omega_{p_1} - \cos\omega_{p_2})/(\sin\omega_{p_1} + \sin\omega_{p_2})} \triangleq \frac{1-k}{1+k}$$

where $k = \tan\frac{\theta_p}{2}\,\frac{\cos\omega_{p_1} - \cos\omega_{p_2}}{\sin\omega_{p_1} + \sin\omega_{p_2}}$.

$$= \tan\frac{\theta_p}{2}\,\frac{2\sin\frac{\omega_{p_2}+\omega_{p_1}}{2}\,.\,\sin\frac{\omega_{p_2}-\omega_{p_1}}{2}}{2\sin\frac{\omega_{p_1}+\omega_{p_2}}{2}\,.\,\cos\frac{\omega_{p_1}-\omega_{p_2}}{2}}$$

$$\therefore \quad \boxed{K = \tan\frac{\theta_p}{2}\,\tan\frac{\omega_{p_2}-\omega_{p_1}}{2} \quad \text{and} \quad \gamma = \frac{1-k}{1+k}} \qquad ...(9.103)$$

Putting this value of k and γ in (6), we get

$$\beta + \underbrace{\left(1 + \frac{1-k}{1+k}\right)}_{=\frac{2}{1+K}}\cos\omega_{p_1} - \cot\frac{\theta_p}{2}\underbrace{\left(1 - \frac{1-k}{1+k}\right)}_{=\frac{2k}{1+k}}\sin\omega_{p_1} = 0$$

$$\therefore \quad \beta = \frac{2}{1+k}\left[\cot\frac{\theta_p}{2}\,.\,k\sin\omega_{p_1} - \cos\omega_{p_1}\right]$$

$$= \frac{2}{1+k}\left[\cot\frac{\theta_p}{2}\,\tan\frac{\theta_2}{2}\,.\,\tan\left(\frac{\omega_{p_2}-\omega_{p_1}}{2}\right).\sin\omega_{p_1} - \cos\omega_{p_1}\right]$$

$$= \frac{2}{1+k}\,\frac{1}{\cos\left(\frac{\omega_{p_2}-\omega_{p_1}}{2}\right)}\left[\sin\frac{\omega_{p_2}-\omega_{p_1}}{2}\sin\omega_{p_1} - \cos\frac{\omega_{p_2}-\omega_{p_1}}{2}\,.\cos\omega_{p_1}\right]$$

$$= \frac{-2}{1+k}\,\frac{1}{\cos\left(\frac{\omega_{p_2}-\omega_{p_1}}{2}\right)}\left[\cos\left(\frac{\omega_{p_2}-\omega_{p_1}}{2} + \omega_{p_1}\right)\right]$$

$$= \frac{-2}{1+k}\,\frac{\cos\frac{(\omega_{p_2}+\omega_{p_1})}{2}}{\cos\frac{(\omega_{p_2}-\omega_{p_1})}{2}}$$

$$\therefore \qquad \boxed{\beta \triangleq \frac{-2\alpha}{1+k}, \text{ where } \alpha = \frac{\cos\frac{(\omega_{p_2}+\omega_{p_1})}{2}}{\cos\frac{(\omega_{p_2}-\omega_{p_1})}{2}}} \qquad ...(9.104)$$

9.10.4 Low-pass to Bandpass Transformations

Given the LPF $H_{LP}(e^{j\theta})$ and we are required to derive $H_{BP}(e^{j\omega})$, *i.e.*, a bandpass filter. The points *A, B, C* and *D* map to points *A′, B′, C′, D′, A″, B″, C″* and *D″* as shown by a retrace of $H_{lp}(e^{j\omega})$

The transformation from $\tilde{z}$ domain to new domain z is

$$\tilde{z}^{-1} = -\frac{z^{-2} - \frac{2\alpha k}{k+1} z^{-1} + \frac{k-1}{k+1}}{1 - \frac{2\alpha k}{k+1} z^{-1} + \frac{k-1}{k+1} z^{-2}} \triangleq -\frac{z^{-2} - \beta z^{-1} + \gamma}{\gamma z^{-2} - \beta z^{-1} + 1}$$

where $$\beta = \frac{2\alpha k}{k+1}, \gamma = \frac{k-1}{k+1} \qquad ...(9.105)$$

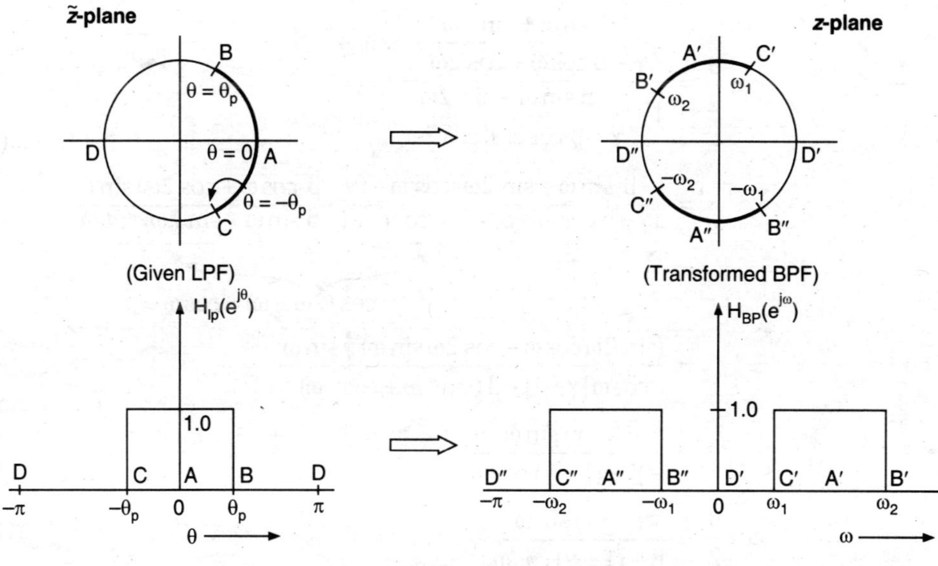

Fig. 9.30. Mapping from LPF to BPF

To make it more generic, we may add a phase factor and have the transformation:

$$\tilde{z}^{-1} = e^{j\xi\pi} \frac{-(z^{-2} - \beta z^{-1} + \gamma)}{\gamma z^{-2} - \beta z^{-1} + 1} \qquad (A)$$

Note that at D, $\tilde{z}^{-1} = -1$ and D to map at $z^{-1} = +1, -1$, (as shown), we must have

$$-1 = e^{j\xi\pi} \frac{-(1 \pm \beta + \gamma)}{(\gamma \pm \beta + 1)} \qquad \text{(Note the step)}$$

$$\therefore \qquad \xi = 0$$

$\therefore$ (A) reduces to

$$\tilde{z}^{-1} = -\frac{z^{-2} - \beta z^{-1} + \gamma}{\gamma z^{-2} - \beta z^{-1} + 1} \quad ...(B)$$

In (B), put $\tilde{z} = e^{j\theta}$ (the given plane) and $z = e^{j\omega}$ (the transformed plane)

$$\therefore \quad e^{-j\theta} = -\frac{e^{-j2\omega} - \beta e^{-j\omega} + \gamma}{\gamma e^{-j2\omega} - \beta e^{-j\omega} + 1}$$

or

$$-e^{j\theta} = e^{-j2\omega}\frac{\gamma - \beta e^{j\omega} + e^{j2\omega}}{\gamma - \beta e^{-j\omega} + e^{-j2\omega}}$$

$$\therefore \quad e^{j(\theta+\pi)} = e^{-j2\omega}\frac{(\gamma - \beta\cos\omega + \cos 2\omega) + j(-\beta\sin\omega + \sin 2\omega)}{(\gamma - \beta\cos\omega + \cos 2\omega) - j(-\beta\sin\omega + \sin 2\omega)}$$

$$\therefore \quad \theta + \pi = -2\omega + 2\tan^{-1}\frac{-\beta\sin\omega + \sin 2\omega}{\gamma - \beta\cos\omega + \cos 2\omega}$$

$$\therefore \quad \tan\frac{\theta+\pi}{2} = \tan\left[\tan^{-1}\frac{-\beta\sin\omega + \sin 2\omega}{\gamma - \beta\cos\omega + \cos 2\omega} - \omega\right]$$

$$\therefore \quad -\cot\frac{\theta}{2} = \frac{\dfrac{-\beta\sin\omega + \sin 2\omega}{\gamma - \beta\cos\omega + \cos 2\omega} - \tan\omega}{1 + \dfrac{-\beta\sin\omega + \sin 2\omega}{\gamma - \beta\cos\omega + \cos 2\omega}.\tan\omega}$$

$$= \frac{(-\beta\sin\omega + \sin 2\omega)\cos\omega - (\gamma - \beta\cos\omega + \cos 2\omega)\sin\omega}{(\gamma - \beta\cos\omega + \underbrace{\cos 2\omega)\cos\omega} + (-\beta\sin\omega + \underbrace{\sin 2\omega)\sin\omega}}$$

$$= \cos(2\omega - \omega) = \cos\omega$$

$$= \frac{(\sin 2\omega\cos\omega - \cos 2\omega\sin\omega)\gamma\sin\omega}{\cos\omega[\gamma + 1] - \beta(\sin^2\omega + \cos^2\omega)}$$

$$= \frac{(1-\gamma)\sin\omega}{-\beta + (1+\gamma)\cos\omega}$$

$$\therefore \quad \cot\frac{\theta}{2} = \frac{(1-\gamma)\sin\omega}{\beta - (1+\gamma)\cos\omega} \quad ...(C)$$

As $$\tan\frac{\theta}{2} = \frac{\beta - (1+\gamma)\cos\omega}{(1-\gamma)\sin\omega} \quad ...(D)$$

Mapping: At B, $\theta = \theta_p$, maps to B' where $\omega = \omega_2$

At C, $\theta = -\theta_p$, maps to C' where $\omega - \omega_1$

Putting $\theta = \theta_p$ and $\omega = \omega_2$, we get

$$\tan\frac{\theta_p}{2} = \frac{\beta - (1+\gamma)\cos\omega_2}{(1-\gamma)\sin\omega_2}$$

$$\therefore \quad \tan\frac{\theta_p}{2}[(1-\gamma)\sin\omega_2] = \beta - (1+\gamma)\cos\omega_2 \quad (E)$$

Similarly, putting $\theta = -\theta_p$ and $\omega = \omega_1$ in (*D*), we will get

$$-\tan\frac{\theta_p}{2}\left[(1-\gamma)\sin\omega_2\right] = \beta - (1+\gamma)\cos\omega_1 \qquad \text{...(F)}$$

[To solve (*E*) and (*F*) for γ and β]

Subtract (*F*) from (*E*)

$$\therefore \quad \tan\frac{\theta_p}{2}\,.\,(1-\gamma)\,.\,[\sin\omega_2 + \sin\omega_1] = (1+\gamma)\,[\cos\omega_1 - \cos\omega_2]$$

$$\therefore \qquad \frac{1-\gamma}{1+\gamma} = \frac{1}{\tan\frac{\theta_p}{2}}\cdot\frac{\cos\omega_1 - \cos\omega_2}{\sin\omega_1 + \sin\omega_2}$$

$$= \frac{1}{k} \qquad = \frac{1}{\tan\frac{\theta_p}{2}}\;\frac{2\sin\frac{\omega_2-\omega_1}{2}\,.\,\sin\frac{\omega_2+\omega_1}{2}}{2\sin\frac{\omega_1+\omega_2}{2}\cos\frac{\omega_1-\omega_2}{2}}$$

$$= \frac{1}{\tan\frac{\theta_p}{2}}\;\tan\frac{\omega_2-\omega_1}{2}$$

Putting $\qquad \gamma = \dfrac{k-1}{k+1} \quad \therefore \quad \dfrac{1-\gamma}{1+\gamma} = \dfrac{2/(k+1)}{2K/(k+1)} = \dfrac{1}{K}$

$$\therefore \qquad k = \cot\frac{\omega_2-\omega_1}{2}\tan\frac{\theta_p}{2} \qquad \text{...(G)}$$

[To determine β]

From (*E*), $\qquad \beta = \tan\dfrac{\theta_p}{2}\,.\sin\omega_2\,.\,(1-\gamma) + \cos\omega_2\,.\,(1+\gamma)$

$$= \tan\frac{\theta_2}{2}\,.\sin\omega_2\,.\,\frac{2}{k+1} + \frac{2k}{k+1}\cos\omega_2$$

$$= \tan\frac{\theta_p}{2}\,.\,\frac{2k}{k+1}\,.\,\frac{\sin\omega_2}{k} + \frac{2k}{k+1}\cos\omega_2 \quad \because\; 1-\gamma = 1-\frac{k-1}{k+1} = \frac{2}{k+1}$$

$$= \frac{2k}{k+1}\left[\tan\frac{\theta_p}{2}\,.\,\frac{\sin\omega_2}{k} + \cos\omega_2\right]$$

$$= \frac{2k}{k+1}\left[\tan\frac{\theta_p}{2}\,.\,\frac{\sin\omega_2}{\cot\frac{\omega_2-\omega_1}{2}\,.\,\tan\frac{\theta_p}{2}} + \cos\omega_2\right]$$

$$= \frac{2k}{k+1}\left[\frac{\sin\frac{\omega_2-\omega_1}{2}\,.\sin\omega_2 + \cos\frac{\omega_2-\omega_1}{2}\,.\cos\omega_2}{\cos\frac{\omega_2-\omega_1}{2}}\right]$$

$$= \frac{2k}{k+1} \frac{\cos(\omega_2 + \omega_1)/2}{\cos(\omega_2 - \omega_1)/2} \triangleq \frac{2\alpha k}{k+1}$$

where $$\alpha = \frac{\cos(\omega_2 + \omega_1)/2}{\cos(\omega_2 - \omega_1)/2}$$

Thus,
$$\boxed{\begin{aligned} \alpha &= \frac{\cos(\omega_2 + \omega_1)/2}{\cos(\omega_2 - \omega_1)/2} \\ k &= \cot \frac{\omega_2 - \omega_1}{2} \tan \frac{\theta_p}{2} \\ \beta &= \frac{2\alpha k}{k+1};\ \gamma = \frac{k-1}{k+1} \end{aligned}} \qquad \text{...(9.106)}$$

All the results derived for various transformations have been given in Table 9.3 for ready reference. In this table, the given domain is $\tilde{z}$ and the transformed domain is z.

Table 9.3. Transformations from a low-pass-digital-filter Prototype of Cut-off Frequency q_p (Constantinides Transformations)

Filter Type	*Transformation*	*Associated Design Formulas*
Low-pass	$\tilde{z}^{-1} = \dfrac{z^{-1} - \alpha}{1 - \alpha z^{-1}}$ (9.95)	$\alpha = \dfrac{\sin\left(\dfrac{\theta_p - \omega_p}{2}\right)}{\sin\left(\dfrac{\theta_p + w_p}{2}\right)}$ ω_p = desired cut-off frequency (9.97)
High-pass	$-\dfrac{z^{-1} + \alpha}{1 + \alpha z^{-1}}$ (9.99)	$\alpha = -\dfrac{\cos\left(\dfrac{\omega_p + \theta_p}{2}\right)}{\cos\left(\dfrac{\omega_p - \theta_p}{2}\right)}$ ω_p = desired cut-off frequency (9.100)
Bandstop	$\dfrac{z^{-2} - \dfrac{2\alpha}{1+k} z^{-1} + \dfrac{1-k}{1+k}}{\dfrac{1-k}{1+k} z^{-2} - \dfrac{2\alpha}{1+k} z^{-1} + 1}$ (9.102)	$\alpha = \dfrac{\cos\left(\dfrac{\omega_2 + \omega_1}{2}\right)}{\cos\left(\dfrac{\omega_2 - \omega_1}{2}\right)}$ (9.104) $k = \tan\left(\dfrac{\omega_2 - \omega_1}{2}\right) \tan \dfrac{\theta_p}{2}$ (9.103) ω_2, ω_1 = desired upper and lower cut-off frequencies, respectivily
Bandpass	$-\dfrac{z^{-2} - \dfrac{2\alpha k}{k+1} z^{-1} + \dfrac{k-1}{k+1}}{\dfrac{k-1}{k+1} z^{-2} - \dfrac{2\alpha k}{k+1} z^{-1} + 1}$ (9.105)	$\alpha = \dfrac{\cos\left(\dfrac{\omega_2 + \omega_1}{2}\right)}{\cos\left(\dfrac{\omega_2 - \omega_1}{2}\right)}$ $k = \cot\left(\dfrac{\omega_2 - \omega_1}{2}\right) \tan \dfrac{\theta_p}{2}$ ω_2, ω_1 = desired upper and lower cut-off frequencies respectivily, (9.106)

Important Result 1

A function defined by

$$F(z) = \frac{Az+B}{B^*z+A^*}, \text{ where } A = a_1 + ja_2,\ B = b_1 + jb_2$$

has
$$F(e^{j\omega}) = \frac{(a_1+ja_2)(\cos\omega + j\sin\omega) + (b_1+jb_2)}{(b_1-jb_2)(\cos\omega + j\sin\omega) + (a_1-ja_2)}$$

$$= \frac{(a_1\cos\omega - a_2\sin\omega + b_1)\ j(a_1\sin\omega + a_2\cos\omega + b_2)}{(b_1\cos\omega + b_2\sin\omega + a_1) + j(b_1\sin\omega - b_2\cos\omega - a_2)}$$

$$\therefore \quad |F(e^{j\omega})|^2 = \frac{\begin{matrix}(a_1^2\cos_2^2\omega + a_2^2\sin^2\omega + b_1^2 - 2a_1 a_2 \sin\omega\cos\omega - 2a_2b_1\sin\omega + 2a_1b_1\cos\omega \\ + a_1^2\sin^2\omega + a_2^2\cos^2\omega + b_2^2 + 2a_1a_2\sin\omega\cos\omega + 2a_2b_2\cos\omega + 2a_1b_2\sin\omega)\end{matrix}}{\begin{matrix}(b_1^2\cos^2\omega + b_2^2\sin^2\omega + a_1^2 + 2b_1b_2\sin\omega\cos\omega + 2a_1b_2\sin\omega + 2a_1b_1\cos\omega \\ + b_1^2\sin^2\omega + b_2^2\cos^2\omega + a_2^2 - 2b_1b_2\sin\omega\cos\omega + 2a_2b_2\cos\omega - 2a_2b_1\sin\omega)\end{matrix}}$$

$$= \frac{(a_1^2+a_2^2+b_1^2+b_2^2) + 2\cos\omega(a_1b_1+a_2b_2) + 2\sin\omega(a_1b_2-a_2b_1)}{(a_1^2+a_2^2+b_1^2+b_2^2) + 2\cos\omega(a_1b_1+a_2b_2) + 2\sin\omega(a_1b_2-a_2b_1)} = 1$$

Thus,

for $F(z) = \dfrac{Az+B}{B^*z+A^*}$
where A and B are complex quantities
$\vert F(e^{j\omega})\vert = 1$
i.e. $F(z)$ is an all pass filter

...(9.107)

Important Result 2

To show that a filter characterized by

$$H(z) = \frac{Az^{-2}+Bz^{-1}+C}{C^*z^{-2}+B^*z^{-1}+A^*}$$

is an all pass filter for $z = e^{j\omega}$.

Proof:

$$H(z) = \frac{Az^{-2}+Bz^{-1}+C}{z^{-2}(C^*+B^*z+A^*z^2)}$$

$$\therefore \quad H(e^{j\omega}) = e^{j2\omega}\cdot\frac{Ae^{-j2\omega}+Be^{-j\omega}+C}{A^*.e^{j2\omega}+B^*e^{j\omega}+C^*}$$

$$= e^{j2\omega}.\ \frac{(Ae^{-j2\omega})+(Be^{-j\omega})+(C)}{(Ae^{-j2\omega})^*+(Be^{j\omega})^*+(C)^*} \triangleq e^{j2\omega}\frac{N(\omega)}{N^*(\omega)}$$

Since, numerator polynomial, $N(\omega)$ and denominator polynomial, is its complex conjugate *viz.* $N^*(\omega)$, therefore, $|N(\omega)| = |N^*(\omega)|$ obviously,

$$|H(e^{j\omega})| = |e^{j2\omega}|\left|\frac{N(\omega)}{N^*(\omega)}\right| = 1$$

Q.E.D.

Corollary:

Any rational function of the form:

$$H(z) = \frac{\sum_{k=0}^{N} A_k z^k}{\sum_{k=0}^{N} A_{N-k}^* z^k} \text{ is an all pass filter} \qquad \ldots(9.108)$$

Proof:

$$H(e^{j\omega}) = e^{-jN\omega} \left. \frac{\sum_{k=0}^{N} A_k z^k}{\sum_{k=0}^{N} A_{N-k}^* z^{-N+k}} \right|_{z=e^{j\omega}}$$

↖ (Put $N-k=l$ ∴ when $k=0, l=N$
when $k=N, l=0$)

$$= e^{-jN\omega} \left. \frac{\sum_{k=0}^{N} A_k z^k}{\sum_{l=0}^{N} A_l^* z^{-l}} \right|_{z=e^{j\omega}} \qquad \text{form } e^{-jN\omega}\frac{N(\omega)}{N^*(\omega)}$$

Clearly, $|H(e^{j\omega})| = 1$.

EXAMPLE 9.23: *Given the low-pass digital-filter function*

$$H(z) = \left(\frac{1}{2}\right)\frac{1+z^{-1}}{2-z^{-1}}$$

Show that the cut-off frequency, (at half power point) is $\theta_p = 0.6435$ rad/s. Use a low-pass transformation to obtain another LPF with $\omega_p = 1$ rad/sec.

SOLUTION: (*a*)

$$H(e^{j\theta}) = \frac{1}{2}\frac{1+e^{-j\theta}}{2-e^{-j\theta}} = \frac{1}{2}\frac{(1+\cos\theta) - j\sin\theta}{(2-\cos\theta)+j\sin\theta}$$

∴

$$H(e^0) = \frac{1}{2}\left(\frac{1+1}{2-1}\right) = 1$$

$$|H(e^{j\theta})|^2 = \frac{1}{4}\frac{(1+\cos\theta)^2+\sin^2\theta}{(2-\cos\theta)^2+\sin\theta} = \frac{2+2\cos\theta}{4(5-4\cos\theta)} = \frac{1+\cos\theta}{2(5-4\cos\theta)}$$

Let at $\theta = \theta_p$, LPF have $|H(e^{j\omega})| = \frac{1}{\sqrt{2}}$ (∵ half power point given)

∴

$$\frac{1}{2} = \frac{1+\cos\theta_p}{2(5-4\cos\theta_p)}$$

i.e. $5 - 4\cos\theta_p = 1 + \cos\theta_p$ ∴ $\cos\theta_p = \frac{4}{5}$ ∴ $\theta_p = 0.6435$ Q.E.D.

(*b*) $\omega_p = 1, \theta_p = 0.6435 \quad \therefore \quad \alpha = \frac{\sin[(\theta_p - \omega_p)/2]}{\sin[(\theta_p + \omega_p)/2]}$

$$\therefore \quad \alpha = \frac{\sin\frac{(0.6435-1)}{2}}{\sin\left(\frac{0.6435+1}{2}\right)} = -\frac{\sin 0.17825}{\sin 0.82175} = -0.2421$$

$\swarrow$ {given domain is $\tilde{z}$; Transformed domain is z}

$$\tilde{z}^{-1} = \frac{z^{-1}-\alpha}{1-\alpha z^{-1}} = \frac{z^{-1}+0.2421}{1+0.2421z^{-1}}$$

$$\therefore \quad H_{LP}(z) = H(\tilde{z})\Big|_{\tilde{z}^{-1}=\frac{z^{-1}+0.2421}{1+0.2421z^{-1}}} = \frac{1}{2}\,\frac{1+\frac{z^{-1}+0.2421}{1+0.2421z^{-1}}}{2-\frac{z^{-1}+0.2421}{1+0.2421z^{-1}}} = \frac{0.3533(1+z^{-1})}{1-0.2934z^{-1}} \qquad \textbf{Ans.}$$

EXAMPLE 9.24: *What will be the transformation required to transform a low pass FIR filter with cut-off at ω_c, to a high pass FIR filter having cut-off at $(\pi - \omega_c)$.*

SOLUTION: This is LPF to HPF transformation LPF has $\omega_c = \theta_p$

HPF has $\omega_p = (\pi - \omega_c)$ (given)

The transformation is

$$\tilde{z}^{-1} = -\frac{z^{-1}+\alpha}{1+\alpha z^{-1}} \qquad \text{(from (9.99))}$$

where

$$\alpha = -\frac{\cos(\omega_p - \theta_p)/2}{\cos(\omega_p + \theta_p)/2}$$

$$= -\frac{\cos[(\pi - \omega_c)]/2}{\cos[(\pi - \omega_c) + \omega_c]/2}$$

$$= -\frac{\cos(\pi/2 - \omega_c)}{\cos(\pi/2)}$$

$$= -\frac{\sin\omega_c}{\cos\pi/2} = -\frac{\sin\omega_c}{0} = \pm\infty$$

$$\therefore \quad \tilde{z}^{-1} = -\frac{\frac{z^{-1}}{\alpha}+1}{\frac{1}{\alpha}+z^{-1}}\Bigg|_{\alpha=\pm\infty} = -\frac{1}{z^{-1}}$$

i.e. $\tilde{z} = -\frac{1}{z}$ is the transformation.

This is also obvious from the frequency responses $(-\theta_p, \theta_p)$ and $(+\omega_p, -\omega_p)$ from the Fig. Ex. 9.24(*b*). **Ans.**

A given LPF filter with passband 0 to ω_c maps to a HPF of band width ω_c (*i.e.* $\pi - \omega_c$ to π) if we change z to $-z$ and vice versa

...(9.109)

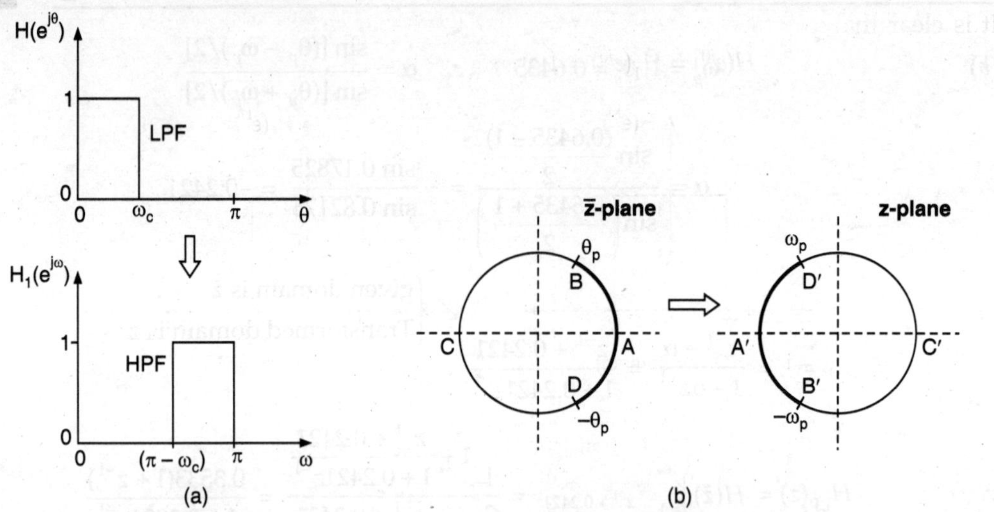

Fig. Ex. 9.24. (*a*) Frequency responses, (*b*) Responses on unit circles

EXAMPLE 9.25: *One method for transforming a low-pass FIR filter with cut-off at* ω_p *to another low-pass filter with cut-off* θ_p *is to use the substitution*

$$\cos\omega = A_0 + A_1 \cos\theta \text{ in } H(e^{j\omega}) = \sum_{k=0}^{M} a_k(\cos\omega)^k$$

thus resulting in the frequency response $H_1(e^{j\theta})$

(*i*) *Plot* $\cos\omega$ *versus* $\cos\theta$

(*ii*) *Show that* $A_0 + A_1 = 1$.

SOLUTION:

(*i*) Given $\cos\omega = A_0 + A_1\cos\theta$ put $\cos\theta = x$, $\cos\omega = y$, then $y = A_0 + A_1 x$. The plot is shown in Fig. 9.25 (*a*) Clearly, $\alpha = \tan^{-1} A_1$.

(*ii*) This is an LPF to LPF transformation as shown from $(-\omega_p, \omega_p)$ to $(-\theta_p, \theta_p)$. The response $H(e^{j\omega})$ is symmetrical about $\omega = 0$ and that $H_1(e^{j\theta})$ is symmetrical about $\theta = 0$.

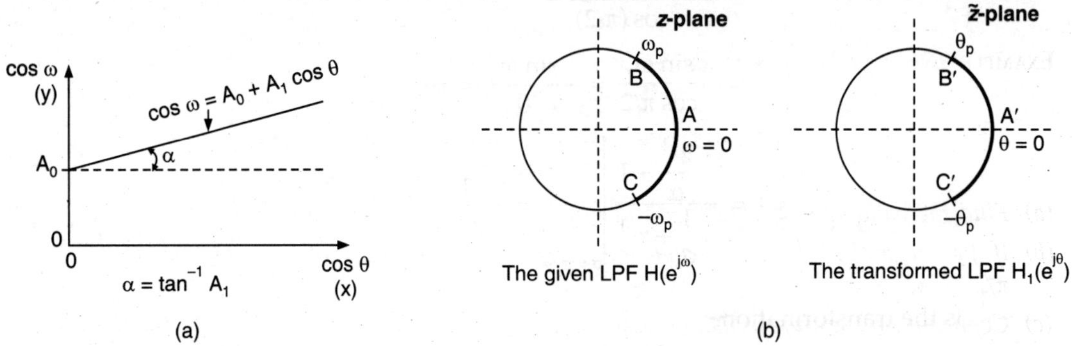

Fig. Ex. 9.25. (*a*) Cos ω versus cos θ curve, (*b*) Transformation from *z* domain to $\tilde{z}$ domain

It is clear that

$$H(e^{j0}) = H_1(e^{j0}) = 1 \qquad \ldots(1)$$

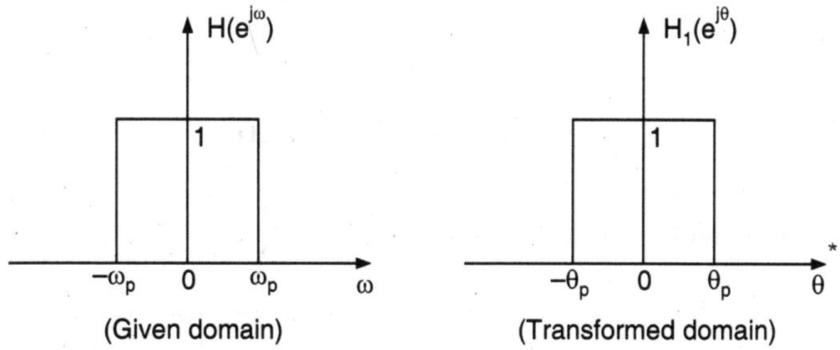

(c)

Fig. Ex. 9.25. (*c*) Transformation as on linear frequency domains

As
$$H(e^{j\omega}) = \sum_{k=0}^{M} a_k(\cos\omega)^k \qquad \ldots(2)$$

$\therefore$
$$H_1(e^{j\theta}) = \sum_{k=0}^{M} a_k(A_0 + A_1\cos\theta)^k \qquad \ldots(3)$$

putting $\cos\omega = A_0 + A_1\cos\theta$.

Putting $\omega = 0$ in (2) and $\theta = 0$ in (3) and equating $H(e^{j0})$ to $H_1(e^{j0})$, we have

$$\sum_{k=0}^{M} a_k(\cos 0)^k = \sum_{k=0}^{M} a_k(A_0 + A_1\cos 0)^k$$

$\therefore$
$$\sum_{k=0}^{M} a_k(1) = \sum_{k=0}^{M} a_k(A_0 + A_1)^k$$

This must hold for any value of A_0 and A_1.

Hence, $1 = (A_0 + A_1)\ \forall\ k$

i.e., $A_0 + A_1 = 1$ **Ans.**

EXAMPLE 9.26: *An IIR digital LPF is characterized by*

$$H_l(z) = \frac{A(1+z^{-1})^2}{(1-0.25z^{-1})(1-0.75z^{-1})}$$

(a) Find the value of A if $H_l(e^{j\omega}) = 1$ *at* $\omega = 0$

(b) If the given LPF has passband $-\pi/2 \le \theta \le \pi/2$, *deduce a high-pass filter with passband* $\pi/2 \le |\omega| \le \pi$

(c) Comment on the transformation results.

SOLUTION: (*a*) The given low-pass filter is defined by the system function

$$H_l(z) = \frac{A(z+1)^2}{(z-0.25)(z-0.75)}$$

$$H_l(e^{j\omega})\,|_{\omega=0} = H_l(z)\,|_{z=1} = \frac{A(1+1)^2}{(1-0.25)(1-0.75)}$$

$$= \left(\frac{4}{\left(\frac{3}{4}\times\frac{1}{4}\right)}\right)A = \frac{64}{3}A$$

To have $H_l(e^{j\omega})\,|_{\omega=0} = 1$, we must have, therefore, $A = \frac{3}{64}$ **Ans.**

(*b*) Here $\theta_p = \pi/2$, $\omega_p = \pi/2$. The LPF to HPF transformation is

$$z^{-1} = -\frac{(\tilde{z}^{-1}+\alpha)}{1+\alpha\tilde{z}^{-1}},$$ where given domain is z transformed domain is $\tilde{z}$

$$\alpha = -\frac{\cos[(\omega_p+\theta_p)/2]}{\cos[(\omega_p-\theta_p)/2]}$$ see (9.100)

Here $$\alpha = -\frac{\cos\left(\frac{\pi}{2}+\frac{\pi}{2}\right)/2}{\cos\left(\frac{\pi}{2}-\frac{\pi}{2}\right)} = -\frac{\cos\left(\frac{\pi}{2}\right)}{\cos 0} = 0$$

$\therefore$ $$z^{-1} = -\frac{\tilde{z}^{-1}+\alpha}{1+\alpha\tilde{z}^{-1}} = -\frac{\tilde{z}^{-1}+0}{1+0\tilde{z}^{-1}} = -\tilde{z}^{-1}$$

The transformed filter is $H_h(\tilde{z}) = H_l(z)|_{z^{-1}=-\tilde{z}^{-1}}$

$$= A\frac{(1+z^{-1})^2}{(1-0.25z^{-1})(1-0.75z^{-1})}\Bigg|_{z^{-1}=-\tilde{z}-1}$$

$$= A\frac{(1-\tilde{z}^{-1})^2}{(1+0.25\tilde{z}^{-1})(1+0.75\tilde{z}^{-1})}$$

$\therefore$ $$H_h(\tilde{z}) = \frac{A(1-\tilde{z}^{-1})^2}{(1+0.25\tilde{z}^{-1})(1+0.75\tilde{z}^{-1})},\ \text{where } A = \frac{3}{64}.$$

Check: $$H_h(e^{j\omega})\,|_{\omega=\pi} = H_h(\tilde{z})\,|_{\tilde{z}=-1} = \frac{\left(\frac{3}{64}\right)(1+1)^2}{\left(1-\frac{1}{4}\right)\left(1-\frac{3}{4}\right)}$$

$$= \frac{3}{64}\times 4\times\frac{4}{3}\times\frac{4}{1} = 1 \text{ as expected.}$$

(*c*) The zeros of $H_l(z)$ are at $(1 + z^{-1})^2 = 0$

i.e., for $z^{-1} = -1, -1$ or $z = -1, -1$, *i.e.,* at $\theta = \pi, \pi$

The zeros of $H_h(\tilde{z})$ are at $(1-\tilde{z}^{-1})^2 = 0$ *i.e.* at $\tilde{z} = 1, 1$, *i.e.,* at $\omega = 0, 0$

Thus, the zeros of a LPF at $z = -1$ get transformed to zeros of the new filter at $\tilde{z} = 1$. This is also expected, since, $z = -1$ means $\omega = \pi$ and a LPF must have a zero at $\omega = \pi$. Similarly, the HPF has zeros at $\omega = 0$.

EXAMPLE 9.27: *A causal linear shift-invariant system is described by the difference equation*

$$y(n) = ay(n-1) + x(n) - bx(n-1).$$

Determine the value of $b(b \neq a)$ such that this system is an all pass filter.

SOLUTION: We have

$$y(n) - ay(n-1) = x(n) - bx(n-1)$$

Taking *ZT* on both sides, we get

$$\frac{Y(z)}{X(z)} = \frac{1-bz^{-1}}{1-az^{-1}}$$

$$= (-b)\frac{\left(-\frac{1}{b}\right)+z^{-1}}{1-az^{-1}} \qquad \ldots(A)$$

For all pass behaviour, we must have $H(z)$ of the form

$$H(z) = \frac{\alpha+\beta z^{-1}}{\beta^* + \alpha^* z^{-1}} \qquad \ldots(B)$$

Here ignoring the scaling factor $(-b)$ in (A) and comparing it with (B)

'β' = 1 here

$$\alpha = -\frac{1}{b}$$

$$-a = \alpha^* = \left(-\frac{1}{b}\right)^*$$

Hence, $$-a = -\frac{1}{b^*} \quad \text{or} \quad b = \frac{1}{a^*}$$ **Ans.**

CHAPTER 10

Effects of Finite Register Length in Digital Signal Processing (Quantization Effect)

10.0 INTRODUCTION

A digital filter may be characterized by a difference equation

$$y(n) = \sum_{i=0}^{N} a_i x(n-i) - \underbrace{\sum_{j=1}^{M} b_j y(n-j)}_{\text{represents feedback}} \qquad \ldots(10.1)$$

Here, we get

$$H(z) = \frac{\sum_{i=0}^{N} a_i z^{-i}}{1+\sum_{j=1}^{M} b_j z^{-j}}, \; N \geq M \text{ for causality} \qquad \ldots(10.2)$$

where

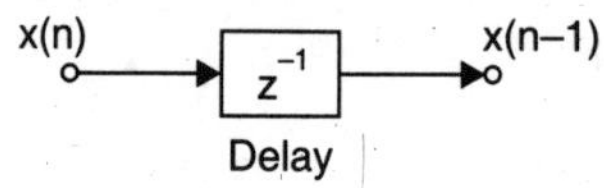

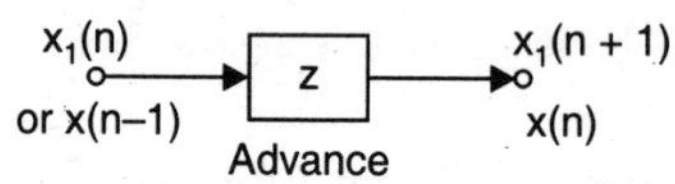

In general, a digital filter may be recursive or non-recursive. Both recursive as well as non-recursive filters can be FIR or IIR types.

A non-recursive filter is of the characteristic system response given by

$$H(z) = 1 + z^{-1} + z^{-2} + \ldots + z^{-(N-1)}$$

i.e.,

$$y(n) = \sum_{i=1}^{N-1} x(n-i), \text{ if } \{h(n)\} = \{1, 1, 1, \ldots, 1\}$$

In general, $\{h(n)\} = \{h(0), h(1), h(2), \ldots, h(N-1)\}$

This can be realized as per the following structure:

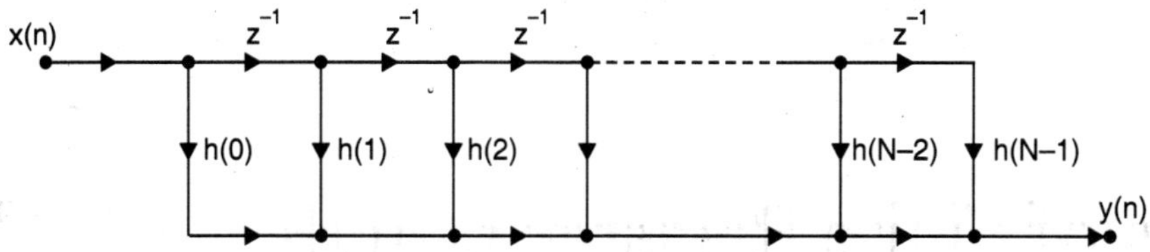

Fig. 10.1. (*a*) A non-recursive realization of $H(z) = \sum_{i=0}^{N-1} h(i)z^{-i}$

Above $H(z)$ may also be realized by, assuming $h(n) = 1 \ \forall \ n$,

$$H(z) = \sum_{i=1}^{N-1} z^{-i} = \frac{1-z^{-N}}{1-z^{-1}} \qquad \text{(using to geometric progression)}$$

$$\therefore \qquad \frac{Y(z)}{X(z)} = \frac{1-z^{-N}}{1-z^{-1}} \qquad ...(10.3)$$

i.e.,
$$Y(z)(1 - z^{-1}) = X(z)(1 - z^{-N})$$

$$\therefore \qquad y(n) - y(n-1) = x(n) - x(n-N)$$

i.e.,
$$y(n) = x(n) - x(n-N) + y(n-1) \qquad ...(10.4)$$

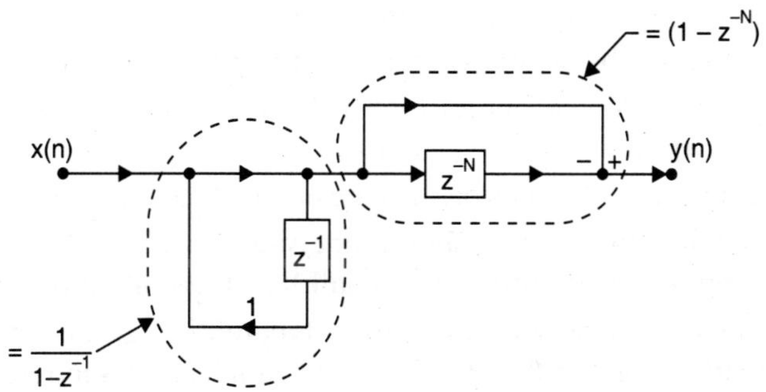

Fig. 10.1. (*b*) A recursive realization of $H(z) = \sum_{i=0}^{N-1} z^{-i} = \frac{1-z^{-N}}{1-z^{-1}}$

Some general points: In digital filter with system response given by

$$H(z) = \frac{\sum_{i=0}^{N} a_i z^{-i}}{1+\sum_{i=1}^{M} b_i z^{-i}}, \ N \geq M \text{ for causality} \qquad ...(10.5)$$

Note that:

(*i*) a_i and b_i have to be binary (0 to 1)

(*ii*) any software/hardware has limited bits and storage memory. This necessitates quantization.

(*iii*) As a result of quantization, the filter may appreciably differ from the original design. The 'quantized' filter may even fail to meet the specifications, or it may even oscillate whereas the 'unquantized' filter does meet the specifications. Thus, the problem of choice of a particular structure (FIR/IIR/cascaded etc.) and the direct design of the filters with quantized coefficients is an important research problem.

(*iv*) Multiplication of (b bits) with (b bits) gives $2b$ bits. In Fig. (10.2), let a_1, a_2 be b bits each. If $x(n)$ is also b bits then $y(n-1)$ is b bits, $a_1 y(n-1)$ is of $2b$ bits. Hence, we must quantize $a_1 y(n-1)$ to b bits. Thus, in multiplication the truncation/rounding off to b bits is a necessity, *i.e.* we must discard the last b bits from the $2b$ bits product, to accommodate it in b bit register.

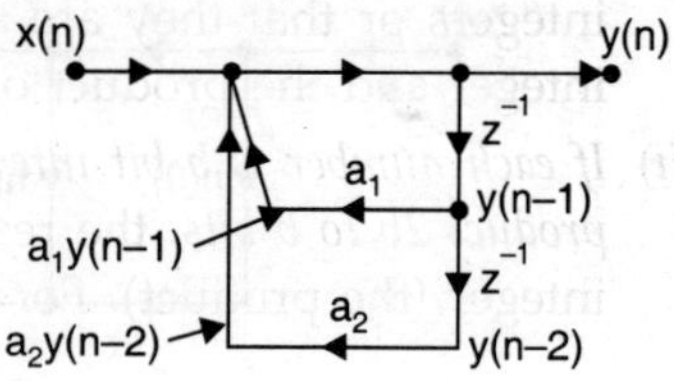

Fig. 10.2. Realization of a second order IIR filter

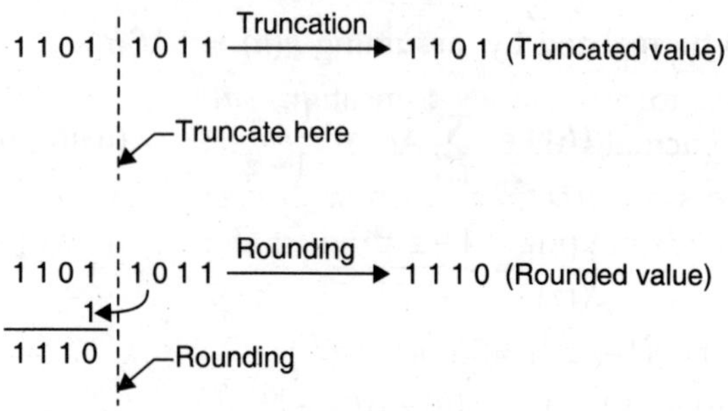

Fig. 10.3. Operations truncation and rounding

While in truncation we abruptly disregard the bits after the truncation point, in rounding off we add the next bit to the last bit where rounding off is performed (see Fig. 10.3).

(*v*) Effect of quantization depends on factors such as whether we use fixed-point arithmetic or floating-point arithmetic in calculations.

(*vi*) Effect of quantization also depends on the type of quantization *i.e.* truncation or rounding off.

(*vii*) In a fixed register length, addition should not cause overflow. This effect can be handled by scaling the inputs, to be sufficiently small that there is no possibility of overflow.

(*viii*) In floating-point arithmetic we have large dynamic range of representation possible. However, in floating-point arithmetic, the quantization error is introduced both in addition as well as in multiplication.

(*ix*) The effect of quantization depends upon the structure *viz.* parallel, cascade, mixed, canonical etc.

10.1 EFFECT OF NUMBER REPRESENTATION ON QUANTIZATION

We first give a brief about fixed-point and floating-point representation of numbers, and some of their salient features.

Fixed-point Representation of Binary Numbers: (Symbol Δ is the binary point)

Consider a binary number

$$1001\ \Delta\ 0110 = (1 \times 2^3 + 0 \times 2^2 + 0 \times 2^1 + 1 \times 2^0) \quad \text{integer part } (= 9 \text{ here})$$

$$\text{Weight: } 2^3 2^2 2^1 2^0 \quad 2^{-1} 2^{-2} 2^{-3} 2^{-4} \qquad + (0 \times 2^{-1} + 1 \times 2^{-2} + 1 \times 2^{-3} + 1 \times 2^{-4}) \quad \text{fraction part } (= 0.375)$$

$$= 9.375 \text{ total}$$

Note:

(*i*) For multiplication, it is generally most convenient to assume either all the numbers as integers or that they are all fractions, since by doing so, the product of integers is an integer and the product of fractions is a fraction.

(*ii*) *If each number is b bit integer,* their product is 2*b* bit integer. If we *truncate/round off the product 2b to b bits,* the resultant *number of b bits may be very different* than the actual 2*b* integer (the product). For example, if we multiply 702 by 301, we get

$$\underset{3\text{ bit}}{702} \times \underset{3\text{ bit}}{301} = \underbrace{211 \vdots 302}_{6\text{ bit}} \quad (\vdots = \text{truncation point})$$

If we scale 211302 to 3 bit (after truncation, say), we obtain 211 which is very very different from the actual value 211302.

(*iii*) If the two numbers are fractions, each with *b* bits, say, their product is generally 2*b* fraction. Truncation/rounding off the product 2*b* to *b* bits will not be so erratic, but will have small error.

For example

$$\underbrace{0.702}_{3\text{ bit}} \times \underbrace{0.301}_{3\text{ bit}} = \underbrace{0.211 \vdots 302}_{\substack{6\text{ bit}\\ \text{product}}} \quad (\vdots = \text{truncation point})$$

Truncation of 0.211302 to 3 bits means we get 0.211 note that 0.211 is very close to 0.211302.

(*iv*) Thus, to facilitate truncation/rounding, it is preferable to have all numbers in fractions, rather than in integers.

(*v*) If two fractions are added, overflow can occur, *i.e.* the sum may exceed unity. For example, $_\Delta 1001$ added to $_\Delta 1000$ yields $1_\Delta 0001$ which is 5 bits. To overcome this problem, we resort to Floating point arithmetic.

Floating-point Representation: We represent a number in floating-point by F given by

$$F = 2^C_\Delta M$$

where M is mantissa normalized such that

$$\frac{1}{2} \leq M < 1 \qquad \text{...(10.6)}$$

and C is called characteristic C may be +ve or –ve.

To multiply two numbers in Floating point

(*i*) Multiply their mantissas *i.e.* $M_1 \times M_2$

(*ii*) Add their characteristics *i.e.* $C_1 + C_2$

$$\therefore \quad (2^{C_1} \Delta M_1)(2^{C_2} \Delta M_2) = 2^{C_1+C_2} \Delta (M_1 \cdot M_2)$$

(*iii*) As M_1, M_2 lie between 1 and $\frac{1}{2}$, therefore

$$\frac{1}{4} \leq (M_1 M_2) < 1 \qquad \text{Call } M_1 M_2 = M$$

Hence, we shall have to normalize the product $(M_1 \cdot M_2)$ to ensure that $\frac{1}{2} \leq M < 1$. If (M_1M_2) is $< \frac{1}{2}$, M is shifted left by one bit and the characteristic decreased by 1 to balance the shift. Note that shifting a binary number to right by one place it makes its value half. Similarly, left shift makes it double.

To add two numbers in Floating-point

(*i*) Sum of two floating-point numbers is carried out by *shifting the bits of the mantissa of the smaller number* to right and increasing its characteristic by 1 for each right shift of the mantissa.

(*ii*) When the two numbers are represented by equal characteristics, add their latest mantissa. An example will make it clear, as follows.

EXAMPLE: *Add* $F_1 = 4$, $F_2 = \frac{5}{4}$ *in floating-point.*

SOLUTION:

$$F_1 = 4 = 2^3_{\Delta}1000 \equiv 2^{11}_{\Delta}\underbrace{1000}_{M_1} \quad (\because 11 \text{ in binary} = 3 \text{ in decimal})$$

$$(\therefore \quad M_1 = 1000, \text{ and } C_1 = 11)$$

$$F_2 = \frac{5}{4} = 2 \times \frac{5}{8} = 2^1_{\Delta}1010 \equiv 2^{01}{}_{\Delta}1010 \quad (\therefore \quad M_2 = 1010, \text{ and } C_2 = 01)$$

As F_2 is smaller with characteristic 01 (*i.e.* 1) to make it 11 and also we shift M_2 to right by two places, to make new M_2 as M_2' equalling ${}_{\Delta}0010100$. Thus

$$\therefore \qquad F_2 = 2^{11}_{\Delta}\underbrace{0010100}_{M_2'}$$

Now we add M_1 and M_2' to obtain ${}_{\Delta}10101$.

$$\begin{array}{ll} {}_{\Delta}10000 & (M_1) \\ {}_{\Delta}00101 & (M_2') \\ \hline {}_{\Delta}10101 & \end{array}$$

Now, we add M_1 and M_2' to obtain ${}_{\Delta}10101$

$$\therefore \qquad F_1 + F_2 = 2^{11}_{\Delta}(M_1 + M_2') = \underset{= 2^3 = 8}{2^{11}} \; \underbrace{{}_{\Delta}10101}_{= 21/32} \quad \textbf{Ans.}$$

$$\left(\text{Check} = 2^3\left(\frac{21}{32}\right) = \frac{21}{4} = 5\frac{1}{4}\right)$$

Thus, in *Floating-point representation, addition as well as multiplication of two numbers can result in mantissa exceeding the register length. Hence, quantization (i.e. truncation/rounding) is necessary* in floating-point representation *both for addition as well as for multiplication.* In case of fixed-point case, truncation/rounding was necessary only after multiplication (and not after addition).

Rule to Multiply two numbers in Floating-point Arithmetic

Let the numbers be $\qquad F_1 = 2^{C_1}_{\Delta}M_1, \; F_2 = 2^{C_2}_{\Delta}M_2$

(*i*) $F_1 \times F_2 = 2^{C_1+C_2} \cdot (M_1 \cdot M_2) \equiv 2^{C}_{\Delta}M$ *i.e.* add characteristic (C_1 and C_2), and multiply mantissas (M_1, M_2).

(*ii*) Normalize $|M_1 \cdot M_2|$ so that $\frac{1}{2} \leq M < 1$ is satisfied.

Rule to Add two numbers in Floating-point Arithmetic

Let the numbers be $F_1 = 2_{\Delta}^{C_1} M_1$, and $F_2 = 2_{\Delta}^{C_2} M_2$, let $F_1 < F_2$

(*i*) Shift the *mantissa of the smaller number* (*i.e.* M_1) to right and increase C_1 by 1 for each right shift of M_1, till the characteristic of F_1 also equals C_2 *i.e.* now $F_1 = 2_{\Delta}^{C_2} \tilde{M}_1 \cdot$ ($\tilde{M}_1$ being the right shifted M_1)

(*ii*) $F_1 + F_2 = 2^{C_2}(\tilde{M}_1 + M_2) \triangleq 2_{\Delta}^{C} M$, where $(\tilde{M}_1 + M_2)$ is normalized to $\frac{1}{2} \leq M < 1$ and C_2 corrected accordingly.

10.2 REPRESENTATION OF NEGATIVE NUMBERS

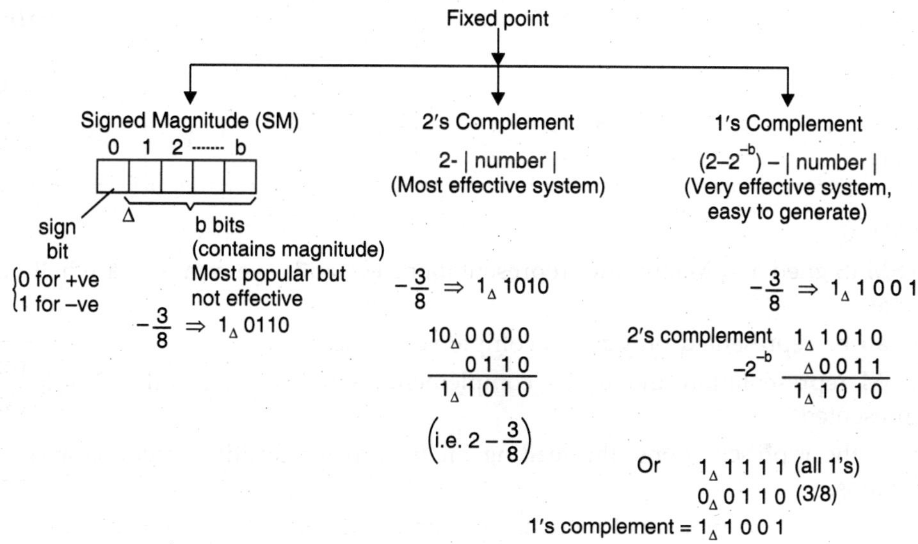

Thus, if we add 2^{-b} to 1's complement, we get 2's complement.
If we subtract 2^{-b} from 2's complement, we get 1's complement

+ve Numbers are the same in SM, 2's complement or 1's complement systems ...(10.7*a*)

–ve Numbers (to obtain the number *N*)

(*i*) In SM case, $N = -\left(\sum_{i=1}^{b} a_i 2^{-i}\right)$ ...(10.7*b*)

(*ii*) In 2's complement case, $N = -\left(2 - \sum_{i=0}^{b} a_i 2^{-i}\right) = -1 + \sum_{i=1}^{b} a_i 2^{-i}$ ...(10.7*c*)

(*iii*) In 1's complement case, $N = -\left(2 - 2^{-b} - \sum_{i=0}^{b} a_i 2^{-i}\right) = -(1-2^{-b}) + \sum_{i=1}^{b} a_i 2^{-i}$ ...(10.7*d*)

Table 10.1. Interpretation of Various Representations (with $b = 3$)

Binary Number (x)	*Value of x (signed magnitude)*	*Value of x (2's comp.)*	*Value of x (1's complement)*
$0_\Delta 111$	7/8	7/8	7/8
$0_\Delta 110$	6/8	6/8	6/8
$0_\Delta 101$	5/8	5/8	5/8
$0_\Delta 100$	4/8	4/8	4/8
$0_\Delta 011$	3/8	3/8	3/8
$0_\Delta 010$	2/8	2/8	2/8
$0_\Delta 001$	1/8	1/8	1/8
$0_\Delta 000$	+0	+0	+0
$1_\Delta 000$	–0	–1	–7/8
$1_\Delta 001$	–1/8	–7/8	–6/8
$1_\Delta 010$	–2/8	–6/8	–5/8
$1_\Delta 011$	–3/8	–5/8	–4/8
$1_\Delta 100$	–4/8	–4/8	–3/8
$1_\Delta 101$	–5/8	–3/8	–2/8
$1_\Delta 110$	–6/8	–2/8	–1/8
$1_\Delta 111$	–7/8	–1/8	–0

Observations

(*i*) In SM (Signed and Magnitude) representation, +ve and –ve numbers are half of its total range.

(*ii*) –1 can be represented only in 2's complement case.

(*iii*) In SM representation and in 1's complement representation, both +0 and –0 can be represented.

(*iv*) In all the representations, the leading bit is zero for positive fractions and 1 for –ve fractions.

(*v*) Negation of 1's complement number case can be accomplished by conjugating all the bits ($1 + b$ bits), *i.e.*, changing 0 to 1 and 1 to 0.

(*vi*) Negation** of 2's complement numbers is accomplished by changing 1 to 0 and 0 to 1 (*i.e.* conjugating) and adding 2^{-b}, and ignoring over flow from the addition.

(*vii*) Negative numbers in Floating point may be represented by giving sign (+ve or –ve) of the number to the associated mantissa, so the mantissa is a signed fraction. Of course one can represent mantissa in 1's complement or 2's complement representation of number also.

****For example:** In 2's complement $-\frac{6}{8} \equiv 1_\Delta 010$

To get $+\frac{6}{8}$, take 1's complement of above $\equiv 0_\Delta 101$

$$\text{add } 2^{-b} \ (i.e., {}_\Delta 001) = \frac{{}_\Delta 001}{{}_\Delta 110} \text{ add}$$

Clearly, ${}_\Delta 110 = \frac{6}{8}$, *i.e.*, negative of $-\frac{6}{8}$.

(*viii*) It can be shown that addition/subtraction in floating point can be accomplished by applying the rules of addition/subtraction used in fixed-point case, to the mantissa of the floating point number.

10.3 EFFECT OF TRUNCATION (IN FIXED POINT REPRESENTATION)

Let the number of bits = $1 + b$

(↗ Reserved as sign bit)

then we must truncate a number after b bits, if the given number exceeds b bits say, upto B bits. Note that the weightage of the bth bit is 2^{-b}, and that of B-th bit is 2^{-B}. If $B > b$ then $2^{-B} < 2^{-b}$.

(*A*) +ve numbers, all systems (SM, 1's complement and 2's complement):

Let the given number $x = a_{0\Delta}\, a_1\, a_2\, a_3 \ldots a_b \,\vdots \ldots a_{b+1}\, a_{b+2} \ldots a_B$

Truncate here

$\therefore$ Value of the given number: $x = \sum_{i=1}^{B} a_i 2^{-i}$, ($a_0$ is 0 for x +ve)

Value of truncated number $= Q[x] = \sum_{i=1}^{b} a_i 2^{-i}$ [Q means quantized value]

$$\text{Truncation error} = E_T \triangleq Q[x] - x \text{ and is always } -\text{ve}$$

$$= \sum_{i=1}^{b} a_i 2^{-i} - \sum_{i=1}^{B} a_i 2^{-i}$$

$$= -\sum_{i=b+1}^{B} a_i 2^{-i}$$

$$= \begin{cases} 0, & \text{if all } a_i = 0 \text{ for } b+1 \le i \le B \\ -(2^{-b} - 2^{-B}), & \text{if all } a_i = 1 \text{ for } b+1 \le i \le B \end{cases}$$

But $2^{-B} \ll 2^{-b}$

Hence,

$$-2^{-b} < E_T \le 0 \quad \text{Truncation error, } x \text{ +ve} \qquad \ldots(10.8)$$

(*B*) –ve numbers, Signed Magnitude Representation

Let $x = a_{0\Delta}\, a_1\, a_2\, a_3 \ldots a_b\, a_{b+1} \ldots a_B$

(↗ 1 here (x being – ve))

$$\text{Value of } x = -\sum_{i=1}^{B} a_i 2^{-i}$$

$$\text{Value of } Q[x] = -\sum_{i=1}^{b} a_i 2^{-i}$$

$$\therefore \qquad E_T = Q[x] - x = -\sum_{i=1}^{b} a_i 2^{-i} + \sum_{i=1}^{B} a_i 2^{-i}$$

$$= \sum_{i=1}^{B} a_i 2^{-i} - \sum_{i=1}^{b} a_i 2^{-i} = \sum_{i=b+1}^{B} a_i 2^{-i}$$

$$= \begin{cases} 0, & \text{for all } a_i = 0 \text{ for } i = b+1 \text{ to } B \\ 2^{-b} - 2^{-B}, & \text{for all } a_i = 1 \text{ for } i = b+1 \text{ to } B \end{cases}$$

Hence, $\quad 0 \le E_T \le 2^{-b} - 2^{-B}$

As $2^{-B} << 2^{-b}$, $\therefore \quad 0 \le E_T < 2^{-b}$ Truncation error, x –ve in SM ...(10.9)

(*C*) –ve numbers, in 2's Complement Representation

Let $\quad x = 1_\Delta a_1 a_2 \ldots a_b a_{b+1} \ldots a_B$

$$E_T = \text{Value of } Q[x] - \text{Value of } x$$

$$= -\left[\cancel{2} - \sum_{i=0}^{b} a_i 2^{-i}\right] - \left[-\left\{\cancel{2} - \sum_{i=0}^{B} a_i 2^{-i}\right\}\right] = -\sum_{i=0}^{B} a_i 2^{-i} + \sum_{i=0}^{b} a_i 2^{-i}$$

$$= -\left(\sum_{i=b+1}^{B} a_i 2^{-i}\right)$$

$$= \begin{cases} 0, & \text{all } a_i = 0 \text{ for } i = b+1 \text{ to } B \\ -(2^{-b} - 2^{-B}), & \text{all } a_i = 0 \text{ for } i = b+1 \text{ to } B \end{cases}$$

$-(2^{-b} - 2^{-B}) \le E_T \le 0$

As $2^{-B} << 2^{-b}$, $\therefore \quad -2^{-b} < E_T \le 0$ Truncation error, x –ve, in 2's complement ...(10.10)

(*D*) –ve numbers, in 1's Complement Representation:

Here $\quad x = 1_\Delta a_1 a_2 \ldots a_b a_{b+1} \ldots a_B$

$$E_T = \text{Value of } Q[x] - \text{Value of } x$$

$$= -\left[(\cancel{2} - 2^{-b}) - \sum_{i=0}^{b} a_i 2^{-i}\right] - \left\{-\left[(\cancel{2} - 2^{-B}) - \sum_{i=0}^{B} a_i 2^{-i}\right]\right\}$$

$$= (2^{-b} - 2^{-B}) - \left(\sum_{i=0}^{B} a_i 2^{-i} - \sum_{i=0}^{b} a_i 2^{-i}\right)$$

$$= (2^{-b} - 2^{-B}) - \sum_{i=b+1}^{B} a_i 2^{-i}$$

$$= (2^{-b} - 2^{-B}) - \begin{cases} 0, & \text{if all } a_i = 0 \text{ for } i = b+1 \text{ to } B \\ 2^{-b} - 2^{-B}, & \text{if all } a_i = 1 \text{ for } i = b+1 \text{ to } B \end{cases}$$

$$= 0 \text{ to } (2^{-b} - 2^{-B})$$

$$0 \le E_T \le 2^{-b} - 2^{-B}$$

As $2^{-B} << 2^{-b}$, $\therefore$ $\quad 0 \le E_T < 2^{-b}$ Truncation error, x –ve in 1's complement ...(10.11)

Summary of Truncation Quantization error in Fixed Point Arithmetic

x +ve $\quad -2^{-b} < Q[x] - x \le 0$, SM, 1's complement or 2's complement

x –ve $\quad -2^{-b} < Q[x] - x \le 0$, 2's complement

$\quad 0 \le Q[x] - x < 2^{-b}$, 1's complement, SM ...(10.12)

where $Q[x] - x = E_T$ the truncation error.

Thus, for 2's complement E_T is always –ve (for x +ve or x –ve), whereas for SM and 1's complement E_T is x –ve for x +ve and E_T is +ve for x –ve.

(E) Effect of Rounding (Fixed point Representation)

(A) +ve numbers
(B) –ve numbers } all systems (SM, 1's complement, 2's complement)

Let $\quad x = 0_\Delta\, a_1\, a_2 \ldots a_b\, a_{b+1} \ldots a_B$

when a_{b+1} is 0, ignore bits $a_{b+1}, a_{b+2}, \ldots, a_B$ (like in truncation)

when a_{b+1} is 1, add 1 to a_b

when a_{b+1} is 0 but $a_{b+2}, a_{b+3}, \ldots a_B$, we have ignored

then $\quad (2^{-(b+1)} - 2^{-B})\text{ max} \approx 2^{-(b+1)} = \frac{1}{2}2^{-b}$, *i.e.* the $Q[x]$ number is short of $\frac{1}{2}2^{-b}$.

Similarly, when $a_{b+1} = 1$, and $a_{b+2}, a_{b+3}, \ldots, a_B$ are all zero. We have added a_b (= 2^{-b}) instead of a_{b+1} (= $2^{-(b+1)}$). Thus, $Q[x]$ is excess by $2^{-b} - 2^{-(b+1)} \approx \frac{1}{2}2^{-b}$. We have the general result for rounding.

$$-\frac{1}{2}2^{-b} \le E_R \le \frac{1}{2}2^{-b} \quad \text{for } x \text{ +ve or } x \text{ –ve}$$

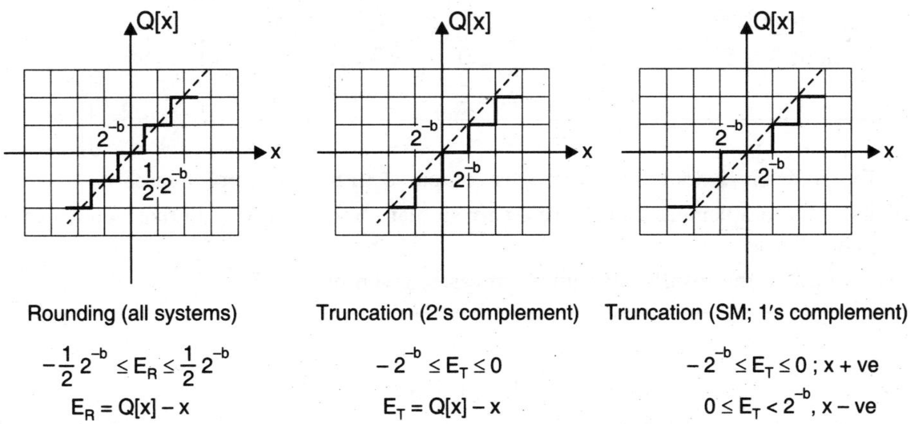

Fig. 10.3. Quantization errors for Rounding and Truncation cases

10.4 QUANTIZATION ERRORS IN FLOATING POINT REPRESENTATION

In floating point rounding/truncation affects only the mantissa. The error in mantissa is multiplied by 2^C since

$$F = 2^C \cdot M, \quad \frac{1}{2} \leq |M| < 1$$

The *error, therefore, is multiplicative rather than additive,* (as was in the case of "fixed point case"). Here, the relative error is important. In fixed point case we had $Q[x] - x = \varepsilon$. But in floating point

$$Q[x] = x(1 + \varepsilon)$$

i.e. $\boxed{Q[x] - x = \varepsilon x}$ (see **) ...(10.13)

so in rounding, we can write

$$\left(-\frac{1}{2}2^{-b}\right) \cdot 2^C \leq Q[x] - x \leq \left(\frac{1}{2}2^{-b}\right)2^C$$

i.e. $$\left(-\frac{1}{2}2^{-b}\right)2^C \leq \varepsilon_R \cdot x \leq \left(\frac{1}{2}2^{-b}\right)2^C \quad ...(A)$$

But $2^{C-1} \leq x < 2^C$ *i.e.* least value of $x = 2^{C-1}$, so we divide (*A*) by 2^{C-1}. This also ensures the maximum possible error.

$$\therefore \quad \left(-\frac{1}{2}2^{-b}\right) \cdot 2 \leq \varepsilon_R \leq \frac{1}{2}2^{-b} \cdot 2 \quad \text{(dividing } (A) \text{ by } 2^{C-1})$$

$\therefore$

$-2^{-b} \leq \varepsilon_R \leq 2^{-b}$ Rounding error in Floating point	...(10.14*a*)
Total (actual) Rounding Error = $x \cdot \varepsilon_R$ in Floating point case	...(10.14*b*)

We cannot divide (*A*) by 2^C since *F* never equals 2^C. But *F* does equal 2^{C-1} $\left(\text{when } M = \frac{1}{2}\right)$.

Moreover, to determine the maximum possible error limits we must divide (*A*) by the smallest value of x $(= 2^{C-1})$.

Summary of Errors in Floating point Quantization

(*i*) **Rounding**	$-2^{-b} < \varepsilon_R \leq 2^{-b}$, all representation	
(*ii*) **Truncation**		
1's complement and SM:	$-2.2^{-b} < \varepsilon_T \leq 0$ x +ve or x –ve	...(10.15)
2's complement:	$-2.2^{-b} < \varepsilon_T \leq 0$, x +ve; $0 \leq \varepsilon_T \leq 2.2^{-b}$, x –ve	

Note :

(*i*) Floating point gives double the errors as compared to the fixed point cases.

(*ii*) Results of 1's complement and SM cases are similar for x +ve, x –ve. In fixed-point case, it was 2's complement case.

Now, we prove the results for truncation cases, given by (10.15).

**As $$x = 2^C_\Delta M$$

$$Q[x] = 2^C_\Delta Q[M] \triangleq x(1 + \varepsilon)$$

$$\therefore \quad Q[x] - x = \varepsilon x.$$

Truncation in Floating Point Representation

(A) x **+ve** (SM, 1's complement or 2's complement for mantissa–all cases)

$$F = 2^C \cdot M = 2^C\,[0_\Delta a_1 a_2 \ldots a_b \cdot a_{b+1} \ldots a_B]$$

$$x = 2^C \cdot \left(\sum_{i=1}^{B} a_i 2^{-i}\right)$$

$$Q[x] = 2^C\left(\sum_{i=1}^{b} a_i 2^{-i}\right)$$

$$Q[x] - x = \varepsilon_T x = 2^C\left[\sum_{i=1}^{b} a_i 2^{-i} - \sum_{i=1}^{B} a_i 2^{-i}\right] = 2^C\left(-\sum_{i=b+1}^{B} a_i 2^{-i}\right)$$

$\therefore$ $\varepsilon_T x$ varies from $2^C[0, -(2^{-b} - 2^{-B})]$

$$\therefore \qquad -2^C(2^{-b} - 2^{-B}) \le \varepsilon_T x \le 0 \qquad \ldots(i)$$

Divide (*i*) by $x = 2^{C-1}$, neglect 2^{-B} w.r.t. 2^{-b}, and we obtain

$$\boxed{-2.2^{-b} < \varepsilon_T \le 0 \text{ Truncation, } x \text{ +ve, Floating point case}} \qquad \ldots(10.16)$$

(B) x **–ve (SM in Floating Point)** $(-2^C < M \le -2^{C-1})$

$$F = 2^C \cdot M = 2^C(1_\Delta a_1 a_2 \ldots a_b a_{b+1} \ldots a_B);$$

$$\text{Value of } M = -\sum_{i=1}^{B} a_i 2^{-i}$$

Minimum value of $x = -2^{C-1}$, maximum value of $x < (-2^C)$

$$\varepsilon_T x = Q[x] - x = \left[-2^C \cdot \sum_{i=1}^{b} a_i 2^{-i} - \left(-2^C \sum_{i=1}^{B} a_i 2^{-i}\right)\right]$$

$$= +2^C \sum_{i=b+1}^{B} a_i 2^{-i} = 2^C[0, (2^{-b} - 2^{-B})]$$

$$\therefore \qquad 0 \le \varepsilon_T x \le 2^C(2^{-b} - 2^{-B}) \qquad \ldots(i)$$

Dividing (*i*) by -2^{C-1}, neglecting 2^{-B} w.r.t. 2^{-b}, we obtain

$$\boxed{-2 \cdot 2^{-b} < \varepsilon_T \le 0\text{: Truncation, } x \text{ –ve, } M \text{ is SM for floating point}} \qquad \ldots(10.17)$$

(C) x **–ve, Floating Point and** M **in 2's Complement**

$$F = 2^C \cdot M = 2^C(1_\Delta a_1 a_2 \ldots a_b a_{b+1} \ldots a_B);$$

$$\text{Value of } M = -\left(2 - \sum_{i=0}^{B} a_i 2^{-i}\right)$$

x varies from -2^{C-1} and $< (-2^C)$ (*i.e.* $-2^C < M \le -2^{C-1}$)

$$\varepsilon_T x = Q[x] - x = \left[-2^C\left(\cancel{2} - \sum_{i=0}^{b} a_i 2^{-i}\right) - \left\{-2^C\left(\cancel{2} - \sum_{i=0}^{B} a_i 2^{-i}\right)\right\}\right]$$

$$= -2^C \sum_{i=b+1}^{B} a_i 2^{-i} = -2^C[0, (2^{-b} - 2^{-B})]$$

$$\therefore \quad -2^C(2^{-b} - 2^{-B}) \leq \varepsilon_T x \leq 0 \qquad \ldots(i)$$

Dividing (*i*) by -2^{C-1}, neglecting 2^{-B} w.r.t. 2^{-b}, we obtain

$$\boxed{0 \leq \varepsilon_T < 2.2^{-b}\text{: Truncation, } x \text{ –ve, } M \text{ in 2's complement-floating point}} \qquad \ldots(10.18)$$

(D) x –ve, Floating point, and M in 1's complement

$$F = 2^C \cdot M = 2^C(1_\Delta a_1 a_2 \ldots a_b a_{b+1} \ldots a_B),$$

$$\text{Value of } M = -\left((2 - 2^{-B}) - \sum_{i=0}^{B} a_i 2^{-i}\right)$$

$$\varepsilon_T x = Q[x] - x$$

$$= \left[-2^C\left\{(\not{2} - 2^{-b}) - \sum_{i=0}^{b} a_i 2^{-i}\right\} + 2^C\left\{(\not{2} - 2^{-B}) - \sum_{i=0}^{B} a_i 2^{-i}\right\}\right]$$

$$= -2^C\left[\sum_{i=b+1}^{B} a_i 2^{-i} - (2^{-b} - 2^{-B})\right] = -2^C[-(2^{-b} - 2^{-B}), 0]$$

$$= 2^C[0, (2^{-b} - 2^{-B})]$$

Dividing by -2^{C-1}, neglecting 2^{-B} w.r.t. 2^{-b}, we get

$$\boxed{-2.2^{-b} < \varepsilon_T \leq 0\text{: Truncation, } x \text{ –ve } M \text{ in 1's complement, Floating point}} \qquad \ldots(10.19)$$

10.5 QUANTIZATION IN SAMPLING ANALOG SIGNALS

As $x(n) = x_a(nT)$, $-\infty < n < \infty$, implies sampling the analog signal $x_a(t)$. The realization in Fig. 10.4 gives the samples. Let $x_a(t)$ be a band limited analog signal, $x_a(nT)$ are the samples with infinite precision, and $\hat{x}(n)$ are the quantized samples (*i.e.* with step-level precision). We may write

$$\hat{x}(n) = x(n) + e(n) \qquad \ldots(10.20)$$

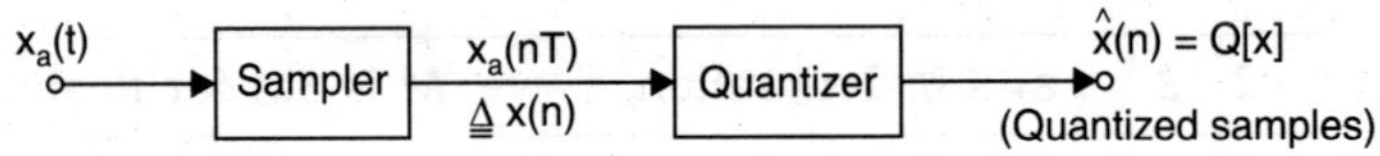

Fig. 10.4. (*a*) A non-linear model of sampling of an analog signal

where $e(n)$ is the quantization error. We can simulate (10.20) by realization given in Fig. 10.4(*b*)

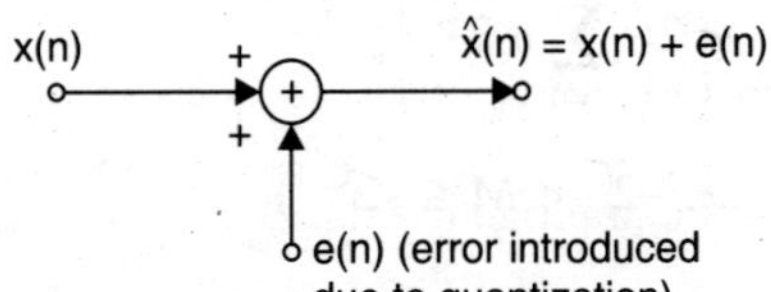

Fig. 10.4. (*b*) Statistical model of Quantization (linear model)

We assume the error $e(n)$ to be additive. Hence, the output noise is a function of

(*i*) Representation: SM/1's complement/2's complement form of the signal

(*ii*) Arithmetic used: Fixed point/Floating point arithmetic

(*iii*) Type of Quantization: Rounding/Truncation method.

If we assume that the unquantized samples are within (1 + b) bits (1 is sign bit; b are useful bits), then the analog waveform is normalized so that

$$-\left(1-\frac{1}{2}2^{-b}\right) < x_a(nT) < \left(1-\frac{1}{2}2^{-b}\right)$$

$$\text{i.e.} \quad |x_a(nT)| < \left(1-\frac{1}{2}2^{-b}\right) \qquad \ldots(10.21)$$

If the exact value of an input sample falls outside this range, an additional distortion will result.

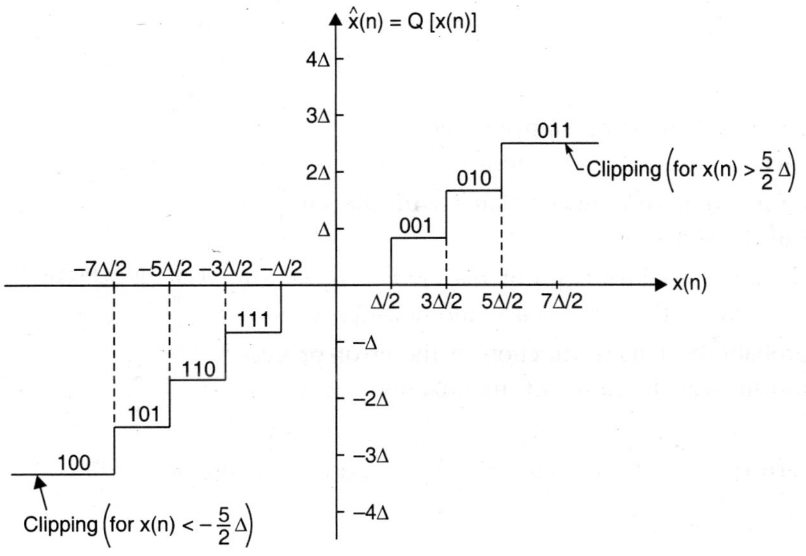

Fig. 10.5. Two's complement rounding of samples for b = 2. Here $x(n)$ is the sampled signal and $\hat{x}(n)$ is the quantized signal after rounding

Note that if the signal exceeds $+\frac{5\Delta}{2}$ or is less than $-\frac{5\Delta}{2}$, then clipping occurs *i.e.* $\hat{x}(n)$ assumes constant (clipped) value when $|x(n)|$ exceeds $\frac{5\Delta}{2}$. In digital signals, clipping is more severe than in analog signals. Hence, we should never allow the signals to exceed these level (where from clipping commences). In general, the analog signals $x_a(t)$ should be in the safe range: $-\left(1-\frac{3}{2}.2^{-b}\right)$ to $\left(1-\frac{3}{2}2^{-b}\right)$ to avoid clipping.

$$x_a(t) \text{ not to exceed } \pm \left(2^b - \frac{3}{2}\right) \cdot \Delta,\ \Delta = 2^{-b} \text{ to avoid clipping}$$

i.e.,
$$|x_a(nT)| \le \left(1 - \frac{3}{2}2^{-b}\right) \text{ for no clipping} \quad \ldots(10.22)$$

Statistical Model of Quantization Effect

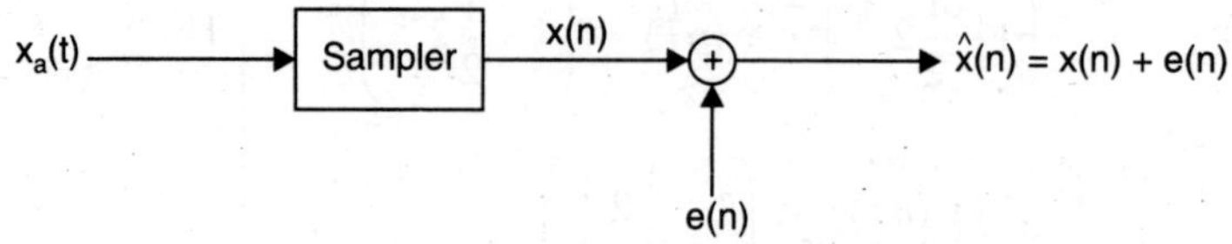

Fig. 10.6. Model of quantization assuming additive error $e(n)$

In rounding, $-\frac{1}{2}2^{-b} \le e(n) \le \frac{1}{2}2^{-b}$, where $e(n)$ is rounding error.

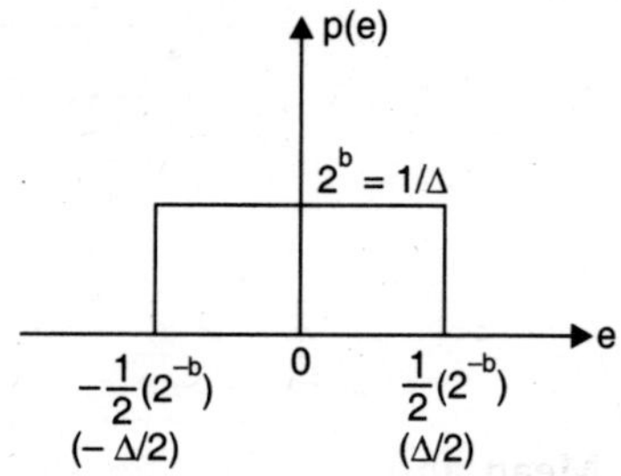

Fig. 10.7. Probability density function (pdf) in rounding, $\Delta = 2^{-b}$, e is error and $p(e)$ is pdf of error

Assume:

1. The sequence of error samples $\{e(n)\}$ is a sample sequence of a stationary random process.
2. The error sequence is uncorrelated with the samples $\{x(n)\}$ of the signal.
3. The random variables (r.v.) of the error process are uncorrelated *i.e.* the error is a white noise process.
4. The probability density function of the error process in uniform over the range of quantization.

Mean of error:
$$m_e = E\{e(n)\} = \int_{-\frac{1}{2}2^{-b}}^{\frac{1}{2}2^{-b}} e \cdot p(e)\, de, \text{ where } p(e) = 2^b$$

$$= 2^b \int_{-\frac{1}{2}2^{-b}}^{\frac{1}{2}2^{-b}} e\, de = 2^b \cdot \frac{1}{2}\left[e^2\right]_{-\frac{1}{2}2^{-b}}^{\frac{1}{2}2^{-b}} = 0 \quad \boxed{m_e = 0} \quad \ldots(10.23a)$$

Variance:
$$\sigma_e^2 = E\{(e(n) - m_e)^2\} = E\{e^2(n)\} - m_e^2, \text{ with } m_e = 0 \text{ here}$$

$$= \int_{-\Delta/2}^{\Delta/2} e^2 p(e)\, de = \frac{1}{\Delta}\int_{-\Delta/2}^{\Delta/2} e^2\, de = \frac{1}{3\Delta}[e^3]_{-\Delta/2}^{\Delta/2}$$

$$= \frac{1}{3\Delta} \cdot \frac{\Delta^3}{4} = \frac{1}{12}\Delta^2 = \frac{1}{12}2^{-2b}$$

$$\boxed{\sigma_e^2 = \frac{1}{12}2^{-2b}} \quad \ldots(10.23b)$$

An Important Result: If x is a uniformly distributed r.v. in the range from $x = a_1$ to $x = a_2$, then

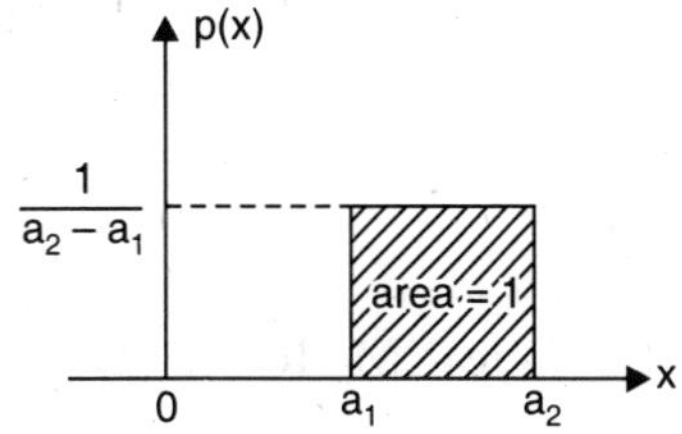

Fig. 10.8. Showing uniform distribution of random variable x

$$p(x) = \frac{1}{a_2 - a_1}$$

$$m_x = \int_{a_1}^{a_2} x\,p(x)\,dx = \frac{1}{a_2 - a_1}\int_{a_1}^{a_2} x\,dx$$

$$= \frac{1}{a_2 - a_1}\left[\frac{x^2}{2}\right]_{a_1}^{a_2} = \frac{a_1 + a_2}{2}$$

$$\sigma_x^2 = E\{x^2\} - (m_x)^2$$

$$= \frac{1}{a_2 - a_1}\int_{a_1}^{a_2} x^2\,dx - \left(\frac{a_1 + a_2}{2}\right)^2$$

$$= \frac{1}{a_2 - a_1}\cdot\frac{1}{3}(a_2^3 - a_1^3) - \left(\frac{a_1 + a_2}{2}\right)^2$$

$$\boxed{m_x = \frac{a_1 + a_2}{2} \qquad \sigma_x^2 = \frac{(a_2 - a_1)^2}{12}} \qquad \text{...(10.24)}$$

$$= \frac{1}{3}(a_2^2 - a_1a_2 + a_1^2) - \frac{a_1^2 + 2a_1a_2 + a_2^2}{4} = \frac{1}{12}(a_2^2 - 2a_1a_2 + a_1^2) = \frac{(a_2 - a_1)^2}{12}$$

$$\boxed{\text{If } a_1 = -2^{-b} \text{ and } a_2 = 2^{-b}, \text{ then } \sigma^2 = \frac{1}{3}2^{-2b}} \qquad \text{...(10.24a)}$$

Mean and Variance for the two cases of Truncation Error ε_T

(*A*) $-2^{-b} \le \varepsilon_T < 0$, here $a_1 = -2^{-b}$, $a_2 = 0$

$$\therefore \quad m_{\varepsilon_T} = \frac{a_1 + a_2}{2} = -\frac{1}{2}2^{-b}$$

$$\sigma_{\varepsilon_T}^2 = \frac{1}{12}(a_2 - a_1)^2 = \frac{1}{12}(0 - 2^{-b})^2 = \frac{1}{12}2^{-2b}$$

(*B*) $0 \le \varepsilon_T < 2^{-b}$, here $a_1 = 0$, $a_2 = 2^{-b}$

$$\therefore \quad m_{\varepsilon_T} = \frac{a_1 + a_2}{2} = \frac{0 + 2^{-b}}{2} = \frac{1}{2}2^{-b}$$

$$\sigma_{\varepsilon_T}^2 = \frac{1}{12}(a_2 - a_1)^2 = \frac{1}{12}(2^{-b} - 0)^2 = \frac{1}{12}2^{-2b}$$

Note that the variance σ^2 for cases (*A*) and (*B*) discussed above is the same equalling $\frac{1}{12}2^{-2b}$ since the range of uniform non-zero error ε_T is the same (equal to 2^{-b}).

10.6 INPUT SIGNAL TO NOISE RATIO (SNR)

(*A*) Without scaling

Let the signal power $= \sigma_x^2$

input noise power $= \sigma_e^2 = \frac{1}{12}2^{-2b}$ in quantization fixed point arithmetic cases

$$\text{Input SNR} = \frac{\sigma_x^2}{\sigma_e^2} = (12.2^{2b})\sigma_x^2$$

$$\begin{aligned}\text{SNR}|_{\text{dB}} &= 10 \log (12.2^{2b} \cdot \sigma_x^2) \\ &= 10 \log_{10} 12 + (20)b \log_{10} 2 + 20 \log \sigma_x\end{aligned}$$

$$\text{Input SNR} = 10.8 + 6b + 20 \log \sigma_x \text{ dB} \qquad \text{...(10.25)}$$

$$\text{If } \sigma_e^2 = \frac{1}{3} 2^{-2b}, \text{ then Input SNR} = 4.8 + 6b + 20 \log \sigma_x \text{ dB}$$

Thus, for every one bit increase in b, the input SNR goes up by 6 dB.

(B) With scaling (factor A): If x is scaled to Ax (say to avoid overflow at the output), then

$$\sigma_{Ax}^2 = A^2\sigma_x^2$$

Replace $20 \log \sigma_x$ above by $20 \log (A\sigma_x) = 20 \log \sigma_x + 20 \log A$

$$\text{SNR (with scaling)} = 10.8 + 6b + 20 \log \sigma_x + 20 \log A \text{ dB} \qquad \text{...(10.26)}$$

$$\text{If } \sigma_e^2 = \frac{1}{3}2^{-2b}, \text{ then SNR} = 4.8 + 6b + 20 \log \sigma_x + 20 \log A \text{ dB}$$

In general, A is less than unity, *i.e.* $20 \log A$ is a –ve quantity. Hence, scaling (by A) (which weakens the signal $x(n)$ to $Ax(n)$), the input SNR is reduced. Hence, an effort to avoid/reduce clipping causes decrease in the input SNR.

In many analog signals, such as speech, music, which may be viewed as random processes, the signals characterized by probability distribution with mean nearly zero. With increasing amplitude, pdf falls rapidly. In such cases, therefore, the probability of the magnitude of a given sample to exceed 3 or 4 times the root mean square value (*i.e.* σ_x) is very low. *We can set* $A = \frac{1}{4\sigma_x}$ *and the probability of clipping will be very-very small.*

Putting
$$A = \frac{1}{4\sigma_x}$$

$$\begin{aligned}20 \log A &= 20 \log \frac{1}{4\sigma_x} \\ &= -20 \log 4 - 20 \log \sigma_x \\ &= -12 - 20 \log \sigma_x\end{aligned}$$

the previous 'scaling' result obtained in (10.26) reduces to

$$\text{Input SNR (with scaling)} = 10.8 + 6b + \cancel{20 \log \sigma_x} + (-12 - \cancel{20 \log \sigma_x})$$

$$\text{Input SNR}\left(\text{with } A = \frac{1}{4\sigma_x}\right) = 6b - 1.24 \text{ dB}$$

$$\text{Input SNR with } A = \frac{1}{4\sigma_x} \text{ and } \sigma_e^2 = \frac{1}{3}2^{-2b} = 6b - 7.24 \text{ dB} \qquad \text{...(10.27)}$$

For a specific value of required SNR, we can choose the appropriate value of bits b. For example, for prescribed SNR $\geq$ 80 dB.

$$b = \frac{(80 + 1.24)}{6} = 13.54, \text{ say } b = 14 \text{ (an integer) would suffice.}$$

In the computers with $1 + b = 16$ *bits,* $b = 15$, giving $6 \times 15 - 1.24 = 88.76$ *i.e. SNR* $\geq$ *88 dB.*

10.7 RELATION BETWEEN INPUT m_e, σ_e^2 AND OUTPUT m_f AND σ_f^2

Calculation of mean of $f(n)$, *i.e.*, m_f: Assume $h(n)$ to be impulse response of an LTI (linear-time-invariant) system. Let the inputs $x(n)$ and $e(n)$ yield outputs $y(n)$ and $f(n)$, respectively. Then the following relations hold

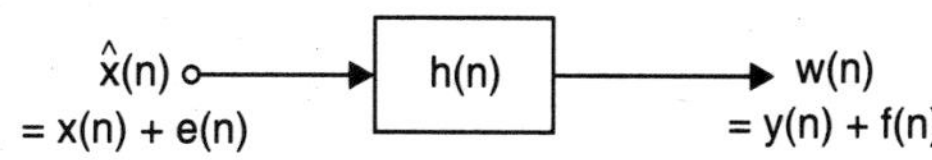

Fig. 10.9. A linear, LTI system

$$y(n) = \sum_{k=-\infty}^{\infty} h(k) \cdot x(n-k) \quad \text{(convolution of } x(n) \text{ and } h(n)) \qquad \text{...(10.28)}$$

and

$$f(n) = \sum_{k=-\infty}^{\infty} h(k) \cdot e(n-k) \quad \text{(convolution of } e(n) \text{ and } h(n)) \qquad \text{...(10.29)}$$

Mean of $f(n) \triangleq m_f = E\{f(n)\}$, *i.e.*, expectation of $f(n)$

$$= E\left\{\sum_{k=-\infty}^{\infty} h(k) e(n-k)\right\} \text{ replacing } f(n) \text{ from (10.29)}$$

$$= \sum_{k=-\infty}^{\infty} h(k) \cdot \underbrace{E\{e(n-k)\}}_{= m_e} \quad (\because e(n) \text{ is random variable } h(k) \text{ is known to us and } \therefore h(k) \text{ is not r.v.})$$

$$= m_e \sum_{k=-\infty}^{\infty} h(k) \quad \text{(Assume } e(n) \text{ stationary} \quad \therefore E\{e(n-k)\} = E\{e(n)\} = m_e)$$

Hence, mean of $f(n) = m_f = m_e \sum_{k=-\infty}^{\infty} h(k)$

As
$$H(z) = \sum_{n=-\infty}^{\infty} h(k) z^{-n}, \text{ i.e., z-transform of } h(n)$$

$\therefore$
$$H(e^{j\omega}) = \sum_{n=-\infty}^{\infty} h(n) e^{-j\omega n}, \text{ i.e., DTFT of } x(n)$$

$$H(e^{j0}) = \sum_{n=-\infty}^{\infty} h(n) e^{-j0 \cdot n} = \sum_{n=-\infty}^{\infty} h(n)$$

Hence,

$$\boxed{m_f = m_e \sum_{k=-\infty}^{\infty} h(k) = m_e \cdot \underbrace{H(e^{j0})}_{\substack{\text{dc} \\ \text{response}}}} \qquad \text{...(10.30)}$$

Note that $H(e^{j0})$ is the dc response of the system $h(n)$. It is zero for band pass/high pass filters but non-zero for low pass filters. Hence, the mean of the output noise (*i.e* m_f) can be zero if mean of the input noise (*i.e* m_e) is zero (as in rounding) or if dc response, $H(e^{j0})$, of the system is zero (as in BPF and HPF's).

Calculation of variance of $f(n)$, i.e., σ_f^2

$$\sigma_f^2 = E[f^2(n)], \text{ assuming } m_f = 0$$

$$= E\left[\left(\sum_{k=-\infty}^{\infty} h(k)\cdot e(n-k)\right)^2\right]$$

$$= E\left[\sum_{k=-\infty}^{\infty}\sum_{l=-\infty}^{\infty} h(k)\cdot h(l)\cdot e(n-k)\cdot e(n-l)\right]$$

$$= \sum_k\sum_l h(k).h(l)\ \underbrace{E[e(n-k)\cdot e(n-l)]}_{=\sigma_e^2\delta(k-l)}$$

for stationary noise

$$\therefore \quad \sigma_f^2 = \sum_k\sum_l h(k).h(l)\cdot\sigma_e^2\delta(k-l)$$

$$= \sigma_e^2\sum_{k=-\infty}^{\infty}|h(k)|^2$$

$$= \frac{1}{2\pi}\sigma_e^2\int_{-\pi}^{\pi}|H(e^{j\omega})|^2\,d\omega \quad \text{(by Parseval's theorem)}$$

If $m_f \neq 0$, then $\sigma_f^2 = E\{[f(n)-m_f]^2\} = E\{f^2(n)\} - m_f^2$

Hence,

$$m_f = m_e\sum_k h(k) \qquad \ldots(10.31a)$$

$$\sigma_f^2 = \sigma_e^2\sum_k|h(k)|^2 - m_f^2 = \frac{\sigma_e^2}{2\pi}\int_{-\pi}^{\pi}|H(e^{j\omega})|^2\,d\omega - m_f^2 \qquad \ldots(10.31b)$$

10.8 FINITE REGISTER LENGTH EFFECT IN REALIZATION OF IIR DIGITAL FILTERS

Due to multiplication and consequent rounding/truncation (*i.e.* quantization), non-linear errors are introduced. If we need $\alpha \cdot x(n)$, each α and $x(n)$ must be appropriately quantized to fit in the given $1 + b$ bits register of the hardware.

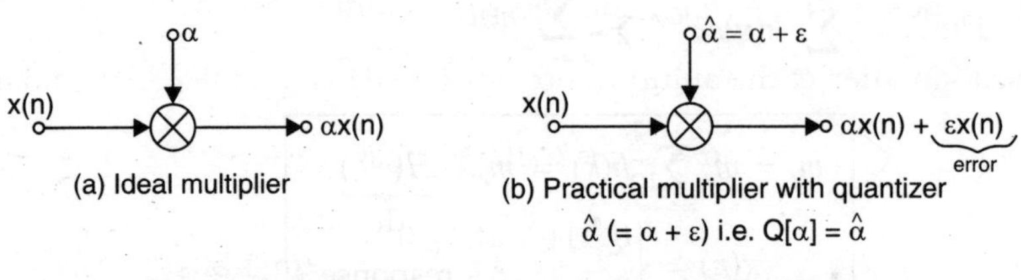

Fig. 10.10. Models of (*a*) ideal and (*b*) practical multipliers

After one multiplication, we get $\hat{\alpha}x(n)$. This quantity is again to be quantized to enable $Q[\hat{\alpha}x(n)]$ fit in the $1 + b$ bit register.

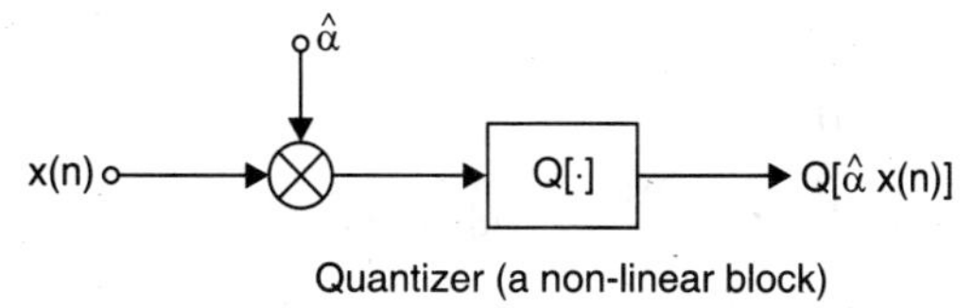

Fig. 10.11. Effect of quantizer

Thus, due to quantization after each multiplication, *non-linearity is inherent at each stage.* In the fixed point there may not be need to round off after the additions. In floating-point case, however, we round off after any addition and after any multiplication, *i.e.* quantization follows after addition as well as after multiplication in the floating point representation.

Truncation and rounding (i.e. quantization) is a non-linear process. Hence, the effect of quantization in the realization of a shift-invariant digital filters is to introduce non-linear elements into certain branches of the filter.

Non-linearity causes a periodic error at the output when the input is set to zero or when the input is constant or when the input is sinusoidal.

Strictly speaking, realization of linear shift-invariant systems are generally non-linear. Non-linearity arises due to quantization. However, we aim at realization of a digital filter that is sufficiently accurate and at the same time requires a minimum of hardware complexity. The analysis of non-linear effects in digital filters is often complex and in many cases is not fully understood, and moreover much of the analysis is very detailed. However, the analysis covered in this chapter gives good insight of the effect of quantization.

10.8.1 Zero-input Limit Cycles in Fixed-point Realization of IIR Digital Filters

One of the effects of quantization is to produce constant or oscillatory output insipite of input having ceased. This is called zero-input limit cycle. It is consequent to non-linear quantization in the feedback loop of the filters.

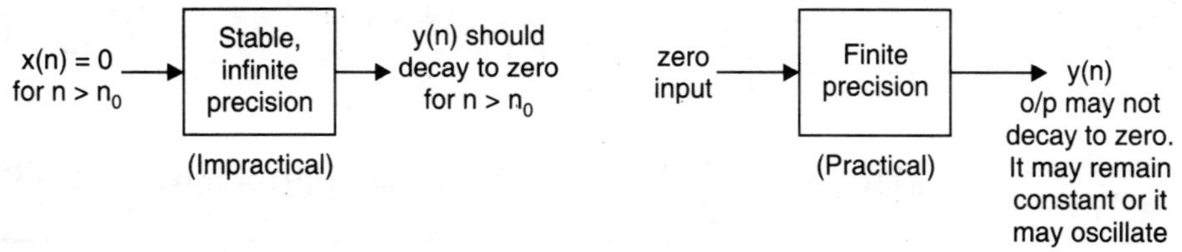

Fig. 10.12. Effect of ideal and practical systems for zero input

Consider a first order IIR system of Fig. 10.13(*a*).

Let $\alpha = \frac{1}{2}$, $b = 3$ bits, $x(n) = \frac{7}{8}\delta(n)$, and signed magnitude is used.

Due to quantization after each multiplication, $\alpha\omega(n-1)$ is quantized. We note that

$$\alpha = \frac{1}{2}, \equiv 0_\Delta 100 \text{ (3 bits)}$$

$$x(n) = \begin{cases} 0_\Delta 111, & \text{at } n = 0 \\ 0, & \text{otherwise} \end{cases} \quad \text{(in 3 bits)}$$

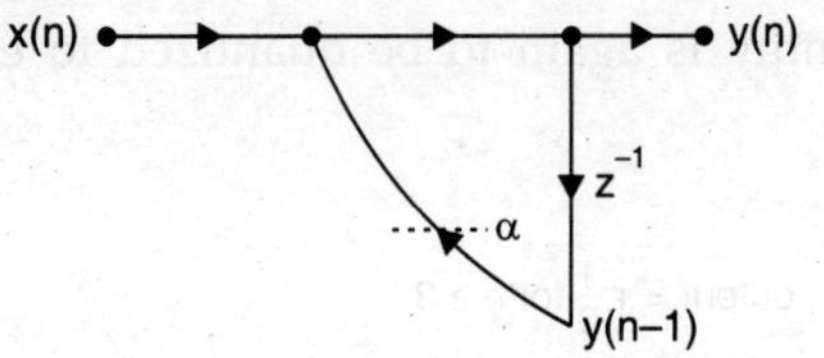

Fig. 10.13. (*a*) Ideal linear filter

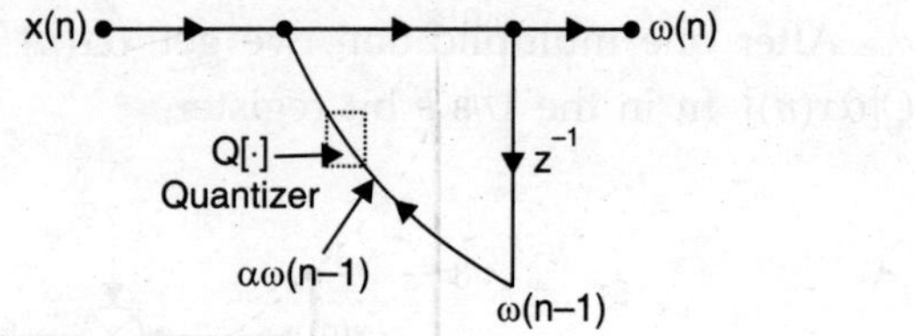

Fig. 10.13. (*b*) Non-linear system due to product quantization

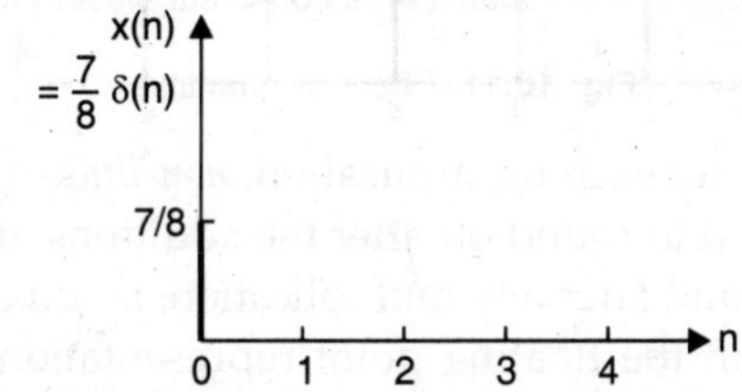

Fig. 10.13. (*c*) Input $x(n) = \frac{7}{8}\delta(n)$

As $x(n)$ and α can be exactly represented in 3 bits, hence these require no quantization for $x(0)$ and α. Assuming rounding

as
$$\omega(n) = x(n) + Q[\alpha\omega(n-1)]$$

$$\omega(0) = x(0) + Q[\alpha \cdot \omega(-1)] = \frac{7}{8} + 0, \text{ assuming } \omega(n) = 0 \text{ for } n < 0$$

$$= 0_\Delta 111$$

$$\omega(1) = 0 + Q\left[\frac{1}{2}\cdot\frac{7}{8}\right] = Q\left[\frac{7}{16}\right]$$

$$= Q[0_\Delta 0111] = 0_D 100 = \frac{1}{2} \qquad (\because \text{ rounding } {}_\Delta 0111 \text{ gives } {}_\Delta 100)$$

$$\omega(2) = 0 + Q\left[\frac{1}{2}\left(\frac{1}{2}\right)\right] = Q\left[\frac{1}{4}\right] = Q[0_\Delta 010] = 0_\Delta 010 = \frac{1}{4}$$

$$\omega(3) = 0 + Q\left[\frac{1}{2}\left(\frac{1}{4}\right)\right] = Q\left[\frac{1}{8}\right] = Q[0_\Delta 001] = 0_\Delta 001 \text{ i.e., } \frac{1}{8}$$

$$\omega(4) = 0 + Q\left[\frac{1}{2}\left(\frac{1}{8}\right)\right] = Q\left[\frac{1}{16}\right] = Q[0_\Delta 0001] = 0_\Delta 001 = \frac{1}{8}$$

$$(\because \text{ rounding } 0_\Delta 0001 \text{ gives } 0_\Delta 001)$$

$$\omega(5) = 0 + Q\left[\frac{1}{2}\left(\frac{1}{8}\right)\right] = Q\left[\frac{1}{16}\right] = Q[0_\Delta 0001] = 0_\Delta 001 = \frac{1}{8}$$

$$\omega(6) = 0 + Q\left[\frac{1}{2}\left(\frac{1}{8}\right)\right] = Q\left[\frac{1}{16}\right] = Q[0_\Delta 0001] = 0_\Delta 001 = \frac{1}{8} \text{ and so on.}$$

The output $\omega(n)$ is shown in Fig. 10.14(*a*). Note that for $n \geq 3$, the output is constant at $\frac{1}{8}$, though the input has ceased. For $\alpha = -\frac{1}{2}$ the output oscillates for $n \geq 3$, as shown in Fig. 10.14(*b*).

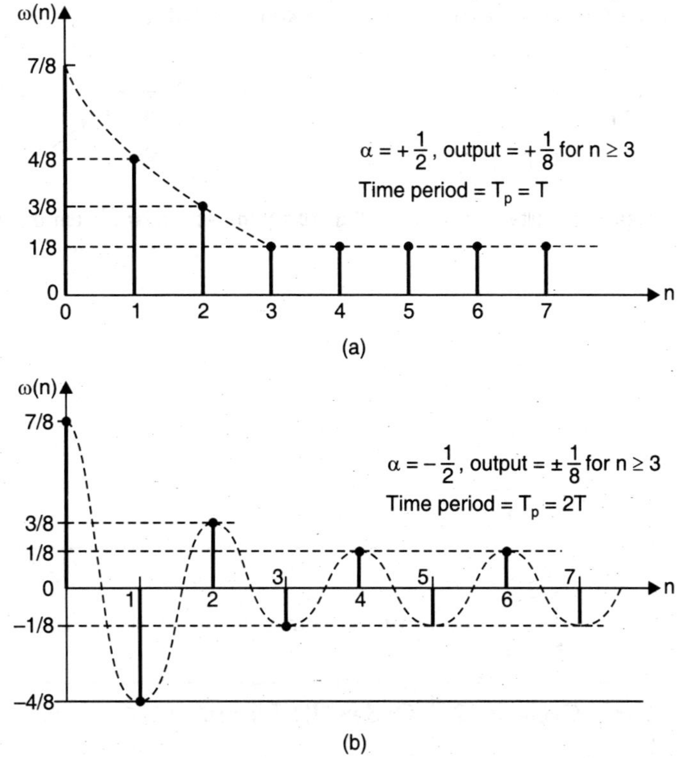

Fig. 10.14. Output $\omega(n)$ for (*a*) $\alpha = \frac{1}{2}$, (*b*) $\alpha = -\frac{1}{2}$ for input $x(n) = \frac{7}{8}\delta(n)$

Zero-input limit cycle exists when the effective value of α reaches unity *i.e.*

$$H(z) = \frac{1}{1-\alpha z^{-1}}$$

which has a pole at $z = \alpha$, gets modified as if $\alpha = \pm 1$ *i.e.* the effective value of α reaches unity due to quantization *viz.* the quantization shifts α from $+\frac{1}{2}$ to + 1 or $\alpha = -\frac{1}{2}$ to –1 in the example considered, and shown in Fig. 10.15.

If the oscillations that result due to quantization are of the order of $\pm 10^{-6}$ (equivalent to bits $b = 20 \because 2^{-20} \approx 10^{-6}$) in amplitude, we need not worry as the noise itself is in that range.

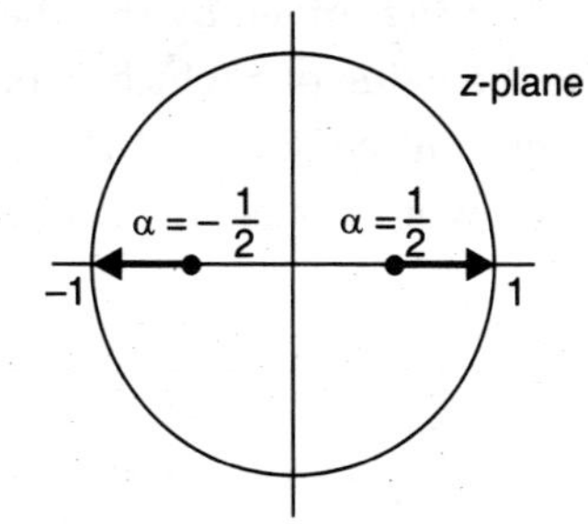

Fig. 10.15. Shifting of poles to ±1

In speech/music signals, there are moments when $x(n) = 0$ for short times. Here, the zero-input limit cycle output will get converted, by *D* to *A* convertor, as unwanted noise. This is an undesirable feature.

However, to design an oscillator, we make use of limit cycle phenomenon to our benefit. The design intentionally allows limit cycle to occur $\left(\text{with } \alpha = -\frac{1}{2}, \text{ say}\right)$ to produce oscillators/clock cycles etc., as shown in Fig. 10.14(*b*).

Derivation of Limit Cycle conditions for 1st order IIR filters

As $|Q[\alpha\omega(n-1)-\alpha\omega(n-1)]| \le \frac{1}{2}2^{-b}$ $\left(\because \text{in rounding we have } -\frac{1}{2}2^{-b} \le \varepsilon_R \le \frac{1}{2}2^{-b}\right)$ ...(10.32)
(quantization error)

When n is in the limit cycle during quantization the effective value of α is unity (As $Q[\alpha\omega(n-1)]$ equals $\omega(n-1)$ *i.e.* $|Q[\alpha\omega(n-1)]| = |\omega(n-1)]|$).

α assuming the value of unity corresponds to the pole at $z = \alpha$ shifting* to $z = 1$, *i.e.*, on the unit circle. The range of values for which this condition is met is given by:

$$Q[\alpha\omega(n-1)] - |\alpha\omega(n-1)| \le \frac{1}{2}2^{-b}$$

i.e. $|\omega(n-1)| - |\alpha\omega(n-1)| \le \frac{1}{2}2^{-b}$ as with quantization $|\alpha| \to 1$

i.e. $|\omega(n-1)|\,(1-|\alpha|) \le \frac{1}{2}2^{-2b}$

$$\therefore \qquad |\omega(n-1)| \le \frac{\frac{1}{2}2^{-b}}{1-|\alpha|} \quad \text{for limit cycle to exist in 1}^{\text{st}}\text{ order IIR filters} \qquad ...(10.33)$$

10.8.2 Zero-input Limit Cycle in 2nd Order IIR Filters

Let $$H(z) = \frac{1}{1-\alpha_1 z^{-1} - \alpha_2 z^{-2}} \qquad ...(A)$$

$$\triangleq \frac{1}{1-2r\cos\theta\, z^{-1} + r^2 z^{-2}} \qquad ...(B)$$

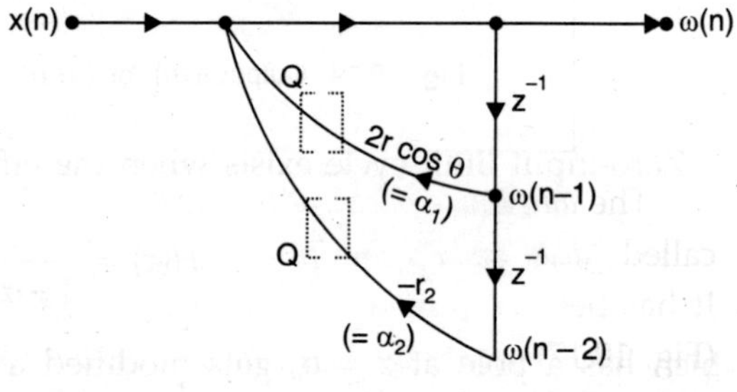

Fig. 10.16. A second order IIR system and the location of quantizers.

For $H(z)$ given by (B), the poles** are at $re^{\pm j\theta}$. It is the value of r which makes the poles to shift to the unit circle, *i.e.*, $|\alpha^2| = 1$ makes $|-r^2| = 1$ which would cause the zero-input limit cycle. As

$$\omega(n) = x(n) + Q[\alpha_1\omega(n-1)] + Q[\alpha_2\omega(n-2)] \qquad ...(10.34)$$

---

* $$H(z) = \frac{1}{1-\alpha z^{-1}}$$

If effect $|\alpha| = 1$, then $H(z) = \frac{1}{1-z^{-1}}$ or $\frac{1}{1+z^{-1}}$

i.e. the pole $\to z = \pm 1$

** **To find poles of $H(z)$:**

$$z^2 - 2r\cos\theta \cdot z + r^2 = 0 \text{ gives us}$$

$$z = \frac{2r\cos\theta \pm \sqrt{4r^2\cos^2\theta - 4r^2}}{2}$$

$$= re^{\pm j\theta} \text{ and } \therefore \ |z| \text{ for poles} = r$$

For limit cycle to occur, $\alpha_2 \to -1$ after quantization.

$$\therefore \quad |Q[\alpha_2\omega(n-2)] - \alpha_2\omega(n-2)| \le \frac{1}{2}2^{-b}$$

i.e., But $Q[\alpha_2\omega(n-2)] \to \omega(n-2)$ for limit cycle to occur

$$\therefore \quad |\omega(n-2) - \alpha_2\omega(n-2)| \le \frac{1}{2}2^{-b}$$

$$\therefore \quad |\omega(n-2)|\,(1-|\alpha_2|) \le \frac{1}{2}2^{-b}$$

$$\therefore \quad \boxed{|\omega(n-2)| \le \frac{\frac{1}{2}2^{-b}}{1-|\alpha_2|} \text{ for limit cycle to occur in 2}^{\text{nd}} \text{ order IIR filters, } |\alpha_2| \to 1} \quad \ldots(10.35)$$

Thus, for starting of the limit cycle, it does not depend upon α_1. The limit cycle solely depends on α_2 ($\because \ \alpha_2 = -r^2$). Once the oscillations start, then α_1 comes into the picture, in deciding the frequency of oscillations. It can be shown that

$$\text{Dead-band during the limit cycle} = \frac{1}{[1-|\alpha_1|-\alpha_2]} \quad \ldots(10.36a)$$

$$\text{Frequency of oscillation: } f = \frac{1}{2\pi T_s}\cdot\cos^{-1}\frac{\alpha_1}{2} = \frac{f_s}{2\pi}\cos^{-1}\frac{\alpha_1}{2} \quad \ldots(10.36b)$$

i.e.

$$\omega_{osc} = f_{\text{sampling}} \times \cos^{-1}\frac{\alpha_1}{2}$$

The *amplitude of the output* during limit cycle behaviour is called *"dead band"*. The poles P_1 and P_2 may shift to ±1 even. It has been observed to take the paths shown by dotted line (Fig. 10.17) when the limit cycle occurs.

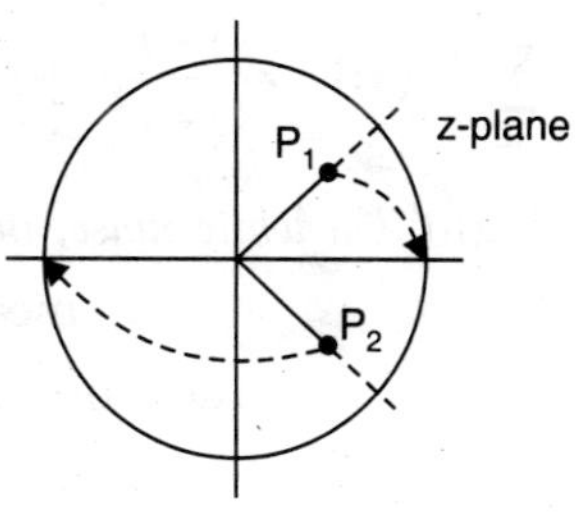

Fig. 10.17. Shifting of poles P_1 and P_2 during limit cycle

In case of parallel and cascade realizations, the analysis is more complex. In case of parallel realizations [Fig. 10.18(*a*)], we can predict limit cycle. Here the outputs of individual 2nd order systems are independent when the input is zero.

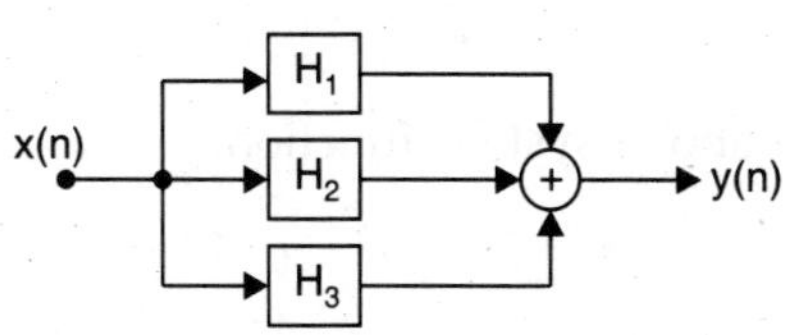

Fig. 10.18. (*a*) Parallel section: $H(z) = \sum_i H_i(z)$

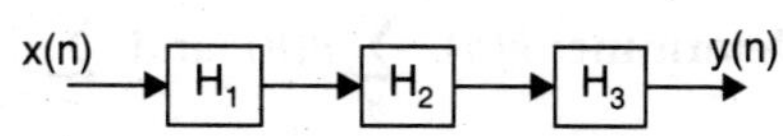

Fig. 10.18. (*b*) Cascaded sections: $H(z) = \prod_i H_i(z)$

In cascade cases [Fig. 10.18(*b*)] only the first section has zero input, the succeeding sections may exhibit limit cycle behaviour, or it may appear to simply decrease the limit cycle output of a previous section. If the limit cycle occurs at the last section/stage, there is no remedy, but a limit cycle at earlier stages may vanish due to the succeeding sections.

Some useful Results

In Fig. 10.19,

$$y(n) = x(n) + \alpha y(n-1) \quad \ldots(10.37a)$$

$$h(n) = \alpha^n u(n) \quad \ldots(10.37b)$$

$$H(z) = \frac{1}{1-\alpha z^{-1}}, \; |z| > |\alpha| \quad \ldots(10.37c)$$

$$\sum_n h(n) = \frac{1}{1-\alpha}, \; |\alpha| < 1 \quad \ldots(10.37d)$$

$$\sum_n |h(n)|^2 = \frac{1}{1-\alpha^2} \quad \ldots(10.37e)$$

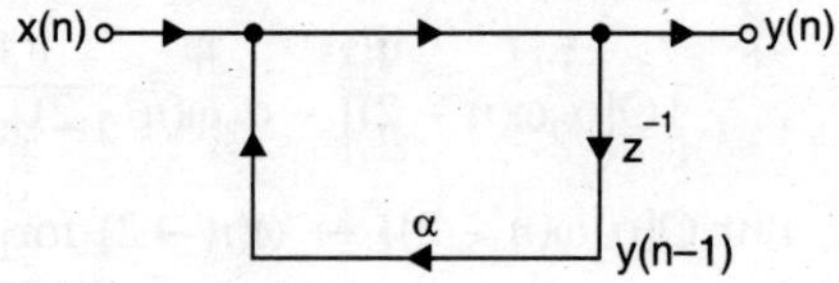

Fig. 10.19. First-order IIR Filter Pole at: $z = \alpha$

In Fig. 10.20,

$$y(n) = x(n) + 2r\cos\theta y(n-1) - r^2 y(n-2) \quad \ldots(10.38a)$$

$$h(n) = \frac{r^n \sin(n+1)\theta}{\sin\theta} u(n) \quad \ldots(10.38b))$$

$$H(z) = \frac{1}{1-2r\cos\theta z^{-1} + r^2 z^{-2}}, \; |z| > r \quad \ldots[10.38(c)]$$

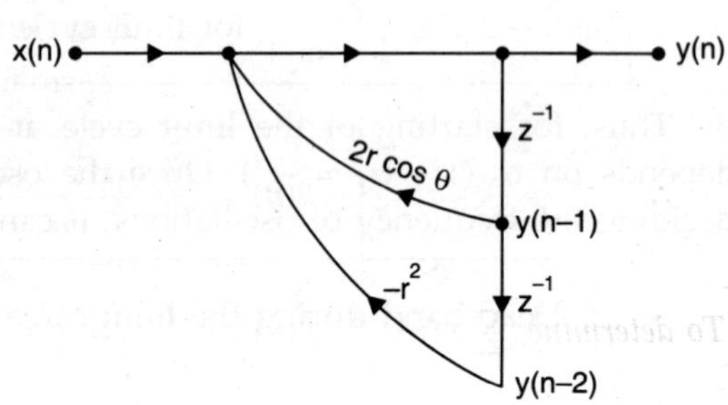

Fig. 10.20. Second-order IIR Filter Poles at: $z = re^{\pm j\theta}$

$$\sum_n h(n) = \frac{1}{1-2r\cos\theta + r^2} \quad \ldots(10.38d)$$

$$\sum_n |h(n)|^2 = \frac{1+r^2}{1-r^2} \cdot \frac{1}{1-2r^2\cos 2\theta + r^4} \quad \ldots(10.38e)$$

If x(n) is a white noise, then

$$\text{mean of } x(n) = m_f = E\{x(n)\} = 0 \quad \ldots(10.39a)$$

$$\text{auto-correlation of } x = \phi_{xx}(l) = E\{x(n) \cdot x(n-l)\} = \sigma_x^2 \delta(l) \quad \ldots(10.39b)$$

$$\text{Variance of } x(n) = \sigma_x^2 \text{ i.e. } \phi_{xx}(l)|_{l=0} = \sigma_x^2 \quad \ldots(10.39c)$$

Given: $H(z) = \dfrac{1}{1-2r\cos\theta z^{-1} + r^2 z^{-2}}$ as the system function.

To determine: $h(n)$, $\sum_n h(n)$ and $\sum_n |h(n)|^2$ for the above system function.

SOLUTION: As

$$H(z) = \frac{1}{1-2r\cos\theta z^{-1} + r^2 z^{-2}} = \frac{1}{(1-re^{j\theta}z^{-1})(1-re^{-j\theta}z^{-1})}$$

$$= \frac{1}{(1-re^{j\theta}z^{-1})(1-re^{-j\theta}\cdot r^{-1}e^{-j\theta})} + \frac{1}{(1-re^{-j\theta}z^{-1})(1-re^{j\theta}\cdot r^{-1}e^{j\theta})}$$

(by partial fractions)

$$= \frac{1}{1-re^{j\theta}z^{-1}}\left(\frac{1}{1-e^{-j2\theta}}\right)+\frac{1}{(1-re^{-j\theta}z^{-1})}\cdot\left(\frac{1}{(1-e^{j2\theta})}\right)$$

$$= \frac{1}{1-re^{j\theta}z^{-1}}\left(\frac{e^{j\theta}}{2j\sin\theta}\right)+\frac{1}{1-re^{-j\theta}z^{-1})}\left(\frac{-e^{-j\theta}}{2j\sin\theta}\right)$$

Taking *IZT*, $$h(n) = [(re^{j\theta})^n\cdot e^{j\theta}+(re^{-j\theta})^n(-e^{-j\theta})]\frac{1}{2j\sin\theta}u(n)$$

$$= \frac{1}{2j\sin\theta}\cdot r^n\cdot(e^{j(n+1)\theta}-e^{-j(n+1)\theta})\cdot u(n)$$

$$= \frac{r^n\cdot 2j\sin(n+1)\theta}{2j\sin\theta}\cdot u(n)$$

$$\therefore \qquad \boxed{h(n) = \frac{r^n\sin(n+1)\theta}{\sin\theta}u(n)} \qquad \ldots(10.40)$$

$\left[\textit{To determine } \sum_n h(n)\right]$, $$h(n) = \frac{r^n}{\sin\theta}\sin(n+1)\theta\cdot u(n)$$

$$\sum_n h(n) = \sum_{n=0}^{\infty}\frac{r^n}{\sin\theta}\sin(n+1)\theta = \frac{1}{r\sin\theta}\sum_{n=0}^{\infty}r^{n+1}\frac{(e^{j(n+1)\theta}-e^{-j(n+1)\theta})}{2j}$$

$$= \frac{1}{j2r\sin\theta}\left[\frac{re^{j\theta}}{1-re^{j\theta}}-\frac{re^{-j\theta}}{1-re^{-j\theta}}\right]$$

$$= \frac{1}{j2r\sin\theta}\frac{(+re^{+j\theta}-re^{-j\theta})}{(1-re^{j\theta})(1-re^{-j\theta})} = j2r\sin\theta = \frac{1}{(1-re^{j\theta})(1-re^{-j\theta})}$$

$$\boxed{= \frac{1}{1-2r\cos\theta+r^2}} \quad \textbf{Ans.} \qquad \ldots(10.41)$$

$\left[\textit{To determine } \sum_n |h(n)|^2\right]$, $$h(n) = \frac{r^n}{\sin\theta}\sin((n+1)\theta\cdot u(n)$$

$$\sum_n |h(n)|^2 = \frac{1}{\sin^2\theta}\sum_{n=0}^{\infty}r^{2n}\sin^2((n+1)\theta) = \frac{1}{\sin^2\theta}\sum_{n=0}^{\infty}r^{2n}\cdot\frac{1}{2}(1-\cos 2(n+1)\theta)$$

$$= \frac{1}{\sin^2\theta}\left[\frac{1}{2}\sum_{n=0}^{\infty}r^{2n}-\frac{1}{2}\frac{1}{r^2}\sum_{n=0}^{\infty}\frac{1}{2}r^{2(n+1)}(e^{j2(n+1)\theta}+e^{-j2(n+1)\theta})\right]$$

$$= \frac{1}{\sin^2\theta}\left[\frac{1}{2}\cdot\frac{1}{1-r^2}-\frac{1}{4r^2}\left\{\frac{r^2e^{j2\theta}}{1-r^2e^{j2\theta}}+\frac{r^2e^{-j2\theta}}{1-r^2e^{-j2\theta}}\right\}\right]$$

$$= \frac{1}{2\sin^2\theta}\left[\frac{1}{1-r^2}-\frac{1}{2}\frac{e^{j2\theta}(1-r^2e^{-j2\theta})+e^{-j2\theta}(1-r^2e^{j2\theta})}{1-2r^2\cos 2\theta+r^4}\right]$$

$$= \frac{1}{2\sin^2\theta}\left[\frac{1}{1-r^2} - \frac{1}{2}\frac{(e^{j2\theta}+e^{-j2\theta})-2r^2}{1-2r^2\cos 2\theta + r^4}\right]$$

$$= \frac{1}{2\sin^2\theta}\left[\frac{1}{1-r^2} - \frac{\cos 2\theta - r^2}{1-2r^2\cos 2\theta + r^4}\right]$$

$$= \frac{1}{2\sin^2\theta}\left[\frac{1-2r^2\cos 2\theta + r^4 - \cos 2\theta + r^2 + r^2\cos 2\theta - r^4}{(1-r^2)(1-2r^2\cos 2\theta + r^4)}\right]$$

$$= \frac{1}{2\sin^2\theta}\frac{(1+r^2)(1-\cos 2\theta)}{(1-r^2)(1-2r^2\cos 2\theta + r^4)}$$

$$\boxed{= \frac{1+r^2}{1-r^2}\cdot\frac{1}{1-2r^2\cos 2\theta + r^4}} \quad \textbf{Ans.} \qquad \ldots(10.42)$$

10.9 STATISTICAL ANALYSIS OF QUANTIZATION IN FIXED POINT REALIZATION OF IIR DIGITAL FILTERS

(A) **1st order IIR system:** Error analysis helps to choose appropriate word length of the register. In general, the addition of one bit to the register reduces the amplitude of the error to half. Thus, the decision concerning register length is sensitive to the accuracies in the error analysis. An analysis correct upto 30–40% is often adequate. Note that the error sequence is given by:

$$e(n) = Q[\alpha\omega(n-1)] - \alpha\omega(n-1) \qquad \ldots(10.43)$$

Assumptions:

(i) Error sequence $e(n)$ is a white noise sequence.

(ii) Error sequence has a uniform distribution over the quantization interval.

(iii) Error sequence $e(n)$ is uncorrelated with $x(n)$ and $\alpha\omega(n-1)$. This implies that $e(n)$ is also uncorrelated with the output $\omega(n)$.

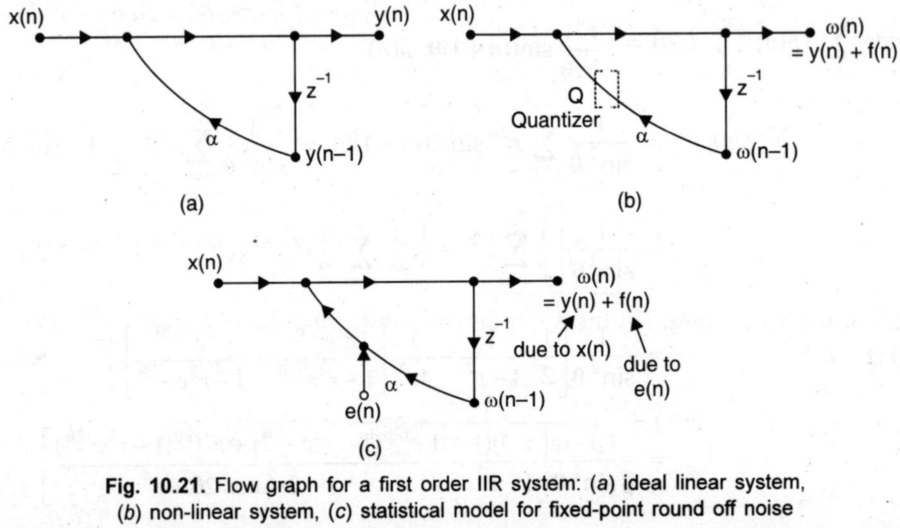

Fig. 10.21. Flow graph for a first order IIR system: *(a)* ideal linear system, *(b)* non-linear system, *(c)* statistical model for fixed-point round off noise

These assumptions hold when $x(n)$ and the resulting node variables (*i.e.* $e(n)$, ...,) vary from sample to sample or in a sufficiently complex manner. These assumptions are clearly not valid for a unit step or a sinusoidal sequence.

Let the register length = $b + 1$ bits

$$\text{Mean of } e(n) = m_e = 0 \text{ for rounding off}$$

$$\text{Variance of } e(n) = \sigma_e^2 = \frac{1}{12}2^{-2b}$$

Output: $$\omega(n) = \underset{\substack{\nearrow \\ \text{due to} \\ x(n)}}{y(n)} + \underset{\substack{\nwarrow \\ \text{due to} \\ e(n)}}{f(n)}$$ [see Fig. 10.21(*b*)]

Let $h_e(n)$ = unit sample response of the system from the node at which $e(n)$ enters the system

$$m_f = m_e \sum_n h_e(n) = 0 \text{ if } m_e = 0 \text{ (rounding off)}$$

$$\sigma_f^2 = \sigma_e^2 \sum_n |h_e(n)|^2$$

Clearly, $$h_e(n) = h(n) = \text{IZT}\left[\frac{1}{1-\alpha z^{-1}}\right] = \alpha^n u(n)$$

$$\therefore \quad \sigma_f^2 = \sigma_e^2 \sum_n |\alpha^n u(n)|^2$$

$$= \sigma_e^2 \sum_{n=0}^{\infty} \alpha^{2n}$$

$$= \sigma_e^2 \cdot \frac{1}{1-\alpha^2} \qquad \because \ |\alpha| < 1, \text{ in general}$$

$$= \left(\frac{1}{12}2^{-2b}\right) \cdot \frac{1}{1-\alpha^2}$$

Thus, we have:

$$\left.\begin{aligned} m_f &= 0 \\ \sigma_f^2 &= \left(\frac{1}{12}2^{-2b}\right)\cdot\frac{1}{1-\alpha^2} \end{aligned}\right\} \text{rounding } (\because m_e = 0) \qquad \text{...(10.44}a\text{)}$$

$$\left.\begin{aligned} m_f &= m_e \cdot \frac{1}{1-\alpha} \\ \sigma_f^2 &= \left(\frac{1}{12}2^{-2b}\right)\cdot\frac{1}{1-\alpha} - m_f^2 \end{aligned}\right\} \text{truncation } (\because m_e \neq 0) \qquad \text{...(10.44}b\text{)}$$

(*B*) 2nd order IIR system: Let the 2nd order system have poles at $z = re^{j\theta}, re^{-j\theta}$ (Fig. 10.22) and (Fig. 10.23)

$$\therefore \quad H(z) = \frac{1}{(1-re^{j\theta}z^{-1})(1-re^{-j\theta}z^{-1})} = \frac{1}{1-2r\cos\theta z^{-1} + r^2 z^{-2}}$$

Using (10.38), we have

$$y(n) = x(n) + 2r\cos\theta y(n-1) - r^2 y(n-2)$$

and
$$h(n) = \frac{r^n}{\sin\theta}\sin((n+1)\theta)\cdot u(n)$$

with rounding of the products, we obtain the difference equation [see Fig. 10.22(*b*)]

$$\omega(n) = x(n) + Q[2r\cos\theta\cdot\omega(n-1)] - Q[r^2\omega(n-2)] \qquad \ldots(10.45)$$

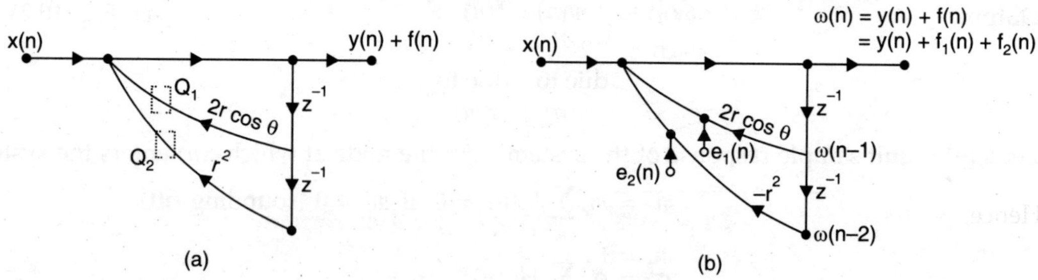

Fig. 10.22. Statistical model for forced point rounding off noise in a 2nd order IIR system

Assumptions:

(*i*) $e_1(n)$ and $e_2(n)$ are uncorrelated

(*ii*) $e_1(n)$, $e_2(n)$ are white noise sequences

(*iii*) $e_1(n)$, $e_2(n)$ have uniform distribution over one quantization interval $\left(-\frac{1}{2}2^{-b}, \frac{1}{2}2^{-b}\right)$

(*iv*) $e_1(n)$, $e_2(n)$ are uncorrelated with $x(n)$, $2r\cos\theta\omega(n-1)$ and $-r^2\omega(n-2)$

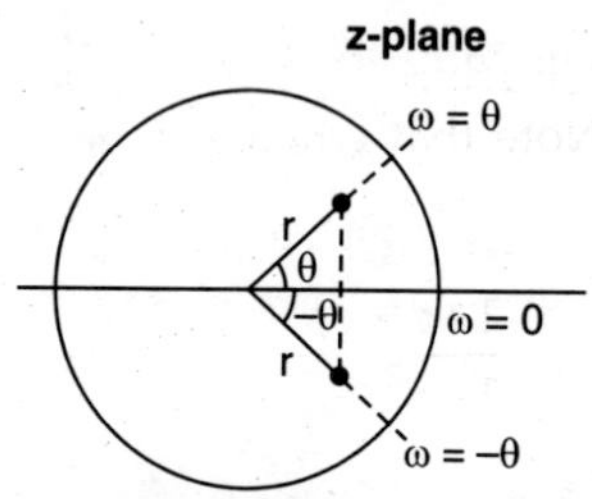

Fig. 10.23. Poles of the given IIR system at $z = re^{\pm j\theta}$ maximum response is at $\omega = 0$

Thus, we have

$$\omega(n) = y(n) + f_1(n) + f_2(n)$$

↗ due to $x(n)$, ↑ due to $e_1(n)$, ↖ due to $e_2(n)$

with the aforementioned assumptions, we have

$$m_f = m_{f_1} + m_{f_1}$$

$$= m_{e_1}\sum h_{e_1}(n) + m_{e_2}\sum h_{e_2}(n)$$

$$= 0 \text{ for rounding since } m_{e_1} = m_{e_2} = 0$$

$$\sigma_f^2 = \sigma_{f_1}^2 + \sigma_{f_2}^2$$

$$= \sigma_{e_1}^2\sum|h_{e_1}(n)|^2 + \sigma_{e_2}^2\sum|h_{e_2}(n)|^2$$

But $$h_{e_1}(n) = h_{e_2}(n) = h(n) = \frac{r^n}{\sin\theta}\sin(n+1)\theta \,.\, u(n)$$

Therefore,

$$\sigma_f^2 = (\sigma_{e_1}^2 + \sigma_{e_2}^2)\sum_n \left|\frac{r^n}{\sin\theta}\sin(n+1)\theta\,.\,u(n)\right|^2$$

$$\nearrow \quad \nwarrow$$

$$\text{each} = \frac{1}{12}2^{-2b}$$

$$= \left(2\frac{1}{12}2^{-2b}\right)\cdot\frac{1+r^2}{1-r^2}\cdot\frac{1}{1-2r^2\cos 2\theta + r^4}$$

Hence, we have

For 2nd order IIR system, with rounding $m_f = 0$ $\sigma_f^2 = 2\left(\frac{1}{12}2^{-2b}\right)\cdot\frac{1+r^2}{1-r^2}\cdot\frac{1}{1-2r^2\cos 2\theta + r^4}$

...(10.46)

Note that when r is near to unity, *i.e.*,

$$r = 1 - \delta, \text{ say, where } |\delta| << 1$$

$$\left.\frac{1+r^2}{1-r^2}\cdot\frac{1}{1-2r^2\cos 2\theta + r^4}\right|_{\theta=0} \to \frac{2}{2\delta}\cdot\frac{1}{1-2(1-\delta)^2+(1-\delta)^4}$$

$$= \frac{1}{\delta}\cdot\frac{1}{\underbrace{1-2+1}_{=0}+\underbrace{4\delta-4\delta}_{=0}\underbrace{-2\delta^2+6\delta^2}_{=4\delta^2}+\text{terms of }\delta^3,\delta^4}$$

$$\approx \frac{1}{4\delta^3}$$

$$\therefore \qquad \boxed{\sigma_f^2 \propto \frac{1}{\delta^3} \text{ if } r = 1-\delta} \qquad \text{...(10.47)}$$

σ_f^2 for 2's complement case of truncation: Here, $e(n)$, assumed to be uniformly distributed in the range

$$-2^{-b} < E_T \le 0 \textit{ i.e. } -2^{-b} \le e(n) \le 0 \text{ [see (10.12)]}$$

i.e. $$m_e = -\frac{1}{2}2^{-b},\ \sigma_e^2 = \frac{1}{12}2^{-2b}$$

$$\therefore \qquad m_f = m_e\sum h(n) \ne 0 \text{ (in general)}$$

$$\sigma_f^2 = \sigma_e^2\sum_n |h(n)|^2 - m_f^2 \text{ and so on}$$

Calculation in 1's complement and in signed magnitude: Truncation we know that for truncation (see 10.12)

2's complement: $-2^{-b} < E_T \le 0, \quad x$ +ve or x –ve

1's complement and SM: $-2^{-b} < E_T \le 0$ for x +ve numbers

$0 \le E_T < 2^{-b}$ for x –ve numbers.

In many examples, the results derived for rounding may be applied in 1's complement and Sign and Magnitude (SM) truncation cases too, although in those cases the correlation between the signal and the truncation error is stronger, *viz.* the polarity of the error is always opposite to the polarity of the signal (x) to which the truncation is applied.

10.10 OVERFLOW PROBLEM

In fixed point arithmetic digital filters, the possibility of overflow is there if proper scaling is not done. If we assume that each fixed-point register represents a signed fraction, each node in the filter must be constrained to maintain a magnitude less than unity, at the output, in order to avoid overflow. Let

k : denotes a particular node (In a 2nd order filter we have $k = 3$ nodes)

$x(n)$: input to the filter

$y_k(n)$: output of the k-th node

$h_k(n)$: unit sample response from the input node to k-th node

$x_{\max}(n)$: maximum value of the absolute value of the input signal $x(n)$.

Then,

$$y_k(n) = \sum_{r=-\infty}^{\infty} h_k(r) \cdot x(n-k) \qquad \text{(convolution)}$$

$$|y_k(n)| \le x_{\max} \sum_{r=-\infty}^{\infty} |h_k(r)| \qquad \because \quad |x(n-k)| \le x_{\max}$$

For no overflow, $|y_k(n)| < 1$. Hence,

$$\boxed{x_{\max} < \frac{1}{\sum_r |h_k(r)|} \quad \forall\, k \text{ for no overflow}} \qquad \ldots(10.48)$$

We might require scaling if above condition is not satisfied.

In case the inequality

$$|y_k(n)| \le x_{\max} \sum_r |h_k(r)|$$

is not satisfied, we require scaling of $x(n)$. In the above relation,

equality is achieved if $x(n-r) = \text{sgn}[h_k(r)]$ and $x_{\max} = \dfrac{1}{\sum_r |h_k(r)|}$

where $\boxed{\text{sgn } x \triangleq \begin{cases} 1, & x \ge 0 \\ -1, & x < 0 \end{cases} \quad \text{Signum function}}$

In general, we need scaling to avoid over flow.

For 1st order filter: $y(n) = \alpha y(n-1) + x(n)$

$$h(n) = \alpha^n u(n) \qquad \text{...(10.37b)}$$

For 2nd order filter: $y(n) = x(n) + 2r\cos\theta y(n-1) - r^2 y(n-2)$

$$h(n) = \frac{r^n}{\sin\theta}\sin(n+1)\theta \cdot u(n) \qquad \text{...(10.38b)}$$

For first order filter, we shall consider two typical cases

(*a*) white noise (extremest possible broad band case)

(*b*) a sinusoid (extremest possible narrow band case) to determine output Noise of Signal Ratio (NSR) if overflow is avoided. Note that the scaling $x(n)$ by, say A makes the signal power A^2. As A is usually less than unity, therefore, scaling reduces the signal power.

10.10.1 1st Order IIR System-white Noise Input *x*(*n*); No Overflow Conditions-Calculation of Output NSR

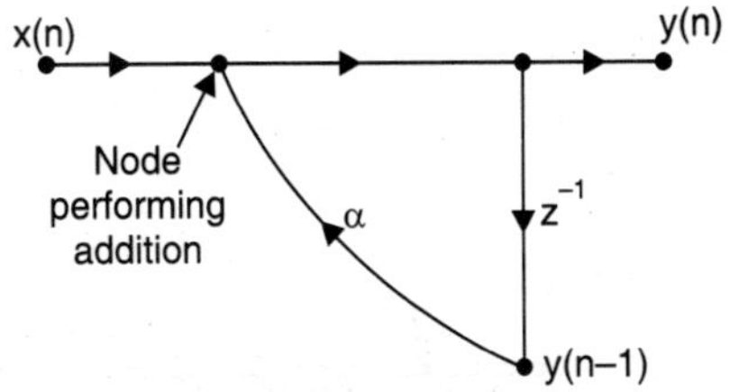

Fig. 10.24. First order IIR system showing the node performing addition

As $h(n) = \alpha^n u(n)$

$$\therefore \quad \sum_r |h(r)| = \sum_{r=0}^{\infty} |\alpha^r|$$

$$= \frac{1}{1-|\alpha|}, \quad |\alpha| < 1$$

For over flow avoidance

$$x_{\max} \le \frac{1}{\sum_r |h_k(r)|} \quad \forall\, k \text{ (Here } k = 1 \text{ i.e. only one node performing addition)}$$

$$\therefore \quad x_{\max} \le (1 - |\alpha|) \qquad \text{...(10.49)}$$

If $x(n)$ is a white noise, assuming it uniformly distributed, pdf is as shown in Fig. 10.25.

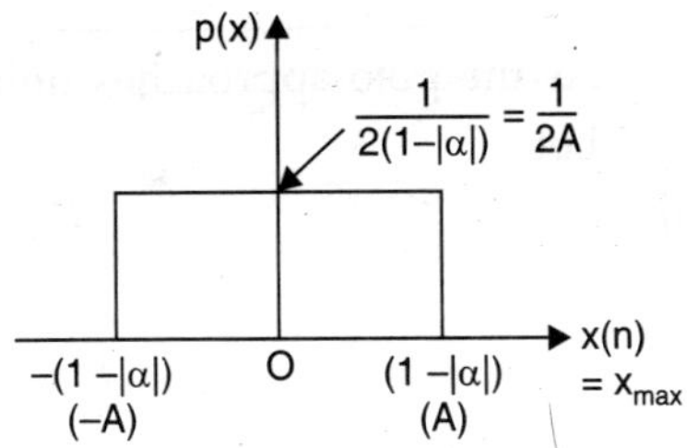

Fig. 10.25. Distribution of x_{max}

$$\therefore \quad \boxed{x(n) \text{ has mean: } m_x = 0, \quad \sigma_x^2 = \frac{1}{3}(1-|\alpha|)^2} \qquad \text{...(10.50)}$$

Proof: Clearly

$$m_x = 0$$

$$\sigma_x^2 = \int_{-A}^{A} \frac{1}{2A} \cdot x^2\, dx$$

$$= \frac{1}{2A}\left(\frac{x^3}{3}\right)_{-A}^{A}$$

$$= \frac{1}{3}A^2 = \frac{1}{3}(1-|\alpha|)^2$$

Output NSR = $\frac{\sigma_f^2}{\sigma_y^2}$ (NSR: Noise to Signal Ratio)

$$= \frac{\sigma_e^2 \sum_n |h_e(n)|^2}{\sigma_x^2 \sum_n |h(n)|^2}$$

$$= \frac{\sigma_e^2}{\sigma_x^2} \qquad \because \; h_e(n) = h(n) \text{ here}$$

= Input NSR

$$= \frac{\frac{1}{12}2^{-2b}}{\frac{1}{3}(1-|\alpha|)^2}$$

$$= \frac{1}{4}2^{-2b}\frac{1}{(1-|\alpha|)^2}$$

$\because \; \sigma_e^2 = \frac{1}{12}2^{-2b} \qquad \sigma_x^2 = \frac{1}{3}(1-|\alpha|)^2$

Output NSR = Input NSR (No overflow condition first order IIR filter) ...(10.51a)

$$\frac{\sigma_f^2}{\sigma_y^2} = \frac{1}{4}\cdot 2^{-2b}\cdot\frac{1}{(1-|\alpha|)^2} \qquad ...(10.51b)$$

$$= \frac{1}{4}\cdot 2^{-2b}\cdot\frac{1}{\delta^2} \qquad ...(10.51c)$$

As the pole approaches unit circle, the filter becomes more selective (sharp)

Let $|\alpha| = 1-\delta, \; |\delta| \ll 1$

then $(1-|\alpha|)^2 = \delta^2$

and
$$\frac{\sigma_f^2}{\sigma_y^2} = \frac{1}{4}2^{-2b}\cdot\frac{1}{\delta^2}$$

$$\propto \frac{1}{\delta^2}$$

Thus, if δ is halved, we must increase 'b' by 1 to maintain the same NSR.

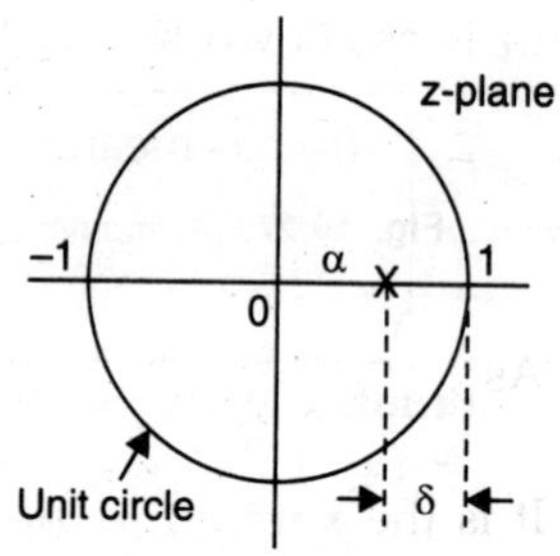

Fig. 10.26. Showing α and δ

10.10.2 2nd order IIR System-white Noise Input $x(n)$: No Overflow Conditions-Calculation of Output NSR

In the 1st IIR system, we had

$$\frac{\sigma_f^2}{\sigma_y^2} = \left(\frac{1}{4}2^{-2b}\right)\left(\frac{1}{(1-|\alpha|)^2}\right) \quad \swarrow \text{ this term} = \left(\sum_n |h(n)|\right)^2$$

By inspection, for 2nd order IIR systems, since, we have two quantizers,

$$\sigma_f^2 = \sigma_{f_1}^2 + \sigma_{f_2}^2$$

$$\therefore \quad \left.\frac{\sigma_f^2}{\sigma_y^2}\right|_{\substack{2^{nd}\text{ order}\\ \text{IIR system}}} = 2\cdot\left(\frac{1}{4}\cdot 2^{-2b}\right)\left[\sum_n \left|\frac{r^n}{\sin\theta}\sin(n+1)\theta\right|\cdot u(n)\right]^2$$

$$= 2\cdot\frac{1}{4}2^{-2b}\cdot\left(\frac{1}{\sin\theta}\cdot\sum_{n=0}^{\infty} r^n\,|\sin(n+1)\theta|\right)^2 \quad \ldots(10.52)$$

It is difficult to evaluate the above expression, but we can find the upper and the lower limits of NSR $\frac{\sigma_f^2}{\sigma_y^2}$.

Note that $\sum_{n=-\infty}^{\infty} |h(n)|$ *is the largest possible output obtainable* (with an input signal $x(n) = 1\ \forall\ n$, *i.e.,* $x_{max} = 1$, for all n. Hence, $\sum_n |h(n)|$ is greater than the output of the signal, at resonance frequency for a sinusoid input. (Note this argument)

(To determine output for $x(n) = \delta(n)$ at $\omega = \theta_0$)

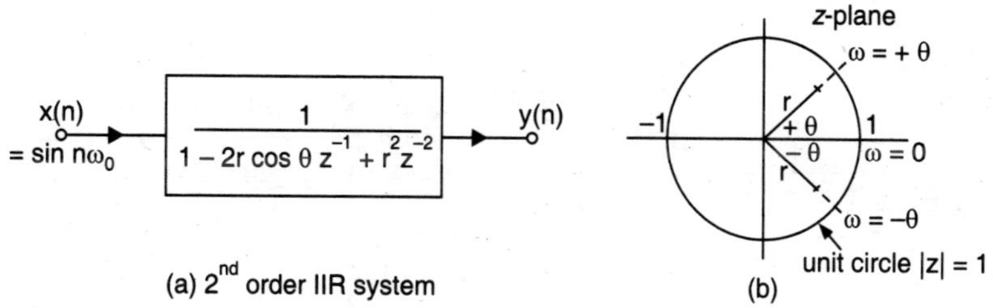

Fig. 10.27. (*a*) Input/output to 2nd order system and (*b*) Location of poles of the 2nd order system

As $$H(z) = \frac{1}{(1-re^{j\theta}z^{-1})(1-re^{-j\theta}z^{-1})}, \text{ poles at } z = re^{j\theta}, re^{-j\theta}$$

It is the output for $x(n) = \delta(n)$ *i.e.* impulse response.

When $\omega = 0$, it becomes a resonator and its output is maximum (but $< \Sigma h(n)$)

As $$y(n) = \sum_k h(k)\cdot x(n-k)$$

For $$x(n-k) \le 1 \qquad (\textit{i.e.}\text{ no overflow})$$

$$|y(n)| \le \sum_k |h(k)||x(n-k)| \le \sum_k |h(k)| \quad \ldots(10.53)$$

As $$H(z) = \frac{1}{(1-re^{j\theta}z^{-1})(1-re^{-j\theta}z^{-1})}$$

To find frequency response at resonance, put $z = e^{j\theta}$

$$\therefore \qquad H(e^{j\theta}) = \frac{1}{(1 - re^{j\theta} \cdot e^{-j\theta})(1 - re^{-j\theta} \cdot e^{-j\theta})}$$

$$= \frac{1}{1-r} \cdot \frac{1}{1 - re^{-j2\theta}}$$

$$|H(e^{j\theta})|^2 = \left(\frac{1}{1-r}\right)^2 \left|\frac{1}{(1 - r\cos 2\theta + jr\sin 2\theta)}\right|^2$$

$$= \left(\frac{1}{1-r}\right)^2 \cdot \frac{1}{1 + r^2 - 2r\cos 2\theta} = (\text{output at resonance})^2$$

Hence, $$\left(\sum_n |h(n)|\right)^2 \geq \frac{1}{(1-r)^2} \cdot \frac{1}{1 + r^2 - 2r\cos 2\theta}$$

Thus, lower* bound for $\dfrac{\sigma_f^2}{\sigma_y^2}$ is

$$\left(\frac{1}{2} \cdot 2^{-2b}\right) \frac{1}{(1-r)^2 (1 + r^2 - 2r\cos 2\theta)} \leq \frac{\sigma_f^2}{\sigma_y^2}$$

$\left(\text{To find upper bound of } \dfrac{\sigma_f^2}{\sigma_y^2}\right)$

As $$\frac{\sigma_f^2}{\sigma_y^2} = \left(\frac{1}{2} 2^{-2b}\right) \cdot \left(\frac{1}{\sin\theta} \sum_{n=0}^{\infty} r^n |\sin(n+1)\theta|\right)^2$$

since $|\sin(n+1)\theta| \leq 1$

$$\therefore \qquad \frac{\sigma_f^2}{\sigma_y^2} \leq \left(\frac{1}{2} 2^{-2b}\right) \frac{1}{\sin^2\theta} \left(\sum_{n=0}^{\infty} r^n\right)^2$$

$$= \left(\frac{1}{2} 2^{-2b}\right) \frac{1}{\sin^2\theta} \cdot \left(\frac{1}{1-r}\right)^2$$

Thus, we can write

$$\frac{1}{2} 2^{-2b} \frac{1}{(1-r)^2 (1 + r^2 - 2r\cos 2\theta)} \leq \frac{\sigma_f^2}{\sigma_y^2} \leq \frac{1}{2} 2^{-2b} \frac{1}{(1-r)^2 \sin^2\theta}$$

$$\text{i.e.} \quad \frac{B}{4} \leq \frac{\sigma_f^2}{\sigma_y^2} \leq B, \text{ where } B = \frac{1}{2} 2^{-2b} \frac{1}{\delta^2 \sin^2\theta} \qquad \ldots(10.54)$$

* Why is it lower bound of NSR. At resonance signal's output response is the highest, hence the NSR would be the least.

If $1 - r = \delta$, $\delta << 1$, then $1 + r^2 - 2r\cos 2\theta \approx 1 + 1 - 2\cos 2\theta = 4\sin^2\theta$

$$\therefore \qquad \frac{1}{2}2^{-2b}\frac{1}{\delta^2}\cdot\frac{1}{4\sin^2\theta} \le \frac{\sigma_f^2}{\sigma_y^2} \le \frac{1}{2}2^{-2b}\cdot\frac{1}{\delta^2\sin^2\theta}$$

$$\frac{1}{4}\left(\frac{1}{2}2^{-2b}\cdot\frac{1}{\delta^2\sin^2\theta}\right) \le \frac{\sigma_f^2}{\sigma_y^2} \le \left(\frac{1}{2}2^{-2b}\frac{1}{\delta^2\sin^2\theta}\right)$$

This is form $\frac{1}{4}B \le \frac{\sigma_f^2}{\sigma_y^2} \le B$, where $B = \frac{1}{2}2^{-2b}\frac{1}{\delta^2\sin^2\theta}$, as given in (10.54)

Note that output NSR $\propto \frac{1}{\delta^2}$, as was for first order IIR system.

Thus, if δ is halved, we must increase bits b by 1 to maintain the same NSR. As $\delta \to 0$, NSR $\to \infty$ and the IIR system becomes more selective.

10.10.3 First Order IIR System with Sinusoid Input

Here, $\qquad h(n) = \alpha^n u(n)$

$\qquad x(n) = A\cos n\omega_0$, (say)

$\qquad y(n) = B\cos(n\omega_0 + \phi)$ where ϕ

is the phase delay due to the system.

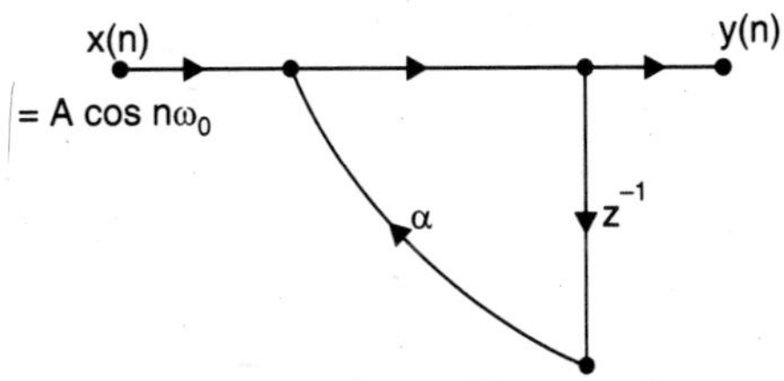

Fig. 10.28. First order IIR system will $x(n)$ a sinusoid

To prevent overflow, $B \le 1$. To maximize output signal energy, B is chosen as large as feasible. Thus, we choose $B = 1$. We may scale the input $A\cos n\omega_0$ so that B does not exceed 1 in the worst case, *i.e.* for which the frequency of the input coincides with the peak gain in the filter transfer function.

For fixed point filters, model for round off case, we have

$$\frac{\sigma_f^2}{\sigma_y^2} = \frac{\sigma_e^2\sum_n |h(n)|^2}{\sigma_y^2} = \frac{\sigma_e^2\sum_{n=0}^{\infty}\alpha^{2n}}{\sigma_y^2} \qquad \because h(n) = \alpha^n u(n)$$

$$= \frac{\left(\frac{1}{12}2^{-2b}\right)\cdot\frac{1}{1-|\alpha|^2}}{\sigma_y^2} = \frac{\left(\frac{1}{12}2^{-2b}\right)\Big/(1-|\alpha|^2)}{\frac{1}{2}} \qquad \left\{\because \; y(n) = 1\cdot\cos(n\omega_0+\phi)\right.$$

$$= \frac{1}{6}2^{-2b}\frac{1}{(1-|\alpha|^2)} \qquad \left.\therefore \; \text{r.m.s. value of } y(n) = \frac{1}{\sqrt{2}} \;\therefore\; \sigma_y^2 = \frac{1}{2}\right\}$$

If $|\alpha| = 1 - \delta$, $\delta \ll 0$, then $1 - |\alpha|^2 = 1 - (1-\delta)^2 \approx 2\delta$

$$\therefore \text{Output NSR} = \frac{1}{6}2^{-2b}\frac{1}{1-|\alpha|^2} \to \frac{1}{12\delta}\cdot 2^{-2b} \qquad \ldots(10.55)$$

i.e., NSR is proportional to $\frac{1}{\delta}$ for sinusoid input for first order IIR system.

Thus, in the case of sinusoids input, the NSR is proportional to $\frac{1}{\delta}$ rather than $\frac{1}{\delta^2}$. *So, if δ is made $\frac{1}{4}$ th, the register length must be increased by one bit so that the NSR remains constant.* In practical cases, where the nature of input $x(n)$ is not known, we may take the most pessimistic case *viz.* NSR $\propto \frac{1}{\delta^2}$.

10.10.4 2nd Order IIR System with Sinusoid Input

Here,

$$\text{NSR} = \frac{\sigma_f^2}{\sigma_y^2} = 2 \cdot \frac{\sigma_e^2 \sum_n |h(n)|^2}{\sigma_y^2}$$ (Factor 2 is due to double error σ_e^2 as there are two quantizations here see Fig. 10.22)

Using value of $\sum_n |h(n)|^2$ from [10.38(e)], we get

$$\text{NSR} = \left(2 \cdot \left(\frac{1}{12} 2^{-2b}\right) \cdot \frac{1+r^2}{1-r^2} \cdot \frac{1}{1-2r^2 \cos 2\theta + r^4}\right) \Big/ \frac{1}{2}$$

$$\sigma_y^2 = \left(\frac{1}{\sqrt{2}}\right)^2 = \frac{1}{2}$$

$$= \frac{1}{3} \cdot 2^{-2b} \cdot \frac{1+r^2}{1-r^2} \cdot \frac{1}{1-2r^2 \cos 2\theta + r^4} \qquad \ldots(10.56)$$

If $r = 1 - \delta$, $\delta \ll 1$,

then $1 + r^2 \approx 2, 1 - r^2 = 1 - (1 - \delta)^2 \approx 2\delta$

$1 - 2r^2 \cos 2\theta + r^4 \approx 1 - 2 \cos 2\theta + 1 = 4 \sin^2 \theta$

$$\text{NSR} = \frac{\sigma_f^2}{\sigma_y^2} = \left(\frac{1}{3} 2^{-2b}\right) \frac{2}{2\delta} \cdot \frac{1}{4 \sin^2 \theta} = \frac{1}{12} \cdot 2^{-2b} \cdot \frac{1}{\delta \sin \theta} \qquad \ldots(10.57)$$

To summarise, we have

$$\text{Output NSR} = \frac{\sigma_f^2}{\sigma_y^2} = \frac{1}{3} 2^{-2b} \frac{1+r^2}{1-r^2} \cdot \frac{1}{1-2r^2 \cos 2\theta + r^4}$$

$$\approx \frac{1}{12} 2^{-2b} \cdot \frac{1}{\delta \sin \theta} \quad \text{For sinusoid input 2nd order IIR systems} \qquad \ldots(10.58)$$

Thus, in 2nd order IIR filter too (as in the 1st order IIR filter) NSR is proportional to $\frac{1}{\delta}$ for sinusoidal input $x(n)$. The two cases *viz.* $x(n)$ = white noise and $x(n)$ = sinusoidal signal represent extreme cases for practical situations.

If the input is a narrow band of frequencies, then the analysis corresponding to sinusoidal input is more relevant. If the input becomes more wide band, the analysis corresponding to white noise is relevant.

For higher-order system analysis, the parallel structure is the simplest to analyses. It may consist of 1st and 2nd order structures.

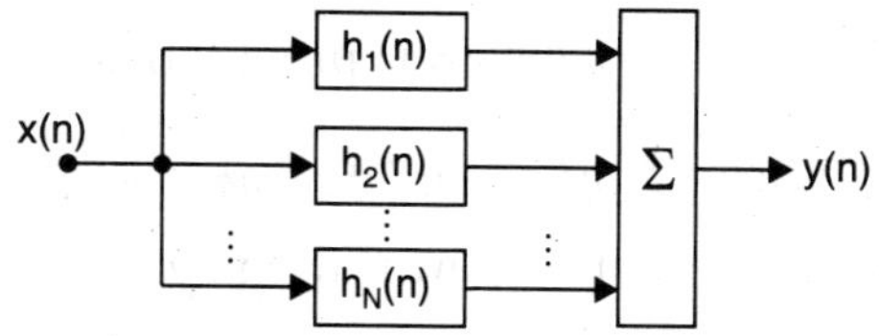

Fig. 10.29. Parallel structures with 1st order and 2nd order IIR blocks

Each structure can be analyzed separately, since, quantization effects can be assumed independent in each section. To get a 3rd order filter we need paralleling a 1st order with a 2nd order. *As we cannot realize imaginary coefficients, hence a 2nd order is a must to realize complex conjugate poles.*

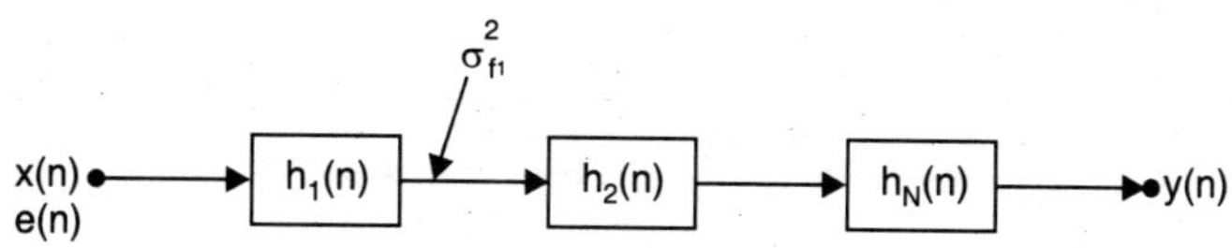

Fig. 10.30. Cascade structure

In cascade realization, noise generated, say, by the first block *viz.* $\sigma_{f_1}^2$, is filtered by subsequent filters and hence the analysis becomes more complicated. The order in which the poles and zeros are arranged in the cascade form can have great effect on the overall NSR. To determine the best pairing of zeros with poles and best ordering of 2nd order sections to have the minimum NSR is yet a research problem.

10.11 STATISTICAL ANALYSIS OF QUANTIZATION IN FLOATING POINT REALIZATION OF IIR DIGITAL FILTERS

We now consider the floating point representation to determine the quantization errors.

10.11.1 1st Order IIR System-Floating Point Realization

There is no scaling problem in the floating point system due its large dynamic range. As the floating point system introduces error both in addition as well as in multiplication, we quantize after addition operation and also after multiplication operation. In the floating point system, we have

$$Q[x(n)] = x(n)[1+\varepsilon(n)] = x(n) + \underbrace{x(n)\cdot\varepsilon(n)}_{\text{total actual error}} \qquad \ldots(10.59)$$

($\varepsilon(n)$: *i.e.* relative error)

$$\boxed{e(n) = \varepsilon(n)\cdot x(n)}$$

By using round off to mantissa, with mantissa $1 + b$ bits, we have

Mean, $m_\varepsilon = 0$, Variance $\sigma_\varepsilon^2 = \frac{1}{3}2^{-2b}$ [see Eqs. [10.14(*a*)] and [10.24(*a*)]]

since the rounding error has the range $-2^{-b} \le \varepsilon(n) \le 2^{-b}$.

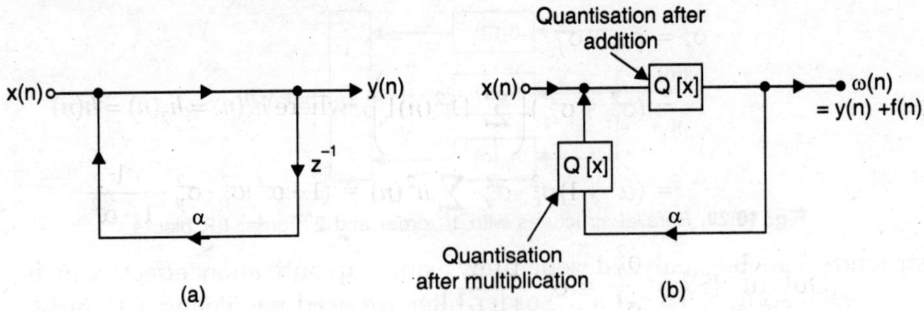

Fig. 10.31. (*a*) Ideal linear system (1st order IIR) and (b) non-linear model of 1st order IIR

Note that the error $\varepsilon(n)$ is relative and the total error $e(n) = \varepsilon(n)\, x$(input signal before quantizer)

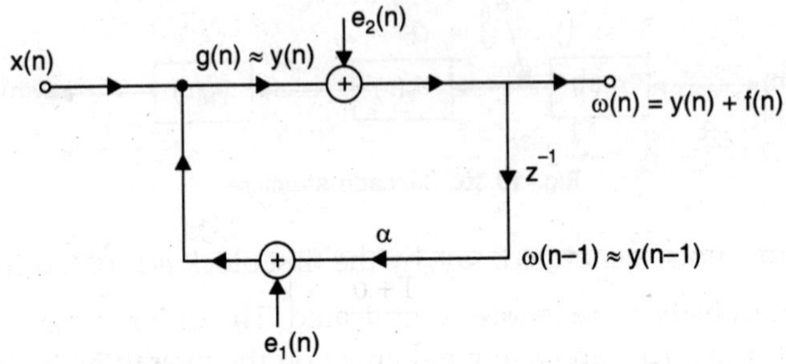

Fig. 10.32. Statistical model for floating-point rounding-off noise

Thus,
$$e_1(n) = \varepsilon_1(n)\,[\alpha\omega(n-1)] \approx \varepsilon_1(n)[\alpha y(n-1)] \quad \ldots(10.60)$$
$$e_2(n) = \varepsilon_2(n)\cdot g(n) \approx \varepsilon_2(n)y(n) \quad \ldots(10.61)$$

Assume:

(*i*) $x(n)$ is random signal

(*ii*) $x(n)$ is zero mean and therefore, $y(n)$ is zero mean

(*iii*) Relative errors $\varepsilon_1(n)$ and $\varepsilon_2(n)$ are

(*a*) White noises

(*b*) uncorrelated with each other

(*c*) uncorrelated with $x(n)$ or any node variable in the system

(*d*) are uniformly distributed in the range $-2^{-b} \le \varepsilon(n) \le 2^{-b}$

i.e.,
$$m_{\varepsilon_1} = m_{\varepsilon_2} = 0, \quad \sigma_{\varepsilon_1}^2 = \sigma_{\varepsilon_2}^2 = \sigma_\varepsilon^2 = \frac{1}{3}2^{-2b}$$

Thus,
$$\sigma_{e_1}^2 = \alpha^2\sigma_{\varepsilon_1}^2 E\{y^2(n-1)\} = \alpha^2\cdot\sigma_\varepsilon^2\cdot\sigma_y^2 \because \ y(n) \text{ is zero mean} \quad \ldots(10.62)$$
$$\sigma_{e_2}^2 = \sigma_{\varepsilon_2}^2 E\{y^2(n)\} = \sigma_\varepsilon^2\cdot\sigma_y^2 \because \ y(n) \text{ is zero mean} \quad \ldots(10.63)$$

The unit sample response of the system for noise $e_1(n)$ and $e_2(n)$ is

$h(n) = \alpha^n u(n)$ [in Fig. [10.31(*a*)] and assume same in Fig. (10.32)]

We have
$$\omega(n) = y(n) + f(n) \quad \text{with } f(n) = f_1(n) + f_2(n)$$

$$\therefore \quad \sigma_f^2 = \sigma_{f_1}^2 + \sigma_{f_2}^2$$

$$= (\sigma_{e_1}^2 + \sigma_{e_2}^2)\left(\sum_n |h^2(n)|\right), \text{ where } h_1(n) = h_2(n) = h(n)$$

$$= (\alpha^2 + 1)\sigma_\varepsilon^2 \cdot \sigma_y^2 \cdot \sum_n h^2(n) = (1+\alpha^2)\sigma_\varepsilon^2 \cdot \sigma_y^2 \cdot \frac{1}{1-\alpha^2}$$

$$\text{Output NSR} = \frac{\sigma_f^2}{\sigma_y^2} = \sigma_\varepsilon^2 \cdot \frac{1+\alpha^2}{1-\alpha^2}$$

$$= \left(\frac{1}{3}2^{-2b}\right)\frac{1+\alpha^2}{1-\alpha^2} \qquad \left(\because \sum_n h^2(n) = \sum_{n=0}^{\infty} \alpha^{2n} = \frac{1}{1-\alpha^2}\right)$$

Putting $\alpha = 1 - \delta, \quad \delta \ll 1, \quad 1 + \alpha^2 \approx 2, \quad 1 - \alpha^2 \approx 2\delta$

Then

$$\text{Output NSR, for } \alpha = 1 - \delta, = \frac{1}{3}2^{-2b} \cdot \frac{2}{2\delta}$$

Hence,

$$\boxed{\text{Output NSR} = \frac{\sigma_f^2}{\sigma_y^2} = \frac{1}{3}2^{-2b} \cdot \frac{1+\alpha^2}{1-\alpha^2} \approx \frac{1}{3}2^{-2b}\frac{1}{\delta}} \qquad \ldots(10.64)$$

This result is independent of type of input $x(n)$ white noise or sinusoidal. Note that the output NSR for first-order filter was derived without particular spectral properties of input $x(n)$. Hence, the result derived above applies to cases whether the input is wide-band such as white noise or narrow band such as sinusoidal input. For more general filters NSR will depend on the form of the input signal $x(n)$.

10.11.2 2nd Order IIR System-Floating Point Realization

Consider the second order IIR system shown in Fig. 10.33(*a*) and redrawn as Fig. 10.33(*b*).

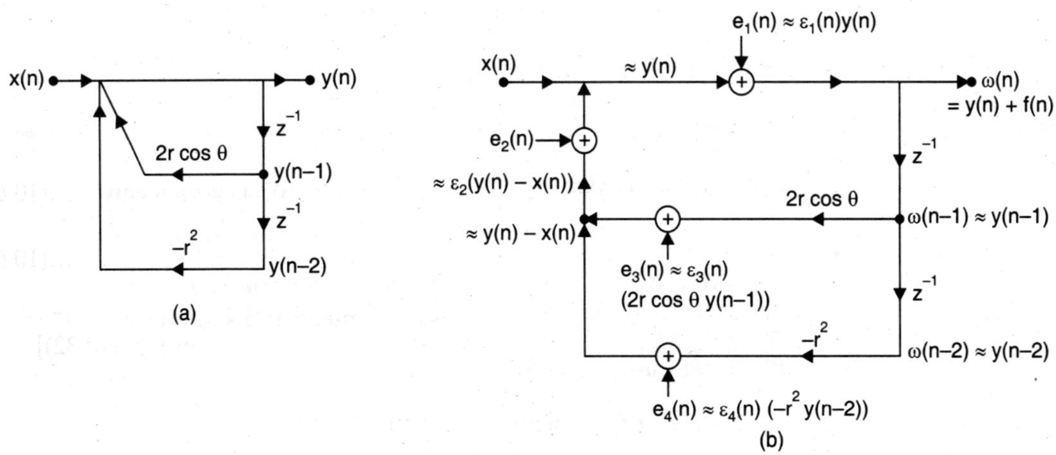

Fig. 10.33. (*a*) 2nd order IIR ideal linear system and (b) 2nd order IIR system-statistical model for floating point rounding off noise

Note that in Fig. 10.33(*a*), we first add the rounded products $2r\cos\theta\cdot\omega(n-1)$ and $-r^2\,\omega(n-2)$. After adding these two, we may have to again round off and hence the error $e_2(n)$ occurs as shown. The noises $e_1(n)$ and $e_2(n)$ represent noises due to rounding after additions and the noises $e_3(n)$ and $e_4(n)$ represent noises due to rounding after multiplications. With assumptions as for in 1st order case, and neglecting the 2nd order terms, we have:

$$e_1(n) = y(n)\cdot\varepsilon_1(n)$$
$$e_2(n) = [y(n) - x(n)]\varepsilon_2(n)$$
$$e_3(n) = [2r\cos\theta\cdot y(n-1)]\varepsilon_3(n)$$
$$e_4(n) = [-r^2 y(n-2)]\varepsilon_4(n) \qquad \text{...(10.65)}$$

Assuming $\varepsilon_1(n)$, $\varepsilon_2(n)$, $\varepsilon_3(n)$ and $\varepsilon_4(n)$ uncorrelated with each other and with $x(n)$; also $\varepsilon_i(n)$ assumed to be white noise sequences having uniform density functions. This will result in $m_{\varepsilon_i} = 0$, $i = 1, 2, 3, 4$ and $\sigma_{\varepsilon_i}^2 = \sigma_\varepsilon^2 = \frac{1}{3}2^{-2b}$. As $\varepsilon_i(n)$ are white and uncorrelated with $x(n)$ (and hence uncorrelated with $y(n)$ also), we can assume that $e_i(n)$, $i = 1, 2, 3, 4$ as white noises. Thus

$$\sigma_{e_1}^2 = E[y^2(n)]\sigma_{\varepsilon_1}^2, \qquad \sigma_{f_1}^2 = \sigma_{e_1}^2\sum_n h_1^2(n)$$

$$\sigma_{e_2}^2 = E[(y(n)-x(n))^2]\sigma_{\varepsilon_2}^2, \qquad \sigma_{f_2}^2 = \sigma_{e_2}^2\sum_n h_2^2(n)$$

$$\sigma_{e_3}^2 = E[4r^2\cos^2\theta\, y^2(n-1)]\sigma_{\varepsilon_3}^2, \qquad \sigma_{f_3}^2 = \sigma_{e_3}^2\sum_n h_3^2(n)$$

$$\sigma_{e_4}^2 = E[r^4 y^2(n-1)]\sigma_{\varepsilon_4}^2, \qquad \sigma_{f_4}^2 = \sigma_{e_4}^2\sum_n h_4^2(n) \qquad \text{...(10.66)}$$

Here $\sigma_{\varepsilon_1}^2 = \sigma_{\varepsilon_2}^2 = \sigma_{\varepsilon_3}^2 = \sigma_{\varepsilon_4}^2 = \sigma_\varepsilon^2$ (say)

$$= \frac{1}{3}2^{-2b} \text{ (in floating point quantization)}$$

$$h_1(n) = h_2(n) = h_3(n) = h_4(n) = h(n) = \frac{r^n}{\sin\theta}\sin(n+1)\theta\,.\,u(n)$$

$$\therefore \quad \sum_n h_i^2(n) = \sum_n h^2(n) = \frac{1+r^2}{1-r^2}\cdot\frac{1}{1-2r^2\cos 2\theta + r^4} = G \text{ (say)} \qquad \text{...(10.67)}$$

$$\therefore \quad \sigma_f^2 = G[\sigma_{e_1}^2 + \sigma_{e_2}^2 + \sigma_{e_3}^2 + \sigma_{e_4}^2] \qquad \text{...(10.68)}$$

But

$$\sigma_{e_1}^2 = \sigma_\varepsilon^2\cdot\sigma_y^2 \qquad \text{...(10.69a)}$$

$$\sigma_{e_3}^2 = \sigma_\varepsilon^2\cdot 4r^2\cos^2\theta\cdot\sigma_y^2 \qquad \because E[y^2(n-1)] = \sigma_y^2 \text{ as } y(n) \text{ is zero mean and stationary} \quad \text{...(10.69b)}$$

$$\sigma_{e_4}^2 = \sigma_e^2 r^4\sigma_y^2 \qquad \because E[y^2(n-2)] = \sigma_y^2 \text{ as } y(n) \text{ is zero mean and stationary} \quad \text{...(10.69c)}$$

and

$$\sigma_{e_2}^2 = \sigma_\varepsilon^2 E[(y(n)-x(n))^2] \qquad \text{...(10.69d)}$$

$$= \sigma_\varepsilon^2 E[y^2(n) - 2y(n)\,x(n) + x^2(n)]$$

$$= \sigma_\varepsilon^2\left[\sigma_y^2 + \sigma_x^2 - 2E\left[\sum_k h(k)\cdot x(n-k)\cdot x(n)\right]\right] \qquad \text{...(10.69e)}$$

White noise input $x(n)$: If $x(n)$ is white noise then $m_x = 0$, $\sigma_x^2 = E[x^2(n)]$

and $E[x(n) \cdot x(n-k)] = \sigma_x^2 \delta(x)$

$$\therefore \quad \sigma_{e_2}^2 = \sigma_\varepsilon^2 \left[\sigma_y^2 + \sigma_x^2 - 2E\left[\sum_k h(k) \underbrace{x(n)x(n-k)} \right] \right] \quad \text{[from [10.69(e)]]}$$

$$= \sigma_\varepsilon^2 \left[\sigma_y^2 + \sigma_x^2 - 2\sum_k h(k) \cdot \sigma_x^2 \delta(k) \right] \quad (\because \; E\{x(n) \cdot x(n-k)\} = \sigma_x^2 \delta(k))$$

$$= \sigma_\varepsilon^2 [\sigma_y^2 + \sigma_x^2 - 2\sigma_x^2 h(0)] \quad (\because \; \delta(k) = 1 \text{ only for } k = 0)$$

But
$$h(0) = \frac{r^n}{\sin\theta} \sin(n+1)\theta \, u(n) \Big|_{n=0} = \frac{r^0 \sin\theta}{\sin\theta} u(0) = 1$$

$$\therefore \quad \sigma_{e_2}^2 = \sigma_\varepsilon^2 [\sigma_y^2 - \sigma_x^2]$$

$$= \sigma_\varepsilon^2 \left[\sigma_y^2 \left(1 - \frac{1}{G} \right) \right] \quad [\because \sigma_y^2 = G \cdot \sigma_x^2, \text{ where } G \text{ is given in (10.67)}]$$

$$\approx \sigma_\varepsilon^2 \sigma_y^2 \quad \because \text{ usually } \frac{1}{G} \ll 1$$

Hence, putting the values of $\sigma_{f_i}^2$ in (10.68) as found above, we get

$$\sigma_f^2 = \sigma_\varepsilon^2 \cdot \sigma_y^2 [1 + 1 + 4r^2 \cos^2\theta + r^4] \cdot G$$

$$= \sigma_y^2 \cdot \sigma_\varepsilon^2 (2 + 4r^2 \cos^2\theta + r^4) G$$

$$\boxed{\begin{aligned} &\text{Output NSR} = \frac{\sigma_f^2}{\sigma_y^2} = \left(\frac{1}{3} 2^{-2b} \right) (2 + 4r^2 \cos^2\theta + r^4) G, \\ &\text{where} \quad G = \frac{1+r^2}{1-r^2} \cdot \frac{1}{1 - 2r^2 \cos 2\theta + r^4} \end{aligned}} \quad \ldots(10.70)$$

If $|r| = 1 - \delta$, $|\delta| \ll 1$

then
$$G \approx \frac{2}{2\delta} \cdot \frac{1}{2 - 2\cos 2\theta} = \frac{1}{(4\sin^2\theta)\delta}$$

and $2 + 4r^2 \cos^2\theta + r^4 \approx 3 + 4\cos^2\theta$

$$\therefore \quad \boxed{\frac{\sigma_f^2}{\sigma_y^2} \approx \left(\frac{1}{3} 2^{-2b} \right) \cdot \frac{3 + 4\cos^2\theta}{4\sin^2\theta} \cdot \frac{1}{\delta}, \text{ if } r = 1 - \delta, \delta \ll 1} \quad \ldots(10.71)$$

Comments:

1. Compared to the fixed point arithmetic, where the white noise NSR $\propto \frac{1}{\delta^2}$ and for sinusoidal input NSR $\propto \frac{1}{\delta}$, the NSR for the case of floating-point arithmetic is proportional to $\frac{1}{\delta}$. *This implies a smaller NSR for the floating-point case resulting in a better filter.*

2. In fixed-point case, NSR's were computed on the basis of that the input signal was as large as possible (the only limitation was to avoid overflow). If the input signal level decreases, the output SNR also decreases $\left(\because \text{ output NSR} = \frac{\sigma_f^2}{\sigma_y^2} = \frac{\sigma_f^2}{G \cdot \sigma_x^2}\right)$ and if $x(n)$ level and hence σ_x^2 decreases, σ_y^2 also decreases thus, decreasing SNR. However, *in the floating point case, $\sigma_f^2 \propto \sigma_y^2$ i.e. the output noise variance is proportional to the σ_y^2 i.e.* $\sigma_f^2 \propto \sigma_x^2$ ($\because \sigma_y^2 = G \cdot \sigma_x^2$). This implies the output noise decreases with scaling down the input signal level and vice versa.
3. Above comparision assumes that the floating-point mantissa bits are equal to the entire bits of the fixed point word length. It does not account for extra bits needed for the characteristic of the floating point word.
4. Analysis of higher-order systems becomes very complicated. The quantization noise is **dependent** on the system parameters and also on the structure of the system. Since there **is essentially** no dynamic range problem with the **floating** point arithmetic, cascade **realizations are** probably not too sensitive to the **ordering of** poles and zeros.

10.12 FINITE-REGISTER LENGTH EFFECT-FIR DIGITAL FILTERS

The analysis of FIR filters is simpler than that of the IIR filters. There is no limit cycle effect with non-recursive realizations such as in direct and cascade form of non-recursive FIR realizations. This is so because if, say, the unit sample response of an FIR filter is of length N samples, then the output of a direct or cascade form of non-recursive filter, after the input has been zero for N consecutive samples, would be zero.

But recursive realizations of FIR systems *e.g.* frequency sampling structure are subject to problems of limit cycle etc.

Dynamic range and rounding off noise are important in FIR filters just as in IIR systems.

10.12.1 Statistical Analysis of Quantization in Fixed-Point Realizations of FIR Digital Filters

Case A: Discrete Form Realization of FIR Filters: The impulse response, $h(n)$, for a linear shift invariant (LTI) systems is non-zero for $0 \le n \le N-1$, and

$$y(n) = h(n) * x(n) = \sum_{k=0}^{N-1} h(k) \cdot x(n-k) \qquad \ldots(10.72)$$

This can be realized as follows:

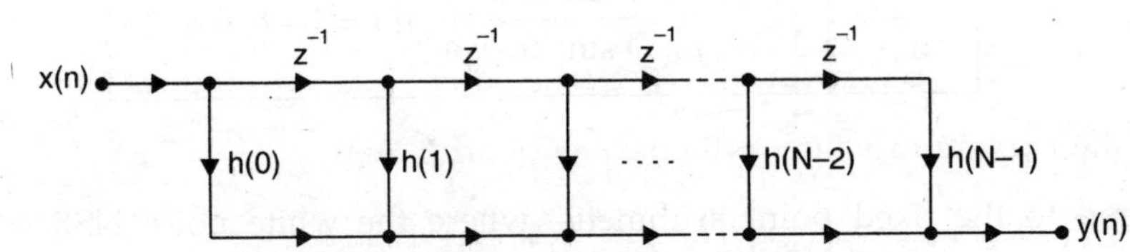

Fig. 10.34. (*a*) Realization of an FIR filter-idea case

Filter length = N, Filter order = $N - 1$

As $$H(z) = \sum_{n=0}^{\infty} h(n)z^{-n}\text{, in general}$$

$$= \sum_{n=0}^{N-1} h(n)z^{-n}\text{, [here in Fig. 10.34(a)]}$$

$$= h(0)z^{-0} + h(1)z^{-1} + h(2)z^{-2} + \ldots + h(0)z^{-0} \qquad \ldots(10.73)$$

Realization in Fig. 10.34(*a*) shows N multipliers *viz.* $h(0), h(1), \ldots, h(N-1)$ and $(N-1)$ delays. Therefore, filter length = N and filter order = $N - 1$.

Due to quantization after each multiplication, and probable scaling factor A, we have the equivalent realization shown in Fig. 10.34(*b*).

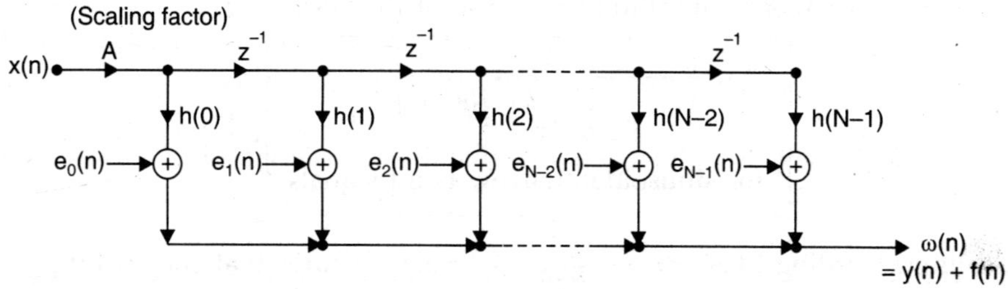

Fig. 10.34. (*b*) Equivalent diagram with addition of quantization errors $e_i(n)$, $i = 0, 1, 2, \ldots, N-1$ after each multiplication. Assume $A = 1$

With $A = 1$, assumed for simplicity,

$$f(n) = \sum_{i=0}^{N-1} e_i(n)$$

$$\sigma_f^2 = N \cdot \sigma_e^2 \quad \text{assuming } e_i(n) \text{ uncorrelated}$$

$$= \left(\frac{1}{12}2^{-2b}\right)N\text{, for rounding} \qquad \ldots(10.74)$$

Thus, the output noise depends on the filter length N. Thus, in Direct Form of FIR filter realization ('A' may have any value).

(*i*) Output noise level is independent of filter parameters $h(n)$ as the noise $e_i(n)$ is not processed by the system at all.

(*ii*) Noise is proportional to the filter length N of the impulse response $h(n)$.

As

$$y(n) = \sum_{k=-\infty}^{\infty} h(k)x(n-k)$$

If x_{max} is the maximum value of the sequence $x(n)$, then

$$|y(n)| \leq x_{max} \sum_{k=-\infty}^{\infty} |h(k)| \qquad \ldots(10.75)$$

In order to avoid overflow, we must ensure $|y(n)| < 1$ we may, therefore, choose appropriate value of scaling factor A, such that

$$(Ax_{max}) \sum_{k=-\infty}^{\infty} |h(k)| < 1$$

i.e. Scaling factor $$A < \frac{1}{x_{max} \sum_{k=0}^{N-1} |h(k)|} \quad \ldots(10.76)$$

for proper scaling in wide band signal $x(n)$.

For a narrow band signal, the above scaling is too conservative for example for the case of a sine wave (being of narrowest band signal). In such a narrow band cases, we should scale in terms of peak of the frequency amplitude response of the system *i.e.*

$$A < \frac{1}{x_{max} \max\limits_{0 \le \omega \le \pi} [|H(e^{j\omega})|]} \quad \ldots(10.77)$$

for sinusoidal/narrow band signals.

Input scaling according to $A < \frac{1}{x_{max} \sum_{k=0}^{N-1} |h(k)|}$ also ensures that correct outputs for direct form realization are obtained without any overflow. (with 2's complement arithmetic, when more than two numbers are added together, and overflow can occur in computing partial sums, yet the correct final result will be obtained if the final result is (theoretically) less than one *i.e.* no overflow).

Case B: Cascade form Realization of FIR Filters

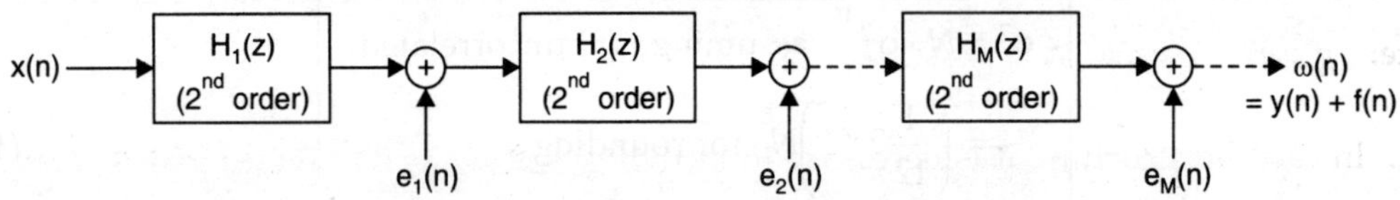

Fig. 10.35. (*a*) Cascade realization of FIR system

In this figure, let overall filter order = $N - 1$, N odd

Let $$M = \frac{(N-1)}{2}$$

so, we require M blocks of 2nd order filters in cascade. Errors $e_1(n)$, $e_2(n)$, ..., $e_M(n)$ are added due to blocks $H_1(z)$, $H_2(z)$, ..., $H_M(n)$, respectively. A typical $H_i(z)$ block is of the form, shown in Fig. 10.35(*b*).

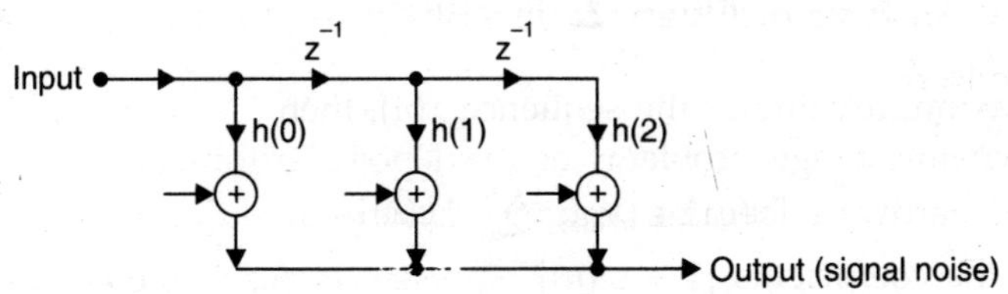

Fig. 10.35. (*b*) Each 2nd order block for the cascade of FIR system shown in Fig. 10.35(*a*) is like this

Clearly, variance of noise at output $= 3\times\frac{1}{12}2^{-2b} = \frac{1}{4}2^{-2b}$. The typical noise $e_i(n)$ in Fig. 10.35(*a*) is processed through the succeeding blocks following $e_i(n)$ *i.e.* by $M - i$ blocks. The $\sigma_{f_i}^2$ at output due to $e_i(n)$ will depend on the processing $e_i(n)$ through $M - i$ blocks.

The order of the filter succeeding $e_i(n) = 2(M - i) = N - 1 - 2i$.

Number of multipliers, $g_i(n)$, say, for the filter of order $N - 1 - 2i$ is $N - 2i$ *viz.*, $g_i(0)$, $g_i(1)$, $g_i(2)$, ..., $g_i(N - 1 - 2i)$.

$$\therefore \quad \sigma_{f_i}^2 = \sigma_{i_1}^2 \sum_{k=0}^{N-1-2i} g_i^2(k) \qquad \left(\because \ \sigma_f^2 = \sigma_e^2 \sum_n |h(n)|^2, \text{in general}\right)$$

Overall noise at output is, therefore, given by

$$\sigma_f^2 = \sum_{i=1}^{M} \sigma_{f_i}^2$$

$$= \sum_{i=1}^{M} \sigma_{i_1}^2 \sum_{k=0}^{N-1-2i} g_i^2(k)$$

$$\sigma_f^2 = \frac{2^{-2b}}{4}\left(\sum_{i=1}^{M}\sum_{k=0}^{N-1-2i} g_i^2(k)\right)$$

where $g_i(n)$ is the unit sample response from i^{th} source of error to output point.

$$M = \frac{(N-1)}{2} \qquad \ldots(10.78)$$

Note: $g_M(n) = 1\,\delta(n)$, $\therefore \quad \sum_{k=0}^{0} g_M^2(k) = 1$

1. In cascade structure, it is necessary to introduce scaling at the input to each section to avoid overflow.
2. If scaling is done at the very beginning, SNR will degrade much more. We may do distributed scaling, *i.e.*, scaling before each section. Here, SNR will not decrease so much as compared to 'bulk scaling' at the very beginning.
3. Output noise σ_f^2 depends on pattern of cascading section placement. There are $M!$ possible ways of ordering the placement. A good ordering is one for which sections having higher gain are in the beginning and those with lower gain in later sections.

10.12.2 Statistical Analysis of Quantization Effect in Floating Point Realization of FIR Digital Filters

To overcome the dynamic range problems of fixed point arithmetic, floating point arithmetic proposed though the hardware, becames more complicated and costly.

In Fig. 10.36(*b*), the coefficients $[1 + \varepsilon_k(n)]$ represent effect of multiplication by $h(k)$ [to the input signal $x(n - k)$] being rounded off.

The coefficients $[1 + \eta_k(n)]$ represent rounding off after each addition.

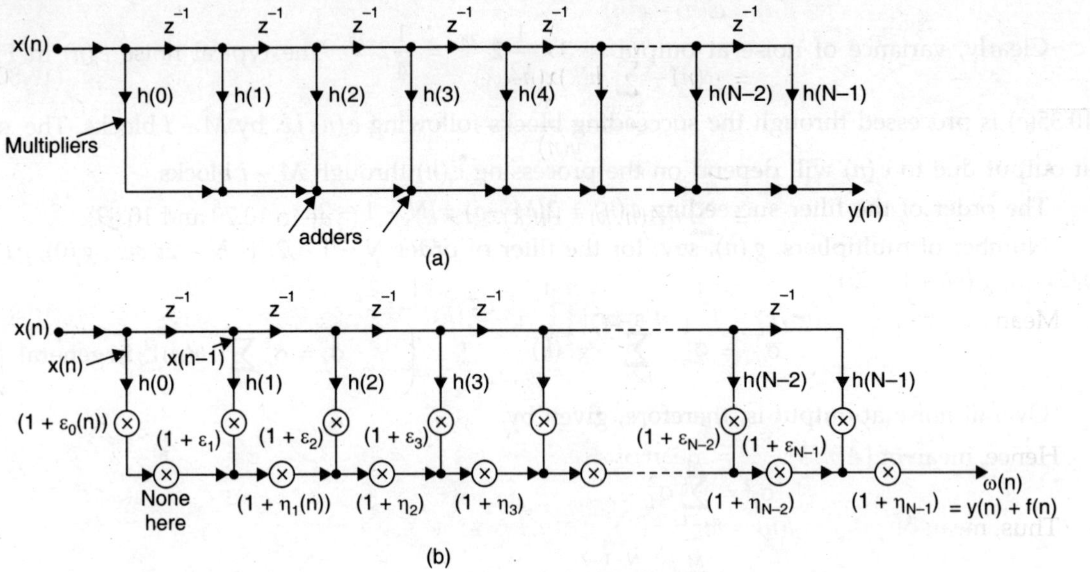

Fig. 10.36. (*a*) Ideal linear FIR system and (b) Statistical model for floating-point rounding off noise for FIR system Fig. 10.36(*a*)

We assume $\varepsilon_k(n)$ and $\eta_k(n)$ independent and uniformly distributed for all k

$$\omega(n) = y(n) + f(n)$$

$$y(n) = \sum_{k=0}^{N-1} h(k)x(n-k)$$

But

$$\omega(n) = x(n)\cdot h(0)[1+\varepsilon_0(n)]\prod_{r=1}^{N-1}[1+\eta_r(n)] \qquad (1^{\text{st}} \text{ term})$$

$$+\, x(n-1)\, h(1)[1+\varepsilon_1(n)]\prod_{r=1}^{N-1}[1+\eta_r(n)] \qquad (2^{\text{nd}} \text{ term})$$

$$+\, x(n-2)\, h(2)[1+\varepsilon_2(n)]\prod_{r=2}^{N-1}[1+\eta_r(n)] \qquad (3^{\text{rd}} \text{ term})$$

$$\vdots$$

$$+\, x(n-i)\, h(i)[1+\varepsilon_i(n)]\prod_{i=i}^{N-1}[1+\eta_r(n)] \qquad (i^{\text{th}} \text{ term } i.e. \text{ general term})$$

$$\vdots$$

$$+\, x(n-N+1)\, h(N-1)[1+\varepsilon_{N-1}(n)][1+\eta_{N+1}(n)] \qquad (\text{last term})$$

$\therefore$

$$\omega(n) = \sum_{k=0}^{N-1} A(n,k)\cdot h(k)\cdot x(n-k) \qquad \ldots(10.79)$$

where

$$A(n,k) \triangleq \begin{cases} [1+\varepsilon_0(n)]\prod_{r=1}^{N-1}[1+\eta_r(n)], & k=0 \\ [1+\varepsilon_k(n)]\prod_{r=k}^{N-1}[1+\eta_r(n)], & k=1,2,\ldots,N-1 \end{cases}$$

$$f(n) = \omega(n) - y(n)$$

$$= \omega(n) - \underbrace{\sum_{k=0}^{N-1} h(k)x(n-k)}_{y(n)} \qquad \ldots(10.80)$$

$$= \sum_{k=0}^{N-1} [A(n,k)-1]h(k)x(n-k) \qquad \text{(due to 10.79 and 10.89)}$$

Mean of $$A(n,k) = E\left[\underset{\text{zero mean}}{[1+\varepsilon_k(n)]}\prod_{r=k}^{N-1}\underset{\text{zero mean}}{[1+\eta_r(n)]}\right] = 1 \qquad \ldots(10.81)$$

Hence, mean of $[A(n,k)-1]$ = mean of $A(n,k) - 1 = 1 - 1 = 0$

Thus, mean of $$f(n) = m_f = E\left[\sum_{k=0}^{N-1} [A(n,k)-1]\, h(k)\cdot x(n-k)\right]$$

$$= \sum_{k=0}^{N-1} h(k)\, x(n-k)\underbrace{E[A(n,k)-1]}_{=0} = 0$$

$\therefore$ $$\boxed{m_f = 0} \qquad \ldots(10.82)$$

Now $$\sigma_f^2 = E\left\{\left[\sum_{k=0}^{N-1} [A(n,k)-1]\cdot h(k)\cdot x(n-k)\right]^2\right\} - m_f^2$$

Put $m_f = 0$ (found above)

$$\therefore \quad \sigma_f^2 = \sum_{k=0}^{N-1}\sum_{l=0}^{N-1} h(k)h(l)\cdot E\{[A(n,k)-1][A(n,l)-1]\}\cdot \underbrace{E\{x(n-k)\cdot x(n-l)\}}_{=\phi_{xx}(l-k)} \qquad \ldots(10.83)$$

i.e. auto-correlation of x

Assume $x(n)$ as random signal with flat power spectrum *i.e.* $x(n)$ as white noise. We may therefore, put $\phi_{xx}(l-k) = \sigma_x^2\delta(l-k)$.

Doing so, equation (10.83) reduces to

$$\sigma_f^2 = \sigma_x^2 \sum_{k=0}^{N-1} h^2(k)\, E\{[A(n,k)-1]^2\}$$

$$= \sigma_x^2 \sum_{k=0}^{N-1} h^2(k)\,\{E[A^2(n,k)] - \underbrace{E2[A(n,k)]}_{=2} + 1\}$$

$$= \sigma_x^2 \sum_{k=0}^{N-1} h^2(k) E\{[A^2(n,k)] - 1\}$$

$[\because E\{A(n,k)\} = 1$ found in 10.81$]$ ...(10.84)

But $$E[A^2(n,0)] = E\left[\left\{[1+\varepsilon_0(n)]\prod_{r=1}^{N-1}[1+\eta_r(n)]\right\}^2\right]$$

Assuming $\varepsilon_i(n)$ and $\eta_i(n)$ uncorrelated, $\sigma^2_{\varepsilon_i} = \sigma^2_{\eta_i} = \frac{1}{3}2^{-2b}$ for all i

$$\therefore \quad E[A^2(n,0)] = \left(1+\frac{1}{3}2^{-2b}\right)^{*}\prod_{r=1}^{N-1}\left(1+\frac{1}{3}2^{-2b}\right)$$

$$= \left(1+\frac{1}{3}2^{-2b}\right)^{N}$$

Again $$E[A^2(n,k)] = E\left[\left\{[1+\varepsilon_k(n)]\prod_{r=k}^{N-1}[1+\eta_k(n)]\right\}^2\right], k \neq 0$$

$$= E\left[[1+\varepsilon_k(n)]^2\prod_{r=k}^{N-1}[1+\eta_k(n)]^2\right], k \neq 0$$

$$= \left(1+\frac{1}{3}2^{-2b}\right)\prod_{r=k}^{N-1}\left(1+\frac{1}{3}2^{-2b}\right), k \neq 0$$

$$= \left(1+\frac{1}{3}2^{-2b}\right)^{N+1-k}, k \neq 0$$

Thus, if we use $E[A^2(n, k)]$ to calculate $E[A^2(n, 0)]$, there is not much error. So we assume, for simplicity

$$E[A^2(n,k)] = \left(1+\frac{1}{3}2^{-2b}\right)^{N+1-k} \quad \text{for all } k = 0, 1, \ldots, N-1$$

$$\approx 1+(N+1-k)\cdot\frac{1}{3}2^{-2b} \quad \left(\text{as } \frac{1}{3}2^{-2b} << 1, \text{ we use } (1+x)^n \approx 1+nx\right)$$

$$\therefore \quad E\{[A^2(n,k)]\} \approx (N+1-k)\cdot\frac{1}{3}2^{-2b}$$

---

*

$$\because \quad E\{[1+\varepsilon_k(n)]^2\} = E\{1+2\varepsilon_k(n)+\varepsilon_k^2(n)\}$$

$$= 1+2\times 0+\frac{1}{3}2^{-2b}$$

$$= \left(1+\frac{1}{3}2^{-2b}\right)$$

$$\therefore \quad \sigma_f^2 = \sigma_x^2 \sum_{k=0}^{N-1} h^2(k) \cdot E\{[A^2(n,k)] - 1\} \quad \text{[From (10.84)]}$$

$$= \sigma_x^2 \sum_{k=0}^{N-1} h^2(k) \cdot (N+1-k) \cdot \frac{1}{3} 2^{-2b}$$

$$\therefore \quad \boxed{\sigma_f^2 = \frac{1}{3} 2^{-2b} \cdot (N+1)\, \sigma_x^2 \sum_{k=0}^{N-1} h^2(k) \left(1 - \frac{k}{N+1}\right) \text{ and } m_f = 0 \text{ for rounding off quantization in Floating point case}} \quad \ldots(10.85)$$

Comments: We have found that

(i) Noise σ_f^2 at output is proportional to N in fixed point arithmetic.

(ii) In floating point FIR filter of length N ($\therefore$ order $N - 1$)

$$\sigma_f^2 = \frac{1}{3} 2^{-2b} (N+1) \sigma_x^2 \sum_{k=0}^{N-1} h^2(k) \left(1 - \frac{k}{N+1}\right) \text{ as given in (10.85)}$$

As $\quad \sigma_x^2 \sum_{k=0}^{N-1} h^2(k) = \sigma_y^2 \qquad \therefore \ \sigma_x^2 \sum_{k=0}^{N-1} h^2(k) \left(1 - \frac{k}{N+1}\right) < \sigma_y^2$

Hence $\quad \sigma_f^2 \leq \frac{1}{3} 2^{-2b} (N+1) \cdot \sigma_y^2$

or $\quad \text{Output NSR} = \dfrac{\sigma_f^2}{\sigma_y^2} \leq \left(\dfrac{1}{3} 2^{-2b} (N+1)\right) \quad \ldots(10.86)$

Hence, RHS of (10.86) is the upper limit of NSR in this case.

(iii) The products were computed and partial sums were accumulated in order to increasing k, *i.e.*, when k is small, *i.e.*, the earlier products are high. Hence, *the products formed first are the ones that are most heavily weighted by the factor* $\left(1 - \frac{k}{N+1}\right)$. To minimize the noise variance, therefore, we should have

$$|h(0)| < |h(1)| < |h(2)| < \ldots < |h(N-1)| \quad \ldots(10.87)$$

Then we expect to achieve the smallest average error in floating point realization. This is in contrast to a fixed-point realization where the error is independent of the placement order of the additions.

(iv) If $|h(0)| < |h(1)| < \ldots |h(N-1)|$ is not satisfied, we may arrange $h(n)$ in ascending order, say, $|h(1)| < |h(0)| < |h(10)| < |h(7)| \ldots$, then add $x(1)h(1)$ to $x(0)h(0)$ and to $x(10)h(10)$ to $x(7)h(7)\ldots$ and so on. This strategy may result in smaller NSR than otherwise possible.

10.13 EFFECT OF FINITE REGISTER LENGTH IN DISCRETE FOURIER TRANSFORM (DFT)

We now, analyses the quantization effect when we compute DFT by conventional method and compute DFT by FFT algorithm.

10.13.1 Analysis of Quantization in Computation of the DFT (Conventional Method to Compute DFT)

We know that

DFT: $$X(k) \triangleq \sum_{n=0}^{N-1} x(n)W_N^{nk}\ , k = 0, 1, 2, \ldots, N-1$$

where $$W_N = e^{-j2\pi/N}$$

Inverse DFT, $$\text{IDFT}\{X(k)\} = x(n) = \frac{1}{N}\sum_{n=0}^{N-1} X(k)W_N^{-nk}\ , n = 0, 1, \ldots, N-1 \quad \ldots(10.88)$$

DFT is generally evaluated by an algorithm, known as FFT (Fast Fourier Transform). When k is small, then straightforward accumulation of product is most reasonable. For a given value of k, Eqn. (10.88) is analogous to the series

$$y(n) = \sum_{k=0}^{N-1} h(k)\cdot x(n-k) \quad (i.e.\ \text{the convolution expressions}) \quad \ldots(10.89a)$$

$$= \sum_{k=0}^{N-1} h(n-k)\cdot x(k) \quad \ldots(10.89b)$$

Here, in DFT, the quantities W_N^{nk} play the role of unit sample response and $X(k)$ play the role of the output.

Each term in the series for DFT (and for IDFT) is, in general, complex. Assume some specific value of k. Then $F(k)$ is the noise/error in computation of kth value of $X(k)$. The model is as shown in Fig. 10.37.

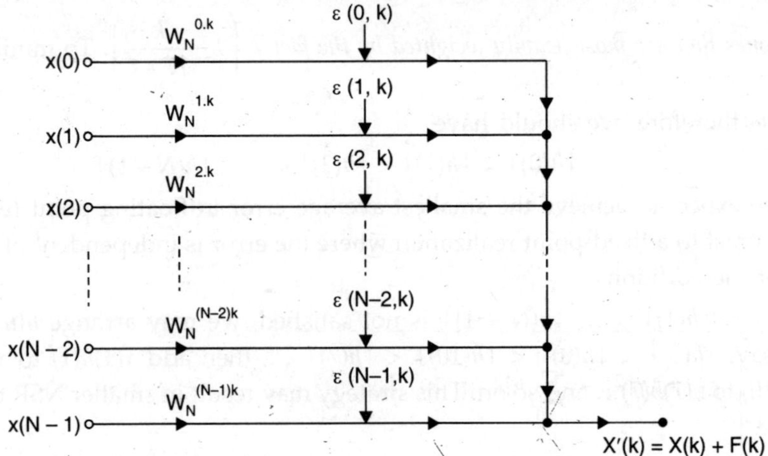

Fig. 10.37. Statistical model for fixed-point round off noise in computation of DFT

Let $\varepsilon(n, k)$ represent the additive error due to rounding off the product $x(n) \cdot W_N^{nk}$. (It is the case of Fixed-Point Arithmetic).

From the above diagram, clearly

$$F(k) = \sum_{n=0}^{N-1} \varepsilon(n, k) \qquad \text{...(10.90)}$$

But the product $x(n) \cdot W_N^{nk} = [\text{Re } x(n) + jI_m x(n)]\left[\cos\left(\frac{2\pi}{N}nk\right) - j\sin\left(\frac{2\pi}{N}nk\right)\right]$

$$= \left[\text{Re } x(n) \cdot \cos\frac{2\pi nk}{N} + I_m x(n) \cdot \sin\frac{2\pi nk}{N}\right]$$

$$+ j\left[I_m x(n) \cos\frac{2\pi nk}{N} - \text{Re } x(n) \sin\frac{2\pi nk}{N}\right]$$

With finite precision and fixed-point arithmetic, after each multiplication we round off and hence we proceed as follows:

$$Q[x(n) \cdot W_N^{nk}] = \text{Re } x(n) \cdot \cos\frac{2\pi nk}{N} + \varepsilon_1(n, k) + I_m x(n) \cdot \sin\frac{2\pi nk}{N} + \varepsilon_2(n, k)$$

$$+ j\left[I_m x(n) \cos\frac{2\pi nk}{N} + \varepsilon_3(n, k) - \text{Re } x(n) \sin\frac{2\pi nk}{N} + \varepsilon_4(n, k)\right]$$

$$\equiv x(n) \cdot W_N^{nk} + [\varepsilon_1(n, k) + \varepsilon_2(n, k)] + j[\varepsilon_3(n, k) + \varepsilon_4(n, k)] \qquad \text{...(10.91)}$$

Assume that:

(*i*) The errors $\varepsilon_i(n, k)$ are uniformly distributed random variables over the range $-\frac{1}{2}2^{-b}$ to $\frac{1}{2}2^{-b}$ *i.e.* $m_{\varepsilon_i} = 0$, $\sigma_{\varepsilon_i}^2 = \frac{1}{12}2^{-2b}$.

(*ii*) All errors are uncorrelated.

(*iii*) All errors are uncorrelated with input $x(n)$ and hence with output '$y(n)$'.

(*iv*) Means of errors = $m_{\varepsilon_i} = 0$, variance of errors: $\sigma_{\varepsilon_i}^2 = \frac{1}{12}2^{-2b}$. Therefore, the mean of error due the complex multiplication is

$$\text{mean } [\varepsilon_1(n, k) + \varepsilon_2(n, k) + j(\varepsilon_3(n, k) + \varepsilon_4(n, k))] = 0 + 0 + j(0 + 0) = 0$$

Also

$$|\varepsilon(n, k)|^2 = [\varepsilon_1(n, k) + \varepsilon_2(n, k)]^2 + [\varepsilon_3(n, k) + \varepsilon_4(n, k)]^2$$

$\therefore$ $$E[\varepsilon(n, k)]^2 = 4 \cdot \frac{1}{12}2^{-2b} = \frac{1}{3}2^{-2b}$$ $\because E[\varepsilon_i(n, k) \cdot \varepsilon_j(n, k)] = 0, i \neq j$ since ε_i, ε_j are uncorrelated.

Hence $$E[|F(k)|^2] = \sum_{n=0}^{N-1} E[|\varepsilon(n, k)|^2] = \sum_{n=0}^{N-1} \frac{1}{3}2^{-2b} \qquad \text{...(10.92)}$$

$\therefore$ $$\sigma_F^2 = \frac{N}{3}2^{-2b} \quad \textit{i.e. } \text{output noise power} \propto N$$

We know that to avoid over flow at the output, we may need scaling by $A(A < 1)$. Since

$$|X(k)| \le \sum_{n=0}^{N-1} |x(n)| < N, \text{ if } x(n) \text{ is unscaled.}$$

In the worst case, we may have to scale by $A = \frac{1}{N}$. For example, for

$$x(n) = 1, 0 \le n \le N-1$$

Then
$$X(k) = \sum_{n=0}^{N-1} 1 \cdot W_N^{nk}, \quad k = 0, 1, 2, \ldots, N-1$$

$$= \begin{cases} N, & k = 0 \\ 0, & k \ne 0 \end{cases}$$

So, it is necessary to scale by $A = \frac{1}{N}$ to have $X(k) \le 1 \ \forall\ k$

Hence
$$x(n) \le \frac{1}{N} \text{ after scaling ensures } X(k) \le 1. \quad \ldots(10.93)$$

If we ensure $x_{max} \le \frac{1}{N}$ then $\sigma_x^2 = \frac{1}{3} \cdot \frac{1}{N^2}$

$$E[X^2(k)] = N \cdot \sigma_x^2 = \frac{N}{3N^2} = \frac{1}{3N}$$

$$\text{Output NSR} = \frac{E[F(k)]}{E[X^2F(k)]} = \frac{N\sigma_B^2}{\frac{1}{3} \cdot \frac{1}{N}} = 3N^2\sigma_B^2 \text{ i.e.} \propto N^2 \quad \ldots(10.94)$$

The above scaling is conservative scaling (or a little over-scaling). Thus, $|x_{max}| < \frac{1}{N}$ ensures no overflow for all values of k.

Note x_{max} may, at times be almost unity and even then no overflow may occur. For example,

$$x(n) = A\delta(n),\ A \approx 1, \text{ will give us } X(k) = \sum_{n=0}^{N-1} A\delta(n)W_N^{nk} = A\ \forall\ k, \text{ i.e., no overflow.}$$

We may not like to scale to $\frac{1}{N}$ at the input stage since the output SNR deteriorates. We may adopt scaling by $\frac{1}{2}$ after each stage. This strategy is called *Block Floating Point* method of scaling.

10.13.2 Quantization Effect in Fixed Point FFT Algorithm

There are many different FFT algorithms, and detailed effect of quantization depends upon specific algorithm used. Most commonly used algorithm for FFT is *Radix-2 form*, as the size of the transform that is computed is an integer power of 2 (*e.g.* 2^v, v an integer). Analysis for decimation-in-time is similar to that of the decimation in frequency. Also, most of the ideal employed in error analysis of the radix-2 algorithm can be utilized in other algorithms.

We note in the typical graph for implementation of FFT, say DIT type.

(*i*) Input signal $x(n)$ forms the $m = 0^{th}$ array

(*ii*) An mth arrays generates an $(m + 1)^{st}$ array

(*iii*) Each array has N signal lines ($N = 8$ in Fig. 10.37(*a*) considered, for example)

(*iv*) the νth array contains the FFT as desired *viz.*, $X(k)$

(*v*) m^{th} array yields $(m + 1)^{st}$ array by using the linear mixing:

$$\left.\begin{aligned} X_{m+1}(p) &= X_m(p) + W_N^r X_m(q) \\ X_{m+1}(q) &= X_m(p) - W_N^r X_m(q) \end{aligned}\right\} \text{ Decimation-in-time} \quad \ldots(10.94a)$$

integers varies with p, q and m depending on manner of FFT computation

$$\left.\begin{aligned} X_{m+1}(p) &= X_m(p) - X_m(q) \\ X_{m+1}(q) &= [X_m(p) - X_m(q)]W_N^r \end{aligned}\right\} \text{ Decimation-in-frequency} \quad \ldots(10.90b)$$

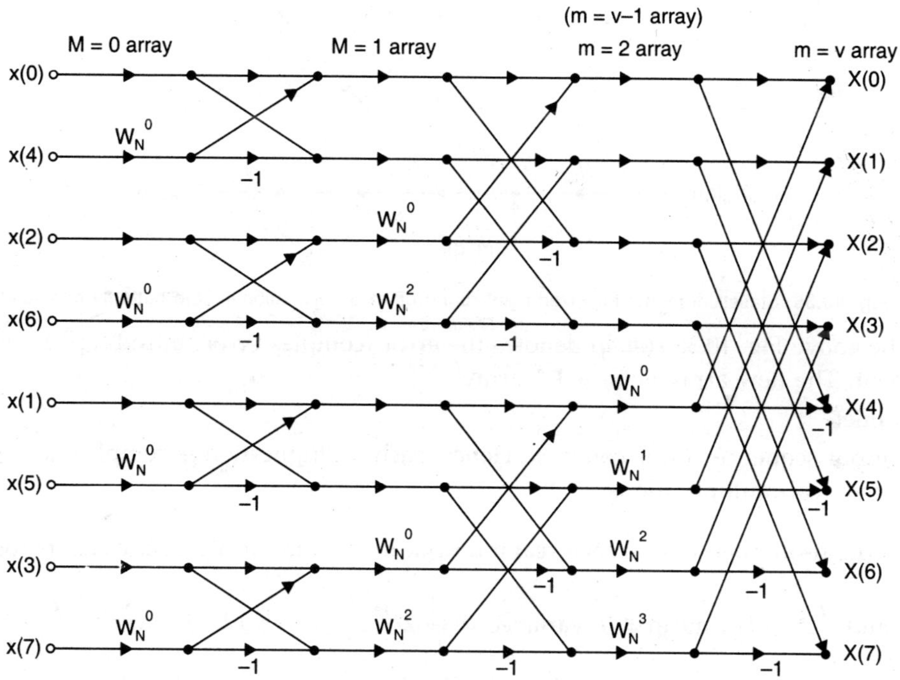

Fig. 10.37. (*a*) Flow graph for decimation in time (DIT) FFT Algorithm

Some Important Results in FFT graph $\nu = 3$ here, $N = 2^{\nu} = 8$

1. Number of butterflies originating at each stage $= \dfrac{N}{2}$ (4 here, since $N = 8$)
2. Number of stages in the FFT algorithm $= \nu = \log_2 N$ (3 here)

3. Total number of butterflies in the complete implementation = $\frac{N}{2}\cdot\nu$ (12 here)
4. Signal arrays = $\nu + 1$. Zeroth array given $x(n)$; ν^{th} array gives $X(k)$
5. Total butterflies connected to each output $X(k)$ are equal to (*i.e.* $2^{\nu} - 1$) = $N - 1 \approx N$, for N large
6. Number of butterflies originating at m^{th} array which get connected to output node $= 2^{\nu-m-1}$, $m = 0, 1, \ldots, \nu - 1$ (*i.e.* here 4 from 0th array, 2 from 1st array and 1 from $(\nu - 1)^{th}$ array)
7. (*a*) Number of butterflies connected to an "output" at m^{th} array = $2^m - 1$ butterflies from previous stages.
   (*b*) Number of signal lines from $x(n)$ connected to each signal of m-th array = 2^m.
8. $(N - 1)$ butterflies contribute $(N-1)\sigma_B^2$ noise at the output node, where $\sigma_B^2 = \frac{1}{3}2^{-2b}$ ...(10.94*c*)

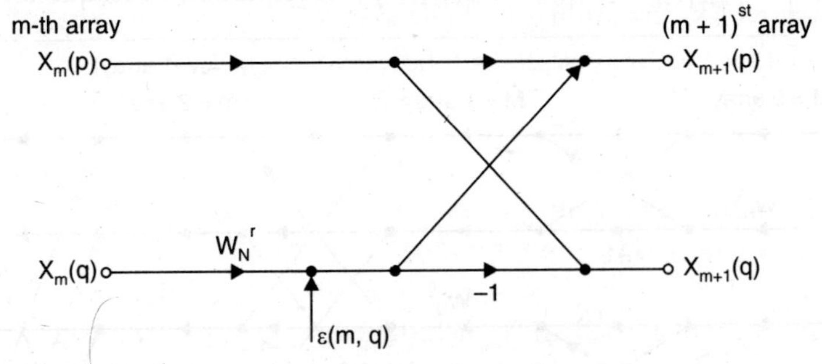

Fig. 10.38. Statistical model for Fixed-point round off in a decimation-in-time butterfly computation.

In the above Fig. 10.38 $\varepsilon(m, q)$ denotes the error (complex error) introduced in m^{th} array for q^{th} element. The new array is $(m + 1)^{st}$ array.

Assume:

(*i*) Input sequence $x(n)$ is complex. Hence, each multiplication is complex *i.e.* equivalent to four real multiplications.

(*ii*) Round-off noise due to each real multiplication is uniformly distributed between $-\frac{1}{2}2^{-b}$ and $\frac{1}{2}2^{-b}$, *i.e.*, mean = 0, variance = $\frac{1}{12}2^{-2b}$.

(*iii*) All noise sources due to each multiplication are uncorrelated with each other.

(*iv*) All the noise sources are uncorrelated with inputs, $x(n)$, and consequently also uncorrelated with the results of computation in each array.

Thus,

$$E[|\varepsilon(m, q)|^2] = 4\times\frac{1}{12}2^{-2b} = \frac{1}{3}2^{-2b}$$

Butterfly noise due to multiplications (rounding off): $\sigma_B^2 = \frac{1}{3}2^{-2b}$ ...(10.94*d*)

Essentiality of Scaling

Note that:

(*i*) The transmission function from any node in the graph to any other node, to which it is connected, is multiplication by a complex constant W_N^r of unity magnitude.

(*ii*) Each output node connects $(N - 1)$ butterflies. (Note the output $X(0)$ and similarly each output node is fed from $(N - 1)$ previous butterflies)

Thus, at each output node, the output noise $= (N - 1)\sigma_B^2$

$$E[|F(k)|^2] \approx N\sigma_B^2,\ N \text{ large:} \quad \text{where } \sigma_B^2 = \frac{1}{3}2^{-2b} \qquad \ldots(10.94e)$$

(*iii*) As

$$\max(|X_m(p)|,\ |X_m(p)|) \le \max(|X_{m+1}(p)|,\ |X_{m+1}(q)|) \qquad \ldots(10.94f)$$

and also

$$\max(|X_{m+1}(p)|,\ |X_{m+1}(p)|) \le 2 \cdot \max(|X_m(p)|,\ |X_m(q)|) \qquad \ldots(10.94g)$$

It simply means that the maximum modulus is non-decreasing from stage to stage. In order to ensure the magnitude at each output point to be < unity, the magnitude of the points in each array must be ensured less than unity, *i.e.* there should be no overflow in any of the array points. To ensure no over flow, we may scale as follows:

(*i*) Scale $x(n)$ in the very beginning *i.e.*, $x(n) < \frac{1}{N}$, $n = 0$ to $N - 1$. This is necessary and sufficient condition to ensure no over flow *i.e.*, to ensure $|X(k)| < 1,\ 0 \le k \le N - 1$.

(*ii*) We may do distributed scaling *i.e.*, scale 1/2 each signal line before computing $(m + 1)^{th}$ array from m^{th} array. Here, we scale by 1/2 the signal lines at $m = 0$ to $m = v - 1$ array stages. Then output at each array, including $m = v$ (*i.e.*, final outputs) would be guarantedly less than unity in magnitude.

(A) Bulk Scaling at array $m = 0$ (*i.e.*, Scaling $x(n)$ only)-Fixed Point FFT

This approach is also called Lumped scaling

(*i*) Assume white noise input $x(n)$, which is uncorrelated with successive sequence values

(*ii*) Real part of $x(n)$ and imaginary part of $x(n)$ are uncorrelated and each has an amplitude density uniformly distributed between $-\frac{1}{\sqrt{2}N}$ and $\frac{1}{\sqrt{2}N}$

As
$$|x(n)| = \frac{1}{N} \qquad \ldots(10.95a)$$

$\therefore$
$$|x(n)|^2 = \frac{1}{N^2} \qquad \ldots(10.95b)$$

i.e.,
$$|\text{Re}\, x(n)|^2 + |I_m x(n)|^2 = \frac{1}{N^2} \qquad \ldots(10.95c)$$

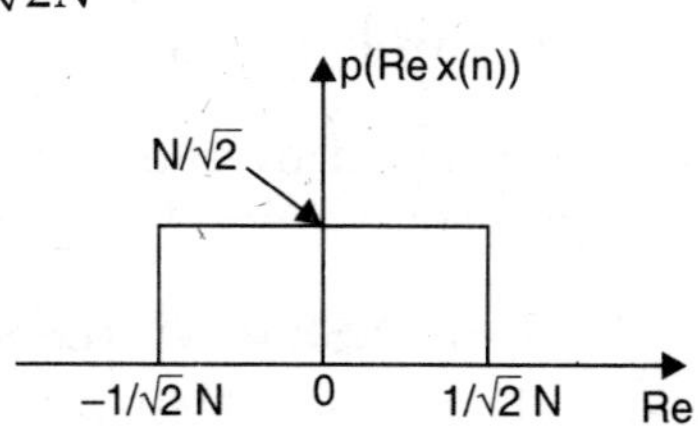

Fig. 10.39. Showing distribution of Re [$x(n)$]

mean = 0 variance = $\frac{1}{3} \cdot \frac{1}{2N^2}$

Assuming Re $x(n)$ and $I_m x(n)$ equally likely we can take

$$|\text{Re}\, x(n)|^2 = |I_m x(n)|^2 = \frac{1}{2} \cdot \frac{1}{N^2} = \left(\frac{1}{\sqrt{2}N}\right)^2 \quad \text{(Note this step)}$$

$$\therefore \quad E[|x(n)|^2] = E[|\text{Re}\,x(n)|^2 + |I_m x(n)|^2]$$

$$= E[|\text{Re}\,x(n)^2|] + E[|I_m x(n)^2|] \quad (\because \text{ Real and imaginary parts have been assumed uncorrelated})$$

$$= \frac{1}{3}\left(\frac{1}{\sqrt{2N}}\right)^2 + \frac{1}{3}\left(\frac{1}{\sqrt{2N}}\right)^2$$

$$= \frac{1}{3N^2}$$

Thus, after necessary bulk scaling (at the very beginning) $x(n)$

$$\left.\begin{aligned} m_x &= 0 \\ \sigma_x^2 &= \frac{1}{3N^2} \end{aligned}\right\} \text{ for scaling by } \frac{1}{N} \text{ at } x(n) \text{ itself} \qquad \ldots(10.96)$$

As
$$X(k) = \sum_{n=0}^{N-1} x(n)\,.\,e^{-j\frac{2\pi nk}{N}}$$

$$\text{mean of } X(k) = 0 \quad \text{as} \quad m_x = 0 \qquad \text{(white noise input)}$$

$$E[|X(k)|^2] = \sum_{n=0}^{N-1} E[|x(n)|^2\,.\,|(e^{-j2\pi nk/N})^2|]$$

$$\nearrow = 1$$

$$= \sum_{n=0}^{N-1} E[|x(n)|^2]$$

$$= \sum_{n=0}^{N-1} \sigma_x^{2*} = N\sigma_x^2 = N\,.\,\frac{1}{3N^2} = \frac{1}{3N}$$

$$\text{Output NSR} = \frac{E[|F(k)|^2]}{E[|X(k)|^2]} = \frac{N\,.\,\sigma_B^2}{(1/3N)} = 3N^2\sigma_B^2 \qquad \ldots(10.97)$$

$$\text{where} \quad \sigma_B^2 = \frac{1}{3}2^{-2b} \quad \text{Bulk scaling of } x(n) \text{ by } N.$$

(B) Distributed Scaling-Fixed Point FFT: We have seen that for bulk scaling *i.e.*, making $x(n)$ to $\frac{1}{N}$ $x(n)$ to avoid overflow of $X(k)$ outputs, the output NSR = $3N^2\sigma_B^2$ (Eqn. 10.57) (where $\sigma_B^2 = \frac{1}{3}$ 2^{-2b}) *i.e.*, NSR $\propto N^2$. The increase of N by a factor of 2 require increasing b to $b + 1$ to maintain the same NSR. The assumption of a white noise input $x(n)$ is not critical for this result.

---

* $$E\{|x(k)|^2\} = E\left\{\left(\sum_{n=0}^{N-1} x(n)^2\right)\right\} = E\left\{\sum_{n=0}^{N-1}\sum_{k=0}^{N-1} |x(n)\,.\,x(k)|\right\}$$

$$= \sum_n \sum_k \sigma_x^2\,\delta(x-k) = \sum_k \sigma_x^2 = N\sigma_x^2$$

In fact, for a variety of other inputs, the NSR is still proportional to N^2, with only the constant of proportionality changing. Also, when we make $x(n)$ to $\frac{1}{N}$ $x(n)$ by scaling, the input signal '$\frac{1}{N}x(n)$' has very low power $\left(=\frac{1}{N^2}\sigma_x^2\right)$, which implies deterioration of SNR due to bulk scaling.

If input is kept at a level $x(n) < 1$, we may scale $x(n)$ to $\frac{1}{2}x(n)$ before computing the outputs for $m = 1$ array. We may scale each signal line by $\frac{1}{2}$ before we use these signal to compute the $(m + 1)^{st}$ array from m-th array. Hence, we scale by $\frac{1}{2}$ (each signal line) every time at an array where butterflies originate.

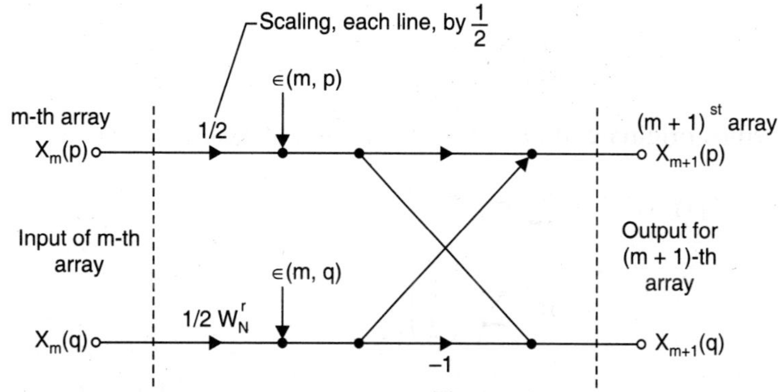

Fig. 10.40. Scaling of m-th stage (array) outputs by 1/2. Butterfly showing scaling multipliers and associated fixed-point round off noise $\varepsilon(m, p)$, $\varepsilon(m, q)$

We know that

$$E[|\varepsilon(m, p)|^2] = E[|\varepsilon(m, q)|^2] = \sigma_B^2 = \frac{1}{3}\ 2^{-2b} \quad \text{(assuming all complex multiplications)}$$

Noise power going each node due to scaling as above = $2\sigma_B^2$. (Note this step)

A noise source originated at m-th array (when we compute signals for $(m + 1)^{st}$ array – as shown in Fig. 10.40) will propagate to the output array (v-th array) after further multiplication by a complex constant with magnitude $\left(\frac{1}{2}\right)^{v-(m+1)}$ (scaling at $m + 1$, $m + 2$, ... till $v - 1$ array stages, and no scaling at v-th, the output, array stage).

No. of butterflies originating at m-th array which contribute to the output node = 2^{v-1-m}

(When $m = 0$, 2^{v-1} butterflies originating here connect to output) ...(10.98)

∴ Noise contributed to output node due m-th array originated butterflies

$$= (2\sigma_B^2)\ 2^{v-1-m} \quad ...(10.99)$$

(∵ in scaling here $2\sigma_B^2$ noise is contributed to each node of $(m + 1)$-th array)

Thus, due to scaling in each line of m-th array signal to compute $(m + 1)$-th array signals the result are

Number of butterflies originating here, connected to final output = 2^{v-m-1} ...(10.100)

Amount of noise to each node of $(m + 1)$-th array = $2\sigma_B^2$ ...(10.101)

This noise undergoes subsequent scaling by a factor $= \left(\frac{1}{2}\right)^{v-m-1}$ ...(10.102)

Thus, total noise contributed to final output due to m-th stage butterflies origination is

$$\sigma_m^2 = \left(\underbrace{2\sigma_B^2}_{\substack{\text{one butterfly}\\\text{inject noise}\\\text{in a node}}} \cdot \underbrace{2^{v-m-1}}_{\substack{\text{butterfly}\\\text{from here to}\\\text{output node}}} \right) \cdot \underbrace{\left(\frac{1}{2}\right)^{2(v-m-1)}}_{\substack{\text{subsequent}\\\text{scaling}\\\text{effect}^*}}$$

$$= 2\sigma_B^2 \cdot \left(\frac{1}{2}\right)^{v-m-1}$$

$$= 4\sigma_B^2 \cdot \left(\frac{1}{2}\right)^{v-m}$$

As the butterflies originate at $m = 0, 1, 2, ..., v - 1$ stages, we have

$$E[|F(k)|^2] = \sum_{m=0}^{v-1} \sigma_m^2 \qquad ...(10.103)$$

$$= 4\sigma_B^2 \sum_{m=0}^{v-1} \left(\frac{1}{2}\right)^{v-m}$$

$$= 4\sigma_B^2 \cdot \frac{1}{N} \sum_{m=0}^{v-1} 2^m \qquad \because \left(\frac{1}{2}\right)^v = \frac{1}{2^v} = \frac{1}{N}$$

$$= 4\sigma_B^2 \cdot \frac{1}{N}\left(\frac{2^v - 1}{2-1}\right)$$

$$= 4\sigma_B^2 \cdot \frac{N-1}{N} \approx 4\sigma_B^2$$

$$\text{Output NSR} = \frac{E[|F(k)|^2]}{E[|X(k)|^2]^{**}} = \frac{4\sigma_B^2}{\frac{1}{3N}} = \underset{\substack{\uparrow\\(= 4.2^{-2b} \,.\, N)}}{(12\sigma_B^2) \,.\, N} \qquad ...(10.104)$$

Distributed scaling

---

* If variance of $x(n) = \sigma_x^2$

Then variance of $Ax(n) = A^2\sigma_x^2$

** As $|x(n)| \leq 1 \quad \therefore \quad \sigma_x^2 = \frac{1}{3} \quad \sigma_y^2$ (unscaled) $= N.\, \sigma_x^2 = N/3$. Due to enroute scaling by $(1/N)$, it gets reduced by $(1/N)^2$

$\therefore \quad \sigma_y^2$ (after distributed scaling) $= (1/N)^2.\, N/3 = \frac{1}{3N}$

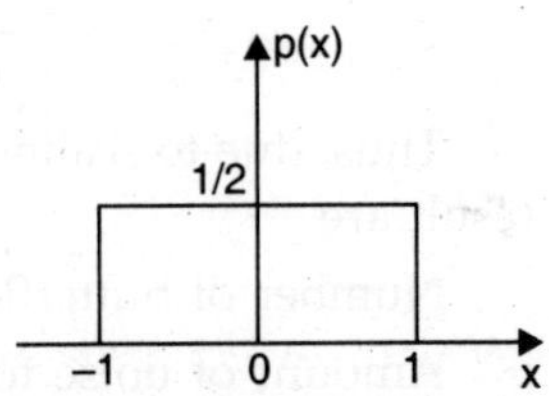

Discussion on Distributed Scaling at each Stage

(*i*) The output NSR is $\propto N$ rather at N^2 as was in the scaling at the beginning (bulk scaling or lumped scaling) where we ensure $x(n) < \frac{1}{N}$.

(*ii*) The actual noise contents are $E[|F(k)|^2] = 4\sigma_B^2 = \frac{4}{3}2^{-2b}$, which is of very small value.

(*iii*) Due to scaling by $\frac{1}{2}$ at each array stage ($m = 0, 1, \ldots v - 1$) to avoid overflow, the output signal power is $E[|X(k)|^2] = \frac{1}{3N}$. However, the input signal level in distributed scaling is N times higher these for the lumped/bulk scaling. Here, it is $x(n) \leq 1$, there it was $x(n) \leq \frac{1}{N}$. Most of the noise has been shifted off by distributed scalings.

(*iv*) The assumption of white noise signal $x(n)$ is not essential in the analysis. The basic result of half a bit per stage increase holds. (Note that Number of stages are v. If v is increased by 1 *i.e.*, $N' = 2^{v+1} = 2N$, then now NSR will be 2 × (NSR for N) *i.e.*, $\text{NSR}|_{\text{new}} = 2 \times (4N \cdot 2^{-2b})$. Similarly, if we increase stages by 2, $N'' = 2^{v+2} = 4N$ and "$\text{NSR}|_{\text{new}}$" $= 4(4N2^{-2b})$. We need to increase b to $b + 1$ *i.e.*, by 1 bit to maintain old NSR, $\because 4(4N2^{-2(b+1)}) = 4N2^{-2b}$. Hence, we **have half a bit per stage increase**). The basic result of half a bit per stage increase holds for a broad class of signals, only the constant 4×2^{-2b}, in NSR $= 4N2^{-2b}$, would change for different signals.

(*v*) In another approach called block floating point, we decide to divide by 2 at only those stages where overflow occurs. Originally, $x(n)$ is normalised such that $x(n) < 1$. For every addition if any overflow is detected, the entire array is divided by 2 and the computation continues. The number of necessary shifts (*i.e.*, division by 2) is counted to determine a ratio factor (or exponent) for the entire final array. Output NSR depends strongly on how many overflows occur and at what stages of the computation they occur. The position and timing of overflow are determined by the signal being transformed.

(*vi*) Obviously, the distributed scaling is preferred to lumped/bulk scaling due to much lower NSR here.

10.13.3 Quantization Effect in Floating-Point FFT Algorithm (DIT Case)

$$X_{m+1}(p) = X_m(p) + W_N^r X_m(q) \quad \ldots(10.105a)$$

$$X_{m+1}(q) = X_m(p) - W_N^r X_m(q) \quad \ldots(10.105b)$$

As $X_m(p), X_m(q), \ldots, W_N^r$ are complex, we can write the relation:

$$\text{Re } X_{m+1}(p) + j\, I_m X_{m+1}(p) = [\text{Re } X_m(p) + jI_m X_m(p)] + [\text{Re } W_N^r + jI_m W_N^r]\,[\text{Re } X_m(q) + j\, I_m X_m(q)]$$

i.e.,

$$\text{Re } X_{m+1}(p) = \text{Re } X_m(p) + (\text{Re } W_N^r)(\text{Re } X_m(q)) - (I_m W_N^r)(I_m X_m(q))$$

$$I_m X_{m+1}(p) = I_m X_m(p) + (\text{Re } W_N^r)(I_m X_m(q)) + (I_m W_N^r)(\text{Re } X_m(q))$$

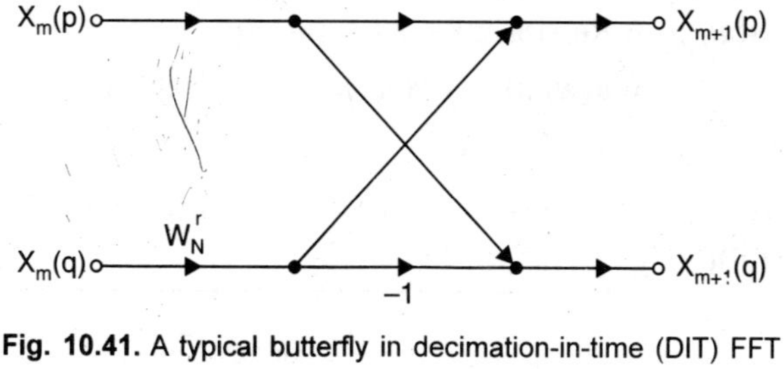

Fig. 10.41. A typical butterfly in decimation-in-time (DIT) FFT

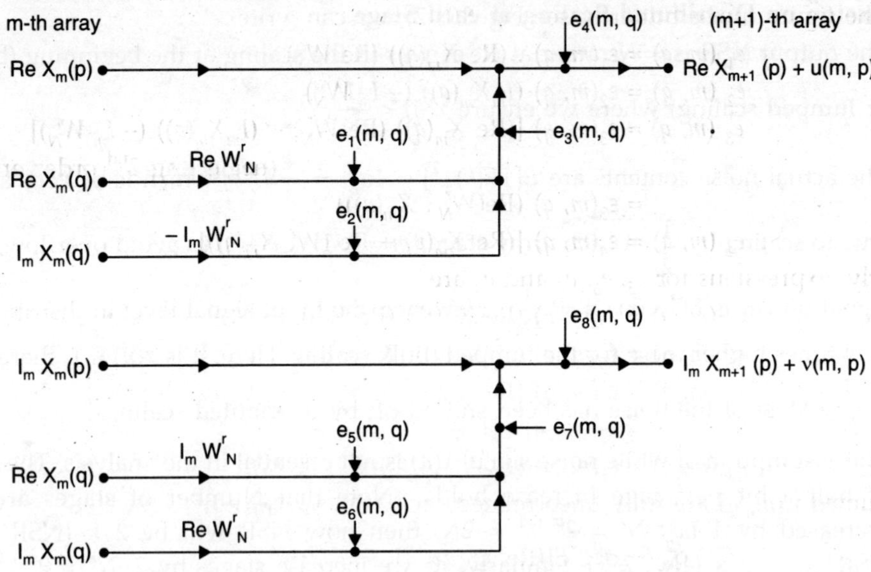

Fig. 10.42. Noisy butterfly computation for Floating point arithmetic.

Assumptions:

(*i*) Rounding off noise/noises are introduced, they have zero means.

(*ii*) Neglect the second-order error terms so that noise sources are introduced after each multiplication and addition.

(*iii*) We add only two quantities at a time (and that is how a computer does).

(*iv*) Noise sources are uncorrelated and their variance is proportional to the variance of the signal at the node.

(*v*) Input $x(n)$ is a white noise.

Other Useful Assumptions/Results

1. $E[(W_N^r)^2] = 1 \quad \because \quad |e^{-j2\pi r/N}| = 1$

2. $E[(\text{Re } W_N^r)^2] = E[(I_m\, W_N^r)^2] = \dfrac{1}{2}$

3. $E[(\text{Re } X_m(p))^2] = E[(I_m\, X_m(p)^2] = \dfrac{1}{2} E[(X_m(p))^2]$

4. $E[(X_m(p))^2] = E[(X_m(q))^2]$

5. $\sigma_s^2 = \sigma_u^2 + \sigma_v^2$, and $|s|^2 = |u|^2 + |v|^2$

6. Noisy output $X'_{m+1}(p)$ = actual non-noisy output $X_{m+1}(p)$ + Noise $s(m, p)$

   where $\qquad s(m, p) = \text{Re } s(m, p) + j\, I_m\, s(m, p)$

   $\qquad\qquad \triangleq u(m, p) + j\, v(m, p)$

   and hence $\qquad |s|^2 = |u|^2 + |v|^2$

7. $X_m(p)$ and $X_m(q)$ are uncorrelated *i.e.*, $E[X_m(p) \,.\, X_m(q)] = E[X_m(p)].\, E[X_m(q)] = 0 \times 0 = 0$ for white noise inputs.

...(10.106)

From the figure (noise butterfly see Fig. 10.42), we can write

$$e_1\,(m, q) = \varepsilon_1(m, q)\ .\ (\text{Re}\ X_m(q))\ (\text{Re}\ W_N^r)$$
$$e_2\,(m, q) = \varepsilon_2(m, q)\ (I_m X_m(q))\ (-\ I_m\ W_N^r)$$
$$e_3\,(m, q) \approx \varepsilon_3(m, q)\ [(\text{Re}\ X_m(q))\ (\text{Re}\ W_N^r) + (I_m X_m(q))\ (-\ I_m\ W_N^r)]$$

(neglecting 2nd order error terms)

$$= \varepsilon_3(m, q)\ (\text{Re}(W_N^r\ .\ X_m(q)))$$
$$e_4\,(m, q) = \varepsilon_4(m, q)\ [(\text{Re}\ X_m(p) + \text{Re}\ (W_N^r\ X_m(q))]$$

Similarly, expressions for e_5, e_6, e_7 and e_8 are

$$e_5\,(m, q) = \varepsilon_5(m, q)\ (\text{Re}\ X_m(q))\ (\text{Re}\ W_N^r)$$
$$e_6\,(m, q) = \varepsilon_6(m, q)\ (I_m\ X_m(q))\ (\text{Re}\ W_N^r)$$
$$e_7\,(m, q) = \varepsilon_7(m, q)\ [\text{Re}\ X_m(q)\ .\ I_m\ W_N^r + I_m\ X_m(q)\ .\ \text{Re}\ W_N^r]$$
$$= \varepsilon_7\,(m, q)\ .\ (I_m\ W_N^r\ X_m(q))$$
$$e_8\,(m, q) = \varepsilon_8(m, q)\ [I_m\ W_N^r\ X_m(q) + I_m\ X_m(p)]$$

As assumed $\varepsilon_i(m, q)$ are fully uncorrelated each with variance σ_ε^2.

$$\sigma_{e_1}^2 = \sigma_\varepsilon^2\ .\ E[(\text{Re}^2 X_m(q))^2\ (\text{Re}\ W_N^r)^2] \quad \text{...(10.107}a\text{)}$$

$$= \sigma_\varepsilon^2\ .\ \frac{1}{2}\ E[X_m^2(q)]\ .\ \frac{1}{2} = \frac{1}{4}\ \sigma_\varepsilon^2\ E[X_m^2(q)]$$

$$\sigma_{e_2}^2 = \sigma_\varepsilon^2\ .\ \frac{1}{2}\ E[X_m^2(q)]\cdot\frac{1}{2} = \frac{1}{4}\ \sigma_\varepsilon^2\ E[X_m^2(q)] \quad \text{...(10.107}b\text{)}$$

$$\sigma_{e_3}^2 = \sigma_\varepsilon^2\ .\ 2\ .\ \left[\frac{1}{4} E\,\{X_m^2\,(q)\}\right] = \frac{1}{2}\ \sigma_\varepsilon^2\ E[X_m^2(q)] \quad \text{...(10.107}c\text{)}$$

$$\sigma_{e_4}^2 = \sigma_\varepsilon^2\ .\ E[\{\text{Re}\ X_m(p) + \text{Re}(W_N^r\ X_m(q))\}^2]$$

$$= \sigma_\varepsilon^2\ .\ E\Big[\{\text{Re}^2\ X_m(p) + \text{Re}^2(W_N^r\ X_m(q)) + \underbrace{2\ .\ \text{Re}\ X_m(p)..\ \text{Re}(W_N^r\ X_m(q))}_{\text{uncorreleted}\ \therefore\ E[.]=0}\Big]$$

$$= \sigma_\varepsilon^2\ .\ \left[\frac{1}{2} E[X_m^2(p)] + \frac{1}{2} E[X_m^2(q)] + 0\right]$$

$$= \sigma_\varepsilon^2\ .\ E[X_m^2(q)]\ (\text{using}\ E[X_m^2(p)] = E[X_m^2(q)]) \quad \text{...(10.107}d\text{)}$$

Similarly, we can write

$$\sigma_{e_5}^2 = \frac{1}{4}\ \sigma_\varepsilon^2\ .\ E[X_m(q)] \quad \text{...(10.108}a\text{)}$$

$$\sigma_{e_6}^2 = \frac{1}{4}\ \sigma_\varepsilon^2\ .\ E[X_m^2(q)] \quad \text{...(10.108}b\text{)}$$

$$\sigma_{e_7}^2 = \frac{1}{2}\ \sigma_\varepsilon^2\ .\ E[X_m^2(q)] \quad \text{...(10.108}c\text{)}$$

$$\sigma_{e_8}^2 = \sigma_\varepsilon^2\ .\ E[X_m^2(q)] \quad \text{...(10.108}d\text{)}$$

Hence,

$$E[u^2(m, p)] = \sigma_{e_1}^2 + \sigma_{e_2}^2 + \sigma_{e_3}^2 + \sigma_{e_4}^2$$
$$= 2\sigma_\varepsilon^2\ .\ E[X_m^2(q)] \quad \text{...(10.109}a\text{)}$$

Similarly, $E[v^2(m, p)] = \sigma_{e_5}^2 + \sigma_{e_6}^2 + \sigma_{e_7}^2 + \sigma_{e_8}^2$

$= 2\sigma_\varepsilon^2 \,.\, E[X_m^2(q)]$ ...(10.109b)

i.e., $E[s^2(m, p)] = E[u^2(m, p)] + E[v^2(m, p)]$ as u, v are uncorrelated

$= 4\sigma_\varepsilon^2 \,.\, E[X_m^2(q)]$ ...(10.109c)

Thus, we note that the variance of noise $E[s^2(m, p)]$ generated for computing $(m + 1)^{st}$ array is $4\sigma_\varepsilon^2$ times the mean square magnitude of m-th array signal. But each signal of m-th array is connected to 2^m signals from $x(n)$ array (i.e. $m = 0$ array)

$\therefore$ Variance of signal at each line of m-th array $E[X_m^2(q)] = 2^m\, \sigma_x^2$ ...(10.110)

No. of butterflies originating at m-th array that contribute to each output node $= 2^{v-m-1}$ ...(10.111)

$\therefore$ Noise contributed to each output node due to butterflies originating at m-th array

$$= \underbrace{(2^m\sigma_x^2)}_{E[X_m^2(q)]}\, 4\sigma_\varepsilon^2,\, 2^{v-m-1}$$

$$\therefore \quad E[F(k)^2] = \sum_{m=0}^{v-1} (2^m \sigma_x^2)\, (4\sigma_\varepsilon^2)\, (2^{v-m-1})$$

$$= 4\sigma_\varepsilon^2 \,.\, \sigma_x^2 \,.\, \frac{1}{2} \sum_{m=0}^{v-1} N \;=\; 2\sigma_\varepsilon^2\, 2\sigma_x{}^2\, N \,.\, v \qquad ...(10.112)$$

We have found that

$$E[|F(k)|^2] = 2\sigma_\varepsilon^2 \,.\, \sigma_x^2 \,.\, \mathrm{N} \,.\, v$$

Also,
$$E[|X(k)|] = E\left[\left|\sum_{n=0}^{N-1} x(n) \,.\, W_N^{nk}\right|^2\right]$$

$$= E\left[\sum_{n=0}^{N-1} |x(n)|^2\right] \qquad \because\; E[|W_N^{nk}|^2] = 1$$

$$= N\sigma_x^2$$

$$\therefore \quad \text{output NSR} = \frac{E[|F(k)|^2]}{E[|X(k)|^2]}$$

$$= \frac{2\sigma_\varepsilon^2\, \sigma_x^2\, Nv}{N\sigma_x^2}$$

$$= 2v\, \sigma_\varepsilon^2$$

Thus,

in floating-point, rounding off FFT computation output NSR $= 2v\, \sigma_\varepsilon^2$; $\sigma_\varepsilon^2 = \frac{1}{3} 2^{-2b}$

...(10.113)

Discussion:

(i) Whereas in fixed-point case (with scaling by $\frac{1}{2}$ at each stage) NSR is $\propto$ N, but in floating point NSR $\propto v$ i.e., to $\log_2 N$. As $\sigma_\varepsilon^2 \propto 2^{-2b}$, quadrupling v i.e., making v to $4v$ (i.e., making N to N^4), NSR increases, which can be restored to previous value of NSR by increasing bits b by one. Thus, in floating point arithmetic NSR increases very little (significantly milder) as compared to fixed-point arithmetic. If N is increased to N^4, we need only 1 bit more to maintain the same NSR. Even though in floating-point, the errors are generated both after addition and multiplication, the overall output NSR $\propto \log_2 N$. Increasing N = 256 to $(256)^4$ would need only one bit extra to maintain the same NSR.

(*ii*) (Afore—mentioned) observation clearly shows the superiority of floating-point arithmetic system over the fixed-point arithmetic system.

Solved Examples

EXAMPLE 10.1: *The first-order filter shown in figure is implemented in four-bit (including sign) fixed-point two's-complement fractional arithmetic. Products are rounded to four-bit representation. Using $x(n) = 0.10\ \delta(n)$, determine:*

(a) The first five outputs if $\alpha = 0.75$. Does the filter go into a limit cycle?

(b) The first five outputs if $\alpha = 0.50$. Does the filter go into a limit cycle?

(c) The first five outputs if $\alpha = 0.40$. Does the filter go into a limit cycle?

SOLUTION: $y(n) = Q[x(n)] + Q[\alpha y(n-1)]$

Note that $x(n)$ also needs quantization.

(*a*) $\alpha = 0.75$, $x(n) = 0.1\delta(n)$

$$\therefore \quad y(n) = Q[0.1\delta(n)] + Q[0.75\ y(n-1)]$$

$$\therefore \quad y(0) = Q[0.1] + Q[0.75\underbrace{y(-1)}_{=0}] = \frac{1}{8} \qquad \left(0.1 \equiv \Delta\ 000\vdots 110 \xrightarrow{Q[.]} \Delta\ 001 = \frac{1}{8}\right)$$

$$y(1) = Q[0.75\ y(0)] = Q\left[0.75 \times \frac{1}{8}\right] = Q\left[\frac{3}{32}\right] = \frac{1}{8} \qquad \left(\frac{3}{32} \equiv \Delta\ 000\vdots 11 \xrightarrow{Q} 001 = \frac{1}{8}\right)$$

$$y(2) = Q[0.75\ y(1)] = Q\left[0.75 \times \frac{1}{8}\right] = \frac{1}{8}$$

$$y(3) = y(4) = \frac{1}{8}$$

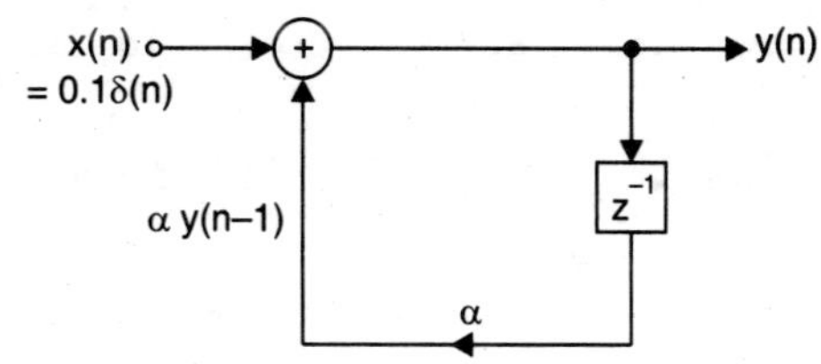

Fig. Ex. 10.1. The given filter. $1 + b = 4$ $\therefore\ b = 3$

$\therefore$ Limit cycle occurs settling at $\frac{1}{8}$. **Ans.**

(*b*) $\alpha = 0.50$, $x(n) = 0.1\delta(n)$

$$y(n) = Q[0.1\delta(n)] + Q[0.50\ y(n-1)]$$

$$\therefore \quad y(0) = Q[0.1] + 0 = \frac{1}{8} \text{ as in the case } (a)$$

$$y(1) = Q[0.50\ y(0)] = Q\left[0.50 \times \frac{1}{8}\right] = Q\left[\frac{1}{16}\right] = \frac{1}{8}$$

$$\left(\frac{1}{16} \equiv \Delta\ 000\vdots 100 \xrightarrow{Q[.]} \Delta 001 = \frac{1}{8}\right)$$

$$y(2) = y(3) = y(4) = \frac{1}{8} \quad \therefore \text{ limit cycle settles at } \frac{1}{8} \textbf{ Ans.}$$

(c) Here, $\alpha = 0.40$, $x(n) = 0.1\delta(n)$

$$y(n) = Q[x(n)] + Q[\alpha y(n-1)]$$

$$y(0) = Q[0.1] + 0 = \frac{1}{8} \text{ as in earlier case}$$

$$y(1) = Q[x(1)] + Q[0.40\, y(0)]$$

$$= 0 + Q\left[0.40 \times \frac{1}{8}\right]$$

$$= Q[0.05] = Q\left[\frac{1}{20}\right] = 0 \qquad \left(\frac{1}{20} \equiv \Delta\, 000 \vdots 01100 \cdots \xrightarrow{Q[.]} = 0\right)$$

$$y(2) = Q[x(2)] = Q[0.40 \times y(1)]$$

$$= 0 + 0 = 0 \qquad \because x(2) = 0, y(1) = 0$$

$$\therefore \qquad y(3) = y(4) = y(5) = \ldots = 0$$

i.e., there are no oscillations of a limit cycle here. **Ans.**

Or directly: For zero cycle to occur, we must have

$$|\omega(n-1)| \le \frac{\frac{1}{2}.2^{-b}}{1-|\alpha|} \qquad \text{[From (10.33)]}$$

Here
$$\frac{\frac{1}{2}.2^{-b}}{1-|\alpha|} = \frac{\frac{1}{2} \times 2^{-3}}{(1-0.4)}$$

$$= \frac{1}{16} \times \frac{10}{16} = \frac{5}{48} < \frac{1}{8}$$

For $b = 3$, $|\omega(n-1)|$ minimum is $\frac{1}{8}$ $\left(\Delta\, 000 \vdots, \text{ weight of 3rd bit is } \frac{1}{8}\right)$

since $|\omega(n-1)|$ cannot be less than $\frac{5}{48}$ but zero.

$\therefore$ $|\omega(n-1)| = 0$ *i.e.*, no limit cycle exist here.

EXAMPLE 10.2: *What is meant by zero-input limit-cycle as observed in the IIR digital systems? Illustrate your answer by taking system's impulse response: $h(n) = (0.75)^n u(n)$*

Input to the system: $x(n) = 0.50\ \delta(n)$

Shift registers of the system here $1 + b = 1 + 4$ bits (i.e., $b = 4$ bits)

SOLUTION: $y(n) = Q[x(n)] + Q[\alpha y(n-1)]$

$$= Q[x(n)] + Q[0.75\,.\,\omega(n-1)]$$

$$\omega(0) = Q[x(0)] + Q[0.75\,.\,\omega(n-1)]$$

↑

assumed zero (relaxed system)

$$= Q[0.5] + 0 = \frac{1}{2} = \frac{4}{8}$$

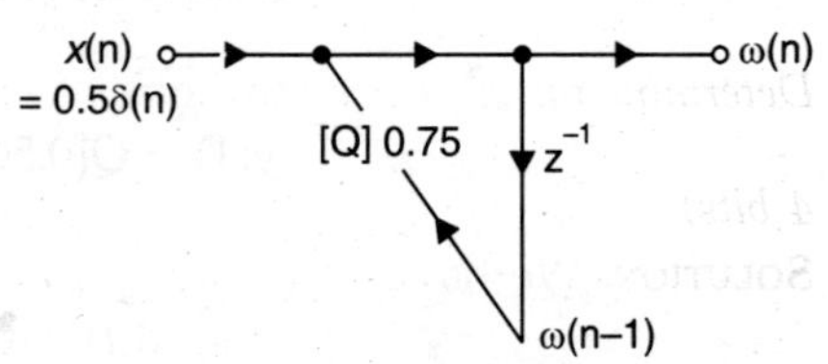

Fig. Ex. 10.2. (*a*) $b = 4$, rounding quantization

$$\omega(1) = 0 + Q\left[0.75 \times \frac{4}{8}\right] + Q\left[\frac{12}{32}\right] = \frac{3}{8} \qquad \left(\Delta\, 0011 \vdots (4 \text{ bits}) = \frac{3}{8}\right)$$

$$\omega(2) = 0 + Q\left[\frac{3}{4} \times \frac{3}{8}\right] + Q\left[\frac{9}{32}\right] = \frac{5}{16} \qquad \left(\Delta\, 0100 \vdots 1 = \Delta\, 0101 = \frac{5}{16}\right)$$

$$\omega(3) = 0 + Q\left[\frac{3}{4} \times \frac{5}{16}\right] + Q\left[\frac{15}{64}\right] = \frac{1}{4} \qquad \left(\Delta\, 0011 \vdots 11 = \Delta\, 0100 = \frac{1}{4}\right)$$

$$\omega(4) = 0 + Q\left[\frac{3}{4} \times \frac{1}{4}\right] + Q\left[\frac{3}{16}\right] = \frac{3}{16} \qquad \left(\Delta\, 0011 \vdots = \Delta\, 0011 = \frac{3}{16}\right)$$

$$\omega(5) = 0 + Q\left[\frac{3}{4} \times \frac{3}{16}\right] + Q\left[\frac{9}{64}\right] = \frac{1}{8} \qquad \left(\Delta\, 0010 \vdots 01 = \Delta\, 0010 = \frac{1}{8}\right)$$

$$\omega(6) = 0 + Q\left[\frac{3}{4} \times \frac{1}{8}\right] + Q\left[\frac{3}{32}\right] = \frac{1}{8} \qquad \left(\Delta\, 0001 \vdots 1 = \Delta\, 0010 = \frac{1}{8}\right)$$

$$\omega(n) = \left\{\underset{\uparrow}{\frac{1}{2}}, \frac{3}{8}, \frac{5}{16}, \frac{1}{4}, \frac{3}{16}, \frac{1}{8}, \frac{1}{8}, \ldots\right\}$$ **Ans.**

Check: $\omega(n-1) \geq \dfrac{\frac{1}{2}2^{-b}}{1-|\alpha|} = \dfrac{\frac{1}{2} \times 2^{-4}}{1-\frac{3}{4}} = \dfrac{\frac{1}{2} \times \frac{1}{16}}{\frac{1}{4}} = \dfrac{1}{8}$

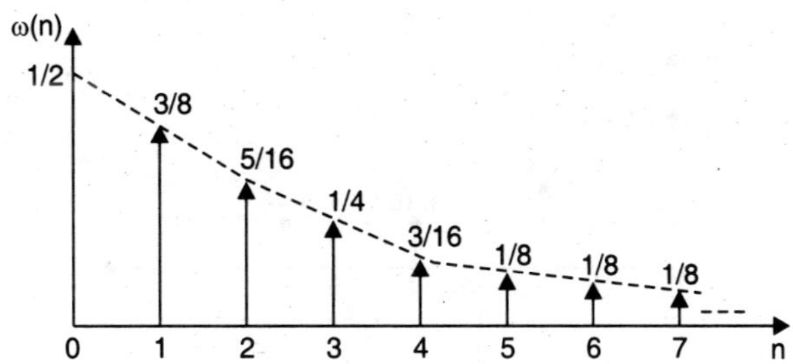

Fig. Ex. 10.2. (*b*) Showing ω(*n*). The limit cycle starts at *n* = 5

EXAMPLE **10.3:** *Explain the existance of zero-input limit cycle as observed in IIR digital filters. Assuming the first order IIR filter characterized by*

$$y(n) = x(n) + \alpha y(n-1)$$

Determine the sequence y(n), given $x(n) = \frac{7}{8}\delta(n)$, $\alpha = -\frac{1}{2}$ *and register bits = 1 + b = 1 + 4 (i.e., b = 4 bits).*

SOLUTION: We have

$$\omega(n) = x(n) + Q[\alpha\, \omega(n-1)]$$

$$\omega(0) = \frac{7}{8} + Q\left[\left(-\frac{1}{2}\right).0\right] = \frac{7}{8}, \quad \text{assuming } \omega(-1) = 0$$

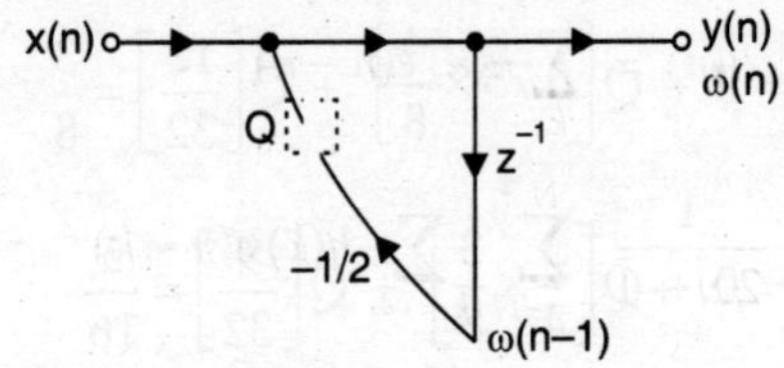

Fig. Ex. 10.3(*a*) The given system

$$\omega(1) = Q\left[-\frac{1}{2}\cdot\frac{7}{8}\right] = Q\left[-\frac{7}{16}\right] = -\frac{7}{16} \qquad (\Delta\ 0\ 1\ 1\ 1)$$

$$\omega(2) = Q\left[-\frac{1}{2}\cdot-\frac{7}{16}\right] = Q\left[\frac{7}{32}\right] = \frac{1}{4} \qquad (\Delta\ 0\ 0\ 1\ 1\ 1)$$

$$\omega(3) = Q\left[-\frac{1}{2}\cdot\frac{1}{4}\right] = Q\left[-\frac{1}{8}\right] = -\frac{1}{8} \qquad (\Delta\ 0\ 0\ 1\ 0)$$

$$\omega(4) = Q\left[-\frac{1}{2}\cdot-\frac{1}{8}\right] = Q\left[\frac{1}{16}\right] = \frac{1}{16} \qquad (\Delta\ 0\ 0\ 0\ 1)$$

$$\omega(5) = Q\left[-\frac{1}{2}\times\frac{1}{16}\right] = Q\left[-\frac{1}{32}\right] = -\frac{1}{16} \qquad (\Delta\ 0\ 0\ 0\ 0\ 1)$$

$$\omega(6) = Q\left[-\frac{1}{2}\cdot-\frac{1}{16}\right] = Q\left[\frac{1}{32}\right] = +\frac{1}{16}$$

Thus $\omega(n) = \left\{\underset{\uparrow}{\frac{7}{8}}, \frac{-7}{16}, \frac{1}{4}, \frac{-1}{8}, \frac{1}{16}, \frac{-1}{16}, \frac{1}{16}, \ldots\right\}$ and is shown in Fig. Ex. 10.3(*b*)

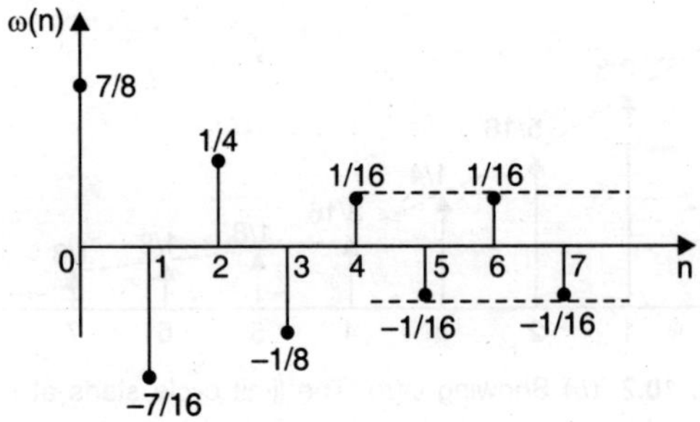

Fig. Ex. 10.3. (*b*) The output ω(*n*). Limit cycle occurs at *n* = 4

EXAMPLE 10.4: *(a) If quantization error e(n) of a random variable with mean m_e and variance σ_e^2 is inputted to a digital system with impulse response h(n), what are the values of mean and variance of the output noise sequence f(n).*

(b) If $h(n) = 0.2(0.8)^n\, u(n)$ in part (a) show that $\sigma_f^2 = 11\%$ of σ_e^2.

SOLUTION: m_e = average (or mean) of $e(n)$

$$= \lim_{N\to\infty}\frac{1}{2N+1}\sum_{n=-N}^{N} e(n)$$

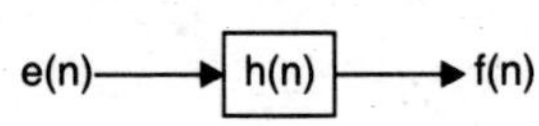

and
$$\sigma_e^2 = \lim_{N\to\infty}\frac{1}{2N+1}\sum_{n=-N}^{N} |e(n)-m_e|^2$$

$$f(n) = e(n) * h(n) = \sum_k h(k)\, e(n-k) \qquad \text{(convolution of } e(n) \text{ and } h(n))$$

$$\therefore \quad m_f = \lim_{N\to\infty} \frac{1}{2N+1} \sum_{n=-N}^{N} \sum_{k=-\infty}^{\infty} h(k)\, e(n-k)$$

$$= \sum_{k=-\infty}^{\infty} h(k) \left(\lim_{N\to\infty} \frac{1}{2N+1} \sum_{n=-N}^{N} e(n-k) \right) \swarrow = m_e$$

[as $e(n)$ is assumed time invariant]

$$= \sum_{k=-\infty}^{\infty} h(k)\,.\, m_e \qquad \therefore \quad \boxed{m_f = m_e \,.\, H(0) = m_e \sum_{k=-\infty}^{\infty} h(k)}$$

Ans.

$$\sigma_f^2 = \lim_{N\to\infty} \frac{1}{2N+1} \sum_{n=-N}^{N} |f(n) - m_f|^2$$

$$= \lim_{N\to\infty} \frac{1}{2N+1} \sum_{n=-N}^{N} \left(\sum_{k=-\infty}^{\infty} h(k)\, e(n-k) \right)\left(\sum_{m=-\infty}^{\infty} h(m)\, e(n-m) \right)$$

$$= \sum_m \sum_k h(k)\,.\,h(m)\,.\left[\lim_{N\to\infty} \frac{1}{2N+1} \sum_{n=-N}^{N} e(n-k)\,.\,e(n-m) \right] \swarrow = \sigma_e^2 \delta(k-m)$$

$(m_e = m_f = 0$ assumed)

$$= \sum_m \sum_k h(k)\,.\,h(m)\,.\,\sigma_e^2\,.\,\delta(k-m)$$

$$\sigma_f^2 = \sum_k |h(k)|^2\,.\,\sigma_e^2$$

($e(n)$ assumed uncorrelated, and time invariant white noise)

$$\therefore \quad \boxed{\sigma_f^2 = \sigma_e^2 \sum_k |h(k)|^2 = \sigma_e^2 \,.\, \frac{1}{2\pi} \int_{-\pi}^{\pi} |H(e^{j\omega})|^2\, d\omega} \qquad \text{(using Parseval's theorem)}$$

Ans.

(b) Given $\quad h(n) = 0.2\,(0.8)^n\, u(n)$

As

$$\sigma_f^2 = \sigma_e^2\,.\, \sum_n |h(n)|^2$$

$$= \sigma_e^2 \sum_{n=0}^{\infty} (0.2)^2\, (0.8)^{2n}$$

$$= \sigma_e^2\,.\,(0.2)^2 \cdot \frac{1}{1-(0.8)^2}$$

$$= \sigma_e^2\,.\,\frac{0.04}{0.36}$$

$$= \sigma_e^2 \times 0.1111$$

$$\therefore \quad \sigma_f^2 = 11\% \text{ of } \sigma_e^2.$$

EXAMPLE 10.5: *For an IIR digital filter cascaded $H(z) = H_1(z) \,.\, H_2(z)$, draw the Product Quantization model of the system. Determine the overall output noise power. Given $H_1(z) = \dfrac{1}{(1-0.9z^{-1})}$, and $H_2(z) = \dfrac{1}{(1-0.8z^{-1})}$.*

SOLUTION:

$$H_1(z) = \frac{1}{1-0.9z^{-1}}$$

$$\therefore \quad h_1(n) = (0.9)^n\, u(n)$$

$$\therefore \quad \sum_n |h_1(n)|^2 = \sum_{n=0}^{\infty} (0.9)^{2n} = \frac{1}{1-0.81} = 5.263$$

$$H_2(z) = \frac{1}{1-0.8z^{-1}}$$

$$\therefore \quad h_2(n) = (0.8)^n\, u(n)$$

$$\therefore \quad \sum_n |h_2(n)|^2 = \sum_{n=0}^{\infty} (0.8)^{2n} = \frac{1}{1-0.64} = 2.777$$

For

$$H(z) = \frac{1}{(1-0.9z^{-1})(1-0.8z^{-1})} = \frac{9}{1-0.9z^{-1}} + \frac{-8}{1-0.8z^{-1}}$$

$$\therefore \quad h(n) = [9(0.9)^n - 8(0.8)^n]u(n)$$

$$\therefore \quad \sum_n |h_2(n)|^2 = \sum_{n=0}^{\infty} 81(0.9)^{2n} + \sum_{n=0}^{\infty} 64(0.8)^{2n} - 2\sum_{n=0}^{\infty} 72\times(0.72)^n$$

$$= 81\times\frac{1}{1-0.81} + 64\times\frac{1}{1-0.64} - 144\frac{1}{1-0.72}$$

$$= (81)\,(5.263) + 64(2.777) - 144(3.571)$$

$$= 426.3 + 177.73 - 514.29 = 89.74$$

Case I. ($H_1(z)$ followed by $H_2(z)$)

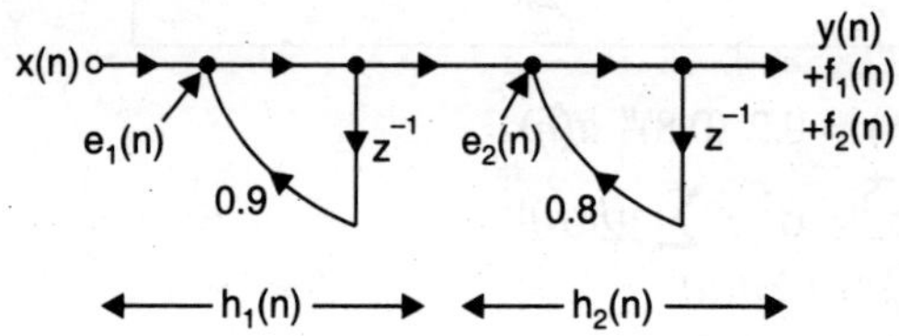

$$\sigma_{f_1}^2 + \sigma_{f_2}^2 = \frac{1}{12}2^{-2b}[89.74 + 2.77]$$

↖ contributed by $h_2(n)$

$$= (7.71) \times 2^{-2b} \text{ (least noise)}$$

Case II. ($H_2(z)$ followed by $H_1(z)$)

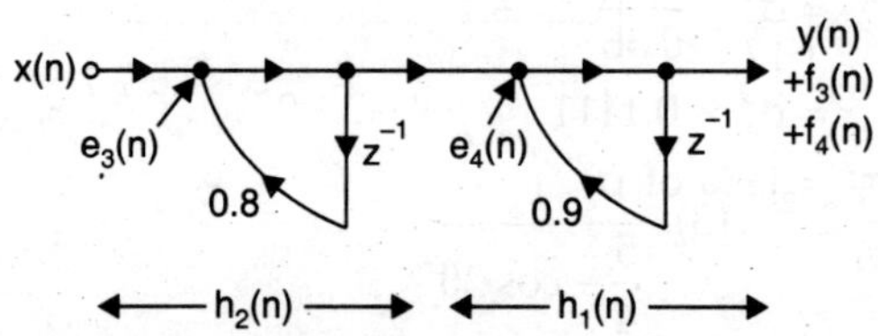

$$\sigma_{f_3}^2 + \sigma_{f_4}^2 = \frac{1}{12} 2^{-2b}[89.74 + 5.263]$$

↖ $e_4(n)$ is contributed only due to $h_1(n)$

$$= (7.92)\ 2^{-2b}$$

Case III. ($H_1(z)$ as canonic realization)

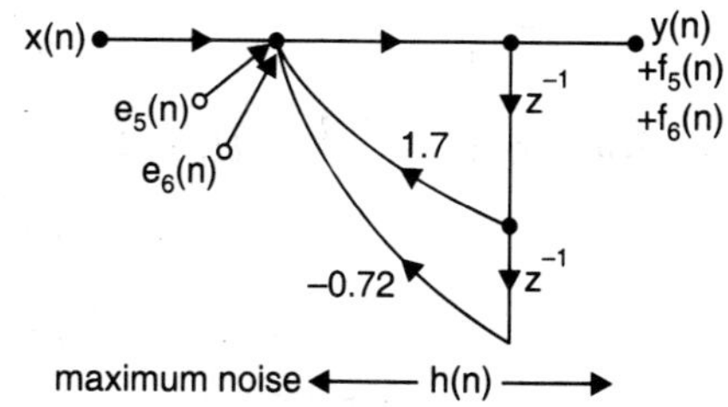

$$H(z) = \frac{1}{(1-0.9z^{-1})(1-0.8z^{-1})}$$

$$= \frac{1}{1-1.7z^{-1}+0-0.72z^{-2}}$$

$$\sigma_{f_5}^2 + \sigma_{f_6}^2 = (\sigma_{e_5}^2 + \sigma_{e_6}^2)(\sum_n |h(n)|^2)$$

$$= \left(2\times\frac{1}{12}2^{-2b}\right)\times 89.74 = (14.96)(2^{-2b}) \text{ maximum noise.}$$

EXAMPLE 10.6: *In a second order IIR digital system, the poles are at $z = re^{\pm j\theta}$. We wish to have the output noise, f(n), having noise power ≤ –80 dB. Determine the minimum value of bits b required for the system if $r = \frac{1}{\sqrt{2}}$. Use fixed point system.*

SOLUTION: Given
$$H(z) = \frac{1}{(1-re^{j\theta}z^{-1})(1-re^{-j\theta}z^{-1})}$$

$$= \frac{1}{1-2r\cos\theta z^{-1}+r^2z^{-1}}$$

Clearly, here
$$h(n) = \frac{r^n}{\sin\theta}\sin(n+1)\,\theta\, u(n)$$

$$f(n) = [e_1(n) + e_2(n)]\ \Sigma h(n)$$

Assuming rounding off, statistically independent white zero mean noise

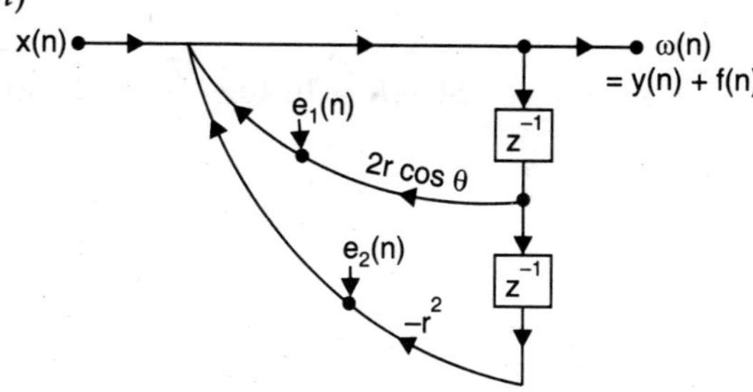

Fig. Ex. 10.6

$$m_{e_1} = m_{e_2} = 0,$$

$$\sigma_{e_1}^2 = \sigma_{e_2}^2 \triangleq \sigma_e^2 = \frac{1}{12}\ 2^{-2b}$$

$$f(n) = 2e(n)\ \Sigma h(n)$$

$$m_f = 2m_e\ \Sigma h(n) = 0$$

$$\sigma_f^2 = 2\ \sigma_e^2\ \Sigma|h(n)|^2 = 2\ .\ \sigma_e^2\ \frac{(1+r^2)}{(1-r^2)(r^4-2r^2\cos 2\theta+1)}$$

$$\sigma_f^2\Big|_{r=\frac{1}{\sqrt{2}}} = 2\times\left(\frac{1}{12}2^{-2b}\right)\frac{\left(1+\frac{1}{2}\right)}{\left(1-\frac{1}{2}\right)}\frac{1}{\frac{1}{4}-2.\frac{1}{2}\cos 2\theta+1}$$

$$= \frac{1}{6}2^{-2b}.(3).\frac{1}{\frac{5}{4}-\cos 2\theta}$$

$$= (2^{-2b+1}) \cdot \frac{1}{5 - 4\cos 2\theta}$$

As $$\sigma_f^2 = \text{Noise power} = 2^{-2b+1} \frac{1}{5 - 4\cos 2\theta}$$

θ can vary from 0 to π. σ_f^2 is maximum when $\theta = 0$

$$\therefore \quad \sigma_f^2 |_{max} = 2^{-2b+1} \frac{1}{5-4}, \text{ putting } \theta = 0$$

$\sigma_f^2 |_{max}$ in dB should not exceed –80 dB $\qquad - 80 \text{ dB} = 10 \log_{10} 10^{-8}$

or $$10 \log_{10} \sigma_{f\,max}^2 \leq -80 \text{ dB}$$

or $$\sigma_{fmax}^2 \leq 10^{-8}$$

$$\therefore \quad 2^{-2b+1} \leq 10^{-8}$$

$$2^{2b-1} \geq 10^8$$

$$(2b-1) \log_{10} 2 \geq 8$$

$$(2b-1)(0.3) \geq 8$$

$$\therefore \quad b \geq 13.8 \qquad \text{Choose } b = 14$$

Ans.

$\therefore$ The system has $1 + b$ *i.e.*, 1 + 14 bits registers. Practically, 16 bits (*i.e.*, 1 + 15 bits) registers are available commercially.

EXAMPLE 10.7: *For an A to D converter, show that*

$$SQNR = 6.02\, b + 16.81 - 20 \log(R/\sigma_x) \text{ dB}$$

where R = dynamic range, b = Register bits, σ_x^2 = *signal power.*

SOLUTION: For analog to digital conversion, we assume the quantization noise, e, uniformly distributed, say, between $-\Delta/2$ and $\Delta/2$.

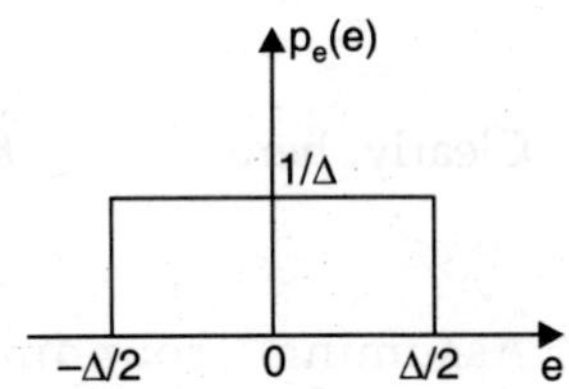

Fig. Ex. 10.7. pdf for uniformly distributed quantization noise *e*.

$$SQNR = 10 \log \frac{\sigma_x^2}{\sigma_e^2} = 10 \log \frac{\text{Signal power}}{\text{Noise power}}$$

But $$\sigma_e^2 = \int_{-\Delta/2}^{\Delta/2} e^2 . P_e(e)\, de = \int_{-\Delta/2}^{\Delta/2} \frac{1}{\Delta} . e^2 . de$$

$$= \frac{1}{\Delta} . \left[\frac{e^3}{3} \right]_{-\Delta/2}^{+\Delta/2} = \frac{\Delta^2}{12}$$

For dynamic range R and register bits b (besides the sign bits)

$$\boxed{\Delta = \frac{R}{2^{b+1}}}, \text{ where } R = \text{range of variation} \equiv -2^b \text{ to } 2^b$$

$$\therefore \text{ Span} = 2\, 2^b = 2^{b+1}. \text{ Range per bit} = \Delta = \frac{R}{2^{b+1}}$$

$$\therefore \quad \sigma_e^2 = \frac{1}{12} \cdot \left(\frac{R}{2^{b+1}} \right)^2 = \frac{1}{48} \frac{R^2}{2^{2b}}$$

$$SQNR = 10 \log \left(\frac{\sigma_x^2}{\frac{1}{48} \frac{R^2}{2^{2b}}} \right) = 10 \log \left(\sigma_x^2 \times \frac{48 \times 2^{2b}}{R^2} \right)$$

$$= 10 \log \left(\frac{\sigma_x}{R} \right)^2 + 10 \log 48 + 10 \log 2^{2b}$$

$$= -20 \log \frac{R}{\sigma_x} + 16.81 + 20\, b \log 2$$

$$= 6.02\, b + 16.81 - 20 \log \frac{R}{\sigma_x}$$ **Ans.**

EXAMPLE 10.8: *For a second order IIR digital system with unit sample response given by*

$$h(n) = [r^n \sin(n + 1)\, \theta / \sin \theta]\, u(n)$$

assume that r is 0.90 and we have fixed point arithmetic with rounding off as the quantization. The system has 1 + b bits. The input signal, x(n), appears as y(n) at the output with zero dB. We wish to have an SNR ≥ 80 dB at the output

(i) Determine the minimum value of b.

(ii) If r in made 0.95, the other parameters remaining the same, compute the value of b then.

SOLUTION: For
$$h(n) = \frac{r^n}{\sin \theta} \sin(n + 1)\theta\, \mu(n)$$

$$H(z) = \frac{1}{1 - 2r \cos \theta\, z^{-1} + r^2 z^{-2}}$$

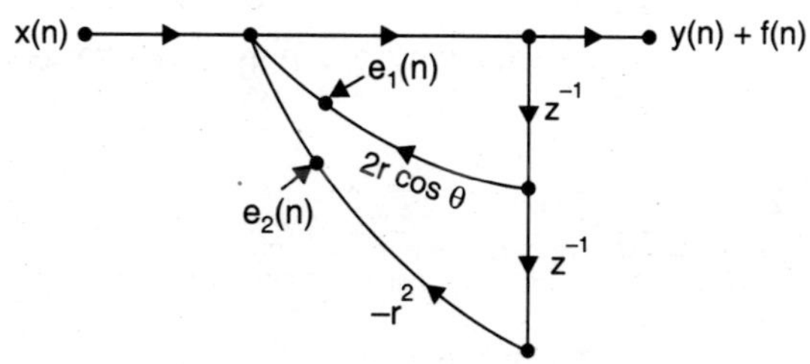

Fig. Ex. 10.8. The given 2nd order system

and the system is realized as shown. For rounding off, fixed-point arithmetic system, we have

$$m_f = 0,$$

$$\sigma_f^2 = (\sigma_{e_1}^2 + \sigma_{e_2}^2) \times \Sigma |h(n)|^2$$

$$= 2\sigma_e^2 \cdot \frac{(1 + r^2)}{(1 - r^2)(r^4 - 2r^2 \cos 2\theta + 1)}$$ [assuming uncorrelated noise $e_i(n)$]

Take the worst case, when cos 2θ = 1, since, it yields highest σ_f^2 then

$$\sigma_f^2|_{max} = \frac{(1 + r^2)\, 2\sigma_e^2}{(1 - r^2)(r^2 - 1)^2} = \frac{1 + r^2}{(1 - r^2)^3} \cdot 2\sigma_e^2$$

An $SNR \geq 80$ dB implies

$$10 \log_{10} \frac{\sigma_y^2}{\sigma_f^2} \geq 80 \text{ dB}$$

i.e., $$10 \ (\log_{10} \sigma_y^2 - \log_{10} \sigma_f^2) \geq 80$$

$= 0$ given

$\therefore$ $$-\log_{10} \sigma_f^2 \geq 80/10$$

or $$\sigma_f^2 \leq 10^{-8}$$

(*i*) $r = 0.90$

$$\frac{(1+r^2) . 2. \left(\frac{1}{12} 2^{-2b}\right)}{(1-r^2)^3} \leq 10^{-8}$$

$\therefore$ $$\frac{(1+0.81) \frac{1}{6} . 2^{-2b}}{(1-0.81)^3} \leq 10^{-8}$$

i.e., $$2^{-2b} \leq \frac{(0.19)^3 \times 6 \times 10^{-8}}{1.81} = 0.022737 \times 10^{-8}$$

$\therefore$ $$2^{2b} \geq \frac{10^8}{0.022737}$$

$$2b \underbrace{\log 2}_{=0.3} \geq 8 - \log 0.022737 = 8 - (-1.6433) = 9.6433$$

$\therefore$ $$b \geq 9.6433/(2 \times 0.3) = 16.072 \text{ say } b = 16$$ **Ans.**

(*ii*) $r = 0.95$*

Here $$\frac{(1+0.9025) \times \frac{1}{6} 2^{-2b}}{(1-0.9025)^3} \leq 10^{-8}$$

$\therefore$ $$2^{-2b} \leq \frac{(0.0975)^3 \times 6 \times 10^{-8}}{(1.9025)} = 0.002923 \times 10^{-8}$$

$\therefore$ $$2^{2b} \geq \frac{10^8}{0.002923} = 10^8 \times 342.105$$

---

* **Note 1.** For $r = 0.95$, $SNR \geq 60$ dB

$$b \geq (6 + 2.534)/(2 \times 0.3) = 14.22$$

$\therefore$ $$b = 15$$ **Ans.**

2. For $r = 0.90$, $SNR \geq 60$ dB

$$\frac{(1+0.81) \times \frac{1}{6} 2^{-2b}}{(1-0.81)^3} \leq 10^{-6}$$

$\therefore$ $$2^{-2b} \leq 10^{-6} \times 6.859 \times 10^{-3} \times 6 \frac{1}{1.81} = 0.022737 \times 10^{6}$$

$$2^{2b} = 43.98 \times 10^6 \quad \therefore \quad b \geq 11.64$$

$$b = 12$$ **Ans.**

$$2b \log 2 \geq 8 + \log 342.105 = 8 + 2.534 = 10.534$$

$$\therefore \quad b \geq \frac{10.534}{(2 \times 0.3)} = 17.56 \quad \therefore \quad b = 18$$ **Ans.**

EXAMPLE 10.9: *For quantization noise/error of a sigma-delta system used for analog to digital conversion, obtain the expression for noise power (sigma-delta system).*

SOLUTION: Noise power in sigma-delta system, for the system shown below; we have

$$x(n) = \hat{x}(n) + \omega(n) \quad \text{...(A)}$$

where $\hat{x}(n)$ = predicted value

$\omega(n)$ = error in prediction

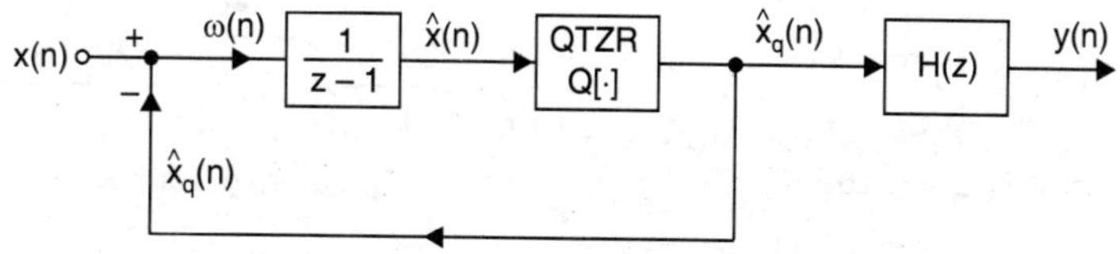

Fig. Ex. 10.9. (*a*) A typical sigma-delta system

For an accurate system we have

$\hat{x}(n) \approx x(n-1)$ with high sampling A to D conversion

$\therefore$ $x(n) = x(n-1) + \omega(n)$ (replacing $\hat{x}(n)$ by $x(n-1)$ on (*A*))

or $X(z) = z^{-1} X(z) + W(z)$

or $$X(z) = \frac{W(z)}{1 - z^{-1}} = \frac{z}{z-1} \cdot W(z) \quad \text{...(B)}$$

Also, $\hat{X}(z) = z^{-1} X(z)$ ($\because$ We have assumed $\hat{x}(n) = x(n-1)$)

$$= \frac{1}{z-1} \cdot W(z) \quad \text{...(using (B))}$$

This relation agrees with the Fig. Ex. 10.9(*a*) sigma-delta converter shown above.

The quantizer effect is to add error $e(n)$. Hence, Fig. Ex. 10.9(*a*) can be replaced by Fig. Ex. 10.9(*b*) shown here.

$$y'(n) = y(n) + \varepsilon(n)$$

where $\varepsilon(n)$ is error due to quantization.

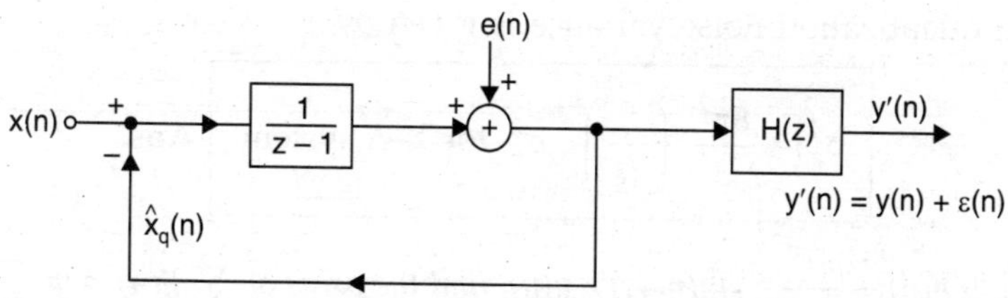

Fig. Ex. 10.9. (*b*) Effect of quantizer

Assuming that $y(n)$ is the desired output, we are interested in the value (variance) of the noise $\varepsilon(n)$ appearing along with $y(n)$.

We can draw the noise flow (in z-transform domain) as shown in Fig. Ex. 10.9 (*c*)

$$\frac{\varepsilon(z)}{H(z)} = E(z) - \left(\frac{\varepsilon(z)}{H(z)}\right)\left(\frac{1}{z-1}\right)$$

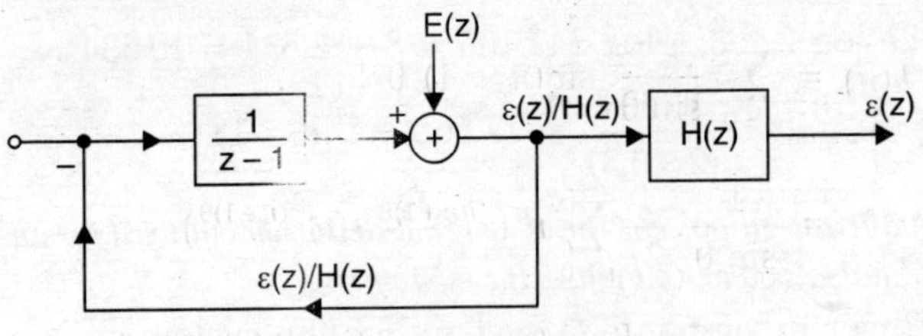

Fig. Ex. 10.9. (c) Calculation for ε(n), ∴ ε(n)

$$\therefore \quad \varepsilon(z) \cdot \frac{1}{H(z)}\left(1+\frac{1}{z-1}\right) = E(z)$$

$$\therefore \quad \varepsilon(z) \cdot \frac{1}{H(z)}\left(\frac{1}{z-1}\right) = E(z)$$

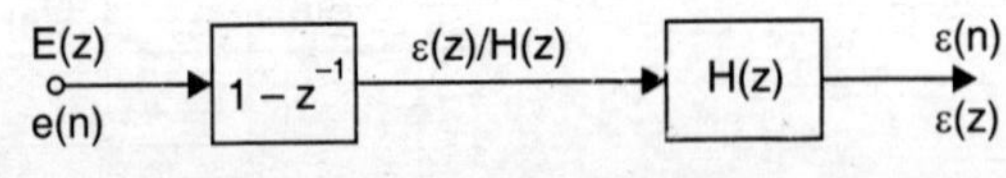

Fig. Ex. 10.9. (d) Simplified circuit to find ε(n)

or $\varepsilon(z) = H(z) \cdot [1 - z^{-1}] \cdot E(z)$, where $H(z)$ is a LPF with cut off frequency f_B such that

$$\therefore \quad \omega_B = \frac{2\pi f_B}{f_s}, \text{ normalised cut off radian frequencies of } H(z)$$

$$\therefore \quad \sigma_\varepsilon^2 = \left(\frac{1}{2\pi}\int_{-\omega_B}^{\omega_B} |1 - e^{-j\omega}|^2 \, d\omega\right) . \sigma_e^2$$

$$\left(\text{“}\because \ \sigma_f^2 = \sigma_e^2 \cdot \frac{1}{2\pi}\int_{-\pi}^{\pi} |H(e^{j\omega})|^2 \, d\omega\text{” From (10.31)}\right)$$

But $\quad |1 - e^{j\omega}| = |e^{-j\omega/2}\,(e^{+j\omega/2} - e^{-j\omega/2})| = 2 \sin \dfrac{\omega}{2} \approx \omega$ for small ω (Note this step)

$$\therefore \quad \sigma_\varepsilon^2 = \sigma_e^2 \cdot \frac{1}{2\pi}\int_{-\omega_B}^{\omega_B} \omega^2 \, d\omega$$

$$= \sigma_e^2 \frac{1}{2\pi}\frac{1}{3}\left[\omega^3\right]_{-\omega_B}^{\omega_B}$$

$$= \sigma_e^2 \frac{1}{6\pi} 2\omega_B^3$$

$$= \sigma_e^2 \frac{1}{3\pi} \cdot \frac{8\pi^3 f_B^3}{f_S^3}$$

Hence, output quantization noise variance is given by

$$\boxed{\sigma_\varepsilon^2 = \frac{8\pi^2}{3} \cdot \left(\frac{f_B}{f_S}\right)^3 . \sigma_e^2 \text{ for } \Sigma\text{–}\Delta \text{ system.}} \quad \textbf{Ans.}$$

EXAMPLE 10.10: *If* $h(n) = \dfrac{r^n}{\sin\theta}\sin(n+1).\ u(n)$, *find the value of* $\sum_n h(n)$ *and* $\sum_n |h(n)|^2$. *Assume* $|r| < 1$. *Find these values by three different approaches.*

SOLUTION: *(a)* ***1st Method***

$$. h(n) = \frac{r^n}{\sin\theta}\sin(n+1)\,\theta \cdot u(n)$$

$$\therefore \quad \sum_{n=-\infty}^{\infty} h(n) = \sum_{n=0}^{\infty} \frac{r^n}{\sin\theta} \sin(n+1)\theta$$

$$= \frac{1}{\sin\theta}\cdot\frac{1}{2j}\sum_{n=0}^{\infty} r^n (e^{j(n+1)\theta} - e^{-j(n+1)\theta})$$

$$= \frac{1}{2j\sin\theta}\left[\frac{e^{j\theta}}{1-re^{j\theta}} - \frac{e^{-j\theta}}{1-re^{-j\theta}}\right] \qquad \because \; |re^{\pm j}| < 1$$

$$= \frac{1}{2j\sin\theta}\frac{e^{j\theta}(1-re^{-j\theta}) - e^{-j\theta}(1-re^{j\theta})}{(1-re^{j\theta})(1-re^{-j\theta})}$$

$$= \frac{1}{2j\sin\theta}\frac{(e^{j\theta}-e^{-j\theta})}{1-2r\cos\theta+r^2}$$

$$\therefore \quad \sum_n h(n) = \frac{1}{1-2r\cos\theta+r^2} \textbf{ Ans.} \qquad \ldots(A)$$

2nd Method:

$$\sum_n h(n) = I_m \text{ part of } \frac{1}{\sin\theta}\sum_{n=0}^{\infty} r^n e^{j(n+1)\theta} \qquad \because \sin(n+1)\theta = I_m \text{ part of } e^{j(n+1)\theta}$$

$$= I_m\left[\frac{1}{\sin\theta}\frac{e^{j\theta}}{1-re^{j\theta}}\right] \qquad \because \; |re^{j\theta}| < 1$$

$$= I_m\left[\frac{1}{\sin\theta}\frac{\cos\theta + j\sin\theta}{1-r\cos\theta - jr\cos\theta}\right]$$

$$= I_m \cdot \frac{1}{\sin\theta}\frac{(\cos\theta + j\sin\theta)[1-r\cos\theta+jr\sin\theta]}{1+r^2-2r\cos\theta}$$

$$= \frac{1}{\sin\theta}\frac{\sin\theta + (1-r\cos\theta) - r\sin\theta\cos\theta}{1-2r\cos\theta+r^2}$$

$$= \frac{1}{1-2r\cos\theta+r^2} \text{ As earlier } \textbf{Ans.} \qquad \ldots(B)$$

To find $H(z)$ given $h(n) = \dfrac{r^n}{\sin\theta}\sin(n+1)\theta\, u(n)$

$$H(z) = \sum_{n=0}^{\infty}\frac{r^n}{\sin\theta}\frac{(e^{j(n+1)\theta} - e^{-j(n+1)\theta})z^{-n}}{2j}$$

$$= \frac{1}{2j\sin\theta}\sum_{n=0}^{\infty} e^{j\theta}(re^{j\theta}z^{-1})^n - e^{-j\theta}(re^{-j\theta}z^{-1})^n$$

$$= \frac{1}{2j\sin\theta}\left\{\frac{e^{j\theta}}{1-re^{j\theta}z^{-1}} - \frac{e^{-j\theta}}{1-re^{-j\theta}z^{-1}}\right\}$$

$$= \frac{e^{j\theta}(1 - r e^{-j\theta} \cancel{z^{-1}}) - e^{-j\theta}(1 - r e^{j\theta} \cancel{z^{-1}})}{2j \sin\theta (1 - 2r\cos\theta\, z^{-1} + r^2 z^{-2})}$$

$$= \frac{1}{1 - 2r\cos z^{-1} + r^2 z^{-2}}, \; |z| > r \qquad \text{...(C)}$$

Putting $z = 1$ in (C), we readily obtain the same result as in (A) or (B).

(b) ***I*** st ***Method:***

$$\sum_n |h(n)|^2 = \frac{1}{\sin^2\theta} \sum_{n=0}^{\infty} r^{2n} \sin^2 (n+1)\theta$$

$$= \frac{1}{\sin^2\theta}\left[\sum_n r^{2n} (1 - \cos 2(n+1)\theta)/2\right]$$

$$= \frac{1}{\sin^2\theta}\left[\sum_{n=0}^{\infty} r^{2n} - \sum_{n=0}^{\infty} r^{2n} \frac{1}{2}(e^{j2(n+1)\theta} + e^{-j2(n+1)\theta}\right]$$

$$= \frac{1}{2\sin^2\theta}\left[\frac{1}{1-r^2} - \frac{1}{2}\left\{\frac{e^{j2\theta}}{1 - r^2 e^{j2\theta}} + \frac{e^{-j2\theta}}{1 - r^2 e^{-j2\theta}}\right\}\right]$$

$$= \frac{1}{2\sin^2\theta}\left[\frac{1}{1-r^2} - \frac{1}{2}\left\{\frac{e^{j2\theta}(1 - r^2 e^{j2\theta}) + e^{-j2\theta}(1 - r^2 e^{2\theta})}{(1 - r^2 e^{j2\theta})(1 - r^2 e^{-j2\theta})}\right\}\right]$$

$$= \frac{1}{2\sin^2\theta}\left[\frac{1}{1-r^2} - \frac{1}{2}\frac{2\cos 2\theta - 2r^2}{1 - 2r^2\cos 2\theta + r^4}\right]$$

$$= \frac{1}{2\sin^2\theta}\left[\frac{(1 - 2r^2\cos 2\theta - r^4) - (1 - r^2)(\cos 2\theta - r^2)}{(1 - r^2)(1 - 2r^2\cos 2\theta + r^4)}\right]$$

$$= \frac{1}{2\sin^2\theta}\left[\frac{1 - 2r^2\cos 2\theta + \cancel{r^4} - \cos 2\theta + r^2 + r^2\cos 2\theta - \cancel{r^4}}{(1 - r^2)(1 - 2r^2\cos 2\theta + r^4)}\right]$$

$$= \frac{1}{2\sin^2\theta}\frac{(1 + r^2) - \cos 2\theta(1 + r^2)}{(1 - r^2)(1 - 2r^2\cos 2\theta + r^4)}$$

$$= \frac{1}{2\sin^2\theta}\frac{2\sin^2\theta(1 + r^2)}{(1 - r^2)(1 - 2r^2\cos 2\theta + r^4)}$$

$$= \frac{1 + r^2}{1 - r^2}\frac{1}{1 - 2r^2\cos 2\theta + r^4}$$

Ans.

2nd ***Method*** to find $\sum_n |h(n)|^2$

We know that $\sum_n |h(n)|^2 = \frac{1}{2\pi j}\oint_C H(z)\,H(z^{-1}).z^{-1}\,dz$

(by Parseval theorem in complex domain)

$$= \sum_{\text{Residues}} H(z)\,H(z^{-1}).z^{-1}$$

As $$H(z) = \sum_{n=0}^{\infty} \frac{r^n}{\sin\theta}\sin(n+1)\,\theta\, z^{-n}$$

$$= \frac{1}{(1-re^{j\theta}z^{-1})(1-re^{-j\theta}z^{-1})} \qquad \text{(A well known result)}$$

$\therefore$ $$\sum_n |h(n)|^2 = \sum_{\text{Residues}} \frac{z^{-1}}{(1-re^{j\theta}z^{-1})(1-re^{-j\theta}z^{-1})(1-re^{j\theta}z)(1-re^{-j\theta}z)}$$

$$= \sum_{\text{Residues}} \frac{z}{r^2(z-re^{j\theta})(z-re^{-j\theta})\left(z-\frac{1}{re^{j\theta}}\right)\left(z-\frac{1}{re^{-j\theta}}\right)}$$

Assuming $|r| < 1$, we consider the poles $p_{1,2} = re^{\pm j\theta}$ being inside the unit circle to contribute towards residues

$\therefore$ $$\sum_n |h(n)|^2 = \text{Residues of } H(z)H(z^{-1})\,z^{-1} \text{ at } re^{j\theta} \text{ and at } re^{-j\theta}$$

$$= \frac{re^{j\theta}}{r^2(re^{j\theta}-re^{-j\theta})\left(re^{j\theta}-\frac{1}{re^{j\theta}}\right)\left(re^{j\theta}-\frac{1}{re^{-j\theta}}\right)}$$

$$+ \frac{re^{-j\theta}}{r^2(re^{-j\theta}-re^{j\theta})\left(re^{-j\theta}-\frac{1}{re^{j\theta}}\right)\left(re^{-j\theta}-\frac{1}{re^{-j\theta}}\right)}$$

$$= \frac{1}{\cancel{r^2}\,(2j\sin\theta)}\left[\frac{e^{j\theta}\,.\,\cancel{re^{j\theta}}\,.\,\cancel{re^{-j\theta}}}{(r^2e^{j2\theta}-1)(r^2-1)} + \frac{-e^{-j\theta}\,.\,\cancel{re^{j\theta}}\,.\,\cancel{re^{-j\theta}}}{(r^2-1)(r^2e^{-j2\theta}-1)}\right]$$

$$= \left(\frac{1}{2j\sin\theta}\right)\left(\frac{1}{1-r^2}\right)\left[\frac{e^{j\theta}}{1-r^2e^{j2\theta}} - \frac{e^{-j\theta}}{(1-r^2e^{-j2\theta})}\right]$$

$$= \frac{1}{(2\,j\sin\theta)(1-r^2)}\cdot\frac{e^{j\theta}-r^2e^{-j\theta}-e^{-j\theta}+r^2e^{j\theta}}{1-2r^2\cos 2\,\theta+r^4}$$

$$= \frac{(1+r^2)\cdot 1}{(1-r^2)(1-2\,r^2\cos 2\,\theta+r^4)}$$

Ans.

3rd ***Method*** of find $\sum_n |h(n)|^2$

$$\sum_n |h(n)|^2 = \sum_{n=0}^{\infty} \frac{r^{2n}}{\sin^2\theta} . \sin^2(n+1)\theta = \sum_{n=0}^{\infty} \frac{r^{2n}}{\sin^2\theta} \frac{1-\cos 2(n+1)\theta}{2}$$

$$= \sum_{n=0}^{\infty} \frac{r^{2n}}{2\sin^2\theta} - \frac{1}{2\sin^2\theta} \sum_{n=0}^{\infty} r^{2n} \cos 2(n+1)\theta$$

$$= \frac{1}{2\sin^2\theta}\left[\sum_{n=0}^{\infty} r^{2n} - \text{Real part of} \sum_{n=0}^{\infty} r^{2n} e^{j2(n+1)\theta}\right]$$

$$= \frac{1}{2\sin^2\theta}\left[\frac{1}{1-r^2} - \text{Re}\frac{e^{j2\theta}}{1-r^2e^{j2\theta}}\right]$$

$$= \frac{1}{2\sin^2\theta}\left[\frac{1}{1-r^2} - \text{Re}\frac{\cos 2\theta + j\sin 2\theta}{1-r^2\cos 2\theta - jr^2\sin 2\theta}\right]$$

$$= \frac{1}{2\sin^2\theta}\left[\frac{1}{1-r^2} - \text{Re}\frac{(\cos 2\theta + j\sin 2\theta)[(1-r^2\cos 2\theta) + jr^2\sin 2\theta]}{(1-r^2\cos 2\theta)^2 + (r^2\sin 2\theta)^2}\right]$$

$$= \frac{1}{2\sin^2\theta}\left[\frac{1}{1-r^2} - \frac{\cos 2\theta + (1-r^2\cos 2\theta) - \sin 2\theta\,(r^2\sin 2\theta)}{1-2r^2\cos 2\theta + r^4}\right]$$

$$= \frac{1}{2\sin^2\theta}\left[\frac{1}{1-r^2} - \frac{\cos 2\theta - r^2}{1-2r^2\cos 2\theta + r^4}\right]$$

$$= \frac{1}{2\sin^2\theta}\left[\frac{1-2r^2\cos 2\theta + \cancel{r^4} - \cos 2\theta + r^2 + r^2\cos 2\theta - \cancel{r^4}}{(1-r^2)(1-2r^2\cos 2\theta + r^4)}\right]$$

$$= \frac{1}{2\sin^2\theta}\,\frac{1}{1-r^2}\,\frac{1-r^2\cos 2\theta - \cos 2\theta + r^2}{1-2r^2\cos 2\theta + r^4}$$

$$= \left(\frac{1}{\cancel{2\sin^2\theta}}\right)\left(\frac{1}{1-r^2}\right)\frac{(1+r^2)\,\cancel{(1-\cos 2\theta)}}{1-2r^2\cos 2\theta + r^4}$$

$$= \frac{1+r^2}{1-r^2}\,\frac{1}{1-2r^2\cos 2\theta + r^4}$$ **Ans.**

EXAMPLE 10.11: *For the 2nd-order system with impulse response*

$$h(n) = \frac{r^n}{\sin\theta}\sin(n+1)\,\theta\, u(n)$$

quantization is performed by rounding. Let the input to the system be x(n) and its output y(n) plus additive noise f(n). Determine the maximum value of r (the pole length) so that the output SNR σ_y^2/σ_f^2 *≥ 60 dB. Assume* $\sigma_y^2 = 1$ *and assume standard bits b.*

SOLUTION: Using (10.46), we get

Here $$\sigma_f^2 = 2 \times \sigma_e^2 \times \frac{(1+r^2)}{(1-r^2)(1-2r^2\cos 2\theta + r^4)}$$

where $$\sigma_e^2 = \frac{1}{12} 2^{-2b}$$

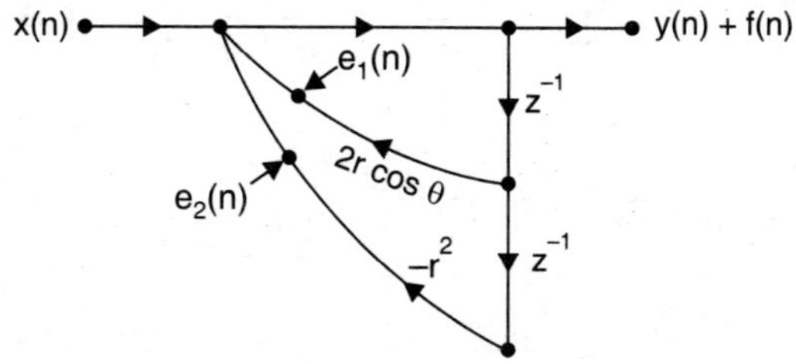

Fig. Ex. 10.11 The given 2nd order system

For the worst case *i.e.*, maximum noise power σ_f^2, take cos 2 θ = +1 (Note this step)

$$\therefore \quad \sigma_f^2 = \frac{1}{6} 2^{-2b} \frac{1+r^2}{(1-r^2)(1-2r^2+r^4)}$$

$$= \frac{1}{6} 2^{-2b} \frac{(1+r^2)}{(1-r^2)^3} \triangleq \frac{1}{6} 2^{-2b} \frac{1+x}{(1-x)^3}; \; x = r^2$$

Also, $\sigma_y^2 = 1$, output SNR = 60 dB

$$\therefore \quad \frac{\sigma_y^2}{\sigma_f^2} = 10^6 \qquad \left(\because \; 10 \log \frac{\sigma_y^2}{\sigma_f^2} = 60\right)$$

Let 1 + *b* = 8 ∴ $b = 7$, with the above given data

$$\frac{\sigma_y^2}{\sigma_f^2} = 10^6$$ ALSO $x = r^2$ *cannot exceed unity for stability constraints.*

(Note this step)

$$\therefore \quad \frac{1}{6} 2^{-2(7)} \times \frac{1+x}{(1-x)^3} = 10^{-6}$$

$$\therefore \quad \frac{1+x}{(1-x)^3} = 6 \times 2^{+14} \times 10^{-6} = 0.098304 \qquad \ldots(A)$$

[To solve for *x*] if $b = 7$

x	*LHS of (A)*
For $x = 1$,	∞
$x = 0.5$	12
$x = 0.25$	2.9629
$x = 0.10$	1.5089
$x = 0.01$	1.0409

(*A*) is satisfied only for extremely small value of $x(= r^2)$ less than 0.01. A system for $r < 0.5$ is considered inefficient. Therefore, $b = 7$ is not suitable.

Now let 1 + b = 16: $b = 15$ (a standard value of bits)

To find the value of x from the equation (*B*)

$$\therefore \quad \frac{1}{6} 2^{-2(7)} \cdot \frac{1+x}{(1-x)^3} = 10^{-6} \qquad \ldots(B)$$

1st iteration

Assume $x \approx 1 \quad \therefore \quad 1 + x = 2, \quad \therefore$ (*B*) gives us

$$(1-x)^3 = \frac{1}{6} 2^{-30} \times 10^6 (1+x)$$

$$= \frac{1}{6} 2^{-30} \times 10^6 (1+1) \text{ for } x \approx 1$$

$$= \frac{1}{3} (9.3132257 \times 10^{-10}) . 10^6 = 3.1044086 \times 10^4$$

$$\therefore \quad (1-x) = 0.067711$$

$\therefore$ $x = 0.9322889$ *i.e.*, x is less than 1

2nd iteration

Put $1 + x = 1 + 0.9322889$ in (*B*) to get

$$(1-x)^3 = \frac{1}{6} 2^{-30} \times 10^6 (1+0.9322889) = 2.9993071 \times 10^{-4}$$

$$\therefore \quad (1-x) = 0.06693814$$

$\therefore$ $x = 0.9330618$ *i.e.*, x is more than the previous value

3rd iteration

Put $1 + x = 1 + 0.9330618$ in (*B*) to get

$$(1-x)^3 = \frac{1}{6} 2^{-30} \times 10^6 (1+0.9330618) = 3.0005068 \times 10^{-4}$$

$\therefore$ $(1 - x) = 0.066947$ or $x = 0.9330529$ *i.e.*, x is less than the previous value

4th iteration

Put $1 + x = 1 + 0.9330529$ in (*B*) to get

$$(1-x)^3 = \frac{1}{6} 2^{-30} \times 10^6 (1+0.9330529) = 3.000493 \times 10^{-4}$$

$\therefore$ $(1 - x) = 0.0669469$ or $x = 0.9330530$ *i.e.*, x is more than the previous value

Choose $x = 0.933053 \quad \therefore \quad r = \sqrt{x} = 0.9659466$, say, 0.96

Check: For $x = 0.933053, \ \frac{1}{6} 2^{-30} \times 10^6 \times \frac{1+0.933053}{(1-0.933053)^3} = 0.99999834$

≈ 1 (as desired)

Hence, we choose $1 + b = 16$ bits (*i.e.*, $b = 15$ bits)
More $r = 0.96$ **Ans.**

EXAMPLE 10.12: *Given an IIR digital filter as shown in the figure, the system uses fixed-point arithmetic and rounding off as the quantization.*

(a) Determine the variance of the noise at the output

(b) If the system is implemented in parallel form, find the variance of output noise due to quantization.

SOLUTION: (*a*) Clearly

$$H(z) = \frac{1}{1-\frac{1}{2}z^{-1}} \cdot \frac{1}{1-\frac{1}{4}z^{-1}} = \frac{2}{1-\frac{1}{2}z^{-1}} - \frac{1}{1-\frac{1}{4}z^{-1}}$$

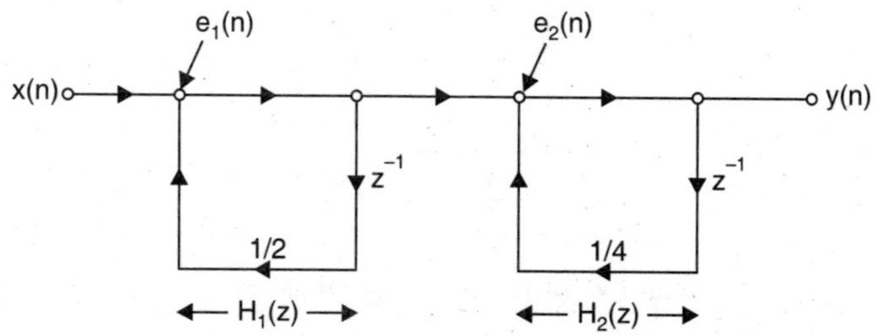

Fig. Ex. 10.12. (a) The given IIR filter

$$\therefore \qquad h(n) = 2\left(\frac{1}{2}\right)^n u(n) - \left(\frac{1}{4}\right)^n u(n)$$

Also, $$h_1(n) = \left(\frac{1}{2}\right)^n u(n) \quad \text{and} \quad h_2(n) = \left(\frac{1}{4}\right)^n u(n) \qquad \ldots(A)$$

$$\sum_n |h_2(n)|^2 = \sum_{n=0}^{\infty} \left(\frac{1}{4}\right)^{2n} u(n) = \frac{1}{1-\frac{1}{16}} = \frac{16}{15}$$

$$\sum_n |h(n)|^2 = \sum_{n=0}^{\infty} \left[2\left(\frac{1}{2}\right)^n - \left(\frac{1}{4}\right)^n\right]^2 u(n)$$

$$= \sum_{n=0}^{\infty} \left[4.\left(\frac{1}{2}\right)^{2n} + \left(\frac{1}{4}\right)^{2n} - 4\left(\frac{1}{8}\right)^n\right]$$

$$= 4\frac{1}{1-\frac{1}{4}} + \frac{1}{1-\frac{1}{16}} - \frac{4}{1-\frac{1}{8}} = \frac{16}{3} + \frac{16}{15} - \frac{32}{7} = \frac{64}{35} \qquad \ldots(B)$$

Now $$\sigma_f^2 = \sigma_e^2 \,.\, [\Sigma |h(n)|^2 + \Sigma |h_2(n)|^2]$$

$$= \sigma_e^2 \left[\frac{64}{35} + \frac{16}{15}\right] = \frac{304}{105}\sigma_e^2 = 2.89\,\sigma_e^2 \qquad \textbf{Ans.}$$

(*b*) For parallel realization of *H*(*z*), we get the following configuration:

$$H(z) = \frac{2}{1-\frac{1}{2}z^{-1}} - \frac{1}{1-\frac{1}{4}z^{-1}} \triangleq H_3(z) + H_4(z)$$

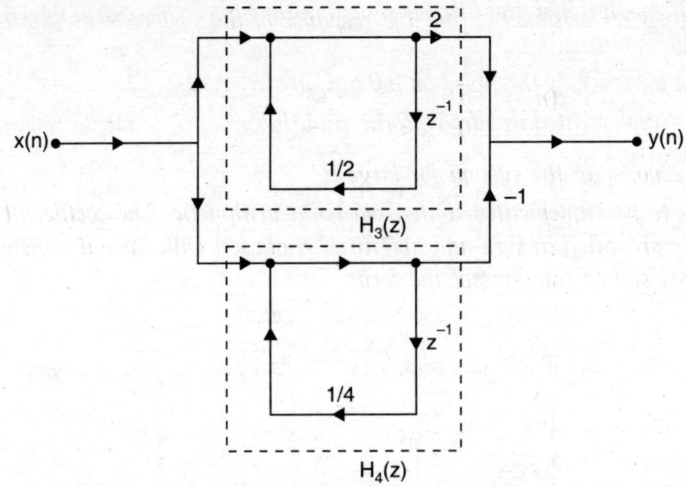

Fig. Ex. 10.12. (*b*) The given IIR filter

where $$H_3(z) = \frac{2}{1-\frac{1}{2}z^{-1}} \quad \therefore \quad h_3(n) = 2\,.\left(\frac{1}{2}\right)^n u(n)$$

$$\sum_n |h_3(n)|^2 = \sum_{n=0}^{\infty} 4\,.\left(\frac{1}{2}\right)^2 = 4\,.\frac{1}{1-\frac{1}{4}} = \frac{16}{3}$$

$$H_4(z) = \frac{-1}{1-\frac{1}{4}z^{-1}} \quad \therefore \quad h_4(z) = -\left(\frac{1}{4}\right)^n u(n)$$

$$\therefore \quad \sum_n |h_4(n)|^2 = \sum_{n=0}^{\infty} \left(\frac{1}{4}\right)^{2n} = \frac{-1}{1-\frac{1}{16}} = \frac{16}{15}$$

$$\sigma_f^2 = \sigma_e^2 \left[\sum_n |h_3(n)|^2 + \sum_n |h_4(n)|^2\right]$$

$$= \sigma_e^2 \left[\frac{16}{3} + \frac{16}{15}\right] = \frac{32}{5}\sigma_e^2 = 6.4\,\sigma_e^2$$ **Ans.**

Note: Had we reversed $H_1(z)$ and $H_2(z)$ with $H_2(z)$ as first filter we would get $\sigma_f^2 = \sigma_e^2 \left[\frac{64}{35} + \frac{4}{3}\right]$ $= \frac{332}{105}\sigma_e^2 = 3.16\,\sigma_e^2$ which is more than that we obtained in part (*a*)

EXAMPLE 10.13: *The flowgraph of the first-order system is shown in Fig. Ex. 10.13(a)*

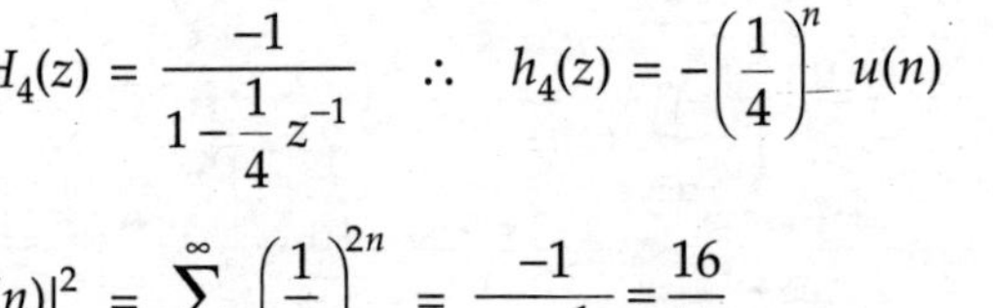

Fig. Ex. 10.13. (*a*)

(a) Assuming perfect arithmetic, find the response of the system to as input

$$x(n) = \begin{cases} \dfrac{1}{2}, & n \geq 0 \\ 0, & < 0 \end{cases}$$

What is the response of the system for large n?

The system is to be implemented with fixed-point arithmetic. The coefficient and all variable in the network are to be represented in sign-and magnitude notation with five-bit registers. That is, all numbers are to be considered signed fractions of the form.

s	a	b	c	d

s = signal bit

$$\text{Register value} = a \times 2^{-1} + b \times 2^{-2} + c \times 2^{-3} + d \times 2^{-4}$$

where a, b, c, d are either 0 or 1.

The result of a multiplication is truncated; i.e., only the sign and the most significant four bits are retained.

(b) Compute the responses of the quantized system to the input of part (a) and plot the responses of both the quantized and unquantized system for $0 \leq n \leq 5$. How do the responses compare for large n?

(c) Now consider the system depicted in Fig. Ex. 10.13(b) where

$$x(n) = \begin{cases} \dfrac{1}{2}(-1)^n, & n \geq 0 \\ 0, & n < 0 \end{cases}$$

Repeat parts (a) and (b) for the system and input

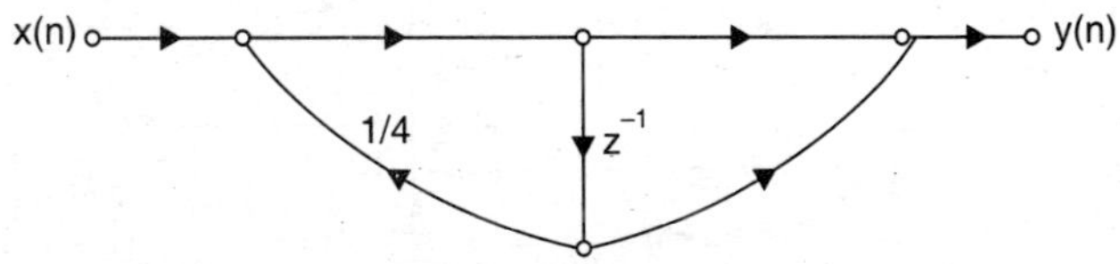

Fig. Ex. 10.13. (*b*)

SOLUTION: (*a*) $y(n) = x(n) + \frac{1}{4}\, y(n-1)$

As $$x(n) = \begin{cases} \dfrac{1}{2}, & n \geq 0 \\ 0, & n < 0 \end{cases}$$

$\therefore$ $$y(0) = x(0) + \frac{1}{4}\,\underset{\nearrow = 0}{y(1)}$$

$$= \frac{1}{2} + 0 = \frac{1}{2}$$

$$y(1) = x(1) + \frac{1}{4}\, y(0)$$

$$= \frac{1}{2} + \frac{1}{4} \cdot \frac{1}{2} = \frac{5}{8}$$

$$y(2) = x(2) + \frac{1}{4}\, y(1)$$

$$= \frac{1}{2} + \frac{1}{4} \cdot \frac{5}{8} = \frac{21}{32}$$

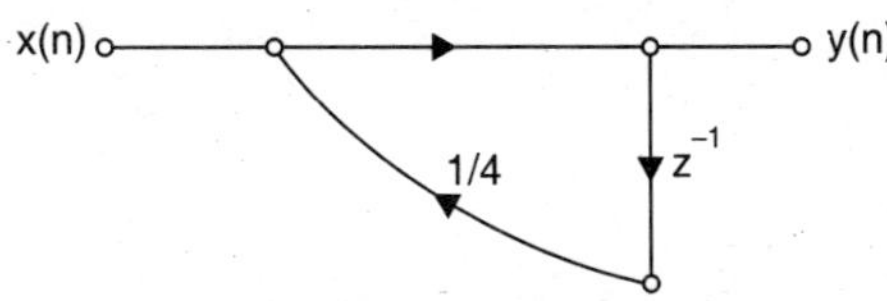

Fig. Ex. 10.13. (*c*)

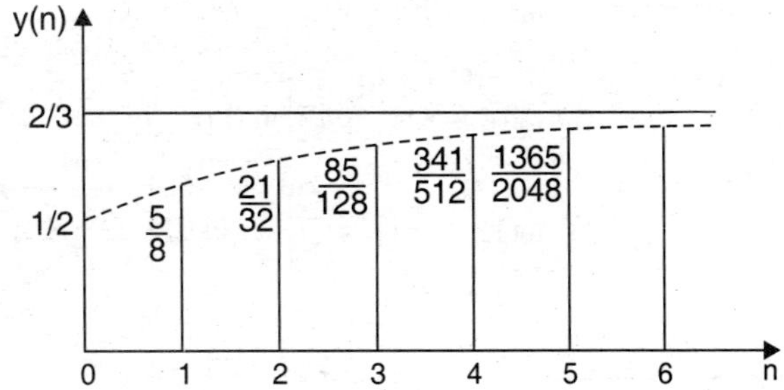

Fig. Ex. 10.13. (*d*)

$$y(3) = x(3) + \frac{1}{4}\, y(2) = \frac{1}{2} + \frac{1}{4}.\frac{21}{32} = \frac{85}{128}$$

$$y(4) = x(4) + \frac{1}{4}\, y(3) = \frac{1}{2} + \frac{1}{4}\left(\frac{85}{128}\right) = \frac{341}{512}$$

$$y(5) = x(5) + \frac{1}{4}\, y(4) = \frac{1}{2} + \frac{1}{4}\frac{341}{512} = \frac{1365}{2048}$$

$$\lim_{n\to\infty} y(n) = \frac{2}{3}$$ **Ans.**

Otherwise

As $$y(n) = x(0) + \frac{1}{4}\, y(n-1),\ x(n) = \begin{cases}\frac{1}{2}, & n \geq 0\\ 0, & n < 0\end{cases}$$

$$\therefore \quad H(z) = \frac{1}{1-\frac{1}{4}z^{-1}}, \qquad X(z) = \frac{1}{2}\frac{1}{1-z^{-1}}$$

$$Y(z) = X(z)\ .\ H(z)$$

$$= \frac{1}{2}\frac{1}{1-z^{-1}}.\frac{1}{1-\frac{1}{4}z^{-1}}$$

$$= \frac{1}{2}\left[\frac{1}{(1-z^{-1})}\left(\frac{1}{1-\frac{1}{4}}\right) + \frac{1}{1-\frac{1}{4}z^{-1}}\left(\frac{1}{1-4}\right)\right]$$

$$= \frac{1}{2}\left[\frac{4/3}{1-z^{-1}} - \frac{1/3}{1-\frac{1}{4}z^{-1}}\right]$$

$$= \frac{2}{3}.\frac{1}{1-z^{-1}} - \frac{1}{6}.\frac{1}{1-\frac{1}{4}z^{-1}}$$

$$\therefore \quad y(n) = \frac{2}{3}u(n) - \frac{1}{6}\left(\frac{1}{4}\right)^n u(n) = \left(\frac{2}{3} - \frac{1}{6}\left(\frac{1}{4}\right)^n\right)u(n)$$

$$\underset{n\to\infty}{y(n)} = \frac{2}{3}$$ **Ans.**

(*b*) Here $$\omega(n) = x(n) + Q\left[\frac{1}{4}\,\omega(n-1)\right]$$

$$\omega(0) = x(0) + Q\left[\frac{1}{4}0\right] = \frac{1}{2}$$

$$\omega(1) = x(1) + Q\left[\frac{1}{4}.\,\omega(0)\right]$$

$$= \frac{1}{2} + Q\left[\frac{1}{4}.\frac{1}{2}\right] = \frac{1}{2} + \frac{1}{8} = \frac{5}{8}$$

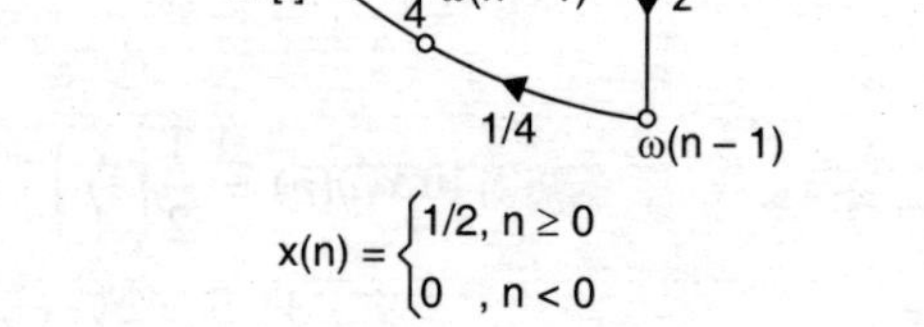

Fig. Ex. 10.13. (*e*)

$$\omega(2) = x(2) + Q\left[\frac{1}{4}\cdot\frac{5}{8}\right] = \frac{1}{2} + \theta\left[\frac{5}{32}\right]$$

$$= \frac{1}{2} + Q\,[0_\Delta 0010\vdots 1]$$

$$= \frac{1}{2} + \frac{1}{8} = \frac{5}{8}$$

$$\omega(3),\ \omega(4)\ \ldots = \frac{5}{8}$$

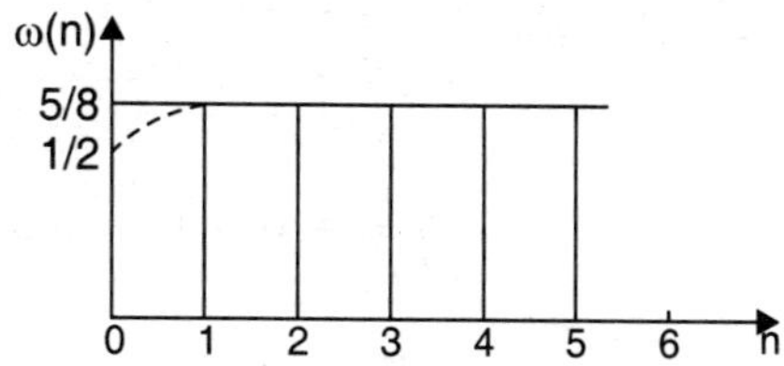

Fig. Ex. 10.13. (*f*)

(*c*) (*i*) (Unquantized case)

$$x(n) = \begin{cases} \frac{1}{2}(-1)^n, & n \ge 0 \\ 0, & \text{otherwise} \end{cases}$$

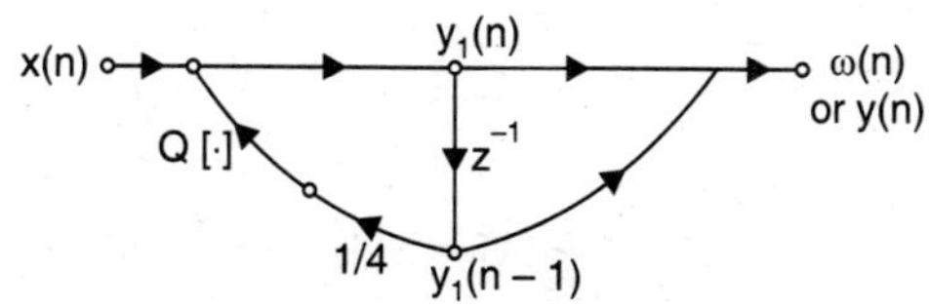

$$y_1(n) = x(n) + \frac{1}{4}y_1(n-1)$$

$$y(n) = y_1(n) + y_1(n-1)$$

Fig. Ex. 10.13. (*g*)

$$\therefore \quad X(z) = \frac{1}{2}\frac{1}{1-(-1)z^{-1}} = \frac{1}{2}\frac{1}{1+z^{-1}}$$

$$H(z) = \frac{1+z^{-1}}{1-\frac{1}{4}z^{-1}}$$

$$\therefore \quad Y(z) = X(z)\,.\,H(z) = \frac{1}{2}\frac{1}{1+z^{-1}}\cdot\frac{1+z^{-1}}{1-\frac{1}{4}z^{-1}} = \frac{1}{2}\frac{1}{1-\frac{1}{4}z^{-1}}$$

$$\therefore \quad y(n) = \frac{1}{2}\cdot\left(\frac{1}{4}\right)^n u(n)$$

$$\therefore \quad y(0) = \frac{1}{2},\ y(1) = \frac{1}{8},\ y(2) = \frac{1}{32}$$

$$y(3) = \frac{1}{128},\ y(4) = \frac{1}{512},\ y(5) = \frac{1}{2048}$$

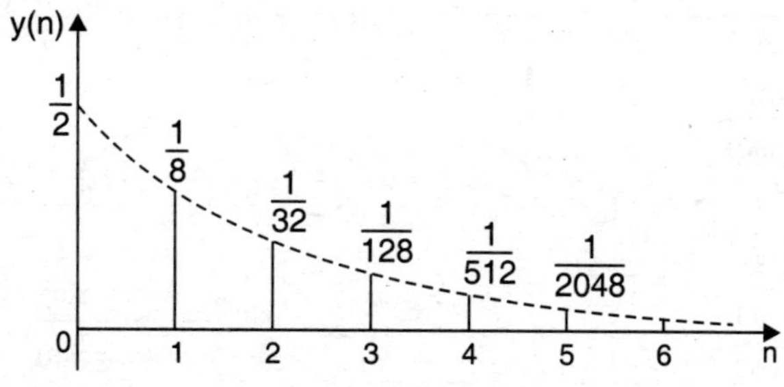

Fig. Ex. 10.13. (*h*)

$$\lim_{n\to\infty} y(n) = \frac{1}{2}\left(\frac{1}{4}\right)^{\infty} = 0$$ **Ans.**

Otherwise

$$y_1(n) = x(n) + \frac{1}{4}\, y_1(n-1)$$

$$\therefore \qquad y_1(0) = x(0) + 0 = +\frac{1}{2}$$

$$y_1(1) = x(1) + \frac{1}{4}\, y_1(0) = -\frac{1}{2}+\frac{1}{4}.\frac{1}{2} = -\frac{3}{8}$$

$$y_1(2) = x(2) + \frac{1}{4}\, y_1(1) = \frac{1}{2}+\frac{1}{4}\left(\frac{-3}{8}\right) = \frac{13}{32}$$

$$y_1(3) = x(3) + \frac{1}{4}\, y_1(2) = -\frac{1}{2}+\frac{1}{4}\left(\frac{13}{32}\right) = -\frac{51}{128}$$

$$y_1(4) = x(4) + \frac{1}{4}\, y_1(3) = \frac{1}{2}+\frac{1}{4}\left(\frac{-51}{128}\right) = \frac{205}{512}$$

$$y_1(5) = x(5) + \frac{1}{4}\, y_1(4) = -\frac{1}{2}+\frac{1}{4}\left(\frac{205}{512}\right) = -\frac{819}{2048}$$

As $\quad y(n) = y_1(n) + y_1(n-1)$

$$y(0) = y_1(0) + y_1(-1) = \frac{1}{2}+0 = \frac{1}{2}$$

$$y(1) = y_1(1) + y_1(0) = -\frac{3}{8}+\frac{1}{4} = \frac{1}{8}$$

$$y(2) = y_1(2) + y_1(1) = \frac{13}{32}-\frac{3}{8} = \frac{1}{32}$$

$$y(3) = y_1(3) + y_1(2) = -\frac{51}{128}+\frac{13}{32} = \frac{1}{128}$$

$$y(4) = y_1(4) + y_1(3) = \frac{205}{512}-\frac{51}{128} = \frac{1}{512}$$

$$y(5) = y_1(5) + y_1(4)$$

$$= -\frac{819}{2048}+\frac{205}{512} = \frac{1}{2048}$$

which are same value find

(*c*) (*ii*) (Quantized case)

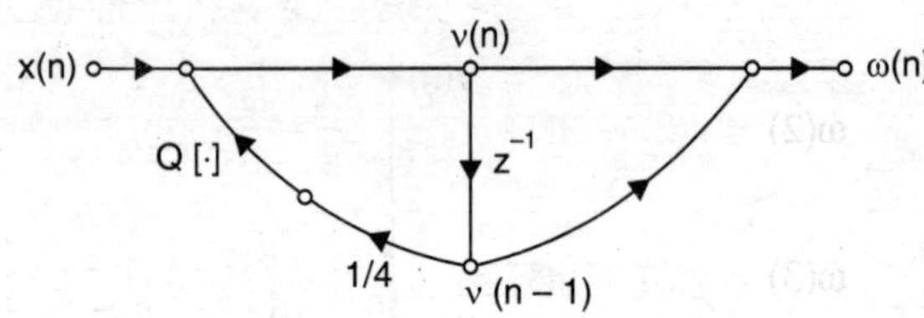

$$\nu(n) = x(n) + Q\left[\frac{1}{4}\,\nu(n-1)\right]$$

$$\omega(n) = \nu(n) + \nu(n-1)$$

$$x(n) = \begin{cases} \frac{1}{2}(-1)^n & n \geq 0 \\ 0 & n < 0 \end{cases}$$

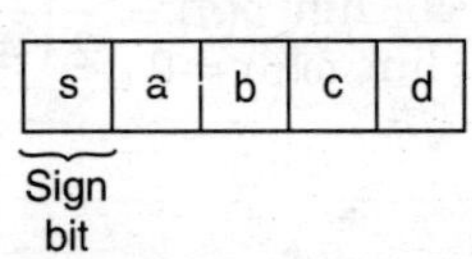

$$\nu(n) = x(n) + Q\left[\frac{1}{4}\,\nu(n-1)\right]$$

$$\nu(0) = x(0) + 0 = \frac{1}{2}$$

$$\nu(1) = x(1) + Q\left[\frac{1}{4}\,\nu(0)\right]$$

$$= -\frac{1}{2}+Q\left[\frac{1}{4}.\frac{1}{2}\right] = -\frac{1}{2}+\frac{1}{8} = -\frac{3}{8}$$

$$\nu(2) = x(2) + Q\left[\frac{1}{4}\nu(1)\right]$$

$$= \frac{1}{2} + Q\left[\frac{1}{4}\cdot\left(-\frac{3}{8}\right)\right] = \frac{1}{2} + \underbrace{Q[1_\Delta 0001\vdots 10]}_{=-\frac{1}{16}} = \frac{1}{2} - \frac{1}{16} = \frac{7}{16}$$

$$\nu(3) = x(3) + Q\left[\frac{1}{4}\nu(2)\right]$$

$$= -\frac{1}{2} + Q\left[\frac{1}{4}\frac{7}{16}\right]$$

$$= -\frac{1}{2} + Q[0_\Delta 0001\vdots 11] = -\frac{1}{2} + \frac{1}{16} = -\frac{7}{16}$$

$$\nu(4) = x(4) + Q\left[\frac{1}{4}\nu(3)\right]$$

$$= \frac{1}{2} + Q\left[\frac{1}{4}\frac{-7}{16}\right] = \frac{1}{2} + Q[1_\Delta 0001\vdots 11] = \frac{1}{2} - \frac{1}{16} = \frac{7}{16}$$

$$\nu(5) = -\frac{7}{16},$$

$$\nu(6) = \frac{7}{16} \text{ and so on.}$$

As $\omega(n) = \nu(n) + \nu(n-1)$

$$\therefore \quad \omega(0) = \nu(0) + 0 = \frac{1}{2}$$

$$\omega(1) = \nu(1) + \nu(0) = -\frac{3}{8} + \frac{1}{2} = \frac{1}{8}$$

$$\omega(2) = \nu(2) + \nu(1) = \frac{7}{16} - \frac{3}{8} = \frac{1}{16}$$

$$\omega(3) = \nu(3) + \nu(1) = -\frac{7}{16} + \frac{7}{16} = 0$$

$$\omega(4) = \nu(4) + \nu(3) = -\frac{7}{16} - \frac{7}{16} = 0$$

$$\omega(5) = \nu(5) + \nu(4) = -\frac{7}{16} + \frac{7}{16} = 0$$

and thus $\quad \omega(6), \omega(7) \ldots = 0$

Thus, $\quad \lim_{n\to\infty} \omega(6) = 0$

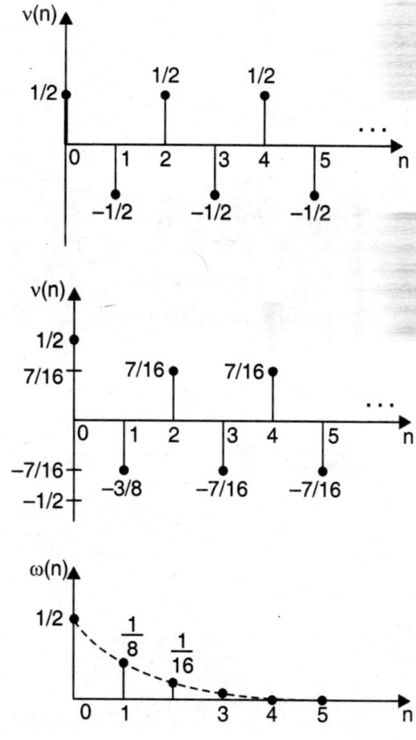

Fig. Ex. 10.13. (i)

Ans.

EXAMPLE 10.14: *Consider the first-order filter shown in Fig. 10. Ex. 14(a). The quantizer Q[] represents the fact that the result of the multiplication by* α *is rounded. All number are fixed-point fractions with a word length of b bits (excluding sign bit)*

The input is zero, but the filter is started with some initial condition, say $y(-1) = A$. *Because of the quantizer, there is a range of values of A referred to as the dead band, for which the effective value of the coefficients* α *is + or – unity, i.e.,* $|Q[\alpha A]| = A$. *Once the output falls into that range, it will either oscillate or remain a constant, depending on whether the effective coeff. is +ve or –ve.*

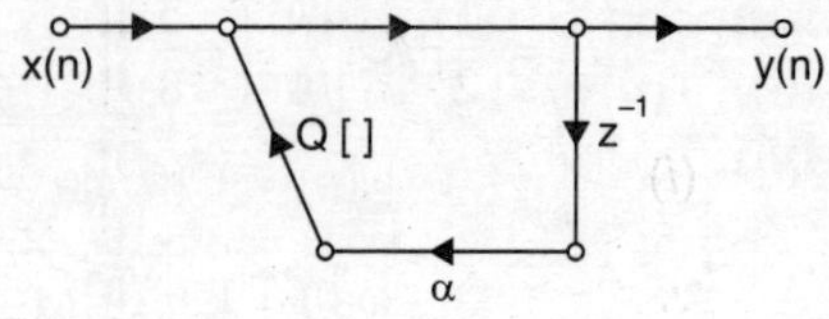

Fig. Ex. 10.14. (a)

(a) Determine in terms of α *and b the range of values of A corresponding to the dead band.*

(b) For $b = 6$ *bits and* $A = \frac{1}{16}$, *sketch y(n) for* $\alpha = +\frac{15}{16}$ *and* $\alpha = -\frac{15}{16}$.

SOLUTION: (*a*) For rounding, the effective values of α is ± 1. When $|Q\,\omega[n-1] - \alpha\,\omega(n-1)| \le \frac{1}{2}2^{-b}$.

i.e., $|\omega(n-1)| - |\alpha|\;|\omega(n-1)| \le \frac{1}{2}\,2^{-b}$

i.e., $$|\omega(n-1)| \le \frac{\frac{1}{2}2^{-b}}{1-|\alpha|}$$

$\therefore$ $$|A| \le \frac{\frac{1}{2}2^{-b}}{1-|\alpha|}$$ gives range of A for zero cycle to occur

[Lower limit of A]

As can be seen from above $|A| \le \dfrac{\frac{1}{2}2^{-b}}{1-|\alpha|}$. For a case, where suppose $|\alpha|$ can be varied in the permissible range $|\alpha| < 1$, the lower limit of $|A|$ will to $|A| = 2^{-b}$ *i.e.,* least significant bit below this value of $|A|$, the register will not store at all, instead it would show 0 in all its bits

When $|A| = 2^{-b}$, then

$$|A| \le \frac{\frac{1}{2}2^{-b}}{1-|\alpha|} \text{ gives } 2^{-b} \le \frac{\frac{1}{2}2^{-b}}{1-|\alpha|}$$

i.e., $$1 - |\alpha| < \frac{1}{2} \text{ i.e. } |\alpha| \ge \frac{1}{2} \text{ which is feasible}$$

Then we can write

$$\boxed{2^{-b} \le |A| \le \frac{\frac{1}{2}2^{-b}}{1-|\alpha|}}$$

(*b*) Given $b = 6$ bits besides sign bit

$$A = \frac{1}{16} \text{ i.e., } \omega(-1) = \frac{1}{16}$$

$$\alpha = \pm\frac{15}{16}$$

(*i*)
$$\omega(n) = Q[\alpha\, \omega(n-1)] + x(n)$$

$$\therefore \quad \omega(0) = Q\left[\frac{15}{16}\,\omega(-1)\right] + x(0)$$

($\omega(-1) = \frac{1}{16}$ given; $x(0) = 0$ given)

$$= Q\left[\frac{15}{16}\cdot\frac{1}{16}\right] = Q\,[0_\Delta 1111\,.\,0_\Delta 0001]$$

$$= Q[0_\Delta 000011\vdots 11] = 0_\Delta 0001 = \frac{1}{16} \text{ (by rounding)}$$

$$\omega(1) = Q\left[\frac{15}{16}\,\omega(0)\right] = Q\left[\frac{15}{16}\cdot\frac{1}{16}\right]$$

$$= \frac{1}{16} \text{ as earlier}$$

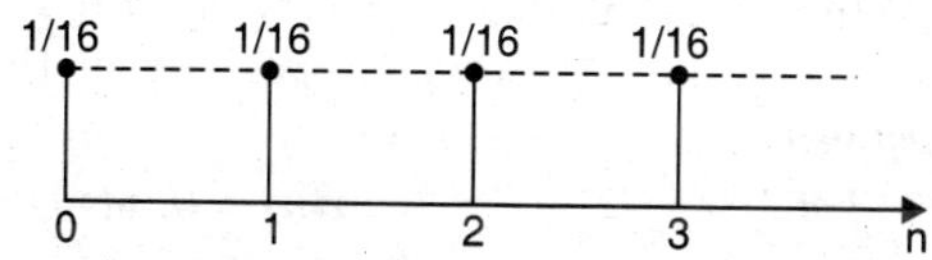

Zero-cycling with Dead band $= \frac{1}{16}$ and frequency (time period) $= 1T$ **Ans.**

(*ii*)
$$\alpha = -\frac{15}{16}$$

$$A = \frac{1}{16} \quad \text{i.e. } (\omega - 1)$$

$$b = 6 \text{ bits}$$

$$\omega(n) = Q[\alpha\, \omega(n-1)] + x(n)$$

$$\omega(0) = Q\left[-\frac{15}{16}\cdot\frac{1}{16}\right] + 0 \qquad \because\ x(0) = 0, \text{ zero input}$$

$$= Q[1_\Delta 000011\vdots 11]$$

$$= 1_\Delta 00010 = -\frac{1}{16}$$

$$\omega(1) = Q[\alpha\omega(0)]$$

$$= Q\left[-\frac{15}{16}\cdot\frac{-1}{16}\right]$$

$$= Q\left[\frac{15}{256}\right] = Q[0_\Delta 000011\vdots 11]$$

$$= 0_\Delta 00010 = \frac{1}{16}$$

Similarly, $\omega(2) = \omega(4) = \ldots -\dfrac{1}{16}$

$\omega(3) = \omega(5) = \ldots +\dfrac{1}{16}$

In general, $\omega(n) = (-1)^{n+1}\,\dfrac{1}{16}$

Dead band $= \pm\,\dfrac{1}{16}$

time period $= 2T$.

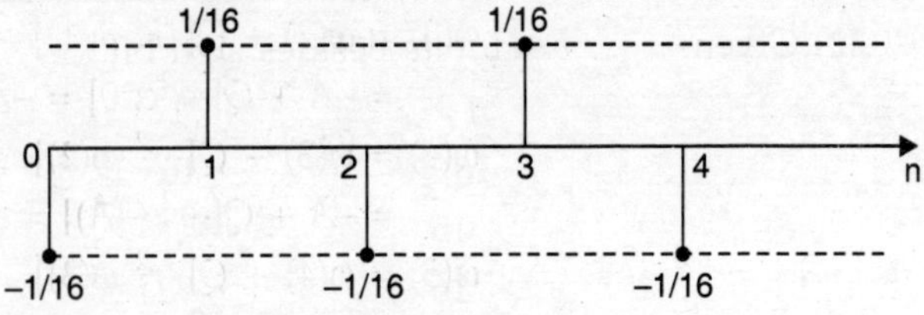

Fig. Ex. 10.14. (*b*)

EXAMPLE 10.15: *Consider the 2nd-order system shown. The filter is to be realized with fixed-point arithmetic and the result of all multiplications are rounded. All numbers are fixed-point fractions with a word length b bits. There is a dead-band region for y(n) for which the 'effective' value of the coefficient $-r^2$ is 1. When this range of y(n) is reached, the effective pole position can be considered to be on the unit circle and the angular position of the poles changed.*

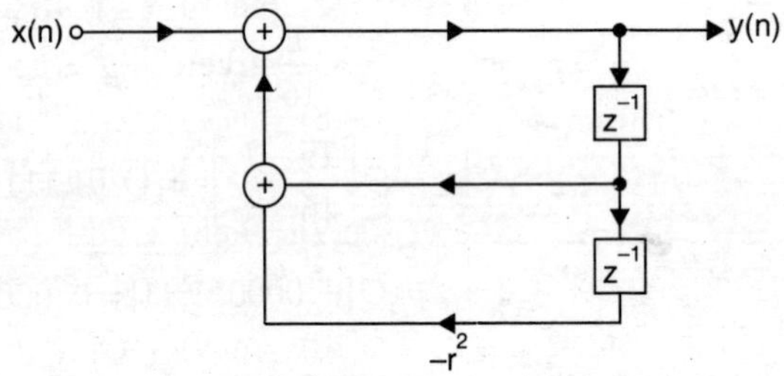

Fig. Ex. 10.15. (*a*)

Let $x(n) = 0,\ y(-1) = A,\ y(-2) = 0,\ A \neq 0$

(*a*) *Find the dead band for A i.e., the values of A for which* $Q[-r^2A] = -A$

(*b*) *By obtaining a lower bound on A, find the range of values of r for which it is possible to have a dead band.*

SOLUTION: Here $y(n) = x(n) + y(n-1) - r^2\,y(n-2)$ ...(1)

Compare this with a 2nd order recursive filter

$$H(z) = \frac{1}{(1 - z^{-1}\,re^{j\theta})(1 - z^{-1}\,re^{-j\theta})}$$

i.e., $$y(n) = x(n) + 2r\cos\theta\; y(n-1) - r^2\,y(n-2) \quad \ldots(2)$$

From (1) and (2), $2r\cos\theta = 1 \;\therefore\; \theta = \cos^{-1}\dfrac{1}{2r}$

Due to quantization (rounding off), the filter can be assumed as shown in Fig. Ex. 10.15(*b*).

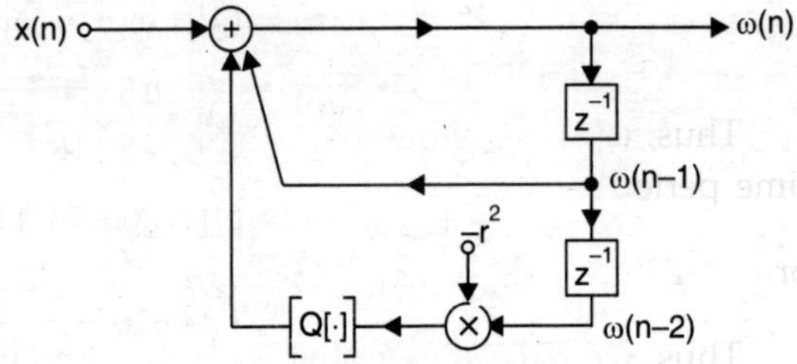

Fig. Ex. 10.15. (*b*)

i.e., effective $r^2 = 1$

Hence, $\omega(n) = x(n) + \omega(n-1) + Q[-r^2\,\omega(n-2)]$

$\omega(0) = x(0) + \omega(-1) + Q[-r^2\,\omega(-2)]$

↗ zero input $\quad \therefore\; x(n) = 0$ function all n

$\omega(-1) = A$ given

Let $\quad Q[-r^2\,\omega(n-2)] = -\omega(n-2)$

$$\therefore \quad \omega(0) = 0 + A + Q[-r^2 \times 0] = A$$

$$\omega(1) = \omega(0) + Q[-r^2\,\omega(-1)]$$

$$= A + Q[r^2A] = A - A = 0$$

$$\omega(2) = \omega(1) + Q[-r^2\,\omega(0)]$$

$$= 0 + Q[-r^2A] = -A$$

$$\begin{aligned}
\omega(3) &= \omega(2) + Q[-r^2\,\omega(1)] \\
&= -A + Q[-r^2\alpha\ 0] = -A \\
\omega(4) &= \omega(3) + Q[-r^2\,\omega(2)] \\
&= -A + Q[-r^2\,(-A)] = -A + A = 0 \\
\omega(5) &= \omega(4) + Q[-r^2\,\omega(3)] \\
&= 0 + Q[-r^2(-A)] = A \\
\omega(6) &= \omega(5) + Q[-r^2\,\omega(4)] \\
&= A + Q[-r^2(0)] = A \\
\omega(7) &= \omega(6) + Q[-r^2\,\omega(5)] \\
&= A + Q[-r^2A] = A - A = 0 \\
\omega(8) &= \omega(7) + Q[-r^2\,\omega(6)] \\
&= 0 + Q[-r^2A] = -A \\
\omega(9) &= \omega(8) + Q[-r^2\,\omega(7)] \\
&= -A + Q[-r^2\times 0] = -A \\
\omega(10) &= \omega(9) + Q[-r^2\,\omega(8)] \\
&= -A + Q[-r^2(-A)] = -A + A = 0
\end{aligned}$$

In general, we find that

$$\omega(n) = \begin{cases} 1, & n = 6M, 6M+5, \quad M = 0 \text{ to } \infty \\ 0, & n = 3M+1, \quad M = 0 \text{ to } \infty \\ -1, & n = 6M+2, 6M+3, \quad M = 0 \text{ to } \infty \end{cases}$$

If we draw this output sequence

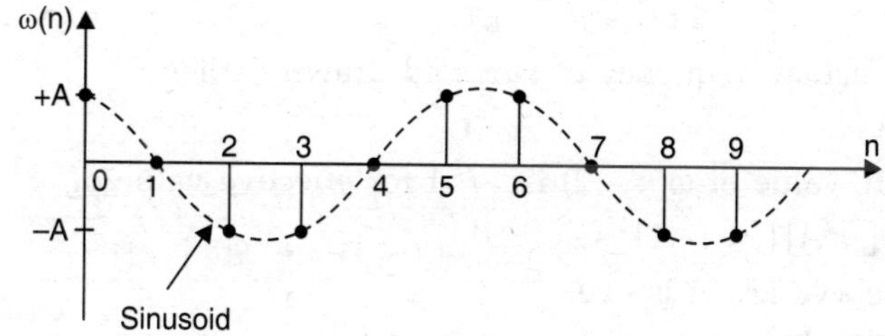

Fig. Ex. 10.15. (*c*)

Thus, $\omega(n)$ is a sinusoid

time period $\tau = 6T$

or $f = \dfrac{1}{6T}$

Thus, we have shown that with zero input $x(n)$ and some value of A (+ve or –ve) a sinusoid will exist which can be viewed as zero input limit cycle.

Lower bound for A

Let b = no. of bits (excluding bit) of register

Then minimum storable value = 2^{-b}

Since, value A (or $-A$) must be present at $\omega(n-1)$ or at $\omega(n-2)$ to sustain limit cycle, the minimum value of A is naturally 2^{-b} *i.e.*, only LSB of the register being 1 and all other 1 bits zero.

Thus, lower bound for A is $\boxed{2^{-b} \le |A|}$

If at least this value of A is initially present at $\omega(n-1)$ or at $\omega(n-2)$, zero input limit cycle can be sustained.

Calculation of sinusoid time period

In the given structure

$$2r \cos \theta = 1$$

But $\quad r^2 = 1 \quad \because$ due to quantization effect r^2 as effectively unity

$\therefore \quad r = +1$

i.e., $$2 \cos \theta = \frac{1}{r} = +1$$

$$\therefore \quad \cos \theta = +\frac{1}{2}$$

$$\therefore \quad \cos \theta = +\frac{\pi}{3}$$

Also $$\omega = \frac{1}{T} \cos^{-1} \frac{2r \cos \theta}{2} \qquad \left[\because \ \omega = \frac{1}{T} \cos^{-1} \frac{\alpha}{2}\right]$$

$$\therefore \quad \omega = \frac{1}{T} \cos^{-1} (r \cos \theta)$$

$$= \frac{1}{T} \cos^{-1} \left(1 \cos \frac{\pi}{3}\right)$$

$$= \frac{\pi}{3T} \cos^{-1} \left(\frac{1}{2}\right)$$

i.e., $$f = \frac{1}{2\pi} \cdot \frac{\pi}{3T} = \frac{1}{6T}$$

which agrees with the actual frequency of sinusoid drawn earlier.

(a) Dead band for A

Before quantization, value of $\omega(n - 2)$ is, $-r^2A$ for effective value of $-r^2$ to be -1,

$$|Q[-r^2A]| = |-A|$$

Case A: Let $-r^2A$ be +ve *i.e.,* A is −ve

$$\therefore \quad Q[-r^2A] = -A$$

But $-\frac{1}{2} 2^{-b} < Q(x) - x < \frac{1}{2} 2^{-b}$ (for fixed point, rounding off)

$$\therefore \quad -\frac{1}{2} 2^{-b} < -A - (-r^2A) \leq \frac{1}{2} 2^{-b}$$

i.e., $$-\frac{1}{2} 2^{-b} < -A \underbrace{(1 - r^2)}_{+\text{ve}} \leq \frac{1}{2} 2^{-b}$$ which is always feasible

i.e., $$\frac{-\frac{1}{2} 2^{-b}}{1 - r^2} < (-A) \leq \frac{\frac{1}{2} 2^{-b}}{1 - r^2}$$

Case B: If $-r^2A$ is −ve *i.e.,* A is +ve

then $$Q[-r^2A] = -A$$

But $\quad -\frac{1}{2}2^{-b} < Q(x) - x \leq \frac{1}{2}2^{-b}$ (for fixed points rounding)

$\therefore \quad -\frac{1}{2}2^{-b} < -A - (-r^2A) \leq \frac{1}{2}2^{-b}$

i.e., $\quad -\frac{1}{2}2^{-b} < -A \underbrace{(1-r^2)}_{+\text{ve}} \leq \frac{1}{2}2^{-b}$

i.e., $\quad \dfrac{-\frac{1}{2}2^{-b}}{1-r^2} < -A \leq \dfrac{\frac{1}{2}2^{-b}}{1-r^2}$

Thus, $\quad \boxed{\dfrac{-\frac{1}{2}2^{-b}}{1-r^2} \leq (-A) \leq \dfrac{\frac{1}{2}2^{-b}}{1-r^2}}$ are bounds of A *i.e.,* dead band of A.

(b) Range of value, of r for lower bound of A

When r is not unity, the least value of A is given by $|A| = 2^{-b}$ the LSB of the register. But $|A| \leq \dfrac{\frac{1}{2}2^{-b}}{1-r^2}$ gives the relation of A and r within the possible range of values, and putting $|A| = 2$ the lower bound of A

$$2^{-b} \leq \frac{1}{2}\cdot\frac{2^{-b}}{1-r^2}$$

$\therefore \quad 2(1 - r^2) \leq 1$

$\therefore \quad 2 - 1 \leq 2r^2$

or $\quad r^2 \geq \frac{1}{2}$

$\therefore \quad |r| \leq \frac{1}{\sqrt{2}}$

Thus, $|r|$ lies between $\frac{1}{\sqrt{2}}$ and 1

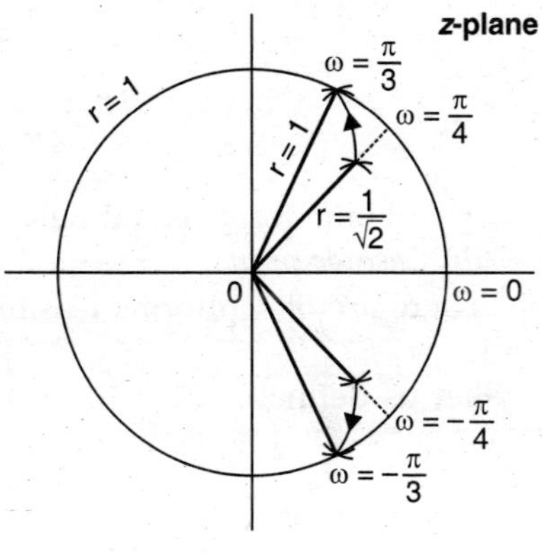

Fig. Ex. 10.15. (*d*)

when $\quad |r| = \frac{1}{\sqrt{2}}$, then $2r\cos\theta = 1$ gives

$$\cos\theta = \frac{1}{\sqrt{2}} \quad i.e., \quad \theta = \pm\frac{\pi}{4}$$

Thus, for the given structure for minimum value of $A(= 2^b)$ r may lie between $\frac{1}{\sqrt{2}}$ and 1 and the poles will shift along the line shown, by arrows in Fig. Ex. 10.15(*d*).

Conclusion

For $\quad |r| = \frac{1}{\sqrt{2}}$, poles are $\frac{1}{\sqrt{2}} e^{\pm j\frac{\pi}{4}}$

For $\quad |r| = 1$, poles are $e^{\pm j\frac{\pi}{3}}$

For minimum (lower bound) of $A = 2^{-b}$, $\frac{1}{\sqrt{2}} \le r < 1$ for limit cycle to exist.

EXAMPLE 10.16: *We wish to implement a digital filter having a transfer function.*

$$H(z) = \frac{1 - \frac{1}{4}z^{-1}}{\left(1 - \frac{1}{2}z^{-1}\right)\left(1 + \frac{1}{2}z^{-1}\right)}$$

(a) Draw a flow graph of the digital network that implements this filter in canonic form

(b) Draw flow graphs of the digital network that implement this filter in each possible cascade realization containing only first-order networks.

(c) The filter is to be implemented using fixed-point arithmetic. Data are represented by sign-and-magnitude fractions with a word length b bits excluding sign. Determine for each of the seven networks in (a) and (b) the variance of the multiplier round off at the output. Indicate which of the configurations leads to the lowest output noise.

SOLUTION: *(a) The canonic form* structure of

$$H(z) = \frac{1 - \frac{1}{4}z^{-1}}{\left(1 - \frac{1}{2}z^{-1}\right)\left(1 + \frac{1}{2}z^{-1}\right)}$$

can be found by writing

$$H(z) = \frac{1 - \frac{1}{4}z^{-1}}{1 - \frac{1}{4}z^{-2}}$$

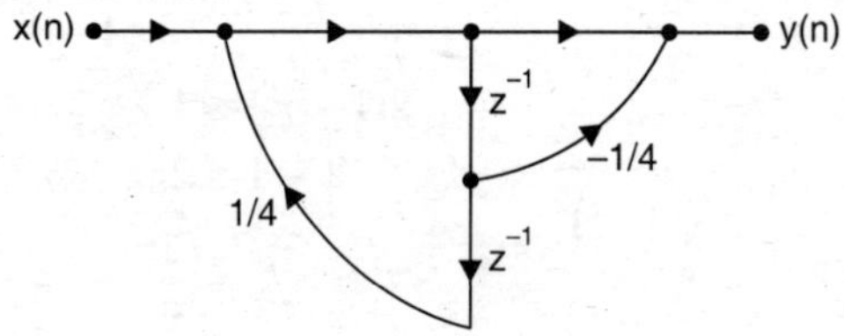

Fig. Ex. 10.16. *(a)*

Canonic form uses 2 delays only.

(b) Cascade form

There are 3! = 6 forms feasible

Let us define
$$H_1(z) = \left(1 - \frac{1}{4}z^{-1}\right)$$
$$H_2(z) = \frac{1}{1 - \frac{1}{2}z^{-1}}$$
$$H_3(z) = \frac{1}{1 + \frac{1}{2}z^{-1}}$$

Then

(i) H_1 H_2 H_3 form

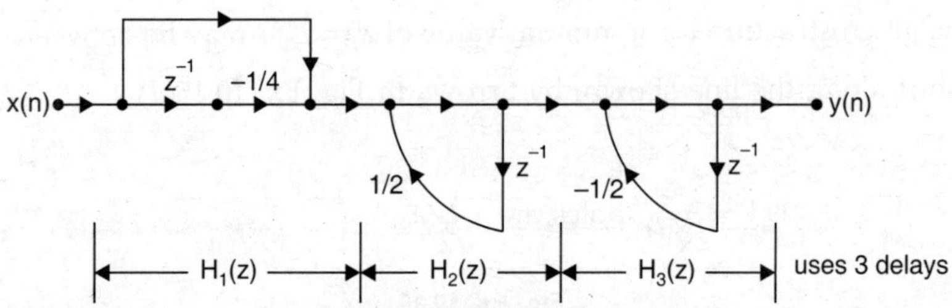

Fig. Ex. 10.16. *(b)*

(ii) $H_1\, H_3\, H_2$ *form*

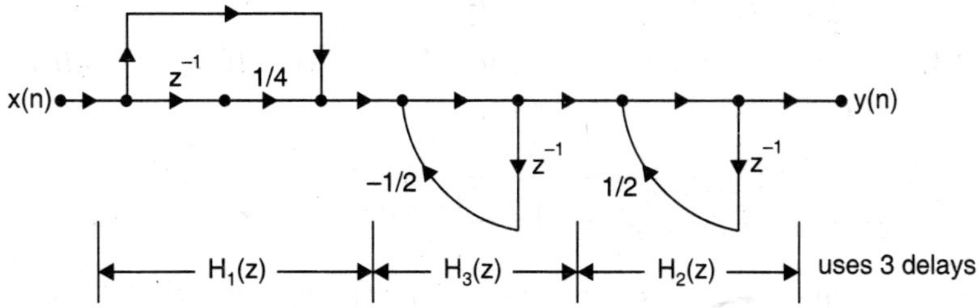

Fig. Ex. 10.16. *(c)*

(iii) $(H_2\, H_1)\, H_3$ *form*

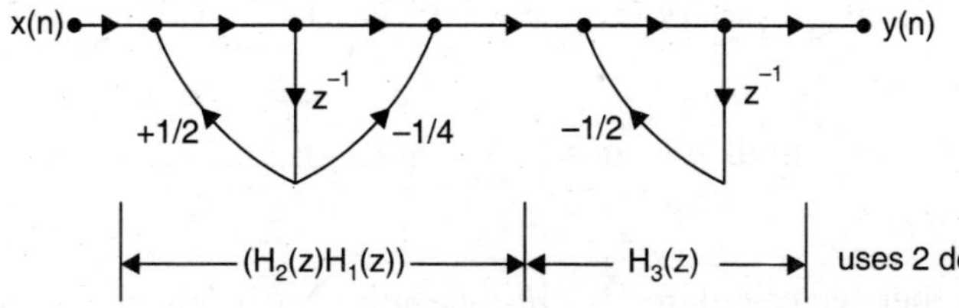

Fig. Ex. 10.16. *(d)*

(iv) $H_2\, (H_3\, H_1)$ *form*

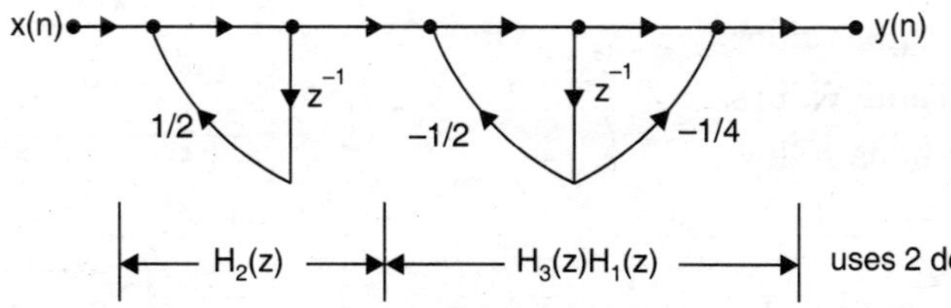

Fig. Ex. 10.16. *(e)*

(v) $(H_3\, H_1)\, H_2$ *form*

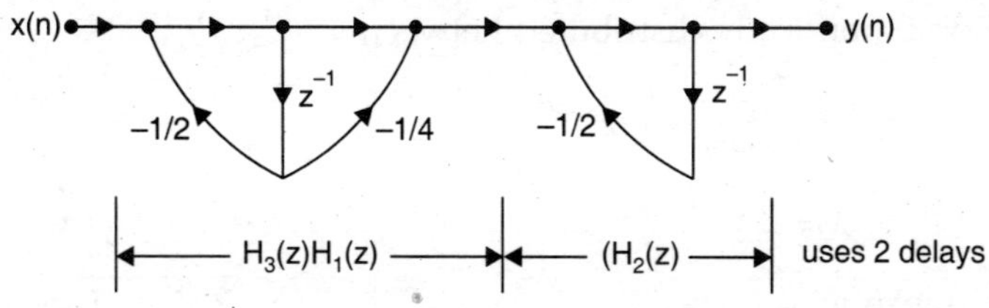

Fig. Ex. 10.16. *(f)*

(vi) $H_3\, (H_2\, H_1)$ *form*

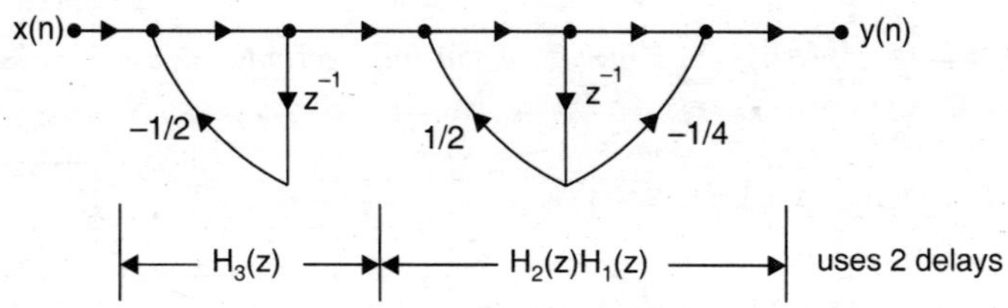

Fig. Ex. 10.16. *(g)*

Thus, the following configurations use 2 delays:

1. Canonic form
2. $(H_2 H_1) H_3$
3. $H_2 (H_3 H_1)$
4. $(H_3 H_1) H_2$
5. $H_3 (H_2 H_1)$

The following forms use 3 delays:

1. $H_1 H_2 H_3$
2. $H_1 H_3 H_2$ *i.e.*, when $H_1(z)$ comes as first section.

(c) To find Rounding off Errors-fixed Point Arithmetic

To calculate the errors at output points, we shall need $\sum_{n=0}^{\infty} |h(n)|^2$ of various sections. To calculate $y_{\max_k}$ at nodes k, we shall also need $\sum_{n=0}^{\infty} |h(n)|$ of various section.

Thus to proceed further we calculate $\sum_{n=0}^{\infty} |h(n)|^2$ and $\sum_{n=0}^{\infty} |h(n)|$ of all sections, individually and as combination of 2 sections

$H_1 H_2$, $H_2 H_1$, give same values

$H_1 H_3$, $H_3 H_1$, give same values

$H_2 H_3$, $H_3 H_2$, give same values.

The detailed calculations follow

$\sigma_{e_i}^2$

We assume that noises introduced are

1. Uncorrelated to $x(n)$ and hence to $y(n)$
2. Uncorrelated to each other
3. Are white noise, uniformly distributed between

$$-\frac{1}{2}2^{-b} < e \le +\frac{1}{2}2^{-b}$$

i.e., between $-\frac{1}{2}2^{-b}$ and $+\frac{1}{2}2^{-b}$

$\therefore$ mean $m_e = 0$

Variance $\sigma_e = \frac{1}{12}2^{-2b}$

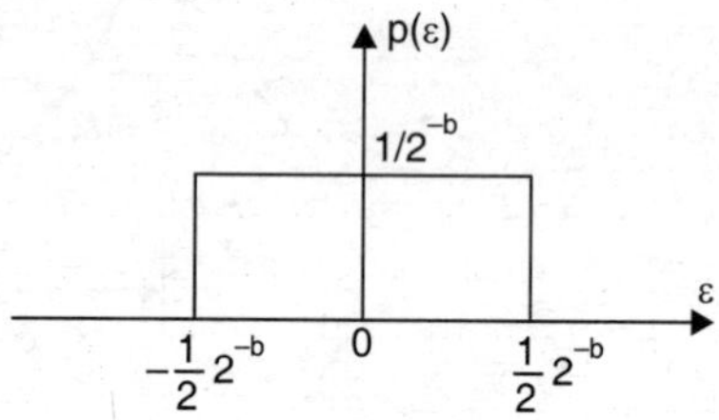

Calculations of h(n), $\sum_{n=0}^{\infty} |h(n)|$, $\sum_{n=0}^{\infty} |h(n)|^2$ *of various sections*

(*i*) $H_1(z) \triangleq \left(1 - \frac{1}{4}z^{-1}\right)$

$$h(n) = \delta(n) - \frac{1}{4}\delta(n-1)$$

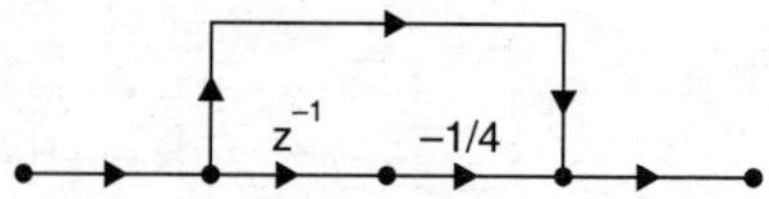

Fig. Ex. 10.16. (*h*)

$$\sum_{n=0}^{\infty} |h_1(n)| = 1 + \left|-\frac{1}{4}\right| = \frac{5}{4}$$

$$\sum_{n=0}^{\infty} |h_1(n)|^2 = \sum_{n=0}^{\infty} \left| \delta^2(n) + \frac{1}{16}\delta^2(n-1) - \underbrace{2\delta(n).(n-1)}_{=0} \right|$$

$$= 1 + \frac{1}{16} = \frac{17}{16}$$

$$H_1(z) = 1 - \frac{1}{4}z^{-1}$$

$$\sum_{n=0}^{\infty} |h_1(n)| = \frac{5}{4}$$

$$\sum_{n=0}^{\infty} |h_1(n)|^2 = \frac{17}{16}$$

(ii) $$H_1(z) \triangleq \frac{1}{1-\frac{1}{2}z^{-1}}$$

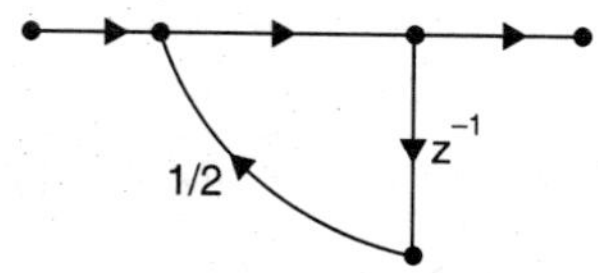

Fig. Ex. 10.16. (*i*)

$$h(n) = \left(\frac{1}{2}\right)^n u(n)$$

$$\sum_{n=0}^{\infty} |h_2(n)| = \sum_{n=0}^{\infty} \left(\frac{1}{2}\right)^n u(n)$$

$$= \frac{1}{1-\frac{1}{2}} = 2$$

$$\sum_{n=0}^{\infty} |h_2(n)|^2 = \sum_{n=0}^{\infty} \left(\frac{1}{4}\right)^n u^2(n)$$

$$= \sum_{n=0}^{\infty} \left(\frac{1}{4}\right)^n u(n)$$

$$= \frac{1}{1-\frac{1}{4}} = \frac{4}{3}$$

$$H_2(z) = \frac{1}{1-\frac{1}{2}z^{-1}}$$

$$\sum_{n=0}^{\infty} |h_2(n)| = 2$$

$$\sum_{n=0}^{\infty} |h_2(n)|^2 = \frac{4}{3}$$

(iii) $$H_3(z) \triangleq \frac{1}{1+\frac{1}{2}z^{-1}}$$

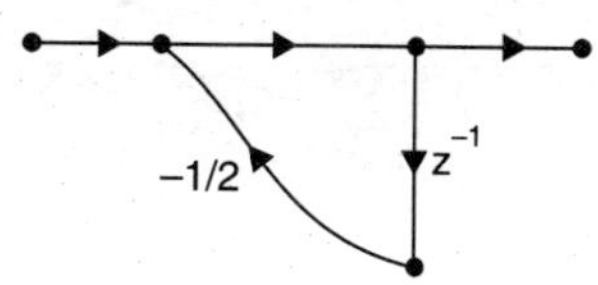

Fig. Ex. 10.16. (*j*)

$$h_3(n) = \left(-\frac{1}{2}\right)^n u(n)$$

$$\sum_{n=0}^{\infty} |h_3(n)| = \sum_{n=0}^{\infty} \left| \left(-\frac{1}{2}\right)^n u(n) \right|$$

$$= 1 + \left|-\frac{1}{2}\right| + \left|\frac{1}{4}\right| + \left|-\frac{1}{8}\right| + \ldots = \frac{1}{1-\frac{1}{2}} = 2$$

$$\sum_{n=0}^{\infty} |h_3(n)|^2 = \sum_{n=0}^{\infty} \left(\frac{1}{4}\right)^n \underset{\downarrow = u(n)}{u^2(n)}$$

$$= 1 + \frac{1}{4} + \frac{1}{16} + \ldots = \frac{1}{1-\frac{1}{4}} = \frac{4}{3}$$

$$H_3(z) = \frac{1}{1+\frac{1}{2}z^{-1}}$$

$$h_3(n) = \left(-\frac{1}{2}\right)^n u(n)$$

$$\sum_{n=0}^{\infty} |h_3(n)| = 2$$

$$\sum_{n=0}^{\infty} |h_3(n)|^2 = \frac{4}{3}$$

(iv) $H_4(z) \triangleq \dfrac{1-\frac{1}{4}z^{-1}}{\left(1-\frac{1}{2}z^{-1}\right)\left(1+\frac{1}{2}z^{-1}\right)}$

$$= \frac{\frac{3}{4}}{1+\frac{1}{2}z^{-1}} + \frac{\frac{1}{4}}{1-\frac{1}{2}z^{-1}}$$

$$\therefore \quad h_4(n) = \frac{3}{4}\left(-\frac{1}{2}\right)^n u(n) + \frac{1}{4}\left(\frac{1}{2}\right)^n u(n)$$

$$\sum_{n=0}^{\infty} |h(n)| = \sum_{n=0}^{\infty} \left|\left(\frac{3}{4}\left(-\frac{1}{2}\right)^n + \frac{1}{4}\left(\frac{1}{2}\right)^n\right)u(n)\right|$$

$$= 1 + \left|-\frac{1}{4}\right| + \left|\frac{1}{4}\right| + \left|-\frac{1}{16}\right| + \left|-\frac{1}{16}\right| + \ldots$$

$$= 1 + 2\left(\frac{1}{4} + \frac{1}{16} + \frac{1}{64} + \ldots\right)$$

$$= 1 + 2\frac{\frac{1}{4}}{1-\frac{1}{4}} = 1 + \frac{1}{2} \times \frac{4}{3}$$

$$= 1 + \frac{2}{3} = \frac{5}{3}$$

$$\sum_{n=0}^{\infty} |h(n)|^2 = \sum_{n=0}^{\infty} \left(\frac{9}{16}\left(\frac{1}{4}\right)^n + \frac{1}{16}\left(\frac{1}{4}\right)^n + \frac{3}{8}\left(-\frac{1}{4}\right)^n\right)u(n)$$

$$= \sum_{n=0}^{\infty} \left|\left(\frac{10}{16}\left(\frac{1}{4}\right)^n + \frac{3}{8}\left(-\frac{1}{4}\right)^n\right)\right| u(n)$$

$$= \frac{5}{8}\frac{1}{1-\frac{1}{4}} + \frac{3}{8}\frac{1}{1+\frac{1}{4}}$$

$$= \frac{5}{8} \times \frac{4}{3} + \frac{3}{8} \times \frac{4}{5}$$

$$= \frac{5}{6} + \frac{3}{10} = \frac{25+9}{30} = \frac{17}{15}$$

$$H(z) = \frac{1-\frac{1}{4}z^{-1}}{\left(1-\frac{1}{2}z^{-1}\right)\left(1+\frac{1}{2}z^{-1}\right)}$$

$$h(n) = \frac{3}{4}\left(-\frac{1}{2}\right)^n u(n) + \frac{1}{4}\left(\frac{1}{2}\right)^n u(n)$$

$$\sum_{n=0}^{\infty} |h(n)| = \frac{5}{3}$$

$$\sum_{n=0}^{\infty} |h(n)|^2 = \frac{17}{15}$$

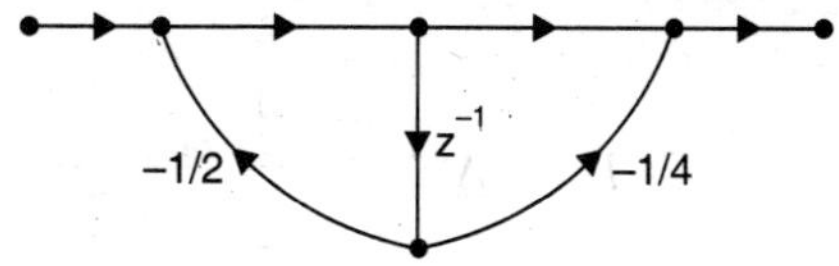

Fig. Ex. 10.16. (*k*)

(*v*) $H_4(z) \triangleq (H_1 H_3) = \dfrac{1-\frac{1}{4}z^{-1}}{1+\frac{1}{2}z^{-1}}$

$$H_4(z) = \frac{-\frac{1}{2}\left(1+\frac{1}{2}z^{-1}\right)+\frac{3}{2}}{1+\frac{1}{2}z^{-1}}$$

$$= -\frac{1}{2} + \frac{3}{2} \cdot \frac{1}{1+\frac{1}{2}z^{-1}}$$

$$\therefore \quad h_4(n) = -\frac{1}{2}\,\delta(n) + \frac{3}{2}\left(-\frac{1}{2}\right)^n u(n)$$

$$\sum_{n=0}^{\infty} |h_4(n)| = \sum_{n=0}^{\infty}\left|-\frac{1}{2}\delta(n)+\frac{3}{2}\left(-\frac{1}{2}\right)^n u(n)\right|$$

$$= \left|-\frac{1}{2}+\frac{3}{2}\right| + \left|-\frac{3}{4}\right| + \left|\frac{3}{8}\right| + \left|-\frac{3}{16}\right| + \ldots$$

$$= 1+\frac{3}{4}+\frac{3}{8}+\frac{3}{16}+\ldots$$

$$= 1+\frac{3}{4}\frac{1}{1-\frac{1}{2}} = 1+\frac{3}{4}.\frac{2}{1}$$

$$= 1+\frac{3}{2} = \frac{5}{2}$$

$$\sum_{n=0}^{\infty} |h_4(n)|^2 = \sum_{n=0}^{\infty}\left(\frac{1}{4}\delta^2(n)+\frac{9}{4}\left(\frac{1}{4}\right)^n u^2(n) - \frac{3}{2}\delta(n)\left(-\frac{1}{2}\right)^n u(n)\right)$$

$\nearrow = u(n)$

$$= \sum_{n=0}^{\infty}\left(\frac{1}{4}\delta(n)+\frac{9}{4}\left(\frac{1}{4}\right)^n u(n) - \frac{3}{2}\left(-\frac{1}{2}\right)^n \delta(n)\right)$$

$$= \frac{1}{4}+\frac{9}{4}\frac{1}{1-\frac{1}{4}}-\frac{3}{2}$$

$$= \frac{1}{4}+\frac{9}{4}\times\frac{4}{3}-\frac{3}{2}$$

$$= \frac{1}{4}+3-\frac{3}{2}$$

$$= \frac{1}{4}+\frac{3}{2}$$

$$= \frac{7}{4}$$

$$H_4(z) = \frac{1-\frac{1}{4}z^{-1}}{1+\frac{1}{2}z^{-1}}$$

$$h_4(n) = -\frac{1}{2}\,\delta(n) + \frac{3}{2}\left(-\frac{1}{2}\right)^n u(n)$$

$$\sum_{n=0}^{\infty} |h_4(n)| = \frac{5}{2}$$

$$\sum_{n=0}^{\infty} |h_4(n)|^2 = \frac{7}{4}$$

(vi) $$H_5(z) \triangleq (H_1\, H_2) = \frac{1-\frac{1}{4}z^{-1}}{1-\frac{1}{2}z^{-1}}$$

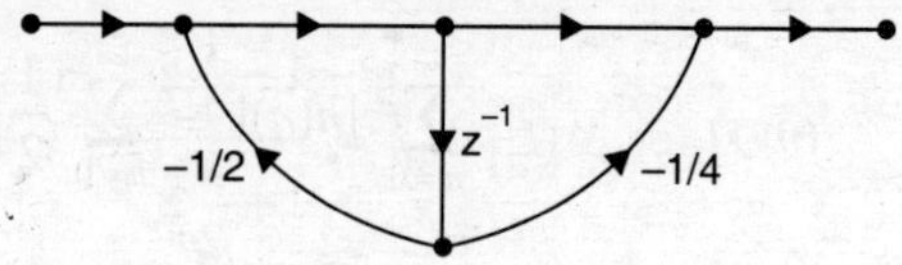

Fig. Ex. 10.16. (l)

$$H_5(z) = \frac{\frac{1}{2}\left(1-\frac{1}{2}z^{-1}\right)+\frac{1}{2}}{1-\frac{1}{2}z^{-1}}$$

$$= \frac{1}{2}+\frac{1}{2}\frac{1}{1-\frac{1}{2}z^{-1}}$$

$\therefore$ $$h_5(n) = \frac{1}{2}\,\delta(n) + \frac{1}{2}\left(\frac{1}{2}\right)^n u(n)$$

$$\sum_{n=0}^{\infty} |h(n)| = \sum_{n=0}^{\infty}\left[\frac{1}{2}\,\delta(n)+\frac{1}{2}\left(\frac{1}{2}\right)^n u(n)\right]$$

$$= \frac{1}{2}+\frac{1}{2}\frac{1}{1-\frac{1}{2}} = \frac{1}{2}+1=\frac{3}{2}$$

$$\sum_{n=0}^{\infty} |h(n)|^2 = \sum_{n=0}^{\infty}\left[\frac{1}{4}\,\delta^2(n)+\frac{1}{4}\left(\frac{1}{4}\right)^n u(n)+\frac{1}{2}\left(\frac{1}{2}\right)^n \delta(n)\,u(n)\right]$$

$$= \sum_{n=0}^{\infty} \frac{1}{4}\,\delta(n)+\frac{1}{4}\left(\frac{1}{4}\right)^n u(n)+\frac{1}{2}\left(\frac{1}{2}\right)^n \delta(n)$$

$$= \frac{1}{4}+\frac{1}{4}\frac{1}{1-\frac{1}{4}}+\frac{1}{2} = \frac{1}{4}+\frac{1}{4}\times\frac{4}{3}+\frac{1}{2} = \frac{3}{4}+\frac{1}{3} = \frac{9+4}{12} = \frac{13}{12}$$

$$H_5(z) = \frac{1-\frac{1}{4}z^{-1}}{1-\frac{1}{2}z^{-1}}$$

$$h_5(n) = \frac{1}{2}\,\delta(n) + \frac{1}{2}\left(\frac{1}{2}\right)^n u(n)$$

$$\sum_{n=0}^{\infty} |h(n)| = \frac{3}{2}$$

$$\sum_{n=0}^{\infty} |h(n)|^2 = \frac{13}{12}$$

(vii) $$H_6(z) \triangleq H_2(z)\, H_3(z)$$

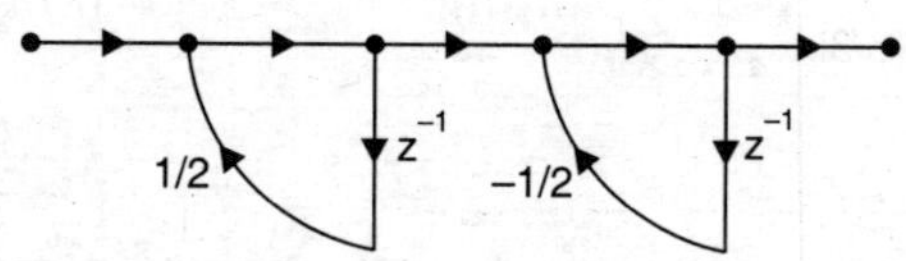

Fig. Ex. 10.16. (m)

$$= \frac{1}{\left(1-\frac{1}{2}z^{-1}\right)\left(1+\frac{1}{2}z^{-1}\right)}$$

$$= \frac{1}{2}\frac{1}{1-\frac{1}{2}z^{-1}}+\frac{1}{2}\frac{1}{1+\frac{1}{2}z^{-1}}$$

$\therefore$ $$h(n) = \frac{1}{2}\left[\left(\frac{1}{2}\right)^n u(n)+\left(-\frac{1}{2}\right)^n u(n)\right]$$

$$= \frac{1}{2}\left[\left(\frac{1}{2}\right)^n+\left(-\frac{1}{2}\right)^n\right]u(n)$$

$$H_6(z) = \frac{1}{\left(1-\frac{1}{2}z^{-1}\right)\left(1+\frac{1}{2}z^{-1}\right)}$$

$$h_6(n) = \frac{1}{2}\left(\left(\frac{1}{2}\right)^n+\left(-\frac{1}{2}\right)^2\right)u(n)$$

$$\sum_{n=0}^{\infty} |h_6(n)| = \frac{4}{3}$$

$$\sum_{n=0}^{\infty} |h_6(n)|^2 = \frac{16}{15}$$

$$\sum_{n=0}^{\infty} |h(n)| = \sum_{n=0}^{\infty} \frac{1}{2}\left(\left(\frac{1}{2}\right)^n + \left(\frac{-1}{2}\right)^n\right)u(n)$$

$$= \frac{1}{2}\left[(1+1) + \left|\frac{1}{2} - \frac{1}{2}\right| + \left|\frac{1}{4} + \frac{1}{4}\right| + \left|\frac{1}{8} - \frac{1}{8}\right| + \left|\frac{1}{16} + \frac{1}{16}\right| + \ldots\right]$$

$$= \frac{1}{2}\left[2 + 2 + \left(\frac{1}{4} + \frac{1}{16} + \frac{1}{64} + \ldots\right)\right] = 1 + \frac{1}{4} + \frac{1}{16} + \frac{1}{64} + \ldots$$

$$= \frac{1}{1 - \frac{1}{4}} = \frac{4}{3}$$

$$\sum_{n=0}^{\infty} |h(n)|^2 = \sum_{n=0}^{\infty} \frac{1}{4}\left(\left(\frac{1}{4}\right)^n + \left(\frac{1}{4}\right)^n + 2\left(\frac{-1}{4}\right)^n\right)u(n)$$

$$= \frac{1}{4}\left[2 \cdot \frac{1}{1 - \frac{1}{4}} + 2 \cdot \frac{1}{1 + \frac{1}{4}}\right] = \frac{1}{2}\left(\frac{4}{3} + \frac{4}{5}\right) = \frac{1}{2} \cdot 4 \cdot \frac{5+3}{15} = \frac{16}{15}$$

Table showing $h(n)$, $\Sigma|h(n)|$ and $\Sigma|h(n)|^2$

S.No.	Transfer Fn	Value of $H_i(z)$	$h_i(n)$	$\sum_{n=0}^{\infty} \lvert h_i(n)\rvert$	$\sum_{n=0}^{\infty} \lvert h_i(n)\rvert^2$
1.	$H_1(z)$	$\left(1 - \frac{1}{4}z^{-1}\right)$	$\delta(n) - \frac{1}{4}\delta(n-1)$	$\frac{5}{4}$	$\frac{17}{16}$
2.	$H_2(z)$	$\frac{1}{1 - \frac{1}{2}z^{-1}}$	$\left(\frac{1}{2}\right)^n u(n)$	2	$\frac{4}{3}$
3.	$H_3(z)$	$\frac{1}{1 + \frac{1}{2}z^{-1}}$	$\left(-\frac{1}{2}\right)^n u(n)$	2	$\frac{4}{3}$
4.	$H_4(z)(= H_1 \cdot H_3)$	$\frac{1 - \frac{1}{4}z^{-1}}{1 + \frac{1}{2}z^{-1}}$	$-\frac{1}{2}\delta(n) + \frac{3}{2}\left(-\frac{1}{2}\right)^n u(n)$	$\frac{5}{2}$	$\frac{7}{4}$
5.	$H_5(z)$ $(= H_1 \cdot H_2)$	$\frac{1 - \frac{1}{4}z^{-1}}{\left(1 - \frac{1}{2}z^{-1}\right)}$	$\frac{1}{2}\delta(n) + \frac{1}{2}\left(\frac{1}{2}\right)^n u(n)$	$\frac{3}{2}$	$\frac{13}{12}$
6.	$H_6(z)$ $(= H_2\, H_3)$	$\frac{1}{\left(1 - \frac{1}{2}z^{-1}\right)\left(1 + \frac{1}{2}z^{-1}\right)}$	$\frac{1}{2}\left(\left(\frac{1}{2}\right)^n + \left(-\frac{1}{2}\right)^n\right)u(n)$	$\frac{4}{3}$	$\frac{16}{15}$
7.	$H(z)$ $(= H_1\, H_2\, H_3)$	$\frac{1 - \frac{1}{4}z^{-1}}{\left(1 - \frac{1}{2}z^{-1}\right)\left(1 + \frac{1}{2}z^{-1}\right)}$	$\left(\frac{3}{4}\left(-\frac{1}{2}\right)^n + \frac{1}{4}\left(\frac{1}{2}\right)^n\right)u(n)$	$\frac{5}{3}$	$\frac{17}{15}$

Add noise source after each multiplication.

(i) *Canonic form*

$$\sigma_f^2 = \sigma_{e_1}^2 \, \Sigma |h(n)|^2 + \sigma_{e_2}^2$$

$$= \sigma_e^2 \left(\frac{17}{15} + 1\right)$$

$$\therefore \quad \sigma_f^2 = \frac{32}{15}\sigma_e^2$$

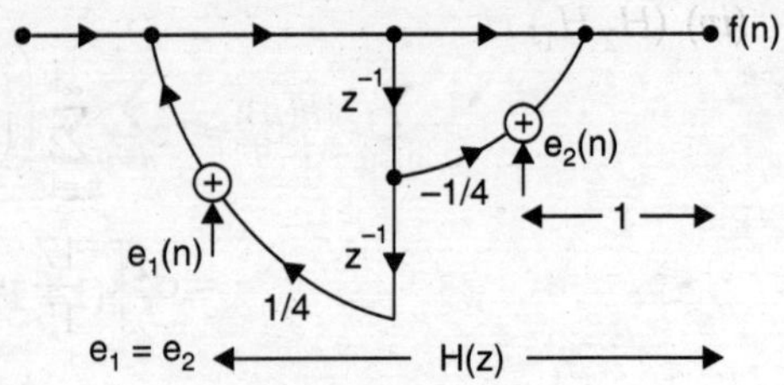

Fig. Ex. 10.16. (*n*)

(ii) $H_1 H_2 H_3$

$$\sigma_f^2 = \sigma_{e_1}^2 \sum_{n=0}^{\infty} |h_6(n)|^2 + \sigma_{e_2}^2 \sum_{n=0}^{\infty} |h_6(n)|^2 + \sigma_{e_3}^2 \sum_{n=0}^{\infty} |h_3(n)|^2$$

$$= 2\sigma_e^2 \, \frac{16}{15} + \sigma_e^2 \, \frac{4}{3} = \frac{52}{15}\sigma_e^2$$

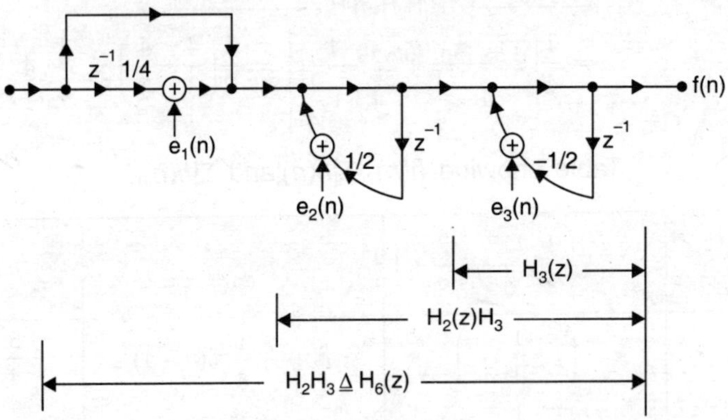

Fig. Ex. 10.16. (*o*)

(iii) $H_1 H_3 H_2$

$$\sigma_f^2 = \sigma_{e_1}^2 \sum_{n=0}^{\infty} |h_6(n)|^2 + \sigma_{e_2}^2 \sum_{n=0}^{\infty} |h_6(n)|^2 + \sigma_{e_3}^2 \sum_{n=0}^{\infty} |h_2(n)|^2$$

$$= 2\sigma_e^2 \cdot \frac{16}{15} + \sigma_e^2 \cdot \frac{4}{3} = \frac{52}{15}\,\sigma_e^2$$

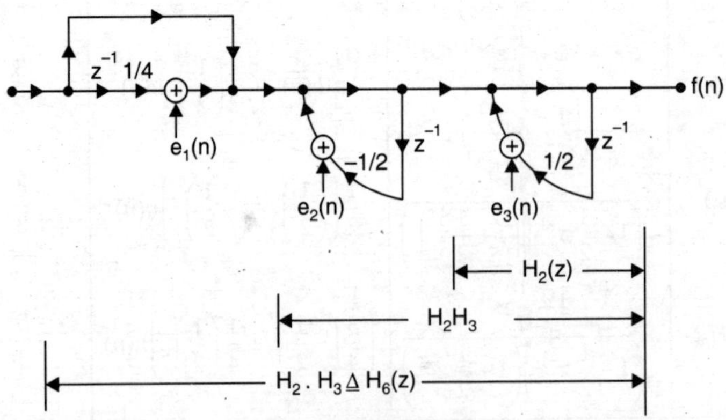

Fig. Ex. 10.16. (*p*)

(*iv*) $(H_2 H_1) H_3$

$$\sigma_f^2 = \sigma_{e_1}^2 \sum_{n=0}^{\infty} |h(n)|^2 + \sigma_{e_2}^2 \sum_{n=0}^{\infty} |h_3(n)|^2 + \sigma_{e_3}^2 \sum_{n=0}^{\infty} |h_3(n)|^2$$

$$= \sigma_e^2 \cdot \frac{17}{15} + 2\sigma_e^2 \cdot \frac{4}{3} = \frac{19}{5}\sigma_e^2$$

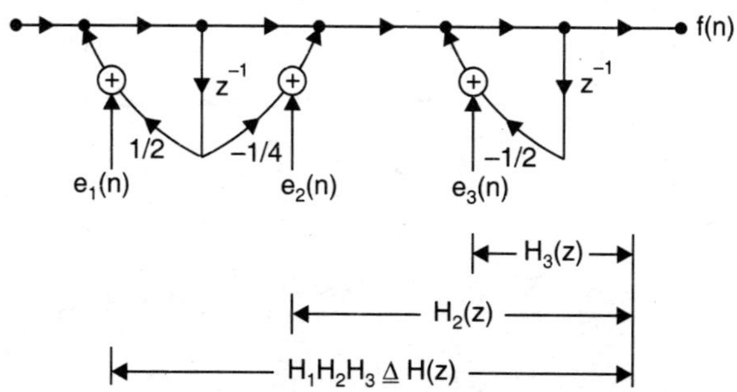

Fig. Ex. 10.16. (*q*)

(*v*) $H_2 (H_3 H_1)$

$$\sigma_f^2 = \sigma_{e_1}^2 \sum_{n=0}^{\infty} |h(n)|^2 + \sigma_{e_2}^2 \sum_{n=0}^{\infty} |h_4(n)|^2 + \sigma_{e_3}^2$$

$$= \sigma_e^2 \left(\frac{17}{15} + \frac{7}{4} + 1\right) = \frac{233}{60}\sigma_e^2$$

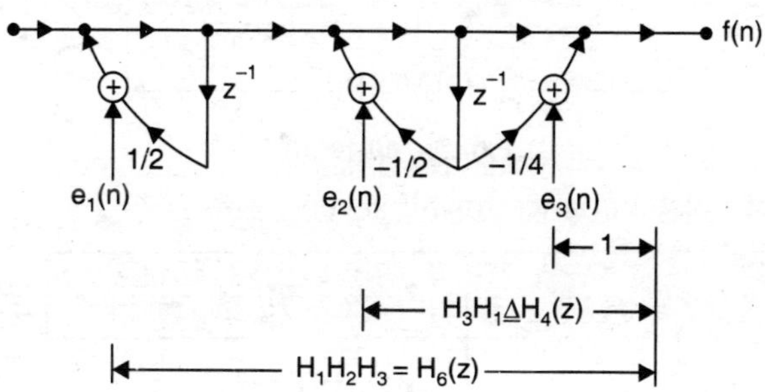

Fig. Ex. 10.16. (*r*)

(*vi*) $(H_3 H_1) H_2$

$$\sigma_f^2 = \sigma_{e_1}^2 \sum_{n=0}^{\infty} |h(n)|^2 + \sigma_{e_2}^2 \sum_{n=0}^{\infty} |h_2(n)|^2 + \sigma_{e_3}^2 \sum_{n=0}^{\infty} |h_2(n)|^2$$

$$= \sigma_e^2 \left(\frac{17}{15} + 2 \cdot \frac{4}{3}\right)$$

$$= \sigma_e^2 \left(\frac{17}{15} + \frac{8}{3}\right)$$

$$= \frac{19}{5}\sigma_e^2$$

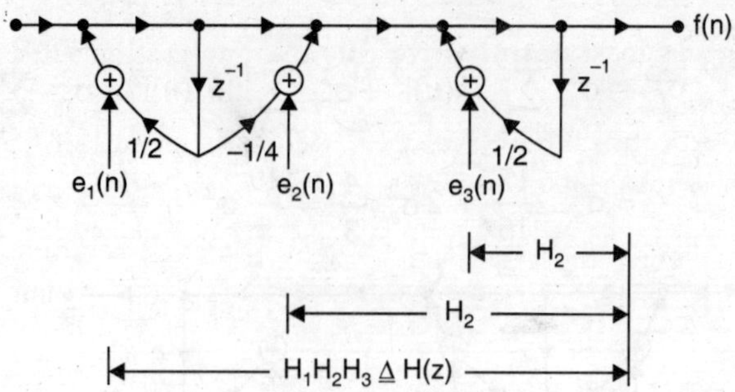

Fig. Ex. 10.16. *(s)*

(vii) $H_3\,(H_2\,H_1)$

$$\sigma_f^2 = \sigma_{e_1}^2 \sum_{n=0}^{\infty} |h(n)|^2 + \sigma_{e_2}^2 \sum_{n=0}^{\infty} |h_5(n)|^2 + \sigma_{e_3}^2\,.1$$

$$= \sigma_e^2\left(\frac{17}{15}+\frac{13}{12}+1\right) = \frac{193}{60}\sigma_e^2$$

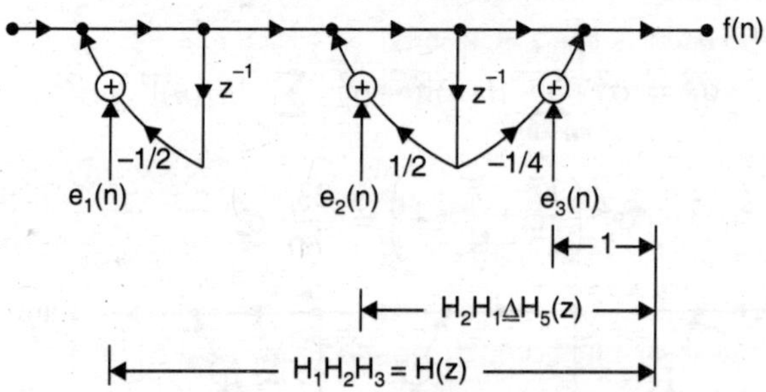

Fig. Ex. 10.16. *(t)*

To summarise output noise variance for all seven forms

S.No.	*Form*	σ_f^2
1.	Canonic $H(z)$	$\frac{32}{15}\sigma_e^2 = 2.133\ \sigma_e^2$
2.	$H_1\,H_2\,H_3$: 3 delays	$\frac{52}{15}\sigma_e^2 = 3.467\ \sigma_e^2$
3.	$H_1\,H_3\,H_2$: 3 delays	$\frac{52}{15}\sigma_e^2 = 3.467\ \sigma_e^2$
4.	$(H_2\,H_1)H_3$: 2 delays	$\frac{19}{5}\sigma_e^2 = 3.8\ \sigma_e^2$
5.	$H_2\,(H_3\,H_1)$: 2 delays	$\frac{233}{60}\sigma_e^2 = 3.833\ \sigma_e^2$
6.	$(H_3\,H_1)H_2$: 2 delays	$\frac{19}{5}\sigma_e^2 = 3.8\ \sigma_e^2$
7.	$H_3\,(H_2\,H_1)$: 2 delays	$\frac{193}{60}\sigma_e^2 = 3.127\ \sigma_e^2$

Minimum error

Inference

(*i*) Canonic form gives least output error due to quantization with roundings in Fixed point arithmetic.

(*ii*) Maximum noise occurs where we use 2 delays is cascade form

(*iii*) Cascaded form with 3 delays give relatively lesser error σ_f^2 as compared to cascade with 2 delays.

UNSOLVED PROBLEMS ON QUANTIZATION EFFECTS

10.1 In an *A* to *D* convertor we want to achieve SNR of at least 90 dB. Assume input $x(n)$ to be Gaussian with variance of σ_x^2. The range of quantizer is from $-3\sigma_x$ to $+3\sigma_x$. Find the number of bits needed.

[**Hint:** Let *A* to *D* have $b + 1$ bits quantizer

Then $$\text{SNR} = 10.8 + 6b + 20 \log \sigma_x + 20 \log A \text{ [see (10.26)]}$$

Put $$\text{SNR} = 90,\ A = \frac{1}{3\sigma_x} \text{ (we scale by } A \text{ to avoid overflow of } x(n) \text{ beyond } \pm 3\sigma_x)$$

∴ $$90 = 10.8 + 6b - \log 3$$

Solving for *b*, we obtain $b = 14.75$, say 15

Hence, least bits needed is $b + 1 = 16$ bits] **Ans.**

10.2. If a signal varies in the range 0 to 1 (say an image signal), how many bits are needed to obtain SNR ≥ 80 dB, assuming uniform distribution of the signal.

[**Hint:** Signal has mean $= \dfrac{(0+1)}{2} = \dfrac{1}{2} = m_x$

$$\text{signal has variance} = \frac{1}{3}\left(\frac{1-0}{2}\right)^2 = \frac{1}{12} = \sigma_x^2$$

$$\text{use } 80 \text{ dB} = 10.8 + 6b + 20 \log \sigma_x + 20 \log \frac{1}{m_x}$$

$$= 10.8 + 6b + 10 \log\left(\frac{1}{12}\right) + 20 \log \frac{1}{0.5}$$

Solving we obtain $b = 12.29 = 13$ say. Hence $b + 1 = 14$] **Ans.**

10.3. For the *IIR* structure shown in the Figure, what should be the maximum value $x_{\max}$ of input $x(n)$ to avoid overflow.

[**Hint:** Unit sample response $h_1(n)$ from input to Node 1 is

$$h_1(n) = (0.8)^n u(n)$$

Unit sample response $h_2(n)$ from input to Node 2 is

$$h_2(n) = (0.8)^n u(n) - 0.9(0.8)^{n-1} u(n-1)$$
$$= \delta(n) - (0.1)\,(0.8)^{n-1}\, u(n-1)$$

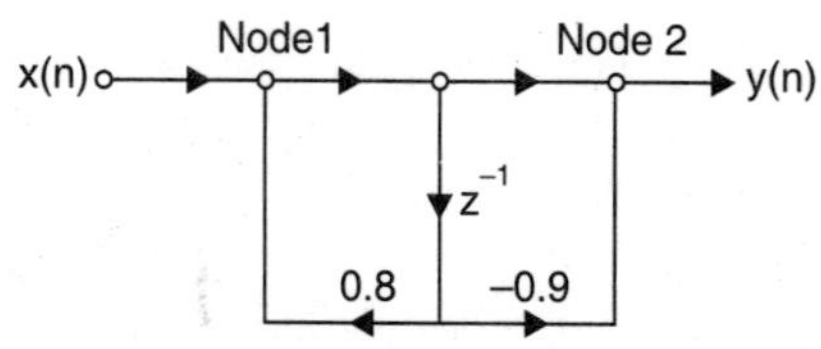

Fig. Prob. 10.3.

$$\sum |h_1(n)| = \frac{1}{1-(0.8)} = 5, \quad \sum_n |h_2(n)| = 1.5$$

∴ Sufficient condition for no overflow is $x_{\max} \leq \dfrac{1}{5} = 0.2$] **Ans.**

10.4. For the IIR structure shown in the figure

(*a*) determine the variance of output noise $f(n)$

(*b*) If $H(z)$ is implemented as a parallel structure, then repeat part (*a*).

[**Hint:** Errors are added as $e_1(n)$ and $e_2(n)$.

$$\sigma_f^2 = \sigma_1^2 \sum_n |h(n)|^2 + \sigma_2^2 \approx 6\sigma_e^2 \textbf{ Ans.}$$

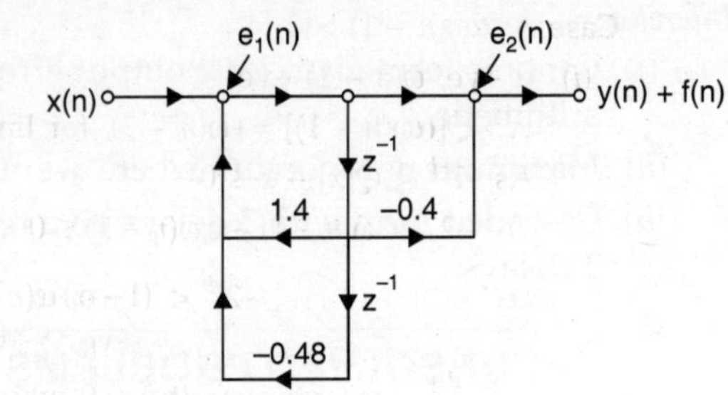

Fig. Prob. 10.4. (*a*) *H*(*z*) as canonic form

In parallel form

$$\sigma_f^2 = \sigma_3^2 \sum_{n=0}^{\infty} |0.8|^2 + \sigma_4^2 \sum_{n=0}^{\infty} |0.6|^2 \approx 4.34\, \sigma_e^2 \textbf{ Ans.}$$

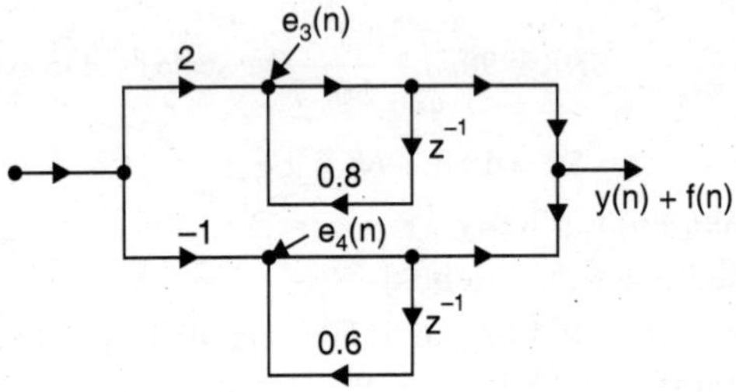

Fig. Prob. 10.4. (*b*) *H*(*z*) is parallel form

Take $\sigma_1^2 = \sigma_2^2 = \sigma_3^2 = \sigma_4^2 = \sigma_e^2$.

10.5. Consider the first-order system of the form

$$y(n) = \alpha y(n-1) + x(n)$$

Assume that all variables and coefficients are represented in signed magnitude form with the results of multiplications being truncated. Thus, the actual difference equation is

$$\omega(n) = Q[\alpha\omega(n-1)] + x(n)$$

where $Q[\cdot]$ represents sign and magnitude truncation.

(*a*) Consider the possibility of a zero-input limit cycle of the form $|\omega(n)| = |\omega(n-1)|$ for all n. Show that if the ideal system is stable, then no zero input limit cycle can exist.

[**Hint:** In signed and Magnitude arithmetic:

The given difference equation with truncation is

$$\omega(n) = \underset{\substack{\uparrow \\ \text{quantization}}}{Q}[\alpha\omega(n-1)] + x(n)$$

For zero input, $x(n) = 0$ for all n

$$\omega(n) = Q[\alpha\omega(n-1)]$$

To limit cycle to occur, *effective value of* α *becomes 1*

i.e. $|Q[\alpha\omega(n-1)]| = |\omega(n-1)|$

If the ideal system is stable than $|\alpha| < 1$

For truncation in SM arithmetic

$$-2^{-b} < Q[x] - x \le 0 \text{ if } x > 0$$
$$0 \le Q[x] - x \le 2^{-b} \text{ of } x < 0$$

Let a limit of cycle exist.

Case A: $\alpha\omega(n-1) > 0$

(*i*) α +ve, $\omega(n-1)$ +ve

$\therefore$ $Q[\alpha\omega(n-1)] = +\omega(n-1)$ for limit cycle to occur $\because$ $'x' = \alpha\omega(n-1)$ is > 0

As $-2^{-b} < Q[x] - x \le 0$

$\therefore$ $-2^{-b} < \omega(n-1) - \alpha\omega(n-1) \le 0$ $\because$ $Q[x] = Q[\alpha\omega(n-1)] = \omega(n-1)$ for limit cycle to occur

i.e. $$-2^{-b} < \underset{+\text{ve}}{(1-\alpha)}\,\underset{+\text{ve}}{\omega(n-1)} \le 0$$

i.e. -2^{-b} < (a +ve quantity) ≤ 0 which is a contradiction

$\therefore$ limit cycle cannot exist

(*ii*) α –ve, $\omega(n-1)$ –ve; $\alpha\omega(n-1)$ +ve

$\therefore$ $Q[\alpha\omega(n-1)] = -\omega(n-1)$ $\because$ $\omega(n-1)$ is –ve

As $-2^{-b} < Q[x] - x \le 0$ for x +ve $-\omega(n-1)$ is +ve

$\therefore$ $$-2^{-b} < -\omega(n-1) - \alpha\omega(n-1) \le 0$$

or $$-2^{-b} < -\underbrace{(1+\alpha)}_{+\text{ve}}\cdot\underbrace{\omega(n-1)}_{-\text{ve}} \le 0$$

i.e. -2^{-b} < (+ve quantity) ≤ 0, which is a contradiction.

$\therefore$ limit cycle cannot exist.

Case B: $\alpha\omega(n-1) < 0$

(*i*) α +ve, $\omega(n-1)$ –ve

$\therefore$ $Q[\alpha\omega(n-1)] = \omega(n-1)$

As $0 \le Q[x] - x < 2^{-b}$ ...truncation of –ve x

$\therefore$ $$0 \le \omega(n-1) - \alpha\omega(n-1) < 2^{-b}$$

i.e. $$0 \le \underbrace{(1-\alpha)}_{+\text{ve}}\cdot\underbrace{\omega(n-1)}_{-\text{ve}} < 2^{-b}$$

$\therefore$ $0 \le$ (a –ve quantity) $< 2^{-b}$ which is a contradiction

$\therefore$ limit cycle cannot exist.

(*ii*) α –ve, $\omega(n-1)$ +ve

$Q[\alpha\omega(n-1)] = -\omega(n-1)$

As $0 \le Q[x] - x < 2^{-b}$ ... truncation of –ve x

$$0 \le -\omega(n-1) - \alpha\omega(n-1) < 2^{-b}$$

i.e. $$0 \le \underbrace{-\omega(n-1)}\cdot\underbrace{(1+\alpha)} < 2^{-b} \text{ which is a contradiction}$$

$\therefore$ limit cycle cannot exist.

Hence in SM arithmetic, zero input limit cycle cannot exist.

10.6. The system described by the difference equation

$$y(n) - \alpha y(n-1) = x(n) - \frac{1}{\alpha^*}x(n-1)$$

is an allpass system. We want to compare the effect of arithmetic round off for a fixed-point and a floating-point realizations of the allpass system. Consider all fixed-point numbers as fractions, so that the fixed-point numbers are between ±1, with a register length of b bits, excluding the sign bit. For the following point case, let t represents the number of bits in the mantissa, excluding sign. The input to filter $x(n)$ is considered to be white random process, with a uniform amplitude distribution between $\pm x_0$. Assume that α is real and $\frac{1}{2} < \alpha < 1$.

(*a*) The maximum input signal level must be small enough so that there is no overflow in the fixed-point realization of the filter. Determine the output NSR of the fixed-point realization in both the direct and canonic forms *i.e.*

(*b*) Determine the output NSR for the canonic form of the filter realized with floating-point arithmetic.

(*c*) Assume that α is close to unity, so that $\alpha = 1 - \delta$, $\delta \ll 1$. Express your results from parts (*a*) and (*b*) in terms of δ, making reasonable approximations.

[**Hint:** (*a*) $y(n) - \alpha y(n-1) = x(n) - \frac{1}{\alpha}x(n-1)$

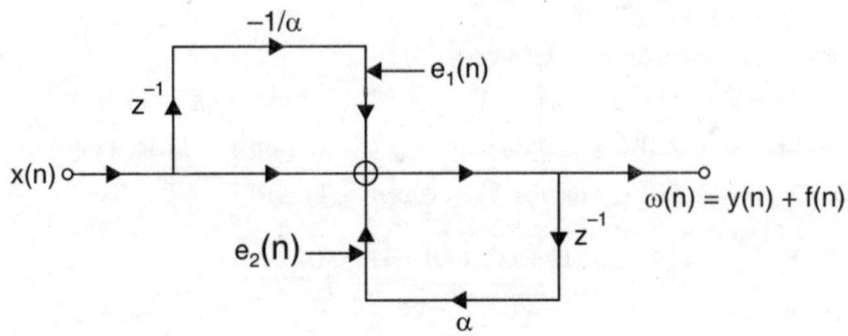

Fig. Prob. 10.6. (*a*)

$$\therefore \quad \frac{Y(z)}{X(z)} = H(z) = \frac{1-\frac{1}{\alpha}z^{-1}}{1-\alpha z^{-1}} = \frac{(1-\alpha z^{-1})\frac{1}{\alpha^2}+1-\frac{1}{\alpha^2}}{1-\alpha z^{-1}}$$

$$= \frac{1}{\alpha^2}+\left(1-\frac{1}{\alpha^2}\right)\frac{1}{1-\alpha z^{-1}}$$

$$h(n) = \frac{1}{\alpha^2}\delta(n)-\left(\frac{1}{\alpha^2}-1\right)\alpha^n u(n)$$

$$\sum_{n=0}^{\infty} h^2(n) = \sum \frac{1}{\alpha^4}\delta(n)+\left(\frac{1}{\alpha^2}-1\right)^2\alpha^{2n}u(n)-2\frac{1}{\alpha^2}\left(\frac{1}{\alpha^2}-1\right)\delta(n)$$

$$= \frac{1}{\alpha^4}+\left(\frac{1-\alpha^2}{\alpha^2}\right)^2\frac{1}{1\cdot\alpha^2}-2\cdot\frac{1}{\alpha^2}\left(\frac{1-\alpha^2}{\alpha^2}\right)$$

$$= \frac{1}{\alpha^4}[1+(1-\alpha^2)-2(1-\alpha^2)] = \frac{1}{\alpha^2}$$

$$\boxed{\therefore \quad \sum_{n=0}^{\infty} h^2(n) = \frac{1}{\alpha^2}}$$

$$\sum_{n=0}^{\infty} |h(n)| = \sum_{n=0}^{\infty}\left|\frac{1}{\alpha^2}\delta(n)-\left(\frac{1-\alpha^2}{\alpha^2}\right)\alpha^n u(n)\right|$$

$$= \left|\frac{1}{\alpha^2}-\frac{1-\alpha^2}{\alpha^2}\right|+\frac{1-\alpha^2}{\alpha^2}(\alpha+\alpha^2+\alpha^3+\ldots)$$

$$= 1+\frac{1-\alpha^2}{\alpha^2}\cdot\alpha\cdot\frac{1}{1-\alpha} = 1+\frac{1+\alpha}{1}$$

$$= 2+\frac{1}{\alpha}$$

$$\boxed{\therefore \quad \sum_{n=0}^{\infty} |h(n)| = 2+\frac{1}{\alpha}}$$

(*a*) **Direct form-NSR (Fixed point arithmetic)**

$$H_1(z) = 1-\frac{1}{\alpha}z^{-1} \qquad H_2(z) = \frac{1}{1-\alpha z^{-1}}$$

$$\therefore \quad h_1(n) = \delta(n)-\frac{1}{\alpha}\delta(n-1) \qquad \therefore\ h_2(n) = \alpha^n u(n)$$

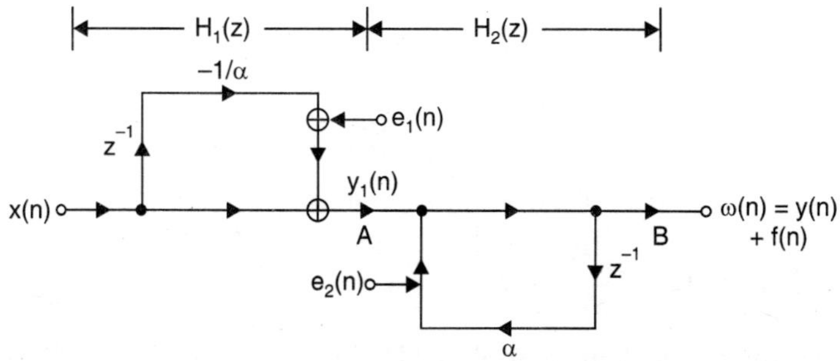

Fig. Prob. 10.6. (*b*)

$$\sum_{n=0}^{\infty} |h_1(n)| = 1+\frac{1}{\alpha}$$

$$\sum_{n=0}^{\infty} h_1^2(n) = \sum_{n=0}^{\infty} \delta^2(n)+\frac{1}{\alpha^2}\delta^2(n-1)$$

$$= 1+\frac{1}{\alpha^2}$$

$$\boxed{\sum_{n=0}^{\infty} |h_1(n)|=1+\frac{1}{\alpha} \qquad \sum_{n=0}^{\infty} h_1^2(n)=1+\frac{1}{\alpha^2}=\frac{1+\alpha^2}{\alpha^2}}$$

$e_1(n)$, $e_2(n)$ pass through filter $H_2(z)$ with $\sum_{n=0}^{\infty} h_2^2(n) = \frac{1}{1-\alpha^2}$

$$\therefore \quad \sigma_f^2 = (\sigma_1^2+\sigma_2^2)\cdot\frac{1}{1-\alpha^2}$$

$$= 2\sigma^2\cdot\frac{1}{1-\alpha^2}$$

$$\boxed{\sum_{n=0}^{\infty} |h_2(n)|=\frac{1}{1-\alpha} \qquad \sum_{n=0}^{\infty} h_2^2(n)=\frac{1}{1-\alpha^2}}$$

[To choose x_0]

As for $h_1(n)$, $\sum_{n=0}^{\infty} |h_1(n)| = 1+\frac{1}{\alpha}$ for node A

for $h(n)$, $\sum_{n=0}^{\infty} |h(n)| = 2+\frac{1}{\alpha}$ for output node

$$\boxed{\sum_{n=0}^{\infty} |h(n)|=2+\frac{1}{\alpha} \qquad \sum_{n=0}^{\infty} h^2(n)=\frac{1}{\alpha^2} \qquad H(z)=H_1(z)\cdot H_2(z)}$$

$$\therefore \quad x_{max} \le \frac{1}{\sum_{n=0}^{\infty} |h_k(n)|} \quad \forall\ k \text{ to avoid overflow}$$

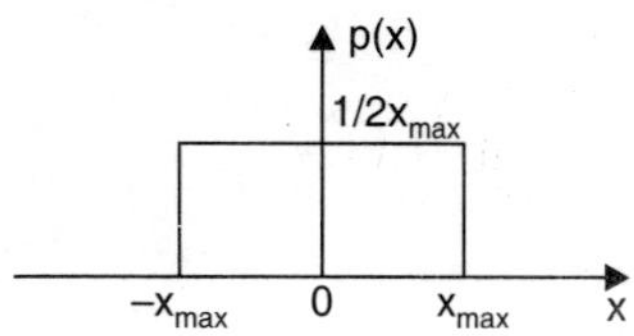

$$\therefore \quad x_{max} = \frac{1}{2+\frac{1}{\alpha}} = \frac{\alpha}{2\alpha+1} \quad \text{to avoid overflow}$$

$$\sigma_x^2 = \frac{1}{3}x_{max}^2 = \frac{1}{3}\frac{\alpha^2}{(2\alpha+1)^2} \qquad x_0 = \frac{\alpha}{2\alpha+1}$$

$$\sigma_y^2 = \frac{1}{\alpha^2}\sigma_x^2$$

$$= \frac{1}{\alpha^2}\cdot\frac{1}{3}\frac{\alpha^2}{(2\alpha+1)^2} = \frac{1}{3}\cdot\frac{1}{(2\alpha+1)^2}$$

$$\text{NSR}\Big|_{\text{output}} = \frac{\sigma_f^2}{\sigma_y^2} = \frac{\dfrac{2\sigma^2}{1-\alpha^2}}{\dfrac{1}{3}\cdot\dfrac{1}{(2\alpha+1)^2}}$$

$$= \frac{6(2\alpha+1)^2}{1-\alpha^2}\sigma^2 = \frac{6(2\alpha+1)}{1-\alpha^2}\cdot\frac{1}{12}2^{-2b} = \frac{(2\alpha+1)^2}{2(1-\alpha^2)}2^{-2b}$$

For $\alpha = 1 - \delta,\ 2\alpha + 1 \approx 3,\ 1 - \alpha^2 \simeq 1 - (1 - \delta) = 2\delta$

$\therefore$ $$\text{Output NSR} = \frac{6\times 3^2}{2\delta}\cdot\frac{1}{12}2^{-2b} = \frac{9}{4\delta}2^{-2b}$$ **Ans.**

Direct form–Floating Point Arithmetic: We add noise sources after each addition and multiplication. Then

$$e_1(n) = \varepsilon_1(n)\left(-\frac{1}{\alpha}x(n-1)\right)$$

$$e_2(n) = \varepsilon_2\left[x(n) - \frac{1}{\alpha}x(n-1)\right]$$

$$e_3(n) = \varepsilon_3(n)[\alpha y(n-1)]$$

$$e_4(n) = \varepsilon_4(n)[y(n)]$$

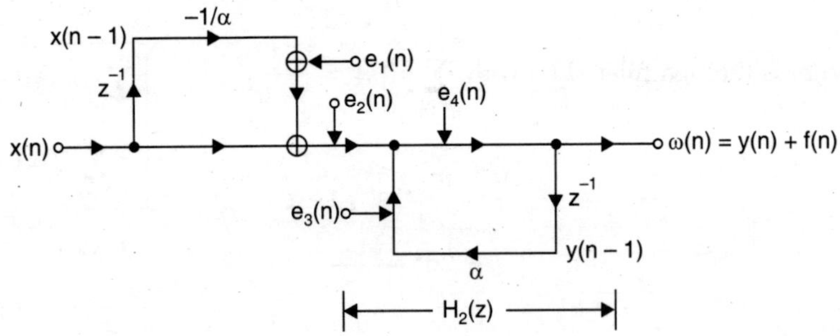

Fig. Prob. 10.6. (*c*)

$$\sigma_{e_1}^2 = \sigma_\varepsilon^2\cdot E\left[\left(-\frac{1}{\alpha}x(n-1)\right)^2\right] = \frac{1}{\alpha^2}\sigma_\varepsilon^2\sigma_x^2 \quad \because\ Ex^2(n-1) = \sigma_x^2$$

$$\sigma_{\varepsilon_2}^2 = \sigma_\varepsilon^2 E\left[x^2(n) + \frac{1}{\alpha^2}x^2(n-1) - 2\frac{1}{\alpha}x(n)\,x(n-1)\right]$$

$$= \sigma_\varepsilon^2\left[\sigma_x^2 + \frac{1}{\alpha^2}\sigma_x^2 + 0\right] \quad \because\ Ex(n)x(n-1) = 0 \text{ assuming } x(n) \text{ white noise}$$

$$= \left(1 + \frac{1}{\alpha^2}\right)\sigma_\varepsilon^2\sigma_x^2$$

$$\sigma_{e_3}^2 = \sigma_\varepsilon^2 E[\alpha^2 y^2(n-1)] = \sigma_\varepsilon^2 \alpha^2 \sigma_y^2$$

$$\sigma_{e_4}^2 = \sigma_\varepsilon^2 E[y^2(n)] = \sigma_\varepsilon^2 \sigma_y^2$$

All noise sources $e_1(n)$, $e_2(n)$, $e_3(n)$ and $e_4(n)$ pass through filter with impulse response $h_2(n) = \alpha^n u(n)$

$$\therefore \quad \sum_{n=0}^{\infty} h_2^2(n) = \frac{1}{1-\alpha^2}$$

$$\therefore \quad \sigma_f^2 = (\sigma_{e_1}^2 + \sigma_{e_2}^2 + \sigma_{e_3}^2 + \sigma_{e_4}^2) \cdot \frac{1}{1-\alpha^2}$$

$$= \sigma_\varepsilon^2 \cdot \frac{1}{1-\alpha^2}\left[\frac{\sigma_x^2}{\alpha^2} + \left(1+\frac{1}{\alpha^2}\right)\sigma_x^2 + \alpha^2\sigma_y^2 + \sigma_y^2\right]$$

Put $\dfrac{\sigma_x^2}{\alpha^2} = \sigma_y^2$.

$$\therefore \quad \sum_{n=0}^{\infty} h^2(n) = \frac{1}{\alpha^2} \text{ as found earlier}$$

$$\therefore \quad \sigma_f^2 = \sigma_\varepsilon^2 \cdot \frac{1}{1-\alpha^2}\left[\sigma_y^2 + \sigma_y^2\alpha^2\left(1+\frac{1}{\alpha^2}\right) + \alpha^2\sigma_y^2 + \sigma_y^2\right]$$

$$= \sigma_\varepsilon^2 \cdot \sigma_y^2 \cdot \frac{1}{1-\alpha^2}[1+\alpha^2+1+\alpha^2+1]$$

$$= \sigma_y^2 \frac{\sigma_\varepsilon^2}{1-\alpha^2} \cdot (3+2\alpha^2)$$

$$\therefore \quad \text{Output NSR} = \frac{\sigma_f^2}{\sigma_y^2} = \frac{\sigma_\varepsilon^2}{1-\alpha^2}(3+2\alpha) = \frac{1}{3}2^{-2b}\left(\frac{3+2\alpha^2}{1-\alpha^2}\right)$$

Put $\alpha = 1 - \delta$, $\sigma_\varepsilon^2 = \dfrac{1}{3}2^{-2b}$

$$\therefore \quad \text{Output NSR} = \frac{1}{3}2^{-2b} \cdot \frac{1}{2\delta}(5) = \frac{5}{6\delta}2^{-2b}$$

$$\therefore \quad \text{Output NSR} = \frac{5}{6\delta} \cdot 2^{-2b}$$

(*b*) Canonic form (Fixed point arithmetic)

$$\sigma_f^2 = \sigma_{e_1}^2 \cdot \sum_{n=0}^{\infty} h^2(n) + \sigma_{e_2}^2$$

$$= \sigma_e^2\left(\frac{1}{\alpha^2} + 1\right)$$

(To choose $x_{\max}$)

$$\sum_{n=0}^{\infty} |h_2(n)| = \frac{1}{1-\alpha}$$

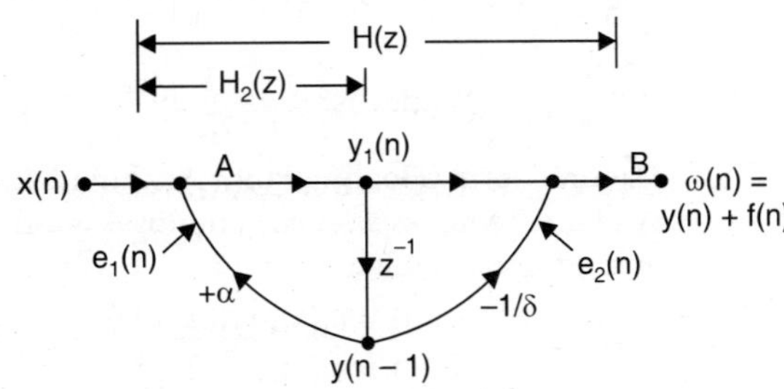

Fig. Prob. 10.6. (*d*)

$\therefore$ for node A, $y_{\max} = \dfrac{1}{1-\alpha}$

for node B, take overall $h(n)$

$$H_2(z) = \frac{1}{1-\alpha z^{-1}}$$

$$\therefore\ h_2(n) = \alpha^n u(n)$$

$$\sum_{n=0}^{\infty} \alpha^n u(n) = \frac{1}{1-\alpha}$$

$$\sum_{n=0}^{\infty} |h(n)| = 2+\frac{1}{\alpha}, \text{ therefore, for node } B\ y_{\max} = 2+\frac{1}{\alpha}$$

As $\frac{1}{2} < \alpha < 1$ (given)

$\therefore$ Maximum value of the signal can be at node A when $\alpha = 1 - \delta$, $\delta \ll 1$

$$\therefore \qquad x_{\max} \le \frac{1}{\sum |h_2(n)|} = (1-\alpha)$$

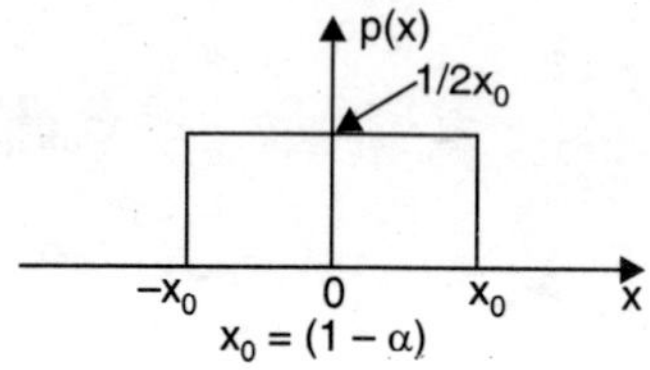

i.e. $$\sigma_x^2 = \frac{1}{3}x_0^2 = \frac{1}{3}(1-\alpha)^2$$

$\therefore$ For no overflow $\sigma_x^{\,2} = \frac{1}{3}(1-\alpha)^2$

$$\therefore \qquad \sigma_y^2 = \sigma_x^2 \sum_{n=0}^{\infty} h^2(n)$$

$$= \frac{1}{3}(1-\alpha)^2 \cdot \frac{1}{\alpha^2}$$

$$\text{Output NSR} = \frac{\sigma_f^2}{\sigma_y^2}$$

$$= \frac{\sigma_e^2 \dfrac{1+\alpha^2}{\alpha^2}}{\dfrac{(1-\alpha)^2}{3\alpha^2}} = 3\sigma_e^2 \frac{1+\alpha^2}{(1-\alpha)^2} = 3\frac{1}{12}2^{-2b}\frac{1+\alpha^2}{(1-\alpha)^2} = \frac{1+\alpha^2}{4(1-\alpha)^2}2^{-2b}$$

For $\alpha = 1 - \delta$, $\delta \ll 1$, and $\sigma_e^2 = \frac{1}{12}2^{-2b}$ (fixed point arithmetic)

$$\text{Output NSR} = 3\cdot\left(\frac{1}{12}2^{-2b}\right)\cdot\frac{1+(1+\delta)^2}{(\delta)^2}$$

$$\therefore \qquad \text{Output NSR} = \frac{1}{2\delta^2}2^{-2b}$$ **Ans.**

Canonic form (Floating Point Arithmetic):
Add error sources after each multiplication and adder as shown

$$e_1(n) = \varepsilon_1(n)[\alpha y_1(n-1)]$$
$$e_2(n) = \varepsilon_2(n)[y_1(n)]$$
$$e_3(n) = \varepsilon_3(n)\left[-\frac{1}{\alpha}y_1(n-1)\right]$$
$$e_4(n) = \varepsilon_4(n)[y(n)]$$

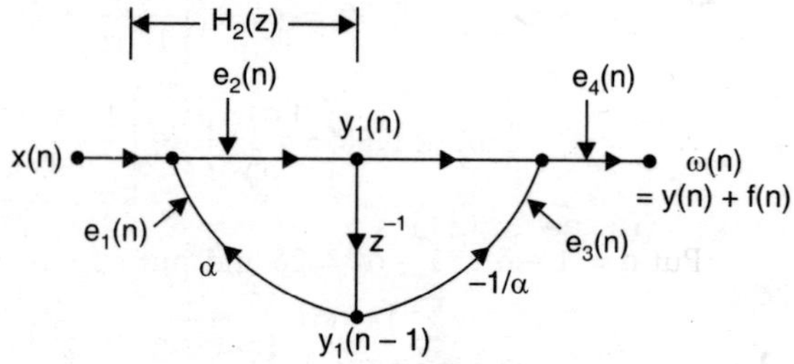

Fig. Prob. 10.6. (*e*)

$$H_2(z) = \frac{1}{1-\alpha z^{-1}}$$

$$\therefore h_2(n) = \alpha^n u(n)$$

$$\sum_{n=0}^{\infty} h_2^2(n) = \frac{1}{1-\alpha^2}$$

$$\therefore \quad \sigma_{e_1}^2 = \sigma_\varepsilon^2\, E[\alpha^2 y_1^2(n-1)] = \sigma_\varepsilon^2 \cdot \alpha^2 \sigma_{y_1}^2$$

$$= \sigma_\varepsilon^2 \cdot \alpha^2 \cdot \frac{1}{1-\alpha^2} \cdot \sigma_x^2$$

$$\because \quad \sigma_{y_1}^2 = \sigma_x^2 \sum |h_2(n)|^2 = \frac{\sigma_x^2}{1-\alpha^2}$$

$$\sigma_{e_2}^2 = \sigma_\varepsilon^2 \cdot E[y_1^2(n)] = \sigma_\varepsilon^2 \cdot \sigma y_1^2 = \sigma_\varepsilon^2 \cdot \frac{\sigma_x^2}{1-\alpha^2}$$

$$\sigma_{e_4}^2 = \sigma_\varepsilon^2 \cdot E[y^2(n)] = \sigma_\varepsilon^2\, \sigma_{y_1}^2$$

$$\sigma_{f_2}^2 = \sigma_\varepsilon^2\, E\left[\frac{1}{\alpha^2} \cdot y_1^2(n-1)\right] = \sigma_\varepsilon^2 \cdot \frac{1}{\alpha^2} \cdot \alpha_{y_1}^2$$

$$= \sigma_\varepsilon^2 \cdot \frac{1}{\alpha^2} \cdot \frac{\sigma_x^2}{1-\alpha^2}$$

$$\sigma_{e_3}^2 = \sigma_\varepsilon^2\, E\left[\frac{1}{\alpha^2}\, y_1^2(n-1)\right] = \sigma_\varepsilon^2 \frac{1}{\alpha^2} . \alpha_{y_1}^2$$

$$\sigma_{x_4}^2 = \sigma_\varepsilon^2 . E[y^2(n)] = \sigma_\varepsilon^2 \sigma_y^2$$

$$\sigma_{f_1}^2 = \sigma_{e_1}^2 \cdot \sum_{n=0}^{\infty} |h(n)|^2 = \frac{1}{\alpha^2} \sigma_{e_1}^2$$

$$\sigma_{f_2}^2 = \sigma_{e_2}^2 \cdot \sum_{n=0}^{\infty} h^2(n) = \frac{1}{\alpha^2} \sigma_{e_2}^2$$

$$\sigma_{f_3}^2 = \sigma_{e_3}^2$$

$$\sigma_{f_4}^2 = \sigma_{e_4}^2$$

$$\therefore \quad \sigma_f^2 = \sum_{i=1}^{4} \sigma_{f_i} = \frac{1}{\alpha^2}(\sigma_{e_1}^2 + \sigma_{e_2}^2) + \sigma_{e_3}^2 + \sigma_{e_4}^2$$

$$= \frac{1}{\alpha^2}\left[\frac{\sigma_\varepsilon^2 \alpha^2 \sigma_x^2}{1-\alpha^2} + \frac{\sigma_\varepsilon^2 \sigma_x^2}{1-\alpha^2}\right] + \frac{\sigma_\varepsilon^2 \sigma_x^2}{\alpha^2(1-\alpha^2)} + \sigma_\varepsilon^2 \sigma_y^2$$

Put $$\frac{\sigma_x^2}{\alpha^2} = \sigma_y^2$$

$$\therefore \quad \sigma_f^2 = \sigma_\varepsilon^2\left[\frac{\alpha^2}{1-\alpha^2} + \frac{1}{1-\alpha^2}\right]\sigma_y^2 + \sigma_\varepsilon^2 \sigma_y^2\left[\frac{1}{1-\alpha^2} + 1\right]$$

$$= \sigma_\varepsilon^2 \cdot \sigma_y^2\left[\frac{1+\alpha^2}{1-\alpha^2} + \frac{2-\alpha^2}{1-\alpha^2}\right]$$

$$\therefore \quad \text{Output NSR} = \frac{\sigma_f^2}{\sigma_y^2} = \sigma_\varepsilon^2\left[\frac{1+\sigma^2+2-\alpha^2}{1-\alpha^2}\right] = \sigma_\varepsilon^2 \frac{3}{1-\alpha^2} = \frac{2^{-2b}}{1-\alpha^2}$$

Put $\alpha = 1 - \delta \therefore 1 - \alpha^2 = 2\delta$ and put $\sigma_\varepsilon^2 = \frac{1}{3}2^{-2b}$ (floating point arithmetic)

$$\therefore \quad \text{Output NSR} = \frac{1}{3}2^{-2b} \cdot \frac{3}{2\delta} = \frac{2^{-2b}}{2\delta}$$

(c) **To summarize the results:**

Structure	*Actual Relation*	$\alpha = 1 - \delta,\ \delta \ll 1$
(A) Direct form structure		
(i) Fixed point (bits = b)	$\dfrac{(2\alpha+1)^2}{2(1-\alpha^2)}2^{-2b}$	$\dfrac{9}{4\delta}2^{-2b}$
(ii) Floating point (bits in mantissa = t)	$\dfrac{(3+2\alpha^2)}{3(1-\alpha^2)}2^{-2t}$	$\dfrac{5}{6\delta}2^{-2t}$
(B) Canonic form structure		
(i) Fixed point (bits = b)	$\dfrac{1+\alpha^2}{4(1-\alpha)^2}2^{-2b}$	$\dfrac{1}{2\delta^2}2^{-2b}$
(ii) Floating point (bits in mantissa = t)	$\dfrac{2^{-2t}}{1-\alpha^2}$	$\dfrac{2^{-2t}}{2\delta}$

10.7. Consider the DFT

$$X(k) = \sum_{n=0}^{N-1} x(n)\,.\,W_N^{kn},\ 0 \le k \le N-1$$

where $W_N = e^{-j2\pi/N}$. Suppose that the sequence values $x(n)$ are N consecutive values of a stationary white-noise sequence with zero mean *i.e.,*

$$E[x(n)\,.\,x(r)] = \sigma_x^2\,\delta(n-r)$$
$$E[x(n)] = 0$$

(a) Determine the variance of $|X(k)|^2$

(b) Determine the cross correlation between value of the DFT *i.e.,* determine $E[X(k)\,.\,X^*(r)]$ as a function of k and r.

[Hint: (a) As $\quad X(k) = \sum_{n=0}^{N-1} x(n)\,.\,W_N^{kn},\quad$ where $\quad W_N = e^{-2\pi/N}$

$$X^*(k) = \sum_{m=0}^{N-1} x^*(m)\,.\,W_N^{-km} \qquad \because\ (W_N^{km})^* = W_N^{-km}$$

$$\therefore\quad E[|X(k)|^2] = E[X(k)\,.\,X^*(k)]$$

$$= E\left[\left(\sum_{n=0}^{N-1} x(n)\,.\,W_N^{kn}\right)\left(\sum_{m=0}^{N-1} x^*(m)\,.\,W_N^{-km}\right)\right]$$

$$= \sum_{n=0}^{N-1}\sum_{m=0}^{N-1} E[x(n)\,x^*(m)]\,W_N^{k(n-m)}$$

$$= \sum_{n=0}^{N-1}\sum_{m=0}^{N-1} \sigma_x^2\,\delta(n-m)\,.\,W_N^{k(n-m)}$$

Put $n - m = 0$ *i.e.,* $\delta(n - m) = 1$ and $W_N^{k(n-m)} = W_N^{\ 0} = 1$

$$= \sum_{n=0}^{N-1} \sigma_x^2 \, \delta(0) \,.\, 1 = \sum_{n=0}^{N-1} \sigma_x^2$$

$\therefore$ $E[\,|X(k)|^2] = N\sigma_x^2$ **Ans.**

(*b*) As $X(k) = \sum_{n=0}^{N-1} x(n)\, W_N^{kn} \quad 0 \le k \le N-1$

$$\therefore \quad X(r) = \sum_{m=0}^{N-1} x(m)\, W_N^{rm}$$

$$\therefore \quad E[X(k) \,.\, X^*(r)] = E\left[\sum_{n=0}^{N-1} x(n)\, W_N^{kn} \,.\, \sum_{m=0}^{N-1} x^*(m)\, W_N^{-rm}\right]$$

$$= \sum_{n=0}^{N-1} \sum_{m=0}^{N-1} E[x(n)\, x^*(m)] \,.\, W_N^{kn - rm}$$

$$= \sum_{n=0}^{N-1} \sum_{m=0}^{N-1} \sigma_x^2 \, \delta(n-m) \,.\, W_N^{kn - rm}$$

Put $n - m = 0 \quad \therefore \quad m = n$ *i.e.,* $W_N^{kn - rm} = W_N^{kn - rn} = W_N^{(k-r)n}$

$$\therefore \quad E[X(k) \,.\, X^*(r)] = \sum_{n=0}^{N-1} \sigma_x^2 \, \delta(0) \,.\, W_N^{(k-r)n}$$

$$= \sigma_x^2 \sum_{n=0}^{N-1} W_N^{(k-r)n}$$

When $k - r = 0$ *i.e.,* $k = r$, then $E[X(k)\, X^*(r)] = E[X(k)\, X^*(r)] = \sigma_x^2 \sum_{n=0}^{N-1} W_N^0$

$$= N\sigma_x^2 \text{ as found earlier}$$

When $k \ne r$, then

$$E[X(k) \,.\, X^*(r)] = \sigma_x^2 \sum_{n=0}^{N-1} W_N^{(k-r)n}$$

Now $\sum_{n=0}^{N-1} W_N^{(k-r)n} = \begin{cases} N, & \text{for } k = r \\ 0, & \text{otherwise} \end{cases}$ (This is a standard result)

i.e., $\sum_{n=0}^{N-1} W_N^{(k-r)n} = N\, \delta(k - r)$

$\therefore$ $E[X(k)\, X^*(r)] = \sigma_x^2 \,.\, N \,.\, \delta(k - r)$

Thus, $E[\,|X(k)|^2] = N\sigma_x^2$

$E[X(k) \,.\, X^*(r)] = N\sigma_x^2\, \delta(k - r)$ **Ans.**

10.8. Consider direct computation of the DFT using fixed-point arithmetic with rounding.

Assume that the register length is b bits plus sign bit and that the round off noise introduced by multiplication is independent of that introduced by any other multiplication. Assuming that $x(n)$ is real, determine the variance of the round off noise in both the real part and the imaginary part of each spectrum point $X(k)$.

[**Hint:** DFT is defined as $X(k) = \sum_{n=0}^{N-1} x(n)\, W_N^{kn}$, $W_N = e^{-j2\pi/N}$

In direct computation, all N multiplications are performed and addition made as shown in Fig. Prob. 10.8.

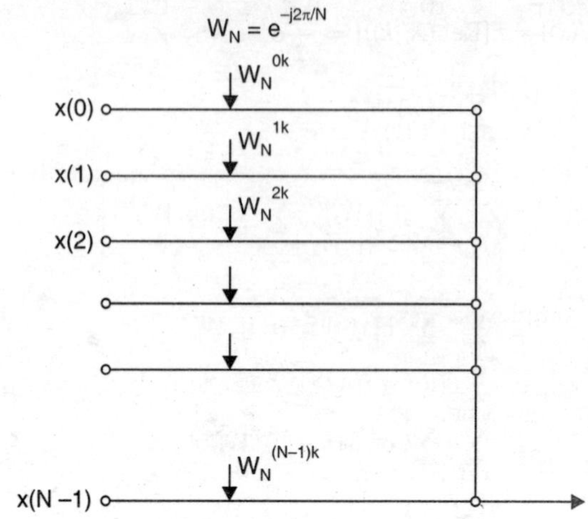

Fig. Prob. 10.8. Direct computation of DFT

If $x(n)$ is a real sequence then $x(n)\,.\,W_N^{kn} = x(n)\,[\text{Re } W_N^{kn}] + j\,x(n)\,[I_m W_N^{\ kn}]$

$$\therefore \qquad \text{Re } X'(k) = \sum_{n=0}^{N-1} x(n)\,.\,\text{Re}\,[W_N^{kn}] + e(n)$$

$$I_m\, X'(k) = \sum_{n=0}^{N-1} x(n)\, I_m\,[W_N^{kn}] + e(n)$$

$$E[(\text{Re } X'(k))]^2 = E\left[\left(\sum_{n=0}^{N-1} x(n)\,\text{Re}\,[W_N^{kn}] + e(n)\right)\left(\sum_{m=0}^{N-1} x(m)\,\text{Re}\,[W_N^{km}] + e(m)\right)\right]$$

$$= \sum_{n=0}^{N-1}\sum_{m=0}^{N-1} E\,[x(n)\;x(m)\cdot \text{Re } W_n^{kn}\ \text{Re } W_N^{km} + e(n)e(m) + e(m)x(n)\ \text{Re } W_N^{kn} + e(n)x(m)\ \text{Re } W_N^{km}$$

$$= \sum_{n=0}^{N-1}\sum_{m=0}^{N-1} \phi_{xx}(n-m)E\,\text{Re}\,W_N^{kn+km} + \sigma_e^2\delta(n-m) + 0 + 0$$

$$= \sum_{n=0}^{N-1} (\sigma_x^2 E\,\text{Re}\,[W_N^{2kn}] + \sigma_e^2) \qquad \because \quad E[x(n)\cdot e(m)] = \text{uncorrelated}$$

But $\qquad E\ \text{Re}\ [W_n^{2kn}] = E[\cos^2\,(km)] = E\left[\dfrac{(1-\cos 2\,km)}{2}\right] = \dfrac{1}{2}$

Hence, $\qquad E[(\text{Re } X'(k))^2] = \sum_{n=0}^{N-1}\left(\sigma_x^2\cdot\dfrac{1}{2} + \sigma_e^2\right)$

$$\therefore \qquad E[\text{Re } (X'(k))] = \frac{N}{2}\sigma_x^2 + N\sigma_e^2$$

As mean of Re $(X'(k))$

$$= E[\text{Re } X'(k)]$$

$$= E\left[\sum_{n=0}^{N-1} x(n)\cdot \text{Re}\,[W_N^{kn}] + e(n)\right]$$

$$= \sum_{n=0}^{N-1} E[x(n)]E[\text{Re}\,W_N^{kn}] + E[e(n)] = 0 \qquad \because x(n) \text{ and } e(n) \text{ are zero mean}$$

$\therefore$ Variance of $\quad (\text{Re } X'(k)) = E[\text{Re}^2\,(X'(k))] = \dfrac{N}{2}\sigma_x^2 + N\sigma_e^2$

Variance of noise in Re $[X'(k)] = N\sigma_e^2$

Similarly variance of noise in $I_m[X'(k)] = N\sigma_e^2$

i.e. Variance of noise in Re $[X(k)]$ = Variance of noise in magnitude part of $X'(k) = N\sigma_e^2$

$$= \left(N\cdot\frac{1}{12}2^{-2b}\right) \quad \textbf{Ans.}$$

Note: If $x(n)$ were a complex sequence

then $\qquad \text{Re}\,[X'(k)] = \sum_{n=0}^{N-1} (\text{Re}\,x(n)\cdot \text{Re}\,W_N^{kn} - I_m x(n)\cdot I_m W_N^{kn} + e_1(n) + e_2(n))$

$\because$ there are two multiplications

$$E[(\text{Re } X'(k))^2] = E\left[\left(\sum_{n=0}^{N-1}\sum_{m=0}^{N-1} (\text{Re}\,x(n)\,\text{Re}\,W_N^{kn} - I_m x(n) I_m W_N^{kn} + e_1(n) + e_2(n))\right.\right.$$

$$\left.\left.(\text{Re}\,x(m)\,\text{Re}\,W_N^{km} - I_m x(m) I_m W_N^{km} + e_1(m) + e_2(m)\right)\right]$$

$$= \sum_{n=0}^{N-1}\sum_{m=0}^{N-1} \frac{1}{2}\sigma_x^2\,\delta(n-m)\delta[\text{Re}\,W_N^{kn}\,\text{Re}\,W_N^{km}] + \frac{1}{2}\sigma_x^2\,\delta(n-m)E[I_m W_N^{kn} I_m W_N^{km}]$$

$$+\sigma_{e_1}^2\,\delta(n-m) + \sigma_{e_2}^2\,\delta(n-m) + 0 + 0 + 0 + 0$$

$$= \sum_{n=0}^{N-1} \frac{1}{2}\sigma_x^2\,E(\text{Re}\,W_N^{kn})^2 + \frac{1}{2}\sigma_x^2\,E(I_m W_N^{kn})^2 + 2\sigma_e^2$$

$$= \sum_{n=0}^{N-1} \frac{1}{2}\sigma_x^2\cdot\frac{1}{2} + \frac{1}{2}\sigma_x^2\cdot\frac{1}{2} + 2\sigma_e^2 = \frac{N}{2}\sigma_x^2 + 2N\sigma_e^2$$

Thus, variance of noise in Re $(X'(k))$ = Variance of noise in $I_m(X'(k)) = 2N\sigma_e^2$ here **Ans.**

Some Books and Papers on Quantization Effects

(*a*) **Books**

1. A.V. Oppenheim and R.W. Schafer, 'Digital Signal Processing' Prentice Hall Inc., New Jersey–1975.
2. Andreas Antoniou, 'Digital Filters: Analysis and Design', TMH, New Delhi–1979.
3. Lawrence R. Rabiner and Bernard Gold, 'Theory and Application of Digital Signal Processing', PHI–1978.
4. Athanasios Papoulis, 'Signal Analysis', McGraw Hill International Book Company–1977.
5. J.G. Proakis, D.G. Manolakis, 'Digital Signal Processing', 3rd edn., Prentice Hall of India–1996.

(b) Papers

1. C. J. Weinstein, 'Round off noise in floating point FFT computation', IEEE Trans. on Audio and Electroacoustic, Vol. AU–17, No. 3, pp. 209–215, Sep., 1969.
2. Ebert, Mazo, and Tylor, 'Overflow oscillations in digital filters', BELL Systems Technical Jr. Vol. 48, pp. 2999–3020, Nov., 1969.
3. A.V. Oppenheim, 'Realization of digital filters using block floating point arithmetic', IEEE Trans. on Audio and Electro Acoustic, Vol. AU–18, No. 2, pp. 130–136, June, 1970.
4. A.V. Oppenheim and Clifford Weinstein, 'Effects of finite register length of digital filtering and Fast Fourier Transform', Proc. IEE, Vol. 60, pp. 957–976, August, 1972.
5. A.V. Oppenheim (editor) et al, 'Selected papers in Digital Signal Processing-II', IEEE Press-IEEE Acoustics, Speech and Signal Processing Society–1976.
6. Barnes and Fam, 'Minimum norm recursive digital filters that are free of overflow limit cycles', IEEE Trans. on Circuits and Systems, Vol. CAS–24, No. 10, pp. 569–574, October, 1977.
7. L.B. Jackson, 'Limit cycles in state-space structure for digital filters', IEEE Trans. on Circuits and Systems, Vol. CAS–26, pp. 67–68, Jan., 1979.
8. A.G. Bolton, 'A two's complement overflow limit cycle free filter structure', IEEE Trans. on Circuits and Systems, Vol. CAS–31, No. 12. pp. 1045–46, December, 1984.

Random Variables and Signals

CHAPTER 11

11.0 INTRODUCTION

The discrete-time signals and systems have both a time-domain and a frequency domain representation. In deterministic (*i.e.,* non-random) signals, its each sample value is uniquely determined by a mathematical expression, or a table of data, or a rule of some type. The deterministic signals can also be represented by z-transform or Fourier transform *sequences that have ZT representation must have finite energy or it must be possible to multiply by an exponential sequence so that the product has finite energy.* This requirement corresponds to the essentiality that the *ZT* converges, (in some specified area, called ROC). A periodic sequence cannot have *ZT* since here the condition of finite energy cannot be satisfied. However, the periodic signals are, by definition, identical from period to period and consequently they can be uniquely represented in terms of a single period. *And a single period of a periodic sequence has finite-length and consequently finite-energy sequence.* This property of periodic sequence (*i.e.,* finite energy of one period sequence) can be exploited by using *DFT of one period.*

Many practical signals do not have finite energy sequence nor are they periodic. Many communication signals are, for example, of indefinite duration and are, therefore, best modelled in terms of infinite-duration, infinite-energy signals. In many situations, signal-generation processes are so complex as to make precise description/model extremely difficult, if not impossible. Many of the effects encountered in implementing *DSP algorithms with finite register length can be represented by additive "noise", which can be reckoned as a sequence with infinite energy.* Many mathematical systems generate acoustic or vibratory signals which can often be processed to diagnose potential failure and such signals are also modelled in terms of *infinite-energy, non-periodic signals.* Speech signals to be processed for automatic recognition or bandwidth compression and music to be processed for quality enhancement are also two more of many possible examples.

The key to the mathematical representation of such (infinite-energy/non-periodic but having infinite energy/random) signals lies in their description in terms of averages (mean, variance...). Many, though not all, of the properties of such signals can be summarized in terms of a finite-energy sequence, called *the auto-correlation or auto-covariance sequence, for which the z-transform or the Fourier transform often exists.* We will see that, the Fourier transform of the auto-covariance sequence has a useful intepretation in terms of the frequency distribution of the power in the signal. Also, by using auto-covariance sequence and its transform has the important advantage that the effect of processing infinite-energy signals (*i.e.*, a random variable sequence) with a discrete linear system can be conveniently described in terms of the effect of the system on the auto-covariance sequence.

To tackle infinite-energy signals, it is convenient to work within the framework of non-deterministic *i.e.*, random or stochastic signals. Here, the signal is considered to be a member of an ensemble or discrete-time signals which are characterized by a set of probability density functions.

11.1 A DISCRETE-TIME RANDOM PROCESS (RP)

The fundamental concept in the mathematical representation of infinite-energy signals is that of a random process (RP). We assume in DSP that the RP's are modelled as infinite-energy discrete-time signals.

11.1.1 Simple Example: The Bernoulli Process

We use the notation of the sequences by $x(n)$ and the value of $x(n)$ sample at n by x_n.

Suppose that a sequence of numbers is generated as follows:

At a given time n, a coin is tossed, and if the result is head the value of the sequence at n is given by

Head: $x(n) = +1$; and if a tail results, the value is denoted by

$x(n) = -1$. A typical sequence is as shown in Fig. 11.1

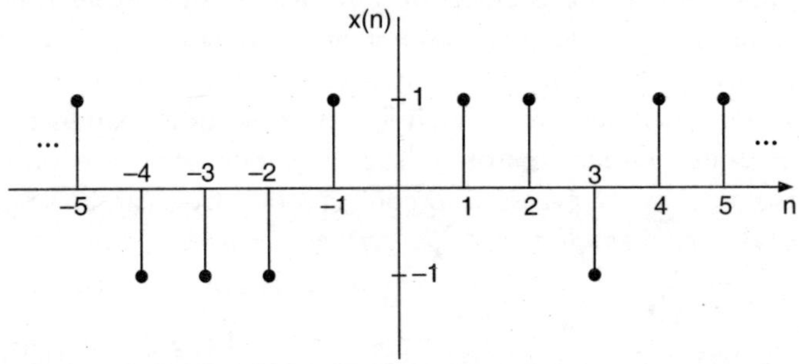

Fig. 11.1. Sequence of +1's and –1's (a sample sequence of a random process). Here, x_n = 1 or –1

If we assume that this process has been operating for all time, *i.e.*, $-\infty < n < \infty$, then we obtain a sequence of infinite duration. Such a sequence has infinite energy and neither the z-transform nor the Fourier transform exists. Also, we have no mathematical formula, except a table, to give the sequence values, since it is assumed infinite-length. It would be impossible to determine the next sample in the sequence with any certainty. This uncertainty leads us, in general, to a characterization of the sequence in terms of probabilities and thus to averages/expectations.

Let us suppose that the probability of head is p and, therefore, the probability of tail is $1 - p$.

The nth sequence value, $x(n)$, thus has an interpretation as a particular value of a random variable, x_n, *i.e.*, a function of the outcome of the experiment of tossing a coin. (Random variables with this probability law are known as Bernoulli random variables). Specially, each event may be viewed by assigning a number to outcome of the coin-tossing experiment. Here, we call the event "a head tossed" by a value $x_n = +1$ and the event "a tail tossed" by a value $x_n = -1$. In this experiment, there being only two types of events (head or tail), we have only two possible values $x(n) = +1$ or $x(n) = -1$. We, therefore, say

$x_n = +1$ with a probability p for head as the outcome
$x_n = -1$ with a probability $(1 - p)$ for tail as the outcome.

The set of *random variables* $\{x_n\}$ *for* $-\infty < n < \infty$, *together with the probabilistic description of each random variable, constitutes the definition of a random process.*

In the above experiment, the ensamble x_n (+1 or –1) are called Bernoullis random variables and description of $\{x_n\}$ with their probabilities (*i.e.*, p and $(1 - p)$) is called *Bernoullis random process.*

A given sequence $\{x(n)\}$, $-\infty < n < \infty$ is a realization of the random process and is called a sample sequence of the RP. Note that the number of possible ensambles, *i.e.*, sample sequences, for a random process, is infinite. The collection of all the sequences (one such sequence is given in Fig. 11.1) as a result of realizing the random process is called an ensamble of sample sequence. Several, all different, sequences result due to tossing the coin. Only when either $p = 1$ or $p = 0$, we shall have only one unique sample sequence (of all +1's for $p = 1$ and of all –1's for $p = 0$). But for $p = 1$ or $p = 0$, the process is no more random but fully deterministic one.

For applying the RP model in practical signal processing applications, we take a particular one sequence out of the ensemble of sample sequences corresponding to the random process. Since any sample sequence is, in general, of infinite duration, thus we call the RP has infinite energy signal $x(n)$. For discrete-time-signal (*i.e.* digital signal) which assume to be one of an ensemble of sample sequences, the law of probability governing the RP (of which the sample sequences are) may not be known in general. We make possible assumption about the structure of the 'mother' RP or we may *estimate the properties* of a random-process representation from a finite segment of a typical sample sequence. For example, given fairly long sample sequence of Fig. 11.1, we may estimate p and therefore $(1 - p)$, mean of the samples, auto-correlation and variance of the sample sequence. These parameters are then taken as quite accurate values of the actual parameters governing the random process.

11.1.2 Random Process Descriptions

Formally, a random process is an indexed family of random variables $\{x_n\}$. The family of RVs' is characterized by a set of probability distribution functions that, in general, may be a function of the index n. This index is associated with time or some other physical dimension (*e.g.* space, pressure, ...).

We define *Cumulative Probability Distribution Functions* (CDF or cdf) by

$$P_{\bar{x}_n}(x_n, n) = \text{Probability}\,[\bar{x}_n \le x_n] \qquad \text{...(11.1)}$$

where $\bar{x}_n$ denotes the generic random variables values and x_n is a particular value of the variable $\bar{x}_n$.*

If $\bar{x}_n$ takes a continuous range of values, we define

Probability Density Function (pdf) by

$$\text{pdf: } p_{\bar{x}_n}(x_n, n) = \frac{\partial P_{\bar{x}_n}(x_n, n)}{\partial x_n} \quad \text{for analog RV case} \qquad \text{...(11.2)}$$

$$\text{cdf: } P_{\bar{x}_n}(x_n, n) = \int_{-\infty}^{x_n} p_{\bar{x}_n}(x, n)\, dx \quad \text{for analog RV case} \qquad \text{...(11.3)}$$

* The bar variables, *i.e.*, $\bar{x}_n$, is used to denote the generic values for the random variables and the regular (unbarred) letter x_n denotes dummy one particular value of the variables of probability functions.

In the example of RV (outcome 'head' or 'tail') the random variables were quantized *i.e.* they take on a countable set of values (and not continuous values). In this case we have the distribution

$$P_{\bar{x}_n}(x_n, n) = \begin{cases} 1, & x_n \geq 1 \quad (\because \text{ both possible values, } -1, 1 \text{ are covered here}) \\ 1-p, & -1 \leq x_n < 1 \quad (\text{Only one value, } -1, \text{ is covered here}) \\ 0 & x_n < -1 \quad (\text{no value of } x_n \text{ lies below } -1) \end{cases} \qquad \text{...(11.4)}$$

Note that in such cases derivative, (11.2) type, does not exist. Here, we define

$$\text{Probability mass function, (of a discrete RV) } p_{\bar{x}_n}(x_n, n) = \text{Probability}\,[\bar{x}_n = x_n] \qquad \text{...(11.5)}$$

For discrete/quantized random variables, the probability distribution (*i.e.* cdf), $P_{\bar{x}_n}(x_n, n)$ is related to the probability density function (pdf) $p_{\bar{x}_n}(x_n, n)$ is

$$\begin{aligned} P_{\bar{x}_n}(x_n, n) &= \text{Probability}\,[\bar{x}_n \leq x_n] \\ \text{cdf} &= \sum_{\bar{x}_n \leq x_n} p_{\bar{x}_n}(x_n, n) \qquad \text{for discrete RV case} \\ \text{and} & \qquad \nwarrow \text{probability mass function} \\ p_{\bar{x}_n}(x_n, n) &= P_{\bar{x}_n}(x_n, n) - P_{\bar{x}_n}(x_{n-1}, n) \end{aligned} \qquad \text{...(11.6)}$$

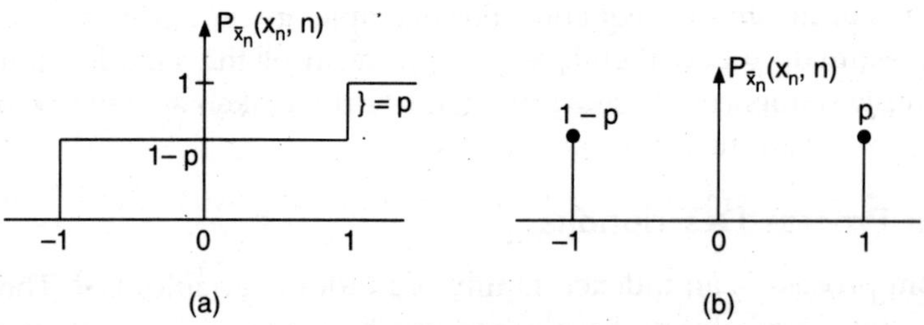

Fig. 11.2. (*a*) cdf (*i.e.* probability distribution) for a Bernoullis RV and (*b*) corresponding pdf (*i.e.*, probability-mass function)

We define interdependence of two RV's, by the joint pdf

$$\underset{\text{(joint pdf)}}{p_{\bar{x}_n, \bar{x}_m}(x_n, n, x_m, m)} = \frac{\partial^2 P_{\bar{x}_n, \bar{x}_m}(x_n, n, x_m, m)}{\partial x_n \, \partial x_m} \quad \text{(for a continuous RP)} \qquad \text{...(11.7)}$$

and

$$\underset{\text{(joint cdf)}}{P_{\bar{x}_n, \bar{x}_m}(x_n, n, x_m, m)} = \text{Probability}\,[\bar{x}_n \leq x_n \text{ and } \bar{x}_m < x_m] \qquad \text{...(11.8)}$$

Similarly, in the case of discrete (*i.e.*, quantized) random variables, the joint density mass function (pdf) is defined as

$$\underset{\text{joint pdf – discrete RV's}}{p_{\bar{x}_n, \bar{x}_m}(x_n, n, x_m, m)} = \text{Probability}\,[\bar{x}_n = x_n \text{ and } \bar{x}_m = x_m] \qquad \text{...(11.9)}$$

A complete characterization/description of an RP requires specification of all possible joint pdf's. These pdf's may be functions of time index *n*. If all the probability functions are independent of a shift of time origin, then the random process is said to be *Stationary*. For example, the second-order distribution of a stationary process satisfies the following condition.

$$P_{\bar{x}_{n+k}\bar{x}_{m+k}}(x_{n+k}, n+k, x_{m+k}, m+k) = P_{\bar{x}_n \bar{x}_m}(x_n, n, x_m, m) \quad \text{Stationarity condition} \quad \ldots(11.10)$$

The Bernoulli process is an example of a stationary RP, since it was assumed that in flipping the coin, probability (head) was always equal to p and each RV (*i.e.* head and tail) was assumed independent of all the others.

To many of the applications in DSP, random variables, and random processes serve as models for signals in the sense that a particular infinite-energy signal can be considered a sample sequence of a random process. Although the complete details of such signals are unpredictable–making our previous approach to signal representation inappropriate–but certain average properties of the ensamble can be predicted if we are given the probability law of the process. These average properties (*viz.*, the mean, variance, moments, ..., etc.) often serve as a useful, although incomplete, characterization of signals for which the Fourier transform (of the 'raw' random variable's ensamble) does not exist.

11.2 AVERAGES

It is often useful to characterize a random variable by averages such as mean, variance, etc. Since an RP is an indexed set of random variables, we may likewise characterize the process by statistical averages of the RVs, comprising the random process. Such averages are called ensemble averages.

11.2.1 Definitions

The average or mean of the random process is defined as:

Mean

$$m_{\bar{x}_n} = E\{\bar{x}_n\} = \int_{-\infty}^{\infty} x p_{\bar{x}_n}(x, n)\, dx, \text{ for analog RV}$$

$$m_{\bar{x}_n} = \sum_x x p_{\bar{x}_n}(x, n), \text{ for discrete RV} \quad \ldots(11.11)$$

where E denotes mathematical expectation. We note that, in general, the mean (expected value) may depend upon n. In addition, if $g(\cdot)$ is a single valued functions, then $g(\bar{x}_n)$ is a random variable and the set of random variables $\{g(\bar{x}_n)\}$ defines a new random process. For example: $g(x) = 1 + a_1 x + a_2 x^2$, if x is a RV then $g(x)$ is also RV. In order to compute averages of this new random process, we may first derive pdf of the new random variables and then use (11.11) to determine the mean of the new random process. Alternatively, we may use (11.12) given below:

$$\text{Mean of } g(\bar{x}_n) = E\{g(\bar{x}_n)\} = \int_{-\infty}^{\infty} g(x) p_{\bar{x}_n}(x, n)\, dx \quad \text{(for analog RV case)} \quad (11.12)$$

and in the case of quantized/discrete case, the integral is replaced by summation over all possible values of the RV, *i.e.*, $E\{g(x)\}$ has the form

$$E\{g(\overline{x}_n)\} = \sum_x g(x) p_{\overline{x}_n}(x, n) \text{ (for discrete RV case)*} \quad ...(11.13)$$

In cases where we are interested in the relationship between two (or more) random processes, there we have two (or more) sets of random variables $\{\overline{x}_n\}$ and $\{\overline{y}_m\}$. Here we define

$$E\{g(\overline{x}_n, \overline{y}_m)\} = \int_{-\infty}^{\infty}\int_{-\infty}^{\infty} g(x, y) p_{\overline{x}_n, \overline{y}_m}(x, n, y, m)\, dx\, dy \quad ...(11.14)$$

where $p_{\overline{x}_n, \overline{y}_m}(x_n, n, y_m, m)$ is the joint pdf of the RV's $\{\overline{x}_n\}$ and $\{\overline{y}_m\}$.

Some other useful properties of averages are as below:

1. $E\{\overline{x}_n + \overline{y}_m\} = E\{\overline{x}_n\} + E\{\overline{y}_m\}$, *i.e.*, average of sum = sum of averages
2. $E\{a\overline{x}_n\} = aE\{\overline{x}_n\}$ *i.e.* average of constant times $\overline{x}_n$ = the constant times the average of $\overline{x}_n$. ...(11.15)

In general, the average of a product of two random variables is *not equal* to the product of the averages. Two random variables are said to be linearly independent or uncorrelated if the average of their product is equal to the product of their (individual) averages.

i.e.,

linearly independent or uncorrelated $\{\overline{x}_n\}$, $\{\overline{y}_m\}$ have: $E\{\overline{x}_n \cdot \overline{y}_m\} = E\{\overline{x}_n\} \cdot E\{\overline{y}_m\}$ (relation for means) ...(11.16)

Thus a sufficient condition for linear independence is

$$p_{\overline{x}_n, \overline{y}_m}(x_n, n, y_m, m) = p_{\overline{x}_n}(x_n, n) \cdot p_{\overline{y}_m}(y_m, m) \quad \text{(relation for pdf's)} \quad ...(11.17a)$$

or

$$P_{\overline{x}_n, \overline{y}_m}(x_n, n, y_m, m) = P_{\overline{x}_n}(x_n, n) \cdot P_{\overline{y}_m}(y_m, m) \quad \text{(relation for cdf's)} \quad ...(11.17b)$$

Statistically independent $\{\overline{x}_n\}, \{\overline{y}_n\}$

It can be shown that Eqn. (11.17) is a stronger statement of independence than Eqn. (11.16). If Eqn. (11.17) holds for all values of n and m, the random variables $\{\overline{x}_n\}$ and $\{\overline{y}_m\}$ are said to be statistically independent. *Statistically, independent random processes are also linearly independent, but linear independent RP's may or may not be statistically independent.*

---

* **Example:** Let $p_{\overline{x}_n}(x, n) = 0.25$ for $x = 1$

0.50 for $x = 2$

0.25 for $x = 4$

For $g(\overline{x}_n) = x^2 + 2x + 2$

$g(x)|_{x=1} = 1 + 2 + 2 = 5$

$g(x)|_{x=2} = 4 + 4 + 2 = 10$

$g(x)|_{x=4} = 16 + 8 + 2 = 26$

$\therefore \quad E\{g(\overline{x}_n)\} = \sum_x g(x) p_{\overline{y}_n}(x, n) = 5 \times 0.25 + 10 \times 0.5 + 26 \times 0.25 = 12.75$

Though averages, Eqns. (11.12) to (11.14) are, in general, functions of time, but for stationary RP's this is not true. Thus, the mean of a stationary RP is a constant, denoted by m_x, and m_x is not a function of time. Delaying or advancing a stationary RP does not change its mean.

In addition to the mean of a random process, there are a number of averages which are of particular importance in DSP, besides in Communication and Parameter Estimation.

Mean square value of $\bar{x}_n$ is average of $|\bar{x}_n|^2$, *i.e.*,

$$E\{|\bar{x}_n|^2\} = \text{mean square value} = \int_{-\infty}^{\infty} |x|^2 p_{\bar{x}_n}(x, n)\, dx : \text{(continuous RP)} \quad \ldots(11.18a)$$

$$= \sum_x |x|^2 p_{\bar{x}_n}(x, n) \quad \text{(discrete RP)} \quad \ldots(11.18b)$$

called Average Power or Mean Square Value of $\{\bar{x}_n\}$.

The variance, $\sigma^2_{\bar{x}_n}$, of $\bar{x}_n$ is the average of $|\bar{x}_n - m_x|^2$ *i.e.* the mean square value of $\{\bar{x}_n - m_x\}$

$$\text{Variance: } \operatorname{var}[\bar{x}_n] \triangleq E\{|\bar{x}_n - m_x|^2\} = E\{|\bar{x}_n|^2\} - |m_x|^2 \triangleq \sigma^2_{\bar{x}_n} \quad \ldots(11.19)$$

i.e.,

$$\text{Variance} = \text{mean square value} - |\text{(mean)}|^{2**} \quad \ldots(11.20)$$

In general, mean square value and variance are functions of time. However, there are constants, w.r.t. time, for stationary processes.

The mean (m_x), mean square (*i.e.*, average power) and the variance ($\sigma^2_{\bar{x}_n}$) are simple averages and provide only a small amount of information about the process. A more useful average is the auto-correlation sequence, which is defined as

$$\phi_{xx}(n, m) \triangleq E\{\bar{x}_n \bar{x}_m^*\} = \sum_{x_n}\sum_{x_m} x_n x_m^* p_{\bar{x}_n, \bar{x}_m}(x_n, n, x_m, m) \quad \text{for discrete RV} \quad \ldots(11.21)$$

(auto-correlation sequence):

$$\phi_{xx}(n, m) = \int_{-\infty}^{\infty}\int_{-\infty}^{\infty} x_n x_m^* p_{\bar{x}_n, \bar{x}_m}(x_n, n, x_m, m)\, dx_n\, dx_m \quad \text{for analog RV} \quad \ldots(11.22)$$

where $*$ denotes complex conjugation. We also define

auto-covariance sequence: $\gamma_{xx}(n, m) \triangleq E\{(x_n - m_{x_n})(x_m - m_{x_m})^{**}\}$ $\quad \ldots(11.23)$

**** Proof:**

$$\sigma^2_{\bar{x}_n} = E\{|\bar{x}_n - m_x|^2\} \quad \text{by definition of variance}$$

$$= E\{\bar{x}_n^2 - 2m_x\bar{x}_n + m_x^2\}$$

$$= E\{|\bar{x}_n|^2\} - 2m_x \underbrace{E\{\bar{x}_n\}}_{=m_x} + m_x^2 = E\{|\bar{x}_n|^2\} - m_x^2$$

More rigorously:

$$\sigma^2_{\bar{x}_n} = E\{(\bar{x}_n - m_x)(\bar{x}_n - m_x)^*\}$$

$$= E\{\bar{x}_n\bar{x}_n^* - \bar{x}_n m_x^* - m_x\bar{x}_n^* + m_x m_x^*\}$$

$$= E\{|\bar{x}_n|^2\} - m_x^* E\{\bar{x}_n\} - m_x E\{\bar{x}_n^*\} + |m_x|^2$$

$$= E\{|\bar{x}_n|^2\} - m_x^* m_x - m_x m_x^* + |m_x|^2$$

$$= E\{|\bar{x}_n|^2\} - |m_x|^2$$

which can be written as

$$\gamma_{xx}(n, m) = \phi_{xx}(n, m) - m_{x_n} m^*_{x_m} \;** \qquad ...(11.24)$$

Note that in general, both the auto-correlation and auto-covariance are two dimensional sequences.

The auto-correlation sequence is a measure of the dependence between values of the random process at different times n, m. In this sense it partially describes the time variation of a random signal.

Similarly, a measure of the dependence between two different random processes is their cross-correlation given by:

$$\text{Cross-correlation: } \phi_{xy}(n, m) \triangleq E\{\overline{x}_n \cdot \overline{y}^*_m\} \text{ (definition)} \qquad ...(11.25a)$$

$$\phi_{xy}(n, m) = \sum_{x_n}\sum_{y_m} x_n y^*_m \, p_{\overline{x}_n, \overline{y}_m}(x_n, n, y_m, m) \text{ (discrete RV)} \qquad ...(11.25b)$$

$$\phi_{xy}(n, m) = \int_{-\infty}^{\infty}\int_{-\infty}^{\infty} x_n y^*_m p_{\overline{x}_n, \overline{y}_m}(x, n, y_m, m)\, dx\, dy \text{ (analog RV)} \qquad ...(11.25c)$$

We define cross-covariance by:

$$\text{Cross-covariance: } \gamma_{xy}(n, m) \triangleq E\{(\overline{x}_n - m_{x_n})(\overline{y}_m - m_{y_m})^*\} \; ***$$

$$= \phi_{xy}(n, m) - m_{x_n} m^*_{y_m} \; *** \qquad ...(11.26)$$

For stationary processes, (which are characterized by an equilibrium conditions; since these don't change with time, *i.e.*, these have past 'transient state'), the statistical properties are invariant to a shift of time origin.

Stationarity implies that the first-order probability distribution is independent of time. Similarly, all the joint probability functions are also invariant to a shift in time origin *i.e.* the second-order pdf satisfies Eqn. (11.10). From (11.10), it also follows that the *second-order joint distributions depend only on the time difference (m – n)*. First order averages such as mean and variance are independent of time. Second-order averages such as auto-correlation $\phi_{xx}(n, m)$, or auto-covariance $\gamma_{xx}(n, m)$ are dependent on the time difference (n, m). Thus for a stationary process, we have

---

** **Proof:**

$$E\{(x_n - m_{x_n})(x_m - m_{x_m})^*\} = E\{(x_n - m_{x_n})(x^*_m - m^*_{x_m})\}$$

$$= E\{x_n x^*_m - x_n m^*_{x_m} - m_{x_n} x^*_m + m_{x_n} m^*_{x_m}\}$$

$$= \phi_{xx}(n, m) - \cancel{m_{x_n} m^*_{x_m}} - m_{x_n} m^*_{x_m} + \cancel{m_{x_n} m^*_{x_m}}$$

$$= \phi_{xx}(n, m) - m_{x_n} m^*_{x_m}$$

Note that

If $E\{x_n\} = m_x$ then $E\{x^*_n\} = m^*_x$

*** **Proof:**

$$\gamma_{xy}(n, m) = E\{(\overline{x}_n - m_{x_n})(\overline{y}_m - m_{y_m})^*\} = E\{(\overline{x}_n - m_{x_n})(\overline{y}^*_m - m^*_{y_m})\}$$

$$= E\{\overline{x}_n \overline{y}^*_m - \overline{x}_n m^*_{y_m} - m_{x_n} \overline{y}^*_m + m_{x_n} m^*_{y_m}\}$$

$$= \phi_{xy}(n, m) - m_{x_n} m^*_{y_m} - \cancel{m_{x_n} m^*_{y_m}} + \cancel{m_{x_n} m^*_{y_m}}$$

$$= \phi_{xy}(n, m) - m_{x_n} m^*_{y_m}$$

$$m_x = E\{\overline{x}_n\} \text{ valid for stationary random processes} \quad \text{...(11.27)}$$

$$\sigma_x^2 = E\{|\overline{x}_n - m_x|^2\} \quad \text{...(11.28)}$$

i.e., independent of n (the time). If we denote the time difference by m, then we have

$$\phi_{xx}(n + m, n) = \phi_{xx}(m) = E\{\overline{x}_{n+m} \cdot \overline{x}_n^*\} \quad \text{...(11.29)}$$

i.e., the auto-correlation sequence of a stationary random process is a one-dimensional sequence, *viz.* a function of the time difference m.

In many instances we encounter RP's that are not time-invariant, *i.e.* not stationary in the strict sense, their pdf not being time-invariant, and yet they might have mean as constant and auto-correlation sequence satisfying Eqn. (11.29). Such RP's are said to be *stationary in the wide sense.*

11.2.2 Time Averages

In a signal processing context, the notion of an ensamble of signals is a convenient mathematical representation. But, in a practical sense, we would prefer to deal with a single sequence rather than an infinite ensamble of sequences. For example, we might wish to determine the probability law of certain averages of the RP from measurements on a single member of the ensamble. When the probability distributions are time-invariant, we might feel intuitively that the amplitude distribution of a long segment of a single-sample sequence (*i.e.*, only one sample sequence out of the ensamble of sample sequences) should approximately equal to the pdf. Similarly, the arithmetic average of a large number of samples of a single sample-sequence should very closely amount to the mean of the RP. Mathematically, we can, therefore, write the time average by:

$$\langle \overline{x}_n \rangle \triangleq \lim_{L \to \infty} \frac{1}{2L+1} \sum_{n=-L}^{L} x_n \quad \text{...(11.30)}$$

Similarly, the time auto-correlation sequence in time is defined as

$$\langle \overline{x}_n^* \, \overline{x}_{n+m} \rangle \triangleq \lim_{L \to \infty} \frac{1}{2L+1} \sum_{n=-L}^{L} \overline{x}_n^* \, \overline{x}_{n+m} \quad \text{...(11.31)}$$

time auto-coorelation

It can be shown that the *limits in (11.30) and (11.31) exist if* $\{\overline{x}_n\}$ *is a stationary process with finite mean* (m_x). Note that the time-averages defined in (11.30) and (11.31) are functions of an infinite set of random variables (since $L \to \infty$) and thus may be properly (*i.e.*, faithfully, truly) viewed as the random variables themselves. Under certain conditions known as ergodicity, the time averages in Eqns. (11.30) and (11.31) are equal to constants and that the time averages of almost all possible sample-sequences are equal to the same constant. Furthermore, *for ergodic RP's the time averages (being constants) are equal to the corresponding ensamble averages.*

A more precise statement is that:

$$\langle \overline{x}_n \rangle = m_x$$

$$\langle \overline{x}_n^* \, \overline{x}_{n+m} \rangle = \phi_{xx}(m)$$

i.e., Variance of $\langle \overline{x}_n \rangle$ as well as that of $\langle \overline{x}_n^* \, \overline{x}_{n+m} \rangle$ are zero *i.e.* time averages as defined are consistent.

Thus, for any single sample sequence $\{x(n)\}$, *i.e.*, time domain sequence

$$\langle x(n)\rangle \triangleq \lim_{L\to\infty}\frac{1}{2L+1}\sum_{n=-L}^{L} x(n) = E\{\bar{x}_n\} = m_x \quad \ldots(11.32)$$

$$\text{and } \langle x^*(n)\,x(n+m)\rangle = \lim_{L\to\infty}\frac{1}{2L+1}\sum_{n=-L}^{L} x^*(n)\,x(n+m)$$

$$= E\{\bar{x}_n^*\,\bar{x}_{n+m}\} = \phi_{xx}(m) \quad \ldots(11.33)$$

For ergodic random processes.

The time average operator $\langle\cdot\rangle$ has the same properties as the ensamble average operates $E\{\cdot\}$. Thus, we generally do not distinguish between the RV $\bar{x}_n$ and its value in a sample-sequence, $x(n)$. In other words

$$E\{x(n)\} \equiv E\{\bar{x}_n\} = \langle x(n)\rangle \quad \ldots(11.34)$$

$E\{x(n)\}$ ↗	$E\{\bar{x}_n\}$ ↗	$\langle x(n)\rangle$ ↖
Expectation of a time random variable	Ensamble average	Time average

A random process for which time averages equal the ensamble averages is called an *Ergodic Process.* In practice, it is common (and also convenient) to assume that a given sequence is a sample-sequence of an ergodic random process, so that the ensamble averages of the RP can be computed from a single sequence. We generally cannot compute the limits in Eqns. (11.32) and (11.33), but the quantities or similar quantities are often computed.

$$\hat{m}_x = \frac{1}{L}\sum_{n=0}^{L-1} x(n) \text{ sample mean (estimate)} \quad \ldots(11.35)$$

$$\hat{\sigma}_x^2 = \frac{1}{L}\sum_{n=0}^{L-1} |x(n)-\hat{m}_x|^2 \text{ sample variance (estimate)} \quad \ldots(11.36)$$

$$\langle x^*(n)\,x(n+m)\rangle_L = \frac{1}{L}\sum_{n=0}^{L-1} x^*(n)\,x(n+m) \text{ sample auto-correlation (estimate)} \quad \ldots(11.37)$$

These are estimates of the mean, variance and auto-correlation. *The estimation of averages of an RP from a finite segment of data is a problem of statistics, also known as parameter estimation.*

11.3 SPECTRUM REPRESENTATION OF INFINITE-ENERGY SIGNALS

Although the z-transform of an infinite-energy signal does not exist, the *auto-covariance and auto-correlation sequences of such a signal are aperiodic sequences* for which the z-transform and Fourier transform often do exist. The spectral representation of these averages plays an important role in describing the input-output relations for a linear, time-invariant system when the input is an infinite-energy signal. We, therefore, consider the properties of correlation and covariance sequences and their corresponding z-transforms.

11.3.1 Properties of Correlation and Covariance Sequences

Consider two stationary random processes $\{\overline{x}_n\}$ and $\{\overline{y}_n\}$ with their statistical parameters:

auto-correlation:	$\phi_{xx}(m) = E[\overline{x}_{n+m}\,\overline{x}_n^*]$	...(11.38)
auto-covariance:	$\gamma_{xx}(m) = E[(\overline{x}_{n+m} - m_x)(\overline{x}_n - m_x)^*]$	...(11.39)
cross-correlation:	$\phi_{xy}(m) = E[\overline{x}_{n+m}\,\overline{y}_n^*]$	...(11.40)
cross-covariance:	$\gamma_{xy}(m) = E[(\overline{x}_{n+m} - m_x)(\overline{y}_n - m_y)^*]$	...(11.41)

where m_x and m_y are the means of the two processes, respectively.

Property 1:

$$\gamma_{xx}(m) = \phi_{xx}(m) - |m_x|^2 \quad \text{...(11.42}a\text{)}$$
$$\gamma_{xy}(m) = \phi_{xy}(m) - m_x m_y^* \quad \text{...(11.42}b\text{)}$$

Property 2:

$$\phi_{xx}(0) = E[|x_n|^2] = \text{Mean square value} \quad \text{...(11.43}a\text{)}$$
$$\gamma_{xx}(0) = \sigma_x^2 = \text{Variance} \quad \text{...(11.43}b\text{)}$$

Hence, mean square value and variance are obtained from $\phi_{xx}(m)$ and $\gamma_{xx}(m)$ by putting $m = 0$.

Property 3:

auto-correlation sequence:	$\phi_{xx}^*(m) = \phi_{xx}(-m)$	$\phi_{xx}(-m) = \phi_{xx}^*(m)$	...(11.44*a*)
auto-covariance sequence:	$\gamma_{xx}^*(m) = \gamma_{xx}(-m)$	$\gamma_{xx}(-m) = \gamma_{xx}^*(m)$	...(11.44*b*)
cross-correlation sequence:	$\phi_{xy}^*(m) = \phi_{yx}(-m)$	$\phi_{xy}(-m) = \phi_{yx}^*(m)$	...(11.44*c*)
cross-covariance sequence:	$\gamma_{xy}^*(m) = \gamma_{yx}(-m)$	$\gamma_{xy}(-m) = \gamma_{yx}^*(m)$	...(11.44*d*)

Note: For real valued RPs, $\phi_{xx}(m) = \phi_{xx}(-m)$; $\gamma_{xx}(m) = \gamma_{xx}(-m)$; $\phi_{xy}(m) = \phi_{yx}(-m)$; $\gamma_{xy}(m) = \gamma_{yx}(-m)$.

Property 4:

$$|\phi_{xy}(m)| \le [\phi_{xx}(0)\cdot\phi_{yy}(0)]^{1/2} \quad \text{...(11.45}a\text{)}$$
$$|\gamma_{xy}(m)| \le [\gamma_{xx}(0)\cdot\gamma_{yy}(0)]^{1/2} \quad \text{...(11.45}b\text{)}$$

In particular, then

$$|\phi_{xx}(m)| \le \phi_{xx}(0) \quad \text{...(11.46}a\text{)}$$
$$|\gamma_{xx}(m)| \le \gamma_{xx}(0) \quad \text{...(11.46}b\text{)}$$

Property 5: If $\overline{y}_n = \overline{x}_{n-n_0}$, then

i.e., $x(n)$ and $y(n)$ are similar random sequences but shifted by time n_0.

$$\phi_{yy}(m) = \phi_{xx}(m) \quad \text{...(11.47}a\text{)}$$
$$\gamma_{yy}(m) = \gamma_{xx}(m) \quad \text{...(11.47}b\text{)}$$

Property 6: For many random processes, the random variables become less correlated (*i.e.*, more uncorrelated) as they become more separated in time. This implies that:

$$\lim_{m\to\infty} \phi_{xx}(m) = E[|x_n|^2] = |m_x|^2 \quad \text{...(11.48a)}$$

$$\lim_{m\to\infty} \gamma_{xx}(m) = 0 \quad \text{...(11.48b)}$$

$$\lim_{m\to\infty} \phi_{xy}(m) = m_x m_y^* \quad \text{...(11.48c)}$$

$$\lim_{m\to\infty} \gamma_{xy}(m) = 0 \quad \text{...(11.48d)}$$

This implies that the auto-correlation and cross-correlation and auto-variance and cross-covariance sequences are aperiodic sequences which tend to die out for large values of m. Thus, it is often possible to represent these sequences in terms of their z-transforms.

Proof of Results in Eqn. (11.48)

$$\lim_{m\to\infty} \phi_{xx}(m) = \lim_{m\to\infty} E\{x^*(n)\cdot x(n+m)\}$$

$$= E\{x^*(n)\}\cdot E\{x(n+m)\} = m_x^* \cdot m_x = |m_x|^2$$

(Due to high degree of uncorrelation as $m \to \infty$)

$$\lim_{m\to\infty} \phi_{xy}(m) = \lim_{m\to\infty} E\{x(n+m)\cdot y^*(n)\} = E\{x(n+m)\}\cdot E\{y^*(n)\} = m_x \cdot m_y^*$$

Due to $m \to\infty$ the sequence $x(n + m)$ and $y^*(n)$ become highly uncorrelated

$$\lim_{m\to\infty} \gamma_{xx}(m) = \lim_{m\to\infty} [\phi_{xx}(m) - |m_x|^2] = |m_x|^2 - |m_x|^2 = 0$$

Similarly,

$$\lim_{m\to\infty} \gamma_{xy}(m) = \lim_{m\to\infty} [\phi_{xy}(m) - m_x m_y^*]$$

$$= \lim_{m\to\infty} \phi_{xy}(m) - m_x m_y^* = m_x m_y^* - m_x m_y^* = 0$$

11.3.2 *Z*-Transform Representations

Let $\Phi_{xx}(z)$, $\Gamma_{xx}(z)$, $\Phi_{xy}(z)$ and $\Gamma_{xy}(z)$ be the z-transforms of $\phi_{xx}(m)$, $\gamma_{xx}(m)$, $\phi_{xy}(m)$ and $\gamma_{xy}(m)$, respectively.

(Pronounce ϕ as phee, Φ as PHAI, γ as gamma and Γ as GAY)

From [11.48(a)] and [11.48(c)] we *note that z-transforms of* $\phi_{xx}(m)$ *and* $\phi_{xy}(m)$ *exist only when* $m_x = 0$ *(because* then $\phi_{xx}(m) = \phi_{xy}(m) = 0$ as $m \to \infty$). In this case, $\Phi_{xx}(z) = \Gamma_{xx}(z)$ and $\Phi_{xy}(z) = \Gamma_{xy}(z)$.

A number of other properties of these z-transforms follow from the properties of correlation and covariance sequences summarized in Sec. 11.3.1. These properties are as below:

Property 1: From property [11.43(b)], we have

$$\sigma_x^2 = \frac{1}{2\pi j} \oint_C \Gamma_{xx}(z) z^{-1}\, dz$$

$= \text{Inverse } ZT \text{ of } \Gamma_{xx}(z)$ for $n = 0$,

$= \gamma_{xx}(0)$, ...(11.49)

where C is a closed contour in the ROC of $\Gamma_{xx}(z)$.

Proof: Let $\Gamma_{xx}(m) \xrightarrow{ZT} \Gamma_{xx}(z)$ and $\gamma_{xy}(m) \xrightarrow{ZT} \Gamma_{xy}(z)$

$$\therefore \quad \gamma_{xx}(m) = \frac{1}{2\pi j}\oint_C \Gamma_{xx}(z)z^{m-1}\,dz$$

or

$$\sigma_x^2 = \gamma_{xx}(0) = \frac{1}{2\pi j}\oint_C \Gamma_{xx}(z)z^{-1}\,dz \qquad \text{Q.E.D.}$$

Property 2:

$\Gamma_{xx}(z) = \Gamma^*_{xx}\left(\frac{1}{z^*}\right)$, and	$\phi_{xx}(z) = \phi^*_{xx}\left(\frac{1}{z^*}\right)$ ...(11.50*a*)
$\Gamma_{xy}(z) = \Gamma^*_{yx}\left(\frac{1}{z^*}\right)$, and	$\phi_{xy}(z) = \phi^*_{yx}\left(\frac{1}{z^*}\right)$ ...(11.50*b*)

Proof: As

$$\Gamma_{xx}(z) = \sum_{m=-\infty}^{\infty} \gamma_{xx}(m)z^{-m}$$

and

$$\Gamma^*_{xx}(z^{-1*}) = \left[\sum_{m=-\infty}^{\infty} \gamma_{xx}(m)(z^{-1*})^{-m}\right]^* = \left[\sum_{m=-\infty}^{\infty} \gamma^*_{xx}(m)z^{m}\right]$$

$$= \sum_{m'=-\infty}^{\infty} \gamma^*_{xx}(-m')z^{-m'} \qquad \text{putting } m = -m'$$

$$= \sum_{m'=-\infty}^{\infty} \gamma_{xx}(m')z^{-m'} \qquad [\because \ \gamma_{xx}(m) = \gamma^*_{xx}(-m)]$$

$$= \Gamma_{xx}(z) \qquad \text{Q.E.D.}$$

> **Important Note:** When $\{x_n\}$ and $\{y_n\}$ are complex valued, then
> $$\gamma_{xy}(m) \triangleq E[x_{n+m}\, y^*_n] = (E[y_n x^*_{n+m}])^* = \gamma^*_{yx}(-m)$$

Also,

$$\Gamma^*_{yx}\left(\frac{1}{z^*}\right) = \left(\sum_{m=-\infty}^{\infty} \gamma_{yx}(m)\left(\frac{1}{z^*}\right)^{-m}\right)^*$$

$$= \left(\sum_{m=-\infty}^{\infty} \gamma_{yx}(m)z^{m}\right) \qquad \left(\because \ \left(\frac{1}{z^*}\right)^* = \frac{1}{z} = z^{-1}\right)$$

$$= \sum_{m'=-\infty}^{\infty} \gamma^*_{yx}(-m')z^{-m'} \qquad \text{putting } m = -m'$$

$$= \sum_{m=-\infty}^{\infty} \gamma_{xy}(m)z^{-m} \qquad \because \ \gamma^*_{yx}(-m) = \gamma_{xy}(m)$$

$$= \Gamma_{xy}(z) \qquad \text{Q.E.D.}$$

As a consequence of results (11.50), it follows that the ROC of $\Gamma_{xx}(z)$ and of $\phi_{xx}(z)$ must be of the form**

$$R_a < |z| < \frac{1}{R_a}.$$

Further, since $\gamma_{xx}(m) \to 0$ as $m \to \infty$, the ROC must include the unit circle***, *i.e.*, $0 < R_a < 1$.

In the important case when $\Gamma_{xx}(z)$ is a rational function of z, this implies that its poles and zeros must occur in complex-conjugate reciprocal pairs as shown in the Fig. 11.3.

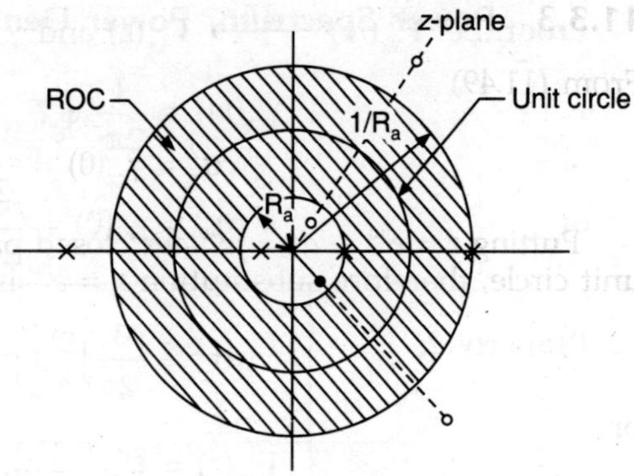

Fig. 11.3. Region of convergence and pole and zero locations of a typical z-transform of a covariance sequence

The major advantage of the z-transform representation is that integrals as Eqn. (11.49) may be evaluated by using the Residue theorem

$\Big\{$ Let $F(z) = \dfrac{(z-a)(z-b)}{(z-c)(z-d)}$ having zeros at $z = a, b$ and poles at $z = c, d$, then

$F\left(\dfrac{1}{z^*}\right) = \dfrac{ab\,(z^*-a^{-1})(z^*-b^{-1})}{cd\,(z^*-c^{-1})(z^*-d^{-1})}$, *i.e.*, $F\left(\dfrac{1}{z^*}\right)$ has poles at $z = \dfrac{1}{c^*}, \dfrac{1}{d^*}$; zeros at $z = \dfrac{1}{a^*}, \dfrac{1}{b^*}$.

As $F(z) = F^*\left(\dfrac{1}{z^*}\right)$ $\therefore$ we must have $b = \dfrac{1}{a^*}$ and $d = \dfrac{1}{c^*}$, *i.e.*, zeros and poles occur in complex-conjugate reciprocal pairs $\Big\}$

** $\Gamma^*_{xx}\left(\dfrac{1}{z^*}\right)$ converges in region where $\Gamma_{xx}\left(\dfrac{1}{z^*}\right)$ converges and $\Gamma_{xx}\left(\dfrac{1}{z^*}\right)$ converges in the region where $\Gamma_{xx}\left(\dfrac{1}{z}\right)$ converges. But $\Gamma\left(\dfrac{1}{z}\right)$ converges where $\left|\dfrac{1}{z}\right| > R_a$.

If $\Gamma_{xx}(z)$ converges for some values (ROC) of $|z|$, say, $|z| > R_a$ and $\Gamma^*_{xx}\left(\dfrac{1}{z^*}\right) = \Gamma_{xx}(z)$, therefore $\Gamma_{xx}\left(\dfrac{1}{z}\right)$ also converges for ROC: $\left|\dfrac{1}{z}\right| > R_a$.

Hence, ROC of $\Gamma_{xx}(z)$ is of the form $R_a < |z| < \dfrac{1}{R_a}$.

*** Suppose $\gamma_{xx}(m) = b^{+m}$ which $\to 0$ as $m \to \infty$ if $|b| < 1$.

$\therefore\ \Gamma_{xx}(z) = \dfrac{1}{1-bz^{-1}}$ and ROC is $|z| > |b|$ *i.e.* $|z| = 1$ forms ROC since $|b| > 1$ *i.e.* ROC includes the unit circle. Even for $\gamma_{xx}(m) = b^{-m}$, $|b| > 1$, it is seen that the ROC includes the unit circle.

11.3.3 Power Spectrum, Power Density Spectrum (PDS)

From (11.49)

$$\sigma_x^2 = \gamma_{xx}(0) = \frac{1}{2\pi j}\oint_C \Gamma_{xx}(z)z^{-1}\,dz$$

Putting $z = e^{j\omega}$ $\therefore$ $dz = je^{j\omega}\,d\omega$, closed path C traverses angle $-\pi$ to π. As the ROC contains the unit circle, therefore substitution $z = e^{j\omega}$ is justified*

$$\therefore \qquad \sigma_x^{\,2} = \frac{1}{2\pi}\int_{-\pi}^{\pi}\Gamma_{xx}(e^{j\omega})\,d\omega$$

or

$$\sigma_x^{\,2} = \frac{1}{2\pi}\int_{-\pi}^{\pi}P_{xx}(e^{j\omega})\,d\omega, \qquad \text{...(11.51)}$$

where $P_{xx}(e^{j\omega}) = \Gamma_{xx}(e^{j\omega})$ for $m_x = 0$ ...(11.52)

($P_{xx}(e^{j\omega})$ also written as $P_{xx}(\omega)$)

when $m_x = 0$, the variance is equal to the mean-square or the average power. Hence the area under $P_{xx}(\omega)$ for $-\pi \le \omega \le \pi$ is proportional to the average power in the signal (when $m_x = 0$). In fact, the $\int P_{xx}(\omega)\,d\omega$ over a band of frequencies is proportional to the power in the signal in that band or in the spectrum. Thus, it is common to call $P_{xx}(\omega)$ as the power density spectrum (PDS) or simply the power spectrum.

We commonly define the power spectrum as the Fourier transform of the auto-correlation sequence rather than the auto-covariance sequence. This is OK if $m_x = 0$. However, when $m_x \neq 0$, then since $\phi_{xx}(m) \to m_x^2$ when $m \to \infty$, the Fourier transform of the auto-correlation sequence does not exist.** In this case ($m_x \neq 0$ case) the Fourier transform of $\phi_{xx}(m)$ has an impulse in the power spectrum at $\omega = 0$.

When $m_x = 0$, the auto-correlation and auto-covariance sequences are identical and so are their Fourier transforms and then

$$\boxed{P_{xx}(\omega) = \Gamma_{xx}(e^{j\omega})} \qquad \text{for } m_x = 0 \text{ case}$$

Also, since $\Gamma_{xx}(z) = \Gamma_{xx}^{*}(z^{-1*})$ due to [11.50(*a*)]

$$\boxed{P_{xx}(\omega) = P_{xx}(-\omega)}$$

Moreover, the Power Spectrum Density (PSD) is a non-negative function.

Similarly, the cross-power density spectrum is defined as

$$P_{xy}(\omega) = \Gamma_{xy}(e^{j\omega}) \qquad \text{for } m_x = 0 \text{ or } m_y = 0 \qquad \text{...(11.53)}$$

Also $$P_{xy}(\omega) = P_{yx}^{*}(\omega) \qquad \text{(due to property [11.50(}b\text{)]} \qquad \text{...(11.54)}$$

(*For a stable sequence, the poles lie strictly INSIDE the unit circle)

(**because for $\phi_{xx}(m) \to m_x^2$ for $m \to \infty$, the ZT $\Phi_{xx}(z) = \sum_{m=-\infty}^{\infty}\phi_{xx}(m)z^{-m}$ will not converge).

$$\because \quad \Gamma_{xy}(z) = \Gamma_{yx}^*\left(\frac{1}{z^*}\right) \quad \therefore \quad \Gamma_{xy}(e^{j\omega}) = \Gamma_{yx}^*(e^{j\omega}) \text{ giving } \Gamma_{xy}(\omega) = \Gamma_{yx}^*(+\omega)$$

$$= \Gamma_{xy}(e^{-j\omega}) \qquad i.e., P_{xy}(\omega) = P_{yx}^*(\omega)$$

$$\therefore \quad P_{xy}(\omega) = P_{yx}(-\omega)$$

Let us define $\Phi_{xx}(e^{j\omega})$, $\Gamma_{xx}(e^{j\omega})$, $\Phi_{xy}(e^{j\omega})$ and $\Gamma_{xy}(e^{j\omega})$ as the Fourier transforms of $\phi_{xx}(m)$, $\gamma_{xx}(m)$, $\phi_{xy}(m)$ and $\gamma_{xy}(m)$, respectively.

As $\quad \gamma_{xx}(m) = \phi_{xx}(m) - |m_x|^2$ from [11.42(a)]

$$\therefore \quad \Phi_{xx}(e^{j\omega}) = \Gamma_{xx}(e^{j\omega}) + 2\pi|m_x|^2\,\delta(\omega), \ |\omega| < \pi \qquad \text{...(11.55a)}$$

and

$$\Phi_{xy}(e^{j\omega}) = \Gamma_{xy}(e^{j\omega}) + 2\pi m_x m_y^*\,\delta(\omega), \ |\omega| < \pi \qquad \text{...(11.55b)}$$

In the case of zero mean processes, ($m_x = 0$, $m_y = 0$), we have

$$\left.\begin{aligned}\Phi_{xx}(e^{j\omega}) &= \Gamma_{xx}(e^{j\omega})\\ \Phi_{xy}(e^{j\omega}) &= \Gamma_{xy}(e^{j\omega})\end{aligned}\right\} \text{ if } m_x = m_y = 0 \text{ or if only } m_x = 0 \text{ and } m_y \neq 0 \qquad \text{...(11.56)}$$

From the inverse Fourier transform equation, it follows that

$$\gamma_{xx}(m) = \frac{1}{2\pi}\int_{-\pi}^{\pi} \Gamma_{xx}(e^{j\omega})e^{j\omega m}\,d\omega \qquad \text{...(11.57)}$$

$$\phi_{xx}(m) = \frac{1}{2\pi}\int_{-\pi}^{\pi} \Phi_{xx}(e^{j\omega})e^{j\omega m}\,d\omega \qquad \text{...(11.58)}$$

and consequently,

$$E\{|x(n)|^2\} = \phi_{xx}(0) = \frac{1}{2\pi}\int_{-\pi}^{\pi} \Phi_{xx}(e^{j\omega})\,d\omega \qquad \text{...(11.59)}$$

$$\sigma_x^2 = \gamma_{xx}(0) = \frac{1}{2\pi}\int_{-\pi}^{\pi} \Gamma_{xx}(e^{j\omega})\,d\omega \qquad \text{...(11.60)}$$

It is convenient to define the quantity $P_{xx}(\omega)$ as

$$P_{xx}(\omega) = \Phi_{xx}(e^{j\omega}) \qquad \text{...(11.61)}$$

Hence, we can write

$$E\{|x(n)|^2\} = \frac{1}{2\pi}\int_{-\pi}^{\pi} P_{xx}(\omega)\,d\omega \qquad \text{...(11.62)}$$

$$\sigma_x^2 = \frac{1}{2\pi}\int_{-\pi}^{\pi} P_{xx}(\omega)\,d\omega - |m_x|^2 \qquad \text{...(11.63)}$$

Thus, the area under $P_{xx}(\omega)$ for $-\pi \le \omega \le \pi$ is proportional to the average power in the signal *viz.* $E\{|x(n)|^2\}$. The integral of $P_{xx}(\omega)$ over a band of frequencies is proportional to the power in the signal in that band. For this reason the function $P_{xx}(\omega)$ is called power density spectrum or simply the power spectrum. When $P_{xx}(\omega)$ is a constant, *i.e.* independent of ω, it is referred to as a white process or *white noise*. When $P_{xx}(\omega)$ is constant over a band and zero otherwise, we refer to it as *band limited white noise*.

From Eqn. [11.44(*b*)] it follows that $P_{xx}(\omega)$ is always real-valued,** and for real RP $\phi_{xx}(m) = \phi_{xx}(-m)$, so $P_{xx}(\omega)$ is both real and even; *i.e.****

$$\boxed{\begin{array}{l} P_{xx}(\omega) = P_{xx}(-\omega) \text{ true only for real RP even} \\ \text{and } P_{xx}(\omega) \text{ is real valued true for all cases of RP} \end{array}} \quad ...(11.64)$$

The cross power density spectrum is defined as

$$P_{xy}(\omega) \triangleq \phi_{xy}(\omega) \quad ...(11.65)$$

This function is generally complex and from Eqn. [11.44(*c*)], it follows that

$$\boxed{P_{xy}(\omega) = P_{yx}^*(\omega)} \quad ...(11.66)$$

11.4 RESPONSE OF LINEAR SYSTEMS TO RANDOM SIGNALS

Let $h(n)$ be the unit-sample response of a stable, linear, shift-invariant system. Let $x(n)$ be a real input sequence *i.e.* a sample sequence of a wide-sense stationary discrete-time random process.

The system output, $y(n)$, is given by

$$y(n) = h(n) * x(n)$$

$$= \sum_{k=-\infty}^{\infty} h(n-k)\, x(k) = \sum_{k=-\infty}^{\infty} h(k)\, x(n-k) \quad ...(11.67)$$

If the system is stable then $y(n)$ will be bounded of $x(n)$ is bounded. Let m_x and $\phi_{xx}(m)$ be the mean and auto-correlation function of the input random variable sequence $\{x_n\}$. The output $y(n)$ is also a random variable sequence $\{y_n\}$. We wish to derive m_y and $\phi_{yy}(m)$ in terms of $h(n)$, m_x, and $\phi_{xx}(n)$.

The mean of the output process $\{y_n\}$ is given by

$$m_y = E\{y(n)\} = E\left\{\sum_{k=-\infty}^{\infty} h(k)\, x(n-k)\right\}$$

$$= \sum_{k=-\infty}^{\infty} h(k) \underbrace{E\{x(n-k)\}}_{=m_x}$$

As $E\{x(n-k)\} = m_x$ since $x(n)$ is a stationary *RP*, hence we can write:

** **Proof:** $\Gamma_{xx}(e^{j\omega}) = \sum_{m=-\infty}^{+\infty} \gamma_{xx}(m)e^{-j\omega m}$ (by definition of Fourier Transform)

$\therefore \quad \Gamma_{xx}^*(e^{j\omega}) = \sum_{m=-\infty}^{\infty} \gamma_{xx}^*(m)e^{+j\omega m}$. Put $m = -m'$ drop dashes also put $\gamma_{xx}^*(-m) = \gamma_{xx}(m)$ due to [11.44(*b*)]

$= \sum_{m} \gamma_{xx}(m)e^{-j\omega m} = \Gamma_{xx}(e^{j\omega})$ *i.e.* $\Gamma_{xx}(e^{j\omega})$ is purely real, *i.e.*, $P_{xx}(\omega)$ is real valued.

*** $P_{xx}(\omega) = \phi_{xx}(e^{j\omega}) \sum_{m=\infty}^{\infty} \phi_{xx}(m)e^{-j\omega m}$. Put $m = m'$, drop dashes

$= \sum_{m=-\infty}^{\infty} \phi_{xx}(-m)e^{-j(-\omega)m}$. Put $\phi_{xx}(-m) = \phi_{xx}(m) = P_{xx}(-\omega)$

$$m_y = m_x \sum_{k=-\infty}^{\infty} h(k) \quad \text{...(11.68)}$$

$$= m_x \cdot H(e^{j0}) \quad \text{...(11.69)}$$

Since the input is stationary, we see that the mean of the output is also constant (just as the mean of the input was constant).

Now assume that the output is non-stationary, then the auto-correlation of the output $y_n(n)$, assuming $x(n)$ stationary, is given by:

$$\phi_{yy}(n, n+m) = E\{y^*(n) \cdot y(n+m)\} \quad \text{for } y(n) \text{ complex valued sequence}$$

$$= E\left\{\sum_{k=-\infty}^{\infty} h^*(k)\, x^*(n-k) \cdot \sum_{r=-\infty}^{\infty} h(r) \cdot x(n+m-r)\right\}$$

$$= \sum_{k=-\infty}^{\infty} h^*(k) \sum_{r=-\infty}^{\infty} h(r) \cdot E\{x^*(n-k) \cdot x(n+m-r)\} \quad \text{...(11.70)}$$

As we have assumed $x(n)$ as stationary, therefore $E\{x^*(n-k) \cdot x(n+m-r)\}$ depends on only the time difference $m + k - r$ and it equals $\phi_{xx}(m + k - r)$. Therefore, (11.70) reduces to

$$\phi_{yy}(n, n+m) = \sum_{k=-\infty}^{\infty} h^*(k) \cdot \sum_{r=-\infty}^{\infty} h(r) \cdot \phi_{xx}(m+k-r)$$

= a function of m only, and not a function of n

$$\triangleq \phi_{yy}(m) \quad \text{...(11.71)}$$

Thus, the output auto-correlation sequence also depends only on the time difference m. *Hence, for a linear shift-invariant system that is excited by a stationary input, the output is also stationary.*

Put $l = r - k$ in Eqn. (11.71)

$\therefore$ $r = l + k$, and we get [eliminating r from Eqn. (11.71)]

$$\phi_{yy}(m) = \sum_{k=-\infty}^{\infty} h^*(k) \cdot \sum_{l=-\infty}^{\infty} h(l+k)\phi_{xx}(m-l)$$

$$= \sum_{l=-\infty}^{\infty} \phi_{xx}(m-l) \sum_{k=-\infty}^{\infty} h^*(k)\, h(l+k)$$

$$\therefore \quad \phi_{yy}(m) = \sum_{l=-\infty}^{\infty} \phi_{xx}(m-l) \cdot \nu(l) \quad \text{...(11.72)}$$

$$= \phi_{xx}(m) * \nu(m)$$

where $$\nu(l) \triangleq \sum_{k=-\infty}^{\infty} h(k)\, h(l+k) \quad \text{with } h(k) \text{ real valued} \quad \text{...(11.73)}$$

↗ Aperiodic auto-correlation sequence $h(n)$, assuming $h(n)$ real valued

A sequence of the form $\nu(l)$ is called an aperiodic auto-correlation sequence or simply the auto-correlation sequence of $h(n)$. It should be noted that $\nu(l)$ is the auto-correlation of an aperiodic *i.e.* finite-energy sequence $h(n)$ and should not be confused with the auto-correlation of an infinite energy sequence. Note that *$\nu(l)$ is simply the discrete convolution of $h(n)$ and $h(-n)$*.**

Thus we have the result

$$\phi_{yy}(m) = \phi_{xx}(m) * \nu(m)$$
auto-correlation of $y(n)$ = Convolution of [auto-correlation of $x(n)$ and auto-correlation of $h(n)$] ...(11.74)

Equations (11.71) and (11.72) further suggest that if $m_x = 0$ and therefore $m_y = 0$ [due to (11.68)]

$$\therefore \quad \phi_{xx}(m) = \gamma_{xx}(m); \; \phi_{yy}(m) = \gamma_{yy}(m)$$

From (11.72) and (11.73), using *z*-transforms, we have

$$\Phi_{yy}(z) = \Phi_{xx}(z) \cdot V(z)^{***}$$
$$= \Phi_{xx}(z) \cdot H(z) \cdot H(z^{-1})$$

or
$$P_{yy}(\omega) = |H(e^{jw})|^2 \, P_{xx}(\omega) \qquad ...(11.75)$$

where $P_{yy}(\omega) = \Phi_{yy}(e^{j\omega})$, $P_{xx}(\omega) = \Phi_{xx}(e^{j\omega})$. Equation (11.75) provides the motivation for the term "power density spectrum" for $P_{yy}(\omega)$. If $m_x = 0$ and therefore $m_y = 0$, then

$$\phi_{yy}(0) = \phi_{yy}(n)|_{n=0} = \text{IFT of } \Phi_{yy}(e^{j\omega})|_{n=0}$$

$$\therefore \quad \phi_{yy}(0) = \frac{1}{2\pi}\int_{-\pi}^{\pi} P_{yy}(\omega)\, d\omega \text{ average power in the output, } y(n) \qquad ...(11.76)$$

Note that $\phi_{yy}(0) = \sigma_y^2$ if $m_y = 0$.

Therefore, using (11.75) in (11.76) we obtain

$$\phi_{yy}(0) = \frac{1}{2\pi}\int_{-\pi}^{\pi} |H(e^{j\omega})|^2 \, P_{xx}(\omega)\, d\omega \qquad ...(11.77)$$

** **Proof:** $$h(n) * h(-n) = \sum_{k=-\infty}^{\infty} h(k)\, h(-(n-k))$$

Put $-n + k = r$

$$\therefore \quad = \sum_{r=-\infty}^{\infty} h(r+n) \cdot h(r)$$
$$= \sum_{k=-\infty}^{\infty} h(k) \cdot h(n+k) \text{ replacing dummy variable } r \text{ by } k$$
$$\triangleq \nu(n)$$

*** **Proof:** $$V(z) = ZT[\nu(l)] = \sum_{l=-\infty}^{\infty}\left\{\sum_{k=-\infty}^{\infty} h(k)\cdot h(l+k)\right\} z^{-l}$$
$$= \sum_{k=-\infty}^{\infty} h(k) \sum_{l=-\infty}^{\infty} h(l+k) \cdot z^{-(l+k)} \cdot z^k$$
$$= \sum_{k=-\infty}^{\infty} h(k) \cdot H(z) \cdot z^k$$
$$= H(z) \cdot H(z^{-1}) \qquad ...(11.73)$$

As an example, consider the bandpass filter shown below:

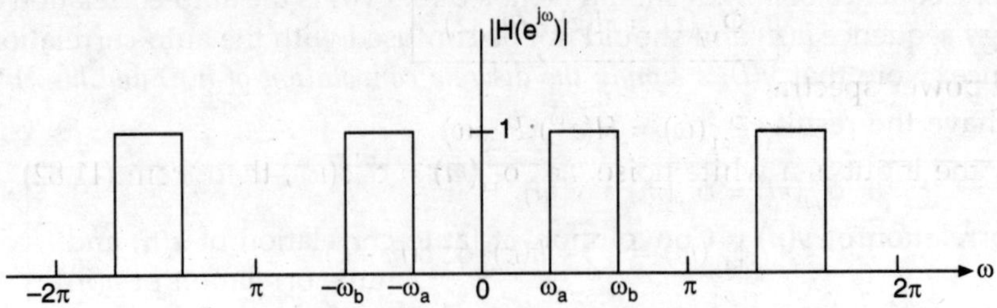

Fig. 11.4. Frequency response of an ideal BPF

As $\phi_{xx}(m)$ is an even function of m, *i.e.*, $\phi_{xx}(m) = \phi_{xx}(-m)$ therefore

$$P_{xx}(\omega) = P_{xx}(-\omega) \qquad \text{...(11.78)}$$

Likewise, $|H(e^{j\omega})|^2$ is also an even function of ω. Therefore

$$\phi_{xx}(0) = \text{average power in output sequence}$$

$$= \frac{1}{2\pi}\int_{-\pi}^{\pi} |H(e^{j\omega})|^2 \cdot P_{xx}(\omega)\, d\omega$$

$$\nwarrow = 1$$

$$= \frac{1}{\pi}\int_{\omega_a}^{\omega_b} P_{xx}(\omega)\, d\omega \qquad \text{...(11.79)}$$

Thus, the area under $P_{xx}(\omega)$ between ω_a to ω_b can be taken to represent the mean-square value of the output power in that frequency band.

Also, we observe that the output power must remain non-negative, *i.e.*,

$$\lim_{(\omega_b - \omega_a)\to 0} \phi_{yy}(0) \geq 0 \qquad \text{...(11.80)}$$

using above inequality, (11.79) yields, by implication that

$$P_{xx}(\omega) \geq 0 \qquad \text{...(11.81)}$$

Thus, we observe that the power density function of a real signal is real, even and positive. [see (11.64) and (11.81)]

Power density spectrum is always real valued for real or complex signals Power density spectrum is also positive for real or complex signals But Power density spectrum is even (*i.e.*, $P_{xx}(\omega) = P_{xx}(-\omega)$) *only for real valued signal x(n)*

Again note that *the cross-correlation between the input and output of a linear time-invariant system*

$$\phi_{xy}(m) = E\{x^*(n) \cdot y(n+m)\}$$

$$= E\left\{x^*(n) \cdot \sum_{k=-\infty}^{\infty} h(k)\, x(n+m-k)\right\}$$

$$= \sum_{k=-\infty}^{\infty} h(k)\, \phi_{xx}(m-k) \qquad \text{...(11.82)}$$

Cross-correlation between input and output = Convolution of input signal's auto-correlation and unit-sample response of the system.

If we assume $m_x = 0$, so that z-transforms of $\phi_{xx}(m)$ and $\phi_{xy}(m)$ exist, then we have

$$\boxed{\Phi_{xy}(z) = H(z) \cdot \Phi_{xx}(z)} \quad \text{...(11.83)}$$

or In terms of power spectra,

$$P_{xy}(\omega) = H(e^{j\omega})\, P_{xx}(\omega) \quad \text{...(11.84)}$$

If, say $x(n)$, the input is a white noise, *i.e.*, $\phi_{xx}(m) = \sigma_x^2 \delta(m)$, then from (11.82)

$$\phi_{xy}(m) = \sum_{k=-\infty}^{\infty} h(k) \cdot \sigma_x^2\, \delta(m-k)$$

$$= \sigma_x^2\, h(m) \quad \text{...(11.85)}$$

i.e., for a white-noise input, the cross-correlation between input and output of a linear system is proportional to the impulse response of the system.

Similarly, the power spectrum of a white-noise input is

$$P_{xx}(\omega) = \sigma_x^2, \; -\pi \le \omega \le \pi \quad \text{...(11.86)}$$

From (11.84),

$$P_{xy}(\omega) = \sigma_x^2 H(e^{j\omega}) \quad \text{...(11.87)}$$

i.e., the cross power spectrum in this case is proportional to the frequency response of the system.

Equations (11.85) and (11.87) may serve as the basis for estimating the impulse response or frequency response of a linear time-invariant system if it is possible to observe the output of the system in response to a white-noise input.

Procedure to Estimate $h(n)$ and $H(e^{j\omega})$ of an Unknown System $h(n)$

1. Generate white noise with its

$$\begin{cases} \text{mean:} & m_e = 0 \\ \text{auto-correlation:} & \phi_{ee}(m) = \sigma_e^2 \delta(m) \end{cases}$$

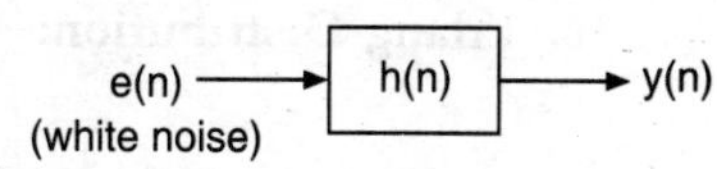

2. Excite the unknown system by the white noise $e(n)$.
3. Let the output be $y(n)$. Then, first find cross-correlation between $e(n)$ and $y(n)$ *i.e.* find $\phi_{xy}(m)$. Then we can write:

(*i*) $\phi_{ey}(m) = \sigma_e^2\, h(m) \quad \therefore\ h(m) = \dfrac{1}{\sigma_e^2} \phi_{ey}(m)$ can be computed

(*ii*) $P_{ey}(m) = \sigma_e^2\, H(e^{j\omega}) \quad \therefore\ H(e^{j\omega}) = \dfrac{1}{\sigma_e^2} P_{ey}(\omega)$ can also be computed

Thus, $h(n)$ and $H(e^{j\omega})$ can be estimated by observing the cross-correlation $\phi_{ey}(m)$ and its power spectrum by inputting a white noise to the unknown system, $h(n)$.

Appendix-A

Some Important Density Functions/Distribution Functions

1. Normal Distribution:

$$f(x) = \frac{1}{\sigma} g\left(\frac{x-m}{\sigma}\right) = \frac{1}{\sigma\sqrt{2\pi}} \exp.\left[-\frac{(x-m)^2}{2\sigma^2}\right] \quad \text{...(A-1)}$$

written as $N(m;\, \sigma)$.

2. Rayleigh Distribution:

$$f(x) = xe^{-x^2/2} \cdot u(x),\ i.e.,\ x \geq 0 \quad \ldots(A\text{-}2)$$

3. Maxwell Distribution:

$$f(x) = \sqrt{\frac{2}{\pi}}\, x^2 e^{-x^2/2} \quad \ldots(A\text{-}3)$$

4. Chi-square Distribution:

$$f(x) = \left(\frac{1}{(2^{n/2} \cdot \Gamma(n/2))}\right) \cdot x^{n/2-1} \cdot e^{-x/2} u(x)\ ;\ x \geq 0 \quad \ldots(A\text{-}4)$$

denoted as $\chi^2(n)$, Chi-square with n degrees of freedom.

5. Gamma Distribution:

$$f(x) = \gamma_x^{b-1} e^{-cx} U(x),\ \gamma = \frac{c^b}{\Gamma(b)} \quad \ldots(A\text{-}5)$$

b, c are +ve and

$$\Gamma(b+1) = \int_0^\infty y^b e^{-y}\, dy,\ b > -1$$

Also

$$\Gamma(b+1) = b\,\Gamma(b);$$

$$\Gamma\left(\frac{1}{2}\right) = \int_0^\infty y^{-1/2} e^{-y}\, dy = 2\int_0^\infty e^{-z^2}\, dz = \sqrt{\pi} \quad \ldots(A\text{-}5a)$$

6. Erlang Distribution:

$$f(x) = \frac{c^n}{(n-1)!} x^{n-1} e^{-cx} u(x) \quad \ldots(A\text{-}6)$$

7. Cauchy Distribution:

$$f(x) = \frac{\alpha/\pi}{x^2 + \alpha^2};\ f(y) = \frac{1/(\alpha\pi)}{y^2 + 1/\alpha^2} \quad \ldots(A\text{-}7)$$

8. Exponential Distribution:

$$f(x) = \lambda e^{-\lambda x} u(x) \quad \ldots(A\text{-}8)$$

9. Poisson Distribution:

$$f(x) = e^{-a} \sum_{k=0}^{\infty} \frac{a^k}{k!} \delta(x-k) \quad \ldots(A\text{-}9)$$

$$P(x = k) = e^{-a} \frac{a^k}{k!} \quad \ldots(A\text{-}10)$$

10. Geometric Distribution:

$$P(\overline{X} = k) = pq^k,\ k = 0, 1, \ldots, \text{ where } p + q = 1 \quad \ldots(A\text{-}11)$$

Here

$$m_x = \frac{q}{p},\quad \sigma_x^2 = \frac{q}{p^2}$$

11. Pascal/Negative Binomial Distribution:

$$P(x = k) = \binom{-n}{k} p^n (-q)^k = \binom{n+k-1}{k} p^n q^k, \; k = 0, 1, \ldots \qquad \ldots(A\text{-}12)$$

Here, $m_x = \dfrac{nq}{p}, \quad \sigma_x^2 = \dfrac{nq}{p^2}$

12. Laplace Distribution:

$$f(x) = e^{-|x|} \qquad \ldots(A\text{-}13)$$

$$m_x = 0$$

13. Lognormal Distribution:

$$f_x(x) = \frac{1}{\sigma x\sqrt{2\pi}} \exp.\left[-\frac{(\ln x - m_x)^2}{2\sigma^2}\right] \qquad \ldots(A\text{-}14)$$

14. Snedecor-*F* Distribution:

$$\overline{z} = \frac{\overline{X}/m}{\overline{Y}/m}, \; f_z(z) = \gamma \frac{x^{m/2-2}}{\sqrt{(1+mx/n)^{m+n}}} u(x) \qquad \ldots(A\text{-}15)$$

This distribution is denoted by $F(m, n)$ and is called the Sendecor F distribution. It is used in hypothesis testing.

15. Uniform Distribution:

$$f(x) = \begin{cases} \dfrac{1}{x_2 - x_1}, & x_1 \le x \le x_2 \\ 0, & \text{otherwise} \end{cases} \qquad (A\text{-}16)$$

16. Weibull Distribution:

$$f(x) = cx^{b-1} \exp.\left\{\frac{-cx^b}{b}\right\} \qquad \ldots(A\text{-}17)$$

17. Yule-Furry Distribution:

$$p_n(t) = e^{-ct}(1 - e^{-ct})^{n-1} \qquad \ldots(A\text{-}18)$$

For a specific t, the RV $\overline{X}(t) - 1$ has a geometric distribution with ratio $(1 - e^{-ct})$.

$$E\{\overline{X}(t)\} = e^{ct}, \quad E\{\overline{X}^2(t)\} = 2e^{2ct} - e^{-ct} \qquad \ldots(A\text{-}18a)$$

The graphs of some of the above distribution functions are given in Fig. Appendix–A.

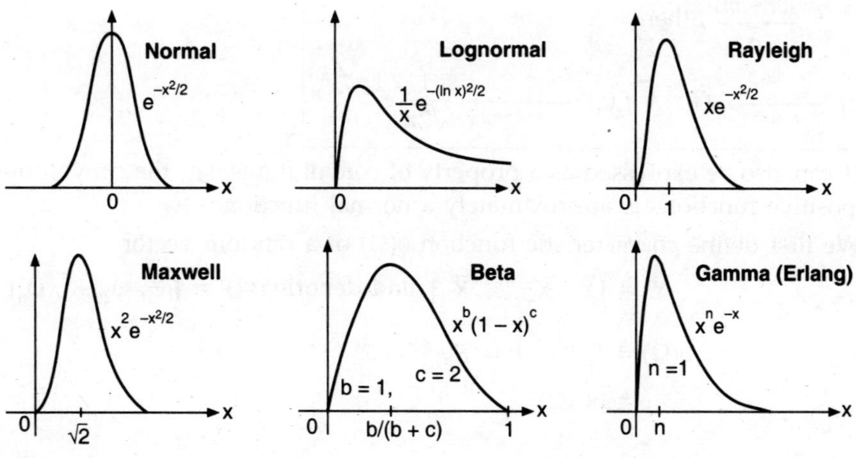

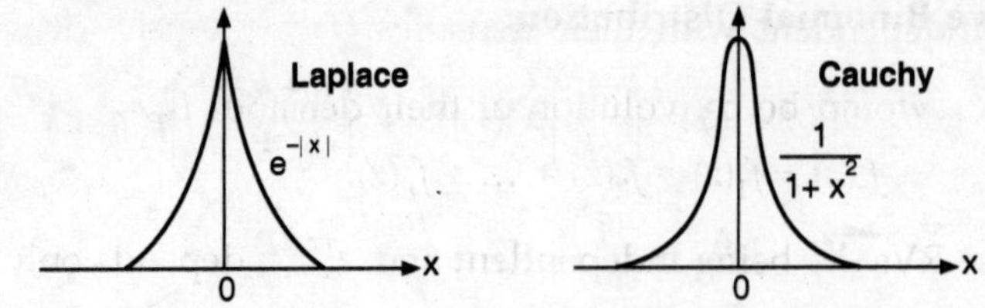

Fig. Appendix A. Graphs of some popular distribution functions

Appendix-B

Central Limit Theorem (CLT): Let n be independent RVs $\overline{X}_i$, we form their sum

$$\overline{X} = \sum_{i=1}^{n} \overline{X}_i$$

The $\overline{X}$ is also a RV with mean m, such that

$$m_{\overline{X}} \triangleq m = \sum_{i=1}^{n} m_i \text{ (Sum of individual means)}$$

where m_i is the mean of RV, $\overline{X}_i$ and σ_i^2 = variance of $\overline{X}_i$ RV, *i.e.*, $\sigma_i^2 = E\{(x - m_i)^2\}$ (sum of individual variances).

The central limit theorem states that under certain general conditions the distribution $F(x)$ of $\overline{X}$ approaches a normal distribution with the same mean and variance, *i.e.*,

$$\boxed{F(x) \approx G\left(\frac{x-m}{\sigma}\right)} \text{ (Cumulative Density Function)} \quad \ldots(B\text{-}1)$$

as n increases. If the random variables $\overline{X}_i$ are of continuous type then the density $f(x)$ of $\overline{X}$ approaches a normal density, *i.e.*,

$$\boxed{f(x) \approx \frac{1}{\sigma\sqrt{2\pi}} e^{-(x-m)/2\sigma^2}} \text{ (Density Function)} \quad \ldots(B\text{-}2)$$

This theorem can also be stated as a limit

$$\boxed{\begin{array}{l} \text{If } \overline{Z} = \dfrac{(\overline{X} - \overline{m})}{\overline{\sigma}}, \text{ then} \\ F_z(z) \xrightarrow[n\to\infty]{} G(z), \; f_z(z) \xrightarrow[n\to\infty]{} \dfrac{1}{\sqrt{2\pi}} e^{-z^2/2} \end{array}} \quad \ldots(B\text{-}3)$$

The CLT can also be expressed as a property of convolutions, *i.e.*, the convolution of a large number of positive functions is approximately a normal function.

Proof: We first define characteristic function $\phi(\Omega)$ of a random vector

$$\overline{X} = [\overline{X}_1, \overline{X}_2, \ldots, \overline{X}_n] \text{ and denoting } \overline{\Omega} = [\omega_1, \omega_2, \ldots, \omega_n]$$

$$\phi(\Omega) \triangleq E\{e^{j\overline{\Omega}\overline{X}^t}\} = E\{e^{j(\omega_1\overline{X}_1 + \omega_2\overline{X}_2 + \ldots + \omega_n\overline{X}_n)}\}$$

$$\triangleq \overline{\phi}(j\,\Omega)$$

If RVs' $\overline{X}_i$ are independent with their densities $f_i(x_i)$, then the density $f_z(z)$ of their sum $\overline{z} = \overline{X}_1 + \overline{X}_2 + \ldots + \overline{X}_n$ would be convolution of their densities *i.e.*

$$f_z(z) = f_1(z) * f_2(z) * \ldots * f_n(z). \qquad \ldots(B\text{-}4)$$

This is so because RVs $\overline{X}_i$ being independent and $e^{j\omega_i \overline{X}_i}$ depends only on $\overline{X}_i$. We can write

$$E\{e^{j(\omega_1 \overline{X}_1 + \omega_2 \overline{X}_2 + \ldots + \omega_n \overline{X}_n)}\} = E\{e^{j\omega_1 \overline{X}_1}\} \cdot E\{e^{j\omega_2 \overline{X}_2}\} \ldots E\{e^{j\omega_n \overline{X}_n}\}$$

Hence

$$\phi_z(\omega) = E\{e^{j(\omega_1 \overline{X}_1 + \omega_2 \overline{X}_2 + \ldots + \omega_n \overline{X}_n)}\} = \phi_1(\omega) \cdot \phi_2(\omega) \ldots \phi_n(\omega) \qquad \ldots(B\text{-}5)$$

where $\phi_i(\omega)$ is the characteristic function of $\overline{X}_i$. Applying the convolution theorem for Fourier transforms to (*B*-5), we readily get (*B*-4). (*i.e.*, multiplication in the "Fourier domain" is equivalent to convolution in "time domain"). Hence convolution property of a large number of positive functions $[f_1(z) * f_2(z) * f_3(z) * \ldots * f_n(z)]$.

EXAMPLE 11.1: *For the Bernoulli process with probability of x_n as head as p and x_n as a tail as $1 - p$, determine mean m_x, means square value $E\{|\overline{x}_n|^2\}$, the auto-correlation sequence $\phi_{xx}(m)$ and variance σ_x^2.*

SOLUTION: We call x_n as head when variable x_n assumes value 1 and x_n as tail when variable x_n assume value –1

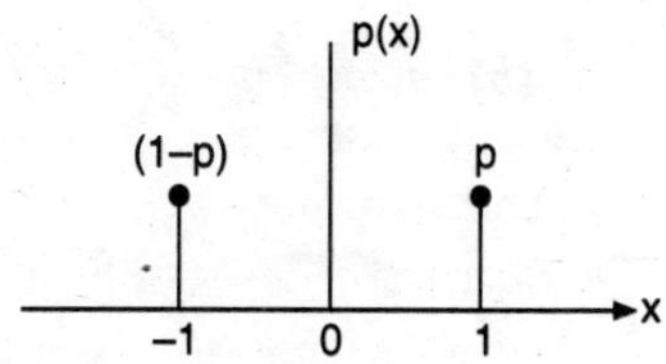

Fig. Ex. 11.1.

$\therefore$ Probability $[x_n = +1] = p$

and Probability $[x_n = -1] = 1 - p$

Mean: $m_x = E\{x_n\} = \sum_x x\, p_{\overline{x}_n}(x)$

$= +1 \cdot p + (-1)(1 - p) = 2p - 1$

Mean square value:

$$E\{|\overline{x}_n|^2\} = \sum_x |x|^2\, p_{\overline{x}_n}(x)$$

$$= (+1)^2 \cdot p + (-1)^2\,(1 - p) = 1$$

Variance: $\sigma_x^2 = E\{|\overline{x}_n|^2\} - (E\{\overline{x}_n\})^2$

$= 1 - (2p - 1)^2 = -4p^2 + 4p = 4p(1 - p)$

Since statistically heads and tails outcome is independent, therefore

Auto-correlation: $\phi_{xx}(m) \triangleq E\{\overline{x}_n^* \cdot \overline{x}_{n+m}\} = \underbrace{E\{\overline{x}_n^*\}}_{= m_x^*} \cdot \underbrace{E\{\overline{x}_{n+m}\}}_{m_x \text{ (being stationary RP)}}$

↖ (The sequences x_n and x_{n+m} are uncorrelated as head's and tail's outcome is independent)

$= m_x^* \cdot m_x = m_x^2$ for $m \neq 0$

If $m = 0$, then $\phi_{xx}(0) = E\{\overline{x}_n^*\, \overline{x}_n\} = E\{|\overline{x}_n|^2\} = 1$ (found above)

Hence $$\phi_{xx}(m) = \begin{cases} E\{|\bar{x}_n|^2\} = 1, & m = 0 \\ E\{\bar{x}_n\} \cdot E\{\bar{x}_{n+m}\} = m_x^2, & m \neq 0 \end{cases}$$

Note here that if $p = \frac{1}{2}$, then $m_x = 0$ and $\therefore\ \phi_{xx}(m) = \delta(m)$, *i.e.*, a white noise sequence.

EXAMPLE 11.2: *Prove the following properties of averages:*

(a) $E[x_n + y_m] = E[x_n] + E[y_m]$

(b) $E[ax_n] = aE[x_n]$.

SOLUTION: *(a)* $E[x_n + y_n] = \int_{-\infty}^{\infty}\int_{-\infty}^{\infty} (x+y)\, p_{xy}(x, y)\, dx\, dy$ (by definition)

$$= \int_{-\infty}^{\infty}\int_{-\infty}^{\infty} x\, p_{xy}(x, y)\, dx\, dy + \int_{-\infty}^{\infty}\int_{-\infty}^{\infty} y\, p_{xy}(x, y)\, dx\, dy$$

$$= \int_{x=-\infty}^{\infty} x\left(\int_{y=-\infty}^{\infty} p_{xy}(x, y)\, dy\right) dx + \int_{y=-\infty}^{\infty} y\left(\int_{x=-\infty}^{\infty} p_{xy}(x, y)\, dx\right) dy$$

$$= \int_{x=-\infty}^{\infty} x\, p_x(x)\, dx + \int_{y=-\infty}^{\infty} y\, p_y(y)\, dy \qquad \textit{(Note this step)}$$

$$= E[x_n] + E[y_m] \qquad \text{Q.E.D.}$$

(b) $$E[ax_n] = \int_{-\infty}^{\infty} (ax)\, p_x(x)\, dx \qquad \text{(by definition)}$$

$$= a\int_{-\infty}^{\infty} x\, p_x(x)\, dx$$

$$= aE[x_n] \qquad \text{Q.E.D.}$$

EXAMPLE 11.3: *Let x(n) and y(n) be uncorrelated random signals. Show that if*

$$\omega(n) = x(n) + y(n)$$

then $$m_\omega = m_x + m_y$$

and $$\sigma_\omega^2 = \sigma_x^2 + \sigma_y^2.$$

SOLUTION:

$$m_\omega = E[\omega_n] = E[x_n + y_n]$$

$$= E[x_n] + E[y_n] \qquad \text{(due to result (a) of Problem 8.1)}$$

$$= m_x + m_y \qquad \text{Q.E.D.} \quad \text{since } x \text{ and } y \text{ are uncorrelated}$$

$$\sigma_\omega^2 = E[(\omega_n - m_\omega)^2]$$

$$= E[\omega_n^2] - (m_\omega)^2$$

$$= m_x + m_y \swarrow$$

$$= E[(x_n + y_n)^2] - (m_\omega)^2$$

$$= E[x_n^2] + 2E[x_n \cdot y_n] + E[y_n^2] - (m_x^2 + 2m_x m_y + m_y^2)$$

$$= \underbrace{(E[x_n^2] - m_x^2)}_{\sigma_x^2} + \underbrace{(E[y_n^2] - m_y^2)}_{\sigma_y^2} + 2[\underbrace{E[x_n]}_{m_x} \cdot \underbrace{E[y_n]}_{m_y} - m_x m_y]$$

$$= \sigma_x^2 + \sigma_y^2 \qquad \text{Q.E.D.}$$

EXAMPLE 11.4: *In modelling the effects of round off and truncation in digital filter implementation, we represent quantized variables as*

$$y(n) = Q[x(n)] = x(n) + e(n)$$

where Q[·] denotes either rounding or truncation and e(n) is the quantization error. Suppose that the sequence e(n) is a white-noise sequence, i.e.

$$E[(e(n) - m_e)\,(e(n+m) - m_e)] = \sigma_e^2\delta(m)$$

The first-order probability distribution for rounding is uniform, Fig. 11.4(a). For truncation, the first-order probability distribution is shown in Fig. 11.4(b).

(a) Find the mean and variance for the noise due to rounding.

(b) Find the mean and variance for the noise due to truncation.

SOLUTION:

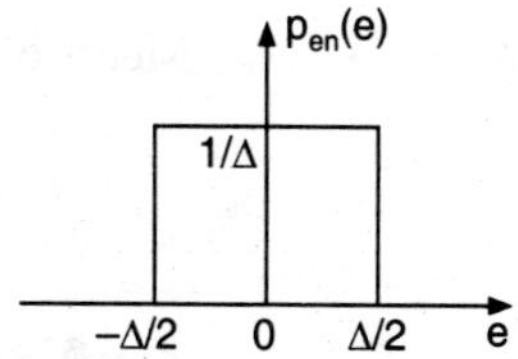

Fig. Ex. 11.4. (*a*) Rounding off

(*a*) $m_e = \dfrac{1}{\Delta}\displaystyle\int_{-\Delta/2}^{\Delta/2} e\, de = \dfrac{1}{\Delta}\left[\dfrac{e^2}{2}\right]_{-\Delta/2}^{\Delta/2} = 0$

$$\sigma_e^2 = \frac{1}{\Delta}\int_{-\Delta/2}^{\Delta/2} e^2\, de = \frac{1}{3\Delta}[e^3]_{-\Delta/2}^{\Delta/2} = \frac{\Delta^2}{12}$$

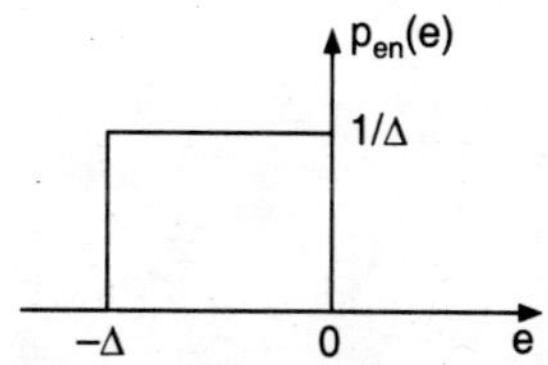

Fig. Ex. 11.4. (*b*) Truncation

(*b*) $m_e = \dfrac{1}{\Delta}\displaystyle\int_{-\Delta}^{0} e\, de = \dfrac{1}{2\Delta}[e^2]_{-\Delta}^{0} = -\dfrac{\Delta}{2}$

$$\sigma_e^2 = \frac{1}{\Delta}\int_{-\Delta}^{0} e^2\, de - m_e^2 = \frac{1}{3\Delta}[e^3]_{-\Delta}^{0} - \left(-\frac{\Delta}{2}\right)^2$$

$$= \frac{1}{3\Delta}(0+\Delta^3) - \frac{\Delta^2}{4} = \frac{1}{12}\Delta^2 \text{ (as in the rounding off case)}$$

EXAMPLE 11.5: *Let e(n) denote a white-noise sequence and let s(n) denote a sequence that is uncorrelated with e(n). Show that the sequence*

$$y(n) = s(n)\cdot e(n)$$

is white, i.e.,

$$E[y(n)\cdot y(n+m)] = A\delta(m)$$

where A is a constant.

SOLUTION: As $e(n)$ is a white noise sequence, let $e(n)$ be zero mean

∴ Mean of a sequence $s(n)\cdot e(n) = E[s(n)\cdot e(n)] = E[s(n)]\cdot E[e(n)]$ (being uncorrelated)

$= m_e \cdot E[s(n)] = 0\ \forall\ n, m$ (with $m_e = 0$)

∴ $m_y = 0$

Now $E[y(n)\cdot y(n+m)] = E[(s(n)\, e(n))\cdot(s(n+m)\cdot e(n+m))]$

$= E[s(n)\, s(n+m)\cdot e(n)\, e(n+m)]$

$= E[s(n)\, s(n+m)]\cdot E[e(n)\cdot e(n+m)]$ [$e(n)$ and $s(n)$ being uncorrelated]

where $E[s(n)\,s(n+m)] = \phi_{ss}(m)$ (by definition of correlation) and $E[e(n)\cdot e(n+m)] = \sigma_e^2\delta(m)$ (being white noise)

$$E[y(m)\cdot y(n+m)] = [\phi_{ss}(m)\sigma_e^2)]\delta(m)$$
$$= \phi_{ss}(0)\cdot\sigma_e^2\delta(m) = \sigma_s^2\sigma_e^2\delta(m)$$
$$\triangleq A\delta(m) \text{ where } A = \sigma_s^2\sigma_e^2$$

Q.E.D.

EXAMPLE 11.6: *Consider a random process in which the sample sequences x(n) are of the form*

$$x(n) = \cos(\omega_0 n + \theta)$$

where θ is an uniformly distributed random variable with the probability density function shown in the given Figure Compute the mean and auto-correlation sequence $\phi_{xx}(m, n)$. Is this a wide-sense stationary process?

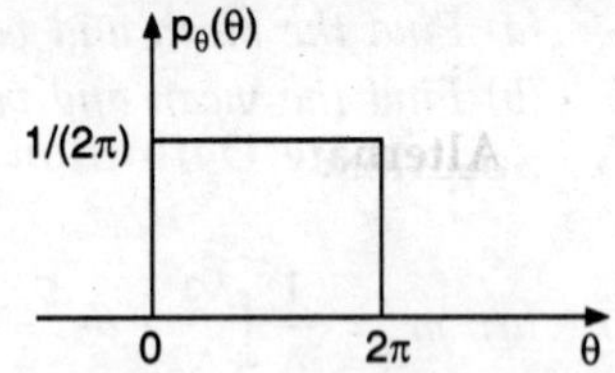

Fig. Ex. 11.6. PDF of θ (given)

SOLUTION:

$$\text{Mean of } x(n) = E[x_n] = \int_0^{2\pi} \cos(\omega_0 n + \theta)\frac{1}{2\pi}\,d\theta$$

$$= \frac{1}{2\pi}[\sin(\omega_0 n+\theta)]_0^{2\pi} = 0$$

$$\phi_{xx}(m, n) = E[x(m)\cdot x(n)]$$

$$= \int_0^{2\pi} x(m).x(n)\left(\frac{1}{2\pi}\right)d\theta \qquad \left(p_\theta(\theta) = \frac{1}{2\pi}\right)$$

$$= \frac{1}{2\pi}\int_0^{2\pi} \cos(\omega_0 m+\theta)\cos(\omega_0 n+\theta)\,d\theta$$

$$= \frac{1}{4\pi}\int_0^{2\pi} [\cos\{\omega_0(m-n)\} + \cos\{\omega_0(m+n)+2\theta\}]\,d\theta$$

$$= \frac{1}{4\pi}[\{\cos\omega_0(m-n)\}\theta]_0^{2\pi} + \frac{1}{2}[\sin[\omega_0(m+n)+2\theta]_0^{2\pi}]$$

$$= \frac{1}{2}\cos\{\omega_0(m-n)\}$$

If we define $m - n = k$, then $\phi_{xx}(k) = \frac{1}{2}\cos(\omega_0\cdot k)$, then the process is wide sense stationary.

EXAMPLE 11.7: *Consider two real stationary random processes, $\{x_n\}$ and $\{y_n\}$, with means m_x and m_y, respectively, and variance σ_x^2 and σ_y^2, respectively. Show that*

(a) $\gamma_{xx}(m) = \phi_{xx}(m) - m_x^2$

$\gamma_{xy}(m) = \phi_{xy}(m) - m_x m_y$

(b) $\phi_{xx}(0) = \textit{mean square}$

$\gamma_{xx}(0) = \sigma_x^2$

(c) $\phi_{xx}(m) = \phi_{xx}(-m)$

$\gamma_{xx}(m) = \gamma_{xx}(-m)$

$\phi_{xy}(m) = \phi_{yx}^*(-m)$

$\gamma_{xy}(m) = \gamma_{yx}^*(-m).$

SOLUTION: *(a) (i)* $\gamma_{xx}(m) = E[(x_n - m_x)(x_{n+m} - m_x)]$, for x a real RV

↖ (auto-covariance)

$$= E[x_n x_{n+m}] - m_x E[x_{n+m}] - m_x E[x_n] + m_x^2$$

$$= \phi_{xx}(m) - m_x \cdot m_x - m_x \cdot m_x + m_x^2$$

$$= \phi_{xx}(m) - m_x^2 \qquad \because \{x_n\} \text{ is a stationary RP}$$

(ii) $\gamma_{xy}(m)$ (cross-variance) $= E[(x_n - m_x)(y_{n+m} - m_y)]$, for x, y real RVs

$$= E[x_n\, y_{n+m}] - E[x_m m_y] - E[m_x \cdot y_{n+m}] + m_x m_y$$

$$= \phi_{xy}(m) - m_x m_y - m_x m_y + m_x m_y$$

$$= \phi_{xy}(m) - m_x m_y \qquad \because \{y_n\} \text{ is a stationary RP}$$

Alternate Definition

$$\gamma_{xy}(m) = E\{(x_{n+m} - m_x)(y_n - m_y)\}$$

$$= E\{x_{n+m}\, y_n\} - m_y E[x_{n+m}] - m_x E[y_n] + m_x m_y$$

$$= \phi_{xy}(m) - \cancel{m_y m_x} - m_x m_y + \cancel{m_x m_y}$$

$$= \phi_{xy}(m) - m_x m_y, \text{ as obtained above}$$

(b) (i) $\phi_{xx}(0) = E[x_n \cdot x_{n+0}] = E[x_n^2] =$ mean square ($\because m = 0$)

(ii) $\gamma_{xx}(0) = E[(x_n - m_x)(x_{n+m} - m_x)]\,|_{m=0}$, for x real RV

$$= E[\,|x_n - m_x|^2]$$

$$= \sigma_x^2 \qquad \text{(due to definition of variance)}$$

(c) (i) $\phi_{xx}(-m)$ (auto-correlation) $= E[x_n\, x_{n-m}]$, for x real RV

Put $n - m = n'$ $\therefore n = n' + m$

$$= E[x_{n'+m}\, x_{n'}]$$

$$= E[x_{n'}\, x_{n'+m}] = \phi_{xx}(m)$$

(ii) $\gamma_{xx}(-m)$ (auto-covariance) $= E[(x_n - m_x)(x_{n-m} - m_x)]$

Put $n - m = n'$ $\therefore$ $n = n' + m$

$$= E[(x_{n'+m} - m_x)(x_{n'} - m_x)]$$

$$= \gamma_{xx}(m)$$

(iii) $\phi_{yx}^*(+m)$ (cross-correlation) $= (E[y_n \cdot x_{n-m}^*])^*$ for complex valued RPs

$$= (E[y_{n'+m}\, x_{n'}^*])^* \quad (\text{putting } n = n' + m)$$

$$= (E[x_{n'}^*\, y_{n'+m}])^*$$

$$= E[x_{n'}\, y_{n'+m}^*]$$

$$= \phi_{xy}(-m) \qquad \text{[by definition, see (11.40)]}$$

$$\therefore \quad \phi_{yx}^*(-m) = \phi_{xy}(m) \qquad \text{(changing } m \text{ to } -m \text{ both sides)}$$

(iv) $\gamma^*_{yx}(-m)$ (cross-covariance) $= (E[(y_n - m_y)(x_{n+m} - m_x)^*])^*$

$= (E[(y_{n'-m} - m_y)(x_{n'} - m_x)^*])^*$ (changing n to $n' - m$)

$= E[(x_{n'} - m_x)(y_{n'-m} - m_y)^*]$

$= \gamma_{xy}(m)$ [by definition of $\gamma_{xy}(m)$, see (11.41)]

EXAMPLE 11.8: *Consider an ergodic random process so that time averages are equal to probability averages. Let x(n) be a particular sample sequence of the random process defined by the set of random variables $\{x_n\}$, $-\infty < n < \infty$, where $p_x(x)$ is the first-order probability density for all the random variables x_n.*

(a) *Consider the time average of the function $u(a - x_n)$; i.e., $\langle u(a - x_n)\rangle$. (The function $u(\cdot)$ is the unit step). Express in words the meaning of this time average.*

(b) *Consider the probability average of the function $u(a - x_n)$. What is $E[u(a - x_n)]$ in terms of $p_x(x)$?*

(c) *Is your result in part (b) consistent with your interpretation of part (a); i.e., is it reasonable that $E[u(a - x_n)] = \langle u(a - x_n)\rangle$?*

SOLUTION: (a) The function $u(a - x_n)$ is defined as

$$u(a - x_n) = \begin{cases} 1, & x_n \le \alpha \\ 0, & x_n > a \end{cases}$$

since $u(n)$ is a unit step function.

Typically, sequence $\{x_n\}$ and $u\{a - x_n\}$ are as shown thus, the function $u(a - x_n)$ counts the occurrences of values of x_n such that $x_n \le a$. Thus, the time average $\langle u(a - x_n)\rangle$ of the function $u(a - x_n)$ gives the probability of $x_n \le a$.

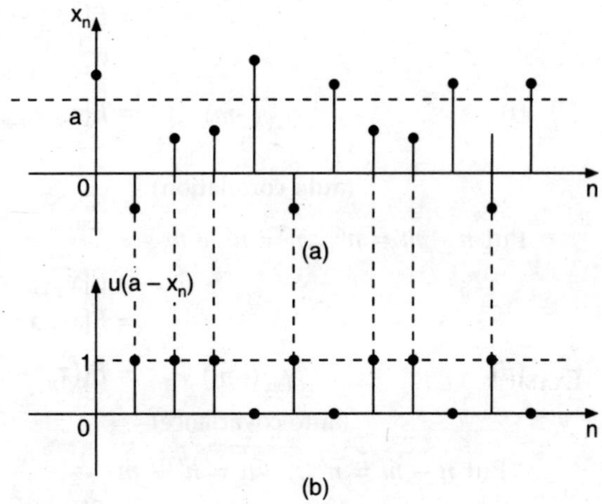

Fig. Ex. 11.8. Typical sequences (a) $\{x_n\}$ and (b) $u(a - x_n)$

(b) $E[u(a - x_n)] = \int_{-\infty}^{\infty} u(a - x_n)\, p_x(x)\, dx$

$= \int_{-\infty}^{\infty} p_x(x)\, dx$

$\because$ $u(a - x_n) = 1$ only for $x_n \le a$ and zero otherwise

$= P_x(a)$

$=$ Probability $[x_n \le a]$

(c) Thus we see that the two results are consistent.

i.e., $E[u(a - x_n)] = \langle u(a - x_n)\rangle$

In fact this simple result is often used as the basis for estimating probability function for random processes that are assumed to be ergodic.

EXAMPLE 11.9: *Let x(n) be a real stationary white-noise process, with zero mean and variance σ_x^2. Let y(n) be the corresponding output when x(n) is the input to a linear shift-invariant system with impulse response h(n).*

(a) *Show that* $E[x(n)\, y(n)] = h(0)\, \sigma_x^2$

(b) *Show that* $\sigma_y^2 = \sigma_x^2 \sum_{n=-\infty}^{\infty} h^2(n)$

SOLUTION: (*a*)

$$E[x(n)\ y(n)] = E\left[x(n)\cdot\sum_{k=-\infty}^{\infty} h(k)\cdot x(n-k)\right]$$

$$= \sum_{k=-\infty}^{\infty} h(k)\, E[x(n)\cdot x(n-k)]$$

$$= \sum_{k=-\infty}^{\infty} h(k)\cdot\sigma_x^2\delta(k)$$ [$\because$ $x(n)$ is a stationary white noise with σ_x^2 as its variance]

$$= h(0)\cdot\sigma_x^2 \quad \textbf{Ans.}$$

(*b*)

$$\sigma_y^2 = E[(y(n) - m_y)^2]$$

But

$$m_y = E[y(n)] = E\left[\sum_{k=-\infty}^{\infty} h(k)\,x(n-k)\right]$$

$$= \sum_{k=-\infty}^{\infty} h(k)\,\underbrace{E[x(n-k)]}_{=0} = 0$$

(being stationary white noise's mean)

$\therefore$

$$\sigma_y^2 = E[y^2(n)] = E\left[\sum_{m=-\infty}^{\infty} h(m)\,x(n-m)\cdot\sum_{k=-\infty}^{\infty} h(k)\,x(n-k)\right]$$

$$= \sum_m\sum_k h(m)\,h(k)\,E[x(n-m)\cdot x(n-k)]$$

$$= \sum_m\sum_k h(m)\,h(k)\cdot\sigma_x^2\delta(m-k)$$

$$= \sigma_x^2\sum_{m=-\infty}^{\infty} h^2(m) \quad \textbf{Ans.}$$

EXAMPLE 11.10: *Show that the z-transform of*

$$v(n) \triangleq \sum_{k=-\infty}^{\infty} h(k)\,h(k+n)$$

is

$$V(z) = H(z)\,H(z^{-1}).$$

SOLUTION: Given

$$v(n) = \sum_{k=-\infty}^{\infty} h(k)\,h(k+n)$$

$\therefore$

$$V(z) = \sum_{n=-\infty}^{\infty} v(n)\cdot z^{-n}$$

$$= \sum_{n=-\infty}^{\infty}\sum_{k=-\infty}^{\infty} h(k)\,h(k+n)\cdot z^{-n}$$

$$= \sum_{k=-\infty}^{\infty} h(k)\cdot\sum_{n=-\infty}^{\infty} h(k+n)z^{-n}$$

Put $k + n = m$ ∴ when $n = -\infty$, $m = -\infty$

$n = +\infty$, $m = +\infty$

∴

$$V(z) = \sum_{k=-\infty}^{\infty} h(k) \sum_{m=-\infty}^{\infty} h(m) z^{-(m-k)}$$

$$= \sum_{k=-\infty}^{\infty} h(k) \cdot z^{k} \underbrace{\sum_{k=-\infty}^{\infty} h(m) z^{-m}}_{= H(z)}$$

$$= H(z) \sum_{k=-\infty}^{\infty} h(k) (z^{-1})^{-k}$$

$$= H(z) \cdot H(z^{-1}) \quad \textbf{Ans.}$$

Note: Note that $\sum_{k=-\infty}^{\infty} h(k) h(n+k) = h(n) * h(-n)$

∴ Clearly, $V(z) = H(z) \cdot H(z^{-1})$**

EXAMPLE 11.11: *An ideal Hilbert transformer with unit sample response*

$$h(n) = \begin{cases} \dfrac{2}{\pi}, \dfrac{\sin^2(n\pi/2)}{n}, & n \neq 0 \\ 0 & n = 0 \end{cases} \qquad \text{...(1)}$$

is excited by a discrete-time random signal $x_r(n)$ as shown

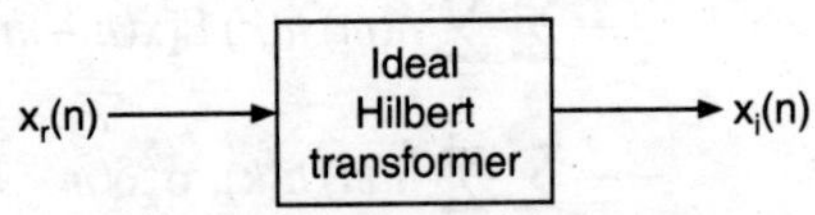

(a) *Find the expression for the auto-correlation sequence $\phi_{x_i x_i}(m)$.*

(b) *Find an expression for the cross-correlation sequence $\phi_{x_r x_i}(m)$. Show that in this case $\phi_{x_r x_i}(m) = -\phi_{x_r x_i}(-m)$.*

(c) *Find the power spectrum $P_{xx}(\omega)$ and the auto-correlation sequence for the complex analytic signal defined by $x(n)$ such that*

$$x(n) = x_r(n) + j x_i(n) \qquad \text{...(2)}$$

SOLUTION: (*a*) $\phi_{x_i x_i}(m) = E[x_i(n) \cdot x_i(n + m)]$

We also known that for the Hilbert transform

$$H(e^{j\omega}) = \begin{cases} -j, & 0 < \omega < \pi \\ +j, & -\pi < \omega < 0 \end{cases} \qquad \text{Hilbert Transformer} \qquad \text{...(3)}$$

** $\quad h(n) * h(-n) = \sum_{k} h(k) \cdot h(-(n-k)) = \sum_{R} h(k) \cdot h(k-n)$

Put $k - n = m$ ∴ $k = n + m$

$$= \sum_{m} h(n+m) \cdot h(m)$$

$$= \sum_{k} h(k)\, h(n+k)$$

and $$P_{x_ix_i}(\omega) = |H(e^{j\omega})|^2 \cdot P_{x_rx_r}(\omega) = P_{x_rx_r}(\omega)$$

$\therefore$ $$\boxed{\phi_{x_ix_i}(m) = \phi_{x_rx_r}(m)} \quad \ldots(4)$$

(*b*) $$\phi_{x_rx_i}(m) = E[x_r(n)\, x_i(n+m)]$$

$$= E\left[x_r(n) \sum_{k=-\infty}^{\infty} h(k)\, x_r(n+m-k)\right]$$

$$= \sum_{k=-\infty}^{\infty} h(k)\, E[x_r(n) \cdot x_r(n+m-k)]$$

$$= \sum_{k=-\infty}^{\infty} h(k)\, \phi_{x_rx_r}(m-k) \quad \ldots(5)$$

Now $$\phi_{x_rx_i}(-m) = \sum_{k=-\infty}^{\infty} h(k)\, \phi_{x_rx_r}(-m-k) \quad \text{[changing } m \text{ to } -m \text{ in (5)]}$$

Put $k = -l$

$$= \sum_{l=-\infty}^{\infty} h(-l)\, \phi_{x_rx_r}(-m+l)$$ ($\because$ auto-correlation for a real sequence is an even function.)

where $h(-l) = -h(+l)$ from (1), and $\phi_{x_rx_r}(-m+l) = \phi_{x_rx_r}(m-l)$

$$= -\sum_{l=-\infty}^{\infty} h(l)\, \phi_{x_rx_r}(m-l)$$

$$= -\phi_{x_rx_i}(m) \quad \text{[due to (5)]}$$

Hence,

$$\boxed{\phi_{x_rx_i}(m) = -\phi_{x_rx_i}(-m)} \quad \ldots(6)$$

(*c*) Given $x(n) = x_r(n) + jx_i(n)$

$\therefore$ $$\phi_{xx}(m) = E[x(n) \cdot x^*(n+m)]$$

$\therefore$ $$\phi_{xx}(m) = E[(x_r(n) + jx_i(n))(x_r(n+m) - jx_i(n+m))]$$

$$= E[x_r(n)\, x_r(n+m)] + E[x_i(n)\, x_i(n+m)] + jE[x_i(n)\, x_r(n+m) - x_r(n)\, x_i(n+m)]$$

$$= \phi_{x_rx_r}(m) + \phi_{x_ix_i} + j[\phi_{x_ix_r}(m) - \phi_{x_rx_i}(m)]$$

where $\phi_{x_ix_i} = \phi_{x_rx_r}(m)$ due to (4), and $\phi_{x_ix_r}(m) = \phi_{x_rx_i}(-m) = -\phi_{x_rx_i}(m)$ due to (6)

$$= 2\phi_{x_rx_r}(m) - 2j\phi_{x_rx_i}(m)$$

Hence,

$$\phi_{xx}(m) = 2[\phi_{x_rx_r}(m) - j\phi_{x_rx_i}(m)] \quad \ldots(7)$$

(*d*) $$2[P_{x_r x_r}(\omega) - jP_{x_r x_i}(\omega)]$$

$$= 2[P_{x_r x_r}(\omega) - j\overbrace{H(e^{j\omega})\,P_{x_r x_r}(\omega)}]$$ [see proof after (8)]

$$= 2P_{x_r x_r}(\omega)[1 - jH(e^{j\omega})] \quad \text{using (3)}$$

$$\therefore \quad = \boxed{P_{xx}(\omega) = \begin{cases} 4P_{x_r x_r}(\omega), & -\pi < \omega < 0 \\ 0, & 0 < \omega < \pi \end{cases}} \quad \ldots(8)$$

[To show that $P_{x_r x_i}(\omega) = H(e^{j\omega})P_{x_r x_r}(\omega)$]

Proof: As $$\phi_{x_r x_i}(m) = \sum_{k=-\infty}^{\infty} h(k)\cdot\phi_{x_r x_i}(m-k)$$ [due to (5)]

$$\therefore \quad P_{x_r x_i}(\omega) = FT[\phi_{x_r x_i}(m)]$$

$$= \sum_{m=-\infty}^{\infty}\left(\sum_{k=-\infty}^{\infty} h(k)\,\phi_{x_r x_r}(m-k)\right)e^{-j\omega m}$$

$$= \underbrace{\sum_{k=-\infty}^{\infty} h(k)e^{-j\omega k}}_{=H(e^{j\omega})}\ \underbrace{\sum_{m=-\infty}^{\infty}\phi_{x_r x_r}(m-k)\,e^{-j\omega(m-k)}}_{=P_{x_r x_r}(\omega)}$$

$$\therefore \quad P_{x_r x_i}(\omega) = H(e^{j\omega})\cdot P_{x_r x_r}(\omega).$$

EXAMPLE 11.12: *Consider a linear shift-invariant digital network with two inputs as depicted in Fig. Ex. 11.12. Let $h_1(n)$ and $h_2(n)$ be the unit-sample responses from nodes 1 and 2, respectively, to the output. Show that if $x_1(n)$ and $x_2(n)$ are uncorrelated, then their corresponding outputs are also uncorrelated.*

SOLUTION: As the system is linear

$$\therefore \quad y(n) = y_1(n) + y_2(n)$$

where

$$y_1(n) = \sum_{k=-\infty}^{\infty} h_1(k)x_1(n-k)$$

$$y_2(n) = \sum_{k=-\infty}^{\infty} h_2(k)x_2(n-k)$$

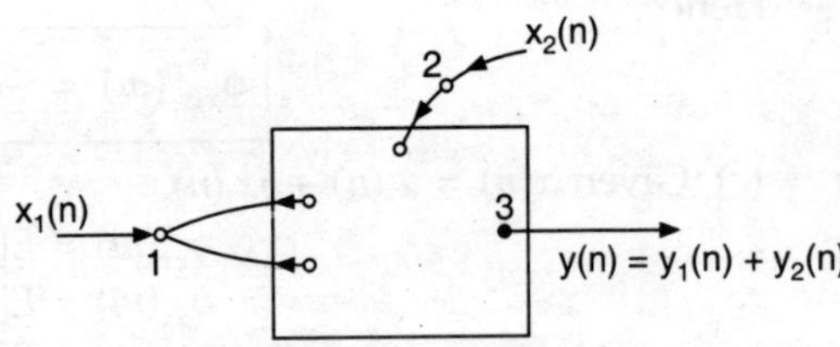

Fig. Ex. 11.12. The given network

$$\therefore \quad E[y_1(m)\cdot y_2(n)] = E\left[\sum_{k=-\infty}^{\infty} h_1(k)x_1(m-k)\cdot\sum_{l=-\infty}^{\infty} h_2(l)x_2(n-l)\right]$$

$$= \sum_k\sum_l h_1(k)h_2(l)\,E[x_1(m-k)\cdot x_2(n-l)]$$

If $x_1(n)$ and $x_2(n)$ are uncorrelated, then $E[x_1(m-k)\,x_2(n-l)] = 0$

$$\therefore \quad E[y_1(m)\cdot y_2(n)] = 0$$

i.e $y_1(n)$ and $y_2(n)$ are uncorrelated.

This means that $\sigma_y^2 = \sigma_{y_1}^2 + \sigma_{y_2}^2$ (Result of Example 11.3)

EXAMPLE 11.13: *Let $x(n)$ be a random white sequence, with zero mean and variance σ_x^2. Let $x(n)$ be the input to the cascade of two linear discrete-time shift invariant systems as shown in Fig. Ex. 11.13:*

(a) Is $\sigma_y^2 = \sigma_x^2 \sum_{k=0}^{\infty} h_1^2(k)$

(b) Is $\sigma_\omega^2 = \sigma_y^2 \sum_{k=0}^{\infty} h_2^2(k)$

(c) Let $h_1(n) = a^n u(n)$ and $h_2(n) = b^n u(n)$. Determine the unit sample response of the overall system in given Fig. Ex. 11.13 and from this determine σ_ω^2. If your answer to part (b) was yes, is that consistent with your answer to part (c)?

SOLUTION:

(a) $\sigma_y^2 = \sigma_x^2 \sum_{k=0}^{\infty} h_1^2(n)$, yes since $x(n)$ is a white noise sequence

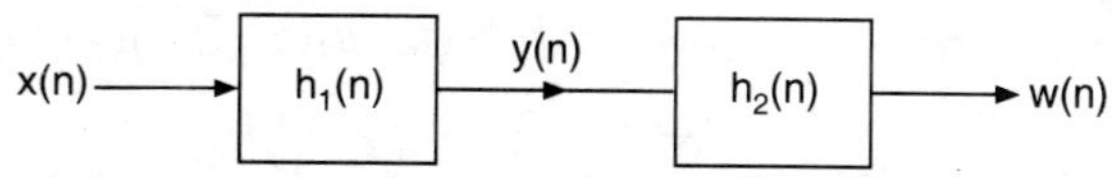

Fig. Ex. 11.13. (*a*) The given cascade system

(b) $\sigma_\omega^2 = \sigma_y^2 \sum_{k=0}^{\infty} h_2^2(n)$ because $y(n)$ is no longer a white noise sequence having been filtered by the system $h_1(n)$

(c) If $h_1(n) = a^n u(n)$ and $h_2(n) = b^n . u(n)$

∴ Overall
$$h(n) = h_1(n) * h_2(n)$$
$$= \sum_{k=0}^{\infty} a^k u(k) \cdot b^{n-k} u(n-k) = \sum_{k=0}^{\infty} a^k b^{n-k}$$

As
$$h(n) = \sum_{k=0}^{n} a^k b^{n-k}, \ n \geq 0$$
$$= b^n \sum_{k=0}^{n} (ab^{-1})^k$$

∴
$$h(n) = \begin{cases} b^n \dfrac{1-(ab^{-1})^{n+1}}{1-ab^{-1}}, & n \geq 0 \\ 0, & n < 0 \end{cases}$$

i.e.
$$h(n) = \frac{b^n(1-(ab^{-1})^{n+1})}{1-ab^{-1}} u(n)$$

$\sigma_\omega^2 = \sigma_x^2 \sum_{k=0}^{\infty} h^2(k)$ ** (surely which is $\neq \sigma_y^2 \sum_{k=0}^{\infty} h_2^2(n)$ so, we were right in answering part (*b*))

** **Note that:**

$$\sigma_x^2 \sum_{k=0}^{\infty} h^2(k) = \sigma_x^2 \sum_{k=0}^{\infty} (b^{2n} - 2a^{n+1}b^{n-1} + a^{2(n+1)}b^{-2})/(1-ab^{-1})^2$$
$$= \frac{\sigma_x^2}{(1-ab^{-1})^2}\left[\frac{1}{1-b^2} - \frac{2ab^{-1}}{1-ab} + \frac{a^2b^{-2}}{1-a^2}\right] = \frac{(1+ab)\sigma_x^2}{(1-a^2)(1-b^2)(1-ab)} \text{ (as expected).}$$

Alternatively

$$\Phi_{\omega\omega}(z) = H(z) \cdot H(z^{-1})\sigma_x^2 \text{ (proved later on)}$$

where $\quad H(z) = H_1(z) \cdot H_2(z) = \dfrac{1}{1-az^{-1}} \cdot \dfrac{1}{1-bz^{-1}}$

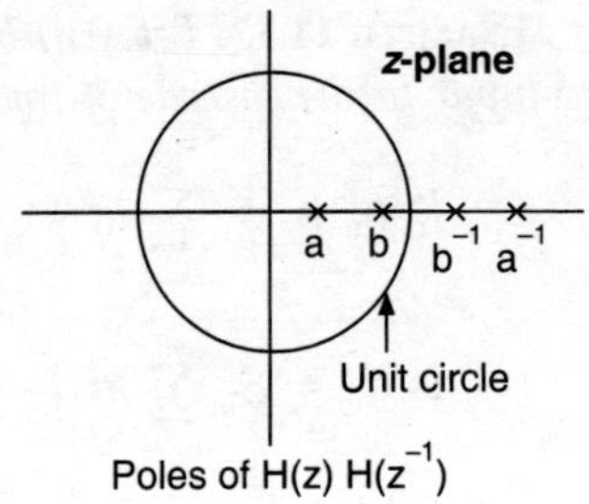

Fig. Ex. 11.13. (*b*) Poles of $H(z)$ $H(z^{-1})$

$$\therefore \quad \Phi_{\omega\omega}(z) = \frac{\sigma_x^2}{(1-az^{-1})(1-az)(1-bz^{-1})(1-bz)}$$

$$\phi_{\omega\omega}(0) = \gamma_{\omega\omega}^2 = \frac{1}{2\pi j}\oint_C \frac{\sigma_x^2\, z^2 \cdot z^{n-1}}{ab(z-a)(z-a^{-1})(z-b)(z-b^{-1})}\, dz \Bigg|_{n=0}$$

$\nearrow$

σ_ω^2

$$= \frac{\sigma_x^2}{ab} \cdot \frac{1}{2\pi j}\oint_C \frac{z\, dz}{(z-a)(z-a^{-1})(z-b)(z-b^{-1})}$$

$$= \frac{\sigma_x^2}{ab}\left[\frac{a}{(a-a^{-1})(a-b)(a-b^{-1})} + \frac{b}{(b-a)(b-a^{-1})(b-b^{-1})}\right]$$

Residues taken only for poles $z = a$, $z = b$ (Note this step)

$$= \frac{\sigma_x^2(1+ab)}{(1-a^2)(1-b^2)(1-ab)}$$

[To show that for $x(n)$ white noise sequence and $h(n)$ real valued, we have $ZT[\gamma_{ww}(m) = \sigma_x^2 H(z) \cdot H(z^{-1})]$

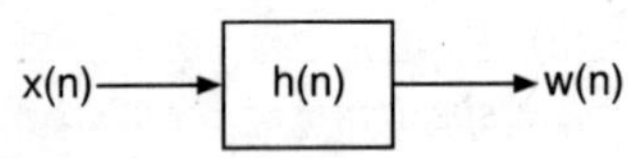

$$m_x = 0 \text{ (white noise)}$$

$$\therefore \quad m_w = m_x \sum_k h(k) = 0$$

Clearly,

$$\omega(n) = x(n) * h(n)$$

$$= \sum_k h(k) \cdot x(n-k)$$

$$\gamma_{ww}(m) \triangleq E[\omega(m+n) \cdot \omega^*(n)]$$

$$= E\left[\sum_k h(k)\, x(m+n-k) \cdot \left(\sum_l h(l)\, x(n-l)\right)^*\right]$$

$$= \sum_k \sum_l h(k) \cdot h^*(l)\, E[x(m+n-k) \cdot x^*(n-l)]$$

$$= \sum_k \sum_l h(k) h^*(l) \sigma_{xx}^2 \cdot \delta(m-k+l)$$

$$ZT[\gamma_{ww}(m)] = \sum_{m=-\infty}^{\infty} \gamma_{ww}(m) z^{-m}$$

$$= \sum_{m=-\infty}^{\infty} \sum_k \sum_l h(k)\, h^*(l)\, \sigma_{xx}^2 \delta(m-k+l)\, z^{-m}$$

$$= \sigma_{xx}^2 \sum_k \sum_l h(k)\, h^*(l) \cdot z^{-(k-l)}$$

$$= \sigma_{xx}^2 \sum_l h^*(l) \underbrace{\left(\sum_{k=-\infty}^{\infty} h(k) z^{-k} \right)}_{H(z)} z^l$$

$$= \sigma_{xx}^2 H(z) \sum_{l=-\infty}^{\infty} h(l)(z^{-1})^{-l}$$

$$= \sigma_{xx}^2 H(z) \cdot H(z^{-1}) \quad \text{taking } h^*(l) = h(l) \text{ being real valued}$$

$\therefore$ $$\boxed{\Phi(z) = \sigma_x^2 H(z) \cdot H(z^{-1})}$$ Q.E.D.

EXAMPLE 11.14: *Consider a continuous-time random process defined by the random variable $\{x_a(t)\}$, where t is a continuous time variable. The auto-covariance function is defined as (assuming zero mean)*

$$\gamma_{x_a x_a}(\tau) = E[x_a(t) \cdot x_a^*(t+\tau)]$$

and the power spectrum is

$$P_{x_a x_a}(\Omega) = \int_{-\infty}^{\infty} \gamma_{x_a x_a}(\tau)\, e^{-j\Omega\tau}\, d\tau .$$

A discrete-time random process obtained by periodic sampling is defined by the set of random variables $\{x(a)\}$ where $x(n) = x_a(nT)$ and T is the sampling period.

(a) What is the relationship between $\gamma_{xx}(n)$ and $\gamma_{x_a x_a}(\tau)$?

(b) Express the power density spectrum of the discrete-time process in terms of the power density spectrum of the continuous process.

(c) Under what condition is the discrete-time power spectrum a faithful representation of the continuous-time power spectrum?

SOLUTION: We have

$$\gamma_{x_a x_a}(\tau) \triangleq E[x_a(t)\, x_a^*(t+\tau)]$$

$$P_{x_a x_a}(\Omega) = \int_{-\infty}^{\infty} \gamma_{x_a x_a}(\tau) e^{-j\Omega\tau}\, d\tau$$

and $$x(n) = x_a(nT)$$

(a) $\gamma_{xx}(m) = E[x(n)x^*(n+m)]$

$$= E[x_a(nT) \cdot x_a^*(nT + mT)]$$

$$= \gamma_{x_a x_a}(mT), \text{ i.e., the sampled auto-covariance.}$$

Thus, $$\gamma_{xx}(m) = \gamma_{x_a x_a}(\tau)\big|_{\tau = mT} \quad \textbf{Ans.}$$

(b) As $\gamma_{xx}(m)$ is just a sampled version of $\gamma_{x_a x_a}(\tau)$, therefore,

$$P_{xx}(\omega) = \frac{1}{T} \sum_{k=-\infty}^{\infty} P_{x_a x_a}\left(\frac{\omega}{T} + \frac{2\pi k}{T} \right) \quad \text{where } \omega = \Omega T$$

(c) If $P_{x_a x_a}(\Omega)\Big|_{\Omega = \frac{\omega}{T}} = 0$ for $|\omega| \geq \pi$

$\omega =$ has max value $\omega_{max} = \pi$

then $P_{x_a x_a}(\Omega)$ is bandlimited to $|\Omega| \leq \frac{\pi\omega}{T}$

i.e., $|\Omega| \leq \frac{2\pi f_s}{2}$

i.e., f_s = twice the highest frequency content of $P_{x_a x_a}(\Omega)$.

Then we have the relation

$$P_{xx}(\omega) = \frac{1}{T} P_{x_a x_a}\left(\frac{\omega}{T}\right), \quad |\omega| \leq \pi$$

and $x(n)$ can reconstruct $x_a(t)$ faithfully with no error.

EXAMPLE 11.15: *Consider a mixed (i.e., ARMA) linear process y that satisfies the difference equation:*

$$y(n) = \sum_{k=1}^{N} a_k y(n-k) + \sum_{k=0}^{M} b_k x(n-k), \; b_0 = 1$$

Sometimes it is of interest to "whiten" the spectrum of y(n) by processing y(n) with a linear filter; i.e. we wish to find a system such that its output power spectrum will be flat for input y(n).

Suppose we know the auto-covariance function $\gamma_{yy}(m)$ and its z-transform $\Gamma_{yy}(z)$ but not the a_k's and the b_k's.

(a) Discuss a procedure or find a system function $H_\omega(z)$ of the whitening filter.

(b) Is the whitening filter unique?

(c) How do the Hilbert transform relations enter into this problem?

SOLUTION: From the given difference equation, we obtain

$$H(z) = \frac{\sum_{k=0}^{M} b_k z^{-k}}{1 - \sum_{k=1}^{N} a_k z^{-k}} \qquad \ldots(1)$$

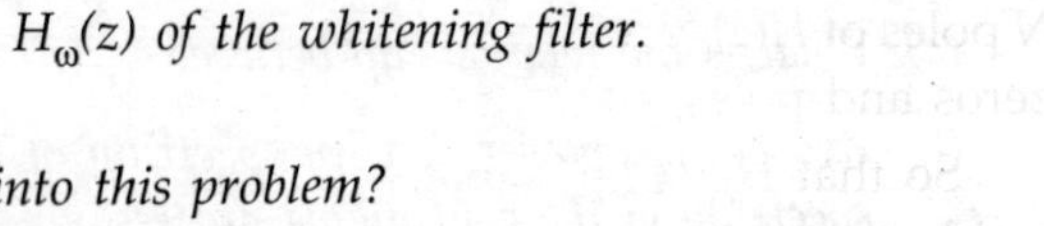

Fig. Ex. 11.15. (*a*) Whitening filter $h_w(n)$ for input $y(n)$.

we do not know a_k's and b_k's: Only $\gamma_{xx}(m)$ and its z-transform $\Gamma_{yy}(z)$ are known. Also the power spectrum of $\omega(n)$ is flat (white noise).

We can put $H(z)$ in the form

$$H(z) = A\frac{\prod_{k=1}^{M}(1 - c_k z^{-1})}{\prod_{k=1}^{N}(1 - d_k z^{-1})}$$

where for stability of the system $H(z)$, $|d_k| < 1$ because then only all the poles of $H(z)$ lie inside the unit circle.

(*a*) z-transform of $\gamma_{yy}(m)$ *viz.* $\Gamma_{yy}(z)$ (which is known) is of the form

$$\Gamma_{yy}(z) = H(z) \cdot H(z^{-1}) \cdot \sigma_x^2$$

$$= A^2\sigma_x^2 \frac{\prod_{k=1}^{M} (1 - c_k z^{-1})(1 - c_k z)}{\prod_{k=1}^{N} (1 - d_k z^{-1})(1 - d_k z)} \quad \text{is known}$$

To whiten the signal $y(n)$, *i.e.*, spectrum of $\omega(n)$ to be a constant, we need a system $H_\omega(z)$ such that

$$H_\omega(z)\, H_\omega(z^{-1}) = \frac{1}{H(z) \cdot H(z^{-1})}$$

Hence, we have

$$H_\omega(z)\, H_\omega(z^{-1}) = \frac{\prod_{k=1}^{M} (1 - d_k z^{-1})(1 - d_k z)}{\prod_{k=1}^{N} (1 - c_k z^{-1})(1 - c_k z)} \quad \text{is known}$$

i.e. the poles of $H_\omega(z)$ are the zeros of $H(z)$ and the zeros of $H_\omega(z)$ are the poles of $H(z)$. Thus we must decide which N of $2N$ poles of $H(z) \cdot H(z^{-1})$ are to become zeros of $H_\omega(z)$ and which M of $2M$ zeros of $H(z) \cdot H(z^{-1})$ are to become poles of $H_\omega(z)$. The remaining N poles of $H(z) \cdot H(z^{-1})$ and its remaining M zeros would become zeros and poles, respectively, of $H_\omega(z^{-1})$.

So that $H_\omega(z)$ be stable, we must choose all its poles to be inside the unit circle. Thus for a given pair of c_k and c_k^{-1}, we must choose the one which is inside the unit circle as the pole point for $H_\omega(z)$. This way all the poles of the whitening filter can be determined from zeros of $\Gamma_{yy}(z)$.

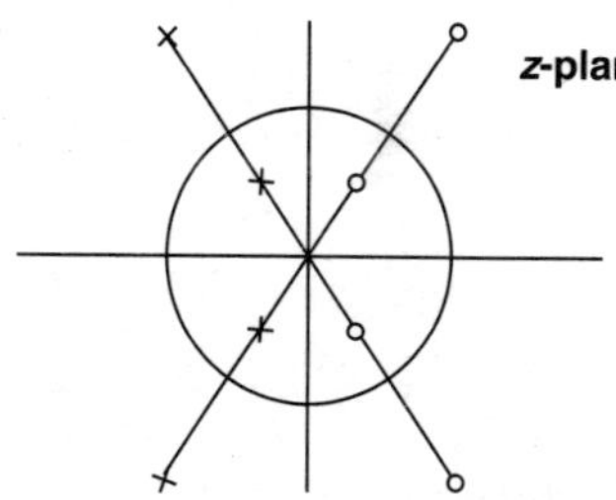

Fig. Ex. 11.15. (*b*) Typical poles and zeros of $H_\omega(z) \cdot H_\omega(z^{-1})$

(*b*) There is no real constraint on the zeros of $H_\omega(z)$ so, we are free to select d_k or d_k^{-1} as its zero. Hence the whitening filter is not unique.

(*c*) If $H(z)$ has all its zeros as well as poles inside the unit circle, then we can easily choose

$$H_\omega(z) = \frac{1}{H(z)}$$

Then $H_\omega(z)$ will also have its poles (which are the zeros of $H(z)$) and its zeros (which are the poles of $H(z)$) inside the unit circle. Hence, if $H(z)$ is minimum phase, then so is $H_\omega(z)$ also a maximum phase system.

EXAMPLE 11.16: *Let $x(n)$ be a stationary white-noise process. Then the input to the system is $\omega(n)$*

$$\omega(n) = x(n) \cdot u(n)$$

and $\omega(n)$ is a non-stationary process. Let $y(n)$ be the output.

(*a*) *Derive an expression for the mean of the output in terms of the mean of the input.*

(*b*) *Derive an expression for the auto-correlation sequence $\phi_{yy}(n_1, n_2)$ of the output.*

(*c*) *Show that for large n, the formulas derived in parts (a) and (b) approach the results for stationary inputs.*

(d) Assume that $h(n) = a^n u(n)$. Find the mean and mean-square values of the output in terms of the mean and mean-square values of the input. Sketch the dependence of these parameters as a function of n.

(Note: The problem here enables us to determine the statistical behaviour of a linear shift-invariant system when the input is a suddenly applied random signal)

SOLUTION: Here

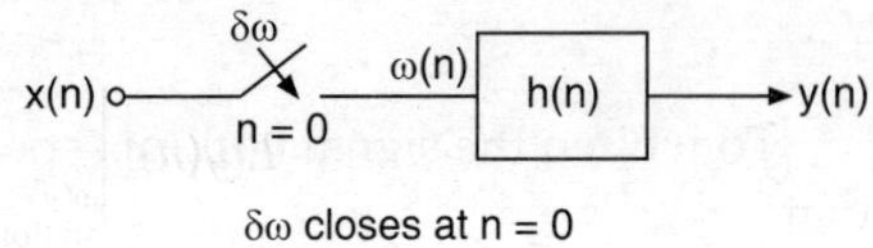

Fig. Ex. 11.16. (*a*) The given system

$$\omega(n) = \begin{cases} x(n), & n \geq 0 \\ 0, & n < 0 \end{cases}$$

(*a*)
$$y(n) = \omega(n) * h(n)$$
$$= (u(n) \cdot x(n)) * h(n)$$

$$\therefore \quad y(n) = \sum_{k=-\infty}^{\infty} h(k) \cdot (x(n-k) \cdot u(n-k)) \quad \text{(convolutions of } h(k) \text{ and } \omega(n))$$

$$= \sum_{k=-\infty}^{\infty} h(k) \cdot x(n-k), \; n \geq 0$$

$$E[y(n)] = E\left[\sum_{k=-\infty}^{n} h(k) \cdot x(n-k)\right], \; n \geq 0$$

$$= \sum_{k=-\infty}^{n} h(k)\, E[x(n-k)], \; n \geq 0$$

$$= m_x \sum_{k=-\infty}^{n} h(k), \; n \geq 0, \quad \text{where } m_x = E[x(n)]$$

Thus,

$$\underset{\nearrow \text{ mean of } y(n)}{E[y(n)]} = \begin{cases} m_x \sum_{k=-\infty}^{n} h(k), & n \geq 0 \\ 0, & n < 0 \end{cases} \quad \textbf{Ans.}$$

(*b*) Auto-correlation: $\phi_{yy}(n_1, n_2) = E[y(n_1) \cdot y(n_2)]$

$= 0$ if n_1 or n_2 or both n_1, n_2 are less than zero

If $n_1, n_2 \geq 0$ then

$$\phi_{yy}(n_1, n_2)\Big|_{n_1, n_2 \geq 0} = E\left[\sum_{k=-\infty}^{n_1} h(k)\, x(n_1 - k) \cdot \sum_{l=-\infty}^{n_2} h(l)\, x(n_2 - l)\right]$$

i.e.,
$$\phi_{yy}(n_1, n_2)\Big|_{n_1, n_2 \geq 0} = \sum_{k=-\infty}^{n_1} \sum_{l=-\infty}^{n_2} h(k) h(l) E[x(n_1 - k) \cdot x(n_2 - l)]$$

$$= \sum_{k=-\infty}^{n_1} \sum_{l=-\infty}^{n_2} h(k) h(l) \phi_{xx}(n_1 - k, n_2 - l)$$

$$\therefore \quad \phi_{yy}(n_1, n_2) = \begin{cases} 0, & n_1 \text{ and or } n_2 < 0 \\ \sum_{k=-\infty}^{n_1} \sum_{l=-\infty}^{n_2} h(k) h(l) \cdot \phi_{xx}(n_1 - k, n_2 - l), & n_1, n_2 \geq 0 \end{cases} \quad \textbf{Ans.}$$

(*c*) Let the input $\omega(n)$ be a stationary random process, then

$$E[y(n)]\Big|_{\substack{\omega(n)\\ \text{stationary}}} = \left(\sum_{k=-\infty}^{\infty} h(k)\right) m_x = m_y, \text{ (say)} \qquad \ldots(A)$$

We have found that for non-stationary input, $\omega(n)$, see part (*a*)

$$E[y(n)]\Big|_{\substack{\omega(n)\\ \text{stationary}}} = \begin{cases} m_x \sum_{k=-\infty}^{n} h(k), & n \geq 0 \\ 0, & n < 0 \end{cases}$$

$$\lim_{n\to\infty} E[y(n)]_{\substack{\omega(n)\\ \text{non-stationary}}} = m_x \sum_{k=-\infty}^{\infty} h(k)$$

$$= m_y \text{ due to } (A)$$

$$= E[y(n)]_{\substack{\omega(n)\\ \text{stationary}}} \qquad \text{Q.E.D.}$$

(*d*) Here $h(n) = a^n u(n)$

$$\therefore \quad E[y(n)]_{n\geq 0} = m_x \sum_{k=-\infty}^{n} (a^k u(k)) \quad \text{from part } (a)$$

$$= m_x \sum_{k=0}^{n} a^k$$

$$= m_x \frac{1-a^{n+1}}{1-a}$$

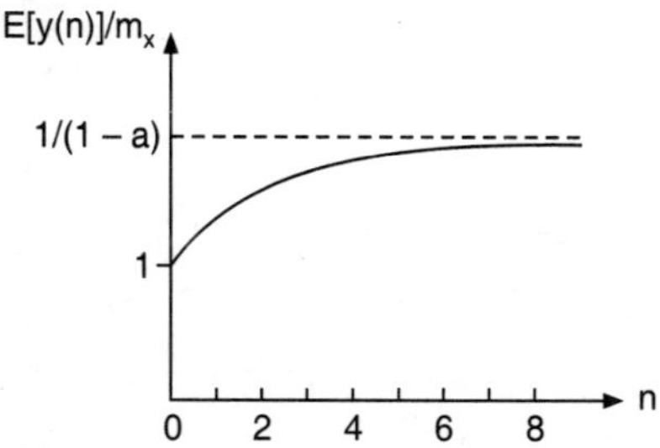

Fig. Ex. 11.16. (*b*) Dependence of $E[y(n)]$ on n for $h(n) = a^n u(n)$

If $|a| < 1$, then $E[y(n)]$ varies with n as shown in Fig. Ex. 11.6(*b*). For $n = 0$, $E[y(n)] = m_x$ and for $n \to \infty$, $E[y(n)]$ $\to \dfrac{m_x}{(1-a)}$.

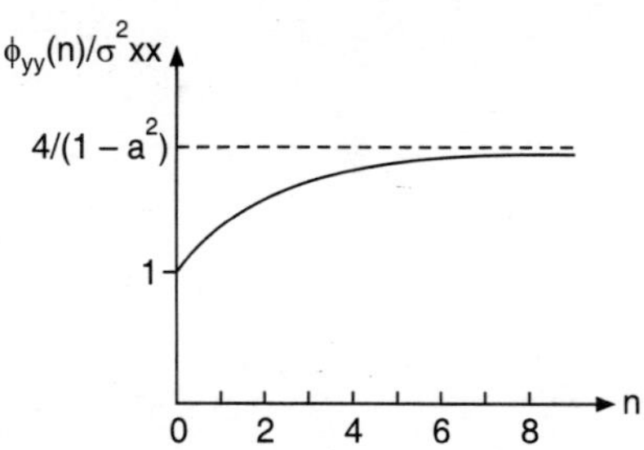

Fig. Ex. 11.16. (*c*) Variation of $\phi_{yy}(n)$ with n if $|a| < 1$.

Now

$$E[y^2(n)]\Big|_{n\geq 0} = E \sum_{k=-\infty}^{n} h(k)x(n-k) \cdot \sum_{l=-\infty}^{n} h(l)\, x(n-l)$$

$$= \sum_{k=-\infty}^{n} \sum_{l=-\infty}^{n} h(k)h(l)\, \phi_{xx}(k,l) \quad \text{for any } h(n)$$

with $h(n) = a^n u(n)$ we, therefore, have

$$E[y^2(n)] = \sum_{k=-\infty}^{n} \sum_{l=-\infty}^{n} a^k a^l\, u(k)u(l)\, \phi_{xx}(k,l),\ n \geq 0$$

$$= \sum_{k=0}^{n} \sum_{l=0}^{n} a^{k+l}\, \phi_{xx}(k,l),\ n \geq 0 \qquad \ldots(c)$$

Assuming $x(n)$, and therefore, $\omega(n)$ as white Gaussian noise with $\phi_{xx}(k, l) = \sigma_{xx}^2 \delta(k-l)$, above (*c*) gives us

$$\phi_{yy}(n) = \sigma_{xx}^2 \sum_{k=0}^{n} a^{2k} = \sigma_{xx}^2 \left(\frac{1-a^{2(n+1)}}{1-a^2} \right)$$

with $|a| < 1$, $\phi_{yy}(n)$ varies as shown in above Figure in Fig. Ex. 11.16(*c*).

EXAMPLE 11.17: *Defining cross correlation of x(n) and y(n) as*

$$\gamma_{yx}(m) = E\{y(n) \cdot x^*(n-m)\}$$

determine the value of $\gamma_{yx}(m)$ *and the Fourier transform of* $\gamma_{yx}(m)$ *for the linear time invariant system having the unit sample response h(n) and input, x(n), as random signal with mean* m_x *and variance* σ_x^2. *Assume output, y(n) as x(n) ∗ h(n).*

SOLUTION: The given data is $E\{x\} = m_x$

$$E\{x^2\} = \sigma_x^2 - m_x^2$$

$$y(n) = x(n) * h(n)$$

$$= \sum_{k=0}^{\infty} h(k)\, x(n-k) \qquad \text{(causal system)}$$

$$E\{y(n)\} = m_x \sum_{k=0}^{\infty} h(k)$$

$$E\{y^2(n)\} = \sigma_x^2 \sum |h(k)|^2 - m_y^2$$

As $$\gamma_{yx}(m) = E\{y(n) \cdot x^*(n-m)\} \qquad \text{(by definition)}$$

$$= E\left\{ \left(\sum_{k=0}^{\infty} h(k) \cdot x(n-k) \right) x^*(n-m) \right\}$$

$$= \sum_{k=0}^{\infty} h(k)\, E\{x(n-k) \cdot x^*(n-m)\}$$

$$= \sum_{k=0}^{\infty} h(k) \cdot \gamma_{xx}(m-k) \qquad \because \; (n-k) - (n-m) = m-k$$

∴ $$\gamma_{yx}(m) = \sum_{k=0}^{\infty} h(k) \cdot \gamma_{xx}(m-k) \qquad \ldots(A) \quad \textbf{Ans.}$$

As $$\gamma_{yx}(m) = \sum_{k=0}^{\infty} h(k) \cdot \gamma_{xx}(m-k) \qquad \text{[due to } (A)]$$

$$= h(m) * \gamma_{xx}(m) \qquad \text{(convolution)}$$

∴ $$FT[\gamma_{yx}(m)] = FT[h(m)] \cdot FT[\gamma_{xx}(m)]$$

But $$FT[h(m)] = H(e^{j\omega})$$

and $$FT[\gamma_{xx}(m)] = \Gamma_{xx}(e^{j\omega})$$

$$= \sigma_x^2 \qquad \text{[if } x(n) \text{ is a random signal of white noise]}$$

Thus, $$FT[\gamma_{yx}(m)] = \Gamma(e^{j\omega}) \cdot H(e^{j\omega}) \qquad \text{[in case } x(n) \text{ is any random signal]}$$

$$= \sigma_x^2 H(e^{j\omega}) \qquad \text{[if } x(n) \text{ is a white noise]} \quad \textbf{Ans.}$$

Problems with Answers

PROBLEM 11.1: *For two real stationary random processes $\{x_n\}$ and $\{y_n\}$, with means m_x and m_y respectively and variances σ_x^2 and σ_y^2, respectively, show that:*

(a) (i) $|\phi_{xy}(m)| \le [\phi_{xx}(0) \cdot \phi_{yy}(0)]^{1/2}$

(ii) $|\gamma_{xy}(m)| \le [\gamma_{xx}(0) \cdot \gamma_{yy}(0)]^{1/2}$

(iii) $|\phi_{xx}(m)| \le \phi_{xx}(0)$

(iv) $|\gamma_{xx}(m)| \le \gamma_{xx}(0)$

$$\left[\textit{Hint: Consider the inequality } 0 \le E\left\{\left(\frac{x_n}{(E\{x_n^2\})^{1/2}} - \frac{y_{n+m}}{(E\{y_{n+m}^2\})^{1/2}}\right)^2\right\}\right]$$

(b) If $y_n = x_{n-n_0}$, *then*

(i) $\phi_{yy}(m) = \phi_{xx}(m)$

(ii) $\gamma_{yy}(m) = \gamma_{xx}(m)$.

SOLUTION: (*a*) (*i*) Consider the inequality

$$E\left[\left(\frac{x_n}{(E[x_n^2])^{1/2}} - \frac{y_{n+m}}{(E[y_{n+m}^2])^{1/2}}\right)^2\right] \ge 0 \qquad \ldots(1)$$

This is so because the quantity inside the $E[\ldots]$ is > 0, being expectation of a square, for all n and m, (power cannot be negative) opening the bracket on LHS of above we have

$$E\left[\underbrace{\frac{x_n^2}{E[x_n^2]}}_{\phi_{xx}(0)} + \underbrace{\frac{x_n^2}{E[y_{n+m}^2]}}_{\phi_{yy}(0)} - 2\frac{x_n y_{n+m}}{\underbrace{(E[x_n^2])^{1/2}}_{\phi_{xx}^{1/2}(0)} \cdot \underbrace{(E[y_{n+m}^2])^{1/2}}_{\phi_{yy}^{1/2}(0)}}\right] \ge 0$$

using the fact that $E[x_n^2] = \phi_{xx}(0)$, $E[y_{n+m}^2] = \phi_{yy}(0)$

and $\underbrace{E[x_n\, y_{n+m}]}_{} = \phi_{xy}(m)$ for real-valued RPs

we have

$$\underbrace{\frac{\phi_{xx}(0)}{\phi_{xx}(0)}}_{=1} + \underbrace{\frac{\phi_{yy}(0)}{\phi_{yy}(0)}}_{=1} - \frac{2\phi_{xy}(m)}{(\phi_{xx}(0)\cdot\phi_{yy}(0))} \ge 0$$

$$\therefore \quad 1 - \frac{\phi_{xy}(m)}{[\phi_{xx}(0)\,\phi_{yy}(0)]^{1/2}} \ge 0$$

$$\therefore \quad |\phi_{xy}(m)| \le [\phi_{xx}(0)\,\phi_{yy}(0)]^{1/2} \qquad \ldots(2)$$

$\therefore \quad |\phi_{xy}(m)| \le [\phi_{xx}(0) \cdot \phi_{yy}(0)]^{1/2} \Rightarrow$ desired result (*ii*) Now consider the inequality

$$E\left\{\left(\underbrace{\frac{(x_n - m_x)}{(E[x_n - m_x]^2)^{1/2}}}_{=\gamma_{xx}^{1/2}(0)} - \underbrace{\frac{(y_{n+m} - m_y)}{(E[(y_{n+m} - m_y)^2])^{1/2}}}_{\gamma_{yy}^{1/2}(0)}\right)\right\} \geq 0 \qquad \ldots(3)$$

$$\therefore \qquad E\left\{\frac{(x_n - m_x)^2}{\gamma_{xx}(0)} + \frac{(y_{n+m} - m_y)^2}{\gamma_{yy}(0)} - 2\frac{(x_n - m_x)(y_{n+m} - m_y)}{(\gamma_{xx}(0)\,\gamma_{yy}(0))^{1/2}}\right\} \geq 0$$

or

$$\underbrace{\frac{\gamma_{xx}(0)}{\gamma_{xx}(0)} + \frac{\gamma_{yy}(0)}{\gamma_{yy}(0)}}_{=2} - 2\frac{\gamma_{xy}(m)}{(\gamma_{xx}(0)\,\gamma_{yy}(0))^{1/2}} \geq 0$$

$$\therefore \qquad |\gamma_{xy}(m)| \leq [\gamma_{xx}(0) \cdot \gamma_{yy}(0)]^{1/2} \qquad \ldots(4)$$

(*iii*) If we put $y_n = x_n$ in (1), proceeding similarly, we get

$$|\phi_{xx}(m)| \leq \phi_{xx}(0)$$

(*iv*) If we put $y_n = x_n$ and $m_y = m_x$ in (4), (3) proceeding as earlier, we get

$$|\gamma_{xx}(m)| \leq \gamma_{xx}(0)$$

(*b*) (*i*) Let $y_n = x_{n-n_0}$ (given)

$$\therefore \qquad \phi_{yy}(m) = E[y_n\, y_{n+m}] = E[x_{n-n_0} \cdot x_{n-n_0+m}]$$

$$= \phi_{xx}(m)$$

(*ii*)

$$\gamma_{yy}(m) = E[(y_n - m_y)(y_{n+m} - m_y)]$$

$$= E[(x_{n-n_0} - m_x)(x_{n-n_0+m} - m_x)] \qquad \text{here } m_y = m_x \text{ due to } y_n = x_{n-n_0}$$

$$= \gamma_{xx}(m).$$

PROBLEM 11.2: *Consider the mean-square sample-to-sample variation of a real signal, defined as*

$$E[(x(n+1) - x(n))^2]$$

consider a zero mean signal x(n) which has a band limited power spectrum such that

$$P_{xx}(\omega) = 0, \quad \omega_c < |\omega| \leq \pi$$

(*a*) *Show that*

$$E[(x(n+1) - x(n)^2] = 2[\phi_{xx}(0) - \phi_{xx}(1)]$$

(*b*) *Show that*

$$[\phi_{xx}(0) - \phi_{xx}(1)] \leq \frac{\omega_c^2}{2}\phi_{xx}(0)$$

and thus

$$E[(x(n+1) - x(n))^2] \leq \omega_c^2\, E[x^2(n)]$$

$$\left[\textit{Hint: Use the fact that } \sin^2\left(\frac{\omega}{2}\right) \leq \frac{\omega_c^2}{4} \text{ for } 0 \leq \omega \leq \omega_c\right]$$

A very important inequality is known as the Chebyshev inequality. It states that

$$\boxed{Prob.[|x(n) - E[x(n)]| \geq \varepsilon] \leq \frac{\sigma_x^2}{\varepsilon^2},\ \varepsilon > 0}$$

The inequality gives us a way of expressing how much a signal can be expected to differ from its mean, i.e. the greater the mean-square value the higher the probability that a particular sequence value will differ from the mean by an amount greater than ε

(c) *Use the result of part (b) and the Chebyshev inequality to show that*

$$Probability\ [|x(n+1) - x(n)| > \varepsilon] \leq \frac{\omega_c^2 E[x^2(n)]}{\varepsilon^2},\ \varepsilon > 0.$$

Interpret this result in light of your knowledge of the relationship between time variation of a signal and its bandwidth.

SOLUTION:

(a) $E[(x(n+1) - x(n))^2] = E[x^2(n+1)] - 2E[x(n+1)\cdot x(n)] + E[x^2(n)]$

$$= \phi_{xx}(0) - 2\phi_{xx}(1) + \phi_{xx}(0)$$
$$= 2[\phi_{xx}(0) - \phi_{xx}(1)]$$

(b) We know that

$$\phi_{xx}(m) = \frac{1}{2\pi}\int_{-\infty}^{\infty} P_{xx}(\omega)e^{j\omega n}\,d\omega$$

$$\therefore \quad \phi_{xx}(0) - \phi_{xx}(1) = \frac{1}{2\pi}\left[\int_{-\omega_c}^{\omega_c} P_{xx}(\omega)\,d\omega - \int_{-\omega_c}^{\omega_c} P_{xx}(\omega)e^{j\omega}\,d\omega\right]$$

[$\because P_{xx}(\omega) = 0$ for $\omega_c < |\omega| < \pi$ (given)]

$$= \frac{1}{\pi}\int_0^{\omega_c} P_{xx}(\omega)\,d\omega - \frac{1}{2\pi}\int_0^{\omega_c} P_{xx}(\omega)(e^{-j\omega} + e^{j\omega})\,d\omega \quad [\because P_{xx}(-\omega) = P_{xx}(\omega)]$$

$$= \frac{1}{\pi}\int_0^{\omega_c} P_{xx}(\omega)(1 - \cos\omega)\,d\omega$$

i.e.,

$$\phi_{xx}(0) - \phi_{xx}(1) = \frac{1}{\pi}\int_0^{\omega_c} P_{xx}(\omega)(1 - \cos\omega)\,d\omega$$

$$= \frac{1}{\pi}\int_0^{\omega_c} P_{xx}(\omega)\left(2\sin^2\frac{\omega}{2}\right)d\omega \quad \ldots(A)$$

As $\sin^2\frac{\omega}{2} \leq \left(\frac{\omega}{2}\right)^2$ in $0 \leq \omega \leq \pi$ $\quad \therefore$ (A) gives us

$$\phi_{xx}(0) - \phi_{xx}(1) \leq \frac{1}{\pi}\int_0^{\omega_c} P_{xx}(\omega)\cdot 2\cdot\frac{\omega_c^2}{4}\,d\omega$$

$$= \frac{\omega_c^2}{2\pi}\underbrace{\int_0^{\omega_c} P_{xx}(\omega)\,d\omega}_{=\phi_{xx}(0)}$$

$$= \frac{\omega_c^2}{2}\phi_{xx}(0)$$

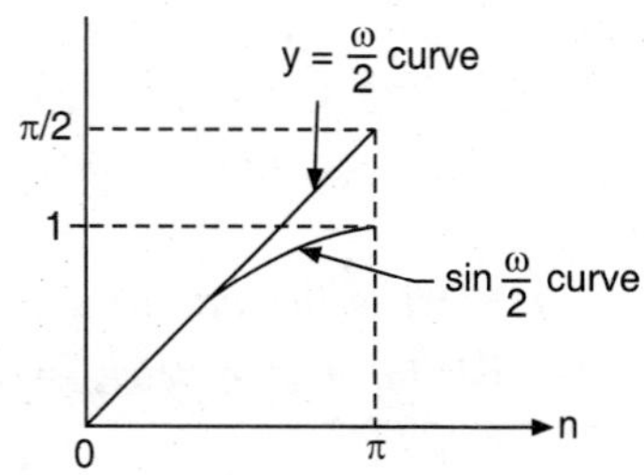

Fig. Prob. 11.2. Curves showing $\sin\frac{\omega}{2} < \frac{\omega}{2}$ for $0 < \omega < \pi$

$$\because \qquad \phi_{xx}(0) = \frac{1}{2\pi}\int_{-\omega_c}^{\omega_c} P_{xx}(\omega)\, d\omega$$

$$= \frac{1}{\pi}\int_{0}^{\omega_c} P_{xx}(\omega)\, d\omega \qquad \text{...}(B)$$

Hence $[\phi_{xx}(0) - \phi_{xx}(1)] \leq \frac{\omega_c^2}{2}\phi_{xx}(0)$ **Ans.**

As $\phi_{xx}(0) - \phi_{xx}(1) = \frac{1}{2}E[(x(n+1) - x(n))^2]$ (result of part (*a*))

and $\phi_{xx}(0) = E[x^2(n)]$

$\therefore$ (*B*) yields $\frac{1}{2}E[(x(n+1) - x(n))^2] \leq \frac{\omega_c^2}{2}E[x^2(n)]$

i.e., $E[(x(n + 1) - x(n))^2] \leq \omega_c^2 E[x^2(n)]$ **Ans.**

(*c*) As $x(n)$ is zero mean stationary sequence

$\therefore \qquad E[x(n + 1) - x(n)] = E[x(n + 1)] - E[x(n)] = m_x - m_x = 0$

Probability $[|x(n + 1) - x(n)| \geq \varepsilon]$ = Prob.$[|x(n + 1) - x(n) - 0| \geq \varepsilon]$

$$= \text{Prob.}[|x(n+1) - x(n) - E\overbrace{[x(n+1) - x(n)]}| \geq \varepsilon]$$

$$\triangleq \text{Prob.}[|y(n) - E[y(n)]| \geq \varepsilon]$$

where $y(n) = x(n + 1) - x(n)$ ...(C)

But Prob.$[|y(n) - E[y(n)]| \geq \varepsilon] \leq \frac{\sigma_y^2}{\varepsilon^2}$ ...(*D*) (due to Chebyshev inequality)

But $\sigma_y^2 = E[(x(n + 1) - x(n))^2]$

$\leq \omega_c^2 \cdot E[x^2(n)]$ ...(*E*) [Proved in part (*b*)]

Putting the values of $y(n)$ and σ_y^2 from (C) and (*E*) in (*D*), we get

$$\text{Prob. } [|x(n + 1) - x(n)| \geq \varepsilon] \leq \frac{\omega_c^2 E[x^2(n)]}{\varepsilon^2}, \ \varepsilon > 0 \qquad \text{Q.E.D.} \qquad \text{...}(F)$$

Thus the absolute sample-to-sample variation of the signal (*i.e.,* LHS of (*F*)) is directly proportional to the mean square value or variance (*viz.* $E[x^2(n)]$, as mean = 0 here) of the signal (RHS of (*F*)) and increases as the square of the bandwidth (ω_c). Thus if bandwidth, ω_c, is small and $E[x^2(n)]$ is small, we would, on the average expect to see small variation from sample to sample.

PROBLEM 11.3: *Consider a continuous-time random process $\{x_a(t)\}$ with its bandlimited power spectrum as depicted in Fig. Prob. 11.3(a). Suppose that we sample $\{x_a(t)\}$ to obtain the discrete-time random process $\{x(n) = x_a(nT)\}$*

(*a*) *What is the auto-covariance sequence of the discrete-time random process.*

(*b*) *For the analog power spectrum above, how should T be chosen so that the discrete-time process is white?*

(*c*) *If the analog power spectrum is as shown in Fig. Prob. 11.3(b), how should T be chosen so that the discrete-time process is white?*

(*d*) *What is the general requirement on the analog process and the sampling period such that the discrete-time process be white?*

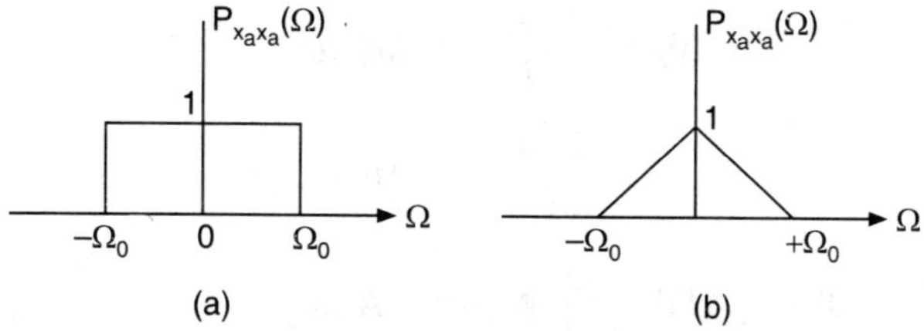

Fig. Prob. 11.3.

SOLUTION:

(*a*) $x(n) \triangleq x_a(nT)$

The auto-correlation function of $x_a(t)$ is

$$\phi_{x_a x_a}(\tau) = E[x_a(t) \cdot x_a(t+\tau)] \qquad \ldots(1)$$

The auto-correlation function of $x(n)$ is

$$\begin{aligned}\phi_{xx}(m) &= E[x(n) \cdot x(n+m)] \\ &= E[x_a(nT) \cdot x_a(nT+mT)] \\ &= \phi_{x_a x_a}(\tau)\Big|_{\tau=mT}\end{aligned}$$

Thus, the discrete-time auto-correlation function $\phi_{xx}(m)$ is a sampled version of the analog auto-correlation function $\phi_{x_a x_a}(\tau)$. Similar is the case of relationship between the auto-covariance $\gamma_{x_a x_a}(\tau)$ of the analog signal $x_a(t)$ and the auto-covariance $\gamma_{xx}(m)$ of the discrete-time sequence.

(*b*) By the sampling theorem, here $x_a(t)$ being a bandlimited signal, we have

$$P_{xx}(e^{j\omega}) = \frac{1}{T}\sum_{r=-\infty}^{\infty} P_{x_a x_a}\left(\frac{\omega}{T} + \frac{2\pi r}{T}\right)$$

$$\because \qquad \Omega T = \omega$$

$$\therefore \qquad \Omega = \frac{\omega}{T}$$

Thus as with the deterministic signals, we require that the sampling period must satisfy

$$\frac{1}{T} \geq 2f_0$$

i.e.,
$$\frac{\pi}{T} \geq \Omega_0 \qquad (\because \; 2\pi f_0 = \Omega_0)$$

(*c*) For the analog spectrum shown in Fig. Prob. 11.3(*b*), if we take

$$f_s = f_0 \quad \text{(sampling at half the mandatory Nyquist criteria)}$$

i.e.,
$$T = \frac{2\pi}{\Omega_0}$$

then due to aliasing the power spectrum of the sampled version would look like as in Fig. Prob. 11.3(*c*). Here the periodicity of ω is 2π but one lobe (corresponding to some *r*, say, *r* = 0) speeds 4π (and not 2π as in unaliased cases). The overall output (top curve) is constant and hence is a white process's spectrum.

(*d*) In discrete-time signals, we require for 'white' case

$$\phi_{xx}(m) = 0,\ m \neq 0$$
$$= \phi_{x_a x_a}(mT) \text{ should be zero at } t = mT,\ m \neq 0$$

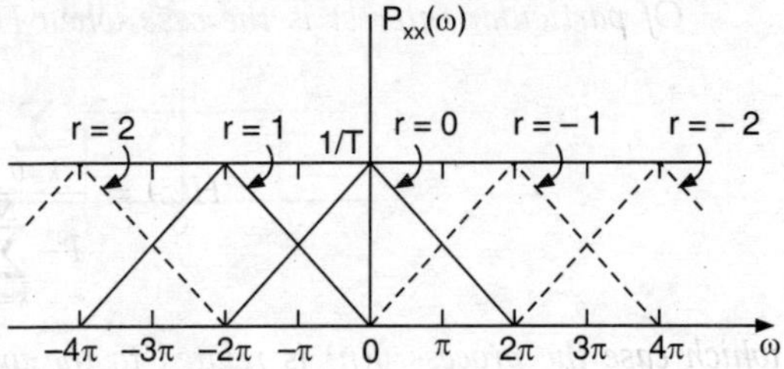

Fig. Prob. 11.3. (*c*) Aliased frequency responses add to give a constant $P_{xx}(\omega)$ red curve

> Hence, any analog signal whose auto-correlation function has zeros equally spaced at intervals of *T* will yield a white discrete-time sequence if sampled with period *T*.

For example, for Fig. Prob. 11.3(*a*)

$$\phi_{x_a x_a}(\tau) = \frac{\sin \Omega_0 t}{\pi\tau}$$
$$\phi_{xx}(m) = \phi_{x_a x_a}(mT)$$
$$= \frac{\sin \Omega_0 mT}{\pi mT},\ -\infty < m < \infty$$

If $$T = \frac{\pi}{\Omega_0},\ i.e.,\ f_s = \frac{\Omega_0}{\pi} = \frac{2\pi f_0}{\pi} = 2f_0$$

which implies that we are observing the Nyquist criteria (not to allow aliasing), then

$$\phi_{xx}(m)\Big|_{T=\frac{\pi}{\Omega_0}} = \frac{\sin m\pi}{\pi m \cdot \dfrac{\pi}{\Omega_0}}$$
$$= \frac{\sin m\pi}{\left(\dfrac{\pi}{\Omega_0}\right)\pi m}$$
$$= \begin{cases} \dfrac{\Omega_0}{\pi}, & m = 0 \\ 0, & m \neq 0 \end{cases}$$

Thus, $\phi_{xx}(m) = \dfrac{\Omega_0}{\pi}\delta(m)$

This implies $P_{xx}(\omega)$ having white spectrum.

PROBLEM 11.4: *It is often appropriate to assume that a wide-sense stationary random process arises as the result of exciting a linear system with a white-noise process. Such processes are called linear processes. Consider a stable linear system as depicted in Fig. prob. 11.4 shown, where x(n) is white noise with zero mean and variance* σ_x^2.

(*a*) *Express the auto-covariance of y(n) in terms of the impulse response, h(n), of the system.*

(*b*) *Use the result of part (a) to express the power spectrum of y(n) in terms of the frequency response of the system.*

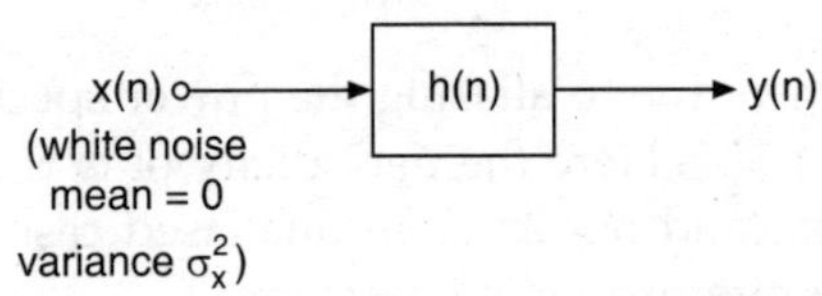

Fig. Prob. 11.4. The given linear system

Of particular interest is the case when H(z) is a rational function of the form

$$H(z) = \frac{\sum_{k=0}^{M} b_k z^{-k}}{1 - \sum_{k=1}^{N} a_k z^{-1}} \qquad \text{...(1)}$$

in which case the process y(n) is related to the white-noise process x(n) by the difference equation

$$y(n) = \sum_{k=1}^{N} a_k y(n-k) + \sum_{k=0}^{M} b_k x(n-k) \qquad \text{...(2)}$$

If all that a_k's are zero, y is called a finite moving-average process. (MA process)
If all the b_k's, except b_0, are zero and $a_N \neq 0$, then y is called an auto-regressive process. (AR process)
If both a_N and b_M are non zero, the process is mixed. (i.e. ARMA process)

(c) Show that the auto-variance sequence $\gamma_{yy}(m)$ of a moving-average process is non-zero only in the interval $|m| \le M$.

(d) Find a general expression for the auto-covariance sequence of an auto-regressive process.

(e) Show that if $b_0 = 1$, the auto-covariance function of an auto-regressive process satisfies the difference equation

$$\gamma_{yy}(0) = \sum_{k=1}^{N} a_k \gamma_{yy}(k) + \sigma_x^2 \qquad \text{...(3)}$$

$$\gamma_{yy}(m) = \sum_{k=1}^{N} a_k \gamma_{yy}(m-k),\ m \ge 1 \qquad \text{...(4)}$$

(f) Use the result of part (e) and the symmetry of $\gamma_{yy}(m)$ to show that the following set of equations is true

$$\sum_{k=1}^{N} a_k \gamma_{yy}(|m-k|) = \gamma_{yy}(m),\ m = 1, 2, \ldots, N \qquad \text{...(5)}$$

Thus, given the first N + 1 covariance values, it can be shown that we can always solve uniquely for the values of a_k and σ_x^2 that characterizes the process.

SOLUTION: Given $x(n)$ a white noise with $m_x = 0$ mean and variance σ_x^2

$\therefore$
$$\phi_{xx}(m) = \sigma_x^2 \delta(m)$$

(a)
$$y(n) = h(n) * x(n)$$

$$= \sum_{k=-\infty}^{\infty} h(k) \cdot x(n-k)$$

$\therefore$
$$m_y = E[y(n)] = \sum_{k=-\infty}^{\infty} h(k) \cdot E[x(n-k)]$$

$$= m_x \sum_{k=-\infty}^{\infty} h(k)$$

$$= 0 \qquad \because m_x = 0 \text{ (given)}$$

$$\phi_{yy}(m) = E[y(n)\, y(n+m)]$$

$$= E\left[\sum_k h(k)\, x(n-k) \cdot \sum_l h(l)\, x(n+m-l)\right]$$

$$= \sum_k \sum_l h(k)\, h(l)\, E[x(n-k) \cdot x(n+m-l)]$$

$$= \sum_k \sum_l h(k)\, h(l)\, \sigma_x^2 \delta(m+k-l)$$

$$= \sum_{k=-\infty}^{\infty} h(k) \cdot h(m+k) \cdot \sigma_x^2$$

$\therefore$
$$\boxed{\begin{aligned}\phi_{yy}(m) &= \sigma_x^2 \sum_{k=-\infty}^{\infty} h(k) h(m+k) \\ &= \sigma_x^2 [h(n) * h(-n)]\end{aligned}} \qquad \text{...(6)}$$

(*b*) Taking *z*-transform on both side of (*b*), we have

$$ZT[\phi_{yy}(m)] = ZT[h(n) * h(-n)] \cdot \sigma_x^2$$

$\therefore$
$$\boxed{\Phi_{yy}(z) = \sigma_x^2 H(z) \cdot H(z^{-1})}$$

(*c*) For a moving average process, a_k's = 0 in $H(z)$ of (1)

$\therefore$
$$H(z)\,|_{MA \text{ case}} = \sum_{k=0}^{M} b_k z^{-k}$$

$\therefore$
$$\Phi_{yy}(z) = \sigma_x^2 H(z) \cdot H(z^{-1})$$

$$= \sigma_x^2 \left(\sum_{k=0}^{M} b_k z^{-k}\right)\left(\sum_{k=0}^{M} b_k z^{k}\right) \qquad \text{...(7)}$$

$$\triangleq \sigma_x^2 \sum_{m=-M}^{M} \phi_{yy}(m)\, z^{-m} \,** \qquad \text{...(8)}$$

Thus $\phi_{yy}(m)$ is non-zero only for $|m| \le M$ and $\phi_{yy}(m) = 0$ for $|m| > M$.

(*d*) For an auto-regressive process, all b_k's except b_0 are zero

$\therefore$
$$H(z) = \frac{b_0}{1 - \sum_{k=1}^{N} \alpha_k z^{-k}}$$

$$\triangleq \frac{b_0}{\prod_{k=1}^{N} (1 - \alpha_k z^{-1})}$$

where $|a_k| < 1$ for stability of $H(z)$.

** **Note:** In the expression of (7), minimum power of *z* is z^{-M} and maximum power of *z* is z^{+M}. Thus we can always write (7) in the form of (8) where

$$\phi_{yy}(m) = \sum_{r=0}^{M} b_r\, b_{m+r}.$$

As
$$\Phi_{yy}(z) = \sigma_x^2 \cdot H(z) \cdot H(z^{-1})$$
$$= \frac{\sigma_x^2 \cdot b_0^2}{\prod_{k=1}^{N}(1-\alpha_k z^{-1})(1-\alpha_k z)}$$

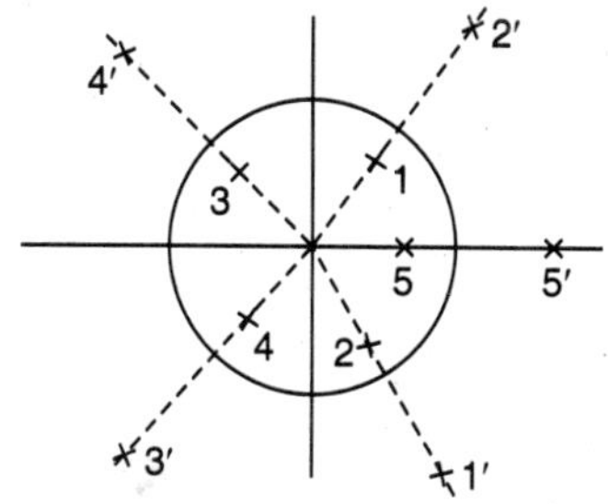
Fig. Prob. 11.4. (a) Typical pole pairs of $\phi_{yy}(z)$

Thus the pole-zero plot of $\Phi_{yy}(z)$ as shown in Fig. Prob. 11.4(a). A pair of pole $z = a_k$, $z = a_k^{-1}$ contributes a sequence of the form $a_k^m u(m)$ and $a_k^{-m}u(-m)$** and collectively, a sequence of the form $a_k^{|m|}$**. Thus we expect

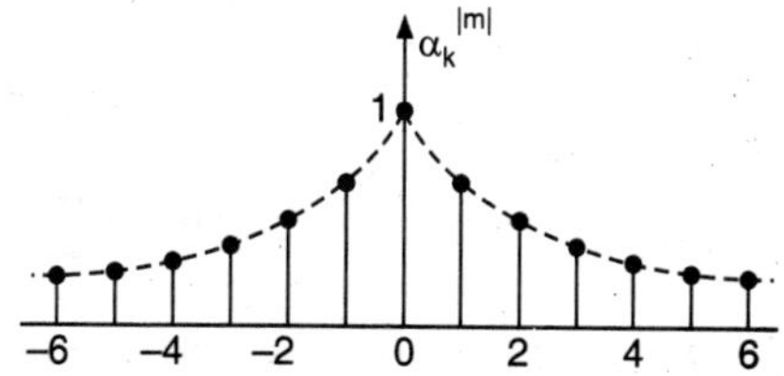
Fig. Prob. 11.4. (b)

$$\phi_{yy}(m) = \sum_{k=1}^{N} A_k \alpha_k^{|m|}$$

Thus, in general

$$\boxed{\phi_{yy}(m) = \sum_{k=1}^{N} A_k \alpha_k^{|m|}} \quad \text{for AR process case} \qquad \ldots(9)$$

(e) If $b_0 = 1$ then for AR case $H(z) = \dfrac{1}{1-\sum_{k=1}^{N} a_k z^{-k}}$

$$\therefore \qquad y(n) = x(n) + \sum_{k=1}^{N} a_k y(n-k)$$
$$\phi_{yy}(m) = E[y(n)\ y(n+m)] = \phi_{yy}(-m)$$
$$= E\left[\left(x(n) + \sum_{k=1}^{N} a_k y(n-k)\right)(y(n+m))\right]$$
$$= E\sum_{k=1}^{N} a_k y(n-k)\cdot y(n+m) + E[x(n)\cdot y(n+m)]$$

If $m = 0$,

$$\phi_{yy}(0) = \sum_{k=1}^{N} a_k E[y(n-k)\ y(n)] + E\left[x(n)\cdot\left\{x(n) + \sum_{k=1}^{N} a_k y(n-k)\right\}\right]$$
$$= \sum_{k=1}^{N} a_k \phi_{yy}(k) + \sigma_x^2 \quad \because x(n) \text{ and } y(n-k) \text{ are fully uncorrelated}$$
$$\therefore \quad E[y(n)\cdot y(n-k)] = 0$$

** **Note:** that factorization of $\Phi_{yy}(z)$ would have pairs $\dfrac{\overline{A}_k}{1-\alpha_k z^{-1}} + \dfrac{\overline{B}_k}{1-\alpha_k z}$ which inverse z-transform to $\alpha_k^m u(m)$ and $\alpha_k^{-m}(-m)$ and collectively to $(\alpha_k^m u(m) + \alpha_k^{-m}(-m)) = \alpha_k^{|m|}$

If $m \neq 0$, then

$$\phi_{yy}(m) = \sum_{k=1}^{N} a_k E[y(n-k) \cdot y(n+m)]$$

$$+ E\left[x(n)\left\{x(n+m) + \sum_{k=1}^{N} a_k y(n+m-k)\right\}\right], \ m \geq L$$

$$= \sum_{k=1}^{N} a_k \phi_{yy}(-m-k) + 0 + 0, \ m \geq 1 \quad \because E[x(n) \cdot x(n+m)] = 0 \text{ and}$$

$E[x(n)\, y(n + m - k)] = 0$
being uncorrelated

$$\therefore \quad \phi_{yy}(m) = \sum_{k=1}^{N} a_k \phi_{yy}(m-k), \ m \geq 1 \ \because \phi_{yy}(m) = \phi_{yy}(-m)$$

As $m_y = 0 \quad \therefore \quad \phi_{yy}(m) = \gamma_{yy}(m) \ \forall \ m$

Hence

$$\gamma_{yy}(0) = \phi_{yy}(0) = \sum_{k=1}^{N} a_k \gamma_{yy}(k) + \sigma_x^2 \quad \text{...[10(a)]}$$

$$\gamma_{yy}(m) = \phi_{yy}(m) = \sum_{k=1}^{N} a_k \gamma_{yy}(m-k), \ m \geq 1 \quad \text{...[10(b)]}$$

Ans.

(*f*) As $\gamma_{yy}(m) = \gamma_{yy}(-m)$, therefore, [10(*b*)] yields

$$\gamma_{yy}(m) = \sum_{k=1}^{N} a_k \gamma_{yy}(|m-k|), \ 1 \leq k \leq N$$

Ans.

Thus, gives $N + 1$ first auto-covariance values, we use these in $N + 1$ equation in [10(*a*)] and [10(*b*)] to determine all a_k's, $k = 1, 2, \ldots, N$ and σ_x^2.

CHAPTER 12

Multirate Digital Signal Processing

12.1 PRELUDE

In various practical applications of digital signal processing, we are required to change the sampling rate of the signal. The new sampling rate may be higher (up conversion or interpolation) or lower (down conversion or decimation), than the original sampling rate. In telecommunication systems, for example, which handle different types of signals such as speech, video, teletype, fascimile or multi-media, to mention a few, there is a need to transmit these signals at different sampling frequencies to cater for the necessary bandwidth of those signals. Also, a complex system may be getting its inputs from various sources/sensors, each (or some) of them sending data of different sampling rates (f_{s_1}, f_{s_2}, ...,). There is essential requirement to mix the data of diverse inputs, and this needs a common sampling frequency, say f_s, before further processing. Hence, the various signals sampled at f_{s_1}, f_{s_2}, ..., must be converted to a common sampling rate f_s. The process of converting a signal from one sampling frequency to another (different) sampling frequency is called multirate digital signal processing.

The sampling rate conversion of a digital signal may be done by one of the following methods:

(*i*) Pass the digital signal through a *D* to *A* convertor and obtain equivalent analog signal $x_a(t)$. Thereafter, we can sample $x_a(t)$ at a desired sampling rate by passing it through an *A* to *D* convertor.

(*ii*) Direct sampling rate conversion, entirely in digital domain (*i.e.*, multirate digital signal processing).

The main advantage in the first method is ease of selection of any desired new sampling rate. There is no necessity of special relationship between the old and the new sampling rates. (We shall explain this relationship as we progress). However, there is a major disadvantage as the signal gets distorted due to *D* to *A* conversion and then *A* to *D* conversion followed by quantization. The sampling rate conversion performed entirely in digital domain is relatively free from aforementioned distortions.

We, in this chapter, shall describe sampling rate conversion and multirate signal processing in digital domain. We shall cover sampling rate conversion first/decimation (*i.e.*, down conversion), followed by interpolation (*i.e.*, up conversion) and thereafter sampling rate conversion by a rational factor $\frac{I}{D}$. Several applications of multirate DSP are also covered which include implementation of narrow band filters, digital filter banks and quadrature mirror filters used in sub-band coding.

12.2 INTRODUCTION

The sampling rate conversion in digital domain may be viewed as a linear filtering operation. The operation is shown in Fig. 12.1.

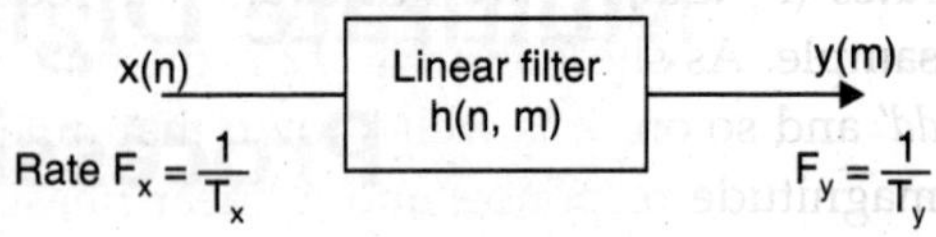

Fig. 12.1. Block diagram for a Sampling Rate Convertor (SRC)

Let $x(n)$ be the given digital signal obtained by sampling analog signal $x_a(t)$ at sampling rate F_x. Then the inter-sample interval is $T_x = \frac{1}{F_x}$, *i.e.*, $F_x = \frac{1}{T_x}$. After the sampling rate conversion from sampling rate F_x to F_y, we obtain the digital signal $y(m)$. Clearly, $F_y = \frac{1}{T_y}$, where T_y is the inter-sample interval for the signal $y(m)$. We assume

$$\frac{F_y}{F_x} = \frac{I}{D} = \frac{T_x}{T_y} \qquad \ldots(12.1)$$

where $\frac{I}{D}$ is a rational number, *i.e.*, I and D are relatively prime integers. The system shown in the block diagram, (Fig. 12.1) which performs sampling rate conversion from F_x to F_y, on the signal $x(n)$ to yield $y(m)$, is a time-variant impulse linear filter. The overall filter $h(n, m)$ may be a single filter or may constitute a number of linear-phase (polyphase) filters. This aspect will be explained in the subsequent Sections. The output $y(m)$ is the convolution of input signal $x(n)$ and $h(n, m)$.

To understand the process of sampling rate conversion, consider a signal $x_a(t)$ sampled by sampling rates F_x, and then by sampling rate F_y to obtain samples $x(n)$ and $y(m)$, respectively.

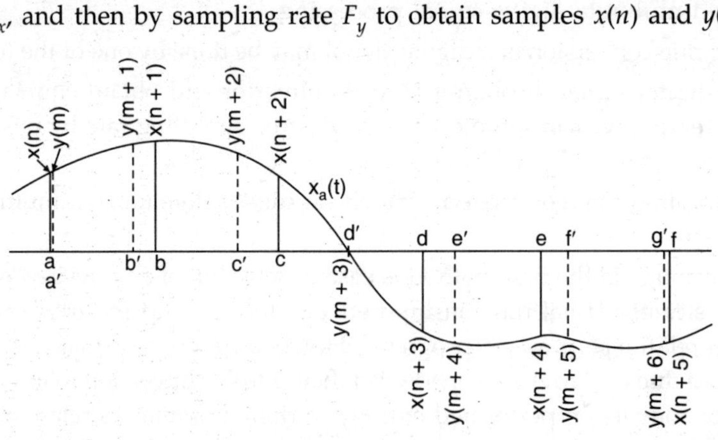

Fig. 12.2. SRC viewed as a Linear Filtering Process (SRC: Sampling Rate Converter)

In Fig. 12.2, the signal $x_a(t)$ is the analog (continuous) signal. It has been sampled first by sampling rate F_x. Such samples are shown by $x(n)$, $x(n + 1)$, …, $x(n + 5)$, by solid lines. The signal

$x_a(t)$ is also sampled by sampling rate F_y. In Fig. 12.2, we have assumed F_y greater than F_x. Signal sampled at sampling rate F_y are shown by $y(m)$, $y(m + 1)$, ..., $y(m + 6)$, as dashed lines. To drive home our point, we take samples $x(n)$ and $y(m)$ at same time instant (shown as a, a'). We indicate time instances a, b, c, d, e, f for samples $x(n)$, $x(n + 1)$, ..., etc. We indicate time instances a', b', c', d'... etc. for new samples $y(m)$, $y(m + 1)$, $y(m + 2)$..., etc. Note that the instances b', c', d'..., etc. appear before the instances b, c, d, ..., respectively, since T_y is lesser than T_x ($\because$ $F_y > F_x$ here). It can, therefore, be stated that $y(m)$ sequence is a time-shifted version of $x(n)$. If the two sampling rates (F_x and F_y) are not equal, the required amount of time shifting will vary from sample to sample. As shown in Fig. 12.2, the time shift $b'b$ is lesser than $c'c$. The time shift cc' is lesser than dd' and so on. It is well known that time shift can be realized by an all-pass filter (which has flat magnitude response) and a linear phase response. This implies that a time delay of, say, τ_i, can be obtained by a filter having frequency response $e^{-j\omega\tau_i}$.

Hence, the rate conversion can be achieved by using a set of linear phase all-pass filters that have the same flat magnitude response but generate different time delays τ_i.

For understanding the general case of sampling rate conversion: $F_y = F_x \cdot \frac{I}{D}$, where $\frac{I}{D}$ is a rational number, it would be appropriate to consider the cases of $F_y = \frac{F_x}{D}$, *i.e.*, F_y lower than F_x (down sampling) and $F_y = IF_x$, *i.e.*, F_y higher than F_x (up sampling). We also assume that I and D are relative prime integers.

12.3 DECIMATION BY A FACTOR D: (DOWN CONVERSION: D TO 1)

Assume a digital signal $x(n)$ with spectrum $X(\omega)$ to be down sampled by an integer D. We also assume that $X(\omega)$ is non-zero in the frequency interval $0 \le |\omega| \le \pi$. This implies that $|F_{max}|$ for $x(n)$ is equal to $\frac{F_x}{2}$, as per the sampling theorem. Here, F_x is the sampling rate of $x_a(t)$ to yield $x(n)$ and the highest frequency of $x(n)$ is $\frac{F_x}{2}$. If we decrease the sampling rate from F_x to $\frac{F_x}{D}$, the resulting signal will be an aliased version of $x(n)$ with a folding frequency of $\frac{1}{2} \cdot \frac{F_x}{D}$. To avoid aliasing, we must first reduce the bandwidth of $x(n)$ from F_{max} to $F'_{max} = \frac{1}{D} F_{max} = \frac{F_x}{2D}$, *i.e.*, $\omega'_{max} = \frac{\pi}{D}$. It is also assumed that the vital information is not lost (or minimally affected). When we shorten the bandwidth of $x(n)$ from F_{max} to $\frac{F_{max}}{D}$. Now down sampling the bandwidth reduced signal by a factor D will not cause aliasing.

Thus, the decimation process requires passing $x(n)$ through a low-pass filter, $h(n)$, characterized by .

$$H_D(\omega) = \begin{cases} 1, & |\omega| \le \frac{\pi}{D} \\ 0, & \text{otherwise} \end{cases} \qquad \text{...(12.2)}$$

The filter $H_D(\omega)$ (or $h(n)$) eliminates the spectrum of $X(\omega)$ in the range $\frac{\pi}{D} \le \omega \le \pi$. We have assumed that the information of $x(n)$ in the range $|\omega| \le \frac{\pi}{D}$ is of main interest.

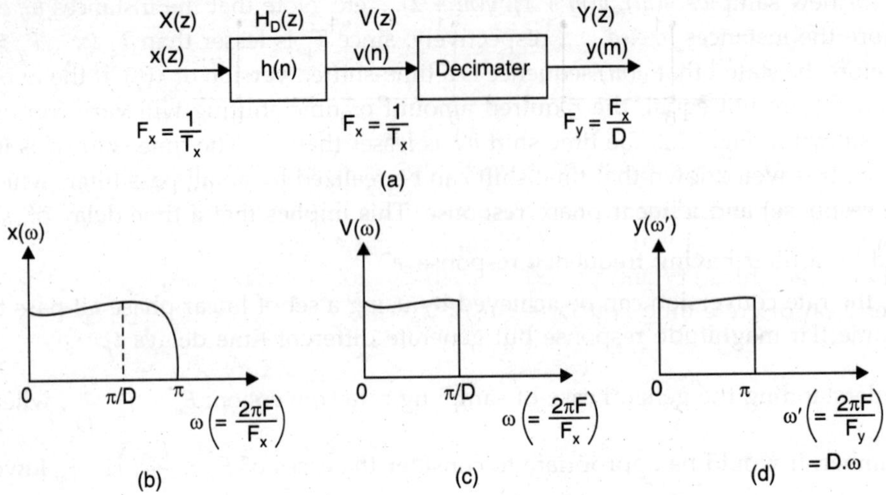

Fig. 12.3. (*a*) Decimation by a factor *D*: block diagram (*b*), (*c*), (*d*) frequency spectra of applied signal *x*(*n*), signal v(*n*) and the decimated signal *y*(*m*)

Figure 12.3(*a*) shows the basic Decimation system. Spectrum of the applied signal $x(n)$ which is non-zero for $0 \le |\omega| \le \pi$ is shown in Fig. 12.3(*b*).

After band limiting $x(n)$ to $0 \le |\omega| \le \frac{\pi}{D}$, and denoting it by $v(n)$, its spectrum $V(\omega)$ in shown in Fig. 12.3(*c*). As $h(n)$ is a low-pass signal with its characteristic as given in (12.2), the spectrum $V(\omega)$ is a replica of $X(\omega)$ for $0 \le |\omega| \le \frac{\pi}{D}$. Now we decrease the sampling rate of $v(n)$ from F_x to $\frac{F_x}{D}$, and obtain $y(m)$. The scale ω on x-axis is always a normalized value given by $\frac{(2\pi \times \text{actual frequency } F)}{(\text{sampling rate})}$. Hence, in Fig. 12.3(*d*), $\omega' = \frac{2\pi F}{F_y} = \frac{2\pi F}{(F_x/D)} = D\left(\frac{2\pi F}{F_x}\right) = D\omega$. Thus, when $\omega = \frac{\pi}{D}$ in Fig. 12.3(*c*) where sampling rate is F_x, it maps to $\omega' = D\left(\frac{\pi}{D}\right) = \pi$ in Fig. 12.3(*d*), where the sampling rate is $\frac{F_x}{D}$.

The output $v(n)$ of the LPF $h(n)$ is given by

$$v(n) = x(n) * h(n) \text{ (i.e., convolution)}$$

$$= \sum_{k=0}^{\infty} h(k)x(n-k) \qquad \ldots(12.3)$$

when $v(n)$ is down sampled by a factor D, we get

$$y(m) = v(mD) \qquad \ldots(12.4)$$

$$= \sum_{k=0}^{\infty} h(k) \cdot x(mD-k) \quad \text{(replacing } n \text{ by } mD \text{ on both sides of 12.3)} \qquad \ldots(12.5)$$

Note that conversion of the form (12.4) is a linear operation and is time-variant. Hence, the overall linear operation (*i.e.*, linear filtering followed by down sampling) on $x(n)$ is NOT time-invariant.

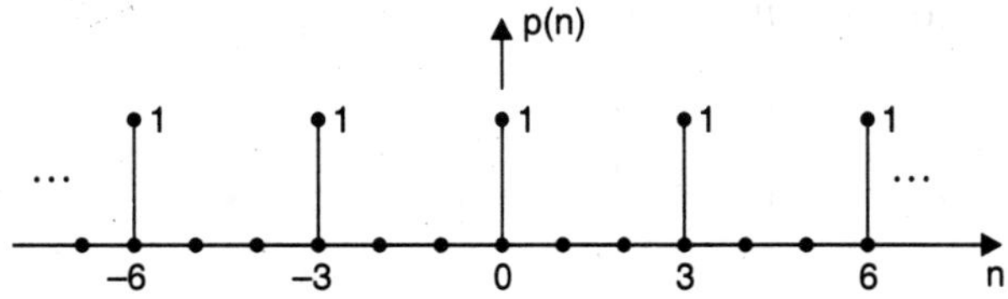

Fig. 12.4. $p(n)$ is a train of unit-time impulses with period $D = 3$ here

We are interested in finding the complete spectrum of decimated signal $y(m)$ in terms of the spectrum of the input signal $x(n)$. For this purpose, we need an expression of a periodic discrete-time impulses of height unity and period D, such as shown in Fig. 12.4. It can be easily shown (see Chapter 2 on discrete-time Fourier series) that

$$p(n) = \frac{1}{D}\sum_{k=0}^{D-1} e^{j\omega_0 kn}, \; \omega_0 = \frac{2\pi}{D} \qquad \text{...(12.6)}$$

$$= \frac{1}{D}\sum_{k=0}^{D-1} e^{j2\pi kn/D} \qquad \text{...(12.7)}$$

The train of unit samples is defined by

$$p(n) = \begin{cases} 1, & n = 0, \pm D, \pm 2D \ldots \\ 0, & \text{otherwise} \end{cases} \qquad \text{...(12.8)}$$

Note that $p(mD) = 1$, where m and D are integers, for all m. Hence, the signal $\tilde{v}(n)$ defined by $v(n) \cdot p(n)$ satisfies

$$\tilde{v}(n) = v(n) \cdot p(n) \qquad \text{...(12.9a)}$$

$$= \begin{cases} v(n), & n = 0, \pm D, \pm 2D, \ldots, \\ 0, & \text{otherwise} \end{cases} \qquad \text{...(12.9b)}$$

This implies that $\tilde{v}(n)$ is a decimated version of $v(n)$ with decimation factor D. Note that we can write

$$\begin{aligned} y(m) &= v(mD) && \text{(due to (12.4))} \\ &= v(mD) \cdot p(mD) && (\because \; p(mD) = 1 \text{ for all } m) \\ &= \tilde{v}(mD) \; \text{(using 12.9(a))} && \text{...(12.10)} \end{aligned}$$

In order to determine spectrum of $y(m)$, we first find z-transform, $Y(z)$ of $y(m)$ and then evaluate $Y(z)$ on the unit circle $|z| = 1$, to obtain $Y(e^{j\omega_y})$ or $Y(\omega_y)$.

Z-transforms of $y(m)$:

$$Y(z) = \sum_{m=-\infty}^{\infty} y(m) z^{-m} \text{ (by definition)}$$

$$= \sum_{m=-\infty}^{\infty} \tilde{v}(mD) \cdot z^{-m} \quad \because \; y(m) = \tilde{v}(mD) \text{ due to (12.10)} \qquad \text{...(12.11)}$$

Put $mD = m'$ ∵ when $m = \pm\infty$, $m' = \pm\infty$

Hence (dropping dashes)

$$Y(z) = \sum_{m=-\infty}^{\infty} \tilde{v}(m)\, z^{-m/D}$$

$$= \sum_{m=-\infty}^{\infty} [v(m) \cdot p(m)] \cdot z^{-m/D} \qquad \text{[due to 12.9(}a\text{)]}$$

$$= \sum_{m=-\infty}^{\infty} \left[v(m) \cdot \left(\frac{1}{D} \sum_{k=0}^{D-1} e^{j2\pi km/D} \right) \right] z^{-m/D} \qquad \text{(due to 12.7)}$$

i.e.,

$$Y(z) = \frac{1}{D} \sum_{k=0}^{D-1} \sum_{m=-\infty}^{\infty} v(m)(e^{-j2\pi k/D} \cdot z^{1/D})^{-m}$$

$$= \frac{1}{D} \sum_{k=0}^{D-1} V(e^{-j2\pi k/D} \cdot z^{1/D}) \qquad \text{...(12.12)}$$

Using $V(z) = H_D(z) \cdot X(z)$, where $H(z)$ is system function of the low pass filter shown in Fig. 12.3(a), (12.12) gives us

$$Y(z) = \frac{1}{D} \sum_{k=0}^{D-1} H_D(e^{-j2\pi k/D} z^{1/D})\, X(e^{-j2\pi k/D} \cdot z^{1/D}) \qquad \text{...(12.13)}$$

We denote

F: actual frequency in Hz of the analog signal

F_x; rate of sampling of $x(n)$. $F_x = \dfrac{1}{T_x}$

F_y; rate of sampling of $y(m)$. Also, $F_y = \dfrac{F_x}{D} = \dfrac{1}{T_y}$

ω_x: radian frequency of $x(n)$ *i.e.* $\omega_x = \dfrac{2\pi F}{F_x}$

ω_y: radian frequency of $y(m)$ *i.e.* $\omega_y = \dfrac{2\pi F}{F_y}$

Hence

$$\omega_y = \frac{2\pi F}{F_y} = \frac{2\pi F}{F_x/D} = D\frac{2\pi F}{F_x} = D\omega_x$$

i.e.,

$$\omega_y = D\omega_x \qquad \text{...(12.14)}$$

This implies that the frequency range $0 \le |\omega_x| \le \dfrac{\pi}{D}$ is stretched into the corresponding frequency range $0 \le |\omega_y| \le \pi$, by decimation (down sampling D to 1) $x(n)$ as expected.

Putting $z = e^{j\omega_y}$ in (12.13), we can write

$$Y(\omega_y) = \frac{1}{D}\sum_{k=0}^{D-1} H_D\left(\frac{\omega_y - 2\pi k}{D}\right) X\left(\frac{\omega_y - 2\pi k}{D}\right) \quad \text{...(12.15)}$$

If the decimation filter $H_D(\omega)$ is properly designed, the aliasing is eliminated and consequently all but the first term in (12.15) will vanish. Hence, we have

$$Y(\omega_y) = \frac{1}{D} H_D\left(\frac{\omega_y}{D}\right) X\left(\frac{\omega_y}{D}\right)$$

$$\boxed{Y(\omega_y) = \frac{1}{D} X\left(\frac{\omega_y}{D}\right)} \qquad \because H_D(\omega) = 1 \text{ for } |\omega| \le \frac{\pi}{D}$$

$$\text{or } H_D\left(\frac{\omega_y}{D}\right) = 1 \text{ for } |\omega_y| \le \pi \quad \text{...(12.16)}$$

The spectra of various signals $x(n)$, $v(n)$, $y(m)$ and of the LPF $h(n)$ are shown in Fig. 12.5.

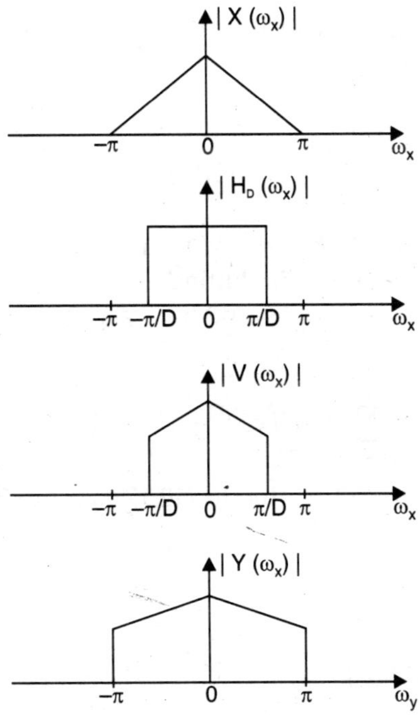

Fig. 12.5. Spectra of signals in the Decimation of $x(n)$ by a factor D to obtain $y(m)$. $H_D(\omega_x)$ is the frequency response of the low-pass filter $h(n)$ and this LPF is ideal

12.4 INTERPOLATION BY A FACTOR I (UP CONVERSION 1 TO I)

The increase in sampling rate F_x to F_y, such that $F_y = IF_x$ is termed as interpolation by a factor I. To do so, we add $I - 1$ new samples in between two successive samples of $x(n)$. We first add (interpolate) $I - 1$ zeros between two successive samples of $x(n)$. Then passing such interpolated (by $I - 1$ zeros) $x(n)$ through a low pass filter, the $I - 1$ zeros become the samples of desired height as if the analog version of $x(n)$ (*i.e.* $x_a(t)$) were sampled at sampling rate of F_y such that $F_y = IF_x$.

Figure 12.6 shows the steps followed to get interpolated signal $y(m)$ from the input signal $x(n)$.

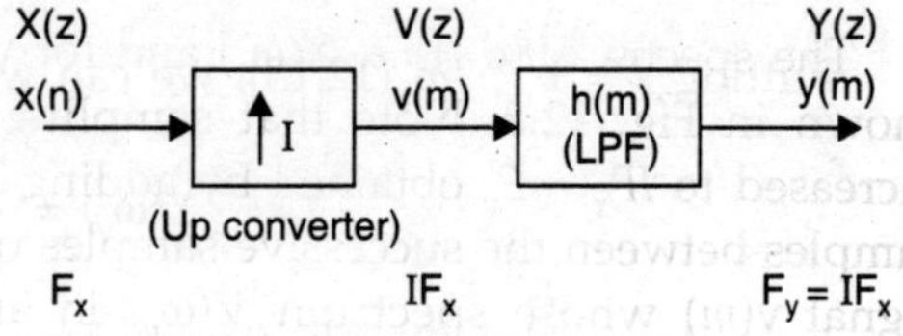

Fig. 12.6. Steps in Interpolation

The up convertor block shown by $\boxed{\uparrow I}$ adds $I - 1$ zeros between successive samples of $x(n)$, to obtain $\nu(m)$ see Figs. 12.7(*a*) and (*b*). The low pass filter $h(m)$ converts $\nu(m)$ to $y(m)$ thus converting $I - 1$ zeros of $\nu(m)$ to appropriate heights of desired interpolated samples. Thus, we obtain $y(m)$ as shown in Fig. 12.7(*c*). The LPF $h(m)$ operates at sampling rate $F_y = IF_x$. Let

$$\nu(m) = \begin{cases} x\left(\dfrac{m}{I}\right), & m = 0, \pm I, \pm 2I, \ldots, \\ 0, & \text{otherwise} \end{cases} \qquad \ldots(12.17)$$

The sampling rate of $\nu(m)$ is IF_x which is the same as we desire for the output signal $y(m)$. The z-transform of $\nu(m)$ is obtained by

$$V(z) = \sum_{m=-\infty}^{\infty} \nu(m) z^{-m} \qquad \ldots(12.18)$$

Note that m is multiple of I in (12.18) since $\nu(m) = 0$ when m is not multiple of I due to (12.17). Putting $m = Im'$ in (12.18), the limits of summation would be $m' = -\infty$ to $+\infty$. We get

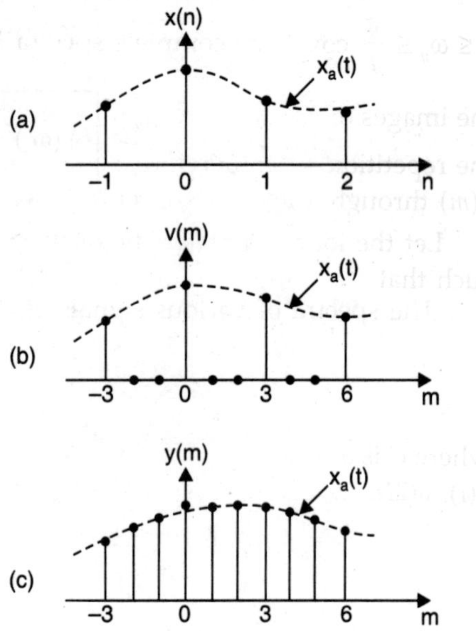

Fig. 12.7. Signals $x(n)$, $x_a(t)$, $\nu(m)$ and $y(m) \cdot I = 3$

$$V(z) = \sum_{m'=-\infty}^{\infty} \nu(m'I) z^{-m'I} \qquad \ldots(12.19)$$

Nothing that $\nu(m'I) = x(m')$ for all m' due to (12.17), and dropping dashes from (12.19), we finally get

$$V(z) = \sum_{m=-\infty}^{\infty} x(m) z^{-mI} \qquad \ldots(12.20)$$

$$= X(z^I) \qquad \ldots(12.21)$$

The corresponding spectrum of $\nu(m)$ is obtained by putting $z = e^{j\omega_y}$ on both sides of (12.21), *i.e.*

$$V(\omega_y) = X(\omega_y I) \qquad \ldots(12.22)$$

where $\omega_y = \dfrac{2\pi F}{F_y}$. As $F_y = IF_x$, we readily get

$$\omega_y = \frac{2\pi F}{IF_x}$$

i.e..

$$\omega_y = \frac{\omega_x}{I} \qquad \ldots(12.23)$$

The spectra of $x(n)$ *i.e.* $X(\omega_x)$ and for $v(m)$ *i.e.* $V(\omega_y)$ are shown in Fig. 12.8. Note that sampling rate F_x for $x(n)$ increased to $IF_x = F_y$ obtained by adding $I - 1$ zero valued samples between the successive samples of $x(n)$ results in a signal $v(m)$ whose spectrum $V(\omega_y)$ in an I-fold periodic repetition of input signal spectrum $X(\omega_x)$.

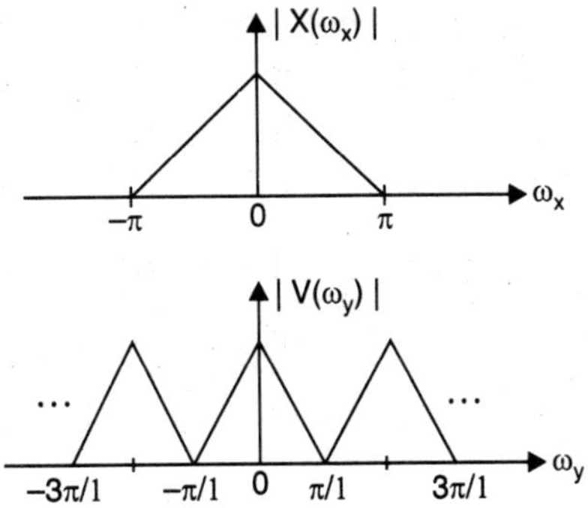

Fig. 12.8. Spectra of $x(n)$ and $v(m) \cdot V(\omega_y) = X(\omega_y I)$

As only the frequency components of $X(\omega_x)$ in the range $0 \le \omega_y \le \frac{\pi}{I}$ cover the complete spectra $X(\omega_x)$ *viz.* $0 \le \omega_x \le \pi$, the images of $X(\omega_x)$ above $\omega_y = \frac{\pi}{I}$ are of no use (being only the repetition) and, therefore, should be rejected by passing $v(m)$ through a low pass filter $h(m)$ as shown in Fig. 12.6.

Let the ideal characteristic of the frequency response of the LPF $h(m)$ be denoted by $H_I(\omega_y)$ such that

$$H_I(\omega_y) = \begin{cases} C, & 0 \le |\omega_y| \le \dfrac{\pi}{I} \\ 0, & \text{otherwise} \end{cases} \qquad \ldots(12.24)$$

where C is a scale factor, and is required to normalize the interpolated output $y(m)$ such that $y(0)$, $y(I)$, $y(2I)$, ..., equals, respectively, $x(0)$, $x(1)$, $x(2)$, ... Using (12.22) and (12.24) we have

$$Y(\omega_y) = \begin{cases} CV(\omega_y) = CX(\omega_y I), & 0 \le |\omega_y| \le \dfrac{\pi}{I} \\ 0, & \text{otherwise} \end{cases} \qquad \ldots(12.25)$$

To find the value of C

As $$y(m) = \frac{1}{2\pi}\int_{-\pi}^{\pi} Y(\omega_y)e^{jm\omega_y}\, d\omega_y \qquad \text{(by taking IDTFT)}$$

i.e., $$y(m) = \frac{1}{2\pi}\int_{-\pi/I}^{\pi/I} CX(\omega_y I)\cdot e^{jm\omega_y}\, d\omega_y \qquad \ldots(12.26)$$

because $Y(\omega_y) = 0$ outside the range $-\frac{\pi}{I} \le \omega_y \le \frac{\pi}{I}$ due to relation (12.25)

Putting $\omega_y I = \omega_x$, when $\omega_y = \pm\frac{\pi}{I}$, then $\omega_x = \pm\pi$ and only $d\omega_y = \frac{1}{I}d\omega_x$. Doing so, (12.26) reduces to

$$y(m) = \frac{C}{2\pi I}\int_{-\pi}^{\pi} X(\omega_x)e^{jm\omega_x/I}\, d\omega_x \qquad \ldots(12.27)$$

putting $m = 0$ both sides, we get

$$y(0) = \left(\frac{C}{I}\right)\cdot\frac{1}{2\pi}\int_{-\pi}^{\pi} X(\omega_x)\cdot e^{j0\omega_x}\, d\omega_x$$

or $$y(0) = \frac{C}{I}x(0) \qquad \ldots(12.28)$$

To make $y(0) = x(0)$, we must have $C = 1$. Check that, putting $C = I$, in (12.27), we can write

$$y(mI) = \frac{1}{2\pi}\int_{-\pi}^{\pi} X(\omega_x)\, e^{jm\omega_x}\, dx$$

$$\therefore \quad y(mI) = x(m) \qquad \text{...(12.29)}$$

i.e. $\quad y(0), y(I), y(2I), \ldots = x(0), x(1), x(2), \ldots$, respectively.

Hence, putting $C = I$, each I-th sample of $y(m)$ becomes equal to the respective (m/I-th) sample of $x(n)$, as is desired in interpolation process.

Since the output $y(m)$ from the LPF $h(m)$ can be expressed as a convolution of $v(m)$ and $h(m)$

$$\therefore \quad y(m) = v(m) * h(m)$$

or

$$y(m) = \sum_{\substack{k=-\infty \\ k,\ \text{multiple of } 1}}^{\infty} h(m-k)\cdot v(k) \qquad \text{...(12.30)}$$

We have taken $k = -2I, -I, 0, I, 2I, \ldots$ (*i.e.* multiple of I) because $v(k) = 0$, whenever k is not multiple of I, due to relation (12.17).

Put $k = Ik'$ in (12.30), then the limit of series will have $k' = \ldots, -2, -1, 0, 1, 2, \ldots$ (*i.e.* continuous integers).

$$\therefore \quad y(m) = \sum_{k'=-\infty}^{\infty} h(m - Ik')v(Ik') \qquad \text{...(12.31)}$$

Putting $v(Ik') = x(k')$, due to (12.17) and finally, dropping dashes, we obtain

$$y(m) = \sum_{k=-\infty}^{\infty} h(m - kI)x(k) \qquad \text{...(12.32)}$$

This is the convolution relation between input $x(n)$ and the time invariant LPF $h(m)$.

12.5 SAMPLING RATE CONVERSION BY A RATIONAL FACTOR *I/D*

If we wish to achieve sampling rate conversion from F_x to F_y by a rational factor $\frac{I}{D}$ *i.e.* $F_y = \left(\frac{I}{D}\right)F_x$, it is equivalent to up sampling by a factor I and down sampling by a factor D. It is possible to achieve this sampling rate conversion by first performing interpolation (up conversion) by factor I followed by decimation (down conversion) by the factor D. Hence, we cascade the interpolator ($\uparrow I$) by a decimator ($\downarrow D$) as shown in Fig. 12.9.

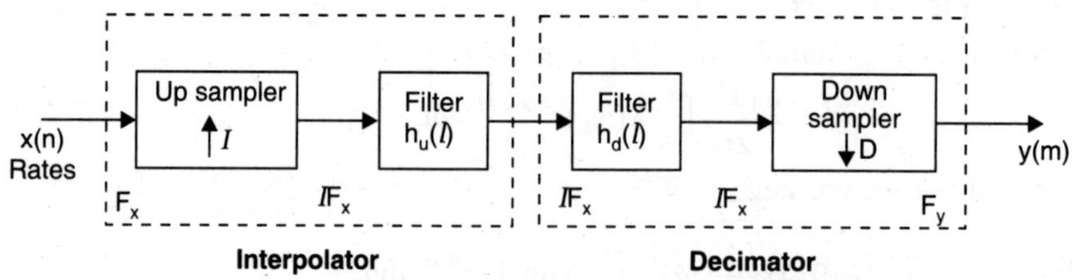

Fig. 12.9. How to achieve sampling rate conversion by a rational factor *I/D*

As upsampler is followed a LPF, say, $h_u(l)$ and a down sampler is preceded by a LPF, say, $h_d(l)$, as shown in Fig. 12.9. Both the LPF's operate at the same rate namely IF_x, and hence can be combined into a single LPF filter with impulse response, say, $h(l)$. The revised and efficient arrangement is shown in Fig. 12.10. The frequency response of $h(l)$ must incorporate the filtering operations/requirement of both the filters $h_u(l)$ and $h_d(l)$.

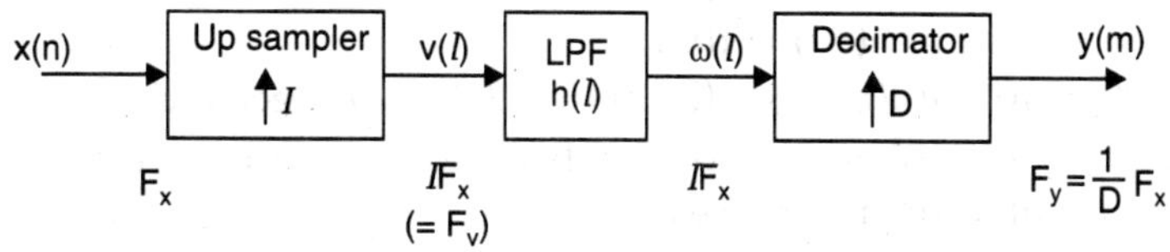

Fig. 12.10. Combining LPFs $h_u(l)$ and $h_d(l)$ of Fig. 12.9 by a composite LPF, $h(l)$, method to achieve sampling rate conversion by a factor I/D

Hence $h(l)$ should have the frequency characteristic given by

$$H(\omega_v) = \begin{cases} I, & 0 \le |\omega_v| \le \min\left(\dfrac{\pi}{D}, \dfrac{\pi}{I}\right) \\ 0, & \text{otherwise} \end{cases} \qquad \text{...(12.33)}$$

where

$$\omega_v = \frac{2\pi F}{F_v} = \frac{2\pi F}{IF_x} = \frac{\omega_x}{I}$$

We can write in time domain, the output of the up sampler as

$$v(l) = \begin{cases} x\left(\dfrac{l}{I}\right), & l = 0, \pm I, \pm 2I, \ldots, \\ 0, & \text{otherwise} \end{cases} \qquad \text{...(12.34)}$$

The output of the linear time-invariant filter $h(l)$ is

$$\omega(l) = h(l) * v(l)$$

$$= \sum_{k=-\infty}^{\infty} h(l-k)\cdot v(k) \qquad \text{...(12.35)}$$

$\therefore$

$$\omega(l) = \sum_{k=-\infty}^{\infty} h(l-kI)\, x(k) \qquad \text{...(12.36)}$$

Equation (12.36) is obtained like we obtained (12.32) from (12.30).

The final output $y(m)$ is obtained by down sampling $\omega(l)$ by a factor D. Thus

$$y(m) = \omega(mD)$$

$$= \sum_{k=-\infty}^{\infty} h(mD-kI)\, x(k) \quad \text{[replacing } l \text{ by } mD \text{ in (12.36)]} \qquad \text{...(12.37)}$$

If we replace, in (12.37), k given by

$$k = \left\lfloor \frac{mD}{I} \right\rfloor - n \qquad \text{...(12.38)}$$

where the notation $\lfloor r \rfloor$ denotes the largest integral value of r. For example $\lfloor 3.2 \rfloor$ is equal to 3, we discard 0.2 part.

We also use the symbol for modulo *i.e.*

$$A \text{ modulo } B \triangleq (A)_B \qquad \text{...(12.39)}$$

It implies that divide A by B, ignore the quotient, if any, and retain the remainder part. For example,

$$23 \text{ modulo } 5 = (23)_5 = 3 \text{ (quotient 4 is ignored)}$$

Also, $$(23 - 5)_5 = (18)_5 = 3$$

and $$(23 + 5)_5 = (28)_5 = 3$$

Note that $$\left\lfloor \frac{23}{5} \right\rfloor = \lfloor 4.6 \rfloor = 4 \text{ (integral part)}$$

$$\left\lfloor \frac{23}{5} \right\rfloor \times 5 + (23)_5 = 4 \times 5 + 3 = 23$$

Hence, in general

$$\lfloor A \rfloor_B \times B + (A)_B = A \qquad \text{...(12.40)}$$

In normal parlance $\lfloor A \rfloor_B$ = quotient part, and $(A)_B$ = remainder part when we divide A by B. Now replacing k by $\left\lfloor \frac{mD}{I} \right\rfloor - n$ in (12.37), and using new variable n in lieu of k, we get

$$y(m) = \sum_{n=-\infty}^{\infty} h\left(mD - \left(\left\lfloor \frac{mD}{I} \right\rfloor - n\right)I\right) \cdot x\left(\left\lfloor \frac{mD}{I} \right\rfloor - n\right)$$

$$= \sum_{n=-\infty}^{\infty} h\left(mD - \left\lfloor \frac{mD}{I} \right\rfloor I + nI\right) \cdot x\left(\left\lfloor \frac{mD}{I} \right\rfloor - n\right) \qquad \text{...(12.41)}$$

We note that

$$mD - \left\lfloor \frac{mD}{I} \right\rfloor I = (mD)_I \qquad \text{...(12.42)}$$

[Compare (12.40) and (12.42), here $A = mD$, $B = I$]

Hence, (12.41) can be written as

$$y(m) = \sum_{n=-\infty}^{\infty} h(nI + (mD)_I) \cdot x\left(\left\lfloor \frac{mD}{I} \right\rfloor - n\right) \qquad \text{...(12.43)}$$

Above equation shows that the output $y(m)$ can be obtained by passing $x(n)$ through a time-variant filter with impulse response $g(n, m)$ given by

$$g(n, m) = h(nI + (mD)_I), \quad -\infty < m, n < \infty \qquad \text{...(12.44)}$$

where $h(k)$ is the impulse response of the time-variant low-pass filter operating at sampling rate IF_x (see Fig. 12.10, where LPF is indicated by $h(l)$), we note that for any integer k,

$$g(n, (m + kI)) = h[nI + ((m + kI)D)_I]$$
$$= h[nI + (mD)_I]$$

$$\therefore \quad g(n, (m + kI)) = g(n, m) \quad \text{[due to (12.44)]} \qquad \text{...(12.45)}$$

Equation (12.45) shows that the LPF $g(n, m)$ is periodic in the variable m with period I.

We have used the notation (12.38), as it leads us to the impulse response $g(n, m)$ which turns out to be time-variant and periodic in m (with period I) as proved by (12.45). Also, we shall develop the concept of polyphase filters, when we discuss the realization to implement the sampling-rate conversion, using $g(n, m)$.

To find the frequency response of $y(m)$, we combine the relationships of interpolation and decimation. From Fig. 12.10, we can write, using interpolation result (12.25),

$$W(\omega_v) = H(\omega_v) \cdot X(\omega_v I)$$

$$= \begin{cases} I \cdot X(\omega_v I), & 0 \le |\omega_v| \le \min\left(\frac{\pi}{D}, \frac{\pi}{I}\right) \\ 0, & \text{otherwise} \end{cases} \quad \text{...(12.46)}$$

The spectrum of $y(m)$ is the decimated version of $\omega(l)$ by a factor D, using the result (12.15), replacing $X(\cdot)$ by $W(\cdot)$ and $H_D(\cdot)$ by a LPF with gain unity in the range 0 to $\frac{\pi}{D}$, we get

$$Y(\omega_y) = \frac{1}{D}\sum_{k=0}^{D-1} W\left(\frac{\omega_y - 2\pi k}{D}\right) \quad \text{...(12.47)}$$

Now $\omega(l)$ is the interpolated sequence from $x(n)$

$$\therefore \quad W(\omega_v) = I \cdot X(I\omega_v),\ 0 \le |\omega_v| \le \min\left(\frac{\pi}{D}, \frac{\pi}{I}\right) \quad \text{...(12.48a)}$$

Changing ω_v to ω_y on both sides of [12.48(*a*)], we get

$$W(\omega_y) = IX(I\omega_y),\ 0 \le |\omega_y| \le \min\left(\frac{\pi}{D}, \frac{\pi}{I}\right) \quad \text{...(12.48b)}$$

As the linear filtering by $h(l)$ prevents aliasing, as in apparent from (12.46), we can write

$$Y(\omega_y) = \frac{1}{D}W\left(\frac{\omega_y}{D}\right) \quad \text{...(12.49)}$$

leaving the remaining terms in (12.47) when $k \ne 0$. From [12.48(*b*)], we get

$$W\left(\frac{1}{D}\omega_y\right) = IX\left(I \cdot \frac{\omega_y}{D}\right),\ 0 \le |\omega_y| \le \min\left(\pi, \frac{\pi D}{I}\right) \quad \text{...(12.50)}$$

Using (12.50) in (12.49), we finally obtain

$$\boxed{Y(\omega_y) = \begin{cases} \frac{I}{D}X\left(\frac{I}{D}\omega_y\right), & 0 \le |\omega_y| \le \min\left(\pi, \frac{\pi D}{I}\right) \\ 0, & \text{otherwise} \end{cases}} \quad \text{...(12.51)}$$

This relation gives the spectrum of $y(m)$, given the spectrum of $x(n)$.

12.6 IMPLEMENTATION OF SAMPLING RATE CONVERSION

We obtain SRC by a factor $\frac{I}{D}$ by first increasing the sampling by I, by inserting $I - 1$ zeros between values of the input signal $x(n)$, then followed by linear filtering. This linear LPF eliminates the unwanted images of $X(\omega)$, which result due to up sampling. Thereafter, down sampling the resultant by a factor D. This approach is implemented by linear filter, in various structures.

12.6.1 Direct-form FIR Filter Structures

We know that for a filter $h(n)$ with system function

$$H(z) = \sum_{k=0}^{M-1} h(k) \cdot z^{-k} \quad \ldots(12.52)$$

where $h(k)$ or $h(n)$ is the unit sample response of the FIR structure. The LPF can be designed to have linear phase, a prescribed band widths (pass and stop bands), and may be equiripple. We may use window method, frequency sampling method. Butterworth, Chebyshev or Elliptic type of filters are not possible as FIR ones.

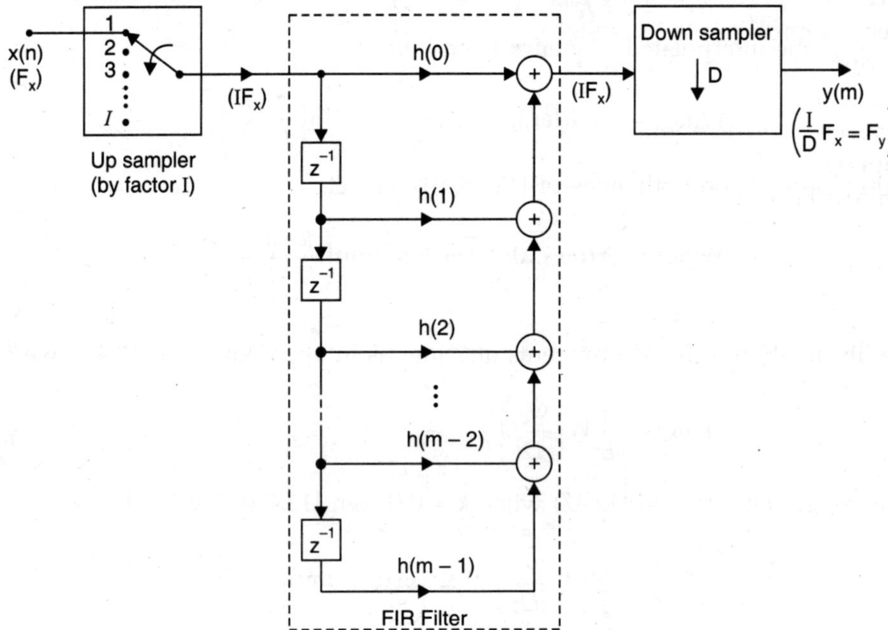

Fig. 12.11. Direct-form realization of FIR filter used in SRC by factor I/D

An implementation of direct-form realization of FIR filter used in sampling rate converter (SRC) by factor $\frac{I}{D}$ is shown in Fig. 12.11. The up sampler adds $I - 1$ zeros between successive samples of $x(n)$. The sampling rate after the up sampler is IF_x as shown in brackets at its output in Fig. 12.11. After passing through the LPF, we have a down sampler, by a factor D, and the sampling rate of the final output is $\frac{I}{D}F_x$. The rotating viper shown in the up sampler covers I contacts in time $T_x = \frac{1}{F_x}$.

The direct-form FIR filter shown in Fig. 12.11 is very simple but very inefficient. Note that out of each I input samples to the FIR filter $I - 1$ are zeros, and only one sample out of every I samples comes from $x(n)$. If I is large (as is true in many practical situations), most of the components in the input sequence to the FIR filter are zero. Hence, most of the multiplications and additions result in zeros. Also, in down sampling process, after the output of the FIR filter, we take only one sample out of D output samples, and call it $y(m)$. This suggests that we can save computation effort if we only compute *those D-th* outputs sample which the down sampler is going to pick up for $y(m)$ sequence.

We have shown a decimator by factor D in Fig. 12.12, as it appears in Fig. 12.11. (The input '$x(n)$' shown in Fig. 12.12 is the output of up sampler of Fig. 12.11 and not $x(n)$ of Fig. 12.11). In Fig. 12.12, the filter is operating at high frequency sampling rate F_x, while only one out of every D output samples is actually needed. To remove this inefficiency, we incorporate the down sampling operation within the filter, as shown Fig. 12.13.

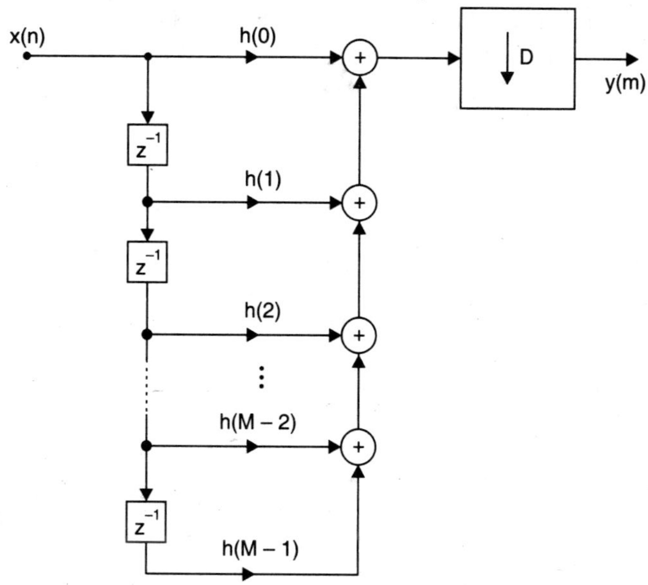

Fig. 12.12. Decimation by factor D (as in Fig. 12.11)

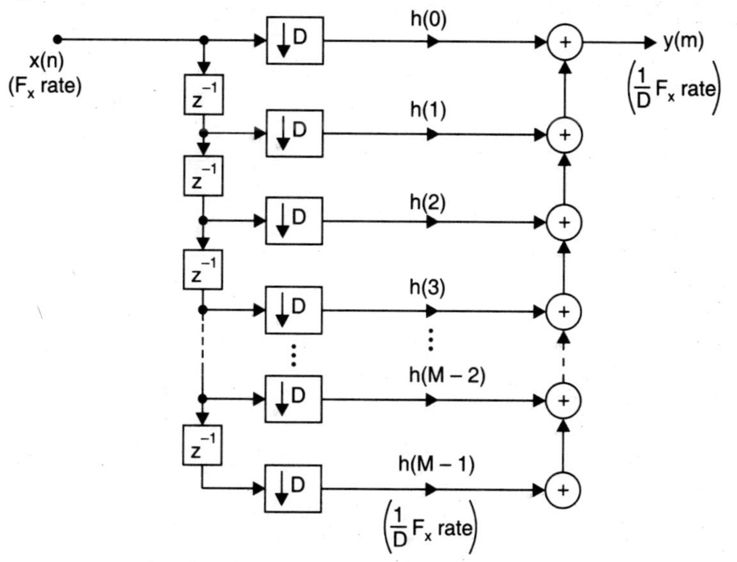

Fig. 12.13. Fig. 12.12 structure realized as an efficient structure for Decimation by factor D

In Fig. 12.13 of filter structures, all the multiplications [by $h(0)$, $h(1)$, ..., $h(M - 1)$] and all additions are performed at the lower sampling rate $\frac{F_x}{D}$. Thus, we save time of computation, and the realization is efficient. Additional reduction in computation can be achieved if the FIR filter is linear phase, where $h(n) = h(N - 1 - n)$.

Now we consider efficient implementation of the Interpolation by factor I. The interpolator of Fig. 12.11 is drawn in Fig. 12.14. Note that sequence $v(n)$ has $I - 1$ zeros in between adjoining samples of input $x(n)$. The computation is performed at high sampling rate IF_x. We desire to simplify this structure to an efficient one. We first use the transposed form of the FIR filter and obtain the structure as shown in Fig. 12.15(a) and then we embed the up sampler with in the FIR filter and get structure shown in Fig. 12.15(b).

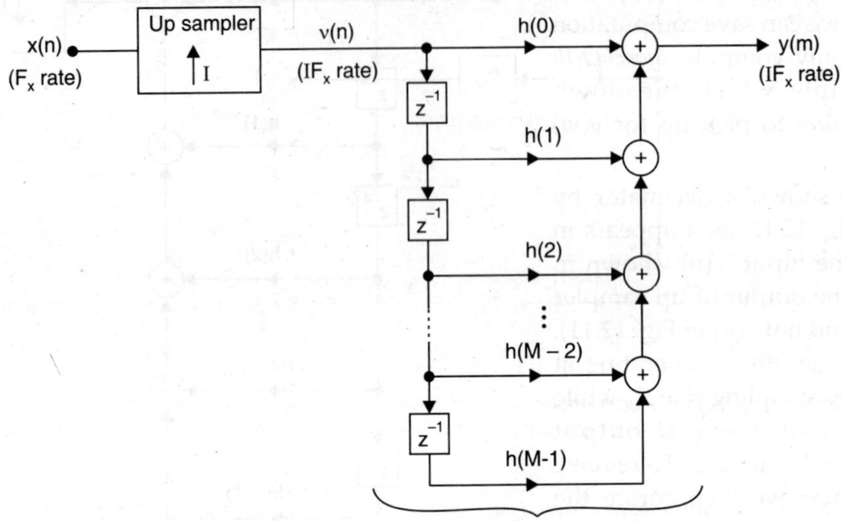

Fig. 12.14. Direct-form realization of FIR filter in interpolation by a factor I (as in Fig. 12.11)

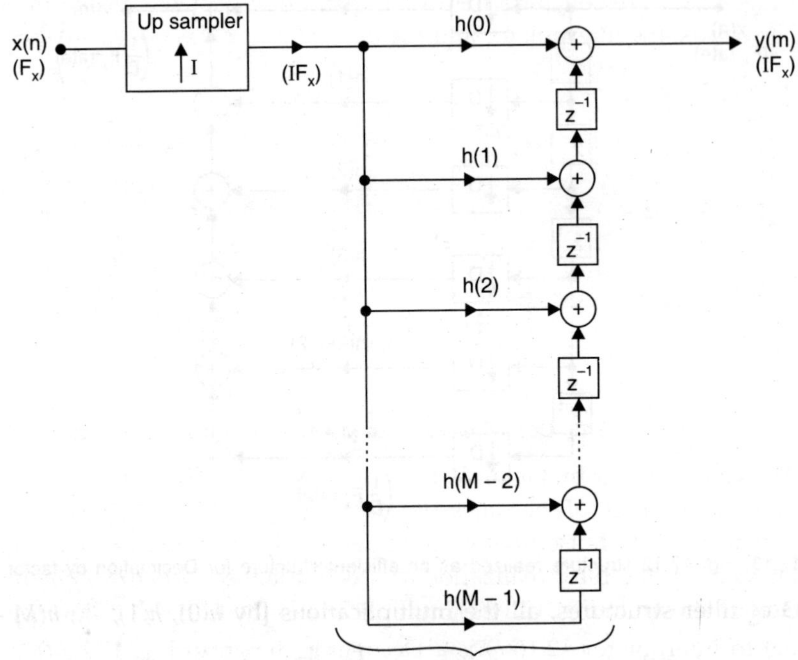

Fig. 12.15. (a) Structure obtained when we transpose the FIR filter of Fig. 12.14. This is a step towards obtaining an efficient version of structure shown in Fig. 12.14. The final efficient structure is shown in Fig. 12.15(b).

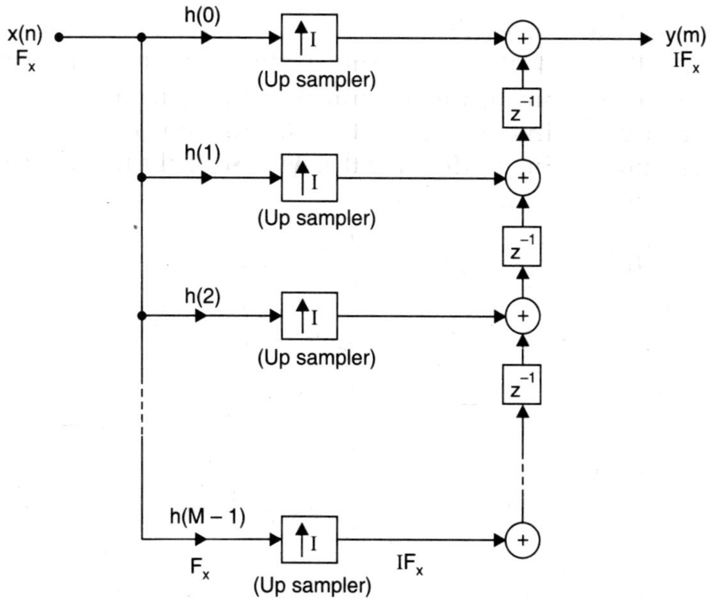

Fig. 12.15. (*b*) Shifting the up sampler in Fig. 12.15(*a*) inside the FIR filter results in an efficient interpolator structure. All up samplers are synchronized

In the structure shown in Fig. 12.15(*b*), all the filter multiplications are performed at the low rate F_x, and the up samplers introduce $I - 1$ zeros in each filter branch of the structure. This, therefore, is an efficient structure of an interpolator.

Note that the structure of interpolator, Fig. 12.15(*a*) can be obtained by transposing the structure of the decimator Fig. 12.12. We conclude that the transpose of decimator is an Interpolator and vice versa. In other words, the interpolator and the decimator are dual to each other as indicated in Fig. 12.16.

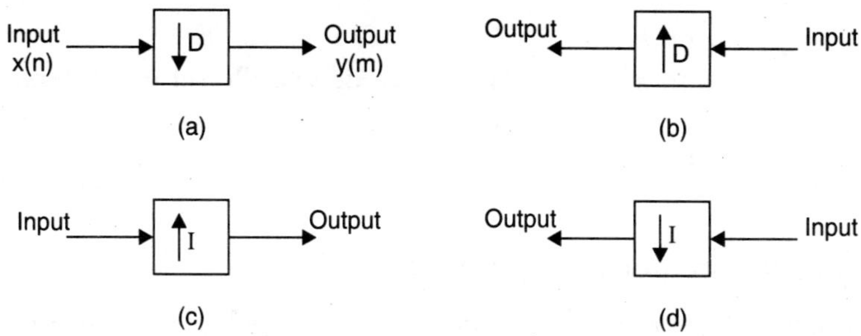

Fig. 12.16. Duality relationships using Transposition

Figure 12.16(*a*) is a decimator by factor *D*. If we reverse all the directions, the input becomes output, the output becomes input, $\downarrow D$ becomes $\uparrow D$, and we get Fig. 12.16(*b*) which is an Interpolator by factor *D*. Note that in the LPF used before the down sampler (not shown) in Fig. 12.16(*a*) for decimator, the delays z^{-1} in the filter realization are NOT changed, when we obtain the dual *i.e.* Interpolator by factor *I* shown in Fig. 12.16(*b*). In Fig. 12.16(*b*) the LPF will follow the up sampler.

Similarly, dual to Interpolator 12.16(*c*) is a Decimator shown in Fig. 12.16(*d*).

The duality property is often used in design problems.

12.7 POLYPHASE FILTER STRUCTURES

We can also achieve the computational efficiency of the structure shown in Fig. 12.15(*a*), by another approach. In Figs. 12.15(*a*) and (*b*), the FIR filter has length M [*i.e.* $h(0)$, $h(1)$, ..., $h(M-1)$]. M is usually large we make $M = KI$, and split the LPF $h(n)$ into I filters, each of length K.

Consider the interpolator given in Fig. 12.14. As the up sampler introduces $I-1$ zeros valued samples in between successive values of $x(n)$, only K out of M input samples $v(n)$, which are fed to the LPF filter are non-zero at any one time. For example, these non-zero values coincide and are multiplied by the filter coefficients $h(0)$, $h(I)$, $h(2I)$, ..., $h(M-I)$. In the following time instant $\left(i.e. \text{ after time } \dfrac{1}{IF_x}\right)$, the non-zero values of $v(n)$ coincide and are multiplied by the filter coefficients $h(1)$, $h(I+1)$, $h(2I+1)$, ..., $h(M-I+1)$, and so on. Thus the input zero padded sequence $v(n)$ gets its K non-zero samples [which came from $x(n)$] multiplied by the filter coefficients at one time which are one of the following

$$\{h(0), h(1I), h(2I), h(3I), \ldots, h(M-I)\}\ldots \quad \ldots(A)$$

then by $\{h(1), h(I+1), h(2I+1), h(3I+1), \ldots, h(M-I+1)\}\ldots, \quad \ldots(B)$

then by $\{h(2), h(I+2), h(2I+2), h(3I+2), \ldots, h(M-I+2)\},\ldots \quad \ldots(C)$

and so, and lastly by

$$\{h(I-1), h(2I-1), h(3I-1), \ldots, h(M-1)\} \quad \ldots(D)$$

Each set of filter coefficients in (*A*), (*B*), (*C*) and (*D*) is of length K, and there would be I different sets like (*A*), (*B*), ..., (*D*). This observation leads us to define I FIR filters each of coefficients K only we name

$$p_0(n) = h(0), h(I), h(2I), \ldots, h(M-I) \quad \ldots\text{from } (A)$$

$$p_1(n) = h(1), h(I+1), h(2I+1), \ldots, h(M-I+1) \quad \ldots\text{from } (B)$$

and so on.

$$p_{I-1}(n) = h(I-1), h(2I-1), h(3I-1), \ldots, h(M-1) \quad \ldots\text{from } (D)$$

To put above definitions in an elegent form, we denote the set of I filters, called *polyphase filters* by

$$\boxed{\begin{aligned} p_k(n) = h(k+nI),\ k &= 0, 1, \ldots, I-1 \\ n &= 0, 1, \ldots, K-1 \end{aligned}} \quad \ldots(12.53)$$

12.7.1 Realization of Interpolator by Polyphase Filters

From afore-mentioned discussion it follows that the set of I polyphase filters (each of length K) can be arranged as parallel realization and output of each filter can be selected by a commutator, as shown in Fig. 12.17.

The commutator makes contact at Ⓐ to yield $y(m)$ for $m = 0, I, 2I, \ldots, y(M-I)$. Contact at Ⓑ yields $y(m)$ for $m = 1, I+1, 2I+1, \ldots, M-I+1$ and so on. Finally, contact at Ⓘ yields $y(m)$ for $m = I-1, 2I-1, 3I-1, \ldots, M-1$. Thus in one round of rotation, making contacts at Ⓐ, Ⓑ, ... Ⓘ, I samples of $y(m)$ are generated. This is done in time $I \times \dfrac{1}{IF_x} = \dfrac{1}{F_x}$ *i.e.* in time T_x we obtain I samples at output. Note that in time T_x, only one sample from $x(n)$ is delivered to the polyphase filters. The polyphase filters, therefore operate at rate F_x.

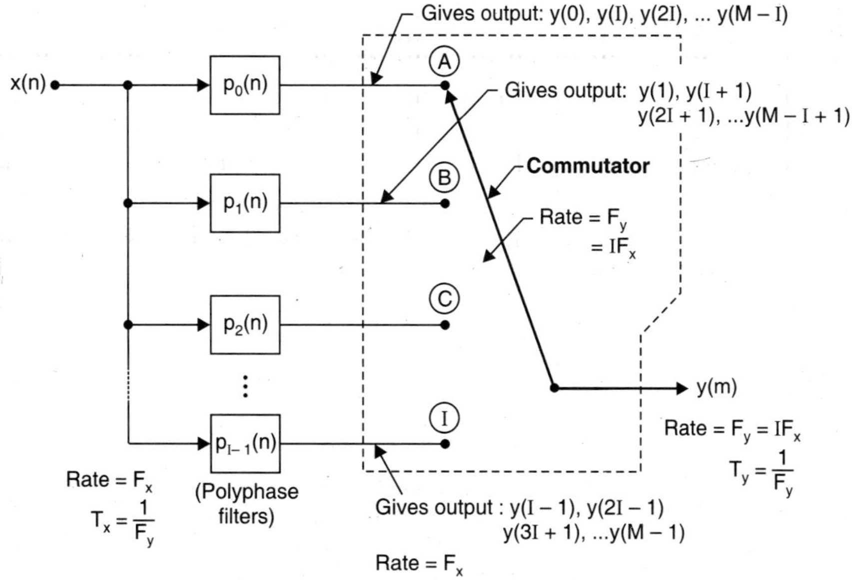

Fig. 12.17. Interpolation achieved by using *I* polyphase filters, and commutator (counter-clockwise)

It may be noted that the polyphase filters is a set of I subfilters, and we have decomposed the filter $\{h(k)\}$, with M filter coefficients, into I subfilters, each having K filter coefficients. The impulse response of each of the subfilters: $p_0(n)$, $p_1(n)$, ..., $p_{I-1}(n)$, is different *i.e.* the input signal $x(n)$ passes through a time variant filter, constituting I subfilters. The time variant filter was denoted by us as $g(n, m)$ in (12.44). We can write

$$p_k(m) \triangleq g(n, m) = h(nI + k) \text{ due to (12.53)}$$

$$\therefore \qquad g(n, m) = h(nI + (mD)_I) \qquad \text{...(12.54)}$$

since $h(nI + k)$ is periodic in k with periodicity I. $D = I$ for the case of interpolation. As $g(n, m)$ varies periodically with period I, consequently a different set of coefficients are used to generate the set I output samples $y(m)$, $m = 0, 1, 2, ..., I - 1$, as shown in Fig. 12.17.

12.7.2 Properties of the Polyphase Filters $p_k(n)$

We know that the set of polyphase subfilters $p_k(n)$ are obtained from $h(n)$ by decimation with a factor I. If the original filter $h(n)$ has frequency response of

$$H(\omega) = \begin{cases} C, & 0 \le |\omega| \le \dfrac{\pi}{I} \\ 0, & \text{otherwise} \end{cases} \qquad \text{...(12.55)}$$

where C is a constant equalling I, (see (12.24) and (12.28)), for an interpolator I. Thus each of the polyphase subfilter has a flat response over the range $0 \le |\omega| \le \pi$. Hence, all the polyphase filters are basically all pass filters and these differ primarily in their phase characteristics. Hence, these are called the polyphase filters. To summarise:

Property 1: Polyphase filters approximate all-pass functions.

Property 2: Each polyphase filter $p_k(n)$, $k = 0, 1, ..., I - 1$, corresponds to a different phase shift, depending on k.

Property 3: If $h(n)$ is length $N = K \cdot I$, and is an FIR filter, then $p_k(n)$ will also be FIR filters for $k = 0, 1, ..., I - 1$ and each $p_k(n)$ will have length K.

Property 4: If $h(n)$ is symmetric (*i.e.* linear phase), then at the most, only one of the $p_k(n)$ will by symmetric.

Property 5: Polyphase filters $p_k(n)$, $k = 0, 1, ..., M - 1$, for M to 1 decimation are equal to the time varying coefficients $g(n, m)$ corresponding to interpolation of 1 to M.

Thus, due to property 1, the frequency responses of the network filters $h(n)$ and the typical polyphase filter $p_k(n)$ are as shown in Fig. 12.18, *i.e.*,

$$H(\omega) = \begin{cases} C, & 0 \le |\omega| \le \dfrac{\pi}{I} \\ 0, & \text{otherwise} \end{cases} \quad \text{...(12.56a)}$$

$$P_k(\omega) = \begin{cases} C, & 0 \le |\omega| \le \pi \\ 0, & \text{otherwise} \end{cases} \quad \text{...(12.56b)}$$

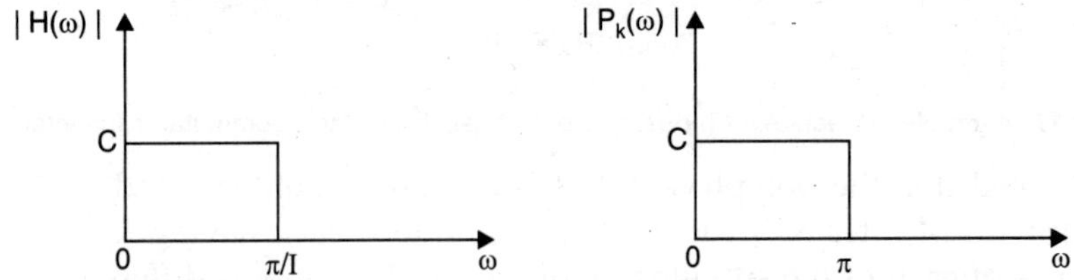

Fig. 12.18. Frequency responses of Polyphase network filters: $p_k(n)$

To visualize the meaning of property 2 and 4, let us consider the basic LPF $h(n)$ with $N = 9$, and assume $I = 3$. Let $h(n)$ be a symmetric (*i.e.* linear-phase) filter with symmetry at $n = \dfrac{(9-1)}{2} = 4$.

Each of the resulting polyphase filter $p_k(n)$, $k = 0, 1, 3$ will have length $\dfrac{9}{3} = 3$

i.e.

$$p_0(n) = h(0), h(3), h(6)$$
$$p_1(n) = h(1), h(4), h(7)$$
$$p_2(n) = h(2), h(5), h(8)$$

Note the impulse response samples as shown in Fig. 12.19. Since point of symmetry of $p_0(n)$ is at $n = \dfrac{4}{3}$, it has a flat delay of $\dfrac{4}{3}$ samples.

Similarly, $p_1(n)$ has flat delay of one sample and $p_2(n)$ has flat delay of $\dfrac{2}{3}$ samples. Thus, different fractional delays and therefore, different phase shifts, are associated with the different filter $p_k(n)$. The fact that different phases are associated with different paths of the network is the reason for the term *polyphase network*. Note that only $p_1(n)$ is symmetric out of all filters $p_k(n)$.

The polyphase filter may be viewed as a set of I subfilters connected to a common delay line. Ideally, the k-th subfilter will generate a forward time shift of $\left(\dfrac{k}{I}\right) \cdot T_s$ for $k = 0, 1, ..., I - 1$, relative to the zeroth subfilter $p_0(n)$. Therefore, if the zeroth filter generates zero delay, the frequency response of the k-th subfilter is

$$P_k(\omega) = e^{j\omega k/I} \text{ assuming constant } C = 1 \text{ in [12.56(b)]} \quad \text{...(12.57)}$$

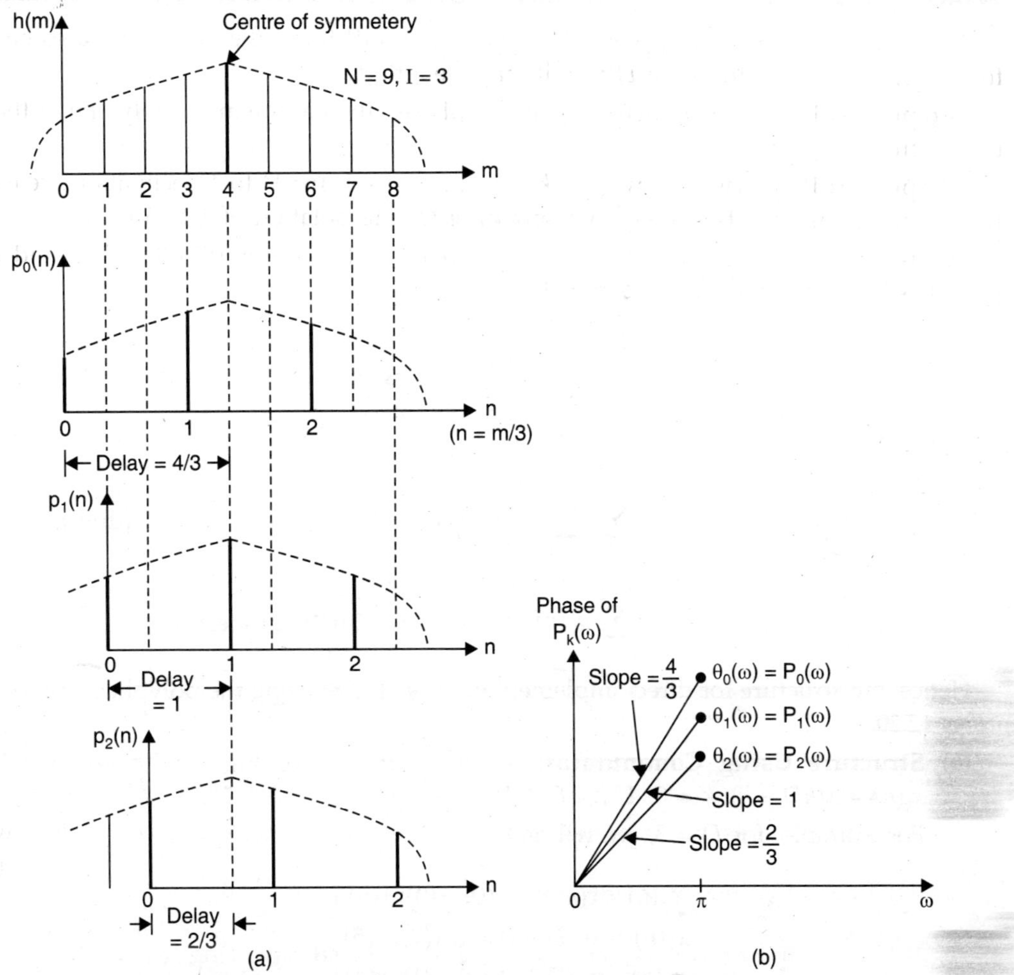

Fig. 12.19. (*a*) Samples of polyphase filters $p_0(n)$, $p_1(n)$ and $p_2(n)$ obtained from the parent filter $h(m)$. (*b*) Different fractional delays and consequent different phase shifts for the polyphase filters $p_0(n)$, $p_1(n)$ and $p_2(n)$

A time shift of an integer number of input sampling interval (*i.e.* lT_s) can be generated by shifting the input data in the delay line by l samples and using the same subfilters $p_k(n)$. By combining these two methods, we can obtain an output that in shifted forward (*i.e.* delayed) by an amount $(l + i)T_s$, relative to the previous outputs.

12.7.3 Realization of Decimator by Polyphase Filters

(*a*) Structure Without Commutator: From (12.5), we know that for a decimator of $D : 1$, we have for a generic $h(n)$, having infinite samples.

$$y(n) = \sum_{k=-\infty}^{\infty} h(k)x(nD-k) \quad \ldots(A)$$

Define $\qquad x_k(n) = x(nD - k),\ k = 0, 1, \ldots, D - 1 \quad \ldots(B)$

$$p_k(n) = h(nD + k),\ k = 0, 1, \ldots, D - 1 \qquad \text{[see also (12.53)]} \ldots(C)$$

change the dummy variable k to l in (A), to avoid confusion with (B) and (C) where k varies from 0 to $D - 1$. Then we can write $y(n)$ as

$$\therefore \quad y(n) = \sum_{l=-\infty}^{\infty} h(l)x(nD-l) \qquad \ldots(D)$$

Put $l = rD + k,\ r = 0, \pm 1, \pm 2, \ldots,$
$k = 0, 1, \ldots, D-1$ in (D) above

$$\therefore \quad y_k(n) = \sum_{r=-\infty}^{\infty} h(rD+k)\cdot x(nD-rD-k),\ k = 0, 1, \ldots, D-1$$

$$\therefore \quad y(n) = \sum_{k=0}^{D-1} y_k(n)$$

$$= \sum_{k=0}^{D-1}\sum_{r=-\infty}^{\infty} h(rD+k)\cdot x(nD-rD-k)$$

$$= \sum_{k=0}^{D-1}\sum_{r=-\infty}^{\infty} p_k(r)\cdot x_k(n-r) \qquad \text{[due to } (B) \text{ and } (C)]$$

$$\therefore \quad y(n) = \sum_{k=0}^{D-1} p_k(n) * x_k(n) \text{ (convolution property)} \qquad \ldots(12.58)$$

Hence, the structure for direct implementation of (12.58) using the polyphase filters is shown in Fig. 12.20.

***(b)* Structure Using Commutator:** In the structure of Fig. 12.20, we have defined $x_k(n) = x(nD-k),\ k = 0, 1, \ldots, D-1$.

For example, for $D = 3$, we will get

$$\left.\begin{aligned} x_0(n) &= x(nD) = x(0), x(3), x(6) \\ x_1(n) &= x(nD-1) = 0, x(2), x(5) \\ x_2(n) &= x(nD-2) = 0, x(1), x(4) \end{aligned}\right\} \qquad \ldots(A)$$

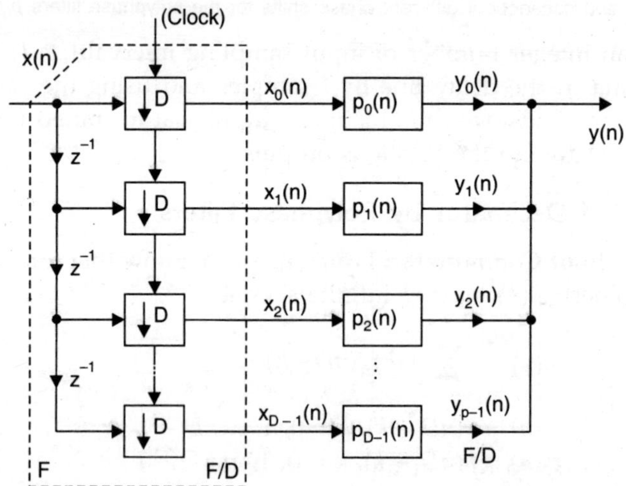

Fig. 12.20. Decimator D to 1 using the Equation (12.58). Decimator realization using polyphase filters

We can efficiently replace the network shown in dashed area in Fig. 12.20, by the network shown in dashed area of Fig. 12.21. whereas the structure of Fig. 12.20 is a version of Fig. 12.13 with slight modification to use polyphase filters $p_k(n)$, the structure given by Fig. 12.21 is obtained by transposing the interpolator structure shown in Fig. 12.17. Note that the commutator shown in dashed area of Fig. 12.21 rotates in counter-clockwise direction.

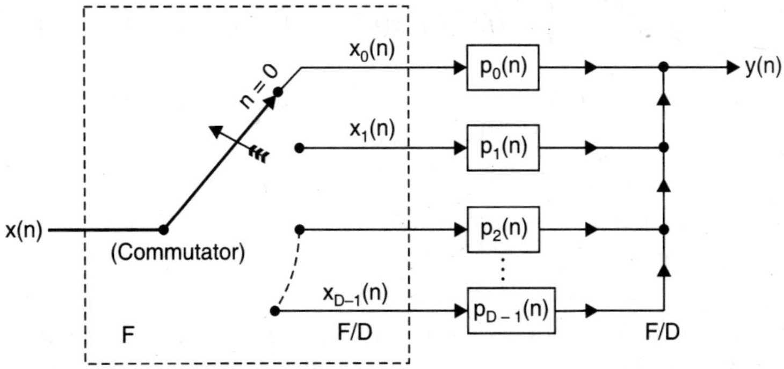

Fig. 12.21. *D* to 1 Decimation by polyphase filters $p_k(n)$ and Commutator (counter-clockwise)

The reason for this will be clear as follows. The speed of the commutator is such that one delay time (z^{-1}) is taken to cover from $p_i(n)$ to $p_{i-1}(n)$ for $i = D - 1, D - 2, \ldots, 0$. It also takes only one delay time to rotate from $p_0(n)$ to $p_{D-1}(n)$. Assume that we have decimator from 3 to 1. This would result Fig. 12.20 to Fig. 12.22

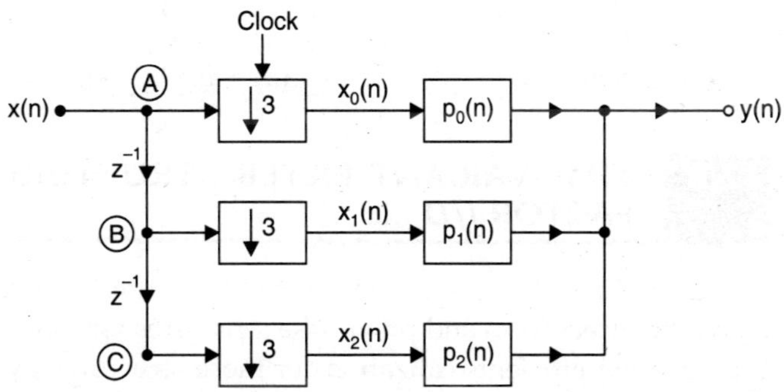

Fig. 12.22. For *D* = 3, Fig. 12.20 redrawn

In Fig. 12.22, we have

$$\left.\begin{aligned} x_0(n) &= x(0), x(3), x(6) \quad \text{fed to filter } p_0(n) \\ x_1(n) &= 0, x(2), x(5) \quad \text{fed to filter } p_1(n) \\ x_2(n) &= 0, x(1), x(4) \quad \text{fed to filter } p_2(n) \end{aligned}\right\} \qquad \ldots(B)$$

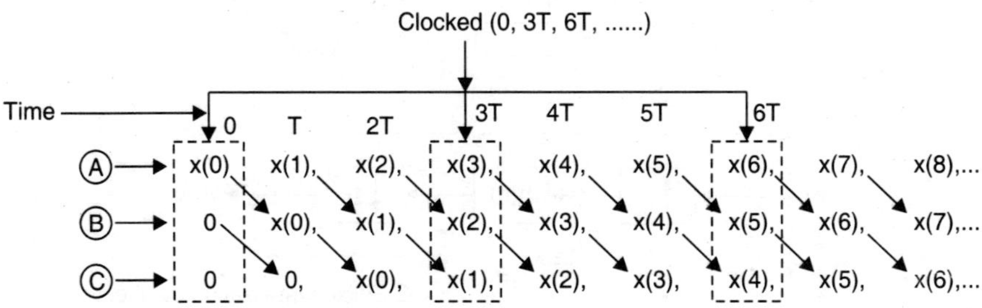

The samples appear LHS to RHS at time interval $T = \dfrac{1}{F}$.

The samples captured by clock, at time interval $3T$ are shown in dashed boxes. Note that the top samples of shaded boxes which are fed to $p_0(n)$ are $x(0)$, $x(3)$, $x(6)$. Similarly, those fed to $p_1(n)$ are middle samples of the shaded boxes and these are 0, $x(2)$, $x(5)$. The last samples of three shaded boxes form a set, 0, $x(1)$, $x(4)$, and these are fed to filter $p_2(n)$. Thus, the sequences fed to filters $p_0(n)$, $p_1(n)$ and $p_2(n)$ are respectively, $x_0(n)$, $x_1(n)$ and $x_2(n)$ as needed by (*B*).

From the commutator shown in Fig. 12.21, assuming $D = 3$, hence only $p_0(n)$, $p_1(n)$ and $p_2(n)$ are there, the samples fed to, if the commutator rotates in counter-clockwise, are:

$$\left.\begin{array}{l} \text{to } p_0(n) \text{ are} : x(0), x(3), x(6) \\ \text{to } p_2(n) \text{ are} : 0, x(1), x(4) \\ \text{to } p_1(n) \text{ are} : 0, x(3), x(5) \end{array}\right\} \quad \ldots(C)$$

The signal sequences fed to polyphase filters $p_0(n)$, $p_1(n)$ and $p_2(n)$ as given by (*B*) and (*C*) agree. Thus, the realizations of Figs. 12.20 and 12.21 (with counter-clockwise commutator rotation) are equivalent.

Although the two commutator structures for interpolator and the decimator, just covered in sections 12.7.1 and 12.7.3 rotate in a counter-clockwise direction, it is possible to derive an equivalent pair of commutator structures having a clockwise rotation. In such cases the polyphase filters would be defined by the impulse responses.

For Interpolator, $\quad p_k(n) = h(nI - k),\ k = 0, 1, \ldots, I - 1 \quad \ldots(12.59a)$

For Decimator: $\quad p_k(n) = h(nD - k),\ k = 0, 1, \ldots, D - 1 \quad \ldots(12.59b)$

12.8 TIME-VARIANT FILTER STRUCTURES FOR RATE CONVERSION BY FACTOR I/D

In the previous sections, we have considered implementation of Interpolation and Decimation by using the direct-form and polyphase structures for the case of *integer changes* in the sampling rate. We obtained efficient realizations of these structures by commutating the filtering operations to occur at the low sampling rate. For the case of network to realize a change in sampling rate by a factor $\frac{I}{D}$, it is difficult to achieve such efficiencies.

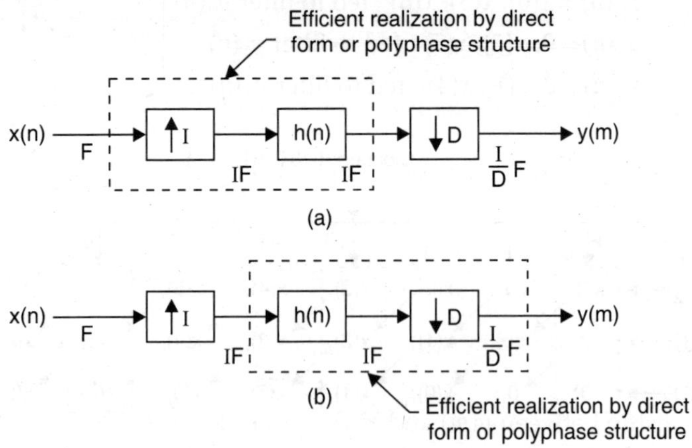

Fig. 12.23. Possible realization of an $\frac{I}{D}$ sampling rate convertor

The difficulty is illustrated in Fig. 12.23. If we realize the 1 to I interpolation part of the structure using the techniques described earlier, then we are faced with the problem of commuting D-to-1 sampling rate compressor into the network [Fig. 12.23(*a*)]. If we realize the D-to-1 decimator first, then the 1-to-I sampling rate expander must be commuted into the structure [Fig. 12.23(*b*)]. In both the cases difficulties arise, and we are faced with a network that cannot be implemented efficiently, simply using the techniques of commutation, and transposition.

Efficient structures exist for implementing a sampling rate converter with a ratio in sampling rate of $\frac{I}{D}$. We, in this section, discuss one such class of FIR structures with time-varying coefficients. We have derived in (12.43) and (12.44) that

$$y(m) = \sum_{n=-\infty}^{\infty} g(n, m) \cdot x\left(\left\lfloor \frac{mD}{I} \right\rfloor - n\right) \qquad \ldots(12.60)$$

where, due to (12.44)

$$g(n, m) = h(nI + (mD)_I) \quad \text{for all } m \text{ and all } n \qquad \ldots(12.61)$$

Here, $h(l)$ corresponds to the low-pass FIR prototype filter. We assume the length of the filter $h(l)$ as a multiple of I, *i.e.*,

$$N = KI \qquad \ldots(12.62)$$

Then all the coefficient sets $g(m, n)$, $m = 0, 1, 2, \ldots, I - 1$ contain exactly K coefficients. Also, we know that $g(n, m)$ is periodic in m with period I (see (12.45)) *i.e.*

$$g(n, m) = g(n, (m + kI)),\ k = 0, \pm 1, \pm 2, \ldots, \qquad \ldots(12.63)$$

Using the results (12.62) and (12.63), we can write (12.60) as

$$y(m) = \sum_{n=0}^{K-1} g(n, (m)_I) \cdot x\left(\left\lfloor \frac{mD}{I} \right\rfloor - n\right)$$

$$= \sum_{n=0}^{K-1} g\left(n, m - \left\lfloor \frac{mD}{I} \right\rfloor I\right) \cdot x\left(\left\lfloor \frac{mD}{I} \right\rfloor - n\right) \qquad \ldots(12.64)$$

Equation (12.64) shows that the computation of an output $y(m)$ is obtained as a weighted sum of K sequential samples of $x(n)$ starting at $x\left(\left\lfloor \frac{mD}{I} \right\rfloor\right)$, when $n = 0$, and going backward in n sequentially, till the sample $x\left(\left\lfloor \frac{mD}{I} \right\rfloor - (K-1)\right)$. The weighting coefficients $g(n, m)$ are periodically time-varying so that $(m)_I$ coefficients $g(n, (m)_I)$, $n = 0, 1, \ldots, K - 1$ are used for the m-th output sample.

Timing relationship between $y(m)$ and $x(n)$ will be clear by taking an example, for $D = 2$, and $I = 3$. This has been explained in Fig. 12.24.

$y(m)$ m	$x\left(\left\lfloor \frac{mD}{I} \right\rfloor\right)$ $\left\lfloor \frac{2}{3}m \right\rfloor$	$g(0, (m)_I)$ $(m)_I$
0	0	0
1	0	1
2	1	2
3	2	0
4	2	1
5	3	2
6	4	0

(*a*)

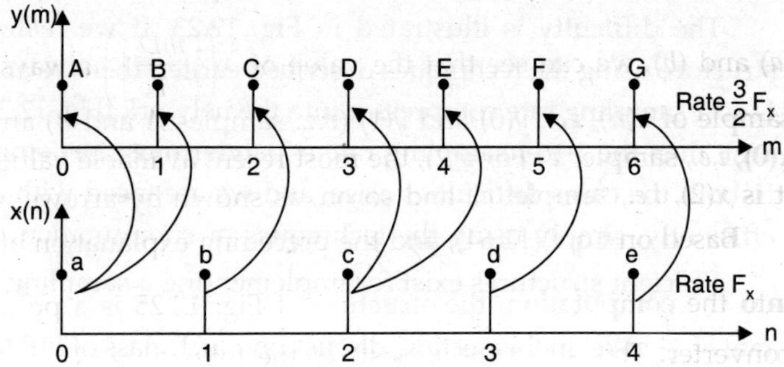

Fig. 12.24. Timing relationships between $y(m)$ and $x(n)$ for the case $D = 2$, $I = 3$ (*a*) For $n = 0$ values of $\left\lfloor \frac{2}{3}m \right\rfloor$ and $(m)_3$ for $m = 0, 1, \ldots, 6$ (*b*) Relative timing position of $x(n)$ and $y(m)$ on absolute time scale

Fig. 12.24(*a*) gives the value of m, $\left\lfloor \frac{2}{3}m \right\rfloor$, $(m)_I$ for $m = 0$ to 6. Figure 12.24(*b*) gives the relative timing position of $x(n)$ and $y(m)$ on absolute time scale for $D = 2$ and $I = 3$. By comparison of parts

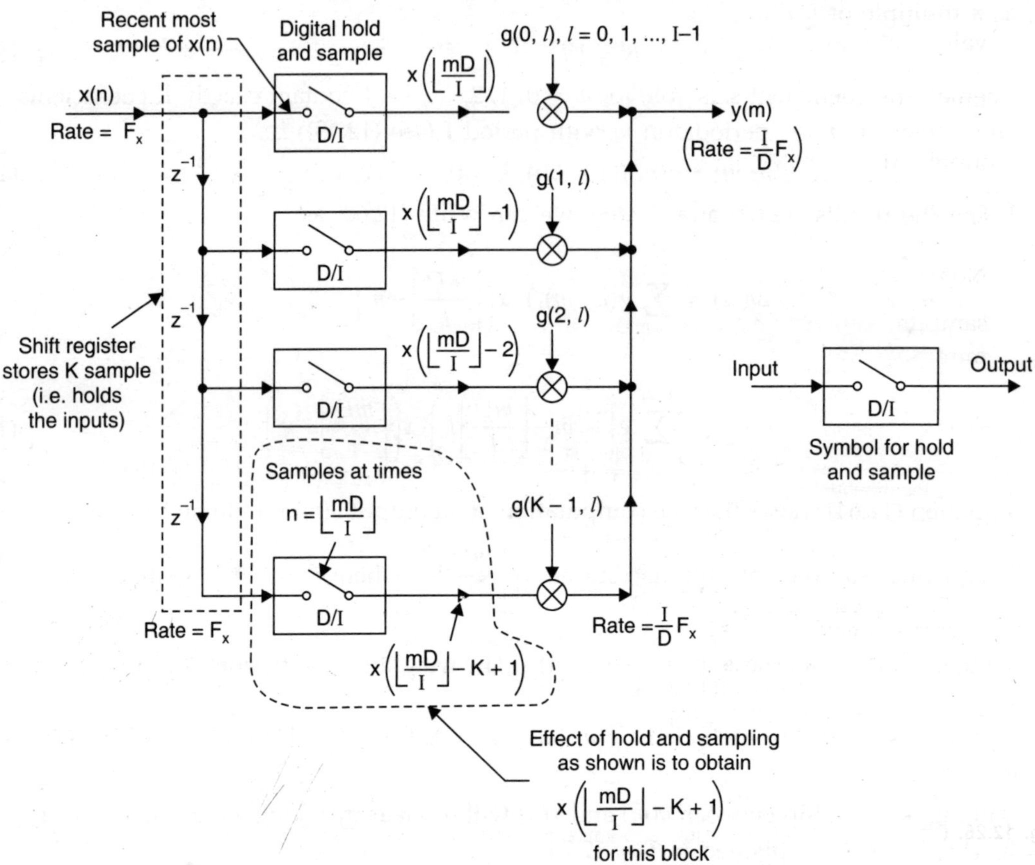

Fig. 12.25. Efficient structure for realizing an $\frac{I}{D}$ sampling rate convertor

(*a*) and (*b*), we can see that the value of $x\left(\left\lfloor \frac{mD}{I} \right\rfloor\right)$ always represents the most recent available sample of $x(n)$, *i.e.*, $y(0)$ and $y(1)$ (*viz.* samples *A* and *B*) are computed on the basis of $x(0 - n) = x(0)$, *i.e.*, sample '*a*'. For $y(2)$, the most recent available value of $x(n)$ is $x(1)$, *i.e.*, sample '*b*', for $y(3)$ it is $x(2)$, *i.e.*, sample '*c*', and so on, as shown by arrows in Fig. 12.24(*b*).

Based on Eqn. (12.64), and the preceding explanation of how the input, and coefficients enter into the computation, the structure of Fig. 12.25 is a possible realization for $\frac{I}{D}$ sampling rate converter. This structure consists of the following:

1. A *K*-sample 'shift register' operating at the input sampling rate F_x, which stores sequential samples of the input signal.
2. A direct-form FIR structure with time-varying coefficients $g(n, l)$, $n = 0, 1, \ldots, K - 1$, that operates at the output sampling rate $\left(\frac{I}{D}\right)F_x$. Here l varies from 0 to $I - 1$.
3. A series of digital 'hold-and-sample' boxes that couple the two sampling rates. The input side of the box *'hold' the most recent input value* of $x(n)$, $x(n - 1)$, …, $x(n - K + 1)$ fed to it until the next input value comes along: the output side of the box 'samples' the input values at time $n = m\frac{D}{I}$. For times when $m\frac{D}{I}$ is an integer (*i.e.*, input and output sampling time/instants are the same), the input changes first and the output samples the changed input. All the hold and sample shown as boxes are synchronized by a clock at $\left(\frac{I}{D}\right)F_x$ cycles per second.

Note that the structure of Fig. 12.25 is an efficient realization for implementing an $\left(\frac{I}{D}\right)$ sampling rate converter as the operations are all performed at output sampling rate with minimum required number of coefficients $g(n, m)$ used to generate each output.

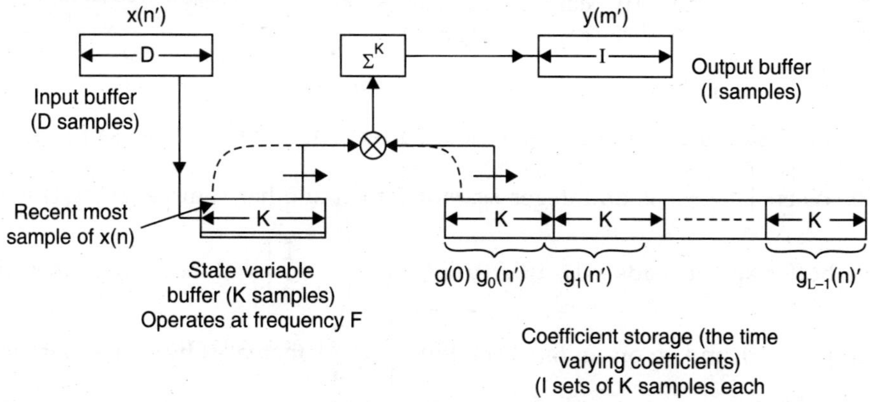

Fig. 12.26. Diagram of a program structure to implement the flow graph of Fig. 12.25 in a block-by-block manner

Fig. 12.26 shows a diagram of a program configuration to implement the structure given in Fig. 12.25, in a block-by-block manner. The program takes in a block of *D* samples of the input signal, denoted by $x(n')$, $n' = 0, 1, 2, \ldots, D-1$, and computes a block of I output samples, $y(m')$, $m' = 0, 1, 2, \ldots, I-1$. For each output sample time of m', $m' = 0, 1, 2, \ldots, I-1$, the K samples from the state-variable buffer are multiplied, respectively with K coefficients from one of the coefficient sets $g_{m'}(n')$ and the products are accumulated to give the output $y(m')$. Each time the quantity $\left\lfloor \frac{m'D}{I} \right\rfloor$ increases by 1, one sample from the input buffer in shifted into the state-variable buffer. (This information can be stored in a control array). Thus, after I output values are computed, D input samples have been shifted into the state-variable buffer and the process can be repeated for next block of data. In the course of processing one block of data (D input samples and I output samples), the state-variable buffer is sequentially addressed I times and the coefficient storage buffer is sequentially addressed once, *i.e.*, all the $K \times I$ coefficients of the coefficient storage buffer have been used once. m' increases by one when $\boxed{\sum_{1}^{K}}$ has down summation 1 to K. Multiplication of K samples of state-variable buffer by $g(n')$ completes in time of one sample period of m'. One summation $\sum_{1}^{K}$ yields one sample $y(m')$.

Fig. 12.27 shows the diagram, redrawn for $D = 2$, $I = 3$ and $K = 4$.

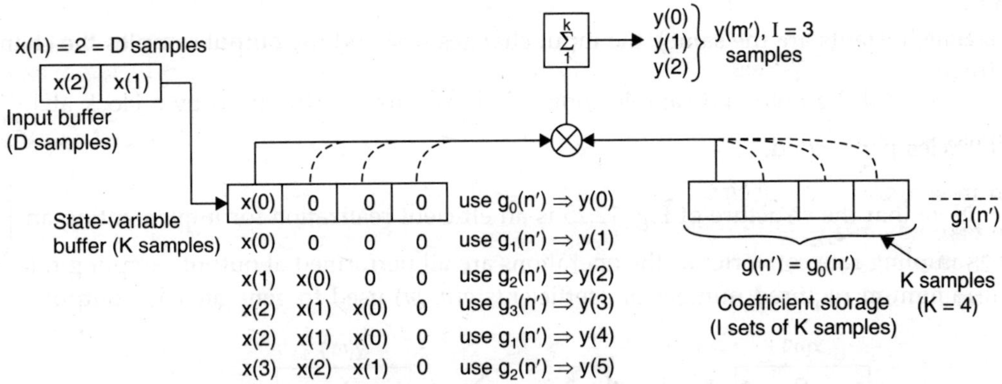

Fig. 12.27. A practical program of Fig. 12.26 for $D = 2$, $I = 3$, $K = 4$

We store $K = 4$ samples in the state-variable buffer. The register stores samples $x(0)$, 0, 0, 0 at $n = m = 0$. When $\left\lfloor m \times \frac{2}{3} \right\rfloor$ is an integer *i.e.* $m = 2$ then another sample, *i.e.*, $x(1)$ is fed to the state variable buffer and it reads $x(1)$, $x(0)$, 0, 0. When $\left\lfloor m \times \frac{2}{3} \right\rfloor = 2$, *i.e.*, $m = 2$, then this buffer reads $x(2)$, $x(1)$, $x(0)$, 0, and so on. In fact each time $\left\lfloor m \cdot \frac{2}{3} \right\rfloor$ increases by 1, one sample from the input buffer is shifted into the state variable buffer. For each two input signals $x(n')$. We obtain three output signal $y(m')$.

12.9 COMPARISON OF STRUCTURES

We have discussed three principal classes of FIR structures for Decimators and Interpolation. We covered direct form FIR structures in Section 12.5, Polyphase structures in section 12.7 and Time-varying structures in Section 12.8. Which of these structures in superior-most is difficult to decide. Some insight and direction, however, can be provided by observing a few general properties of the afore-mentioned structures.

The direction form structures have the advantages that these can be easily modified to exploit the symmetry in the system function to gain additional reduction in computation by a factor of approximately two. The polyphase structures have the advantage that the filters $p_k(n)$ can be easily realized with efficient techniques such as the fast convolution methods based on FFT. As such this structure has been found useful for filter banks. The structures with time-varying coefficients are particularly useful when considering conversions by factor $\frac{I}{D}$.

It may be mentioned here that multistage cascades of afore-mentioned structures can lead to additional gains in computations efficiency when conversion ratios are large.

12.10 SAMPLING RATE CONVERSION OF BANDPASS SIGNALS

In many cases we may deal with a bandpass signal such as in speech, TV or music signals. In analog signals, by heterodyning, we bring the band width of interest to IF (intermediate frequency). As the frequency goes up, its stability also deteriorates. Therefore, in digital signals too, we bring a bandpass signal of interest, say $\frac{2\pi}{D}$ to $\frac{3\pi}{D}$, to a lower level: 0 to $\frac{\pi}{D}$ in ω domain, *i.e.*, 0 to π domain in ω′ domain by decimation.

We take advantage of the inherent properties of decimation and interpolation *viz.* aliasing. Fig. 12.28 shows decimation by integer D. The input signal is first filtered by a bandpass filter, *i.e.*, a filter $h_{BP}(n)$ having ideal spectrum

$$H_{BP}(\omega) = \begin{cases} 1, & \frac{k\pi}{D} < |\omega| < \frac{(k+1)\pi}{D} \\ 0, & \text{otherwise} \end{cases} \qquad \text{...(12.65)}$$

where $k = 0, 1, 2, \ldots, D-1$, *i.e.*, the $H_{BP}(\omega)$ is restricted to bands $\omega = \frac{k\pi}{D}$ to $\frac{(k+1)\pi}{D}$, where $\frac{\pi}{D}$ is the band width. Note that when $k = 0$, the band of interest is already 0 to $\frac{\pi}{D}$ in ω domain (*i.e.* 0 to π in ω′ domain). In general, band pass filter $h_{BP}(n)$ filters the frequencies of the interested band, *i.e.* we obtain the resulting signal $x_{BP}(n)$, as shown in Fig. 12.28(*a*), which is bandlimited to, say, $\frac{2\pi}{D}$ to $\frac{3\pi}{D}$. Fig. 12.28(*d*).

The decimation by D to 1 reduces the sampling rate by a factor D. The resultant is $y(m)$ with spectrum $Y(\omega')$ where in $\left(\frac{2\pi}{D} - \frac{3\pi}{D}\right)$ band pass appears as 0 to π in ω′ domain. In fact, each of the bands, 0 to $\frac{\pi}{D}$; $\frac{\pi}{D}$ to $\frac{2\pi}{D}$; $\frac{2\pi}{D}$ to $\frac{3\pi}{D}$, ..., traces 0 to π in ω' domain due to decimation. Since there is no signal from 0 to $\frac{\pi}{D}$, $\frac{\pi}{D}$ to $\frac{2\pi}{D}$, [see Fig. 12.28(*d*)] in $X_{BP}(\omega)$, and the only signal exists in $\frac{2\pi}{D}$ to $\frac{3\pi}{D}$ in ω domain. Therefore, only this signal, shown 'hashed' in Fig. 12.28(*d*), appears 0 to π in ω' domain, as shown in Fig. 12.28(*e*), after decimation $D : 1$. This system will thus function satisfactorily only by choosing the interested band $\frac{k\pi}{D}$ to $\frac{(k+1)\pi}{D}$ in ω domain. This tentamounts to the fact that only specific frequency bands are allowed by this method to translate to band 0 to π in ω' domain. Clearly, when $k = 0, 2, 4, \ldots$, the translation to $0 - \pi$ in ω' domain is for upper side band. When $k = 1, 3, 5, \ldots$, the lower side band is traced from 0 to π in ω' domain. This corresponds to 'inverted band' having been traced in 0 to π in ω' domain. To achieve the upper side band from the inverted band, we take $\tilde{y}(m) = (-1)^m y(m)$. The spectrum of $\tilde{y}(m)$ will correspond to the inversion of spectrum $y(m)$ *i.e.* inversion of inverted spectrum *i.e.* the upper side band. This method is based on the fact that

$$FT(-1)^m y(m) = Y(\omega - \pi) \qquad \ldots(12.66)$$

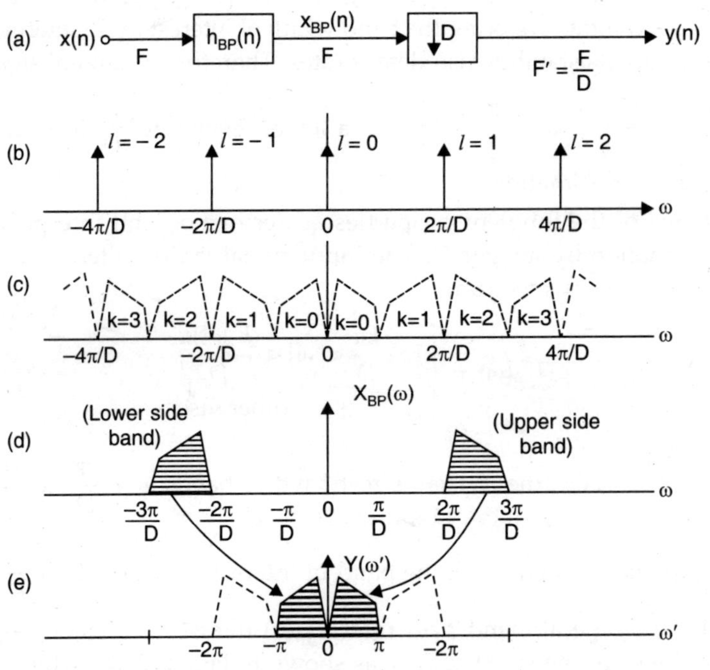

Fig. 12.28. Decimation of a band pass signal (*a*) The decimation using a band pass filter $h_{BP}(n)$ before the down rate converter *D* to 1 to select the bandpass signal to be used (*b*) The train of unit samples: $\sum_{l=-\infty}^{\infty} \delta\left(\omega - \frac{2\pi l}{D}\right)$ in ω domain (*c*) Convolution of $X_{BP}(\omega)$ and the samples given in (*b*), Eqn. (12.68) (*d*) A typical bandpass signal to be down sampled (*e*) The spectrum of $y(m)$ resulting from (*d*)

Figures 12.28(*b*), (*c*) show that

As $$X(\omega) * \delta\left(\omega - \frac{2\pi l}{D}\right) = X\left(\omega - \frac{2\pi l}{D}\right)$$

$$\therefore \quad X(\omega) * \sum_{l=-\infty}^{\infty} \delta\left(\omega - \frac{2\pi l}{D}\right) = \sum_{l=-\infty}^{\infty} X\left(\omega - \frac{2\pi l}{D}\right) \quad \ldots(12.67)$$

Hence, heterodyning leads to

$$X(\omega) * \sum_{l=0}^{D-1} \delta\left(\omega - \frac{2\pi l}{D}\right) = \sum_{l=0}^{D-1} X\left(\omega - \frac{2\pi l}{D}\right) \quad \ldots(12.68)$$

RHS of (12.68) shows that $X(\omega)$ appears as aliased version, repeated at an interval of $\frac{2\pi}{D}$ as shown in Fig. 12.28(*c*). In case we replace $H_D\left[(\omega_y - 2\pi k)/D\right]$ by $H_{BP}\left[(\omega' - 2\pi l)/D\right]$ and $X\left[(\omega_y - 2\pi k)/D\right]$ by $X\left[(\omega' - 2\pi l)/D\right]$, where $\omega' = D\omega$, in (12.15), we get

$$Y(\omega') = \frac{1}{D}\sum_{l=0}^{D-1} H_{BP}\left[(\omega' - 2\pi l)/D\right] X\left[(\omega' - 2\pi l)/D\right] \quad \ldots(12.69)$$

Note that $Y(\omega')$ in composed of D aliased components of $X(\omega')$. $H_{BP}(\omega')$, modulated by factor $\frac{2\pi l}{D}$. Figure 12.28(*b*) shows D possibie modulating frequencies which would result as a consequence of D to 1 sampling rate reduction.

There are digital sampling functions, (a periodic train of unit samples spaced D sample apart) has spectral components spaced $\frac{2\pi l}{D}$ apart.

Figure 12.28(*c*) shows the side bands that are associated with the spectrals spaced $\frac{2\pi l}{D}$ apart, which correspond to D choices of bands. It implies that any of the bands among these D choices would be translated to $0 - \pi$ in ω' (*i.e.*, ω_y) domain after decimation. To summarise the above discussion, we have the following significant results:

(*i*) There are D possible frequency bands, which would translate 0 to π in ω' (*i.e.*, ω_y) domain after decimation. These possible bands are $\left(0 - \frac{\pi}{D}\right), \left(\frac{\pi}{D} - \frac{2\pi}{D}\right), \ldots, \left(\frac{k\pi}{D} - \frac{(k+1)\pi}{D}\right)$, where $k = 0, 1, \ldots, D-1$.

(*ii*) Decimation by $D : 1$ amounts to convolution of spectra $[X_{BP}(\omega)]$ with sampling function $\delta\left(\omega - \frac{2\pi l}{D}\right)$, $l = 0, 1, \ldots, D-1$.

(*iii*) Modulation ('heterodyning') and sampling rate reduction are achieved simultaneously by D to 1 sampling reduction.

12.11 SOME APPLICATIONS OF MULTIRATE DIGITAL SIGNAL PROCESSING (MDSP)

Applications of Multirate DSP

1. Sub-band coding (*i.e.* speech, image)
2. Voice privacy using analog phone lines
3. Signal compression by sub-sampling
4. A/D, D/A converters etc.

Areas of use of MDSP

1. Speech and audio processing systems
2. Antenna systems
3. Communication systems
4. Radar, Sonar systems
5. Bio medical, geophysical
6. Graphics/imaging
7. Instrumentation
8. Control engineering
9. Consumer, industrial automation.

Advantages of MDSP

1. Computational requirements are less
2. Storage for filter coefficients are less
3. Finite arithmetic effects are less
4. Filter order required in multirate applications are low
5. Sensitivity to filter coefficient lengths are less. When we design multirate systems, effects of aliasing in decimation and pseudo images for interpolators must be avoided.

12.11.1 Design of Phase Shifters (by Application of Multirate DSP)

We wish to design a network that delays the signal $x(n)$ by a fraction of a sample. Assume that the delay is a rational function of a sampling interval T_x (T_x is the inter sample time of samples $x(n)$, *i.e.*, $T_x = 1/F_x$); we assume that delay time

$$d = \left(\frac{k}{I}\right)T_x \qquad \text{...(12.70)}$$

In the frequency domain, the delay d above corresponds to a linear phase shift of the forms

$$\theta(\omega) = -\left(\frac{k}{I}\right)\omega \qquad \text{...(12.71)}$$

The design of an ideal all-pass filter is some what difficult. However, we can use the method of sample-rate conversion to achieve a delay of $\left(\frac{k}{I}\right)T_x$ exactly without significant distortion in the signal. Consider the system shown in Fig. 12.29. First, we increase the sampling rate of $x(n)$ by a factor I to obtain $v(m)$. Each sample of $v(m)$ is time spaced by $\frac{T_x}{I}$. The low pass filter $h(n)$

removes the images of $X(\omega_x)$ beyond $|\omega_y| \geq \frac{\pi}{I}$. It implies that, as in interpolation cases [see (12.24)].

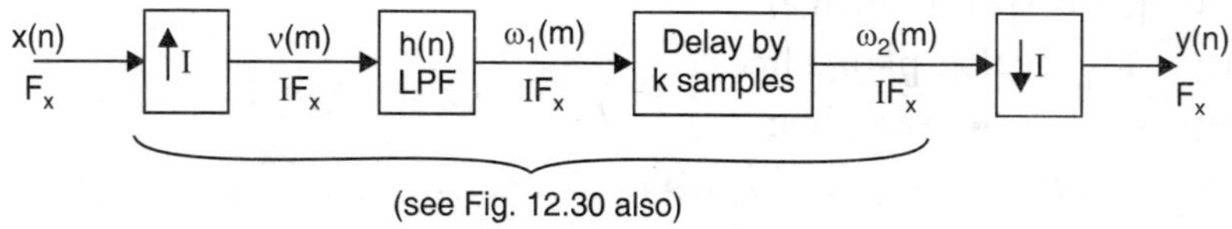

Fig. 12.29. System to generate a delay of $\left(\frac{k}{I}\right)T_x$ for $x(n)$

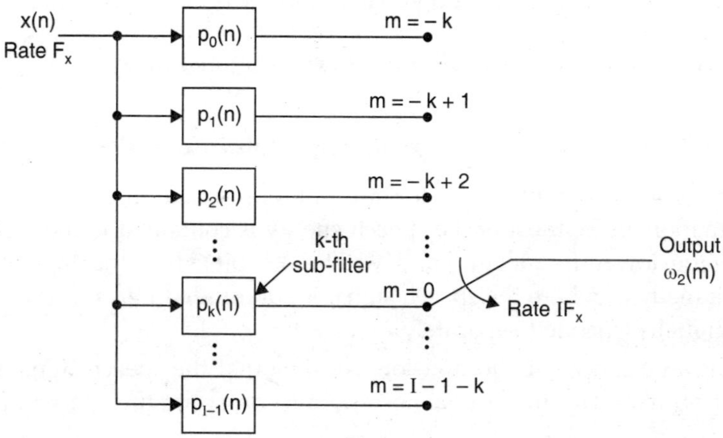

Fig. 12.30. Polyphase filter structure for implementing the system shown in Fig. 12.29 (the first three blocks)

$$H(\omega_y) = \begin{cases} I, & 0 \leq |\omega_y| \leq \dfrac{\pi}{I} \\ 0, & \text{otherwise} \end{cases} \qquad \ldots(12.72)$$

Thereafter, we delay $v(m)$ by k samples, *i.e.*,

$$\omega_2(m) = \omega_1(m - k) \qquad \ldots(12.73)$$

Note that $\omega_2(m)$ is delayed version of $\omega_1(m)$ by k samples, *i.e.*, in time domain, $\omega_2(m)$ is delayed version of $\omega_1(m)$ with a time delay of $\left(\frac{k}{I}\right)T_x$. The delayed signal $\omega_2(m)$ is decimated by a factor $D = I$. Thus we achieve the desired delay of $\left(\frac{k}{I}\right)T_x$ for the signal $x(n)$, now available as $y(n)$. Hence

$$y(nT_x) = x\left[\left(n - \frac{k}{I}\right)T_x\right] \qquad \ldots(12.74a)$$

or

$$y(n) = x\left(n - \frac{k}{I}\right) \qquad \ldots(12.74b)$$

An efficient implementation of the interpolator, for causing a fractional delay of $\left(\frac{k}{I}\right)T_x$, is the polyphase filter, shown in Fig. 12.30. The delay of k samples (in IF_x rate) is achieved by placing the initial position of the commutator at the output of the k-th polyphase sub-filter. This causes delaying $x(nT_x)$ to result $x\left(nT_x - \frac{k}{I}T_x\right) = x\left(\left(n - \frac{k}{I}\right)T_x\right)$ as given by [12.74(*a*)].

Since decimation by $D = I$, as implemented by the fourth block in Fig. 12.29, means that we take one out of every I samples from the polyphase filter, the commutator position can be fixed to the output of the k-th subfilter. Thus a delay in $\frac{k}{I}$ can be achieved *by using only the k-th subfilter of the* polyphase filter. We note that each polyphase subfilter is an all pass filter. If each subfilter has M samples, the polyphase subfilter will introduce additional delay of $\frac{(M-1)}{2}$ samples.

12.11.2 Subband Coding of Speech Signals (by Multirate DSP)

Speech signal coding is an important subject for efficient representation, storage and transmission of the speech information. Since most of the speech energy is contained in the lower frequencies, we always encode the lower frequency band with more bits than the high-frequency band. Subband coding is a method, where the speech signal is subdivided into several frequency bands and each band is digitally encoded separately.

Figure 12.31(*a*) is an example of sub division. Assume that the speech signal is sampled at a rate F_x samples per second. The first frequency subdivision splits the spectrum $X(\omega)$ into two equal-width segments, a low pass signal $\left(0 \le F \le \frac{F_x}{4}\right)$ and a high pass signal $\left(\frac{F_x}{4} \le F \le \frac{F_x}{2}\right)$. Note that the signal $x(n)$, assuming a full band, has highest frequency $F_{\max} = \frac{F_x}{2}$.

The second frequency subdivision splits the low pass signal from the first into two equal bands, a low pass signal $\left(0 \le F \le \frac{F_x}{8}\right)$ and a high pass signal $\left(\frac{F_x}{8} \le F \le \frac{F_x}{4}\right)$. Finally, the third frequency subdivision splits the low pass signal from the second stage into two equal bandwidth signals. The signal, thus subdivided into four frequency bands covering three octaves is shown in Fig. 12.31(*b*).

Decimation by a factor of 2 is performed after each frequency sub division. This makes the subdivided (to half the bandwidth of π) to appear as a signal covering full bandwidth in the decimated ω scale. Note that a signal covering the bandwidth 0 to $\frac{\pi}{2}$ when sampled at the rate F_x (*i.e.*, upto normalized frequency: $\omega/F_x = 2\pi F/F_x = 2\pi \cdot (F_{\max}/2)/2F_{\max} = \pi/2$ for lower half band) will cover a band 0 to π when decimated by a factor of 2, for new sampling frequency being $F_x/2$. Hence, each decimation by a factor 2 makes lower half band $\left(0 \text{ to } \frac{\pi}{2}\right)$ translate into

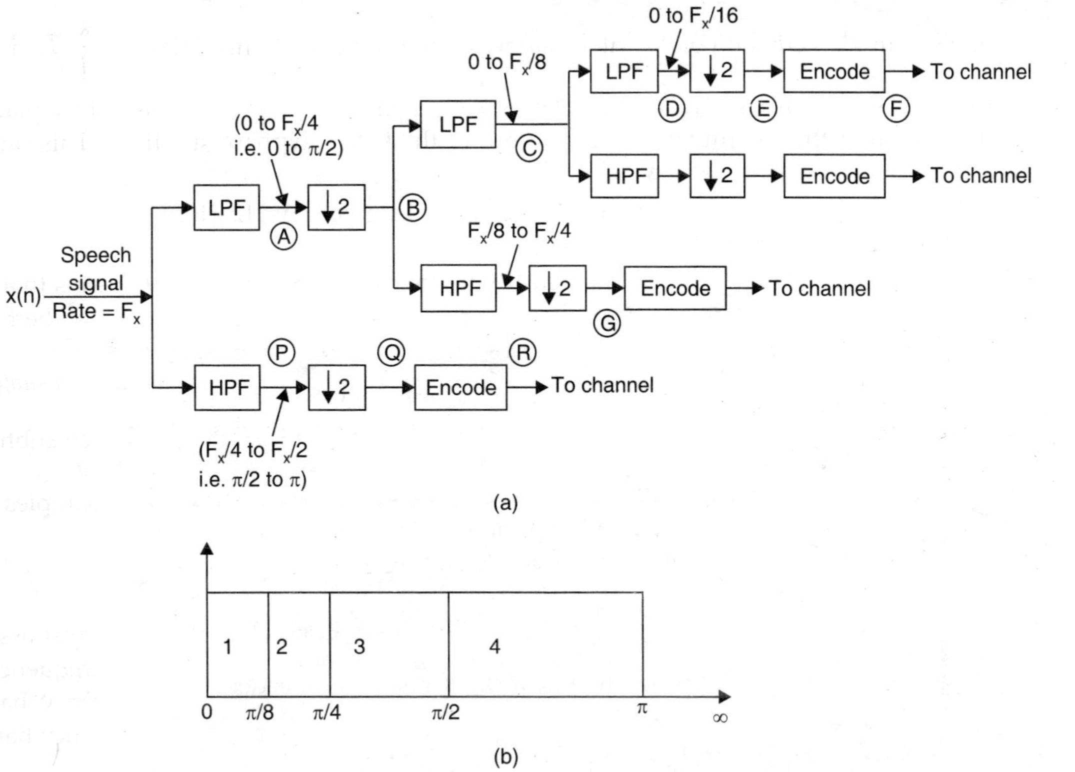

Fig. 12.31. Block diagram of a sub band coder (*a*) Procedure to obtain subband and (*b*) The subbands obtained in three octaves by three sub-divisions

full band (0 to π). Also, if the signal covers upper half band $\left(\frac{\pi}{2} \text{ to } \pi\right)$, if decimated by a factor $D = 2$, will cover full band (0 to π) after decimation. In short, by decimation 2 to 1, each half band spectrum 0 to $\frac{\pi}{2}$ or $\frac{\pi}{2}$ to π gets translated to full band (0 to π) spectrum in the decimated sampling rate. Thus spectrum at (*A*) is 0 to $\frac{\pi}{2}$ radians or 0 to $\frac{F_x}{4}$, and the spectrum at (*B*) is 0 to π (0 to $2\pi F_x/4(F_x/2)$, *i.e.*, 0 to π) at new sampling rate of $\frac{F_x}{2}$. In short the spectra at each point (*B*), (*E*), (*G*) and (*Q*) is 0 to π radians. This enables us to separate lower and upper half band signals by LPF and HPF efficiently by using half band filters.

We allocate different number of bits per sample to the signal in the four subbands, while encoding before sending the signals to channel. We achieve a reduction in the bit rate of the digitized speech signal besides giving more importance to low frequency signal (since the most of speech energy is contained in lower frequency).

To achieve good performance in sub band coding, the filter design is particularly important. Aliasing resulting from decimation of the sub band signals has to be negligible. The ideal, brick wall half-band signals as shown in Fig. 12.32(*a*) are physically unrealizable. A practical solution to the aliasing problem is to use *Quadrature Mirror Filters* (QMF), which have frequency characteristics as shown in Fig. 12.32(*b*). Efficient design of QMFs are available in the literature.

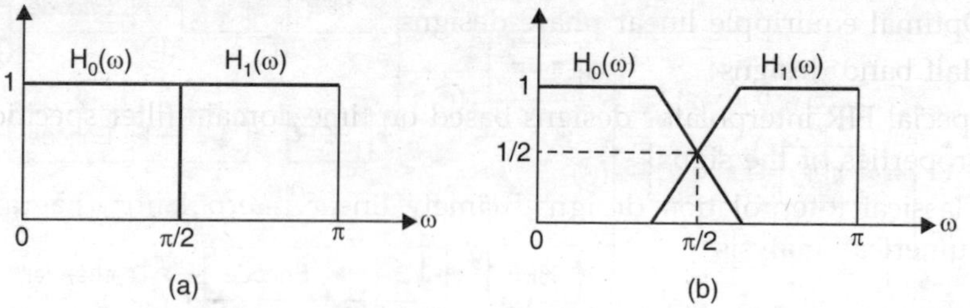

Fig. 12.32. Filter characteristics for subband-coding filters (a) Brickwall filters and (b) QMF filters

The synthesis method for the subband coded speech signal is the reverse of the encoding process. Fig. 12.33 shows block diagram of a synthesis system of subband coded signal. The signals in adjacent low pass and high pass frequency bands are interpolated (by factor of 2), filtered, and combined as shown by ⊕ in Fig. 12.33. A pair of QMF is used in the signal synthesis for each octave of the signal. Subband coding is an effective method to achieve data compression in image signal processing. By combining subband coding and vector quantization for each sub band, coded images with as low as $\frac{1}{2}$ bit per pixel of the image can be achieved. This compares favourably where 8 bits per pixel for the uncoded of image are needed.

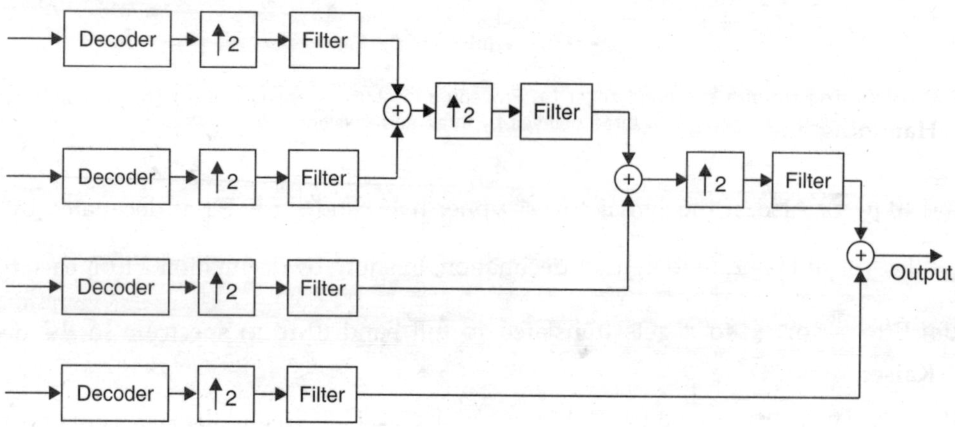

Fig. 12.33. Synthesis of a subband coded signal

In general, sub band coding of signals is an effective method for achieving bandwidth compression in a digital representation of the signal, when the signal energy is concentrated in a particular region of the frequency band. Multirate signal processing properties give us efficient implementation of the subband encoder and decoder.

12.12 FILTER DESIGN PROCEDURES

Nearly all the networks in digital signal processing can be solved by low pass (or band pass) filter design procedures.

Main categories of filter design procedures are:

(*i*) Window designs

(*ii*) Optimal equiripple linear phase designs

(*iii*) Half band designs

(*iv*) Special FIR interpolator designs based on time-domain filter specifications or stochastic properties of the signal

(*v*) Classical interpolation designs, namely linear interpolation, Lagrangian interpolation, numerical analysis

12.12.1 FIR Filters Based on Window Designs

One straight forward approach to design FIR filter for Decimators and Interpolators is by well-known method of windowing or truncating the ideal prototype response $\tilde{h}(k)$. But this leads to Gibb's phenomenon, which gives about 9% ripple in the frequency behaviour of the filter in the vicinity of filter magnitude discontinuities, *i.e.,* near the edges of the pass band and stop band. Also, the amplitude of this ripple does not decrease with increasing duration of the filter, (it only becomes narrower in width). Hence direct truncation or a rectangular windowing of $\tilde{h}(k)$ is rarely used in practice.

Rectangular Window

$$W_R(n) = \begin{cases} 1, & |n| \le \dfrac{N-1}{2} \\ 0, & \text{otherwise} \end{cases} \quad \ldots(12.75)$$

Hamming and Hann Window (Generalized Hamming Window)

$$W_H(k) = \begin{cases} \alpha + (1-\alpha)\cos\dfrac{2\pi k}{N-1}, & |k| \le \dfrac{N-1}{2} \\ 0, & \text{otherwise} \end{cases} \quad \ldots(12.76)$$

$\alpha = 0.54$ for Hamming
$= 0.5$ for Hann

Kaiser Window

$$W_K(k) = \begin{cases} \dfrac{I_0\left(\beta\sqrt{1-\left(\dfrac{2k}{N-1}\right)^2}\right)}{I_0(\beta)}, & |k| \le \dfrac{N-1}{2} \\ 0, & \text{otherwise} \end{cases} \quad \ldots(12.77)$$

The windowed filter $h(k)$ is then given by

$$h(k) = \tilde{h}(k)\cdot\omega(k), \quad \frac{-(N-1)}{2} \le k \le \frac{N-1}{2} \quad \ldots(12.78)$$

where we have assumed that $\omega(k)$ is a symmetrical, N point (N odd) window.

The window designs have the property that they preserve the zero crossing pattern of $\tilde{h}(k)$ in the actual filter design $h(k)$. Hence if $\tilde{h}(k)$ is obtained as $\tilde{h}(k) = \dfrac{\sin(\pi k/L)}{(\pi k/L)}$, $k = 0, \pm 1, \pm 2, \ldots$ then time domain properties of $\tilde{h}(k)$ *viz.* symmetry, every L-th sample of $\tilde{h}(k)$ being zero, zeroth polynomial $p(n) = p_0(n) = \delta(n)\ldots$ etc. apply to $h(k)$ as well.

Advantages of window design are:

(*i*) It is simple, easy to use.

(*ii*) Can be readily implemented in a direct manner.

(*iii*) Closed form expressions for window coefficients are available. Hence window and filter responses can be obtained readily.

(*iv*) It preserves the zeros of $\tilde{h}(k)$ and hence saving in computations time continues for $h(k)$ too.

Disadvantages:

(*i*) Only limited control in choosing cut off frequencies.

(*ii*) Pass band and stop band errors for most cases.

(*iii*) Resulting filter design are sub optimal (or conservative).

12.12.2 Equiripple (Optimal) FIR Designs

Windowing technique is a straight forward approach to design digital filters, in all sampling rate conversions. There are more sophisticated techniques too available. One such method is based on Chebyshev approximation methods. Filter designed by this technique are optimal in the sense that peak (weighted) approximation error in the frequency domain (over the frequency range of interest) is minimised.

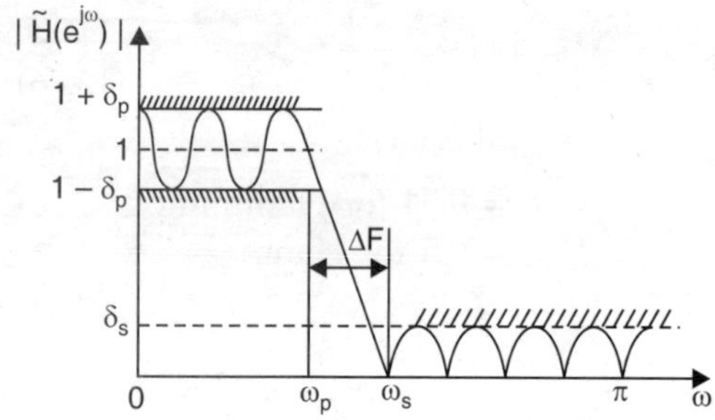

Fig. 12.34. Illustration of tolerance scheme for a practical LP filter

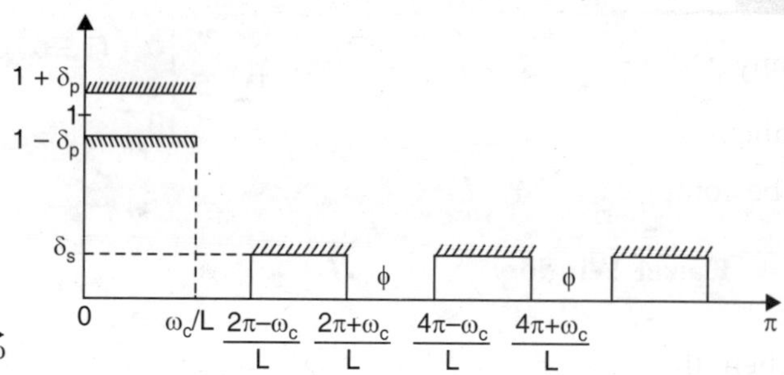

Fig. 12.35. Illustration of a tolerance scheme for multiband interpolator filter

Standard tolerance scheme is as shown in Fig. 12.34 for a low pass filter where

δ_p = ripple (deviation) in the pass band from the ideal response

δ_s = ripple (deviation) in the stop band from the ideal response

F_p = pass band edge frequency $= \dfrac{\omega_p}{2\pi}$

F_s = stop band edge frequency $= \dfrac{\omega_s}{2\pi}$

N = Number of taps in the FIR filter.

Figure 12.34 shows a practical tolerance scheme for a multiband design of a 1 to L interpolator when input spectrum is $\omega_c(< \pi)$.

Given the above tolerance scheme, filter approximation problem can be solved by using standard techniques for Chebyshev approximation. Computer programs are also available for such designs. Multiple exchange Remez Algorithm or a single exchange linear programing solutions are also useful for the designs. Equiripple in pass band as well as in stop band is truly an Elliptic approximation. This is also called Jacobian approximation.

Kaiser windows are also very much popular for efficient and quick approximations. The value of filter length M is given by

$$\boxed{M = \frac{(-10 \log (\delta_1 \cdot \delta_2) - 13)}{(14.6\, \Delta F)} + 1} \qquad ...(12.79)$$

where
$$\delta_1 = \text{Pass band ripple}$$
$$\delta_2 = \text{stop band ripple}$$
$$\Delta F = \frac{(F_s - F_p)}{(\text{Sampling Frequency})}$$
$$= \text{normalized transition bandwidth}$$
$$F_p = \text{Pass band } (\textit{i.e.} \text{ pass band cut off})$$
$$F_s = \text{Stop band (start of stop band)}$$
$$M = \text{Filter length or taps.}$$

12.13 MULTISTAGE IMPLEMENTATION OF SAMPLING RATE CONVERSION

In many practical applications, we have decimation factors (D) and interpolation factors (I) which are much larger than unity. For example, if $\frac{I}{D} = \frac{260}{63}$, we shall require 260 polyphase filters. This may be computationally inefficient. If we have $D \gg 1$ and $I \gg 1$, we use cascades. Assume that

$$I = \prod_{i=1}^{L} I_i \qquad ...(12.80)$$

Then, the interpolation factor I can be achieved in L cascaded stages as shown in Fig. 12.36.

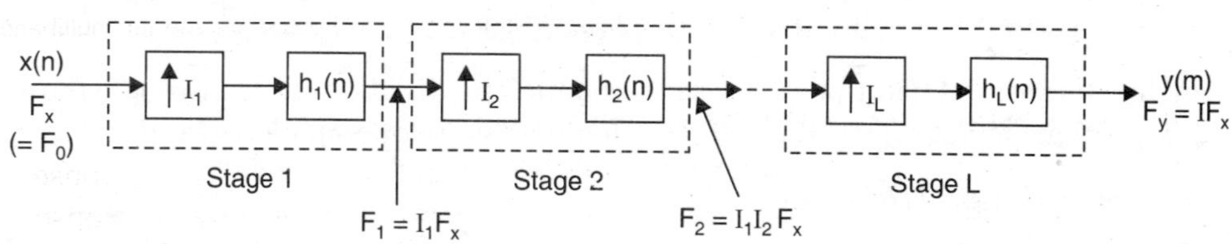

Fig. 12.36. Multistage implementation of Interpolation by a factor $I = I_1 \cdot I_2 \ldots I_L$

In a similar manner, for decimation by a factor $D \gg 1$, we factorize D as

$$D = \prod_{i=1}^{M} D_i \qquad ...(12.81)$$

Assume that the input sampling rate $F_x = F_0$ for $x(n)$.

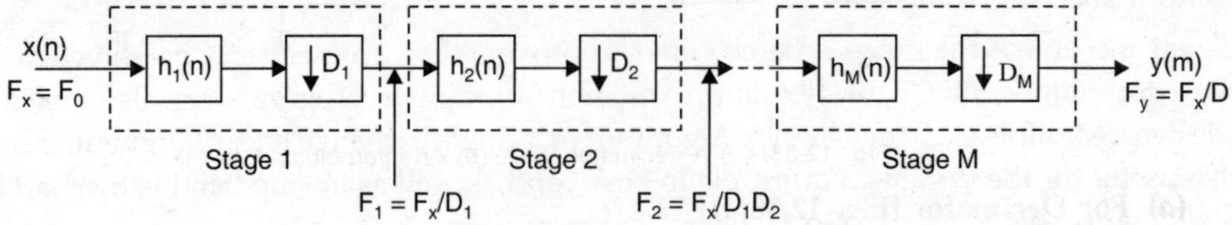

Fig. 12.37. Multistage implementation of Decimation by a factor $D = D_1 \cdot D_2 \ldots D_M$

Then the decimation of D can be implemented as multistage as shown in Fig. 12.37 in M cascade stages note that the sampling rate at the output of i-th stage is given by

$$F_i = \frac{F_{i-1}}{D_i},\ i = 1, 2, \ldots, M \qquad \ldots(12.82)$$

As decimation can cause aliasing if factor D causes the overall sampling rate $F_y = \frac{F_x}{D}$ less than twice the pass band frequency of $x(n)$, we must design each filter stage to avoid aliasing with in the frequency band of interest.

Suppose the signal at $x(n)$ is sampled at a rate F_x. We wish to design the filter $h_i(n)$ at the i-th decimation stage. Suppose overall decimation required is to fulfill

$$\left.\begin{array}{l}\text{Pass band}: 0 \le F \le F_p \\ \text{Transition band}: F_p \le F \le F_s\end{array}\right\} \qquad \ldots(12.83)$$

It is assumed that final sampling frequency $\frac{F_x}{D}$ is greater than twice the F_s, *i.e.*, $F_s \le \frac{1}{2}\frac{F_x}{D}$.

Then to avoid aliasing of frequency band of each stage, we design for the i-th stage which results sampling frequency F_s, we assume

$$\left.\begin{array}{l}\text{Pass band}: 0 \le F \le F_p \\ \text{Transition band}: F_p \le F \le F_i - F_s \\ \text{Stop band}: F_i - F_s \le F \le F_{i-1}/2\end{array}\right\} \qquad \ldots(12.84)$$

For example, in the first stage of decimation of D_1, the filter $h_1(n)$ is designed to meet the specifications:

$$\left.\begin{array}{l}\text{Pass band}: 0 \le F \le F_p \\ \text{Transition band}: F_p \le F \le F_1 - F_s \\ \text{Stop band}: F_1 - F_s \le F \le F_x/2 \ (\because\ \ F_0 = F_x)\end{array}\right\} \qquad \ldots(12.85)$$

Normalized transition band in each case in obtained by dividing the transition bandwidth by the sampling frequency at which the LPF $h(n)$ for that stage operates.

Rule to Design Multirate FIR Filters

Assume the given specifications as:

Pass band : $0 \le F \le F_p$

Transition band : $F_p \le F \le F_s$

Pass band ripple : δ_1

Stop band ripple : δ_2

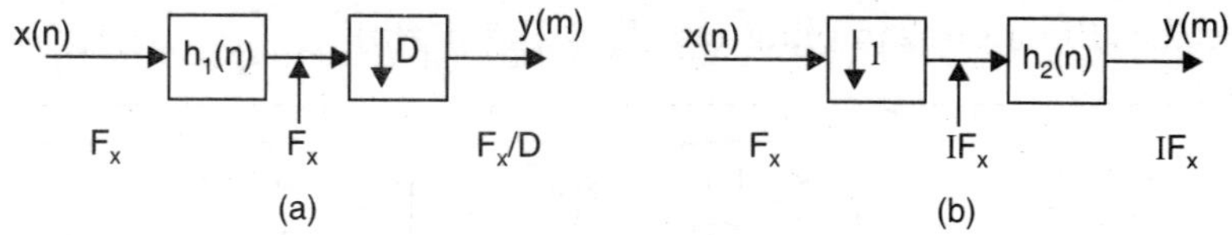

Fig. 12.38. (*a*) A decimator D : 1 (*b*) An interpolator 1 to I

(*a*) For Decimator [Fig. 12.38(*a*)]

$$\text{Revised stopband } F_s = \frac{F_x}{D} - F_s \triangleq F_{s1}$$

$$\text{Revised } \Delta F_1 = \frac{(F_{s1} - F_p)}{F_x} \qquad (F_x \text{ is rate of } h_1(n))$$

(*b*) For Interpolator [Fig. 12.38(*b*)]

$$\text{Revised stopband } F_s = F_x - F_s \triangleq F_{s2}$$

$$\text{Revised } \Delta F_2 = \frac{(F_{s2} - F_p)}{IF_x} \qquad (IF_x \text{ is rate of } h_2(n))$$

(*c*) Revised ($\delta_1\delta_2$) product (both cases)

$$\text{Revised } (\delta_1\delta_2) = \frac{(\delta_1\delta_2)}{2} \text{ if only one stage used}$$

$$\text{Revised } (\delta_1\delta_2) = \frac{(\delta_1\delta_2)}{4} \text{ if two stages in cascade used}$$

$$\text{Tap (Multiplications) : } M = \frac{-10\log(\text{revised } \delta_1\delta_2) - 13}{14.6\,(\text{Revised } \Delta F)} + 1 \qquad \text{(by Kaiser formula)}$$

Solved Examples in Multirate Digital Signal Processing

EXAMPLE 12.1: *Show that the up-sampler is a time-varying system.*

SOLUTION: For an up sampler, we have

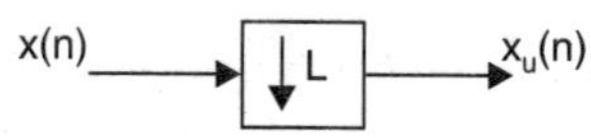

$$x(n) = \begin{cases} x\left(\dfrac{n}{L}\right), & n = 0, \pm L, \pm 2L, \ldots \\ 0, & \text{otherwise} \end{cases} \qquad \ldots(A)$$

i.e., calling outputs as $x_{u1}(n)$ and $x_{u2}(n)$ for inputs $x_1(n)$ and $x_2(n)$

$$x_{u1}(n) = \begin{cases} x_1\left(\dfrac{n}{L}\right), & n = 0, \pm L, \pm 2L \\ 0, & \text{otherwise} \end{cases} + \ldots, \qquad \ldots(B)$$

and

$$x_{u2}(n) = \begin{cases} x_2\left(\dfrac{n}{L}\right), & n = 0, \pm L, \pm 2L, \ldots \\ 0, & \text{otherwise} \end{cases} \qquad \ldots(C)$$

Let $x_2(n) = x_1(n - n_0)$. If $x_{u2}(n) = x_{u1}(n - n_0)$, then the system would be time-invariant, otherwise not. Putting $x_2(n) = x_1(n - n_0)$ in (C), we get

$$x_{u2}(n) = \begin{cases} x_1\left(\left(\frac{n}{L}\right) - n_0\right), & n = 0, \pm L, \pm 2L, \ldots \\ 0, & \text{otherwise} \end{cases} \quad \ldots(D)$$

Also, $x_{u1}(n - n_0)$ from (B) is obtained as

$$x_{u1}(n - n_0) = \begin{cases} x_1\left(\frac{(n - n_0)}{L}\right), & (n - n_0) = 0, \pm L, \pm 2L, \ldots \\ 0, & \text{otherwise} \end{cases} \quad \ldots(E)$$

From (D) and (E), $x_{u2}(n) \neq x_{u1}(n - n_0)$, hence the up sampler is NOT time invariant *i.e.* it is time-variant system.

EXAMPLE 12.2: *Show that up-sampler and the down-sampler are linear systems.*

SOLUTION: Up-Sampler:

As $$y(n) = \begin{cases} x\left(\frac{n}{L}\right), & n = 0, \pm L, \pm 2L, \ldots \\ 0, & \text{otherwise} \end{cases}$$

Let inputs be $x_1(n)$, $x_2(n)$ and $\alpha x_1(n) + \beta x_2(n)$. The outputs will be

Input Output

$x_1(n)$ $$y_1(n) = \begin{cases} x_1\left(\frac{n}{L}\right), & n = 0, \pm L, \pm 2L, \ldots \\ 0, & \text{otherwise} \end{cases}$$

$x_2(n)$ $$y_2(n) = \begin{cases} x_2\left(\frac{n}{L}\right), & n = 0, \pm L, \pm 2L, \ldots \\ 0, & \text{otherwise} \end{cases}$$

$\alpha x_1(n) + \beta x_2(n)$ $$y_3(n) = \begin{cases} \alpha x_1\left(\frac{n}{L}\right) + \beta x_2\left(\frac{n}{L}\right), & n = 0, \pm L, \pm 2L, \ldots \\ 0, & \text{otherwise} \end{cases}$$

$$= \begin{cases} \alpha x_1\left(\frac{n}{L}\right) \\ 0, \end{cases} + \begin{cases} \beta x_2\left(\frac{n}{L}\right), & n = 0, \pm L, \pm 2L, \ldots \\ 0, & \text{otherwise} \end{cases}$$

i.e., $$y_3(n) = \alpha y_1(n) + \beta y_2(n)$$ $\therefore$ up sampler is linear.

Down-sampler: Here $y(n) = x(Mn)$

Let inputs be $x_1(n)$, $x_2(n)$, $\alpha x_1(n) + \beta x_2(n)$. The outputs will be

$$y_1(n) = x_1(Mn)$$
$$y_2(n) = x_2(Mn)$$
$$y_3(n) = \alpha x_1(Mn) + \beta x_2(Mn)$$

i.e., $$y_3(n) = \alpha y_1(n) + \beta y_2(n)$$ $\therefore$ down sampler is linear.

EXAMPLE 12.3: *Prove the identity*

$$C(n) = \begin{cases} 1, & n = 0, \pm M, \pm 2M \\ 0, & otherwise \end{cases}$$

$$= \frac{1}{M}\sum_{k=0}^{M-1} W_M^{kn}, \; W_M = e^{-j2\pi/M}.$$

SOLUTION: If

$$C(n) = \frac{1}{M}\sum_{k=0}^{M-1} W_M^{kn}$$

$$= \frac{1}{M}\left(\frac{1-W_M^{nM}}{1-W_M^{n}}\right) = \frac{1}{M}\left(\frac{1-e^{(-j2\pi/M)nM}}{1-e^{-j2\pi n/M}}\right)$$

$$= \frac{1}{M}\frac{1-e^{-j2\pi n}}{1-e^{-j2\pi n/M}} = 0 \text{ if } n \text{ is not multiple of } M$$

$= 1$ if n is multiple of M (by L'Hospital's rule)

$\therefore$ $$C(n) = \begin{cases} 1, & n = 0, \pm M, \pm 2M, \ldots, \\ 0, & \text{otherwise} \end{cases}$$ Q.E.D.

EXAMPLE 12.4: *Show that* $y(n) = x(n-1)$ *in the system shown.*

SOLUTION:

$$V(z) = \frac{1}{2}X(z^{1/2}) + \frac{1}{2}X(-z^{1/2})$$

$$W(z) = \frac{1}{2}z^{-1/2}X(z^{1/2}) + \left[\frac{1}{2}(-z^{-1/2})X(-z^{1/2})\right]$$

$$V_u(z) = \frac{1}{2}X(z) + \frac{1}{2}X(-z) \quad (\text{changing } z^{1/2} \text{ to } z \text{ in } V(z)) \quad \ldots(1)$$

$$W_u(z) = \frac{1}{2}z^{-1}X(z) - \frac{1}{2}z^{-1}X(-z) \quad (\text{changing } z^{1/2} \text{ to } z \text{ in } W(z)) \quad \ldots(2)$$

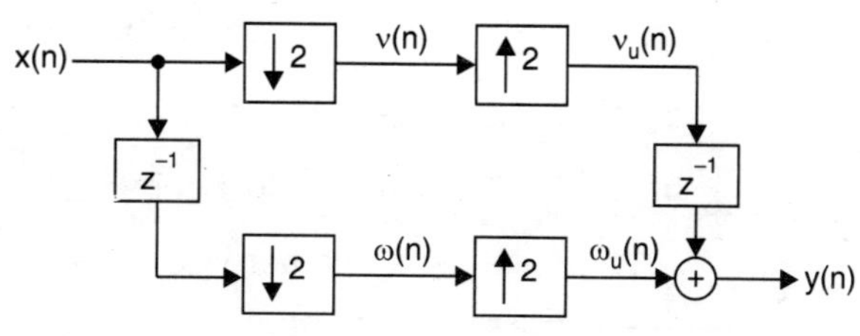

Fig. Ex. 12.4. The given system.

For	$M = 2,\ Y(z) = \frac{1}{2}[X(z^{1/2}) + X(-z^{1/2})]$
For	$L = 2,\ X_u(z) = X(z^2)$

$$Y(z) = z^{-1}V_u(z) + W_u(z)$$

$$= z^{-1}\left[\frac{1}{2}X(z) + \frac{1}{2}X(-z)\right] + \frac{1}{2}z^{-1}X(z) - \frac{1}{2}z^{-1}X(-z) = z^{-1}X(z)$$

$\therefore$ $$y(n) = x(n - 1)$$ Q.E.D.

EXAMPLE 12.5: *We wish to convert the data sampled at a sampling frequency of 44.1 KHz (as in a Compact Disc) to a sampling frequency of 48.0 KHz (as in a Digital Audio Tape) to facilitate data transfer from a CD to DAT. Suggest a suitable multirate system.*

SOLUTION: Clearly, we want to up convert a sampling rate of 44.1 KHz to 48.0 KHz. The system shown in Fig. Ex. 12.5 is, therefore suitable

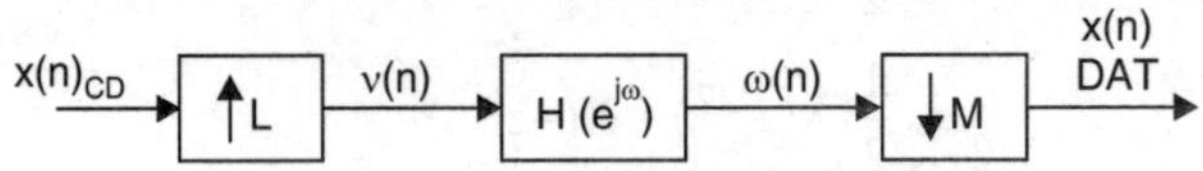

Fig. Ex. 12.5. The up conversion by $\frac{L}{M}$ ratio

Here,
$$44.1 \text{ KHz} = 44100 = 2^2 \times 3^2 \times 5^2 \times 7^2$$
$$48.0 \text{ KHz} = 48000 = 2^7 \times 3 \times 5^3$$

$$\therefore \quad \frac{L}{M} = \frac{2^7 \times 3 \times 5^3}{2^2 \times 3^2 \times 5^2 \times 7^2} = \frac{2^5 \times 5}{3 \times 7^2} = \frac{160}{147}$$

Therefore, if we up sample by $L = 160$, and then down sample by $M = 147$, we would achieve the desired rate conversion.

The low-pass filter $H(e^{j\omega})$ required is such that its cut off frequency

$$\omega_c = \min\left(\frac{\pi}{L}, \frac{\pi}{M}\right) = \min\left(\frac{\pi}{160}, \frac{\pi}{147}\right) = \frac{\pi}{160}$$

The gain of the LPF = L = 160 **Ans.**

EXAMPLE 12.6: *Consider the sequence $x(n) = a^n u(n)$, $|a| < 1$*

(a) Determine the spectrum $X(\omega)$

(b) The signal $x(n)$ is applied to a decimator that reduces the rate by a factor of 2. Determine the output spectrum.

(c) Show that the spectrum in part (b) is simply the Fourier transform of $x(2n)$.

SOLUTION:

(a)
$$X(e^{j\omega}) = \sum_{n=-\infty}^{\infty} x(n)e^{-j\omega n} \quad \text{(by definition of Fourier transform)}$$

$$= \sum_{n=0}^{\infty} a^n \cdot e^{-j\omega n} \quad \text{(as here)}$$

$$= \frac{1}{1 - ae^{-j\omega}} \quad \because |a| < 1 \therefore |ae^{-j\omega}| < 1$$

(b) Note that here

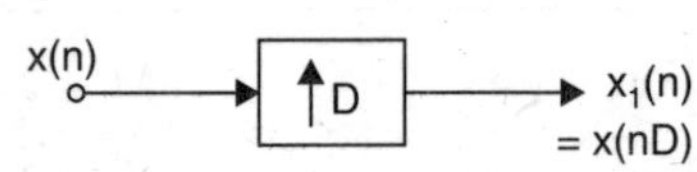

$$X(z) = \frac{1}{1 - az^{-1}}$$

After passing through the decimator by D, we have

$$X_1(z) = \frac{1}{D}\sum_{l=0}^{D-1} X(z^{1/D}W_D^l) \quad \text{where } W_D = e^{-j2\pi/D}$$

Here $D = 2$

$$\therefore \quad X_1(z) = \frac{1}{2}\sum_{l=0}^{1} X\left(z^{1/2} \cdot e^{-j\frac{2\pi l}{2}}\right)$$

$$= \frac{1}{2}[X(z^{1/2}) + X(z^{1/2}X(-1))]$$

$$= \frac{1}{2}[X(z^{1/2}) + X(-z^{1/2})]$$

As $$X(z) = \frac{1}{1-az^{-1}}$$

$$\therefore \quad X_1(z) = \frac{[X(z^{1/2}) + X(-z^{1/2})]}{2}$$

$$= \frac{1}{2}\left[\frac{1}{1-az^{-1/2}} + \frac{1}{1+az^{-1/2}}\right]$$

$$= \frac{1}{2}\frac{(1+az^{-1/2}) + (1-az^{-1/2})}{1-a^2z^{-1}}$$

$$= \frac{1}{1-a^2z^{-1}}$$

$$\therefore \quad X_1(e^{j\omega}) = X_1(z)\Big|_{z=e^{j\omega}}$$

i.e., $$X_1(e^{j\omega}) = \frac{1}{1-a^2e^{-j\omega}} \quad \textbf{Ans.}$$

(c) $$F.T.[x(2n)] = \sum_{n=-\infty}^{\infty} x(2n)\, e^{-j\omega n}$$

Putting $$x(2n) = a^n u(n)\Big|_{'n'=2n} = a^{2n}u(2n)$$

$$\therefore \quad F.T.[x(2n)] = \sum_{n=-\infty}^{\infty} a^{2n}u(2n)\, e^{-j\omega n}$$

$$= \sum_{n=0}^{\infty} a^{2n}\, e^{-j\omega n}$$

$$= \frac{1}{1-a^2e^{-j\omega}} \qquad \because \ |a^2e^{-j\omega}| < 1 \text{ due to } |a| < 1 \text{ (given)}$$

Thus, $$X_1(e^{j\omega}) = F.T.[x(2n)]$$ Q.E.D.

EXAMPLE 12.7: *Prove that the Fig. Ex. 12.7 (a) and (b) shown below are equivalent.*

SOLUTION: This is a useful Identity. The cascade structure as shown in Fig. Ex. 12.7 appears in a number of applications.

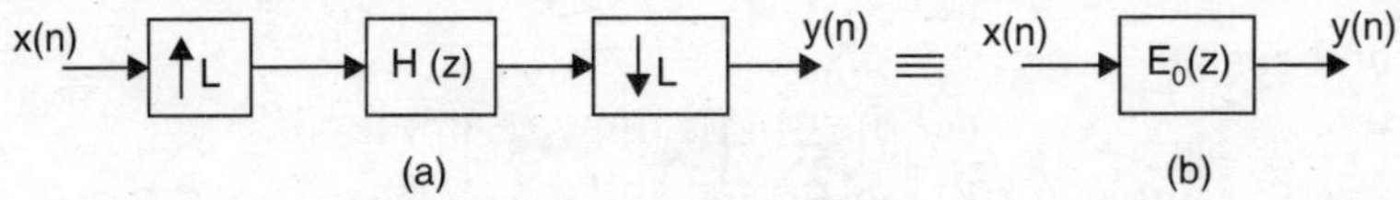

Fig. Ex. 12.7. (*a*) A cascade multirate structure, (*b*) its equivalent form

Proof:

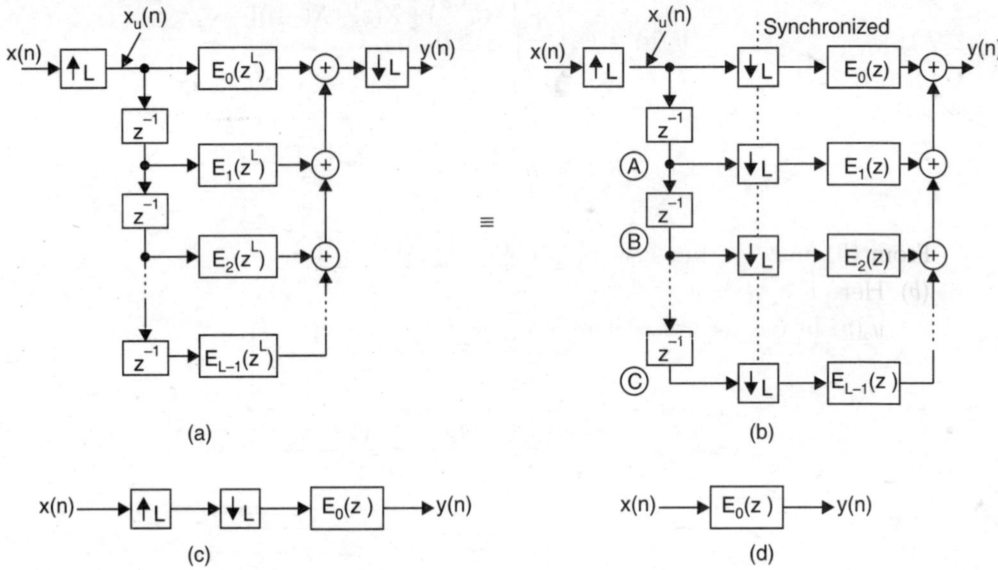

Realize structure of Fig. Ex. 12.7(*a*) by Fig. Ex. 12.7 (*a*) above using polyphase filters of type *I*. Using equivalence relation, we get Fig. (*b*). In Fig. Ex. 12.7 (*b*) when down sampler picks up, say $x(1)$ then signals at locations (*A*), (*B*), ..., (*C*) are $L - 1$ zeros. So $E_1(z)$, $E_2(z)$, ..., $E_{L-1}(z)$ have inputs zeros. These always are fed by zeros. Hence $E_1(z)$, $E_2(z)$, ..., $E_{L-1}(z)$ contribute zeros towards $y(n)$. Figure Ex. 12.7 (*b*), therefore, reduces to Fig. Ex. 12.7 (*c*) and hence to Fig. Ex. 12.7 (*d*). This proves the identity. Q.E.D.

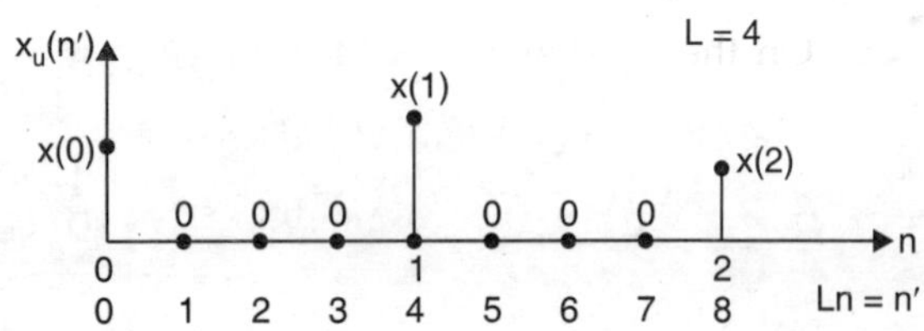

EXAMPLE 12.8: *In the following two different systems*

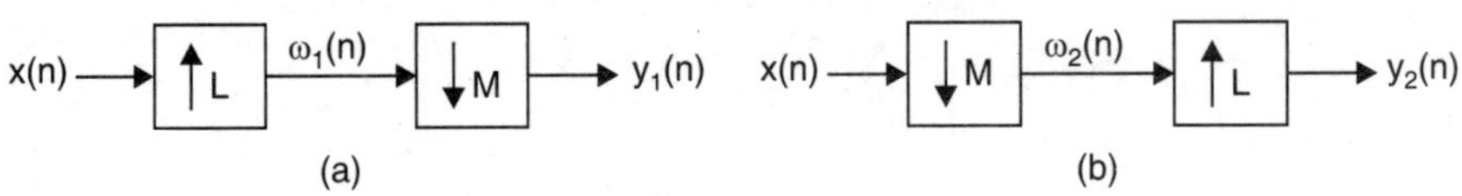

(a) If M = L, show that the two systems are not identical.

(b) Under what conditions will the two systems be identical?

SOLUTION:

(*a*) $L = M$ case

In first system $$\omega_1(n) = x\left(\frac{n}{L}\right) \quad ...(A)$$

$$y_1(n) = \omega_1(Mn) = x\left(\frac{n}{L}M\right)$$

$$\therefore \quad y_1(n) = x(n) \qquad (\because L = M) \quad ...(B)$$

In the second system

$$\omega_2(n) = x(nM) \text{ (down sampling)} \qquad \ldots(C)$$

Only every M-th sample of $x(n)$ is extracted and the other $M-1$ samples of $x(n)$ are discarded. The upsampler inserts $L-1$ zeros between each value of $\omega_2(n)$. Thus

$$y_2(n) = \omega_2\left(\frac{n}{L}\right), \; n = 0, \pm L, \pm 2L, \ldots,$$

$$= \begin{cases} x\left(\dfrac{nM}{L}\right), & n = 0, \pm L, \pm 2L, \ldots \\ 0, & \text{otherwise} \end{cases} \qquad \ldots(D)$$

From (B) and (D), the systems are not same as $y_1(n) \neq y_2(n)$.

(*b*) Here $L \neq M$

$y_2(n)$ in the second system, given by (B) is shown in Fig. (*a*) below

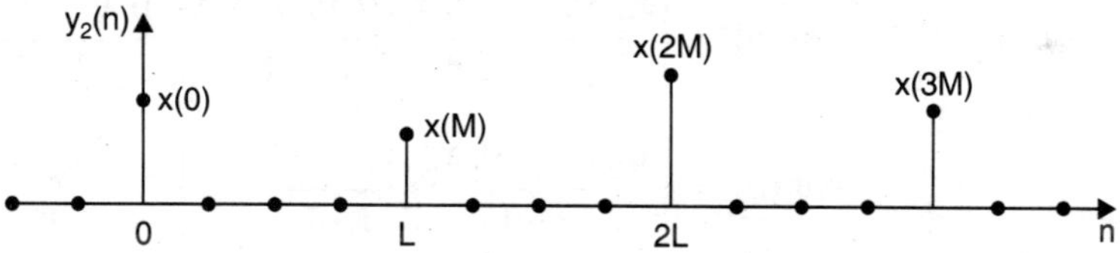

Fig. (*a*) Sequence $y_2(n)$ from second system

On the other hand $\omega_1(n)$ in the first system in Fig. (*b*).

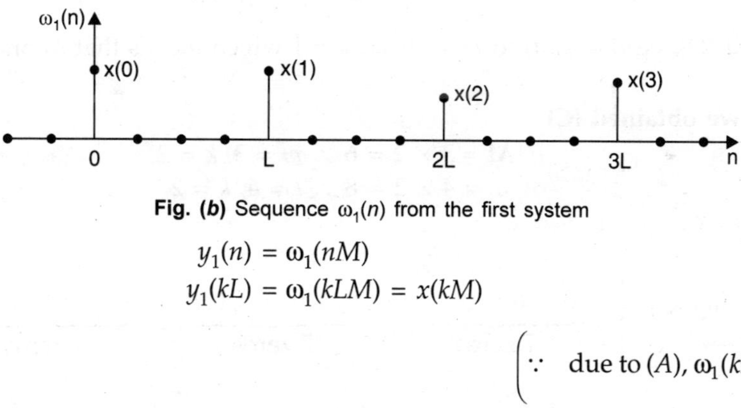

Fig. (*b*) Sequence $\omega_1(n)$ from the first system

As $\qquad y_1(n) = \omega_1(nM)$

$\therefore \qquad y_1(kL) = \omega_1(kLM) = x(kM) \qquad \ldots(E)$

$$\left(\because \text{ due to } (A), \; \omega_1(kLM) = x\left(\frac{kLM}{L}\right)\right)$$

But $\therefore \qquad y_2(kL) = x\left(kL\dfrac{M}{L}\right)$

i.e., $\qquad y_2(kL) = x(kM) \qquad \ldots(F)$

From (E) and (F), $y_1(kL) = y_2(kL)$

However, in order of $y_1(n)$ to be equal $y_2(n)$, we require that

$$y_1(n) = \omega_1(nm) = 0, \text{ for } n \neq kL \quad [\because y_2(n) \text{ holds this condition from } (D)]$$

This will be true iff M and L are relatively prime. **Ans.**

Alternative Solution

(*a*) Let $L = M = 2$

In Fig. (*a*), interpolation by $L = 2$ gives us

$$\omega_1(n) = \{x_0, 0, x_1, 0, x_2, 0, \ldots\}$$

Decimation of $\omega_1(n)$ by $M = 2$, gives us

$$y_1(n) = \{x_0, x_1, x_2, \ldots\} \quad \ldots(A)$$

In Fig. (*b*), decimation by $M = 2$, gives

$$\omega_3(n) = \{x_0, x_2, x_4, \ldots\}$$

Interpolation of $\omega_3(n)$ by $L = 2$, gives us

$$y_2(n) = \{x_0, 0, x_2, 0, x_4, 0, \ldots\} \quad \ldots(B)$$

(*A*) and (*B*) show that $y_1(n) \neq y_2(n)$, when $L = M$

(*b*) Let $M = mk$ and $L = lk$, with m, l relatively prime.

Let $x(n) = \{x_0, x_1, x_2, \ldots\}$

$\therefore$ From Fig. (*a*),
$$\omega_1(n) = \left\{ x_0, \underbrace{0, 0, \ldots 0}_{lk-1}, x_1, \underbrace{0, 0, \ldots 0}_{lk-1}, x_2, \underbrace{0, 0, \ldots 0, \ldots}_{lk-1} \right\}$$

$$y_1(n) = \left\{ x_0, \underbrace{0, \ldots, 0}_{l-1}, x_m, \underbrace{0, \ldots, 0}_{l-1}, x_{2m} \right\} \quad \ldots(C)$$

From Fig. (*b*)
$$\omega_2(n) = \{x_0, x_{mk}, x_{2mk}, \ldots\}$$

$$y_2(n) = \left\{ x_0, \underbrace{0, \ldots 0}_{lk-1}, x_{mk}, \underbrace{0, \ldots, 0}_{lk-1}, x_{2mk}, \ldots \right\} \quad \ldots(D)$$

From (*C*) and (*D*), $y_1(n) = y_2(n)$ iff $m = mk$ *i.e.* $k = 1$ which means that M and L are relatively prime. **Ans.**

Note: How we obtained (*C*)

Suppose
$$M = 3 \times 2 = 6 \;\therefore\; m = 3,\ k = 2$$
$$L = 4 \times 2 = 8 \;\therefore\; l = 4,\ k = 2$$

Let $x(n) = \{x_0, x_1, x_2, \ldots\}$

$$\omega_1(n) = \left\{ \overset{\swarrow}{x_0}, \underbrace{0, 0, 0, \overset{\swarrow}{0}, 0, 0, 0}_{7\text{ zeros}}, x_1, \underbrace{0, 0, 0, 0, \overset{\swarrow}{0}, 0, 0}_{7\text{ zeros}}, x_2, \underbrace{0, 0, \overset{\swarrow}{0}, 0, 0, 0, 0}_{7\text{ zeros}} \right.$$

$$x_3, \underbrace{0, 0, 0, 0, 0, 0, 0}_{7\text{ zeros}}, x_4, \underbrace{0, 0, 0, 0, 0, 0, 0}_{7\text{ zeros}}, x_5, 0, 0, 0, 0, 0, 0, 0, x_6, \ldots$$

Decimation of $\omega_1(n)$ by 6, gives us

$$y_1(n) = \left\{ x_0, \underbrace{0, 0, 0,}_{l-1\text{ zeros}} x_3, \underbrace{0, 0, 0,}_{l-1\text{ zeros}} x_6, \ldots \right.$$

$$= \left\{ x_0, \underbrace{0, 0, \ldots,}_{l-1} x_m, \underbrace{0, 0, \ldots,}_{l-1} x_{2m}, \underbrace{0, 0, \ldots,}_{} x_{3m}, \ldots \right\}$$

So, the decimation of $\omega_1(n)$, to obtain $y_1(n)$ as given by (C) is obtained for generic m and l and not $m = 3$, $l = 4$, as assumed in above explanation.

EXAMPLE 12.9: *Prove the equivalence of the two decimator and interpolator configurations shown in the Fig. Ex. 12.9. (These equivalent relations are called the* ***Noble identities****).*

SOLUTION:

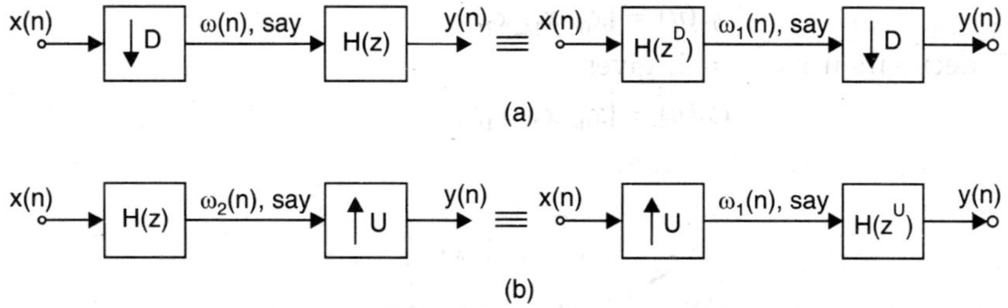

Fig. Ex. 12.9. The given configurations

(*a*) Let output of down counter in LHS figure be called $\omega(n)$

Then
$$W(z) = \frac{1}{D}\sum_{l=0}^{D-1} X(z^{1/D}e^{-j2\pi l/D})$$

$$\triangleq \frac{1}{D}\sum_{l=0}^{D-1} X(z^{1/D}W_D^l) \text{ where } W_D = e^{-j2\pi/D} \text{ (as in DFT)}$$

$$Y(z) = W(z)\cdot H(z)$$

$$= \left[\frac{1}{D}\sum_{l=0}^{D-1} X(z^{1/D}W_D^l)\right][H(z)]$$

$$= \frac{1}{D}H(z)\sum_{l=0}^{D-1} X(z^{1/D}\cdot W_D^l) \qquad \ldots(A)$$

RHS of (*a*) yields $W_1(z) = X(z)\cdot H(z^D)$

$$Y(z) = \frac{1}{D}\sum_{l=0}^{D-1} W_1(z^{1/D}\cdot W_D^l)$$

$$= \frac{1}{D}\sum_{l=0}^{D-1} X(z^{1/D}W_D^l)\cdot H((z^{1/D}\cdot W_D^l)^D)$$

$$= \frac{1}{D}\sum_{l=0}^{D-1} X(z^{1/D}W_D^l)H(z) \qquad \because W_D^{lD} = 1$$

$$= \left[\frac{1}{D}\sum_{l=0}^{D-1} X(z^{1/D}W_D^l)\right][H(z)] = \text{RHS of } (A)$$

(*b*)
$$W_2(z) = X(z)\cdot H(z)$$
$$Y(z) = W_2(z^U)$$
$$= X(z^U)\cdot H(z^U) \qquad \ldots(B)$$

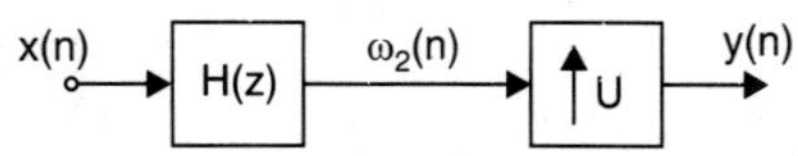

Here

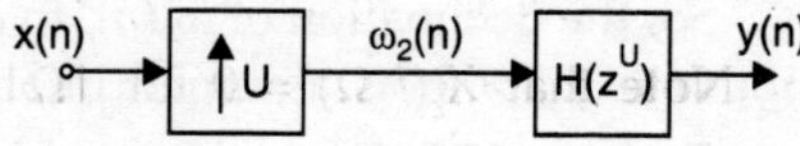

$$W_3(z) = X(z^U)$$
$$Y(z) = W_3(z) \cdot H(z^U)$$
$$= X(z^U) \cdot H(z^U)$$
$$= \text{RHS of } (B)$$

Q.E.D.

Thus, the Noble identities are proved.

EXAMPLE 12.10: *In the system in Fig. Ex. 12.10*

$$X_c(j\,\Omega) = 0,\ |\Omega| \geq \frac{\pi}{T}$$

and

$$H(e^{j\omega}) = \begin{cases} e^{-jw}, & |\omega| < \dfrac{\pi}{L} \\ 0, & \dfrac{\pi}{L} < |\omega| \leq \pi \end{cases}$$

How is y(n) related to the input signal $x_c(t)$ (Fractional delay circuit).

SOLUTION:

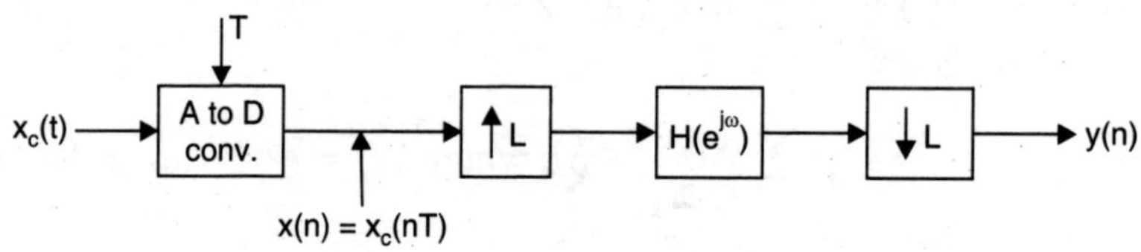

Fig. Ex. 12.10. The Fractional delay circuit

Let us split $H(e^{j\omega})$ into an ideal LPF and a delay, *i.e.*,

$$H(e^{j\omega}) = H_{LP}(e^{j\omega}) \cdot e^{-j\omega}$$

where

$$H_{LP}(e^{j\omega}) \triangleq \begin{cases} 1, & |\omega| < \dfrac{\pi}{L} \\ 0, & \dfrac{\pi}{L} < |\omega| \leq \pi \end{cases}$$

Redrawing again, we get the following configuration.

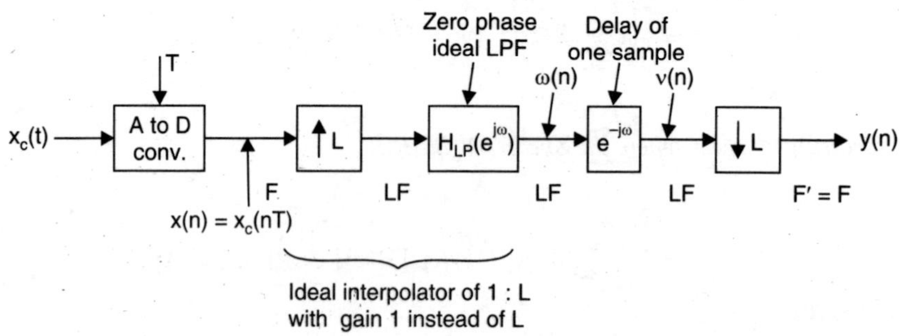

Note that $X_c(j\,\Omega) = 0$ for $|\Omega| \geq \frac{\pi}{T}$ means that $X_c(j\,\Omega)$ = non-zero for $|\Omega| \leq \frac{\pi}{T} = \frac{\omega_s}{2}$, $\omega_s = \frac{2\pi}{T}$. Hence, $X_c(j\,\Omega)$ is a full band signal for frequency range of $0 \leq \Omega \leq \frac{\omega_s}{2}$. Hence, there is no aliasing while converting $x_c(t)$ to digital signal $x(n) = x_c(nT)$.

$\therefore$ $$x(n) = x_c(nT), \text{ no aliasing} \qquad \ldots(A)$$

$\omega(n)$ = output of ideal interpolator will LPF having a gain of unity and not L

$\therefore$ $$\omega(n) = \frac{1}{L}x\left(\frac{n}{L}\right) : \text{(interpolation)} \qquad \ldots(B)$$

$$v(n) = \omega(n-1)' : \text{(delay of one sample)}$$

$$= \frac{1}{L}x\left(\frac{n-1}{L}\right) : [\text{changing } n \text{ to } n-1 \text{ in } (B)] \qquad \ldots(C)$$

Now $y(n) = v(nL)$

$$= \frac{1}{L}x\left[\frac{nL-1}{L}\right] : [\text{changing } n \text{ to } nL \text{ in } (C)]$$

$$= \frac{1}{L}x\left(n-\frac{1}{L}\right)$$

$$= \frac{1}{L}x_c\left[\left(n-\frac{1}{L}\right)T\right] : (\text{using } (A))$$

$$= \frac{1}{L}x_c\left(nT-\frac{T}{L}\right)$$ **Ans.**

$\therefore$ this is a circuit for fractional delay of $\frac{T}{L}$.

EXAMPLE 12.11: *A signal x(n) is sampled at a frequency (1/T). From x(n), a new signal y(n) is obtained by sampling frequency of (2/T) by use of a linear interpolation method described by the equation*

$$y(n) = \begin{cases} x\left(\dfrac{n}{2}\right), & n \text{ even} \\ \dfrac{1}{2}\left[x\left(\dfrac{n-1}{2}\right)+x\left(\dfrac{n+1}{2}\right)\right], & n \text{ odd} \end{cases}$$

Determine spectrum of y(n) when the spectrum of x(n) is

$$X(\omega) = \begin{cases} 1, & 0 \leq |\omega| \leq 0.2\pi \\ 0, & otherwise \end{cases}.$$

SOLUTION: Assume $F_x = \frac{1}{T}$

$$\omega' = \frac{F}{F_x} \text{ and } \omega'' = \frac{F}{F_y} = \frac{F}{2F_x} = \frac{1}{2}\omega' \qquad \because F_y = \frac{1}{T_y} = \frac{1}{T/2} = 2F_x$$

$$\therefore \qquad Y(\omega'') = \sum_n y(n)e^{-j\omega'' n}$$

$$= \sum_{n\text{ even}} x\left(\frac{n}{2}\right)e^{-j\omega'' n} + \frac{1}{2}\sum_{n\text{ odd}}\left[x\left(\frac{n-1}{2}\right) + x\left(\frac{n+1}{2}\right)\right]e^{-j\omega'' n}$$

$$\nearrow \text{Put } n = 2p \qquad\qquad \nearrow \text{Put } n = 2q+1$$

$$\therefore \qquad Y(\omega'') = \sum_p x(p)e^{-j2\omega''\cdot n} + \frac{1}{2}\sum_q [x(q) + x(q+1)]e^{-j\omega''(2q+1)}$$

$$= X(2\omega'') + \frac{1}{2}\left[\sum_q e^{-j\omega''}x(q)e^{-j2\omega'' q} + \sum_q e^{j\omega''}x(q+1)e^{-j2\omega''(q+1)}\right]$$

$$= X(2\omega'') + \frac{1}{2}e^{-j\omega''}X(2\omega'') + \frac{1}{2}e^{j\omega''}X(2\omega'')$$

$$= X(2\omega'')\,[1 + \cos\omega'']$$

$$X(2\omega'') = \begin{cases} 1, & 0 \le |2\omega''| \le 0.2\pi \\ 0, & \text{otherwise} \end{cases}$$

$$\equiv \begin{cases} 1, & 0 \le |\omega''| \le 0.1\pi \\ 0, & \text{otherwise} \end{cases}$$

Hence $$Y(\omega'') = \begin{cases} 1 + \cos\omega'', & 0 \le |\omega''| \le 0.1\pi \\ 0, & \text{otherwise} \end{cases}$$ **Ans.**

EXAMPLE 12.12: *(a) Determine the ideal frequency domain properties of Interpolation Filter used in 1 to L interpolation system.*

(b) Find the group delay of the corresponding polyphase filters $p_k(n)$.

SOLUTION: *(a)* $x(n)$ is sampled at the sampling frequency of F and $y(m)$ at the sampling frequency of $F' = LF$. Clearly, $\omega' = \dfrac{\omega}{L}$

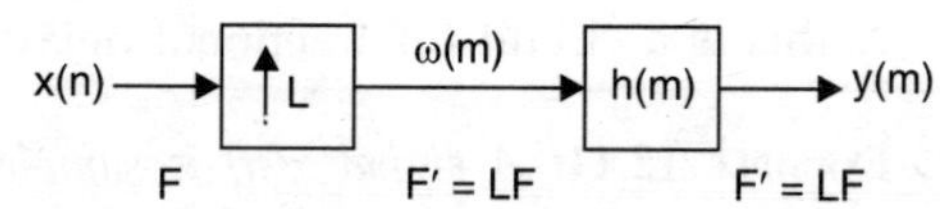

Fig. Ex. 12.12. *(a)* An interpolation system 1 to *L*

Ideal LPF used has spectrum (practical LPF, $h(m)$, is an approximation of $\tilde{h}(m)$)

$$\tilde{H}(e^{j\omega'}) = \begin{cases} L, & |\omega'| \le \dfrac{\pi}{L} \\ 0, & \text{otherwise} \end{cases} \qquad \ldots(A)$$

If $\tilde{p}_k(n)$ are the ideal polyphase filters, $k = 0, 1, 2, \ldots, L-1$, then ideal

$$\tilde{P}_k(e^{j\omega}) = \frac{1}{L}\sum_{l=0}^{L-1} e^{j(\omega-2\pi l)k/L}\cdot\tilde{H}(e^{j(\omega-2\pi l)/L}) \quad k = 0, 1, 2, \ldots, L-1 \qquad \ldots(B)$$

The above result is proved in Example 12.13 (solved)

As $$\tilde{H}(e^{j\omega'}) = 0 \text{ for } |\omega'| > \frac{\pi}{L}$$

$$\therefore \quad \tilde{H}(e^{j\omega'}) = 0 \text{ for } \left|\frac{\omega}{L}\right| > \frac{\pi}{L} \qquad \because \quad \omega' = \frac{\omega}{L}$$

Hence in (*B*), we take summation only for $l = 0$, the other factors being all zero. Thus

$$\tilde{P}_k(e^{j\omega}) = \frac{1}{L} e^{j\omega k/L} \cdot \tilde{H}(e^{j\omega/L}) \qquad \ldots(C)$$

Putting $\omega = \omega' L$, (*C*) gives us

$$\tilde{P}_k(e^{j\omega}) = \frac{1}{L} e^{j\omega k/L} \cdot \tilde{H}(j\omega')$$

$$= \frac{1}{L} e^{j\omega k/L} \cdot L \text{ due to } (A)$$

$$\therefore \quad \tilde{P}_k(e^{j\omega}) = e^{j\omega k/L},\ k = 0, 1, 2, \ldots, L-1 \qquad \ldots(D)$$

(*D*) gives the ideal polyphase filter $\tilde{p}_k(n)$. Note that $|\tilde{P}_k(e^{j\omega})| = 1$ *i.e.* an ideal polyphase filter is an all pass linear phase filter.

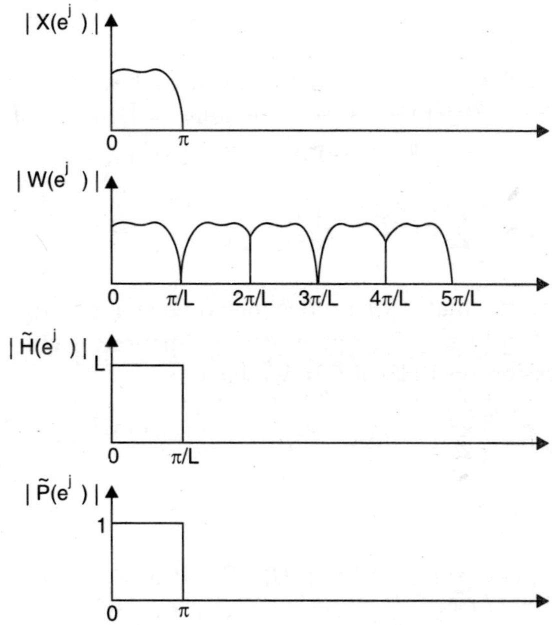

Fig. Ex. 12.12. (*b*) Illustration of Fourier Transforms of $x(n)$, $\omega(m)$, $\tilde{h}(m)$ and $\tilde{p}_p(n)$

(*b*) The frequency responses of $x(n)$, $\omega(m)$, $\tilde{h}(m)$ and $\tilde{p}_k(n)$ are shown in Fig. Ex. 12.12(*b*).

Result (*D*) shows that the fractional advances $\frac{k}{L}$, $k = 0, 1, 2, \ldots, L-1$, for the ideal polyphase filters $\tilde{p}_k(n)$ will give different phases for different values of k. As

$$\tilde{P}_k(e^{j\omega}) = e^{j\omega k/L},\ k = 0, 1, 2, \ldots, L-1 \text{ from } (D)$$

$$\therefore \quad \theta_k(\omega) = \frac{\omega k}{L},\ k = 0, 1, 2, \ldots, L-1$$

$$\frac{d\theta_k(\omega)}{d\omega} = \frac{k}{L}$$

$$\therefore \quad \text{Group delay} - \frac{d\theta(\omega)}{d\omega} = -\frac{k}{L} \qquad \text{...(E)}$$

The negative sign for group delay means that this a 'group advance' and not delay. We know that (in fact) $p_k(n)$ has its first sample delayed by $\frac{k}{L}$. But in time scale each sample of $p_k(n)$ is advanced by $\frac{k}{L}$ to synchronise with zeroth sample of each $p_k(n)$ at $t = 0$. See Fig. 12.19 where the first sample of each $p_k(n)$ (*i.e.* of $p_0(n)$, $p_1(n)$, $p_2(n)$) is at $n = 0$. These have to be advanced by 0, $\frac{1}{3}, \frac{2}{3}$ for $k = 0, 1, 2$ (as here $L = 3$) to synchronise each $p_k(n)$ with $h(m)$.

EXAMPLE 12.13: *Show that the polyphase filter $p_k(n)$ has the spectrum given by*

$$P_k(e^{j\omega}) = \frac{1}{I}\sum_{l=0}^{I-1} (e^{j(\omega-2\pi l)k/I}) \times H(e^{j(\omega-2\pi l)/I})$$

SOLUTION: Define a function

$$g(n) \triangleq h(n+k) \text{ i.e. } h(n) \text{ advanced by } k \text{ samples} \qquad \text{...(A)}$$

$$\therefore \quad G(z) = z^k H(z) \text{ by } ZT \text{ on both sides of } (A) \qquad \text{...(B)}$$

$$\text{But} \quad p_k(n) = h(nI + k),\ k = 0, 1, \ldots, I-1 \text{ (from Eqn. 12.53)} \qquad \text{...(C)}$$

$$\therefore \quad P_k(z) = \frac{1}{I}\sum_{l=0}^{I-1} G(e^{-j2\pi l/I} z^{1/I}) \qquad \text{...(D)}$$

Above result is due to the fact that $p_k(n)$ is a decimated version of $h(n)$ by ratio I to 1. We used result (12.12) by changing D to I since $y(n)$ there was decimation of $v(n)$ by D to 1. Using $G(z)$ as given in (B) in the expression on RHS of (D), we have

$$P_k(z) = \frac{1}{I}\sum_{l=0}^{I-1} (e^{-j2\pi l} z)^{k/I} \cdot H(e^{-j2\pi l/I} \cdot z^{1/I}) \qquad \text{...(E)}$$

put $z = e^{j\omega}$ on both sides of (E), Hence

$$P_k(e^{j\omega}) = \frac{1}{I}\sum_{l=0}^{I-1} (e^{j(\omega-2\pi l)k/I}) \cdot H(e^{j(\omega-2\pi l)/I}),\ k = 0, 1, \ldots, I-1$$

which is required frequency spectrum of polyphase filters $p_k(n)$ which are decimated version of the core LPF $h(n)$. Q.E.D.

Note: The above result has also been obtained by an alternate approach given in Example 12.14 (solved)

EXAMPLE 12.14: *Determine z-transform of $p_k(n)$ i.e. $P_k(z)$, given $H(z)$, where $h(n)$ is the core LPF used in interpolation.*

SOLUTION: Define

$$\delta_k(n) = \begin{cases} 1, & n = k, k \pm I, k \pm 2I, \ldots, \\ 0, & \text{otherwise} \end{cases}$$

$$= \frac{1}{I}\sum_{l=0}^{I-1} e^{j2\pi l(n-k)/I} \qquad \text{...(A)}$$

Then the sampling rate expanded sequence $\hat{p}_k(n)$ (*i.e.*, the sequence $p_k(n)$ with zero padding by $I - 1$ zeros between two samples) can be expressed as

$$\hat{p}_k(n) = \delta_k(n) \cdot h(n)$$

$$= h(n) \cdot \frac{1}{I}\sum_{l=0}^{I-1} e^{j2\pi l(n-k)/I} \quad \text{[due to (A)]} \qquad \ldots(B)$$

ZT of $p_k(n)$ is given by

$$P_k(z) = \sum_n p_k(n) z^{-n}$$

$$= \sum_n \hat{p}_k(nI + k) \cdot z^{-n} \qquad \because \; p_k(n) = \hat{p}_k(nI+k)$$

Put $\quad nI + k = m, \; \because \; n = \dfrac{m-k}{I}$

$$\therefore \quad P_k(z) = \sum_m \hat{p}_k(m) z^{-(m-k)/I}$$

$$= \sum_m \left[h(m) \cdot \frac{1}{I}\sum_{l=0}^{I-1} e^{j2\pi l(m-k)/I} \right] z^{-(m-k)/I} \quad \text{[using (B)]}$$

i.e.,
$$P_k(z) = \frac{1}{I}\sum_m \sum_{l=0}^{I-1} h(m) \cdot e^{j2\pi l(m-k)/I} \cdot z^{-(m-k)/I} \qquad \ldots(C)$$

Put $z = e^{j\omega}$ on both sides of (C), we obtain

$$P_k(e^{j\omega}) = \frac{1}{I}\sum_{l=0}^{I-1} \sum_m e^{j2\pi l(m-k)/I} \cdot h(m) e^{-j\omega(m-k)/I}$$

$$= \frac{1}{I}\sum_{l=0}^{I-1} e^{j(\omega - 2\pi l)k/I} \cdot \underbrace{\sum_m h(m) e^{-j(\omega-2\pi l)m/I}}_{= H(e^{j(\omega-2\pi l)/I})}$$

$$\therefore \quad \boxed{P_k(e^{j\omega}) = \frac{1}{I}\sum_{l=0}^{I-1} e^{j(\omega-2\pi l)k/I} \cdot H(e^{j(\omega-2\pi l)/I}), \quad k = 0, 1, \ldots, I-1} \qquad \ldots(D)$$

Above result gives frequency response of a polyphase filter $p_k(n)$ in terms of frequency response $H(e^{j\omega})$ of the core filter. In terms of ZT, replacing $e^{j\omega}$ by z in (D), we get

$$P_k(z) = \frac{1}{I}\sum_{l=0}^{I-1} (e^{-j2\pi l} \cdot z)^{k/I} \cdot H(e^{-j2\pi l} \cdot z)^{1/I}$$

which is the required expression to derive ZT of a polyphase filter $p_k(z)$, given $H(z)$.

EXAMPLE 12.15: *Consider an arbitrary digital filter with transfer function:*

$$H(z) = \sum_{n=-\infty}^{\infty} h(n)z^{-n}$$

(a) Perform a two-component polyphase decomposition of H(z) by grouping the even-numbered samples $h_0(n) = h(2n)$ and odd-numbered samples $h_1(n) = h(2n + 1)$. Thus show that H(z) may be expressed as

$$H(z) = H_0(z^2) + z^{-1}H_1(z^2)$$

and determine $H_0(z)$ and $H_1(z)$.

(b) Generalize the result in part (a) by showing that H(z) can be decomposed into D-component polyphase filter structure with transfer function

$$H(z) = \sum_{k=0}^{D-1} z^{-k}H_k(z^D)$$

Determine $H_k(z)$.

(c) For the IIR filter with transfer function

$$H(z) = \frac{1}{(1 - az^{-1})}$$

determine $H_0(z)$ and $H_1(z)$ for the two-component decomposition.

SOLUTION:

(*a*) As

$$H(z) = \sum_{n=-\infty}^{\infty} h(n)z^{-n}$$

$$= \sum_{\substack{n=-\infty \\ n\text{ even}}}^{\infty} h(n)z^{-n} + \sum_{\substack{n=-\infty \\ n\text{ odd}}}^{\infty} h(n)z^{-n}$$

As $\sum_{\substack{n=-\infty \\ n\text{ even}}}^{\infty} h(n)z^{-n}$, putting $n = 2m$, equals $\sum_{m=-\infty}^{\infty} h(2m)z^{-2m}$

and $\sum_{\substack{n=-\infty \\ n\text{ odd}}}^{\infty} h(n)z^{-n}$, putting $n = 2m' + 1$, equals $\sum_{m'=-\infty}^{\infty} h(2m'+1)z^{-(2m'+1)}$

$\therefore$

$$H(z) = \sum_{m=-\infty}^{\infty} h(2m)z^{-2m} + z^{-1}\sum_{m'=-\infty}^{\infty} h(2m'+1)z^{-2m'}$$

$$\triangleq H_0(z^2) + z^{-1}H_1(z^2)$$

then we must have:

$$H_0(z^2) = \sum_{m=-\infty}^{\infty} h(2m)z^{-2m}$$

i.e.,

$$H_0(z) = \sum_{m=-\infty}^{\infty} h(2m)z^{-m} \quad \textbf{Ans.}$$

and also we must have:

$$H_1(z^2) = \sum_{m'=-\infty}^{\infty} h(2m'+1)z^{-2m'}$$

i.e.,

$$H_1(z) = \sum_{m=-\infty}^{\infty} h(2m+1)z^{-m} \quad \textbf{Ans.}$$

(b) $H(z) = \sum_{n=-\infty}^{\infty} h(n)z^{-n}$

$$= \sum_{\substack{n \\ n=rD}} h(n)z^{-n} + \sum_{\substack{n \\ n=rD+1}} h(n)z^{-n} + \sum_{\substack{n \\ n=rD+2}} h(n)z^{-n} + \ldots + \sum_{\substack{n \\ n=rD+D-1}} h(n)z^{-n}$$

(Note this step)

Put $n = rD$ ↗, r varies $-\infty$ to ∞; Put $n = rD + 1$ ↗, r varies $-\infty$ to ∞

$$\therefore \quad H(z) = \sum_{r=-\infty}^{\infty} h(rD)z^{-rD} + \sum_{r=-\infty}^{\infty} h(rD+1)z^{-(rD+1)} + \ldots + \sum_{r=-\infty}^{\infty} h(rD+D-1)z^{-(rD+D-1)}$$

$$= \sum_{k=0}^{D-1} z^{-k} \sum_{r=-\infty}^{\infty} h(rD+k)z^{-rD}$$

$$\triangleq \sum_{k=0}^{D-1} z^{-k} H_k(z^D), \quad \text{where } H_k(z) = \sum_{r=-\infty}^{D-1} h(rD+k)z^{-r} \quad \textbf{Ans.}$$

(c) For $H(z) = \dfrac{1}{(1-az^{-1})}$, we have

$$h(n) = a^n u(n)$$

$$\therefore \quad H_0(z) = \sum_{m=-\infty}^{\infty} h(2m)z^{-m} = \sum_{m=0}^{\infty} a^{2m}z^{-m} = \frac{1}{1-a^2z^{-1}} \quad \textbf{Ans.}$$

$$H_1(z) = \sum_{m=-\infty}^{\infty} h(2m+1)z^{-m} = \sum_{m=0}^{\infty} a^{2m+1}z^{-m} = \frac{a}{1-a^2z^{-1}} \quad \textbf{Ans.}$$

Alternative approach

(a) $h_0(n) = h(2n)$

$$\therefore \quad H_0(z) = \sum_{n=-\infty}^{\infty} h(2n)z^{-n} \qquad \text{(definition of } ZT\text{)}$$

Put $2n = m$ $\therefore$ when $n = -1, 0, 1, 2, \ldots$, then $m = -2, 0, 2, 4, \ldots$

$$\therefore \quad H_0(z) = \sum_{m=0,\pm2,\pm4,\ldots} h(m)z^{-m/2} \qquad \ldots(A)$$

We know that $\boxed{\dfrac{1}{M}\sum_{l=0}^{M-1} e^{j2\pi lm/M} = \delta(m - nM),\ n = 0, \pm1, \pm2, \ldots}$

Put $M = 2$

$$\therefore \quad \frac{1}{2}\sum_{l=0}^{1} e^{j2\pi lm/2} = \delta(m - 2n),\ n = 0, \pm1, \pm2, \ldots$$

$$= 1 \text{ only for } m = 0, \pm2, \pm4, \ldots \qquad \ldots(B)$$

Using (*B*) in (*A*) and then letting $m = 0, \pm 1, \pm 2, \ldots$, *i.e.*, all values $-\infty$ to ∞

$$H_0(z) = \frac{1}{2}\sum_{l=0}^{1}\sum_{m=-\infty}^{\infty} h(m)\cdot \underbrace{z^{-m/2}\cdot e^{j\pi lm}}_{} \triangleq (z')^{-m} \text{ where } z' = z^{1/2}e^{-j\pi l}$$

$$= \frac{1}{2}\sum_{l=0}^{1} H(z^{1/2}e^{-j\pi l})$$

$$= \frac{1}{2}[H(z^{1/2}) + H(-z^{1/2})]$$

Now $h_1(n) = h(2n + 1)$

$$\therefore \qquad H_1(z) = \sum_{n=-\infty}^{\infty} h(2n+1)z^{-n} \qquad \text{Put } 2n + 1 = m$$

$$\therefore \quad n = -1, 0, 1, \ldots \Rightarrow m = -1, 1, 3, \ldots = \pm 1, \pm 3, \pm 5, \quad \ldots(C)$$

$$= \sum_{m=\pm 1, \pm 3, \ldots} h(m)z^{-(m-1)/2}$$

$$= z^{1/2} \sum_{m=\pm 1, \pm 3, \ldots} h(m)z^{-m/2}$$

Using $\frac{1}{M}\sum_{l=0}^{M-1} e^{j2\pi l(m-1)/M} = \delta(m - 1 - nM),\ n = 0, \pm 1, \pm 2, \ldots$

$= 1$ for $m = 1, M + 1, 2M + 1, \ldots -M + 1, -2M - 1$

Putting $M = 2$, we have the relation

$$\frac{1}{2}\sum_{l=0}^{1} e^{j\pi l(m-1)} = \begin{cases} 1, & m = \pm 1, \pm 3, \ldots \\ 0, & \text{otherwise} \end{cases} \qquad \ldots(D)$$

Using (*D*) in (*C*) and letting $m = 0, \pm 1, \pm 2, \ldots$, *i.e.*, all values, we get

$$H_1(z) = \frac{z^{1/2}}{2}\sum_{l=0}^{1}\sum_{m=-\infty}^{\infty} h(m)\cdot z^{-m/2} \underbrace{e^{j\pi l(m-1)}}_{=(-1)^l e^{j\pi lm}}$$

$$= \frac{z^{1/2}}{2}\sum_{l=0}^{1}(-1)^l \sum_{m=-\infty}^{\infty} h(m)(z^{1/2}\cdot e^{-j\pi l})^{-m}$$

$$= \frac{z^{1/2}}{2}\sum_{l=0}^{1}(-1)^l H(z^{1/2}\cdot e^{-j\pi l})$$

$$= \frac{z^{1/2}}{2}[H(z^{1/2}) - H(-z^{1/2})]$$

Hence

$$H_0(z) = \frac{1}{2}[H(z^{1/2}) + H(-z^{1/2})]$$

$$H_1(z) = \frac{z^{1/2}}{2}[H(z^{1/2}) - H(-z^{1/2})] \quad \textbf{Ans.}$$

(c) Here $H(z) = \dfrac{1}{1-az^{-1}}$

$$\therefore \qquad H(z^{1/2}) = \frac{1}{1-az^{-1/2}}$$

Hence
$$H_0(z) = \frac{1}{2}\left[\frac{1}{1-az^{-1/2}} + \frac{1}{1+az^{-1/2}}\right]$$

$$= \frac{1}{1-a^2z^{-1}} \quad \textbf{Ans.}$$

$$H_1(z) = \frac{z^{1/2}}{2}\left[\frac{1}{1-az^{-1/2}} - \frac{1}{1+az^{-1/2}}\right]$$

$$= \frac{a}{1-a^2z^{-1}} \quad \textbf{Ans.}$$

EXAMPLE 12.16: *(a) Find the time domain impulse response of ideal Interpolation filter $\tilde{h}(m)$. Give important properties of $\tilde{h}(m)$. Assume interpolation factor 1 to L.*

(b) From $\tilde{h}(n)$ found in part (a) determine the time-domain impulse response of ideal polyphase filters $\tilde{p}_k(n)$, $k = 0, 1, \ldots, L-1$.

(c) Show that $\tilde{p}_0(n) = \delta(n)$ for all n.

(d) Show that $\tilde{p}_k(n) = \tilde{p}_{L-k}(-n-1)$, i.e., mirror symmetry.

SOLUTION:

(a) We know that the ideal interpolation filter $\tilde{h}(m)$ (see Fig. 12.6), for interpolation factor 1 to L, has frequency response given by (12.24), replacing I by L and C by L,

$$\tilde{H}(e^{j\omega'}) = \begin{cases} L, & 0 \le |\omega'| \le \dfrac{\pi}{L} \\ 0, & \text{otherwise} \end{cases} \qquad \ldots(A)$$

Taking inverse Fourier transform, we get

$$\tilde{h}(n) = \frac{1}{2\pi}\int_{-\pi}^{\pi} \tilde{H}(e^{j\omega'})e^{j\omega' n}\, d\omega'$$

$$= \frac{1}{2\pi}\int_{-\pi/L}^{\pi/L} L \cdot e^{j\omega n}\, d\omega \qquad \text{[Using (A) and dropping dashes]}$$

$$= \frac{L}{2\pi}\left[\frac{e^{j\omega n}}{jn}\right]_{-\pi/L}^{\pi/L}$$

$$\therefore \qquad \boxed{\tilde{h}(n) = \frac{\sin(\pi n/L)}{(\pi n/L)}, \; n = 0, \pm 1, \pm 2, \ldots,} \qquad \ldots(B)$$

(*i*) Note that $\tilde{h}(n) = \tilde{h}(-n)$ *i.e.* $\tilde{h}(n)$ is an even function of n.

(*ii*) When $n = 0$, $\tilde{h}(0) = \left.\dfrac{\sin(\pi n/L)}{(\pi n/L)}\right|_{n=0}$

$\therefore$ $\tilde{h}(0) = 1$ (Using L' Hospital's rule)

(*iii*) When $n = rL$, *i.e.*, n is a multiple of L, then the numerator $\sin\left(\dfrac{\pi n}{L}\right) = \sin(\pi r) = 0$ always for all $r \neq 0$

$$\therefore \quad \tilde{h}(n) = \begin{cases} 1, & n = 0 \\ 0, & n = rl, r = \pm 1, \pm 2, \ldots, \end{cases} \quad \ldots(B\text{–}1)$$

Above three properties of $\tilde{h}(n)$ are useful and important ones.

(*b*) Polyphase filter is given by

$$\tilde{p}_k(n) = h(nL + k) \text{ from (12.53), changing } I \text{ to } L$$

Changing argument n to $nL + k$ in (*B*), we obtain

$$\tilde{p}_k(n) = \left.\tilde{h}(n)\right|_{n=nL+k} = \frac{\sin(\pi(nL+k)/L)}{(\pi(nL+k)/L)}$$

$$\therefore \quad \tilde{p}_k(n) = \frac{\sin[\pi(n+k/L)]}{\pi(n+k/L)} \quad k = 0, 1, 2, \ldots, L-1 \quad \ldots(C)$$

(*c*) Putting $k = 0$ in (C), we have

$$\tilde{p}_0(n) = \frac{\sin(\pi(n+0)/L)}{\pi(n+0)/L}$$

$$= \frac{\sin(n\pi L)}{n\pi L} = 0 \text{ for all } n \neq 0$$

$p_0(0) = 1$ (Using L' Hospital's rule)

Hence, we can write

$$\tilde{p}_0(n) = \delta(n) \text{ for all } n \quad \ldots(D)$$

i.e. $\tilde{p}_0(n) = 1$ only when $n = 0$, otherwise $\tilde{p}_0(n) = 0$.

This also implies that the zeroth polyphase filter, $p_0(n)$ has an impulse response that is a unit pulse $\delta(n)$. It also implies that $y_0(m)$ of the zeroth polyphase branch, as shown in Fig. Ex. 12.16 is identical to the input signal $x(n)$, filled with $L - 1$ zeros.

$$\therefore \quad y_0(n) = x(n) * p_0(n)$$

$$= x(n) * \delta(n)$$

$$= x(n)$$

As
$$y_0(n) = x(n)$$
$$y_0(m) = \begin{cases} x\left(\dfrac{m}{L}\right), & m = 0, \pm L, \pm 2L, \ldots, \\ 0, & \text{otherwise} \end{cases} \qquad \ldots(E)$$

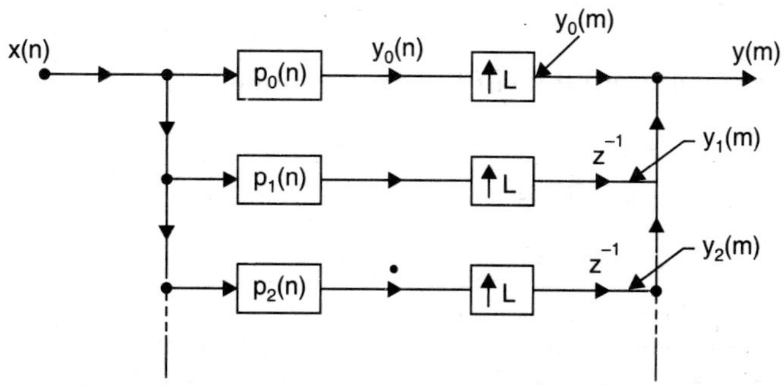

Fig. Ex. 12.16. Showing use of polyphase filters $p_k(n)$ to get $y(m)$ for interpolation

Comments

(*i*) Hence, $y_0(m)$ is $x(n)$ filled with $(L - 1)$ zeros between each sample of $x(n)$. In other words, $y_0(m)$ is always known with the knowledge of the input signal $x(n)$. The unfilled samples of $y(m)$, *i.e.* for $m = 1, 2, \ldots, L - 1$, are filled by other polyphase filters $p_k(n)$, $k = 1, 2, \ldots, L - 1$.

(*ii*) Theoretically filters $\tilde{p}_k(n)$ are infinite in duration, as clear from (*C*). But these ideal polyphase filters are not realizable. Hence, "interpolation error" between the outputs of a practical system and an ideal system can be zero for $m = 0, \pm L, \pm 2L, \ldots$, but in between the samples the error will always be non-zero.

By choosing a design such that it does not satisfy the requirement (*B* – 1), and (*D*), a trade-off can be made between the errors that occurs at samples $m = 0, \pm L, \pm 2L, \ldots$, and the errors that occur between these samples.

(*d*) As
$$\tilde{h}(n) = \frac{\sin(\pi n/L)}{(\pi n/L)}$$
and
$$\tilde{h}(n) = \tilde{h}(-n)$$

For practical systems, $\tilde{h}(n)$ might be symmetrical about some fixed delay (a non-zero delay). The symmetry of $\tilde{h}(n)$ does not automatically imply that $\tilde{p}_k(n)$ is also symmetrical, since $\tilde{p}_k(n)$ are the sampled versions of $\tilde{h}(n)$. However, there exists a form of mirror image symmetry between the pairs of polyphase filters $\tilde{p}_k(n)$ and $\tilde{p}_{L-k}(n)$, as proved below. We know that

$$\tilde{p}_k(n) = \tilde{h}(nL+k) \quad \text{...(F)}$$

$$= \tilde{h}(-nL-k) \quad \because \quad \tilde{h}(n) = \tilde{h}(-n)$$

$$= \tilde{h}(L-k-L-nL) \quad \text{(Note this step)}$$

$$= \tilde{h}\,(L - k - (n + 1)\,L) \quad \text{...(G)}$$

But $\tilde{p}_{L-k}(n) = \tilde{h}(nL+(L-k))$ Changing k to $L - k$ in (F) ...(H)

Changing n to $(-n - 1)$ on both sides of (H), we obtain

$$\tilde{p}_{L-k}(-n-1) = \tilde{h}[(-n-1)L+L-k]$$

$$= \tilde{h}[L-k-(n+1)L]$$

$$= \tilde{p}_k(n) \quad \text{due to (G)}$$

Hence $\boxed{\tilde{p}_k(n) = \tilde{p}_{L-k}(-n-1)}$ ...(I)

(I) shows the mirror symmetry between the polyphase filter $\tilde{p}_k(n)$ and $\tilde{p}_{L-k}(n)$, shifted by one sample delay. Q.E.D.

Note: In the case of Decimation, it is not possible to identify the outputs of specific polyphase branches with specific polyphase output samples of the network. Note that we concluded here in comments to part (C) of the question that the samples $y(m)$, for $m = 0, L, 2L, \ldots$, are associated with the outputs of polyphase filter $p_0(n)$ due to (E).

In decimation, all the polyphase branches contribute to each output. So, a meaningful interpretation in time domain $m = 0, 1, 2, \ldots$, is not feasible.

For decimation D to 1, the ideal time responses of $\tilde{h}(n)$ and $p_k(n)$ are similar to as for interpolation *i.e.*

For decimation, D to 1

$$\tilde{h}(n) = \frac{\sin(\pi n/D)}{(\pi n/D)}, \; n = 0, \pm 1, \pm 2, \ldots,$$

$$\tilde{p}_k(n) = \tilde{h}(nD+k) = \frac{\sin[\pi(n+k/D)]}{\pi(n+k/D)} \quad k = 0, 1, 2, \ldots, D-1 \text{ for all } n \quad \text{...(J)}$$

EXAMPLE 12.17: *An audio-band signal with band width of 4 KHz is sampled at 8 KHz. Design a LPF to isolate the signal content with frequency components*

Pass band : $0 \le F \le 75$ *Hz*

Transition band : $75 \le F \le 80$ *Hz*

Pass band ripple = $\delta_1 = 10^{-2}$

Stop band ripple = $\delta_2 = 10^{-4}$.

SOLUTION: As the F_{max} for the separated signal is 80 Hz. Hence minimum sampling frequency needed is 160 samples per second. We can bring $F_x = 8 \times 10^3$ to $F_y = 160$, *i.e.*,

$$\therefore \quad \text{Maximum decimation ratio } D = \frac{8 \times 10^3}{160} = 50$$

One FIR Filter Design: $h(n)$

$$\Delta F = \frac{\text{Transition band width}}{\text{Sampling frequency of } h(n)}$$

$$= \frac{(80-75)}{8\times10^3} = \frac{5}{8}\times10^{-3} = 6.25 \times 10^{-4}$$

By Kaiser formula (12.79), we have

$$M = \frac{-10\log(\delta_1\delta_2)-13}{14.6\cdot\Delta F}+1$$

$$= \frac{-10\log(10^{-2}\cdot10^{-4})-13}{14.6\times6.25\times10^{-4}}+1 = \frac{47\times10^4}{14.6\times6.25}+1$$

$$= 5150.6 + 1 = 5152$$

Thus, a single FIR filter followed by a decimator of $D = 50$, requires a high filter length of 5152. We now cascade two decimators, *i.e.*, $D_1 = 25$ in first stage and $D_2 = 2$ in second stage.

Design by two filters $h_1(n)$ and $h_2(n)$

For designing $h_1(n)$, use the data

Pass band: $0 \le F \le 75$

Transition band: $75 \le F \le F_1 - 80$ *i.e.* $75 \le F \le 240$

$$\Delta F_1 = \frac{240-75}{F_x} = \frac{165}{8000}$$

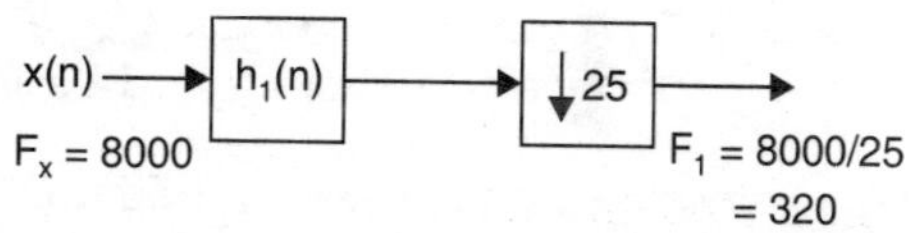

Fig. Ex. 12.17. (*a*) First stage of Decimation

We normalize ΔF_1 by F_x at which $h_1(n)$ works

$$\delta_{11} = \frac{\delta_1}{2},\ \delta_{21} = \delta_2 \qquad \text{(Note this step)}$$

Note that we have reduced the pass band ripple δ_1 by a factor of 2, so that the total pass band ripple in the cascade of the two filters does not exceed δ_1. On the other hand, the stop band ripple is maintained at δ_2.

By Kaiser formula, $$M_1 = \frac{-10\log(\delta_{11}\delta_{21})-13}{14.6\times\Delta F_1}+1$$

$$= \frac{-10\log(10^{-2}\times10^{-4}/2)-13}{14.6\times165/8000}+1$$

$$= \frac{3+60-13}{14.6\times165}\times8000+1$$

$$= \frac{50\times8000}{14.6\times165}+1 = 166 + 1 = 167$$

2nd stage $h_2(n)$ with decimator of 2: Here, we use the data

Pass band, $0 \le F \le 75$

Transition band: $75 \le F \le F_2 - 80$

i.e., $75 \le F \le 80$

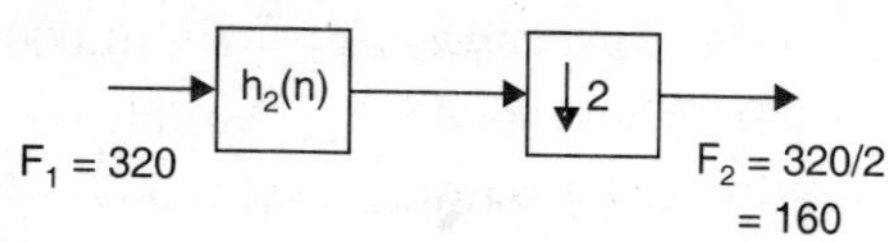

Fig. Ex. 12.17. (*b*) Second stage of Decimation

$$\Delta F_2 = \frac{\text{Transition bandwidth}}{\text{Sampling frequency of } h_2(n)}$$

$$= \frac{(80 - 75)}{320} = \frac{5}{320}$$

$$\delta_{12} = \frac{\delta_1}{2}, \; \delta_{22} = \delta_2$$

The reason for making the pass band ripple to $\frac{\delta_1}{2}$ is the same as for the design of $h_1(n)$, explained above.

By using Kaiser window, (12.79), we get

$$M_2 = \frac{-10 \log (\delta_{12} \cdot \delta_{22}) - 13}{14.6 \cdot \Delta F_2} + 1$$

$$= \frac{-10 \log (10^{-2} \times 10^{-4}/2) - 13}{14.6 \times (5/320)} + 1$$

$$= \frac{3 + 60 - 13}{14.6 \times 5} + 1$$

$$= \frac{50 \times 320}{14.6 \times 5} + 1 = 219 + 1 = 220$$

Hence $M_1 + M_2 = 167 + 220 = 387$. The saving in filter length $= \frac{5152}{387} = 13.3$.

In general, we save in the filter length by using cascade of decimation filters in stead of a single stage decimator. In fact, by decimating in multistage we are able to increase the width of the transition region, ΔF, due to the reduction in the sampling rate at which individual LPF $h_1(n)$, $h_2(n)$, ..., operate.

EXAMPLE 12.18: *A linear phase FIR digital filter is required to meet the specifications*

Pass band : $0 \le F \le 60$

Transition band : $60 \le F \le 65$

Ripple, $\delta_1 = 10^{-1}$, $\delta_2 = 10^{-3}$

Sampling rate : 10,000 Hz

Use two-stage multirate structure.

SOLUTION: *Single stage Design* would give us

$$\Delta F = \frac{65 - 60}{10,000} = 5 \times 10^{-4} \quad \left(\frac{\text{Transition band width}}{\text{Filter's sampling rate}}\right)$$

By Kaiser's formula $\quad M = \dfrac{-10 \log (\delta_1 \cdot \delta_2) - 13}{14.6 \times \Delta F} + 1$

$$= \frac{-10\log(10^{-1}\times10^{-3})-13}{14.6\times5\times10^{-4}}+1$$

$$= \frac{40-13}{73}\times10^{4}+1 = 3698.6 + 1 = 3700 \quad \textbf{Ans.}$$

Two-stage Design (by decimation followed by interpolation): As maximum frequency of transition band is 65 Hz. Assume the minimum sampling rate after decimation as 200.

$$\therefore \qquad D = \frac{10{,}000}{250} = 50$$

Assume $D_1 = 25$, $D_2 = 2$,
Hence $I_1 = 2$, $I_2 = 25$

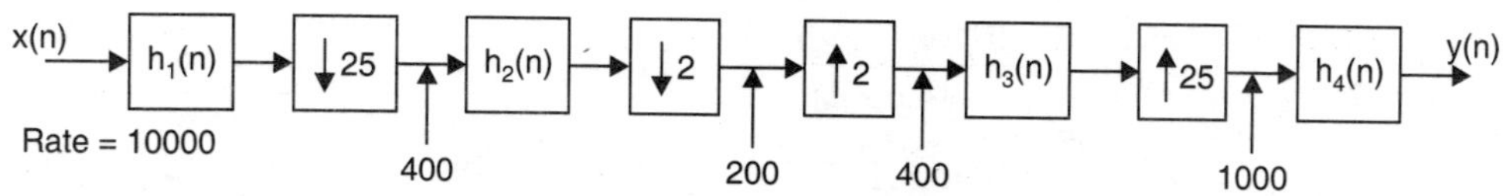

Fig. Ex. 12.18. Design by decimation followed by interpolation

For Filter $h_1(n)$
Pass band : $0 \le F \le 60$
Transition band : $60 \le F \le (400 - 65)$ *i.e.* $60 \le F \le 335$

$$\delta_{11} = \frac{\delta_1}{4} = \frac{1}{4}\times10^{-1},\ \delta_{12} = \delta_2 = 10^{-3}$$ (Note this step, we take δ_{11} as 1/4 of δ_1 to reduce ripples)

$$\Delta F_1 = \frac{335-60}{10{,}000} = \frac{275}{10^4}$$

$$\therefore \qquad M_1 = \frac{-10\log(10^{-4}/4)-13}{14.6\times275/10000}+1 = \frac{(46-13)\times10^2}{40.15}+1 = 83$$

For filter $h_2(n)$
Pass band : $0 \le F \le 60$
Transition band : $60 \le F \le (200 - 65)$, *i.e.,* $60 \le F \le 135$

$$\Delta F_2 = \frac{135-60}{400} = \frac{75}{400} = 0.1875$$

$$\therefore \qquad M_2 = \frac{-10\log((\delta_1\delta_2)/4)-13}{14.6\times0.18.75}+1 = \frac{(46-13)\times10^2}{2.738}+1 = 13$$

Filter $h_3(n)$: It is similar to filter $h_2(n)$ $\therefore$ $M_3 = 13$
Filter $h_4(n)$: It is similar to filter $h_1(n)$ $\therefore$ $M_4 = 83$
Total multiplications by decimation-interpolation design 2(83 + 13) = 192

$$\text{Saving factor over direct design} = \frac{3700}{192} = 19.3$$

Thus filter design by multirate structure is highly efficient. **Ans**

EXAMPLE 12.19: *Design a LPF satisfying the specifications,*
Sampling frequency : 8000 Hz
Pass band : $0 \le F \le 75$
Transition band : $75 \le F \le 80$
Stop band : $80 \le F \le 4000$
Pass band ripple : $\delta_1 = 10^{-2}$
Stop band ripple : $\delta_2 = 10^{-4}$.
What is reduction in design taps when we design this filter via. multirate.

SOLUTION: Single rate linear phase filter

$$\Delta F = \frac{(80-75)}{8000} = \frac{5}{8000}$$

$$M = \frac{-10\log(\delta_1\delta_2)-13}{14.6\times\Delta F}+1$$

$$= \frac{-10\log(10^{-6})-13}{14.6\times(5/8000)}+1 = \frac{60-13}{14.6\times 6.25\times 10^{-4}}+1$$

$$= 5150.6 + 1 = 5152 \quad \textbf{Ans.}$$

Design by multirate: We can safely take $D = 40 = I$ or $D_1 = 20$, $D_2 = 2$, $I_1 = 2$, $I_2 = 2$.

By choosing $D = 40$, the revised down sampled rate would be $\frac{8000}{10} = 200$ which is greater than 80 Hz of transition band end.

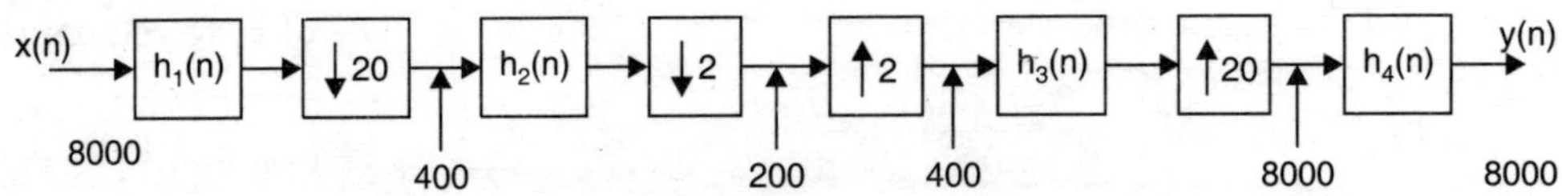

Fig. Ex. 12.19. Design steps

Design of $h_1(n)$

Take transition band : $75 \le F \le (400 - 80)$, *i.e.*, $75 \le F \le 320$

Take $$\Delta F_1 = \frac{320-75}{8000} = \frac{245}{8000}$$

$$\text{Take } (\delta_1\delta_2) \text{ revised} = \frac{(\delta_1\delta_2)}{4} = \frac{10^{-6}}{4}$$

$$\therefore \quad M_1 = \frac{-10\log(10^{-6}/4)-13}{14.6\times(245/8000)}+1$$

$$= \frac{66-13}{14.6\times 245}\times 8000+1 = 118.5 + 1 = 120$$

Design of $h_2(n)$

Take transition band : $75 \le F \le (200 - 80)$, *i.e.*, $75 \le F \le 120$

Take $$\Delta F_2 = \frac{120-75}{400} = \frac{45}{400}$$

Take $(\delta_1\delta_2)$ revised $= \dfrac{(\delta_1\delta_2)}{4} = \dfrac{10^{-6}}{4}$

$$\therefore \qquad M_2 = \frac{-10\log(10^{-6}/4)-13}{14.6\times(45/400)}+1 = \frac{53\times 400}{14.6\times 45}+1 = 32.26 + 1 = 34$$

Hence $M_3 = 34$, $M_4 = 120$

Total taps $= (120 + 34) \times 2 = 308$

$\therefore$ Reduction by multirate approach $= \dfrac{5152}{308} = 16.8$ **Ans.**

EXAMPLE 12.20: *Realize a Decimator by polyphase filters assuming the core filter h(n) as linear phase and length N = 12.*

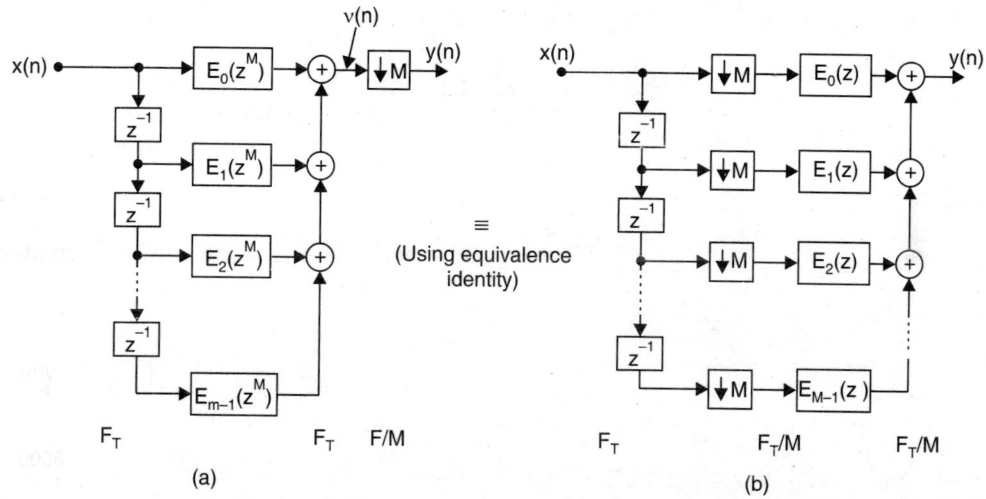

Fig. Ex. 12.20. (*a*) Decimator implementation based on polyphase decomposition

SOLUTION: The complete decimator realization using Type *I* polyphase components $E_k(z^M)$ is shown in Fig. Ex. 12.20(*a*). By using equivalence identity it reduces to Fig. Ex. 12.20(*b*) which is more efficient compared to Fig. 12.20(*a*).

If an FIR filter say, $N = 12$, is also linear phase, then we have say

$$H(z) = \overset{\checkmark}{h(0)} + \overset{\times}{h(1)z^{-1}} + h(2)z^{-2} + \overset{\checkmark}{h(3)z^{-3}} + \overset{\times}{h(4)z^{-4}} + h(5)z^{-5}$$

$$+ \overset{\checkmark}{h(5)z^{-6}} + \overset{\times}{h(4)z^{-7}} + h(3)z^{-8} + \overset{\checkmark}{h(2)z^{-9}} + \overset{\times}{h(1)z^{-10}} + h(0)z^{-11}$$

$\therefore$

$E_0(z) = h(0) + h(3)z^{-1} + h(5)z^{-2} + h(2)z^{-3}$ $\quad$ ($\because$ ✓ marked are $E_0(z^3)$)

$E_1(z) = h(1) + h(4)z^{-1} + h(4)z^{-2} + h(1)z^{-3}$ $\quad$ ($\because$ ✗ marked are $z^{-1} \cdot E_1(z^3)$)

$E_2(z) = h(2) + h(5)z^{-1} + h(3)z^{-2} + h(0)z^{-3}$ $\quad$ ($\because$ unmarked are $z^{-2}E_2(z^3)$)

Note $E_1(z)$ has a symmetric response whereas $E_0(z)$ and $E_2(z)$ are mirror to each other. $H(z)$ can be split in three polyphase filters and Fig. 12.20(*b*) type implementation is shown in Fig. Ex. 12.20(*c*) here. It has only six multiplications and eleven two-point adders.

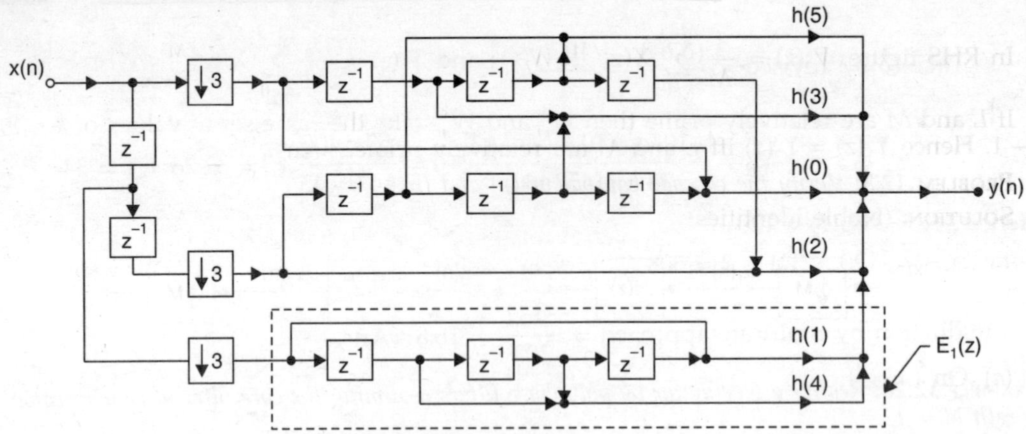

Fig. Ex. 12.20. (c) A computationally efficient decimator (M = 3), exploiting linear phase symmetry of length = 12

Additional Problems

PROBLEM 12.1: *Consider the multirate system shown in Figure, and show that it is a delay of one sample time.*

SOLUTION:

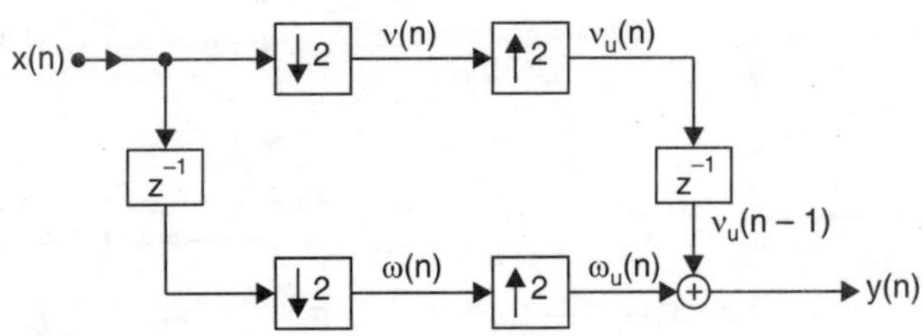

Consider signal $x(n)$ and other output signals. Then

n	0	1	2	3	4	5	6	7	8
$x(n)$	$x(0)$	$x(1)$	$x(2)$	$x(3)$	$x(4)$	$x(5)$	$x(6)$	$x(7)$	$x(8)$
$\nu(n)$	$x(0)$	$x(2)$	$x(4)$	$x(6)$	$x(8)$	$x(10)$	$x(12)$	$x(14)$	$x(16)$
$\omega(n)$	$x(-1)$	$x(1)$	$x(3)$	$x(5)$	$x(7)$	$x(9)$	$x(11)$	$x(13)$	$x(15)$
$\nu_u(n)$	$x(0)$	0	$x(2)$	0	$x(4)$	0	$x(6)$	0	$x(8)$
$\omega_u(n)$	$x(-1)$	0	$x(1)$	0	$x(3)$	0	$x(5)$	0	$x(7)$
$\nu_u(n-1)$	0	$x(0)$	0	$x(2)$	0	$x(4)$	0	$x(6)$	0
$y(n)$	$x(-1)$	$x(0)$	$x(1)$	$x(2)$	$x(3)$	$x(4)$	$x(5)$	$x(6)$	$x(7)$

Clearly, $y(n) = x(n-1)$. Hence the given system acts as a one sample delay.

PROBLEM 12.2: *Show that two possible cascade configurations of a factor-of-L up sampler and a factor-of-M down sampler are as shown iff L and M are relatively (mutually) prime.*

SOLUTION:

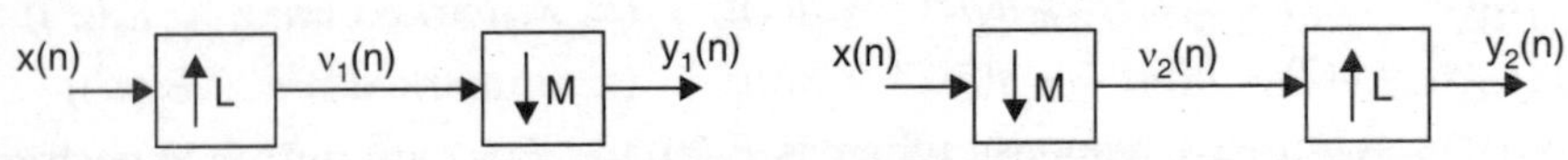

[We shall show that if L and M are relatively prime then $y_1(n) = y_2(n)$.]

In LHS figure, $V_1(z) = X(z^L)$ and $Y_1(z) = \dfrac{1}{M}\sum_{k=0}^{M-1} X(z^{L/M} \cdot W_M^k)$ ...(A)

In RHS figure, $V_2(z) = \dfrac{1}{M}\sum_{k=0}^{M-1} X(z^{1/M}\cdot W_M^k)$; and $Y_2(z) = \dfrac{1}{M}\sum_{k=0}^{M-1} X(z^{L/M}\cdot W_M^{kL})$ ...(B)

If L and M are relatively prime then W_m^k and W_m^{kL} take the same set of values of $k = 0, 1, \ldots M-1$. Hence $Y_1(z) = Y_2(z)$ iff L and M are relatively prime. **Ans.**

PROBLEM 12.3: *Verify the cascade equivalent (a) and (b).*

SOLUTION: (Noble identities)

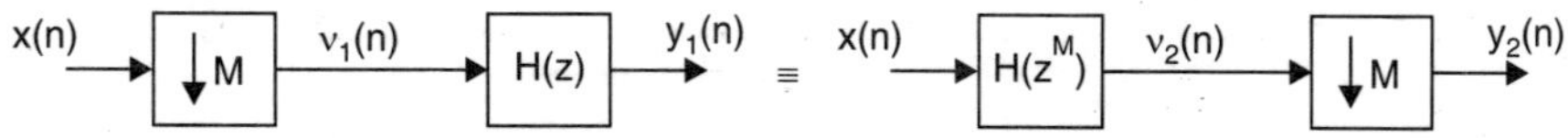

(*a*) On LHS, figure $V_1(z) = \dfrac{1}{M}\sum_{k=0}^{M-1} X(z^{1/M}\cdot W_M^k)$, $\therefore Y_1(z) = \dfrac{1}{M}\sum_{k=0}^{M-1} X(z^{1/M}\cdot W_M^k)\cdot H(z)$

On RHS figure, $V_2(z) = H(z^M)\cdot X(z)$ $\therefore Y_2(z) = \dfrac{1}{M}\sum_{k=0}^{M-1} H(z^{M/M}W_M^{kM})\cdot X(z^{1/M}\cdot W_M^k)$

$$= \frac{1}{M}\sum_{k=0}^{M-1} H(z)X(z^{1/M}\cdot W_M^k) \qquad \therefore \quad Y_1(z) = Y_2(z) \text{ Q.E.D.}$$

(*b*)

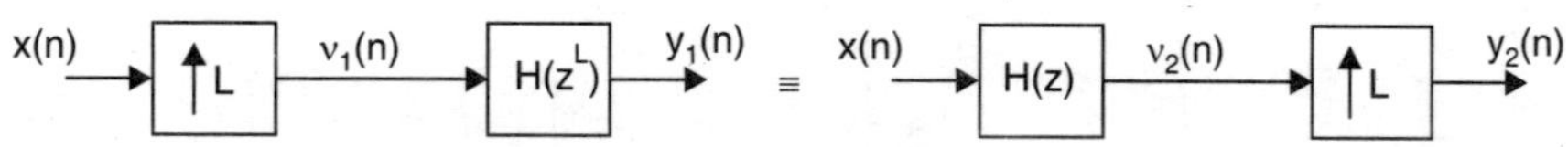

For LHS, $V_1(z) = X(z^L)$, $Y_1(z) = X(z^L)\cdot H(z^L)$

For RHS, $V_2(z) = X(z)\cdot H(z)$, $Y_2(z) = X(z^L)\cdot H(z^L)$

$\therefore$ $Y_1(z) = Y_2(z)$ *i.e.* equivalence of RH and LH systems hold Q.E.D.

PROBLEM 12.4: *Decompose* $H(z) = \dfrac{1-2z^{-1}}{1+3z^{-1}}$ *in polyphase form.*

SOLUTION:
$$H(z) = \frac{1-2z^{-1}}{1+3z^{-1}}$$

$$= \frac{(1-2z^{-1})(1-3z^{-1})}{(1+3z^{-1})(1-3z^{-1})} = \frac{1-5z^{-1}+6z^{-2}}{1-9z^{-2}} \qquad \text{(Note this step)}$$

$$= \frac{1+6z^{-2}}{1-9z^{-2}} + z^{-1}\frac{(-5)}{1-9z^{-2}} \triangleq E_0(z^2) + z^{-1}E_1(z^2)$$

where $E_0(z^2) = \dfrac{1+6z^{-2}}{1-9z^{-2}}$ $\therefore E_0(z) = \dfrac{1+6z^{-1}}{1-9z^{-1}}$

and $E_1(z^2) = \dfrac{-5}{1-9z^{-2}}$ $\therefore E_1(z) = \dfrac{-5}{1-9z^{-1}}$ **Ans.**

PROBLEM 12.5: *Derive z-transform H(z) of the core LPF in terms of z-transforms of polyphase filters* $p_k(n)$, $k = 0, 1, \ldots, I-1$.

SOLUTION: The polyphase filters $p_k(n)$ are decimation I to 1 version of the core LPF $h(n)$, as shown in Fig. Pro. 12.5

$$p_k(n) = h(nI + k),\ k = 0, 1, \ldots, I-1$$

If we zero pad each $p_k(n)$ by $I - 1$ zeros between samples of $p_k(n)$ (as typically shown for $p_0(n)$), then adding of such zero padded $p_k(n)$, which we name as $\hat{p}_k(n)$, would give us $h(n)$.

Define

$$\hat{p}_k(n) = \begin{cases} p_k\left(\dfrac{n}{I}\right), & n = 0, \pm I, \pm 2I, \ldots, \\ 0, & \text{otherwise} \end{cases}$$

Then $$h(n) = \sum_{k=0}^{I-1} \hat{p}_k(n-k) \text{ (Note this step)} \qquad \ldots(A)$$

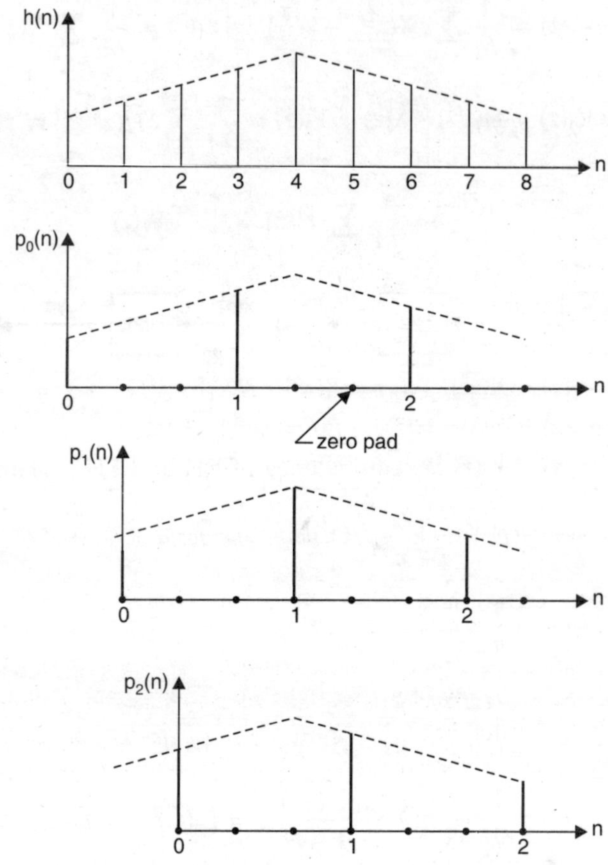

Fig. Prob. 12.5. Generation of $p_k(n)$ from $h(n)$ assuming $I = 3$

Taking ZT of $h(n)$, we have

$$H(z) = \sum_{n=-\infty}^{\infty} h(n) z^{-n}$$

$$= \sum_{n} \left[\sum_{k=0}^{I-1} \hat{p}_k(n-k) \right] z^{-n} \text{ due to } (A)$$

$$= \sum_{k=0}^{I-1} \sum_{n} \hat{p}_k(n-k) z^{-n}$$

Put $n - k = m$

$$\therefore \qquad H(z) = \sum_{k=0}^{I-1} \sum_{m} \hat{p}_k(m) z^{-(m+k)}$$

$$= \sum_{k=0}^{I-1} z^{-k} \hat{P}_k(z) \qquad \ldots(B)$$

But

$$\hat{P}_k(z) = \sum_{n} \hat{p}_k(n) z^{-n}$$

$$= \sum_{n=0,\pm I,\pm 2I,\ldots,} p_k\left(\frac{n}{I}\right) z^{-n}$$

$$\because \qquad \hat{p}_k(n) = \begin{cases} p_k\left(\dfrac{n}{I}\right), & n = 0, \pm I, \pm 2I, \ldots \\ 0, & \text{otherwise} \end{cases}$$

Put $\dfrac{n}{I} = l \;\therefore$ when $n = 0, \pm I, \pm 2I, \ldots,$

then $l = 0, \pm 1, \pm 2, \ldots$

$$\therefore \qquad \hat{P}_k(z) = \sum_{l=-\infty}^{\infty} p_k(l) z^{-(Il)}$$

$$= P_k(z^I)$$

Putting this value of $\hat{P}_k(z)$ on RHS of (B), we finally obtain

$$\boxed{H(z) = \sum_{k=0}^{I-1} z^{-k} P_k(z^I),} \quad \text{where } P_k(z) \text{ is the ZT of } p_k(n).$$

This is the relation to derive $H(z)$, and hence $h(n)$ given the polyphase filters $p_k(n)$, $k = 0, 1, 2, \ldots, I - 1$. **Ans.**

PROBLEM 12.6: *Design a sample-rate convertor that increases the sampling rate by a factor 2.5. Use the Remez Algorithm to determine the coefficients of the FIR filter that has 0.1 dB ripple in the pass band and is down by at least 30 dB in the stop band. Specify the sets of time-varying coefficient g(n, m) used in the realization of the sampling-rate convertors according to the structure shown.*

SOLUTION:

$$\frac{L}{M} = \frac{2.5}{1} = \frac{5}{2}$$

We write $g(n, m)$ as $g_m(n)$.

The FIR filter that meets the specifications in this problem has pass band from 0 to $\dfrac{\pi}{5}$.

$$\therefore \qquad H_{LPF}(e^{j\omega}) = \min\left(\frac{\pi}{L}, \frac{\pi}{M}\right)$$

Here $L = 5$, $M = 2$ we, can find $h(n)$ for such a LPF by using Remez Algorithm.

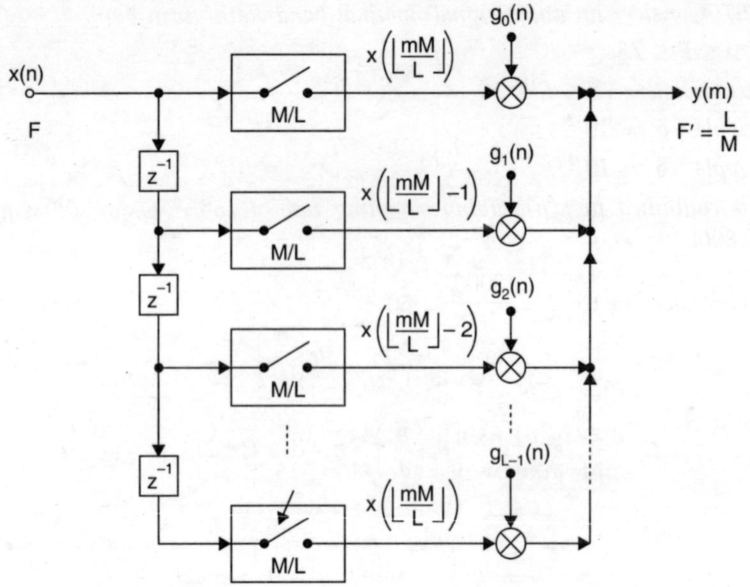

Fig. Prob. 12.6. Efficient realization of sampling rate conversion from F to $\frac{L}{M}F$

As
$$g_m(n) = h(nL + mM \oplus L)$$
$$= h\left(nL + mM - \left\lfloor \frac{mM}{L} \right\rfloor L\right)$$
$$= h\left(5n + 2m - \left\lfloor \frac{2m}{5} \right\rfloor 5\right) \qquad \because \; L = 5, M = 2 \text{ here}$$

Now $g_m(n) = g_{m+rL}(n)$, *i.e.*, $g_m(n)$ is periodic in m with period $L(=5)$. So we need only to calculate $g_0(n), g_1(n), \ldots, g_4(n)$. We assume that $n = 0, 1, 2, \ldots, 5$.

$$\therefore \quad g_m(0) = h\left(2m - \left\lfloor \frac{2m}{5} \right\rfloor 5\right) = \{h(0), h(2), h(4), h(1), h(3)\}$$

$$g_m(1) = h\left(5 + 2m - \left\lfloor \frac{2m}{5} \right\rfloor 5\right) = \{h(5), h(7), h(9), h(6), h(8)\}$$

$$g_m(2) = h\left(10 + 2m - \left\lfloor \frac{2m}{5} \right\rfloor 5\right) = \{h(10), h(12), h(14), h(11), h(13)\}$$

$$g_m(3) = h\left(15 + 2m - \left\lfloor \frac{2m}{5} \right\rfloor 5\right) = \{h(15), h(17), h(19), h(16), h(18)\}$$

$$g_m(4) = h\left(20 + 2m - \left\lfloor \frac{2m}{5} \right\rfloor 5\right) = \{h(20), h(22), h(24), h(21), h(23)\}$$

$$g_m(5) = h\left(25 + 2m - \left\lfloor \frac{2m}{5} \right\rfloor 5\right) = \{h(25), h(27), h(29), h(26), h(28)\}$$

A polyphase filter implementation would employ $L(=5)$ sub filter each of length 6, *e.g.*, $p_0(n)$ has samples $h(0), h(5), h(10), \ldots, h(25)$ and so on. **Ans.**

PROBLEM 12.7: *Consider an audio signal nominal bandwidth given by*

Pass band : $0 \le F \le 75$

Transition bandwidth : $75 \le F \le 80$

Pass band ripple : $\delta_1 = 10^{-2}$

Stop band ripple : $\delta_2 = 10^{-4}$

The signal is contained in x(n) having sampling rate of 160. Design LPF required if the revised sampling rate is 8000.

[**HINT:** Interpolation factor $I = \dfrac{8000}{160} = 50$

Use $I_1 = 2$, and $I_2 = 25$

$$\left.\begin{array}{l}\text{Filter } h_1(n) \text{ will have } M_1 = 220 \\ \text{Filter } h_2(n) \text{ will have } M_2 = 167 \\ \text{Single filter will have } M = 5152\end{array}\right\} \textbf{Ans.}$$

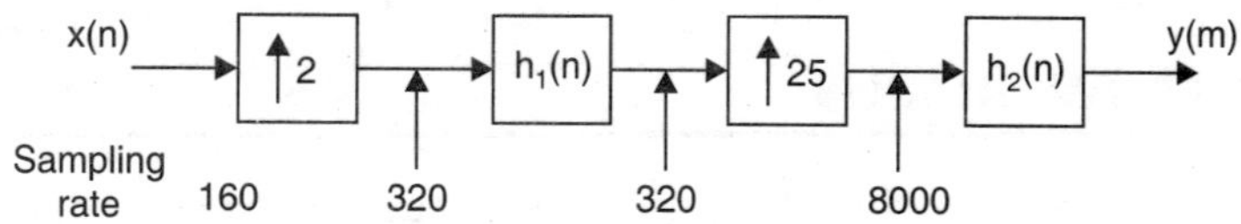

Fig. Prob. 12.7. Design steps

For filter $h_1(n)$ use, $$\Delta F_1 = \frac{[(160-80)-75]}{320} = \frac{5}{320}$$

$$\delta_{11} \cdot \delta_{12} = \frac{1}{2}\delta_1 \cdot \delta_2$$

For filter $h_2(n)$, use: $$\Delta F_2 = \frac{[(320-80)-75]}{8000} = \frac{165}{8000}.$$

PROBLEM 12.8: *Prove the following expressions for an interpolator of order of I*

(a) The impulse response h(n) can be expressed as

$$h(n) = \sum_{k=0}^{I-1} p_k(n-k)$$

where $$p_k(n) = \begin{cases} p_k\left(\dfrac{n}{L}\right), & n = 0, \pm I, 2I, \ldots, \\ 0, & \text{otherwise} \end{cases}$$

(b) H(z) may be expressed as

$$H(z) = \sum_{k=0}^{I-1} z^{-k} P_k(z)$$

(c) $$P_k(z) = \frac{1}{I}\sum_{n=-\infty}^{\infty}\sum_{l=0}^{I-1} h(n)e^{j2\pi l(n-k)/I} \cdot z^{-(n-k)/I}$$

$$P_k(\omega) = \frac{1}{I}\sum_{l=0}^{I-1} H\left(\omega - \frac{2\pi l}{I}\right) \cdot e^{j(\omega-2\pi l)k/I}$$

[**HINT:** See solved Examples–12.13 and 12.14].

CHAPTER 13

Signal Flow Graphs and Tellegen's Theorem

13.1 SIGNAL FLOW GRAPHS

A signal flow graph is a diagram which represents a set of simultaneous linear algebraic equations. Thus, while applying signal flow graph method to control systems or digital systems, we must transform linear differential/difference equations in s/z domains (*i.e.* Laplace transforms or z-transforms).

A signal flow graph consists of a network in which nodes represent system variables and branches connected between nodes act as signal multiplier. The signal flow is only in one direction thus we always have directed branches.

Node: It represents a system/signal variable, which is equal to the sum of all incoming signals at that node. Outgoing signals from the node do not affect the value of the node variable.

Branch: It is a directed line segment joining two nodes (direction indicated by an arrow on the branch). In the process of flow of the signal through the branch, the signal gets multiplied by the gain or transmittance between the two nodes.

Input node or Source: An input node or source is a node which has only outgoing branches. This corresponds to an *independent variable.*

Output node or Sink: An output node or sink is a node which has only incoming branches. This corresponds to a *dependent variable.*

Mixed node: A mixed node is a node which has both incoming and outgoing branches.

Path: It is the traversal of connected branches in the direction of the branch arrows. If no node is crossed more than once, the path is open. If the path ends at the same node from which it began and does not cross any other node more than once; the path is closed. If a path crosses some nodes more than once (and other nodes only once) but ends at different node from which it began, then the path is neither open nor closed. a, b, c, d, 1 are transmittances in Fig. 13.1.

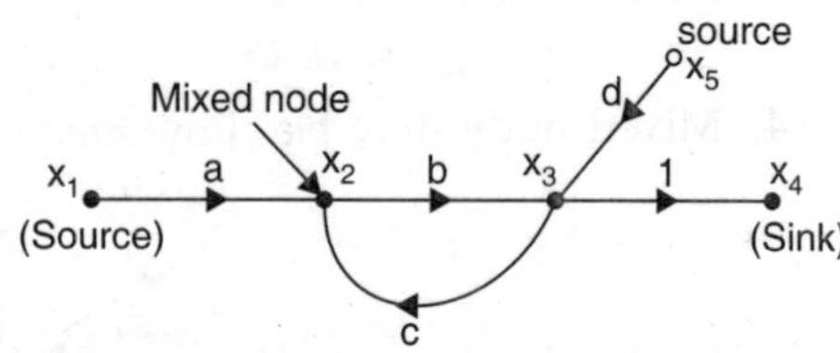

Fig. 13.1. Different types of nodes

Loop: A closed path is called a loop.

Loop gain: It is the product of branch transmittances of all the branches constituting the loop.

Non-touching loops: Two loops having non common nodes (and no common branches) are non-touching loops.

Forward path: A forward path is a path from an input node (source) to an output (sink) which does not cross any nodes more than once.

Forward path gain: A forward path gain is the product of the branch transmittances of the branches constituting the forward path.

Properties of Signal flow Graphs:

1. A branch indicates the functional dependence of one signal upon another. A signal passes through only in the arrow marked side.
2. A node adds all the incoming signals and transmits this sum to all outgoing branches.
3. A mixed node, (having both incoming and outgoing branches), may be treated as an output node (sink) by adding an outgoing branch of unity transmittance (see x_4 from x_3 in Fig. 13.1). However, we cannot change a mixed node to a source node by this method.
4. For a given system, the signal flow graph is NOT UNIQUE. Many graphs for the same system are feasible.

13.2 SIGNAL FLOW GRAPH ALGEBRA

We usually bring the input nodes (sources) to the left and the output nodes (sinks) to the right. The independent (dependent) variables of the equations become the input nodes (output nodes), The branch transmittances can be obtained from the coefficients of the equations.

To determine the input-output relationships, we may use Mason's formula or we may reduce the signal flow graph to a graph containing only input and output nodes. We use the following simple rules, (see Fig. 13.2):

1. $x_2 = ax_1$

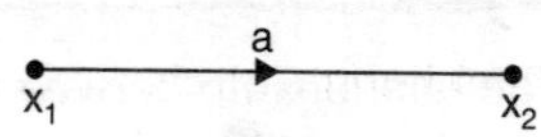

2. Cascading is multiplication

$$x_3 = ab \cdot x_1$$

Equivalent

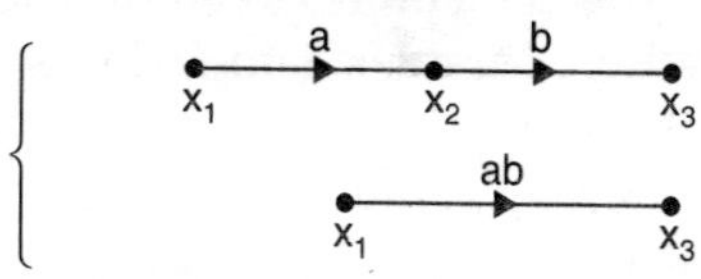

3. Paralleling is adding

$$x_2 = (a + b)x_1$$

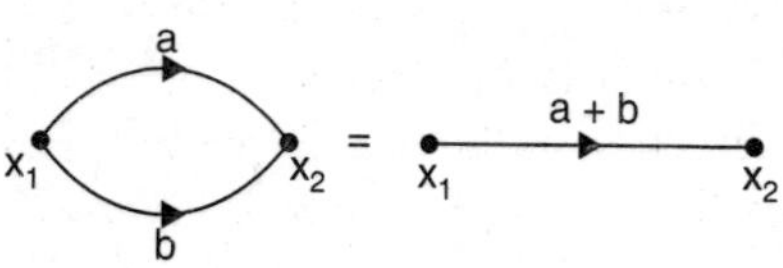

4. Mixed node may be eliminated

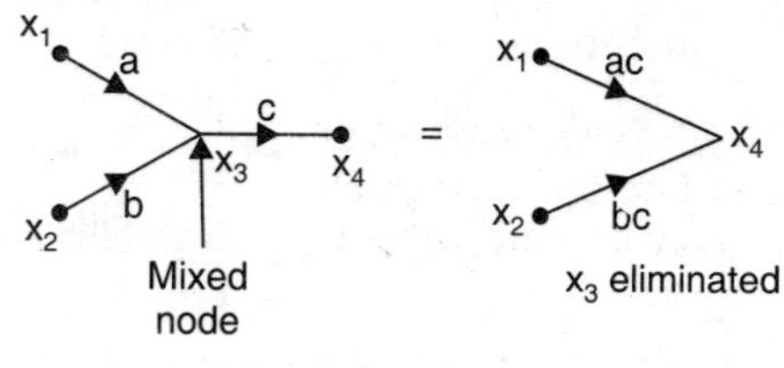

Fig. 13.2. (*a*)

5. A loop may be eliminated [see Fig. 13.2(*b*)]

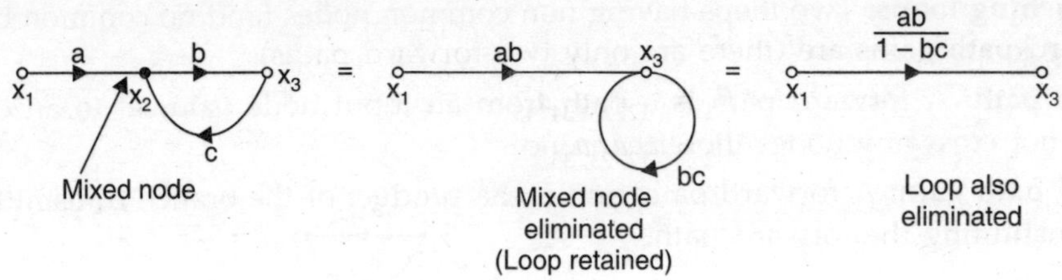

Fig. 13.2. (*b*)

Proof:

$$x_2 = ax_1 + cx_3 \qquad \text{...(A)}$$

$$x_3 = bx_2 \qquad \text{...(B)}$$

Eliminate x_2 from (*A*) and (*B*).

From (*B*), $x_2 = \dfrac{x_3}{b}$, putting this value in (*A*), we have

$$\frac{x_3}{b} = ax_1 + cx_3$$

$$\therefore \qquad x_3\left(\frac{1}{b} - c\right) = ax_1$$

or $$x_3 = \frac{ab}{1-bc}x_1$$ hence the above graph.

Thus, the loop shown on LHS flow graph has been eliminated in the equivalent flow graph drawn on RHS of Fig. 13.2(*b*).

13.3 MASON'S GAIN FORMULA FOR SIGNAL FLOW GRAPHS

The relationship between an input variable and an output variable of a signal flow graph is given by the net gain between the input and the output nodes and is known as the overall gain of the system. Mason's gain formula gives this overall gain, *T* as

Overall gain, $$T = \frac{1}{\Delta}\sum_k P_k \Delta_k \qquad \text{...(13.1)}$$

where P_k = path gain of *k*-th forward path

Δ = determinant of the graph

= 1 – (Sum of loop gain of all individual loops) + (Sum of gain products of all possible combinations of two non-touching loops) – (Sum of gain products of all possible combinations of three non-touching loops) + ...

i.e., $$\Delta = 1 - \sum_m L_{m1} + \sum_m L_{m2} - \sum_m L_{m3} + \ldots \qquad \text{...(13.2)}$$

where L_{mr} = gain product of *m*-th possible combination of *r* non-touching loops

Δ_k = Value of Δ for that part of the graph not touching the *k*-th forward path = Δ – (gain of loops touching P_k made zero)

Note that the Mason's Gain formula becomes involved if a system has loops numbering higher than five.

EXAMPLE 13.1: *Find TF for the given signal flow graph, by using Mason's Gain formula.*

SOLUTION:

1. Forward path gains are (there are only two forward paths)

$$P_1 = a_{12}a_{23}a_{34}a_{45}$$
$$P_2 = a_{12}a_{23}a_{35}$$

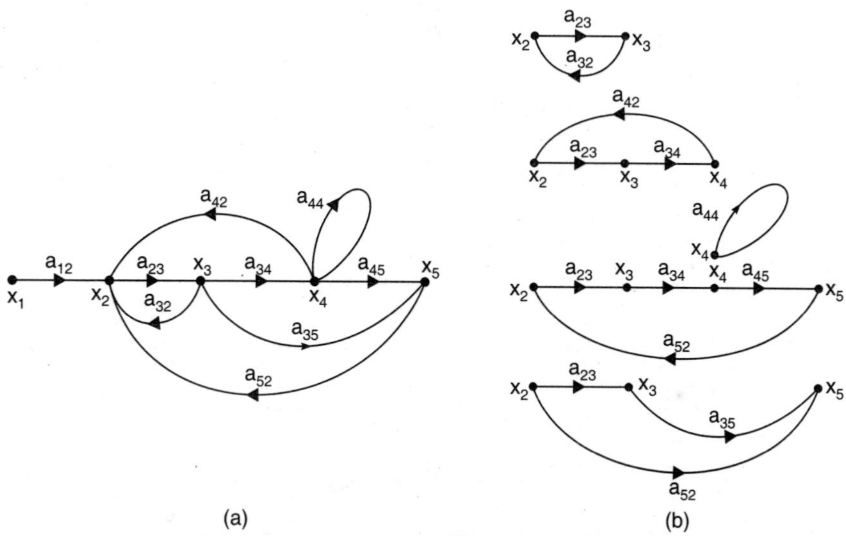

Fig. Ex. 13.1. The given signal flow graph

2. Individual loops are five in number

$\therefore$

$$L_{11} = a_{23}a_{32}$$
$$L_{21} = a_{23}a_{34}a_{42}$$
$$L_{31} = a_{44} \text{ (a self loop)}$$
$$L_{41} = a_{23}a_{34}a_{45}a_{52}$$
$$L_{51} = a_{23}a_{35}a_{52}$$

3. There are two possible combinations of two non-touching loops *viz.*

L_{11} and L_{13} are non-touching $\quad \therefore \quad L_{12} = (a_{23}a_{32})(a_{44})$

L_{31} and L_{51} are non-touching $\quad \therefore \quad L_{22} = (a_{44})(a_{23}a_{35}a_{52})$

4. There are no combination of three or more than three non-touching loops.

5. $\Delta = 1 - (a_{23}a_{32} + a_{23}a_{34}a_{42} + a_{44} + a_{23}a_{34}a_{45}a_{52} + a_{23}a_{35}a_{52}) + (a_{23}a_{32}a_{44} + a_{23}a_{35}a_{52}a_{44})$

$$\Delta_1 = \Delta\Big|_{\substack{\text{(gain of all touching}\\ \text{loops to path } P_1 \text{ made zero)}}} = 1$$

$\because$ P_1 touches all the loops hence make all loop gain zero

$$\Delta_2 = \Delta\Big|_{\substack{\text{putting gain of loops}\\ \text{touching } P_2 \text{ zero}}}$$

$\because$ All loops except L_3 (with gain a_{44}) touch P_2

$$= 1 - a_{44}$$

$$\therefore \quad T = \frac{P_1\Delta_1 + P_2\Delta_2}{\Delta} = \frac{a_{12}a_{23}a_{34}a_{45} + a_{12}a_{23}a_{35}(1 - a_{44})}{1 - (a_{23}a_{32} + a_{23}a_{34}a_{42} + a_{44} + a_{23}a_{34}a_{52} + a_{23}a_{35}a_{52}) + (a_{23}a_{35}a_{52}a_{44} + a_{23}a_{32}a_{44})}$$

EXAMPLE 13.2: *Consider the system shown in the Figure. Obtain the transfer function* $\frac{C(s)}{R(s)}$ *by using Mason's Gain formula.*

SOLUTION: The given system is shown in Fig. Ex. 13.2(*a*).

Draw the signal flow graph as (*b*) Forward path is only one

$$P_1 = G_1G_2G_3$$

Different loops are

$$L_1 = G_1G_2H_1$$
$$L_2 = -G_1G_3H_2$$
$$L_3 = -G_1G_2G_3$$

None of these is non-touching type

$$\therefore \quad \Delta = 1 - (L_1 + L_2 + L_3)$$
$$= 1 - G_1G_2H_1 + G_2G_3H_2 + G_1G_2G_3$$

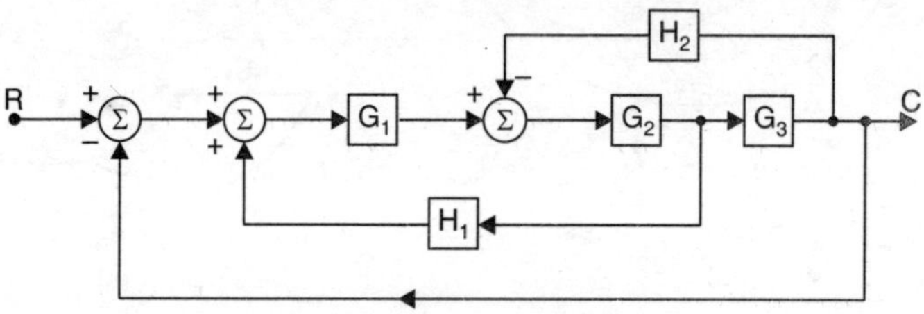

(a) The given figure

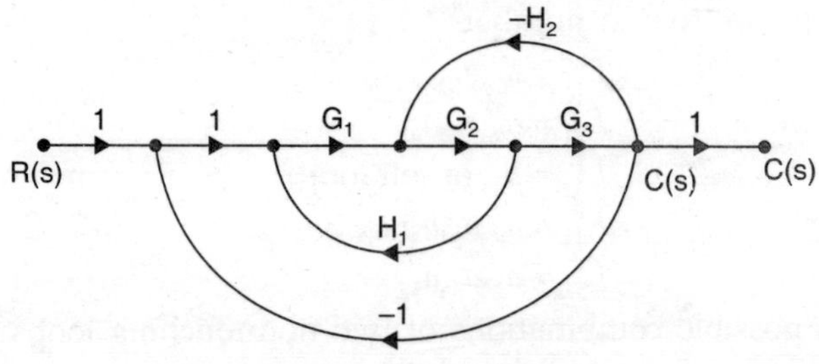

(b) Signal flow graph of figure given above

Fig. Ex. 13.2.

$$\Delta_1 = \Delta \Big|_{\substack{\text{putting gains of loops} \\ \text{touching path } P_1 \text{ to zero}}}$$

$$= 1 - (0 + 0 + 0) = 1 \text{ since all loops touch } P_1$$

$$\therefore \quad T(s) = \frac{C(s)}{R(s)} = \frac{P_1\,\Delta_1}{1 - G_1G_2H_1 + G_2G_3H_2 + G_1G_2G_3}$$

$$\therefore \quad \frac{C(s)}{R(s)} = \frac{G_1G_2G_3}{1 - G_1G_2H_1 + G_2G_3H_2 + G_1G_2G_3}$$ **Ans.**

EXAMPLE 13.3: *For the signal flow graph shown obtain* $\frac{C(s)}{R(s)}$ *by using Mason's gain formula.*

SOLUTION: The forward paths are

$$P_1 = G_1G_2G_3G_4G_5$$
$$P_2 = G_1G_6G_4G_5$$
$$P_3 = G_1G_2G_7$$

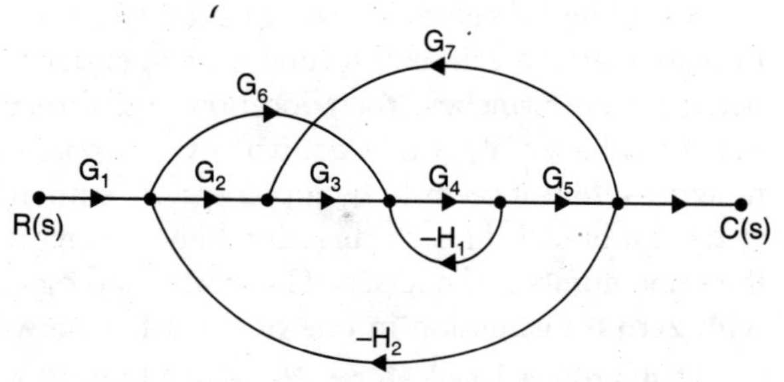

Fig. Ex. 13.3. The given signal flow diagram

The loop gains are

$$L_1 = -G_4H_1$$

Here L_1 does not touch L_2, as there is no branch common to L_1 and L_2

$$L_2 = -G_2G_7H_2$$

All other loops are touching all, as there is at least one branch common between other pairs of loops (except the pair L_1 and L_2)

$$L_3 = -G_6G_4G_5H_2$$
$$L_4 = -G_2G_3G_4G_5H_2$$
$$\Delta = 1 - (L_1 + L_2 + L_3 + L_4) + (L_1L_2)$$
$$= 1 + G_4H_1 + G_2G_7H_2 + G_4G_5G_6H_2 + G_2G_3G_4G_5H_2 - G_2G_4G_7H_1H_2$$

$$\Delta_1 = \Delta\Big|_{\substack{\text{gains of loops touching}\\ P_1 \text{ put to zero}}} = 1 \qquad (\because \text{ all loops touch } P_1)$$

$$\Delta_2 = \Delta\Big|_{\substack{\text{gains of loops touching}\\ P_2 \text{ put to zero}}} = 1 \qquad (\because \text{ all loops touch } P_2)$$

$$\Delta_3 = \Delta\Big|_{\substack{\text{gains of loops touching}\\ P_3 \text{ put to zero}}}$$

$$= 1 - (L_1) = 1 + G_4H_1 \qquad (\text{Only } L_1 \text{ does not touch } P_3 \therefore \text{ gain of } L_1 \text{ is not put to zero})$$

$$\therefore \quad \frac{C(s)}{R(s)} = \frac{P_1\Delta_1 + P_2\Delta_2 + P_3\Delta_3}{\Delta}$$

$$= \frac{G_1G_2G_3G_4G_5 + G_1G_6G_4G_5 + G_1G_2G_7(1 + G_4H_1)}{1 + G_4H_1 + G_2G_7H_2 + G_4G_5G_6H_2 + G_2G_3G_4G_5H_2 - G_2G_4G_7H_1H_2}$$ **Ans.**

13.4 TELLEGEN'S THEOREM FOR DIGITAL FILTERS AND ITS APPLICATIONS

Tellegen's theorem is an important basic theorem of conventional network theory. Many network theorems, such as conservation of energy, reciprocity, etc. can be developed from Tellegen's theorem.

Digital filters/networks are not subject to (*i.e.*, donot obey) *Kirchhoff's Laws,* and hence the Tellegen's theorem in its most general form does not apply. However, a restricted form of Tellegen's theorem, referred to the difference form, can be derived. From this theorem, a number of useful properties of digital networks can also be developed.

In classical networks, Tellegen's theorem is in the form of a relationship between the voltage distribution in one network and the current distribution a second network, when the two networks have the same topology.

So, in digital networks, we consider two flow graphs with the same topology. Same topology implies that there is one to one correspondence between the nodes in the two networks and between the branches (their location and direction only). Note that the requirement that two networks be topologically equivalent is rather minor and can be easily met even if two given networks do not seem to be topologically similar. In particular, if we consider every flow graph to have a branch in each direction between every pair of nodes, then any two flow graphs with the same number of nodes can be made topologically equivalent provided we add a few branches with zero transmission in one or the other network.

Convention Used Here: We adopt the following convention:

1. Each network is drawn in such a way that each network has a source node connected to it by a branch of unit transmittance.
2. The source node is not connected to any other network nodes.
3. The *source node is numbered to coincide with the associated network node, e.g.* the source x_k is the input to network node k.
4. If source node and the corresponding branch are not drawn, this implies that the source node value is zero.

13.4.1 Tellegen's Theorem

Consider two signal flow-graphs with the same topology each having N nodes. If the network node variables, branch outputs and source node values in the first network are denoted by ω_k, v_{jk} and x_j, respectively, and in the second network by ω'_k, v'_{jk} and x'_j, then

$$\sum_{k=1}^{N}\sum_{j=1}^{N}(\omega'_k v_{jk} - \omega_k v'_{jk}) + \sum_{k=1}^{N}(\omega'_k x_k - \omega_k x'_k) = 0 \qquad \text{...(13.3)}$$

Proof: Note that the branch outputs are related to the node variable by the relation

$$\underbrace{\omega_k}_{k \text{ node's variable}} = \underbrace{x_k}_{\text{Source to } k \text{ node}} + \underbrace{\sum_{j=1}^{N} v_{jk}}_{\text{Sum of branch outputs coming to } k\text{-node}} \qquad \text{...(13.4)}$$

where branch output $v_{jk} = w_j \times$ transmittance of branch F_{jk} of branch j to k

We know that

$$\sum_{k=1}^{N}(\omega_k\omega'_k - \omega'_k\omega_k) = 0 \qquad \text{(a trivial equation)} \qquad \text{...(13.5)}$$

i.e.,

$$\sum_{k=1}^{N}\left[\left(\underbrace{x_k}_{\text{From the source}} + \underbrace{\sum_{j=1}^{N} v_{jk}}_{\text{From the branches}}\right)(\omega'_k) - \left(x'_k + \sum_{j=1}^{N} v'_{jk}\right)(\omega_k)\right] = 0 \qquad \text{[using (13.4) for } \omega_k]$$

$$\therefore \quad \sum_{k=1}^{N}\sum_{j=1}^{N}(\omega_k' v_{jk} - \omega_k v_{jk}') + \sum_{k=1}^{N}(\omega_k' x_k - \omega_k x_k') = 0 \qquad \text{Q.E.D.}$$

Note that derivation of Tellegen's theorem, Eqn. (13.3) depends only on Eqn. (13.4) and it does not require that the flow graph be linear. Moreover, if variables W_k, W_k', V_{jk}, V_{jk}', X_k *and* X_k' are derived through a linear operation from ω_k, ω_k', v_{jk}, v_{jk}', x_k and x_k', respectively, then

$$\boxed{\sum_{k=1}^{N}\sum_{j=1}^{N}(W_k' V_{jk} - W_k V_{jk}') + \sum_{k=1}^{N}(W_k' X_k - W_k X_k') = 0} \qquad \text{...(13.6)}$$

where capital letters refer to the z-transforms of corresponding signals.

Thus, Tellegen's theorem applies either to the sequence values [Eqn. (13.3)] or to the z-transforms [Eqn. (13.6)].

As an example, to illustrate the idea of identical topologies and primed and unprimed variables (networks), consider two networks shown in Fig. 13.3. To have ditto equivalence of topologies, we have indicated by dashed branches with zero transmittances. Normally, such branches are not drawn.

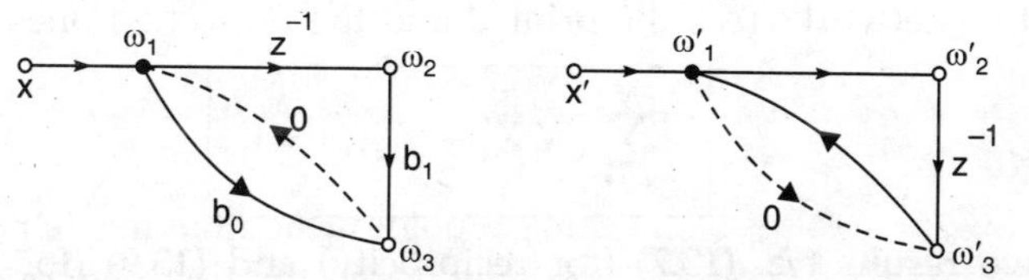

Fig. 13.3. Example of two networks that are topologically equivalent and thus satisfy Tellegen's theorem

13.5 RECIPROCAL AND INTERRECIPROCAL DIGITAL NETWORKS

In passive analog networks consisting of interconnections of resistors, inductors and capacitors, the idea of reciprocity plays an important role. In digital networks, there exists corresponding notions of reciprocity and interreciprocity.

Reciprocal Digital Networks: Consider two different sets of sources X_k and X_k' exciting a given network.

Let W_k = k-th node value when the network is excited by the sources X_k, in unprimed network.

W'_k = k-th node value when the network is excited by the sources X'_k, in primed network.

The given network is said to be reciprocal if

$$\boxed{\sum_{k=1}^{N}(W_k X_k' - W_k' X_k) = 0} \qquad \text{...(13.7)}$$

As one consequence of reciprocity consider all X_k except X_a to be zero. Also, in primed sources, assume that all X_k' except X_b' are zero [see Fig. 13.3 (*a*)]. Then (13.7) yields

$$W_b X'_b - W'_a X_a = 0$$

or
$$\boxed{W_b = W'_a, \text{ if } X_a = X'_b} \qquad \text{...(13.8)}$$

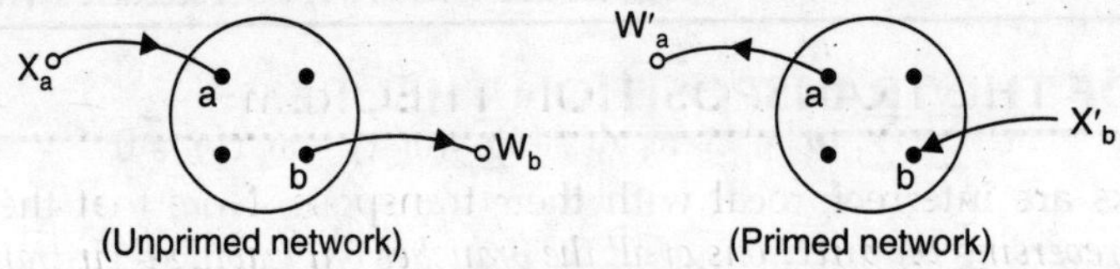

Fig. 13.3. (*a*)

Hence, if a network is reciprocal, if we excite the graph at network node '*a*' and observe the output at node '*b*', then the same excitation at node '*b*' would give the same output at node '*a*'.

Note that whereas most analog networks are reciprocal, *most digital networks are not reciprocal* (due to directional quality of digital signal flow graph!). For digital networks, the concept of interreciprocity is more useful, which we define as follows:

13.5.1 Interreciprocal Digital Networks

Consider two distinct signal flow graphs (unprimed and primed, say).

Let X_k be the sources feeding unprimed network, having node values W_k, and X'_k be the sources exciting primed network, having node values W'_k.

Then the given two networks (*i.e.*, the primed and the unprimed ones) are interreciprocal if

$$\sum_{k=1}^{N} (W_k X'_k - W'_k X_k) = 0 \qquad ...(13.9)$$

Note that the two results *viz.* (13.7) (for reciprocity) and (13.9) (for interreciprocity) look similar. However, it is important to keep in mind that *for reciprocity* the primed and unprimed networks differ only in the sources, *i.e., the network is one,* excited by X_k (to give W_k) or excited by X'_k (to give W'_k). *For interreciprocity, there are two different networks, i.e.,* both the sources and the branch transmittances can differ in the primed and unprimed networks. It is clear that: two networks that are individually reciprocal are also interreciprocal; whereas two interreciprocal networks may not be individually reciprocals, *i.e,.* two reciprocal networks (*i.e.* two networks are individually reciprocal as per (13.7)) are also interreciprocal networks as per (13.9). Whereas two interreciprocal networks, obeying (13.9), may not necessarily be intra (*i.e.,* self) reciprocals.

Note that For analog networks, passive reciprocal networks obey the conditions given below:

Parameter	*Condition for Passive Network Reciprocity*	*Condition for Electrical Symmetry*
z	$z_{12} = z_{21}$	$z_{11} = z_{22}$
y	$y_{12} = y_{21}$	$y_{11} = y_{22}$
$ABCD$	$AD - BC = 1$, *i.e.*, $\Delta_T = 1$	$A = D$
$A'B'C'D'$	$A'D' - B'C' = 1$, *i.e.*, $\Delta_{T'} = 1$	$A' = D'$
h	$h_{12} = -h_{21}$	$\Delta_h = 1$, *i.e.*, $h_{11}h_{22} - h_{12}h_{21} = 1$
g	$g_{12} = -g_{21}$	$\Delta_g = 1$, *i.e.*, $g_{11}g_{22} - g_{12}g_{21} = 1$

13.6 PROOF OF THE TRANSPOSITION THEOREM

The digital networks are interreciprocal with their transpose. Note that the *transpose of a flow graph is generated by reversing the directions of all the branches but leaving their transmittances the same.* Let,

X_k be source input to k-th node,

W_k be node variable (Node value) of k-th node,

V_{jk} output of branch between nodes j and k and from node j to node k,

F_{jk} transmittance ('multiplying factor') between nodes j and k (*i.e.*, from node j node k)

Hence, V_{jk} = node variable W_j at node j multiplied by F_{jk} (the enroute scaling).

The primed values indicate similar respective parameters in the primed network. Then we have

$$V_{jk} = W_j F_{jk} \quad \text{...(13.10)}$$

$$V'_{jk} = W'_j F'_{jk} \quad \text{...(13.11)}$$

$$F'_{jk} = F_{kj}, \quad \text{if primed network is the transpose of unprimed network.}$$

To show that the two networks (primed and unprimed ones) are interreciprocal, i.e., to show that Eqn. (13.9) holds here. As the unprimed network and its transpose (the primed network) have the same number of nodes, say, N hence Tellegen's theorem holds, *i.e.*,

$$\sum_{j=1}^{N}\sum_{k=1}^{N}(W_kV'_{jk} - W'_kV_{jk}) + \sum_{k=1}^{N}(W_kX'_k - W'_kX_k) = 0 \quad \text{...(13.12)}$$

Put $V_{jk} = W_j F_{jk}$, $V'_{jk} = W'_j F'_{jk}$ in (13.12), we get

$$\sum_{j=1}^{N}\sum_{k=1}^{N}(W_kW'_jF'_{jk} - W'_kW_jF_{jk}) + \sum_{k=1}^{N}(W_kX'_k - W'_kX_k) = 0$$

i.e.,

$$\sum_{j=1}^{N}\sum_{k=1}^{N}W_kW'_jF'_{jk} - \sum_{j=1}^{N}\sum_{k=1}^{N}W'_kW_jF_{jk} + \sum_{k=1}^{N}(W_kX'_k - W'_kX_k) = 0 \quad \text{...(13.13)}$$

Interchanging the dummy variables, calling j to k and k to j and therefore $F'_{jk} \overset{j \text{ to } k}{\underset{k \text{ to } j}{\Rightarrow}} F'_{kj}$ becomes F_{jk}, W_k becomes W_k; W'_j becomes W'_k in the first double summation in (13.12), we have

$$\underbrace{\sum_{k=1}^{N}\sum_{j=1}^{N}}_{\text{Interchanging summation order}} W_jW'_kF_{jk} - \sum_{j=1}^{N}\sum_{k=1}^{N}W'_kW_jF_{jk} + \sum_{k=1}^{N}(W_kX'_k - W'_kX_k) = 0$$

$$\therefore \quad \sum_{j=1}^{N}\sum_{k=1}^{N}(\cancel{W_jW'_kF_{jk}} - \cancel{W'_kW_jF_{jk}}) + \sum_{k=1}^{N}(W_kX'_k - W'_kX_k) = 0$$

i.e.,
$$\sum_{k=1}^{N}(W_k X'_k - W'_k X_k) = 0 \quad \text{...(13.14)}$$

which shown that the unprimed and the primed networks are interreciprocal to each other, *i.e.*, a digital network and its transposed network are interreciprocal.

Corollary: For a single-input-single output networks, a network and its transpose have the same transfer function.

Proof: Consider any two nodes a and b, let all sources X_k, except X_a, be zero for the original (unprimed) network. Also, let all sources X'_k except X'_b, be zero for the transposed (primed) network. Then from Eqn. (13.14), we have

$$W_b X'_b - W'_a X_a = 0$$

If $X_a = X'_b$ then $W_b = W'_a$

i.e., for input X_a, output is W_b in original network on node b.

For input X'_b equalling X_a on node b of transpose network, the output at its node a is also equal to W_b.

Thus, for same excitations in one branch/single input-single output network and its transpose yield the same outputs; *i.e.*, a single-input-single-output network and its transpose have the same transfer functions.

13.7 NETWORK-SENSITIVITY FORMULA

In parameter quantization, the following results are of vital importance. The students may see Chapter 10 on Quantization.

(*i*) The effect of coefficient quantization is highly dependent on the structure used to implement the system.

(*ii*) No systematic method has yet been developed for determining the best realization, given constraints on the number of multipliers, word length, and the number of delays.

(*iii*) The understanding of the relationship between network structure and coefficient sensitivity is indeed meagre.

(*iv*) One measure of the sensitivity of a given network realizations to parameter quantization is the error in the location of the poles (or zeros) cause by an error in the constant multipliers in the network. *If the poles and zeros are tightly clustered, it is possible that small errors in the coefficients can cause large shifts of the poles (or zeros).*

(*v*) Cascade and parallel forms are to be preferred over the direct form from the view point of parameter quantization. This is particularly true in the case of narrow-band frequency selective filters with tightly clustered poles and zeros.

It is often more desirable to implement linear-phase FIR filters as a cascade of second-order sections or in direct form.

****Or directly

$$\frac{W_b}{X_a} = \frac{W'_a}{X'_b}, \textit{ i.e., } T_{ab} = T'_{ba}.$$

The afore-mentioned results/statements are based on parameter sensitivity from the point of view of the movement of the poles and zeros. For more complex networks, it is not easy to obtain a general relationship between the poles and zeros and the network parameters.

With the help of Tellegen's theorem, it is possible to obtain a general expression for the sensitivity of the system function, $T(z)$, of a given network, to changes in the parameters of the network. This facilitates computer-aided design and analysis of digital networks.

Assume that the source X_a feeds the node 'a' and the output is taken at node 'b', *i.e.*,

$$W_b(z) = T_{ab}(z)\, X_a(z) \qquad \text{...(13.15)}$$

where

$T_{ab}(z)$ = Transfer function from node 'a' to node 'b'

$W_b(z)$ = Output at node 'b'

$X_a(z)$ = Input at node 'a'.

The sensitivity of this system function ($T_{ab}(z)$) w.r.t. change in a branch transmittance, $F_{nm}(z)$, is defined as: $\dfrac{\partial T_{ab}(z)}{\partial F_{nm}(z)}$.

[To show that]

$$\boxed{\frac{\partial T_{ab}(z)}{\partial F_{nm}(z)} = T_{an}(z) \cdot T_{mb}(z)} \qquad \text{...(13.16)}$$

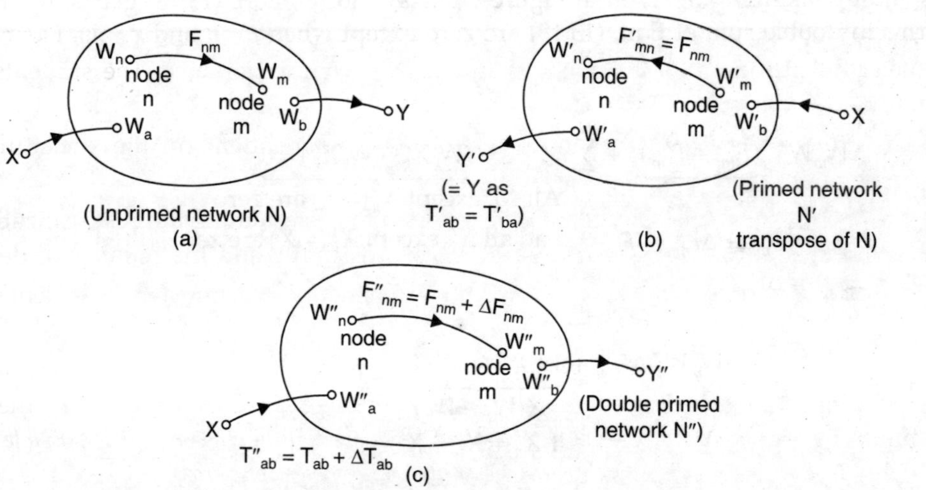

Fig. 13.4. (*a*) Original network (*b*) Transposed network from Fig. (a) and (*c*) Original system with error in branch transmittance F_{nm}

Proof: Primed and double primed networks have the same number of nodes, hence we can apply Tellegen's theorem to networks of Figs. 13.4(*b*) and (*c*). Thus

$$\sum_{k=1}^{N}\sum_{j=1}^{N}(W_k' V_{jk}'' - W_k'' V_{jk}') + \sum_{k=1}^{N}(W_k' X_k'' - W_k'' X_k') = 0 \qquad \text{...(13.17)}$$

i.e.

$$\sum_{k=1}^{N}\sum_{j=1}^{N} W_k' V_{jk}'' - \sum_{k=1}^{N}\sum_{j=1}^{N} W_k'' V_{jk}' + \sum_{k=1}^{N}(W_k' X_k'' - W_k'' X_k') = 0$$

We interchange j and k and change the summation order in

$$\underbrace{\sum_{k=1}^{N}\sum_{j=1}^{N} W'_k V''_{jk}} - \underbrace{\sum_{k=1}^{N}\sum_{j=1}^{N} W''_k V'_{jk}} + \sum_{k=1}^{N}(W'_k X''_{jk} - W'' X'_k) = 0$$

Change j to k and k to j

$$\sum_{j=1}^{N}\sum_{k=1}^{N} W'_k V''_{jk} \qquad \sum_{j=1}^{N}\sum_{k=1}^{N} W''_j V'_{kj}$$

(Interchanging summation order) (Note this step)

$$= W''_k V'_{jk} \text{ (changing } j \text{ to } k \text{ and } k \text{ to } j) \qquad = W'_k F'_{kj}$$

We finally obtain

$$\therefore \quad \sum_{j=1}^{N}\sum_{k=1}^{N} W'_k(W''_j F''_{jk}) - \sum_{j=1}^{N}\sum_{k=1}^{N} W'_j(W'_k F'_{kj}) + \sum_{k=1}^{N}(W'_k X''_k - W''_k X'_k) = 0$$

or

$$\sum_{j=1}^{N}\sum_{k=1}^{N} W'_k W''_j(F''_{jk} - F'_{kj}) + \sum_{j=1}^{N}(W'_k X''_k - W''_k X'_k) = 0 \qquad \text{...(13.18)}$$

As $F''_{jk} = F'_{kj}$ for all k and j except for branch nm in double primed and branch mn in primed networks and by taking $j = n$, $k = m$ in Figures. 13.4(b) and (c), Eqn. (13.18) gets simplified, and all the terms in double sum of Eqn. (13.18) are zero except when $j = n$ and $k = m$. Hence (13.18) yields

$$W'_m W''_n \underbrace{(F''_{nm} - F'_{mn})} + \sum_{k=1}^{N} \underbrace{(W'_k X''_k - W''_k X'_k) = 0}$$

All X''_k except $X''_a(= X)$ are zero and all X'_k except $X'_b(= X)$ are zero

$$= F_{nm} + \Delta F_{nm} - F_{nm}$$
$$= \Delta F_{nm}$$

$$\therefore \quad W'_m W''_n \Delta F_{nm} + \underbrace{W'_a X''_a - W''_b X'_b}_{= X(W'_a - W''_b)} = 0$$

if $X''_a = X'_b \triangleq X$

$$\therefore \quad W'_m W''_n \Delta F_{nm} + X(W'_a - W''_b) = 0 \qquad \text{...(13.19)}$$

But $\quad W'_a = X'_b T'_{ba} = X T_{ab} \qquad (\because \; X'_b = X)$

...(unprimed and primed networks being each other's transposes $T'_{ba} = T_{ab}$)

$$W''_b = X''_a T''_{ab} = X(T_{ab} + \Delta T_{ab}) \qquad (\because \; X''_a = X)$$

...(in double primed network, $W''_b = X(T_{ab} + \Delta T_{ab}$ due to $F''_{nm} = F_{nm} + \Delta F_{nm})$

$$W'_m = X'_b T'_{bm} = X T_{mb} \qquad (\because \; X'_b = X)$$
$$W''_n = X''_a T''_{an} = X T''_{an} \qquad (\because \; X''_a = X)$$

Putting these values in (13.19), we get

$$(XT_{mb})\,(XT''_{an})\cdot\Delta F_{nm}+X[XT_{ab}-X(T_{ab}+\Delta T_{ab})]=0$$

or

$$[T_{mb}T''_{an}\,\Delta F_{nm}-\Delta T_{ab}]X^2=0 \qquad \text{...(13.20)}$$

The above equation holds for all X, therefore,

$$T_{mb}T''\,\Delta F_{nm}=\Delta T_{ab} \qquad \text{...(13.21)}$$

$$\therefore \qquad \frac{\Delta T_{ab}}{\Delta F_{nm}}=T''_{an}T_{mb} \qquad \text{...(13.22)}$$

Taking limits of Eqn. (13.22), as $\Delta F_{nm}\to 0$, we obtain

$$\lim_{\Delta F_{nm}\to 0}\left[\frac{\Delta T_{ab}}{\Delta F_{nm}}\right]=\lim_{\Delta F_{nm}\to 0}[T''_{an}T_{mb}] \qquad \text{...(13.23)}$$

$$\therefore \qquad \frac{\partial T_{ab}}{\partial F_{nm}}=T_{an}T_{mb} \qquad \left(\because \lim_{\Delta F_{nm}\to 0}T''_{an}=T_{an}\right) \qquad \text{...(13.24)}$$

Q.E.D.

Such form of computation of sensitivity can also easily be done when the network is represented in matrix form. If the change ΔF_{nm} in F_{nm} is large, then we can use Taylor's series to find ΔT_{ab} as follows:

$$\boxed{\Delta T_{ab}=\frac{\partial T_{ab}}{\partial F_{nm}}\cdot\Delta F_{nm}+\frac{1}{2}\frac{\partial^2 T_{ab}}{\partial F_{nm}^2}(\Delta F_{nm})^2+\ldots} \qquad \text{...(13.25)}$$

The higher-order derivatives (sensitivities) of T_{ab} w.r.t. F_{nm} can be obtained from Eqn. (13.24) by the chain rule of differentiation. Such as approach yields.

$$\boxed{\Delta T_{ab}=\frac{T_{an}T_{mb}\,\Delta F_{nm}}{1-T_{mn}\Delta F_{nm}}} \qquad \text{...(13.26)}$$

EXAMPLE 13.4: *Find the sensitivities, $S_{b_1}^{H}(z)$ and $S_{b_2}^{H}(z)$ for the given network.*

SOLUTION: We have two multipliers *viz.* by b_1 and b_2 in the network we find the sensitivities:

$$S_{b_1}^{H}(z)\triangleq\frac{\partial H(z)}{\partial b_1}$$

$$S_{b_2}^{H}(z)\triangleq\frac{\partial H(z)}{\partial b_2}$$

Number the nodes are as shown. Clearly,

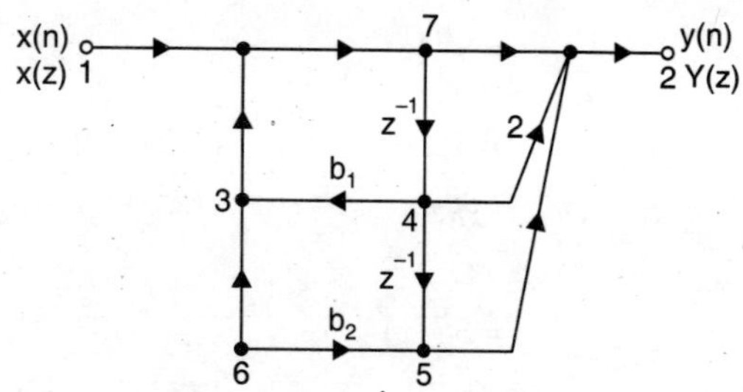

Fig. Ex. 13.1. The given network

$$H(z)=\frac{1+2z^{-1}+z^{-2}}{1-b_1z^{-1}-b_2z^{-2}} \quad \text{(by inspection)}$$

$$H_{32}=H_{62}(z)=H(z)=\frac{1+2z^{-1}+z^{-2}}{1-b_1z^{-1}-b_2z^{-2}} \quad \text{(by inspection)}$$

$$\text{As} \quad H_{17}(z)=\frac{1}{1-b_1z^{-1}-b_2z^{-2}} \qquad \left(H_{17}(z)=H(z)\Big|_{\substack{\text{(feed forward from nodes}\\ \text{4, 5 assuming to be zero)}}}\right)$$

$$\therefore \qquad H_{14}(z) = z^{-1}H_{17}(z) = \frac{z^{-1}}{1 - b_1 z^{-1} - b_2 z^{-2}} \qquad \text{['delaying' } H_{17}(z) \text{ by } z^{-1}]$$

$$H_{15}(z) = z^{-2}H_{17}(z) = \frac{z^{-2}}{1 - b_1 z^{-1} - b_2 z^{-2}} \qquad \text{['delaying' } H_{17}(z) \text{ by } z^{-2}]$$

Now
$$S_{b_1}^H(z) = H_{14}(z) \cdot H_{32}(z)$$

$$= \frac{z^{-1}}{1 - b_1 z^{-1} - b_2 z^{-2}} \cdot \frac{1 + 2z^{-1} + z^{-2}}{1 - b_1 z^{-1} - b_2 z^{-2}}$$

$$= \frac{z(z+1)^2}{(z^2 - b_1 z - b_2)^2}$$ **Ans.**

$$S_{b_2}^H(z) = H_{15}(z) \cdot H_{62}(z)$$

$$= \frac{z^{-2}}{1 - b_1 z^{-1} - b_2 z^{-2}} \cdot \frac{(1 + 2z^{-1} + z^{-2})}{1 - b_1 z^{-1} - b_2 z^{-2}}$$

$$= \frac{(z+1)^2}{(z^2 - b_1 z - b_2)^2}$$ **Ans.**

Check:

As
$$H(z) = \frac{1 + 2z^{-1} + z^{-2}}{1 - b_1 z^{-1} - b_2 z^{-2}} = \frac{(z+1)^2}{z^2 - b_1 z - b_2}$$

$$\frac{\partial H(z)}{\partial b_1} = (z+1)^2 \frac{(-1)(-z)}{(z^2 - b_1 z - b_2)^2} = \frac{z(z+1)^2}{(z^2 - b_1 z - b_2)^2}$$

$$\nearrow$$

$$= S_{b_1}^H(z)$$

Again
$$\frac{\partial H(z)}{\partial b_2} = (z+1)^2 \frac{(-1)(-1)}{(z^2 - b_1 z - b_2)^2} = \frac{(z+1)^2}{(z^2 - b_1 z - b_2)^2}$$

$$\nearrow$$

$$\triangleq S_{b_2}^H(z)$$

Thus, we get the same values of sensitivity by direct computation as by Tellegen's theorem, as expected. **Ans.**

EXAMPLE 13.5: *The gain and phase-shift sensitivities of a digital filter are defined as*

$$S_{m_i}^M \triangleq \frac{\partial M(w)}{\partial m_i}, \; S_{m_i}^\phi = \frac{\partial \phi(w)}{\partial m_i}$$

Assuming that $\left.\frac{\partial H(z)}{\partial m_i}\right|_{z=e^{j\omega}} = Re\, S_{m_i}^H(e^{j\omega}) + jI_m S_{m_i}^H(e^{j\omega})$ *derive expressions for* $S_{m_i}^M$ *and* $S_{m_i}^\phi$, *where* $H(e^{j\omega}) = M(\omega)\, e^{j\phi(\omega)}$.

SOLUTION: We can write $H(z)\big|_{z=e^{j\omega}}$ as

$$H(e^{j\omega}) = M(\omega)\cdot e^{j\phi(\omega)} \text{ where } M(\omega) \text{ is purely real}$$

$$\frac{\partial H(e^{j\omega})}{\partial m_i} = \frac{\partial M(\omega)}{\partial m_i}\cdot e^{j\phi(\omega)} + M(\omega)\cdot je^{j\phi(\omega)}\cdot\frac{\partial \phi(\omega)}{\partial m_i}$$

$$= \frac{\partial M(\omega)}{\partial m_i}[\cos\phi(\omega) + j\sin\phi(\omega)] + \frac{\partial \phi(\omega)}{\partial m_i}[-\sin\phi(\omega) + j\cos\phi(\omega)]\times M(\omega)$$

$$\triangleq \text{Re } S^H_{m_i}(e^{j\omega}) + jI_m S^H_{m_i}(e^{j\omega})$$

where
$$\text{Re } S^H_{m_i}(e^{j\omega}) = \cos\phi(\omega)\cdot\frac{\partial M(\omega)}{\partial m_i} - M(\omega)\sin\phi(\omega)\cdot\frac{\partial \phi(\omega)}{\partial m_i} \quad \ldots(A)$$

$$I_m S^H_{m_i}(e^{j\omega}) = \sin\phi(\omega)\frac{\partial M(\omega)}{\partial m_i} + M(\omega)\cos\phi(\omega)\cdot\frac{\partial \phi(\omega)}{\partial m_i} \quad \ldots(B)$$

$$\left[\text{To solve } (A) \text{ and } (B) \text{ for } \frac{\partial M(\omega)}{\partial m_i} \text{ and } \frac{\partial \phi(\omega)}{\partial m_i}\right]$$

Multiplying (A) by $\cos\phi(\omega)$ and (B) by $\sin\phi(\omega)$ and adding, we get

$$\cos\phi(\omega)\text{ Re } S^H_{m_i}(e^{j\omega}) + \sin\phi(\omega) I_m S^H_{m_i}(e^{j\omega}) = \underbrace{\left[\cos^2\phi(\omega) + \sin^2\phi(\omega)\right]}_{=1}\frac{\partial M(\omega)}{\partial m_i}$$

$$\therefore \quad \underset{\substack{\nearrow \\ \triangleq S^M_{m_i}(e^{j\omega})}}{\frac{\partial M(\omega)}{\partial m_i}} = \cos\phi(\omega)\cdot\text{Re } S^H_{m_i}(e^{j\omega}) + \sin\phi(\omega)\, I_m S^H_{m_i}(e^{j\omega})$$ **Ans.**

Now multiplying (A) by $-\sin\phi(\omega)$ and (B) by $\cos\phi(\omega)$ and adding, we have

$$-\sin\phi(\omega)\cdot\text{Re } S^H_{m_i}(e^{j\omega}) + \cos\phi(\omega)\, I_m S^H_{m_i}(e^{j\omega}) = M(\omega)\underbrace{(\sin^2\phi + \cos^2\phi)}_{=1}\cdot\frac{\partial \phi(\omega)}{\partial m_i}$$

$$\therefore \quad \underset{\substack{\swarrow \\ \triangleq S^{\phi}_{m_i}(e^{j\omega})}}{\frac{\partial \phi(\omega)}{\partial m_i}} = \frac{1}{M(\omega)}[\cos\phi(\omega)\cdot I_m S^H_{m_i}(e^{j\omega}) - \sin\phi(\omega)\text{ Re } S^H_{m_i}(e^{j\omega})]$$ **Ans.**

EXAMPLE 13.6: *(a) Verify that Tellegen's theorem in the form of Eqn. (13.3) holds for the two networks given.*

(b) Repeat part (a) for Tellegen's theorem in the form of Eqn. (13.6).

SOLUTION: *(a)* Eqn. (13.3) form of Tellegen's theorem is

$$\sum_{k=1}^{N}\sum_{j=1}^{N}(\omega'_k v_{jk} - \omega_k v'_{jk}) + \sum_{k=1}^{N}(\omega'_k x_k - \omega_k x'_k) = 0$$

Here $N = 3$ (*i.e.* three nodes excluding source)

$$(k = 1): \omega_1'v_{11} - \omega_1 v_{11}' + \omega_1' v_{21} - \omega_1 v_{21}' + \omega_1' v_{31} - \omega_1' v_{31} + (\omega_1' x_1 - \omega_1 x_1')$$
$$(k = 2): \omega_2'v_{12} - \omega_2 v_{12}' + \omega_2' v_{22} - \omega_2 v_{22}' + \omega_2' v_{32} - \omega_2' v_{32} + (\omega_2' x_2 - \omega_2 x_2')$$
$$(k = 3): \omega_3'v_{13} - \omega_3 v_{13}' + \omega_3' v_{23} - \omega_3 v_{23}' + \omega_3' v_{33} - \omega_3' v_{33} + (\omega_3' x_3 - \omega_3 x_3')$$

Writing the non-zero terms, since $v_{11}, v_{11}', v_{22}, v_{22}', v_{33}, v_{33}', x_2, x_2', x_3, x_3', v_{21}, v_{21}', v_{32}, v_{32}', v_{31}, v_{13}'$ are all zero.

$$\therefore \quad \text{LHS} = \omega_2' v_{12} - \omega_2 v_{12}' + \omega_3' v_{13} + \omega_3' v_{23} - \omega_3 v_{23}' - \omega_1 v_{31}' + \omega_1' x_1 - \omega_1 x_1'$$

$$= -\omega_1 \underbrace{[x_1' + v_{31}']}_{\omega_1'} - \omega_2 \underbrace{[v_{12}']}_{\omega_2'} - \omega_3 \underbrace{[v_{23}']}_{\omega_3'} + \omega_1' \underbrace{[x_1]}_{\omega_1} + \omega_2' \underbrace{[v_{12}]}_{\omega_2} + \omega_3' \underbrace{[v_{13} + v_{23}]}_{\omega_3}$$

$$= -\omega_1\omega_1' - \omega_2\omega_2' - \omega_3\omega_3' + \omega_1'\omega_1 + \omega_2'\omega_2 + \omega_3'\omega_3 = 0 \qquad \text{Q.E.D.}$$

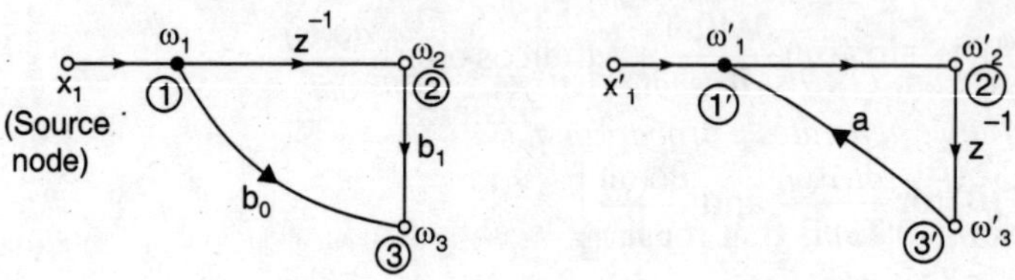

Fig. Ex. 13.3. The two given networks

(*b*) Similar method as followed in part (*a*)

EXAMPLE 13.7: *Show that the change in the transfer function (T_{ab}) of a linear signal flow graph due to a large-scale change in a branch nm transmittance F_{nm} is given by*

$$\Delta T_{ab} = \frac{T_{an}\, T_{mb} \Delta F_{nm}}{1 - T_{mn} \Delta F_{nm}}.$$

SOLUTION: Expressing ΔT_{ab} in a Taylor's series expansion, we have

$$\Delta T_{ab} = \sum_{k=1}^{\infty} \frac{1}{k!} \frac{\partial^k T_{ab}}{\partial F_{nm}^k} [\Delta F_{nm}]^k \qquad \ldots(A) \text{ (Note this step)}$$

As

$$\frac{\partial^2 T_{ab}}{\partial F_{nm}^2} = \frac{\partial}{\partial F_{nm}} \left(\frac{\partial T_{ab}}{\partial F_{nm}} \right) = \frac{\partial}{\partial F_{nm}} [T_{an} \cdot T_{nb}] \qquad \text{(from sensitivity formula)}$$

$$= \frac{\partial T_{an}}{\partial F_{nm}} \cdot T_{mb} + T_{an} \frac{\partial T_{mb}}{\partial F_{nm}}$$

$$= (T_{an} T_{mn}) T_{mb} + T_{an} (T_{mn} T_{mb}) = 2T_{mn} T_{an} T_{mb} \qquad \ldots(B)$$

Again

$$\frac{\partial^3 T_{ab}}{\partial F_{nm}^3} = \frac{\partial}{\partial F_{nm}} \left(\frac{\partial^2 T_{ab}}{\partial F_{nm}^2} \right) = \frac{\partial}{\partial F_{nm}} [2T_{mn} T_{an} T_{mb}] \qquad \text{[due to } (B)]$$

$$= 2\left[\frac{\partial T_{mn}}{\partial F_{nm}} T_{an} T_{mb} + T_{mn} \frac{\partial T_{an}}{\partial F_{nm}} T_{mb} + T_{mn} T_{an} \frac{\partial T_{mb}}{\partial F_{nm}} \right]$$

$$= 2[(T_{mn} T_{mn}) \cdot T_{an} T_{mb} + T_{mn} (T_{an} T_{mn}) T_{mb} + T_{mn} T_{an} (T_{mn} T_{mb})]$$

$$= 3!T_{mn}^2 T_{an} T_{mb} \qquad \text{...(C)}$$

Generalising
$$\frac{\partial^k T_{ab}}{\partial F_{nm}^k} = k!T_{mn}^{k-1} T_{an} T_{mb} \qquad \text{...(D)}$$

Using (*D*) in (*A*), we get

$$\Delta T_{ab} = \sum_{k=1}^{\infty} \frac{1}{k!} \cdot k! T_{mn}^{k-1} T_{an} T_{mb} [\Delta F_{nm}]^k$$

$$= T_{an} T_{mb} \Delta F_{nm} \sum_{k=1}^{\infty} (T_{mn} \Delta F_{nm})^{k-1}$$

$$= T_{an} T_{mb} \Delta F_{nm} \cdot \left[\frac{1}{1 - T_{mn} \Delta F_{nm}} \right] = \frac{T_{an} T_{mb} \Delta F_{nm}}{1 - T_{mn} \Delta F_{nm}}$$ **Ans.**

EXAMPLE 13.8: *Use Eqn. (13.26) to show that for a non-recursive digital filter, a large-scale change in one branch transmittance generates a proportional change in the overall transfer function; i.e., show that ΔT_{ab} is proportional to ΔF_{nm}.*

SOLUTION: Equation (13.26) is that for large-scale change ΔF_{nm} in F_{nm}, the change in the transfer function T_{ab} is

$$\Delta T_{ab} = \frac{T_{an} T_{mb} \Delta F_{nm}}{1 - T_{mn} \Delta F_{nm}}$$

The above result is true for any generic network, *i.e.*, recursive as well as non-recursive. In the case of non-recursive digital filters, if F_{nm} represents a transmittance in branch *n* to *m*, $n \circ \xrightarrow{F_{nm}} \circ m$, the transmission from *m* to *n* is necessarily zero since there is no feedback path between any nodes. (Note that a recursion in a recursive filter implies the existence of a feedback path as a necessity). Thus if F_{nm} is non-zero, T_{mn} (Transfer function from *m* to *n*) is zero in a non-recursive filter. Putting $T_{mn} = 0$ in (13.26), we get

$$\Delta T_{ab} \Big|_{\substack{\text{non-recursive} \\ \text{filters}}} = T_{an} T_{mn} \cdot \Delta F_{nm} \propto \Delta F_{nm}$$ Q.E.D.

CHAPTER 14

Applications of Digital Signal Processing

14.1 INTRODUCTION

Digital Signal Processing (DSP) is exploited in various practical applications. The growth of efficient, high speed and economical digital computers has further facilitated the preference of DSP over the analog processing. Though it is not feasible to enlist all the applications using DSP technology however, a few important areas are mentioned here.

(*i*) Telecommunications: Modems, speaker phones, cellophones, I-phones, I-pad
(*ii*) Speech processing: Speech synthesis, speech recognition
(*iii*) Music: Generation of echoes and reverberations, music synthesis, HI-FI and stereo systems
(*iv*) Control systems: Robots machine tools, CNC, satellite control
(*v*) Medical systems: ECG, X-ray, hearing aids, MRI, EEG, DNA matching
(*vi*) Image processing: Image enhancement, image compression
(*vii*) Geology: Seismic analysis, underwater search
(*viii*) Forensic: Lie detector, finger print matching, etc.

We shall cover a few applications in this chapter.

14.2 DIGITAL SINE-COSINE GENERATOR

We can realize digital sinusoidal oscillator, say a digital sine-cosine generator. These circuits have many applications, such as in the computation of the Discrete Fourier Transform (DFT) and certain communication systems. In some applications, it is more convenient to use numerical algorithms for computation of the sine-cosine functions.

Let
$$s_1(n) = \alpha \sin(\omega_0 n) \qquad \text{...(14.1}a\text{)}$$
$$s_2(n) = \beta \cos(\omega_0 n) \qquad \text{...(14.1}b\text{)}$$

Then
$$s_1(n+1) = \alpha \sin((n+1)\omega_0)$$
$$= \underbrace{\alpha \sin(n\omega_0)}_{s_1(n)} \cos\omega_0 + \underbrace{\alpha \cos(n\omega_0)}_{(\alpha/\beta)s_2(n)} \sin\omega_0 \qquad \text{...(14.2}a\text{)}$$

and
$$s_2(n+1) = \beta \cos((n+1)\omega_0)$$

$$= \underbrace{\beta \cos(n\omega_0)}_{s_2(n)}\cos\omega_0 - \underbrace{\beta \sin(n\omega_0)}_{(\beta/\alpha)s_1(n)}\sin\omega_0 \qquad \ldots(14.2b)$$

Using Eqn. [14.1(*a*)] and [14.1(*b*)], we can write Eqn. [14.2(*a*)] and [14.2(*b*)] in matrix form as follows

$$\begin{bmatrix} s_1(n+1) \\ s_2(n+1) \end{bmatrix} = \begin{bmatrix} \cos\omega_0 & \frac{\alpha}{\beta}\sin\omega_0 \\ -\frac{\beta}{\alpha}\sin\omega_0 & \cos\omega_0 \end{bmatrix} \begin{bmatrix} s_1(n) \\ s_2(n) \end{bmatrix} \qquad \ldots(14.3)$$

To generate $s_1(n)$ from $s_1(n+1)$, we need a delay, and similarly, to generate $s_2(n)$ from $s_2(n+1)$ we need a delay. Thus the structure must have at least two delays to realize matrix (14.3). We, now envolve the structure using above results.

Consider the following equations

$$\begin{bmatrix} s_1(n+1) \\ s_2(n+1) \end{bmatrix} = \begin{bmatrix} 0 & A \\ 0 & 0 \end{bmatrix} \begin{bmatrix} s_1(n+1) \\ s_2(n+1) \end{bmatrix} + \begin{bmatrix} C & D \\ E & F \end{bmatrix} \begin{bmatrix} s_1(n) \\ s_2(n) \end{bmatrix} \qquad \ldots(14.4)$$

This have five multipliers

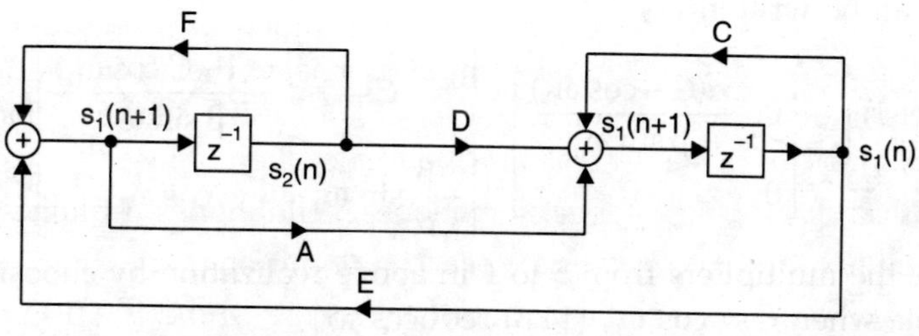

Fig. 14.1. A general second-order digital filter with no input node (5 multipliers: *A*, *C*, *D*, *E* and *F*)

In Fig. 14.1, we see that

$$s_2(n+1) = Es_1(n) + Fs_2(n)$$

and

$$\begin{aligned} s_1(n+1) &= Cs_1(n) + Ds_2(n) + As_2(n+1) \\ &= Cs_1(n) + Ds_2(n) + A[Es_1(n) + Fs_2(n)] \\ &= [AE + C]s_1(n) + (AF + D)s_2(n) \end{aligned}$$

i.e.,

$$\begin{bmatrix} s_1(n+1) \\ s_2(n+1) \end{bmatrix} = \begin{bmatrix} AE + C & AF + D \\ E & F \end{bmatrix} \begin{bmatrix} s_1(n) \\ s_2(n) \end{bmatrix} \qquad \ldots(14.5)$$

Comparing (14.3) and (14.5), we have

$$E = -\frac{\beta}{\alpha}\sin\omega_0,\ F = \cos\omega_0,$$

$$AE + C = \cos\omega_0;\ AF + D = \frac{\alpha}{\beta}\sin\omega_0 \qquad \ldots(14.5a)$$

We wish to express the variables *A*, *D*, *E*, *F* in terms of *C*, α, β, $\sin\omega_0$, $\cos\omega_0$ from above four relations. This would simplify the need of coefficients.

Note that

$$C = \cos\omega_0 - AE \qquad \ldots(14.5b)$$

$$D\cdot\frac{\beta}{\alpha} = \sin\omega_0 - \frac{\beta}{\alpha}AF \qquad \ldots(14.5c)$$

$$\therefore \quad C\cos\omega_0 + D\cdot\frac{\beta}{\alpha}\sin\omega_0 = \left[\cos^2\omega_0 - \cos\omega_0\, AE + \sin^2\omega_0 - \frac{\beta}{\alpha}AF\sin\omega_0\right]$$

$$= \left[1 - A\left(E\cos\omega_0 + \frac{\beta}{\alpha}F\sin\omega_0\right)\right]$$

$$= \left[1 - A\left(-\frac{\beta}{\alpha}\sin\omega_0\cos\omega_0 + \frac{\beta}{\alpha}\cos\omega_0\sin\omega_0\right)\right]$$

$$\therefore \quad C\cos\omega_0 + D\frac{\beta}{\alpha}\sin\omega_0 = 1 \qquad \text{...(14.6)}$$

Equation (14.4) can now be expressed in terms of C, α, β, $\sin\omega_0$ and $\cos\omega_0$ since

$$E = -\frac{\beta}{\alpha}\sin\omega_0,\; F = \cos\omega_0,\; A = \frac{(\cos\omega_0 - C)}{E} = \frac{(C - \cos\omega_0)}{\left(\frac{\beta}{\alpha}\sin\omega_0\right)}$$

$$D = (1 - C\cos\omega_0)\cdot\frac{\alpha}{\beta\sin\omega_0} \quad \text{(using [14.5(a)] and (14.6))} \qquad \text{...(14.7)}$$

Hence, (14.4) can be written as

$$\begin{bmatrix} s_1(n+1) \\ s_2(n+1) \end{bmatrix} = \begin{bmatrix} 0 & \frac{\alpha(C - \cos\omega_0)}{\beta\sin\omega_0} \\ 0 & 0 \end{bmatrix} + \begin{bmatrix} C & \frac{\alpha(1 - C\cos\omega_0)}{\beta\sin\omega_0} \\ -\frac{\beta}{\alpha}\sin\omega_0 & \cos\omega_0 \end{bmatrix}\begin{bmatrix} s_1(n) \\ s_2(n) \end{bmatrix} \qquad \text{...(14.8)}$$

We can reduce the multipliers from 5 to 4 in above realization by choosing $C = 0, +1, -1$ or $\cos\omega_0$. For example when $C = \cos\omega_0$, (14.8) reduces to

$$\begin{bmatrix} s_1(n+1) \\ s_2(n+1) \end{bmatrix} = \begin{bmatrix} \cos\omega_0 & \frac{\alpha}{\beta}\sin\omega_0 \\ -\frac{\beta}{\alpha}\sin\omega_0 & \cos\omega_0 \end{bmatrix}\begin{bmatrix} s_1(n) \\ s_2(n) \end{bmatrix} \qquad \text{...(14.9)}$$

which for $\beta = \pm\alpha$, leads to four multiplier sine-cosine generator.

If we set $\alpha\sin\omega_0 = \pm\beta$, then $\frac{\alpha}{\beta}\sin\omega_0 = \pm 1$, then (14.2) reduces to

$$\begin{bmatrix} s_1(n+1) \\ s_2(n+1) \end{bmatrix} = \begin{bmatrix} \cos\omega_0 & 1 \\ -\sin^2\omega_0 & \cos\omega_0 \end{bmatrix}\begin{bmatrix} s_1(n) \\ s_2(n) \end{bmatrix} \qquad \text{...(14.10)}$$

$$\because \quad -\frac{\beta}{\alpha}\sin\omega_0 = -(\sin\omega_0)\sin\omega_0 = -\sin^2\omega_0$$

The final realization is shown in Fig. 14.2, giving $s_1(n) = \alpha\sin(\omega_0 n)$ and $s_2(n) = \beta\cos(\omega_0 n)$.

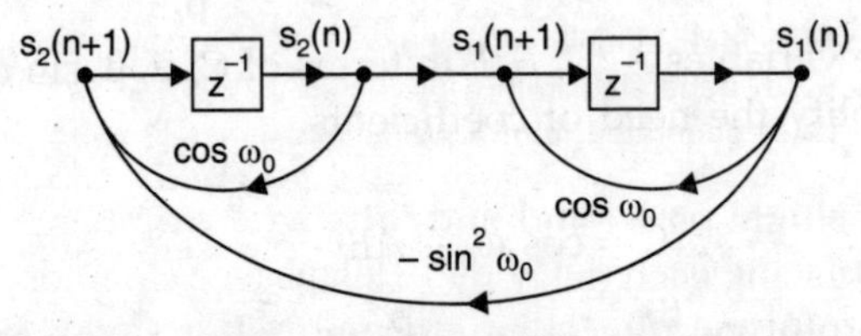

Fig. 14.2. Three multiplier sine-cosine Generator

A Single Multiplier Structure for Sine-cosine Generator

If we get $(\beta \sin \omega_0) = \alpha(1 - \cos \omega_0)$ in (14.9) then

$$\frac{\beta}{\alpha} \sin \omega_0 = 1 - \cos \omega_0$$

and
$$\frac{\alpha}{\beta} \sin \omega_0 = \left(\frac{\sin \omega_0}{1-\cos \omega_0}\right) \sin \omega_0 = \frac{1-\cos^2 \omega_0}{1-\cos \omega_0} = 1 + \cos \omega_0,$$

We obtain from (14.9)

$$\begin{bmatrix} s_1(n+1) \\ s_2(n+1) \end{bmatrix} = \begin{bmatrix} \cos \omega_0 & 1+\cos \omega_0 \\ \cos \omega_0 - 1 & \cos \omega_0 \end{bmatrix} \begin{bmatrix} s_1(n) \\ s_2(n) \end{bmatrix} \quad \ldots(14.11)$$

Other single-multiplier realization can be derived by setting $-\beta \sin \omega_0 = \alpha(1 + \cos \omega_0)$.

To start recursion at least one variable $s_1(n)$ or $s_2(n)$ should be initially non-zero value. Single multiplier structures retain their poles on the unit circle even for finite word length constraint. The other (non-single multiplier) structures may cause oscillation to decay or explode due to quantization effect.

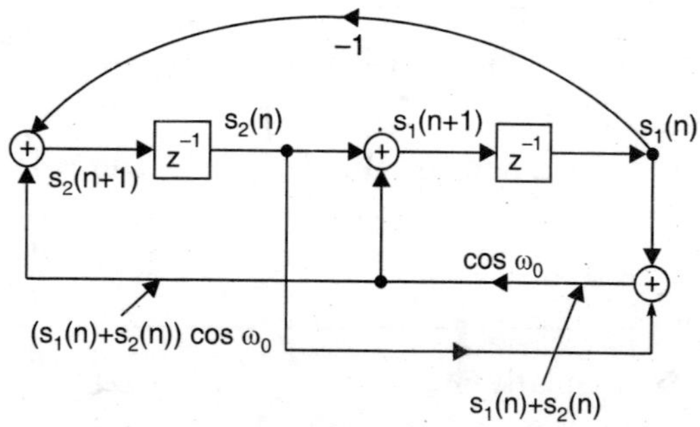

Fig. 14.3. A single multiplier (cos ω_0) sine-cosine generator

14.3 COMB FILTERS

There are a number of applications where filters with multiple pass bands and stop bands are required. Comb filters can be used for such applications. In most general form, a comb filter has a periodic frequency response function of ω with a period of $\frac{2\pi}{L}$, (L a +ve integer).

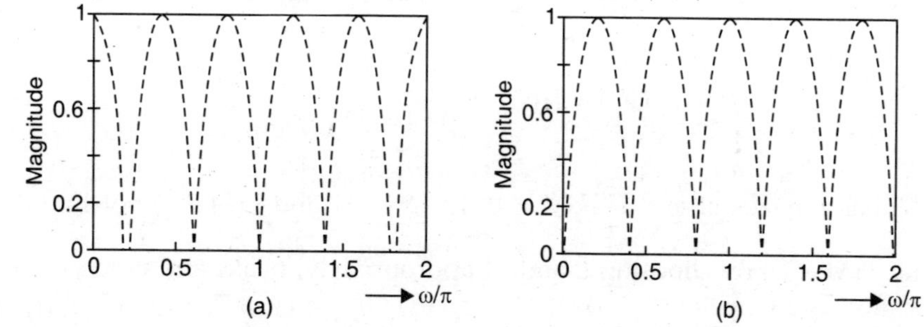

Fig. 14.4. Magnitude responses of FIR Comb filters:
(*a*) generated from a prototype, LPF with $L = 5$
(*b*) generated from a prototype HPF, with $L = 5$.

If $H(z)$ is a filter with single pass band and/or single stop band, a comb filter can be easily generated from $H(z)$ by replacing each delay by L delays (see Chapter 12, upsampling by factor L). $H(z)$ may be FIR or IIR prototype filter, then a Comb Filter $G(z)$ is given by

$$\boxed{G(z) = H(z^L)} \text{ (up sampling by } L) \quad ...(14.12)$$

If the magnitude response $|H(e^{j\omega})|$ has its peak at $\omega_p = \frac{\pi}{2}$, then the magnitude response $|G(e^{j\omega})|$ will have peaks at $\frac{\pi}{2}\frac{k}{L}$, $k = 1, 2, ..., L$. Similarly if $|H(e^{j\omega})|$ has a notch at $\omega_0 = \frac{\pi}{2}$, then $|G(e^{j\omega})|$ will have L notches at $\frac{\pi}{2}\cdot\frac{k}{L}$, $k = 1, 2, ..., L$.

For example, if $\quad H(z) = \frac{1}{2}(1+z^{-1})$ (a LPF, FIR type)

then $\quad G_0(z) = \frac{1}{2}(1+z^{-L})$, is a comb filter [Fig. 14.4 (*a*)] ...(14.13)

$G_0(e^{j\omega})$ has L peaks at:	$\omega = \frac{2\pi k}{L}$, $k = 0, 1, ..., L-1$
and L notches at:	$\omega = \frac{2\pi}{L}\frac{2k+1}{2}$, $k = 0, 1, ..., L-1$
i.e.	at $\omega = \frac{\pi}{L}, \frac{3\pi}{L}, \frac{5\pi}{L}, ...$ ...(14.14)

Similarly, if $\quad H(z) = \frac{1}{2}(1-z^{-1})$ (a HPF, FIR type)

then $\quad G_1(z) = \frac{1}{2}(1-z^{-L})$ is a comb filer, [Fig. 14.4(*b*)] ...(14.15)

> $G_1(z)$ has $G_1(e^{j\omega})$ has its notches are at $\omega = \frac{2\pi k}{L}$, $k = 0, 1, ..., L-1$ and has peaks at $\frac{\pi}{L}\cdot(2k+1)$, $L = 0, 1, ..., L-1$ ...(14.16)

If $\quad H(z) = \frac{1-z^{-M}}{M(1-z^{-1})}$, an M-point moving average filter

then $\quad G(z) = H(z^L) = \frac{1-z^{-LM}}{M(1-z^{-L})}$

And $G(e^{j\omega})$ has L peaks at $\omega = \frac{2\pi}{L}k$, $k = 0, 1, ..., L-1$ and $L(M-1)$ notches at $\omega = \frac{2\pi}{LM}k$, for $k = 1, 2, ..., L(M-1)$. By choosing L and M appropriately, peaks and notches can be created at desired locations.

Applications of Comb filters:

1. Cancellation of periodic interferences. At notch points the response is zero, hence the interference signals at notch frequencies are removed.
2. In creating special audio effects in musical sound processing.
3. In LORAN navigation systems for suppression of cross-rate interference.
4. In digital colour TV receivers.

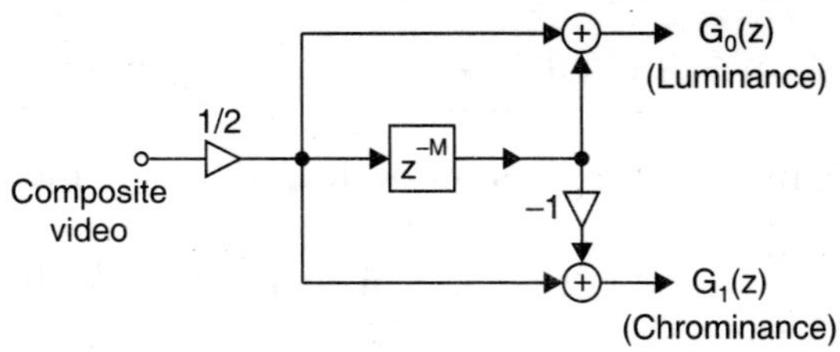

Fig. 14.5. Use of comb filter (Chrominances) for TV receivers.

$$G_0(z) = \frac{1}{2}(1+z^{-M}) \text{ : luminance (intensity signal)}$$

$$G_1(z) = \frac{1}{2}(1-z^{-M}) \text{ : chrominance (colour signal)}$$

Delay chain is chosen to get line-delay of z^{-M}. (The time taken to cover one line is M sample time. It is called line delay of z^{-M}) $G_0(z)$ acts as LPF by averaging two successive horizontal lines of video signal. It also blurs the luminance signal. $G_1(z)$ gives the information of chrominance *i.e.* colour signal.

14.4 SHORT-TIME FOURIER TRANSFORM (STFT)

In many practical situations, the signals are non-stationary whose vital parameters such as frequency, amplitude and phase changes vary with time. In such cases a single DFT of the complete signal is not possible. Speech signal, radar and sonar signals are the examples of non-stationary signals. For such cases, we view the incoming signal sequence with windows, centred at different times. The "viewing window" is of length, say, L where the complete signal sequence $x(n)$ has length many times L. As the signal $x(n)$ is time-varying, the frequency-dome representation of $x(n)$ under different window movement will also vary. Hence, we use a part of signal viewed by the window to determine the Discrete-Time Fourier Transform (DTFT). Such a DTFT is called Short-Time Fourier Transform (STFT). We defined STFT of $x(n)$ using the window $\omega(m)$ by

$$\text{STFT: } X(e^{j\omega}, n) = \sum_{m=-\infty}^{\infty} x(n+m)\cdot\omega(m)\cdot e^{-j\omega m} \quad \text{...(14.16}a\text{)}$$

$$= \sum_{m=0}^{L-1} x(n+m)\omega(m)e^{-j\omega m} \quad \text{...(14.16}b\text{)}$$

The symbol $X(e^{j\omega}, n)$ includes n, and it indicates that the STFT is time (*i.e.* n) dependent. For example if STFT of $x(n)$ at $n = n_0$ is taken and window $\omega(m)$ has length L, then the STFT would amount to DTFT for L samples given by the sequence:

$x(n_0)\cdot\omega(0),\ x(n_0+1)\cdot\omega(1),\ x(n_0+2)\cdot\omega(2),\ \ldots,\ x(n_0+L-1)\cdot\omega(L-1)$.

As DFT : $X(k)$ of a sequence $x(n)$ is obtained by taking discrete samples of $X(e^{j\omega})$ at $\omega = \frac{2\pi k}{N}$, $k = 0, 1, \ldots, N-1$, similarly, we obtain DFT of STFT of a non-stationary sequence by replacing ω by $\frac{2\pi k}{N}$, $k = 0, 1, \ldots, N-1$, *i.e.*,

$$X(k, n) \triangleq X(e^{j\omega}, n)\Big|_{\omega=2\pi k/N}$$

where N is the DFT length and $N \geq L$ (L being the window length). Thus, we can write

$$\therefore \quad \boxed{X(k, n) = \sum_{m=0}^{L-1} x(n+m)\omega(m)e^{-j2\pi km/N}, \; k = 0, 1, \ldots, N-1} \qquad \ldots(14.16c)$$

Taking inverse DFT of $X(k, n)$, we get

$$x(n + m) \cdot \omega(m) = \frac{1}{N}\sum_{k=0}^{N-1} X(k, n)\, e^{j2\pi km/N}$$

$$\therefore \quad \boxed{x(n + m) = \frac{1}{N\omega(m)}\sum_{k=0}^{N-1} X(k, n)e^{j2\pi km/N}} \qquad \ldots(14.16d)$$

The signal $x(n)$ can be fully recovered only if none of the values of $\omega(m)$ is zero.

To appreciate the use of STFT as a tool for frequency-domain conversion of a non-stationary sequence $x(n)$, it will be appropriate to learn a few important properties of STFT. We cover these properties by giving a few solved examples.

EXAMPLE 14.1: *Show that if $X_1(e^{j\omega}, n)$ and $X_2(e^{j\omega}, n)$ are the STFTs of $x_1(n)$ and $x_2(n)$, respectively, then*

(i) STFT $[ax_1(n) + bx_2(n)] = aX_1(e^{j\omega}, n) + bX_2(e^{j\omega}, n)$

(ii) STFT $[x_1(n - k)] = X_1(e^{j\omega}, n - k)$

(iii) STFT $[e^{j\omega_0 n}x_1(n)] = e^{j\omega_0 n}X_1(n, e^{j(\omega-\omega_0)})$.

SOLUTION:

(i) STFT $[ax_1(n) + bx_2(n)] = \sum_{m=-\infty}^{\infty} [ax_1(n+m) + bx_2(n+m)\omega(m)e^{-j\omega n}]$

$$= a\sum_{m=-\infty}^{\infty} x_1(n+m)\omega(m)e^{-j\omega m} + b\sum_{m=-\infty}^{\infty} x_2(n+m)\omega(m)\cdot e^{-j\omega m}$$

$$= aX_1(e^{j\omega}, n) + bX_2(e^{j\omega}, n)$$ **Ans.**

(ii) STFT $[x_1(n - k)] = \sum_{m=-\infty}^{\infty} x_1(n-k+m)\cdot\omega(m).e^{-j\omega n}$

$$= \sum_{m=-\infty}^{\infty} x_1(n'+m)\cdot\omega(m)\cdot e^{-j\omega m}, \text{ where } n' = n - k$$

$$= X_1(e^{j\omega}, n'), \quad n' = n - k$$

$$= X_1(e^{j\omega}, n - k)$$ **Ans.**

(iii) STFT $[e^{j\omega_0 n}x_1(n)] = \sum_{m=-\infty}^{\infty} [e^{j\omega_0(n+m)}\cdot x_1(n+m)]\omega(m)e^{-j\omega m}$

$$= e^{j\omega_0 n} \sum_{m=-\infty}^{\infty} x_1(n+m)\cdot \omega(m)\cdot e^{-j(\omega-\omega_0)m} \qquad \ldots(A)$$

$$= e^{j\omega_0 n} X_1(n, e^{j(\omega-\omega_0)}) \text{ comparing } (A) \text{ with } (14.1) \quad \textbf{Ans.}$$

EXAMPLE 14.2: *Show that*

$$\sum_{m=-\infty}^{\infty} x(m)\cdot \omega(m-n)e^{-j\omega m} = e^{-j\omega n} X(e^{j\omega}, n).$$

SOLUTION:

$$\text{LHS} = \sum_{m=-\infty}^{\infty} x(m)\omega(m-n)e^{-j\omega n} \qquad \ldots(A)$$

Put $m = n + m'$ $\therefore$ $m - n = m'$

$$(A) = \sum_{m'=-\infty}^{\infty} x(n+m')\omega(m')\cdot e^{-j\omega(n+m')}$$

$$= e^{-j\omega n} \sum_{m'=-\infty}^{\infty} x(n+m')\omega(m')e^{-j\omega m'} \qquad \ldots(B)$$

$$= e^{-j\omega n} \sum_{m=-\infty}^{\infty} x(n+m)\omega(m)e^{-j\omega m} \text{ dropping dashes from } m' \text{ in } (B)$$

$$= e^{-j\omega n} X(e^{j\omega}, n) \qquad \text{Q.E.D.}$$

EXAMPLE 14.3: *An FIR causal LTI system with impulse response $h(n)$ such that $h(n) = 0$ for $n < 0$ and for $n > m$, has input $x(n)$ and output $y(n)$. Show that:*

$$Y(e^{j\omega}, n) = h(n) * X(e^{j\omega}, n)$$

where $X(e^{j\omega}, n)$ and $Y(e^{j\omega}, n)$ are the STFTs of $x(n)$ and $y(n)$, respectively. The convolution is computed for variable n.

SOLUTION: We know that

$$y(n) = x(n) * h(n) \text{ (convolution operation)}$$

$$= \sum_{k=0}^{m} h(k)\cdot x(n-k) \qquad (\text{as } x(k) = 0 \text{ for } k < 0 \text{ and } k > m)$$

$$\therefore \quad y(n+m) = \sum_{k=0}^{m} h(k)x(n+m-k) \qquad \ldots(A)$$

$$\therefore \quad Y(e^{j\omega}, n) = \sum_{m=-\infty}^{\infty} y(n+m)\omega(m)\cdot e^{-j\omega n} \text{ (by definition of STFT)}$$

$$= \sum_{m=-\infty}^{\infty} \left[\sum_{k=0}^{m} h(k)\cdot x(n+m-k)\right]\omega(m)\cdot e^{-j\omega n} \text{ [using } (A) \text{ for } y(n+m)]$$

$$= \sum_{k=0}^{m} h(k)\left\{\sum_{m=-\infty}^{\infty} x(n-k+m)\omega(m)e^{-j\omega m}\right\}$$

$$= \sum_{k=0}^{m} h(k) \cdot X(e^{j\omega}, n-k)$$

$$= h(n) * X(e^{j\omega}, n) \qquad \text{(Convolution for variable } n\text{)}$$

Thus, the STFT computation obeys the law of convolution as for LTI systems.

14.4.1 Auto-correlation Function in STFT Domain

Auto-correlation function $r(n, m)$ for the time varying sequence $x(n)$ is also termed as time-dependent auto-correlation and is defined as

$$\boxed{r(n, m) \triangleq \sum_{l=-\infty}^{\infty} [x(n+l)\omega(l)][x(m+n+l) \cdot \omega(m+l)]} \qquad \ldots(14.16e)$$

To show that

$$\boxed{R(e^{j\omega}, n) = |X(e^{j\omega}, n)|^2} \qquad \ldots(14.16f)$$

where $R(e^{j\omega}, n)$ is the DTFT of $r(n, m)$ defined by

$$R(e^{j\omega}, n) = \sum_{m=-\infty}^{\infty} r(n, m)e^{-j\omega n}.$$

Proof:

$$r(n, m) = \sum_{l=-\infty}^{\infty} x(n+l)\omega(l) \cdot x(m+n+l)\omega(m+l) \quad \text{(by definition)}\ldots(A)$$

Replace l by $-k$ in (A) (Note this step)

$$\therefore \quad r(n, m) = \sum_{k=-\infty}^{\infty} \underbrace{x(n-k)\omega(-k)}_{x_2(n,k)} \cdot \underbrace{x(m+n-k) \cdot \omega(m-k)}_{x_1(n, m-k)} \qquad \ldots(B)$$

Define $\quad x_1(n, k) = x(n + k) \cdot \omega(k) \qquad \ldots(C)$

and $\quad x_2(n, k) = x(n - k) \cdot \omega(-k) \qquad \ldots(D)$

$$\therefore \quad r(n, m) = \sum_{k=-\infty}^{\infty} x_2(n, k) \cdot x_1(n, m-k)$$

$$= x_1(n, m) * x_2(n, m) \qquad \ldots(E)$$

As,

$$\text{DTFT } [x_1(n, m)] = \sum_{m=-\infty}^{\infty} x_1(n, m)e^{-j\omega m}$$

$$= \sum_{m=-\infty}^{\infty} x(n+m) \cdot \omega(m)e^{-j\omega m} \qquad \text{[Changing } k \text{ to } m \text{ in (C)]}$$

$$= X(e^{j\omega}, n) \qquad \text{(by definition of STFT)}$$

Also,

$$\text{DTFT } [x_2(n, m)] = \sum_{m=-\infty}^{\infty} x_2(n, m)e^{-j\omega m}$$

$$= \sum_{m=-\infty}^{\infty} x(n-m) \cdot \omega(-m)e^{-j\omega m} \qquad \text{[Changing } k \text{ to } m \text{ in (D)]}$$

Replacing m by $-p$, we have from above

$$\text{DTFT}\,[x_2(n, m)] = \sum_{p=-\infty}^{\infty} x(n+p)\omega(p)e^{j\omega p}$$

$$= \left[\sum_{p=-\infty}^{\infty} x(n+p)\cdot\omega(p)e^{-j\omega p}\right]^* \quad \ldots(F)$$

We have assumed $x(n)$ and $\omega(n)$ as real valued in (F).

From (F) $\quad \text{DTFT}\,[x_2(n, m)] = X^*(e^{j\omega}, n) \quad \ldots(G)$

$$R(e^{j\omega}, n) = \text{DFT}\,[r(m, n)]$$
$$= \text{DFT}\,\{x_1(n, m) * x_2(n, m)\} \qquad [\text{using } (E) \text{ for } (r, m)]$$
$$= \text{DFT}\,[x_1(n, m)]\cdot\text{DFT}\,[x_2(n, m)]$$
$$= X(e^{j\omega}, n)\cdot X^*(e^{j\omega}, n) \text{(as DTFT obeys law of convolution)}$$
$$= |X(e^{j\omega}, n)|^2 \qquad \text{Q.E.D.}$$

Thus, the power spectrum of a time varying sequence can be obtained by using STFT of sub sequence of a lengthy time varying random sequence $x(n)$.

14.5 A NOTE ON DISCRETE-TIME HILBERT TRANSFORM (DHT)

Discrete-time Hilbert Transform (DHT) finds extensive use in digital communication and other digital processing units. The DHT is also called a $\frac{\pi}{2}$ (*i.e.* 90°) phase shifter, since its frequency response is given by

$$\text{DTFT}\,[h_{HT}(n)] = \begin{cases} -j, & 0 < \omega \le \pi \\ +j, & -\pi \le \omega < 0 \end{cases} \quad \ldots(14.16g)$$

where

$$h_{HT}(n) = \begin{cases} \frac{2}{\pi n}\sin^2\frac{\pi n}{2}, & n \neq 0 \\ 0, & \text{otherwise} \end{cases} \quad \ldots(14.16h)$$

[see solved Example 8.17(*b*) for above derivation]

We are interested in a spectrum $X(e^{j\omega}) = 0$ for $-\pi \le \omega < 0$. Clearly, $x(n)$ cannot be a real sequence, since for $x_r(n)$ real, [see results in Eqns. (8.79)]

$$X_r(e^{j\omega}) = X_r^*(e^{-j\omega}) \quad \ldots(14.16i)$$

Hence, we can have a complex sequence, $x(n)$ give by

$$x(n) = x_r(n) + jx_i(n) \quad \ldots(14.16j)$$

with $\quad X(e^{j\omega}) = X_r(e^{j\omega}) + jX_i(e^{j\omega}) \quad \ldots(14.16k)$

such that $\quad X(e^{j\omega}) = 0$ for $-\pi \le \omega < 0 \quad \ldots(14.16l)$

We shall show that $X_r(e^{j\omega})$ and $X_i(e^{j\omega})$ form Hilbert transform pair *i.e.* we aim of proving the relation:

$$X_i(e^{j\omega}) = \begin{cases} -jX_r(e^{j\omega}) \text{ for } 0 < \omega \le \pi \\ +jX_r(e^{j\omega}) \text{ for } -\pi \le \omega \le 0 \end{cases} \quad \ldots(14.16m)$$

or $\quad X_i(e^{j\omega}) = H(e^{j\omega})\cdot X_r(e^{j\omega}) \quad \ldots(14.16n)$

Conversely,

$$X_r(e^{j\omega}) = -H(e^{j\omega}) \cdot X_i(e^{j\omega}) \qquad \text{...(14.16o)}$$

Proof of Equation (14.16*n*): As $x_r(n)$ and $x_i(n)$ are real sequences and their DTFTs obey

$$\text{DTFT } [x_r(n)] = X_r(e^{j\omega}) = X_r^*(e^{-j\omega}) \qquad \text{...(14.16p)}$$

$$\text{DTFT } [x_i(n)] = X_i(e^{j\omega}) = X_i^*(e^{-j\omega}) \qquad \text{...(14.16q)}$$

Taking DTFT on both sides of (14.16*j*), we have

$$\therefore \quad X(e^{j\omega}) = X_r(e^{j\omega}) + jX_i(e^{j\omega}) \qquad \text{...(14.16r)}$$

where $X_r(e^{j\omega})$ is DTFT of $x_r(n)$ and $X_i(e^{j\omega})$ is DTFT of $x_i(n)$. Taking complex conjugate on both sides of (14.15), we get

$$X^*(e^{j\omega}) = X_r^*(e^{j\omega}) - jX_i^*(e^{j\omega})$$

$$= X_r(e^{-j\omega}) - jX_i(e^{-j\omega}) \qquad \text{due to (14.16)}$$

Changing ω to –ω in above equation, we get

$$X^*(e^{-j\omega}) = X_r(e^{j\omega}) - jX_i(e^{j\omega}) \qquad \text{...(14.16s)}$$

Adding and subtracting (14.16*r*) and (14.16*s*), we get

$$X_r(e^{j\omega}) = \frac{1}{2}[X(e^{j\omega}) + X^*(e^{-j\omega})] \qquad \text{...(14.17)}$$

$$jX_r(e^{j\omega}) = \frac{1}{2}[X(e^{j\omega}) - X^*(e^{-j\omega})] \qquad \text{...(14.18)}$$

As $X(e^{j\omega}) = 0$ for $-\pi \le \omega < 0$, therefore $X^*(e^{-j\omega}) = 0$ for $0 < \omega \le \pi$. Hence, from (14.17) and (14.18), we have

$$\left.\begin{aligned} X_r(e^{j\omega}) &= \frac{1}{2}X(e^{j\omega}),\ 0\ \omega \le \pi \\ &= \frac{1}{2}X^*(e^{-j\omega}),\ -\pi \le \omega < 0 \end{aligned}\right\} \qquad \text{...(14.19)}$$

and

$$\left.\begin{aligned} jX_i(e^{j\omega}) &= \frac{1}{2}X(e^{j\omega}),\ 0,\ \omega \le \pi \\ &= -\frac{1}{2}X^*(e^{-j\omega}),\ -\pi \le \omega < 0 \end{aligned}\right\} \qquad \text{...(14.20)}$$

From (14.19) and (14.20), we get the relation

$$\left.\begin{aligned} X_r(e^{j\omega}) &= jX_i(e^{j\omega}),\ 0 < \omega \le \pi \\ &= -jX_i(e^{j\omega}),\ -\pi \le \omega < 0 \end{aligned}\right\} \qquad \text{...(14.21)}$$

and

$$\left.\begin{aligned} X_i(e^{j\omega}) &= -jX_r(e^{j\omega}),\ 0 < \omega \le \pi \\ &= jX_r(e^{j\omega}),\ -\pi \le \omega < 0 \end{aligned}\right\} \qquad \text{...(14.22)}$$

In other words

$$\boxed{\begin{aligned} X_r(e^{j\omega}) &= -H_{HT}(e^{j\omega})\ X_i(e^{j\omega}) \\ X_i(e^{j\omega}) &= H_{HT}(e^{j\omega}) \cdot X_r(e^{j\omega}) \end{aligned}} \qquad \text{...(14.23)}$$

14.6 APPLICATION OF DSP FOR OBTAINING SSB (USING DHT)

The DSP is vastly used in the field of communication due to advantages of digital communication over the analog one. Some powerful DSP microprocessors besides FFT chips have resulted in use of DSP principle for implementation of different modulation schemes such as Amplitude

Modulation (AM), Frequency Modulation (FM), Frequency and Phase Shift Keying (FSK, PSK) Cellular phone services and Pulse Code Modulation (PCM) etc. DSP applications in communication are limited by the maximum sampling rate, as a number of instructions are to be executed between the samples.

One of the important applications of DSP is for obtaining SSB in Amplitude Modulation (AM) communication systems.

Consider a real signal $x_r(n)$, with its Fourier transform $X_r(e^{j\omega})$ shown in Fig. 14.6(*a*). We wish to obtain a single side band signal $x_{SSB}(n)$, modulated by carrier ω_c, as shown in Fig. 14.6(*b*).

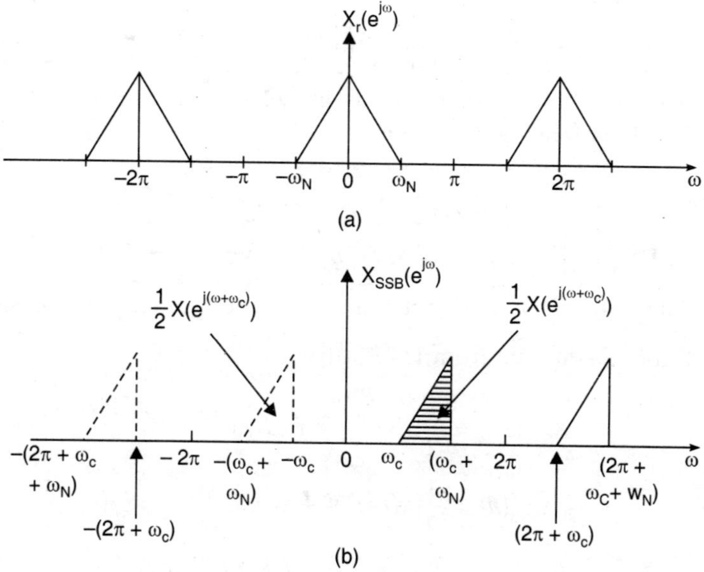

Fig. 14.6. (*a*) Spectrum of double side band signal $x_r(n)$. Note that $X_r(e^{j\omega}) = X_r^*(e^{-j\omega})$ or $|X_r(e^{j\omega})| = |X_r(e^{-j\omega})|$ and (*b*) Single side band signal $X_{SSB}(e^{j\omega})$ shown shifted by carrier frequency ω_c to right (dashed) and shifted by $-\omega_c$, *i.e.*, to left of origin (shown by dashed boundary). Periodicity of $X_{SSB}(e^{j\omega})$ is 2π.

A new time sequence of the form

$$x(n) = x_r(n) + jx_i(n) \qquad \text{...(14.24)}$$

can have a one sided (*i.e.*, single side) band such that $X(e^{j\omega}) = 0$ for $-\pi \le \omega < 0$, as given in [14.11(*b*)]. It has been shown that if this condition holds then

$$X_r(e^{j\omega}) = -H_{HT}(e^{j\omega})X_i(e^{j\omega}) \qquad \text{...(14.25)}$$

and

$$X_i(e^{j\omega}) = H_{HT}(e^{j\omega})X_r(e^{j\omega}) \qquad \text{...(14.26)}$$

Above results are proved in Section 14.5.

where

$$H(e^{j\omega}) = \begin{cases} -j, & 0 < \omega \le \pi \\ 0, & -\pi \le \omega < 0 \end{cases} \qquad \text{...(14.27)}$$

$H(e^{j\omega})$ is called *Hilbert transform.* A signal such as $x(n)$ given by (14.24) is called an *Analytic signal.* Note that $x_r(n)$ as well $x_i(n)$ both are real valued sequences. Obviously $x(n) = x_r(n) + jx_i(n)$ is a complex sequence.

As

$$\begin{aligned} X(e^{j\omega}) &= X_r(e^{j\omega}) + jX_i(e^{j\omega}) \\ &= X_r(e^{j\omega}) + jX_{HT}(e^{j\omega}) \cdot X_r(e^{j\omega}) \qquad \text{[due to (14.26)]} \\ &= X_r(e^{j\omega}) + j(-jX_r(e^{j\omega})),\ 0 < \omega \le \pi \end{aligned}$$

i.e.,

$$X(e^{j\omega}) = 2X_r(e^{j\omega}),\ 0 < \omega \le \pi \qquad \text{...(14.28)}$$

For $-\pi \le \omega < 0$, we have

$$X(e^{j\omega}) = X_r(e^{j\omega}) + j(jX_r(e^{j\omega})),\ -\pi \le \omega < 0$$
$$= 0,\ -\pi \le \omega < 0 \qquad \text{...(14.29)}$$

Combining (14.28) and (14.29), we get

$$\boxed{X(e^{j\omega}) = \begin{cases} 2X_r(e^{j\omega}), & 0 < \omega \le \pi \\ 0, & -\pi \le \omega < 0 \end{cases}} \qquad \text{...(14.30)}$$

Now consider another analytic signal

$$x_1(n) = x_r(n) - jx_i(n) \qquad \text{...(14.31)}$$

where $x_r(n)$ and $x_i(n)$ are real valued sequences and $x_i(n)$ is the Hilbert transform of $x_r(n)$. The relations (14.25) and (14.26) hold. Proceeding as in Eqns. (14.28) and (14.29), we shall obtain relation similar to (14.30) as follows:

$$\boxed{X_1(e^{j\omega}) = \begin{cases} 0, & 0 < \omega \le \pi \\ 2X_r(e^{j\omega}), & -\pi \le \omega < 0 \end{cases}} \qquad \text{...(14.31a)}$$

The SSB, modulated signal *i.e.* a signal with only upper side band present, is written as

[$\because$ $X_1(e^{j(\omega+\omega_c)}) = 0$ for $\omega + \omega_c$ +ve from (14.31*a*)]

$$X_{SSB}(e^{j\omega}) = \frac{1}{2}[X(e^{j(\omega-\omega_c)}) + X_1(e^{j(\omega+\omega_c)})] \qquad \text{...(14.32)}$$

or in time domain

$$x_{SSB}(n) = \frac{1}{2}[x(n)e^{j\omega_c n} + x_1(n)e^{-j\omega_c n}]$$

$$= \frac{1}{2}[\{x_r(n) + jx_i(n)\}e^{j\omega_c n} + \{x_r(n) - jx_i(n)\}e^{-j\omega_c n}]$$

$$= \frac{1}{2}[x_r(n)\{e^{j\omega_c n} + e^{-j\omega_c n}\} - x_i(n)\{e^{j\omega_c n} - e^{-j\omega_c n}\}]$$

$$\therefore \qquad \boxed{x_{SSB}(n) = x_r(n)\cos\omega_c n - x_i(n)\sin\omega_c n} \qquad \text{...(14.33)}$$

Realization of $x_{SSB}(n)$ from $x_r(n)$ and $x_i(n)$ is shown in Fig. 14.7.

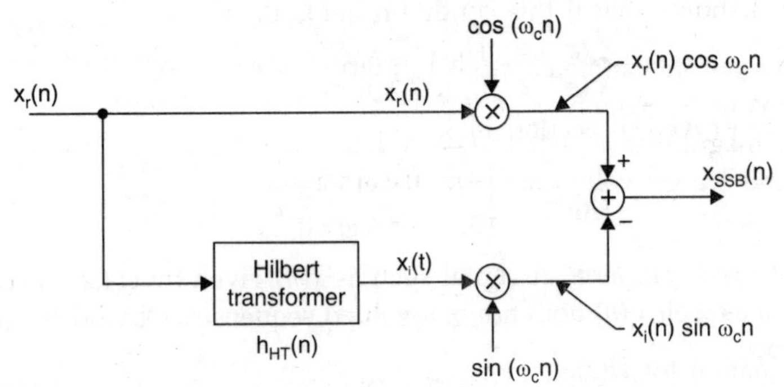

Fig. 14.7. Realization of $x_{SSB}(n)$ from $x_r(n)$ as per Eqn. (14.33) $h_{HT} = \begin{cases} \left(\dfrac{2}{n\pi}\right)\sin^2\dfrac{n\pi}{2}, & n \ne 0 \\ 0, & \text{otherwise} \end{cases}$

Suppose $x_r(n) = \cos \omega_m n$, then $x_i(n) = \sin \omega_m n$, ω_m being the modulating frequency. Assume ω_c as the carrier frequency.

Then
$$x_{SSB}(n) = \cos \omega_m n \cdot \cos \omega_c n - \sin \omega_m n \cdot \sin \omega_c n$$
$$= \cos (\omega_c + \omega_m)n$$

Hence realization in Fig. 14.7 gives upper side band. For lower side band, SSB, we choose

$$\boxed{x_{SSB}(n) = x_r(n) \cos \omega_c n + x_i(n) \sin \omega_c n} \quad ...(14.34)$$

Putting $x_r(n) = \cos \omega_m n$ and $x_i(n) = \sin \omega_m n$, we obtain

$x_{SSB}(n) = \cos (\omega_c - \omega_m)n$ being the lower side band in SSB.

Hence, we can obtain upper or lower SSB by using 90° phase shifter or a Hilbert transformer.

14.7 GENERATION OF ECHOS

In entertainment electronics, we often require generation of echos to produce various effects, say in music or in cinema pictures or in TV serials. It is possible to simulate echo generation using DSP principles. We can generate echos of decaying intensity or of constant magnitude, as explained in the following.

14.7.1 Echos of Decaying Intensity/Magnitude

Consider the comb filter system function

$$H(z) = \frac{1}{1 - az^{-T}} \quad ...(14.35)$$

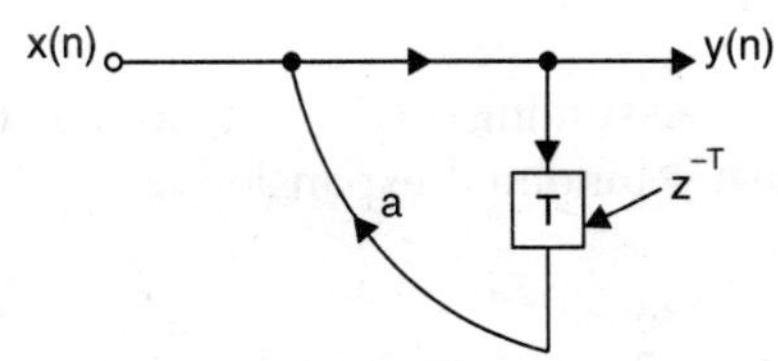

Fig. 14.8. Realization of an Echo Generator

Realization of (14.35) is shown in Fig. 14.8.

As
$$\frac{Y(z)}{X(z)} = H(z) = \frac{1}{1 - az^{-T}}$$

∴
$$H(z) = \sum_{n=0}^{\infty} (az^{-T})^n \quad |az^{-T}| < 1$$
$$= 1 + (az^{-T}) + (az^{-T})^2 + (az^{-T})^3 + ... \quad ...(14.36)$$

For input $x(n)$, we obtain

$$y(n) = x(n) + ax(n - T) + a^2x(n - 2T) + a^3x(n - 3T) + ... \quad ...(14.37)$$

Hence, $y(n)$ the output can be expressed in terms of $x(n)$, $x(n)$ delayed by T, $x(n)$ delayed by $2T$, ..., etc. with intensity given by a^k, $k = 0, 1, 2, ...$,. These are the replicas of $x(n)$, appearing at delays of kT and magnitude a^k, where $k = 0, 1, ...$,. As $|a| < 1$, therefore, echos of decaying intensity occur, and we get coloration of musical sounds.

The system function

$$H(z) = \frac{1}{1 - az^{-T}} \quad ...(14.38)$$

and difference equation for $H(z)$.

$$y(z) = ay(n - T) + x(n) \quad ...(14.39)$$

is a comb filter.

14.7.2 Echos of Constant Magnitude

Consider a system function

$$H(z) = \frac{z^{-T} - a}{1 - az^{-T}}, \; |a| < 1 \qquad \text{...(14.40)}$$

As
$$H(e^{j\omega}) = \frac{e^{-j\omega T} - a}{1 - ae^{-j\omega T}}$$

$$|H(e^{j\omega})|^2 = \left| \frac{(\cos \omega T - a) - j \sin \omega T}{(1 - a \cos \omega T) + ja \sin \omega T} \right|^2$$

$$= \frac{(\cos \omega T - a)^2 + (\sin \omega T)^2}{(1 - a \cos \omega T)^2 + (a \sin \omega T)^2}$$

Hence,
$$|H(e^{j\omega})|^2 = 1 \qquad \text{...(14.41)}$$

i.e., $H(z)$ given by (14.40) is an all-pass system.

[To find y(n) for input x(n)]

As
$$H(z) = \frac{Y(z)}{X(z)} = \frac{z^{-T} - a}{1 - az^{-T}} \qquad \text{...(14.42)}$$

Assuming $|az^{-1}| < 1$, so that $H(z)$ represents a stable system, we can expand RHS of (14.42) using binomial expansion.

Hence,
$$\frac{Y(z)}{X(z)} = z^{-T} \sum_{k=0}^{\infty} (az^{-T})^k - a \sum_{k=0}^{\infty} (az^{-T})^k$$

$$= \sum_{k=0}^{\infty} a^k z^{-(k+1)T} - \sum_{k=0}^{\infty} a^{k+1} z^{-kT}$$

$\therefore$
$$y(n) = \sum_{k=0}^{\infty} a^k x[n - (k+1)T] - \sum_{k=0}^{\infty} a^{k+1} x(n - kT)$$

$$= \sum_{k=0}^{\infty} [a^k x(n - (k+1)T) - a^{k+1} x(n - kT)] \qquad \text{...(14.43)}$$

Thus for
$$k = 0, \; y(n) = x(n - T) - ax(n)$$
$$k = 1, \; y(n) = ax(n - 2T) - a^2 x(n - T)$$
$$k = 2, \; y(n) = a^2 x(n - 3T) - a^3 x(n - 2T)$$

and so on, for $k = m - 1$, $\quad y(n) = a^{m-1} x(n - mT) - a^{m+1} x[n - (m - 1)T]$.

Thus, m-th echo has gain of $(a^{m-1} - a^{m+1})$. The magnitude response of each echo is constant due to the relation proved in (14.41). This results in more pleasant sounds as compared to decaying intensity echos.

Some other system functions can also be used for generating echo signals. Consider two systems

$$H_1(z) = \frac{a + z^{-T_1}}{1 - az^{-T_1}} \qquad \text{...(14.44a)}$$

$$H_2(z) = \frac{b + z^{-T_2}}{1 - bz^{-T_2}} \quad \text{...(14.44b)}$$

Proceeding as for $H(z)$, given by (14.42), we find the values of outputs $y_1(n)$ and $y_2(n)$, as follows:

$$y_1(n) = \sum_{k=0}^{\infty} a^{k+1} x(n - kT_1) + \sum_{k=0}^{\infty} a^k x[n - (k+1)T_1] \quad \text{...(14.44c)}$$

$$y_2(n) = \sum_{k=0}^{\infty} b^{k+1} x(n - kT_2) + \sum_{k=0}^{\infty} b^k x[n - (k+1)T_2] \quad \text{...(14.44d)}$$

If we use only [14.44(*a*)] or [14.44(*b*)], the echo outputs will be as given by [14.44(*c*)] or [14.44(*d*)], just as given by (14.43) with echo delays of m_1T_1 or m_2T_2. However, if we cascade $H_1(z)$ and $H_2(z)$, there will be echos at time $n = mT_1 + kT_2$ (m, n integers). The cascaded system produces more densely (more rich) packed echo. For example, if $T_1 = 3$ and $T_2 = 5$, then the cascaded system will produce echos at time instances $n = 3, 5, 6, 8, 9, 10, \ldots$. However, each time the echo appears, its magnitude will not be constant as is for the case of $H(z)$ given by (14.42).

14.8 MATCHED FILTER

In various communication systems and in Radars, Sonars using linear FM (chirp) pulse for transmission, we need a receiver for optimum results. When the channel through which the signal is passed is corrupted by noise, the detection of received signal requires some special techniques. In DSP, the matched filter is one of the most preferred ones when the goal is to maximize the signal to noise ratio (SNR) at the filter output, particularly when uncertainty is very high.

In developing mathematical results to determine the impulse response, $h(n)$ of an LTI match filter, we shall need the following results:

1. *Schwarz's inequality*

$$\left| \int_{-\pi}^{\pi} X_1(e^{j\omega}) \cdot X_2(e^{j\omega})\, d\omega \right|^2 \le \int_{-\pi}^{\pi} |X_1(e^{j\omega})|^2\, d\omega \int_{-\pi}^{\pi} |X_2(e^{j\omega})|^2\, d\omega$$

The equality holds when $X_1(e^{j\omega}) = kX_2^*(e^{j\omega})$

2. $\int_{-\pi}^{\pi} |H(e^{j\omega})e^{j\omega N}|^2\, d\omega = \int_{-\pi}^{\pi} |H(e^{j\omega})|^2\, d\omega$ where N is real number

3. White noise has average power, for sample n, given by $E\{\omega^2(n)\}$, where $\omega(n)$ is a white noise sequence. Also, $E\{\omega^2(n)\} = \frac{1}{2\pi}\int_{-\pi}^{\pi} \phi_{\omega\omega}(e^{j\omega})\, d\omega$, where $\phi_{\omega\omega}(e^{j\omega})$ is the PSD of $\omega(n)$.

...(14.44*e*)

Note the following symbols used for the derivation here.

(*i*) $g(n)$: the transmitted signal through the channel

(*ii*) $\omega(n)$: the channel noise

(*iii*) $x(n)$: the received signal, being noise corrupted, *i.e.*, $x(n) = g(n) + \omega(n)$

(*iv*) $y(n)$: the output of the matched filter, *i.e.*, $y(n) = x(n) * h(n)$

(*v*) $h(n)$: the impulse response of LTI match filter

(*vi*) $g_0(n)$: the output produced by the signal component of $x(n)$, *i.e.*, $g_0(n) = g(n) * h(n)$

(*vii*) $\omega_0(n)$: the output produced from the filter due to the noise component of $x(n)$, *i.e.*, $\omega_0(n) = \omega(n) * h(n)$

(*viii*) $\phi_{\omega\omega}(e^{j\omega})$: the power spectrum density of white noise $\omega(n)$ and $\phi_{\omega\omega}(e^{j\omega}) = \sigma_\omega^2$ for $\omega(n)$ a white noise.

(*ix*) $\phi_{\omega_0\omega_0}(e^{j\omega})$ = the power spectrum density of output $\omega_0(n)$ due to input white noise $\omega(n)$

to the matched filter $h(n) \cdot \phi_{\omega_0\omega_0}(e^{j\omega}) = \phi_{\omega\omega}(e^{j\omega}) \cdot |H(e^{j\omega})|^2$

(*x*) $|g_0(n)|^2$: instantaneous power $g_0(n)$ at sample n

(*xi*) $E\{\omega_0^2(n)\}$: average power of output noise $\omega_0(n)$ ...(14.45)

We know that

$$y(n) = x(n) * h(n)$$
$$= \{g(n) + \omega(n)\} * h(n)$$
$$= g(n) * h(n) + \omega(n) * h(n)$$
$$\therefore \quad y(n) = g_0(n) + \omega_0(n)$$

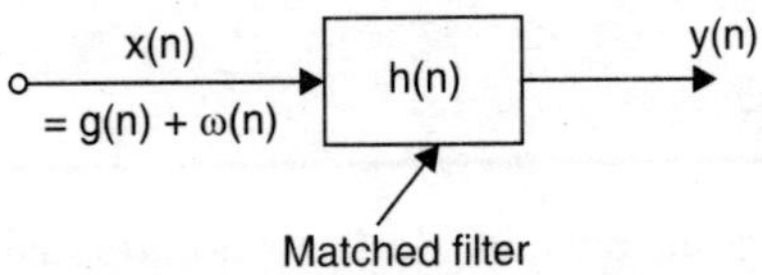

Fig. 14.9. Showing input and output signals

The receiver, $h(n)$ (called the matched filter) is to detect the useful signal *i.e.* $g(n)$. The effect of the noise is to so minimized at the receiver output. By appropriate choice of the receiver's impulse response $h(n)$, the receiver achieves the goal by maximizing the signal to noise ratio at its output. We shall prove that $h(n)$ of the receiver is matched to the transmitted signal $g(n)$, and hence it is called the **Matched Filter**.

The SNR at the receiver output is given by

$$\text{SNR} = \frac{\text{Power of } g_0(n)}{\text{Power of noise } \omega_0(n)} = \frac{|g_0(n)|^2}{E\{\omega_0^2(n)\}} \qquad ...(14.46)$$

$$= \frac{\left|\dfrac{1}{2\pi}\displaystyle\int_{-\pi}^{\pi} G_0(e^{j\omega})e^{jn\omega}\, d\omega\right|^2}{\dfrac{1}{2\pi}\displaystyle\int_{-\pi}^{\pi} \phi_{\omega_0\omega_0}(e^{j\omega})\, d\omega} \quad \text{[using IDFT of } G_0(e^{j\omega}) \text{ for } g_0(n)]$$

$$\therefore \quad \text{SNR} = \frac{\left|\dfrac{1}{2\pi}\displaystyle\int_{-\pi}^{\pi} G(e^{j\omega}) \cdot H(e^{j\omega})e^{j\omega n}\, d\omega\right|^2}{\dfrac{1}{2\pi}\displaystyle\int_{-\pi}^{\pi} \phi_{\omega\omega}(e^{j\omega}) \cdot |H(e^{j\omega})|^2\, d\omega} \quad \text{[using 14.45(ix)]} \qquad ...(14.47)$$

We have used the property

$$FT[g_0(n)] = FT[g(n) * h(n)]$$
$$= G(e^{j\omega}) \cdot H(e^{j\omega})$$

If a random signal $\omega(n)$, with power spectrum $\phi_{\omega\omega}(e^{j\omega})$, when inputted to the system $h(n)$, the output $\omega_0(n)$ has power spectrum given by $\phi_{\omega_0\omega_0}(e^{j\omega}) = \phi_{\omega\omega}(e^{j\omega})\,|H(e^{j\omega})|^2$.

The value of SNR at the filter output at sample $n = N$ is given by, putting $\phi_{\omega\omega}(e^{j\omega}) = \sigma_\omega^2$ for the white noise in (14.47),

$$\therefore \qquad \text{SNR} = \frac{1}{2\pi}\frac{\left|\int_{-\pi}^{\pi} G(e^{j\omega})\cdot H(e^{j\omega})e^{j\omega N}\,d\omega\right|^2}{\int_{-\pi}^{\pi}\sigma_\omega^2\,|H(e^{j\omega})|^2\,d\omega} \qquad \ldots(14.48)$$

Using Schwarz's inequality [see (14.44)]

$$\left|\int_{-\pi}^{\pi} G(e^{j\omega})\cdot H(e^{j\omega})e^{j\omega N}\,d\omega\right|^2 \le \int_{-\pi}^{\pi}|G(e^{j\omega})|^2\,d\omega\int_{-\pi}^{\pi}|H(e^{j\omega})e^{j\omega N}|^2\,d\omega$$

$$= \int_{-\pi}^{\pi}|G(e^{j\omega})|^2\,d\omega\cdot\int_{-\pi}^{\pi}|H(e^{j\omega})|^2\,d\omega \qquad \ldots(14.49)$$

$\therefore$ Maximum SNR, at $n = N$ is given by using (14.49) in (14.48),

$$(\text{SNR})_{\max} = \frac{1}{2\pi}\frac{\int_{-\pi}^{\pi}|G(e^{j\omega})|^2\,d\omega\cdot\int_{-\pi}^{\pi}|H(e^{j\omega})|^2\,d\omega}{\sigma_\omega^2\int_{-\pi}^{\pi}|H(e^{j\omega})|^2\,d\omega}$$

$$= \frac{1}{2\pi}\frac{\int_{-\pi}^{\pi}|G(e^{j\omega})|^2\,d\omega}{\sigma_\omega^2} \qquad \ldots(14.50)$$

To obtain maximum SNR, we use the Schwarz's inequality

$$\therefore \qquad G(e^{j\omega}) = K\{H(e^{j\omega})\cdot e^{j\omega N}\}^*, \text{ where } K \text{ is a constant}$$

$$= KH^*(e^{j\omega})\cdot e^{-j\omega N}$$

$$\therefore \qquad H(e^{j\omega}) = \left(\frac{1}{K}\right)G^*(e^{j\omega})e^{-j\omega N} \qquad \ldots(14.51)$$

$$\therefore \qquad h(n) = \text{IDTF of } \frac{1}{K}G^*(e^{j\omega})e^{-j\omega N}$$

$$= \frac{1}{K}\cdot\frac{1}{2\pi}\int_{-\pi}^{\pi}G^*(e^{j\omega})\cdot e^{-j\omega N}e^{j\omega n}\,d\omega$$

$$= \frac{1}{K}\cdot\frac{1}{2\pi}\left[\int_{-\pi}^{\pi}G(e^{j\omega})e^{j\omega(N-n)}\,d\omega\right]^*$$

$$= \frac{1}{K}[g(N-n)]^*$$

$$\therefore \qquad h(n) = \frac{1}{K}g^*(N-n)$$

If $g(n)$ is a real signal, then $h(n) = \frac{1}{K}g(N-n)$ ...(14.52)

Typical sequences $g(n)$ and $h(n) = g(-n + N)$, for $g(n)$ real are shown in Fig. 14.10. It can be readily seen that maximum value of $g(n) * h(n) = g_0(n)$ is $a^2 + b^2 + c^2 + d^2 + e^2 + \ldots$ ...(14.53)

No other combination of a, b, c, d, e would give value more than that given by (14.53). So the matched filter maximizes the output signal power $|g_0(n)|^2$.

Matched filters are particularly useful in pulse compression radars, multiuser spread spectrum communication, and other digital communication systems.

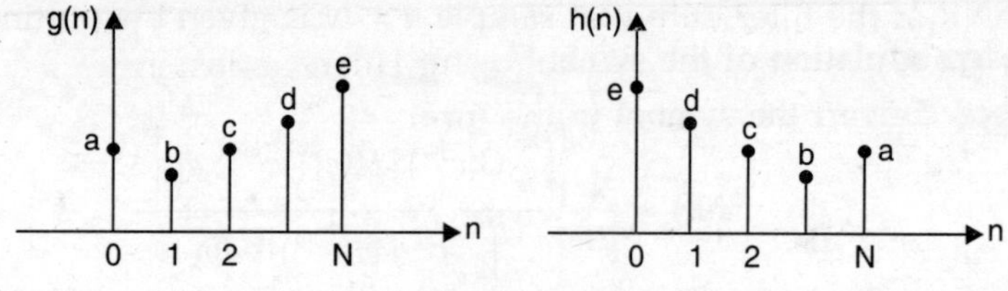

$h(n) = g(-n + N)$

Fig. 14.10. Showing typical sequences $g(n)$ and $h(n)$

As in another example, consider two other signals $x_1(n)$ and $x_2(n)$ as shown in Fig. 14.11.

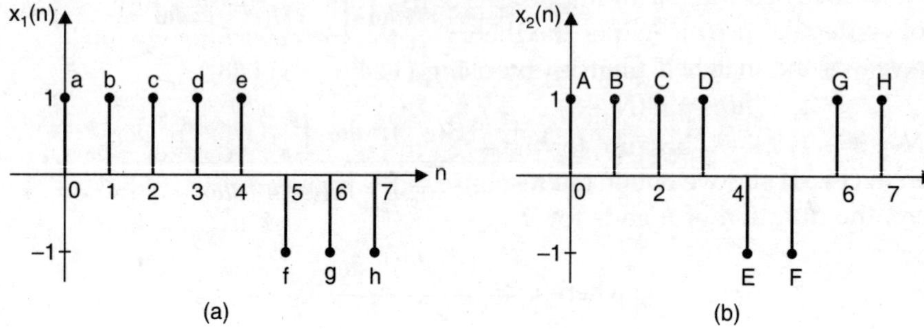

Fig. 14.11. Two possible discrete time signals

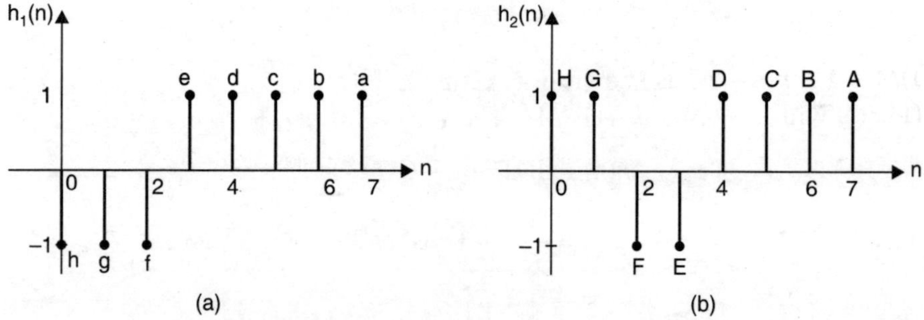

Fig. 14.12. Impulse responses for the corresponding matched filters (*a*) for $x_1(n)$, (*b*) for $x_2(n)$

The impulse responses $h_1(n)$ and $h_2(n)$ for $x_1(n)$ and $x_2(n)$, respectively, of the corresponding matched filters are shown in Fig. 14.12. Note that with delay ($N = 7$ here), the values

$$x_1(n) * h_1(n) = x_2(n) * h_2(n) = 8$$

$$x_1(n) * h_2(n) = 2 \text{ and } x_2(n) * h_1(n) = 2$$

This example also shows that impulse response of the matched filter is different for different signals. This is a serious limitation for hardware designs meant for generic use.

14.8.1 Use of Digital Matched Filter in FSK System

For demodulation of FSK modulated signals in FSK systems, discrete-time Matched Filter are usually used. In FSK systems, different frequencies are allotted to the symbols to be transmitted. On the receiver end, the demodulation involves:

(*a*) Conversion of Radio Frequency (RF) to Intermediate Frequency (IF) of the received signal by analog means.

(*b*) Complex demodulation of the symbol using Hilbert transform.

Above two steps convert the symbol in the form

$$\left. \begin{array}{l} r(n) = e^{jx}, \text{ where } x = \pi \dfrac{a(k)(n - kM)}{M} \\ \text{for } kM \le n \le (k+1)M - 1 \end{array} \right\} \qquad \ldots(14.54)$$

and $a(k)$ represents data for the k-th symbol.

Note in (14.54) that $(n - kM)$ varies from (0) to $(M - 1)$ as n varies from kM to $(k + 1)M - 1$. This implies that the sequence $r(n)$ is of length M for each received symbol.

Discrete-time matched filter with impulse response $h(n)$ can be efficiently used for detection of the symbol contained in $r(n)$. As per the theory of the matched filter the matched filter. The impulse response of the matched filter is given by:

$$h(n) = r^*(N - n) \qquad \ldots(14.55)$$

Putting $N = (k + 1) M - 1$, because for the *k-th* symbol, the variation of n is $kM \le n \le (k + 1) M - 1$ as given in (14.54) and we obtain the response of the matched filter at the end of the symbol duration. Here, the duration of n ends for $n = (k + 1) M - 1$ and we denote $N = (k + 1) M - 1$.

$$\left. \begin{array}{l} r(-n) = e^{jk}, \text{ where } u = \pi \dfrac{a(k)\,(-n - kM)}{M}, \\ -(k+1)M + 1 \le n \le -kM \end{array} \right\} \qquad \ldots(14.56)$$

We obtained (14.56) by changing n to $-n$ in (14.54),

i.e.,
$$kM \le -n \le (k + 1)M - 1 \text{ becomes}$$
$$-kM \ge n \ge -(k + 1) M + 1$$

i.e., $-(k + 1)M + 1 \le n \le -kM$ as shown in (14.56)

From (14.56), with $N = (k + 1) M - 1$, changing $-n$ to $N - n$ both sides

$$r(N - n) = e^{jz}\ , \text{ where } z = \pi \frac{a(k)\,\{(k+1)\,M - 1 - n - kM\}}{M}$$

$$= \pi \frac{a(k)\,\{M - 1 - n\}}{M}$$

and in the limits of n in (14.56), *i.e.*,

$$-(k + 1)M + 1 \le n \le -kM$$

Adding $(k + 1)M - 1$ on both sides of limits, we obtain

$$0 \le n \le M - 1$$

Hence we can write

$$\left. \begin{array}{l} r(N - n) = e^{jz}, \text{ where } z = \pi \dfrac{a(k)\,\{M - 1 - n\}}{M} \\ 0 \le n \le M - 1 \end{array} \right\} \qquad \ldots(14.57)$$

$$r^*(N - n) = e^{jz}$$

or
$$h(n) = r^*(N - n) = r[(k + 1)\,M - 1 - n] = e^{-jz}$$

where
$$z = \frac{a(k)\,[M - 1 - n]}{M}$$

for
$$0 \le n \le M - 1 \qquad \ldots(14.58)$$

If $a(k) = i$, say, *i.e.*, the symbol $a(k)$ equalling i-th level, then the impulse response $h_i(n)$ for the i-th matched filter is given by

$$h_i(n) = e^{jy}, \text{ where } y = -z = -\pi \frac{i[M-1-n]}{M}, \; 0 \leq n \leq M-1 \quad \text{...(14.59)}$$

It will give the maximum output if the symbol $a(k) = i$.

14.8.2 Removal of Echos from the Received Signal

It is also possible to remove the known echos from the incoming signal by appropriately using an inverse filter. Consider the system as follows:

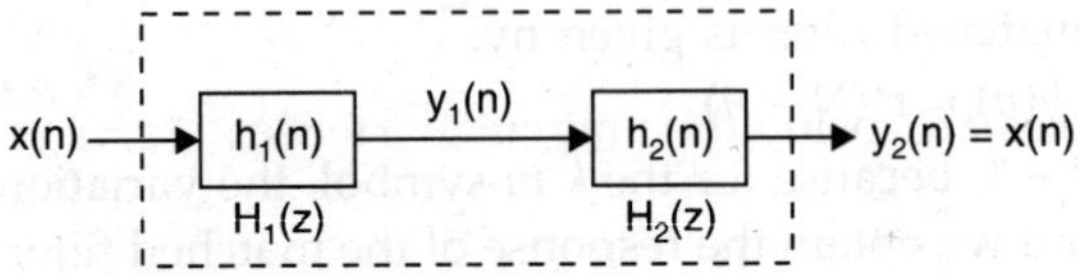

Fig. 14.13. Use of inverse filter $H_2(z)$ to recover $x(n)$

Here,

$$Y_1(z) = X(z) \,.\, H_1(z)$$
$$Y_2(z) = Y_1(z) \,.\, H_2(z)$$
$$= X(z) \,.\, H_1(z) \,.\, H_2(z) \quad \text{...(14.60)}$$

If we let $H_1(z) \,.\, H_2(z) = 1$ on (14.60), we obtain $Y_2(z) = X(z)$ or $y_2(z) = x(n)$. Putting $H_1(z) \,.\, H_2(z) = 1$ implies that the overall system, shown by dashed lines in Fig. 14.13, acts as an all pass filter. Consider the received signal $y(n)$ with echos at delays n_0 and $2n_0$,

$$y(n) = x(n) + \frac{1}{2} x(n - n_0) + \frac{1}{4} x(n - 2n_0) \quad \text{...(14.61)}$$

Taking z-transform on both sides of (14.61), we get

$$Y(z) = X(z)\left[1 + \frac{1}{2} z^{-n_0} + \frac{1}{4} z^{-2n_0}\right] \quad \text{...(14.62)}$$

Note that if we multiply $Y(z)$ by an expression

$$F(z^{n_0}) = \frac{1}{1 + \frac{1}{2} z^{-n_0} + \frac{1}{4} z^{-2n_0}} \quad \text{...(14.63)}$$

then $$Y(z) \,.\, F(z^{n_0}) = X(n) \quad \text{...(14.64)}$$

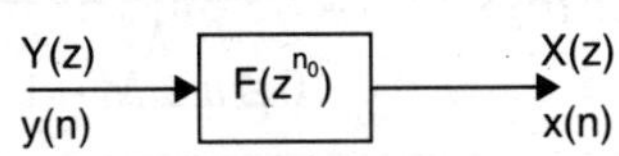

Fig. 14.14. The output $x(n)$ obtained from $y(n)$

i.e., the output is $x(n)$. Hence, the echos appearing in $y(n)$ as $\frac{1}{2}$ $x(n - n_0)$ and $\frac{1}{4}$ $x(n - 2n_0)$ have been removed by the filter $F(z^{n_0})$.

If we define

$$G(z) \triangleq F(z^{n_0})\Big|_{z^{n_0}=z}$$

$$\therefore \qquad G(z) = \frac{1}{1+\frac{1}{2}z^{-1}+\frac{1}{4}z^{-2}} \qquad \text{...(14.65)}$$

Then the poles of $G(z)$ are at

$$z_{1,2} = -\frac{1}{4}(1 \pm j\sqrt{3})$$

$$\therefore \qquad |z_{1,2}| = \frac{1}{2}$$

i.e., $G(z)$ is stable as its poles are inside the unit circle. Hence, $F(z^{n_0}) = G(z^{n_0})$ is also realizable.

14.9 PRODUCTION OF CHORUS EFFECT IN MUSIC USING DSP

It is possible, by using DSP techniques, to make a music piece, though sung by one singer, to appear as having been sung by a chorus of singers. It is economical to engage one singer and yet produce the chorus effect. When a group of musicians play the same music simultaneously, it is not possible for them to play the notes at exactly the same time with exactly same amplitude. This property of chorus singing or chorus of instrument playing can be simulated using DSP techniques.

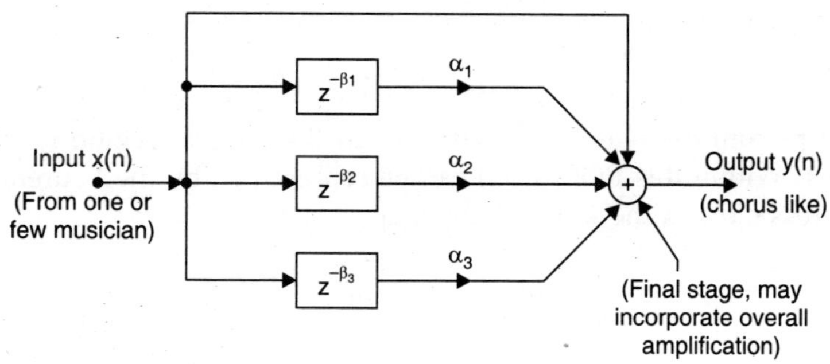

Fig. 14.15. A block diagram showing implementation of Chorus effect

Figure 14.15 shows a block diagram for implementation of chorus effect. The delays are shown by $z^{-\beta_i}$, $i = 1, 2, ...$ and these represent delays of music input at $x(n)$. α_i, $i = 1, 2, ...$, represent the amplitude of the music from 'different musicians' with respect to the reference $x(n)$. For digital realization the delays: $z^{-\beta_1}, z^{-\beta_2}, ...$, can be easily implemented. Typical delays are 10 to 50 milli seconds. If the sampling rate for $x(n)$ is F_s, then

$$\beta_i = \text{Delay coefficient} = (\text{Delay needed})/T_s$$

where $$T_s = \frac{1}{F_s} \qquad \text{...(14.66)}$$

If we wish to simulate a randomly varying delay (it is more realistic for a chorus), then

$$\beta_i = \beta_i(n) \qquad ...(14.67)$$

i.e., we make the value of β_i which depends on a number n where n, is pseudo random noise that varies slowly. Pseudo random digital n can also be generated by DSP techniques.

For actual delay of 10 m sec and F_s = 8 kHz, the value of $\beta = (10 \times 10^{-3})/(1/8000) = 80$ and so.

We may also vary the gain α_i randomly for different tastes of the chorus effect.

Even if one singer's voice is inputted at $x(n)$, the addition of delayed (by $\beta_1, \beta_2, ...$) and scaled (by $\alpha_1, \alpha_2, ...$) versions of $x(n)$ when added in the final stage, the output $y(n)$ will be of the form

$$y(n) = x(n) + \alpha_1 x(n - \beta_1) + \alpha_2 x(n - \beta_2) + ... \qquad ...(14.68)$$

By appropriate choice of delays and scaling factors, the final signal $y(n)$ will be a chorus type music piece.

14.10 A NOTE ON COMPLEX CEPSTRUM

Let $x(n)$ be a stable sequence with its z-transform

$$X(z) = \sum_{n=-\infty}^{\infty} x(n)\, z^{-n} \qquad ...(14.69)$$

We define complex cepstrum of $x(n)$ by

$$c_x(n) \triangleq \text{Complex cepstrum of } x(n)$$

$$C_x(z) = \ln[X(z)] = \sum_{n=-\infty}^{\infty} c_x(n)\, z^{-n} \qquad ...(14.70)$$

The complex cepstrum exists if $C_x(z)$ converges in the annular region $r_1 < |z| < r_2$ where $0 < r_1 < 1$ and $r_2 > 1$. Within this ROC, $C_x(z)$ can be represented by the Laurent series given by (14.70) we can express $c_x(n)$ as the IZT of $\ln X(z)$, *i.e.*,

$$c_x(n) = \frac{1}{2\pi j} \oint_C \ln X(z) \,.\, Z^{n-1}\, dz \qquad ...(14.71)$$

where C is a closed contour (in the counter-clock direction) and lies within the ROC: $r_1 < |z| < r_2$, and the origin is enclosed in C.

If $C_x(z)$ can be represented by the Laurent series shown in (14.70), then the sequence $\{C_x(n)\}$ is stable. Also, if the complex cepstrum $c_x(n)$ exists then its *ZT* $C_x(z)$ converges on the unit circle $|z| = 1$ and hence we have the relation (changing z to $e^{j\omega}$) as follows:

$$C_x(\omega) = \ln X(\omega) = \sum_{n=-\infty}^{\infty} c_x(n)\, e^{-j\omega n} \qquad ...(14.72)$$

where
$$c_x(n) = \frac{1}{2\pi} \int_{-\pi}^{\pi} \ln X(\omega)\, e^{j\omega n}\, d\omega \qquad ...(14.73)$$

Note the notations $C_x(\omega) \triangleq C_x(e^{j\omega})$ and $X(\omega) \triangleq X(e^{j\omega})$. We can express $X(\omega)$ in terms of magnitude and phase by

$$X(\omega) = |X(\omega)|\, e^{j\theta(\omega)} \quad ...(14.74)$$

then
$$\ln X(\omega) = \ln|X(\omega)| + j\theta(\omega) \quad ...(14.75)$$

Putting ln $X(\omega)$ expression from (14.75) in (14.73), we obtain the cepstrum $c_x(n)$ in the form

$$c_x(n) = \frac{1}{2\pi}\int_{-\pi}^{\pi} [\ln|X(\omega)| + j\theta(\omega)]e^{j\omega n}\, d\omega \quad ...(14.76)$$

Separating (14.76) in two parts we can write IFT of magnitude part ln $|X(\omega)|$ and IFT of phase part as

Magnitude: $$c_m(n) = \frac{1}{2\pi}\int_{-\pi}^{\pi} \ln|X(\omega)|\, e^{j\omega n}\, d\omega \quad ...(14.77)$$

Phase: $$c_\theta(n) = \frac{1}{2\pi}\int_{-\pi}^{\pi} \theta(\omega)\, e^{j\omega n}\, d\omega \quad ...(14.78)$$

In various applications, such as in speech signal processing, the component $c_m(n)$ in useful and the component $c_\theta(n)$ is ignored. Note that the sequence $x(n)$ cannot be recovered from $c_m(n)$. In various speech signal processing, the real part of $c_x(n)$, *i.e.*, $c_m(n)$ is separated to estimate the spectral content of the speech from the pitch frequency of the speech. The complex cepstrum is used to separate two signals, say $x_1(n)$ and $x_2(n)$ if $x_1(n) * x_2(n)$ is available. This is called deconvolution and the use of complex cepstrum for separation is called **Homomorphic Deconvolution.**

14.10.1 Homomorphic Deconvolution

The complex cepstrum is a useful tool for processing deconvolution in many applications such as in seismic, speech and space signal processing, to mention a few.

Suppose a signal $y(n)$ is the output sequence of a linear time-invariant system which is excited by the input $x(n)$. Therefore

$$Y(z) = X(z)\,.\,H(z) \quad ...(14.79)$$

where $H(z)$ is the system function. Then we can write

$$c_y(z) = \ln\,[Y(z)] \quad \text{[from definition (14.70)]}$$
$$= \ln X(z) + \ln H(z) \quad ...(14.80\ a)$$
$$= c_x(z) + c_h(z) \quad ...(14.80\ b)$$

This leads to, by taking IZT on both sides of [14.80 (*a*)],

$$c_y(n) = c_x(n) + c_h(n) \quad ...(14.81)$$

Thus, convolution of two sequences in time domain [the sequences here are $x(n)$ and $h(n)$] leads to summation of the cepstrum sequences [here these are $c_x(n)$ and $c_h(n)$] in the cepstral domain. Figure 14.16 shows a homomorphic system performing these transformations.

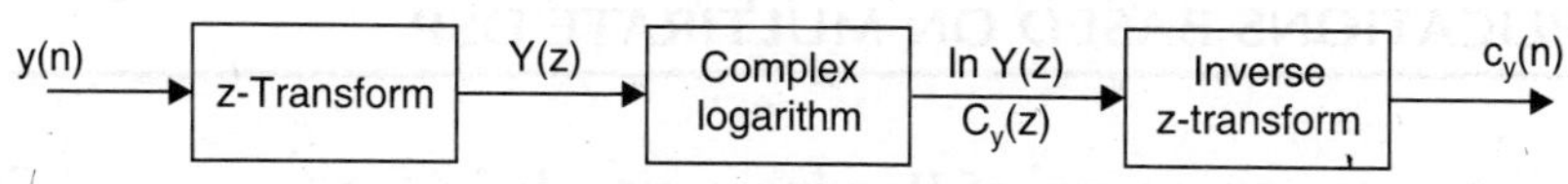

Fig. 14.16. Homomorphic system for obtaining the cepstrum sequence $c_y(n)$ from the sequence $y(n)$

In some applications such as seismic or speech signal processing, the properties of their cepstral sequences $c_x(n)$ and $c_h(n)$ are sufficiently different, and therefore these can be separated in the cepstral domain. Suppose the cepstrum $c_h(n)$ has its main components, *i.e.*, the main energy in the vicinity of small values of n, whereas the cepstrum $c_x(n)$ has its main components concentrated at large values of n. In this case we may say that $c_h(n)$ is "low-pass" and $c_x(n)$ is "high-pass". We can easily separate $c_h(n)$ and $c_x(n)$ by using "low-pass" and "high-pass" windows as shown in Fig. 14.17. Here the outputs $\hat{c}_h(n)$ and $\hat{c}_x(n)$ are almost equal to $c_h(n)$ and $c_x(n)$.

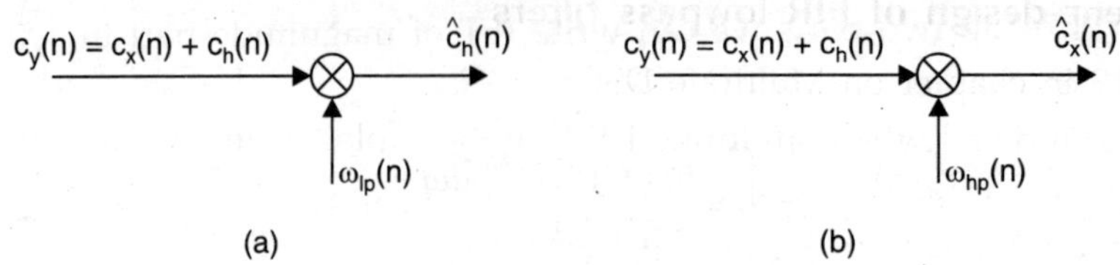

Fig. 14.17. Obtaining (*a*) $\hat{c}_h(n)$ and (*b*) $\hat{c}_x(n)$ from $c_x(n) + c_h(n)$ by using low-pass window $\omega_{lp}(n)$ and high-pass window $\omega_{hp}(n)$

The low-pass and high-pass windows used in Fig. 14.17 have the characteristics

$$\omega_{lp}(n) = \begin{cases} 1, & |n| \le N_1 \\ 0, & \text{Otherwise} \end{cases} \quad \ldots(14.82a)$$

$$\omega_{hp}(n) = \begin{cases} 0, & |n| \le N_1 \\ 1, & \text{Otherwise} \end{cases} \quad \ldots(14.82b)$$

Having extracted $\hat{c}_h(n)$ and $\hat{c}_x(n)$, and these being the cepstra, we obtain the sequence $\hat{h}(n)$ and $\hat{x}(n)$, respectively, by passing these through the inverse homomorphic system, such as shown in Fig. 14.18.

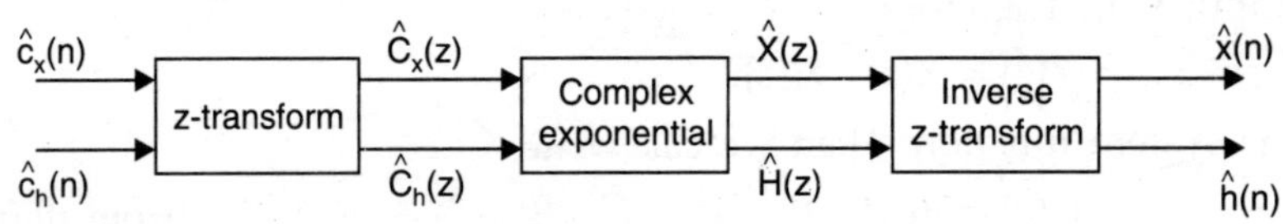

Fig. 14.18. Inverse homomorphic system for recovering $\hat{x}(n)$ and $\hat{h}(n)$ from their corresponding cepstra $\hat{c}_x(n)$ and $\hat{c}_h(n)$ respectively

In general, digital computer is used to compute cepstrum and the inverse cepstrum. To perform z-transform and inverse z-transform DFT and FFT techniques are applied. In short, homomorphic processes are highly useful in practical applications.

14.11 APPLICATIONS BASED ON MULTIRATE DSP

14.11.1 Sampling rate conversion of Bandpass signals:

See Section 12.10 in chapter on Multirate DSP.

14.11.2 Design of phase shifters (fractional sample delay)

See Section 12.11.1 in chapter on Multirate DSP.

14.11.3 Subband coding of speech signals

See Section 12.11.2 in chapter on Multirate DSP.

14.11.4 Efficient design of FIR lowpass filters

See Section 12.13 in chapter on Multirate DSP.

A list giving in detail where multirate DSP can be exploited in various areas of application is given in Section 12.11.

Also, the students may go through the solved Examples 12.17, 12.18 and 12.19 regarding efficient design of FIR lowpass.

References

1. A.V. Oppenheim and R.W. Schafer, *Digital Signal Processing*, Prentice-Hall, 1975.
2. A.V. Oppenheim and R.W. Schafer, *Discrete-time Signal Processing*, Prentice-Hall, 1999 (2nd edition).
3. L.R. Rabiner and B. Gold, *Theory and Application of Digital Signal Processing*, Prentice-Hall, 1975.
4. S. K. Mitra, *Digital Signal Processing*, Tata McGraw-Hill Publishing Company, 2008 (3rd edition).
5. J. G. Proakis and D. G. Manolakis, *Digital Signal Processing*, Pearson Education, 2009 (4th Edition).
6. J. G. Proakis, Rader, Ling and Nikias, *Advanced Digital Signal Processing*, Maxwell Macmillan, 1992.
7. P. P. Vaidyanathan, *Multirate Systems and Filter Banks*, Prentice-Hall, 1993.
8. R. E. Crochiere and L. R. Rabiner, *Multirate Digital Signal Processing*, Prentice-Hall, 1983.
9. M. H. Hayes, *Digital Signal Processing*, Tata McGraw-Hill, 2007.
10. Johnny R. Johnson, *Introduction to Digital Signal Processing*, Prentice-Hall International Editions, 1989.

Index

A

B

C

D

E

F

G

H

I

J

K

L

M

S

T

U

V

W

X

Y

Z